INTRODUCTION TO THE LAW AND LEGAL SYSTEM OF THE UNITED STATES

Second Edition

By

William Burnham
Professor of Law
Wayne State University Law School

WEST
GROUP

ST. PAUL, MINN., 1999

COPYRIGHT © 1999 By WEST GROUP
                    610 Opperman Drive
                    P.O. Box 64526
                    St. Paul, MN 55164–0526
                    1–800–328–9352

ISBN 0–314–23587–6

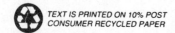 TEXT IS PRINTED ON 10% POST
CONSUMER RECYCLED PAPER

PREFACE

This introductory book on the law and legal system of the United States is intended for people interested in the U.S. legal system who have not completed law school at a U.S. law school. Within that category, I have three primary groups in mind: (1) law students, lawyers and legal scholars from foreign countries, (2) U.S. graduate and undergraduate college students, and (3) members of the general reading public in the United States. This book can be used either as the text for an introductory course on U.S. law, as a reference or for self-study.

In the process of writing the book, I have come to realize the difficulty of producing a book that will "work" for three such diverse groups. In places, readers will find some compromises and special efforts to accommodate one or another group. I hope readers from the other groups are not put off by them. For reasons set out below, the first group — foreign lawyers — is the primary group I had in mind when writing. Nonetheless, undergraduate students, whether "pre-law" or not, should find it useful as an overview of the primary topics and methodology covered in law school. Graduate students in non-law disciplines should find the book useful if they are working in a field that intersects with law. Layperson members of the general public may wish to skip footnotes and parts of the text that are too specialized, but should find the book useful. In addition, non-legal professionals who work regularly with lawyers or law will find this book a useful insight into both.

The original idea for this book grew out of two frustrations. The first was my effort to find a text for a course, "Introduction to American Law," that I was called upon to teach while on a faculty exchange at the University of Utrecht Law School in the Netherlands in 1990 and 1992. Books for U.S. lawyers and law students were clearly unsuitable because they are too detailed. In any event, they are narrowly focused on one or two major substantive law areas. Books intended for undergraduate college students, primarily business law and constitutional law books, are useful only for teaching those two areas of the law and, in any event, are often overly simplistic and "un-lawyerlike" in their presentation. There did not seem to be anything in between. I also heard complaints from foreign law graduates studying for an advanced law degree at U.S. law schools. They often want to get an overview of U.S. law, but the one year they are in residence at their U.S. law school does not afford them the time to take a sufficient variety of courses to get a broad exposure to U.S. law. This is especially so if they fill the larger part of their schedule with courses in their speciality area.

The second frustration that led me to attempt this project comes from the opposite perspective — my difficulties as a *student* of foreign law trying to learn about other legal systems. Books on other countries' systems written for foreign audiences tend to deal in generalities that make it hard to picture how the system actually operates and what the principal legal concepts are. At the same time, many such books are quick to give the author's own impressions of the differences in systems based on those generalities, without giving sufficient detail to allow me, as the reader, to decide for myself how that system fits into my own frame of reference.

Accordingly, my approach in this book has been to try to provide a sufficiently detailed summary of the principal features of the law and the operation of the legal system in the United States to allow readers to get a real "feel" for it and to make their own judgments. I have largely dispensed with my own comparative observations, though there are some. When U.S. institutions or laws have been the subject of criticisms, I have sought to provide an outline of both sides of the question. To aid readers who wish to find out even more about particular areas of the law, I have put in many citations to original materials, particularly cases and statutes, and to books and articles that will provide more detailed information. The Reader's Guide and Bibliographic Introduction that follows this Preface generally explains the books and cases cited and makes some general comments on the organization of the book. It should help in reading and using the book.

Acknowledgments During this project, I have come to realize how understated acknowledgments in the preface of a book are. I simply could not have written this book without the interest and assistance of my colleagues and friends. Primary among those who provided assistance on various chapters were G. Thomas Munsterman, Martin Kriegel, Kathryn Heidt, Marcia Major, Leroy Lamborn, Robert Sedler, Jonathan Weinberg, Janet Findlater, George Feldman, Steven Calkins, Joseph Grano, Frederica Lombard, Suellyn Scarnecchia, Kingsley Brown, Stephen Schulman, Diana Pratt, Edward Wise, Peter Henning, Vincent Wellman, Alan Schenk, Michael Sinclair, John Dolan, Margaret Mahoney, Peter Bal, Helen Kabatova and Hans Pijls. Prominent among the student assistants who worked on this project were Damon Whitmore, Mary Kosmalski, Kathy Murphy, Tom Bishoff, David Zack, and Dmitri Shevtsov. Editorial assistance was provided by Susan Hartman, Marilyn Preston, Frank DeMita and Nancy Shafer. Diagrams are by Laura Kootsillas. I also owe a special word of thanks to Tom Berreman, now retired from West Publishing, who maintained his interest in this project through several interruptions and difficulties.

I would also like to thank my Dutch and other European Erasmus Program students at the University of Utrecht for inspiring me to write this book and then suffering through early editions. Similarly exposed to a prior temporary edition were my foreign lawyer LL.M. students in my class at the University of Michigan Law School, who provided constructive feedback. Several Russian judges and lawyers were also exposed to previous versions of some chapters in a temporary Russian edition produced for the Federal Judicial Center and the American Bar Association's Central and East-European Law Initiative. In addition, I tried out lecture forerunners of several chapters on Russian law students at the law department of Moscow State Institute for International Relations, at the Moscow Law Institute and at the Russian State Humanities University, where I lectured while I was on a Fulbright teaching fellowship in Moscow in 1991.

I have written in several areas of law in which I am not a specialist. The noted comparativists Zweigert and Kötz have observed how, when non-specialists venture into unfamiliar territory, certain dangers lurk — "natives" with sharp arrows in the thickets on whose turf I am treading. But if my fellow "non-native" friends here and abroad get something worthwhile from this work, it will have been worth it.

March, 1995   William Burnham

PREFACE TO THE SECOND EDITION

The second edition has undergone a thorough up-dating in all areas and considerable expansion in many, particularly those on private law subjects. Case law is current through the United States Supreme Court's 1997-98 term and partially into the 1998-99 term.

Major Additions There were four major additions to the text: (1) a section on environmental law, including toxic substance clean-ups, federal environmental impact statements and the Endangered Species Act, added to the business law chapter; (2) expanded treatment of Article 2 of the Uniform Commercial Code and federal and state consumer protection laws, including Truth in Lending, credit reporting, bill collection practices and Federal Trade Commission rules, reflected in a change of name of the contracts chapter to "Contracts and Commercial Law"; (3) a section on intellectual property — copyright, patents and trademarks — added to the property chapter; and (4) a new chapter on tax law, added as Chapter XVI.

Other Additions and Changes Other additions and changes of note are the following: in constitutional law, updating the "new federalism" balance that has been struck by Supreme Court cases in the last two terms and inclusion of the latest cases on civil liberties; in business law, adding the new federal legislative changes regulating stockholder derivative actions, and expanding treatment of limited liability companies (LLCs), in light of their continued growth and approval by tax authorities; in torts, including discussions of the latest cases from the Supreme Court regarding constitutional limits on punitive damages, and more extended treatment of strict liability, including contributions of the Third Restatement of Torts on Product Liability; in criminal law, expanding coverage of duress, necessity and entrapment, adding new material on the federal Racketeer-Influenced and Corrupt Organizations (RICO) law, corporate criminal liability and "white collar" crime, and more detail on strict liability offenses, including a discussion of corporate criminal liability; in family law, adding sections on adoption of children, guardianships over and civil commitment of the mentally ill and retarded, and updating family law cases dealing with advances in reproductive technology.

Stylistic Changes General editorial changes have been made, as well. Some sections have been shortened or rewritten to make them more readable. Case citations and examples have been expanded to better illustrate the concepts being discussed.

Index The index has been expanded considerably to make the book easier to use as a reference book on the law. Additional multiple finding aids have been added and every effort has been made to cover not just topical, but also conceptual entries. In addition, many of the additions are of a type that permit the book to be used as a legal "dictionary." There are numerous new separate entries of legal terms, concepts, institutions and doctrines with cites to the pages on which the entry is defined. In addition, when there is more than one subentry under an entry, the "defined" subentry is listed first.

Internet Sources Since the first edition was published, the availability of primary legal sources on the Internet has expanded considerably. Because many readers, both foreign and domestic, do not have access to full and up-to-date collections of

U.S. law books in their local libraries, cites to sources for U.S. legal materials on the Internet have been added in Appendix B, in addition to updated and electronic access information on the major publishers of printed legal materials.

A New Audience? As stated in the original preface, this book is primarily for foreign law students and lawyers, U.S. undergraduate college students, and the general U.S. reading public. However, law students *in the U.S.* have told me that they have used the book to give them "the big picture" of the law, as a general reference and as an information source for deciding what elective courses to take. Recent graduates have told me that they find it to be a useful compendium of "what you would have learned in law school had you been paying attention." The most commented-on use is by first-year law students who come to law school with an undergraduate, family or personal background devoid of law and lawyers. They find that the book gives them an essential context for better handling the rigors and complete immersion of the first year.

Acknowledgments Providing assistance in helping me understand the intricacies of environmental law — yet another area in which I am not an expert — were Professors Robert H. Abrams, Zygmunt Plater and Kathryn Heidt. New colleagues who have been extraordinarily helpful are Eric Kades, Peter Henning, Dennis Devaney and Katherine White. John Dolan, an old colleagues whom I was unable to corner for the first edition, graciously assisted on the expanded commercial law sections of the second. And Tom Munsterman of the National Center for State Courts was his usual helpful self in updating materials on state courts and pointing out new trends related to jury trials. Shela Khan worked tirelessly to track down updates of various materials, legal and non-legal, for the second edition. My secretary, Nancy Shafer, provided useful editing help and kept me organized.

The assistance of Martin Kriegel, J.D., LL.M., was absolutely essential in putting together the tax chapter. In addition, he took a keen interest in the rest of the book and helped in clarifying my thinking in many other areas.

I would also like to thank the participants and administrators of various programs and institutions that have invited me to teach using the book. Among them are law students in my classes at the Universities of Utrecht and Maastricht in the Netherlands, foreign lawyers and law-students participating in the Orientation in American Law and Orientation in American Business Law held each summer in Ann Arbor by the American Institute of Legal Education, and several groups of young law teachers from Russia, Ukraine, Byelorus, Georgia, Moldova, Armenia, Azerbaijan Kazakstan, Uzbekistan, Tajikistan, Turkmenistan and Kirgizia whom I taught in programs sponsored by the Institute for Constitutional and Legislative Policy in Budapest (COLPI). Zaza Namoradze of COLPI has been particularly helpful in arranging these latter training sessions.

I welcome comments on any aspect of this book. Please address them to me at Wayne State University Law School, 468 West Ferry Mall, Detroit, Michigan 48202; william.burnham@wayne.edu; 313-577-3928 (voice) or 313-577-2620 (fax).

April 19, 1999   William Burnham
Detroit, Michigan

READER'S GUIDE AND BIBLIOGRAPHIC INTRODUCTION

Organization of Chapters   The chapters are arranged in an order that makes sense to me. But readers or teachers may wish to use a different order. In general, there is no great disadvantage to doing so. In most situations where knowledge from an earlier chapter is needed, there are references to the appropriate pages.

In general, the organization of the book is as follows. Chapters I through VI deal with matters of constitutional, administrative and judicial structure of the legal system and general legal methodology, including caselaw method, the adversary system of adjudication and legal education and the legal profession. Chapters VII and VIII deal with procedural law in civil and criminal cases. Chapter IX, on constitutional law, starts the remainder of the book's focus on substantive law topics. Chapters X through XV cover most of the major substantive private law areas, plus criminal law.

Within chapters, organization varies. But I have tried to place the more difficult material at the end of each chapter. A teacher who wishes to spare students some of these complexities could have them stop at the appropriate point and go on to the next chapter.

Citations to Cases and Other Authorities   There are many citations to original sources in this book. These citations should facilitate the use of this book as a reference. However, readers who plan to use it in this way should make sure that they consult the original sources cited. A table of case citations is provided in Appendix C.[1]

In most instances where a case is cited in this book, the facts of the case will either be apparent from the text or will be set out in a parenthetical summary following the citation in the footnote. Part of the reason for citing cases is because caselaw is an important source of law in a common law system. But even aside from their precedential value, the fact situations of cases serve as concrete illustrations of how the legal concepts, doctrines or laws discussed in the text are applied in practice. In addition, judicial opinions are often helpful for reference purposes because they tend to be encyclopedic, at least in important cases. In such cases, the reader can often find useful citations to more general caselaw, law review articles and treatises.

It is essential that foreign law students or lawyers planning to study in the United States look up and read a few of the principal cases cited here since much of their time studying in U.S. law schools will be taken up by reading and analyzing appellate opinions in preparation for class. Moreover, cases give one a real sense of what kinds of legal disputes arise in the United States and how they arise. I would strongly urge even the casual reader to look up a case that seems interesting from the description in the text and read it.

I would also suggest that teachers using this book edit, copy and hand out one or two cases in each subject matter area for students to read after they have had an overview from the narrative description of the law in the book. Especially useful would be recent cases that have come out since the book was published, especially a case that takes the law in a new direction. Another way to work cases in is to give

---

1   Omitted from citations in both the book and the table of cases is any denial of review of the case by a higher court, including denials of certiorari by the U.S. Supreme Court.

students or groups of students find and read a particular case in the library and report to the class on their impressions of it.

Case Citation Form Information on citation form and legal research is set out last section of Chapter II.[2] However, a few preliminary comments should be made here to facilitate reading. The basic citation form for a case decision is in the following: case name, volume number, abbreviated reporter name, page number where the case begins, and then the court and year of the decision in parentheses. For example, the case set out in the Appendix on page A1 would be cited as *Hoffman v. Jones*, 280 So.2d 431 (Fla. 1973). This indicates that it is found in volume 280 of West's Southern Reporter, 2d Series, starting on page 431, and that it is a 1973 decision of the Florida Supreme Court. Had the case been from the Florida Court of Appeals, the intermediate appellate court in that state, the abbreviation "Fla.App." would have appeared in the parentheses with the year. United States Supreme Court cases are reported in an official United States Reports (U.S.), so any case with U.S. as the reporter citation is the U.S. Supreme Court. Lower federal court cases are published in the Federal Reporter (F.2d or F.3d) and Federal Supplement (F.Supp. or F.Supp.2d).

States often publish official state reporters. However, the official citations are not included because foreign law libraries and general libraries in the United States are more likely to have the West regional reporters than the official state reporters. The official reporter citation is used for United States Supreme Court Reports since this is the almost universal practice among lawyers and judges. However, since libraries often have only the unofficial commercial reporters of United States Supreme Court cases, parallel citations are set out in the table of cases in Appendix C.

Appendix A reproduces a sample common law case decision and the U.S. Constitution. Following them are diagrams of the structure of the federal government, the court system and the floor plan of a trial courtroom.

Books Cited The first footnote or so in each chapter or section of this book will contain references to more specialized books on that particular topic. Most of these books are from the "big five" in the educational legal publishing business: West Group, Aspen Law and Business (formerly the law book division of Little, Brown & Co.), Foundation Press, Matthew Bender & Co. and the Lexis Law Publishing. Appendix B sets out the full addresses, Web pages and other means of contacting these publishers. Consequently, when a book published by any of these five is cited in the text, only the name of the publisher appears. For other books cited, if they are in print or likely to be available in general libraries, I have included the name of the publisher and place of publication to aid in finding the book.

I have limited books citations to those likely to be useful to the foreign law-trained or U.S. non-law-trained reader. Extended multi-volume treatises exist in most of the subject-matter areas of law addressed in this book, but these will usually tell readers more than they ever wanted to know. "Casebooks," sometimes called "cases and materials," are by far the most numerous educational publications of legal publishers and there is at least one for every area of the law discussed here. But casebooks are designed to be used by law students taking a course on the subject. As the title implies, casebooks are primarily full of cases. The cases are then followed

---

2 *See* pp. 75-78.

by a series of questions which, in the traditional style of such books, are largely unanswerable and designed primarily to stimulate classroom discussion. For the non-specialist reader, casebooks are an unnecessarily difficult and frustrating way to gain an overview of an area of law.[3]

For these reasons, I generally cite two classes of books that are likely to be helpful: (1) one-volume treatises and (2) law student aids. The one-volume treatises are written by prominent scholars in the given area of law and are the authors' attempts at a single-volume narrative treatment of the subject matter area. Treatises of this type are used by law students to review for an examination in a course or for clarification while a course is being taught. They are also used by teachers and practicing lawyers as a departure point for research in an area of law with which they are not familiar. Typically treatises have extensive citations to cases and other authorities for further information and research. The paradigm treatise of this type is West Group's "Hornbook Series," though the other law publishers have some as well.[4] Law student aids take various forms: the "Nutshell Series" and "Black Letter Law Series" published by West Group; "Examples and Explanations" published by Aspen; and the "Understanding the Law" series published by Matthew Bender. Nutshells are intended to condense an entire law school course into a small pocket-sized paperback usually consisting of less than 300 pages. The Black Letter Series does much the same thing in a larger outline format. "Examples and Explanations" contain just that, with some introductory text. The "Understanding the Law" series is somewhere between a Nutshell or Outline and a one-volume treatise.

There is great variation in the quality of writing and clarity of all the books mentioned, and in their suitability for the nonspecialist reader. Single-volume treatises and student aids often assume too much knowledge on the part of the lay reader. This is because these books are at least partly intended for review reading for a course the intended law-student reader has just finished. Another shortcoming of some student aids, particularly outlines, is that they do not provide regular citations to cases or statutes. This can make them frustrating if the reader wants to clarify some generalization about the law by looking at the appropriate caselaw or statute. The "examples and explanations" approach has the benefit of giving the reader both textual material and concrete problems to work through to learn basic concepts and variations on them. However, these books are often not as comprehensive as some other sources since they must limit themselves to those areas of the law that can be approached *via* the problem method. They are also designed for supplemental reading in a course or for review and, like nutshells and outlines, may be too detailed and assume too much knowledge. "Understanding the Law" texts are written in narrative form. They are generally not as detailed and comprehensive as hornbooks, though they are more so than nutshells or outlines.

Introductory multi-volume works not cited in this book may be found in the library. Three encyclopedias are WEST'S ENCYCLOPEDIA OF AMERICAN LAW (West, 12 vols., 1998); CORPUS JURIS SECUNDUM (West, 101 vols., updated with supplements); and AMERICAN JURISPRUDENCE, 2D (Lawyers Co-op, New York, updated with supplements). The first of the three is designed for the lay reader, while the second two are used by

---

3   Law school classes and the use of casebooks are explained in Chapter IV, pp. 136-137.
4   For the origin of the term "hornbook," *see* Chapter II, p. 77 note 178.

some lawyers as a departure point for research.

Access to U.S. Legal Materials on the Internet   Since the first edition of this book was published, there has been sustained growth in the amount of U.S. legal materials that are available on the Internet. For this reason, the reader will find in Appendix B, along with the contact information about legal publishers, the more prominent Web Sites for obtaining legal materials. A major improvement on the Web has been the recent introduction of search engines for doing legal research, such as Findlaw, that allow the researcher to do key word searches. While Internet sources are important, they are limited. The most important limitation is that they contain only the most recent case law. Only rarely finds court decisions before 1990. Statutes are available only from selected states. And, even if the material one seeks is available, there is no guarantee that it is current. As a result, for any kind of comprehensive research, it is still necessary to gain access to a U.S. law collection in a library or to use the Westlaw or Lexis computerized libraries of materials.[5]

Unfamiliar Terminology   There is no glossary of terms in this book as such. However, the index is designed in part to be used as one. It has the usual topical listing of subjects and terms discussed. However, there are separate alphabetized entries for important legal terms and concepts used, as well as identification of the names of agencies whose names are commonly abbreviated. If the reader encounters an unfamiliar term, the index can be consulted and an explanation is provided under the "defined" entry. To assist in finding the term, specialized terms are placed in quotation marks the first time they are used. Where there are multiple entries under a main heading, "defined" appears as the first entry.

An alternative solution is to keep handy one of the many excellent legal dictionaries that have been published over the years. The traditional comprehensive work is BLACK'S LAW DICTIONARY, 6TH ED. (West 1990). More succinct dictionaries are West's student edition of Black's, BLACK'S LAW DICTIONARY, ABRIDGED 6TH ED. (West 1991), MELLINKOFF'S DICTIONARY OF AMERICAN LEGAL USAGE (West 1992), BRYAN A. GARNER, A DICTIONARY OF MODERN LEGAL USAGE (Oxford U. Press, N.Y. 1987) and ORAN'S DICTIONARY OF THE LAW, 2D ED. (Delmar Publishing 1991). There are several smaller and different legal dictionaries, including a "pocket" version of Black's. In addition, the West Legal Directory provides an electronic version of Oran's on the Web in the form of a free term search service at www.wld.com/client/clawinfo/orans.asp.

---

5   Westlaw and Nexis are explained in Chapter II, *infra* p. 75. While these services are available on the Internet as well, one must subscribe to them in order to use them.

SUMMARY OF CONTENTS

TABLE OF CONTENTS

CHAPTER I

HISTORY AND GOVERNMENTAL STRUCTURE

It is impossible to understand the legal system of the United States without understanding its structure of government. Consequently, it is appropriate to begin this book with that topic.

The governmental structure was established by the Constitution of 1789. The two characteristics of that structure that most directly affect the legal system are "separation of powers" and "federalism." Separation of powers principles assure that none of the three branches of federal government — legislative, executive or judicial — oversteps the bounds of its proper constitutional role and usurps power belonging to the others. We will see later in this chapter that the primary effect on the *legal system* that separation of powers has is on the role of the federal courts.

Federalism means that there are two levels of government in the country, federal and state. In the version of federalism found in the United States, the 50 states of the United States have a great deal of independence and power. In a real sense, the United States is a country of 51 different governments — 50 states and the federal government. Each of these governments has its own legal system. Indeed, the title of this book is misleading to the extent that it suggests that there is a *single* "legal system of the United States." It would be more accurate to call it an introduction to "the legal *systems* of the United States."

We will first discuss briefly the historical circumstances that led to the adoption of the Constitution and the reasons why the Framers of that document chose the governmental structure they did.[1] Then we will trace the development of the constitutional structure by amendment, governmental practices and court cases since 1789. In reviewing trends and developments since 1789, we will focus first on separation powers and then on the states and federalism. Finally, there will be an overview of the impact of the governmental structure on the legal system.

A. Some Constitutional History

1. Independence From Colonial Rule and Efforts to Achieve Union

The country started out as 13 colonies of Great Britain. During the period 1760-1775, there was much strife and then actual violent clashes between British colonial authorities and the dissatisfied American colonists over a variety of taxation measures and other grievances against colonial rulers.

The dissident colonists identified strongly with their own colony and concentrated on resistance to British authority at the local level. However, they made an effort in 1774 to take collective action in Philadelphia at the "First Continental Congress." In response to measures adopted at this Congress, King George III sent troops and the American War of Independence, also called the American Revolution, began in 1775.[2]

---

1   It is traditional to refer to the Constitution's authors as "the Framers."
2   For a short summary of the events of this time, *see* JAMES CURRY, RICHARD B. RILEY & RICHARD M. BATTISTONI, CONSTITUTIONAL GOVERNMENT: THE AMERICAN EXPERIENCE 41-54 (West 1988).

By July of 1776, the Second Continental Congress was ready to adopt unanimously a "Declaration of Independence," which it did on July 4, 1776.[3] Also adopted was a resolution that a "plan of confederation be prepared and transmitted to the respective colonies for their consideration." In June 1776, a committee was appointed to draft what would later become the Articles of Confederation. After considerable debate, the states agreed to the Articles of Confederation, which were finally ratified by all the states in 1781.

2. The Articles of Confederation

Governmental Structure Under the Articles   The Articles of Confederation were doomed from the start as a viable blueprint for governing the country. Indeed, no real national government was provided for — only a Congress of representatives from the states. When the Congress was not in session, executive power was to be exercised by committees set up by the Congress. Moreover, though the Articles granted several powers to Congress, that body could act in most important matters only on the agreement of 9 of the 13 states. Unanimous approval was needed to amend the Articles themselves. States agreed in the Articles to abide by decisions of the Congress, but Congress was given no power to enforce its decisions. It could only request that states comply. The Articles did not give Congress the power to regulate commerce or to tax, undoubtedly as a result of the experience of the colonists with the British Parliament's abuse of those powers.

Overall, the Articles established a confederation of separate states — a "firm league of friendship" in which "[e]ach State retains its sovereignty, freedom and independence, and every power, jurisdiction and right, which is not by this confederation expressly delegated to the United States . . . ."[4] As George Washington once remarked, the Articles of Confederation bound the states together with a "rope of sand."

Sources of Disharmony Among the States   Underlying the difficulties with the Articles were differences among the inhabitants of the states over philosophy and social and economic structure, as well as territorial disputes. These differences and disputes pre-dated the Revolution, but had been temporarily forgotten for the duration of the war. They quickly resurfaced once the common enemy of the British crown was defeated. The south was largely rural and agricultural; both economic and social life revolved around large plantations run with slave labor. The northernmost states, called New England, were more oriented toward manufacturing and milling, fishing, shipbuilding, and overseas trade. These kinds of activities led to the creation of urban centers, which were the focus of social and economic life. The middle states engaged in many of the same activities as did New England, but had agricultural activity as well. However, farming was carried out generally on smaller farms without slave labor.

As a direct result of the inadequacies of the Articles, things deteriorated quickly after the end of the War of Independence. Congress negotiated and approved a treaty with Britain in 1784 ending the war, but many states ignored its provisions and Congress could do nothing to force them to honor the treaty. State interference

---

[3] This Declaration occupies an important place in political history of the United States and expresses the enlightened political theory of the time: a belief in "natural rights" of human beings, the right of people to throw off an oppressive government, the right of citizens to be free to develop their talents and resources — the right to the "pursuit of happiness" in the document's own words — and other important ideas. .

[4] Articles of Confederation, Art. II.

provided Britain with a justification for refusing to carry out many of its obligations under the treaty. More important, it caused friendly foreign countries, which could have provided needed trade and other assistance, to decline to enter into treaties with the largely ineffective national government. Domestically, there was no effective central regulator of disputes about interstate commerce, so trade wars erupted between states. The resulting prohibitively high tariff barriers erected by states caused a sharp drop in trade at a particularly difficult time. States also refused to provide promised funding for the national government. With the army near mutiny because it had not been paid, Congress sought to amend the Articles to allow it to impose a 5% tariff on foreign imports, but the opposition of one state (Rhode Island, the smallest of the 13 states) was sufficient to defeat that proposal.

During the time of the Articles, some states sought to mediate disputes by meeting in conferences, and it was out of one such conference that the idea for a new charter of government emerged. James Madison, a Virginia delegate to a conference on navigation on interstate rivers suggested that the delegates at that conference call for a convention in Philadelphia in 1787 to discuss the question. All states but Rhode Island sent delegations.[5]

3. The Constitutional Convention

The delegates to the convention were convinced that a stronger national government was necessary, but they sharply disagreed on just how strong it should be. They had learned the vices of *insufficient* governmental power from their experience with the Articles of Confederation. But they also had clear memories of the vices of too much governmental power from their struggles against the Crown. One group of delegates favored a strong national government capable of rising above regional differences. Others mistrusted strong central control and argued against any greater encroachment on the powers of the states than was minimally necessary to avoid the problems that had arisen under the Articles of Confederation. The "national-ists" ironically and, in a stroke of political genius, chose to be called "Federalists." The "states' rights" delegates, who ultimately opposed the ratification of the constitution as written by the Convention, inherited the label "Anti-Federalists."

For the most part, the Federalists' views prevailed at the 1787 convention. However, as will be seen, significant compromises had to be made to accommodate states' rights advocates. The debates among the delegates were repeated during the ratification process at ratification conventions in the states. Despite substantial initial opposition, the Constitution was ratified and the new government commenced on March 4, 1789.[6]

---

5 James Madison (1751-1836) is considered the "father" of the Constitution (a title he himself rejected), because he played a pivotal role in drafting the 1789 Constitution. His notes, taken at the convention, are the primary source of information about the proceedings at the convention. In addition, Madison, Alexander Hamilton and John Jay authored a series of essays, called collectively *The Federalist Papers*, arguing in favor of ratification of the Constitution. *See* THE FEDERALIST (Jacob E. Cooke, ed., Wesleyan U. Press, Middletown, Conn. 1961). *The Federalist Papers* are a classic in the political literature of the United States and are regularly used even today by the Supreme Court as a guide to interpreting the Constitution. After ratification of the Constitution, Madison became a member of Congress and in 1808 was elected the fourth President of the United States.

6 For an in-depth discussion of the circumstances surrounding the framing and ratification of the Constitution with excerpts from the original sources and special attention paid to the Constitution's intellectual origins, *see* DANIEL FARBER AND SUSANNA SHERRY, A HISTORY OF THE AMERICAN CONSTITUTION (West 1990). *See also* MAX FARRAND, THE FRAMING OF THE CONSTITUTION OF THE UNITED STATES (Yale U. Press 1913). For a collection of documents related to the convention, *see* THE RECORDS OF THE FEDERAL CONVENTION OF 1787 (Max Farrand, ed., Yale U. Press 1913). The debates in the states are collected in JONATHAN ELLIOT,

4. Ratification of the Bill of Rights

A large part of the reason the Anti-Federalists and others opposed the Constitution was because it did not contain a list of individual rights that citizens would have against the new stronger central government. Bills of Rights were a feature of many state constitutions. The Federalists resisted discussing the issue, believing that the most important goal was to establish a basic structure for governing the country as quickly as possible. They urged proponents of a Bill of Rights to wait until the Constitution was ratified and to add such a Bill by way of amendment — a measure the Federalists agreed to support. The depth of feeling in favor of a Bill of Rights was demonstrated by the fact that 5 of the 13 states submitted demands for a Bill of Rights along with their ratifications. James Madison, one of the Federalists who argued for delaying the question until ratification, drafted a Bill of Rights, which became the first 10 amendments to the Constitution when it was ratified by the people in 1791, shortly after being proposed.

Except for the 10th Amendment, the guarantees of the Bill of Rights relate only indirectly to the structure of government. Consequently, discussion of them is delayed until the later chapters on constitutional rights.[7]

B. The Governmental Structure Provided for in the 1789 Constitution

The Constitution has six substantive articles.[8] The most important in terms of governmental structure are Articles I, II and III, which constitute the legislative, executive and judicial branches of government. Article IV contains miscellaneous provisions that relate mainly to the states and their relationship to each other. Article V sets out the complicated and difficult process needed to amend the Constitution. Article VI sets out miscellaneous provisions, the most important of which declares the supremacy of federal over state law.

1. Legislative Power

"Enumerated" Powers of Congress Article I vests "[a]ll legislative Powers herein" in the Congress and later (in §8) lists those powers. This list of powers was a compromise resulting from one of the major differences of opinion at the convention. The Virginia delegation proposed — in direct response to the problems that had been experienced under the Articles of Confederation — that Congress be given the power "to legislate in all cases to which the separate states are incompetent, or in which the harmony of the United States may be interrupted by the exercise of individual legislation."[9] However, other delegates objected that this gave too much power to Congress. The final compromise language listed particular subject-matter areas in which it was *anticipated* that individual state legislation would be disruptive of the "harmony of the United States." Because the powers are set out individually in a list, they are often referred to as Congress's "enumerated powers."

The major powers listed in §8 are those one would expect a national government to have: the powers to issue money, to establish a postal system, to create federal courts, to raise an army and navy, to declare war, to collect taxes and spend money

---

THE DEBATES OF THE SEVERAL STATE CONVENTIONS ON THE ADOPTION OF THE FEDERAL CONSTITUTION (J.B. Lippincott Co. 1836).

7 *See* Chapter VIII, pp. 270-303 (4th, 5th, 6th and 8th Amendments as constitutional requirements in criminal procedure) and Chapter IX, pp. 343-365 (1st Amendment freedoms).

8 A copy of the Constitution is set out in the Appendix, pp. A14-A29.

9 *Quoted in* JOHN E. NOWAK & RONALD D. ROTUNDA, CONSTITUTIONAL LAW, 5TH ED. 119 (West 1995).

for the general welfare, and the like. As it has developed, the most important of the powers granted is the one empowering Congress to regulate interstate commerce.[10]

Compromise on Representation   Another major disagreement among the Framers arose over the composition and the method of selection of the national legislature provided for under Article I. The Federalists wanted representation in the legislature based on population, rather than on equal state representation. This would prevent states representing a minority of the population from blocking national legislation, as had happened under the Articles of Confederation. However, strong opposition from the smaller states forced the Framers to compromise. A dual system of representation in a bicameral or two-chamber Congress was agreed to. One "house," the House of Representatives, would have proportional representation based on population, while the other house, the Senate, would have equal representation from each state. To assure that the House of Representatives would better reflect the prevailing sentiment of the voters, its members, called "representatives" or simply "members of Congress," were made subject to re-election every 2 years. Senators would be elected to 6-year terms so as to provide some stability. Both houses would have to agree to legislation before it could become law.

In accordance with this system, today there are 100 Senators (two from each of 50 states) and 435 members of the House of Representatives representing the residents of as many districts throughout the country. The 435 House seats are divided among the states based on total population (250,000,000 in 1990), but allowing every state a minimum of one representative. The average size of districts is approximately 570,000 residents. Accordingly, California has 52 representatives, Michigan has 16 and Wyoming (with a population of total of only 435,588) has only one.

Compromise on Slavery   In the southern states, an agricultural economy based on slavery had developed and the question of slavery came up several times at the convention. Slavery was not abolished by the Constitution nor was Congress given the power to abolish it. Despite viewing slaves as property rather than human beings, southern delegates insisted that they be counted the same as citizens in determining the number of representatives in Congress. A compromise was reached to count slaves as three-fifths of a free person.[11] Southerners also insisted on a provision requiring the return of escaped slaves from other states.[12] However, many of the Framers hoped that slavery would eventually be abolished and, in another compromise, Congress was authorized to outlaw further *importation* of slaves after the year 1808.[13]

Assuring the Supremacy of Federal Law Another area of disagreement that arose during discussions of the legislative power was how to deal with conflicts between federal legislation and state law. Under the Articles of Confederation serious problems had arisen when states simply ignored federal laws and treaties which they did not like. Originally, Madison's plan called for a veto procedure whereby Congress could pass resolutions that would annul the effect of particular state laws. Others

---

10 In §9 and §10, the Framers listed miscellaneous prohibitions. Most are of little consequence today except prohibitions on retroactive or *ex post facto* criminal laws and laws retroactively "impairing the Obligation of Contracts."

11 Art. I §2 cl. 3.

12 Art. IV §2 cl. 3.

13 Art. I §9. Congress duly passed such a prohibition. The embarrassment of some of the Framers about slavery is reflected in the fact that the Constitution never uses the words "slavery" or "slaves," euphemistically referring to slaves as "other Persons" and "Person held to Service or Labor in one State."

argued that this means of assuring federal supremacy would be too direct an affront to the states and unwieldy. The Framers settled upon a clause, set out in Article VI, which is referred to as the "supremacy clause":

> This Constitution and the Laws of the United States which shall be made in Pursuance thereof; and all Treaties made, or which shall be made, under the Authority of the United States, shall be the supreme Law of the Land; and Judges in every State shall be bound thereby, any Thing in the Constitution or Laws of any State to the Contrary notwithstanding.[14]

Congress's "Power of the Purse" A power of Congress about which the Framers did not disagree was the "power of the purse." They resolved that the sole power to decide whether and to what extent to tax and fund governmental programs must be lodged in Congress.[15] Further, Article I gives the sole power to originate revenue bills to the House of Representatives, the house most directly representative of the people.[16] This clause assured that there would be "no taxation without representation" — a major complaint about British colonial taxes. In addition, the "power of the purse" would serve as a democratic curb on presidential excesses and adventures, since both would likely need funding. The Framers also gave Congress the ultimate check on executive and judicial power — the power of impeachment and removal from office of any "civil Officers of the United States," including the President and any federal judge.[17]

2. Executive Power

There was little in the Articles of Confederation to use as a departure point for discussion of the executive branch, since the Articles did not provide for an executive at all. The language of Article II of the Constitution is not much more help in determining the structure and powers of the executive. Most of Article II is taken up by qualifications for the office of President and the complicated method of election.[18]

The President as Chief Executive Article II §1 does declare generally that "[t]he executive Power shall be vested in a President of the United States of America," and §3 imposes on the President the duty "to take Care that the Laws be faithfully executed." Article II §3 also gives the President the power, with the "Advice and Consent" of the Senate, to appoint ambassadors, judges, "public Ministers and Consuls" and "all other Officers of the United States" who staff the executive branch of government. Originally the Framers intended to specify in the Constitution various departments of the executive branch, but they changed their minds and decided to leave that to Congress to accomplish by statute. Currently, Congress has created fourteen departments: Agriculture, Commerce, Education, Energy, Housing and Urban Development, Interior, Labor, State, Defense, Transportation, Treasury, Justice, Veterans Affairs and Health and Human Services. The heads of these departments are called "secretaries"

---

14 Art. VI cl. 2.

15 Art. I §8 cl. 1.

16 Art. II §7 cl. 2.

17 Art. II §4.

18 Under this method, instead of direct election by popular vote, "electors" from each state are chosen by vote of the people of that state and those electors then meet and elect the President. The original idea was that the electors could exercise some independent judgment when they voted as a check on extremism or bad judgment of the populace, but the practice has grown up that the presidential candidate who wins the popular vote in a state automatically wins the votes of all the electors from that state.

and they are appointed by the President with the advice and consent of the Senate. Collectively, they are referred to as the President's "cabinet."[19]

Veto Power of the President   One of the most important and most specific powers of the President, the power to veto legislation, is set out in Article I §7, not Article II.   In the discussions over the shape of the powers to be accorded the executive branch, the Framers divided themselves into two camps.   Some feared tyranny from a too-powerful executive.   Others feared that, without a powerful executive to counterbalance Congress, there would be *legislative* tyranny, which had happened already with some state legislatures. It was the latter group whose ideas prevailed. The delegates determined that there should be a single President, elected independently of the Congress for 4-year terms, who would have limited veto power over legislation. Similar to the veto power enjoyed by governors in many states, the President could veto legislation, but that veto could be overridden by a two-thirds majority vote of the entire Congress.[20]

The presence of a President with his own direct electoral mandate and veto power makes the U.S. system different from some parliamentary systems. A stalemate between the chief executive officer and the chief legislative body cannot be resolved by a vote of "no confidence" by the legislature, the resignation of the government and a new election. Under the system provided for in the Constitution, an adamant President exercising his veto power liberally against an equally stubborn Congress unable to muster a two-thirds majority could in many instances result in stalemate, called "gridlock." Because of this potential, there is a great need for cooperation between Congress and the President.[21]

Presidential Power in Foreign Affairs   The powers granted the President by Article II are the most specific in the area of foreign affairs. The President has the power to "receive Ambassadors and other public Ministers" (and thus the power to choose whether to recognize foreign governments) and to make treaties with Senate concurrence.[22] The President is also made "Commander in Chief" of the armed forces.[23] The relative specificity of duties in the area of foreign affairs and the fact that the President is head of state show that, at least in foreign affairs, the President has broad authority. An 1816 statement by the Senate Committee on Foreign Relations observed that "[t]he President is the Constitutional representative of the United States with regard to foreign nations. He manages our concerns with foreign nations." The statement emphasizes that the executive power is particularly appropriate for international relations since "[t]he nature of transactions with foreign nations . . . requires caution and unity of design, and their success frequently depends on secrecy

---

19 A chart showing the organization of federal government and its principal agencies and departments is set out on pp. A30-A31 of the Appendix.

20 Art. I §7 cl. 2-3.

21 The need for cooperation and accommodation has been great in recent years: until the 1992 election, in only 4½ of the last 27 years have federal elections produced a President and a majority of Congress from the same political party. In general, in recent years, Presidents have been Republican, while Democrats controlled the Congress. In 1992, the voters changed this history by electing a Democratic President and a Democratic Congress. But then, just two years later, they voted in a Republican Congress in both houses. Recent research has shown that stalemate has not been a problem and that the common juxtaposition of a Democratic Party-controlled Congress and a Republican President has not stopped major legislation from being passed. *See* DAVID MAYHEW, DIVIDED WE GOVERN (Yale U. Press, New Haven 1991).

22 Art. II §2.

23 Art. II §2.

and dispatch."[24]   However, the Framers provided for a shared responsibility with Congress for foreign policy.   They gave Congress the power to regulate foreign commerce and to decide whether and to what extent to maintain and regulate the armed forces, to ratify treaties, or to fund foreign involvements. In addition, Congress has the sole power to declare war.[25]

3. Judicial Power

The Supreme Court and Lower Federal Courts   Article III provides: "The judicial Power of the United States, shall be vested in one supreme Court, and in such inferior Courts as Congress may from time to time ordain and establish."[26]   The quoted language was the source of a major dispute among the Framers. Some delegates, particularly Madison, felt that the Constitution should *establish* lower federal courts as well as a Supreme Court to assure an effective check on the excesses of the states and the legislative and executive branches of the federal government. Other delegates objected and argued that state courts were sufficient to enforce federal law. They feared that a full complement of federal courts would lead to greater interference in state prerogatives. As a compromise, the Framers agreed that lower federal courts would not be created by the Constitution itself, but that the Constitution would give *Congress* the power to create them if it thought they were needed.

Limited Subject-Matter Jurisdiction of Federal Courts   This mistrust of federal courts also led the Framers to limit the types of cases the federal judiciary could handle. Federal courts were limited to cases of two principal types: controversies between citizens of different states or aliens, and cases "arising under" the federal Constitution and laws. The first type of jurisdiction, called "diversity" jurisdiction, was relatively uncontroversial, undoubtedly because it was thought appropriate to avoid possible bias by state courts against persons from other states. The second category, commonly referred to as "federal question" jurisdiction, was conceded to be appropriate to assure sympathetic and consistent treatment of issues of federal law — but only if Congress thought that necessary. It is some indication of the mistrust of the lower federal courts in federal question cases that Congress gave federal courts diversity jurisdiction almost immediately in 1789, but did not vest them with general federal question jurisdiction until 1875.[27]

The Framers did agree that it was important that the Supreme Court be established in the Constitution itself. However, consistent with separation of powers principles, the Court's[28] appellate jurisdiction was established "with such Exceptions, and under such Regulations as the Congress shall make."[29]

---

24   Quoted in *United States v. Curtiss-Wright Export Corp.*, 299 U.S. 304, 319 (1936).

25   Art. I §8 cl. 3, 11-16. The President's and Congress's powers in foreign affairs are discussed in Chapter IX, pp. 316-318.

26   For a more complete discussion of the jurisdiction of the United States Supreme Court and the lower federal courts, *see* Chapter V, pp. 170-173.

27   Details of federal question and diversity jurisdiction are discussed in Chapter V, pp. 183-185.

28   When referring to the United States Supreme Court in short form, it is common to call it "the Court," with a capital "C," which distinguishes it from references to all other courts.

29   Art. III §2 cl. 2. The meaning of this clause and its possible use as a means of controlling the Supreme Court's power of judicial review are discussed in the chapter on constitutional law, Chapter IX, pp. 314-316. The power of judicial review, which is not explicitly referred to in the Constitution, is also discussed in Chapter IX, pp. 304-309, and later in this chapter where developments since 1789 are considered. *See infra* pp. 9-11.

Judicial Selection Perhaps the most important difference of opinion among the delegates regarding the judicial power was the issue of judicial independence. Judicial independence was thought necessary to assure immunity from pressure from the political branches to decide cases a particular way. Much of the discussion focused on the method of selection and the tenure of federal judges. Many delegates wanted Congress to elect federal judges. Others feared that this would make judges too dependent on Congress's will. Ultimately the question was decided by a compromise that spread the responsibility between the President and the Congress: the President would appoint federal judges for life terms with the advice and consent of the Senate, though they could be removed by the entire Congress through the impeachment process.[30]

C. Separation and Balance of Powers Among the Branches of the Federal Government

Separation of powers and "checks and balances" among the three branches of government were a matter of conscious design. The concept derives from the writings of Baron de Montesquieu and John Locke, with whose works the delegates to the convention were familiar.[31] However, the idea as understood in the United States is less one of strictly *separating* powers than it is of *spreading* power among the branches. As Madison observed, the "necessary partition of power among the several departments" in the Constitution will assure that "its several constituent parts may, by their mutual relations, be the means of keeping each other in their proper places."[32] A contemporary commentator has described the Constitution as establishing "separate institutions sharing power."[33] Consequently, it is more appropriate to understand the scheme of the Constitution as a *balancing* of powers — as it is referred to commonly, a system of "checks and balances."

Since 1789, governmental structure and relationships between components of government have evolved. Supreme Court decisions have caused some changes. Others have resulted from the natural growth of the size of the country and changes in technology and in the types of challenges facing government. We will discuss four major developments affecting the balance and separation of powers: judicial review, greater presidential power, the growth of administrative agencies, and Congress's modern investigatory oversight role.

1. Establishment and Vigorous Exercise of the Power of Judicial Review

As the discussion of the basic provisions of the 1789 Constitution indicates, the Constitution's "checks and balances" provide means for the executive and legislative branches to check the power of the judicial branch, primarily through selection of judges and control of federal court jurisdiction. The constitutional text does not clearly set out what checks the *judicial* branch was to have on *legislative* and *executive* power. Today, we know it is the power of judicial review — the power of the

---

30 Art. III §1 and Art. II §4. The modern impact of the lifetime tenure requirement is discussed in Chapter VI, pp. 212-214. Impeachment of federal judges is discussed in Chapter V, pp. 179-180.

31 *See* MONTESQUIEU, THE SPIRIT OF THE LAWS 151-152 (Nugent trans. 1949)(originally published 1748) ("there can be no liberty where the legislative and executive powers are united in the same person or body of magistrates"); John Locke, SECOND TREATISE ON GOVERNMENT: AN ESSAY CONCERNING THE TRUE ORIGIN, EXTENT AND END OF CIVIL GOVERNMENT (1690). *See generally* M.C.J. VILE, CONSTITUTIONALISM AND THE SEPARATION OF POWERS 64-67 (Oxford U. Press 1967) (discussing Locke's role in developing this theory).

32 *Federalist No. 51, supra* note 5, at 347-348.

33 RICHARD NEUSTADT, PRESIDENTIAL POWER: THE POLITICS OF LEADERSHIP 3 (Wiley & Sons 1960).

Supreme Court to pass on the constitutionality of laws and actions of the other two branches. But such power is not explicitly set out in the Constitution. Instead, it was held to be implicit in the Constitution in the 1803 case of *Marbury v. Madison*.[34]

The Basis for Judicial Review   The Court in *Marbury*, speaking through Chief Justice John Marshall, found judicial review implicit in the nature of a written constitution, in the supremacy clause and in Article III's grant of judicial power. He reasoned as follows. First, the Constitution is *law* and must be followed; indeed, the supremacy clause makes the Constitution the *supreme* law of the land. Second, the judges of the judicial branch, being vested by Article III with the "judicial Power of the United States," have the power to say *what the law is* in cases that come before them. It follows then that judges, in deciding an issue to which both a statute and the Constitution apply, must follow the hierarchy of law set out in the supremacy clause: they must apply the constitutional provision and disregard the statute. *Marbury* involved a federal statute, but the reasoning of *Marbury* was applied to invalidate a state enactment in 1810 in *Fletcher v. Peck*.[35]

Vigorous Exercise of Judicial Review in Modern Times   Judicial review was used sparingly in the first century of the country's history. Today, it is a major force in law and government that profoundly affects the balance of federalism, separation of powers and the relationship between individuals and all levels of government. The greatest surge in judicial review has been since 1953, when Earl Warren became Chief Justice of the United States.

In the 75 years from 1789 until 1864, the Court held only two Acts of Congress unconstitutional. From 1789 to 1953, a period of 164 years, the total climbs to only 76 invalidations. But during the period 1953 to 1995, a period of only 42 years, it held 70 Acts of Congress unconstitutional, or almost two per year. Interestingly enough, though the surge in cases began with the "liberal" Warren Court (1953-1969), the more "conservative" Burger Court (1969-1986) was no less "activist."[36] While the tenures of the two Chief Justices were approximately the same length (16 years), Chief Justice Burger presided over 34 invalidations of federal law, while Chief Justice Warren presided over only 25. The Rehnquist Court (since 1986) has proceeded at an only slightly lower rate of 11 federal laws in 9 years.[37]

A similar trend can be seen with state laws, though the Court has invalidated more state laws than federal laws. In the first 100 years of the existence of the Constitution, the Supreme Court invalidated 79 state laws, while in the second 100

---

34 5 U.S. (1 Cranch.) 137 (1803).

35 10 U.S. (6 Cranch.) 87 (1810) (Georgia state law unconstitutional for violation of prohibition against passing any "Law impairing the Obligation of Contract"). Judicial review is discussed in more detail in Chapter IX, pp. 304-306.

36 Historians generally divide the various eras of Supreme Court history into periods of time defined by the tenures of the fourteen Chief Justices. For a brief, readable excerpt dividing the Court's history into four principal periods, *see* DANIEL A. FARBER, WILLIAM N. ESKRIDGE, JR. & PHILIP P. FRICKEY, CONSTITUTIONAL LAW: THEMES FOR THE CONSTITUTION'S THIRD CENTURY, 2D ED. 7-28 (West 1998). Although the cited book is a casebook, it has more than the average amount of narrative explanation and analysis.

37 These statistics are taken from DAVID M. O'BRIEN, STORM CENTER: THE SUPREME COURT IN AMERICAN POLITICS, 4TH ED. 54 (W.W. Norton 1996). The figures do not include federal laws effectively invalidated by Court decisions because they are identical in all relevant respects to the law involved in a decided case. For example, *Immigration & Naturalization Service v. Chadha*, 462 U.S. 919 (1983), is counted only once despite the fact that the decision effectively meant that 212 other federal statutes with the offending legislative veto provision were unconstitutional. Nor do the statistics include the decisions of the lower federal courts, which also have the power to hold Acts of Congress and state laws unconstitutional and often do so in cases that never reach the Supreme Court level.

years, it invalidated over ten times as many — 865. Of these 865 decisions, 457 or almost half were rendered after 1953. Again, the "conservative" Burger Court accounted for more decisions striking down state laws (192) than did the "liberal-activist" Warren Court (150).

Numbers do not tell the entire story. But it is as true qualitatively as quantitatively that in the modern era, the federal courts — and the Supreme Court in particular — have become a greater influence on the life of the average citizen in the United States than ever before. Constitutional considerations play a major role in many areas of the law. The era since 1953 has been one marked by unprecedented attention to constitutional issues in general and to individual rights and liberties in particular. Some recent decisions of the Court have shown a less accommodating approach to certain individual rights. However, it would take a radical retreat to return to the situation before 1953.[38]

Dangers in Activist Judicial Review While judicial review has generally won praise, it has not always served progressive interests. Some "low points" in legal history demonstrate the dangers of activist judicial review. One low point that will be discussed shortly was the Court's infamous 1857 decision in *Dred Scott v. Sandford*,[39] which held that Congress had no power to end slavery. Thus, the Court did not get off to a very good start in its exercise of judicial review: *Dred Scott* was only the Court's second invalidation of a federal law, the first being *Marbury v. Madison*.[40]

The most recent difficult period for the Court was the period from around 1900 to 1937. During this time, the Court repeatedly used three bases — the due process clause of the 5th and 14th Amendments, a limited view of Congress's power to regulate interstate commerce, and the doctrine against delegation of legislative power — to deny to Congress and the states the power to enact progressive laws regulating business. The Court struck down a New York state law limiting the hours bakers could work per week,[41] federal laws prohibiting child labor,[42] federal laws regulating industry through taxation,[43] federal laws to regulate the economy in the wake of the Great Depression of the 1930s,[44] and a New York law setting minimum wages for women.[45]

Viewing these decisions as a continuing obstacle to further legislation treating the serious social and economic needs of the country, President Franklin Roosevelt and Congress in 1937 considered the possibility of legislation to "pack" the Court, that is, to authorize the President to appoint additional justices to the Court in order to change the balance of power. In the alternative, the President considered the possibility of simply disregarding the Supreme Court's decisions. Neither the "Court-packing" plan

---

38 Supreme Court decisions on individual rights are discussed in Chapter IX, pp. 327-365, and decisions affecting rights of criminal suspects and defendants are discussed in Chapter VIII, pp. 270-303.

39 60 U.S.(19 How.) 393 (1857).

40 *See* discussion *infra* p. 23.

41 *Lochner v. New York*, 198 U.S. 45 (1905).

42 *Hammer v. Dagenhart*, 247 U.S. 251 (1918).

43 *Bailey v. Drexel Furniture Co.*, 259 U.S. 20 (1922) (child labor tax); *Hill v. Wallace*, 259 U.S. 44 (1922) (tax on grain future contracts).

44 *See, e.g., A.L.A. Schechter Poultry Corp. v. United States*, 295 U.S. 495 (1935) (improper delegation of power to develop trade code for industry); *Railroad Retirement Board v. Alton R. Co.*, 295 U.S. 330 (1935) (act setting up retirement program for railroad employees exceeded Congress's commerce clause powers); *Carter v. Carter Coal Co.*, 298 U.S. 238 (1936) (maximum hour labor standards for coal industry beyond commerce clause power).

45 *Morehead v. New York ex rel. Tipaldo*, 298 U.S. 587 (1936).

nor disobedience to the Court was necessary, however. In the Spring of 1937, one Justice switched his vote to favor upholding economic and social welfare programs. Over the next four years, death or retirement of Justices allowed President Roosevelt to appoint seven new justices, all of whom were committed to a more expansive view of Congress's power.[46]

The due process decisions of the Court during this disastrous 1900-1937 period starkly illustrate the nature of the crisis in judicial review then and what many consider to be a continuing problem with judicial review today. Due process doctrine developed toward the end of the 19th century, when the Court began to define the concept of "liberty" in the 14th Amendment due process clause as including the "freedom of contract." In *Lochner v. New York*[47] the Court held that a New York law that limited the hours that bakers could work to sixty per week violated the due process clause. Such a law, the Court concluded, was an undue burden on "the freedom of the master and employee to contract with each other in relation to their employment."[48] In his dissent in the case, Justice Oliver Wendell Holmes, Jr., protested that the majority's concept of "liberty" imposed its own concept of what was proper economic policy on states. Referring to a popular book by a 19th-century English philosopher of *laissez faire* economic policy, he observed wryly: "[t]he fourteenth amendment does not enact Mr. Herbert Spencer's Social Statics."[49]

The Court has regularly referred to the period before 1937 as providing important lessons for its role today. The most recent occasion for discussion of this history and its meaning for the Court's role was in the Court's 1992 decision to stick by its 1973 abortion decision despite considerable opposition on the part of the public.[50] The *Lochner* Era teaches that, while the Court is a counter-majoritarian check on political forces, it cannot allow itself and its decisions to stray too far from the mainstream of thought in the country. Its power and influence ultimately depend not on coercion, but on the degree to which its decisions are voluntarily respected by society. Despite the bad experience of the *Lochner* Era, it is fair to say that the Court has recovered the prestige and moral power it lost in the pre-1937 period and the vigorous exercise of judicial review is a feature of the governmental structure that is fully accepted today.

2. Growth of Presidential Power

Many Framers were concerned with the *legislative* branch becoming too powerful. If anything, the modern era has demonstrated their concerns in reverse. The President's function in the 19th century — described as "carrying out the will of Congress"[51] — has been supplanted in the 20th century by a model of presidential primacy. A good part of the responsibility for the emergence of what some have called the "Imperial Presidency" falls on Congress, which has largely cooperated in

---

46 This history is related in NOWAK & ROTUNDA, *supra* note 9, at 147-154.

47 198 U.S. 45 (1905).

48 *Id.* at 75. There were several other decisions invalidating state laws on due process grounds.

49 198 U.S. at 64. Holmes, known during his tenure on the Court as the "great dissenter," is discussed in another connection in Chapter II, p. 41.

50 *See Planned Parenthood of Southeastern Pennsylvania v. Casey*, 505 U.S. 833 (1992).

51 HARRY A. BAILEY, JR. AND JAY M. SHAFRITZ, EDS., THE AMERICAN PRESIDENCY: HISTORICAL AND CONTEMPORARY PERSPECTIVES vii (Dorsey Press, Chicago 1988).

establishing and maintaining it.[52] There have been "power grabs" by strong Presidents, but there have been many more willing delegations of power by Congress.[53]

Factors in the Growth of Presidential Power Perhaps the primary factor leading to greater presidential power has been the succession of strong personalities who have occupied the White House in the 20th century, starting with President Theodore Roosevelt in 1901 and continuing with Franklin Roosevelt in the 1930s and 1940s, followed by several strong post-World War II Presidents. Although responsibility for foreign policy is shared between the President and Congress, the different nature and organization of the two branches makes the executive branch more capable of reacting to modern crises than Congress. United States participation in two world wars and its emergence as a world power, and numerous other international incidents have generated the need for quick decisions and responses — something a branch headed by one person and a staff of advisors can do better than a 535-member pluralistic legislature. All this, plus the President's control of information about unfolding crises, has allowed the President to seize the initiative in formulating foreign policy, often leaving Congress with no other choice but to follow along.

On the domestic front, much of the impetus behind presidential primacy came from the Great Depression of the 1930s. That crisis called for the decisive action of a strong national leader. President Franklin Roosevelt, in response, presented a comprehensive legislative program for Congress to enact. There have also been "spill-over" effects from the primacy of the President in wars and foreign affairs. For all these reasons, voters today look to the President for a domestic legislative agenda as much as for foreign policy. A large part of Congress's legislative role when an active President is in the White House has been reacting to the President's proposed legislative programs.[54]

Power Over Implementation of Legislative Programs Even if the President cannot implement his own legislative program, he can affect the implementation of Congress's or earlier Presidents' programs. The Constitution directs the President to "take Care that the Laws be faithfully executed,"[55] and the President is required to implement Congressional programs.[56] But there is no requirement that he implement them enthusiastically. There are many opportunities for undermining legislative commands. There is usually much room for interpretation of statutory directives. This room for interpretation is most directly felt when the statutory scheme is the typical delegation of authority to a secretary in the President's cabinet or the head of an

---

52 *See* ARTHUR M. SCHLESINGER, JR., THE IMPERIAL PRESIDENCY (Houghton, Mifflin 1973). The impact of this growth in presidential power on separation of powers is discussed in Philip D. Kurland, *The Rise and Fall of the "Doctrine" of Separation of Powers*, 85 MICH. L. REV. 592, 607-613 (1986). In the 20th century, Congress has also *gained* much power as the result of the Supreme Court's willingness to read its powers broadly. But, as will be discussed, that gain in power has been at the expense of the states rather than the President.

53 Recently and in reaction to some perceived excesses of the Presidents, Congress has made some efforts to reclaim some of its power from the executive branch. This has raised some interesting separation of powers questions. *See* Chapter VI, p. 210 (legislative veto) and Chapter IX, p. 317-318 (war powers).

54 Only members of Congress may introduce legislation, but the President has no trouble convincing members of his party in Congress to lend their names to legislation he would like to propose.

55 Art. II §3.

56 *See Train v. City of New York*, 420 U.S. 35 (1975) (President may not impound money Congress has directed to be spent).

administrative agency answerable to the President or cabinet secretary.[57]

Limits on Presidential Power   Despite the growth in presidential power, the President's power must give way when it conflicts with the constitutional powers of the other branches. Two cases illustrate this. One involved a conflict with Congress's legislative power and the other was a conflict with the judicial power.

The first case was the *Steel Seizure Case* or *Youngstown Sheet & Tube v. Sawyer*,[58] decided in 1952. In that case, labor strikes at steel mills during the Korean War caused concern because they might interfere with steel production needed for U.S. troops in Korea. Consequently, President Truman issued an executive order instructing the Secretary of Commerce to seize the privately-owned steel mills and begin to operate them under government control. The Supreme Court held the order unconstitutional. Congress had passed, at an earlier time, general labor-management legislation and in the process had rejected the possibility of government seizures of plants in cases of emergency caused by labor strife. Thus, the executive order was invalid because it conflicted with a policy that Congress had already declared.

The second case on presidential prerogatives was *United States v. Nixon*,[59] which involved the Watergate Scandal. During the campaign for the 1972 presidential election, several men identified with the Republican Party national organization were caught breaking into the national headquarters of the Democratic Party located in a building called "The Watergate." President Nixon, who was re-elected after that campaign, sought to withhold various tape recordings and documents that had been subpoenaed by a Special Prosecutor investigating the matter. Nixon claimed "executive privilege" as the basis for withholding the tapes and documents — the power of the President to protect from disclosure information and material regarding the discharge of executive functions that the President believes should not be disclosed. While acknowledging that executive privilege existed, the Supreme Court unanimously affirmed a district court order to produce the tapes. Thus, the Court confirmed that Presidents, no less than the average citizen, must comply with court orders to turn over evidence.

In the President's favor, the Court in the *Nixon* case recognized that executive privilege exists as an implied power of the President. Despite absence of explicit text in Article II, "[c]ertain powers and privileges flow from the nature of enumerated powers; the protection of confidentiality of presidential communications has similar constitutional underpinnings." To the extent that such confidentiality "relates to the effective discharge of a President's powers, it is constitutionally based." However, outside the context of military and diplomatic discussions, the privilege must give way to the needs of the parties and courts in criminal cases to obtain all relevant evidence. Most important, the Court made it clear that the decision whether material was protected by executive privilege was one that only the *courts* could make. The Court noted that "[a]ny other conclusion would be contrary to the basic concept of separation of powers and checks and balances that flow from the scheme of tripartite government."[60]

---

57 In fact many influences come to bear on administrative agencies. *See* Chapter VI, pp. 206-211, where congressional and presidential means of controlling agency action are discussed.

58 343 U.S. 579 (1952).

59 418 U.S. 683 (1974).

60 Since the *Nixon* case, Presidents Nixon, Ford, Carter, Reagan and Clinton have all testified in cases under litigation, usually by way of videotaped depositions. *See* NOWAK & ROTUNDA, *supra* note 9, at 231, n. 28.

3. The Advent and Growth of Administrative Agencies

Development of Agencies Administrative agencies are nowhere mentioned in the Constitution. Yet, today they occupy an important place in governmental structure.[61] The first powerful federal administrative agency, the Interstate Commerce Commission, was established as early as 1887. But the greatest growth in the power of administrative agencies came in the 1930s. At the request of President Roosevelt, Congress readily delegated a great deal of power to administrative agencies to provide the expertise and swift action necessary to regulate the economy and provide relief to victims of the Great Depression. This was only the beginning of a transformation of the country into what some have called "the administrative state."[62] This change has been true of states as well as the federal government. Today federal and state administrative agencies operate in a wide variety of areas, from banking to social security to occupational health and safety to labor organizing.[63]

The principal impact agencies have is through their enactment of substantive law in the form of rules through delegated legislative power.[64] One can get a rough idea of the impact of agency rules by looking in the law library: the shelf space in the library taken up by federal regulations is some ten times that of federal statutes. A person or company engaged in an activity controlled by federal law will often find little useful guidance from the statute and will instead have to consult masses of administrative rules and interpretive guidelines. But agencies not only enact rules. They have enforcement divisions that investigate and prosecute violations of those rules and administrative hearing officers that adjudicate the disputes resulting from enforcement (subject to judicial review). In many areas of the law, the only hearing of consequence the litigants will get will be an administrative hearing, not a court hearing. Even though there will be judicial review, in most instances that review is limited in scope.[65]

"Independent" Federal Administrative Agencies There are two types of federal agencies: "executive" agencies and "independent" agencies. Executive agencies are under the general supervision and control of a cabinet officer responsible to the President. Consequently, the growth of the power of executive administrative agencies can be considered part of the growth of presidential power discussed earlier, though there are limits to how much control Presidents can effectively exercise over them. Independent agencies, on the other hand, are not even formally subject to supervision by a cabinet member or the President. They are typically headed by collegial bodies. Members of these bodies are appointed by the President, with Senate advice and consent, but the appointments are for set terms of office that overlap presidential and congressional elections. Such members cannot be removed except for good cause. Among the independent agencies are the Securities and Exchange Commission, which regulates matters related to sales of financial securities

---

61 *See* Chapter VI, where the law of administrative agencies is outlined.

62 A diagram of the structure of the modern federal government showing many of the major agencies is set out in the Appendix to this book on pp. A30-A31.

63 The phenomenon is international. *See* MAURO CAPPELLETTI, THE JUDICIAL PROCESS IN COMPARATIVE PERSPECTIVE 16-24 (Oxford U. Press 1989).

64 In general, delegation is proper so long as Congress provides sufficient standards to guide the agency in its rule-making. Many standards that have been approved are very general. *See* Chapter VI, pp. 211-212.

65 Separation of powers objections to this mixing of legislative, executive and judicial power in administrative agencies have been largely rejected or ignored by the Court. *See* Chapter VI, pp. 211-215.

of corporations, the Federal Communications Commission, which regulates and decides on licensing of television and radio stations, the Federal Reserve Board, which controls monetary policy, and the Federal Trade Commission, which regulates certain business practices.[66]

Independent agencies regulate in important areas that are thought to need more continuity of policy and insulation from political control than would be the case if they were subject to the effects of different presidential administrations, shifting majorities in Congress, and the influences of congressional committees. However, Congress has not shown a great deal of consistency in its judgment about what subject matter areas should be under the control of independent agencies; in fact, it has left many areas of regulation partially in the hands of an independent agency and partially in the hands of a more conventional cabinet-controlled agency.

The size and practical independence of administrative agencies have led some commentators to refer to them as a "fourth branch of government."[67] In view of the fact that unelected administrative agencies exercise a great deal of independent power over citizens, their growth may well signal a net loss for democratic values in government.[68] However, at least some democratic control is reasserted through congressional and presidential influences on agency action.[69]

4. Congress's Investigatory Oversight Role

As legislating in the modern world has become more complex, there has been greater need for professional assistance and for legislative work to be done by committees. Proposals for legislation, budgets, approval of Presidential appointments, and all manner of other legislative business must generally survive intensive committee scrutiny before it can be brought forward for a vote on the floor. And on the floor, the relevant committee's recommendations have weight among busy members of Congress who may be only vaguely aware of the details of much legislation outside their areas of concern and expertise.[70] There are now 298 standing, special and select committees and subcommittees. The subject matters of some of the more important standing committees that both houses of Congress have are agriculture, appropriations, armed services, banking, education, energy, foreign affairs, governmental operations, judiciary, labor, small business, and science and technology. Within each committee are standing subcommittees devoted to particular areas.

The original purpose of committees and Congressional agencies was to deal with the increased complexity and specialized nature of legislation in the modern world. But with the changing nature of legislation and the growth of administrative agencies, committees have taken on the more general task of overseeing the operations of government.

President Woodrow Wilson, before he became President, remarked on the

---

66 Others include the National Labor Relations Board, the Federal Maritime Commission, the Consumer Product Safety Council, the Commodity Futures Trading Commission, and the Nuclear Regulatory Commission.

67 *See* Peter Strauss, *The Place of Administrative Agencies in Government: Separation of Powers and the Fourth Branch*, 84 COLUM. L. REV. 573 (1984).

68 *See* CAPPELLETTI, *supra* note 63.

69 *See* Chapter VI, pp. 206-211.

70 A side effect of the committee system and the requirement that all proposed legislation go through committees has been to give extraordinary power to those members of Congress who chair important committees and therefore have considerable control over what bills get discussed and reported out and what bills do not.

importance of Congress's role in overseeing government and exposing inadequacies, noting that the "informing function of Congress should be preferred even to its legislative function."[71] Committee investigative hearings are nowhere mentioned in the Constitution, but the connection to Congress's legislative power that investigations have is that they are undertaken to determine whether there is a need for legislation. On this basis the Court has upheld Congress's right to investigate, including the power to issue subpoenas and to punish disregard of those subpoenas as a "contempt of Congress."[72] However, for some committee hearings in recent years, the legislative agenda potentially involved has not always been obvious. The fact that the investigators are politicians and there is often intense press and television coverage of the hearings has caused many such investigations to take on a life of their own. The primary product of many such committee investigations is publicity, but that is all to the good if the investigations create greater public awareness of the shortcomings of the government and its officials.

To undertake such oversight functions, the legislative branch cannot be dependent on the executive to provide it with information, so with the growth of the congressional investigative function has come a growth in congressional staff and other professional assistance.[73] Providing information and assistance essential to Congress's oversight role is the General Accounting Office (GAO). The GAO, which has more than 4,000 professional employees, conducts regular audits of agency expenditures and more broadly seeks out fraud, waste and mismanagement in agencies. It also performs particular studies at the request of congressional committees. Its suggested "corrective measures" instantly get the attention of both Congress and the agency involved and its finding that a particular expenditure would be improper will make even the most intrepid, independent-minded agency administrator hesitant to spend those funds.[74]

Investigations can take on political overtones and the more political congressional investigations are, the more controversial they are. Some such investigations have had laudatory results, but others have not. The Senate committee investigation of the Watergate scandal, which ultimately led to President Nixon's resignation, is placed by most in the positive category.[75] In that scandal, the Senate committee in 1974 began investigating to see if officials at the highest levels of the Republican White House were involved in and later tried to cover up a burglary of the Democratic National Headquarters. Ultimately, the incriminating evidence was laid out on national television and the President, who had denied any involvement, resigned in disgrace.

---

71 WOODROW WILSON, CONGRESSIONAL GOVERNMENT 303-04 (Houghton-Mifflin, Boston 1885).

72 *McGrain v. Daugherty*, 273 U.S. 135, 177 (1927). *See* NOWAK & ROTUNDA, *supra* note 9, §§7.4-7.5.

73 In 1989, there were 2,999 Congressional staff members assigned to Congressional committees. Personal staff for all members of Congress totaled 11,406, averaging 38 for each Senator and 18 for each house member. This represents a 400% growth in personal staff and a 650% growth in committee staff since 1946. In addition to these permanent staff, committees also hire investigative aides each year who, while nominally temporary, often remain with a given committee year after year. CONGRESSIONAL QUARTERLY GUIDE TO CONGRESS 483-484 (1991). *See also* HARRISON W. FOX, JR. & SUSAN W. HAMMOND, CONGRESSIONAL STAFFS: THE INVISIBLE FORCE IN AMERICAN LAWMAKING (Free Press, N.Y. 1977).

74 For a general discussion of the GAO, *see* ERASMUS KLOMAN, ED., CASES IN ACCOUNTABILITY: THE WORK OF THE GAO (Westview, Boulder Colo. 1979). Another important congressional agency, the Congressional Budge Office, has since 1974 enabled Congress to prepare its own budget proposals and to assist budget committees in analyzing the effect of budget proposals coming from the White House. For a lucid description of the machinery of government with a specific focus on agencies, *see* PETER STRAUSS, AN INTRODUCTION TO ADMINISTRATIVE JUSTICE IN THE UNITED STATES (Carolina Academic Press 1989).

75 *See supra* p. 14.

Perhaps the most widely known abuse of the committee investigatory process involved the activities of Senator Joseph McCarthy, who chaired a committee in a 1954 investigation of "Communists" allegedly working in the Army and the State Department. No substantial evidence was ever produced, but the accusations of McCarthy, assisted by a brewing anti-Communist hysteria in the country at the time, cost hundreds of people their reputations and careers. For better or for worse, the Congressional investigatory power is well established and has become a real force in government.

D. The States and Federalism

As discussed earlier, the principle of separation of powers and "checks and balances" between the branches of the federal government was carefully planned. Federalism had a different basis. As the brief discussion of history of the Constitution's formation suggests, the federal structure of government resulted from political necessity. Few in the newly independent states would have voted for ratification of any constitution that did not provide a vigorous and meaningful role for the states.

Federalism has two dimensions. "Vertical" federalism describes the relationship between the states and the federal government. "Horizontal" or interstate federalism describes the relationship of the states to each other. Both relationships have changed considerably since 1789. The history of vertical federalism has largely been a story of the growth of federal power over state power. Horizontal federalism has been marked by a steady decrease in the legal significance of state boundaries.

It is an interesting question whether the delegates to the constitutional convention would have approved of these developments. Before reviewing those changes and considering that question, however, we should discuss more generally the nature of state power and the governments of the states and their political subdivisions.

1. State Government Structure and Powers

The Nature of State Governmental Power   States were not created by the Constitution, though it often refers to them. There was no need to create them because they already existed in 1787. In fact, states wrote and ratified their own constitutions quickly — all had them by the end of 1776. This fact of states' "aboriginal" existence makes the nature of the power of states significantly different from that of the federal government. The thirteen colonies emerged from the War of Independence as separate sovereign nation-states and this status was modified only to the extent that they gave up certain rights in the Constitution of 1789 and later amendments to it. Thus, states need not search the federal Constitution for some positive grant of power to act or to make law: they have the power and inherent competence of separate, independent and sovereign nations and may pass legislation on any subject they choose, except as limited by the federal Constitution or their own constitutions.[76]

State Governmental Structure   The governmental structure of many states is a state-sized version of federal governmental structure and powers, at least in broad outline. Many concepts were "borrowed" from state constitutions and placed in the 1789 federal Constitution. In turn, as states framed new constitutions periodically after the ratification of the federal Constitution, they borrowed from it to some extent.

---

76 The principle that all states are equal and admitted to the union on the same basis preserves this same status for later-admitted states.

Like federal governmental structure, state constitutions provide for three branches of government, with the chief executive officer having veto power over the legislative branch and the supreme court of the state having the power of judicial review. State legislatures are bicameral (i.e., there are two "houses," usually a "house of representatives" and a "senate"), except for one state, Nebraska, which is unicameral. However, many of the names of state governmental offices and institutions differ from those of their corresponding federal office. The chief executive officer of the state is called the Governor and the person next in line to succeed the Governor is called the Lieutenant Governor. There is generally a Secretary of State, an Attorney General, commonly an Auditor General, and department heads for departments that sound similar to those of the federal government. The chief legislative body is generally referred to as the "state legislature" or "general assembly." The court of last resort is usually called the state supreme court.

The constitutions of states sometimes reflect their citizens' feeling that the best government is the one that governs least. In many states, governors have been restricted to short terms of office and cannot seek consecutive terms of office.[77] Legislatures have historically been limited as well. One device is to limit legislative sessions to only one every two years and then for only a given number of days. Another is to allow only one house of the legislature to meet one year, the other the next. Many states limit the number of bills each member may introduce. However, the tremendous growth of the responsibilities of states in the last 30 years has caused most state governments to reorganize along more realistic lines.[78]

Executive power in most states is more diffused than federal executive power. On the federal level, the President appoints the members of his cabinet and other high-level executive officials with the advice and consent of the Senate. By contrast, in many states, the heads of some major divisions of state government, such as the Attorney General or the Secretary of State or the Auditor General, are directly elected by the people. As such, they neither owe their office to the Governor nor can they be dismissed by the Governor. In many states, these officials are members of a different political party from the governor. It is even the case in some states that the Lieutenant Governor of the state is from a different political party than the Governor.[79] Such independently-elected officers will often act independently of, and sometimes in opposition to, the Governor. State judges tend to be elected rather than appointed. Election systems were present in some states around the time the Constitution was adopted, but elections became more prevalent during the first half of the 19th century. Nonetheless, many states have appointment systems and some have combined systems.[80]

Constitutional Limits on State Governmental Structure　　Having seen that state governments have a structure somewhat similar to the federal government, it is fair to wonder whether states are required to have any particular form of government.

77　For example, in Virginia, governors serve a four year term and consecutive terms are not allowed. BOOK OF THE STATES: 1998-1999 EDITION 17, Table 2-1 (The Council of State Governments, Lexington, Ky.) Term limits in Alabama led the governor of that state to run his wife for Governor with the understanding that he would really be in charge. His wife was elected in 1967, but she died halfway through her term in 1968.

78　*See generally* BOOK OF THE STATES, *id.* at 124-208.

79　The 12th Amendment to the U.S. Constitution makes it impossible for the President and Vice President to be members of different political parties.

80　Methods of judicial selection are discussed in Chapter V, pp. 176-179.

The answer is "yes and no." Article IV §4 of the Constitution provides that "[t]he United States shall guarantee to every State in this union a Republican Form of Government." However, even assuming one could define precisely the characteristics of a "republican" form of government, the Court has held that this clause is not enforceable by the courts in the same manner as other guarantees in the Constitution, since it presents a non-justiciable "political question."[81] Nevertheless, the Supreme Court has not hesitated to assure that boundaries of state election districts are fairly drawn so as not to dilute the voting strength of people in some parts of the state. A system that assures "one man, one vote" is said to be necessary because of the right to equal protection of the laws under the 14th Amendment to the Constitution.[82] The basis for distinguishing these redistricting cases from the republican form of government case is that redistricting does not affect basic state governmental structure; it simply assures that the *existing* election structure already chosen by the people of that state does not discriminate.

Local Governmental Structure   The basic political subdivisions of states are counties and cities or villages, though in rural areas, the intermediate township level is also important. All these levels are subsumed under the term "local government" or "municipal government." The governmental entities on these levels are generally considered to be creatures of the state and subject to overall state control. However, in many states large cities enjoy a certain independence from state government. This is sometimes the result of political reality (a large percentage of the members of the state legislature may be elected from the largest city in the state) and sometimes it is the result of the state constitutions granting more independence and "home rule" rights to large cities.

On the city level, the chief executive officer is generally called the mayor and the legislative body is called the "city council." It is common on the local level to have a relatively weak executive in comparison to the legislative body. The laws passed by cities are generally referred to as "ordinances" rather than statutes. They have legal effect only within the city. There is often no judicial branch, since courts that are part of the state judicial system will have jurisdiction over offenses within the city limits, including violations of city ordinances.

Powers of Local Governments   Local governments provide many of the services needed to maintain communities and urban centers. One of the most important and traditional functions of local government is law enforcement. Law enforcement was originally conducted solely by local police forces, which were raised and supported through the revenue of local governments. Then in the 20th century, state governments created state police forces to assist in the enforcement of laws.

Another important function of local governments is the control of land use through zoning. Local governments also provide various services for their populations, including sewage and garbage disposal, and water supply. A major function of local government is public education on the elementary and secondary school level — schools which the vast majority of children attend. These school systems, while they must generally meet requirements imposed by a state department of education, are usually run by local school boards. Local governments are given the authority to

---

81 *See Luther v. Borden*, 48 U.S. (7 How.) 1 (1849). The political question doctrine is discussed in Chapter IX, pp. 313-314.

82 *See Baker v. Carr*, 369 U.S. 186 (1962); *Reynolds v. Sims*, 377 U.S. 533 (1967). The 14th Amendment's guarantee of equal protection of the laws is discussed in Chapter IX, pp. 328-338.

raise revenues by taxation in order to pursue all these programs. By far the largest portion of the local tax burden in most communities is the school tax imposed to support elementary and secondary education. Often local governments fund local community colleges or vocational training centers as well.

2. Changes in Vertical Federalism: The Growth of the Federal Power

The understanding of federal and state power that many had from reading the "enumerated powers" of Congress in the Constitution was that described by James Madison in the debates on ratification:

> The powers delegated . . . to the federal government are few and defined. Those which are to remain in the State governments are numerous and indefinite. The former will be exercised principally on external objects, as war peace, negotiation, and foreign commerce; with which last the power of taxation will, for the most part, be connected. The powers reserved to the several States will extend to all the objects which, in the ordinary course of affairs, concern the lives, liberties, and properties of the people; and the internal order, improvement, and prosperity of the State.[83]

To emphasize the narrow scope of those powers, the 10th Amendment of the Bill of Rights provided that "[t]he powers not delegated to the United States by the Constitution, nor prohibited by it to the States, are reserved to the States respectively, or to the people."

The Implied Powers Doctrine   Despite this view of the limited powers of the federal government, Chief Justice John Marshall upheld an expansive view of the Congress's power on a theory of "implied powers" in the 1819 case of *McCulloch v. Maryland*.[84] The issue in *McCulloch* was the constitutionality of Congress's establishment of a Bank of the United States. Chief Justice Marshall admitted that the federal government was one of limited powers and that there was no specific mention in Article I of any power to constitute a bank. But he held that the grant of explicit enumerated powers necessarily implied the power to do what was appropriate to carry out those powers. Thus, since Congress had explicit power to lay and collect taxes, to borrow money, to regulate commerce and to raise armies, and a bank would clearly assist in carrying out these powers, it had the implied power to create a bank. In reaching this result, Marshall found support in the "necessary and proper" clause, the last of the enumerated powers, giving Congress the power "[t]o make all Laws which shall be necessary and proper for carrying into Execution the foregoing Powers."[85]

Supreme Court Power to Review State Court Judgments   Federal judicial power *vis-a-vis* the states was also solidified early. As noted earlier, in the 1810 case of *Fletcher v. Peck*, the Court extended its power of judicial review to acts of state governments. Then, in 1816, it made clear that it had appellate jurisdiction over state

---

83 Federalist No. 45 at 313, *supra* note 5. As with all statements made during ratification debates, there is no guarantee that Madison really thought this or was saying what was expedient to calm those who were opposed to ratification based on a fear of a strong central government.

84 17 U.S. (4 Wheat.) 316 (1819). Chief Justice John Marshall (1755-1835), the fourth and most famous of the fourteen Chief Justices who have headed the Court, was a strong Federalist in favor of a strong central government. In his 34 years on the Court, he had a great impact on the shape of federal power, writing many of the opinions in landmark cases, including the case that established the power of judicial review, *Marbury v. Madison*, discussed *supra* p. 10 and in Chapter IX, p. 304.

85 Art. I §8 cl. 18.

court decisions that interpret federal law. In *Martin v. Hunter's Lessee*,[86] the Virginia Supreme Court, while acknowledging that it was bound by the supremacy clause of the Constitution to *follow* federal law, denied that the United States Supreme Court could review its *interpretation* of federal law. The United States Supreme Court held that its appellate jurisdiction applied to *all* cases raising issues of federal law, whether those cases came from the lower federal courts or the state courts. Otherwise, the Court noted that great "public mischief" would result as the Constitution or a treaty could mean one thing in Virginia and another in New York. The power to review state *criminal* cases where the conviction was alleged to violate federal law was made clear in *Cohens v. Virginia*.[87]

State Resistance to Federal Power   In the period 1800-1860, the growing power of the federal government disturbed many in the southern states who believed in states' rights and who were concerned that the federal government was largely controlled by the more populous, more urban, anti-slavery, Northern states. What frustrated southern states' rights proponents most about federal action displacing state authority was that the limits of the federal government's power were being decided solely by its own departments without any meaningful participation by the states.

Starting in the 1830s, resistance to federal authority became increasingly strident. A characteristic incident was South Carolina's attempt to "nullify" a federal tariff law that hurt the interests of southern planters. John C. Calhoun, a former Vice President of the United States, became the head of the South Carolina States' Rights party and called a convention to adopt an "ordinance of nullification" declaring the offending tariffs passed by Congress "null, void, and no law, nor binding on this state, its officers or citizens." The federal government responded to South Carolina's actions with a show of force and the state had to back down.

The southern states also deeply resented the Supreme Court's assertion of appellate power, set out in *Martin v. Hunter's Lessee* and *Cohens v. Virginia*, discussed above.[88] The depth of the animosity toward the Supreme Court and Congress is illustrated by an incident in 1830. Georgia had convicted an Indian named George Tassell of murder and had sentenced him to death. This was a violation of a federal statute prohibiting states from exercising jurisdiction over Indians in certain areas of the state. Tassell appealed his death sentence to the Supreme Court, which was sure to apply the federal statute and reverse the conviction. However, the appeal had to be dismissed as moot when Georgia, in defiance of the Supreme Court's exercise of jurisdiction, executed Tassell, an act that Chief Justice Story labeled "indecorous."[89]

---

86   14 U.S.(1 Wheat.) 304 (1816). At issue in *Martin* was a Virginia law prohibiting aliens from inheriting property in the state, which was challenged on the ground that it violated the 1794 treaty with Great Britain, which guaranteed the rights of British subjects in the United States.

87   19 U.S.(16 Wheat.) 264 (1821). Article III does not give the United States Supreme Court the power to review state supreme court decisions on issues of *state* law, however. Consequently, after *Martin*, state supreme courts have the final say as to the meaning of *their own* law, but the Supreme Court must in all cases be the final arbiter of the meaning of federal law, whether the issue arises in state or federal court. *See* Chapter V, pp. 188-189 and the diagram of federal and state court systems in the Appendix, p. A32. *See also* Chapter II, p. 35 and note 3.

88   Seven states enacted laws denying the Supreme Court's appellate power over their courts. *See* Charles Warren, *Legislative and Judicial Attacks on the Supreme Court of the United States — A History of the Twenty-Fifth Section of the Judiciary Act*, 47 AM.L.REV. 1, 3-4 (1913).

89   *Id.* at 167. In reaction to a case holding the state liable for breach of contract, Georgia enacted a statute in which it declared that anyone enforcing the Court's ruling was "hereby declared to be guilty of a felony, and shall suffer death, without benefit of clergy by being hanged." That decision, *Chisholm v. Georgia*, 2 U.S. (Dall.) 419 (1793), was eventually overruled by the ratification of the Eleventh

The Slavery Question and Civil War   The southern states' system of agricultural economy based on slave labor spread into other new southern states. The south's resentment of federal government's was magnified by the gradual westward expansion of the remainder of the United States. A major expansion added states in the Northwest Territory, now roughly the states of Indiana, Illinois, Wisconsin, Ohio and Michigan. Congress had prohibited slavery in these states and the citizens of many of these new states were "abolitionists," meaning that they favored the abolition of slavery. Moreover, these and other Northern states became points on an "underground railroad" that assisted slaves to escape to free states or to Canada. Thus, slavery came up as a national issue in Congress during the first half of the 19th century primarily in relation to the admission of new states into the Union. Each new state's admission raised the question of whether it would be admitted as a "slave" or "free" state. Unable to resolve the question otherwise, Congress compromised and sought to balance the number of new "free" and "slave" states.

One such compromise was the Missouri Compromise of 1820, which admitted the states of Missouri ("slave") and Maine ("free"). The enactment went further and broadly declared that the whole Northern part of Louisiana Territory would be "free" — an immense territory extending as far North and West as the present state of Montana. In an apparent attempt to placate the southern states and head off their secession from the Union, the Supreme Court issued its now-infamous 1857 decision in *Dred Scott v. Sanford*.[90] In that case, a slave, Dred Scott, had sued for his freedom on the ground that he had lived in "free" areas for years as a result of accompanying his "owner" there. The Court rejected Scott's claim on several grounds in several opinions, but the case is taken to stand, among other things, for the proposition that Congress had no power to outlaw slavery in the territories. This ringing endorsement of slavery in *Dred Scott* was not enough for the south. Eleven states seceded (withdrew) from the Union and formed the Confederate States of America. Civil war broke out in 1861 and ended in 1865 with the surrender of the south.[91]

The "Civil War" Amendments to the Constitution   The fact that the south lost the Civil War established that the states were in the Union for better or for worse and that the interests of the union would prevail where they conflicted with those of the states.[92] The legal impact of the war on states' rights was spelled out in the three so-called "Civil War Amendments" to the Constitution, the provisions of which altered significantly the relationship established by the original Constitution. The 13th Amendment (1865) ended slavery. The 15th Amendment (1870) assured voting rights to the newly freed slaves. The 14th Amendment (1868) made clear that former slaves were citizens of the United States and of the state in which they reside, thus overruling a part of *Dred Scott v. Sanford* that asserted that blacks were not citizens. More broadly, the 14th Amendment provided that a state could not "make or enforce any law which shall abridge the privileges or immunities of citizens of the United States," nor "deprive any person of life, liberty or property, without due process of law," nor

---

Amendment to the Constitution. *See infra* p. 34 and Chapter VI, pp. 217-218.

90   60 U.S.(19 How.) 393 (1857).

91   The rebel "Confederate States of America" were Alabama, Arkansas, Florida, Georgia, Louisiana, Mississippi, North Carolina, South Carolina, Tennessee, Texas, and Virginia. As might be expected from the name chosen, the confederate constitution emphasized states' rights much more than did the United States Constitution.

92   In a case decided after the Civil War was over, the Supreme Court held that the states had no constitutional right to secede and that, for the entire time of the war, they remained states of the Union. See *Texas v. White*, 74 U.S. (7 Wall.) 700 (1869).

"deny to any person within its jurisdiction the equal protection of the laws." All three amendments gave Congress broad power to "enforce" these amendments "by appropriate legislation."

Congress has used some of its power under the Civil War amendments.[93] But the greatest impact of those amendments has been felt through court decisions. The due process and equal protection clauses of the 14th Amendment have been used by the Supreme Court and lower federal courts to "constitutionalize" many areas of law traditionally considered to be matters solely of state concern. Two of the most important have been the areas of criminal due process rights and racial discrimination.[94]

Expansion of Federal Power in the 20th Century   The greatest gains in federal power over state power have taken place in the 20th century as a result of the Court taking a broad view of Congress's power to regulate interstate commerce set out in Article I. After a series of decisions reading the commerce power narrowly,[95] the Court switched to a much broader view.

Today federal legislation will be sustained under the commerce clause if Congress had a rational basis for concluding that the regulated activity would affect interstate commerce.[96] Under this test, the Court has upheld Congressional regulation of many local activities that only indirectly relate to movement of commerce across state lines. This is so even if the activity occurs completely within a state and its effect on the national economy can be demonstrated only as a matter of economic theory. Thus, in one case the Court allowed Congress to regulate the amount of wheat a farmer could grow for his own consumption and local sale on a small farm in Ohio on the theory that the "cumulative effect" of *many* small farmers doing the same could have a depressing effect on wheat prices.[97] Racial discrimination may be prohibited based on its effect on interstate commerce, because discrimination even in small local hotels and restaurants make it difficult for black citizens to travel on business.[98] Matters as minuscule as the shape and color of oleomargarine sold in grocery stores are not beyond the scope of Congress's attention under this test.[99] The 10th Amendment to the Constitution, which reserves to the states all powers not delegated the federal government, has been urged as a limitation on Congress's commerce clause power. However, the Court's reply has been that it "states but a truism, that all is retained that has not been surrendered."[100]

---

93 Expansive notions of the commerce power, discussed next, have made it largely unnecessary for Congress to use its powers under the Civil War Amendments.

94 *See* Chapter VIII, pp. 270-303 (criminal due process rights) and Chapter IX. pp 328-332 (racial discrimination). Many have unthinkingly heaped praise on the "genius" of the 1789 Constitution without considering the fact that it set the country on course for civil war through its vagueness about state-federal relations and its failure to deal with the question of slavery. See Thurgood Marshall, *Reflections of the Bicentennial of the United States Constitution*, 101 HARV. L. REV. 1, 2 (1987). Justice Thurgood Marshall (1908-1993) was the first black justice to sit on the Supreme Court.

95 *See, e.g., United States v. E.C. Knight Co.*, 156 U.S. 1 (1895) (manufacturing is not "commerce"); *Veazie Bank v. Fenno*, 75 U.S. (8 Wall) 533 (1869) (insurance contracts are not "commerce").

96 *Heart of Atlanta Motel v. United States*, 379 U.S. 241 (1964); *Katzenbach v. McClung*, 379 U.S. 294 (1964) (accepting Congress's conclusion that racial discrimination affects interstate commerce).

97 *Wickard v. Filburn*, 317 U.S. 111 (1942).

98 *See* cases cited *supra* note 96.

99 *See* 21 U.S.C.A. §347.

100 *United States v. Darby*, 312 U.S. 100, 124 (1941). Limitations of the 10th Amendment are more substantial when Congress seeks to regulate the states themselves. *See* Chapter IX, pp. 319-321.

Nonetheless, some recent cases suggest a possible return to a more limited view of the commerce clause power. In *United States v. Lopez*,[101] the Court struck down as not within the commerce power a federal criminal law punishing possession of a handgun in or near any school. In *Printz v. United States*,[102] the Court invalidated a federal law that required local police officials to investigate the backgrounds of prospective handgun purchasers. This, the Court held, was an improper "commandeering" of state governments. However, it may be that the real problem underlying this seeming narrowing of the commerce power is that Congress has gotten too lax in its findings of the interstate commerce aspects of the activities it seeks to regulate. In *Lopez*, the Court complained that there was no adequate record created by Congress that pinpointed the interstate commerce underpinnings of its regulation of handgun possession.

Conditional Spending   Any assessment of the federal government's power *vis-a-vis* states must take into account "conditional spending." Congress cannot *directly* "commandeer" state legislatures and require states to enact particular laws.[103] However, it can effectively do so through use of the device of "conditional spending" — offering financial grants to states on the condition that they set up programs that comply with federal requirements. The power source for this kind of measure is not the commerce clause, but the power to tax and spend to "provide for the General Welfare."[104] This power of Congress, referred to as the "spending power," was greatly enhanced by ratification of the 16th Amendment to the Constitution (1913), which for the first time established the right of the federal government to impose a direct tax on income. Federal income tax is generally the most significant tax that inhabitants of the United States pay. Today, it ranges from 15% to around 40% of income. Federal income tax receipts have led to an enormous imbalance in tax revenues received by the federal government on the one hand and the states on the other. It is true, as the Court remarked in a 1947 case, that a state can resist the temptation of federal money by the "'simple expedient' of not yielding."[105] But few states are in a position to do so. Refusing federal money means that the state will, to that extent, experience a disadvantageous "balance of payments" with the federal government: the state will receive less back in federal money than its citizens pay in federal taxes. Thus, Congress as a practical matter has the power to force states to pass many laws or conform to other federal directives through the state's "voluntary" agreement to comply with federal grant conditions.[106]

One can see examples of the effects of federal conditional spending programs in the minimum drinking age of 21 imposed by all states. This was among the conditions attached to federal highway construction money. In addition, the principal

---

101 514 U.S.549 (1995).

102 521 U.S. 98 (1997).

103 *New York v. United States*, 505 U.S. 144 (1992) (federal law vesting states with ownership of privately produced toxic waste unless they enact certain laws to provide for disposal of such waste held to be an unconstitutional). This case, *Lopez* and *Prinz* are discussed in Chapter IX, pp. 320-322.

104 Art. I §8 cl. 1.

105 *Oklahoma v. Civil Service Commission*, 330 U.S. 127, 143-144 (1947).

106 To be constitutional, conditions for receipt of particular federal money must be clear to the states and must have some rational relationship to the use of the federal grant. *See South Dakota v. Dole*, 483 U.S. 203 (1987) (conditioning receipt of highway funding money on state having certain minimum drinking age is rational). In *Dole*, the Court acknowledged that financial inducements to states might amount to unconstitutional coercion in some circumstances, but adhered to its position in earlier cases that "to hold that motive or temptation is equivalent to coercion is to plunge the law into endless difficulties." *Id.* at 213.

reason many states have had strong social welfare programs for the poor is that Congress has passed legislation making federal funds available to set up such programs, but only if states follow federal requirements.[107]

3. Changes in Horizontal Federalism: The Blurring of State Boundaries

There has been a psychological blurring of state boundaries resulting from greater urbanization, mobility of the population, and advances in communication and transportation. Crossing a state boundary is a barely noticed event. Accompanying this psychological blurring has been a *legal* blurring of boundaries. While the legal consequences of state borders are still significant, several constitutional provisions and doctrines make them less significant than they have been in the past.

The Right to Travel The right of interstate travel was explicitly protected by the Articles of Confederation, but inexplicably no such provision was included in the 1789 Constitution. Nonetheless, the right has been recognized by the Supreme Court based on a number of sources in the Constitution. One of the principal cases involved a Nevada law that imposed a tax on persons leaving the state by means of public transportation. In *Crandall v. Nevada*,[108] the Court held the tax unconstitutional, calling the unrestricted right of interstate travel inherent in the very nature of the federal system.[109] In more recent times, the Court has spoken of the right to travel to travel as a "fundamental right" and has invalidated more indirect burdens on exercise of that right. In *Shapiro v. Thompson*,[110] it held unconstitutional a state requirement that all applicants for welfare benefits be able to show that they had resided in the state for at least 6 months. The effect of this law, the Court said, was to prevent the migration of people who might need those benefits to survive in their new state of residence.[111]

The "Dormant" Commerce Clause A doctrine with even greater impact on state barriers to trade and travel is the doctrine of the "dormant" commerce clause. The "active" commerce clause has been discussed. It is a source of expansive federal power to reach most any private conduct or transaction taking place within the states. But even in its unexercised "dormant state," the commerce clause has an effect. Its mere presence in the Constitution was intended to guarantee the free flow of commerce between the states. As the Court observed in one case, "this Nation is a common market in which state lines cannot be made barriers to the free flow of both raw materials and finished goods in response to the economic laws of supply and demand."[112] From early in the history of the country, the Court has used the dormant commerce clause to invalidate state economic protectionist legislation that discriminates against or unduly burdens the commercial activities of out-of-state businesses. "Out-of-state businesses" include international firms. In recent years, the instances of use of the dormant commerce clause have increased.[113]

---

107 Federal-state cooperative assistance programs are discussed in Chapter IX, p. 320.

108 73 U.S. (6 Wall.) 35, 18 L.Ed. 745 (1867).

109 A state or municipality may nonetheless charge *all* travelers a nominal amount for the use of state-provided transportation facilities (such as an airport) to help pay for the cost of those facilities. See *Evansville-Vandenburgh Airport Authority District v. Delta Airlines*, 405 U.S. 707 (1972).

110 394 U.S. 618 (1969).

111 *Shapiro* was decided as a "fundamental rights" equal protection case. *See* Chapter IX, p 332.

112 *Hughes v. Alexandria Scrap Corp.*, 426 U.S. 794, 803 (1976)

113 The dormant commerce clause is discussed at greater length in Chapter IX, pp. 324-327.

Expanded Interstate Reach of State Court Power As traditionally understood, the territorial boundaries of a state defined the limits of the power of its courts over defendants. Thus, a court of one state generally had no power to handle a suit against a defendant from another state, unless that defendant was present or owned property in the first state at the time suit was commenced.[114] A state court's ability to bind a defendant to its judgments is called "personal jurisdiction" and the ability to bind an out-of-state defendant is called "long-arm" jurisdiction. The Court expanded this power in the second half of the 20th century. Starting in 1945, the "long arm of the law" got longer. The Court expanded the circumstances under which out-of-state residents, particularly out-of-state corporations, are amenable to suit. In *International Shoe v. Washington*,[115] the Court approved subjecting out-of-state defendants to personal jurisdiction so long as the defendant had sufficient "minimum contacts" with the state — in the form of having done business there — such that subjecting the defendant to personal jurisdiction would not be "unfair." Thus today, despite state boundaries that ordinarily would prevent extraterritorial operation of the process of a state court, the courts of California may properly decide a civil case against New York defendants if they have conducted business in California and the suit relates to that business.[116]

The "Full Faith and Credit" Requirement Article IV requires that states give "full faith and credit" to the judicial proceedings, records, and public acts of other states. This assures that a birth certificate issued or marriage concluded in one state will be considered valid in every other state. The main application of the full faith and credit clause in legal matters has to do with the validity and scope of judgments rendered by out-of-state courts. Here the Court has taken a strict view that a state must give the judgment of a court of another state the same effect that it gives the judgments of its own courts. Only if the courts of the first state did not have the constitutional prerequisite of personal jurisdiction can the courts of a second state refuse to enforce that judgment.[117] It does not matter if the first state's judgment is clearly in error or that it is based on a law that violates the public policy or laws of the second state. It must be honored by the second state.[118] The combination of long-arm jurisdiction and full faith and credit concepts makes it impossible for people to use state boundaries to evade legal responsibility in a civil case.

Extradition of Fugitives from Justice The extradition clause of the Constitution assures the validity of a state's criminal convictions in other states.[119] Extradition is the process by which someone charged with or convicted of a crime in one state and arrested in another state may be sent back to or "extradited" to the first state upon request. The request must be complied with. Reversing an old precedent, the Supreme Court in 1987 held that if all the necessary paperwork is completed, there

---

114 *Pennoyer v. Neff*, 95 U.S. (5 Otto) 714 (1877).

115 326 U.S. 310 (1945).

116 The fairness limitations on personal jurisdiction are enforced by way of the due process clause of the 14th Amendment. Details of the circumstances under which personal jurisdiction can be constitutionally obtained are discussed in Chapter VII, pp. 245-248.

117 *Durfee v. Duke*, 375 U.S. 106 (1963).

118 *See Fauntleroy v. Lum*, 210 U.S. 230 (1908) (Holmes, J.) (Missouri court judgment for gambling debt that arose in Mississippi and was illegal under Mississippi law must be enforced by Mississippi because of full faith and credit). This area is dealt with in more detail in Chapter V, pp. 250-252.

119 Art. IV §2 cl. 2.

can be no other proper ground to refuse to extradite and that, if necessary, an action can be filed against a state governor in federal court to compel extradition.[120]

E. The Impact of Governmental Structure on the Legal System: An Overview

Separation of powers and federalism have their advantages in diffusing power among several components of the governmental structure. However, they make for a complex legal system. In later chapters of this book, we will discuss many of those complications, but a few points by way of an overview should be made here.

1. The Effects of Vertical Federalism: Concurrent Power to Make Laws and Adjudicate Disputes on the Same Territory

a. Concurrent Federal and State Lawmaking Power

Reasons for Concurrent Lawmaking Power   As already discussed, Madison's suggestion that federal power is limited and that federal and state power occupy mutually exclusive spheres has not been accepted by the Supreme Court. Instead, it has allowed federal power to expand to the point that the federal government today under its commerce powers can probably regulate most any subject matter anywhere in the country that can be shown to have some economic impact. At the same time, states have retained their traditional sovereign power to make laws for persons and transactions within their borders. The result is that two different sovereigns — state and federal governments — have overlapping or concurrent power to make law governing transactions and occurrences taking place on the same geographical territory.

Where Congress has chosen to legislate, conflicting state law must give way under the supremacy clause. Some areas of federal law have little occasion to conflict with state law, as where Congress has created a whole new body of law, such as federal tax law or laws dealing with administration of the federal government. But there are many other areas of federal legislative activity that are more general and have the potential of displacing state law. Yet, despite the great increase in federal legislative activity in the last 70 years, Congress has followed a longstanding policy of legislating incompletely — asserting federal power only as far as necessary for the success of some national policy or program — and thus acting in a way that has not disturbed the continued application of state law in most areas which state law has traditionally controlled.

State Law's Traditional Domain Because of Congress's restraint, there are many areas of law that remain overwhelmingly state law. For example, Congress probably has the power to pass a national commercial code for the entire country and a national law for incorporating companies, but it has shown little interest in doing so. As a result, most of the law that governs most ordinary transactions among private citizens or companies remains state law. Contract, tort, property, family and commercial law are virtually all state law. Professions, from law and medicine to barbers and morticians, are regulated by state law. Corporations and other business entities are established and regulated primarily in accordance with state law. Public utilities supplying gas or electric power to homes and businesses are generally state-regulated private monopolies. Most ordinary crimes, such as murder, robbery, larceny, rape, and assault, are state law.

---

120 *See Puerto Rico v. Branstad*, 483 U.S. 219 (1987), *overruling Kentucky v. Dennison*, 65 U.S.(24 How.) 66 (1860).

Incomplete Federal Legislative Intervention When Congress does choose to intervene in an area traditionally governed by state law, the result is most often a mix of federal and state law on the same topic. One typical pattern occurs when Congress decides that the resources of the federal government should be brought to bear on a traditionally local problem that has become a national one. An example of this is the problem of collection of child support from responsible parents. Since the 1970s, when the low rate of child support collection became a national disgrace, Congress provided funding and imposed certain minimum standards for child support collection.[121] A second pattern consists of Congress deciding that there is a need for a uniform national rule for some category of transactions that states will have already regulated for years. An example of this is consumer credit transactions. The enormous growth in the number of credit cards and other forms of credit, combined with the welter of conflicting state requirements for advertising the terms of credit, led Congress to conclude that it was difficult for consumers to compare credit terms and shop among lenders, so it passed the federal "Truth-in-Lending" Act.[122] Typically, federal law does not completely preempt state law, so a layer of federal law is simply superimposed on existing state law.

The coexistence of both state and federal law on the same subject matter is made all the more likely by the Supreme Court's doctrine on "preemption" of state law by federal law. While the supremacy clause invalidates state laws that conflict with federal laws, there is a presumption *against* federal preemption. Thus, state law will be displaced only if there is a direct conflict between state and federal law or Congress has clearly expressed an intent to "occupy" an entire "field" of law.[123]

The Mix of State and Federal Law Two examples will illustrate typical mixes of federal and state law. Taking an example from civil law, in a simple real estate sales transaction where homeowners are selling their house, state contract and property law (usually common law and a few special statutes) will govern the transfer of the property and the rights and obligations of the parties on the contracts for sale of the property and the bank's loan of the money to purchase it. State law or local city or county ordinances will regulate the liability of the buyer and seller for property taxes, the zoning of the property for particular uses and whether the building's structure and sanitation are proper. However, federal consumer protection laws regulate the bank's disclosure of the terms of its loan and any report of the problems with the buyer's creditworthiness. If the buyers are eligible for any of the various federal housing assistance programs, the parties will have to follow applicable federal regulations. Federal banking laws control some bank operations while state laws control others.

On the criminal side, bank robbery violates state criminal laws against robbery and larceny. State law would govern the robbery and any assaults on police or local inhabitants committed in the process of the robbery and the theft of any "getaway" car. However, the federal government has, since the Great Depression of the 1930s,

---

121 *See* 42 U.S.C.A. §§651 *et seq.*, discussed in Chapter XIII, p. 492.

122 15 U.S.C.A. §1601 *et seq.* The same is true of other federal consumer legislation. *See generally* Chapter X, pp. 394-401, where state and federal consumer protection statutes are discussed.

123 *See Pacific Gas & Elec. Co. v. State Energy Resources Conservation & Dev. Comm'n*, 461 U.S. 190, 203-204 (1983) (California law prohibiting construction of nuclear power plants until nuclear fuel could be disposed of was valid even though it had the effect of preventing the building of federally-approved nuclear power plants); *Silkwood v. Kerr-Magee Corp.*, 464 U.S. 238 (1984) (state suit for damages against federally-regulated nuclear materials processor for leak of nuclear materials not preempted). *See also Medtronics, Inc. v. Lohr*, 518 U.S. 470 (1996) (state tort suit seeking civil damages for defective heart pacemaker device not preempted by federal law regulating such devices).

insured bank deposits against loss and has made robbery of any federally-insured bank a federal crime. If the getaway car the bank robbers stole has moved in interstate commerce, they could be in violation of federal law. Moreover, interstate flight to avoid prosecution, even for a state crime, is a federal offense. Any attack on federal law enforcement agents involved in apprehending the robbers would violate federal criminal laws. City ordinances may even be applicable if the robbers speed away in their getaway car or discharge their firearms within the city limits, though prosecution would not be likely in view of the other offenses committed. If the robbers are prosecuted in state court, applicable criminal procedure would be governed by state law, but a large body of quite specific federal constitutional requirements would also apply. If prosecuted in federal court, both federal statutory and constitutional law would govern the procedure.[124]

The reasons why both state and federal government might choose to regulate the same subject matter vary with the area involved. Sometimes one government deems the measures adopted by the other to be inadequate to protect its interests. But often overlapping regulation is a result of inertia.

The mix of state and federal law can present a challenge to the lawyer seeking to find all the applicable law. Experienced lawyers will have a good sense of whether a given area is one in which Congress has decided to intervene, but this is not always obvious. Unless already familiar with the area of law, a lawyer will have to do a thorough search of both state and federal law, and then seek to determine how they intersect on the issue in question.

b. Concurrent Federal and State Adjudicatory Power

Concurrent Subject-Matter Jurisdiction   Not only do both state and federal governments exercise concurrent *lawmaking* power; two coordinate *judicial systems* — state and federal — coexist on the same territory. Often federal and state courts in a state are literally across the street from each other. Federal courts naturally have jurisdiction over all federal-law claims and criminal prosecutions, just as state courts have jurisdiction over all state law claims and crimes. At the same time, however, *state* courts are required by the supremacy clause to adjudicate most *federal* law claims[125] and *federal* courts routinely handle *state* law claims between citizens of different states under their "diversity of citizenship" jurisdiction. The result is that a plaintiff who has a federal claim or who has a state-law claim against a citizen of a different state, has a choice of filing either in state or federal court. The defendant also has a choice: if the plaintiff files a federal question or diversity case in state court, the defendant can in most situations "remove" those cases to federal court if so desired.[126]

What Law is Applied by State and Federal Courts   When a *federal* court handles a *state* claim, it must apply *state substantive* law, though it may use its own *federal procedural* law. The federal court must follow state law as declared by the highest

---

124 A person whose single criminal act constitutes both a state and a federal crime may in most situations be prosecuted for both violations despite the prohibition against "double jeopardy" for the same offense, guaranteed by the Constitution's 5th Amendment. *See* Chapter VIII, p. 298.

125 *Testa v. Katt*, 330 U.S. 386 (1947) (invalidating state court's refusal to adjudicate a federal claim because the state's conflicts of law rule provided that the states were not required to entertain penal actions of "foreign sovereign").

126 Details of the subject-matter jurisdiction of state and federal courts is set out in Chapter V, pp. 183-185. Of course, because most state law claims involve parties from the same state, the bulk of state law claims will only be allowed to be asserted in state court.

court of the relevant state. For example, a federal court handling a diversity medical malpractice case (a state law claim) will follow state law as to the nature of the claim and any defenses, but will apply its own federal rules of procedure.[127] When a *state* court handles a *federal* claim, an approximate reverse mirror image results. The supremacy clause requires that the state court apply *federal substantive* law, but the state court may use its own *state procedural* rules so long as they do not conflict with federal law. Thus, a state court handling a federal civil rights claim will follow federal law as to the substance of that claim, but will apply its own state court rules on matters of procedure.[128]

2. The Effects of Horizontal Federalism: Concurrent Adjudicatory and Lawmaking Powers Among the States

In the typical case involving state-law claims, the law and the courts of only one state are involved. However, if the case involves parties, transactions or occurrences connected with more than one state — as a great and increasing number of cases do — "horizontal" federalism complicates matters. In such interstate disputes, the courts of more than one state may have jurisdiction to decide the dispute and more than one state may claim an interest in the dispute sufficient to have its law applied to resolve it. This proceeds from the broadened personal jurisdiction powers of state courts and the variety of state choice of law rules.

Multiple State Forums for Adjudication As discussed briefly earlier in this chapter, a state has the power of "personal jurisdiction" over all its residents and other persons present within its borders, meaning that all such persons are properly subject to suit in its courts. A state's power over non-residents was for years limited to cases where the person had property in the forum state. However, in the last 50 years that understanding has changed. Anyone who has certain "minimum contacts" with a state may be subject to suit in its courts.[129] Since a given defendant — especially a corporation — may have the appropriate "minimum contacts" with several states, it may be subject to suit in the courts of more than one state.

Choice of Law Among Multiple State Sources The law can vary from state to state. In interstate litigation, "choice of law" issues can arise — questions of which state's law will govern the dispute. Unfortunately, there is no uniform body of federal choice-of-law rules to mediate between the competing state interests involved. Instead, the choice-of-law rules of the state where the case is pending apply to determine the question. One difficulty with this is that state choice-of-law rules are in a great state of flux, so it is difficult to predict what law will be applied to a given dispute.[130]

An equally difficult problem is that many states' choice of law rules have tended in recent years to favor application of their own law. This trend, when combined with the wider personal jurisdiction powers of state courts, makes it more likely that the choice of *where* one litigates a dispute will often affect *what law* will be applied to resolve the dispute.[131] Interstate cases governed by state law can present the lawyer with a wide variety of courts and bodies of law to choose from. The decision of where

---

127 *See* 28 U.S.C.A. §1652.

128 For more detail on state claims in federal court and federal claims in state court, *see* Chapter V, pp. 186-188.

129 *See International Shoe v. Washington*, discussed *supra* p. 27.

130 The variety of choice of law rules is discussed in Chapter VII, pp. 252-258.

131 Details of personal jurisdiction are set out in Chapter VII, pp. 245-248.

to file suit is often a complicated one. So, for example, in choosing to file suit in Minnesota, one must take into account not only the questions of convenient location and other such issues relevant to the deciding where to litigate, but also the possibility that Minnesota law will be applied to the dispute simply because the dispute is filed in its courts.

3. The Effects of Separation of Powers and Federalism on the Federal Courts

Limitations on federal court power under the double banners of separation of powers and federalism are on the rise today as a more conservative Supreme Court reacts to the federal court "activism" of the 1960s and 1970s. Whether one agrees with the Supreme Court's formulation of these limitations on federal court power or not — many of them are controversial — they are consistent with concerns of some of the Framers that a system of lower federal courts parallel to state courts was unnecessary and presented the potential for interference with the states.[132]

The "Cases" and "Controversies" Limitation of Article III This limitation relates to justiciability of a suit — whether a dispute is of a type that should be decided by the federal court. Article III states that federal "judicial power" extends to "cases" and "controversies." These terms have been read by the Supreme Court to limit federal courts to deciding only traditional lawsuits in which there are opposing parties who have a legal claim between them and a concrete "stake" in the controversy. As a result, federal courts may not render advisory opinions or otherwise declare what the law is in some abstract, non-judicial context. In addition, a federal court must check closely in all cases to determine whether the plaintiff has "standing" to raise an issue or whether the case presents a "political" as opposed to a legal question.[133]

Since justiciability limits arise from the special nature of federal courts as defined by Article III, they have no effect on state courts. Some state constitutions have similar limitations on the power of their courts, but others do not. For example, it is not uncommon for state supreme courts to have the power to issue advisory opinions, even on federal constitutional issues.[134]

Federal Common Law-Making Federal courts, like state courts, have the power to make "common law." As will be discussed in the next chapter, the term "common law," when used in this sense, means law that is made completely by judicial decision or caselaw, as opposed to statutory law or even caselaw interpreting statutes.[135] Courts exercising common law powers might be thought of as performing a "legislative" function, since they are creating substantive rules of law that will govern people's conduct in the future. The fact that courts perform such "legislative" functions is not a problem in a common law system as a general matter. However, federal courts are said to be different from state courts: federal courts' common law-making powers are affected by separation of powers and the grant of "[a]ll legislative Powers" to Congress. As the Court noted in a recent case, the common law-making process "involves

---

132 *See supra* p. 8. *See generally* ERWIN CHEMERINSKY, FEDERAL JURISDICTION, 3D ED. (Aspen 1999) for a discussion of the intricacies of federal court jurisdiction.

133 These justiciability limitations are discussed in more depth in Chapter IX, pp. 309-314.

134 *See* Chapter IX, p. 305. *See also Doremus v. Board of Education*, 342 U.S. 429 (1952) (appeal from state court to U.S. Supreme Court on issue of 1st Amendment freedom of religion dismissed for lack of standing under Art. III; irrelevant that plaintiff had standing in state court under state law).

135 *See* Chapter II, p. 37.

the balancing of competing values and interests, which in our democratic system is the business of elected representatives."[136]

Federal courts were long ago denied the power to punish common law crimes.[137] Their power to make common law in civil cases, while it exists, is more limited than for the courts of the states. Federal judicial lawmaking is proper only in a few areas where there are clear and strong uniquely federal interests or Congress directs its application. Thus, federal common law-making is generally limited to cases concerning property and rights and obligations of the United States government (such as government checks and bonds), international disputes, and admiralty cases, plus those instances where there is clear congressional intent that federal common law be created or that gaps in federal legislation be filled.[138]

This limitation on federal court common law power also has federalism underpinnings. *Erie, Lackawanna R.R. v. Tompkins*[139] established that federal courts must follow state common law decisions when they handle state law claims and have no right to make their own determinations of what state law is. The *Erie* decision relied in part on the reserved powers of the states over their common law and the fact that common law-making by federal courts interfered with those state powers.[140]

Implied Private Rights of Action When a statute creates a right, but provides no remedy, a common law court will generally create one in the form of an action for damages. The power to do so is inherent in the ancient maxim *ubi jus ibi remedium*.[141] Congress has created many federal rights by statute, but often has failed to provide a private right of action to enforce those rights. If so, federal courts may not create a remedy unless Congress expressly authorizes it to do so or there is some implied congressional direction to do so.[142] According to the Supreme Court, free judicial creation of remedies not only might invade the legislative function generally, but would also allow federal courts effectively to expand their own jurisdiction, a function the Constitution gives solely to Congress in Article III.[143]

---

136 *See Texas Industries, Inc. v. Radcliff Materials, Inc.*, 451 U.S. 630, 647 (1981), quoting *Diamond v. Chakrabarty*, 447 U.S. 303, 317 (1980).

137 *United States v. Hudson & Goodwin*, 11 U.S. (7 Cranch.) 32 (1812).

138 *See generally* CHEMERINSKY, *supra* note 132, §§6.1-6.3.

139 304 U.S. 64 (1938).

140 *Erie* was decided at a time when the Court's view of federal power was more restricted than it is today. Consequently, it is not so clear today that the Court would hold that federal courts are *constitutionally* incapable of making common law outside of the limited federal areas listed earlier.

141 "For every right, there is a remedy." *See also* RESTATEMENT (SECOND) OF TORTS §874A (1979) (when a statute "protects a class of persons," but provides no civil remedy, a "new cause of action analogous to an existing tort action" may be accorded a person injured by violation of a statute if the court "determines that the remedy is appropriate in furtherance of the purpose of the legislation and needed to assure the effectiveness of the provision").

142 *See Touche Ross & Co v. Redington*, 442 U.S. 560 (1979). *See generally* CHEMERINSKY, *supra* note 132, §6.3.3.

143 *See* Article III §2 and discussion *supra* p. 8. The most complete statement of the rationale for this restrictive rule for federal courts is Justice Powell's dissent in *Cannon v. University of Chicago*, 441 U.S. 677, 730-749 (1979), a position effectively adopted by the majority in the *Touche Ross, supra*. This apparently constitutionally-based incapacity of federal courts to create rights of actions from federal statutes is a recently "discovered" incapacity. *See Middlesex Sewerage Authority v. National Sea Clammers Assoc.*, 453 U.S. 1, 23-25 (1981) (Stevens, J., dissenting) and *Marbury v. Madison*, 5 U.S. (1 Cranch.) 137, 163 (1803) ("[I]t is a general and indisputable rule, that where there is a right, there is also a legal remedy by suit, or action at law, whenever that right is invaded.")

If state courts show a hesitancy to make common law, the disability is one imposed by their own sense of restraint or by their own state constitutions or laws. They are unaffected by federal separation of powers or Article III considerations.

The Anti-Injunction Act and Federal Court Abstention   Under the supremacy clause, federal courts enforcing federal law necessarily enjoy primacy over state institutions, including state courts. However, Congress's concern about federal court interference with state court proceedings caused it to reverse this normal effect of federal supremacy as part of the first legislation enacted under the new Constitution. In 1789, it passed the "Anti-Injunction Act," a statutory prohibition on federal courts enjoining state court litigation (ordering that state court litigation cease). Some exceptions to the ban on injunctions have developed over the years, but the general prohibition exists to this day. In addition, the Supreme Court in the 20th century has developed in recent years several complete or partial "abstention" doctrines. These doctrines, which appear to be in part constitutionally based, independently require federal courts to abstain from exercising jurisdiction to avoid interference with pending state proceedings or otherwise to avoid a direct affront to the exercise of state judicial, administrative and legislative power.[144]

State Sovereign Immunity from Suit in Federal Court   Article III originally provided for federal court jurisdiction over some categories of suits against a *state*. When the Constitution was being debated, the question arose whether this provision of Article III served to abolish state sovereign immunity from suit at least when suit was brought in federal court. In the 1791 case of *Chisholm v. Georgia*,[145] the Supreme Court decided that Article III did abolish such immunity. It held that the state of Georgia was liable on a contract for supplies that it had entered into during the Revolutionary War. Congress and the states responded with passage and ratification of the 11th Amendment in 1793, overruling *Chisholm*. State sovereign immunity continues to exist today despite the intervening ratification of the Civil War Amendments, particularly the 14th Amendment's clear limitations on state power. Various fictions have developed to allow suits in federal court to compel states to follow federal law, but suits for money damages remain barred unless the relevant state consents to suit.[146]

---

144 Some of these are discussed in when the judicial system is discussed in Chapter V, pp. 189-191. For more detail, *see* CHEMERINSKY, *supra* note 132, §§12-14.

145 2 U.S. (2 Dall.) 419 (1793). The decision was not well-received in Georgia. *See supra* note 89.

146 The complicated fictions allowing injunctive relief are necessary because the Supreme Court has declined to hold or even to rule on the argument of many that the 14th Amendment (ratified in 1868) of its own force repealed the 11th Amendment (ratified in 1798). For more on the 11th Amendment, *see* Chapter VI, pp. 217-218. *See also generally* Chapter VI, pp. 215-220, where judicial remedies against state and federal governments and officials are discussed.

CHAPTER II

LEGAL METHODOLOGY

The first task of this chapter is to inventory the various forms that sources of law take in the United States and place them in the appropriate hierarchy of authoritativeness. We will then examine in depth the two most frequently encountered sources of law — common law and statutes — and will explore their interrelationship and methodology. Finally, we will examine briefly the practical questions of how lawyers find and research the law and argue legal points.

A. Sources of Law and Their Hierarchy

1. Enacted Law

Constitutions The structural provisions of the federal Constitution were discussed in Chapter I, as was the increased "constitutionalization" of the law that has taken place since 1953. As will be evident from later chapters, there is scarcely any area of the law that has not been touched by the growth of federal constitutional limitations on government action. Federal constitutional law is discussed in more detail later in this book.[1]

Challenges to state laws and practices based on *state* constitutional grounds have been increasingly successful. For years, close examination of state constitutional rights was overshadowed and rendered largely unnecessary by vigorous enforcement of federal constitutional guarantees. However, some state courts have chosen to provide their residents with greater protections.[2] Even where federal and state constitutional provisions have exactly the same wording, state supreme courts have sometimes interpreted their state's versions to provide more protection than their federal counterparts.[3] Since the United States Supreme Court has no power to decide any issue of state law, such state constitutional rulings are immune from reversal by the United States Supreme Court unless they violate some federal law, which is unlikely.

Statutes Statutes are laws enacted by federal, state and local legislative bodies. Generally proposed statutes, called "bills," must survive close scrutiny from specialized legislative committees and gain the approval of the appropriate head executive official. The collection of federal statutes is called the United States Code, while collections of state statutes are called compiled laws or statutes. Statutes and statutory interpretation are discussed in more depth later in this chapter.[4]

Treaties Treaties with foreign nations, concluded by the President and ratified by the Senate, and executive agreements — treaty-like documents that need not be ratified — are another source of law, though not a major one. All treaties are federal law, as states are prohibited by the federal Constitution from entering into treaties with

---

1 *See* Chapter IX.

2 William Brennan, *State Constitutions and the Protection of Individual Rights*, 90 Harv.L.Rev. 489 (1977); Jennifer Friesen, *Recovering Damages for State Bills of Rights Claims*, 63 Tex. L. Rev. 1269 (1985).

3 *Compare Michigan Dept. of State Police v. Sitz*, 496 U.S. 444 (1990) *with Sitz v. Dept. of State Police*, 506 N.W.2d 209 (Mich. 1993), discussed in Chapter VIII, p. 282, note 122 (unreasonable searches). *See also* Chapter XII, p. 448 (equal protection clause). *See* Utter, State Constitutional Law, the U.S. Supreme Court and Democratic Accountability, 64 Wash.L.Rev. 19 (1989) (finding 450 such decisions).

4 *See infra* pp. 46-60.

foreign nations.[5] Unlike the situation in some other countries, treaties in the United States are on the same hierarchical level as federal statutes, meaning that Congress can change a treaty by simply passing a contrary statute — arguably not a firm basis on which to build good international relations. In addition, some treaties are not "self-executing" and cannot be enforced unless Congress has passed implementing legislation.[6]

Court Rules Court rules govern the procedures to be followed in courts. For example, the federal courts are governed by the following bodies of court rules adopted in the following years: Federal Rules of Civil Procedure (1938), the Federal Rules of Criminal Procedure (1946), Federal Rules of Appellate Procedure (1968), and the Federal Rules of Evidence (1975).

Federal court rules are the primary responsibility of the Judicial Conference of the United States, a supervisory and administrative arm of the federal courts. The Conference appoints an Advisory Committee of legal academics, judges and practitioners who draft the rules. The rules are then reviewed and revised by the United States Supreme Court and, if Congress does not intervene, they become law. Federal court rules have the same force as federal statutes. Some of the federal rules related to civil and criminal procedure and evidence are discussed in later chapters.[7]

States also have court rules, which are adopted by various means, usually by the supreme court of the state. Often in states, the court rule (if it truly deals with matters of procedure) has higher status than a statute passed by the legislature and, if there is a conflict, the court rule will prevail.[8]

Administrative Agency Rules and Decisions Administrative agencies make law primarily through rules they promulgate. In addition, administrative hearing decisions may have some lawmaking effect in the same manner as judicial caselaw, discussed next. Some federal administrative agencies make policy almost exclusively by way of case-by-case adjudication. Agency rule-making and adjudication are discussed in the chapter on administrative law.[9]

2. Caselaw

In a common law system, caselaw court decisions of individual cases are a source of law and are referred to as a whole as "caselaw." Thus, court decisions not only resolve past controversies; a decision of a case is considered to be a "precedent" that has legal effect in the future. This effect comes from the principle of *stare decisis* — the idea that future cases should be decided the same way as past cases.[10]

---

5   Art. I §10. States may, however, with Congressional approval, enter into "compacts" with foreign nations, as they may with sister states. Pursuant to this authorization, some American states have entered into compacts with neighboring Canadian provinces.

6   *See Frolova v. U.S.S.R.*, 761 F.2d 370 (7th Cir. 1985) (U.N Charter and Helsinki Accord concerning the reunification of married couples were not self-executing, so American wife of a Russian citizen could not sue the Soviet Government for its refusal to allow her husband to emigrate).

7   *See* Chapters VII, pp. 163, 185, 192, 211, 221-234 (Federal Rules of Civil Procedure) and Chapter III, pp. 106-112 (Federal Rules of Evidence).

8   See, e.g. *Winberry v. Salisbury*, 74 A.2d 406 (N.J. 1950) (court rule governing the time period within which an appeal could be taken governed over a contrary statute) and *Ammerman v. Hubbard Broadcasting, Inc.*, 551 P.2d 1354 (N.M. 1976) (since evidence law in New Mexico was considered procedural rather than substantive, statute establishing a privilege in favor of newspaper reporters was ineffective).

9   *See* Chapter VI, pp. 193-198.

10   *Stare decisis* is discussed in greater detail *infra* pp. 61-63.

Caselaw is sometimes referred to as "unwritten" law, because the rule established by the court decision is often only implicit in the decision.

There are two kinds of caselaw: common law caselaw and caselaw interpreting enacted law. The two types of caselaw occupy different places in the hierarchy of sources of law, so they are treated separately here.

Common Law Caselaw The term "common law" is sometimes used to refer to *all* judicial decisions in a system where those decisions have precedential effect. In this book, the term is used in a more narrow sense to mean only that body of law developed and articulated *solely* through judicial decisions which began in England in the 11th century. As such, unlike caselaw interpreting statutes, common law constitutes a separate and distinct source of law independent of enacted law. The history and nature of common law and its relationship to statutory law are discussed in more detail below.[11]

Common law is on the lowest level of the hierarchy of sources of law. At one point in history, there was a suggestion that the common law prevailed over contrary statutory law.[12] However, the principle of legislative supremacy has won out. Consequently, a legislature has the power to abolish or modify the common law as it sees fit. Common law may also be displaced by a constitutional provision or by an administrative agency rule properly promulgated and within the agency's statutory authority.

Caselaw Interpreting Enacted Law Caselaw interpreting enacted law, like common law caselaw, follows the rule of *stare decisis*. Consequently, a case decision interpreting a statute is a source of law and will control later cases arising under the statute that involve similar facts.

Caselaw construing enacted law is listed here as a separate source of law apart from the enacted law it interprets. This reflects the understanding that a case decision interpreting and applying enacted law adds something to the law beyond the effect of the enactment standing alone. The amount of law that is added by judicial decision depends on how much interpretation of the enacted law is needed. But that is only a matter of degree. Some lawmaking is taking place.

As a *source of law*, however, caselaw interpreting enacted law is considered to be derivative of the law it interprets. As such, this form of caselaw takes on the hierarchical level of the enacted law that it interprets. Thus, caselaw interpreting the Constitution prevails over a conflicting statute, caselaw interpreting a statute prevails over common law, and so on. Caselaw interpreting a statute can be overruled by later action of the legislature, just as the statute itself can be amended. Caselaw interpreting the Constitution is reversible only by amending the Constitution.

Common law and caselaw interpreting statutes employ much the same reasoning process. For that reason, the two are discussed together when the nature of caselaw reasoning is discussed.[13]

---

11 *See infra* pp. 40-45 and 46-51.

12 *See Dr. Bonham's Case*, 77 Eng. Rep. 646 (C.P. 1610) (Coke, J.).

13 *See infra* pp. 63-70. The precise boundary between common law caselaw and statutory interpretation is sometimes difficult to discern. There are at least three "hybrid" forms. The legislature may delegate the power to make common law without limitations. *See* Federal Rule of Evidence (FRE) 501 (privilege of witnesses from testifying, e.g. doctor-patient privilege, "shall be governed by the principles of the common law as they may be interpreted by the courts of the United States in the light of reason and experience."). Or the legislature may so delegate with the understanding that such

3. The Hierarchy of Sources of Law

Adding the supremacy clause of the Constitution to the points about hierarchy mentioned above, a complete hierarchy of sources of law can be constructed. From highest to lowest, they are (1) the federal Constitution, (2) federal statutes, treaties and court rules, (3) federal administrative agency rules, (4) federal common law, (5) state constitutions, (6) state statutes and court rules, (7) state agency rules, and (8) state common law. It is understood that each level of enacted law includes the caselaw interpreting that enacted law. If two sources of law on the same level of the hierarchy conflict, then the later in time will govern.

This hierarchy of law should be viewed with caution. First, a law's superior position in the hierarchy is not an indication of its importance or the frequency of its use. As discussed in Chapter I, while there is more federal law now than ever before, it is still true that most everyday transactions and occurrences affecting most people and companies in the United States are governed by state law.[14]

A second caveat regarding this hierarchy is that some conflict combinations in the hierarchy are more likely than others. It is not uncommon for courts to find that a state statute or regulation conflicts with a federal statute and is consequently invalid. It would be rare that a federal administrative rule would override a right guaranteed by a state constitution. The subject matters addressed by the typical federal agency rule and the typical state constitution are so dissimilar that such a conflict is unlikely.

In the next sections, we will focus in more depth on common law and statutes. There are several reasons to do this. First, common law and statutory law together govern the overwhelming majority of legal questions that arise in the legal system. Second, the relationship between common law and statutory law is important, as the role of one affects the nature of the other. Third, the judicial processes involved in common law and statutory interpretation serve as paradigms for dealing with other sources of law: reasoning applied in common law caselaw applies generally to all caselaw, and statutory interpretation principles have applicability to interpretation of other forms of enacted law.

B. Common Law

1. A Very Brief History

After the Norman Invasion of Britain in 1066, the first royal courts developed from the King's Council. The first royal judges then were the King's closest advisors who traveled the country checking on local administration and, as part of their duties, deciding disputes. Later their tasks became primarily judicial. They separated from the Council and began to acquire their own jurisdiction as royal courts. These royal judges held court both in Westminster and while traveling throughout the country. Local courts controlled by local nobles continued to resolve most disputes. However, the more important cases were reserved for the King's courts.

---

common law will be consistent with prevailing legislative principles in the area. *See Textile Workers Union v. Lincoln Mills*, 353 U.S. 448 (1957) (construing §301 of the Taft-Hartley Act as a congressional direction to federal courts to make a federal common law of collective bargaining contracts that is responsive to federal legislative policy on labor-management relations). Or the legislature may use general statutory language and signal its intent that courts interpret that language in accordance with pre-existing common law understandings of its meaning. *See* Sherman Antitrust Act, 15 U.S.C.A. §1, and *National Society of Professional Engineers v. United States*, 435 U.S. 679, 688 (1978) (Congress intended that §1, prohibiting all agreements "in restraint of trade or commerce," would be "shape[d]" by "drawing on common law tradition").

14 *See* pp. 28-30.

The royal judges through their travels acquired in-depth knowledge of local customary law in all parts of the country. However, they believed that cases of "national" interest should be decided — not according to local customary law as applied by the local courts — but in accord with a single national body of law common to the entire country. Meeting in Westminster, they developed such a body of law by selecting from, combining or modifying the local customs that they had learned about. The law thus determined and applied became known as the "common law." This was because it was law that was "common" to the entire country, as opposed local law, which varied from place to place. Eventually, the royal courts grew and common law displaced a large part of local law.

The instinct of the early common law judges was to keep their decisions as consistent as possible. This principle, called *stare decisis*, dates at least to the 1170s when Richard Fitz-Nigel wrote: "There are cases where the course of events, and the reasons for decisions are obscure; and in those it is enough to cite precedents."[15] A system of precedent is difficult without some written records of earlier decisions, but the small number of common law judges during this period and their central location in Westminster made it possible to maintain some consistency.[16] In addition, lawyers who appeared in the common law courts would assist by reminding the judges of prior cases. This rough system of precedent later gave way to a more sophisticated one once reliable reports of decisions became available.[17]

One might wonder why judge-made law survived in England at a time when it was abandoned in the rest of Europe. The common law survived two major threats to its existence. The first came during the 16th and 17th centuries when the common law faced competition from more accessible Roman-canon law. However, this was also the time of the struggle for supremacy between the King and Parliament — a struggle which Parliament eventually won. The losing Royalists favored Roman-canon law, which was simpler and its procedure and content more easily controlled by the King. The common law, which Parliament favored, represented a guarantee of freedom, in large part because its ponderous, formalistic procedures and strong judges made the courts more difficult for the King to control.[18]

The second threat to the common law's existence was the French Revolution. Its democratic theory maintained that the legislature was the only proper source of positive law in an enlightened democratic age. This strong feeling against judge-made law was largely prompted by the fact that aristocratic pre-revolutionary French judges of the *parlements* had used their independence and broad power to sabotage statutory reforms sought by the French Crown in efforts to pass moderate reforms to stave off revolution.[19] The reaction to this in France was to limit strictly the powers of judges in order to assure that they could never again have the power to do anything

---

15 RICHARD FITZ-NIGEL, DIALOGUS DE SCACCARIO (written 1177-1179), quoted in HENRY J. ABRAHAM, THE JUDICIAL PROCESS, 6TH ED. 9 (Oxford U. Press 1993).

16 The three courts at Westminster were the Court of Exchequer, the Court of Common Pleas and the Court of King's Bench.

17 *See generally* JOHN P. DAWSON, THE ORACLES OF THE LAW 1-80 (U. of Michigan Law School 1968) and KONRAD ZWEIGERT AND HEIN KÖTZ, AN INTRODUCTION TO COMPARATIVE LAW, 2D ED. 189-191 (Clarendon Press 1992) and authorities cited therein. Assisting in the insularity and cohesiveness of the system was the eventual requirement that common law judges be selected exclusively from the ranks of the lawyers who practiced in their courts. *See* Harry Jones, *Our Uncommon Common Law*, 42 TENN.L.REV. 443, 450-452 (1975); ZWEIGERT & KÖTZ, *id.* at 189-204 and authorities cited therein.

18 ZWEIGERT & KÖTZ, *supra* note 17, *id.*

19 *See* DAWSON, *supra* note 17, at 368-371 and authorities cited therein.

more than strictly apply the law as set out by the legislature. This idea spread to other parts of continental Europe as a result of the great influence of the ideas of the French Revolution.[20]

English common law was well developed when the North American colonies were being settled, primarily by English colonists. Around the time of the Declaration of Independence and thereafter it was formally "received" from England by the newly independent states.[21] Since then, after 200 years of separate existence, common law in the United States has taken on a life of its own. Though common law method is largely the same, there are numerous differences in substantive common law rules in the United States and England and it is rare that courts in the United States rely on English decisions today.[22]

2. The Nature of the Judicial Process in Common Law Adjudication

Common law decisions and rules are based on precedent. However, all cases differ somewhat from prior cases. Consequently, a judge deciding a case must, to a greater or lesser degree, rely on considerations and principles beyond what is set out in prior cases. Moreover, when a court is faced with making the *first* decision in a given area of the law — the "case of first impression" — there is often little precedent on which to rely. This gives rise to the question: what is the ultimate source of common law rules and the nature of the judicial process in common law adjudication? This question has been answered differently at different times.

Current Theory Today, we know that the creative component of the common law comes from judges. Judges "make" common law by applying their conception of what is appropriate public policy. If there is law from prior caselaw to be applied, it should be applied. But whether in applying prior caselaw or striking out in a completely new direction, it is unavoidable that judges infuse notions of public policy when they choose a new rule of law or decide a case that is not exactly controlled by precedent. Thus, it is customary today to describe judges as "creating" common law or engaging in "lawmaking" activities when they develop common law.

An example of this is *Hoffman v. Jones*,[23] a Florida Supreme Court opinion that is set out in the appendix.[24] *Hoffman* involved a major doctrinal change in the common law of torts — the change from "contributory negligence" to "comparative negligence." Under contributory negligence, an injured plaintiff's negligence, however slight, operated as a complete bar to recovery from even a clearly negligent defendant. Under comparative negligence, the negligence of the plaintiff serves to

---

20 *See* John H. Merryman, The Civil Law Tradition, 2d ed. 15-16 (Stanford U. Press 1985); Dawson, *supra* note 17, at 362-379. An important development not discussed here is the appearance of "equity" courts that grew up in England. Equity and law are now combined in one court and equity primarily concerns the form and mode of giving relief in a civil case and whether there is a right to a jury trial in civil cases. Consequently, the development of equity is discussed in the chapter on civil procedure. *See* Chapter VII, pp. 234-235 and 237-239.

21 *See* West's Fla. Stat. Ann. §2.01, quoted in *Hoffman v. Jones*, 280 So.2d 431 (Fla. 1973), set out on p. A11 of the Appendix. *See generally* Harry Jones, *supra,* note 17, at 452-454. Some states received English statutes as well. *See* Ford W. Hall, *The Common Law: An Account of Its Reception in the United States*, 4 Vand.L.Rev. 791, 816, 818 (1951).

22 Close examination reveals some significant differences in caselaw methodology as well. *See* P.S. Atiyah & Robert Summers, Form and Substance in Anglo-American Law 116-127 (Clarendon Press 1987). This interesting book makes comparisons between English and American legal methodology in several areas, concluding that English law tends to be "formal" and American law "substantive."

23 280 So.2d 431 (Fla. 1973).

24 *See* Appendix, pp. A1-A13.

reduce the amount of damages recovered, but will not stand as a complete bar.[25] In reaching this decision, the majority opinion in *Hoffman* freely considered and weighed considerations of history, economics and philosophy. It observed that the old rule was developed at a time when tort recovery was thought to pose a serious threat to the development of industry, that today industry is stronger and widespread insurance coverage has made damage awards much less a threat to its existence, and that it is considered unfair and inhumane today to deny recovery for injury because of only slight contributory fault of the injured person.

Consistent with the notion that what is taking place is lawmaking, these kinds of considerations are commonly referred to as "legislative facts" — the kinds of data and public policy considerations a legislature would discuss in deciding whether to pass a statute. This is in contrast to "adjudicatory facts," facts that courts must ascertain to decide whether a particular fact situation fits a settled rule of law.[26]

Past Theories of Common Law Judicial Process We acknowledge today that judges make common law, but this was not always the case. In the 18th and 19th centuries, many suggested that the common law existed independently of human action. According to Sir William Blackstone, a judge was simply an "oracle of the law."[27] As such, judges did not *make* law. The law already existed "out there." Judges *discovered* and *declared* it. A past case was not law, but only "evidence of the existing applicable rule."[28] Judges "declared the true common law." In overruling a case, Blackstone noted, "if it be found that the former decision is manifestly absurd or unjust, it is declared not that such was bad law, but that it was not law."[29] Thus, a court overruling a case simply "recognized that the common law has changed" or that the prior case "evinced an incorrect understanding of what the common law rule is."

Complementing this discovery theory of law was a large dose of formalism. The notion was that, if the court found the applicable precedents and they were correct, then the correct resolution of a case could be determined through the proper application of a "scientific" methodology of logic and reasoning from those prior precedents.[30] Christopher Langdell, who introduced the "case method" of law study at Harvard Law School in 1870 and later became Dean, is associated with this view.[31]

Justice Oliver Wendell Holmes, Jr., was largely responsible for changing this conception of common law. He mocked the discovery approach as perceiving the

---

25 *See* Chapter XI, p. 413.

26 *See generally* WILLIAM REYNOLDS, JUDICIAL PROCESS IN A NUTSHELL §§4.22-4.26 (West 1991). Courts are assisted in fully exploring all the relevant considerations in an important case by permitting *amicus curiae* briefs. Several *amici* appeared in *Hoffman*. *See* Appendix, p. A2. *Amici curiae*, literally "friends of the court," are persons or organizations with an interest in the legal issues being developed in a case, who are permitted to state their views on one side or the other. Their appearance in cases is a recognition that the rights of more than just the formal parties to the case are at stake.

27 WILLIAM BLACKSTONE, COMMENTARIES ON THE LAW OF ENGLAND 69 (William S. Hein & Co. 1992) (originally published 1765-1769).

28 *Black & White Taxicab Co. v. Brown & Yellow Taxicab Co.*, 276 U.S. 518, 529-30 (1928). *See also Swift v. Tyson*, 41 U.S. 1 (1842) ("it will hardly be contended that the decisions of Courts constitute laws. They are, at most, only evidence of what the laws are; and are not of themselves laws.")

29 BLACKSTONE, *supra* note 27, at 70.

30 See GRANT GILMORE, THE AGES OF AMERICAN LAW 62 (Yale U. Press 1977).

31 Although the "scientific" method of Langdell's formalism is now largely discredited, his case method of teaching in law school remains. *See* Chapter IV, p. 127.

common law as a "brooding omnipresence in the sky"[32] or as the antiseptic product of logic. His view in 1881 — considered shocking at the time — was that:

> The life of the [common] law has not been logic; it has been experience. The felt necessities of the time, the prevalent moral and political theories, intuitions of public policy, avowed or unconscious, even the prejudices which judges share with their fellow-men, have had a good deal more to do than the syllogism in determining the rules by which men should be governed. . . . The very consideration which judges most rarely mention, and always with an apology, are the secret root from which the law draws all the juices of life. I mean, of course, consideration of what is expedient for the community concerned.[33]

Whatever other purposes the discovery myth and formalism of the common law served, they made judicial lawmaking appear more legitimate. If judges discover the law or use a scientific method to apply it or extend it beyond existing law, then judicial decisions are objective and dictated by "the law" rather than policy choices made by judges. The persistence of the myth that judges do not make law can probably be attributed to the fact that judicial lawmaking threatens a basic notion that underlies all legal systems: the fundamental principle that decisions should be made in accord with *preexisting rules* and not by fiat. This notion undoubtedly explains the persistence of a parallel myth in civil law countries — that judicial decisions are not a source of law and that judges simply apply code provisions to the case at hand and come up with a decision.[34] Such "folklore," as Professor Merryman has called it, is difficult to eradicate.[35]

The most comprehensive attack on the "folklore" of the common law in the United States was by the Legal Realists in the 1930s, led by Professor Karl Llewellyn and Judge Jerome Frank. The Realists developed both points made by Holmes: first, that the law in judicial opinions is not discovered and declared, it is made; and second, that its content is affected by all manner of social, political, economic, historical and other trends in thinking that operate consciously or unconsciously through the judge making it.[36]

---

32 *Southern Pacific Co. v. Jensen*, 244 U.S. 205, 222 (1917) (Holmes, J., dissenting).

33 OLIVER W. HOLMES, JR., THE COMMON LAW 1-2 (1881). Oliver Wendell Holmes, Jr. (1841-1935) was among the most famous of American judges, serving as Chief Justice of the Supreme Judicial Court of Massachusetts and as an Associate Justice of the U.S. Supreme Court. For similar views, *see* BENJAMIN N. CARDOZO, THE JUDICIAL PROCESS 98-141 (Yale U. Press 1921) (discussing the "judge as legislator"). *See generally* KENNETH J. VANDEVELDE, THINKING LIKE A LAWYER 109-140 (Westview Press 1996); BAILEY KUKLIN & JEFFREY W. STEMPEL, FOUNDATIONS OF THE LAW: AN INTERDISCIPLINARY AND JURISPRUDENTIAL PRIMER 1 17-158 (West 1994).

34 The development of a complex body of tort law in France from only 40 or so words in the French Code Civil demonstrate that civil law judges have just as creative a role as common law judges. *See* MARTIN SHAPIRO, COURTS 136-143 (University of Chicago Press 1981) (discussing French tort law). The fact that a very different body of tort law has developed in the province of Quebec in Canada from essentially the same words shows how codes hardly dictate decisions. *See* H.R. Hanlo, *Here Lies the Common Law: Rest in Peace*, 30 Modern L. Rev. 341, 245-256 (1967).

35 MERRYMAN, *supra* note 20, at 47 ("the important distinction between civil law and common law judicial processes does not lie in what courts in fact do, but in what the dominant folklore tells them they do."); ZWEIGERT & KÖTZ, *supra* note 17, at 272-273. *See also* MAURO CAPPELLETTI, THE JUDICIAL PROCESS IN COMPARATIVE PERSPECTIVE 3-56 (Clarendon Press 1989) (exploring the spread of the domain of judge-made law in civil law countries and the possible reasons for it).

36 *See generally* LAURA KALMAN, LEGAL REALISM AT YALE 1927-1960 (U. North Carolina Press, Chapel Hill 1986). Many of these ideas had been promoted earlier by Roscoe Pound and others in the Sociological Jurisprudence camp. *See* Roscoe Pound, *The Scope and Purpose of Sociological Jurisprudence*, 25 Harv. L. Rev. 489 (1912).

Practical Effects of Legal Realism   The demise of the discovery theory of common law and formalism has had its effects on modern judges. First, judges are much more self-conscious and reticent about their creative functions. Whether at public gatherings or in opinions, judges tend to emphasize their role as law-*interpreter* and to downplay their law-*making* functions. They are often more hesitant to exercise common law-making functions even in areas that are traditionally the common law's domain. Their self-consciousness and reticence flows in part from the notion that lawmaking in a democracy is a function to be performed by a representative legislature, not by unelected judges. It also flows from a practical consideration: recognition that the legislature has the greater relative institutional competence to investigate and assess the public policy considerations underlying lawmaking. Courts simply do not have access to the legislative hearing process or staff assistance from public policy experts that legislatures employ when statutory changes in the law are considered.

Judicial reticence about lawmaking is apparent in many modern common law decisions. Judicial opinions often begin with a discussion of whether it is proper for the *court* to alter a common law rule or whether it is the province of the legislature. An example of this can be found in the *Hoffman v. Jones* case discussed above and set out in the appendix. Considerable time was spent in the majority opinion and a dissent was sparked on the question of whether it fell to the court or the legislature to change the rule on contributory negligence.[37]

A second effect of greater realism about common law-making has been more candor in opinions when a court decides to develop new rules. Instead of trying to hide policy choices behind strained discussions of precedents, the authors of the modern common law opinions which make new law are more likely to recognize publicly what they are doing and forthrightly support the rule chosen with arguments based on public policy considerations. This greater candor is reflected in the majority opinion in *Hoffman v. Jones*, which, as discussed earlier, openly relies on considerations of history, sociology, economics and philosophy.[38] A demonstration of the older approach of hiding public policy choices behind masterful feats of recasting and distinguishing precedents is Judge Cardozo's opinion in the 1916 case of *McPherson v. Buick Motor Co.*[39] *McPherson* is often cited as a paradigm of the judicial process in common law. But even though the *McPherson* decision makes radical changes in the nature of liability for defective products, Cardozo's opinion for the court reads as if it were making only the smallest incremental change in the law.

The Limits of the Realist Critique and the "Legal Process" Reaction   Although we are all Legal Realists now, that same realism requires that we recognize grains of truth in both the discovery theory of common law and formalism. Judges are products of the society in which they live and their attitudes and actions reflect more than personal predilections. They reflect *society's* values in their opinions and decisions. And, to the extent that society's values and a judge's values conflict, most judges try to discover and choose society's values rather than their own. Practical considerations also support common law rules that reflect widespread customs and conventional morality. Such rules best serve expectation interests of the people governed by

---

37 *See* pp. A7, A10-A13.

38 *See supra* p. 40. This greater candor has been referred to as evidence of the greater overall "substantive" nature of the American as compared to the English approach to law. *See generally* ATIYAH & SUMMERS, *supra* note 22.

39 111 N.E. 1050 (N.Y. 1916).

them and lessen the concern about notice of the common law's "unwritten" rules. To this extent, much of the law *does* already exist "out there" in society waiting to be "discovered" by judges.[40]

We must also recognize that, despite the bad name that "formalism" has today, judges *are* restrained by formalistic requirements. They are expected to write opinions justifying their decisions. Those opinions are expected to conform to long-standing judicial conventions regarding reasoning and justification. "We just felt like it" is not a sufficient justification for a judicial decision. The Legal Process School of jurisprudence which grew up in the 1950s explored the nature of these justificatory constraints on judicial creativity and demonstrated how they are real.[41] According to Legal Process adherents, the common law tradition's demand for "reasoned elaboration" of precedent and other standards of "craftsmanship" in reasoning and opinion writing limit the freedom of judges to decide cases in whatever way they want. Consistent with the Legal Process view, judges in real life sometimes complain that they personally feel inclined to decide a case a particular way, but that "the opinion won't write" that way.

Opinions of judges in real cases reflect the lessons of both the Legal Realism and Legal Process schools of thought. While freely discussing historical, economic, social and philosophical considerations, judges also pay attention to "craftsmanship." Regardless of what other modern justifications there might be for a new rule, links to the past are honored and dealt with in a principled way. Again, *Hoffman v. Jones* illustrates this. The candid Legal Realist side of the opinion has already been mentioned: the court's candor in justifying the rule it adopted with sources other than precedent. However, the *Hoffman* court also had to deal with the threshold issue of whether it should decide the issue of comparative negligence. It determined that it should do so in part based on a close analysis of precedent.[42]

Some Perspective on Judicial Creativity The question of judges making law is interesting, but the creative aspects of the judicial process should be put into perspective. Virtually all cases decided by trial courts, many cases decided by intermediate appellate courts and the majority of cases decided by the highest state courts involve simple application of settled authority or, at the most, choosing between two divergent lines of authority. At a time when the common law still reigned supreme in many areas, Benjamin Cardozo, a judge known to be creative with the common law,

---

40 *See generally* RONALD DWORKIN, TAKING RIGHTS SERIOUSLY 22-45 (Harvard U. Press 1977) (discussing how fundamental principles that exist in society and are recognized as binding are themselves law and are used to decide cases that are not directly covered by prior rules).

41 HENRY HART & ALBERT SACKS, THE LEGAL PROCESS: BASIC PROBLEMS IN THE MAKING AND APPLICATION OF LAW (Foundation 1994) (originally released 1958). This casebook, labeled by the authors a "tentative edition" and distributed for years only in duplicated form, has been widely used to teach courses on legal process and is among the most influential books on the subject. *See also* KARL LLEWELLYN, THE COMMON LAW TRADITION: DECIDING APPEALS (Little Brown 1960).

42 *See* p. A4. *See also* A10-A13 (dissent on the issue). Some believe that the constraints imposed by the need for justification are illusory. Among the most critical are those of the Critical Legal Studies movement, principally Duncan Kennedy and Robert Unger. Adherents of the Law and Economics (identified with Richard Posner), assert that courts should strive to develop and effectuate legal rules that are economically efficient. Followers of Feminist Jurisprudence (identified with Catherine MacKinnon), question legal doctrine and all the jurisprudential movements for their failure to reflect the experiences of women. For a review of recent trends in jurisprudence, *see* Gary Minda, *The Jurisprudential Movements of the 1980s*, 50 OHIO ST. L.J. 599 (1989). *See also* KUKLIN & STEMPEL, *supra* note 4, at 174-176. For a short collection of readings outlining the principal tenets of these and other contemporary jurisprudential movements, *see* STEPHEN B. PRESSER & JAMIL S. ZAINALDIN, MATERIALS ON LAW AND JURISPRUDENCE IN AMERICAN HISTORY, 3D ED. 879-1063 (West 1995).

remarked while a member of the highest court of New York that the majority of the cases that came before the court "could not, with semblance of reason, be decided in any way but one."[43]

3. The Problem of Retroactivity

Any system that considers judicial decisions to be a source of law should be concerned about problems of retroactive lawmaking.[44] Retroactivity did not trouble Blackstone and other adherents to the "discovery" theory of common law. The announcement of a "new" rule did not change the law; it only declared what the true common law rule was all along. But once one admits that caselaw really does change the law, one must be concerned with the fairness of applying that rule retroactively.

The primary concern about retroactivity is with the rule's application to persons other than the parties to that case. Courts in the United States often resort to the technique of giving decisions prospective effect only or only partial retroactivity.[45] In deciding whether to do so, they evaluate the extent of reliance on the old rule and the degree to which the new rule represents "a clear break with the past."[46] The most common form of prospective application is to apply the new rule to the parties in that case, to other cases pending on the date of the decision, and to all cases arising in the future. This is what the Florida Supreme Court did in *Hoffman v. Jones*, the comparative negligence case in the appendix discussed earlier.[47]

But in a strict sense, the parties in the very case that changes the law are subject to retroactive lawmaking. The appellate decision in a case is made some period of time (often years) after the conduct in question in the lawsuit took place. If the standard of conduct is a new one and especially if the decision overrules some prior clear rule, it would seem unfair to apply it even to the parties in the case, who would have had no notice of such a rule when they engaged in the conduct.[48] Recognizing this, a few cases have given *solely* prospective effect to new caselaw rules, thus not even giving the "winning" party in that case the benefit of the new rule.[49] However, this technique is rarely used as it gives rise to a host of other objections. Among them is the fact that, without some prospect of gaining some benefit from an appeal, few parties would seek changes in the law, and it would become stagnant. The prevailing view today is that the winning party should get the benefit of the decision, even if it is

---

43 CARDOZO, *supra* note 33, at 164. *See also* Jon O. Newman, *Between Legal Realism and Neutral Principles: The Legitimacy of Institutional Values*, 72 CAL. L. REV. 200, 204 (1984) (in all cases decided in a one year period in 1982-1983, dissenting votes were cast in only 3.7% of them).

44 Retroactivity is a problem with common law, where rules are completely judge-made, but it is also a problem with caselaw interpreting statutes in new directions and particularly with caselaw interpreting the Constitution.

45 English courts generally follow a rule of full retroactivity. But English courts adhere to *stare decisis* more rigidly and are generally not as activist as American courts, thus reducing the unfair effects or retroactivity. *See* ATIYAH & SUMMERS, *supra* note 22, at 147-148.

46 *Desist v. United States*, 394 U.S. 244 (1969).

47 *See* Appendix, p. A9.

48 Jeremy Bentham, a strong supporter of codification of law, explained the problem in a colorful way in answering the question of how judges make common law: "Do you know how they make it? Just as a man makes laws for his dog. When your dog does anything you want to break him of, you wait till he does it, and then beat him for it. This is the way you make laws for your dog and this is the way the judges make law for you and me." Jeremy Bentham, *Truth v. Ashhurst*, 5 WORKS 233, 235 (W. Tait, Edinburgh 1923) (first published 1838).

49 *See Great Northern Ry. Co. v. Sunburst Oil & Refining Co.*, 287 U.S. 358 (1932) (affirming Montana Supreme Court decision reversing case rule for future, but refusing to give appellant benefit of new rule).

prospective in all other respects, and that this is an unavoidable cost of a caselaw system.[50]

The retroactivity problem should not be exaggerated, however. As just discussed, changes in doctrine are not that common because of the strength of *stare decisis*. A court must decide that the policies supporting adherence to the established rule — predictability, certainty, fairness and efficiency — are outweighed by the need to overrule an established precedent. Even when there are changes in doctrine, most changes effected by caselaw are incremental and are hardly surprises.

Moreover, although retroactivity is a disadvantage of judge-made law, many argue that the benefits of its flexibility outweigh any such disadvantage. Judge-made law can react to the multitude of situations that could not be foreseen by even the most conscientious legislature. Judges can thus make exceptions to general rules as needed or even rethink and change a rule if it is causing unjust results. And, in any event, any major judicial "mistakes" are subject to change by the legislature.[51]

It should be noted as well that retroactivity is no less a problem in code-based systems with statutory law, since "interpretations" of statutes can change. The sparse 45 or so words of the French Civil Code dealing with civil wrongs have undoubtedly provided little notice to those affected by the judicially created twists and turns of French tort law. Certainly the parties in French tort cases that developed in the law in new directions were no less unfairly surprised than was the defendant in *Hoffman v. Jones*.[52]

C. Statutory Law in a Common Law System

1. Growth of Statutory Law

Calling the United States a "common law" country is misleading to the extent that it suggests that the most prevalent form of law is common law. While this might have been true at one point, it is emphatically not true today. Since the turn of the 20th century and particularly since the 1930s, there has been an "orgy of statute-making"[53] ushering in what has been called the "Age of Statutes." [54] The "center of gravity" of state law has also shifted to statutes. Indeed, it is probably fair to say that the average state in the United States has as many statutes as the average civil law country in Europe. If one multiplies that amount of statutory law by 50 states, one can see just how prevalent statutory law is in the United States.

Some statutes have replaced common law, but many more have created entirely new areas of law. On the federal level, volumes of federal taxation, social security, environmental, financial securities and banking law fill the United States Code. On the

---

50 *See Stovall v. Denno*, 388 U.S. 293 (1967). Other objections to solely prospective effect are discussed in REYNOLDS, *supra* note 26, §4.29.

51 In England, legislative change is spearheaded by various law reform commissions that keep track of the law in particular areas and report needs for changes to the legislature. This is not generally true in the United States, where the likelihood of legislative intervention in the event of judicial "mistakes" is much lower. *See* ATIYAH & SUMMERS, *supra* note 22, at 29-30, 134-141, 148-149. For a good discussion of the limits and weaknesses of judicial law-making, *see* CAPPELLETTI, *supra* note 35, at 35-46.

52 *See Jand'heur c. Les Galeries Belfortaises*, D.P. 1930.I. 57 (words of the Civil Code imposing liability upon persons for damage caused by "things under their guard" meant that there would be strict liability in automobile accidents), discussed in SHAPIRO, *supra* note 34, at 140-143. *See also* Ruth Redmond-Cooper, *The Relevance of Fault in Determining Liability for Road Accidents: the French Experience*, 38 INT. & COMP. L.Q. 502-509 (1989).

53 GILMORE, *supra* note 30, at 95.

54 *See* GUIDO CALIBRESI, A COMMON LAW FOR THE AGE OF STATUTES (Yale U. Press 1985).

state level, numerous statutes regulating businesses, consumer rights, commercial transactions, and family relations have been enacted. Common law has not disappeared. Many areas of private law in the states — contracts, torts and property law — are governed primarily by common law with some statutory modifications. In most areas of the law, however, statutes are the rule rather than the exception.

2.   The Common Law Attitude Toward Statutes

The prevalence of statutory law in the United States does not mean that statutes in the United States and continental Europe are applied the same way or even look the same. A quick glance at federal or state statute books will disclose that U.S. statutes are longer and infinitely more complex than the average civil law code or even most "special legislation" that has grown up in civil law countries outside the codes.[55] Underlying this formal difference is an important conceptual difference in attitudes about statutes.

The Civil Law Approach to Statutes   Because of the influence of the French Revolution throughout continental Europe, the idea of legislative supremacy that developed was really one of legislative *exclusivity* — that legislation was the *sole* legitimate source of law. Judicial lawmaking was formally denied. When legislatures passed codes, they intended those codes to be a comprehensive statement of the entire law on the subject addressed. Thus, when gaps in code coverage inevitably developed, whether through oversight of the drafters or simple obsolescence, judges supplied an answer, but were compelled by the principles of comprehensiveness and legislative exclusivity to justify that answer as an interpretation of the code. This led to a flexible approach to the interpretation of statutes. Flexible interpretation was in turn aided by the fact that the codes, intended as they were to be comprehensive and enduring for years to come, tended to be written in general terms.

The Common law Approach to Statutes   There is a distinctive "common law attitude" toward statutes that differs from the approach taken in most civil law countries. Common law judges see statutes as containing specific *rules of law* that will be applied fairly according to their terms, but not beyond. Subject matter outside the terms of the statute remains governed by the common law. This means that, as a general rule, U.S. courts will not interpret statutes in two ways that are routine in civil law countries.

First, courts in civil law systems treat the codes as containing germinating principles from which specific rules can be generated. An entire body of French tort law, for example, has been derived from only a few lines of general text in the civil code.[56] Courts in the United States are not likely to find — nor are legislatures likely to write — broad principles in legislation that can be used for the germination of

---

55 An interesting comparison in this respect can be made between the "Model Uniform Product Liability Act" promulgated by the U.S. Department of Commerce as a suggestion for state enactment, U.S. Dept. of Commerce, Uniform Products Liability Act: A Model For the States (U.S. Govt. Printing Off., Washington 1979) and the Federal Republic of Germany's Act of December 15, 1989, on Liability for Defective Products (Product Liability Act — ProdHaftG) (eff. January 1, 1990). Anyone who doubts the potential for complexity of U.S. statutes and has access to federal laws should examine the Clean Air Act, particularly 42 U.S.C.A. §7511a, or most any section of the Internal Revenue Code, 26 U.S.C.A. §1 *et seq.*.

56 The principal section is §1383, which provides: "Everyone is liable for damage he has caused not only by his intentional acts, but also by his negligence or imprudence."

rules.[57] Broad principles suitable for germinating rules exist for common law judges, but they are found in the common law.

Second, courts in civil law countries may reason by analogy from a statute and apply it to situations not within its literal terms. For example, in a recent decision the German Federal Constitutional Court interpreted a statute protecting the rights of a surviving *spouse* of a deceased tenant to continue living in an apartment to grant the same rights to a live-in male companion of a deceased tenant. In doing so, it emphasized the propriety and even the obligation of courts to reason by analogy where appropriate.[58] The average U.S. court will interpret a statute to apply to the extent of its terms, but will generally decline to reason by analogy to a different rule. Indeed, it is likely that a U.S. court considering a statute like the German statute just mentioned would probably use the maxim of *expressio unius est exclusio alterius* and hold that the statute, by specifically including spouses, impliedly excluded persons in less official cohabitation relationships.

3. Reasons for the Common Law Approach to Statutes

The common law attitude toward statutes is somewhat ironic, given that common law courts regularly reason analogically from prior cases and germinate specific rules from general common law principles, as discussed later in this chapter.[59] There would not seem to be any logical reason why legislative principles could not *also* be used to germinate rules.[60] To the extent that judges give a reason for the narrow approach to statutes, it is said to be compelled by legislative supremacy: any judicial effort to extend a statute beyond a fair reading of its terms would add something to the statute that the legislature apparently did not wish. Had the legislature wished something else to be the rule, it would have so provided in the text of the statute. Thus, any court that makes law on the subject of the statute beyond what is fairly traceable to its text is invading the province of the legislature. But it is equally plausible to assume that the legislature would have wished that unanticipated gaps be filled by reasoning analogically from the rules set out in the statute and any underlying principles.[61]

The common law approach to statutes strikes some as a singularly unhelpful judicial attitude. Where it came from, however, is understandable. It is the result of the lack of any necessity to view statutes any differently, the basic conception of the

---

57 It is more likely that the legislature will simply delegate the power to make common law. *See infra* p. 63.

58 *See Constitutional Complaint of Building Cooperative "X,"* BVerfGE 82, 6 (First Panel, April 30, 1990). *See also Harty v. Ville de Châlon-sur-Marne*, S. 1878.II. 48 (French Court of Appeals) (interpreting §1386 of the French Code Civil, which makes owners of buildings liable for any damage caused by collapse of their buildings, to apply by analogy to owner of a rotten tree which collapsed causing personal injury) and D. NEIL MACCORMICK AND ROBERT S. SUMMERS EDS, INTERPRETING STATUTES: A COMPARATIVE STUDY 471-472 (Dartmouth Publishing, Brookfield, Vermont 1991). Reasoning by analogy is inappropriate to expand the reach of criminal or tax statutes, however.

59 *See infra* pp. 66-69.

60 As long ago as 1908, Dean Roscoe Pound noted the distinctive common law attitude and urged U.S. courts to consider statutes in a more expansive manner. *See* Roscoe Pound, *Common Law and Legislation*, 21 HARV.L.REV. 383 (1908). *See also* Harlan Fiske Stone, *The Common Law in the United States*, 50 HARV. L.REV. 4, 12-15 (1936) and Roger Traynor, *Statutes Revolving in Common law Orbits*, 17 CATH. L.REV. 401, 405-409 (1968). Stone later became Chief Justice of the United States Supreme Court, serving from 1941 to 1946. Traynor was Chief Justice of the California Supreme Court.

61 The common law approach to statutes is especially ironic in the United States, where constitutional interpretation is marked by an extremely flexible view of the text of the Constitution somewhat similar to continental European courts' approaches to their codes. *See* Chapter IX, pp. 306-308.

relationship between statutes and common law, and a historical judicial hostility toward statutes.

Lack of a Need for Expansive Statutory Interpretation   As discussed earlier, a complete system of judge-made common law was developed relatively quickly, over about 100 years.[62] Since the common law was understood to be the repository of any "broad and comprehensive principles" that existed in the law,[63] there was no need for statutes to state any enduring principles. Instead, statutes were enacted on an *ad hoc* basis as needed to address particular problems thought not to be sufficiently addressed by the common law. Thus, common law judges did not search for basic principles in statutes, nor did legislators deem it necessary to set out such principles in the statutes they passed.

Relationship Between Statutes and Common Law   Because common law developed first and statutes dealt with relatively narrow subjects, the common law mind views statutes as being enacted against the comprehensive backdrop of the common law. As a result, there is no need to fill any statutory gaps by extending the reach of the statute. Any gaps have already been filled by the common law. Enacting a statute in a common law system, then, is like placing a rock in a pail of water: the rock displaces the water as far as it goes, but the water immediately fills any space not occupied by the rock. Judges deciding a case not covered by the statute simply resort to the common law. As a result, common law judges have had no need to resort to a flexible view of the statutory language, to germinate a rule from the statute's underlying principles, or to reason by analogy from the rule it states.

Historical Judicial Hostility   The common law developed and reigned supreme for centuries before there were any significant statutory intrusions. Common law judges wielded a great deal of power and resented statutory infringements on their domain. In their modest view, statutes were quite unnecessary since the common law had an answer for all important legal questions. Judges viewed Parliament's occasional forays into lawmaking as mistaken and amateurish, and therefore calling for a narrow interpretation. As Pollock observed, "Parliament generally changes the law for the worse, and . . . the business of the judge is to keep the mischief of its interference within the narrowest possible bounds."[64] The maxim that "a statute in derogation of the common law should be strictly construed" is a product of this attitude.[65] In turn, Parliament reacted to narrow and grudging judicial interpretations of its statutes by spelling out its intentions in detail in the statutory language. This then resulted in a complex and specific legislative product unsuitable for expansive interpretation.[66]

Common Law and Statutes in the United States   The above relates to the experience in England. In the United States, discomfort with statutes was perhaps less from the very beginning. States formally "received" English common law by constitutional or statutory enactment, but they freely modified it by statute from the beginning,

---

62 DAWSON, *supra* note 17, p. 6.

63 *Norway Plains Co. v. Boston & Maine R.R.*, 67 Mass. 263 (1854) (Shaw, C.J.).

64 SIR FREDERICK POLLOCK, ESSAYS ON JURISPRUDENCE AND ETHICS 85 (1882).

65 *See* Jefferson B. Fordham & J. Russel Leach, *Interpretation of Statutes in Derogation of the Common Law*, 3 VANDERBILT L. REV. 438, 440-441 (1950).

66 *See* ZWEIGERT & KÖTZ, *supra* note 17, at 273-278.

sometimes in a fit of anti-English pique.[67] However, the notion of strictly construing statutes in derogation of the common law experienced a surge at the turn of the century in the United States when politically conservative judges narrowly interpreted progressive state social legislation. American legislatures reacted much as Parliament did, by spelling out their intentions specifically.[68]

Courts in both England and the United States long ago abandoned their hostility to statutes. However, the basic idea that "the law" means "the common law with a few statutes added in" continues in the United States. Returning to the conceptual analogy of the statutory "rocks" in a pail of common law "water," the fact that today — in the "Age of Statutes" — the pail is now more full of rocks than water does not alter the basic concept.

4. Attempts at Codification in the United States

Given the common law attitude toward statutes, it should not be surprising that efforts at comprehensive legislative codification of the law have failed in the United States. The first codification opportunity presented itself when Jeremy Bentham, a proponent of codification in England, wrote to President James Madison in 1811 offering to codify law in the United States. His offer was politely refused.[69]

The Field Codes Somewhat more fruitful efforts were undertaken in the latter half of the 19th century. This movement was led by David Dudley Field of New York, who in 1847 persuaded the New York legislature to constitute a commission to codify the law. In 1865, the commission presented five codes to the legislature for passage: civil procedure, criminal procedure, penal, civil and political. However, New York enacted only the civil and criminal procedure codes. Much of the reason for the lack of success was the opposition of the organized bar. Another factor was that much of the driving force behind codes — the claim that unwritten caselaw was difficult to understand and apply — had been undercut by the appearance of commentaries on the law, books that summarized caselaw, particularly those of James Kent and Joseph Story.[70]

Field's codes had greater success in the Western United States, where frontier attitudes about law made the apparent simplicity and accessibility of a code more appealing. Five Western states passed forms of his Civil Codes and still have them today (California, North Dakota, South Dakota, Idaho and Montana). However, any

---

67 It is reported that a common toast during the immediate post-Revolutionary United States was: "The Common Law of England: may wholesome statutes soon root out this engine of oppression from America." EVAN HAYNES, THE SELECTION AND TENURE OF JUDGES 96 (Fred B. Rothman & Co., Littleton, Colo. 1981) (originally published in 1944). *See also* Eric Stein, *The Attraction of the Civil Law in Post-Revolutionary America*, 52 VA.L.REV. 403 (1966). New Jersey and Kentucky statutes prohibited citation of any English common law authorities. LAWRENCE FRIEDMAN, HISTORY OF AMERICAN LAW, 2D ED., 97-98 (Touchstone Books, N.Y. 1985)

68 *Jones v. Milwaukee Elec. Ry. & Light Co.*, 133 N.W. 636 (Wis. 1911) (statute imposing liability on "every railroad company" does not include an "electric interurban railroad company"). It was this conservative judicial attitude that constitutionalized free enterprise that led to the problems generated by the *Lochner* Era discussed in Chapter I, pp. 11-12.

69 ZWEIGERT & KÖTZ, *supra* note 17, at 250. Bentham's view of judge-made law was mentioned *supra* note 48.

70 James Kent (1763-1847) was a judge for many years and then retired to become a professor at Columbia University in 1823, when he published his *Commentaries on American Law*, which went through several editions between 1826 and 1830. Joseph Story (1779-1845) was a Justice of the Supreme Court who taught at Harvard Law School while still a Justice. He published nine commentaries on various subjects of private and constitutional law from 1832 to 1845. Many continued to be updated after his death. These great commentaries inspired many imitators and commentaries became a principal means of gaining access to the law in a system that relied principally on case decisions.

hope that these codes would be like the European codes were dashed on the rocks of the common law attitude toward statutes. Legislators — themselves imbued with the common law view of statutes — made them too specific and courts treated them the same way common law courts have always treated statutes: as statements of rules to be applied according to their terms, not as containing germinating principles.[71]

Despite the pervasive common law attitude toward statutes, recent times have seen some move away from it and toward a more expansive view similar to the European approach. Some of those unusual cases are discussed after the following discussion of more traditional approaches to statutory interpretation.[72]

D. Statutory Interpretation Methods

What follows is a mixture of approaches and "maxims" of statutory interpretation commonly encountered in judicial opinions interpreting statutes.[73] In reading this description, two things should be kept in mind. First, there is no single official approved list of approaches or maxims.[74] Although most of the cases cited here are from the United States Supreme Court, this is done primarily for ease of referencing the opinions cited. State courts are not compelled to follow the Supreme Court's approach except as to *federal* statutes. However, state court approaches are generally similar in any event. Second, many of the maxims discussed contradict each other. In some cases, the court's choice of one maxim over another is left unexplained.[75]

If pressed to give an overall generalization about statutory interpretation in the United States, one could say that courts in the United States generally believe they should interpret the language of the statute in such a way as to give effect to the purpose the legislature sought to accomplish, keeping in mind that ordinarily the best evidence of purpose is the text of the statute. Yet, there are many approaches used that ignore or run counter to this goal.[76]

1. The Plain Meaning Rule

According to this rule, a court should construe a statute so as to give its words their ordinary meaning, unless the result would be absurd. Resort to legislative history

---

71 FRIEDMAN, *supra* note 67, at 351-354; *See also* ARTHUR T. VON MEHREN, LAW IN THE UNITED STATES 20-21 (Kluwer 1989).

72 *See infra* pp. 58-60.

73 For a taxonomy of methods used in the U.S., *see* MACCORMICK & SUMMERS, *supra* note 58, at 407-459. This excellent book contains chapters on many other countries and a concluding comparative discussion. *See also* HART & SACKS, *supra* note 41, pp. 1111-1380; F. REED DICKERSON, THE INTERPRETATION AND APPLICATION OF STATUTES (Little, Brown 1975) (a classic though theoretical book); and WILLIAM N. ESKRIDGE, JR. & PHILIP P. FRICKEY, LEGISLATION (Foundation 1999). A useful book containing drafting exercises and problems is WILLIAM P. STATSKY, LEGISLATIVE ANALYSIS AND DRAFTING, 2D ED. (West 1984).

74 Some state legislatures have attempted to compile a list of rules. *See, e.g.*, Minn. Stat. Ann. §645.16. However, courts tend to ignore them. *See Comment*, "The Effect of the Statutory Construction Act in Pennsylvania," 12 U. PITT. L. REV. 283 (1951 (act used in fewer than 3% of cases involving statutory interpretation). There is also a MODEL STATUTORY CONSTRUCTION ACT, 14 UNIF. L. ANN. 513, promulgated by the Uniform Law Commissioners.

75 The "thrust" and "parry" of a whole host of competing maxims are outlined in Karl Llewellyn, *Remarks on the Theory of Appellate Decision and the Rules of Canons About How Statutes are to be Construed*, 3 VANDERBILT L. REV. 395, 401-406 (1950). One commentator has noted with alarm the Supreme Court's increased use of formal maxims of statutory construction. *See* Daniel A. Farber, *Revival of the Canons*, TRIAL, p. 82 (June 1992). *See also* Daniel A. Farber, *The Inevitability of Practical Reason: Statutes, Formalism and the Rule of Law*, 45 VANDERBILT L. REV. 533, 535 (1992).

76 No attempt will be made here to distinguish between legislative "purpose" and "intent." *See* REYNOLDS, *supra* note 26, §5.5.

or aids to understanding beyond the text is ordinarily not appropriate. The "plain meaning" rule is returning to favor after a period of disfavor.[77]

Proponents of the plain meaning approach argue two points in its favor. First, what the legislature passed and the executive signed were the words of the statute, not the committee report or speeches of supporters or opponents. As Justice Jackson put it, "[i]t is the business of Congress to sum up its debates in its legislation." He viewed going beyond the words of the statute in any case but one where they are "inescapably ambiguous" as allowing the courts to inject themselves and take sides in the "political controversies" that accompanied the enactment, thus subverting the democratic process.[78] Second, ordinary people and most lawyers rely solely on the statutory language and do not have ready access to legislative history materials: "[t]o accept legislative debates to modify statutory provisions is to make the law inaccessible to a large part of the country."[79]

Opponents of a plain meaning rule argue that plain meaning "rests on the erroneous assumption that words have a fixed meaning," pointing out that "[w]ords are symbols used for communication — means, not ends, in the legislative process."[80] As Justice Holmes stated, "[a] word is not a crystal, transparent and unchanged, it is the skin of a living thought and may vary greatly in color and content according to the circumstances and the time in which it is used."[81] Moreover, the plain meaning rule can make for worse judicial meddling than that it seeks to avoid: "Why should a judge be permitted to impose his own reference or that of some hypothetical average person on statutory words instead of inquiring in the first instance as the reference of the enactors?"[82]

The Supreme Court has at one time or another approved the use of the plain meaning rule. A classic application was in *Caminetti v. United States*.[83] There the Court held that the language of a federal criminal statute that prohibited transportation of women across state lines for prostitution or "any other immoral purpose" was clear, and therefore applied to non-commercial debauchery. The decision came over a strong protest that the sole aim of the statute was to stop *commercialized* vice.

Some commentators and judges see a trend in the late 1980s back toward plain meaning in the Supreme Court, largely as a result of Justice Antonin Scalia's influence. In the 1981 Supreme Court term the Court always checked the text against the legislative history.[84] Yet, in the 1989 and 1990 terms, 10 out of 65 and 19 out of 55 statutory interpretation cases were decided without *any* reference to legislative history.[85]

---

77 *See* Phillip P. Frickey, *The New Textualism*, 37 U.C.L.A. L.Rev. 621 (1990).

78 *Schwegmann Brothers v. Calvert Distillers Corp.*, 341 U.S. 384, 395 (1951).

79 *Id.*

80 *Note, A Re-evaluation of the Use of Legislative History in the Federal Courts*, 52 Colum. L. Rev. 125, 134 (1952).

81 *Towne v. Eisner*, 245 U.S. 418, 425 (1918).

82 John M. Kernochan, *Statutory Interpretation, An Outline of Method*, 3 Dalhousie L. J. 333, 342 (1975).

83 242 U.S. 470 (1917).

84 Patricia Wald, *Some Observations on the Use of Legislative History in the 1981 Supreme Court Term*, 68 Iowa L. Rev. 195, 197 (1983). Judge Wald was Chief Judge of the Court of Appeals for the District of Columbia Circuit.

85 Stephen Breyer, *The Uses of Legislative History in Interpreting Statutes*, 65 S. Cal. L.Rev. 845, 846 (1992). The author, a proponent of using legislative history, is the most recently appointed justice of United States Supreme Court. *See also* MacCormick & Summers, *supra* note 58, at 457-458. For a

2. Plain Meaning and Legislative History

The Court has recently *said* that the plain language of the statute governs when it is unambiguously applicable to the problem[86] and that "[t]he starting point of every case involving construction of a statute is the language itself."[87] It has also cautioned that reliance on legislative history as a means of ascertaining congressional intent is a "step to be taken cautiously"[88] and at one time emphasized Justice Oliver Wendell Holmes's admonition that "[w]e do not inquire what the legislature meant; we ask only what the statute means."[89]

However, the Court has also gone to the opposite extreme. In 1976, it unanimously reversed the Court of Appeals for its invocation of plain meaning and refusal to consult legislative history.[90] Moreover, statutory language apparently has rarely been so clear that the Court does not at least "peek" at that history to verify its reading of the language. Such a "peek" would seem to be required even when the statutory language is clear: one formulation of the plain meaning rule has it that the language of the statute controls "absent a clearly expressed legislative intention to the contrary."[91] Thus, the Civil Rights Act of 1964 was interpreted in *United Steelworkers of America v. Weber*[92] to allow some race-based disadvantageous treatment of white employees (through use of an affirmative action program for minorities) despite the statute's literal prohibition against discriminating "because of . . . race." The legislative history disclosed a purpose to permit reasonable race-conscious attempts to remedy "conspicuous racial imbalance in traditionally segregated categories" of employment.

When legislative history is used, there is a hierarchy of probative value of the various items of that history. Of greatest importance are legislative committee reports.[93] These are descriptions of the legislation written by the legislative committees that have studied it, heard testimony and arguments for and against it, and have voted to send it to the floor for a vote by the relevant house of Congress. Committee reports are thought to be important for statutory interpretation because busy legislators often rely on those reports for their information about the bill in order to decide whether to vote for it or against it. Also important if they exist are conference committee reports. Conference committees are committes with both House and Senate members on them that are set up to work out the differences between versions of bills passed by the House and Senate.[94]

---

discussion pros and cons of using legislative history, *see* Breyer, *supra*, at 861-869.

86 *American Tobacco Co. v. Patterson*, 456 U.S. 63, 68 (1982).

87 *Ernst & Ernst v. Hochfelder*, 425 U.S. 185, 197 (1976).

88 *Piper v. Chris-Craft Industries, Inc.*, 430 U.S. 1, 26 (1977).

89 Oliver W. Holmes, *The Theory of Legal Interpretation*, 12 Harv.L.Rev. 417, 419 (1899), quoted in *S&E Contractors v. United States*, 406 U.S. 1, 14 n.1 (1972).

90 *Train v. Colo. Public Interest Research Group*, 426 U.S. 1 (1976). Indeed, in one case the Court seemed to reverse the usual order of things *See Citizens to Preserve Overton Park, Inc. v. Volpe*, 401 U.S. 402 (1971) ("Because of this ambiguity [in the *legislative history*], it is clear we must look primarily to the *statutes* themselves to find the legislative intent.") (emphasis supplied).

91 *Maine v. Thiboutot*, 448 U.S. 1, 6 n.4 (1980), citing cases.

92 443 U.S. 193 (1979). The substance of *Weber* is discussed in Chapter XV, p. 571.

93 *Lewis v. United States*, 445 U.S. 55, 63 (1980); *Wright v. Vinton Branch Bank*, 300 U.S. 440, 463-64 (1937).

94 *See* Chapter I, p. 16. "Standing" committees of the whole Congress also issue reports, such as the Joint Committee on Taxation, which is active in studying various proposals for tax reform and issues frequent studies and reports describing the current law as well as the reform proposals. At least the Committee's analysis of current reform proposals are used by courts much like other legislative history. Senate and House reports are numbered sequentially for each year without reference to the originating

Of a value equal to committee reports are statements of individual legislators responsible for the preparation or drafting of the bill.[95] A statement on the floor of Congress by a representative immediately after introducing an amendment to a bill, which later became part of the final legislation, was held to be "clearly probative of a legislative judgment."[96] Statements in debates on the floor of Congress are considered as somewhat persuasive, "though [they are] not entitled to the same weight" as committee reports.[97] Statements "other than by persons responsible for the preparation and drafting of a bill, are entitled to little weight"[98] and "the fears and doubts of the opposition are no authoritative guide to the construction of legislation."[99]

On the subject of legislative history, Justice Scalia has added a conspiratorial angle to his arguments in favor of plain meaning. Legislative history is unreliable, he says, because legislators can manipulate its content. There are many opportunities to "plant" sentences or case citations in committee reports or to engage in rehearsed exchanges on the floor of Congress. This would be bad enough if done out of the legislator's philosophical disagreement with the majority. But the chances are great that such activities would be done at the behest of a lobbyist employed by some special interest group to influence the legislation.[100]

There is considerably less reliance on legislative history in state court decisions construing state statutes. The reason for this is that state legislative histories are usually not published and are otherwise difficult to find and compile. Thus, state courts are more likely to use the plain meaning rule or to resort to the other aids to interpretation discussed here.[101]

3. The Social Purpose Rule

Under the "social purpose" rule, a statute will be construed to effectuate the social purpose it was designed to accomplish. Traceable to the 1584 English case, *Heydon's Case*,[102] it was used by the United States Supreme Court in the famous case of *Holy Trinity Church v. United States*.[103]

In *Holy Trinity Church*, a federal statute made it unlawful for anyone to assist in the migration of "any alien . . . under contract or agreement . . . to perform labor or

---

committee. Thus, the 175th committee report in the Senate in the year 1997 would bear a formal citation "S. Rep. 97-175," while the 493rd House report of 1997 would be cited "H.R. Rep. 97-493." Conference reports bear a House number.

95 *Federal Energy Administration v. Algonquin SNG, Inc.*, 426 U.S. 548, 564 (1976); *United States v. International Union*, 352 U.S. 567, 573-75 (1957).

96 *Simpson v. United States*, 435 U.S. 6, 13 (1978).

97 *Chandler v. Roudebush*, 425 U.S. 840, 858 n.36 (1976).

98 *Ernst & Ernst v. Hochfelder*, 425 U.S. 185, 203 n.24 (1976).

99 *Gulf Offshore Co. v. Mobil Oil Co.*, 453 U.S. 473, 483 (1981). Uniform laws, such as the Uniform Commercial Code, have official comments written by the drafters. These can be highly probative of the meaning of the text, and often give examples and cite other authorities, such as prior caselaw.

100 *Blanchard v. Bergeron*, 489 U.S. 87, 98-99 (1989) (Scalia, J., concurring); *Thompson v. Thompson*, 484 U.S. 174 (1988) (Scalia, J., concurring). *See* William S. Moorhead, *A Congressman Looks at the Planned Colloquy and Its Effect on the Interpretation of Statutes*, 45 A.B.A.J. 1314 (1959).

101 The official English view before 1993 was not to examine legislative history, although English courts before then could consider committee reports and other preparatory material to determine the evil against which the Act in question was directed. See GLANVILLE WILLIAMS, LEARNING THE LAW 102 (11th ed. 1982) and RUPERT CROSS, STATUTORY CONSTRUCTION 42-52 (1976). This changed in *Pepper v. Hart*, [1993] 1 All E.R. 42, in which the House of Lords adopted the view that it was proper to consider parliamentary legislative history materials in ascertaining the meaning of the statute.

102 76 Eng. Rep. 637 (Exchequer 1584).

103 143 U.S. 457 (1892).

service of any kind in the United States." Holy Trinity Church was prosecuted when it hired an Englishman to come to the United States to be its pastor. Despite the wording of the statute, the Supreme Court held that the church had not violated the statute. It observed that the "evil" at which the statute was directed was importation "an ignorant and servile class of foreign laborers" who agreed to work "at a low rate of wages," thus "break[ing] down the labor market." Since "it was cheap unskilled labor that was making the trouble" and that it was never suggested that "the market for the services of Christian ministers was depressed by foreign competition," the statute would not apply, despite its clear terms. Clearly the "social purpose" rule can conflict with application of the "plain meaning" rule.

A version of the social purpose rule is the "absurdity" limit on the plain meaning rule. The Court has cautioned that the absurdity exception should be utilized only in "rare and exceptional circumstances."[104] The absurdity limit was used, however, in *United States v. Kirby*,[105] a case in which a state sheriff was prosecuted for violating a federal statute which made it a crime to "knowingly and willfully obstruct or retard the passage of the mail, or of any driver . . . carrying the same." The defendant sheriff had arrested a federal postal service letter carrier on a warrant issued by a state court. The Supreme Court found that this was an absurd application of the law that could not have been intended by Congress.

In a recent case, a literal reading of the word "defendant" would have meant that in a civil case evidence of a prior criminal conviction could be introduced to attack the *defendant's*, but not the plaintiff's credibility, a distinction that was simply irrational.[106] The Court declined to read the rule literally, relying in part on the absurdity exception. The case is also notable for the fact that it one of the rare instances when Justice Scalia agreed that use of legislative history was proper.

4. The Context of Statutory Language

The Immediate Context of Terms Two maxims are used for discerning the meaning of statutory terms from their immediate context. The first is the canon *ejusdem generis*, the concept that "where general words follow an enumeration of specific items, the general words are read as applying to other items akin to those specifically enumerated."[107] For example, in *McBoyle v. United States*,[108] the Supreme Court held that the National Motor Vehicle Theft Act did not apply to airplanes. The definition of motor vehicle listed "an automobile, automobile truck, automobile wagon, motorcycle, or any other self-propelled vehicle not designed for running on rails." Although an airplane met the literal definition of the statutory language, the Court held that this definition covered vehicles *running on land only*.

A second, similar rule is *noscitur a sociis* — the notion that "a word may be known by the company it keeps." It was used in *Jarecki v. G.D. Searle & Co.*,[109] in which the Court held that inventions of drugs and photographic devices were not, despite their great novelty, within the definition of "discovery" where the statute used "exploration" and "prospecting" in conjunction with the word "discovery." According

---

104 *Howe v. Smith*, 452 U.S. 473, 483 (1981) (no reason to depart from language of federal statute on prisoner transfer).

105 74 U.S. (7 Wall.) 482 (1868).

106 *Green v. Bock Laundry*, 490 U.S. 504 (1989) (interpreting Federal Rule of Evidence 609(a)).

107 *Harrison v. P.P.G. Industries, Inc.*, 446 U.S. 578, 588 (1980).

108 283 U.S. 25 (1931).

109 367 U.S. 303 (1961).

to the Court, the context indicated that Congress intended to describe income-producing activity in the oil and gas and mining industries, not in the development of manufactured products, such as drugs and cameras. However, the maxim may not be used to narrow any distinctive meaning intended by the legislature.[110]

Statutes In Pari Materia and Contextual Harmonization   On a broader level of harmonization, courts are supposed to interpret statutes *in pari materia* — "on the same subject" — in a way that is consistent. This device was employed by the Court in *Bowen v. Massachusetts,*[111] in which it held that an action for "damages" included an action for *injunctive* relief that would require payment of money, a form of relief not technically within the definition of "damages."[112] The suit was one against the United States. Another federal statute defining jurisdiction in suits against the United States, had long been construed to include such injunctive actions. The Court consequently found support for its reading from the settled meaning of the other statute. Other harmonization efforts might include intersectional harmony within the same statute or harmonization with a general public policy applicable to that subject matter area.

5. Presumptions About the Use of Language

The Negative Implication Rule   An important maxim close to the heart of the limited common law view of statutes is *expressio unius est exclusio alterius*: the expression of one thing implies the exclusion of others. An example of the *expressio unius* canon is *Tennessee Valley Authority v. Hill*, in which the Court upheld an injunction against completion of a $100 million dam. The injunction was to prevent possible extinction of an endangered species of fish, called "snail darters," in accord with the Endangered Species Act, an act prohibiting destruction of species shown to be on the verge of extinction. The federal agency in charge of the dam argued that there should be a "hardship exemption" from the strict protections afforded to endangered species by the Act, but the Court disagreed. The Act listed several other exemptions, and the Court presumed that the list was exhaustive.[113] *Holy Trinity Church*, discussed earlier, was distinguished.[114]

Specific Language Controls Over the General   Another maxim of statutory construction is that specific statutes take precedence over general statutes. For example, in *People v. Ruster*,[115] the defendant was convicted of felony theft under a general theft statute for falsifying his identity in order to receive unemployment benefits. The California Supreme Court reversed the conviction, however, because there existed a more specific statute that made the falsification of unemployment applications a less serious misdemeanor.

---

110 *See Babbitt v. Sweet Home Chapter of Communities for a Great Oregon*, 515 U.S. 587, 702 (1995) (in defining "take" to mean only the direct application of force against an endangered species, the lower court ignored surrounding words, such a "harm,"that contemplated indirect effects).

111 487 U.S. 879 (1988).

112 Though both forms of relief require payment of money, one is "legal" while the other is "equitable." *See* Chapter VII, pp. 234-235, 237-239.

113 437 U.S. 153, 184 (1978). *Hill* is discussed in another respect in Chapter XV, p. 585.

114 *See also Leatherman v. Tarrant County Narcotics and Intelligence Coordination Unit*, 507 U.S. 163 (1993) (federal court rule's requirement of higher pleading standard for certain types of claims precludes its application to other types not listed); *Chan v. Korean Airlines, Ltd.*, 490 U.S. 122, 133 (1989) (Warsaw Convention's specifying one sanction for defective notice of limited liability on airline ticket impliedly excluded the sanction of making airline fully liable for damages).

115 548 P.2d 353 (Cal. 1976).

6. External Influences on Statutory Interpretation

The Rule of Lenity for Criminal Statutes Another canon of construction that likely underlay the *McBoyle* case, discussed above as an example of *ejusdem generis*, is the "rule of lenity." Under this concept, basic fairness requires that criminal laws give clear notice to possible violators of what conduct is prohibited, so any ambiguity or lack of clarity will be interpreted in favor of the accused. This rule was applied in the early case of *United States v. Wiltberger*,[116] in which the Court interpreted a federal statute extending jurisdiction of American courts over crimes committed on the "high seas" as not extending to crimes committed on rivers in foreign countries.[117]

Deference to Administrative Interpretations The interpretation of a statute by an administrative agency charged with administering that statute is entitled to deference by the courts. If the intent of Congress is clear and the interpretation contradicts that intent, legislative intent controls and a contrary agency interpretation will be struck down. But where the statute or its legislative history is ambiguous or silent on the precise question involved, then a court "does not simply impose its own construction on the statute." Instead, it must uphold the agency's position so long as it is a "permissible construction of the statute."[118] To qualify for this kind of deference, it makes a difference whether the agency interpretation is long-standing or one only recently formulated.[119]

Interpretation to Avoid Unconstitutionality A court should avoid an interpretation of a statute that might result in its being unconstitutional. In *Kent v. Dulles*,[120] the Court interpreted passport laws as not authorizing the State Department to prohibit persons with "communist backgrounds" from traveling, since such an application would infringe on the fundamental right to travel. In *Webster v. Doe*,[121] the federal Administrative Procedures Act was construed to allow a suit for violation of constitutional rights "in part to avoid the 'serious constitutional question' that would arise if a federal statute were construed to deny any judicial forum for a colorable constitutional claim." Also included in this category are various "clear statement" rules imposed by the Supreme Court that require that Congress make absolutely clear its intentions to alter certain aspects of state sovereignty.[122]

---

116 18 U.S. (5 Wheat.) 76, 95 (1820) (Marshall, C.J.).

117 *See also United States v. Thompson/Center Arms* Co., 504 U.S. 505, 517-518, 112 S.Ct. 2102, 119 L.Ed.2d 308 (1992) (rule applied to scope of definition of prohibited weapons). But *see United States v. Alpers*, 338 U.S. 680 (1950) (statute prohibiting any "book, pamphlet, picture, motion-picture film, paper, letter, writing, print, or other matter of indecent character" was not limited to articles comprehended by sight alone; it included obscene phonograph records).

118 *Chevron, U.S.A., Inc. v. Natural Resources Defense Council, Inc.*, 467 U.S. 837 (1984). *See also E.I. duPont de Nemours and Co. v. Collins*, 432 U.S. 46, 54-55 (1977) (construction of statute "by those charged with its execution should be followed unless there are compelling indications that it is wrong"). For a discussions of this question by sitting justices of the Court, *see* Antonin Scalia, *Judicial Deference to Administrative Interpretations of Law*, 1989 DUKE L. J. 511 and Stephen Breyer, *Judicial Review of Questions of Law and Policy*, 38 ADMIN. L.REV. 363, 373 (1986).

119 *North Haven Board of Education v. Bell*, 456 U.S. 512, 522 n.12 (1982) (little deference due agency interpretation that was not a long-standing one and had fluctuated). Even greater deference is accorded "legislative" regulations — regulations exercising delegated legislative power. They are upheld unless "arbitrary, capricious or irrational." *Batterton v. Francis*, 432 U.S. 416 (1977).

120 357 U.S. 116 (1958).

121 486 U.S. 592, 603 (1988).

122 *See* Chapter I, p. 29, and Chapter IX, p. 319 (statutes preempting state control over core functions) and Chapter VI, p. 218 and note 159 (statutes abrogating 11th Amendment immunity). *See also* Chapter IX, p. 326 note 124 (clear statement required for Congress to approve state regulation that burdens interstate commerce).

Interpretation in Light of Fundamental Values Courts sometimes base a statutory interpretation in whole or in part on the assumption that the legislature did not mean to enact a rule that violates fundamental societal values absent some clear statement. Part of the basis for the Court in *Trinity Church* decision interpreting the statute to permit the church to bring in the English pastor was a supposed policy favoring religion.[123] A more specific fundamental policy may also affect interpretation. In *Santa Clara Pueblo v. Martinez*,[124] the Court declined to imply a private right of action under a federal statute because of the long-standing special policy against judicial interference in Indian affairs.

7. Less Traditional Approaches to Statutory Interpretation

The above aids and approaches to statutory interpretation are generally consistent with the limited "common law attitude" toward statutes identified earlier. However, there has been some movement in recent years toward a more "civil-law" style of reasoning from statutes.[125]

a. Legislatively-Inspired Common Law

Filling "gaps" in statutes with common law is nothing new. This is fully consistent with the conception that statutes are enacted against a common law background. The common law rule that fills the gap may be one that runs counter to the general thrust of the statutory rule.[126] But when a new common law rule must be developed, there is no reason why it could not be consistent with the statute. Thus, courts have sometimes chosen a *complementary* common law rule analogous to the statutory rule. For example, in *University of Tennessee v. Elliott*,[127] a federal statute required that state *court judgments* be respected by other states and the federal courts. The statute did not by its terms apply to decisions of *administrative agencies*, but the Court was inspired by the principles underlying the statute to create a complementary common law rule analogous to the one stated in the statute that would govern administrative agency decisions.[128]

Other cases involving legislatively-inspired common law move further away from complementary gap-filling cases like *Elliott* and closer to direct reasoning by analogy. In these cases, the "gap" being filled is quite large (if indeed it can be described as a "gap"), and legislative policy is used to *displace* an inconsistent, well-settled common law rule.

A pair of California cases illustrates this. The California legislature had passed Married Women's Property Acts, which abrogated common law disabilities of married women related to property rights.[129] The California Supreme Court relied on the policies underlying those Acts to abolish two common law doctrines that were not

---

123 *See supra* p. 54.

124 436 U.S. 49 (1978).

125 A broader approach to statutes has been championed by some scholars and judges. *See supra* note 60.

126 *See, e.g., Norfolk Redevelopment and Housing Authority v. Chesapeake and Potomac Telephone Co.*, 464 U.S. 30 (1983) (telephone company that was required to relocate equipment because of street realignment was not a "displaced person" entitled to relocation benefits within the meaning of federal statute; court applied common law principle that a utility forced to relocate from public right-of-way must do so at its own expense).

127 478 U.S. 788 (1986).

128 It is interesting that the Court in the *Elliott* case did not consider the possible application of the *expressio unius* maxim, which would have dictated the opposite result. *See supra* p. 56.

129 *See* Chapter XIII, p. 476, for a discussion of Married Women's Property Acts.

within the sweep of the statutes. In one case, the court abolished the doctrine prohibiting tort suits between spouses[130] and in the other, it abolished the rule deeming that husband and wife were incapable of a criminal conspiracy.[131] The court found that the statutes abrogating common law property ownership disabilities had undercut the principle underlying the tort and criminal law doctrines — the fiction that a married woman's person merged with that of the husband upon marriage. The new statutory principle of separate personhood in property matters was applied in a non-property context.

A U.S. Supreme Court case, *Moragne v. States Marine Lines, Inc.*,[132] involved similar reasoning. In that case, an 1886 common law precedent stood in the way of a wrongful death suit by the widow of a longshoreman killed in coastal waters off Florida. Although the common law authorized suits for *injuries*, the 1886 precedent established that *wrongful death* suits by survivors were not permitted unless provided for by statute.   Neither Florida nor federal statutes authorized suit in the case. However, the Court overruled the troublesome common law precedent and permitted the suit. It based its decision on the fact that federal and state legislatures in several statutes had consistently granted a statutory right to recover for wrongful death in analogous situations. Justice Harlan's unanimous opinion spoke expansively of the propriety of drawing on legislative policy as a basis for lawmaking.[133]

Legislatively-inspired common law should not seem alien to a common law court. When choosing a common law rule, a court considers *all* possible input into the question of what that rule should be. Public policy choices made by democratically elected legislators are certainly a legitimate part of that data. Indeed, to the extent that courts are concerned that judicial lawmaking is undemocratic,[134] legislative sources for common law-making should be all the more attractive to courts.[135]

b. Reasoning by Analogy Without the Common Law Medium

There are a few examples of true application of statutory provisions by analogy without using the medium of common law doctrine. In *Cintrone v. Hertz Trucking Leasing and Rental Service*,[136] and *Newmark v. Gimbel's, Inc.*,[137] the New Jersey Supreme Court found that an implied warranty of fitness for purpose, as set out in the Uniform Commercial Code (UCC) for *sales* of *goods*, applied to the *lease* of a truck and to *services* rendered in a beauty parlor. In the lease case, the court observed that the "development of the warranty doctrine in sales should point the way by suggestive analogy to similar results in cases where a commodity is leased" in view of the fact that the same business ends that can be achieved by selling and buying can be achieved by leasing.[138] The aftermath of the UCC analogy cases, however, shows just

---

130 *Self v. Self*, 376 P.2d 65 (Cal. 1962).

131 *People v. Pierce*, 395 P.2d 893 (Cal. 1964).

132 398 U.S. 375 (1970).

133 *See Comment*, "The Legitimacy of Civil Law Reasoning in Common Law: Justice Harlan's Contribution," 82 YALE L.J. 258 (1972).

134 *See supra* p. 43.

135 The development of common law from legislative principles was pointed out several years ago in an essay. *See* James Landis, "Statutes and the Sources of Law," in HARVARD LEGAL ESSAYS 213 (1934).

136 212 A.2d 769 (N.J. 1965).

137 258 A.2d 697 (N.J. 1969).

138 This is consistent with the Uniform Commercial Code's drafters' suggestion that the Code's underlying principles should be applied to decide cases not expressly included in the language of the act. *See* Comment to UCC § 1-102, SELECTED COMMERCIAL STATUTES (West 1998).

how strong a pull the typical common law attitude still has. Other courts have followed the *result* of these cases, but not surprisingly have understood the cases as extending a *common law* rule of strict liability in *tort*. They do not rely on or even mention the Uniform Commercial Code.[139]

One U.S. Supreme Court opinion has reasoned directly by analogy, though over a strong protest from Justice Scalia. In *Agency Holding Corp. v. Malley Duff & Associates*,[140] the Court had to determine what the time limitation period was for filing actions under the federal Racketeer Influenced and Corrupt Organizations (RICO) statute.[141] The majority opinion applied the limitation period of a different federal statute, an antitrust act, believing that it provided the "closest analogy" to the RICO statute based on its similar structure and purpose. Justice Scalia, voicing the traditional common law attitude, viewed this form of reasoning as illegitimate. If the statute did not provide a limitations period, he argued, then either state law applied or there simply was *no* limitation period. He objected strongly to the Court's "prowling hungrily through the Statutes at Large for an appetizing federal limitations period," absent legislative direction to apply an analogous federal statute. He could "find no legitimate source for the new rule" and argued that picking a limitation period of a certain length was "quintessentially the kind of judgment to be made by the legislature."[142]

The above cases should not lead one to conclude that American courts reason analogically from statutes on a regular basis. Justice Scalia's dissenting position in the *Agency Holding* case is clearly the traditional view. Further, the maxim of *expressio unius est exclusio alterius*, which has seen a resurgence in use by the Supreme Court in recent years, remains an obstacle to much analogical reasoning from statutes. So far, it remains an exotic form of reasoning that is more often rejected than accepted.

E. The Form and General Nature of Caselaw

Having considered statutes in depth, we will now consider caselaw in this and the next section of this chapter. This section will consider the form that caselaw generally takes and the principle of *stare decisis*. In the next section, we will discuss the legal reasoning process used in applying caselaw.

1. Judicial Opinions and Their Structure

Types of Opinions The most important judicial opinions are appellate court opinions. Appellate courts have multiple judges — usually 3, 5, 7, or 9 judges — and the case is decided by a majority vote of the judges on the court. There is an "opinion of the court" which states the decision and detailed reasons for that decision agreed to by a majority of the judges.[143] This opinion is written and signed by an individual

---

139 *See Martin v. Ryder Truck Rental, Inc.*, 353 A.2d 581 (Del. 1976). Analogical application of the UCC to leases was rendered largely moot when a new Article 2A covering leases was added in 1990 and adopted in 43 states.

140 483 U.S. 143 (1987).

141 The statute failed to specify any period. Typically, the Court has applied state-law limitation periods of the state where the federal action is brought. This has been justified either on a theory that state law applies of its own force where Congress has not preempted it or because Congress has implicitly directed that courts "borrow" state law.

142 *But see* Traynor, *supra* note 60, at 405-409 (collecting examples from between 1300 and 1800 of English common law courts analogizing from limitation periods in otherwise inapplicable statutes). Traynor was Chief Justice of the California Supreme Court.

143 The general form of appellate opinions can be seen from *Hoffman v. Jones*, reprinted in the Appendix A.

judge who is a member of that majority.[144] Unless the decision is unanimous, one or more "dissenting opinions" may be filed by judges who disagree with the majority's conclusion and reasoning, or a judge may simply indicate the fact of dissent without an opinion. There may also be "concurring opinions" written by judges who agree with the conclusion of the majority, but disagree with its reasoning. Clearly, the majority opinion is the most important opinion, but the attentive lawyer will wish to read concurring and dissenting opinions to clarify the impact of the majority opinion.

The assignment to write the majority opinion is usually made by the chief justice or judge. Drafts of proposed majority, dissenting and concurring opinions are circulated among members of the court. In the process, the majority opinion writer often gets suggestions from other members of the majority and may include responses to criticisms by dissenting and concurring opinions. Sometimes there is a need to "bargain" to accommodate demands from members of the majority. This will force the writer to include ideas that are not his or her own, thus sometimes making for a less than completely coherent or consistent opinion. If a majority agrees on the proper result, but less than a majority agrees on a rationale for the decision, no one opinion receives the approval of a majority. The opinion supporting the result in the case that has the most votes is referred to as a "plurality opinion." The precise precedential value of a plurality opinion is not well defined and depends to a large extent on how later majority opinions of the same court treat it. Some have been cited and treated almost like majority opinions while others have been given little weight or have been completely ignored.

Structure and Content of Opinions There is no set structure for a majority opinion, but it will usually start with a statement summarizing the case and its procedural posture, a statement of the facts and the legal issues presented, a section discussing in detail the reasons supporting the decision, and the action to be taken in the case. The discussion of the reasoning behind the decision will often be encyclopedic, including extensive citations to and discussions of all prior relevant cases and many secondary authorities, such as law review articles and treatises. Thus, as noted in the Reader's Guide and Bibliographic Introduction to this book, the judicial opinions of some courts — and of the U.S. Supreme Court in particular — are often helpful as references for discovering useful sources in the general area of law to which the case relates.

2. Precedential Effect of Court Decisions

Stare Decisis The essence of the system by which court decisions are a source of law for later cases is the rule of *stare decisis*. The precise meaning of *stare decisis* is best expressed by the full Latin phrase from which the term comes: "*stare decisis et non quieta movere*," which means "to stand by precedents and not to disturb settled points."

The rationales for having a caselaw or precedential law system have been variously stated.[145] Perhaps the most often-stated justification for following precedent is what Karl Llewellyn called "that curious, almost universal sense of justice which

---

144 The English style in the 1700s, inherited by American appellate courts, was to have *seriatim* opioions by each judge, giving the reader the task of figuring out who was in the majority and what their reasoning was. Chief Justice John Marshall of the United States Supreme Court, who served from 1801 to 1836, was responsible for breaking with the English practice and requiring a single opinion of the Court.

145 *See* LLEWELLYN, *supra* note 41 at 26, where several are discussed..

urges that all men are properly to be treated alike in like circumstances."[146] This equality of treatment in turn serves to limit bias and arbitrariness and allows parties to rely with some certainty on how the system has dealt with cases similar to theirs. In addition, following precedent is efficient since similar cases need not be reasoned through "from the ground up." Since statutes can be subject to differing interpretations, the rationales for a system of precedent apply with equal force to judicial decisions interpreting enacted law.

Court decisions can have two types of *stare decisis* effect. The effect can be "binding" or it can be only "persuasive."

Binding Stare Decisis Effect Binding effect on a court means that the court is obligated to follow the rule established by an earlier case. The decisions of a superior court have binding effect on all lower courts in the same court system. Thus, a decision of the Florida Supreme Court, the highest court in the state, has binding effect on all other state courts in Florida. This form of binding effect is sometimes referred to as "vertical" *stare decisis*. Prior decisions of a court will also bind that *same* court in later cases. This is sometimes referred to as "horizontal" *stare decisis*. However, horizontal binding effect is more flexible than vertical binding effect. It is not unusual that a court would sometimes overrule its own precedent.[147]

Persuasive Stare Decisis Effect If a court is not obligated to follow precedents established in earlier cases, but may do so if it is persuaded by the reasoning used, the precedential effect is only "persuasive." The decision of a legal question by the courts of one state will have only persuasive effect on the courts of another state. For example, New York courts will follow a Florida Supreme Court decision only if they believe it is correctly reasoned. Similarly, as noted in Chapter I, federal courts must apply state law in suits between citizens of different states [148] However, their interpretations of state law have only persuasive effect on the state courts of that state, since authoritative interpretations of a state's law may only be rendered by those state courts.

Stare Decisis Effect of Statutory Interpretations Some have argued for a rule of absolute *stare decisis* effect for caselaw interpreting statutes.[149] Among the factors urged in favor is the ease with which the legislature can notice and correct any misunderstanding of legislative intent. In addition, the greater specificity of statutes often means that there are greater reliance interests involved. This has not been the Supreme Court's approach, however.[150]

Stare Decisis Effect of Constitutional Decisions Legislatures have the ability to change both common law caselaw and caselaw interpreting statutes. However, legislative "correction" of *constitutional* caselaw can only take place through the

---

146 LLEWELLYN, *id.* See also EDGAR BODENHEIMER, JURISPRUDENCE: THE PHILOSOPHY AND METHOD OF THE LAW 425-430 (Harvard U. Press 1974).

147 *Stare decisis* is more closely adhered to in England than in the United States. Indeed, it was only in 1966 that the House of Lords, the highest court in England, formally adopted the principle that it should feel free in appropriate cases to depart from its own prior decisions. 1 W.L.R. 1234 (H.L. 1966) (Lord Gardner L.C.).

148 *See* p. 30.

149 *See* Lawrence C. Marshall, *"Let Congress Do It": The Case for an Absolute Rule of Statutory Stare Decisis*, 88 MICH. L. REV. 177 (1989) (arguing for an absolute rule and suggesting that *stare decisis* as used today is a "mere rhetorical device").

150 *See, e.g. Monell v. New York Department of Social Services*, 436 U.S. 658 (1978) *overruling Monroe v. Pape*, 365 U.S. 167 (1961) (confessing error in construing the word defining suable defendant "persons" as not including municipalities).

process of amending the Constitution — rarely a successful option. For this reason, the Supreme Court has been somewhat more amenable to overruling cases interpreting the Constitution that have been called into serious question.[151]

F. The Legal Reasoning Process in Caselaw

Two basic types of legal reasoning are used with caselaw: deductive reasoning and analogical reasoning.[152] Deductive reasoning takes caselaw "rules" and applies them in a manner similar to statutes. Analogical reasoning directly compares the facts of the prior precedent to the facts of the case to be decided.[153]

1. Deductive Reasoning from Caselaw Rules

The deductive reasoning process used in caselaw, like the process used with statutes, begins with a rule. However, caselaw involves an added step, because one must first determine just what "rule" has been established by prior caselaw. When dealing with one prior case, that "rule" is the "holding" of a case. In England, the term "ratio decidendi" is used.

a. Determining the Holding or Rule of a Case

The "holding" or "rule" of a case is a one or two sentence statement that summarizes the broader, more abstract principle for which the case stands, and for which the case can be used to decide later cases. A holding must be stated in such a way that it will make sense to a person who has not read the case, so a proper holding will contain shorthand references to the facts which were deemed most important for the decision.

For example, assume A owns a boat. B steals the boat. B then sells the boat to C. C pays B fair market value for it and does not know the boat is stolen. A finds out that C has the boat and sues C for possession.[154] Assume the judge decides for A, the owner. The opinion states in part: "It is argued that C paid fair market value for the boat and had no notice that it had been stolen and therefore acquired title. We do not agree. The seller B acquired the boat by illegal means and thus did not gain any right or title to it. Having no title himself, he was powerless to convey any to C. Moreover, there is benefit in a rule that serves to make it more difficult for thieves to dispose of stolen property. Judgement for A." The holding of the case might be as follows: "Where property is stolen from the owner and sold by the thief to a third person, the owner can recover that property from the third-party purchaser even if the purchaser paid full value and had no knowledge that the property was stolen." This rule can then be applied in the same manner as a statute.[155]

---

151 *See Burnet v. Colorado Oil & Gas Co.*, 285 U.S. 393, 406-08 (1932) (Brandies, J., dissenting) ("in cases involving the Federal Constitution, where correction through legislative action is practically impossible, this Court has often overruled its earlier decisions"). *But see Planned Parenthood of Southeastern Pennsylvania v. Casey*, 505 U.S. 833 (1992) (declining to overrule its 1973 decision establishing a constitutionally-secured right to an abortion, largely on *stare decisis* grounds).

152 For discussions of the modes of legal reasoning, *see* STEVEN BURTON, AN INTRODUCTION TO LAW AND LEGAL REASONING, 2D ED (Aspen 1995); MELVIN A. EISENBERG, THE NATURE OF THE COMMON LAW (Harvard U. Press 1988); RUGGERO ALDISERT, LOGIC FOR LAWYERS (Clark, Boardman 1989). *See also* Vincent Wellman, *Practical Reasoning and Judicial Justification: Toward an Adequate Theory*, 57 U. COLO.L.REV. 45 (1985).

153 The legal reasoning process is the same for common law caselaw as for caselaw interpreting statutes or other enacted law. Consequently, the two are treated together in this section.

154 These illustrations are adapted from Lon Fuller, *The Forms and Limits of Adjudication*, 92 HARV.L.REV. 353, 375-76 (1978).

155 Note that this statement of the holding largely ignores the reasoning given in the "opinion" in the earlier case. The extent to which the reasons given by the court in the opinion are to be incorporated into the statement of the holding is a matter of some difference of opinion and the American lawyer is much

There can be broad and narrow statements of the holding of a case. A broad statement is on a higher level of generalization, while a narrow one will stick more closely to the precise facts of the decided case. The statement of the holding just given above is probably a relatively narrow statement of it, though a statement confining the holding to boats alone, would be even narrower. A broader one would be: "An owner can recover *unlawfully-obtained* property from a subsequent purchaser, even if the subsequent purchaser did not know of the property's illegal origins."

The danger of broad statements of holdings is that they can turn out to be *overly* broad. This is illustrated by assuming that after the above case is decided, which we will call Case 1, a Case 2 arises in the same court. In this case, the boat was bought with a *fraudulent check* and the defrauding purchaser in turn sold it to a third party. The court holds in Case 2 that the original owner may *not* recover from the third party. Without getting into the reasons why a court might so decide (we will discuss that below), it is clear at least one form of "unlawfully-obtained property" may *not* be recovered from the third party purchaser for value. The court has detected a difference between outright theft and fraud and our statement of the holdings in both cases should reflect that fact.

b. Dictum

Judges are expected to give reasons for their decisions. In the process of doing so, they are conscious of the fact that they are not only deciding a case; they are also making law. As a result, they will often seek to elucidate the impact of their decision for future cases. However, not all statements of legal principles by judges deciding a case are part of the holding. Statements that were not necessary to the decision of that case can have no binding authority in a later case, and should be ignored in stating the holding of the case. A statement that is not necessary for decision of the case is called "*dictum*" or "*obiter dictum*."[156] For example, assume that in Case 1 (outright theft of the boat and later sale; A wins), the court goes on to say that "in a case in which a seller of property obtained that property from the owner fraudulently, the owner could not recover." Or the court might say that "an owner who abandoned his property cannot thereafter sue to recover it from someone who finds it." These comments would not have been necessary to the decision of Case 1 in A's favor and would therefore be *dictum*.

Strictly speaking, *dictum* has no precedential value for future cases. Consequently, it would be improper to say that the above dictum from Case 1 applies to determine later cases of fraudulent sale or abandonment of property. However, no sensible lawyer can ignore *dictum*. It shows that the court has thought about how those other cases should be resolved and would so act if given the chance. The lawyer whose argument in a case is contrary to *dictum* contained in the majority opinion in a recent supreme court case will have a difficult time convincing the court otherwise. On the other hand, it is not unheard of for a court to go against its own earlier *dictum*. The hypothetical nature of *dictum* often means that the court will not

---

more likely to include them than the English lawyer. *See* ATIYAH & SUMMERS, *supra* note 22, at 124-125 and sources cited therein.

156 *Dictum* means literally a statement. *Obiter dictum* means a statement uttered in passing. The practical reason why *dictum* should not be relied upon is that both the court and the parties before it have most comprehensively investigated and considered the question actually before the court, and any side issues are not the product of as thorough a process. *See Cohens v. Virginia*, 19 U.S. (6 Wheat.) 264, 399 (1821) (Marshall, C.J.)

have thought about it as deeply and the parties' arguments will not have addressed it as well as points more central to decision of the case.

c. Multiple and Implied Holdings

It sometimes happens that a court rendering a decision does not explicitly state a holding, but one may be implied from the result and the court's statement of the facts. Assume, for example, in boat Case 2 where the seller procured the boat by fraud and then sold it, the court decides that the purchaser wins instead of the owner. However, instead of explaining its reasons, the court merely states the relevant facts of the case, emphasizing the fact that the purchaser of the boat did not know of the fraud. Any statement of the holding in the case must necessarily include the element of lack of knowledge since the context indicates that the court viewed that as important.

A case can have more than one holding. Thus, in Case 1 above involving the stolen boat, the opinion may have also discussed and decided whether the original owner could get specific recovery of the property (as opposed to recovery of the value of the property) as a remedy. A holding that accounted for this part of the case might be: "An owner of stolen property found in the possession of another may obtain an order for specific relief requiring its return so long as the property can be reasonably identified and the person in possession is subject to the jurisdiction of the court."[157]

d. Synthesizing a Rule From Several Cases

There is a second kind of caselaw rule from which lawyers can argue deductively. It is like the holding or rule of a particular case, but represents a "synthesis" of several cases. By putting together or "synthesizing" the holdings of several cases, the lawyer can come up with an overall legal rule for which a line of decisions stands.

To demonstrate this, assume as before that Case 1 involved a *stolen* boat and the owner was *allowed* to recover. Assume as well that Case 2 involved a *fraudulently-obtained* boat and the court held the owner could *not* recover. Now assume a Case 3, in which X has an oil painting. Y obtains the painting from X through fraud. Y then sells the painting to Z. Before this sale, Z had heard rumors that perhaps Y had obtained the painting through some improper means and the price Y was asking was very low. But Z bought the painting anyway. The original owner X now sues Z for possession of the painting. Assume that the court in Case 3 holds that X *can* recover this time. In so deciding, the court notes that, unlike Case 2 (where fraud was also involved), in Case 3, Z paid much less than market price for the painting and had heard from others that Y might have obtained the painting unlawfully. These facts, the court observed, should have put Z on notice that there was something wrong with the painting. A synthesis of cases 1, 2 and 3 might be stated as follows: "An owner may recover stolen personal property from a subsequent purchaser for value who did not have notice that it was stolen. However, an owner may not recover fraudulently-obtained property from a subsequent purchaser unless the purchaser knew of the fraud or had reason to question the seller's title to the property." This synthesized rule, like the rule derived from a single case, can then be applied deductively to a later case much the same way that a statute might be applied.

---

157 However, if the court had decided that A could *not* recover because A had failed to prove ownership, and then went on to state the circumstances under which an owner *could* obtain an order for specific relief, then such a statement would be *dictum*.

If a synthesis of cases is a broad one and involves the common law, it is sometimes referred to as a "common law rule." Such rules are abstract statements that summarize a "family" of related holdings. The just-stated synthesis of cases 1 through 3 might be treated this way, though most common law rules will cover a broader area. Sometimes a court's opinion will helpfully provide a summarized synthesis of cases.

2. Analogical Reasoning Directly From Prior Caselaw Decisions

There are limits to using holdings and case syntheses deductively like statutes. Deductive reasoning alone is of little use in deciding whether a case *comes within* the rule one has distilled from a prior case, unless the new case involves the same facts as the earlier one. For example, judges who are trying to decide Case 2 (fraudulently obtained boat) can read and reread the *holding* of Case 1, but it will not tell them whether the rule of Case 1 *should* cover Case 2 as well. What the judges need to decide is how Case 2 is similar to or different from Case 1 or any other precedents in the area. To do this requires the application of analogical reasoning directly from the facts of the prior case.

a. The Analogical Reasoning Process

The analogical reasoning process involves a two-step process of (1) identifying the factual similarities and differences between the new case to be decided and the precedent and (2) determining whether the current case is either similar to or different from that precedent in *important* respects relevant to the issue to be decided. If the precedent is deemed similar in those important respects, it will be *followed*. If it is deemed different in important respects, it will be *distinguished*.[158]

Following or distinguishing precedents involves a simple analogical reasoning process used every day. To take an example anyone with children will recognize, assume that you have decided to let your ten-year-old stay up until 10:00 PM (on a non-school night).[159] Your six-year-old feels the sting of injustice when she is forced to go to bed at 8:00 PM. She appeals to you to allow her to stay up until 10:00, arguing that you let the ten-year-old child stay up. In developing her argument from precedent, perhaps the six-year-old will point out the factual similarities between their situations, e.g., that they are both children and that neither of them has school the next day. If you find the younger child's appeal to the precedent involving the older child unpersuasive, it will be because you have determined that the difference in their ages is more important than whatever similarities might exist. This difference is important because age directly relates to the issue to be decided — bedtimes for children. The difference in ages is important to bedtimes because younger children need more sleep.

Clearly the most difficult part of the analogical reasoning process is evaluating the importance of the differences and similarities. This question of importance cannot be determined in the abstract. Importance is situational and depends on the issue that

---

158 *See* BURTON, *supra* note 152, at 26-27. Professor Edward Levi explains analogical reasoning from precedent as involving three steps: "similarity is seen between cases; next the rule of law inherent in the first case is announced; then the rule of law is made applicable to the second case." *See* EDWARD LEVI, AN INTRODUCTION TO LEGAL REASONING 1-2 (University of Chicago Press 1948). Levi is not specific enough about the nature of the "rule of law" involved to judge, but this seems more like deductive, not analogical reasoning. I believe that Burton's and Golding's view more accurately portrays what lawyers and judges actually do, especially in difficult cases: they make direct comparisons between the facts of each case without the intervention of any clearly formulated intermediate "rule." *See* MARTIN GOLDING, LEGAL REASONING 103 (Alfred Knopf 1984); BURTON, *supra* note 152, at 36.

159 This example is adapted from BURTON, *supra* note 152, at 26-27.

is to be decided. In the example with the children, denying the younger child's request to stay up late on the ground that "she's Ann and you're Zelda" is a decision based on an actual difference between them — their names. But different names cannot be a valid basis for deciding the case presented because it is based on a difference that has nothing to do with *bedtimes*. On the other hand, "she's Ann and you're Zelda" *is* a relevant difference in determining where each child should be in a line of children that is arranged alphabetically.

b. Evaluating Factual Variations in Common Law Caselaw

The importance question for common law caselaw is most often determined by examining a "family" of similar cases and principles underlying them. We will return to the example introduced earlier of the dispute between the owners of property and subsequent purchasers to demonstrate the process.

Analogical Reasoning Applied to a Common Law Example Assume that a court has decided Case 1 (boat stolen and sold; owner wins). The Court must now decide Case 2 (boat fraudulently-obtained) where the innocent purchaser has also been sued. On the one hand, underlying Case 1 and similar cases protecting owners of property is the notion that ownership of property is good for society and greater protection will encourage owners to invest in and preserve their property. On the other hand, free commerce in goods is important to society. One could argue that it is unreasonable to burden an innocent purchaser with the risk that the original owner could appear on the scene at any time, even years later, and reclaim the property. The court in Case 1 nonetheless imposed this risk on the purchaser in the case of theft in the name of protecting property ownership and making things more difficult for thieves.[160]

Case 2 is arguably different because owners are more able to protect themselves from fraud than from theft. An owner can prevent fraud by insisting on verification of any tender of payment, while theft can take place at any time and is usually unexpected. At the same time, the subsequent purchaser is *less* able to protect himself from the fraud than from theft. Purchasers in the marketplace in general have limited ability to verify assertions of good title. But purchasers have even more trouble verifying title where their seller has obtained the property by fraud. The transaction has all the outward appearances of a *bona fide* sale, complete with a bill of sale signed by the owner. In fact, but for the fact that the check the owner received for the property later turned out to be worthless, the transaction had all the characteristics of a sale, including the fact that the owner, at the time of transfer of the property, voluntarily parted with possession.

On this analysis, assume that the court decides Case 2 in favor of the purchaser. It concludes that, while no title passes by virtue of a theft, many of the elements of a normal sale are present in the fraudulent transaction, including the owner's intent to transfer title, such that it can be said that the defrauding purchaser obtained at least voidable title. Thus, while the owner might be able to sue the *defrauding party* directly to void the title and regain the property, if the property is resold to an innocent purchaser before title is voided, title passes to that purchaser and the owner cannot recover his property from that purchaser.[161]

---

160 The "opinion" of the court is set out *supra* p. 63.

161 Many jurisdictions have distinguished fraud cases from stolen property cases for the reasons stated, as does the UCC. *See generally* RAY A. BROWN, THE LAW ON PERSONAL PROPERTY §§ 9.4, 9.6 (Callaghan & Co. 1975).

Now assume that Case 3 arises, the case in which the painting was fraudulently obtained and the buyer paid a low price and had heard rumors about the possibly dubious title of the seller. Case 3 is the same as Case 2 except for the fact that the purchaser seems to have some reason to suspect that there is a problem with the painting. The discussion in Case 2 would seem to make this factual difference an important one, since underlying that decision is a concern that buyers in the market have great difficulty finding out about defective title in fraud cases. In terms of this factor, the purchaser in Case 3 is different from the purchaser in Case 2 and should have been on notice from the low price and rumors that there should be further inquiry. A more subtle basis for deciding Case 3 against the purchaser that might be gleaned from the earlier cases deals with the reprehensibility of the conduct of the actors involved. In Case 1, the Court in part justified its decision on the policy of making things more difficult for thieves. In Case 2, it was undisputed that the owner could recover against the *perpetrator* of the fraud. A person who takes advantage of fraud, as the purchaser in Case 3 did, is only slightly better than the thief or the perpetrator of the fraud and should not be allowed to benefit from that conduct.

"Ghost" Precedents The analogical arguments made here suggest that there may be more "precedents" involved than just the decided cases. For example, it was argued in Case 2, not only that the fraudulent transfer situation was *distinguishable* from the *theft* situation in Case 1, but that the fraudulent transfer was *similar* to a *true sale*. We were given no *real* case involving a true sale. But we can assume hypothetically that a court would reject the claim of an owner who received the price he asked and completed a sale, but then had second thoughts and sought to reclaim the property from his purchaser. A similar hypothetical "precedent" was used to support the decision in Case 3. The court in Case 3 necessarily assumed that the owner *would* win in a contest between the owner and the *perpetrator* of the fraud. It then used that "ghost" precedent as one of its reasons for denying recovery to the purchaser who took advantage of the fraud.

Recasting Precedent The arguments made in Case 2 and Case 3 also point out how a court dealing with precedent is not necessarily limited to the rationale given in earlier opinions. The opinion in Case 1 relied in part on a rather formal theory that title had not passed to the thief. The case is recast in the decision of the later cases to fit into a more general theory about safeguarding ownership and purchasers' abilities to protect themselves in the market.[162]

c. Choice of Deductive or Analogical Reasoning: Easy Cases and Hard Cases

Having outlined both deductive and analogical reasoning in caselaw, it is appropriate to consider when judges or lawyer might choose one mode over the other. Some judicial opinions or arguments go through a complete analogical analysis of the factual differences between the case to be decided and various precedents. Others will synthesize a rule out of the applicable precedents and apply that rule deductively like a statute. Which approach is used depends on a number of factors, including the personal decision-making style of the judge.

---

162 A classic recasting of precedent is Judge Cardozo's opinion in *McPherson v. Buick Motor Co.*, 111 N.E. 1050 (N.Y. 1916) (recasting precedents to broaden protection from harm caused by "imminently" dangerous products, such as mislabeled poisons, to harm caused by products that are dangerous because they are negligently made, such as an automobile).

Deductive reasoning from general rules established by cases is particularly useful in deciding *easy* cases or easy parts of cases. For example, returning to the property hypothetical, assume that after Case 3 is decided, a Case 4 arises in which the buyer of stolen property actually helped to facilitate the theft of the property. The court could dispose of the case by citing the common law rule set out earlier, followed by a "string cite" of Cases 1 through 3 and other prominent cases in the particular "family" of cases.[163] Because the matter is so clear, there would be no need for any analogical analysis of the facts of the cases.[164]

In fact, deductive reasoning from statements of holdings or rules of prior cases is useful *only* to decide clear or "easy" cases. Arguments in more difficult cases may start out with deductive reasoning, but soon disagreement arises over whether a particular synthesized rule is applicable to the case at bar, or whether such a "rule" exists at all. When that happens, the arguments turn immediately to analogical reasoning directly from the facts of prior cases, seeking to apply them to or distinguish them from the facts of the case to be decided.

3. Reasoning in Caselaw Interpreting Statutes

a. Deductive and Analogical Reasoning in Statutory Caselaw

As already discussed when statutory interpretation was outlined, a court faced with applying a statute must examine the text of the statute and any permitted aids to interpretation allowed to be consulted. The court must also consider prior caselaw interpreting the statute. These holdings and syntheses of holdings serve as "sub-rules" of the statutory rule being interpreted and can be applied deductively to decide easy cases. For example, it is common that a criminal statute will punish assault "with a deadly weapon" more seriously than a simple assault. A case arises in which the defendant, who was stopped by a policeman for a traffic violation, tried to run over the policeman with his car. If there is caselaw holding that a car does or does not qualify as deadly weapons, then that caselaw rule is as valid as any definition that might have been enacted in the statute.

Courts use caselaw interpreting statutes in much the same way that common law caselaw is used — both deductively and analogically. If the caselaw is clear on the subject of whether a car can be a "deadly weapon" if used to try to kill someone, then the case is an "easy" one and the rule established can be applied deductively without any need for direct analogical reasoning.[165] If there is no prior precedent that provides a suitable sub-rule holding that is directly on point, the court must resort to analogical reasoning. Perhaps there are cases involving assaults using other implements that were not originally designed to be used as deadly weapons, but which could be and were used as such. The court will then have to use the analogical reasoning process already outlined for common law decisions and make the factual comparisons and judgments involved[166]

---

163 A "string cite" is where a court or lawyer simply "strings" together in a list the case names and citations of several cases without discussing their facts or reasoning.

164 Use of deductive application of a rule with string cites is so identified with resolving easy questions that intellectually dishonest or lazy judges or lawyers who want the issue involved to seem easier than it is will often misuse the technique. Examination of the facts and holdings of cases in a "string cite" often turn out not to support the proposition claimed.

165 *See supra* pp. 63-66.

166 *See supra* pp. 66-67.

b. Evaluating Factual Variations in Caselaw Interpreting Statutes

Applying Legislative Policy   The main difference between analogical reasoning in common law and statutory caselaw comes at the point when the court must evaluate the questions of the *importance* of the factual differences and similarities between prior cases and the new case to be decided. In *common law* caselaw, the court refers to principles enunciated in prior cases or in the common law generally. In dealing with caselaw concerning *statutes*, the importance inquiry must generally be confined to criteria set by the *legislature*.

These legislative criteria are usually found by examining the language, purpose and legislative history of the enactment. However, the relevant legislative policy and purpose have often been sifted through several judicial filters. As Professor Shapiro has cogently observed:

> [J]udges [in the United States] often construct their opinions as mosaics of excerpts from, citations of, and comments about earlier judicial decisions. Even when the case is one of statutory interpretation, the wording of the statute may be buried in a footnote. In many instances, of course, the judge will openly proclaim that the source of the basic legal rule being applied is a previous decision rather than a statutory provision.[167]

In the process of this judicial filtering of legislative policy, more general principles sometimes appear.[168]

"Ghost" Precedents in Statutory Interpretation   As we saw earlier when "ghost" common law precedents were discussed, one need not have *actual* prior caselaw to reason by analogy. So strong is the pull of cases and analogical reasoning that judges or lawyers will often create "ghost" cases from which to argue when interpreting a statute. A court will often construct "paradigm cases" that reflect the social ills that the legislature was seeking to eradicate or the kinds of positive behavior it was trying to promote. The court will then compare the instant case with the hypothetical cases and reason from them as if they were real cases. Such "ghost" precedents are especially easy to generate in statutory caselaw because sponsors and supporters of the bill will often themselves create such examples to illustrate the purpose of the legislation.[169]

G. Legal Research Techniques and the Form of Legal Argument

1. Library Resources for Finding Primary Materials

Caselaw   The percentage of appellate court decisions that are published varies widely and has in general been declining in recent years as the number of appeals has increased. Among the federal courts of appeal, fewer than half of their decisions are published. The judges who decided the case make the decision whether to release their decision for publication. Even if not published, opinions are generally available nonetheless from one of the computerized legal research services, discussed below.

---

167 MARTIN SHAPIRO, COURTS: A COMPARATIVE AND POLITICAL ANALYSIS 135 (U. Chicago Press 1981).

168 For a discussion of how general principles operate in both common law and statutory caselaw, *see* DWORKIN, *supra* note 40, at 23-24 (discussing both a common law example and one involving a statute). *Cf. Riggs v. Palmer*, 22 N.E. 188 (N.Y. 1899) (grandson could not inherit from the grandparent he had murdered despite lack of such disqualification in the statute; court presumed that legislature had "maxims of the common law" in mind when it passed the statute). *See also supra*, p. 58 (statutory interpretation in light of fundamental values).

169 This technique was used by the Court in a statutory context in the *Holy Trinity Church* case, *supra* p. 55. *See also supra* p. 68 ("ghost" precedents in common law caselaw).

However, local rules generally state either that unpublished opinions have no precedential effect or that reliance on them is "disfavored."

Published judicial opinions in cases are published in chronological order and can be found in books known as "reporters" or "case reports."[170] Case reporting in the United States began informally and on a selective basis just as it did in England. However, it soon became more systematic with "official" reports issued by states and the United States Supreme Court. West Publishing Company, a private company, began an effort to be more comprehensive and systematic in the 1880s. Today West publishes "regional reporters" covering all the states. In addition, it publishes the only readily available reporters of federal court decisions. Because the West reporters publish all opinions released for publication, many states have abandoned publication of official reports. State trial court decisions are generally not published even on a selective basis except in a few states.

On the federal level, United States Supreme Court opinions are published in three places: the official reporter, United States Reports (U.S.); the Supreme Court Reporter (S.Ct.) published by West Publishing; and U.S. Supreme Court Reports, Lawyer's Edition (L.Ed.), a reporter series published by Lawyer's Cooperative Publishing Company, another private legal publisher.[171] Selected federal district court opinions are reported in reporters entitled Federal Supplement (F. Supp.) and, if they deal with issues of federal court procedure, in the Federal Rules Decisions (F.R.D.). Federal appellate opinions available for publication are published in Federal Reporter, Second Series (F.2d) or Third Series (F.3d). A federal court of appeals opinion might be cited as *Donnelly v. Guion*, 467 F.2d 290 (2d Cir. 1972). The parenthetical material indicates that the court was the U.S. Court of Appeals for the Second Circuit.[172]

Enacted Law State and federal constitutions, statutes, and regulations are published in volumes arranged topically. State and federal statutes are published by governmental publishers and by private publishers in annotated volumes providing reference to cases interpreting the statute, citations to legislative history, pertinent articles in legal periodicals, and references to computer data bases. For example, on the federal level, statutes are contained in the government publication entitled United States Code (U.S.C.) and in two privately published and annotated versions entitled United States Code Annotated (U.S.C.A.) and United States Code Service (U.S.C.S.). Annotations are brief summaries of cases that have been decided that interpret each section of the statute. State statutes are presented in a similar manner, and both federal and state codes are updated regularly by the insertion of a pamphlet known as a "pocket part" into the back of the applicable volume. These pocket parts contain new statutes and summaries of new caselaw explaining existing statutes.

The legislative history accompanying a federal statute is reprinted in two sources. The first is the United States Code Congressional and Administrative News (USCCAN),

---

170 Case citation form was discussed in the Bibliographic Introduction and Reader's Guide *supra* p. viii. For a resource book on doing legal research that contains numerous useful illustrations, *see* MORRIS L. COHEN, ROBERT C. BERRING, KENT C. OLSON., HOW TO FIND THE LAW, 9TH ED. (West 1989). *See also* MORRIS L. COHEN & KENT C. OLSON, LEGAL RESEARCH IN A NUTSHELL, 6TH ED. (West 1996) and RUTH ANN MCKINNEY, LEGAL RESEARCH: A PRACTICAL GUIDE AND SELF-INSTRUCTION WORKBOOK (1996).

171 Only official U.S. Supreme Court cites are given in the text of this book, but for those whose libraries have one of the other reporting services, parallel cites are set out in the table of cases in Appendix C to this book.

172 Rules for all forms of citation are set out in two competing books, the "Blue Book" put out by Harvard Law School and the "Maroon Book" put out by the University of Chicago Law School.

which contains selected documents pertaining to the statute. The second and more exhaustive source is the Congressional Information Service (CIS). It contains transcripts of committee hearings, committee reports, and congressional debates accompanying the passage of federal laws. This source of legislative history is immense and is contained on microfiche.

Federal regulations promulgated by administrative agencies are contained in the Code of Federal Regulations (C.F.R.) where they are arranged by subject matter. Any changes to existing regulations or the addition of new regulations are published daily in the Federal Register and the C.F.R. is completely revised every year.

2. Secondary Authorities

Secondary authorities are used to supplement the primary sources. These include treatises, hornbooks, restatements of the law, law reviews, and other legal periodicals, which summarize, restate, review, analyze, and interpret the law. Secondary sources are only persuasive authority, that is, they can influence a court to the extent that the court is persuaded by the reasoning in them. They are also consulted as a finding aid by lawyers or judges seeking citations to statutes, cases or other primary sources of law.

Attorney General Opinions In many states some state officials have the right to request an opinion of the state's Attorney General on a particular point of law. These opinions are published in a set of books labeled in most states Opinions of the Attorney General (OAG). No such practice exists with the federal Attorney General. These state attorney general opinions are cited and sometimes relied upon by courts and lawyers as secondary authority. However, like other forms of secondary authority, they are influential in courts only to the extent that they demonstrate thorough analysis of the issues involved.

Texts and Treatises Treatises are books written about a particular area of the law with the needs of the practitioner in mind. Many treatises are multi-volume. For example, the treatise on Federal Practice and Procedure by Wright, Miller and Cooper extends to some 23 volumes. Treatises strive to summarize in narrative form all the applicable law touching on a particular area, from statutes and regulations to common law or constitutional law. They also contain analysis and commentary by the authors, including their opinions and criticisms of various rules adopted by courts and legislative bodies.

Restatements Restatements of Law are compilations or summaries in statute form of the common law in designated areas of the law, such as torts, contracts, property, judgments and conflicts of laws.[173] Restatements are prepared by the American Law Institute, an organization of eminent scholars and practitioners in the given fields. The overall form is a set of statements of the "black letter" law on the subject arranged in sections and stated in the form of a statute.[174] After the "black letter" statement of the law on a particular point, there are scholarly comments on the application of each of the rules just stated, complete with appropriate hypotheticals

---

[173] Currently there are Restatements of Torts, Contracts, Property, Judgments, Agency, Conflicts of Laws, Foreign Relations, Restitution, and Trusts.

[174] The expression "black letter" law refers to any clear, simple statement of a rule of law on a particular point without a statement of the reasons for the rule or how to apply the rule to other circumstances. Law students, confused by a conflicting and seemingly endless number of court opinions in a given area of law, often yearn for the professor to give them the applicable "black letter law" on a point, that is, a simple statement of the legal rule established by all those decisions.

drawn from actual cases that illustrate the rule stated. These are followed by annotations, updated regularly, that summarize the cases deemed relevant to the subject matter in the section.

Restatements are supposed to do just that — restate or summarize common law rules derived from caselaw. However, that has not prevented some restatement authors from stating what they believe is the more enlightened rule of law, even if it is not the majority view in current caselaw. Thus, some restatements have been less a reflection of *current* law than a statement of what the authors of them think the rule of law *should* be. Restatements have had an influence on the shape of the law. Particularly influential has been the Restatement of Torts, which was largely responsible for establishing strict liability for injuries caused by defective products.[175]

Law Review Articles Law reviews or law journals, usually published by law schools, contain articles by law teachers and scholars analyzing and discussing issues in various areas of the law. If these articles provide a useful analysis of a particular problem that may be facing a court, they can have an impact on the law. Treatises, law review articles and other works by scholars in the United States generally have a greater impact on the law than their counterparts in England do, and less impact on the law than at least some of their counterparts in continental Europe.[176] Generally, in both England and the United States, a judge searching for authority is more likely to turn to another judge's judicial opinion than to a scholar's work.

One-Volume Treatises and Student Texts Single volume treatises and other student texts were introduced in the Bibliographic Introduction and Reader's Guide following the Preface to this book. The "hornbooks" published by West are the most numerous of the one-volume treatises. These works are written primarily by law teachers for law students and therefore are used in judicial opinions only for relatively general propositions of law.[177] However, they are useful as departure points for research and have footnotes that can be used by the reader to locate more specific authority. There are also student aids, such as "nutshells," outlines and review problems, but these are much less likely to be consulted by a lawyer or judge or cited in a judicial opinion. Casebooks — collections of edited cases and statutes with commentary and discussion questions used in law school courses — are rarely relied upon by courts.[178] If a summary of the pertinent law is desired, a treatise will generally be used.

Other Secondary Authorities Legal encyclopedias can be used as secondary sources of law, but they usually serve as a beginning point of research. Legal encyclopedias in the United States contain short general entries written by unnamed authors. The two national encyclopedia series available, Corpus Juris Secundum (CJS) and American Jurisprudence, Second (Am. Jur. 2d), were discussed in the Bibliographic Introduction and Reader's Guide. Most states also have at least one encyclopedia of its own law. These encyclopedias provide a rudimentary description

---

175 *See* Chapter XI, pp. 417-419.

176 *See* Chapter IV, p. 132, and pp. A4-A7 of the majority opinion and p. A12 of the dissent in *Hoffman v. Jones*, reprinted in the Appendix.

177 The term "hornbook" was originally defined as "A leaf or written or printed paper pasted on a board, and covered with horn, for children to learn letters by, and to prevent their being torn and daubed." *Pardon's New General English Dictionary* (1758). Later, the hornbook was replaced by primers in book form for children to learn basic information.

178 One example of a casebook that gets cited relatively frequently by courts is HART & WECHSLER, *supra* note 143.

of the law by breaking it into subjects which are arranged and presented alphabetically. Their purpose is to provide background on a particular legal topic and direct the researcher to pertinent case law and enacted law as well as secondary sources such as restatements and legal periodicals.

Somewhat similar to the encyclopedia are the American Law Reports (ALR). The ALR contains "annotations" in the form of short articles with summaries of the law and citations for selected legal topics. ALR started originally as a selective reporter of important cases, but is now used principally for its annotations.

3. How Legal Research is Approached

Lawyers doing legal research are usually in one of two positions. The lawyer may have only a general understanding of the law governing the problem and may wish to find the specific cases and statutes that address the problem at hand. Or the lawyer may already have a specific case or statute that addresses the issue involved or at least addresses some aspect of the issue, and must find other cases, statutes or authorities and more general support. While the research tools used in both instances are the same, they are used differently.

If the lawyer has a general idea of the law and wants to narrow the issue and the search, the first step is often to refer to a treatise in the general area involved or, if a treatise cannot be found, to one of several legal encyclopedias or the ALR. The researcher can then obtain citations to some of the principal cases and statutes in the area or to other more specific secondary authorities.

The researcher who already has an applicable case or statute may use one of several finding aids to locate other similar cases. One way to do this is by looking for cases that cite the cases with which the researcher is already familiar. One can do this by referring to Shepard's Citations, a multi-volume set of books filled with citations of court decisions that have cited a particular case, statute, court rule or other source of law. The person must find the appropriate Shepard's set for the reporter or statutory compilation of the case or statute in question and then look it up by its citation. Beneath the citation will be a list of the citations of all the later cases that have cited the case. If these later opinions have discussed the cited case, their treatment of it will be indicated in the margin next to the citation (e.g., criticized, distinguished, followed). Such "Shepardizing" of a case is not just a useful way to find other cases. Before relying on any case, it is essential to "Shepardize" the case to determine whether it has been reversed or overruled.

Another method of finding cases is to use state or federal "digests" published by West, the major reporter of opinions. West publishes "headnotes" with every case. Headnotes are brief summaries of the points of law contained in the case that are written by an editor. The headnotes appear at the beginning of the opinion and are serialized with a "key number" assigned to that particular topic throughout all West's publications. The state and federal digests then contain the listings of these headnotes organized by subject matter with the key numbers. The researcher who has a case need only take the pertinent key number from a known case that deals with the issue to be researched and look it up in the appropriate digest, which lists the headnotes from all the other cases that have addressed the same issue. Key numbers and cases may also be found in the digest by looking up key words or terms in the digest's general index similar to the method used for encyclopedias and ALRs.[179]

4. Computerized Legal Research

Clearly, finding aids like those just described are applied more easily by computer. Such assistance is available through two on-line legal research data: Lexis-Nexis and Westlaw (by West Group). Subscribers to these services can hook up to the computer containing these data bases through telephone lines. In addition to speeding up use of traditional methods of legal research, the computer services allow their own direct search of cases, statutes and regulations for particular words or phrases. The ability of computers to handle a great deal of data efficiently also allows for more complete information about cases. Thus, West has produced "Keycite," a service similar to Shepard's, but which supplies a wider range of more specific information about how the case has been used or treated in other cases.

Beyond the advantages of greater speed and efficiency, computer data bases are also updated more quickly than books. Case opinions or amendments to statutes can be loaded into the data bases within hours after their release, whereas it may take weeks or months for them to appear in print. The disadvantage of computer research services is that they are relatively expensive. In addition to any equipment outlay, there are monthly charges and charges by the minute for time spent doing research.

The two computer research services mentioned and other companies also produce CD-ROM (Compact Disk - Read Only Memory) databases. These look the same as audio compact disks, but instead contain masses of legal material, often specialized databases such as cases and materials on federal taxation or bankruptcy law. One can search these databases the same way as one can search through one of the computerized research services. The advantage of CD-ROM databases, however, is that there are no access fees, monthly charges or need for telephone linkage equipment. CD-ROM libraries are one possible way that libraries with little room for books might be able to acquire and maintain an adequate collection on U.S. law. However, they must be updated periodically and are expensive to purchase.[180]

5. The Form of Legal Argument

There are usually four distinct conceptual components to every legal argument. The lawyer must (1) state the issue involved; (2) state the rule to be applied; (3) apply the rule to the facts of the client's case and (4) state the conclusion reached from the application of the rule to the facts. It is during steps (3) and (4) that the deductive or analogical reasoning processes discussed earlier take place.

The physical form that legal argument generally takes in court is a written "brief," sometimes called a "memorandum of law." There are "trial briefs" submitted to trial courts and "appellate briefs" addressed to appellate courts.[181] Generally, all types of

---

179 Examples of two of the headnotes with key numbers published with *Hoffman v. Jones*, the case in Appendix A, are set out on p. A2. *See also* p. A1, note [4]. It is perhaps a continuing legacy of the common law bias against statutes that there is no similar comprehensive system for nationwide indexing and classification of statutes.

180 A cheaper alternative for those wishing to do research who do not have access to a U.S. law collection is to go on the Internet. Appendix B of this book sets out several sites that offer free access to U.S. legal materials, particularly cases and statutes, which can be downloaded. Few books are available on the Internet as of yet. For readers who have identified a particular book needed, the addresses of the "Big 5" legal education publishers are also listed in Appendix B.

181 For a discussion of the nature of trial and appellate courts, *see* Chapter V, pp. 163-167.

briefs are composed of standard, well defined, sections that correspond with the structure of legal arguments just discussed.

Most argument of legal issues in the United States is in written form. While oral argument of legal points does take place in both trial and appellate courts, it does not serve as a substitute for a written brief in the modern American appellate court. Indeed, it could not so substitute even if the parties wished, since the entire oral argument of the case is customarily limited to 15 or 30 minutes per side. In this respect, American appellate legal argument is very different from that of England, where oral arguments in an appellate court develop much of the argumentation that is contained only in written briefs in the United States and can take hours or even days. Oral argument in U.S. appellate courts is limited to the advocate highlighting the most important aspects of the case and answering questions from the appellate judges. It is not uncommon that the questioning of the advocate will occupy almost the entire time allotted for oral argument.

The prevalence of legal argument in written form has caused some to question the need for any oral argumentation and a few courts have abolished it. However, most judges believe that even short oral argument is important for clearing up questions the court has after reading the parties' written briefing, and many judges assert strongly that it should be retained.[182]

Argument of legal points in trial courts during trial is much more likely to be entirely oral, but even during trial, if the legal point is anticipated and is important, most good lawyers will produce at least a short written memorandum or brief discussing the relevant authorities. Pre-trial motions raising legal issues that are made in trial courts outside the immediate context of the trial itself are invariably required to be in writing and are most often accompanied by a written brief. An example would be a pre-trial motion to dismiss for lack of subject matter jurisdiction. In some jurisdictions, a written brief is required by the relevant court rules for all motions made other than those made during trial, and the clerk of the court will not accept any motion for filing that is not accompanied by a brief.

---

182 *See* William H. Rehnquist, *Remarks on the Process of Judging*, 49 WASH. & LEE L. REV. 263, 269 (1992). Rehnquist is the current Chief Justice of the United States.

CHAPTER III

THE ADVERSARY SYSTEM AND JURY TRIALS

There will be later chapters on civil and criminal procedure in this book, so it may seem somewhat out of place to discuss adversary procedure and jury trials separately here, in the third chapter of the book. The topic is addressed here for two reasons.

First, the adversary trial and juries constitute more than just another step in civil or criminal procedure. These traditions occupy a fundamental place in the United States legal system that is difficult to understate. One reason for this is the high value placed on procedure in general. As Justice Frankfurter has stated, "[t]he history of American freedom is, in no small measure, the history of procedure."[1] It is no coincidence that the overwhelming number of rights the Framers saw fit to include in the Bill of Rights were procedural rights. Moreover, even the more "substantive" freedoms of speech and the press set out in the 1st Amendment have a distinct adversary and procedural component. Thus, a prominent justification for protecting the freedom of expression is the "marketplace of ideas" theory: that "[t]he best test of truth is the power of the thought to get itself accepted in the competition of the market."[2] Even more broadly, an "adversary ethic" prevails in many non-legal contexts. Whether a business management meeting or a political debate, the notion that a particular idea or theory has been exposed to a head-to-head clash with opposing ideas or theories and has been chosen over them gives it real credibility.

Second, discussing the adversary system and jury trials here completes the picture of the tasks that lawyers and judges are called on to perform in the legal system. The last chapter outlined *legal* methodology, that is, how courts in the United States think about and resolve *legal* issues. However, resolving issues of law is only part of the task involved in adjudicating disputes — and it is often the least important part. The facts must also be determined and the law must then be applied to those facts. The process of fact adjudication has particular significance for lawyers who engage in litigation in the United States, since it is the lawyers for the parties who must shoulder the burden of investigating, developing and presenting evidence at trial. The adversary trial process is the core of what might be called the *factual* methodology of the legal system.[3]

We will start with a brief description of adversary theory — the overall characteristics and rationale for an adversary system of adjudication. Then we will examine the institution of the jury in general terms. This will be followed by a relatively detailed description of an adversary jury trial and the lawyer's role in it, including a cursory review of some of the more important limitations on evidence. Thereafter, various criticisms of the adversary system and juries will be considered.

---

[1] *Malinski v. New York*, 324 U.S. 401, 414 (1945).

[2] *Abrams v. United States*, 250 U.S. 616, 630 (1919) (Holmes, J.).

[3] Although it is essential that practicing lawyers know how to develop the facts in a case, legal education in the United States has tended to emphasize legal analysis and knowledge and traditionally has downplayed the importance of how facts are investigated and adjudicated. As a result, new lawyers may be quite skilled at the legal methodology set out in Chapter II, but may have only a rudimentary understanding of how to investigate and present facts. *See* Chapter IV, pp. 134-136.

A. The Characteristics and Rationale of the Adversary System

All legal systems strive for decision-making that is impartial and fully-informed. Proponents of an adversary system believe that this is best achieved (1) where the decision-maker is neutral and passive, and is charged solely with the responsibility of deciding the case; (2) the parties themselves develop and present the evidence and arguments on which the decision will be based; (3) the proceeding is concentrated, uninterrupted and otherwise designed to emphasize the clash of opposing evidence and arguments presented by the parties; and (4) the parties have equal opportunities to present and argue their cases to the decision-maker.

1. The Need for a Passive Decision-Maker

The most fundamental principle of the adversary system is its insistence upon strictly separating the active function of investigating and gathering evidence from the more passive function of considering the evidence and deciding the case. The theory behind the need for this separation is the belief that performance of the former function necessarily taints the latter: decision-makers who gather the evidence lose their impartiality by reason of their active investigatory role in the case.

The root of the problem, in the words of an often-quoted American Bar Association (ABA) Committee Report on the adversary system, is the "natural human tendency to judge too swiftly in terms of the familiar that which is not yet fully known."[4] We all have a natural urge to impose order on chaos by evaluating and categorizing information as we hear it. But decision-makers are under special pressure to do so, since they must decide the case. The result is a strong inclination in the decision-maker early on — while the information is still being gathered — to start theorizing about what the evidence means. Even passive decision-makers may engage in preliminary theorizing. But decision-makers who actively investigate cannot avoid doing so. An investigator cannot possibly determine what questions to ask or what direction to take the investigation next without first assessing the meaning of the information that is already known.[5]

The main danger of preliminary theorizing is that preliminary theories will become fixed, permanent theories long before they should. As the ABA Committee Report explains, "what starts as a preliminary diagnosis designed to direct the inquiry tends, quickly and imperceptibly, to become a fixed conclusion, as all that confirms the diagnosis makes a strong imprint on the mind, while all that runs counter to it is received with diverted attention." The biasing effects of preliminary theorizing are magnified when the investigator controls *what further* evidence will be investigated — as would be the case if the investigator is also the judge. Ego investment in a preliminary theory provides a strong unconscious motivation to nudge the investiga-

---

4 *Professional Responsibility: Report of the Joint Conference*, 44 A.B.A.J. 1159 (1958), quoted in Lon Fuller, *The Forms and Limits of Adjudication*, 92 HARV. L. REV. 353, 382-85 (1978) (emphasis added). *See also* Lon Fuller, "The Adversary System" (Chapter III), in HAROLD BERMAN, ED. TALKS ON AMERICAN LAW, 2D ED. 43-44 (Vintage Books 1971). For further discussion of the theory of the adversary system, see STEVEN LANDSMAN, READINGS ON ADVERSARIAL JUSTICE: THE AMERICAN APPROACH TO ADJUDICATION (American Bar Association Section on Litigation) (West 1988); MONROE FREEDMAN, UNDERSTANDING LAWYERS' ETHICS, 2D ED. 13-42 (Matthew Bender 1998); and BAILEY KUKLIN & JEFFREY W. STEMPEL, FOUNDATIONS OF THE LAW: AN INTERDISCIPLINARY PRIMER 103-129 (West 1994).

5 As Professor Damaska has observed, "You cannot decide which facts matter unless you have already selected, at least tentatively, applicable decisional standards. But most of the time you cannot properly understand these legal standards without relating them to the factual situation of the case." Mirjan Damaska, *Presentation of Evidence and Factfinding Precision*, 123 U.PA. L.REV. 1083, 1087 (1975).

tion in the direction of information that confirms that theory, and away from information that conflicts with it.[6]

2. Party Presentation of Evidence and Arguments

Proponents of an adversary system believe that the only way to avoid the skewing effects of the investigative role is to take the responsibility for investigation away from the decision-maker and give it to the parties themselves. Doing so relieves the decision-maker of any need for preliminary theorizing. The decision-maker can relax and simply follow the parties' presentations of the evidence.

But giving the responsibility of investigation to the parties has another beneficial effect: it improves the quality of the decision-making. It does so in two important ways.

First, party investigation increases the amount of information available to the decision-maker. It gives the responsibility of gathering it to those who have the greatest incentive to develop the evidence in their favor. Moreover, the parties have only half the total job a single investigator would have, since they need only concentrate on the evidence in their favor. Second, party presentation assures that the *full potential weight and value* of the evidence will be explored. It is simply impossible for a single investigator to develop in his or her mind, simultaneously and with equal force, completely contradictory theories of a case, and then to maintain those theories in balance until the end of the investigation. While some people are better at this than others, no single person can hold the opposing positions on an issue as well as the opposing parties themselves. Similarly, the weight and value a decision-maker gives to evidence are often affected by *how* the decision-maker first became acquainted with that evidence. Evidence stumbled across in random pieces is not likely to have as strong an impression on the mind as evidence that is presented forthrightly as a logical and coherent whole. Allowing the parties to prepare and present all the evidence in its best light neutralizes the random factor of how the investigator-decision-maker might have encountered that evidence when it first came to light.

The second benefit of placing the burden of investigation and presentation of evidence on the parties is that it promotes the *appearance* of fairness. This is a crucial factor if the stage at which evidence is officially gathered is to be public, as all trials are in the United States. In a public trial, the active involvement of a decision-maker in the investigation and presentation of the evidence can create the appearance that the decision-maker has prejudged the case. An example of this, which often arises in the trial of cases, is where a witness's testimony at trial contradicts an earlier statement given by the witness. There are several different theories about what this could mean. It could be anything from a simple misunderstanding or lapse in thought to a deliberate lie. One has difficulty imagining a series of questions adequately exploring the issue with the witness that would not communicate a preliminary judgment about the contradiction. The investigating official might "bear down" on the witness, pressing the witness for an explanation, but this would convey the impression that the judge doubts the truth of the witness's testimony. Or, more likely, the interrogating judge might *not* "bear down" on the witness in an effort to maintain the appearance of impartiality. But this would convey the impression of a judgment that

---

6 Some decision-maker bias is counteracted by a system in which an investigator (usually also a member of the judiciary) investigates the case and delivers the evidence produced to judges who will decide the case. However, if the effect just related is correct, the dossier compiled by the investigator for the judges, while not a final decision, is likely to similarly skewed.

the contradiction is not important. It is one thing for the parties, the jury or the public to see a *party's lawyer* take one or the other approach and thus convey one or the other impression. But if the *judge* does it, such action communicates the appearance of prejudging the evidence even if no such prejudgment is meant to be communicated.[7]

3. Structuring the Trial to Induce and Sustain a Clash of Opposing Partisan Views of the Case

The Function of the Adversarial Clash The simple fact of party presentation of opposing versions and interpretations of the evidence results in a clash before the passive decision-maker. But the clash is more than a by-product of partisan presentations. It is an essential element of adversary procedure. Partisan presentation of opposing viewpoints serves to counteract the tendency toward premature decision-making noted earlier. As the ABA Report notes:

> The [presentations and] arguments of counsel hold the case, as it were, in suspension between two opposing interpretations of it. While the proper classification of the case is thus kept unresolved, there is time to explore all of its peculiarities and nuances.

Structuring the Adversarial Clash This "suspending" effect is emphasized by the structure of the adversary trial, which requires that the parties' presentations of evidence and arguments alternate. As will be described shortly, each segment of the trial has its plaintiff's part and its defendant's part and the presentations follow shortly after each other.[8] Within a single segment of the trial, "direct examination" of a witness by the proponent of that evidence is followed immediately by "cross examination" by the opponent. The result of this alternating structure is that any proffered analysis of evidence from one side that seems appealing will be followed shortly by a competing view. The clash of competing views of the case is sustained up to the point of jury deliberation, when jury instructions include party-provided summaries of each side's principal contentions, first the plaintiff's and then the defendant's.

"Immediacy" of the Clash of Evidence and Argument Another important feature of the adversary trial serves to heighten and sustain the clash of evidence. This is the general preference for "immediate" oral evidence and argument rather than "mediate" written evidence and argument. Rules of evidence generally exclude written and other secondary versions of witness observations as "hearsay," thus requiring that the original source of the evidence come to court and testify personally at the trial.[9] Although hearsay is excluded in large part because it is not as reliable as first-hand oral evidence, it is no coincidence that conflicting "immediate" oral first-hand evidence also presents a sharper clash than conflicting written or other secondary

---

7 This final point shows why active judicial development of evidence is problematic even when the important decision-maker, the jury, remains passive. Juries generally want to do the right thing. Since they cannot depend on the parties before them to give them unbiased advice, they are particularly sensitive to any indications from the judge as to what is the right way for them to decide the case. A "solution" to the appearance-of-bias problem might be to exclude the public from the stage of proceedings at which the "raw" facts are gathered and present publicly only a "sanitized" version of the facts. That is not an option in the U.S. system, which generally requires that all judicial proceedings be public. Moreover, it does not eliminate the effect that the appearance of unfairness would have on the parties, lawyers, witnesses or anyone else involved in the closed proceeding.

8 *See infra* pp. 88-106.

9 *See* discussion of evidence law *infra*, pp. 106-112.

evidence.[10] Moreover, the unreliability of hearsay is directly linked to the need for a first-hand adversarial clash. It is mistrusted precisely because the person who uttered it was not subject to a first-hand confrontation in the form of cross examination.[11]

The fact that the parties themselves present and examine the evidence heightens the immediacy of the clash of opposing viewpoints as well. Questions to the witness are not filtered through a judge or other state official, but are put to the witness directly by the lawyers for the parties. In most cases, the most dramatic first-hand clash of competing views of the evidence comes when direct examination of a party by the party's own lawyer is followed by cross examination of that party by the opposing party's lawyer.

The adversary trial's emphasis on immediacy is not restricted to the *content* of oral testimony, but also takes into account the *manner* in which the witnesses testify. It is acceptable and even expected that a fact-finder (judge or jury) will consider nonverbal clues to credibility that a witness's demeanor on the stand might disclose. This cannot be done with written evidence. This point is emphasized constantly by appellate courts. Even with the aid of verbatim transcripts on appeal, appellate courts will defer to the trial court's evaluation of the evidence in recognition of the trial judge's first-hand opportunity to observe the witnesses and to consider the evidence in the context of a living trial rather than upon a "cold paper record."[12]

Concentrated Hearing The clash of opposing views is also heightened by the use of a continuous and concentrated trial. All the evidence is ready and the persons needed to present it and finally decide the case (judge, parties, jury, lawyers and witnesses) are gathered together in one place. The trial continues uninterrupted until final decision of the case. If the trial were scheduled discontinuously with hearings spread out over several weeks or months, the clash would be greatly reduced. Scheduling the trial as one continuous hearing is also necessary to accommodate the jury, which would likely become restless or forget what it had heard if called back for a few hours on scattered days over a span of several weeks. But usually even trials before the judge alone are scheduled continuously. Judges deciding a case alone without a jury often mention how the trial's continuous nature and other adversarial features assist them in keeping an open mind throughout the trial. Indeed, consistent with adversary theory, many judges, upon hearing that the case will be tried to them without a jury, make a point of learning as little as possible about the case so as not to prejudge it and to gain the maximum benefits from the clash of adversary presentations of the parties.[13]

4. Structuring the Trial to Assure Equality of Adversarial Opportunities

Equality of "Forensic Arms" It is inherent in the notion of party presentation that the parties' opportunities to present evidence and persuade the decision-maker should be equal. Such "equality of forensic arms," as it is sometimes called, is fundamental to adversary theory. It applies in both civil and criminal cases in the

---

10 JOHN MERRYMAN, THE CIVIL LAW TRADITION 114 (2d ed.) (Stanford 1985). It should be noted that a large part of the original reason for orality of evidence in the common law trial was that juries were often illiterate and would be unable to read written evidence.

11 *See infra* p. 108.

12 *Gasparini v. Center for the Humanities*, 518 U.S. 415, 421 (1996). The narrow scope of appellate review of facts in the U.S. is discussed in Chapter V, pp. 166-167.

13 In a system of concentrated and continuous trials, the lawyers must prepare their cases thoroughly and completely before the trial starts, since they will be able to make only limited mid-trial corrections.

Anglo-American tradition. Thus, the prosecution and defense in a criminal case face identical limitations on presentation of evidence and argument. The prosecution sits at the same kind of table on the same level as the defense and wears the same ordinary clothes as the defense attorney. Whatever prerogatives the prosecutor may enjoy outside the courtroom, they disappear when the prosecutor appears in court in a criminal trial.[14]

Detailed Procedural Rules Administered in an Insular Way We have already discussed how evidence and trial procedure rules serve to create, heighten and sustain a clash of opposing evidence and arguments. Here we should note how the *nature* of these rules and the *manner in which they are administered* serve to promote equality of adversarial opportunity. First, the procedural and evidence rules applicable to an adversary trial are detailed and relatively rigid.[15] The more detailed and rigid such rules are, the less judicial discretion there is to limit what evidence the parties are allowed to present and how they present it. Second, these procedural and evidence rules are administered in an insular and episodic fashion unrelated to the overall context of the case. This is in part because the rules are detailed and specific and in part because of traditional understandings of the judicial role. It is also a matter of necessity. Given that the parties are responsible for developing the facts at trial, trial judges will usually have only the sketchiest idea of what the facts of the case are. Such a "veil of ignorance" also makes it a virtual necessity that the judge rule in an insular fashion.[16]

This final point on reducing judicial discretion to control what evidence is presented brings us full circle to the first point made with regard to adversary theory. The reason for seeking to limit judicial discretion is to lessen the likelihood of the judge using a premature theory about the merits of the case to control what further evidence is presented, thus skewing the entire direction of the search for evidence. As discussed earlier, this is the most serious danger of judges actively investigating the evidence.[17]

Consistent with this theory, the best trial judges in the U.S. are not those who have the fullest understanding of the facts of the case. The best judges are those who are most knowledgeable about the *rules governing evidence and procedure*, and who administer those rules in an evenhanded fashion *regardless of which side seems to have the better case on the merits*. Trial lawyers in the United States often comment with favor on judges whose ruling on each objection in a trial is made independently of the relative balance of the evidence in the case. Thus, the judge's job in a jury trial might be likened to the job of the referee at a football game, whose job it is to enforce

---

14 In a civil case, both parties have equal access to the means to investigate and prepare the case for trial. In a criminal case, the prosecution has the investigative resources of the police at its disposal in preparing its case, which the defendant does not have. However, other factors compensate for the imbalance somewhat. First, the defense has the right of compulsory process to subpoena any witness it wants who has relevant testimony (including the victim, a member of the police force or someone else in the prosecution "camp"), but the prosecutor may not compel the defendant to testify or even to answer questions informally because of the privilege against "self-incrimination" guaranteed by the Constitution. Second, the Constitution requires the prosecutor to disclose all exculpatory evidence to the defense that the police might uncover. Finally, the defendant is free to use the services of a private detective and many public defender offices (which represent indigent defendants) have private investigators on their staff. *See generally* Chapter VIII for a discussion of criminal procedure rights of defendants.

15 The content of evidence rules is discussed *infra* pp. 106-112.

16 Neither the judge nor the jury has any comprehensive summary or dossier of all the facts in the case before the trial starts.

17 *See supra* p. 78.

the rules to assure that the sides compete fairly and — to return again to the first point on adversary theory — certainly *not* to kick the ball.[18]

B. Juries

It is possible to have an adversary system without juries and to have juries in a non-adversary system. However, the jury fits well in an adversary system because it is the quintessential passive decision-maker. All the jury does is take in the evidence and decide the case. It has no knowledge of the facts of the case and no right to ask questions, to call witnesses, or otherwise direct the examination of the evidence. Before proceeding in the next section to a detailed description of the adversary jury trial, we should examine the institution of the jury more generally.

1. Some History and Comparative Comments

History The historical origins of the jury are obscure and, in any event, a complete history is not needed to understand the modern institution.[19] The jury's origins are considered by many to have been in France, where some form of jury trial was in evidence during the reign of Louis the Pious, circa 829 A.D. It was imported to England by the Normans after the invasion of 1066 and was firmly established as a part of English legal procedure by the twelfth century, probably in reaction to the decline of the medieval forms of procedure, such as trial by battle, ordeal and wager.[20] By the 1400s, the modern characteristic of the jury as a passive and impartial decider of the facts was well established. By 1670, the jury was established as an institution independent of the king and the king's judges, when in *Bushel's Case*[21] it was held that a juror could not be fined or imprisoned for acquitting a defendant. The last characteristic of the modern jury — the need to decide the case based solely on the evidence produced at trial and not on extrajudicial knowledge — was established by the 1700s. The institution of the jury was exported to the United States by English colonists and has been a fundamental part of our jurisprudence ever since despite its decline in recent years in England. Right to trial by jury is guaranteed by the 7th Amendment for civil cases and by Article III and the 6th Amendment for criminal cases.[22]

A Comparative Perspective At one point in Europe, inspired by the French Revolution, juries existed in many civil law countries. Today, they have largely disappeared in those countries for good, except for a recent resurgence in Russia and Spain.[23] But even in civil law countries, the participation of lay persons in deciding

---

18 An excellent comparative work explores, among other things, connections between adversarial litigation and more general attitudes about the purposes and functions of a legal system. *See* MIRJAN R. DAMASKA, EVIDENCE LAW ADRIFT (Yale U. Press 1997).

19 For a discussion of the history of the jury, *see* Stephen Yeazell, *The New Jury and Ancient Jury Conflict*, 1990 U.CHI.LEGAL FORUM 87 *and* THOMAS GREEN, VERDICT ACCORDING TO CONSCIENCE: PERSPECTIVES ON THE ENGLISH CRIMINAL JURY TRIAL, 1200-1800 (U. Chicago Press 1985). For a short popularized history of the jury in both England and the United States, *see* JOHN GUINTHER, THE JURY IN AMERICA 1-35 (Facts on File, N.Y. 1988).

20 *See generally* THEODORE F. T. PLUCKNETT, A CONCISE HISTORY OF THE COMMON LAW (1956) and WILLIAM S. HOLDSWOVTH, I A HISTORY OF ENGLISH LAW (1956). *See also* Stephen A. Landsman, *The Civil Jury in America: Scenes from an Unappreciated History*, 44 HASTINGS L.J. 579, 582-587 (1993).

21 124 Eng. Rep. 1006 (1670). The facts behind the decision in *Bushel's Case* are recounted in GUINTHER, *supra* note 19, at. 24-27.

22 The precise scope of the constitutional right to trial by jury is set on in Chapter VII, pp. 234-235, for civil cases and in Chapter VIII, p. 291, for criminal cases.

23 Stephen C. Thaman, The Resurrection of Trial by Jury in Russia, 32 STANFORD J. INT'L LAW 61 (1995) and Stephen C. Thaman, Spain Returns to Trial by Jury, 21 HASTINGS INT'L & COMP. L. REV. 241 (1998).

cases in court is quite common. In France and Austria, a jury trial of sorts is allowed in some criminal cases and in Germany, there are mixed courts consisting of both law and lay judges. Somewhat parallel to the policies behind juries in the Anglo-American tradition, use of lay judges in these countries is designed to increase the diversity of viewpoints on the proper resolution of cases, to spread the awesome responsibility for decision-making, and to bring a common sense of justice to the legal system.

However, in few systems do lay decision-makers match the degree of independence which the jury enjoys in the Anglo-American tradition. Continental lay judges are fewer in number and are generally screened for service rather than being randomly selected from the population at large. Almost as importantly, they deliberate together with the legally educated judge and must, together with the professional judge, justify their decision in writing.[24] By contrast, the Anglo-American jury numbers up to 12, is randomly chosen for a given case only, deliberates separately from the judge in secret, and generally need not justify its decision.[25]

2. The Division of Labor Between Judge and Jury

Fact vs. Law Division Despite their considerable independence, the common law jury does not have the right to decide all the issues in a case. In general, the judge decides issues of law and the jury decides issues of fact. Even on issues of fact, a jury is not free to come to any conclusion it wants. Except for a verdict of acquittal (not guilty) in a criminal case, the trial judge or an appellate court has the power to set aside the verdict if there is no substantial evidence to support it.[26] This power of the trial judge is not an exception to the general rule that judges determine only issues of law. Whether there is any substantial evidence to support a jury's fact-finding is considered to be an issue of law. Stated another way, the question of whether there is enough evidence *for the jury to decide* a fact question is a question of law for the judge.

It is sometimes difficult to tell what is an issue of fact and what is an issue of law. So-called "mixed fact-law" questions arise. In jury trials, the most common mixed questions are issues of "law application" — where a legal standard must be applied to the facts of the case. For example, the question of how fast the defendant was driving at the time of an automobile accident is a pure fact issue clearly appropriate for the jury to decide. It is a mixed fact-law question whether the defendant's driving that speed under the road and weather conditions the jury finds existed constitutes "negligence," thereby entitling the plaintiff to recover. Juries are generally allowed to decide law application questions and would certainly be permitted to decide the negligence question posed. If the law application question is of a type that requires uniform application, such as applying a standard provision of a contract to determine whether there has been a breach of that contract, it is more likely to be deemed an

---

24 For example, German lay judges are more "professional" than jurors since they are elected for one-year terms by the local legislature and are supposed to be the "most suitable" in terms of "proven judgment and honorableness." They also deliberate with the professional judges. Not surprisingly, their rate of disagreement with the professional judges is low, around 1.4% *See* Gerhard Casper and Hans Zeisel, *Lay Judges in German Criminal Courts*, 1 J. LEGAL STUDIES 138 (1972).

25 A modern-day jury of comparable independence is the Russian jury. *See infra* note 32.

26 See discussion *infra*, p. 105.

issue of law. On the other hand, if the contract provision is one that laypersons are capable of applying, the jury will be allowed to decide the question.[27]

Jury Nullification   Modern juries are told that they must accept the law as given to them by the judge, determine what the relevant facts are, apply the law to those facts and in that manner decide the case. Generally, a verdict at odds with the law will be set aside by the trial judge. However, a jury acquittal in a criminal case is not reviewable on appeal or otherwise. This means that in this one situation juries have the power of "nullification" — the power to acquit a criminal defendant despite clear evidence of guilt. Sometimes jurors may acquit in such circumstances because they do not believe the evidence. But when the jury acquits in the face of compelling evidence of guilt, it does so because it disagrees with the law or its particular application in that case. When it does this, it is judging the law as well as the facts and, by refusing to apply the law, is to that extent "nullifying" it.

There is considerable evidence that the 18th century jury that the Framers of the Constitution had in mind had this right to judge not only the facts, but the law as well.[28] However, the modern view is that they do not.[29] The reason why an acquittal cannot be set aside and a new trial ordered is the Constitution's double jeopardy protection, which prevents the defendant from being tried twice for the same offense.[30] But the double jeopardy clause does not bestow any right of nullification on the jury. Thus, it is said today that the jury has the *de facto power* to nullify, but it does *not* have the *legal right* to do so. Consequently, neither the judge nor the defendant's attorney may inform the jury of its power. In most jurisdictions, jurors are instructed by the judge that it would be a violation of their oath as jurors to ignore the court's instructions and that, if they find from the evidence that the defendant committed the offense charged, then they must convict regardless of their personal feelings.[31]

There are no statistics on how often jury nullification occurs, nor could there be, since the jury is not required to give any reason for its verdict and the question whether the evidence for conviction was compelling is a matter of judgment. When

---

27   *See Nunez v. Superior Oil Co.*, 572 F.2d 1119 (5th Cir. 1978) (discussing the fact-law distinction and allowing a jury to decide whether a contract provision excusing failure to pay royalties if that failure was "justified" would include a mistake in paperwork). There may be constitutional restraints on what mixed issues are given to a jury. *See United States v. Gaudin*, 515 U.S. 506 (1995) (reversing a conviction for making false statements on a loan application on the ground that it deprived the defendant of his right to trial by jury when the judge rather than the jury decided whether the statements were "material"). *But see Markman v. Westview Instruments, Inc.*, 517 U.S. 370 (1996) (meaning of the word "inventory" in patent claim held an issue of law for the judge in part because of the need for consistency).

28   *See* Chief Justice John Jay's charge to the jury in *Georgia v. Brailsford*, 3 U.S. (3 Dall.) 1, 4 (1794) and the dissent in *Sparf v. United States*, 156 U.S. 51 (1895). *See generally* Alan Scheflin & Jon Van Dyke, *Jury Nullification: The Contours of a Controversy*, 43 LAW & CONTEMP. PROBS. 51 (1980).

29   *Sparf, supra.*

30   *See* Chapter VII, pp. 296-299.

31   In *United States v. Krzyske*, 836 F.2d 1013, 1021 (6th Cir. 1988), jurors specifically asked the trial judge to explain nullification to them. The trial judge's decision to be less than candid in answer was upheld on appeal. For different views on whether to tell the jury of its nullification power, *see* David C. Brody, *Sparf and Dougherty Revisted: Why the Court Should Instruct the Jury of Its Nullification Right*, 33 AM. CRIM. L. REV. 89 (1995) and Jack. B. Weinstein, *Considering Jury "Nullification": When May or Should a Jury Reject the Law and Do Justice*, 30 AM. CRIM. L. REV. 239 (1993). A recent article collects sources on nullification and discusses two important ways that trial judges fight against nullification: by keeping potential "nullifiers" off the jury and by keeping information on nullification from the jury. *See* Nancy J. King, *Silencing Nullification Advocacy Inside the Jury Room and Outside the Courtroom*, 65 U. CHI. L. REV. 433 (1998). *See also* Darryl K. Brown, *Jury Nullification Within the Rule of Law*, 81 MINN. L. REV.1149 (1997).

what appears to be nullification takes place, it often attracts great attention from the press, and this makes its frequency seem greater than it probably is. The traditional instructions juries are given tend to assure that nullification will take place only in a few extreme cases.[32]

In civil cases, the jury is subject to greater control by the judge and must often give reasons for its verdict through the use of "special verdict" forms or by answering questions about the reasons for its decision.[33] Yet juries can still express their resentment of a legal rule by using their broad power to determine contested issues of *fact*. Indeed, juries can have an effect on the development of the law by consistently and over a long period of time by finding disputed facts a particular way to avoid an unjust legal rule. For example, in *Hoffman v. Jones*, the Florida case changing state law from contributory to comparative negligence, the court supported its decision in part by noting one scholar's observation that there is "something basically wrong with a rule of law that is so contrary to the settled convictions of the lay community that laymen will almost always refuse to enforce it, even when solemnly told to do so by a judge whose instructions they have sworn to follow."[34]

3. Characteristics of the Modern Jury

Jury Pools and Exemptions from Jury Service The traditional source for jury pools or the "jury venire" — the group of prospective jurors from which jurors are selected — has been voter registration lists.[35] However, usually fewer than 50% of the population in the United States votes in elections, so most jurisdictions use a combination of voter lists and driver's license lists. In a country that relies so heavily on the automobile, driver's license lists will likely include more than 95% of all adults. Whatever list is used for the pool, jurors are selected at random for service.

Traditionally important professionals and others whose services are thought valuable to society, such as physicians, have been exempt from jury duty. Federal law exempts from federal jury service employees of police and fire departments as well as public officials.[36] Lawyers are often exempt from jury service on the theory that their legal knowledge would have a disruptive effect on jury deliberations. However, the trend in recent years has been to abolish all exemptions from jury duty, including any exemption for lawyers or even judges. At the present time, 27 states have no exemptions based on the prospective juror's profession and seven more have only limited exemptions.[37] The idea has emerged that the right of a citizen to a representative jury for decision of court cases overrides any other societal interest and that the burdens and the civic education benefits of jury service should be as widely shared as possible. The concern that lawyers on juries would create problems is thought to

---

32 The Russian jury between 1864 and 1917 often exercised its powers of nullification to acquit revolutionaries. *See generally* SAMUEL KUCHEROV, LAW AND LAWYERS UNDER THE LAST THREE TSARS (Frederick A. Praeger, N.Y. 1953). The power of nullification is retained and made explicit for the modern Russian jury. Set forth in the statute are three separate questions the jury is to answer:"(1) was it proven that the acts charged took place; (2) was it proven that the defendant committed those acts; [and] (3) is the defendant guilty of committing those acts." Art. §449, Crim. Proc. Code of the Russian Federation.

33 *See infra* p. 104.

34 *See Hoffman v. Jones*, Appendix, p. A7.

35 "Venire" comes from the original name of the writ used to command the sheriff to summon jurors. Called a *venire facias*, it meant literally "that you cause to come."

36 28 U.S.C.A. §1863(b)(5).

37 Source: Center for Jury Studies, National Center for State Courts (1993). Conviction for a felony is still a universal disqualification. *See* ABA STANDARDS RELATING TO JUROR USE AND MANAGEMENT, Part A, Standard 4 .

be overstated, since the most important work of juries is in resolving factual issues, a task for which legal training is largely irrelevant and, some argue, a detriment.[38]

Avoiding Jury Service Jury duty is mandatory on all those called to serve, but it does not arise very often for the average person. Frequency of service varies with the area of the country, but for a registered voter, serving more than once in ten years is unusual in most areas and many people go their whole life without ever being called. For the average case, jury duty is not that onerous and many people say that they find performance of their "civic duty" to be interesting. Also, a system of "one day, one trial," used in 40% of the states, has made service much less onerous. Under this system, jurors are in the jury venire for only one day. If they are chosen for a trial, they serve in that trial to conclusion, but if not, they need not return. But some people for one reason or another try to avoid being placed on a jury. Failure to comply with a jury subpoena is contempt of court and is punishable by fine or imprisonment. A prospective juror's statements of an inability to be impartial will be probed by the judge with some disbelief if no concrete reason can be offered. However, obvious non-cooperation by a juror may lead one or the other counsel to dismiss the juror from service through a peremptory challenge. Jurors may be excused for "undue hardship or extreme inconvenience."[39]

Educational Levels of Jurors Beyond the ability to read and write the English language, there are generally no educational requirements for being a juror. It is not uncommon for a professor with a Ph.D. to be seated next to a high-school dropout. Each of their votes on the jury counts the same, though the professor may perhaps be more persuasive with other jurors during deliberations.

Because of the lack of any educational requirements, concern has been voiced about juries not understanding complex cases. It is claimed that some cases are impossible for *any* jury to understand, and the federal Courts of Appeal are split on the issue of whether there is a "complexity exception" to the constitutional right to a civil jury trial in federal court.[40] "Blue ribbon" juries, juries made up solely of college graduates, for example, are a possibility, but they are controversial and constitutional doubts have been raised about them.[41] Another suggestion is to increase the amount of juror pay (and charge it to the litigants) so as to attract the better-educated juror.[42]

But many believe the jury's true capacity for accurate fact-finding has not yet been fully tapped. They point out that many traditional jury trial procedures are inconsistent with modern learning theory. One example is the procedure for jury instruction. Jurors traditionally have been given instructions on the law they must

---

38 In one case with which the author is familiar, a sitting Circuit Court judge of the state of Michigan served as a juror in a criminal case. No problems were reported.

39 28 U.S.C.A. §1863(b)(5) (applicable to federal jury service).

40 *Compare United States Financial Securities Litigation*, 609 F.2d 411 (9th Cir. 1979) (there is no complexity exception to jury trial right in complex securities case) *with In Re Japanese Electronic Products Antitrust Litigation*, 631 F.2d 1069, 1073-74 (3d Cir. 1980)(jury trial request denied in complicated antitrust case where there were millions of documents and jury would be required to analyze Japanese market conditions and business practices over a 30-year period and make price comparisons of many electronic products). These cases and the general problem of jurors' abilities to understand truly complex cases are discussed in SAUL M. KASSIN AND LAWRENCE S. WRIGHTSMAN, THE AMERICAN JURY ON TRIAL: PSYCHOLOGICAL PERSPECTIVES (Hemisphere Publishing, N.Y. 1988).

41 A review of proposals and a general discussion of some of the potential constitutional and other objections is found in Rita Sutton, *A More Rational Approach to Complex Civil Litigation in the Federal Courts: The Special Jury*, 1990 U.CHI.LEGAL FORUM 575.

42 To lighten the financial burden of jury service, Russia provides that jurors are to receive 75% of the salary of a judge.

apply to the case only at the very end of the trial. The result is that they listen to the evidence throughout the trial without knowing which parts of it are important for deciding the case and which parts are not. And then, when the instructions are finally given, it has been traditional for the judge to read them to the jury rather than to give jurors a written copy. A major effort in recent years has been made to conduct psychological research on the effects of particular jury trial procedures and to seek to change those procedures that interfere with comprehension.[43]

Juror Pay Jurors receive pay from the court for their service, but it is not an amount that would make them rich. At the present time in the federal court system, jurors are paid $40 per day, but in some states, they are paid as little as $5 per day. Whether jurors continue to receive pay from their employers varies. All government employees continue to receive their normal pay. Some states require private employers to continue to pay regular wages or a portion of regular wages to jurors for a certain number of days of jury service.[44] In states without this requirement, the issue of employee pay depends on the agreement between employer and employee. Where employees are unionized, collective bargaining agreements commonly require continuation of employee pay during jury service at least for a limited period. For employees without any of these protections or for people who run their own businesses, jury duty in a trial that goes on for weeks or months can be financially costly. However, statistics indicate that only 25% of all trials in federal court last more than one week and 0.6% last more than 30 days. Moreover, the prospect of serious financial consequences constitutes "undue hardship" that can excuse the juror from service.

Avoiding Prejudicial Influences When involved in a case, jurors are generally not sequestered (segregated from the public) except while in attendance at trial. They are generally allowed to go home at the end of the day with the admonition that they are not to talk with anyone about the case. But trial judges have the discretion to order any procedures necessary to shelter them from the effect of publicity. In a notorious case, jurors may be sequestered in a hotel during the trial (or at least during deliberations), their access to television or newspapers may be censored and they may be transported to and from court in a van with its windows taped over to prevent them from seeing newspapers on newsstands or signs of protesters. Pre-trial publicity can also make it difficult to find a jury that has not already heard about the facts of the case and formed an opinion. It is not a disqualification that the juror has heard or read about the case. It is only if they have formed an opinion about it that would make it impossible for them to be impartial that they will be rejected.[45]

C. The Adversary Jury Trial and the Lawyer's Role in It

We will now move into a relatively detailed description of the stages of the typical adversary jury trial, with special attention paid to the responsibilities of the lawyers for

---

43 For an excellent recent collection of such changes and proposed changes, the arguments pro and con and citations to the relevant literature, *see* G. THOMAS MUNSTERMAN, PAULA L. HANNAFORD AND G. MARC WHITEHEAD, EDS, JURY TRIAL INNOVATIONS (Nat'l Center for State Courts, Washington, D.C. 1997).

44 *See, e.g.,* Conn. Gen. Stat. §51-247 (requiring employers to pay regular wages for the first 5 days of jury service) and Mass. Gen. Laws Ann. ch. 234A §48 (1986) (first 3 days). *See also Dean v. Gadsden Times*, 412 U.S. 543 (1973) (holding such statutes constitutional). There are also penalties against employers who discharge employees because of jury service. *See* 28 U.S.C.A. §1875 and ROTHSTEIN ET AL., HORNBOOK ON EMPLOYMENT LAW §4.31 (West 1994) (similar laws in every state but Montana).

45 *See generally* THOMAS R. MURPHY, GENERVA KAY LOVELAND AND G. THOMAS MUNSTERMAN, A MANUAL FOR MANAGING NOTORIOUS CASES (Nat'l Center for State Courts. Washington, D.C. 1993).

the parties in presenting and arguing the case.[46]

Civil vs. Criminal Jury Trials Most of the examples used for illustration in the description that follows are from a criminal case. However, there is little difference between criminal trial procedure and civil trial procedure that would strike the casual observer. The only obvious difference would be that in the criminal trial, the plaintiff's side is referred to as "the prosecution" (or "the government") and the lawyer appearing on that side is employed by the government rather than by a private party. Other differences between civil and criminal trials that would not be immediately obvious are: (1) in a criminal case the standard of proof is stricter, (2) criminal defendants cannot be compelled to take the stand or otherwise testify against themselves, and (3) there can be no appeal from a jury verdict of acquittal in a criminal case.[47]

Bench Trial Procedure A non-jury trial, called a "bench trial" or "court trial," follows essentially the procedure outlined here for a jury trial. The main differences are that the steps that concern only the jury would be missing and that the lawyers would modify their arguments to suit a professional decision-maker.

Trial Courtroom Setting A diagram of a typical trial courtroom designed for jury trials is set out in the Appendix.[48] The judge's dais or bench is at the highest level and the witness stand is generally at the next highest level. The judge wears a robe, but no wig. The lawyers do not wear any special dress to distinguish them from others in the courtroom. They usually wear business suits. The parties sit at counsel table next to their lawyers, the better to consult with them during the course of the trial. This is even true of the defendant in a criminal case.[49]

1. Jury Selection

The Jury Selection Process The purpose of jury selection, sometimes called "voir dire,"[50] is to determine the qualifications of potential members of the jury and to select an impartial jury to try the case. The format used for jury selection varies from jurisdiction to jurisdiction.[51] In almost all jury selections, by the time of trial the jurors have completed and the lawyers have read questionnaires containing basic information about each juror. The panel of prospective jurors or "jury venire" is generally given some brief introduction to the case for which they are being selected. This is then followed by questions to members of the panel about their qualifications to serve.

In some jurisdictions, only the judge is allowed to address questions to the jurors directly. In such jurisdictions, the lawyers must submit any questions in writing to the judge, who may or may not choose to ask the question. In other jurisdictions, the lawyers are allowed to address the jury venire directly and, after a few general questions from the judge, to ask questions of prospective jurors, either as a group or

---

46 For more information on this and other trial techniques of lawyers, *see* STEVEN LUBET, MODERN TRIAL ADVOCACY: ANALYSIS AND PRACTICE, 2D ED. (Nat'l. Inst. for Trial Advocacy 1997); JAMES W. JEANS, TRIAL ADVOCACY, 2D ED. (West 1993); RONALD CARLSON AND EDWARD IMWINKELREID, DYNAMICS OF TRIAL PRACTICE, 2D ED. (West 1995, 1997); THOMAS MAUET, FUNDAMENTALS OF TRIAL TECHNIQUES, 3D ED. (Aspen 1997); and ROGER HAYDOCK AND JOHN SONSTENG, TRIAL: THEORIES, TACTICS AND TECHNIQUES (West 1991). For an overview of English trial techniques, *see* KEITH EVANS, ADVOCACY AT THE BAR (Blackstone Press Ltd. 1992).

47 There are major differences between *pre-trial* procedures in civil and criminal cases. *See* Chapter VII, pp. 221-234 (civil cases) and Chapter VIII, pp. 259-264 (criminal cases).

48 *See* p. A33.

49 For a description of the other aspects of trial courts procedure, *see* Chapter V, pp. 163-165.

50 "Voir dire" comes from the Law French and means "to speak the truth."

51 "Jurisdiction" as used here means the judicial systems of the states and the federal government.

individually. Ultimately the extent of lawyer participation is up to the discretion of the individual judge in a given case. But as a general rule, federal courts tend to have judge-conducted jury selection, while state courts allow lawyer-conducted selection. However, several states have changed over to the federal system.

By whatever method information is obtained, indications that a juror is unable or unwilling to hear and decide the case fairly can be the basis for a "challenge for cause" on which the judge must rule. In addition, the lawyers can make "peremptory challenges," which allow them to exclude a certain number of jurors for no reason at all. The number of peremptory challenges allowed varies from one jurisdiction to another, but for a twelve-person jury, it would be typical to have five challenges for felonies not involving the death penalty or life imprisonment, and perhaps twice as many or more for capital cases.[52]

Trial Lawyer Techniques in Jury Selection The primary aim of the lawyers for the parties is to select a jury that is as sympathetic to their side as possible. The ability of the lawyers to influence the composition of the jury is limited at best: by invoking challenges for cause (which are rarely granted) and a set number of peremptory challenges. The pool of jurors that one begins with, however, is randomly determined and beyond the lawyer's ability to influence. Though lawyers often say they are going to court to "select a jury," jury selection is really "juror exclusion" and only a limited number can be excluded in most cases.

Lawyers question jurors to discover their likely predisposition toward the case to be tried. This is most often explored by asking them about experiences they or their close friends and relatives have had that are similar to the facts in the case to be tried. Any questions on sensitive private issues are handled at a bench conference, out of the hearing of the public and other jurors.[53] However, peremptory challenges are often made without regard to the answers given by jurors during *voir dire* and may even be decided before questioning begins. Often the decision is based on assumptions about the person's likely predisposition toward the case based on age, address, education, employment and other basic characteristics disclosed on written juror questionnaires — a socio-economic "portrait" of a juror.

Just what assumptions are drawn from basic information varies from one lawyer to another. In general, however, civil plaintiffs and criminal defendants will represent "anti-establishment" points of view and will lean toward younger, lower class, and

---

52 England abolished peremptory challenges for prosecutors in 1305 and for the defense in 1988. Although challenges for cause are permitted, they are made in only 1% of cases. *See* Buston, *Challenging and Discharging Jurors*, [1990] CRIM.L.REV. 225. The exercise of peremptory challenges in the United States was essentially unlimited until recently, when the Supreme Court prohibited their use to exclude jurors based on their race, ethnic origin or sex. *See* Chapter VIII, p. 291 (criminal cases) and *Edmondson v Leesville Concrete Co.*, 500 U.S. 614 (1991) (applying rule to civil cases).

53 An issue of recent concern is the juror's right to privacy. In one case, a juror objected to a questionnaire that asked such things as her religious preference, her political party affiliation, television shows she watched, whether she classified herself as a political conservative, liberal or moderate, her typical reading material and whether she belonged o the National Rifle Association. A recent article, David Weinstein, *Protecting A Juror's Right to Privacy: Constitutional Constraints and Policy Options*, 70 TEMPLE L.REV. 1 (1997), explores the issue of how to protect juror privacy while safeguarding a defendant's right to a fair trial and the public's right of access to court proceedings. In 1998, the American Bar Association added a "Standard on Jury Privacy" to its Standards Relating to Juror Use and Management.

ethnically diverse jurors while civil defendants and the prosecution in criminal cases will represent the "establishment" and will generally want the opposite kind of juror.[54]

More sophisticated analysis of potential jurors is available from a growing number of professional jury selection consultants, many of them trained in psychology and other social sciences. They will, for a fee, analyze the lawyer's case and construct a profile of the kinds of jurors to retain or strike, often based on community surveys or the use of focus groups. Use of jury consultants has been touted as very successful in some recent high-profile cases. One was the 1992 Rodney King case where, despite a videotape showing what appeared to be a rather savage beating, state court jurors acquitted Los Angeles policemen of using excessive force on King. Some research indicates limited effectiveness of such "scientific" jury selection techniques.[55]

Following jury selection, the jury is sworn to decide the case impartially and is given some preliminary instructions on the format of the trial.[56] Jurors are told something about the format of the trial and their duties. Most important, they are admonished to keep an open mind and not to discuss the case with anyone (even among themselves) until the evidence, arguments and final instructions have been completed and they have retired to deliberate. Generally, except in the most complex of cases, the jury is not given any instruction at this point on the law of the claim made or offense charged, because of the belief that such instruction would be confusing or incomplete at this point and might interfere with the jury's listening to all the facts.[57]

2. Opening Statements

The Form and Role of Opening Statements After the jury is selected, sworn and seated, the lawyers are permitted to make "opening statements" to the jury. The purpose of the opening statements is to allow the parties to outline the facts in the case and to introduce the jury to their claims or defenses. The evidence in the case will not come before the jury in a clear chronological order, but in a disjointed way dictated by the order in which witnesses testify. Thus, the opening statement is an opportunity to give jurors a clear exposition of the entire "story" of the case. Each side, of course, will have a different "story" to tell. The task facing the lawyers in opening is to set out the story of their case without argument in a way that will appeal to the jury.

Jurors are told that an opening statement is not evidence, only "a guide to the evidence," but studies show just how important a "guide" it is. Research on the decision-making process of jurors shows that they decide cases by constructing a "story" of how the case happened and testing it for accuracy against similar true "stories" from their own lives or experience. Since the opening statement is the

---

54 As noted earlier, peremptory challenges that appear to be based on race, sex or national origin can be contested and will be allowed only if the judge is convinced that the lawyer has a non-discriminatory reason for excluding the juror. *See supra* note 52 and Chapter VIII, p. 291.

55 *See* GUINTHER, *supra* note 19, at 55-58; KASSIN & WRIGHTSMAN, *supra* note 40, at 57-62.

56 A typical form of the oath taken is as follows: "Each of you do solemnly swear (or affirm) that, in this action now before the court, you will justly decide the questions submitted to you, that, unless you are discharged by the court from further deliberation, you will render a true verdict, and that you will render your verdict only on the evidence introduced and in accordance with the instructions of the court, so help you God."

57 This is changing somewhat, however. *See supra* p. 88.

opportunity for the lawyers to present their side's "story" in a coherent manner, it is a particularly powerful tool of persuasion.[58]

Lawyer's Approach to Opening Statement The best opening statement will usually present the facts in chronological order. In whatever order presented, the lawyer is supposed to be limited largely to reciting the *facts* the lawyer plans to prove rather than arguing the case. Indeed, one of the few objections allowed during an opening statement is that "counsel is arguing." Nonetheless, each side is permitted to outline its contentions with regard to the evidence so that the jury clearly understands the basic positions of the parties. This may involve some discussion of the applicable law as well. In a criminal case, for example, defense counsel in many cases will want to spend some time introducing the notion of "reasonable doubt." Clearly, the line between impermissible "argument" and "introducing" one's "contentions" or "position" to the jury is not a clear one.

Because what lawyers say in opening statements is not evidence, but only a guide to the evidence, it has been traditional for lawyers to preface each description of the evidence with the phrase "the evidence will show" or "the prosecution intends to prove that . . . ," instead of just telling the story. Indeed, some judges believe that this is legally required. The modern trend is that it is permissible and much more effective for lawyers to simply tell the story as it will come out. For example an excerpt from an opening in a criminal case might sound like this:

> On Tuesday, May 9th, the defendant John Smith had been drinking beer with his buddies for about four hours at the Dew Drop Inn. At around 10PM, he left his friends at the bar and drove up to the Grand Hotel. He stopped his car in the loading zone and left the motor running. Then, with a loaded pistol in his belt, he walked into the lobby of the hotel and went directly to the hotel night clerk's desk. He passed a note he had written to the night clerk. In the note, he said "I've got a gun. Give me all your 10s and 20s."

3. Presentation of Evidence (Proofs)

Following the opening statements the most important part of the trial starts with the lawyers for the parties presenting their "cases" — the evidence for their side. The plaintiff (or the prosecution in a criminal case) goes first and presents the "plaintiff's case," called the "government's case" or "state's case" in a criminal action. Then the defendant's lawyers present the "defendant's case." Following that, the plaintiff or prosecution has the opportunity to present a "rebuttal case."

It is the responsibility of the lawyers for the parties to assure the attendance of witnesses they need and obtain the appropriate documents for trial. This is generally done by the lawyer simply requesting the court clerk to provide an order requiring the witness to appear, called a "subpoena."[59] The lawyers know what witnesses and other evidence to use at trial because they have investigated the case both through informal means (e.g., talking to witnesses, using private investigators) and through a formal pre-trial process called "discovery." In a civil case, either side in the dispute can compel any member of the public who has knowledge of the case to give "depositions" at the lawyer's office and otherwise to disclose any relevant information

---

58 Nancy Pennington and Reid Hastie, *The Story Model of Juror Decision Making* in REID HASTIE, ED., INSIDE THE JUROR 192-221 (Cambridge U. Press 1993). Judges probably do the same thing.

59 Generally, the court clerk gives the lawyers the requisite subpoenas in blank. A recent change in the rule applicable in federal courts now gives lawyers in civil cases the power to actually issue the subpoenas themselves without any need to go through the court clerk. See FRCP 45(a)(3).

or documents. Discovery applies to compel even the opposing party and the opposing party's witnesses to disclose what they know long before trial. In the process of discovery, lawyers will generally hear testimony from all the witnesses who will be called to testify at trial.[60]

In a criminal case, discovery is more limited. Because of their right against self-incrimination, defendants are generally not required to testify or otherwise provide information before trial.[61] The Constitution requires that the prosecution disclose exculpatory evidence to the defense, but the defendant in the United States does not have full access to the prosecution's investigatory file. However, much of the prosecution's file consists of notes and reports of police personnel who will be witnesses in the case. The prosecution is required to produce for the defendant's inspection any writings used by a witness to prepare for testifying.[62]

The lawyers presenting their evidence have three principal tasks: presenting witness testimony, presenting documents or other tangible evidence, and making and defending against objections to evidence. The law and techniques for these activities are outlined next.

a. Witness Testimony

Witness testimony forms the bulk of the proofs offered at most trial. Witnesses may testify based only on personal knowledge and generally witnesses may not testify to "hearsay" — what someone else told the witness.[63] A court stenographer takes down verbatim all the testimony and everything else said in the proceedings.

How Witness Testimony Is Presented The witness is first "called to the witness stand" by one of the lawyers and takes an oath to tell "the whole truth and nothing but the truth."[64] Despite it being called the witness "stand," the place from which witnesses give evidence is really a chair next to the judge's dais in which the witness sits while testifying. All witnesses testify while seated unless asked to demonstrate something or point something out on a demonstrative aid. This includes the defendant giving testimony in a criminal case.

The side that called the witness questions the witness first on "direct examination." The opposing side is then given the right to conduct a "cross examination" of the witness. Following the cross examination, the side that called the witness then has the opportunity to conduct a "redirect examination." A "recross examination" and even possibly a second redirect examination may follow, but these are discretionary with the judge. In general, the purpose of direct examination is to get before the jury information that supports the proponent's case; the purpose of cross examination is to bring out contrary facts and to cast doubt on the direct examination.[65]

---

60 *See* Chapter VII, pp. 226-231.

61 However, some defenses require special prosecutorial investigation to rebut, such as alibi or insanity, and are required to be disclosed beforehand. Also, criminal defendants must provide the prosecution with samples for testing, such as handwriting or blood. *See* Chapter VIII, p. 265 and note 28.

62 *See supra* note 14. *See* FRE 612 and FRCrP 26.2.

63 Evidence law is discussed *infra* pp. 106-112.

64 If religious scruples prevent swearing an oath, an alternative "affirmation" may be used.

65 In general, jurors cannot ask questions, but some judges have permitted them to do so on a limited basis. The questions had to be submitted to the judge in writing and then would be asked by the judge unless if was not a proper one from the standpoint of the law of evidence or if the judge was sure the lawyers would ask it at a later time. Reactions to the practice during a 1984 study in a federal court were positive reactions on the part of judges and jurors, and even some of the lawyers (plaintiffs' lawyers favored the practice more than defendants' lawyers). GUINTHER, *supra* note 19, at 68. *See also* KASSIN &

Witnesses are generally not permitted to testify in a narrative form on either direct or cross examination. They may testify only in response to questions. One reason for this has been discussed: it is thought desirable for lawyers to be able to control and "shape" the witness's testimony by the questions they ask so that the lawyer can present the testimony to the fact-finder in the best (or worst) possible light. Another reason is efficiency. To have a witness simply state everything the witness thinks is relevant to the case will generally result in much that is not really essential. Finally, question-and-answer format is essential to administer limitations on admissibility of evidence. Requiring that witnesses testify only in response to questions gives opposing counsel time to determine from the question asked whether inadmissible evidence is called for, so that an objection can be interposed before the jury hears the answer.[66]

(1) Direct Examination

A direct examination usually has three parts: (1) *background* of the witness (who he is, where he works, etc.) (2) *setting the scene* by describing the place where the incident occurred, (3) *action*, that is, description of the incident itself. In getting the witness's story out, the witness will usually be answering the five essential "W" questions that any good newspaper story answers — who, what, where, when and why — and most of the lawyer's direct examination questions will begin with one of these five words.

Form of Questions on Direct Examination In general, the lawyer conducting direct examination will want to ask "open" questions that give the witness the opportunity to talk. An example of an "open" question is "What did you see in the lobby of the Grand Hotel around 10PM on Tuesday, May 9th, of last year?" This is in contrast to "closed" questions that contemplate a limited response from the witness. An example of a closed question would be "How far from the night clerk's desk were you when the robbery was taking place?" or any question that can be answered "yes" or "no." Open questions are in general more efficient in that they ask for more information and allow the witness to answer in several sentences at a time. But there is an additional reason why open questions are used on direct examination: longer answers give the jury more of chance to get to know and to get a "feel" for the witness. This is important, since the jury must decide to what extent to believe the witness and what weight to give the witness's testimony.

Closed questions are appropriate on direct and are essential to probe matters of detail. For example, in answer to the open question of what happened in the hotel lobby, the witness may start telling about how he was in the lobby waiting for a friend to arrive; how he was leaning against a table reading a newspaper; and that he noticed a person approach the night clerk's desk and hand the clerk a piece of paper. At that point the direct examiner will wish to ask some closed questions, including the example just given about how close the witness was to the clerk's desk. Other closed questions would probably be "How much of man's body could you see: his entire body or just his face?"; "How tall did he appear to be?"; "How was he dressed?"; "What were his facial features like?"; and so on, going into a detailed description that

---

WRIGHTSMAN, *supra* note 40, at 129-131.

66 The Federal Rules of Evidence contain no blanket prohibition against narrative answers. However, the judge has the general power to "exercise reasonable control over the mode . . . of interrogating witnesses and presenting evidence." FRE 611. Consequently, judges will usually sustain an objection to narrative testimony if it is argued that the witness could well blurt out inadmissible evidence before an objection can be interposed.

obviously matches the defendant, thus showing in the process that the witness was a careful enough observer to notice details.

"Pacing" a Direct Examination The mark of a good direct examiner is knowing when to move forward with open questions, thus allowing the witness to get through the story more quickly, and when to slow down the action and focus on details by way of closed questions. This is called the "pace" of the examination. If there are too many narrow questions, important parts of the story will get buried under a mass of unnecessary detail and the slow pace will bore the jury. If there are too many open questions, the story will go by too quickly for the jury to remember or will be described in such a general way that the jury will conclude that the witness did not see much or did not pay much attention to what was there to be seen.

Leading Questions There is one kind of closed question that is objectionable on direct examination. This is the "leading" question. A leading question is one that suggests to the witness what the answer should be. "Weren't you standing only 10 feet from the night clerk's desk when the defendant walked up?" is a leading question. On direct examination, leading questions are prohibited because it is thought to be unfair to permit the lawyer to "feed" answers to witnesses that support the lawyer's own side. Moreover, the lawyers are permitted and even expected to interview witnesses and review their testimony with them before trial, so leading questions should not be necessary to get the witness's testimony out.[67]

(2) Cross Examination

Purpose of Cross Examination The purpose of cross examination may in some cases be to seek out information, but more often its main purpose is to undermine the credibility of the witness's direct examination testimony. Such "impeachment" of the witness's testimony may include casting doubt on the witness's ability and opportunity to observe (e.g., it was dark and stormy), exposing any bias or prejudice the witness might have (e.g., the witness dislikes one of the parties), pointing out any interest the witness has in the outcome of the case (e.g., the witness has "cut a deal" with the prosecution allowing the witness to avoid prosecution if he testifies in this case), and showing bad character for truth-telling (e.g., the witness has been convicted of perjury). Another form of impeachment is to show that the witness made a prior statement that is inconsistent with the witness's testimony at trial.

Form of Questions Not only are leading questions permitted on cross examination; many lawyers believe that proper technique requires that *all* questions on cross examination be leading. Most questions on cross examination at the very least will be closed questions, will not give the witness to explain anything, and will be answerable only by "yes" or "no." If the witness does try to explain an answer, for example, by answering "yes, but . . . ," the questioner can object that the answer is non-responsive, assuming the question can fairly be answered "yes" or "no."[68]

---

67 Leading questions *are* permitted on direct examination for uncontested material, for foundation material for introducing exhibits into evidence (*see infra* pp. 98-99) and to draw the witness's attention to a particular part of her testimony. They are also permitted in examining a hostile witness, the adverse party or a child or adult witness with impaired communication skills. FRE 611 states a softened version of the rule against leading questions: "Leading questions *should not* be used on direct examination of a witness except as may be necessary to develop his testimony." (emphasis added).

68 As a control tactic, lawyers sometimes begin their cross examination by instructing the witness that all questions will be answerable only with "yes" or "no" and that the witness should not go beyond that answer. This is generally frowned upon and many judges will sustain objections to it on the ground that it is not counsel's place to instruct the witness, but to simply ask the questions.

The idea behind using leading questions is that they allow the cross examiner to bring out only those items of information that are of value to the cross-examiner's case. Effective cross-examiners will generally ask only questions to which they know the answer and will never ask the witness "why" questions or other questions that give the witness a chance to explain. A cross-examining lawyer, however, is not permitted to argue with the witness or to "badger" the witness. What amounts to argument or badgering is not always clear, but asking the same question over and over or insisting that the answer the witness has given is false will in most circumstances fall into this category.

Effective Cross Examination Techniques A mistake that many beginning lawyers make is to try to accomplish too much on cross examination, expecting that they will be able to get the witness to completely agree with their position.[69] For example, after a direct examination in which the witness identifies the defendant as the robber, the defense lawyer might be tempted to ask "Isn't it true that it was so dark in the lobby that you were really unable to get a good look at the robber?" If the issue in the case is eyewitness identification of the defendant by this witness, this is a valid point to make. However, as a *question*, it is of limited use, since the witness will answer "no" or, worse yet, will feel challenged and thus will repeat once again for the jury just how well he or she could see. The point that it was so dark the witness could not see is a *conclusion* that the lawyer should *argue* in the final arguments in the case (when the witness cannot answer the argument). On *cross examination*, the lawyer is generally only looking for the *facts needed* to make the argument later. Thus, the lawyer, having done the appropriate investigation to determine that affirmative answers will be given, will ask instead: "This took place at 10:00 at night, didn't it?" "So, it was dark outside, correct?" "The only source of light in that lobby was a single light fixture, correct?" "And that single light fixture was hanging from the ceiling *behind* the robber's head, wasn't it?" "And isn't it true that, when you described the assailant to police when they arrived just 10 minutes after the robber left, you told them that it was 'pretty dark' in the hotel lobby?"

(3) Redirect Examination

Redirect examination is the opportunity for the direct examiner to return to "repair" any "damage" done on cross examination. Redirect examination, like direct examination, must be conducted by way of non-leading questions. This makes it difficult to "repair damage" done on cross unless the direct examiner has anticipated the damage and has prepared the witness for redirect examination. For example, if the redirect examiner wishes to elicit testimony that a prior inconsistent statement the witness signed was signed under time pressure, the most specific question the examiner can properly ask without leading is: "Why did you sign that statement?"

It is in part because of the difficulty of doing an effective redirect with non-leading question that it is said by some experts in trial advocacy that the "first rule" of redirect examination is "Don't!" Unless there has been damage on cross and that damage can be repaired by way of redirect, redirect will be a waste of time or, worse yet, will serve only to emphasize the damage done on cross.

---

69 This unrealistic attitude is undoubtedly influenced by watching too many movies and television shows about trials. Often in such stories the real murderer is a witness for the prosecution, who is then exposed by defense counsel during cross examination and confesses to the crime in open court.

b. Objections

A jury need not explain the reasons for its verdict. Consequently, the best way to assure that it does not rely on improper evidence in deciding a case is to keep it from hearing that evidence at all.[70] The most common method for doing so in trials is to have the lawyers interpose objections to improper evidence as it is being presented.[71]

Form of Objections Objections are stated orally in open court during the trial. The objecting lawyer is required to state his or her objection and the ground for it, such as "Objection, your honor, hearsay." If in the judge's opinion the objection is clearly well taken or is clearly incorrect, the judge will rule immediately without considering any response from the other side. An objection that is correct will be "sustained" by the judge and one that is not correct will be "overruled."

The judge may choose to hear a brief response to the objection and possibly a brief rejoinder from the objecting lawyer. In the course of argument, an "offer of proof" may need to be made since the judge, in order to rule on the objection, may need to know what answer the witness would give if allowed to answer. Any such offer of proof or extended argument will have to be heard outside the hearing of the jury at a "bench conference" with the judge. When such a conference is needed, the lawyers may ask to "approach the bench." The lawyers then stand close to the judge's bench and may need to speak in whispers if the courtroom is small. If the argument is extensive because the item of evidence is very important and the question of admissibility is a close one, the jury may need to be temporarily removed from the courtroom instead.[72]

Effect of Objections on the Jury Lawyers will seek to avoid unnecessary objections and, when they feel the need to object, will keep in mind that they may be trying the jury's patience. Witness examinations that are constantly interrupted by objections and bench conferences irritate jurors. Not only is the testimony difficult to follow, the jury will think the objecting lawyer is trying to hide something from them.

Motions to Strike Testimony Most objections will be made after a question is asked, but before the witness has a chance to answer. However, sometimes objectionable evidence comes out before an objection can be interposed. If the jury has already heard the evidence, the lawyer should make a motion to "strike the evidence from the record" and ask that the judge give an "instruction to disregard" the "stricken" evidence.[73] Clearly, it is very difficult for jurors to disregard something they have already heard, so some have characterized such instructions to disregard as attempts "to unring a bell." When the evidence is truly crucial and an instruction to disregard it would be inadequate, it may be necessary to order a new trial.

Motions in Liminé Because objections cannot always be interposed in time and instructions to disregard testimony are imperfect, a better means of assuring that evidence is not disclosed is the "motion in liminé." This motion, literally a motion

---

70 *See* FRCP 52; FRCrP 23(c).

71 The grounds for objecting to evidence are discussed later in this chapter. *See* pp. 106-112.

72 This is also called a "sidebar" conference if the judge has to go to the side of the bench to confer with the lawyers.

73 Testimony that is "stricken from the record" still appears in the verbatim transcript of the trial. It will appear. Striking testimony from the record simply means that the court formally declares that it is not proper evidence and must be disregarded by the jury in reaching a decision.

made "at the threshold," seeks to obtain a ruling on the admissibility of evidence before the trial starts or at any other point before the witness takes the stand.

c. Exhibits: Real, Demonstrative and Documentary Evidence

Importance of Exhibits Exhibits are items of tangible evidence that must be formally authenticated and "admitted into evidence" during the trial. Exhibits are important because juries tend to give them greater weight than testimonial evidence. Tangible evidence cannot forget or exaggerate as witnesses can. Moreover, the jury can read or examine them over and over again in the jury room during their deliberation, while witness testimony lingers only in the memory of the jury.

Types of Exhibits Exhibits are generally of three types: "real" evidence, "demonstrative" evidence and documents. Real evidence is actual tangible items involved in the occurrence in dispute, such as the gun or the blood-soaked clothes in a murder case, or the clamp left in the patient during surgery in a medical malpractice case. Demonstrative evidence is anything that is used to represent or demonstrate something that cannot be brought into the courtroom, such as a diagram of the floor plan of a house that was the scene of the crime or a diagram of an intersection where an accident occurred. Documentary evidence comprises any writings relevant to the case. The overall goal for a lawyer seeking to use an exhibit at trial is to get it "admitted into evidence" — formally declared to be part of the official record of the case and thus appropriate for the jury to consider as evidence and take into the jury room at the end of the trial.

Procedures for Exhibits The overall procedural steps that must be followed are that the lawyer must (1) have the court reporter "mark the exhibit for identification" by giving it a number or letter for easy reference, (2) show the exhibit to opposing counsel, (3) "lay a foundation" for its admission and (4) "move the exhibit into evidence." The need to lay a foundation for its admission requires that the lawyer satisfy the judge that the legal prerequisites for its admission into evidence exist. Laying a foundation is usually done by way of witness testimony. After the foundation has been established, to move the exhibit into evidence the attorney simply turns to the judge and says "I move that State's Exhibit No. 34 be admitted into evidence." The judge will then hear any objections to the motion from the other side and will rule.

More than one witness may be necessary to complete the foundation for an exhibit. Thus, for example, if drugs were seized during an arrest, a "chain of custody" must be established to show that the evidence is authentic and was not tampered with from the point that it was seized to the point it is introduced as evidence at the trial. This may involve calling everyone who handled the exhibit as a foundation witness, e.g., the arresting officer, the police courier who delivered the evidence to the police chemist, the chemist, and any custodian of evidence at the police station. As a result, counsel may not be able to complete the last step of moving the exhibit into evidence until after several witnesses are called. Since some of these witnesses will be testifying to matters other than things relating to the particular exhibit, foundation laying can sometimes stretch out over several days of trial.

Effectively Dealing With Exhibits The key to effectively laying foundations for exhibits is to do it as efficiently and unobtrusively as possible. The point of the foundation-laying — and what the jury is looking forward to — is the *content* of the exhibit. Anything seen by the jury as delaying getting to that content will be resented. One way to make the process more efficient is to mark the exhibits for identification and to show them to opposing counsel before the trial starts, thereby eliminating two of the four steps in the process outlined above. The lawyer can then fit the foundation into the normal direct examination. For example, in seeking to introduce the note the robber passed to the night clerk demanding money, the prosecutor can simply go through the night clerk's description the robbery, including reference to the note (something that the prosecutor would do in any event). Then all that need be done further is to draw the witness's attention to the exhibit and to ask the witness whether the exhibit is the note to which he has been referring in his description of the robbery. Having thus laid the foundation, the prosecutor can simply move its admission into evidence.

In civil cases, the availability of extensive discovery opportunities means that almost all issues of the admissibility of exhibits will be determined well in advance of trial. This will be done by way of "stipulation" — an agreement between the parties — or by pre-trial rulings of the trial judge.[74] In criminal cases, discovery is more limited, so pretrial resolution of exhibit issues is less likely.

4. Motions for a Directed Verdict

Following the plaintiff's or prosecution's presentation of evidence, the defense may move for a "directed verdict" on the basis of the plaintiff's evidence, even before presenting the defense case.[75] In a criminal case, a similar motion is made after presentation of the prosecution's evidence and it is often called a "motion for judgment of acquittal."[76] The motion seeks dismissal of the case on the ground that the plaintiff or prosecution has failed to produce sufficient evidence for rational jurors to return a verdict in its favor. The defendant has the right to make a second motion for a directed verdict or judgment of acquittal after all the evidence has been presented. This assures that the case that goes to the jury has been screened one final time to assure that there is sufficient for the jury to decide the case.[77]

5. Closing Arguments

The Nature of Closing Argument After both the plaintiff and defendant have "rested their cases" — meaning that they have presented all their evidence — it is time for "closing arguments."[78] Closing arguments are the opportunity given to the lawyers in the case to address the jury directly and seek to persuade the jury to decide the case in their side's favor. Closing is certainly the most "flashy" of all the things that trial lawyers do in trials, but it is not necessarily the most important. If the evidence has not been presented effectively, a brilliant closing argument will not save the case.

Despite how it might sometimes appear to the casual observer, there are in fact limits on what a lawyer can do and say in argument. Generally not allowed are appeals to passion or prejudice, such as arguing or implying that the defendant in a criminal case is guilty because he is black or that a particular verdict will "clean up the drug problem in this city." Counsel may not misstate evidence or "argue off the record." This means that counsel cannot rely on facts that were not introduced into

---

74 *See* Chapter VII, pp. 221-234, for a discussion of civil pre-trial procedures.

75 In federal court, this motion is called a Motion for Judgment as a Matter of Law (JML). Federal Rule of Civil Procedure (FRCP) 50(a).

76 *See* Federal Rule of Criminal Procedure (FRCrP) 29(a).

77 A similar motion can be made after a verdict is rendered. *See infra* p. 105.

78 As noted earlier, a motion for a directed verdict may be renewed at this time, and the case will be dismissed by the judge at this point if the plaintiff or prosecutor has not presented evidence sufficient for a rational verdict in its favor.

evidence at the trial. Similarly, when evidence is admitted for a limited purpose the lawyer may not argue a broader use of the evidence. For example, the lawyer may not argue that a prior conviction shows general bad character when it was admitted only to impeach credibility.[79] Finally, a lawyer is not permitted to state the lawyer's personal opinion as to the believability of witnesses or of the correctness of his client's case or of the guilt or innocence of the accused. Generally lawyers will not object even if the other side is transgressing some of these limitations during final argument, but this is not a legal restriction, only a traditional courtesy. Objections should be made if violations of the stated limitations are hurting one's case.

Trial Lawyer Techniques in Closing Argument The form of closing argument is not specified and there are a wide variety of styles among lawyers. Some are cool and analytical, while others are emotional and intuitive. However, most effective closing arguments will (1) focus the case by setting aside uncontested or less important issues and pointing out the *real* issues in the case; (2) argue the issues that have been brought into focus by carefully organizing the evidence that supports each of them and, where there is a conflict, explaining to the jury why it should accept the arguing party's version over the opposing party's version; and (3) relate the evidence the jury has just heard to the principles of law the jury must apply as set out in the jury instructions.

Closing argument is sometimes referred to as "summation," but that is misleading. A good closing argument will not just summarize the evidence; it will organize it and argue it. In all but the longest and most complicated trials, lawyers who start out their closing argument by announcing that they will now summarize all the evidence the jury has heard will be greeted by anguished facial expressions and then bored looks from jurors who already know the evidence well. What most jurors want and need is some guidance on what the evidence *means*. That is the primary purpose of closing argument.

Trial lawyers will usually try to construct a "theme" for their case. A theme is a shorthand characterization of the case or a "story" of the case that will be easily accepted by the jury as a valid archetype. It may serve to explain the entire case or only important parts of it. A common theme in a medical malpractice case defense would cast the plaintiff as "the ungrateful patient," who makes unreasonable demands and expects miracles. The Bible, Shakespeare, and proverbs provide material for many case themes, but themes can be found in all kinds of everyday experiences as well. A version of the Biblical saying, "only the wicked flee when no man pursueth," can be used to get the greatest effect out of evidence that the defendant tried to flee. In a similar vein, when a party has overreacted to something the opposing party did, the opposing party may quote Shakespeare: "methinks she doth protest too much." Prosecutors are often faced with trying to prove intent of the defendant circumstantially in the face of believable testimony from the defendant denying that he had such intent. The prosecutor might remind the jury, several times if need be, that "actions speak louder than words."

For a theme to work, it must be anchored in strong evidence, such as an unimpeachable witness or a document.[80] If the evidence on which is it based is weak, the theme will suffer accordingly. For example, the "wicked flee" approach will not work well if there is some doubt that the party *was* in fact fleeing. Moreover, the

---

79 Examples are hearsay statements admitted for a purpose other than their truth. *See infra* p. 109.

80 Other guides for constructing themes are suggested in LUBET, *supra* note 46, at 1-14.

theme must be one with which the jury can readily identify. For example, a trial lawyer who uses stories about or quotations from famous male sports figures is not likely to get far with a jury of all women. Finally, trial lawyers must always check their case theories to see if their theme can be turned around and used against them.

Analogies, sometimes presented in the form of a "personal anecdote" with which the jury can readily identify, are an extension of this form of theme construction. For example, a prosecutor who wants to encourage the jury to use a relatively small amount of circumstantial evidence to tie the defendant to the crime, can use some variant of the "sugar barrel" story:

> We grew up poor in the south. We didn't have much, but one treat that me and my brother had was that, once a week after supper on Saturday, Mama would give us each a spoonful of sugar from a big barrel where she kept it. That sugar sure tasted good! But we'd sometimes have a yearning for it before Saturday and we'd sneak into the kitchen and take some. Every time we did that, no matter how much we denied it, no matter whether we would sneak down there at midnight when my mama was asleep or when she was gone from the house — she would *always* know we'd done it and we would get a whipping. We began to think she could read our minds!

> But later on, when we were grown up, we found out the reason: each time we would take some sugar, no matter *how careful* we were, we would spill the tiniest bit of it — just a few crystals — on the floor. Since Mama kept the floors real clean, she'd see it and would know we'd been somewhere we shouldn't have been.

> Now, the defendant here thought he had been *really careful* in covering up his crime, but he dropped some sugar crystals, too. Like my Mama, we can learn a lot from looking at those tiny crystals.

At this point the lawyer can go into the small clues left by the defendant and how they connect him with the crime.[81]

6. Jury Instructions

Content of Instructions At the end of all the proofs and usually after closing argument,[82] the judge will provide jury instructions on the law applicable to the case. This is sometimes referred to as the "charge" to the jury. This will include the substantive law related to the claim made or offense charged, such as the requirements for a binding contract or the elements of murder. Many jurisdictions have standard or "pattern" jury instructions that are officially approved by the highest court of that state and which must be given in any case where they are applicable. However, not all points of law that arise in a case are covered by standard instructions and it becomes the task of the lawyers to write and submit proposed instructions to

---

81 Some observers have noted that there is often an inverse relationship between the strength of one's case and the amount of theatrics and story-telling that a lawyer engages in. As one trial lawyer confessed, "If the facts of my case are weak, I stand on the law. If the law in my case is weak, I stand on the facts. If both the facts and law of my case are weak, I stand on the *table*." A lawyer facing an entertaining opponent can counter such efforts by arguing that the lawyer is "showing off" to avoid dealing with the serious problems with his case. This can be succinctly illustrated to the jury by using the story of the trial lawyer's confession just related in this footnote.

82 In some jurisdictions, jury instructions may precede the closing arguments. *See, e.g.* FRCP 51; FRCrP 30. The reason for this is to allow the lawyers to refer to the instructions during their argument. However, even in jurisdictions where argument comes before the instructions, the lawyer may freely refer to them because the judge will have gone over the instructions with the lawyers prior to closing argument.

the court.

Instructions will also cover the law governing how the jury is to assess the evidence and decide the case. These instructions are generally not very detailed. The jury is told to elect a "foreperson," who will preside over deliberations and allow everyone a chance to speak, and that they are the sole judges of the credibility and weight of the evidence. But they are generally not given any formula for assessing particular types of evidence.

Standards of Proof   The jury is told what standard of proof it is to apply in deciding the case. In a criminal case, the standard is "proof beyond a reasonable doubt." Thus, the jury is told that it may find the defendant guilty only if it finds beyond a reasonable doubt that the defendant committed the crime and that it must acquit the defendant if it has a reasonable doubt as to the defendant's guilt. In a civil case, the standard of proof is the "preponderance of the evidence," sometimes referred to as the "greater weight of the evidence." There is also an intermediate standard of "clear and convincing evidence" that is used in some civil cases that have very serious consequences, such as terminations of parental rights and involuntary commitments to mental hospitals. According to some, if the criminal and normal civil standards were expressed as percentages, they would be 95% and 51% respectively, with "clear and convincing" weighing in somewhere around 75-80%.

A typical instruction explaining reasonable doubt tells the jury:

> Reasonable doubt means a doubt based upon reason and common sense that arises from a fair and rational consideration of all the evidence or lack of evidence in the case. It is a doubt that is not a vague, speculative or imaginary doubt, but such a doubt as would cause reasonable persons to hesitate to act in matters of serious importance to themselves.

A typical instruction explaining the civil standard is:

> When I use the expression "by a preponderance of the evidence," I mean that you must be persuaded from a consideration of all the evidence in the case that the issue in question is more probably true than not true. Any findings of fact you make must be based on probabilities, not possibilities. It may not be based on surmise, speculation, or conjecture.

Jury instructions are read to the jury and, up until recently, the jury was generally not given a copy of them. Given the inherent weaknesses of reading 15 minutes or more of legal instructions, more and more jurisdictions are allowing or requiring that judges give the jury a copy. Studies show that, while juries are good factfinders, they do less well in getting legal standards straight.[83] There is no direct judicial check on jury misunderstanding of the law, unless the jury asks the judge for assistance. However, the judge can set aside any verdict (other than a criminal acquittal) that is not warranted by the facts or the law.[84]

---

[83] HARRY KALVEN, JR. AND HANS ZEISEL, THE AMERICAN JURY 149-50 (Little, Brown 1966). *See also* R. P. Charrow and V. R. Charrow, *A Psycholinguistic Study of Jury Instructions*, 79 COLUM. L. REV. 1306 (1979) and KASSIN & WRIGHTSMAN, *supra* note 40, at 144-167. A recent study shows that jurors' understanding of instructions is increased significantly when they take the opportunity to ask the judge questions. Alan Reifman, Spencer M. Gusick, and Phoebe Ellsworth, *Real Jurors' Understanding of the Law in Real Cases*, 16 Law & Human Behavior 539 (1992).

[84] *See infra*, p. 105. *See also* Chapter VII, pp. 232-233, where pre-trial screening devices are discussed. Another standard of proof applied in civil cases with serious consequences (e.g. termination of parental rights, involuntary commitment to a psychiatric hospital) is proof "by clear and convincing evidence."

Judicial Comments on the Evidence Generally, judges in the United States do not summarize the evidence for the jury or comment on it. While federal judges at least theoretically have this power, and commenting on the evidence was at one time an accepted custom, the practice has fallen into disuse today as judges are more concerned lest they improperly influence the jury.[85] The only vestige of the judicial summary and comment that remains is that the judge may read to the jury at the parties' request a brief "theory of the case" instruction written by the parties that outlines each side's principal contentions in summary form.

7. Deliberation and Verdict

Because jury deliberations are undertaken in secret and every jury is unique, little of a general nature can be said about what happens in deliberations. However, there are composite descriptions based on observations of mock juries and some jurors have written about their experiences.[86] At some point, often at the very beginning, a tentative vote is taken to determine the extent of disagreement. This is followed by discussion and more votes until the jury either agrees or is "deadlocked."

Deadlocked and Hung Juries If the jury reports that it is deadlocked, the judge will usually send the jurors back to deliberate with the admonition to try to see if they can work out their differences. Sometimes, an additional instruction is given to them that is designed to motivate jurors to reconsider their positions. Called an *Allen* charge or a "dynamite charge," it tells the jurors in essence to think seriously about their position and listen carefully to the arguments of the other jurors.[87]

In criminal cases in federal court and all but 5 states, jury verdicts — whether for conviction or acquittal — must be unanimous.[88] In civil cases, a simple majority or a two-thirds majority is required. Anything less is a "hung jury." If the jury is truly deadlocked, the judge has no choice but to "declare a mistrial." As soon as the jury has reached a verdict, it communicates that to the judge. Everyone assembles in the courtroom, the foreperson of the jury hands the verdict to the judge, who checks it for proper form and then hands it back to the foreperson to read aloud.[89]

Requests for Evidence or Instructions Sometimes the jury will request that certain testimony be read to them or, if written jury instructions are not provided, that certain portions of the instructions be reread. Jurors may request exhibits that have not already been taken into the jury room. Judges are somewhat reluctant to read only the portion of the testimony or instructions that the jury requests for fear that doing so would overemphasize the requested part to the exclusion of other parts. Conse-

---

85 *See Quercia v. United States*, 289 U.S. 466 (1933) conviction because of trial judge's comment to the jury: "I think that every single word that man [the defendant] said, except when he agreed with the Government's testimony, was a lie"). Not all judges agree that judges should be reticent to summarize and comment on the evidence. Detailed proposals for a broader role for the judge are discussed by a federal judge in Jack Weinstein, *The Power and Duty of Federal Judges to Marshall and Comment on the Evidence in Jury Trials and Some Suggestions on Charging Jurors*, 118 F.R.D. 161 (1988).

86 *See* Phoebe Ellsworth, *Are Twelve Heads Better Than One?*, 52 LAW & CONTEMP. PROB. 205 (1989) (describing a composite picture based on observing mock juries). Two juror accounts are MELVYN ZERMAN, CALL THE FINAL WITNESS 122-42 (Harper & Row 1977), reprinted in part in LANDSMAN, *supra* note 4; VICTOR VILLASENOR, JURY — THE PEOPLE VS. JUAN CORONA (Little, Brown 1977).

87 The *Allen* charge is named for the case in which the Supreme Court approved its use, *Allen v. United States*, 164 U.S. 492 (1896). "Dynamite charge" is a play on words. "Charge" can mean both a jury instruction and an explosive device.

88 Constitutional requirements regarding unanimity are discussed in Chapter VIII, p. 291.

89 Mistrials may also be granted whenever continuation of a trial is impossible or unfair for other reasons, such as misconduct of the lawyers, parties, witnesses or jurors that cannot be "cured" by an instruction to the jury.

quently, to the extent possible, the judge will try to give them the entire testimony of the witness they asked about or the entire instructions, adding the admonition to consider the material they requested in the context of all the evidence and instructions.

Polling the Jury There is little that the lawyers can do during deliberations except appear and argue about any supplemental instructions or other problems that arise in deliberations. However, the losing side has the right to "poll the jury." The judge will then require that each juror answer individually whether in fact the verdict read was the one they agreed to. Occasionally this results in a juror blurting out that it was not his or her verdict and the problem must be ironed out by more deliberation and, if necessary, a mistrial will be declared, resulting in a new trial before a new jury.[90]

Form of the Verdict In all criminal cases and in most civil cases, a "general verdict" stating the bare conclusion of the jury is rendered. In a criminal case, the form for a general verdict will allow the jury to check either guilty or not guilty on each of the charges tried. In a civil case, there will similarly be two choices, either "We find for the plaintiff and award damages of $_____" or "We find for the defendant."

In civil cases, the judge may use a "special verdict" or "general verdict with interrogatories."[91] Special verdict forms direct the jury to answer the component questions that are necessary for a general verdict and, based on those answers, the judge determines what the final resolution of the case is. Thus, in a libel case, the jury may be asked such questions as "Did the Defendant accuse the Plaintiff of taking a bribe in the article published in Smithton Observer on January 10, 1997?" "Did this statement defame the Plaintiff?" "Was the statement privileged?" and so on. Components of damages may similarly be subject to a special verdict. The jury would then state separate amounts for each economic loss suffered, such as lost wages, hospital and medical expenses, impairment of future earning capacity, and for non-economic losses, including fear, shock and pain at the time of the injury, pain and suffering thereafter, loss of companionship or consortium, and whatever other components of non-economic harm are allowed in that jurisdiction.

General verdicts with interrogatories are like ordinary general verdicts in that the jury determines the final conclusion of the verdict itself, but the final conclusion is then followed by questions designed to check whether the jury had the correct reasons for that conclusion. Thus, questions similar to those mentioned above for the special verdict might appear.

It is usually the job of the lawyers to draft a special verdict or a general verdict with interrogatories. To the extent that such verdict forms serve to "rationalize" the jury's decision-making process, they are favored by defendants in civil tort cases to counteract feelings of sympathy for the injured plaintiff. The problem with these devices lies in the difficulty of framing precise, yet understandable, questions for the jury. These verdict forms increase the danger that a verdict that is warranted by the evidence would have to be thrown out just because the jury made mistakes in answering the questions.

---

90 A mistrial is declared not just when jurors cannot agree, but whenever the trial process aborts. A mistrial can be declared where there is misconduct of the jury or of counsel that cannot be cured. Mistrials also take place when the trial cannot continue because illness or other disaster has reduced the number of jury members to less than the minimum needed or has otherwise made it impossible to continue the trial. Lawyers may move for a mistrial or the judge may declare one on his or her own initiative.

91 *See* FRCP 49.

8. Post-Trial Motions

Judgment NOV Motions   The defense may make a motion *after* a verdict is rendered on this same grounds that a motion for a directed verdict is made earlier in the proceeding.[92] In civil cases, this is called a motion for "judgment notwithstanding the verdict" or "judgment NOV" for the Latin *non obstante verdicto*.[93] However, a directed verdict or judgment NOV may be granted only if there is a "no legally sufficient evidentiary basis for a reasonable jury" to decide for the plaintiff.[94]

New Trial Motions   The judge in a civil case may also "set aside" the verdict and grant a new trial if it is "against the great weight of the evidence" or if liability is correct, but the verdict is grossly excessive or inadequate. If it is only the amount of the verdict that is improper, the judge may grant a "remittitur" or an "additur" — ordering a new trial on grounds of excessiveness or inadequacy of the verdict conditioned on the parties consenting to either a reduction of or addition to the amount awarded by the jury. However, the judge may not order a new trial simply because the judge disagrees with it. Thus, it is said that the judge may not sit as a "thirteenth juror."

Post-Trial Motions in Criminal Cases   In criminal cases, the defense may also make a motion after a guilty verdict that corresponds to the directed verdict motion or motion for judgment of acquittal made earlier in the trial. It may be called a motion for judgment notwithstanding the verdict or sometimes a renewed motion for judgment of acquittal.[95] The ground for granting such a motion is that the evidence presented at trial was insufficient for the jury to find the defendant guilty beyond a reasonable doubt. The prosecution is not permitted to move to set aside an acquittal.[96]

Impeaching the Verdict   A party may also seek to set aside the verdict on the ground that the jury acted improperly during deliberations or trial. This is called "impeaching a verdict." However, motions to impeach the verdict are looked upon with disfavor. Such a rule serves to preserve the secrecy of the jury room and to prevent lawyers from hounding jurors, trying to discover evidence of irregularities.[97] A typical modern rule on the ability of a juror to impeach a verdict is Federal Rule of Evidence 606. It makes an intrinsic-extrinsic distinction: a court may not receive any evidence as to any matter or statement occurring during the course of the jury's deliberations or the effect of anything on deliberations unless it concerns "extraneous prejudicial information" brought to the juror's attention or some "outside influence"

---

92 *See supra* p. 99.

93 In civil cases in federal court, this motion is called a Renewed Motion for Judgment as a Matter of Law (JML). *See* FRCP 50. This emphasizes the fact that the motion is not a separate motion, but simply delayed consideration of the earlier Motion for JML made before the case was submitted to the jury.

94 FRCP 50(a). As explained by the court in *Boeing Co. v. Shipman*, 411 F.2d 365, 374 (5th Cir. 1969), in considering a motion for judgment NOV, a judge must consider all the evidence "in a light and with all reasonable inferences most favorable to the [plaintiff]," and may reverse the verdict only if the judge "believes that reasonable men could not arrive at a . . . verdict" for the plaintiff. "[I]f there is substantial evidence [for the plaintiff], that is, evidence of such quality and weight that reasonable and fair-minded men in the exercise of impartial judgment might reach" a verdict for the plaintiff, it must be affirmed. The opinion goes on to admonish that "it is the function of the jury as the traditional finder of the facts, and not the Court, to weigh conflicting evidence and inferences, and determine the credibility of witnesses."

95 *See* FRCrP 29(c).

96 Doing so would violate the right against being tried twice for the same offense secured the so-called "double jeopardy" clause of the 5th Amendment. *See infra* Chapter VIII, pp. 296-299.

97 *Vaise v. Delaval*, I.T.R. 11 (1785) (Mansfield, L.J.); *McDonald v. Pless*, 238 U.S. 264 (1915).

on the jury.[98] Thus, testimony would be allowed as to such things as bribery, comments to a juror during deliberation by anyone other than another juror (such as a lawyer, party or court personnel), or exposure of a juror to a newspaper article on the case. The result of this rule is that, so long as there is substantial evidence in the record to support the verdict, it will not be set aside based on misunderstanding of the evidence or the law or on anything else that took place in the jury room.[99]

D. Evidence Law

As already alluded to, the law of evidence is relatively complex. In addition, trial lawyers must be sufficiently familiar with evidence rules to be able to interpose timely objections in the lightening quick pace of the adversary trial. Presented here is a simplified overview of the major evidentiary limitations that apply in jury trials.[100]

1. The Requirement of Personal Knowledge for Testimony

Witnesses may testify only to matters about which they have personal knowledge.[101] In other words, they must have experienced first-hand through one of their senses the events they describe. Personal knowledge may not be assumed. It must be established *by testimony*. Thus, a lawyer who calls a witness to testify to seeing a robber in a hotel lobby will first have to ask questions that show that the witness was *in* the lobby of the hotel and was able to see what was going on there. While all this seems simple in the abstract, it is a problem for many lawyers, because of the natural tendency of people who know the facts of a case well to forget that other people do not share that knowledge.

2. Opinion Evidence

Lay Opinions   Generally layperson (non-expert) witnesses may testify only to facts and may not testify to conclusions. The reason for this is that it is up to the *jury* to decide what conclusions to draw from the facts. Thus, it is improper for a witness to testify that the defendant "was driving too fast for the existing road conditions" because that is for the jury to decide. But it is hard to tell the difference between facts and conclusions since almost any label language places on an event is a conclusion of sorts.

For example, assume a witness testifies, "the defendant threw a brick." Taking only one word in the sentence as an example, "throwing" is a conclusion based on the fact of the defendant's having the brick in his hand, holding his arm extended behind his head, moving his arm over his head swiftly in a forward direction, and letting go of the brick at some point when his hand came in front of his body. Also,

---

98   FRE 606(b). *See In re Beverly Hills Fire Litigation*, 695 F.2d 207 (6th Cir. 1982) (new trial ordered because juror performed his own experiment to test whether the fire could have started as the plaintiff's expert testified and then told other jurors).

99   After the trial is over, jurors may freely talk with whomever they please about what went on in the jury room. Sometimes, lawyers in the case make a point of asking the jurors questions, both to see if there were any extrinsic influences that could lead to impeachment of the verdict and in order to learn from the experience by getting the jurors' impressions of their presentation.

100   For more detailed analysis of the law of evidence, *see* ROGER C. PARK, DAVID P. LEONARD, STEVEN H. GOLDBERG, HORNBOOK ON EVIDENCE LAW (West 1998); JOHN W. STRONG, ET AL., MCCORMICK'S HORNBOOK ON EVIDENCE, 4TH ED. (West 1992); MICHAEL H. GRAHAM, FEDERAL RULES OF EVIDENCE IN A NUTSHELL, 4TH ED. (West 1996); PAUL V. ROTHSTEIN, MYRNA S. RAEDER & DAVID CRUMP, EVIDENCE IN A NUTSHELL: STATE AND FEDERAL RULES, 3D ED. (West 1997); ARTHUR BEST, EVIDENCE: EXAMPLES AND EXPLANATIONS, 2D ED. (Aspen 1997).

101   *See* Federal Rule of Evidence (FRE) 602, reprinted in EVIDENCE RULES: FEDERAL RULES OF EVIDENCE (West 1998). Trials in federal court are governed by the FRE, first promulgated in 1975. Before 1975, evidence law in federal courts was governed by case law, with a few isolated issues governed by statute. Most state courts have followed the lead of federal courts and have evidence rules very similar to the FRE.

calling the object "a brick" is a conclusion based on the facts that it was square, red and about the size of other things that qualify as bricks, appeared to be made of clay, and appeared to be heavy. Clearly, if people were not allowed to use *any* conclusions, their speech would be very strange indeed. These kinds of "everyday" conclusions must be allowed.

Consequently, the rule against conclusions provides an exception for conclusions that are (1) based on the perception of the witness and (2) "helpful to a clear understanding of the witness's testimony."[102] The first condition is simply a restatement of the personal knowledge requirement. The second requirement of "helpfulness" simply means that using the conclusion would avoid cumbersome and abnormal speech. This second requirement is certainly satisfied in the brick-throwing example above. Other lay conclusions that are permitted are statements such as that a person was "drunk" or that a car was going "thirty-five miles per hour."

Expert Opinions If scientific, technical or other specialized knowledge would be useful to understand a case, an expert witness may testify. Experts have special skills, education, training or experience that permit them to testify to conclusions in their field of expertise that laypersons could not.[103] Physicians testifying in personal injury cases, psychiatrists testifying in criminal cases or child custody cases, and engineers testifying in product liability cases are perhaps the most commonly encountered experts. However, more exotic forms of experts, such as accident reconstruction experts, exist as well.[104]

Court-appointed experts are possible.[105] However, they are not often used. Consistent with adversary principles, each side finds, prepares and presents its own expert testimony. This is a recognition that in specialized and scientific fields, just as when "ordinary" facts are involved, there is often more than one perspective on the issue. To the extent possible, it is appropriate that all sides of the question should be explored.

3. Relevance and Character Evidence

General Relevance Standard The federal rules and many state evidence rules set a low threshold of probative value, deeming relevant "evidence having *any tendency* to make the existence of any fact . . . more probable or less probable than it would be without the evidence."[106] But this lax standard of factual relevance must be weighed against other factors, primarily the danger of undue prejudice. The rule states that evidence that is otherwise relevant "may be excluded if its probative value is substantially outweighed by the danger of unfair prejudice, confusion of the issues, or misleading the jury, or by considerations of undue delay, waste of time, or needless presentation of cumulative evidence."[107] For example, gruesome, close-up color photographs of the victim in a murder case probably pass the threshold test of

---

102 FRE 701.

103 *See* FRE 702-706.

104 Recently, the Supreme Court expanded the possibility of a wider variety of experts being permitted to testify by holding that FRE 702 overruled the earlier common law test of expert evidence: whether given evidence meets "general acceptance" in the scientific community. In its place, FRE 702 establishes to a more flexible test of whether the evidence "rests on a reliable foundation and is relevant to the task at hand." *Daubert v. Merrill Dow Pharmaceuticals, Inc.*, 509 U.S. 579 (1993) (admitting testimony of experts that countered published scientific literature that drug Bendectin did not cause birth defects).

105 *See* FRE 706.

106 FRE 401 (emphasis added).

107 FRE 403.

relevancy. However, they are often excluded from evidence in jury cases because their probative value is low (it is uncontroverted that the victim is dead) and there is great danger that they could inflame the jury and interfere with their ability to be fair to the defendant.

Evidence of Character The general rule on character evidence is that "[e]vidence of a person's character is not admissible for the purpose of proving action in conformity therewith on a particular occasion."[108] Thus, in a suit for damages for injuries in an automobile collision, evidence of prior accidents the defendant was involved in will not be admissible to prove he was a "bad driver." Similarly, the prosecution in a criminal case generally cannot introduce evidence of the defendant's bad character.[109] The rationale for excluding bad character evidence is that juries may use it to convict criminal defendants or hold civil defendants liable simply for being "bad" people and not because they in fact did what they are accused of doing in a given case.

The prohibition is not complete, however. The prosecution in a criminal case is allowed to present evidence of the defendant's *bad* character to rebut any evidence the *defendant* has chosen to present that shows his *good* character.[110] Also, witnesses who take the stand to testify — including a criminal defendant who chooses to do so — are subject to the possibility that some of their prior felony convictions and perhaps some other prior bad actions will be admitted into evidence to the extent that they bear on the witness's ability to tell the truth (e.g., a prior conviction for perjury or fraud). However, the court is required to weigh carefully evidence of a witness's or party's criminal record to determine whether its probative value is outweighed by its prejudicial effect.[111]

4. The Rule Against Hearsay and Its Major Exceptions

Hearsay testimony, roughly speaking, is testimony about something someone else said. A more complete definition is that hearsay is evidence of a statement, made earlier out-of-court, that is now being offered to prove the truth of what it asserts.[112] The problem with hearsay is its unreliability based on the lack of opportunity for the party against whom it is offered to confront and to cross-examine the person who made the statement at the time it was made. The rule has ancient beginnings in English law. A common example of hearsay occurs whenever there is an automobile accident, and a witness to the accident describes it to a police officer, but then, in the confusion of the accident, disappears. The police officer generally cannot testify at a later trial as to what the person said. It does not matter that we know the person's

---

108 See FRE 404(a).

109 *See* FRE 404(a). If character is an element of the offense or claim or defense, then it is fully admissible. Thus, in the example given in the text of proving the character of a "bad driver," such evidence is not admissible in a suit to prove the *driver's* negligence. However, it may be admissible in a suit against the *owner of the car* for negligently entrusting the car to a poor driver if the owner knew of the bad driving history. Character evidence in any may properly be considered in determining the sentence for a criminal defendant. However, sentencing hearings are proceedings separate from the trial of the case, where only the question of guilt is determined. *See* Chapter VIII, pp. 265-266.

110 FRE 404(a)(1).

111 See FRE 608, 609 and 403. Evidence of prior bad acts may be admissible to prove something *other than* the character of the person. Thus, evidence of the prior bad acts of a person may be used to show motive, absence of intent, mistake, identity or common scheme or plan. FRE 404(b).

112 FRE 801(c) defines hearsay as "a statement, other than one made by the declarant while testifying at the trial or hearing, offered in evidence to prove the truth of the matter asserted." Note that this includes prior out-of-court statements made by the witness as well, i.e., where the "declarant" and the witness at trial are the same person.

name or that what the person told the police officer is consistent with other admissible evidence.[113]

There are two general categories of out-of-court utterances that are admissible despite the hearsay rule. Since hearsay is defined as an out-of-court statement that is offered to prove the *truth of what it asserts*, the first category of admissible statements consists of those that are *not* hearsay because they are offered for some purpose other than their truth. The second category of admissible statements comprises those that meet the definition of hearsay, but fall within some exception to the rule against hearsay.

a. Statements Not Offered for Their Truth

When a statement is offered for a purpose other than that of proving what the speaker intended to assert in it, then it is not subject to the danger that the speaker is lying. This is so because we are ignoring what the speaker asserts and are instead looking at an *unintended* meaning. For example, assume that George Jones seeks to testify that John Smith called him on the telephone on a particular day and in the course of the conversation Smith said "It is raining in Peoria today." This is hearsay *if* it is offered to prove that it was raining in Peoria at that time. However, if the statement is offered in evidence for *any other* purpose, it is not hearsay. It would be admissible, for example, if it were offered to show that the phone line was working, that John Smith spoke the English language, that John Smith was alive that day, that John Smith had not lost his voice, that John Smith knew George Jones's telephone number, or for some other purpose. The three most common instances of using out-of-court statements indirectly for non-hearsay purposes follow.

Statements Offered to Show an Effect on Hearer Assume Barney is arrested in a building for burglary (breaking into a building with intent to commit a crime therein). He offers evidence that the reason he broke into the building was that a little girl told him that there was a fire in the building and that her mother was trapped inside. Normally what the little girl said would be hearsay.[114] However, Barney is permitted to testify to what she said to him because Barney is *not* offering the statement to prove that there was a fire and that the girl's mother needed to be rescued. He is offering it only to show the *reason* why he broke into the building.

Statements Offered to Attack Credibility Out-of-court statements that are inconsistent with in-court testimony do not violate the rule against hearsay. In telephone example above, assume John Smith, the person who said on the telephone that it was raining in Peoria, testifies at a later trial that it was *not* raining in Peoria on the day in question. Evidence of his inconsistent statement over the telephone (testified to by anyone who heard it) is not hearsay. The theory is that the out-of-court statement is offered *not* to prove that it was in fact raining, but to impeach Smith's credibility — to show that Smith made a statement contrary to his trial testimony and therefore should not be believed.[115]

Legally Operative Language This includes any out-of-court utterance that has overriding legal significance beyond anything asserted in it. For example, one might

---

113 *But see infra* p. 112, where the "catch-all" exceptions to hearsay are discussed.

114 This would be true even if the little girl were available to testify at the trial. *See supra* note 112.

115 It follows that it would not be proper for the jury to use the inconsistent telephone statement as substantive proof that it *was* raining in Peoria. Jurors are often puzzled by an instruction from the judge explaining that, because the prior inconsistent statement was introduced solely for its relevance to Smith's credibility as a witness, they may use it only for that purpose and not for its substantive content.

wonder why the contents of a contract, which are out-of-court statements, are admissible in evidence. Those contents and any words of offer or acceptance are not hearsay because they are said to have *legal significance without regard to what they assert*. It is the fact that the statements were made that is crucial, not any factual assertions they make. In fact, it is likely that the contract sets out only promises, which do not assert any facts. Other examples of legally operative language are the defamatory statement made by the defendant in a defamation case and the words urging the commission of a crime in a conspiracy or incitement case.

b. Exceptions to the Rule Against Hearsay

There are many exceptions to the rule against hearsay. There are twenty-nine in the Federal Rules of Evidence, including an open-ended exception, discussed below.[116] Because the rule against hearsay contains so many exceptions, some have argued that it should be abolished.[117] However, much to the consternation of law students who have to learn its intricacies, the rule remains. The exceptions discussed here are only some of the major ones.

The exceptions discussed below apply to statements that are clearly hearsay, i.e., statements that are offered to prove what the speaker intended to assert and therefore their reliability depends on the credibility of the speaker. Nonetheless, they are admissible in evidence to prove what they assert, generally because (1) there is something about the nature of the statement or the circumstances in which the speaker utters it that provides some *collateral guarantee of reliability* or (2) there is some *necessity for hearing the statement* in view of the difficulty of proving the matter asserted in any other way.

(1) Party Admissions

Any statement made by a party that *the opposing party* seeks to introduce at trial will be allowed.[118] For example, Dan's dog bites Peter. After the attack, Dan states to Wilma: "My dog bit Peter." In a suit by Peter against Dan for damages suffered as a result, Wilma will be allowed to testify to Dan's statement because it is a statement of a party (the defendant) and it is being offered by the plaintiff Peter, an opposing party. Though there are many reasons to allow one party to freely use pre-litigation statements made by the other party, the main one is this. If an *opposing* party is seeking to use the statement, then it must be against the interests of the speaker-party. Therefore, it is likely to be true, since people do not normally say things that are to their detriment unless they are true.[119]

(2) Business Records

Business records potentially include any routinely kept records of any person or organization that keeps such records in the ordinary course of its business activities. Common examples are medical records from doctors' offices or hospitals, records of

---

116 *See* FRE 803 and 804.

117 This was actually proposed, but quickly dropped when the Federal Rules of Evidence were adopted in 1975.

118 *See* FRE 801(d)(2).

119 The Federal Rules of Evidence treat party admissions, not as exceptions to hearsay, but as not being hearsay at all. However, admissions are commonly referred to as an exception and that status makes sense, so that is the way they are classified here.

governmental agencies and accounts and other records of private businesses.[120] The collateral guarantee of reliability for this exception is the *regularity* with which business records are kept. If every time a payment is made, an entry is made in a ledger, then using the ledger to prove payment would seem to be reliable. Necessity is also a consideration, given that it is extremely doubtful a clerk who took the payment would actually remember the amount, when it was made or who made it. However, to protect against falsification or self-serving records, the rule provides that the court can refuse to admit such records if "the source of information or the method or circumstances of preparation indicate lack of trustworthiness."[121]

(3) Excited Utterances

The behavioral assumption behind this exception is that persons who are startled by a sudden event will correctly report that event, since they will not have the time or presence of mind to make up a lie about it. For example, a bomb explodes and Willy, hysterical, screams, "It's a bomb and it was thrown from that car over there!" Willy's statement is an exception to hearsay and a witness who heard it may testify about it to prove that there was a bomb and that it came from a particular car.[122]

(4) Present Sense Impression

The rationale for this exception is similar to the excited utterance, except that there is no requirement of excitement, only a requirement that the description of the event take place while it is going on or shortly thereafter.[123] For example, X and W are standing on the street corner talking to each other with X looking toward the intersection and W facing X. Over W's shoulder, X sees an accident happen and says "That furniture truck just ran the red light." W will be permitted to testify to what X said. Related to present sense impression is the matter of identification of a person after perceiving him, such as a policeman testifying after a lineup that the victim said "that's the man who did it." However, an extra safeguard is provided for identification testimony by the rules, which require that the victim who made the statement be available for cross examination about the circumstances of the statement.[124]

(5) State of Mind

Examples of statements regarding one's state of mind are where the witness reports that the person said at some prior time "my leg hurts," "I feel bad," "I'm going to New York tomorrow." Usually people who make such statements do not think about their possible significance in later litigation, although it is always possible that the statement is staged for that purpose. An additional overriding reason they are permitted is the difficulty of proving state of mind by any other method.[125]

---

120 *See* FRE 803(6). The definition requires that the entry in the records must be made (1) at or near the time the recorded event took place, (2) by, or from information provided by, a person with knowledge of the event recorded, (3) in records kept in the ordinary course of business (4) by an organization which makes it a regular practice to keep such records. *But see* FRE 803(8) (police reports are not admissible in criminal cases).

121 Police reports of criminal investigations are within the business record exception, but in criminal cases they are excluded from the exception and are thus inadmissible hearsay. *See* FRE 803(8).

122 *See* FRE 803(2).

123 *See* FRE 803(1).

124 *See* FRE 801(d)(1)(C).

125 *See* FRE 803(3).

(6) Other Exceptions

Merely naming some of the other exceptions to the hearsay rule will suggest what collateral guarantees of reliability exist that make them admissible: statements made for purposes of medical diagnosis, records of vital statistics, marriage and baptismal certificates, market reports, reputation concerning family history and boundaries of land, dying declarations, and statements against pecuniary or penal interest.[126] The Federal Rules of Evidence also provide a residual hearsay exception that allows a court to admit hearsay that is not covered by any existing exception. The residual exception reflects the two bases underlying rationale of the specific exceptions. It provides that a hearsay statement not covered by the specific exceptions that has "equivalent circumstantial guarantees of trustworthiness" and "is more probative . . . than any other evidence which the proponent can procure" is admissible.[127]

E.   Criticisms of the Adversary System

There have been and continue to be debates about the assumptions underlying the adversary system. Both the justifications and the criticisms are largely based on untested behavioral assumptions and anecdotal evidence. In addition, proposals for radical change are somewhat pointless given that at least some aspects of the adversary system are enshrined in the Constitution.[128] Nevertheless, we should review some of the major criticisms that have been raised and debated.[129]

1.   Abuse of Party-Control

Witness Preparation and Abuse   Critics point to all the opportunities for abuse that exist when the parties are in control of investigating and presenting the case. One target is the accepted practice of lawyers preparing "their" witnesses to testify. There are advantages to proper witness preparation: it makes the testimony more to the point. But it is argued that witness preparation allows for the possibility of lawyers prompting the witness to testify to things that are not true. And, critics point out, cross examination by the other side is hardly a match for a well-prepared witness. The result, they argue, is likely to be that the other side will feel it necessary to attack the witness in any way possible to undermine their credibility, thus turning the witness stand into a "slaughterhouse of reputations" with courts unable to restrain "bullying" of witnesses by lawyers who "forget that they are officers of the court."[130]

Supporters point out that lawyers are prohibited by both professional ethics and the criminal law from suborning perjury or otherwise perpetrating a fraud upon the court. But beyond that, the supposed invincibility of lawyer-prepared witnesses to impeachment ignores the scope and power of cross examination, aided by discovery, to uncover fraud. Moreover, juries are particularly prone to be suspicious of evidence

---

126 These are set out in other sections of FRE 803 and FRE 804.

127 FRE 807. Another important part of evidence law is the law of "privileges" covered by FRE 501. Information communicated in the course of certain special relationships, such as lawyer-client, doctor-patient, priest-penitent and between spouses is said to be "privileged" and may not be divulged under compulsion at any time. *See also infra* Chapter VII, p. 229 (exemption from discovery) and Chapter IV, p. 160 (attorney-client privilege).

128 *See Herring v. New York*, 422 U.S. 853 (1975) (the constitutional right to counsel "has been understood to mean that there can be no restriction on the function of counsel in defending a prosecution in accord with the traditions of the adversary fact-finding process that has been constitutionalized in the Sixth and Fourteenth Amendments").

129 For a more complete, but somewhat partisan account of criticisms of the adversary system and responses to those criticisms, *see* LANDSMAN, *supra* note 4, at 24-76 and FREEDMAN, *infra* note 136, at 26-42.

130 Roscoe Pound, *The Causes of Popular Dissatisfaction with the Administration of Justice*, 29 ABA REPORTS 395, 405 (1906).

that sounds "too good." Indeed, many lawyers are careful not to "over-prepare" witnesses for this reason. And the amount of preparation the witness has been through can be explored on cross-examination. As for abusive cross-examination tactics, lawyers who conduct themselves in this manner will be admonished by a good trial judge. But the most effective restraint on lawyers is the fact that such tactics are usually counterproductive in front of a jury, which is far more likely to identify with the hapless witness than with the bullying lawyer.

Benefits of Party Control   Supporters of the adversary system emphasize that, even if party control may have its risks, it has important benefits. When the parties have extensive and direct input into the process by which their case is decided, they are more likely to feel that their point of view was fully aired and was understood as well as it could be — even if it was ultimately rejected. In this way, party control does two things. First, it promotes the legitimacy of judicial decisions, which depend first and foremost on voluntary acceptance by society as legitimate and only secondarily on state coercion. Second, a system that gives individuals direct participation in and control over litigation affecting their lives affirms human dignity and value. Even if one loses a hearing, active party participation at that hearing "express[es] the elementary idea that to be a *person*, rather than a *thing*, is at least to be consulted about what is done with one."[131] The greater the opportunity to be heard fully in the manner that one wishes to be heard, the greater the respect that is paid to human dignity and worth. Given the threat to individuality posed by expanding governmental power and the pressures of "efficiency" in modern society, supporters of party control argue that there is a greater need today than ever before for individuality-reinforcing institutions.[132]

The Government as Partisan Litigant   Special difficulties can arise in an adversary system when the *government* is involved as a party. In many countries, the prosecutor is a quasi-judicial official who is above the partisan fray and "sleeps well even after an acquittal."[133] The prosecutor in the United States is supposed to be an exception to the general rule of partisan representation in that the prosecutor has the duty "to seek justice, not merely to convict."[134] But a realist would have to recognize that once the case reaches the trial stage, prosecutors in the United States see their role as that of a partisan advocate for their client and it is a matter of mere coincidence that that "client" is a powerful government. Thus, prosecutors will in the overwhelming majority of cases do everything in their power to win the case for their client, i.e., to secure the defendant's conviction to the highest possible charge. There have been isolated instances in recent years of overzealous prosecution by prosecutors who take a "win at all costs" attitude toward their role.

---

131 LAWRENCE TRIBE, AMERICAN CONSTITUTIONAL LAW, 2D ED. 666 (Foundation Press 1988).

132 In an interesting study in JOHN THIBAULT AND LAURENS WALKER, PROCEDURAL JUSTICE: A PSYCHOLOGICAL ANALYSIS 77-80, 94-96 (John Wiley & Sons 1975), the authors found that a majority of the subjects of multinational studies thought that adversary procedures were fairer than investigatory procedures for resolving disputes.

133 *See* William J. Pizzi and Luca Marafioti, *The New Italian Code of Criminal Procedure: The Difficulties of Building an Adversarial Trial System on a Civil Law Foundation*, 17 YALE J.INT'L.L. 1, 31 (1992).

134 ABA STANDARDS FOR CRIMINAL JUSTICE, Standard 3-1.1(ABA 1991). These standards are supposed to be "guidelines that have long been adhered to by the best prosecutors and best defense counsel." Federal prosecutors are admonished to "see that justice is done." DEPARTMENT OF JUSTICE MANUAL, Title 9, Chapter 27, §9-27.000 et seq., "Federal Principles of Criminal Prosecution," pp. 9-495-9-559.

The ABA Model Rules of Professional Conduct, which have been adopted in three-fourths of the states, have something to say on the subject, but they equivocate somewhat. Rule 3.8 provides that a prosecutor must refrain from pressing groundless charges, must assure that defendants are advised of their right to counsel, may not take advantage of unrepresented defendants, and must disclose exculpatory information they have to defendants. The official "comment" to this rule explains in general terms that a "prosecutor has a responsibility as a minister of justice and not simply that of an advocate. This responsibility carries with it specific obligations to see that the defendant is accorded procedural justice and that guilt is decided upon the basis of sufficient evidence." However, it concludes unhelpfully, "[p]recisely how far the prosecutor is required to go in this direction is a matter of debate and varies in different jurisdictions."[135]

2. Inadequate Focus on the Truth

This criticism is related to concerns about abuse of party control. It asserts that, contrary to adversary theory, party control of litigation is not likely to result in a fully-informed decision-maker because not all the relevant information will be uncovered. As Judge Frankel, a long-standing critic of the adversary system, has observed, it is a rare case in which either side yearns to have the witness, or anyone, give the *whole truth*.[136] To the extent that incomplete information is supplied, the court will be making a decision based on something other than the real truth about a case. A slightly different version of this critique has it that our "sporting theory of justice" never asks what the truth is; it only asks "have the rules of the game been carried out strictly?"[137] Two responses are usually given to these points.

The Misconceived Quest for "The Truth" The first response admits that the adversary system has a relativistic attitude toward truth, but argues that this is more consistent with reality than any search for "*the* truth." For all the talk in some systems that the "objective truth" must be discovered in legal proceedings, an event cannot be reproduced in court. After it has taken place, unless there is a videotape of it, all that we can rely on are *perceptions* of the event and then only to the extent that those perceptions can be *remembered* by *people* and then *communicated* by them. Given the weaknesses of perception, memory and communication, there are often as many "truths" about an event as there are witnesses to it. The idea is not to find "*the* truth" of an event, but to find *which communicated perception* of an event is the *most plausible account* of that event. A system that gives full leeway to competing perceptions of an event throughout the trial and right up until the time for decision is one that accurately reflects reality. By contrast, pursuit of "*the* truth" is not only naive, but ultimately impossible. Defenders of the adversary system would point out that the cause of truth is routinely *better* served in an adversary system since in every case at least two versions of the truth get presented — one more version than would routinely be unearthed in a less adversarial system.[138] In fact, the adversary system *is* con

---

135 Rule 3.8 of the ABA Model Rules of Professional Conduct and comment (ABA 1991).

136 *See* Marvin Frankel, Partisan Justice 10-20 (Hill & Wang 1980). This book is a succinct, but thorough critique of most all aspects of the adversary system. It is interesting to note that many of the critics of the adversary system and juries are judges with extensive experience with the intricacies of adversary trials. As discussed *infra*, Judge Jerome Frank was also a vigorous critics of the jury system. *See* Jerome Frank, Courts on Trial (Princeton 1949).

137 Pound, *supra* note 60, p.406.

138 Some support for the adversary system's more relativistic view of truth can be found in the psychological literature which shows that much of what people perceive is a particular interpretation of the events, rather than a true reflection. *See* David J. Schneider, Albert H. Hasdorf, Phoebe Ellsworth, cerned with determining the truth, at least as just defined. One has difficulty imagining a case in which the parties collectively would not have the incentive to discover and present all information that is truly relevant to a decision in the matter.

Allocating the Power to Declare Truth Given that there can be competing versions of the truth, it is *equally* important in finding the truth to be concerned about *who has the power to investigate and declare truth*. Given the often elusive nature of truth, the adversary system sees serious dangers if one entity — the state — has a monopoly on the power to discover and declare it. Borrowing from the concept of separation of powers in constitutional theory, proponents of the adversary system believe that the cause of truth is better served if the responsibility for discovering and declaring it is spread between the state, the parties and, where applicable, the jury. While one might doubt how often governments fail their citizens and abuse their power in this respect, mistrust of government is a strong theme in American political history. And one could point to several instances just in the 20th century where governments, unrestrained by countervailing forces, have declared rather monstrous versions of "the truth."

3. The Inefficiency of Adversary Litigation

Complexity, Speed and Values Beyond Efficiency A major criticism of the adversary system, which relates in part to problems with party control, is its slow pace. While some things go quickly, the actual progress of the trial is a slow and complicated process. First-hand oral and other "immediate" evidence presented in a question-and-answer format can take a long time to develop, objections based on complex rules of evidence arise and must be decided, and the judge must remain passive throughout and assure that both sides are heard fully.[139]

It is no secret that all this takes time. However, it does increase the amount of information available to the decision-maker. Any proposal to truncate the inquiry in the interests of efficiency would bear the burden of showing that what would be excluded would truly be surplusage. Moreover, efficiency is not everything. As the Supreme Court has observed:

> The establishment of prompt efficacious procedures to achieve legitimate state ends is a proper state interest worthy of cognizance in constitutional adjudication. But the Constitution recognizes higher values than speed and efficiency. Indeed, one might fairly say of the Bill of Rights in general, and the Due Process Clause in particular, that they were designed to protect the fragile values of a vulnerable citizenry from the overbearing concern for efficiency and efficacy that may characterize praiseworthy government officials no less, and perhaps more, than mediocre ones.[140]

Some Efficiencies of Adversary Procedure Adversary systems have efficiencies absent from some other systems. Party control over litigation confers the right to litigate vigorously, but it also permits parties to choose not to litigate. Many civil law systems, at least in criminal cases, require that a trial be held regardless of whether

---

PERSON PERCEPTION (Addison-Wesley Pub. Co., Reading, Mass. 1979).

139 Of course, much of the extra time it takes to try a case is not caused by the adversary system as much as by the right to a jury trial. Criticisms of juries are discussed in the next section of this chapter.

140 *Stanley v. Illinois*, 405 U.S. 645 (1972). In *Stanley*, the Court held unconstitutional an Illinois law that provided that unwed fathers need not be given a hearing before their parental rights were terminated. For more on the issue of custody of children of unwed parents, *see* Chapter XIII, p. 483, note 45, and Chapter IX, p. 338.

the affected parties want one. In an adversary system, when defendants plead guilty and waive their right to further proceedings, there is no need for a trial. All that is necessary is that they understand that they are waiving their right to a trial and that they admit on the record facts showing that they in fact committed the offense charged.[141] In civil cases, settlements are even easier. Unless a minor or other person in need of special protection is affected, parties have the absolute right to settle whenever and on whatever terms they wish. In the 75 largest counties in the U.S. in 1992, 75% of all civil tort cases were disposed of through an agreed settlement or voluntary dismissal. In criminal cases, 92% of convictions obtained were the result of a guilty plea.[142]

Recent Anti-Adversarial Reforms There have been efforts in recent years to limit some "adversarial excesses" and to make litigation more efficient. Among the efforts in federal court are limits on excessive discovery, amendments of pre-trial procedures to encourage more active case management by judges, the introduction of serious sanctions on lawyers who assert groundless positions in litigation, and the increase in the responsibilities of "magistrate judges," who can keep closer track of litigation. Many of these measures are part of a general trend in recent years toward more "managerial judging."[143] There have also been major efforts to urge alternatives to judicial resolution of disputes.[144]

4. The Costs of Litigation and Inequality of Financial Resources

A Special Problem for Adversary Systems Inequality in litigation because one side has superior resources is undoubtedly a problem in all legal systems. But inequality of resources is a special problem in an adversary system where the parties have so many responsibilities for gathering evidence and presenting the case. Though parties have the right to represent themselves, a party without a lawyer is much more likely to be completely lost in an adversary system. Consequently, it is perhaps much more likely in an adversary system that the party with the more skilled lawyer and more resources for litigation support, such as investigators and experts, will have an advantage. This is exacerbated as well by the "American rule" with regard to litigation costs, under which winning parties may not recover their attorneys fees if they win.[145]

Mitigating Factors The practical need for a lawyer has been met to a certain extent. The 6th Amendment to the Constitution requires that the government provide lawyers and other assistance for the unrepresented in all criminal cases where jail is

---

141 *See* Chapter VIII, pp. 268-270, for a description of guilty pleas. The efficiencies gained by guilty pleas were part of what caused Italy to introduce a more adversarial style criminal procedure in 1989. *See* Pizzi & Marafioti, *supra* note 133. Serious limitations on plea bargaining and legal cultural differences have made implementation of the summary guilty plea procedures difficult. Spain and Denmark have enacted similar procedures and informal practices approximating plea bargaining have grown up in France and Germany. *See id.* at 35-37.

142 Source: Bureau of Justice Statistics, U.S. Dept. of Justice. *See* Chapter VII, p. 242 (settlements in civil cases) and Chapter VIII, p. 268 (guilty pleas in criminal cases).

143 *See* Chapter VII, pp. 231, 233. For an account of the move toward greater judicial control over fact-finding, *see* John Langbein, *The German Advantage in Civil Procedure*, 52 U. CHI. L.REV. 823, 866 (1988) and Judith Resnick, *Managerial Judges*, 96 HARV.L.REV. 374 (1982). This trend is, to say the least, controversial in the United States. *See* LANDSMAN, *supra* note 4, at 77-121.

144 *See* Chapter VII, pp. 242-244.

145 The "American rule" regarding attorney fees is so called to distinguish it from the "English rule," which normally shifts the burden to the losing side. *See* Chapter VII, p. 239.

a possibility.[146] In civil cases, there is no such constitutional right, but efforts have been made since 1964 to provide federal funding for legal services for the poor, and prepaid legal insurance and other plans have grown in recent years.[147] Moreover, the availability of the contingent fee serves as a powerful incentive for good lawyers to handle personal injury civil cases of clients otherwise unable to afford an attorney.[148] In addition, some statutes have changed the "American rule" on litigation costs to one that allows a winning party to recover attorneys fees and court costs from the losing party in some kinds of cases.[149]

In civil cases, many procedural devices are designed to make the outcome in a case less dependent on the skills of the lawyer at trial. The discovery process in civil litigation allows parties to obtain most of the opposing party's evidence well before trial, thereby making it easier for the less well-equipped or less expert lawyer to respond to what greater financial resources or talent may have amassed on the other side of a case. To the extent that a more powerful opponent can use discovery and other procedural devices to "wear down" or increase the litigation costs of a party with fewer resources, the recent changes imposing limits on discovery and sanctions for misuse of the courts for these purposes, mentioned earlier, are specifically designed to prevent this.[150]

Built-In Safeguards There are also built-in features of the adversary system in the United States that equalize parties with disparate amounts of resources. The presence of a jury makes the trial somewhat more equal since jury members are much more likely to identify with the poor litigant than with the rich corporation or the powerful state. Less well-off parties' lawyers regularly take advantage of the "underdog" status of their client to considerable effect.

But even with all these factors at work, candor requires the admission that inequality based on wealth remains a problem in courts in the United States. It is probably true that, to a certain extent, "what kind of justice a person gets depends on how much money he has."[151] How much more of a problem this is in the United States than anywhere else is hard to say.

F. Criticisms of the Jury System

Most of the criticisms of the jury system are of two types. Critics either point to the relative inefficiency and high cost of jury trials or they question the ability of juries to decide cases properly.[152]

---

146 *See* Chapter VIII, p. 293. *See also* Chapter IV, p. 153, for a discussion of public defenders. The criminal defendant also has the right to any necessary experts or investigators at government expense. *See Ake v. Oklahoma*, 470 U.S. 68 (1988) (Defendant has right to a psychiatric evaluation and expert witness assistance where his sanity is at issue in case) and Criminal Justice Act, 18 U.S.C.A. §3006A(c)(1) (providing for payment for defense experts).

147 *See* Chapter IV, pp. 152-153, for a discussion of civil legal services for the poor.

148 In a contingent fee arrangement, the lawyer will not charge the client a fee unless the client wins, in which case the lawyer will take the fee out of the recovery, usually to one-third of the recovery. For a lawyer to be attracted to such a case, of course, there must be a good chance of winning a large enough verdict. Consequently, it is only in personal injury cases where several thousands of dollars or more are at stake that a lawyer will agree to such an arrangement. *See* Chapter IV, p. 142.

149 *See* Chapter VII, p. 240.

150 *See* Chapter VII, p. 231.

151 *Griffin v. Illinois*, 351 U.S. 12, 18 n.16 (1956).

152 Among the severest critics of juries was Judge Jerome Frank. *See* JEROME FRANK, COURTS ON TRIAL (Princeton 1949). There has been much interest in and criticism of the jury system in recent years. Two recent books are JEFFREY ABRAMSON, WE, THE JURY: THE JURY SYSTEM AND THE IDEAL OF DEMOCRACY (Basic Books 1994) and STEPHEN J. ADLER, THE JURY: DISORDER IN THE COURTS (Doubleday 1994).

The Expense and Inefficiency of Juries   Trials with juries take about 40% longer than bench trials. Enforcing the rules of evidence strictly takes time and the lawyers are more deliberate in presenting their cases. Jurors, not being the "professional listeners" judges are, get tired and need more frequent breaks. And it goes without saying that the decision making process of juries is more protracted. While this may seem like a great loss of efficiency, it should be remembered that around 90% of cases filed do not go to trial at all, and only some of the trials in the 10% of cases that do go to trial are jury trials.

In addition, some of the "anti-adversarial" reforms mentioned earlier have served to make jury trials more efficient. More vigorous pre-trial judicial supervision has the effect of forcing the parties to agree on more facts, thus leaving less for the jury to decide. The use of special verdicts, as discussed earlier in this chapter, can improve efficiency. Such verdicts, instead of just "dumping" the entire case on jurors with no direction other than instructions, can spell out the issues for them by way of specific questions and thus streamline their decision making process.[153] Moreover, the trial judge has always had the power to limit unnecessary proof and to exclude even relevant evidence to prevent "undue delay, waste of time, and needless presentation of cumulative evidence."[154] Many trial judges are exercising this power to a greater degree than before and the result has been improved efficiency.

The Abilities of Juries as Decision-Makers   Critics often argue that only legal specialists, not laypeople, should be involved in decision-making in the legal system. However, it must be remembered that the *legal* issues in a case *are* decided by a judge. The division of labor between judge and jury involves juries in deciding only disputed issues of fact — a task for which a legal education is not necessarily an advantage.[155]

Lawyers who try cases before juries often remark how impressed they are with the abilities of juries at determining fact issues. Though individual jurors may know very little and as *individuals* may not even be particularly good decision-makers, many comment on how the jury, when it sits as a group, is far more than the sum of its parts — how the entire jury seems to acquire abilities that would not be expected from looking at its members individually.

Psychological research on the dynamics of group decision-making tends to support this intuitive observation. One particularly telling study is by Barnlund, who tested the effect of group dynamics on reasoning ability.[156] College students were tested on their syllogistic reasoning ability. Then researchers pitted the *best individual* reasoners against *groups* of the *poorest* reasoners. When it came to dealing with syllogisms whose premises and conclusions were statements that awakened strong emotions and value preferences, such as assertions about Communism, college rule systems, and the like, the *best individual* reasoners did *worse* at solving them than the

---

153 *See supra* p. 104. Some of these reforms are addressed in William W. Schwarzer, *Reforming Jury Trials*, 1990 U.Chi.Legal Forum 119, 121-125. Judge Schwarzer is the Director of the Federal Judicial Center, a research agency for the federal court system. *See also* Munsterman et al., *supra* note 43.

154 FRE 403; FRCP 16. The wide-spread use of smaller juries in civil cases makes jury trial somewhat easier. Civil juries of between 6 and 12 may be used in federal court since 1991 and attempts to restore the 12-person jury were defeated in 1996. Close to 40 states provide for juries of fewer than 12 in civil cases.

155 *See supra* pp. 84, 86.

156 Dean C. Barnlund, *A Comparative Study of Individual, Majority and Group Judgment*, 58 J. Ab. & Soc. Psych. 55 (1959). Similar studies are cited in Richard Lempert, *Uncovering "Nondiscernable" Differences: Empirical Research and the Jury-Size Cases*, 73 Mich.L.Rev. 643-708 (1975).

groups of *poor* reasoners. The explanation was that the individual good reasoners were misled by their emotional responses. Members of the groups of *poor* reasoners were also misled initially, but in different directions. As a result, the group was able to set them straight. Those misled in one direction were corrected or balanced out by others who had a different reaction. The operation of this group dynamic is supported by other studies that indicate that accuracy in jury deliberations is increased more by increasing the *social diversity* of jurors than by increasing their average educational level.[157]

Comparing the Alternatives   In evaluating the abilities of the jury, we must remember exactly what fact-finding institutions we are comparing. In all situations other than a criminal acquittal, the judge has the power to set aside lawless or arbitrary jury verdicts. Even if it is reasonable to assume that the average judge would be superior to the average juror, that is not what is being compared. The appropriate comparison is between the judge alone on the one hand and the *entire* jury with the *judge's assistance and control* on the other.

It is interesting to compare the level of judge and jury disagreement in decision-making, especially since the alternative to juries deciding cases is to have judges decide them. In a now-classic study, Kalven and Zeisel found that judges agreed with jury verdicts in 78% of civil and criminal cases.[158] Perhaps more important than the rate of agreement is the fact that many of the 22% of cases where there was disagreement related to a probable different perception of what "justice" required.[159] Among the examples of cases where the jury acquitted, but the judge would have convicted were the case of a larceny defendant who had stolen $2.50 worth of lumber and who had been in jail for two months awaiting trial and the case of a drunk driving defendant charged with manslaughter in an accident that killed his wife and left him paralyzed for life. And it is possible, given the psychological studies by Barnlund discussed above, that at least in some of the remaining cases where there was disagreement, the jury could have reached the more accurate conclusion.

Juries in Civil Damages Cases   There have been special concerns raised about the abilities of juries in civil cases in recent years. It has been argued vigorously by defense attorneys and insurance companies that "run-away" juries have been awarding outrageous amounts to plaintiffs in personal injury cases. Similar reasons were given for effectively abolishing the right to a civil jury in England.[160] Headlines in newspapers tend to support the charge. However, a different picture emerges when one considers the average case. One study of a sample of cases does indicate that judges would have given less than the jury awarded in 52% of cases, about the same in 10%, and more in 38%. However, the average dollar amount of disagreement in cases where juries gave more money was 10%, placing judges and juries rather close to each other. And where the amounts awarded are clearly out of line with the damages proven, the fault is not so much with the jury as it is with the judge, who clearly has the power to reduce such awards or to order a new trial, as previously

---

157 *See* Fred L. Strodtbeck, Rita M. James and Charles Hawkins, *Social Status in Jury Deliberations*, 22 Am. Sociological Rev. 713 (1957).

158 KALVEN & ZEISEL, *supra* note 148, at 55-65.

159 *Id.*, p. 116.

160 *See Ward v. James*, [1965] 1 Q.B. 273, 1 All Eng. Rep. 563. Juries are now available only if provided for by statute or in the judge's discretion "in exceptional circumstances." Currently, only twelve or so civil jury trials a year take place.

discussed.[161] In addition, there may be some issues that a jury is inherently better at deciding. Particularly in civil cases where such things as the value of a human life are being decided, there is no reason to believe that a judge has the superior ability to make that judgment.[162]

Another common criticism of juries in civil cases is that they are biased in favor of injured plaintiffs in personal injury cases. Kalven and Zeisel's study does not bear this out. Though the juries in the study tended to side with the defense more than the prosecution in criminal cases, in the 22% of civil cases where judge and jury disagreed, they were almost evenly split. A more recent study examining products liability cases between 1979 and 1988 showed that in nine of the ten years examined, *plaintiffs* won more *bench* trials than jury trials. In 1986, plaintiffs won as many as 58% of all federal products liability cases tried before *judges* and only 29% of federal products liability cases tried before *juries*.[163]

Benefits of Juries Beyond Factual Accuracy   Some supporters of juries believe that one of the benefits of juries is their very "erroneous" ways in that their decision reflects something more than cold logic. As explained by one federal judge:

> The law can become rigid. Rules that made sense when adopted may be foolish and unjust in particular cases. The jury can give flexibility to the law, ensuring that it is applied in a way that is consistent with the standards of the community. Because it does not have to explain its reasons, it is able to arrive at appropriate decisions that avoid irrational results but may be difficult for a judge to explain.[164]

Sometimes juries' consistent "tempering" of a legal rule can point the way for law reform. An example of this is *Hoffman v. Jones*, the Florida case changing from contributory negligence to comparative negligence, which was discussed in Chapter II. The Florida Supreme Court relied in part on the fact that it was apparent that juries consistently judged plaintiffs' conduct by a less harsh comparative negligence standard even when told to apply the more strict contributory negligence standard.[165]

Many heros of American political history have been saved by "erroneous" jury verdicts. Peter Zenger, the publisher of criticism against the British Crown who was

---

161 *See supra* p. 105.

162 GUINTHER, *supra* note 19, at 170. In considering increased amounts of jury awards in recent years, it is relevant that medical costs constitute the bulk of personal injury damages awards and that medical costs rose by 600% from 1955 to 1985 at a time when per capita income only doubled. Some studies suggest that juries may not be awarding enough damages. In one state, contrary to expectations, where professional decision-makers with medical knowledge were substituted for the jury trial system, the average award *increased* by one-third. *See* Michael Saks, *Do We Really Know Anything About the Behavior of the Tort Litigation System — and Why Not?* 140 U.PA.L.REV. 1147, 1273-1274 (1992).

163 Theodore Eisenberg & James A. Henderson, *The Quiet Revolution in Products Liability: An Empirical Study of Legal Change*, 37 U.C.L.A. L.REV 479 (1990). *But see* Kevin Clermont & Theodore Eisenberg, *Do Case Outcomes Really Reveal Anything About the Legal System? Win Rates and Removal Jurisdiction*, 83 CORNELL L. REV. 581 (1998) (advising caution in relying on raw win statistics, since cases that go to trial are a small and skewed sample of all cases). Supposed difficulties with civil juries in tort cases, particularly those with punitive damages, are discussed in Chapter XI, pp. 431-437. The Saks article, *supra* note 162, reviews the major empirical data on the subject. A concern voice by foreigners doing business in the U.S. has been that they are at a disadvantage before U.S. courts, in part because juries have a bias against them. A recent article dispels this myth. Kevin Clermont & Theodore Eisenberg, *Xenophilia in American Courts*, 109 HARV. L. REV. 1120 (1996) (foreigners, whether as plaintiff or defendant, win 63% of the cases, whereas natives win only 37%).

164 William W. Schwarzer, "Some Observations on the Values of the Jury System" (address at Federal Judicial Center Seminar for Russian Judges and Court Administrators, July 1993).

165 *See* discussion *supra* p. 86.

acquitted by a New York colonial jury in 1734, was probably factually guilty of seditious libel.[166] Later, Northern abolitionists who hid escaped slaves before the Civil War would benefit from jury "inaccuracy." More recently, protesters against the Vietnam War, draft resisters and citizens who hid illegal asylum seekers from El Salvador, whom juries acquitted, were probably factually guilty. Of course, the vast majority of cases are not ones that demand that "the truth" be slighted in favor of justice. But in those cases where truth *and* justice both point toward conviction, the government has ample resources and good lawyers of its own who can make the case for conviction before the jury, if there is one to be made.[167]

Consistent with this, the Supreme Court observed in a 1970 case that the Founders "knew from history and experience that it was necessary to protect against unfounded criminal charges brought to eliminate enemies and against judges too responsive to the voice of higher authority." The right to trial by a jury gives the citizen:

> an inestimable safeguard against the corrupt or overzealous prosecutor and against the compliant, biased, or eccentric judge. [It] reflect[s] a fundamental decision about the exercise of official power — a reluctance to entrust plenary powers over the life and liberty of the citizen to one judge or to a group of judges. Fear of unchecked power, so typical of our State and Federal Governments in other respects, found expression in the criminal law in this insistence upon community participation in the determination of guilt or innocence.[168]

This role of the jury was eloquently stated by a Maryland farmer in the debates over the constitutional right to a jury trial. He agreed that all the structural controls on the federal government contained in the Constitution, such as separation of power and federalism, were needed to keep it from passing unjust legislation infringing on civil liberties of citizens. But he saw a greater threat to freedom in the *misuse* of otherwise *just* laws on the *local* level, from which the structural protections of the constitution gave no protection. "[T]hose usurpations, which silently undermine the spirit of liberty, under the sanctions of law, are more dangerous than direct and open legislative attack." He argued that the only effective protection from this threat was the jury.[169]

The Value of Civic Participation   Aside from standing as a protection against arbitrary government action, juries also promote democratic values and principles of self-government by enlisting ordinary citizens in the business of government. This popular participation has an indirect benefit similar to one mentioned for party-control over litigation: if citizens have more of a stake in their system, they are more likely to support the decisions of courts, which rely first and foremost on voluntary compliance with their decisions. This consideration played a major role in Russia's recent reintroduction of the jury system in that country. It was said to be needed to restore

---

166 An account of the Zenger case is set out in GUINTHER, *supra* note 19, at 28-30.

167 Juries have also nullified based on racist attitudes, as when southern juries in the past acquitted whites accused of murdering blacks. However, blacks were at that time systematically excluded from jury service. Further, the federal government has often later prosecuted the acquitted defendants for violation of the victim's civil rights. This is allowed under the "dual sovereignty" exception to the ban on multiple prosecutions for the same offense, discussed in Chapter VIII, p. 298.

168 *Duncan v. Louisiana*, 391 U.S. 145, 156 (1968).

169 HERBERT J. STORING, THE COMPLETE ANTI-FEDERALIST 18-19 (U. Chicago 1981), quoting Federal Farmer (XV, 2, 8, 90).

public confidence in a judicial system discredited by 70 years of state and Communist Party control.

The Jury's Effect on Judicial Independence   It has been pointed out that juries help to protect the independence of judges. As explained by the federal judge quoted earlier:

> Even under the best of circumstances, a single judge making an unpopular decision comes under public and sometimes official criticism that may have adverse effects on his person, his family and his career. Juries, being anonymous and out of the public eye as soon as the case is over, are well suited to decide controversial cases that could be difficult for judges to decide. And because they hold no office, have no other continuing connection with the government and have no political ambition, they are genuinely independent.[170]

This last point is particularly important for those state courts in the United States whose judges must face reelection, though even federal judges and other appointed judges are not unaffected by these kinds of pressures.[171]

As these last few points suggest, juries may have been retained in the United States long after they had been abolished elsewhere precisely because they reflect peculiarly American values. A jury system could well not work in other systems or might work only with major modifications in attitudes and laws.[172]

---

170 Schwarzer, *supra* note 164. Clearly, there is room for improvement in the jury system. A recent article by the author of the quotation in the text and director of the Federal Judicial Center, a research arm of the federal courts, surveys various points where improvement have been made and suggested. *See* Schwarzer, *supra* note 153. *See also* MUNSTERMAN ET AL., *supra* note 43.

171 Modes of judicial selection are discussed in Chapter V, pp. 176-179.

172 There have also been discussions about resurrecting the right to a jury in Japan, though doubts have been expressed as to whether jury trials would be consistent with that culture. *See* Richard O. Lempert, *A Jury for Japan?*, 40 AM. J. COMP. L. 37 (1992).

CHAPTER IV

THE LEGAL PROFESSION

The Place of the Legal Profession in Society The legal profession in the United States has historically been one of society's most influential professions, if not its most beloved.[1] From the very beginning of the republic, a disproportionate percentage of lawyers have occupied positions of power in political circles. Almost 45% of the Framers of the 1789 Constitution were lawyers. Around 65% of the Senate and well over half the members of the House of Representatives have been lawyers. Alexis de Tocqueville observed in his famous work, *Democracy in America*:

> In America there are no nobles or literary men, and the people are apt to mistrust the wealthy; lawyers consequently form the highest political class and the most cultivated portion of society. . . . If I were asked where I place the American aristocracy, I should reply without hesitation that it is not among the rich, who are united by no common tie, it occupies the judicial bench and the bar.[2]

Given some of the negative public attitudes about lawyers heard today, it is clear that much of the "aristocratic" veneer of the legal profession has worn off.[3] Part of the respect and perhaps a great deal of the dislike of lawyers undoubtedly also comes from the nature of law and procedure in the United States. As demonstrated in Chapter II, the legal methodology involved in a caselaw system is complicated and, as discussed in Chapter III, adversarial procedure requires skilled lawyers to fulfill the obligations imposed on parties to investigate and present their own evidence in court proceedings. To this extent, the need to turn to lawyers for help is greater in the United States than in some other systems. Such dependence doubtless results in lawyers being perceived, not only as powerful helper-friends, but also as irritating reminders of powerlessness.

The Profession in Crisis? Beyond its public relations difficulties, the legal profession has quietly been suffering somewhat of a crisis in the past few years. Two changes have occurred and the final impact of both has yet to be determined.

The first change has been a loss of cohesion in the profession. Even in the most cohesive of times, the legal profession has covered a broad spectrum of lawyers. Defining the legal profession as all persons trained in law who have a license to practice law, it includes solo practitioners, judges, government lawyers on every level

---

1 For a recent description of the profession by a committee of the American Bar Association citing and discussing many sources of information on the profession and making recommendations for change in lawyer education and training, *see Legal Education and Professional Development — An Educational Continuum*, REPORT OF THE TASK FORCE ON LAW SCHOOLS AND THE PROFESSION: NARROWING THE GAP (ABA Section of Legal Education and Admissions to the Bar 1992) (also known as the "MacCrate Report"). *See also* CHARLES W. WOLFRAM, HORNBOOK ON MODERN LEGAL ETHICS (West 1986) and RICHARD ABEL, AMERICAN LAWYERS (Oxford University Press 1989) (statistical information on the legal profession).

2 I ALEXIS DE TOCQUEVILLE, DEMOCRACY IN AMERICA 288 (1835-1840) (Vintage Books, New York 1954).

3 A poll conducted in 1993 by the National Law Journal, a newspaper concentrating on news and other topics of interest to lawyers, found that the image of lawyers with the public, which was already low, has taken a downturn since 1988. *See* 15 NAT'L L.J. 1 (August 9, 1993). *See also* Marc Galanter, *Predators and Parasites: Lawyer-Bashing and Civil Justice*, 28 GA. L. REV. 633 (1994) (offering a taxonomy of anti-lawyer themes (and some jokes) organized into 4 categories: (1) corrupters of discourse; (2) fomenters of strife; (3) betrayers of trust; and (4) economic predators). Polls are difficult to evaluate, however. While having a negative attitude about lawyers in general, 90% of respondents think that *their* lawyer is fine and react positively when asked whether they would want their child to become a lawyer.

of government, in-house counsel for corporations, public defenders and other lawyers for the poor, associates on salary and partners in firms of all sizes with all kinds of clients, and law teachers. Even within the broad category of private practice, lawyers work in such a variety of settings and represent such a broad spectrum of clients that they often have little in common. Some lack of cohesiveness is the result of the great increase in the number of lawyers — an increase of 100% between 1970 and 1990. In addition, in the past 25 years there has been a surge in the diversity of the profession in terms of race, ethnicity and sex as many more racial minorities and women have entered the profession. This diversity has not only changed the traditional "white male face" of the profession; it has also challenged many aspects of how law is or should be practiced, and many assumptions underlying the law itself. All these changes have led some to suggest that the legal profession is no longer a single profession, but many.[4]

Since almost three-fourths of the legal profession is engaged in private practice, a second change that affects many in the profession has been in the nature of the work of lawyers in private practice. The last 40 years have been the era of the law firm, and particularly of the large corporate law firm of more than 250 lawyers. Because of the elite status of such lawyers and the prominence of their firms, the model of the private lawyer has gone from that of the single practitioner or small partnership to that of the associate of a large law firm. With it, the paradigm work setting of today's private practitioner has changed from that of an independent professional who works closely with clients to solve their problems and is responsible for his or her own work, to that of an employee who often has never met his or her client, who is responsible only for some portion of a client's case, and who gauges his or her worth not by the results obtained for the client, but by the number of hours billed. The downturns in the business climate in the early 1990s and skyrocketing salaries paid to attract talented lawyers to large firms have brought a greater attention to the "business" side of law practice. It is not enough today just to be an excellent lawyer. Thus, lawyers in large firms today are under pressure, not only to bill more hours, but also to cultivate and bring in new clients. As a result of some of these changes, many more lawyers are disenchanted with practice at its most elite levels than has ever been the case before.

One experience common to almost all lawyers today is law school. Consequently, it is appropriate to begin with that subject.

A. Legal Education and Admission to the Bar

1. Legal Educational Requirements and the J.D. Degree

Today in the United States, graduation from law school is the only practical route to becoming a lawyer. This was not always the case. Legal education, as it existed from the time of the Constitution until well into the 20th century consisted of reading and apprenticeships with practicing lawyers. Thomas Jefferson, Chief Justice John Marshall and Abraham Lincoln all "read law" and served apprenticeships. In the 20th century, Robert H. Jackson, Attorney General under President Franklin D. Roosevelt, chief U.S. prosecutor at the Nazi war crimes trials at Nuremburg and a justice of the United States Supreme Court, entered the legal profession by way of reading and

---

4　ABEL, *supra* note 1, at 208-211.

apprenticeship in a law office. Though seven states still allow some form of law office study to satisfy educational requirements, few use this method of study today.[5]

Educational requirements for lawyers hit an all-time low point in the mid 19th century. This was largely the result of a surge in populist feeling under President Andrew Jackson from 1830 to 1840 that resisted the notion that the bar constituted an elite. In 1860, a specific period of law study was required in only 9 out of 39 states. Bar examinations were uniformly oral and so easy to pass that they were considered by many to be a joke.[6] The American Bar Association (ABA), a voluntary private organization of lawyers founded in 1878, began a long campaign to establish a uniform educational requirement of attendance at a law school satisfying certain minimum standards as a prerequisite for entry into the legal profession.[7]

There are 179 law schools in the United States that are approved by the American Bar Association (ABA). Other law schools, mostly in California, are not approved by the ABA, but operate under the approval of state government. Approval by the ABA is very important because 43 of the 50 states require bar examinees to graduate from an ABA-approved law school in order to take the bar examination. This is so despite the fact that the ABA, as a private organization, has no government power. Of the 179 ABA-approved law schools, 160 are members of the Association of American Law Schools (AALS), a separate organization interested in quality legal education that maintains a close working relationship with the ABA.[8]

Currently, the required course of study to become a lawyer is 7 years, although only the last 3 years are spent studying law. The first 4 years are spent obtaining an undergraduate degree from a college or university — an almost universal requirement for admission to law school. Although the typical future lawyer will get their undergraduate degree in business, economics, history or political science, there is no requirement regarding one's major subject of study. Some law students have degrees in such areas as electrical engineering, nursing or even music.

After 3 years of law school, the graduate receives a Juris Doctor or J.D. degree.[9] The overall number of J.D. candidate law students enrolled at ABA-approved schools in the 1996-1997 academic year was 128,623. Every year, law schools graduate about almost 40,000 J.D. candidates.

Law schools are called "schools" even when they are, as most are, departments of universities. This is the legacy of the time, in the first half of the 19th century, when

---

5 Correspondence study is generally not possible. For a summary guide to bar admission requirements in all states, *see* COMPREHENSIVE GUIDE TO BAR ADMISSION REQUIREMENTS 1997-98 (ABA Section of Legal Education and Admission to the Bar and the National Committee of Bar Examiners).

6 *See* ROBERT B. STEVENS, LAW SCHOOL: LEGAL EDUCATION IN AMERICA FROM THE 1850'S TO THE 1980'S 25 (U. North Carolina Press, Chapel Hill 1983) and LAWRENCE FRIEDMAN, A HISTORY OF AMERICAN LAW, 2D ED. 652 (Touchstone Books 1985).

7 TASK FORCE REPORT, *supra* note 1, at 105-108. *See also* SUSAN K. BOYD, THE ABA'S FIRST SECTION: ASSURING A QUALIFIED BAR (ABA Section of Legal Education and Admissions to the Bar 1993).

8 Beginning in 1990, a major news magazine began to rank law schools according to their quality. The methodology used has been criticized by a consortium of ABA , AALS and other committees active in legal education as "meaning less or grossly misleading." In reaction, the ABA has published an OFFICIAL GUIDE TO APPROVED LAW SCHOOLS (1999 ed.) which reports accurate data on law schools' faculty, entrance requirements, career placement, bar passage rates and other information. Statistics in this chapter are taken from this guide.

9 Before the 1960s, this degree was called an LL.B., or Bachelor of Laws degree. Nothing has changed about the basic degree except its name and many schools have allowed LL.B. degree-holders to exchange that degree for a J.D.

law schools were not affiliated with universities and were instead separate, vocationally oriented institutions.

2. Admission to Law School

Prerequisites Two requirements are the most important in law school admission: the applicant's undergraduate grade-point average (GPA) and scores on the Law School Aptitude Test (LSAT). These two numbers in general determine both whether the applicant gets into any law school and how prestigious a law school the applicant will be able to enroll in. But in recent years, in an effort to increase the social and ethnic diversity of law students, faculties have been experimenting with different methods of choosing law students. Schools may, for example, choose half their entering class by way of LSAT scores and grades, and the other half in an alternative manner based on factors other than LSAT and GPA. The school forms a "pool" of applicants that is 3 to 4 times larger than the number of places remaining, consisting of applicants with the next highest LSAT scores and grades. Within this pool, students are chosen by considering recommendation letters, work experience, racial identification or ethnic or geographical origin, life experience, a required essay, reasons for wanting to become a lawyer, and any number of other factors deemed relevant.

Competition for Admission There was a surge in applications in the late 1960s and early 1970s when the prospect of social change through law was attractive to many. More recently, many believe that the lawyer market has become saturated and it has been more difficult for law graduates to find jobs, so applications have been declining. However, the level is still quite high, with as many as 18 applicants per place in the first-year class at the most prestigious schools and about half that per position at less prestigious schools.

Women and Minorities in Law School Today women constitute 44% of admitted law students and minority group members constitute 20%. In the general population women are 51% and minorities 22%. While law school student populations even today do not reflect exactly the gender and racial content of the country as a whole, the present situation is a considerable improvement over the past. In 1960, women constituted only 4% of the law student population and minorities were less than 1%.[10]

The Cost of Legal Education The cost of a legal education varies widely from law school to law school. Average yearly tuition at ABA-approved law schools in 1997 was more than $18,000 at private schools, more than $13,000 for non-state residents at state institutions and more than $6,000 for state residents at state institutions. In addition to tuition, a student must pay for living expenses, including room and board and transportation. Average living expenses in 1997-1998 ranged from $8,000 for those living in dormitories to more than $11,000 for those living off-campus. Students with excellent undergraduate college grades and good LSAT scores can expect a certain amount of financial aid from their law school in the form of scholarships. But most students graduate with a significant amount of debt.[11]

For private law schools the tuition is usually the same for every student unless a scholarship is awarded. However, public law schools, which are funded in part by the government of the state in which they are located, charge considerably less for

---

10 As discussed later, the legal *profession* today is made up of 22% women and 3.3% blacks.

11 Source: ABA Section on Legal Education and Admissions to the Bar. For an interesting article and empirical study of the problem of law student debt, *see* David L. Chambers, *The Burdens of Educational Loans: The Impact of Debt on Job Choice and Standard of Living for Students at Nine American Law Schools*, 42 J.LEG. EDUC. 187 (1992).

students who reside in that state. For example, tuition at the University of Michigan Law School for a student who resides in that state is around $9,000 per year — half that charged nonresident students. A state is permitted to favor its own residents in this way and generally justifies such differing treatment on the ground that out-of-state students (or more accurately, the student's parents) have not been paying taxes in that state.[12]

3. The Basic J.D. Curriculum and Degree

Courses   There is no "official" curriculum mandated by the government for the 3 years of study leading to a J.D. degree, but the content in the first year of law school tends to be dictated by tradition and is surprisingly uniform from school to school. In the first year, all the subjects are usually mandatory.

The typical first year student usually takes Civil Procedure, Contracts, Property, Criminal Law, Torts, Constitutional Law and Legal Writing. The subjects in the second and third years are usually all "electives" chosen by the students themselves with the exception of the requirements of a research seminar and a course on professional responsibility.   Thus, there is no specialization in law school except whatever specialization students themselves may choose by selecting particular courses. The majority of law students choose courses on subjects covered on the bar exam and in the specialty area in which they plan to work. A typical student in the second and third years will take four courses a semester. Typical courses of a student taken in those years could be Commercial Transactions, Business Organizations, Tax Law, Labor Law, Wills and Trusts, Evidence, Legal Process, Criminal Procedure, Administrative Law, Legal Ethics, Conflict of Laws, International Law, Environmental Law, Antitrust Law and a research seminar requiring a substantial research paper.[13]

Method of Instruction   The method of instruction in law school varies somewhat among law schools, but in most some form of the "case method" is used. The case method of law study was the invention of Christopher Columbus Langdell who was a professor and dean of Harvard Law School beginning in the 1870s. Before that time the primary method of instruction was summaries of the law provided by way of lecture or assigned readings from treatises.[14] The main change wrought by Langdell's case method was its focus on original sources of the law and on the methods of case analysis and legal reasoning in caselaw. Some of Langdell's theories about how much of a "science" the caselaw has been undercut by new ideas about the nature of the judicial process.[15] But allowing for modification of the caselaw method to reflect those new ideas, Langdell's method is still the basic model for most modern law school courses.

The main focus of the typical law school course is the "casebook" for the course. This casebook, sometimes called "cases and materials," contains judicial opinions and any applicable statutes. It also contains some textual material that links the cases together or summarizes caselaw or statutory law not sufficiently important to have the

---

12   The practice has been held constitutional. *See* Chapter IX, p. 327.

13   Twelve states require that law students have taken certain courses at law school as a prerequisite to being admitted to the bar.   Underlying these educational requirements imposed by the bar is a smoldering conflict over who should control the content of legal education, law schools or the legal profession.

14   The most authoritative of the sources in the 19th century were William Blackstone's 1765-1769 Commentaries on the Laws of England and the treatises on American law of Supreme Court Justice Joseph Story and Chancellor James Kent. *See* Chapter II, p. 50.

15   *See* Chapter II, pp. 40-45.

student read the primary materials. Students must each have a personal copy of the book, since they are assigned appellate opinions to read in preparation for class. Study questions in the book following the cases provide hints as to what aspects of the case are important, confusing or subject to criticism.

Class sessions are devoted primarily to a discussion of the principal cases that were assigned to be read. The first purpose of class discussions is to determine the governing rules of law that those cases stand for. Then the ramifications of those rules as applied to hypothetical facts similar to those in the principal case are explored, which may necessitate a deeper analysis of and a recasting of the rules gleaned from the principal case. In the process of this, a secondary purpose — particularly in the first year of law school — is to teach the techniques of working with caselaw that were outlined in Chapter II. At some point in the discussion, the focus will turn to the social policies behind the rules established by the cases, criticisms of the rules, their social and historical context and economic effects and any number of other issues the case raises. The rationale for using class discussion rather than lecture as a method of instruction is that students will learn more if they learn actively — doing the necessary case analysis and critique themselves rather than listening passively to a teacher's lecture about how to do it. In addition, oral analysis and discussion of legal points are essential skills for a lawyer. To the extent that there is lecture in a class based on this model, it is used to summarize class discussion or to cover additional information not covered in the text or class discussion, particularly the teacher's own insights or criticisms of the cases assigned.

"Socratic" Method   There are many ways to conduct a class discussion, but teachers most often use some variation on a unique method of teaching called the "Socratic method" to engage students in discussion of the cases they have read. According to this method, the teacher calls on a student and asks the student to "state the case," meaning to set out its facts, holding, and reasoning. The student is then asked progressively more difficult questions about the implications of the holding in the case, the relationship of that holding to other cases in that area or about the reasoning employed by the court. "Socratic" interrogation often exposes inadequacies in the student's preparation or thinking and, if conducted aggressively by a domineering teacher, can be emotionally painful experience for the student. Because of the "Socratic" method of instruction and the heavy workload associated with reading cases and preparing for class, students generally report that the law school experience, at least in the first year, is a difficult and trying one somewhat akin to military training.[16]

The use of Socratic method in its purest and more aggressive form has declined in the last 25 years. Some teachers have simply modified it to a gentler form of questioning, which some have called "avuncular" Socratic method — questioning conducted as your uncle might do it. The decline of the Socratic method is especially evident in the second and third year courses, where both students and teachers have less patience for it. There has also been a resurgence in use of the lecture method

---

16 The peculiarities and hardship of the law school classroom have had sufficient popular appeal to be the subject of a film, *The Paper Chase* (1973) starring the late John Houseman. It depicts the difficulties of a Harvard law student facing an old-style "Socratic" contracts teacher. Several books are available that give students tips on how to prepare for and survive the law school classroom experience. *See* GEORGE J. ROTH, SLAYING THE LAW SCHOOL DRAGON: A PRIMER ON HOW TO SURVIVE AND COMBAT LAW SCHOOL INTIMIDATION (Dodd, Mead & Co., New York 1980). *See also* ANN BURKHART & ROBERT STEIN, HOW TO STUDY LAW AND TAKE LAW EXAMS IN A NUTSHELL (West 1996); JOHN MAKDISI, INTRODUCTION TO THE STUDY OF LAW (Anderson Publishing Co., Cincinnati 1990).

among some teachers. Even when there is lecture, however, the lecture is rarely a substitute for doing the assigned readings, since it assumes students have read and understand the readings. Other teachers use a "problem approach" to teaching. They hand out realistic written problems for students to prepare answers to before class and then conduct a class discussion of those problems.[17]

Examinations and Evaluation Examinations are invariably written and traditionally consist of essay questions that present complex fact situations. In the essay answer, students must analyze the facts and state what legal issues are raised and for each issue raised state what the applicable rule of law is, analyze how it should be resolved from all sides of the question and state what conclusion a court should reach.[18] Such essay exams are typically 3 hours long. In recent years there has been more variety in examinations. The "take-home" exam, which allows students to work at home over a given number of hours or days, is increasingly popular. In addition, some teachers have developed objective examinations with multiple choice and true-false questions.[19] Grading must be done on an anonymous basis to the extent possible and grading duties are performed by the teacher of the course rather than being delegated to assistants.

The number of students who drop out of ABA-approved law schools is around 4.5%. More drop out in the first year (around 9%) than do in the third year (less than 1%). However, among some of the weaker and often newer law schools, there is a policy of low admission standards and a high "flunk-out" rate, often resulting in as many as one third of the entering class failing.[20]

Marks of success in law school are good grades and membership on the editorial board of the law review or law journal. The law school's law review edits and publishes articles written by teachers and scholars, and notes and comments on recent cases written by student members of the law review. In order to be admitted to the law review, the student must either receive outstanding grades in the first year (usually law reviews take only those students with first-year grades in the top 5-10%) or do well in a legal writing competition. The students who are selected to work on the law review do so during their second and third years. The most prestigious law firms strongly prefer former editors and members of law reviews and some large firms will interview only graduates who were "on" law review. The majority of the law teachers in the United States were probably members or editors of the law review of their law school.[21]

Summer Clerkships During the summers after the first and second years, law students generally do not take courses. Instead, they try to find some kind of summer work. The preferred work is legal work because it teaches students something about law practice and possibly will assist them in obtaining a job after graduation. Students

---

17 *See* Myron Moskovitz, *Beyond the Case Method: It's Time to Teach with Problems*, 42 J.LEG. EDUC. 241 (1992).

18 This method of approaching essay exam questions has been reduced to the acronym "IRAC" by law students who wish to make sure they remember each step: *I*ssue, *R*ule, *A*nalysis, *C*onclusion.

19 The development of objective examinations in law school has in general paralleled the growth of the multi-state bar examination, which is a multiple choice examination.

20 Source: ABA Section on Legal Education and Admissions to the Bar.

21 There are a few law reviews that are edited by law teachers and scholars. It seems strange to some that *students* are the keepers of the prominent academic journals of the profession. It is especially strange given that the decision of law faculties to give tenure or to promote a teacher is determined in large part based on what law reviews accepted and published the teacher's articles.

who work in such positions are called "law clerks" and their summer job is called a "summer clerkship." Law clerks mainly do legal research in the library and write memoranda summarizing the results. It is relatively difficult for students to find a legal clerkship the summer after their first year, but most all find such legal work in the summer of their second year. In recent years, summer clerkships for the best students at many corporate law firms have not been very demanding and might better be described as a combination orientation to the firm and "courtship" of the best students. Indeed, it is not uncommon for a student at an elite law school to be able to "split" a summer between two different firms, an arrangement more conducive to "courtship" and orientation than to serious work.

4. Advanced Degrees

For the vast majority of lawyers in the United States, legal education ends with the J.D. degree. This is even true of teachers of law, who need not receive any degree beyond the J.D. degree in order to teach or to receive tenure at their university. There are higher degrees in law, the Master's Degree in Law (LL.M.) and the Doctor of Science in Law (S.J.D.), and the majority of those who receive these degrees are teachers. But teachers do this voluntarily, often to "launder" themselves with an LLM from a prestigious law school after receiving a J.D. degree at a less well known university. Each year, there are about 4,000 students enrolled in master's programs and around 2,000 students graduate each year with master's degrees.

The two most common master's degree programs are in the areas of tax law and comparative law. Some schools offer specialized training and master's degrees in other areas, including labor law and corporate practice. All but the master's in comparative law are sought by lawyers practicing in the U.S. who wish to specialize in those areas. The comparative law master's degree (M.C.L. or LL.M.) is sought by foreign lawyers who come to the United States to study law. Such degrees are attractive because of their prestige and because the length of study required is only one year. In addition, it can be a "short cut" for the foreign lawyer who wants to be admitted to the bar in one of the United States. The one year of study for an LL.M. degree at an ABA-approved law school will qualify the foreign law graduate to take the bar examination in 11 states.[22]

5. Law Teachers

Titles The system of titles and ranks for law teachers (and for teachers in other disciplines as well) differs from the European model. The term "professor" is used in the United States as a general term for most all full-time teachers. There are 3 ranks of professor: assistant professor, associate professor and professor.[23] These roughly correspond to the ranks of lecturer, docent and professor in the European system. However, full professors in the U.S. system are more numerous than the European professor. There is no limit on the number of full professors that a law school may have and it often happens that over three-quarters of the members of a faculty will be full professors.

Academic Administration The law school is headed by a single dean. There is also an associate dean in charge of academic affairs and administrative tasks, an assistant dean for student affairs and an assistant dean in charge of admissions. Law

---

22 *See* COMPREHENSIVE GUIDE TO BAR ADMISSION REQUIREMENTS 1997-98, *supra* note 5.

23 There are also "adjunct" professors, generally practitioners teaching a single course at the law school, and "visiting" professors, full-time teachers from other law schools teaching full-time for a semester or a year at the host institution.

schools are typically not divided into different institutes or subdepartments as in Europe (e.g., civil law, criminal law, state law). This lack of different institutes or subdepartments relieves professors from many of the administrative duties that professors in European systems must contend with. Routine administrative matters and the hiring and supervision of support personnel are handled through the dean's office, so that professors can concentrate on teaching and scholarship.

The life of the law teacher is not totally free from administrative burdens, however. Most of the important decisions made at most law schools are not made by the dean, but by the faculty as a whole on the recommendation of various faculty committees. Democracy has its price and that price in law schools is service on these committees. The most important committees are curriculum, faculty appointments, budget, admissions and tenure and promotions. If a teacher wishes to offer a new course, it must first be proposed to and approved by the curriculum committee and then voted on by the faculty. New teachers are hired only after comprehensive screening and recommendation by the faculty appointments committee and a vote of the entire faculty. Current teachers are promoted or granted tenure only if such action is recommended by the tenure and promotions committee. Then the recommendation must be confirmed by a vote of the entire faculty.

Duties and Career Path Teaching duties for the average teacher usually involve teaching two courses a semester or four courses a year.[24] In addition, the teacher is expected to engage in scholarly pursuits resulting in books and articles. Because teachers are not confined to a particular institute or subdepartment within the law school, it is not unusual for teachers to teach and write across what lawyers from civil-law countries would consider basic boundaries in the law. Thus, a teacher might teach and write in the areas of corporations, criminal law, civil procedure and constitutional law.

Typically a teacher will start out as an assistant professor, unless considerable practice or other experience calls for beginning at the associate level. After writing two or three law review articles that prove his or her intellectual mettle and surviving 4 to 6 years in the classroom, the assistant professor will be given "tenure" and promoted to associate professor. This is a serious decision, since tenure assures that the teacher cannot be fired except for the most serious breach or neglect of duties.[25] Then, after 2 or 3 more years of teaching and writing, the teacher will be eligible for promotion to full professor. After reaching full professor, the stimulus to continue to do research and writing and to improve one's teaching is largely financial, since it is the most productive scholars and the best teachers who receive the larger share of discretionary raises in pay that are bestowed each year.

Each step in the promotion process at the better law schools requires a complete evaluation of the teacher's scholarly work-product by "outside" experts — scholars in the teacher's field from other law schools across the country. It was noted earlier that law teachers in the U.S. are not required to and do not generally seek advanced degrees in law. In terms of the intellectual and scholarly writing demands it places on the teacher, the tenure and promotion process is similar to pursuit of an advanced degree.

---

24 Most courses are "three credit-hour" courses, meaning that they meet three hours a week during a semester of 14 or 15 weeks.

25 Tenure is for the purpose of assuring "academic freedom," the right to teach, write and speak out on any public issues without fear of retaliation.

Influence on the Law Articles and books by legal academics have some considerable effect on the development of the law. Law review articles are regularly cited in briefs and judicial opinions and have been responsible for some major changes in the law. In this respect, American academics are more influential on the legal system than their colleagues in England.[26] On the other hand, academic writing does not have the authoritativeness of professors' commentaries in continental Europe. Judges in the United States are more likely to be influenced by court opinions written by other judges than by a law review article. In addition, law review articles of professors from many of the elite law schools have in recent years become oriented toward high theory rather than legal doctrine.[27]

Another way that legal academics affect development of the law is through service in government posts. Many professors are tapped to be judges. Some positions, such as Solicitor General of the United States — the lawyer who argues the position of the United States government before the United State Supreme Court — and head of the antitrust enforcement division of the Department of Justice, have traditionally gone to law professors. Legal academics from leading law schools also occupy general counsel positions for government agencies or serve as members of or consultants to various government commissions. Moreover, it is relatively common for litigants to retain law professors to argue their cases in the appellate courts and particularly in the Supreme Court.[28]

Pay The salaries of law teachers vary somewhat, with private schools tending to pay more than state institutions, though the range is narrower than the range of salaries of private practitioners.[29] In 1997, the average range of pay for assistant professors was between $55,000 and $65,000, for associate professors between $65,000 and $85,000, for full professors between $95,000 to $150,000 and for deans between $120,000 and $180,000. These figures do not reflect the possibilities that exist for supplemental income from special research grants, representing clients, consulting or writing books. In general, private law schools will pay more than public ones.[30]

6. Admission to the Bar

The overwhelming majority of law school graduates in the United States gain admission to the bar and practice law in some form. In this respect, the United States is different from many other countries, in which the study of law is considered to be a general preparation for all kinds of work in the area of business or government service and considerably fewer graduates become practicing lawyers.

Types of State Bar Regulation State rather than federal law governs admission to the practice of law and requirements vary from state to state. States have adopted one of two kinds of agencies to oversee the profession. In some states, the agency

---

26 *See generally* P.S. ATIYAH & ROBERT SUMMERS, FORM AND SUBSTANCE IN ANGLO-AMERICAN LAW 398-407 (Clarendon Press 1987). The authors give several reasons for this, not the least of which is the relative lesser ability of English judges to stray far from precedent and inject public policy considerations into their decisions.

27 *See* Harry T. Edwards, *The Growing Disjunction Between Legal Education And The Legal Profession*, 91 MICH.L.REV. 34 (1992).

28 *See e.g. New York Times v. United States*, 403 U.S. 713 (1971), the "Pentagon Papers" case (discussed in Chapter IX, p. 355) wherein Professor Erwin Griswold of Yale Law School as Solicitor General argued against Professor Alexander Bickel of Harvard.

29 *See infra* p. 144.

30 Unless otherwise indicated, these and other salary figures in this chapter are taken from "What Lawyers Earn," NATIONAL LAW JOURNAL, p. B8 col. 1 (June 1, 1998). They are current as of June 1, 1998.

is an actual governmental one (for example, the supreme court of the state). In others, an "integrated bar" exists and constitutes a form of self-regulation. Under such a system, the state delegates its licensing and regulation authority to an organization, usually called the State Bar Association, which oversees admission to practice and regulates the profession. Membership in the State Bar Association is mandatory in order to practice. In both systems, the supreme court of the state exercises ultimate control over the legal profession.

Bar Examinations All states but one require first-time applicants to the bar to pass a bar examination and most impose specific educational requirements as a precondition to taking the examination.[31] The bar examination is a two-part written examination of approximately two to three days length that is offered twice a year, usually in July and February. One part of the examination consists of objective multiple-choice questions on general law, in all but three states the uniform "multistate" bar examination (MBE).[32] However, each state has the right to set whatever passing score it wishes. The second part of the examination consists of essay questions concerning the law of the particular state. Some states, concerned with testing competence for practice more accurately, have departed from the traditional focus on legal knowledge. For example, Alaska, Colorado, and California have included "performance tests" in their bar exams, which have required examinees to do such things as draft memoranda, write a closing argument for a trial, or outline a deposition.[33]

Before taking the bar exam, almost all graduates take a 6-week "bar review" course. Private companies offer the course to teach students everything they need to succeed on the bar examination. The bar review course is particularly important for the state law part of the bar exam, because most of the better law schools teach only general doctrines and concepts and not the law of any particular state. The percentage of students who pass the bar exam varies from state to state. For example, in July 1991, in California, only 30% passed the bar exam, while in Montana 91% passed. The remaining states fall in between.[34] Often law graduates complain that states make it difficult to pass the bar exam, not so much to guarantee higher competence among lawyers in the state, but as a method of limiting competition with lawyers already practicing in the state.

Interstate Practice Without being admitted to the bar of a given state, a lawyer has no right to practice there. This prohibition includes all aspects of law practice, including giving legal advice and drafting documents. A lawyer from another state may take part in a trial if the judge gives special permission solely for that case (called appearing *pro hac vice*) and the lawyer works together with a local lawyer. Otherwise, in a majority of states, the lawyer wishing to practice in that state must take and pass the bar examination of that state. In some states, a lawyer may be admitted to practice in that state without examination if the lawyer has practiced law in another state for a given period of time, usually 5 to 7 years.

---

31 Wisconsin exempts students who graduate from the University of Wisconsin from any bar examination requirement in that state. *See* ADMISSION REQUIREMENTS, *supra* note 5.

32 *See* COMPREHENSIVE GUIDE, *supra* note 5. There is also a separate multi-state Professional Responsibility Examination (MPRE) which all but four states give.

33 ABA TASK FORCE REPORT, *supra* note 1, at 280-282.

34 Other examples of percentages for the same year were Texas, 87%; Illinois, 83%; and Michigan, 79%.

Federal Court Practice A license to practice in the state courts of a state does not authorize the lawyer to practice in the federal courts — even the federal courts located in that state. Despite the fact that federal law is uniform throughout the country, there is no one central place to obtain such certification. Instead, lawyers admitted to practice in a state must go to the local federal district court and obtain a certificate entitling them to practice in that district. Since some states have more than one district, this may involve getting as many as 4 certificates.[35] Fortunately, there is no separate federal bar examination and in most districts obtaining a certificate to practice is simply a matter of money and the formality of being "sworn in" by a federal judge. It is common to arrange "mass" swearing in ceremonies in both state and federal court shortly after the state bar examination results are announced.[36]

Lawyers As Legal Generalists When a lawyer becomes a member of the bar, that lawyer has the right to fulfill all the duties of the lawyer: consultation, advice, drafting documents, and all other aspects of representation of clients, both in court and out of court. There is no division of lawyers such as exists in England between barristers (who appear in court) and solicitors (who generally may not). There is also no separate branch of the profession equivalent to the civil-law notary.[37] Lawyers do specialize. A general division of many lawyers is the line between "office lawyers" who do transactional work and "litigators" who handle lawsuits in court. But this and more narrow specializations are the result of individual choice and are informal.

The generalist nature of the license to practice law means that lawyers have the freedom to change from one field of law or type of practice to another. It is not uncommon for lawyers to do so one or more times in the course of their professional lives. Studies show a higher rate of mobility in law than in any other profession.[38]

7. Criticism of Legal Education in Law Schools

As stated earlier, the vast majority of law graduates in the United States will practice law. Yet, unlike many other countries, U.S. law graduates are not required to undergo any official apprenticeship period of study before being permitted to practice.[39] Because law school is the only training a new lawyer is required to have before being entrusted with the legal affairs of members of the public, there has been concern that law schools should better prepare their graduates for practice.

Many of the criticisms are longstanding, dating from the 1930s.[40] More recently, Chief Justice Warren Burger in 1973 focused specifically on inadequacies of lawyers

---

35 There are 91 federal districts in the 50 states and Puerto Rice. *See infra* p. 170. U.S. Courts of Appeal also control admission to their own bars, though like the District Courts, admission is *pro forma*. The U.S. Supreme Court bar is open to anyone who has practiced for at least three years.

36 Some districts have used their power to control admission to impose additional educational or experience requirements on lawyers before allowing them to appear in trials.

37 There is a person called a "notary" or "notary public" in the United States, but a U.S. notary is not a legal advisor and indeed has no formal legal education of any kind. All a notary in the U.S. has the power to do is to administer oaths to persons who are to testify or who are to sign sworn documents, and to "notarize" or verify the signatures on such documents. Thus, court reporters, who swear witnesses and take down testimony in court and at depositions, are notaries. Depositions are discussed in Chapter VII, p. 227. The majority of notaries are secretaries in law firms, courts, banks and insurance agencies.

38 *See* ABEL, *supra* note 1, at 175-176.

39 Two exceptions, Vermont and Delaware, are discussed *infra*.

40 *See* Jerome Frank, *Why Not a Clinical Lawyer-School?*, 81 U.PA.L.REV. 907 (1933). Judge Jerome Frank was a judge on the U.S. Court of Appeals for the Second Circuit and is known for his contributions to the school of Legal Realism (*see* Chapter II, p. 42) and criticisms of adversary excesses and the jury system (*see* Chapter III, notes 136 and 152).

in litigation.[41] And, in 1992, the American Bar Association turned its attention to legal education and professional development by publishing a critical Task Force Report on the subject.[42] Consequently, it is appropriate to provide a flavor of the debate that has taken place.

The Law School Curriculum and Lawyering Skills Essentially the criticism of legal education is that it teaches too narrow a range of skills, primarily concentrating on the skill of analyzing the legal doctrine in cases to the exclusion of other tasks that lawyers are called upon to perform.[43] In an adversary system, lawyers must be able to investigate, analyze and present facts in trials. Yet, courses in trial advocacy, fact investigation and pre-trial motion practice have had no place in the traditional curriculum. Some of these courses (particularly trial advocacy) are offered regularly in law schools today, but often not in a sufficient number of sections to satisfy demand. Moreover, no school makes these courses mandatory. Similarly, the non-litigating "office lawyer" must have interviewing, counseling and negotiation skills, and must be able to draft contracts and other documents properly and write opinion letters. Yet, there are few classes that address these skills and where they exist, none are required. A major general problem with law schools preparing their students for practice is their presentation of subjects in an atomized fashion. Few courses integrate several different areas of substantive and procedural law in the way that practitioners must deal with them in real life.

Defenders of the traditional curriculum usually respond that law school is not designed to do anything more than teach legal analysis and provide a public policy or interdisciplinary perspective context for law. Graduates, they assert, will learn everything they need to know about practice once they start practicing. But this response ignores the fact that many graduates do not in fact have the opportunity to learn what they need to know after law school. It is true that the large corporate law firms have training programs for new associates that seek to provide the necessary supplemental legal education. However, almost 70% of lawyers in private practice work either on an individual basis or in a firm of 5 or fewer lawyers — where there is often no senior lawyer to protect clients from mistakes and no training program.

Some progress has been made to make legal education more practical, as law schools have provided more and more "lawyering skills" courses. However, few law teachers have practiced for any length of time and many became academics because of the refuge it offered from practice. But uninterested faculty are not the only problem. Large firms, which tend to have the greatest influence in the profession and on leading law schools, are generally satisfied with the status quo despite the fact — and even agreeing with the fact — that the traditional curriculum does not teach students very much about practice. They have little faith in the abilities of the majority of current teachers to teach practice skills. Moreover, it is not coincidental that the existing system serves their interests: if large corporate firms alone have the resources to provide the supplemental post-law school training necessary to ease the transition to practice, then that gives their lawyers an advantage not enjoyed by those who must practice in less luxurious circumstances.

---

41 *See* Warren Burger, *The Special Skills of Advocacy: Are Specialized Training and Certification of Advocates Essential to Our System of Justice?* 42 FORDHAM L.REV. 227, 230 (1973) (remarking that "we are more casual about qualifying people we allow to act as advocates in the courtrooms than we are about licensing our electricians").

42 *See* ABA TASK FORCE REPORT, *supra* note 1.

43 *Id.* at 236-268.

Clinical Education One of the more interesting developments in legal education has been the introduction of legal clinics in the 1960s. Borrowing the word and idea of a clinic from the medical schools, law schools have established law offices at the law school so students can work as lawyers under the supervision of teachers.[44] Students do everything that a lawyer would do, from consultation with clients to handling trials.[45] The clients in clinics are poor people who otherwise would not be able to afford a lawyer. Clinics provide a valuable service to poor people and teach students how to practice. They also help law students, who are generally from the middle class and upper class of society, to learn something about the position of poor people in society and to introduce students to their future professional obligation to help those who are unable to pay for a lawyer.[46] Law school clinics have grown in number. Eighty percent of 155 law schools surveyed in 1991 had client-contact clinics and the number of clinics increased by 15% from 1986 to 1991.[47]

Simulation Courses A more cost-effective "clinical" approach is the simulation course. In this kind of course, students are forced to deal with realistic problems that clients might face, but those problems are presented as role-play exercises. Thus, in the course in trial advocacy mentioned earlier, students must present evidence from mock casefiles via mock witnesses and exhibits to a mock judge and a jury. Similar courses have been developed to teach appellate advocacy, interviewing and counseling, pre-trial litigation skills, and arbitration. Simulation techniques have also been introduced to teach more traditional course material.

The advent of the computer has also opened new possibilities for simulations. With computer games, students can develop their skills, either inside or outside the classroom, at their own speed, and can then go back and repeat those parts that gave them difficulty. A consortium of law schools, called CALI (for Computer Assisted Legal Instruction) has been established to promote computer-based learning.

It should be added that the above criticism of the inadequacies of U.S. legal education does not mean there is an absence of good lawyers in the United States. However, it does means that the good lawyers became good lawyers in large part *despite* the system of legal education they went through and not because of it. In addition, some readers may be puzzled by the criticisms here in view of the fact that in their home countries, formal legal education at the university is far more abstract and theoretical than in the U.S. However, in such systems, there is generally a post-graduation apprenticeship system that teaches the fundamentals of practice.

8. Legal Education After Law School

Some believe that the best way to improve lawyering skills is through educational efforts after graduation from law school. Most states have "continuing legal education" centers which sponsor programs of instruction for lawyers admitted to the bar who wish to improve their skills or acquire new skills. About two-thirds of the states have made a certain amount of post-law school continuing legal education mandatory and seven states have instituted "transition education" requirements to help smooth

---

44 The word "clinic" comes from the Greek word "klinigos," which means "bed." In the medical sense of the word, clinics have to do with the relationship of the doctor to the patient, who is often lying in bed.

45 Law student practice is allowed pursuant to the court rules of the state. *See, e.g.* Michigan Court Rule 8.120 (providing that students at ABA-approved schools who have completed all first year courses to practice under supervision in a legal aid clinic or prosecutor's or city attorney's office).

46 *See* ABA Model Rules of Professional Responsibility, Rule 6.1 (1983).

47 Task Force Report, *supra* note 1, at 253.

the passage from law school to law practice. The most ambitious is the program in the State of Washington where skills are taught over 9 days in small groups with role-playing exercises. Most other required programs, however, are no more than 3 days long, have a lecture format and do not address lawyering skills. Others may be spread over a three-year period to accommodate the busy schedule of the practicing attorney.

A return to post-law-school apprenticeships has been suggested as a means of assuring better preparation for practice, but it has been largely rejected as infeasible. Among the difficulties are assuring the educational quality of the experience and seeing that it does not become a "form of near-peonage" — problems that have arisen in apprenticeship systems in other countries. Only two states, Vermont and Delaware, require a form of apprenticeship. Delaware's apprenticeship is the only one that must be completed before admission to the bar.[48] Delaware's requirements are quite extensive, requiring the observation of several proceedings in court and completion of a wide variety of lawyering tasks over a 6-month period, from drafting a trial court motion to preparing a will or trust document. However, several other states that have tried apprenticeships have been disappointed in them and have replaced them with required attendance at continuing legal education programs.

B. Issues in the Regulation of Practice

Citizenship and Residency Requirements Constitutional questions have been raised regarding the traditional requirement that lawyers, as "officers of the court," be citizens of the United States. In the case of *Application of Griffiths*,[49] the Court declared that it violated the equal protection clause of the 14th Amendment to exclude someone from the practice of law based solely upon that person's not being a United States citizen. And in the case of *Supreme Court of New Hampshire v. Piper*[50] and *Supreme Court of Virginia v. Friedman*,[51] the Court similarly declared unconstitutional states' insistence that lawyers either be domiciled in the state or have a permanent office in the state as a precondition to being admitted to its bar.

Mandatory Bar Membership and Dues As mentioned earlier, some states have "integrated bar" system, which require all lawyers to be members of and pay dues to an official State Bar Association, and delegate to that Association the power of professional regulation.[52] These organizations have used their delegated power to perform self-regulatory functions, such as formulating rules of professional conduct and disciplining members for misconduct, but have also engaged in activities similar to voluntary organizations like the ABA. Thus, state bars have lobbied legislatures and other governmental agencies, filed *amicus curiae* briefs in pending cases, and held conferences on current legal issues. In *Keller v. State Bar of California*,[53] the Supreme Court held that the state bar's use of compulsory dues to finance political and ideological activities with which members disagreed violated their First Amendment right of free speech. While lawyers can be required to join the organization, they can only be charged an amount as dues that reflects expenditures for the purpose of regulating the profession or improving the quality of legal services.

---

48 Apprenticeships and programs of transition education are discussed in the ABA TASK FORCE REPORT, *supra* note 1, at 287-299.

49 413 U.S. 717 (1973). *See* Chapter IX, p. 332, where discrimination against aliens is discussed.

50 470 U.S. 274 (1985).

51 487 U.S. 59 (1988).

52 *See supra* p. 133.

53 496 U.S. 1 (1990).

Minimum Fee Schedules It was optimistically assumed for some time that the fact that the legal profession had a history of self-regulation as a "learned profession" would exempt it from liability under the federal antitrust laws for "ethical" rules designed to limit certain kinds of competition among lawyers.[54] This assumption was suddenly shattered in the Supreme Court's unanimous decision in *Goldfarb v. Virginia State Bar*.[55] In *Goldfarb*, the Court held that a bar association's enforcement of a mandatory minimum fee schedule that set a minimum fee for title searches for residential property sales violated antitrust laws against price fixing. The Court immediately saw through several justifications for minimum fee schedules, including the argument that without them lawyers would engage in unscrupulous competitive efforts and employ shoddy cost cutting methods to win clients.

Unauthorized Practice of Law Non-lawyers are generally prohibited from practicing law. This was not always the case. For much of colonial history up through the 19th century, many states permitted nonlawyers to practice law and even to represent others in litigation.[56] As the legal profession developed, states made the right to practice law the exclusive province of lawyers to protect the public from legal representation by unqualified persons. However, it is clear that many things that are considered the practice of law can be done by laypersons, such as real estate agents preparing deeds, mortgages and promissory notes and accountants and others preparing tax returns and giving tax advice. Beginning in the 1930s, bar associations, urged on by the ABA, formed committees to aggressively police unauthorized practice. The result was a whole series of agreements with trade organizations for realtors, accountants, law book publishers and others that assured that as much business as possible would be done by lawyers. Much of this came to a halt in 1975 when the *Goldfarb* decision discussed above made it clear that such arrangements would violate antitrust laws.[57]

Lawyer Advertising Before the 20th century, lawyers were largely unregulated and advertising by lawyers was unrestrained. As professional control developed, more efforts were made to preserve public respect for and the dignity of the legal profession. Since advertising made law sound like just any other commercial endeavor, one of the restrictions imposed was a ban on advertising. In general, all that was permitted was a dignified sign on one's office building and a similarly dignified listing in the telephone book. All this was changed by a 1977 U.S. Supreme Court case, *Bates v. State Bar of Arizona*.[58] In that case, the Supreme Court continued its expansion of the protection of "commercial speech" under the 1st Amendment by holding unconstitutional most state regulations prohibiting lawyers from advertising. The Court held that advertising provides consumer information about legal services and that such information is entitled to 1st Amendment protection almost equal to political and other protected speech. Advertising has created considerable competition at least in legal services for moderate income persons and, as discussed below, has spawned some alternative means of delivering legal services that could not have developed without it.[59]

---

54 Antitrust law is discussed in Chapter XV, pp. 557-563.

55 421 U.S. 773 (1975).

56 *See generally* WOLFRAM, *supra* note 1, §15.1.

57 WOLFRAM, *supra* note 1, at 826-827.

58 433 U.S. 350 (1977).

59 The commercial speech doctrine of 1st Amendment law is discussed in Chapter IX, pp. 354-355.

Specialization Among Lawyers in Private Practice Despite the existence of a general license to practice in all areas of the law, lawyers in the U.S. as elsewhere have seen fit to specialize, whether in terms of type of client or area of law.[60] Generally, states have prohibited lawyers from holding themselves out to the public as specialists in any particular areas except trademark, patent or admiralty law. However, the Supreme Court held in *Peel v. Attorney Registration and Disciplinary Comm. of Illinois*,[61] that the 1st Amendment's protection of free speech barred Illinois from prohibiting a lawyer's truthful advertising that he was certified as a specialist by the "National Board of Trial Advocates," a private organization that has promulgated standards for trial lawyers.

The *Peel* case has proved a catalyst to specialization. As of 1991, fifteen states had specialization plans in effect for certification of lawyers in up to 25 specialties. However, it is important to emphasize that states have not prohibited non-certified lawyers from practicing in those specialty areas. Some states have required that non-certified lawyers who practice in specialty areas disclose in all advertising that they are not certified in that area of practice.[62]

Are There Too Many Lawyers? The number of lawyers in the United States is not regulated in any way except by the market. And it is fair to say that there are so many different law schools in the United States that it can be said with some assurance that virtually anyone who has graduated from college, who sincerely wishes to become a lawyer — and who has money — will be able to enroll and in three years become one of the 43,000 new lawyers admitted to practice each year. It has been the subject of some debate in recent years whether there are too many lawyers in the United States. From 1970 to 1990, the number of lawyers grew by 100%. In 1992, there were 777,119 members of the bar in the United States. This works out to one lawyer for every 320 people in the country. Ratios range from a low of one lawyer for every 658 in North Carolina to one in 12 in Washington, D.C.[63]

This *laissez faire* market approach in the U.S. is in stark contrast to other countries. In Japan, the number of *bengoshi* is strictly controlled and kept artificially low. Of the 30,000 who take the entrance exam for the Legal Training and Research Institute (the only route to becoming a licensed lawyer after law school), only 700 pass. Similarly in England, only 1,000 would-be barristers are admitted to the British Bar School per year and the total number of barristers is around 6,000.

A recent report issued by the President's Council on Competitiveness, pointing to statistics on lawyers in other countries, charges that there are too many lawyers in the United States. For example, it argues, the ratio of 28 lawyers per 10,000 population in the United States far exceeds the ratio of 11 per 10,000 in Germany, 8 per 10,000 io England, and only 1 per 10,000 in Japan.[64] But comparisons across legal systems are difficult. The cited figure for Japan counts only the 13,000 or so *bengoshi* — the only lawyers who may open an office and represent clients for a fee. It does not include the many more non-*bengoshi* law graduates and others who do legal work as employees of government agencies and business corporations, doing largely the same

---

60 *See infra* pp. 140-148.

61 496 U.S. 91 (1990) (plurality opinion).

62 *See* ABA TASK FORCE REPORT, *supra* note 1, at p. 44-45.

63 *See* ABA TASK FORCE REPORT, *supra* note 1, at 13-18.

64 *See* AGENDA FOR REFORM IN AMERICA: A REPORT FROM THE PRESIDENT'S COUNSEL ON COMPETITIVENESS (1991), as reported in the NEW YORK TIMES (August 13, 1991).

work that in-house corporate counsel and government lawyers in the U.S. do. The Sony Corporation alone has 150 non-bengoshi lawyers on staff. If these are included, as their U.S. counterparts are in the U.S. figure, the result for Japan is around 32 lawyers per 10,000 population — about 4 more lawyers per 10,000 than in the United States. Similarly, in Germany, only private practitioners were counted. Adding government-employed law providers, the revised figure would be for Germany becomes 34 per 10,000.[65]

C. Types of Practice

The legal profession consists of the following types of practice and percentages of lawyers engaged in each: 71.9% in private practice; 9.8% in-house counsel, 8% in federal, state and local government service, 2.6% judges, 1% in teaching, 1% lawyers engaged in public interest practice, and 5.6% retired or inactive.[66] We will discuss private practice, in-house counsel, government service, and public interest practice in this chapter. The work of judges, who in the United States are also members of the bar, will be described in the chapter on the judicial system.[67] The work of law teachers was described earlier in this chapter when legal education was discussed.

Financially, lawyers do quite well. The median salary of all lawyers and judges in 1991 was around $67,000 per year while the median salary for all American workers was around $25,000 per year.[68] However, as the discussion below indicates, there is considerable variation in pay between types of practice and between geographical areas.

1. Private Practice

Lawyers in private practice are the most numerous category of lawyers, comprising approximately 72% of all lawyers in the country. It has been traditional to organize discussions of private practice by size of law firm and to categorize firms into three basic sizes: small (from 1 to 10 lawyers), medium (from 11 to 50 lawyers) and large (more than 50 lawyers).[69] However, the incredible growth of law firms with more than 250 lawyers and even more than 500 lawyers has made the traditional classifications obsolete, particularly the description of a firm of more than 50 lawyers as "large."

The discussion that follows will be organized under two very rough headings. The first is solo practice and smaller firms, under which the various business and non-business-oriented areas of law in which such firms tend to practice will be discussed. Then large corporate firms will be discussed. Following that will be a brief discussion of non-traditional means of delivery of private legal services that have developed in recent years.

---

65 This and the other cross-cultural comparisons are from Ray August, *The Mythical Kingdom of Lawyers*, 78 ABA JOURNAL 72 (September 1992). One must remember as well that lawyers have comparatively greater responsibilities in an adversary system and do much of the work that investigators, magistrates or judges do in more inquisitorial systems. Thus, one would expect more lawyers and fewer judges in a common law country. *See* John Langbein, *Judging Foreign Judges Badly: Nose-Counting Isn't Enough*, 18 JUDGES' JOURNAL (Fall 1979).

66 These and other statistics in the text are from 1988 and are taken from the ABA TASK FORCE REPORT, *supra* note 1. The original source, which is the latest complete data of this type and contains many other statistics, is BARBARA A. CURRAN ET AL., THE LAWYER STATISTICAL REPORT: A STATISTICAL PROFILE OF THE U.S. LEGAL PROFESSION IN THE 1980S, (ABA, Chicago 1986) and SUPPLEMENT TO LAWYER STATISTICAL REPORT (1988).

67 *See* Chapter V, pp. 173-182.

68 AMERICAN LAWYER, Vol 15, July/August, 1993 (pullout section).

69 See ABA TASK FORCE REPORT, *supra* note 1, at 73.

a. Solo Practice and Smaller Firms

Solo practitioners and small firms have much in common. Indeed, small firms often operate more as an aggregate of solo practitioners sharing rent than as a true firm. Solo or small-firm practitioners may be new lawyers who aspire to grow and add partners or they may be experienced practitioners who like the independence and atmosphere of working alone or with a small group of lawyers.

Of the divisions of private practitioners, the category of the smallest firms — 1-10 lawyer firms — by far accounts for the greatest number and percentage of lawyers in the profession. In 1988, this category represented 51.2% of all lawyers in the country and 71% of all private lawyers. Interestingly enough, though the number of sole and small-firm practitioners declined with the growth of large firms, there has been some recent increase in the number of law graduates going into small-firm or solo practice. Some of this has to do with recent poor economic times that have reduced hiring by some large and medium-sized firms. But some of it has to do with the technology revolution in law practice — primarily computer word processing and electronic assistance in legal research and litigation. These developments have made high-quality legal practice by solo or small firm practitioners much easier. Historically at least, sole practitioners on average have received the lowest pay.[70]

General Practice Many and perhaps most firms of up to 10 lawyers engage in general practice. As sole practitioners often say, "I handle anything that walks through the door."[71] Most of their cases involve representing individual as opposed to business clients. There may be specialization within the firm, but in the aggregate, the firm handles most every kind of legal problem that arises in the life of the average citizen: divorces and related family law matters, residential real estate transactions, wills and trusts, personal injury litigation, consumer disputes, and personal financial problems, such as debt problems or bankruptcy. In addition, some commercial law issues may come up involving small businesses and some criminal work may be done, particular misdemeanor representation in traffic cases.

But both solo practitioners and smaller firms often specialize. One study found that 55% of solo practitioners spent at least 50% of their time in one area.[72] The following paragraphs present the more common areas of specialization. Though grouped here in the "smaller firm" category, some of the specialty firms listed are more likely to be medium-sized firms of up to 50 lawyers.

Personal Injury Personal injury litigation firms tend to be either "plaintiffs' firms" and "defense firms" depending on the side they usually represent. While most plaintiffs' firms would fall into the category of small and many defense firms are small as well, some defense firms are medium-sized or even large firms. Firms get involved in personal injury defense because they represent insurance companies. Most personal injury defense is performed pursuant to insurance policy "duty-to-defend"

---

70 *See* ABEL, *supra* note 1, at 206-207. After 11 years of practice, a 1986 study of graduates of 7 Northeastern law schools showed an average salary of a sole practitioner to be $35,000 and a partner of a firm with over 84 lawyers to be $123,000. After 26 years the figures were $60,000 and $200,000, respectively.

71 *See* JOEL F. HANDLER, THE LAWYER AND HIS COMMUNITY: THE PRACTICING BAR IN A MIDDLE-SIZED CITY (U. of Wisconsin Press., Madison, Wis. 1967) and other sources cited in ABA TASK FORCE REPORT, *supra* note 1, at 36.

72 *See* ABA TASK FORCE REPORT, *supra* note 1, at 41. A 1991 survey of California lawyers indicated that 75% of all lawyers spent at least 50% of their time in one substantive area. In small firms, this sort of specialization is often the result of specialization of individual lawyers within a general practice firm.

clauses. Insurance companies not only agree to pay the damage the insured is liable for, but to defend the insured in court. A large firm will sometimes represent a personal injury plaintiff, but it is not a common specialty.

There is a distinctive entrepreneurial spirit among many plaintiffs' personal injury lawyers that is reflected in the way they get paid. The "American rule" on litigation costs is that the parties must absorb their own legal representation costs.[73] Defendants' lawyers, and almost all other lawyers, bill their clients by the hour. Win or lose, they receive their pay. Plaintiffs' lawyers use what is called a "contingent fee" arrangement. In a contingent fee arrangement, if the matter is resolved against the plaintiff and the plaintiff receives no money, the plaintiff's lawyers receive nothing. But if the plaintiff's lawyers succeed in obtaining monetary damages, either as a result of a trial or through settlement of the case, they take a proportion (usually one-third) of the amount they have won for the client. Of course, in a scheme of contingent fees, it often happens that in a successful case — particularly when the matter is resolved at an early stage of litigation or even without litigation — the lawyer receives a fee that seems large considering the number of hours that the lawyer actually worked on the case. But this is as it must be in such a system, since in those cases that were lost, a great deal of work was done, but no fee was received.

Many believe that the contingent fee is somehow dishonest and in any event encourages groundless lawsuits. Plaintiffs' lawyers respond that many victims of serious accidents do not have the money to pay a lawyer by the hour to get legal representation and would be unable to gain redress for their injuries without the contingent fee.[74]

Plaintiffs' lawyers have a problem that defense lawyers retained by insurance companies are generally not faced with: finding clients. As a result plaintiffs' lawyers are much more likely to resort to advertising. Indeed, one cannot watch daytime television in urban areas of the United States without seeing several such advertisements, some of them in questionable taste.

Criminal Defense One specialty area that is almost always confined to small firms is criminal defense work. Privately retained defense counsel in criminal cases typically are sole or small-firm practitioners who limit their practice to such work. Often the lawyers who start such firms do so after they have gained experience as prosecutors or public defenders, discussed later in this chapter.[75] Most "street crime" defendants have little money and qualify for representation by a public defender. However many others do not qualify and must seek representation from the private bar. Also, some categories of crime — for example, "white collar" crimes, such as embezzlement, tax fraud, securities fraud, illegal currency transactions and "laundering" drug money — will typically involve defendants who have the means to pay for a lawyer.[76] Moreover, in areas where there is no universal public defender system, courts must appoint members of the private bar to represent indigent defendants.

---

73 *See* Chapter VII, p. 255.

74 In England, contingent fees are completely prohibited. But in contrast to the United States, where the parties must absorb their own costs, including attorney fees, the winning party in England has the right to obtain an order requiring the losing party to pay costs, including attorney fees. *See* Herbert M. Kritzer, *The English Rule*, 78 ABA JOURNAL 55 (November 1992).

75 *See* discussions *infra* p. 154 (public defenders) and p. 151 (prosecutors).

76 *See* KENNETH MANN, DEFENDING WHITE-COLLAR CRIME: A PORTRAIT OF ATTORNEYS AT WORK (Yale U. Press, New Haven, CT 1985) "White collar" refers to the fact that perpetrators of crimes of this type are the sort who wear white shirts to work. Such defendants "steal with the pen instead of the gun."

Family Law   Divorce and related family law matters are often the mainstays of sole and small firm practice. It is said that divorce cases "pay the rent," meaning that the fee in any given case is not that high, but the supply of clients is a steady one on which one can depend. But some small firms actually specialize in divorce and particularly in contested divorces. Large firms generally consider that divorce cases are not important enough to bother with because there is not much money involved. But in recent years, some of the larger firms in New York have begun to take divorces where both spouses have high-paying jobs and considerable property.[77]

Labor and Employment Law   Firms in this category often deal with issues related to unions and collective bargaining. As with the personal injury firms, labor firms can be "management-side" labor law firms or "union-side" labor law firms — both to avoid conflicts of interest and because of personal inclinations of the lawyers. Labor law firms advise management or unions about issues of union recognition and elections, assist in the collective bargaining process, advise on strikes or other labor unrest, and deal with grievances processed under collective bargaining agreements. Lawyers specializing in employment law have increasingly been occupied with a new form of claim by employees — claims for "wrongful discharge." Under this legal theory, employees in many situations are able to argue that they should not be fired without "just cause," generally based on an implied covenant of their employment contract.[78] Other areas related to employment that some firms have specialized in have been workmen's compensation (administrative remedies for job-related injury) and employment discrimination.[79]

"Boutique" Business Law Firms   Though small firms are less likely to represent corporate business clients, lawyers who are "refugees" from large business firms often form small firms specializing in corporate law. Because these small firms have experienced and capable corporate law specialists, they are able to attract "big name" clients and charge big firm fees. Accordingly, they are often called "boutique" firms. While "boutique" in French simply means a shop, in American English, it has come to mean a small fancy store selling expensive specialty goods. Often these "boutique" firms specialize in a particular kind of practice related to business, such as antitrust or securities regulation or representation of business corporations before administrative agencies. The growth of such firms has been accelerated by the changing practices of many large corporations seeking legal representation. As noted below, corporations have increasingly spread their work among several legal service providers, often looking for lower fees for the same service. For specialized matters particularly, a large corporation may be as likely to turn to a boutique firm, which will generally have smaller overhead costs than a large firm and therefore somewhat lower fees.

b. Large-Firm Practice

The Era of the Large Firm   In 1949, only five firms in the U.S. had more than 50 lawyers, by 1989 there were more than 287 in this category. Between 1977 and 1989

---

77   Divorce cases may not be handled on a contingency basis. *See* ABA MODEL RULES OF PROFESSIONAL RESPONSIBILITY Rule 1.5(d)(1). *But see Ballesteros v. Jones*, 1998 WL 794834 (Tex.App. 1998) (*en banc*) (contingent fee was not improper in action to establish existence of common law marriage). Even without contingent fees, however, a large amount of money at stake and high incomes mean that the parties to the divorce can spend relatively large amounts of money on lawyers in order to protect their share of the property or child custody rights.

78   *See* Chapter XV, pp. 573-575.

79   *See* Chapter XV, pp. 569-573.

the number of firms with more than *100* lawyers increased five times — from 47 to 245.[80] At the end of 1989 there were more than 100 firms in the United States that had more than 250 lawyers, and from that number, 15 firms had more than 500 lawyers and two had more than 1,000. The largest firm in the United States is Baker & McKenzie, founded in Chicago, which has forty-eight offices throughout the world. In 1992, 1,604 lawyers were working in all its offices.[81] If, as many thought 20 years ago, a "large firm" is one with more than 50 lawyers, then these are "super large" or "megafirms."[82]

Clientele   The largest firms all specialize in representing business corporations. Corporate practice includes both matters of corporate structure and business dealings of the corporation. Large corporate firms have various departments that specialize in tax law, antitrust law, real estate law, litigation, banking law, intellectual property, and labor law. Among the clients of these firms one can find the richest and most well-known corporations. In corporate practice, lawyers largely perform the role of advisor, organizer, and negotiator in business matters and draft the necessary documents related to business deals, but if litigation is necessary, the litigation department of the firm will become involved. When it is necessary to represent the company in administrative or criminal matters that the government has filed against it, there are specialists in these areas as well.

Firm Structure   Lawyers in firms that are partnerships are either partners or associates. In a professional corporation, they will be shareholders or associates.[83] Partners or shareholders own the firm and receive a percentage of the amount that the firm takes in every year. Associates are on salary. The ratio of associates to partners-shareholders is approximately one to one in the largest firms, though there may be more associates in some. The path by which an associate may become a partner or shareholder varies from firm to firm, but usually the decision is made between the fifth and the seventh year of an associate's work. The policy has been an "up-or-out" policy: either the associate becomes a partner or the associate is asked to leave.

Pay and Work Environment   Megafirm lawyers do well financially. In 1997, the median starting salary of lawyers in private firms was $55,000 a year, while the median starting salary in a large New York firm was $86,000 a year. In the large "Wall Street" firms in New York, the 1997 starting pay was more than $100,000. In Boston, the median was $75,000, in Cleveland, $58,000, in Minneapolis, $60,000, and in Seattle, $53,000. Partners in such firms make even more, of course, and the amount they receive depends on how well the firm performed that year. Some partners in large firms in large cities receive over $500,000 a year.[84]

---

80 *See* Stephanie Goldberg, *Then and Now: 75 Years of Change*, 76 A.B.A. JOURNAL 56 (January 1989).

81 The other firm with more than 1,000 lawyers was Jones, Day, Reavis & Pogue of Cleveland, Ohio (1,183 lawyers). These statistics and other information on super large firms are taken from the article *The National Law Journal 250*, NAT'L.L.J. (September 28, 1992).

82 Two recent books provide interesting accounts of the growth of the megafirms. *See* ROBERT NELSON, PARTNERS WITH POWER (U. of Cal. Press, Berkeley, Cal. 1988) and MARC GALANTER & THOMAS PALAY, TOURNAMENT OF LAWYERS (U. of Chicago Press, Chicago, Ill. 1990).

83 The limited liability of corporations is discussed in Chapter XV, p. 539. Professional corporations have limited liability for ordinary kinds of liability, but the lawyer-shareholders remain personally liable for any malpractice they commit.

84 84 ABA JOURNAL 28 (August, 1998). *But see supra* note 68 and *infra* Chapter XVI (income taxes).

Of course, in return for such pay, firms insist that associates and partners work very hard, usually over 60 hours a week and often on evenings and weekends. Often firms use a system under which associates are required to bill a certain number of hours a year. The number of "billable" hours required by firms with such a system is between 2,000 and 2,400 hours a year. Taking two weeks out for vacation, for the fifty working weeks in a year, 2,400 hours a year averages out to 48 hours a week. When one considers that lawyers may spend as much as 15-20% of their time on "non-billable" tasks, a person billing hours at this annual level is working rather hard. And there is pressure to bill even above these levels. In many firms, the number of hours billed is one of the most important criteria for partnership and compensation awarded to those already partner.[85]

The pay of new lawyers in the large firms seems like high pay, but the law firms, like good merchants, "buy low" and "sell high." Taking an average pay among large firms, a mid-level associate who makes $65,000 a year and submits 2,200 billable hours is being paid only about $29 an hour plus fringe benefits. If the average billing rate for the lawyer is even as low as $125, the 2,200 hours billed represent income of $275,000 to the firm.[86]

Prestige and Influence of Large Law Firms As just seen, "megafirm" lawyers are disproportionately better off financially than other lawyers. But more than money is involved. Senior partners of the largest firms often move in powerful governmental and political circles. They regularly serve in governmental positions when their political party is in power and are often tapped for special assignments, such as special counsel to the President or special prosecutors. Big firm lawyers are also disproportionately influential in the legal profession. The number of lawyers working in firms of over 50 lawyers comprises only 14.6% of private lawyers and only 10.5% of all lawyers. But senior lawyers from these firms serve with much greater frequency on bar association committees and commissions than sole practitioners or lawyers from smaller firms or in-house counsel. Both because of the high pay and the elite status of large law firms, they attract some of the more able graduates of the most prestigious law schools.

Recent Difficulties for Large Firms From 1977 to 1990, large firms continued to hire and promote associates because the general business climate was good and companies needed representation. This was the primary reason for the explosion in size of corporate law firms. In turn, to keep all their new associates and partners busy, firms aggressively sought work in order to utilize their growing resources and personnel. However, the economy declined substantially in the period 1990-1993 and this brought changes in large corporate firms. Many cut down on hiring new associates. Others fired or laid off associates and even partners and shareholders whom they believed were not sufficiently productive. Some large firms even went bankrupt.

---

85 Things were not always this way. In the 1960s and 1970s, associates were generally expected to bill 1,600 and partners 1,300. *See* Goldberg, *supra* note 80. It is not surprising in view of this that a "satisfaction" survey seeking to determine how happy lawyers were in their jobs found that of all lawyers in the given regions, lawyers in large firms in the Northeastern and Western United States were the least satisfied with their work situation. They scored 67% and 63% satisfied, respectively. The lawyers with the highest job satisfaction rates were lawyers working in medium-sized firms in the west and southwest. NAT'L. L.J. S2 (May 28, 1990).

86 In 1993, the median hourly billing rate for an associate and partner respectively varied from $90 and $120 per hour in cities of a population less than 100,000 to $120 and $180 an hour in cities with a population of over 1 million.

While the economy has picked up in recent years, there have been two lasting legacies of these difficult years for some large firms. The first has been that partners and shareholders have had to become not just good lawyers, but also good at "rain-making" — attracting new business to the firm. For some associates, partnership became more elusive as some firms created a new position between the positions of partner or shareholder on the one hand and associate on the other. These new positions, generally called "senior associate" or "non-participating partner," are salaried positions that are not intended to lead to an ownership interest in the firm. They are for associates who are "only" good lawyers.

A second result is that bad economic times have made corporate clients more discriminating consumers of legal services. To save costs and improve the quality of the representation they get for the money they spend, corporations have used their own in-house lawyers as sophisticated "shoppers" for legal services, actively negotiating prices and terms of legal representation.[87] No longer can large corporate firms count on being retained as the exclusive provider of legal services for a corporation. Instead, many corporations have switched to contracting with several different firms on an *ad hoc* basis for discrete tasks or cases. They then decide whether to go back to that firm based on how that firm performed for them. And when corporate firms are retained, they can no longer expect that their bills will be paid without question. Clients are much more likely to insist on itemized bills and to require that the firms justify the tasks listed and hours charged.[88]

c. Non-Traditional Forms for Delivery of Private Legal Services

"Legal Clinics" and Other Low-Cost Standardized Legal Services Legal clinics as understood here should not to be confused with the teaching clinics in law schools. The term "clinic" has also been used to describe law offices that specialize in delivery of relatively routine legal services at below-market rates for individuals. Typical types of cases handled are divorce, bankruptcy, real estate transactions, wills and social security cases.

Below-market rates are achieved through a high volume of clients, the routine nature of the services rendered, fixed-rate fees, and standardized and streamlined office procedures.[89] Clinics attract the necessary high volume of clients by means of advertising, convenient location in such non-traditional locations as shopping malls, and projecting an informal office atmosphere. They are targeted at middle-income clients who cannot afford traditional rates of lawyers, but are not poor enough to qualify for government-sponsored legal assistance.[90]

The name "clinic" has gradually been disappearing in reaction to the public perception, because of law school clinics, that the word "clinic" is associated with poor people. In addition, some smaller traditional firms and solo practitioners, in reaction to competition from clinics, have changed their procedures to imitate some of the pricing and advertising characteristics of clinics. Consequently, what is and what is not a "clinic" has become harder to determine.

---

87 In-house counsel are discussed *infra* pp. 148-149.

88 This practice is so widespread that a separate business of auditing legal bills has sprung up. *See* "You Charged How Much?", 85 ABA JOURNAL 20 (1999).

89 *See* GERALD SINGSEN, REPORT ON THE SURVEY OF LEGAL CLINICS AND ADVERTISING LAW FIRMS, ABA Special Committee on Delivery of Legal Services (American Bar Association 1990).

90 Legal services to the poor is discussed *infra* pp. 152-153.

Two national legal services firms that use the clinic-style approach are Jacoby & Meyers and Hyatt Legal Services. Begun with a great flourish in the wake of the Supreme Court's ruling legalizing advertising in 1977, these firms have contracted somewhat since the late 1980s, but are still a substantial presence. Today Hyatt Legal Services has 112 offices in 23 states and a lawyer staff of 302. Jacoby & Meyers has 150 offices in 6 states with 305 lawyers.

Group Discount and Pre-Paid Legal Services Plans These sorts of plans were an outgrowth of the consumer movement of the 1960s and, like legal clinics, seek to make reasonably priced legal services available for middle-income people. Like some other areas of the law related to the legal profession, group legal services were made possible only by decisions of the Supreme Court striking down restrictive state bar regulation on constitutional grounds.[91]

Under a group discount plan, members of a group obtain legal services at below market rates. Under one of the largest of these plans, the Union Privilege Legal Services Plan sponsored by AFL-CIO labor union, union members are eligible for discounts and some free services from a panel of lawyers selected from small firms by the plan administrators. Limitations of the plan are that the eligible person must still go the lawyer's office and pay the discounted price. More important, the person must be able to recognize whether it is necessary to go to a lawyer in the first place — a decision that itself often requires legal advice.

Pre-paid legal services plans are designed to mitigate these problems. This form for delivery of legal services is basically a form of legal insurance that pays for legal services. It has been the joint effort of insurance companies, consumer groups and the organized bar and has grown at a phenomenal rate in the last few years. Such insurance is common in some countries, but has only recently developed in the United States.

The basic benefit under pre-paid plans is unlimited legal advice and consultation by telephone by calling a lawyer's office on an "800" toll-free number. In addition, some plans provide for certain simple document preparation or letter-writing and informal negotiation. If further assistance is required, the same sort of discount arrangement used in group plans is available. Some plans, such as the United Auto Workers' plan employs its own staff attorneys to handle certain routine consumer and real estate matters.

Prepaid plans are usually offered by labor unions or employers. In addition, some credit card companies have been offering a limited legal-advice-only plan to credit card holders for a small monthly fee. It is estimated by an industry group that in mid-1991, there were 17 million Americans covered by some type of prepaid legal services plan.[92]

2. In-House Counsel

In-house counsel are lawyers who constitute a legal department within the corporation and represent that corporation. They must be admitted to the bar of the state in which they are working. The in-house counsel in charge of the legal depart-

---

91 *See NAACP v. Button*, 371 U.S. 415 (1963) (1st Amendment freedom of association protects right of organization to obtain legal counsel for its members); *United Transportation Union v. State Bar of Michigan*, 401 U.S. 576 (1971) (state court injunction against union providing legal services to its members violates 1st Amendment right of access to courts).

92 *See* ABA Task Force Report, *supra* note 1, at 68.

ment of a corporation usually is called the "general counsel" and is often also a vice president of the corporation.

Work   In one sense, in-house counsel have a practice very similar to that of lawyers in corporate firms: they work primarily as advisors and organizers, draft documents and negotiate for the business corporation and, increasingly, handle litigation. However, they have a broader role — that of "managing the legal function of the business enterprise."[93] As already noted above, an increasingly important part of this special management function is the task of negotiating and supervising the relationship of the corporation with "outside counsel," the law firms that represent the corporation in matters that in-house counsel do not handle.

Working Conditions   Many consider that the job of in-house counsel is among the most pleasant forms of private law practice. Salaries are quite adequate: a new lawyer on the legal staff of a large company receives about $50,000 a year and a general counsel could receive from $150,000 to $430,000. It is reported that the vice-president and general counsel for General Electric earned $933,333 plus a $1.1 million bonus in 1996. But what is more important than money from the point of view of a lawyer who is comparing this with practice in a corporate firm, the average in-house counsel rarely has to work in the evenings, weekends or holidays. In part for this reason, many members of the legal staff of companies are former partners or associates of corporate firms, many of whom were undoubtedly looking at least in part for a more relaxed work schedule. In 1988, 75% of the general counsels and 50% of the associates in the legal department of companies worked earlier in large corporate firms.[94] But a lawyer who joins the law department of a corporation does not necessarily avoid all the problems associated with the large size of the typical corporate firm. Although many legal departments of corporations comprise only a few lawyers (for example, a small bank or hospital may have only one or two lawyers), others are larger. In 1988 the legal department of the American Telephone and Telegraph Company had more than 500 lawyers.

Moreover, in recent years, the responsibilities of in-house counsel have grown. Corporations have begun to use in-house counsel more and outside counsel less in an effort to economize, particularly in the area of litigation. The fees charged by the large corporate firms have increased so much in the last few years that companies view it as more efficient to have full-time lawyers as employees.

Notwithstanding in-house counsel performing legal services previously performed by outside counsel, some areas of practice have remained regular candidates for referral to outside counsel. Among them are international legal matters (particularly European Community work), patent and trademark cases, environmental issues, labor law, mergers and acquisitions, bankruptcy and antitrust.[95]

Potential Conflicts of Loyalty   The more active participation of in-house counsel in litigation and generally in contested matters has occasionally led to conflicts between companies and their in-house counsel. Employees of a company are obligated to be loyal to their employer, but when those employees work as lawyers, they must follow the rules of professional responsibility for lawyers. Among those responsibilities is the duty to decline to represent a client or assert a position in a

---

93   J.D. DONNELL, THE CORPORATE COUNSEL: A ROLE STUDY 27-28 (Indiana U. 1970).

94   These and other statistics are taken from *5th Annual Price, Waterhouse Law Department Survey* (Price, Waterhouse Service Group 1988).

95   ABA TASK FORCE REPORT, *supra* note 1, at 94.

lawsuit whenever the lawyer is convinced that position is groundless.[96] It is much easier for a lawyer in a law firm to decline to represent a client or to refuse to take particular action in a case than it is for an employee in-house counsel. Sometimes the company fires its in-house counsel for refusal to handle a matter. In the last few years, occasions have arisen where courts have awarded damages to in-house counsel for wrongful termination where it was based on just such a conflict with the company.[97]

3. Government Service

a. Federal Government Service

U.S. Attorney General The legal department of the federal government is one of the component parts of the executive branch and is called the Department of Justice. The head of the Department of Justice is the Attorney General of the United States. The Attorney General is a member of the President's cabinet and is nominated by the President with the advice and consent of the Senate, as required by the Constitution.

U.S. Attorneys The legal powers of the Attorney General and Department of Justice are carried out primarily by local United States Attorneys, sometimes called District Attorneys. The United States Attorneys oversee 91 districts throughout the 50 states and the District of Columbia. Small and sparsely populated states each comprise one district, but the majority of states have two or more districts. These districts are the same districts that define the territories of the federal district courts.[98]

A U.S. Attorney, like the Attorney General, is a political appointee nominated by the President and confirmed by the Senate. When a President of a different party is elected, it is expected that the U.S. Attorney will resign so that the new President can appoint someone from the new President's party. However, the U.S. Attorney is sometimes court-appointed. When President Bush left office, there were 77 U.S. Attorneys who were appointed by him. President Clinton asked for and received their resignations. The rest of the U.S. Attorney's posts were held by court appointees and they were not asked to resign at that time. It happens occasionally that the President declines to change a particular U.S. Attorney despite the fact that the U.S. Attorney was appointed by a previous President of the opposing political party.

Assistant U.S. Attorneys serve under the United States Attorney and carry out the day-to-day work in district offices. Personnel decisions regarding assistant U.S. Attorneys are not generally made on an explicit political basis, but the ability to work under the policies of the U.S. Attorney and division chiefs in the office is important and those policies may have some political overtones. In many U.S. Attorneys offices, except for the top jobs, there are few turnovers in personnel.[99]

Work of U.S. Attorneys United States Attorneys may file criminal charges only for violations of federal criminal law, not state law. Examples of typical federal criminal cases include robbery of a federally insured bank, assault on a federal agent, criminal conduct on a federal reservation, fraud by way of interstate telephone lines, antitrust violations, fraud in sale of securities, violations of federal narcotics laws, possession

---

96 *See* discussion of lawyer ethics related to adversary representation *infra* p. 171-174.

97 *See Mourad v. Automobile Club Ins. Assoc.*, 465 N.W.2d 395 (Mich.App.1991). Other courts have refused to allow such suits. *See, e.g., Balla v. Gambro, Inc.*, 584 N.E.2d 104 (Ill. 1991).

98 *See* Chapter V, p. 170.

99 In *Rutan v. Republican Party of Illinois*, 497 U.S. 62 (1990) and *Branti v. Finkel*, 445 U.S. 507 (1980), the Supreme Court declared that hiring or firing governmental employees according to party affiliation (except for the highest officials whose personal loyalty is essential) violates the First Amendment by penalizing political affiliation and beliefs.

of certain weapons, and embezzlement of federal funds. As discussed in Chapter I, there is much overlap of state and federal crimes and a violation of federal criminal law in many situations will also be a violation of state criminal law. In the past, the U.S. Attorney in such situations has deferred to state investigation and prosecution in many instances. However, in recent years, there has been much more "federalization" of law enforcement for one category of "ordinary" street crime — illegal sale and distribution of drugs.[100]

Civil actions by or against the United States are also handled by U.S. Attorneys and their assistants or of by lawyers from the Department of Justice in Washington. Lawsuits against the United States and its officials are permitted in many instances.[101] There are also civil actions for judicial review of the actions of various federal administrative agencies. Judicial review of administrative claims for disability insurance benefits available to permanently disabled workers constitutes a large volume of the cases. There are also matters that arise out of contract disputes with companies working on government projects. Civil suits may also contest the constitutionality of a particular statute, regulation or action of the federal government.[102]

Other Federal Government Lawyers In many other departments of the federal government, there are lawyers who handle the specialized legal business of those agencies. Large employers of lawyers include, for example, the Environmental Protection Agency, the Federal Trade Commission, the Internal Revenue Service, the Securities and Exchange Commission, and the National Labor Relations Board. Even the Central Intelligence Agency employs lawyers.

Pay Federal government attorneys receive good salaries, though they are less than those of many private lawyers. U.S. Attorneys themselves make $118,400. supervisory assistant U.S. attorneys make up to $109,000, senior litigation counsel up to $105,050 and non-supervisory attorneys $35,800 to $95,750. The Attorney General of the United States makes $148,400.

b. State Attorneys General

The Office In state government, just as in the federal, a lawyer called the Attorney General is the head of the legal department of the executive branch and represents the state both in and out of court. But most attorneys general of states enjoy a greater degree of independence from their governors than their federal colleague enjoys from the President. In a majority of states, the attorneys general are elected by way of a general vote of the citizenry and may not be dismissed by the governor. Often they are members of a different political party than the governor.

Work The attorney general of a state represents the state in all civil matters and gives advice to officials, legislators and agencies of the state. In this capacity, state attorneys general often have an additional way to affect the public policy of the state: they often may exercise independent judgment in determining what the state's legal position should be and may decline to assert positions in litigation with which they disagree. In addition, state attorneys general often perform quasi-judicial functions

---

100 Charles Bonner, *Federalization of Crime: Too Much of a Good Thing?*, 32 U. RICH. L. REV. 905 (1998). Prosecution by both state and federal authorities is also a possibility and does not violate the 5th Amendment's right against double jeopardy. *See* Chapter VIII, pp. 296-299.

101 *See* Chapter VI, p. 216. In 1990 alone, there were 787 suits filed against the United States and plaintiffs received approximately $304 million in judgments and settlements.

102 The circumstances under which the United States can be sued are discussed in Chapter VI, pp. 215-216.

by issuing formal attorney general opinions.[103] Unlike the federal Attorney General, the attorneys general of states do not prosecute or supervise prosecution of ordinary criminal cases. In most states, such prosecutions are handled by local prosecutors, discussed next, who are independent of the state attorney general's office.[104]

Pay The pay of attorneys general varies considerably from state to state. The California and New York Attorneys General receive $107,100 and $110,000 respectively, while the Attorney General of South Dakota makes $71,972. The pay of lawyers on the staff of the attorney general of a state varies from state to state, but the better paid receive approximately what Assistant United States Attorneys make.

c. Local Prosecutors

Nature of the Office Although local prosecutors act in the name of the state, they are elected by and responsible to the citizens of a given county, are paid their salary by that county, and are not under the supervision of the attorney general of the state. This reflects a policy that the population of the locale suffering the effects of crimes should be able to express their preferences about enforcement policies through their choice of the lawyers who will prosecute those crimes.[105]

Work Criminal statutes of a state include all of the ordinary forms of criminal activity and the job of the local prosecutor in large cities is enormous. This does not necessarily mean that the typical assistant prosecutor is always trying cases in court. Just as with civil cases, more than 90% of criminal cases are settled by agreement of the parties. In the majority of criminal cases, this means that the accused pleads guilty to the charge, usually as a result of a plea bargain.[106] Local prosecutors also have responsibilities in enforcing quasi-criminal laws, such as actions to terminate parental rights for abuse or neglect of children, actions to enforce child support orders, and suits to establish paternity. In some states, prosecutors are even required to make an appearance in all divorce actions where children are involved to insure that the interests of the children are protected. In some areas, prosecutors are active in consumer protection activities, investigating and mediating disputes between consumers and merchants regarding sales of goods or services.

Pay The pay of assistant prosecutors varies widely. A beginning assistant prosecutor in Jefferson County, Kentucky, receives $23,000 per year, while his or her counterpart in Humboldt County, Nevada receives $46,679. The chief prosecutor in Door County, Wisconsin, received $65,494, while the chief in Orange County, California, is paid $26,214. In sparsely populated counties of many states, there is only one lawyer who works as prosecutor. In some of those counties, that single local prosecutor works as a prosecutor only part time and has a private practice in addition.

d. City and County Attorneys

The local prosecutors just discussed handle only criminal and quasi-criminal matters on behalf of the state as a rule. Because of this, counties and cities need another set of lawyers to represent their interests in civil cases and in criminal cases

---

103 *See* Chapter II, p. 77.

104 However, in the majority of states the office of the attorney general has responsibility for criminal appeals and in half of the states the attorney general's office has the authority to initiate prosecutions at least in some instances. *See* BOOK OF THE STATES: 1998-1999 EDITION (The Council of State Governments, Lexington, Ky.).

105 Unlike prosecutors in some other countries, prosecutors in the U.S. are not required to prosecute every violation of the law. *See* Chapter VIII, p. 261.

106 Plea bargaining is discussed in Chapter VIII, pp. 268-270.

involving violations of municipal ordinances. These lawyers are called city attorneys and county attorneys. In large cities, there are large legal departments under the direction of a city attorney. A majority of counties and small towns do not have enough legal business to justify having a full-time lawyer on staff. Instead, they employ an outside attorney from a private firm when advice or representation in court is necessary.

4. Public Interest Practice

The lawyers who work for organizations devoted to public interest practice are not numerous, but they are important to the legal profession and society because much of the litigation and other activities they engage in serve to reform the law. Further, to the extent that public interest lawyers represent clients and points of view that are unpopular or provide representation to persons unable to afford it, they remind the profession one of its highest duties.[107]

a. Legal Services Assistance in Civil Matters

Development of Legal Services Given the complicated character of law and the adversary system of litigation, the assistance of a lawyer is essential in most cases as a practical matter. Persons unable to afford a lawyer then are at a severe disadvantage when dealing with a legal problem. This has led to the establishment and growth of organizations, called "legal services organizations" or "legal aid societies" that are dedicated to providing free civil legal services to the poor.[108]

Legal aid societies have existed since 1876, but they were limited by the fact of their reliance on voluntary donations of money by the public and volunteer efforts of private lawyers. In a scathing report issued in 1917, Reginald Heber Smith reviewed the state of legal services for the poor for the Carnegie Foundation and concluded that existing efforts were grossly inadequate even for minimum access to the legal system for the poor. However, the first major effort to try to meet the need did not come until 1964, when President Lyndon B. Johnson's "war on poverty" included funding for such legal aid societies as an essential part of anti-poverty efforts. In that year, legislation was passed by Congress which appropriated several million dollars to the task of establishing new and strengthening old legal aid societies.

Work Legal services lawyers handle principally two types of cases. Most cases are everyday matters: divorces, custody of children, welfare, consumer disputes, housing (particularly disputes landlord-tenant relations), employment disputes, and so on. The other category of cases consists of so-called "test cases," many of them "class actions" or cases in which a single plaintiff is allowed to represent a group of persons similarly situated.[109] A test case is a case that is brought for the purpose of changing the law, generally to broaden constitutional and other important rights. In one case, the constitutional right to notice and a hearing before termination of public benefits was established.[110] In another, the right of a tenant to withhold rent if the

---

107 *See infra* p. 162, where the *pro bono* ethical duties of lawyers are discussed. It should be kept in mind that many cases handled by private lawyers could be considered "public interest" cases, such as judgments that serve to gain redress for personal injuries caused by corporations or the government. What distinguishes public interest lawyers from others is that they represent clients principally out of non-material motivations and characteristically limit their practice to such representation.

108 Legal services for the poor in criminal cases are provided by public defender programs and private attorneys appointed by the court. *See infra* p. 154.

109 Class actions are described in Chapter VII, p. 225.

110 *See Goldberg v. Kelly*, 397 U.S. 254 (1970), striking down this policy as violative of the due process clause of the Fourteenth Amendment. *Goldberg* is discussed in Chapter VII, p. 200.

landlord has not made necessary repairs to the property was won.[111] In recent years, the frequency of test case litigation has declined as courts and the general atmosphere in the country have become more conservative and there has been more concentration on efficient delivery of everyday legal services.[112]

Funding   By 1981, the amount of the appropriations to the Legal Services Corporation, the agency set up in 1974 to administer legal services programs, had reached $300 million for 1,200 organizations, 5,000 lawyers and 2,500 paralegal assistants.[113] But in the 1980s, the administration of President Ronald Reagan tried several times to completely eliminate federal funding for legal services.[114] Congress prevented its abolition, but agreed to cut funding by a third and thereafter raised the appropriation every year by only a very small amount. The amount of appropriations for 1994 was $376 million and local programs handled 1.5 million cases in 1993.[115] By 1999 the level of funding had dropped to $300 million. Today the Legal Services Corporation funds 4,800 full-time staff attorneys and 2,000 paralegal assistants. Local and non-legal services federal money fund 2,369 additional offices. In addition, private lawyers provided volunteer and reduced-fee *pro bono* services under referral programs set up by legal services and under more than 600 other *pro bono* projects.[116] Despite funding setbacks, legal services programs have the solid support of the organized bar and are established part of the legal landscape.[117]

b. Representation of Indigent Defendants in Criminal Cases

Criminal defendants have a 6th Amendment right to government-provided counsel in all criminal prosecutions in which they face the prospect of being jailed.[118] The government's initial method of discharging this constitutional duty was to assign members of the private bar to represent defendants on an *ad hoc* basis. However, in many parts of the country, federal and state authorities sought to make representation of the poor in criminal cases more effective and its cost more predictable by establishing a system of "public defenders." Under this system, full time lawyers are paid a salary to defend all or most criminal defendants who come before the local courts.

Public defenders working exclusively on criminal cases do not often find themselves involved in class actions.[119] However, important questions of general applicability are decided in criminal appellate cases, in which public defenders often participate. Some states even have a separate defender office that handles criminal

---

111 *Brown v. Southall Realty Co.*, 237 A.2d 834 (D.C.App. 1968).

112 See Alan W. Houseman, *A Short Review of Past Poverty Law Advocacy*, CLEARINGHOUSE REV. 1514 (April 1990). In addition, restrictions have been added by Congress, including prohibitions on legal services lawyers handling desegregation or abortion cases. *See generally* 42 U.S.C.A. §2996f(b).

113 Paralegals are legal workers who do not have a law school education and who do routine lawyering tasks under the supervision of a lawyer. They are widely used in legal services offices and in large law firms.

114 It is said that a good part of President Reagan's dislike for legal services programs was traceable to his experience as Governor of California when he was sued by a legal services organization for taking alleged illegal action in cutting California welfare benefits to the poor.

115 Legal Service Corporation Annual Audit (1994).

116 ABA TASK FORCE REPORT, *supra* note 1, at 53.

117 For a less optimistic view, *see* ABEL, *supra* note 1, at 132-134.

118 *See* Chapter VIII, pp. 285, 293.

119 *But see Gerstein v. Pugh*, 420 U.S. 103 (1975) (class action ordering state sheriff to free all prisoners for whom there has not been a probable cause hearing promptly after their arrest). *See* Chapter VIII, p. 261.

appeals exclusively.[120] But the primary contribution of public defenders to the public interest is found in the collective effect of their representation of individual clients. One study of public defenders in Chicago shows that they represent their clients in court vigorously. However, the perception of the quality of their representation by the public and their client population is more negative.[121]

c. Private Public Interest Organizations

Development of Private Public Interest Groups The "test case" approach to the problems of disadvantaged persons was first employed by civil rights lawyers working for private public interest organizations, who first brought such suits during the struggles against racial segregation in the 1950s. Foremost among those organizations is the NAACP Legal Defense and Education Fund, which handled perhaps the most important test case in history, *Brown v. Board of Education.*[122]

The ACLU as an Example The organization best known for using test cases is the American Civil Liberties Union, or ACLU, founded in 1924. In tens of thousands of cases touching on issues of constitutional rights in the Supreme Court and the lower federal and state courts for the last fifty years, lawyers from the ACLU have appeared either as lawyers for a party or in the capacity of *amicus curiae.*[123] The ACLU has comparatively few lawyers on staff, but has great influence because it is more than just a law firm. It has 250,000 mainly non-lawyer "members." More than 10,000 of these members work as volunteers in offices in all the United States, publicizing civil rights issues and working on concrete projects that concern civil liberties issues in their regions and cities. In addition, the ACLU has more than 5,000 volunteer lawyers.

The work of the ACLU is controversial even among supporters of civil liberties and indeed among its own members. In the 1970s, it represented the American Nazi party when the town of Skokie, Illinois prohibited the Nazis from organizing a demonstration. Skokie was thought by all concerned to be a special location for the demonstration because it was a city where many survivors of World War II Nazi concentration camps lived. When the Nazis were unable to find a private lawyer who would agree to represent them in their efforts to obtain a parade permit, the ACLU filed suit on their behalf and won.[124] The ACLU represented the Nazis just as vigorously as they defended Communists in the 1950s during a time when many of them were being persecuted for their views. In several situations lately, the position of the ACLU in favor of unlimited freedom of speech was subject to criticism by the public and cost it some of its membership.[125]

Other Groups Other public interest organizations, such as the Sierra Club and the Natural Resources Defense Council, fight for ecological causes. There are also

---

120 Criminal defendants have a right to counsel on appeal as well as at trial. *See* Chapter VIII, p. 302.

121 *See* LISA MCINTYRE, THE PUBLIC DEFENDER: THE PRACTICE OF LAW IN THE SHADOW OF REPUTE (U. Chicago Press 1987).

122 347 U.S. 483 (1954). *Brown* held that racial segregation in public schools violates the equal protection clause of the Fourteenth Amendment of the Constitution. *See* Chapter IX, p. 330. For a history of *Brown* and the NAACP's litigation strategy regarding civil rights, *see* RICHARD KLUGER, SIMPLE JUSTICE (Knopf, New York 1976).

123 An *amicus curiae* is not a formal party to the case, but an individual or organization that is permitted to file a brief on one or another side of an issue in a case in which it has an interest. *See* Chapter II, p. 41 note 26.

124 *Collin v. Smith*, 578 F.2d 1197 (7th Cir. 1978). *See* Chapter IX, p. 344

125 For an interesting history of the ACLU that discusses its difficulties with support for some of its positions, *see* SAMUEL WALKER, IN DEFENSE OF AMERICAN LIBERTIES: A HISTORY OF THE ACLU (Oxford U. Press 1990).

groups organized around issues of women's rights, consumer protection, the disabled, education, mass media, health care, children's rights and welfare. Historically, most public interest law firms have represented "liberal" or "left" points of view. But in recent years, organizations of different political persuasions have been formed. For example, the Mountain States Legal Foundation is dedicated to protecting "free enterprise." Similarly, the Washington Legal Foundation and the Pacific Legal Foundation have been active in recent cases.[126]

Pay of Public Interest Lawyers Lawyers who work for either publicly funded or private public interest organizations earn relatively low salaries in comparison with lawyers practicing in private firms. A beginning lawyer in a legal aid society can expect to be paid from $25,000 to $35,000 per year. After five years, that pay might be increased to approximately $35,000 to $45,000, with directors of programs making perhaps as much as $50,000 to $70,000. The pay of a lawyer at the national office of the American Civil Liberties Union in New York varies from $28,700 for a starting salary to $71,800 for the top salary. Considering the fact that living in New York is very expensive and comparing this amount to a beginning associate in a Wall Street firm, this is low pay.[127]

Obviously, lawyers in public interest organizations feel that money is not the most important part of their work. And, despite the fact that high salaries and prestige usually go together, public interest lawyers fighting for civil liberties, rights of minorities or the ecosystem enjoy considerable respect in the eyes of the public.

D. Minorities and Women in the Legal Profession

The Changing Face of the Legal Profession Recent years have seen a great influx of racial minorities and women into the legal profession. In 1960, only 3.5% of all lawyers were women and only 1% of lawyers were black. Today, women comprise approximately 22% of lawyers and blacks comprise 3.3%. A signal that more change may be in store is found in the fact that fully 42.5% of present day law students are women and 12% of the current law school students are black. Treatment of minorities and women in the legal profession has changed for the better over the years, but is still a problem in a profession which for many years has been considered almost exclusively male and white. For example, partnership statistics show women account for only 14.2% of partners and blacks account for only 1%.[128]

Racial and Ethnic Minorities As the profession began to admit women and racial and ethnic minorities in greater numbers in the 1950s, many large firms continued to hire only white males of Anglo-Saxon origin. Black, Hispanic and Jewish lawyers, and generally lawyers from all the immigrant families that came to the United States in the first half of the 20th century, went to work as sole practitioners, for the government, or in small or medium sized firms.[129] The situation for hiring minorities and women

---

126 *Keller v. California*, discussed *supra* p. 138, and *Nollan v. California Coastal Commission*, 483 U.S. 825 (1987), discussed in Chapter XII, p. 450, were sponsored and argued in the Supreme Court by lawyers from the conservative Pacific Legal Foundation.

127 Even the conservative Pacific Legal Foundation pays beginning lawyers only $30,000, though it recently raised its top lawyer's salary to $150,000.

128 Source: National Association of Law Placement. The firms in counted were the 40,000 firms listed in the 1997-1998 National Directory of Legal Employers. For a history of minority admissions to law schools, *see* Edward J. Littlejohn and Leonard S. Rabinowitz, *Black Enrollment in Law Schools: Forward to the Past?*, 12 T. MARSHALL L. REV. 415 (1987). For a suggestion that the presence of excluded groups may result in changes beyond the legal profession, *see* Carrie Menkel-Meadow, *Excluded Voices: Excluded Voices in the Legal Profession Making New Voices in the Law*, 42 U. MIAMI L. REV. 29 (1987).

129 *See generally* ABEL, *supra* note 1, at 85-87, 99-108.

has improved considerably in the last 25 years. The main reason for the change was that Congress passed the Civil Rights Act of 1964. That law prohibits discrimination based on race, sex, or ethnic origin in the hiring, promotion or conditions of work of employees of all private institutions and businesses and provides a right to sue and receive monetary compensation from employers who violate the law.[130]

Women Lawyers Discrimination against women is more complicated because women have for years now been among the best graduates of the best law schools.[131] The hiring situation for women was not always as good. Up until the last quarter of the 19th century, women were prohibited from becoming lawyers in many states. The Supreme Court upheld the constitutionality of that prohibition in 1873 in *Bradwell v. Illinois*, with one justice explaining that "the natural and proper timidity and delicacy which belongs to the female sex unfits it" for law practice.[132] Columbia Law School Dean and later Chief Justice Harlan F. Stone proclaimed in 1927 that women would be admitted to Columbia Law School "over my dead body." Harvard Law School barred women from enrolling until 1950, Washington and Lee Law School barred them until 1972. In the 1970s, though, women began enrolling in substantial numbers.

Yet, as noted above, not many women become partners. And surveys show that they are consistently paid less. Raw data from a recent study showed that, while women who graduated in 1970 started out earning 98% of what their male counterparts earned, after 22 years their pay had shrunk to only 65% of what male 1970 graduates earned. Part of this discrepancy results from choice of type of legal job (more women than men work in public interest jobs) and that women experience more work interruptions than men, but even accounting for these factors, for women in private firms 29% and 37% of the gender wage gap remains unexplained.[133]

Many believe that the whole system of promotion and admission to partnership in a law firm works against women achieving partnership. Partnership selection takes place usually before the seventh year an associate's work. And, as already related, in order to become a partner in many firms, one must bill many hours and work many more. In addition, lawyers are expected to make efforts to bring in new clients for the firm. All this takes up much of the associate's evenings and weekends. For many women, the first 7 years after they finish law school (from the ages of 24 to 31 usually) are also the time when they begin to have children, if they do not already have them. Even in families with relatively progressive views, child care and domestic chores are still done principally by women. In addition, at least the child care part is often desired by women who wish to have a closer relationship to their children than would be permitted were to be gone many evenings and weekends.[134]

---

130 *See* Title VII of the Civil Rights Act of 1964, 42 U.S.C.A. §2000e *et seq.* Title VII is discussed in Chapter XV, pp. 569-573. While Title VII has always applied to initial hiring of associates, it was only in 1984 that the Supreme Court made it clear that Title VII applied to *partnership* decisions in law firms. *See Hishon v. King & Spalding*, 467 U.S. 69 (1984).

131 *See generally* ABEL, *supra* note 1, at 90-99; Patricia M. Wald, *Breaking the Glass Ceiling: Will We Ever Rid the Legal Profession of the "Ugly Residue of Gender Discrimination?,"* 16 HUMAN RTS. 40 (1989). *See also* Nancy Blodgett, Whatever Happened to the Class of '81, 74 A.B.A.J. 56 (1988).

132 83 U.S. 130 (1872) (Bradley, J. concurring). *See* Chapter IX, p. 335.

133 Wynn R. Huang, *Gender Differences in the Earnings of Lawyers*, 30 COLUM. J.L. & SOC. PROBS. 267 (1997).

134 *See* David L. Chambers, *Accommodation and Satisfaction: Women and Men Lawyers and the Balance of Work and Family*, 14 LAW & SOC. INQUIRY 251 (1989) (showing great career and life satisfaction of women who combined career and family life).

A recent suggestion for the problem of balancing career goals and motherhood has been through some version of what has been termed the "mommy track."[135] Under this option, women could arrange alternative work patterns utilizing flexible hours, periods of extended leave and telecommuting. But they would be on a separate track to remain a "permanent" associate rather than become a partner. Some have praised the "mommy track" idea as offering a feasible alternative for women who desire to have a semi-normal relationship with their children, while others have criticized it as institutionalizing "second-class citizen" treatment of women in the firm. It may even spark tensions with male counterparts who desire some form of a "daddy track." However, despite the flaws of a formally recognized "mommy track," some firms recognize the benefit of offering some of its features to women in order to recruit and retain good women lawyers.

Aside from the problems just discussed, women lawyers in law firms face a male-oriented atmosphere and social standards. A common complaint is that men in firms spend their social time with other men and make no effort to include women in their network of informal associations. While these "old boys" associations are ostensibly social, the attachments and interactions that result clearly spill over into work.

E. Legal Ethics

1. Regulating the Legal Profession: Sources of Regulation

The last several decades have witnessed an increase in public and professional interest in the ethics and conduct of the legal profession in the United States.[136] Part of this can be attributed to the dramatic increase in the number of lawyers and part of it to the fact that so many lawyers were implicated in the Watergate scandal of the Nixon Administration.[137] In the United States, the conduct of lawyers is subject to regulation from three sources: the judicial branch, self-regulation by the organized bar, and increasing, albeit indirect, regulation through private malpractice actions.

Role of the Judiciary As discussed earlier, the ultimate power of regulation of the profession generally resides in the supreme courts of the states. The judiciary is deemed to have inherent power and the primary role in regulating the legal profession. The connection between legal practice and the judiciary is seen in the common reference to lawyers as "officers of the court." One direct regulatory tool of courts is their power to hold a lawyer in "contempt" or to institute disciplinary proceedings for misconduct. Recently the primacy of judicial control over the profession has been questioned since a high percentage of lawyers today — especially those in large corporate firms — are "office lawyers" who never appear in court. However, much of the power of the judiciary over the profession has been delegated to the profession itself, where "office lawyers" are well-represented.[138]

Self-Regulation Consistent with a long tradition of self-regulation, the ABA has had a strong role in determining the ethical standards of the profession. In 1908, it

---

135 This notion was spawned by an article in the Harvard Business Review. Felice N. Schwartz, *Management Women and the New Facts of Life*, HARV. BUS. REV. 65 (1989).

136 A standard text for a course on professional responsibility is STEPHEN GILLERS, REGULATION OF LAWYERS: PROBLEMS OF LAW AND ETHICS, 5TH ED. (Aspen 1998). A standard though dated hornbook is WOLFRAM *supra* note 1. A student text by a provocative author is MONROE H. FREEDMAN, UNDERSTANDING LAWYERS' ETHICS, 2D ED. (Matthew Bender 1998). *See also* RESTATEMENT, THIRD, OF THE LAW GOVERNING LAWYERS (American Law Institute 1988).

137 *See* GILLERS, *supra* note 136 at 3. The Watergate affair was discussed in Chapter I, p. 14.

138 *See* ABA Task Force Report, *supra* note 1, at 117-118.

promulgated its Canons of Professional Ethics which were adopted by many state bar associations. These canons were advisory, but several courts eventually began enforcing them as if they were rules of law. The canons remained in effect until 1970, when the ABA promulgated the Model Code of Professional Responsibility (the "Model Code"). In 1983, the ABA replaced the Code with the Model Rules of Professional Conduct ("Model Rules"). Because the ABA is a private organization and lacks the power to impose its rules on anyone, the code and rules are only "models." However, they have been widely adopted by states as law.

Malpractice Suits Suits against lawyers for malpractice were once a rarity. That is no longer so. The level of competence of lawyers is probably no lower today than in the recent past. The growth in legal malpractice claims is probably due to the same changes in attitudes toward professionals that has made suing doctors more acceptable — less awe and greater realism about their work and their place in society. Most of the successful malpractice cases have been for especially egregious conduct, such as the deliberate and willful neglect of a client matter to the extreme detriment of the client or gross incompetence. Part of the reason for this is in the legal requirements for a legal malpractice claim. The dissatisfied former client must show both that the attorney was at fault *and* that, but for the attorney's misconduct, the client would have prevailed on the underlying claim — usually shown by a "trial within a trial" on the mishandled claim.[139]

Most lawyers carry malpractice insurance, but the rate for such insurance is far below that of physicians. Bar organizations maintain "client security funds" that are designed to reimburse clients who lose money as a result of improper conduct of lawyers and who are unable to recover their loss otherwise. However, few of these funds provide full compensation.[140]

2. Defining Ethical Behavior: The Duties of the Attorney

The Code and the Model Rules set forth standards and guidelines in the following areas: the attorney-client relationship; the attorney's role as a counselor and an advocate; transactions with persons other than clients; law firms and association of attorneys; pro bono service; and the integrity of the legal profession. Discussion of all these topics is beyond the scope of this chapter, but some are covered here.

a. The Nature of the Attorney-Client Relationship

The attorney-client relationship is the most important aspect of the practice of law. A rhetorical foundation for the nature of the relationship is Lord Brougham's observation that "an advocate, in the discharge of his duty, knows but one person in all the world, and that person is his client."[141] Less dramatically, the Model Rules set forth several of the lawyer's duties to the client, discussed in the next few paragraphs.

---

139 A developing area of liability is bad settlement recommendations. *See Thomas v. Bethea*, 718 A.2d 1787 (Md. 1998) (defendant recommended settlement of $2,500 with landlords for lead paint poisoning of children; "trial within a trial" on underlying tort claim resulted in $125,000 verdict).

140 Such suits also attract the attention of the bar, which may investigate and discipline the offending attorney. For more on malpractice, *see* JEFFREY M. SMITH & RONALD E. MALLEN, PREVENTING LEGAL MALPRACTICE, 2D ED. (West 1996). Another possible approach is to sue the lawyer for violation of consumer protection statutes. *See Latham v. Castillo*, 972 S.W.2d 66 (Tex. 1998) (lawyer misrepresenting that medical malpractice action had been filed perpetrated consumer fraud). *But see Cripe v. Leiter*, 703 N.E.2d 100 (Ill. 1998) (consumer fraud law did not apply to claim that attorney charged excessive fees; excessive fee issues are exclusively remediable by bar disciplinary proceedings).

141 TRIAL OF QUEEN CAROLINE 8 (J. Nightingale ed. 1821).

Duty of Competent Representation The lawyer has a duty to "provide competent representation" which requires the "legal knowledge, skill, thoroughness, and preparation necessary for the representation."[142] Accordingly, a lawyer whose practice is limited to advising corporations should probably not attempt to try a murder case. Lawyers who do not have sufficient knowledge or experience to handle a matter should either decline representation, associate with an attorney who is knowledgeable on the subject of the representation, or adequately prepare and educate themselves.

Duty to Consult The lawyer has a duty to "abide by a client's decisions concerning the objectives of representation" and "consult with the client as to the means by which they are pursued."[143] The attorney has some authority to make binding decisions for the client, especially concerning technical matters that arise during litigation. But the attorney generally may not make unilateral decisions that will have an impact on the substantial legal rights of the client, such as entering into a settlement without the consent of the client or, in criminal cases, deciding whether the client will testify, plead guilty, or waive the right to a jury trial.[144]

Duty of Diligence An attorney must "act with reasonable diligence and promptness in representing a client."[145] This obligates an attorney to take any action that is legal and ethical to pursue a matter on behalf of a client despite public opposition or personal inconvenience to the lawyer. Procrastination and unreasonable delay must be avoided so that a client's rights are not prejudiced or forfeited due to the expiration of any applicable statute of limitations, the legal time period for filing suit.

Duty to Charge Reasonable Fees The Model Rules require lawyers to charge reasonable fees. Most bar associations provide a fee mediation service to assist in enforcing this provision. The fee should be communicated in writing to the client within a reasonable time after the representation has begun. Contingent fee arrangements are prohibited in domestic relations matters and criminal cases.[146]

Duty of Loyalty and Conflicts of Interest The Model Rules prohibit an attorney from representing a client when the attorney has personal interests that conflict with those of the client, since this would violate the duty of "undivided loyalty."[147] Consequently, an attorney can have no personal interest or stake in the outcome of a suit or matter.[148] Further, if the attorney already has a client whose interests are directly adverse to those of a potential client, the attorney must decline the second representation. Even after an attorney-client relationship ends, an attorney may not later represent a client whose interests are adverse to those of a former client if the attorney obtained confidential information from the former client which relates in a substantial way to the second client's case. As noted next, the attorney owes the first client a continuing duty of confidentiality that survives the termination of the client-attorney relationship.

---

142 MODEL RULES OF PROFESSIONAL CONDUCT, Rule 1.1 (1992). These and other rules are reprinted in JOHN S. DZIERNKOWSKI, ED., PROFESSIONAL RESPONSIBILITY: STANDARDS, RULES AND STATUTES 1998-1999 (West 1998). *See also* ANNOTATED MODEL RULES OF PROFESSIONAL CONDUCT, 3D ED. (ABA 1996).

143 MODEL RULES, Rule 1.2.

144 MODEL RULES, Rule 1.2(a).

145 MODEL RULES, Rule 1.3.

146 MODEL RULES. Rule 5.1. Contingent fees were discussed *supra* p. 142.

147 MODEL RULES, Rules 1.7, 1.8, 1.9.

148 This does not prohibit contingent fees, however. *See supra* p. 142.

Duty of Confidentiality An attorney owes a client the important duty of confidentiality. Generally, an attorney may not disclose any information "relating to representation of a client unless the client consents after consultation, except for disclosures that are impliedly authorized in order to carry out the representation."[149]

Faithful adherence to the duty of confidentiality has resulted in what some people feel are repugnant results. For example, during a criminal case in New York, a defendant charged with murder informed his attorneys of the location of the bodies of two other people he had killed. The father of one of the victims begged the attorneys to reveal this information so that he could give his child a decent burial. The attorneys refused because the disclosure of the information would be a breach of their duty of confidentiality to their client and would prejudice his chances of plea bargaining with the prosecutor. While the actions of the attorneys in this case may seem heartless, the majority of the legal community agreed that the attorneys acted properly in a morally difficult situation. The foundation of such a strict duty of confidentiality is the need for clients to feel that they can disclose all relevant facts to their attorney, so that they receive the best legal representation possible.[150]

The Model Rules provide two exceptions to the strict rule of confidentiality. First, if the attorney believes that the client is intending to commit a crime that is likely to result in imminent death or substantial bodily harm, the lawyer may inform the authorities.[151] Second, an attorney may reveal client confidences where it is necessary to prove a claim or defense in a controversy between the lawyer and the client.[152] In addition, as discussed next, the duty of candor may override confidentiality in some situations.

b. The Attorney's Duty to the Administration of Justice

As was clear from Chapter III, attorneys have major responsibilities in litigation with regard to presentation of evidence and argument before a court on behalf of a client. In performing this public function as an "officer of the court," the lawyer owes duties to the public and to the court that may conflict with some of lawyer's duties to the client. The attorney's responsibility to the court includes a duty of candor.[153] If an attorney discovers that a client intends to commit perjury, the attorney is faced with a potential dilemma: whether to maintain client confidences or to disclose the perjury to the court. The Model Rules prohibit an attorney from committing fraud or perjury upon the court, and from assisting a client in doing so. Failing to reveal that the client plans to commit perjury could be construed as assisting the client in that perjury. Thus, the Rules provide that the duty to the client must give way to the duty of candor

---

149 MODEL RULES, Rule 1.6.

150 *People v. Belge*, 83 Misc. 2d 186, 372 N.Y.S.2d 798 (Co. Ct. 1975), *aff'd*, 376 N.Y.S.2d 771 (App.Div. 1975), *aff'd*, 390 N.Y.S.2d 867 (N.Y. 1976).

151 MODEL RULES, Rule 1.6(b)(1). The exact substance of this rule varies from state to state; some *require* the disclosure while others *permit* it. Further, some states permit the attorney to reveal the client's intention to commit *any* crime. Regardless of what ethical rules might require or permit, lawyers may be required – on pain of paying civil damages – to reveal a client's stated intentions to commit a crime of violence against a particular person. *See Tarasoff v. Regents of the University of California*, 551 P.2d 334 (Cal. 1973) (duty of psychiatrist to warn intended victim of patient's threats of harm).

152 The information is also privileged under evidence law. *See* Chapter III, p. 112, n. 127. The Court recently clarified that the attorney-client privilege even survives the death of the client. *Swidler & Berlin v. United States*, 524 U.S. 399 (1998).

153 MODEL RULES, Rule 3.3.

owed to the court.[154] But some would argue that this view of the duty of candor violates the basic tenets of the accusatorial and adversarial system of justice by requiring or permitting defense counsel to assist the prosecution.[155]

Another difficult issue along these lines is presented when an attorney who knows a witness is providing truthful testimony has an opportunity to impeach the witness by attacking the witness' credibility. For example, may a lawyer vigorously cross-examine an eyewitness about a discrepancy in that witness's testimony and argue that the witness is not telling the truth when the lawyer knows from the client that the witness is telling the truth? At least in criminal cases this is permitted, because it is the defense attorney's duty to cast the prosecution's case in the worst light possible, regardless of what the attorney thinks or knows to be the truth.[156]

Connected with the duty to refrain from fraud or perjury, the attorney must accurately state the law controlling an issue and must disclose legal authority which is adverse to the client's case and which the opposing side has not discovered. This does not prevent the attorney from making creative and good faith arguments to distinguish adverse law in order to persuade the court that existing law is not applicable or sound.

c. Duties to the Profession and Others

Dealing with Represented Parties A lawyer may not communicate on a subject of representation with a person known to be represented by a lawyer without the consent of the other lawyer.[157] An interesting issue arose regarding this rule when the U.S. Attorney General in 1989 announced that government attorneys could contact people represented by attorneys in certain situations. One provision authorized contact if it is "in the process of conducting an investigation, including, but not limited to, an undercover investigation." Another permitted contact with any employee of a corporation unless the employee is a "controlling individual" in the corporate organization.[158] The regulations further announced that all contact issues involving government attorneys were solely within the jurisdiction of the Attorney General and that any contrary state rules were preempted. After the ensuing furor and at least two U.S. Court of Appeals cases holding the rule invalid, Congress passed a law placing government lawyers back under the control of state and local rules applicable to all other attorneys.[159] However, opponents have vowed to change that law.

Pro Bono Service The Model Rules recommend that every lawyer "aspire to render at least (50) hours of *pro bono publico* legal services per year."[160] The *pro bono* services contemplated are legal services for "persons of limited means," for public

---

154 The comment to the Rule states: "If perjured testimony or false evidence has been offered, the advocate's proper course ordinarily is to remonstrate with the client confidentially. If that fails, the advocate should seek to withdraw if that will remedy the situation. If withdrawal will not remedy the situation or is impossible, the advocate should make disclosure to the court. It is for the court then to determine what should be done — making a statement about the matter to the trier of fact, ordering a mistrial or perhaps nothing."

155 *See* FREEDMAN, *supra* note 136, at 109-141 (lawyer should not disclose perjury). Accusatorial and adversarial principles in criminal cases are discussed in Chapter VIII, p. 275.

156 WOLFRAM, *supra* note 1, at 646 (citing *United States v. Wade*, 388 U.S. 218, 257-58 (1967). *See also* FREEDMAN, *supra* note 136, at 161-171.

157 MODEL RULES, Rule 4.2.

158 *See* 28 CFR §77.1 *et seq.* The quoted language is from §77.7 and §77.10..

159 *See United States ex rel. O'Keefe v. McDonnell Douglas Corp.*, 132 F.3d 1252 (8th Cir. 1998) (prohibiting contact with employees and some former employees of corporation) and P.L.105-277 §801.

160 MODEL RULES, Rule 6.1.

service groups or charities, or "for individuals, groups or organizations seeking to secure or protect civil rights, civil liberties or public rights." In some states, the *pro bono* requirement can be satisfied by a generous donation of money to the local legal aid society. In others, the Model Rule's "aspiration" is a requirement.

Issues in Leaving Firms When a lawyer leaves a firm, disputes over "stolen" clients often arise. It is up to clients to decide who will represent them. However, firms take a proprietary attitude toward long-standing clients and losing several of them can have a major economic impact on the firm. One method of dealing with this problem has been to use non-compete agreements like those used with other employees — an agreement barring departing lawyers from practicing law in competition with the firm they have left for some period of time. However, Model Rule 5.6 prohibits such agreements for lawyers, except when conditioned upon the receipt of retirement benefits. The rule is based on the rationale that choice of counsel is up to the client. Courts have for this reason held that non-compete agreements for lawyers are void as against public policy.[161] However, a partner in a firm owes a fiduciary duty to other partners, so soliciting firm clients — especially before announcing one's departure — could be a breach of that duty, and possibly tortious interference with prospective economic advantage.[162]

Client Solicitation, Advertising and Duty to Report The Model Rules prohibit in-person or live telephone contact to solicit employment for pecuniary gain from a potential client with whom the lawyer has no previous relationship. This limitation is intended to protect vulnerable individuals from undue influence, intimidation and overreaching by an attorney.[163] Further, the Rules impose strict requirements on the content of advertising to insure that it is truthful and that the public will not be misled by it.[164] The Model Rules also impose a duty on lawyers to report any "significant violation" of ethical duties by other lawyers "that raise substantial question as to that lawyer's honesty, trustworthiness, or fitness as a lawyer."[165]

---

161 *See Cohen v. Lord, Day & Lord*,550 N.E.2d 410 (N.Y. 1989).

162 *See Dowd & Dowd v. Gleason*, 693 N.E.2d 358 (Ill. 1998) (non-compete agreement is not valid, but breach of fiduciary duty and interference with prospective economic advantage claims possible). Breach of fiduciary duty is discussed in Chapter XV, p. 533, and interference with prospective economic advantage is discussed in Chapter XI, p. 422.

163 MODEL RULES, Rule 7.3.

164 MODEL RULES, Rule 7.1. Some of the ethical restrictions on solicitation and advertising have run afoul of 1st Amendment protections of free speech. *See* Chapter IX, pp. 354-355.

165 MODEL RULES, Rule 8.3.

CHAPTER V

THE JUDICIAL SYSTEM

To speak of "the judicial system" of the United States is misleading, because there are in reality 51 different judicial systems in the country: the federal court system and the court system in each state. As to questions of state law, each of the state systems is a separate closed system. In other words, each state system has its own court of last resort that has the last word on what state law is. Only on issues of federal law, arising originally either in federal or state court, can it be said that there is the semblance of a single national judicial system with one court, the United States Supreme Court, serving as the court of last resort.[1]

PART I: An Overview of Court Systems and Judicial Officials

It is impossible here to go into the structure of the judicial systems of all 50 states and the federal government. State systems tend to be similar in their general outline in any event, so a composite picture is presented of them.[2]

A. Trial Courts and Appellate Courts: Their Basic Characteristics and Interrelationship

All the court systems in the United States, state and federal, have two basic types of courts: trial courts and appellate courts. The two have different functions and characteristics.

1. Trial Courts

Functions and Characteristics Judges who staff trial courts "sit" alone without any other judges. They conduct trials either with or without a jury, depending on the type of case and the wishes of the parties. The overall job of trial courts is to reach a decision in the first instance on all disputes filed in a given judicial system. This involves hearing the evidence and arguments presented by the parties, determining the facts in the case and applying the law to those facts. In the process, the trier of fact, whether judge or jury, must resolve conflicts in the testimony and make judgments about the credibility of witnesses and the believability and weight to be given all the evidence. This is an important function because, as discussed below, the facts of a case cannot be relitigated on appeal.[3]

Trials constitute only part of the activity of a trial judge. Pretrial motions must be heard and decided. A great deal of a trial court's time is spent on this activity, which the judge performs alone without the assistance of a jury. In most courts one or two days a week are set aside as "motion days." In addition, trial judges preside over pre-trial conferences in civil cases slated for trial. In those conferences the judge will attempt to persuade the parties to settle the case or, if they cannot settle it, to narrow the factual and legal issues for trial.[4] In criminal cases, a great deal of time is spent on

---

1   *See* Chapter I, p. 22, and the diagram of the federal and state court systems in set out in the Appendix, p. A32.

2   For an excellent short introduction to U.S. courts written especially for a foreign audience, *see* DANIEL J. MEADOR, AMERICAN COURTS (West 1991) and DANIEL J. MEADOR & JORDANA S. BERNSTEIN, APPELLATE COURT IN THE UNITED STATES (West 1994). *See also* HENRY J. ABRAHAM, THE JUDICIAL PROCESS, 7TH ED. (Oxford U. Press, N.Y. 1998).

3   *See generally* Chapter III, pp. 88-106 for jury trial procedure.

4   *See* Chapter VII, pp. 221-234.

arraignments of criminal defendants (a hearing at which formal charges are presented and bail set) and preliminary hearings (where the prosecution must present enough evidence to warrant binding the defendant over for trial).[5] Judges of trial courts also need time to do legal research and to write the required judicial opinions deciding motions or trials they have already heard. There are also administrative tasks, such as conferences with colleagues on mutual problems, personnel matters, the operation of the clerk's office, and the like.

Trial Judges and Courtrooms Trial judges wear robes, but not wigs as are the case in England. The "bench," i.e., the dais where the judge sits when presiding at a hearing, is raised. The judge's secretary or clerk and the court reporter sit in front or to the side of the judge's bench. A jury box, an area with 12 or 14 seats that is enclosed by a one-meter high partial wall, is located to one side. Further out in front of both the judge's bench and the jury box are the counsel tables and chairs, where the lawyers sit while handling a matter before the judge. Nearby is a lectern which the lawyers may use when arguing or conducting witness examinations. Behind counsel tables is a "bar" about a meter high between the area where the lawyers, judge and jury sit, and the rest of the courtroom where the general public sits. There are also places in the courtroom for the court reporter and the judge's clerk and judge's law clerk, if there is one.[6]

As a show of respect to the judge, all persons present in the courtroom are required to stand when the judge enters and is seated "on the bench." The judge has contempt power to punish summarily any disruption in the courtroom or other display of disrespect to the court. When court is in session, lawyers generally must address the judge from the lectern or counsel table unless they are invited or obtain permission to "approach the bench." This is done usually at trial when matters must be discussed which the jury is prohibited from hearing.

Each judge has a court reporter who takes down verbatim (either in shorthand or by means of a machine) everything that takes place in court at a trial or hearing. In the event of an appeal, this record must be typed up in a transcript that must be filed with the appellate court to apprize it of exactly what happened in the trial court.

Virtually all trial court hearings are open to the public and are in general required to be by state law and as a constitutional matter.[7] However, many trial judges conduct pre-trial conferences "in chambers," meaning the judge's office, usually located behind the courtroom. Also, some matters that are required or permitted to be inquired into confidentially may be heard "*in camera*," i.e., in chambers.

Since trial courts handle all cases filed in a given judicial system, the atmosphere in a trial court in a large city on motion day or the day set for preliminary hearings in criminal cases can be chaotic, with parties, lawyers, policemen and complaining witnesses moving in and out of the courtroom or up to the lectern or bench for conferences with the judge as their cases are called. In the halls, lawyers confer with their clients, worried litigants pace and family members of the litigants gather in

---

5 *See* Chapter VIII, pp. 262-264.

6 A diagram of a trial courtroom is set out in the Appendix to this book on p. A33. The bar between the area where the judge and lawyers the area where the public sits gives us the expression that a lawyer, when admitted to practice, is "called to the bar" (English version) or "admitted to the bar" (American version). Lawyers and judges are so identified with their physical place in the courtroom that it is common to refer to judges collectively as "the bench" and to lawyers collectively as "the bar."

7 *See* Chapter IX, p. 353.

groups. In addition, an air of tension is present in view of the fact that disputes are the business of the day and that delay is inevitable as the court tries to handle everything that has been scheduled.

Trial courts, being at the bottom of the judicial system pyramid, are the most numerous courts in a state or in the federal system. The number of judges staffing them varies from a high of 760 in Illinois to a low of 15 in Delaware.[8]

2. Appellate Courts

Intermediate Appellate Courts and Supreme Courts Above the trial courts of a judicial system, there are usually two layers of appellate courts: an intermediate court of appeals and a supreme court. The intermediate appellate court is usually called the "Court of Appeals" and the court of final resort is called the "Supreme Court."[9] Judges of supreme courts are usually called "justices," while judges of intermediate courts of appeal and trial courts are called "judges." Appellate courts have no jury or other non-lawyer members. When meeting to hear and decide cases, intermediate appellate courts have three judges while supreme courts usually number five, seven, or nine justices.

This two-tiered structure prevails in the federal system and all but twelve of the states. For most types of cases, there is an appeal as of right from the trial court to the court of appeals, while further appeal to the supreme court is discretionary with that court. However, some categories of cases may qualify for review as of right in a state supreme court, such as cases where the death penalty has been imposed. Where two levels of appellate courts exist, the intermediate court of appeals has the task of assuring that trial court errors are corrected. The supreme court in such a system has the broader task of overseeing the development of the law. Thus, it will generally decide only cases in which the law needs to be clarified or some question of overriding public significance is presented. A system of granting discretionary review is established to select such cases. To have a case heard in the supreme court of a system, a party must be "granted leave to appeal" or must obtain a writ of "certiorari," the procedure established at common law for a higher court to review the decision of a lower court.[10] Thus, in the ordinary case in most jurisdictions, litigants must be satisfied with only one appeal. However, the courts of final resort of some states with two-level appellate systems, among them New York, retain relatively large categories of obligatory appellate jurisdiction.

Resolving Conflicts Within the Court of Appeals The "panel" of three judges of intermediate courts of appeal that decides appeals constitutes less than all the judges of that court. This can result in disagreement among different panels of the appellate court. There are many mechanisms for resolving such disagreements. One method, used by the federal courts of appeal and many states, is to convene a court of all of the judges of that court for an *en banc* hearing to resolve the conflict. Sometimes this makes for a very large court. For example, when the U.S. Court of Appeals of the Ninth Circuit meets *en banc*, it has 28 judges.[11] States handle panel conflicts variously.

---

8 This information and other information regarding state courts contained in this chapter are taken from THE BOOK OF THE STATES 204-207 (Council of State Governments, Lexington, Kentucky 1990-91).

9 In some states, among them New York, the court of final resort is called the Court of Appeals and in Massachusetts it is called the Supreme Judicial Court. In Texas and Oklahoma, there are separate supreme courts for criminal and civil appeals.

10 Certiorari practice in the United States Supreme Court is similar and is discussed *infra* p. 182.

11 A recent statutory change allows courts with a large number of judges to take *en banc* action with only 14 judges present. *See* Ct. App. 9th Cir. Rule 35-3 (1994) (limited *en banc* court of 11).

In some, the first panel to decide an issue binds the entire court until and unless it is reversed by the state supreme court. Another method of dealing with conflicts is to make the first panel's decision binding, but to allow the second panel considering the issue to indicate that it is following the first panel's decision only because it is required to do so. This statement then forms the basis for surveying all Court of Appeals judges to determine whether to convene a special enlarged panel to resolve the issue. Further appeal to the state supreme court is possible if the appellate court judges decline to convene the special panel or after the special panel decides the issue.[12]

No such conflict problems attend supreme courts. All judges participate in each case heard unless ill or disqualified. Thus, supreme courts normally sit *en banc*.[13]

3. The Scope of Appellate Review

The scope of appellate review of trial court judgments depends on two factors: whether the issue reviewed is one of fact or one of law and, if one of fact, whether the fact finder was a judge or a jury.[14] An appellate court can review issues of law *de novo* and will reverse for any non-harmless error, but it is much more limited in its review of the factual basis for a trial court judgment.

Fact Review in General   One reason for limited review of facts is one of the tenets of the adversary system discussed in Chapter III: a belief in the superiority of immediate oral evidence over mediate written evidence.[15] Though a verbatim transcript of the entire trial is available to the appellate court, this "cold paper record" of the trial is no substitute for the vantage point of the fact finder on the trial level, who actually saw and heard the witnesses and is therefor in a far superior position to find the facts accurately. Indeed, much of the presumed benefit of the trial-level adversary presentation of the facts would be lost if an appellate court could simply substitute its view of the evidence for that of the trial court.

Standards for Bench Trials and Jury Trials   When a trial judge sits as the fact-finder in a bench trial, the judge's findings of fact will be reversed only if they are "clearly erroneous."[16] Review of jury verdicts is even more limited. If the judgment reviewed is based on a jury verdict, a second reason for great deference to trial level findings emerges. The right to trial by jury would not mean very much if either trial or appellate judges could simply reverse jury findings whenever they disagreed with them. The standard for appellate review of jury verdicts is identical to the standard employed by a trial judge in reviewing a jury verdict: the verdict of the jury can be reversed only if there is a complete absence of any substantial credible evidence to support it. Simple disagreement with the verdict is not sufficient. In determining the sufficiency of the evidence, the appellate court must be careful not to substitute its

---

12 *See* Michigan Court Rules Administrative Order 1994-4, Resolution of Conflicts in Court of Appeals Decisions (April 27, 1994).

13 If one judge cannot hear a particular case for some reason, this can result in an even number on the court and a tie vote. In such a case, the judgment below is affirmed.

14 *See generally* JACK H. FRIEDENTHAL, MARY KAY KANE AND ARTHUR MILLER, HORNBOOK ON CIVIL PROCEDURE 603-608 (West 1993).

15 *See* pp. 80-81.

16 *See* Federal Rule of Civil Procedure 52(a). *See generally Anderson v. Bessemer City*, 470 U.S. 564 (1985).

view for that of the jury. This would be a violation of the fundamental right to a trial by jury.[17]

It follows from what has been said that an appellate court generally may not receive new evidence on the factual issues in the case.[18] Even if the appellate court determines that more evidence is necessary on a point, it will direct the trial court to take such evidence and make a decision in the first instance.

Review of Decisions Committed to Trial Court Discretion   There are numerous decisions that trial courts make that are committed to their discretion. Most often, there are guidelines for the court to follow, but reasonable judges could differ as to their application to a given set of facts. In such cases, a trial court's decision will be reversed on appeal only if the appellate court finds an "abuse of discretion." This question is essentially one of whether the trial judge's decision was among the rational choices a reasonable judge could make under the circumstances. It is not what the appellate court would have done had it been the trial judge. An example of such decisions is whether to issue a preliminary injunction, an order preserving the *status quo* until the merits of a case can be heard.[19]

Civil vs. Criminal Cases   The same narrow scope of appellate review of fact issues applies to criminal appeals except to the extent that the standard of proof affects the question. Thus, a civil judgment of a jury will be reversed only if the evidence was legally insufficient for the jury to find as it did *by a preponderance* of the evidence. In a criminal case, a jury verdict finding the defendant guilty will be reversed on factual grounds only if the record discloses that there was legally insufficient evidence *beyond a reasonable doubt* to support it.[20]

4. Appellate Court Procedure

The issues of law raised on appeal are argued principally through the exchange of written briefs between the parties.[21] Some limited oral argument before the court is permitted. The maximum time for oral argument permitted each side is usually 15 or 30 minutes. Because most of the arguments of a party will be presented well in the written briefs, oral argument generally serves as a time for the attorney to touch on recent developments in the law affecting the case, to highlight the main arguments in their favor and, most important, to respond to questions from the bench.[22]

---

17 An attempt at explaining the precise difference between the standard of review for judge and jury factual findings is set out in *Hersch v. United States*, 719 F.2d 873 (6th Cir. 1983). The standard for trial judge review of jury verdicts is set out in Chapter III, p. 105 and note 94.

18 For a discussion of the history leading to this almost invariable rule, *see* Robert W. Millar, *New Allegations and Proof on Appeal in Anglo-American Civil Procedure*, 47 Nw. L. REV. 427 (1952).

19 *See, e.g.*, *William Inglis & Sons Baking Co. v. ITT Continental BakingCo.*, 526 F.2d 86 (9th Cir. 1976) ("the question is not whether or not [the appeals court] would make or would not have made the order. It was to the discretion of the trial court, not to that of the appellate court, that the law entrusted the granting or refusing of these injunctions").

20 There can be no appellate review of a verdict of acquittal. *See* Chapter VIII, p. 297.

21 The nature of the argumentation style and composition of briefs was discussed in Chapter II, pp. 75-76.

22 Two classic works on the proper purpose and appropriate techniques of oral argument are John W. Davis, *The Argument of an Appeal*, 26 A.B.A.J. 895 (1940), and Robert H. Jackson, *Advocacy Before the Supreme Court: Suggestions for Effective Case Presentations*, 37 A.B.A.J. 801 (1951). Davis was a well-known, and well-connected lawyer who argued many cases in the United States Supreme Court, among them the defense (and losing) side in *Brown v. Board of Education*, 347 U.S. 483 (1954), the school desegregation case. Jackson was a Justice of the Supreme Court.

The fact that only issues of law are involved and that they are addressed primarily in written briefs gives the appellate court a much more quiet and erudite atmosphere than prevails in most trial courts. Only the lawyers and their assistants generally attend court sessions. Clients rarely do, in part because the appellate court is often many miles from where they live and in part because they would not understand much of the argument, which would be confined to the legal issues.

Appellate Court Action An appellate court decides a case by issuing an order or judgment indicating who wins and, usually, an opinion of the court setting out the reasons for the decision. As described in Chapter II, there may also be concurring opinions from judges who agree with the result, but differ in the reasoning behind it, and dissenting opinions from judges who disagree with the result and the reasoning of the majority.[23] There are various actions that an appellate court can take. It can affirm the judgment of the trial court, meaning that it approves of it. It can reverse that judgment and direct entry of judgment for the opposing side. Or if the implications of the appellate court's opinion depend on development of further facts or the appellate court wishes the trial court to take further action consistent with the opinion, the appellate court will "vacate" the trial court's judgment and "remand" the case to the trial court for "further proceedings consistent with" its opinion.

5. Trial Court Actions that are Reviewable

The Final Judgment Rule A final trial court judgment deciding the case on the merits or dismissing it is usually the only kind of judgment or order that can be appealed. The policy behind this final judgment rule is the notion that one appeal at the end of the case is more efficient. One "big" appeal takes less time than multiple appeals and many errors that take place could well be rendered moot if the party complaining of those errors ultimately wins the case or if the case is settled.

Interlocutory Appeals Appeals of non-final orders, called "interlocutory appeals," are often allowed, but they are discretionary. Usually both the trial court and the appellate court must agree that the issue raised by the interlocutory order is a close one and that it would be efficient to address the issue without waiting for a final judgment.[24] For example, if the trial judge denies a motion to dismiss a case for lack of jurisdiction finding that it has jurisdiction, permission to take an interlocutory appeal will often be granted if the issue is a close one, since an appellate finding of lack of jurisdiction at that point could avoid an unnecessary trial. There are a few other exceptions to the final judgment requirement, primarily based on overriding need to have the issue addressed at an early stage of the litigation.[25]

Mandamus A limited path around the final judgment rule is pursuit of an action for a "writ of mandamus" (an order requiring certain trial court action) or "writ of prohibition" (an order prohibiting certain trial court action).[26] In some state courts

---

23 *See* p. 60.

24 For example, 28 U.S.C.A. §1292, applicable in federal court, allows an interlocutory appeal from a non-final order if the trial judge certifies that it presents "a controlling question of law as to which there is substantial ground for difference of opinion and that immediate appeal . . . may materially advance the ultimate termination of the litigation," and the appeals court agrees as well.

25 For example, in the federal system an immediate appeal as of right is provided from interlocutory orders granting or denying injunctive relief. 28 U.S.C.A. §1292(a)(1). In addition, some non-final orders that have a "practical finality" about them may be appealed under the "collateral order: doctrine. *See Cohen v. Beneficial Industrial Loan Co.*, 337 U.S.541 (1949) (order declining to require a bond in stockholder derivative action in which plaintiffs own few shares of stock).

26 *See* 28 U.S.C.A. §1651 (federal statute authorizing writs).

these ancient writs are consolidated under the modern label, "writ of superintending control." These forms of action avoid the final judgment rule because they are considered to be an *original* action filed against the trial judge (often by name) rather than an appeal. The limited nature of mandamus review must be emphasized, however. It is considered to be an "extraordinary writ" and is available generally only to redress clearly illegal action by the trial judge of a particularly serious sort, most often concerning an improper exercise or abdication of jurisdiction. In the federal system, at least, the occasions for mandamus are narrow and it is said that "mandamus will not lie" for any error that could be remedied adequately by appeal.[27] However, many state systems regularly allow such writs as a supplement to interlocutory appeal.[28]

B. State and Federal Court Structure and Characteristics

1. State Court Structure

Trial Courts of General Jurisdiction The basic component of the state court systems of all states is the trial court of general jurisdiction. This court has jurisdiction over major civil disputes and all serious criminal offenses, called "felonies."[29] These courts are called by various names. The most common names for this court are the "Superior Court" or the "Circuit Court," though in some states they are called the "District Court." Strangely enough, in New York these trial courts are called the "Supreme Court" (while the highest court in New York is called the "Court of Appeals"). In general the territorial subdivisions over which these state trial courts preside correspond with the county lines of a state.

In most states, there is a layer of trial courts below the circuit or superior court level which exercise limited general jurisdiction. Typically they have jurisdiction over all types of civil cases up to a certain amount of money in controversy and over all criminal prosecutions of less serious criminal matters, called "misdemeanors."[30] For example, in California the Superior Court handles all felonies and civil cases with more than $25,000 in controversy, while the Municipal and Justice Courts handle criminal misdemeanors and civil disputes of $25,000 or less. Sometimes these lower level courts are the descendants of "Justice of the Peace" or other small claims courts. Those less formal courts were gradually "upgraded" and given greater jurisdiction to relieve the increased workload of the superior or circuit court. Appeals from judgments of these lower courts often go to the circuit or superior court rather than to the regular appeals court. In such cases, the circuit or superior court acts as a single-judge appellate court rather than a trial court.

Trial Courts with Specialized Jurisdiction States have other trial courts with specialized jurisdiction to decide only disputes of a particular type. Among them are probate or surrogate's courts (for overseeing distribution of decedents' estates, for juvenile matters, or for mental commitments and guardianships over adults unable to handle their affairs), juvenile courts (if juvenile matters are not handled by the probate court), and courts of claims (to handle money claims against the state). In some states, some courts with specialized subject-matter jurisdiction are considered the

---

27 *See Kerr v. United States District Court*, 426 U.S. 394 (1976) (disapproving mandamus as means of reviewing discovery order, even though irreparable injury was alleged).

28 For a discussion of all these devices and some other miscellaneous routes around the final judgment rule, *see* FRIEDENTHAL, *supra* note 14, §§13.1-13.3.

29 A felony is generally defined as an offense punishable by more than one year in prison.

30 Misdemeanors are usually crimes punishable by less than a year in jail. *See* Chapter VIII, p. 259.

equal of the superior or circuit courts of general jurisdiction. In other states, specialized courts are considered inferior to the circuit or superior court and the latter are sometimes assigned the task of deciding appeals from the former. This is an instance when a trial court exercises appellate court functions and when an appeal can be decided by a single judge.

Small Claims and Other Informal Courts Most states have established small claims divisions either in the courts of general jurisdiction or in the courts just below them. Disputes are limited to those involving less than a specified amount in controversy, such as $300, $500 or $1,000. Sometimes these courts are called "Justice of the Peace" courts, because that is the name of the official who presides over the proceedings. Sometimes these "justices" are not lawyers and have no particular legal training.[31] Procedure in small claims courts is very informal and there is generally no appeal from a judgment. Sometimes lawyers are prohibited from representing parties in such courts. However, in most jurisdictions, if parties to cases in small claims court wish to utilize a lawyer or to avail themselves of the greater rights afforded by a regular court, they may do so by simply asking that the case be "removed" from small claims court to the regular trial court. In others, there is no right of removal, but the losing party has a right to a "trial *de novo*" in a higher court. A trial *de novo* is a completely new trial that ignores the earlier result in the small claims court.

Appellate Courts The structure of state appellate courts conforms generally to that described above in the general description of appellate courts.[32] However, it bears repeating that the state appellate court of last resort of a state is the final arbiter of the meaning and application of *state* law. While the United States Supreme Court has power to review state court judgments, it may do so only on issues of *federal* law.

2. The Federal Court System

As discussed in Chapter I, federal courts have jurisdiction over federal law claims and state law claims that involve parties from different states. Such claims can arise anywhere, so the federal court system court system covers the entire country. However, the federal court system is much smaller than the aggregate of all the state systems. In one recent year, 272,027 cases were filed in federal courts nationwide.[33] During the same period, almost 90 million cases were filed in state courts.[34] There were 28,560 state judges, as compared to 646 federal district court judges and 179 federal court of appeals judges — about the same number of judges as in the California state judicial system. But the numbers of cases handled by California courts totaled almost a million while the federal courts handled about a quarter that many.

District Courts The basic trial court in the federal system is the United States District Court, which is located in 94 districts.[35] Districts vary in size. In the more populous states, there will be three or even four districts. In the less populous states, the entire state is one district. New York has southern, northern, eastern and western

---

31 *See infra* p. 174 and note 46.

32 *See supra* pp. 165-169.

33 *Judicial Business of the United States Courts: 1997* (Administrative Office of U.S. Courts 1998). This and other statistics come from the Federal Judiciary website set out in Appendix B.

34 *See generally* EXAMINING THE WORK OF STATE COURTS, 1997: A NATIONAL PERSPECTIVE FROM THE COURT STATISTICS PROJECT (Natl Center for State Courts 1998). *See* NSCS's website in Appendix B.

35 28 U.S.C.A. §§81-131. These districts are in the 50 states, the District of Columbia, the Commonwealth of Puerto Rico, and the territories of Guam, the U.S. Virgin Islands, and the Northern Mariana Islands. For more information on the federal court system, *see* CHARLES A. WRIGHT, LAW OF FEDERAL COURTS, 5TH ED. §§1-6 (West 1994).

districts, while the state of Montana is all one district. All district courts have at least two judges and one (the southern district of New York) has as many as 28. Where necessary to provide better access for litigants and witnesses, judges of the district court "sit" (i.e., hold court sessions) in various places in the state.

Although federal law claims are not as numerous as state claims, when issues of federal law arise, they are often very important. Either the federal Constitution is involved or the case involves a problem of sufficient importance that Congress has decided to regulate it by way of a federal statute. The importance of many of the cases that federal judges handle, plus the facts that there are relatively few federal judges and that they are appointed by the President for life, all combine to give federal district judges a certain prestige that does not attach to state trial court judges.

Federal Courts with Specialized Jurisdiction There are several federal courts with specialized jurisdiction. They are the United States Claims Court, which handles exclusively claims against the federal government; the Tax Court, which handles suits involving federal taxes; the Court of International Trade, which handles civil matters related to tariff and trade agreements; and the system of bankruptcy courts housed with the federal district courts. In addition, there are the District of Columbia Superior Court and the District of Columbia Court of Appeals, which act like "state" courts for Washington, D.C. where local law is federal law. There is also a Foreign Intelligence Surveillance Court, which determines applications by the Attorney General for permission to implement domestic wiretaps in the interest of national security and which uses judges from the regular federal courts. Two specialized courts deal with military and veterans matters: the Court of Military Appeals reviews court-martial convictions for military offenses and the Court of Veterans Appeals reviews decisions of the Department of Veterans Affairs on claims for veterans benefits.

The judges of all these specialized courts, except the Court of International Trade and Foreign Intelligence Surveillance Court, are called "Article I judges" and their courts "Article I courts." Unlike "Article III" district judges, they are not appointed for life, but for specific terms. The differences between the two types of judges and the effect these differences have on their powers are considered in the chapter on administrative law, since similar issues arise with administrative agency adjudicators.[36]

The volume of cases these specialized courts handle is insignificant in comparison to district courts. Congress has generally resisted pressures to create more federal courts with specialized jurisdiction, preferring that most federal judicial business be handled by "generalist" Article III judges who handle all kinds of cases.

Federal Courts of Appeals Above the federal district level are the 13 federal courts of appeal. There is a right to appeal all final judgments of district courts to the circuit courts of appeals of the appropriate circuit. In addition, the circuit courts have jurisdiction to hear appeals from decisions of certain administrative agencies, such as the National Labor Relations Board and the Department of Health and Human Services.[37]

---

36 Chapter VI, pp. 212-214. *See also infra* p. 181 and note 71, where federal magistrate judges, also Article I judges, are discussed.

37 The federal courts of appeals are sometimes called "circuit" courts of appeal because the judges at one point had to "ride circuit," i.e., to travel through the states under their jurisdiction along a regular route, usually on horseback, and hold court in various places along that route.

Eleven of these 13 circuits cover several states. For example, the Sixth Circuit covers Ohio, Kentucky, Tennessee and Michigan. The District of Columbia Circuit covers that federal territory. The Federal Circuit is not organized on a geographical basis at all. It has been assigned the task of handling appeals that involve patents and certain damages suits against the United States government from any of the 94 district courts, as well as appeals from the Claims Court and the Court of International Trade. The smallest number of court of appeals judges is in the First Circuit, which has 6, and the largest is in the Ninth Circuit, which has 28.

The federal circuit courts of appeal have the right to disagree with one another and decisions from one circuit only have persuasive precedential effect in another circuit. The result is that there can be and often is a different rule on a point of federal law in New York (a state in the Second Circuit) and in California (a state in the Ninth Circuit). Just such a "split in the circuits" forms one basis for the Supreme Court to exercise its power to review decisions of the circuit courts of appeal, as discussed below.

3. The United States Supreme Court

Nature and Dual Function The Supreme Court of the United States is part of the federal court system, but has a hybrid function. As one might expect, it exercises appellate jurisdiction over cases appealed from the United States Courts of Appeals, but it also exercises appellate jurisdiction over state courts as to *federal issues*.[38]

The Supreme Court is the only court that is specifically created by the Constitution. However, its composition and jurisdiction are determined by Congress. Currently and since 1868, the Court has consisted of a total of 9 judges: 8 associate justices and one "Chief Justice of the United States." It has had as few as 5 and as many as 10 justices. The Court is located in Washington, D.C. and hears every case *en banc*, meaning that all 9 justices sit together and make final decisions in all cases.

Certiorari and Appeals There are two routes to review in the U.S. Supreme Court: an appeal as a matter of right and the discretionary grant of a writ of certiorari. Very few cases fall into the category of appeals as of right, so as a practical matter certiorari is the only way to gain Supreme Court review.[39] Certiorari means to "bring up the record," an essential first step for review of a case by an appellate court. By exercising its appellate certiorari jurisdiction over cases involving issues of federal law coming from the lower federal courts and the highest courts of the states, the Court maintains the supremacy and consistency of federal law.

Certiorari Procedure In a private conference held each week certiorari grants are decided according to the "Rule of Four," meaning that it takes a vote of four Justices to grant certiorari. As is the case with the state supreme courts exercising discretionary jurisdiction, the Supreme Court does not view its role as one of

---

38 *See* 28 U.S.C.A. §§1254, 1257 and *supra* note 1. For a readable and more detailed description of the Supreme Court and how it operates, *see* ABRAHAM, *supra* note 2, 170-244. For even greater detail on how the Court selects and decides case, *see* SUSAN LOW BLOCH & THOMAS G. KRATTENMAKER, SUPREME COURT POLITICS (West 1994).

39 28 U.S.C.A. §§1251-1259. Appeals as of right directly to the Supreme Court are allowed only from special three-judge district court decisions. *See* 28 U.S.C.A. §1253 and §2284. Such three-judge courts are exceptions to the rule that trial courts normally have only one judge. The court is made up of two district judges and one circuit court of appeals judge and is authorized only when reapportionment of legislative districts is ordered and occasionally when Congress desires speedy resolution of a constitutional issue. *See, e.g., United States v. Eichman*, 496 U.S. 310 (1990) (constitutionality federal statute making illegal burning of the U.S. flag), discussed in Chapter IX, p. 351.

correcting error, but as one of serving the broader interests of the law and the legal system. Thus, its rules provide that certiorari will be granted only when a federal appeals court or a state supreme court has decided a federal law question in conflict with another federal appeals court or state supreme court, or where "a state court or a United States court of appeals has decided an important question of federal law that has not been, but should be, settled by this Court, or has decided an important federal question in a way that conflicts with relevant decisions of this Court."[40] Typically, the Supreme Court will receive about 6,000 petitions for certiorari and will grant review in only about 130 of them, or about 2%.[41]

Original Jurisdiction The Supreme Court also has original jurisdiction in a narrow category of cases. These cases form a negligible part of its business, usually less than one-tenth of the number in which certiorari is granted. Virtually all the original jurisdiction cases handled by the Court involve disputes between states. Most such cases concern territorial disputes, usually arising as a result of a river changing its course.[42] A notable non-territorial dispute was the seemingly interminable litigation between Texas, California and Utah over which state had the right to tax the estate of multi-billionaire Howard Hughes.[43] As the court of first instance in these cases, the Supreme Court acts as a trial court. Since a trial before the Supreme Court would be unwieldy, the Court appoints a "special master," usually a retired federal judge, to hear proofs and make a recommended decision in such disputes.

C. Judges and Methods of Judicial Selection

1. Characteristics of Judges

Experience as Members of the Bar Virtually all judges today are members of the bar. As such, they have gone through the same legal education and procedures for acceptance into the bar described in Chapter IV.[44] At one point in United States history, judges were neither members of the bar nor even trained in law. From colonial times until well into the nineteenth century, "lay judges" were not uncommon

---

40 Supreme Court Rule 10.

41 For the 1996 term, the Court decided 158 cases out of 6,695. While the number of certiorari petitions has increased by four times in the last 40 years, the number of cases in which the Court grants review has actually gone down, decreasing from 206 to 158 since 1992. For description and analysis of the Court's certiorari practices, *see* BLOCH & KRATTENMAKER, *supra* note 38, at. 325-380, as well as the process of collegial decision-making on the merits of cases (pp. 381-444) and particularly the role of the Chief Justice (pp. 445-512). A useful annual summary and analysis of the most important decisions of the Court is published in the Harvard Law Review each Fall. *See, e.g., The Supreme Court 1997 Term, Leading Cases*, 112 HARV. L.REV. 122 (1998).

42 *See, e.g., Arkansas v. Tennessee*, 310 U.S. 563 (1940) (holding Arkansas had through acquiescence given up its legal claim to land cut away from Arkansas and attached to Tennessee island by Mississippi River due to avulsion in the early 1800s given Tennessee's unchallenged exercise of governmental authority over land for years).

43 *See California v. Texas*, 437 U.S. 601 (1978) and *California v. Texas*, 457 U.S. 164 (1982). The litigation finally ended in 1991. A recent case of note was litigation between New Jersey and New York over their claims to filled portions of Ellis Island, the famous entry point for many waves of immigrants to the United States. *New Jersey v. New York*, 523 U.S. 767 (1998).

44 *See* pp. 124-136.

in the United States.[45] Things are different today, although there are still a few non-lawyer judges in some rural areas in some states.[46]

Judges in the United States almost always come to the bench following several years of law practice, whether as private lawyers, prosecutors, or public defenders. Because of this, new judges in the United States tend to be older than their counterparts in civil law countries, most of whom start out on the judicial ladder shortly after finishing their legal education.[47] Part of the Anglo-American tradition of preferring older judges has to do with the need for the judge to have gained adequate knowledge of the law and the complexities of court procedure, particularly how to handle the relatively complicated adversary trial process, a task for which law school does not prepare them particularly well. But it is more than that. Experience, not just as a lawyer, but in life, is deemed essential for the exercise of mature judgment, which many view as the hallmark of a good judge in the United States. This is particularly so in a common law system where judges have lawmaking powers.

Career Paths of Judges Career paths of judges in the United States differ from the career paths of judges in civil law countries and of judges in England.[48] Judges in the United States usually do not start at the bottom of the judicial ladder and work their way up to positions on higher courts and more responsibility. A judge in the United States who starts out at the trial level is likely to remain there unless he or she makes some effort to gain the attention of the electorate or political appointing authorities. There is no official "performance review" system. Similarly, a judge can start a judicial career at any level in the judiciary, depending on his or her ability to influence the voters or the inclinations of the appointing authorities. Thus, a lawyer who has no prior judicial experience can become a justice on a court of last resort in a state or even the United States Supreme Court. Felix Frankfurter came to the Court after a 25-year law-teaching career. The current Chief Justice William Rehnquist was Chief of the Office of Legal Counsel at the Department of Justice. In fact, fewer than half of the justices who have served on the United States Supreme Court had prior judicial experience of any kind. Interestingly, there is no legal requirement that federal judges even be lawyers.[49]

---

45 Of the eleven judges of the Massachusetts Superior Court from 1760 to 1774, nine had never practiced law and six had never studied it. New York included the governor and legislators on its highest court until well into the nineteenth century. *See* LAWRENCE FRIEDMAN, A HISTORY OF AMERICAN LAW, 2D ED. 125 (Touchstone Books, New York 1985). Use of lay judges was consistent with English practice of having trial courts run by layperson squires and having a legislative body, the House of Lords, as the court of last resort in the system.

46 The Supreme Court has held that it does not violate the due process clause of the Constitution for a defendant to be tried before a non-lawyer judge in a petty criminal case, at least where there is a right to *de novo* re-trial in a higher court with a lawyer-judge. *North v. Russell*, 427 U.S. 328 (1976). In reaction to erratic and legally questionable behavior of some lay judges, several states have enacted laws requiring that all judges in the state be lawyers. *See generally* ABRAHAM, *supra* note 2, at 21, 138-140.

47 For a further description of courts and judges in the United States with comparisons to other countries, *see* ABRAHAM, *supra* note 2.

48 For a more detailed comparison of the career paths of English and American judges, *see* P. S. ATIYAH AND ROBERT S. SUMMERS, FORM AND SUBSTANCE IN ANGLO-AMERICAN LAW 347-353 (Clarendon Press 1987).

49 A useful summary of the backgrounds of recent United States Supreme Court justices is set out in DANIEL A. FARBER, WILLIAM ESKRIDGE, JR. & PHILIP FRICKEY, CONSTITUTIONAL LAW, 2D ED. 29-32 (West 1998). Justice Frankfurter once remarked that "the correlation between prior judicial experience and fitness for the functions of the Supreme Court is zero." Felix Frankfurter, *The Supreme Court in the Mirror of Justice*, 105 U.PA.L.REV. 781, 795 (1957).

Judges as Political Beings As will be discussed shortly, under most judicial selection systems in the United States, judges either run for election by the general population or are appointed by elected officials. Consequently, whether the post is that of federal or state judge, becoming a judge depends in large part on the candidate's ability to attract political support. Consequently, it is not surprising that many judges in the United States are "political people" — people who have been involved in politics on a regular basis in some capacity, whether as office holders, political organizers, fund-raisers, campaign managers or party chairs. It is sometimes the case, especially for judicial candidates for appellate courts, that any law practice experience they had ended many years ago and was superseded by a much longer political career. Whatever their past political background, however, once on the bench, judges are not supposed to engage in partisan political activity.

But while a judge may have to cease political activity of the partisan sort after going on the bench, the political orientation of candidates continues to make itself felt after appointment through their "judicial philosophy." A central component of that philosophy is a concept of the proper role of courts in society. Judicial philosophy may be a "liberal-activist" one that emphasizes the role of courts in fighting social injustice and expanding individual rights. Or it may be a more "conservative" philosophy of judicial restraint, which maintains that courts should rarely intervene to upset a legislative judgment or interfere with administrative action. More recently, a "conservative activist" philosophy has emerged on the Supreme Court among conservative appointees who have sought to upset or limit liberal precedents.

Other elements of judicial philosophy might involve attitudes about such "non-political" issues as the proper limits of tort recovery for personal injury, the rights of consumers against manufacturers, the rights of criminal defendants or even the rights of shareholders in a corporation against management. More generally, all people — including judges — have a natural tendency to be sympathetic toward one side or the other when they learn of a dispute between the government and the individual, the government and a business, rich and poor, businesses and individuals, or even state and federal governments. This is not to say that judicial decisions can be made on overtly political grounds. However, when the case is a close one and a rational decision either way is possible and supportable by the law and the facts, these general inclinations can have a crucial influence.[50]

It should be emphasized that many of these elements of judicial philosophy are often unconscious or, when conscious, are not thought of as being political. They are in any event no different from the kinds of attitudes that often influence judicial decision-making in other legal systems. But the fact that judges in the United States have a well-developed political "past" makes the connection between political viewpoint and judicial decision more transparent. It is not uncommon for lawyers in an important case to read the judicial opinions and research the political background of the judge before whom they are soon to appear for some insight into the judge's basic political attitudes, so that they may better frame their arguments and assess their chances of success.

Judicial philosophy can grow and change, especially when nurtured by the lifetime tenure guarantees of the federal system and some state systems. For example, U. S. Supreme Court justices have produced surprises for Presidents who

---

50 Of course, when there is a jury present, issues of fact or the application of law to fact are resolved by the jury and the judge has limited power to reverse jury findings. *See* Chapter III, pp. 84, 105.

nominated them. The most notable of these was Earl Warren, a former Republican governor of California who was appointed by Republican President Dwight D. Eisenhower as Chief Justice. Following his appointment, the Warren Court proceeded to issue liberal opinions on civil rights, rights of the accused in criminal cases and in other areas, much to the dismay of conservatives. This led the plain-spoken war hero President Eisenhower to remark that his appointment of Earl Warren was the "worst damn-fool mistake I ever made as President."[51] Both William Brennan, appointed by Eisenhower, and Harry A. Blackmun, appointed by Republican President Richard M. Nixon, were Republicans who turned liberal on the Court. On the other side, Justice Byron White, appointed by Democrat John F. Kennedy, was a disappointment to liberals as he often sided with the conservative faction of the Supreme Court in criminal procedure and other cases involving constitutional rights of the individual.

Judicial Pay　United State district judges earn $136,700, court of appeals judges $145,000, Supreme Court associate justices $167,900 and the Chief Justice of the United States $175,400. Salaries of state judges on the trial courts of general jurisdiction vary from $72,042 to $115,300 with a median of $94,041. Salaries of judges of intermediate state appeals courts range from $79,413 to $124,200, with a median of $102,171. Judges of state supreme courts have salaries that range from $77,092 to $137,314, with a median of $106,110.[52] Although the salaries of judges are certainly not modest, they are less than those of many experienced and established private lawyers, from whose ranks judicial candidates are most often chosen. Clearly, for many lawyers, the attraction of being a judge is found in other aspects of the position, primarily power, prestige and a less-pressured work life.[53]

2. Judicial Selection Methods in the Federal System

As discussed earlier, to assure independence of the federal judiciary, the notion of their election (even by Congress) was rejected in favor of lifetime appointment by the President with "advice and consent" of the Senate.[54] Where the path to the bench is by way of executive appointment, the power of appointment, at least on the federal level, is generally exercised along political lines. More than 90% of judgeships bestowed by recent Presidents have been to members of their own political party, except for Gerald Ford, who appointed only 82% from his own party. The precise way that the appointment process works in the federal system varies depending on whether it is for the lower federal courts or the Supreme Court.

Lower Federal Court Appointments　Generally, the President consults with the Attorney General and other advisors, to come up with a list of nominees. In addition, because of the need for Senate approval, certain customs and practices have arisen with regard to appointments to the lower federal courts. Senators with the same party affiliation as the President have a great deal of power to "suggest" nominees to the President for district court posts in their state and have virtually an absolute right to "veto" nominees the President may be considering if they are "personally obnoxious" to the Senator. Arrangements vary from state to state and there are even compromise agreements in some states that allow a Senator of the opposite political party of the President to "suggest" judicial candidates. The President has more latitude in naming

---

51　JOHN D. WEAVER, WARREN: THE MAN, THE COURT, THE ERA 342-343 (Little, Brown & Co. 1967).

52　National Center for State Courts Survey, current as of January 1, 1998.

53　The salaries of the highest paid private lawyers were discussed in Chapter IV, p. 144.

54　*See* Article II §2 cl. 2 and Chapter I, p. 9. For more information on judicial selection, *see* ABRAHAM, *supra* note 2, at 22-39.

judges for the courts of appeal, since circuits cover more than one state, but even there seats are in practice thought of as "belonging" to one or another state, thereby assuring a major role for the Senators from that state.[55]

United States Supreme Court Appointments   The President's problem with Supreme Court nominees is less one of placating individual Senators than one of surviving the scrutiny of the Senate Judiciary Committee (which conducts hearings on judicial nominees) and the full Senate in its exercise of its right of "advice and consent." For better or for worse, the nomination and confirmation process has been a political one from the beginning. George Washington's nomination of John Rutledge to the Supreme Court in 1795 was rejected by the Senate because of the nominee's opposition to a treaty with Great Britain. Since that time, the Senate has rejected one out of every five nominations, though most of the rejections were before 1900. Earlier in this century, there was opposition to Justice Louis D. Brandeis, the first Jewish member of the Court, from railroad and business interests concerned with his past public interest advocacy activities. This delayed approval of his nomination for some five months. The degree to which there have been complaints about "politicization" of the selection process depends on whose nominee is being held up at any given time. Senator Strom Thurmond, who complained the loudest when Bork was rejected in 1987, had led an ideological campaign in 1967 against appointing Justice Thurgood Marshall, the first black justice on the Court, largely on the basis of Marshall's career as a fighter for "liberal" civil rights causes.

As the Supreme Court has become polarized into liberal and conservative camps and a long line of Republican Presidents has sought to name more and more conservative justices to the Court, Senate "advice and consent" has once again come the forefront of the public consciousness. The defeat before the Senate in 1987 of President Reagan's nomination of Robert Bork caused some of the greatest controversy in recent years.[56]

Recently, in reaction to the political controversy over nominations, Presidents have sought to choose nominees who will not cause a political stir. One way to do that is to pick a nominee about whose attitudes very little is known. President George Bush did this with Justice David Souter. Souter was dubbed the "stealth" candidate by the press, the reference being to the United States warplane that is constructed in such a way as to be undetectable on radar. President Bill Clinton's first appointment, Ruth Bader Ginsburg, while detectable on "political radar," had demonstrated moderate views while serving on the Court of Appeals. The same could be said for Stephen Breyer, the Clinton nominee most recently approved, who was confirmed by an almost unanimous Senate vote.[57]

---

55 A deputy attorney general under President Kennedy once remarked that, in light of the realities of judicial selection, the Constitution "reads backwards" — that it should say "the Senators shall nominate and with the consent of the President appoint judges . . . ." *See* ABRAHAM, *supra* note 2, at 22, n.5.

56 The Bork debacle is all the more notable for the fact that the nominee took his defeat to the public by way of a book and regular newspaper articles seeking to "expose" the process that defeated his nomination as an illegitimate political move by the Senate that has no place in the process. *See* ROBERT BORK, THE TEMPTING OF AMERICA (Touchstone Books 1990) and Chapter IX, p. 308, note 20. The most recent acrimonious debate over a nominee for the Court were the Senate hearings in 1991 involving Clarence Thomas. While the Thomas hearings had some political overtones, they were largely focused on the judges' non-political activities — alleged sexual harassment of a female employee in his office.

57 In this respect, *see* LOUIS FISHER, CONSTITUTIONAL DIALOGUES 135-143 (Princeton U. Press 1988) (arguing that the nomination process is an integral part of the constitutional decision-making process that involves a complex interaction among all three branches of the federal government, the states and the general public).

The fact that political considerations enter into judicial selection should not be taken as an indication that those appointed are not qualified. At the very least, an incompetent judge is a political liability for the appointing politician. Especially as to the federal bench, there exists a convention of appointing highly qualified candidates. Selection based on merit has been aided by the American Bar Association (ABA), which has been active in rating federal judicial candidates. A nominee with an unfavorable rating from the ABA will face hard questions from Senators during confirmation hearings.[58]

3. State Judicial Selection Systems

States have a wide variety of systems for selection of judges. Some are the same for all courts in the state, while others have different selection systems depending on what level of court is involved.[59]

Executive Appointment Systems An executive appointment system, whereby the governor of the state appoints judges, exists in some states. The appointment is sometimes from a pre-screened slate of candidates, sometimes with input from the legislature, and sometimes without any limitation. Judicial terms of office can be for life or for a term of years from as short as 4 or 6 years or as long as 12 to 15 years.

Electoral Systems for Judicial Selection Many state systems provide for the election of judges by a vote of the general populace. Election of judges is based on the notion that judges, no less than any other public official exercising power in a democracy, should ultimately be answerable to the people. Today electoral systems are in decline, but still enjoy widespread use in the states.[60]

There are several different versions of electoral systems for judges. Sometimes judges are elected by a vote of the general populace and sometimes by a vote of the state legislature. In some states where the general electorate chooses judges, judicial candidates run by party affiliation just as executive and legislative candidates do. In others, they run as non-partisan candidates. This requirement is based on the notion that it is unseemly for judges to conduct partisan political campaigns.[61]

Modified "Missouri" Plans An interesting system for judicial selection was developed in the state of Missouri in 1940 and has been adopted in one form or another in almost half the states. The "Missouri Plan" is said to combine the best features of an election system and the best features of an appointment system, with additional measures taken to assure non-partisan selection of candidates based on merit. Under this plan, judicial candidates are screened by a nominating committee composed of lawyers, judges and laypersons. The committee selects three candidates for every judicial vacancy on the basis of their credentials and merits, and submits these nominees to the state's governor who must select one of the three. The appointment is for at least a year and until the next general election, at which time the

---

58 For a discussion of the role of the ABA in federal judicial selection and other aspects of that process, *see* HAROLD W. CHASE, FEDERAL JUDGES: THE APPOINTING PROCESS (U. of Minn. Press 1972).

59 A summary of all the states' systems is set out in BOOK OF THE STATES: 1992-1993 233-234 (Council of State Governments, Lexington, Ky. 1993).

60 Some states have always provided for an electoral system. However, many states began with executive appointment systems and then changed to an electoral system in the mid-19th century, a time of great populism in the country, reflected and magnified by the presidency of Andrew Jackson, a popular general who championed "the common man." *See* FRIEDMAN, *supra* note 45, at 371.

61 States with election systems regulate closely judicial candidates' campaign conduct and other political activity. *See, e.g.,* Michigan Code of Judicial Conduct, Canon 7.

question is placed on the ballot as to whether the judge should be "retained" in office. If the judge is retained, then the judge serves for a 12-year term on the appellate courts and for a shorter term in the trial courts. Statistics show that the electorate votes to retain virtually all judges. Some form of an appointment and retention system has been adopted in almost half the states.

Evaluating Judicial Selection Systems Election of judges has been criticized on several grounds. An obvious one is its failure to assure adequate judicial independence as judges will worry more about popular reaction to their decisions than the proper application of the law. Another concern is that the general population does not know enough about law or judicial qualifications to choose their judges wisely. Often the sophisticated voter and even the average lawyer will not be familiar with all the judicial candidates on the ballot. The question of how to finance judicial election campaigns complicates matters. Lawyers are a natural source of campaign contributions, but there is the danger of judges treating contributing and non-contributing lawyers differently after they are elected. This is possible not only with respect to the decision of cases, but also as to other discretionary functions that judges perform, such appointments of lawyers to represent indigent defendants.

With all its difficulties, however, electoral systems have managed to select qualified judges to many appellate courts. For example, the highest court of New York, the New York Court of Appeals, was elected before 1978 and was known as perhaps the best state court in the nation.[62] And appointment systems are not without problems. While the tradition with federal judges has been generally to avoid the appointment of unqualified candidates, governors of states have sometimes used their appointment powers to reward political supporters without sufficient concern for their judicial qualifications.

It should also be noted that many states that supposedly have electoral systems operate under a *de facto* modified appointment and retention system. The executive has the power to make interim appointments if judges die or resign in the middle of their term. The interim appointed judges who complete the unexpired term are listed as "judge" on the ballot in the upcoming election and they can argue that they have proven that they can do the job. These factors will likely give them an almost insurmountable advantage of other candidates. In some states there is a tradition of elected judges resigning before the end of their terms just so that the governor can appoint a replacement who will then have an advantage in the next election.[63]

4. Removal and Discipline of Judges

Impeachment of Federal Judges The only constitutional method of removing federal judges is impeachment by the House and conviction in the Senate for "Treason, Bribery, or other high Crimes and Misdemeanors."[64] The first judge to be impeached and removed was John Pickering in 1803, who was charged with misconduct in a trial and being drunk while on the bench. Justice Samuel Chase was impeached in 1804 for what could be described as political reasons, but he was

---

62 Chief Judge Stanley H. Fuld, considered an exceptional judge, was so popular that he was nominated by all four political parties for reelection in 1966.

63 Just how much advantage is enjoyed by incumbent judges is testified to by the fact that many of them, particularly trial judges, consistently face no opposition at election time. For a comparative look at American and English judicial appointment practice, *see* ATIYAH & SUMMERS, *supra* note 48.

64 Article II §4. For impeachment, a majority vote in the House is needed. For conviction and removal from office, a two-thirds majority is needed in the Senate. Article I §3 cl. 6.

acquitted in the Senate. Since then, Congress has used impeachment as a means of removing or attempting to remove federal judges from office only 7 times.[65] Hostility to judicial decisions has not been the motivating force in most impeachments. Indeed, most removals of federal judges from office in recent years have followed the judge's conviction of a serious crime in the ordinary courts.

Congress has removed three federal judges recently and each case presented its memorable aspects. Harry Claiborne of Nevada, the first federal judge in some 50 years to be impeached, had been convicted of the crime of federal income tax evasion. He was serving a prison sentence in a Louisiana federal prison, but steadfastly refused to resign from office. He continued to draw his salary until Congress voted by a wide margin to remove him. Judge Alcee Hastings of Florida was acquitted of bribery before a jury in 1983, but Congress felt there was sufficient evidence of guilt to proceed with impeachment. Congress impeached him and removed him from office in 1987. Hastings was subsequently elected to Congress and some people joked that he might get to vote on his own impeachment. Most recently, the 1989 impeachment of Judge Walter Nixon is notable because it resulted in a constitutional challenge to the impeachment process used. The Senate did not convict Nixon by way of a trial before the *entire* Senate. Instead, it appointed a committee of twelve Senators to hear the evidence and to report that evidence to the full Senate, which then voted on the impeachment charge. In *Nixon v. United States*,[66] the Court rejected Nixon's challenges to this procedure, holding that the lawsuit presented a non-justiciable political question solely within the power of Congress to determine.[67]

Removal of State Judges For states with electoral systems or systems providing for electoral retention of judges, removal is theoretically possible at each general election. However, incumbent judges — even more than incumbent legislators — tend to be reelected over and over again with little trouble. A recent exception to matter-of-course retention took place in California. There the Chief Justice Rose Bird and two other justices were ousted by the voters, who did not like their record of voting to overturn death penalty sentences.[68]

Whatever judicial selection system states have, they also provide for midterm removal for criminal behavior, incompetence, "lack of judicial temperament," and other good cause. Review of a judge's behavior is generally undertaken by a state commission on the complaint of a lawyer, litigant or member of the public. The commission has power to take or recommend to the supreme court of the state appropriate disciplinary action, including removal from the bench. Most often these commissions are referred to as the Judicial Tenure Commission or Board of Judicial Standards. Impeachment by the legislature is usually an additional possible alternative.[69]

---

65 However, several more judges have resigned rather than face impeachment.

66 506 U.S. 224 (1993).

67 Three Justices took the position that judicial review of the challenge was not barred by the political question doctrine, but that the practice was constitutionally permissible.

68 *See* ABRAHAM *supra* note 2, at 36.

69 *See generally* BOOK OF THE STATES, *supra* note 59, pp. 235-241. For an account of some of the intricacies of tenure and removal of judges, *see* FISHER, *supra* note 57, at 143-149.

D. Other Judicial Officials and Assistants

1. Magistrates

The term "magistrate" can have a general meaning, referring to any kind of judge. However, it also has a more specific meaning, referring to a lower level judicial officer who is under the supervision of a judge. Thus, in the federal system, the federal Magistrates Act creates the office of "magistrate judge."[70] In contrast to the political selection process for Article III judges, federal magistrate judges are selected on a merit basis after screening by a committee of lawyers and non-lawyers. The district judges in a district make a choice from a list provided by the committee. Magistrate judges serve 8-year terms. If they do well, they are usually offered the opportunity to serve additional 8-year terms.

Magistrate judges can hold hearings on all non-dispositive motions (decisions that do not decide a case on the merits or dismiss it). Without consent of the parties they have the power to hold hearings on dispositive motions and make recommended decisions, which must then be reviewed by the district judge. With consent, they can try civil cases (including jury trials) to final judgment just as a district judge would. The degree to which federal magistrate judges are given responsibility varies from district to district and depends in large part on the attitude of the judges of that district toward delegating judicial duties. Magistrate judges are used much more widely in the federal system today than in the past as the caseload of the federal courts has increased and the need for supervision of pre-trial proceedings has grown.

The limited nature of the duties of federal magistrate judges results from their limited tenure. Article III of the Constitution requires that the "judicial power of the United States" be exercised by federal judges who have lifetime tenure. The theory that permits magistrates to exercise judicial functions at all is the idea that they are "adjuncts" to the "Article III" district judge — helpers who assist the district judge by hearing evidence and making recommendations. Under this arrangement, they may hold hearings and write recommended decisions, but responsibility for the ultimate decision must reside in an Article III judge.[71] Magistrates then are "Article I" judges. The largest category of Article I judges are administrative agency adjudicators. Consequently, the limits on the powers of Article I judges are discussed in more depth in the chapter on administrative law.[72]

Many state trial courts have magistrates and give them similar duties. Sometimes lower level judicial officers in states are called "commissioners" or "referees." Often on the state level, such officers are attorneys in private practice who work part time in their judicial role.

2. Bankruptcy Judges

Bankruptcy law is entirely federal, though state issues arise to the extent that state contract, property and tort law are relevant to the debtor's rights and obligations.[73] Bankruptcy cases are handled by a special corps of federal bankruptcy judges

---

70 28 U.S.C.A. §631 *et seq.* Federal magistrate judges have existed in some form since the first statute setting up the federal court system in 1789, but were called "commissioners" until 1968.

71 *United States v. Raddatz*, 447 U.S. 667 (1980) (Article III not violated by magistrate conducting hearing and making recommended decision on suppression motion in criminal case so long as district judges has *de novo* review power). *But see Gomez v. United States*, 490 U.S. 858 (1989) (absent consent, magistrate may not preside over jury selection in criminal trial).

72 *See* Chapter VI, pp. 212-214.

73 Bankruptcy law is discussed in Chapter XV, pp. 554-556.

attached to federal district court and appointed for 14-year terms by means of a merit selection process similar to that employed for magistrate judges. Because of their term limitations, bankruptcy judges are Article I judges like federal magistrate judges and are subject to some of the same limitations. Thus, absent consent of the parties, bankruptcy judges are limited to rendering recommended decisions on many issues. However, on matters directly concerning bankruptcy discharge and administration of the bankruptcy case, they may render final decisions like any other trial court. Such decisions are subject to a right of appeal to the district court, which then sits as an appellate court and provides the same scope of review and deference to fact-finding due in an appeal to an appellate court.[74]

3. Administrative Adjudicators

Administrative agencies exercise considerable judicial power when they adjudicate disputes arising in the programs they administer. Consequently, no understanding of the "judicial system" of the United States would be complete without consideration of their important functions. As already indicated, their functions and the limits on powers of other Article I judges are discussed in the next chapter on administrative law.

4. Court Clerks, Law Clerks and Other Court Officials

Administrators Each court, trial or appellate, has a chief "clerk of the court" who is in charge of administrative matters and in whose office all litigation documents are filed and kept. In addition, judges are assisted by other clerks or secretaries who run their chambers, do filing and typing and draft routine orders and correspondence. Also important are court reporters who keep a record of all proceedings before the judge.

Law Clerks The person of greatest direct assistance to a judge on any level is a "judicial clerk" or "law clerk," also called "law secretaries" in some jurisdictions. All federal trial and appellate judges and all state appellate judges and justices have full-time law clerks to do legal research and drafting of opinions and memoranda of decisions. Most often judicial law clerks are recent law school graduates who work for the judge (or for the entire court if that is the system) for a short period of time, usually one or two years. Judicial clerks, especially those working for federal judges and state supreme court justices, usually have excellent law school records and often have writing and research experience as members of the law review of their law school. Average pay for such clerks runs between $24,000 and $39,000.[75] While many law clerks could conceivably get higher paying jobs in private practice, they choose to be law clerks because of the experience and education they will gain and because of the prestige attached to such service. The most prestigious of judicial clerkship posts are those held by law clerks for justices of the United States Supreme Court, many of whom go on to impressive careers as private lawyers or law teachers. Some Supreme Court law clerks return later in life to the Supreme Court as Supreme Court justices. For example, the current Chief Justice William Rehnquist was clerk to Justice Robert Jackson.

The vast majority of state trial judges do not have full-time law school graduates as law clerks. However, many state trial court judges in urban areas have at least law-

---

74 28 U.S.C.A. §§157-158. The areas of law in which Article I judges are allowed are explained in Chapter VI, pp. 212-213, in conjunction with *Northern Pipeline Co. v. Marathon Pipeline Co.*, 458 U.S. 50 (1982), a case in which the Supreme Court held the entire bankruptcy judge system unconstitutional.

75 "What Lawyers Earn," NAT'L.L.J., Special Supplement S7 (April 27, 1992).

student law clerks on a regular if only on a part time basis. The reason for not providing clerks (aside from the high cost) is the assumption that state trial judges need them less, since most of their work has less to do with fine legal points than with factual issues and the exercise of discretion within known legal parameters. Many state trial judges disagree and point to the fact that they handle many of the same kinds of cases that their colleagues on the federal trial court bench do.

E. Subject-Matter Jurisdiction of State and Federal Courts

1. State Court Subject Matter Jurisdiction

In Chapter I, when the nature of state power was discussed, we saw how states before the Constitution had all the inherent powers of sovereign international states and, upon ratification, lost only those powers that they gave up in the plan of the Constitution. Consistent with this concept, state courts potentially have general and unlimited subject-matter jurisdiction over disputes of every conceivable type that are not prohibited to them by federal law. The symbol of such broad jurisdiction is the trial court of general jurisdiction of the state — the superior or circuit court — which has power to handle the widest range of cases. State court subject matter jurisdiction definitions may require that certain kinds of disputes be handled by one of its specialized courts, but for every type of case there will be some court of the state that has the power to hear it.[76]

2. Federal District Court Subject Matter Jurisdiction

In contrast to state courts, federal courts are courts of *limited* jurisdiction. As with any other organ of federal power, federal courts must trace their jurisdiction to some affirmative source of power in the Constitution. Federal judicial power is confined to cases "arising under [the] Constitution, the Laws of the United States, and Treaties," and controversies "between Citizens of different states."[77] The first category is generally referred to as "federal question" jurisdiction and the second as "diversity" jurisdiction.

Federal Question Jurisdiction Today, federal question cases comprise by far the most numerous category of cases in federal court. This was not always true. A lingering effect of the mistrust that some Framers had of the lower federal courts was that they were not given general federal question jurisdiction until 1875 — after the Civil War.[78] Before then, state courts were relied upon to enforce what federal law there was. The history of state court enforcement of federal law before the Civil War was marked by evasion, hostility and interference with federal policy at every turn.[79] The rationale for federal question jurisdiction is that federal courts will give a more consistent and more sympathetic interpretation of federal law than state courts. However, state courts retain concurrent jurisdiction over all federal question cases so that, if the parties wish to go to state court, they may. There are a few categories of federal question cases, however, where Congress has made federal court jurisdiction

---

76 States may limit the jurisdiction of their own courts. for example, as a matter of *forum non conveniens*. *See* Chapter VII, pp. 248-250.

77 Art. III §2. For more detail on subject matter jurisdiction, *see* WRIGHT, *supra* note 35, §§17-22A.

78 28 U.S.C.A. §1331. *See* Chapter I, p. 8.

79 *See generally*, John Gibbons, *Enforcement of Federal Law in State Courts 1789-1860*, 36 RUTGERS L. REV. 399 (1984). *See also* Chapter I, p. 22.

exclusive.[80] Federal question jurisdiction is most commonly invoked in such areas as civil rights, antitrust, violations of federal criminal statutes, bankruptcy, patent and copyright infringement, securities violations and labor law.

Article III does not itself bestow jurisdiction. Congress must pass a statute conferring jurisdiction as well. Federal question jurisdiction under Article III might seem to include every case in which a federal issue comes up. However, the federal question jurisdiction *statute* has been interpreted narrowly to mean that jurisdiction exists only for cases where the federal question presented is necessary to make out the *plaintiff's claim*. This rule, called the "well-pleaded complaint" rule, excludes any case where the federal issue is presented as part of a *defense*.[81] It does not matter that a defensively asserted federal issue is the most important or even the only real issue in the case. For example, a state-law defamation claim (a claim for damage to reputation caused by untrue statements) is sometimes met with a defense based on the free speech guarantees of the 1st Amendment to the Constitution.[82] Such a case can be handled only in state court.[83] The wisdom and legitimacy of the "well-pleaded complaint" rule of federal question jurisdiction have been questioned.[84] Clearly the rule abandons many important federal law issues to state courts. However, its advantages are that it is simple to administer and it allows jurisdiction to be determined at the very beginning of the lawsuit by looking only at the plaintiff's complaint.[85]

Diversity Jurisdiction Federal court jurisdiction applies to disputes between citizens of different states or between a citizen and an alien.[86] Congress has always limited diversity cases to major disputes, providing a requisite amount that must be in controversy. In 1789, the amount was $500; today it is $75,000. Diversity cases account for about 20% of the federal district court case load.

The Framers of the Constitution created diversity jurisdiction out of a concern that state courts would favor their own citizens over citizens of a different state or country. It was thought that federal judges would be more neutral in such disputes, in part because they would not identify so strongly with any particular state and in part because lifetime appointment would mean that they would not have to face the wrath of the voters for unpopular decisions. There have been recent attempts by Congress to eliminate diversity jurisdiction based on the argument that state prejudice against

---

80 Exclusive federal jurisdiction is given in admiralty cases (28 U.S.C.A. §1333), bankruptcy cases (28 U.S.C.A. §1334), patent and copyright cases (28 U.S.C.A. §1338), claims arising under the securities exchange laws (28 U.S.C.A. §78aa), federal criminal law (18 U.S.C.A. §3231), and antitrust actions (28 U.S.C.A. §1337), though the exclusion from antitrust cases is only implied.

81 *L&N R.R. v. Mottley*, 211 U.S. 149 (1908).

82 *See* Chapter IX, p. 356, and Chapter XI, pp. 426-428

83 In general, the federal law must create the claim on which the plaintiff sues. Consequently, in most cases where a federal law *issue* arises as part of a *state-law claim*, there is no jurisdiction. *See Merrill Dow Pharmaceuticals v. Thompson*, 478 U.S. 804 (1986) (no federal question jurisdiction just because proof of violation of federal drug labeling law would constitute negligence *per se* under state law). Violation of a regulatory statute as *per se* negligence is discussed in Chapter XI, p. 410.

84 *See* Donald Doernberg, *"There's No Reason For It; It's Just Our Policy": Why the Well-Pleaded Complaint Rule Sabotages the Purposes of Federal Question Jurisdiction*, 38 HASTINGS L.J. 597 (1987).

85 The well-pleaded complaint rule is only an interpretation of 28 U.S.C.A. §1331, the applicable statute. Although Article III uses the very same words, it has been interpreted as potentially including jurisdiction over cases where the federal issue arises in the defense or even in some other context. *See Verlinden B.V. v. Central Bank of Nigeria*, 461 U.S. 480 (1983) (approving statutory grant of jurisdiction where federal issue arose as an anticipation of a defense). *See* WRIGHT, *supra* note 35, §20.

86 28 U.S.C.A. §1332.

outsiders is no longer a problem in the modern, mobile age. Proponents of diversity jurisdiction dispute this and, to date, diversity jurisdiction remains.

Natural persons' citizenship is their place of domicile, or their permanent home, at the time suit is filed.[87] A corporation has dual citizenship: it is considered a citizen both of the state where it is incorporated and the state in which it has its principal place of business. Since diversity cases are based on state law, it goes without saying that there is concurrent jurisdiction of all diversity cases in state court.

Like federal question jurisdiction, diversity jurisdiction is interpreted narrowly by the Supreme Court in a way that does not completely carry out the policies behind it. The phrase, suits "between Citizens of different States," could conceivably mean any suit in which there are some parties from different states involved. However, the Supreme Court has read the applicable jurisdictional statute to require "complete diversity." In other words, *all* the plaintiffs must be from different states from *all* the defendants. Thus, there would be no diversity jurisdiction over a suit in which New York, Ohio and Michigan plaintiffs sued Florida, California and Ohio defendants, despite the fact that several out-of-state parties would be involved regardless of what federal district the suit was filed in.[88]

Removal Where subject matter jurisdiction would exist in either state or federal court, the initial court choice is made by the plaintiff. However, defendants can choose the federal forum as well through a procedure called "removal." A defendant sued in state court on a claim that would have qualified for federal court jurisdiction may remove the case from state court to the local federal court.[89] However, if removal is based solely on diversity of citizenship, the defendant may remove the case only if no defendant is a citizen of the state in whose courts the action was brought. The rationale for this rule is that diversity is designed to ensure that out-of-state parties are treated fairly, so it makes little sense to allow defendants sued in their home state's courts to have access to federal courts. Thus, if a New York plaintiff sues a California defendant in the state court in *California*, the defendant may *not* remove the case, but if the same case is filed in any other state court (e.g., New York), it *is* removable.[90]

PART II: Federalism Complications in the Judicial System

Concurrent overlapping competence of state and federal courts to handle both state and federal claims can give rise to complexities and inefficiencies.[91] We will consider two issues that arise when federal courts adjudicate state-law claims and state courts adjudicate federal-law claims: (1) what law, state or federal, applies to

---

87   In an effort to limit diversity jurisdiction in cases involving aliens, Congress recently amended §1332 to provide that "an alien admitted to the United States for permanent residence shall be deemed a citizen of the state in which such alien is domiciled." This change does not bestow United States citizenship; it only relates to federal court jurisdiction.

88   The same phrase in Article III, suit "between Citizens of different States," has been interpreted as allowing less than complete diversity, so Congress could if it wished define diversity more broadly than the present statute.. *See State Farm Fire and Casualty Co. v. Tashire*, 386 U.S. 523 (1967) (upholding constitutionality of 28 U.S.C.A. §1335).

89   28 U.S.C.A. §1441. The case is removed to the federal court of the district where the state court is located.

90   Federal courts are authorized to include as part of the case they assume jurisdiction over some claims that involve neither diverse parties nor federal questions if those claims arise out of the same facts. *See* 28 U.S.C.A. §1367 and *United Mine Workers v. Gibbs*, 383 U.S. 715 (1966). This concept of jurisdiction, called "supplemental jurisdiction," is based on the notion of economy and fairness.

91   Overlapping jurisdiction in the courts of *different states* also causes complication. This topic discussed in the chapter on civil procedure. *See* Chapter VII, pp. 244-258.

what kinds of issues in such "mixed" cases and (2) the structure for appellate review of issues in mixed cases. Another feature of overlapping jurisdiction is the potential for simultaneous litigation of the same dispute in both state and federal court. That issue will also be examined briefly.

A. Law Applied in Federal and State Courts

1. Law Applied When State-Law Claims Are Adjudicated in Federal Court

The Rules of Decision Act   As already alluded to in Chapter I, Congress has provided since 1789 in the Rules of Decision Act that federal courts handling state-law claims must follow state law.[92] The Act has been interpreted to mean that federal courts must follow state law on all *substantive* issues, but that they may follow their own federal *procedural* law. This is consistent with the traditional conflict-of-laws notion that the forum court is permitted to apply its own procedural rules. The precise scope of the command of the Rules of Decision Act was made clear in the 1938 case of *Erie, Lackawanna R.R. v. Tompkins*, and issues under the Act are referred to as "*Erie* questions."[93]

Erie's dichotomy of substantive state law, but procedural federal law is consistent with general conflict-of-laws principles. But the special policies behind the *Erie* decision may cause the substantive-procedural line to be drawn in a different place than might be expected in the conflicts situation.

Anti-Forum-Shopping Policy The first relevant policy is the policy against "forum-shopping." The Framers of the Constitution made federal courts available as an alternative to state courts to provide a more neutral *forum* for disputes between citizens from different states. They did not intend that federal courts would provide a different *body of law* to decide those disputes. Thus, parties should not be able to "forum-shop" between state and federal court in order to obtain a better result in their cases, based on the state court applying state law and the federal court applying federal law.[94] Consistent with this policy, the substance-procedure question for *Erie* purposes is decided according to the "outcome determinative" test: an issue is considered to be a "substantive" one calling for application of state law if (1) applying federal law would cause the court to come to a different result and (2) that difference

---

92 *See* 28 U.S.C.A. §1652.

93 304 U.S. 64 (1938). *Erie* made clear that federal courts must follow *all* of state law, both statutory and common law. This "corrected" an old case interpreting the Rules of Decision Act that held that the "laws of the several states" that the Act required federal courts to follow meant only state *statutory* law, not common law decisions. *Swift v. Tyson*, 41 U.S.(16 Pet.) 1 (1842). The holding in *Swift* was understandable given the "discovery" view of the common law prevalent at that time: since there could only be one correct common law view, all courts, state and federal, should come to the same result. In Chapter II, we saw how Justice Holmes's realism about common law exploded the discovery myth. His view was ultimately adopted by the Court in *Erie*: that the common law, like any other law, is the command of a particular sovereign and uniformity of decisions is possible only if federal courts are required to follow the state courts *own version* of the common law. *See* Chapter II, pp. 41-42.

94 Such "forum-shopping" was rampant before *Erie* required federal courts to follow state common law as well as statutory law. *See Black & White Taxi Co. v. Brown & Yellow Taxi Co.*, 276 U.S. 518 (1928) (plaintiff Kentucky corporation reincorporated in Tennessee to create the diversity of citizenship that would allow it to sue in the Kentucky federal court and thus avoid Kentucky state common law that would have defeated its claim in state court).

is the kind of difference that would influence the parties to choose federal court over state court.[95]

This test is easy to apply in most situations. For example, the law relating to the standard of conduct by which a court judges the defendant's actions in a tort case is clearly substantive under this standard. Other issues are less clear. For example, the law may provide that the "burden of proof" is on one party or the other in a particular kind of case. Burden of proof sounds "procedural" in an intuitive sense, but it clearly can affect the outcome of the case. Consequently, burden of proof is classified as "substantive," and state rather than federal law on burden of proof must be applied by the federal court.[96] The Court has held that all the following issues are substantive law issues calling for the application of state rather than federal law: time limitation periods within which suit must be filed,[97] a requirement that a bond be posted by shareholders before they may sue their corporation,[98] and laws prohibiting suit by any corporation not licensed to do business in the state.[99] Most importantly for purposes of later discussions, the Court has held that *choice of law* rules are substantive, thus calling for the federal court to apply the choice of law laws of the state where it sits.[100]

It is important to emphasize that the Rules of Decision Act is concerned only with one kind of forum-shopping: parties seeking to take advantage of the difference between *federal and state* law. It has nothing to say about parties taking advantage of a difference between the *law of two different states*. Shopping *between states* for better law, made possible by state choice-of-law rules, does not offend the need for federal and state courts in the same state to apply the same substantive law.

Supremacy of Federal Law   Despite the importance of preventing forum-shopping, that policy may conflict with the supremacy of federal law. Some state laws or practices, regardless of how "substantive" they appear, may disrupt important and well-established federal court procedures. If so, the supremacy of federal requires they be displaced by federal law. In some cases, this is so even if applying federal law might change the outcome of the case and lead to forum-shopping. For example, in one case, state law required that a particular mixed fact-law issue be determined by the judge, while federal law would normally give such an issue to the jury to determine. The Court held that the "strong federal policy against allowing state rules to disrupt the judge-jury relationship in the federal courts" required that the federal

---

95 *Guaranty Trust Co. v. York*, 326 U.S. 99 (1945). Since defendants have the power to remove many diversity cases to federal court, defendants as well as plaintiffs can engage in "forum-shopping." *See* discussion of removal, *supra* p. 185.

96 *Palmer v. Hoffman*, 318 U.S. 109 (1945).

97 *Ragan v. Merchants Transfer & Warehouse Co.*, 337 U.S. 530 (1949); *Walker v. Armco Steel Corp.*, 446 U.S. 740 (1980). These periods are referred to as "statutes of limitations."

98 *Cohen v. Beneficial Indus. Loan Corp.*, 337 U.S. 541 (1949). Shareholder suits are discussed in Chapter XV, p. 545.

99 *Woods v. Interstate Realty Co.* 337 U.S. 535 (1949).

100 *Klaxon Co. v. Stentor Electric Mfg. Co.*, 313 U.S. 487 (1941). *See e.g. Day & Zimmermann, Inc. v. Challoner*, 423 U.S. 3 (1975) (in a diversity suit brought by the parents of a soldier killed in Cambodia against manufacturer of artillery shell, the federal court located in Texas had to apply Cambodian tort law since that is the body of law that Texas choice-of-law rules indicated would be applied had the suit been brought in the Texas state court). *See generally* Chapter VII, pp. 252-258, where choice of law rules are discussed. However, some federal appeals courts have applied *federal* common law conflicts rules to state law claims arising under a federal law giving federal courts jurisdiction over claims arising out of international banking transactions. *See Edelman v. Chase Manhattan Bank*, 861 F.2d 1291 (1st Cir. 1988).

court apply the federal rule.[101] It was also clear that who determined the issue would not in most cases affect how the issue was resolved and the state's choice of the judge was a matter of historical accident. In *Gasperini v. Center for Humanities*,[102] a New York law affected the judge-jury relationship directly by requiring its judges to reduce jury awards that "deviate materially from what would be reasonable compensation." The normal federal standard allows reduction only if the verdict was so excessive as to "shock the conscience" of the court. The Court upheld application of the New York rule by federal courts in diversity cases because it was clearly outcome-determinative and the state had substantive policy reasons for enacting it.

The strongest expression of federal procedural interests occurs when the federal law on the subject is set out in one of the Federal Rules of Civil Procedure or its equivalent. In such cases, the Supreme Court has followed a policy of presumptive application of the federal rule regardless of how "outcome-determinative" its effects might be.[103] This policy has resulted in differing outcomes between state and federal courts and to that extent encourages forum-shopping.[104]

2. Law Applied When Federal Law Claims are Adjudicated in State Court

The procedural-substantive dichotomy arises when a *federal claim* is filed in *state court*, and the Court has imposed a rough "reverse-*Erie*" rule: the forum state court applies its own procedural law even while applying substantive federal law. However, the supremacy of federal law can pre-empt a procedural state rule that "unduly" interferes with assertion of a federal claim. For example, in *Brown v. Western Railway of Alabama*, the plaintiff brought suit on a federal claim in the Georgia state court. The plaintiff's complaint was dismissed based on a Georgia state pleading rule that provided that pleadings would be "construed strictly against the pleader."[105] Despite the fact that rules about pleadings would seem intuitively to be "procedural," the Supreme Court held the Georgia rule invalid as applied to the federal claim on the ground that it "unduly interfered" with assertion of the federal claim. This was so despite the fact that the state court applied the rule evenhandedly to all claims that came before it, whether state or federal.

3. Appeals of Federal Law Issues in State Court and State Law Issues in Federal Court

As can be seen, state courts routinely decide issues of federal law and federal courts routinely decide issues of state law. If a state court is wrong on an issue of federal law, the Supreme Court has the power to review that state court's judgment

---

101 *Byrd v. Blue Ridge Rural Electrical Cooperative*, 356 U.S. 525 (1958) (issue was whether the plaintiff was an "employee" of the defendant; if so, he was only entitled to Workmens Compensation administrative remedy; if he was not an "employee," he could sue in court for damages).

102 518 U.S. 415 (1996).

103 *Hanna v. Plumer*, 380 U.S. 460 (1965). *See generally* FRIEDENTHAL, KANE & MILLER, *supra* note 14, §§4.1-4.3.

104 *See, e.g.*, *Stewart Organization, Inc. v. Ricoh Corp.*, 487 U.S. 22 (1988) (federal statute allowing transfers of cases permits transfer pursuant to forum-selection clause of contract even though applicable state law would render such clause unenforceable as a matter of state contract law); *Business Guides, Inc. v. Chromatic Communications Enterprises, Inc.*, 498 U.S. 533 (1991) (FRCP 11 imposing liability on represented parties for prosecution of a groundless suit will apply to a suit in federal court regardless of whether such liability exists in state law for a suit filed in state court).

105 338 U.S. 294 (1949). *See also Felder v. Casey*, 487 U.S. 131 (1988) (state pre-suit notice of claim requirement when suing the government unduly interferes with assertion of federal civil rights claim).

on issues of *federal* law.[106] However, if a federal court in a diversity of citizenship case is wrong on an issue of *state* law, there is no comparable appeal to a state court with final authority to decide the issue of state law. An appeal to the United States Supreme Court is to no avail, since it has always disclaimed the power to review issues of *state* law arising in either state or federal courts. No appeal from the federal court to the state supreme court of the relevant state is possible. There is no mechanism for it and whole nature of the supremacy of federal law and institutions over the states would seem to deny any such power.[107] Thus, while federal courts are supposed to follow state law as declared by the state's highest court, state law is not always clear and there is no provision for definitive appellate review. Federal courts then are sometimes relegated to a "best guess" as to the content of state law.

The danger of lower federal court mistakes on issues of state law is lessened considerably by the fact that federal district judges are admitted to the bar of the state where the federal court is located, are usually experienced lawyers, and are often former state court judges from that state. In addition, many states have a procedure for federal courts to "certify" unclear issues of state law to the state supreme court.[108] But there is no federal certification law and not all states have a certification procedure. Moreover, certification sometimes does not work very well. One problem is certification is optional with the federal judge, who may resist admitting inability to determine an issue of state law. From the state side, state supreme courts often resist deciding legal issues in the abstract, and may even be prohibited by their constitutions or laws from doing so. Or an abstract answer may be given that is unclear.[109] The result is that mistakes are sometime made in forecasting how an issue would be decided in state court law, especially on an issue of first impression.[110] At the same time, because of the quality of some federal court decisions on state law issues of first impression, those federal decisions are sometimes followed by state courts, even though they technically qualify only as persuasive precedential authority.[111]

B. Simultaneous Litigation in State and Federal Court

Concurrent jurisdiction gives rise to the potential for conflict between state and federal court where both are asked simultaneously to assume jurisdiction over essentially the same dispute. Parties tend not to litigate in two forums at once, so the question does not arise often, but when it does, it raises difficult issues of federalism. Duplicative litigation is wasteful and it may be somewhat surprising that there is no prohibition *per se* against a party litigating in both state and federal court simultaneously.   However, duplicative litigation is seen as one of the costs of federalism. Indeed, the Supreme Court has emphasized that federal courts should not abstain from exercising their jurisdiction in order to avoid duplicative litigation except

---

106 *See Martin v. Hunter's Lessee*, discussed in Chapter I, p. 21.

107 *See infra*, p. 190 and note 114, and Chapter VI, p. 216.

108 *See, e.g.*, Mich. Ct. Rule 7.305(B).

109 *See Sun Insurance Office v. Clay*, 319 F.2d 505, 509-510 (5th Cir. 1963), where the federal court of appeals was somewhat puzzled by the Florida supreme courts answer to a question it had certified, so it went on to interpret state law on its own.

110 *See Pierce v. Cook & Co.*, 518 F.2d 720 (10th Cir. 1975) (setting aside federal court judgment based on state supreme courts overruling of caselaw on which federal court relied).

111 For a positive review of certification, *see*. Lillich and Mundy, *Federal Court Certification of Doubtful State Law Questions*, 18 U.C.L.A.L.Rev. 888 (1971).

in the most exceptional circumstances.[112] Conflicts in the exercise of jurisdiction are determined as follows.

1. Resolution by First Entry of Judgment

Under the requirement of "full faith and credit" federal and state courts must respect each others final judgments. So in the case of simultaneous litigation, the first judgment controls the result in the case and the issue of which court's judgment will prevail is determined by which court wins the "race" to judgment.[113] But the question arises as to what a state or federal court may do — while litigation is pending — to *prevent* a judgment from being entered first in the other court. This raises the question of what power state and federal courts have to enjoin parties from litigating in the other forum.

2. Injunctions Against Litigation in Another Court

Because of the nature of the federal system, particularly the supremacy clause, state courts may not enjoin federal litigation, unless it is necessary to protect state court jurisdiction over real property located in the state.[114] At the same time, since 1789, the federal Anti-Injunction Act has generally prohibited *federal* courts from enjoining state proceedings.[115] This would seem to leave things at an impasse. However, there are three important exceptions in the federal Anti-Injunction Act. Federal courts may enjoin state court proceedings if "expressly authorized by Act of Congress or where necessary in aid its jurisdiction or to protect and effectuate its judgments."[116] Thus, in the event of a clash of jurisdiction, federal courts have substantial power to enjoin state litigation. However, several doctrines of "abstention" have grown up that limit federal courts in their exercise of power under these three exceptions to enjoin state court litigation.[117]

3. Abstention

Given the supremacy of federal law and federal institutions and the fact, as just discussed, that the federal court may even enjoin state court litigation in some circumstances, it may seem surprising that the most common result when the same controversy is pending in both federal and state court is that the federal court must defer to the state court. In such cases, it is said that the federal court must "abstain" from addressing the dispute. There are several different types of abstention and each has a different effect. In some a state case must be pending at the same time as the federal case and in others it is simply sufficient that the action *could* be filed in state court. The four major abstention doctrines are outlined here.

"Younger" Abstention One situation where simultaneous litigation is possible is where a party who has been sued or prosecuted in state court believes that the state proceeding is barred by federal law, but has no confidence that the state court will give proper consideration to the federal-law defense. Most often this involves

---

112 *Moses H. Cone Memorial Hospital v. Mercury Construction Co.*, 460 U.S. 1 (1983).

113 *See* Chapter VII, pp. 250-251. One exception to this rule, however, is a federal suit for writ of *habeas corpus*. A state prisoner convicted in state court whose federal constitutional claims have already been rejected by the state trial and appellate courts can get a fresh hearing of those claims in federal district court under certain circumstances. *Habeas corpus* is discussed in Chapter VIII, pp. 267-268.

114 *Donovan v. Dallas*, 377 U.S. 408 (1964).

115 28 U.S.C.A. §2283.

116 *Id.*

117 For a lucid discussion of these abstentions and others, *see* ERWIN CHEMERINSKY, FEDERAL JURISDICTION, 2D ED. §§11.1-14.4 (Aspen 1994).

situations where a state criminal defendant has a federal constitutional law defense to the state criminal prosecution — for example, when a state prosecutes a person for conduct asserted to be protected by 1st Amendment free speech rights. Federal civil rights laws give the person a claim in federal court to enjoin the prosecution on the ground that it violates federal rights.[118] But if the person seeks an injunction against the state proceeding, the federalism-based abstention doctrine of *Younger v. Harris*[119] will require that the federal court "abstain" in favor of the state court deciding the federal law issue. As a result, the person must rely on the state court to vindicate any federal rights by way of a defense to the state court prosecution. The only way that a federal court will become involved is if the person is able to convince the U.S. Supreme Court to grant *certiorari* after all state appeals are exhausted or if the criminal defendant seeks *habeas corpus* review in the lower federal courts.[120] A narrow exception to the *Younger* doctrine is where it can be shown that the state prosecution is in bad faith.[121]

"Pullman" Abstention Another form of abstention applies when a federal suit challenges a state law as unconstitutional, but there are unclear issues of state law involved. Unclear state-law issues are generally of two types: (1) the challenged state law *could* be interpreted by a state court in a way that would make it constitutional or (2) there is a plausible argument that the law is invalid as a matter of state-law. In either event, clarification of state law would result in a plaintiff victory on state-law grounds, thus rendering federal court decision of the constitutional challenge unnecessary. This form of abstention applies even if no state court action is pending in which clarification of the state law issue could be obtained. Plaintiffs must file another suit in state court to obtain that clarification. Then, if they lose on that issue, than can return to federal court to press their federal constitutional claims.[122]

This form of partial abstention is named for *Pullman v. Texas Railroad Comm'n*,[123] the facts of which illustrate the typical case. In *Pullman*, a regulation of the Texas Railroad Commission segregated railroad employees by race according to their job description and reserved the higher status jobs for whites. Black railroad porters challenged the regulation, claiming that it constituted unconstitutional race discrimination. Texas law appeared to allow a basis for challenging the regulation on the ground that it was beyond the powers of the commission set out in state statutes, but the law was unclear on the point. Because of this, the plaintiffs were required to go to the Texas state courts to resolve that state law issue. If that challenge was rejected, they would be allowed to return to federal court to renew their federal constitutional challenge. Since *Pullman* abstention gives the state the first chance to take care of the plaintiff's problem on the basis of state law, it is said to promote harmony between state and federal courts.

---

118 The claim would be based on 42 U.S.C.A. §1983, discussed in Chapter VI, pp. 218, 219. Section 1983 has been held to be come within the exception to the Anti-Injunction Act for injunctions "expressly authorized by Act of Congress."

119 401 U.S. 37 (1971).

120 *Habeas corpus* is discussed in Chapter VIII, pp. 267-268.

121 The *Younger* doctrine has been extended to some civil cases. Generally, *Younger* applies only to civil judicial and administrative proceedings that seek some coercive remedy *against* the federal plaintiff. *See* Chapter VI, p. 218.

122 *England v. Louisiana Board of Medical Examiners*, 375 U.S. 411 (1964).

123 312 U.S. 496 (1941).

"Colorado River" Abstention   Where there is parallel litigation on the same subject pending in both state and federal courts and neither *Younger* nor *Pullman* abstention applies, *Colorado River* abstention is possible.[124] Unfortunately, this form of abstention is not well-defined. On the one hand, the Court has emphasized that federal courts should abstain only in the most exceptional circumstances. On the other hand, the lower federal courts do not seem to follow this principle, commonly dismissing pending cases before them. The Court has on several occasions had to reverse trial court decisions to abstain from exercising jurisdiction. Major unspoken reasons why lower federal court judges are so quick to abstain are undoubtedly found in the facts that such judges feel that they are overwhelmed with cases, and that duplicative litigation, whatever the reason for it, is not a priority for application of scarce judicial resources.[125]

---

124 *See Colorado River Water Conservation District v. United States*, 424 U.S. 800 (1976) (simultaneous litigation over water rights in state and federal court; federal court abstention warranted).

125 *See, e.g., Moses H. Cone Memorial Hospital v. Mercury Construction*, *supra* note 112.

CHAPTER VI

ADMINISTRATIVE LAW

Administrative law is the study of the law governing administrative agencies and officials.[1] Included are the proper procedures for promulgating legislative rules and adjudicating disputes, legal issues raised by less formal actions of agencies, the problem of improper conduct of administrative officials, and the judicial remedies available in all these areas.[2]

This chapter will focus primarily on the law of federal administrative agencies and the requirements of the federal administrative Procedures Act (APA) and caselaw thereunder. One reason for focusing on federal agencies is their importance in their own right, but another is that much of state administrative law is modeled on the federal experience.[3]

PART I: Law and Procedures of Administrative Agencies

A. Types and Purposes of Administrative Agencies

Types of Agencies Broadly defined, virtually every non-military government organ other than the courts and the legislature is considered an "agency."[4] However, administrative law focuses somewhat more narrowly on the two basic types of agencies: regulatory agencies and social welfare agencies. Regulatory agencies regulate conduct in private relations in various areas, from transportation to food and prescription drugs. An example is the federal Interstate Commerce Commission, the first administrative agency. Social welfare agencies dispense government assistance in the various programs of assistance for veterans, the aged, the disabled and others. An example is the federal Social Security Administration within the Department of Health and Human Services. Both types of agencies exist on both the state and federal level. Both have the power to make rules, to enforce them and to adjudicate disputes arising in matters under their jurisdiction.

Federal agencies are also distinguished by whether they are "executive branch" agencies or "independent" agencies. The former are responsible to a cabinet "Secretary," while independent agencies are headed by administrators, boards or commissions not formally subject to executive branch supervision.

Advantages and Disadvantages of Agencies There are essentially three reasons for having agencies. First, agencies bring expertise to bear on problems in a way that

---

1 The advent and expansion of administrative agencies is one of the major changes in the structure of government since 1789. *See* Chapter I, pp. 14-16.

2 For one-volume treatise treatment of administrative law, *see* ALFRED C. AMAN, JR. & WILLIAM T. MAYTON, HORNBOOK ON ADMINISTRATIVE LAW (West 1993); BERNARD SCHWARTZ, ADMINISTRATIVE LAW, 3D ED. (Aspen 1991); ROBERT J. PIERCE, SIDNEY A. SHAPIRO & PAUL R. VERKUIL, ADMINISTRATIVE LAW AND PROCESS, 2D ED. (Foundation 1992). Student texts are ERNEST GELLHORN & RONALD M. LEVIN, ADMINISTRATIVE LAW AND PROCESS IN A NUTSHELL (West 1997); WILLIAM F. FOX, JR., UNDERSTANDING ADMINISTRATIVE LAW, 3D ED. (Matthew Bender 1997). *See also* PETER STRAUSS, AN INTRODUCTION TO ADMINISTRATIVE JUSTICE IN THE UNITED STATES (Carolina Academic Press, Chapel Hill 1989), a book written especially for the foreign lawyer. *See* Appendix, p. A30-A31, for an outline of governmental structure with major federal agencies shown. Major federal and state laws on administrative agencies are collected in SELECTED FEDERAL AND STATE ADMINISTRATIVE AND REGULATORY LAWS (West 1997).

3` Also having strong influence on state practice is the Uniform Law Commissioners' Model State Administrative Procedure Act (1981).

4 *See* 5 U.S.C.A. §551(1).

generalist executive officials, legislators and judges cannot. The highly technical fields of economic and market regulation require expert knowledge and flexibility to react quickly to changes in conditions. In the social welfare area, programs are complex and the number of recipients is so great that it is only through specialized and expert administration that benefits can be properly distributed. The second reason for agencies is efficiency. Considerable efficiency results naturally from expertise in administration. But further efficiency gains come from the nature of agency structure. It combines legislative, executive and judicial functions "under one roof" rather than relying on the more traditional diffused governmental structure.[5] A third attraction of agencies is that their self-contained structure makes them more independent, insulating them from the "political winds that sweep Washington."[6] Thus, it is hoped, government policy and actions in a given area will be more consistent and more rational than those that would be produced by the political branches.

The disadvantages of agencies grow directly out of the three advantages just stated. Expertise can breed a narrow vision and arrogance. Undue concern for efficiency can trample individual rights. Insulation from political control can lead to a lack of accountability for actions and lawlessness. Much of administrative law struggles to enhance the positive side of agency expertise, efficiency and independence while controlling their more negative consequences.

The first half of the 20th century saw unrestrained growth in the size, number and variety of practices of federal agencies. A scathing report issued in 1937 complained that they had become "a headless 'fourth branch' of government, a haphazard collection of irresponsible agencies and uncoordinated powers."[7] Following a presidential commission investigation, steps were taken in 1946 to deal with such problems though passage of the Administrative Procedures Act (APA), a comprehensive statute regulating federal agency procedure for rule-making, adjudication and other activities.[8]

Agencies have two basic functions beyond their obvious executive mission: rule-making and adjudication. Statutory and constitutional aspects of these two functions will be outlined first.

B. Rule-Making Functions of Agencies

1. Legislative Rules and the Rule-Making Process

"Legislative rules" set substantive and procedural law that must be followed by both the agency and those subject to its jurisdiction. Under the APA, rule-making can be formal or informal, but by far the most common process is informal rule-making. For this, the APA requires a notice-and-comment procedure.[9] A federal agency must first publish a notice of proposed rule-making in the Federal Register, a daily government publication, and invite public comments on its proposal. "[A]n agency's notice must 'provide sufficient detail and rationale for the rule to permit interested parties to comment meaningfully.'"[10] At the end of the notice and comment period,

---

5   The separation of powers problems inherent in such an arrangement are discussed *infra* pp. 211-215.

6   *Commodity Futures Trading Comm. v. Schor*, 478 U.S. 833, 835 (1986).

7   President's Commission on Administrative Management, Report with Special Studies (1937), quoted in AMAN & MAYTON, *supra* note 2, at 3.

8   *See* 5 U.S.C.A. §§551-559, 701-706, 1305, 3105, 3344, 5372, 7521.

9   5 U.S.C.A. §553.

10   *Fertilizer Institute v. Environmental Protection Agency*, 935 F.2d 1303, 1311 (D.C. Cir. 1991).

the agency promulgates and publishes the final version of the rule. In an introduction to the rule, the agency must take into account and discuss the public comments it has received and declare the basis for writing the final rule as it did in light of the comments it received. In the process, the agency must deal meaningfully with the public comments and cannot ignore any point of view.[11] It must respond specifically to significant negative comments either by modifying the proposed rule or explaining why it did not.[12] Overall, the agency must show that it has "genuinely engaged in reasoned decision-making."[13] Otherwise, a reviewing court will vacate the rule.

Congress may require, but rarely does, that formal rule-making procedures be followed. With formal rule-making, testimony and other evidence must be taken "on the record" before final rules can be promulgated.[14] Formal rule-making is generally reserved for such matters as rate-making, in which an agency must make a general decision on what prices or rates to allow in an industry that it regulates. The Court has made it clear that rule-making procedures more formal than the notice-and-comment procedure may only be imposed by *Congress* and that courts do not have any power to impose more stringent procedures where Congress has not.[15]

The public has the right to petition for rule-making. However, there is no requirement that the agency respond with rule-making.[16]

Final federal agency rules are compiled yearly in Code of Federal Regulations (CFR), where they are organized by subject matter. However, CFR compilations are notoriously late in being published, so it is often necessary to find the final rule in the Federal Register.

Both state and federal administrative procedure acts contain "good cause" exceptions to the normal notice and comment procedure. Under the federal APA, "good cause" is said to exist when the notice and comment procedures would be "unnecessary, impracticable or contrary to the public interest." These are generally interpreted as requiring some sort of emergency need for the rule. The rules adopted pursuant to this exception are called "interim final" rules. The agency then goes through the comment procedure before finalizing the rule, although it may take effect upon its first publication.

2. Interpretive Rules and Statements of Policy

Agencies also issue "interpretive rules." As the name suggests, these rules

---

11 *See Kennecott Copper Corp. v. Environmental Protection Agency*, 462 F.2d 846 (D.C. Cir. 1972) (rule sent back to agency for reconsideration of why it reached a particular standard for air quality when tests showed a different standard was sufficient). In addition, Congress has required that all major agency action consider specific items. One is the requirement of an environmental impact statement. *See* 42 U.S.C.A. §4321.

12 *United States v. Nova Scotia Food Products Corp.*, 568 F.2d 240 (2d Cir. 1977) (agency did not respond sufficiently to comments that current health standards were adequate and new rule would make commercial marketing of whitefish unfeasible).

13 *Greater Boston Television Corp. v. Fed. Communications Comm'n*, 444 F.2d 841, 851 (D.C.Cir 1970) (decision on license renewal upheld). If a court vacates a rule, the agency can re-publishes the same rule and follows the proper procedures the second time, but it cannot make the rule retroactive. *Bowen v. Georgetown Univ. Hospital*, 488 U.S. 204 (1988) (retroactive recoupment of Medicare payments already made to hospitals).

14 *See* 5 U.S.C.A. §557.

15 *Vermont Yankee Nuclear Power v. Natural Resources Defense Council, Inc.*, 435 U.S. 519 (1978) (reversing lower court order requiring agency to implement additional procedures, including suggestion of possible cross-examination of agency personnel who produced report on which agency relied).

16 5 U.S.C.A. §553(e). *See WWHT, Inc. v. Fed. Communications Comm'n*, 656 F.2d 807 (D.C.Cir. 1981) (by providing petition procedure, Congress did not mean to compel rule-making).

interpret some existing legal standard. They often deal with the application of legislative rules to particular facts and are expected to apply to a general category of cases of that type. Interpretive rules are exempt from the procedural requirements for rule-making applicable to legislative rules.[17] Interpretive rules may be promulgated in the same rule-style form as legislative rules or they may be in a less formal style, such as a question-and-answer format.[18] It is sometimes difficult to draw the line between an interpretive rule and a new legislative rule, but the basic principle is clear. An interpretive rule is improper if it sets out what is effectively a new requirement.[19]

"Statements of policy" are also issued. They need not follow any particular form. They relate principally to the future intentions of the agency, often with regard to what enforcement action it will take in particular situations. Interpretive rules or policy statements can be disputed as incorrect interpretations of existing law. If this can be shown, the agency has the duty to refrain from applying them to the complaining party and to change them for other similar cases.[20]

Agencies also give advice to the public on how to comply with their regulations. When that advice is correct, it is a great service to the public. When it is incorrect, agencies will seek to protect reliance interests to the extent possible. However, it is clear that in general there is no obligation to do so.[21]

C. Adjudicatory Functions of Agencies

Adjudication determines the rights and obligations of a particular party based on the application of some legal standard to particular facts. Understood in a broad sense, adjudication happens every time an agency takes action that is not in the form of a rule. However, in this section we will focus on *formal* adjudication, by which affected parties are afforded a trial-type hearing before the agency. Examples of formal adjudication by federal agencies are claims before the Social Security Administration for disability insurance benefits, unfair labor practice claims against an employer or union before the National Labor Relations Board or enforcement proceedings before the Securities and Exchange Commission to revoke the license of a securities broker. The formal adjudicatory functions of administrative agencies are an important part of their work. Indeed, Congress has established several agencies whose sole responsibility is adjudication and who do not issue rules.[22]

Whether formal adjudication is called for is determined by examining the relevant statutes. Requirements can vary. For example, while all the proceedings mentioned in the last paragraph require formal adjudication, no such process applies

---

17 *See* 5 U.S.C.A. §553(d).

18 The Equal Employment Opportunity Commission issues both. *See Newport News Shipbuilding and Dry Dock v. Equal Employment Opportunity Comm.*, 462 U.S. 669 (1983), where examples of both forms of interpretive rules (on sex discrimination in medical disability insurance) are quoted.

19 *Compare Cabias v. Egger*, 690 F.2d 234 (D.C.Cir. 1982) (agency letter simply construed the language and intent of statute) *with Chamber of Commerce v. Occupational Safety & Health Admin.*, 636 F.2d 464 (D.C.Cir. 1980) (requirement announced in agency head's speech and later published as an interpretive rule enunciated a new requirement that must be promulgated as a rule). *See also Hoctor v. United States Dep't. of Agriculture*, 82 F.3d 165 (7th Cir. 1996)(discussing what an interpretive rule is).

20 Agencies may also waive their rules in individual cases where it appears the rule is not appropriate, a part of what has been called "administrative equity." *See* Jim Rossi, Making Policy Through the Waiver of Regulations at the Federal Energy Regulatory Commission, 47 ADMIN.L.REV. 255 (1995).

21 *Office of Personnel Management v. Richmond*, 496 U.S. 414 (1990)(incorrect advice caused plaintiff to lose 6 months of his pension; yet, equitable estoppel did not operate against the government).

22 Among them are the Occupational Safety and Health Review Commission, the Federal Mine Safety and Health Review Commission and the National Transportation Safety Board.

to a decision of the Secretary of Transportation to order an automobile manufacturer to recall a particular car for safety defects. Although the primary focus here will be on formal adjudication, more informal agency action will be discussed later when judicial review is considered.[23]

1. Administrative Adjudication Procedure under the APA

Hearing Before the Administrative Law Judge The centerpiece of formal APA administrative adjudication is the hearing before an administrative law judge (ALJ) of the agency in question.[24] The ALJ is well versed in the intricacies of the subject matter of the agency and only decides cases from that agency. To assure a fair hearing, the APA mandates strict separation of ALJs from employees of the agency's investigatory and adjudicatory branches, including prohibitions on *ex parte* contacts and undue influence. In addition, it prohibits any "interested person outside the agency" from engaging in such activity.[25]

Nature of Agency Hearings The ALJ's decision must be made based solely on the "record" compiled by that ALJ.[26] The written decision will include findings of fact and conclusions of law much like the decision of a judge following a bench trial in court. In some agencies, the administrative hearing process resembles traditional courtroom proceedings, while in others it is more inquisitorial. An observer dropping in on a contested hearing before an ALJ from the National Labor Relations Board would probably see little to distinguish it from a bench trial in a courtroom. On the other hand, an observer of most administrative hearings involving Social Security benefits would witness ALJ interrogation of the claimant and other indices of judicial control that would be inappropriate in a courtroom. Indeed, it is said that the Social Security ALJ, as the only government representative present at the hearing, is supposed to "wear three hats": to represent the claimant's interests, to represent the agency and to decide the case.[27] Whatever procedure is afforded by the agency, the standard by which a decision must be made is the same standard as in civil cases in court: whether the factual contentions have been proven by a preponderance of the evidence.[28]

One difference between administrative hearings and court proceedings is that there is no absolute right to an oral hearing or cross examination of witnesses at the administrative hearing. The APA provides that the party "is entitled to present his case or defense by oral or documentary evidence" and "to conduct such cross-examination as may be required for a full and true disclosure of the facts."[29] Cross examination rights will be more likely to be afforded if the issues at the hearing are factual and

---

23 *See infra* pp. 205-206.

24 *See* 5 U.S.C.A. §§554, 556, 557. *See generally* AMAN & MAYTON, *supra* note 2, §§8.1-8.5. The question of what kinds of agency decisions require these formal adjudication standards is one that is often disputed and is not entirely clear from the statute. ALJs are called referees or hearings examiners in some state systems.

25 5 U.S.C.A. §554(d), §557(d) and *infra* p. 215. *Ex parte* contact is contact between adjudicators and others without all the parties to the dispute being present. The prohibition applies to the President and White House staff, *Portland Audubon Society v. Endangered Species Comm.*, 984 F.2d 1534 (9th Cir. 1993), and to members of Congress, *Pillsbury Co. v. Fed. Trade Comm'n*, 354 F.2d 952 (5th Cir. 1966).

26 5 U.S.C.A. §556(e).

27 This is contrary to the basic adversary principles discussed in Chapter III and has been criticized on that ground. However, it has been upheld by the Supreme Court. *See Richardson v. Perales*, 402 U.S. 389, 410 (1971). *See* SCHWARTZ, *supra* note 2, §5.29.

28 *See* Chapter III, p. 102, where standards of proof in civil and criminal cases are discussed.

29 5 U.S.C.A. §556(d).

depend on witness credibility.[30] However, there are many other issues that arise where cross examination would not be useful, such as expositions of technical data. Some courts have required that the necessity for cross examination "be established under specific circumstances by the party seeking it."[31] Pretrial procedures differ, however. In the administrative case, there usually has been a full investigation conducted by the enforcement division of the agency, so there are full statements of witnesses in the file for all parties to see and examine before the hearing.[32]

Rules of Evidence The Federal Rules of Evidence do not generally apply to agency hearings.[33] The APA provides that all oral or documentary evidence is admissible except irrelevant, immaterial or unduly repetitious evidence.[34] So hearsay evidence is fully admissible and a decision may be based solely on hearsay evidence if it is trustworthy.[35] Even when hearsay evidence is suspect, however, it will not be excluded, but will instead be admitted, evaluated and given such weight as appears appropriate.[36] But if hearsay is contradicted by other direct trustworthy testimony, it will not be deemed to be substantial evidence to support a decision.[37] When material evidence relevant to the issues in the case is excluded, reversal is appropriate.[38] Courts have also reversed agency decisions when the agency has not articulated on the record any reason why it did not find certain testimony credible.[39]

The Final Agency Decision The status of ALJ action varies from agency to agency. ALJs are considered the designees of the head of the agency appointed to gather the evidence, but beyond that practice varies. In some agencies the ALJ makes only a recommended decision that is then submitted to the agency head for acceptance, rejection or modification. In others, the ALJ decision is a final initial decision that may be subject to modification by higher authority in the agency. In yet others, the ALJ decision is the final agency action.[40]

By whatever means the decision of an ALJ becomes final, the final adjudicatory decision is deemed the decision of the head of the agency.[41] This does not mean that the head of the agency must personally participate in reviewing the ALJ decision.

---

30 *See* SCHWARTZ, *supra* note 2, §7.7.

31 *Cellular Mobile Systems of Pa. v. Fed. Communications Comm'n.*, 782 F.2d 182, 198 (D.C.Cir. 1985). *Compare Giant Food Inc. v. Fed. Trade Comm'n.*, 322 F.2d 977 (D.C.Cir. 1963) (agencies cannot refuse or limit cross examination).

32 This makes less necessary the formal "discovery" process that is used in civil cases in court. *See* Chapter VII, pp. 226-231.

33 *But see* 29 U.S.C.A. §160(b)(proceedings before the National Labor Relations Board "shall, so far as practicable, be conducted in accordance with the rules of evidence applicable in the district courts of the United States under the rules of civil procedure.") *See* Chapter III, pp. 106-112, for a discussion of evidence rules for courts.

34 5 U.S.C.A. §556(d).

35 *Richardson v. Perales*, 402 U.S. 389 (1971) (medical reports were properly relied on in disability hearing at least where claimant did not subpoena doctor for cross examination).

36 *See Calhoun v. Bailer*, 626 F.2d 145 (9th Cir. 1980) (8 factors to consider in evaluating hearsay).

37 *Hoska v. Dep't. of the Army*, 677 F.2d 131 (D.C.Cir. 1982).

38 *Catholic Medical Center v. Nat'l Labor Relations Board*, 589 F.2d 1166 (2d Cir. 1978) (evidence that employer did not refuse to bargain was improperly excluded).

39 *Tieniber v. Heckler*, 720 F.2d 1251 (11th Cir. 1983) (claimant's testimony as to his disability).

40 Consistent with the movement toward alternative dispute resolution (ADR) in the courts, *see* Chapter VII, pp.242-244, 1990 amendments to the APA require agencies to use ADR in all their functions.

41 *See* 42 U.S.C.A. §405(g) (referring to final social security on appeals taken to the hearing stage as decisions as the "the final decision of the Secretary [of the Department of Health and Human Services]."

Instead, the agency is likely to have an "appeals council" or other body comprising persons at the policy-making level in the agency.

Agency Decisions as Precedents The practice of relying on prior administrative adjudications varies among agencies and is not always clear. Use of administrative decisions as precedent is hampered by the fact that agencies that set out agency policy primarily in rule-making often do not publish their decisions in a form that is easily accessible to the public or even to lawyers. However, if prior decisions can be found, the law of judicial review effectively requires that they be given precedential effect by the agency. This follows from a long-established common law and statutory basis for courts to reverse administrative action on the ground that it is "arbitrary and capricious."[42] If it can be shown that an agency has decided seemingly identical cases in two different ways without distinguishing the prior case, that is the very definition of arbitrary decision-making. However, the facts of prior agency decisions are often unique, thereby making it easy for the agency to distinguish any prior decisions that might be argued. Some types of decisions, such as individual disability adjudications, for example, are so unique that it may not be worth the effort to try to research them.

Case Adjudication As Lawmaking   Despite what was just said, some administrative agencies give full *stare decisis* effect to their adjudicatory decisions and use those decisions to establish agency policy much in the way that courts make law. For example, the National Labor Relations Board (NLRB), makes policy almost exclusively through its administrative hearing decisions — despite pleas from several quarters that it do so by rule.[43] Administrative adjudication as a means of making agency policy raises all the problems that attend judicial lawmaking on a case-by-case basis, including the problem of retroactive lawmaking.[44] However, it has been upheld by the Supreme Court. This is so even when an agency decision clearly announces new principles.[45] As with judicial lawmaking, however, it is easy to overstate the problem.   Even more so than in the judicial context, routine administrative adjudication affords even less opportunity for lawmaking than routine judicial adjudication, since the administrative legal standards applied are relatively more specific than other forms of law, thus providing less room for creativity on the part of the adjudicator.

2. Minimum Due Process Requirements for Agency Action

The APA requirements for hearings apply only to actions of federal agencies. State statutes on administrative procedure impose similar standards on some state agencies. Generally, these requirements provide for hearing rights that are well above the constitutional minimum. However, state statutes may not apply to some state and local administrative actions. And certain federal or state statutory hearing rights may not in some circumstances comport with due process. In these instances, the person affected will have to resort to the minimum procedural due process protections

---

42 5 U.S.C.A. §706(2)(A).

43 *See, e.g.*, Merton C. Bernstein, *The NLRB's Adjudication-Rule Making Dilemma Under the Administrative Procedure Act*, 79 YALE L.J. 571, 589-98 (1970). *See also Nat'l Labor Relations Bd. v. Wyman-Gordon Co.*, 394 U.S. 759 (1969) (plurality, concurring and dissenting opinions addressing the legitimacy of NLRB practices). *But see American Hospital Assoc. v. Nat'l Labor Relations Bd.*, 499 U.S. 606 (1991) (unsuccessful challenge to the first substantive rule issued by the NLRB since 1935).

44 *See* Chapter II, pp. 45-46.

45 *Nat'l Labor Relations Bd. v. Bell Aerospace Co.*, 416 U.S. 267 (1974); *Securities & Exchange Comm'n v. Chenery Corp.*, 332 U.S. 194 (1947). *See generally* AMAN & MAYTON, *supra* note 2, §4.5.

afforded by the due process clauses of the 5th and 14th Amendments to the Constitution as developed in court decisions.

The due process clause states that no person may be "deprived of . . . liberty, or property, without due process of law."[46] There are two steps in the procedural due process analysis. The first is to determine whether there is a "deprivation" of "liberty or property." If there is no such deprivation, the due process clause is inapplicable and no procedural safeguards are required. If there is a deprivation, then due process applies and a second question arises: what "process" is "due," i.e., what procedural safeguards are required to accompany government attempts to bring about such a deprivation?

Defining "Liberty" or "Property" Interests By confining a person or taking away property owned by a person, the government clearly has "deprived" that person of liberty or property. But liberty and property for due process purposes include something less than a vested right to "pure" liberty (i.e., freedom from confinement) or an ownership-type property interest. For example, due process applies to a welfare recipient's "right" to continue to receive welfare benefits. This is so even though the state is not required to have welfare programs for relief of poor people and could abolish them tomorrow if it chose. If the government *has* chosen to have welfare programs and a person is eligible to receive those benefits as long as certain factual conditions are met, then that recipient has a *legitimate claim of entitlement to continue* receiving those benefits. That is sufficient to constitute "property" that cannot be "deprived" without affording due process.[47]

Similarly, prisoners who are granted parole from prison on the condition that they follow certain rules have a liberty interest subject to due process protections.[48] Properly convicted prisoners have already had their liberty seriously and validly restricted in compliance with the highest due process standards when they were convicted and sentenced to prison. While on parole, their liberty interests are clearly less than those of a free person on the street. However, their liberty interest qualifies for protection if they have a *legitimate claim of entitlement* to stay out of prison *unless* they violate the rules of their parole. If they do, as is generally the case with parolees, then they have a liberty interest that is subject to due process protections.[49]

Also treated as protected "deprivations" are revocation of a driver's license[50] and suspensions of school students for misbehavior.[51] On the other hand, a state university teacher who had a one-year contract was held not to have a legitimate claim of entitlement beyond that year.[52] Similarly, temporary public employees would

---

46 The due process clause also protects "life." However, deprivations of life (and the most common form of "pure" liberty deprivations — conviction of a crime) may only be accomplished by way of the criminal process consistent with all the criminal due process safeguards specified in the Bill of Rights. *See* Chapter VIII, pp. 270-303, where constitutional criminal procedural rights are discussed.

47 *Goldberg v. Kelly*, 397 U.S. 254 (1970).

48 *Morrissey v. Brewer*, 408 U.S. 471 (1972).

49 *Compare Sandin v. Conner*, 515 472 (1995) (punitive isolation for prisoner did not affect any liberty interest) *and Meachum v. Fano*, 427 U.S. 215 (1976) (no liberty interest affected by transfer from medium to maximum security prison) *with Vitek v. Jones*, 445 U.S. 535 (1980) (transfer from prison to mental hospital affects liberty interest because of stigma and greater restrictions on activities).

50 *Bell v. Burson*, 402 U.S. 535 (1971). *See also Barry v. Barchi*, 443 U.S. 55 (1979)(jockey's license); *Memphis Light, Gas and Water Div. v. Craft*, 436 U.S. 1 (1978)(right to continued utility service from municipal utility).

51 *Goss v. Lopez*, 419 U.S. 565 (1975).

52 *Roth v. Bd. of Regents*, 408 U.S. 564 (1972).

generally have no legitimate expectation that they would be continued in their positions indefinitely. In the welfare assistance context, there are emergency assistance programs that provide funding for temporary housing and contemplate that that assistance is limited to one week. Termination at the end of that week would not deprive the recipient of any protected property interest (assuming the recipient has been advised of the one-week limit), but termination *before* the end of that week would be subject to some form of due process.

Defining the Content of Procedural Safeguards Required Once it is determined that liberty or property interests have been deprived by administrative action, the next question in the procedural due process analysis is: what "process" is "due" for there to be "due process"? Obviously, there are many procedural protections that might be required. The proper process could range from an informal opportunity to state one's objections in writing to the full range of rights comparable to those enjoyed by a person facing a criminal charge in court — a full adversary hearing with rights to counsel, confrontation, proof beyond reasonable doubt, and so on.[53]

The standard "bundle" of due process rights that have been afforded when a very important property interest is at stake in the administrative context are those set out in the 1970 decision in *Goldberg v. Kelly*,[54] a case involving termination of welfare benefits based on financial need. According to *Goldberg*, a person facing such a loss is entitled to (1) notice of the action a reasonable time *before* it is scheduled to take effect, together with the reasons therefor and (2) the opportunity for a trial-type hearing *before* the deprivation becomes effective. The hearing must be (3) conducted by a neutral administrative official not connected with the original decision. At the hearing, the affected person has (4) the right to have a lawyer or other person present to assist him or her at the hearing, (5) the right to confront and cross-examine the witnesses against him or her when credibility is at issue, (6) the right to a written decision based solely on the evidence produced at that hearing, and (7) the right to have a complete record of the hearing, including a record of the testimony and other evidence offered. By contrast, a secondary school student facing a short suspension from school for misconduct is only entitled to "oral or written notice of the charges against him and, if he denies them, an explanation of the evidence the authorities have and an opportunity to present his side of the story."[55]

While *Goldberg* establishes the baseline due process standard, due process overall is a flexible standard. The test for determining the content of procedural safeguards required is that of *Mathews v. Eldridge*.[56] The *Eldridge* standard imposes a "cost effectiveness" test that balances three factors: (1) how serious the deprivation is, (2) how high the rate of erroneous deprivations using the *current* procedures is and what improvement in that rate *additional* procedural protections would bring about, and (3) the additional cost to the government of the proposed added procedural protections.

---

53 *See generally* Chapter VIII, pp. 290-296.

54 397 U.S. 254 (1970).

55 *Goss v. Lopez, supra* note 51. Expulsion from school or even suspension for a long period would clearly require more process than *Goss* requires. However, a dismissal for academic rather than disciplinary reasons is entitled to much less process — perhaps none at all. *See Bd. of Curators v. Horowitz*, 435 U.S. 78 (1978) (dismissal from medical school, "like the decision of an individual professor as to the proper grade for a student in his course . . . requires expert evaluation of cumulative information and is not readily adapted to the procedural tools of judicial or administrative decision-making").

56 424 U.S. 319 (1976).

Balancing these three factors may involve adding to or subtracting from any of the baseline elements identified in *Goldberg v. Kelly*. An example of this is the fact situation of *Mathews v. Eldridge*. Mr. Eldridge was receiving benefits from the Social Security Administration's disability program and was terminated. Regulations entitled him to a hearing, but only a *post-deprivation* hearing. Although *Goldberg* had held that a *pre-deprivation* hearing was required for *need-based* welfare benefit terminations, the Supreme Court found an important distinction in the fact that Social Security disability benefits are government *insurance* benefits payable regardless of whether the disabled person is financially needy. Thus, the seriousness of the deprivation (factor (1) above) in Eldridge's case was less. The *Eldridge* opinion also relied on factor (2), pointing to the fact that the decision on disability was a medical one. Consequently, according to the Court, a face-to-face hearing before an ALJ would not improve greatly on the accuracy of the initial agency decision, which was made in consultation with medical experts. This was contrasted with situations like *Goldberg*, where factual questions involving credibility are central.[57]

The *Eldridge* factors also explain why the government may act in an emergency without first affording a hearing. The fact of an emergency gives overwhelming weight to factor (3), the government's interest in summary action. Summary action has been allowed to stop strip mining, to seize property for the war effort, to protect against a bank failure and to protect the public from misbranded drugs or contaminated food.[58]

Procedural Due Process and Judicial Proceedings The due process clause provides minimum standards for *all* adjudicatory actions of government — judicial as well as administrative. Consequently, the *Eldridge* test has relevance to civil and criminal cases in courts. For example, procedural due process has been held to require a prior judicial hearing before personal property can be seized by a creditor under an installment sales contract.[59] When "pure" liberty interests are at stake, the protections are even greater. Persons facing imprisonment for civil contempt of court may be entitled, not just to the opportunity to bring a lawyer at their own expense, but to the right to have a lawyer appointed and paid for by the state to act as their representative at the proceeding.[60] Conceptually, the due process continuum reaches all the way up to criminal cases. Criminal cases are generally governed, not by the procedural due process test of *Eldridge*, but by the specific guarantees of the Bill of Rights.[61] But one could well imagine that the *Eldridge* factors, if applied to criminal

---

57 For an application of the *Eldridge* test to dismissal of a public employee, *see Cleveland Bd. of Education v. Loudermill*, 470 U.S. 532 (1985).

58 *See Hodel v. Virginia Surface Mining Assoc.*, 452 U.S. 264, 300 (1981) (strip mining); *Phillips v. Commissioner of Internal Revenue*, 283 U.S. 589 (1931) (tax collection); *Coffin Bros. & Co. v. Bennett*, 277 U.S. 29 (1928) (bank failure); *North American Cold Storage Co. v. Chicago*, 211 U.S. 306 (1908) (contaminated food).

59 *Fuentes v. Shevin*, 407 U.S. 67 (1972) (secured creditor's seizure of debtor's kitchen stove pursuant to state law that did not provide for a pre-seizure hearing violated procedural due process).

60 *See Mead v. Batchlor*, 460 N.W.2d 493 (Mich. 1990). The contempt power is discussed in Chapter VII, p. 238. *But see Lassiter v. North Carolina Dep't. of Social Services*, 452 U.S. 18 (1981) (appointed counsel not *per se* required for parents facing termination of parental rights to their children).

61 *See* Chapter VIII, p. 271, where the sources of criminal due process rights are discussed. As noted there, the 5th and 14th Amendment due process clauses are also sources of procedural rights in criminal cases, but the Court has not applied the *Eldridge* test in criminal cases.

cases, could cause a court to apply many of the same strict safeguards found in the Bill of Rights as a matter of procedural due process.[62]

Criticism of the Eldridge Test The *Eldridge* test has been criticized for its attempt to "balance" completely dissimilar factors. How much weight one gives, for example, to the *individual interests* versus *governmental interests* implicates the most fundamental of political attitudes and cannot be weighed according to any objective legal standard. One could well ask if the test is any better than a judge simply deciding whether a given procedure "sounds fair under the circumstances." Another criticism of the *Eldridge* test is that it is too cold and objective: as a "cost-effectiveness" test of procedural safeguards, it fails to include the intangible concepts of justice and respect for individual autonomy that due process represents.[63] Thus, it fails to consider that forcing the government to justify deprivations it seeks to impose may serve valid constitutional and social purposes regardless of the *result* of the process.[64]

D. Judicial Review of Agency Action

While one major value of administrative agencies is their expertise, they must apply that expertise within the confines of the law. Judicial review is deemed necessary to assure a rational and legally appropriate decision, both when agencies adjudicate and when they make rules. In the United States, this judicial review is undertaken by the ordinary courts — not by special administrative courts, as is the case in some other systems. Review by generalist judges is thought to be a benefit since it counteracts tendencies toward a narrow agency perspective.

1. Right to Judicial Review of Agency Action

Right to Review in General The right to judicial review of agency action is provided by statute, either by the specific statute that governs that agency or by the APA.[65] Where there is no specific statute and the APA is the only possibility, a court will "begin with the strong presumption that Congress intends judicial review."[66] The question of whether there is a *constitutional* right to judicial review of all administrative action is one that has been debated, but not definitively resolved.

Interpretation of Statutes to Permit Review Part of the reason the issue of a constitutional right to judicial review has not been resolved is that courts have tended to interpret statutes in such a way as to permit judicial review even when those statutes appear on their face to preclude it. For example, despite the fact that the

---

62 In actuality, the due process clause *does* result in the application of most Bill of Rights guarantees to state court criminal cases, but it is generally said instead that those right are "incorporated" against the states by the due process clause rather than being the product of a weighing due process factors. *See* Chapter VIII, p. 271.

63 *See* Jerry L. Mashaw, *The Supreme Court's Due Process Calculus for Administrative Adjudication in Mathews v. Eldridge: Three Factors in Search of Value*, 44 U. CHI. L. REV. 28, 46-57 (1976) (offering an alternative "value-sensitive approach"). *Cf. Saleeby v. State Bar*, 702 P.2d 525 (Cal. 1985) (including in California due process "the dignitary interest in informing individuals of the nature, grounds, and consequences of the action" and "freedom from arbitrary adjudicative procedures").

64 *See* Chapter III, text at note 131, where the individuality-reinforcing values of procedural fairness are discussed. Due process hearing rights apply only to adjudicative determinations and not to legislative changes. Thus, if an agency were promulgating a rule the effect of which would be to deprive a person of liberty or property, the trial-type procedures of *Goldberg v. Kelly* are not required before such a rule can be adopted. SCHWARTZ, *supra* note 2, §§5.6-5.8. For more on procedural due process rights, *see* JOHN E. NOWAK & RONALD D. ROTUNDA, HORNBOOK ON CONSTITUTIONAL LAW, 5TH ED. §§13.1-13.10 (West 1995).

65 5 U.S.C.A. §§701-706.

66 *Bowen v. Michigan Academy of Family Physicians*, 476 U.S. 667, 670 (1986).

Immigration and Nationality Act provides that all agency decisions in deportation cases "shall be final," judicial review was held to be available.[67] The statutory interpretations involved have on occasion appeared strained.[68] However, the Court has refused review of agency decisions even when they are alleged to be arbitrary and capricious or in violation of statutes, if Congress has prohibited review.[69] A more difficult question is whether judicial review of *constitutional* issues could ever be denied. This issue is discussed in more depth in the chapter on constitutional law.[70] The Court has never decided the issue, but it has interpreted ambiguous statutes is such a way as to permit review "in part to avoid the 'serious constitutional question' that would arise if a federal statute were construed to deny any judicial forum for a colorable constitutional claim."[71]

2. Procedural Aspects of Judicial Review

Exhaustion of Administrative Remedies Generally, claimants aggrieved by agency action must obtain a final decision of the agency before resorting to judicial review.[72] This means that the claimant faced with a negative action by an agency must exhaust the appeal procedures the agency provides. This is said to assure economical use of judicial and administrative resources, to promote administrative autonomy and responsibility by providing the agency with the opportunity to correct its own mistakes, and to further the legislative purpose of granting authority to the agency by requiring that its procedures be respected. However, exhaustion will not be required if it would be futile, such as where the agency is bound by applicable law to decide against the claimant and the claimant wishes to challenge that law.[73]

Means of Obtaining Review Judicial review may be obtained by any available means. Usually, a petition for review is required to be filed within a certain number of days after the final decision.[74] In other cases, the agency may have to bring an enforcement action in court to gain compliance, at which time review will be provided in that proceeding. This is the case with some decisions of the NLRB, which must bring an action for enforcement in the Court of Appeals.[75] In some cases, review will be by way of defense against administrative enforcement and appeal from any negative decision in that proceeding. In addition, an action for an injunction or for

---

67 *Shaughnessy v. Pedreiro*, 349 U.S. 48 (1955). Congress subsequently provided expressly for review by statute in deportation cases.

68 *Lindahl v. Office of Personnel Management*, 470 U.S. 768 (1985) (statute providing that Navy disability determinations were "final and conclusive and are not subject to review" held not to preclude some judicial review of "misconstruction of the governing legislation" going "to the heart of the administrative determination").

69 *See. e.g. United States v. Wunderlich*, 342 U.S. 98 (1951) (decision of agency in government contract dispute). *But see* SCHWARTZ, *supra* note 2, §8.6 at 485-486 (criticizing lack of review as making agencies "virtual laws unto themselves").

70 *See* Chapter IX, pp. 314-316.

71 *Webster v. Doe*, 486 U.S. 592, 603 (1988). *See also Johnson v. Robison*, 415 U.S. 361, 366 (1974) (prohibition of review of veterans benefit cases did not prohibit review of constitutional issue). *But see* Scalia, J., dissenting in *Webster v. Doe, supra.*

72 5 U.S.C.A. §704. *McKart v. United States*, 395 U.S. 185 (1969) (military draft classification not appealed administratively, so later judicial review is barred). However, exhaustion is not required where the administrative remedies are inadequate to award the relief the plaintiff seeks. *McCarthy v. Madigan*, 503 U.S. 140 (1992) (federal prisoner who sued prison officials for money damages was not required to exhaust prison administrative remedy).

73 *Bethesda Hospital Assoc. v. Bowen*, 485 U.S. 399 (1988) (agency had no power to award reimbursement hospitals sought). *See generally* SCHWARTZ, *supra* note 2, §§8.33-8.40.

74 *See e.g.* 42 U.S.C.A. §405(g) (60 days for Social Security appeals).

75 29 U.S.C.A. §160(e), (f).

declaratory relief may be used.[76] *Habeas corpus* was used in deportation cases until review under the APA was recognized.[77]

Standing A person seeking judicial review of agency action in federal court must have "standing" to contest that action. Standing generally requires that the person be one who is actually injured by the agency action.[78] However, when review is sought under the APA, an additional requirement beyond simple injury must be met. The APA provides for review only if the claimant's injury qualifies as an injury "within the meaning of a relevant statute."[79] This has been understood as requiring that the injury complained of be one that is within the "zone of interests" defined by the statute governing the agency action.

This requirement is most relevant when the injured plaintiff is not the party who was the direct subject of the administrative action. Such plaintiffs must show that the relevant statutes were intended to protect them from the type of injury they complain of. For example, when the Comptroller of Currency approved the applications of two banks to sell securities, the banks did not complain, but stock brokers and dealers who would face competition from the banks did file suit. The Court found that an arguable basis for the National Bank Act limiting securities brokerage activities of banks was to prevent competition with established securities dealers — the precise injury complained of by the plaintiffs.[80] Had the Court found that the sole purpose of the Act was to assure that banks did not fail by overextending their operations, then injury to competitors would not have been within that zone of interests. An example of a negative zone of interests case is one involving the decision of the federal Postal Service to permit certain private courier companies to engage in some international mail delivery. The postal workers' union sued to contest the decision, claiming that it was unlawful. The Court held that the zone of interest test was not satisfied: Congress's purpose in prohibiting private competition with the Postal Service was to assure that the Service received sufficient revenues, not to protect government postal workers' jobs.[81]

3. Scope of Review of Agency Action

Review of Fact Determinations The general rule is that agency determinations of issues of fact made after a trial-type hearing must be affirmed by a reviewing court if they are supported by "substantial evidence."[82] Substantial evidence has been defined as "such relevant evidence as a reasonable mind might accept as adequate to support a conclusion."[83] Many courts have held that this is largely the same standard used when trial judges review jury verdicts or appellate courts review a trial

---

76 An injunction is a court order stopping the defendant from doing something or requiring the defendant to do something. Declaratory relief is a declaration that the defendant's actions are unlawful. Both are discussed in greater detail in the chapter on Civil Procedure. *See* Chapter VII, pp. 237-239.

77 *Shaughnessy v. Pedreiro, supra* note 67. *Habeas corpus* is discussed in Chapter VIII, pp. 267-268.

78 Constitutional aspects of standing are discussed in Chapter IX, pp. 310-312.

79 5 U.S.C.A. §702.

80 *Clarke v. Securities Industry Assoc.*, 479 U.S. 388 (1987). Clearly, application of the zone of interest test can lead to varying results depending on the analysis of the relevant purposes of the statute — an analysis that often comes close to deciding the merits of the case.

81 *Air Couriers Conference of America v. American Postal Workers Union*, 498 U.S. 517 (1991). *See also Block v. Community Nutrition Institute*, 467 U.S. 340 (1984) (denying standing to consumers of milk products to challenge minimum prices set for milk handlers and producers).

82 5 U.S.C.A. §706(2)(E) and *Universal Camera v. Nat'l Labor Relations Bd.*, 340 U.S. 474 (1951).

83 *Consolidated Edison Co. v. Nat'l Labor Relations Bd.*, 305 U.S. 197, 229 (1938).

judge's factual findings to see if they are "clearly erroneous."[84] Courts give great deference to the findings of agencies because of their expertise in the subject matter. Applying the substantial evidence test — like reviewing jury verdicts and trial court findings of fact — is "more of an art than a science."[85]

Some agency decisions may be reviewed *de novo* by a court. This means that the court can examine the record as if it were the finder of fact in the first instance.[86] In some cases, *de novo* judicial review of fact issues is required by the Constitution.[87]

Review of Legal Issues Courts have primary responsibility to say what the law is and thus have the power to determine *legal* issues *de novo* based on their own analysis of the law. Where the statute is clear and the agency has erroneously interpreted it, courts may reverse based on their own independent view of what the law is. However, in many cases the statute is not clear and the agency interpretation is one possible view. In the absence of clear legislative intent to the contrary, a reviewing court "may not substitute its own construction for a reasonable interpretation" by the agency.[88]

Review of Mixed Fact-Law Issues Some issues of law are not "pure" law or fact issues. They seem legal, but have factual aspects to them, as where the legal standard is applied to the facts of the case to reach a conclusion in the statutory language — commonly referred to as "mixed" fact and law issues. In such instances, the reviewing court must affirm the finding if the application is reasonable.[89] Clearly the questions of whether the statute is clear or how "pure" an issue of law is are issues about which there is considerable room for disagreement.[90]

4. Review of Discretionary Agency Actions

Many agency decisions are matters of discretion not dictated by the law or facts. Examples are the numerous decisions on funding, refusals to grant exceptions, "no-action" letters and other refusals to take action. The questions of whether such actions are subject to review and the scope of that review are important.

The APA appears on the surface to provide contradictory answers to the question of reviewability. On the one hand, it provides that a court may set aside agency action that is "arbitrary, capricious, *an abuse of discretion*, or otherwise not in accordance with law."[91] On the other hand, it prohibits judicial review of any matter "committed to agency discretion by law."[92] If action is truly committed to agency discretion, then it is difficult to see how a court is to determine whether the administrator's discretion

---

84 *See* discussion Chapter V, p. 166 and Robert L. Stern, *Review of Findings of Administrators, Judges and Juries: A Comparative Analysis*, 58 HARV. L.REV. 70 (1944).

85 AMAN & MAYTON, *supra* note 2, at 446.

86 This is true of many civil rights claims. *See Chandler v. Roudebush*, 425 U.S. 840 (1976) (employment discrimination).

87 *Agosto v. Immigration and Naturalization Service*, 436 U.S. 748 (1978) (*de novo* trial of citizenship issue in deportation proceeding required both by statute and the Constitution).

88 *See Chevron, U.S.A., Inc. v. Natural Resources Defense Council*, 467 U.S. 837 (1984), discussed in Chapter II, p. 57. For a good discussion of what deference is due and when, *see* STRAUSS, *supra* note 2, at 257-261.

89 *Nat'l Labor Relations Bd. v. Hearst Publications, Inc.*, 322 U.S. 111 (1944) (determination of whether "newsboys" who distributed papers on the street were "employees" within the meaning of the National Labor Relations Act).

90 *See generally* AMAN & MAYTON, *supra* note 2, §13.7. A similar fact-law distinction arises with respect to the division of labor between judge and jury. *See* Chapter III, p. 84.

91 5 U.S.C.A. §706 (emphasis supplied).

92 5 U.S.C.A. §701(a).

was "abused." In other words, if there are *no* statutory standards limiting an administrator's actions, then it is difficult to see how judicial review would be anything more than a court arbitrarily substituting its decision for that of the administrator. The Court has determined that, if there is truly "no law to apply" — no standards by which a reviewing court could judge the propriety of the decision — then the matter is "committed to agency discretion" and is not reviewable. But if there is some law to apply, then the decision is reviewable and those standards are applied to determine whether the decision was an abuse of discretion.[93]

The principal case in the area illustrates how both the question of reviewability is decided and the standard of "abuse of discretion" is applied. In *Citizens to Preserve Overton Park v. Volpe*,[94] the Secretary of Transportation released federal money to local authorities to fund construction of a highway through a park. A provision of the governing statute allowed such construction unless a "feasible and prudent" alternative route existed. If no alternative existed, the statute mandated that all possible steps be taken to "minimize harm" to the park. The Secretary took the position that the question of whether any alternative route was "feasible and prudent" was clearly non-reviewable discretionary action. The Supreme Court held that there was in fact "law to apply." The statute clearly indicated Congress's intent that park land be protected. Consequently, the standard to be applied was whether the Secretary had fully considered alternative routes and had properly determined that there were special problems with them. Thus, while a court in a case involving discretionary action cannot dictate what decision an administrator must reach, it can assure that the decision made is a rational one that takes into account the factors that the law requires to be taken into account.[95]

5. Attorney Fees and Costs

The Equal Access to Justice Act was passed by Congress in recognition of the high cost of contesting actions of agencies and the beneficial effects of redressing lawless agency action or inaction. Consequently, in any case against the United States or one of its agencies, a federal court "shall award" attorney fees to any prevailing private party "unless the court finds that the position of the United States was substantially justified or that special circumstances make an award unjust."[96]

E. Presidential and Congressional Controls on Federal Agency Action

Federal agencies are subject to statutory commands and owe their continued existence to Congress and the President. Consequently, complete control of agencies is always available through legislation abolishing them or limiting their power. However, these means of control are not often resorted to. Instead, Congress and the President use less drastic and less direct means. These efforts are not completely successful in part because many agencies have been set up as independent precisely

---

93 Professor Schwartz disagrees with the premise that there must be statutory standards to apply, citing English practice as support. *See* SCHWARTZ, *supra* note 2, §8.11, at 495. Examples of discretionary actions not subject to review are the President's decision to accept or reject a list of miliary base closings, *Dalton v. Spencer*, 511 U.S. 462 (1994), and an agency's decision to discontinue funding a health program out of its lump sum appropriation. *Lincoln v. Virgil*, 508 U.S. 182 (1993).

94 401 U.S. 402 (1971).

95 It is important to emphasize that the "substantial evidence" rule and great deference to administrative agency fact-finding would not apply to discretionary decisions such as the one in *Overton Park*, because there was no trial-type administrative hearing. Indeed, the problem with the administrator's decision in *Overton Park* was that there was *no* record of reasons for it.

96 28 U.S.C.A. §2412(d)(1)(A). However, the maximum rate for attorney fees is $125 per hour.

to avoid the effects of political influence. In addition, presidential and congressional influences often pull agencies in opposite directions, so they effectively cancel each other out.

1. Power Over Tenure of Agency Officials

Presidential Power of Appointment A major way to influence agency policy and rules is through the power to appoint the agency head or cabinet secretary whose department supervises the agency. The "appointments clause" of the Constitution provides that Congress shall establish the offices of government, that higher-level or "principal officers" will be appointed by the President subject to Senate confirmation, and that "inferior officers" may be appointed by the President, by the courts of law, or by department heads without need for Senate involvement, if Congress so provides.[97] The President's choice and the process of Senate approval of a Cabinet Secretary or agency head present opportunities to pick administrators who have particular views about the way the agency should be run and to extract promises regarding the future direction of the agency.

Presidential Removal Power The Constitution is silent about how federal administrative officers may be removed other than by way of impeachment by the Congress. Any presidential removal power would presumably be part of the grant of executive power in Article II, particularly the power to "take care that the Laws be faithfully executed."[98] But as noted in Chapter I, there are many "independent" administrative agencies. This independence is assured by providing for appointment terms that extend beyond the term of office of the President who appointed them and by limiting the presidential ability to remove them.[99]

The original caselaw on removal drew a distinction between administrative officials who perform "executive" functions and those who performed "quasi-judicial" and "quasi-legislative" functions. While the President retained the right to dismiss "those who are part of the Executive establishment" and who perform purely executive functions, he could not dismiss those "whose tasks require absolute freedom from Executive interference."[100] This test has been replaced by a more flexible functional one under which the President can freely dismiss only those officials who are essential to the President's performance of core presidential functions.[101] Thus, the distinction is drawn between executive branch officials performing "administrative" functions, whose dismissal Congress can regulate, executive officials exercising "political" executive authority, whom the President can dismiss at will.[102]

---

97 Art. II §2 cl. 2.

98 Art. II, §3. *See Myers v. United States*, 272 U.S. 52, 164 (1926) and NOWAK & ROTUNDA, *supra* note 55, at 264. The removal power has been a sore point between the President and Congress. The famous impeachment of President Andrew Johnson and his narrow acquittal in the Senate in 1867 — the only impeachment ever of a President — was based on his refusal to accede to a Tenure in Office Act passed by Congress that would have changed the tenure of all his cabinet officials (most of them inherited from President Lincoln) from service at the pleasure of the President to dismissal only with the concurrence of the Senate. Under *Myers, supra*, the Act violates separation of powers.

99 *See* Chapter I, p. 15.

100 *Humphrey's Executor v. United States*, 295 U.S. 602 (1935) (prohibiting presidential dismissal where Congress had provided by statute that a member of the Federal Trade Commission could be removed mid-term only for poor job performance).

101 *Morrison v. Olson*, 487 U.S. 654 (1988) (appointment and removal procedure for special prosecutor not invalid just because limits were placed on presidential power to dismiss her, since such limits did not "impede the President's ability to perform his constitutional duty").

102 *See* STRAUSS, *supra* note 1, at 68.

Civil Service Employees Below "inferior officers" are employees whose appointment and tenure are not subject to any constitutional restraints.[103] This provides a constitutional justification for the existence of a competitive, merit-based civil service system.[104] It is these individuals, who are protected from dismissal except for cause, who perform the daily functions of government administration.

Congressional Control Over Tenure of Agency Officials Though the Senate must approve presidential agency appointments, it is clear that Congress does not have the power itself to appoint executive officials. In *Buckley v. Valeo*,[105] the Supreme Court considered the constitutionality of provisions of the Federal Election Campaign Act. It authorized a Federal Election Commission to make rules regulating campaign practices and to investigate and prosecute violations of them. In an effort to achieve a political balance on the Commission in this sensitive political area, the Act provided for appointment of some commissioners by the President (without participation of the Senate) and some by the President *pro tempore* of the Senate and the Speaker of the House of Representatives.[106] The Supreme Court held the Commission so constituted violated the appointments clause. Since the Commissioners would be enforcing the law and would therefore be *executive* officers, they could only be appointed by the President with approval of the Senate and could not be appointed by legislative officials. The decision was supported by reference to the policy that underlies all separation of powers problems: the notion that "the same persons should not both legislate and administer the laws."[107]

Just as Congress cannot appoint executive agency personnel, it violates separation of powers for Congress to vest executive power in an official over whose tenure it already has control. In *Bowsher v. Synar*,[108] Congress passed a law intended to reduce the federal deficit. The law assigned certain duties to the Comptroller General, the official in charge of the Government Accounting Office, a legislative bureau that investigates and evaluates internal operations of government. The law instructed the Comptroller, upon being notified of certain fiscal information, to determine what spending cuts to make based on standards set out in legislation. These spending cuts were then to be transmitted to the President who was required to put them into effect. The Comptroller General's exercise of this kind of judgment, the Court held, was clearly executive action. The problem was that the Comptroller General, as head of a legislative agency, was subject to removal by Congress before expiration of his 15-year term. It violated separation of powers for Congress to vest executive decision-making power in an official under its control.[109]

---

103 *Buckley v. Valeo*, 424 U.S. 1, 126, n. 162 (1976).

104 Another reason why the civil service is constitutional is that civil service employees are "inferior officers" whose appointment and dismissal are vested in department heads whose discretion to hire and fire is controlled by the merit requirements of the statute establishing the civil service. *See* STRAUSS, *supra* note 2, at 64 and *United States v. Perkins*, 116 U.S. 483 (1886) (when Congress vests appointment power in department heads, it may restrict the manner of removal).

105 424 U.S. 1 (1976).

106 These officials are the presiding officers of the two houses of Congress elected by their members.

107 424 U.S. at 272. The act had also provided that all appointees would need to be approved not just by the Senate, but by both houses of Congress — a provision that the Court struck down as well.

108 478 U.S. 714 (1986).

109 *See also MWAA v. Citizens for the Abatement of Aircraft Noise*, 501 U.S. 252 (1991) (unconstitutional for members of Congress to serve on a board overseeing administration of federal airports because power they would exercise would be executive power and would be in a form other than legislation).

2. Ongoing Presidential and Congressional Influence on Agency Action

Presidential Means of Control Beyond the power to appoint agency officials, the President has many opportunities to exercise ongoing control over agency policy and action. The degree of a President's control varies with the agency and depends in part on whether the agency is an executive agency, which is responsible to a presidential cabinet Secretary or other presidential appointee, or an independent agency. Actions of executive agencies can be supervised closely. "Major rules" generally must be cleared with the White House's Office of Management and Budget (OMB) and may result in considerable debate, negotiation and compromise.[110] The content and timing of the administrative rules may be affected. Enforcement priorities of agencies can be set that reflect the President's view as to the wisdom or importance of the law. A policy of agency *inaction* is the easiest to implement. Thus, there is a long history of executive branch officials and agencies reading statutory commands narrowly or "dragging their feet" in promulgating needed regulations or in initiating or pursuing enforcement actions in programs with which they disagree. To give a recent example, the Reagan and Bush administrations were repeatedly criticized for failing to enforce vigorously civil rights and environmental protection laws.

Presidential influence should not be overstated, however. Most federal administrative agencies are housed in the executive branch. However, of the approximately 5 million civilian and military personnel in the 14 departments of the government, the President gets to appoint only the top 3,000 or so. The remaining administrators who actually do the work carrying out policy are not so easy to control. They are part of the merit-based civil service system.[111] Generally the President cannot fire them and they have specialized knowledge and strong feelings about "their" agency's policies and practices. Further, the President and his staff or appointees are only one influence on agency personnel. As pointed out below, congressional committees have great influence over agencies.

President Harry S. Truman, who served from 1945 until 1953, was considered by many to have been a very strong President. But in dealing with the bureaucracy, he described his task as being "to bring people in and try to persuade them to do what they ought to do without persuasion. That's what I spend most of my time doing. That's what the power of the President amounts to."[112] Truman also commented on the eve of his successor, former Army General Dwight D. Eisenhower, becoming President: "He'll sit here and he'll say 'Do this! Do that!' and nothing will happen. Poor Ike — it won't be a bit like the Army."[113]

There are some legal limits to presidential intervention in agency matters even in those agencies whose heads the President has appointed. For example, the President may not seek to "impound" funds Congress intended that the agency spend.[114] In *Train v. City of New York*,[115] Congress had passed the Clean Water Act of

---

110 *See* OMB Executive Order No. 12291, 46 Fed. Reg. 13193 Feb. 17, 1981) (requiring that all executive agency action be cleared through OMB).

111 *See supra* p. 208.

112 Quoted in STRAUSS, *supra* note 2, at 61 n.32.

113 ALEX AYRES, ED., THE WIT AND WISDOM OF HARRY S. TRUMAN 43 (Meridian Books 1998).

114 Impoundment dates from 1803, when President Thomas Jefferson refused to spend $50,000 on defense of the Mississippi River. President Nixon was perhaps the biggest impounder of funds, at one point impounding as much as $25 billion.

115 420 U.S. 35 (1975).

1972 over President Nixon's veto, but Nixon continued his opposition to the program and impounded funds by ordering the administrator of the Environmental Protection Agency to withhold several billion dollars that Congress had directed should go to fund construction of sewage treatment plants for New York City. The City of New York sued for release of the money. The Court held that the President had no power to order the agency to withhold the funds and that the agency must spend those funds as Congress directed.[116]

Congressional Power and Influence Over Agencies Congressional oversight of agencies has its source in the "power of the purse" given by the Constitution — the power to decide whether and to what extent to fund government operations.[117] The means by which congressional influence is most commonly exercised is through congressional committees. As noted in Chapter I, the original purpose of committees was to deal with the increased complexity and specialized nature of legislation in the modern world. But with the growth of administrative agencies, committees have developed a strong supervisory influence on their operations. Because committees are organized according to subject matter, their members develop expertise and a strong interest in an area of agency action, making it difficult for agencies to use their superior knowledge to escape scrutiny. Most important, since Congress has control over agency budgets, Congressional committee members can be very persuasive in convincing agency heads to alter the way they are carrying out a particular Congressional program.[118]

To assist it in carrying out this oversight role, Congress has established powerful agencies of its own to do research and investigative work and to make recommendations in particular areas. Among them are the Government Accounting Office (GAO), the Congressional Budget Office and the Library of Congress. The GAO regularly issues reports on the performance of federal agencies.

One device widely used in the past by Congress to control agency action was the "legislative veto." Congress would reserve to itself the right to "veto" certain agency action or proposed rules through the use of a joint resolution or vote of one house or in some cases even a committee vote. This device was declared unconstitutional by the Supreme Court in *Immigration & Naturalization Service v. Chadha*[119] as an encroachment on the power of the executive branch. The Court held that the legislative veto by a single house of Congress provided for in *Chadha* violated the "presentment" clause, which requires that legislation be presented to the President for approval or veto, the "bicameral" clause, which requires that legislation be passed by both houses of Congress, and the implied separation of powers structure of the

---

116 A "settlement" of the impoundment dispute between Congress and the President enacted after *Train* is set out in 2 U.S.C.A. §681 *et seq.* (allowing the President to delay spending and propose recission of budgetary amounts, but prohibiting outright impoundment).

117 *See* Chapter I, p. 6.

118 Even the influence of individual members of Congress on agency decisions have been tolerated at least before the adjudication stage. *DCP Farms v. Yeutter*, 957 F.2d 1183 (5th Cir. 1992). *Compare supra* note

119 462 U.S. 919 (1983).

Constitution.[120] According to the dissent in *Chadha*, the majority decision in that case invalidated some 200 federal statutes.[121]

PART II: Separation of Powers and Federalism Issues Involving Agencies

A. Administrative Agencies and Separation of Powers

From all that has been discussed, it is clear that administrative agencies exercise *executive* power when they enforce the law, exercise *legislative* power when they engage in rule-making and exercise *judicial* power when they adjudicate disputes under governing law. One might suppose that a system that purports to be based on separation of powers would have some difficulty with these mixed features of administrative agencies.[122] In fact, all these separation of powers questions have been settled by the Supreme Court in a way that has permitted longstanding agency practice to continue.

There are three dimensions to the separation of powers critique of federal administrative agencies: (1) that executive agencies are exercising legislative power, (2) that executive agencies are exercising judicial power, and (3) that one governmental organ, regardless of what branch it belongs to, combines executive, legislative and judicial functions "under one roof."

1. Agencies Exercising Legislative Power

The Court has viewed the problem of agencies exercising legislative power by promulgating rules as one of "delegation" of legislative power. The Court's position is that a statute does not improperly delegate legislative power so long as Congress provides "intelligible standards" to limit the discretion of the agency and to provide a basis for meaningful judicial review.[123] Only then can it be assured that the essentials of the legislative function of determining policy are being exercised by Congress and not by the agency. Thus, in *A.L.A. Schechter Poultry v. United States*,[124] the Court unanimously invalidated a statutory grant of administrative authority to establish "codes of fair competition" in various segments of business and industry with no indication of what the content of those codes should be.

The Court has never overruled the *Schechter* case, but the requirement of legislative standards has been diluted to a point of virtual uselessness. The Court has repeatedly upheld the most general of guidelines. For example, it is a sufficient

---

120 *See* Art. I §7 cl. 2 & 3. One method of avoiding presidential veto is to attach a "rider" affecting particular administrative action to a bill the President wants. The President has no "line-item veto" power and must either approve or veto the entire bill presented to him. *See infra* note 123.

121 A new form of legislative veto was enacted in 1996. It provides in general that any "major" agency rule (as defined, there are around 80-100 major rules a year) may not take effect for at least 60 days after it is submitted to Congress to give Congress the chance to pass a joint resolution of disapproval. In accord with *Chadha*, the resolution would be approved by both houses and signed by the President. If this occurs, the agency cannot re-issue the same rule unless Congress enacts legislation allowing it to do so. *See* 5 U.S.C.A. §§601-808. It is to be expected that Congress would not often be able to mobilize itself sufficiently within 60 days to stop most rules. However, it may pass the resolution any time, even after the rule goes into effect.

122 *See* Chapter I, pp. 9-18, 32-34, and Chapter IX, pp. 309-318, where separation of powers is discussed.

123 *Yakus v. United States*, 321 U.S. 414 (1944). *See also Touby v. United States*, 500 U.S. 160 (1991). The Court has consistently rejected the idea that Congress may properly give away whatever power it wants. *See Clinton v. City of New York*, 524 U.S. 417 (1998) (the "line item veto" case, holding unconstitutional Congress's attempt to give the President the power to cancel certain appropriations that have been enacted into law).

124 295 U.S. 495 (1935).

direction from Congress that the Federal Communications Commission regulate broadcast licensing in accord with the "public interest,"[125] that a government department define and recover "excess profits,"[126] and that the federal Price Administrator fix "fair and equitable" commodities prices.[127]

Anti-delegation rules have somewhat more force on the state level, where one can find an occasional case decision striking down a state administrative rule for improper delegation of legislative power. But most states follow an approach similar to that used for the federal government.[128]

2. Agencies Exercising Judicial Power

In a common sense meaning of "judicial power," the hearing divisions of agencies clearly exercise judicial power when they hold hearings and decide disputes. If this is so, a problem arises with Article III of the Constitution, which specifies that "[t]he judicial Power of the United States, shall be vested in" federal courts staffed by "Article III" judges — judges whose independence in decision-making is protected by lifetime tenure subject only to removal by impeachment. Administrative adjudicators, sometimes referred to as "Article I" judges, do not have lifetime tenure.

The Court has had some difficulty with this issue. On the one hand, administrative agencies are a practical necessity in the modern age. On the other, there must be *some* limits on Congress's ability to assign the task of adjudicating disputes to non-lifetime-tenured adjudicators. Otherwise, Congress could give *all* federal judicial business to agencies or other non-life-tenured judges over whom it has greater influence. This would render the lifetime tenure requirements of Article III a nullity and defeat the Framers' purpose to establish a federal judiciary that is independent of Congress's will.[129]

There are three theories under which administrative adjudication by agencies is permitted, none of them entirely satisfying.

Public vs. Private Rights   The traditional approach to the problem has been to divide potential judicial business into two categories: "public rights" and "private rights."[130] According to the Court, Article III judges are required only for adjudication of disputes over *private* rights. "Private rights" cases are tort, contract, property or other suits between private parties, including claims for damages between private parties provided for in federal statutes. The category also includes all criminal cases. These private rights are thought to be at the "core" of "judicial business" that cannot be handled by agencies, but must instead be adjudicated even in the first instance by

---

125 *National Broadcasting Co. v. United States*, 319 U.S. 190, 225-226 (1943).

126 *Lichter v. United States*, 334 U.S. 742, 778-786 (1948).

127 *Yakus v. United States*, 321 U.S. 414, 426-427 (1944). *See generally* Peter H. Aranson, Ernest Gellhorn, Glen O. Robinson, *A Theory of Legislative Delegation*, 68 Cornell L. Rev. 1 (1982). Some have suggested that the *Schechter* case might still be good law on its facts since it involved a grant of open-ended power directly to the President (rather than to an agency) to makes rules in a vast area (reorganization of the economy) without any of the procedural requirements for promulgating rules that agencies must follow today. *See* STRAUSS, *supra* note 2, at 20-21. Others have suggested even more broadly that the anti-delegation doctrine might be on its way back. *See* AMAN & MAYTON, *supra* note 2, at 23-27, and *National Cable Television Assoc., Inc. v. United States*, 415 U.S. 336 (1974).

128 *See* AMAN & MAYTON, *supra* note 2, at 7.

129 Federal magistrate judges, bankruptcy judges and many of the judges on federal courts with specialized jurisdiction are also Article I judges. *See* Chapter V, pp. 181-182 and 171. As such, the same constitutional difficulties and solutions that justify agency adjudicators apply to them.

130 *See Northern Pipeline Co. v. Marathon Pipeline Co.*, 458 U.S. 50 (1982) (legislation authorizing bankruptcy judges with 14-year terms to adjudicate private rights cases violates Article III).

an Article III judge or by a state court. "Public rights" are said to arise in matters between the government and individuals where the rights have been created by Congress and are thus subject to its control.[131] Public rights are said to include all manner of public benefits and privileges, such as Social Security payments, veterans' benefits, food stamps, and licenses. Congress can constitutionally create and assign determinations of public rights to purely administrative determination by Article I adjudicators.

The categories of public rights just listed are certainly the most numerous types of cases that administrative agencies handle and the private rights cases are the kinds of cases judges traditionally handled before the advent of the modern administrative state. However, the public-private rights distinction does not make much sense in terms of the purpose of Article III's lifetime tenure requirement as a safeguard against congressional influences on federal judges.[132] Any test of what cases require an independent Article III judge should include cases that are particularly subject to congressional intervention and should exclude cases that are not. Many *public* rights cases, such as suits to protect and expand government health and welfare assistance or to stop pollution or cutting trees on federal lands, are exactly the kinds of cases that invite political interference. At the same time, many *private* rights cases, such as contract disputes between corporations and suits by creditors on debts, are not likely to attract much political attention and are therefore the least in need of a judge who has lifetime tenure. In many ways, the public-private distinction would make more sense if it were *reversed*.

Agencies as "Adjuncts" to Courts An alternative rationale explains Article I agency adjudicators as "adjuncts" to an Article III court. Under this theory, agencies are allowed to adjudicate many private rights cases on the principle that they are "assisting" a court in deciding the case, with the Article III court making the *ultimate* decision. Thus, in the typical agency arrangement, the agency adjudicates the case in the first instance, but there will be *judicial review* of that decision by an Article III court. Thus, "the essential attributes of judicial power" are reserved to Article III courts, and the rule against non-Article III adjudication of private rights is not offended.[133] The problem with this theory is that it does not comport with reality. Most administrative agency adjudications are really final and binding when rendered without any need for the agency to seek approval of an Article III court.[134] Even when there is judicial review, virtually conclusive effect is given to the Article I adjudicator's administrative fact-finding and courts give great deference even on issues of law.[135]

The Functional Approach Because of difficulties with the public-private right test and the adjunct theories, the Supreme Court has seemed to back off both theories. It has taken a "functional" approach similar to that employed to resolve other separation of powers problems: it has interpreted Article III's judicial qualifications

---

131 *Atlas Roofing v. Occupational Safety and Health Review Comm'n*, 430 U.S. 442, 450 (1977). Thus, under this theory Congress need not afford *any* judicial or administrative hearing remedies in public rights cases other than those required by procedural due process. *See supra*, pp. 198-202.

132 *See* Chapter I, p. 9.

133 *See Commodity Futures Trading Comm'n v. Schor*, 478 U.S. 833 (1986), quoting *Crowell v. Benson*, 285 U.S. 22, 51 (1932).

134 An exception is the NLRB, which must seek enforcement of its decisions. *See supra* p. 203.

135 *See supra* pp. 204-205. The "adjunct" theory works somewhat better in describing federal magistrates, also classified as non-tenured Article I adjudicators, who work under the close supervision of an Article III district judge and for the most part only recommend decisions. *See* Chapter V, p. 181.

requirement in a manner that may not do complete justice to its wording, but generally serves the constitutional *function* it was designed to serve.[136] Applying the functional approach to Article I adjudicators, the Court has sought to balance two opposing factors: (1) Congress's interest in efficiency and expertise in having a particular category of cases adjudicated by an Article I adjudicator and (2) the danger of congressional influence over that category of cases. Using this standard, the Court allowed Congress to assign some private rights disputes to administrative adjudication.[137]

The "functional" approach is subject to the usual criticisms of balancing tests — that it is impossible to balance dissimilar values against each other on any principled basis. Also, it ignores relatively clear text of the Constitution that vests "[t]he judicial Power" in Article III judges. Indeed, the Court's "functional" approach could be seen as nothing more than a device that allows the Court to switch to a higher level of generalization to avoid clear language. As such, it effectively reduces Article III's command to a standardless test of whether a particular arrangement offends the *general idea* of separation of powers as that idea is understood by a given majority of the Court at a given time.[138]

3. Intra-Agency Separation of Powers Problems

Even if the *inter-branch* separation of powers problems just discussed can be resolved, many argue that surely there must be an *intra-branch* separation of powers problem when rule-making, enforcement and adjudication functions are located "under one roof." As James Madison stated in Federalist No. 47, "[t]he accumulation of all powers, legislative, executive, and judiciary, in the same hands, whether of one, a few, or many, and whether hereditary, self-appointed, or elective, may justly be pronounced the very definition of tyranny."[139] In addition there are the fundamental notions that "no man shall be a judge of his own cause" and that "the same persons should not both legislate and administer the laws."[140]

Professor Strauss has observed that "[i]t is hard to say as a theoretical matter why these arrangements satisfy the structural requirements of 'separation of powers,' although it is clear beyond doubt in the eyes of courts that they do."[141] The true reason why agencies have been sustained against constitutional challenge probably lies in the fact that they serve important functions in modern government, and that hobbling them by insisting on purity in separation of powers would not be a wise policy.

However, there is no need to resort to reasons of expediency, since, as just noted, separation of powers cases tend to require only that federal government power

---

136 This approach can be directly traced to Justice White's dissent in *Northern Pipeline*, the last case to take the pure public-versus-private rights approach. *See supra* note 130.

137 *See, e.g., Thomas v. Union Carbide Agricultural Products Co.*, 473 U.S. 568, (1985) (approving administrative system of reimbursement for development costs of chemical); *Commodity Futures Trading Comm'n v. Schor*, 478 U.S. 833 (1986) (approving administrative adjudication of disputes between federally-licensed securities brokers and their clients). Another constitutional objection to administrative adjudication has been that it violates the 7th Amendment right to a jury trial in civil cases. The Court has rejected this argument. *See Atlas Roofing Co. v. Occupational Safety and Health Review Comm'n.*, 430 U.S. 442, 461 (1977); *Granfinanciera, S.A. v. Nordberg*, 492 U.S. 33, 61 (1989). See also AMAN & MAYTON, *supra* note 2, at 143-145 (criticizing the Court's view).

138 *See Morrison v. Olson*, 487 U.S. 654, 697 (Scalia, J., dissenting).

139 THE FEDERALIST PAPERS at 324 (Jacob E. Cooke ed.) (Wesleyan U. Press, Middletown, Conn. 1961) (originally published 1788).

140 *Buckley v. Valeo*, 424 U.S. 1, 272 (1967).

141 STRAUSS, *supra* note 2, at 16.

structures not offend the *functions served* by separation of powers. Applying this functional approach, agencies do not to violate separation of powers because they simply do not present the threat of tyranny that Madison and the other Framers were concerned about. First, modern agencies are relatively independent of all three branches and are not "captives" of any one branch. A greater threat would be presented if legislative, executive and judicial functions were combined in the President, the Congress or the courts. Second, while agencies enjoy a certain independence from any *one* branch, they are subject to the external and often competing influences exerted by *all three* branches noted earlier: the President appoints many agency heads and top officials, supervises their activities and may fire some of them, Congress monitors their operations through committee oversight and legislative mandates, and the courts review the legality of agency actions. This makes agencies less likely to threaten the tyranny Madison feared.[142]

A third reason agencies do not present serious separation of powers problems is said to found in that fact that, in reality, they combine enforcement, rule-making and adjudicative functions *only at the top levels*. The head of the agency and top advisors have the power to decide whether to promulgate a rule, whether and how to enforce the rule, and whether a contested case was properly adjudicated under the rule. Below the top level, functions are separated into different divisions of the agency. The most dangerous threat to fairness is probably influence by the enforcement division on the adjudicative division. Under the APA, however, ALJs may not be "responsible to or subject to" the "supervision or direction" of agency enforcement personnel and there may be no *ex parte* contact between them regarding a pending case.[143]

B. Federalism and Sovereign Immunity Limits on Suits to Redress Illegal Federal and State Agency Action

1. Suits Against Agencies Themselves

When judicial review was discussed, we considered several situations in which agencies were sued by individuals. Suits against agencies, however, can sometimes conflict with sovereign immunity — the notion that a sovereign cannot be sued without its consent. When judicial review is provided for by statute, as in most cases, the relevant sovereign can be said to have given "consent." However, consent does not cover all forms of action against governmental agencies. Further, statutes giving consent may be repealed.

It is somewhat ironic that a country that threw off the yoke of monarchism and ratified a written constitution to assure that the government followed the rule of law, retains the doctrine of sovereign immunity.[144] Since sovereign immunity could effectively make the government unaccountable to the Constitution and laws, the tension between accountability and sovereign immunity has produced caselaw and legislation that modifies immunity concepts sufficiently to allow actions for most forms

---

142 *See* STRAUSS, *supra* note 2, at 14-17. The Supreme Court has also rejected due process challenges to combining investigative and adjudicative functions in one agency. *See Withrow v. Larkin*, 421 U.S. 35 (1975) (rejecting physician's argument that due process was violated because the agency that handled charges of professional misconduct against doctors had the power to investigate those charges, present them, and then rule on their validity, unless a risk of actual bias or prejudgment could be shown).

143 5 U.S.C.A. §554(d) and *supra* p. 196. ALJs are also exempt from agency performance review and have their tenure and compensation determined by the chief civil service commission. *See generally* AMAN & MAYTON, *supra* note 2, §8.5.2.

144 *See* ERWIN CHEMERINSKY, FEDERAL JURISDICTION, 3D ED. §9.2.1 (Aspen 1999).

of *injunctive relief*. This at least allows a court to halt an illegal practice and to order that the government conform its conduct to the law in the future.[145]

Precisely what injunctive relief is allowed varies depending on whether the court handling the suit is a state or federal court and on what level of government is being sued. Consequently, it is necessary to consider all permutations of courts and defendants that are possible as a result of federalism.

a. Suits Against *Federal* Agencies in *Federal* Court

For actions in federal court "seeking relief *other than money damages*," the APA operates as a waiver of sovereign immunity and allows the United States to be named as a defendant.[146] Actions against the United States or its agencies for money damages are generally barred by sovereign immunity, but may be brought pursuant to statute. Primary among them are the Federal Tort Claims Act (FTCA) and the Tucker Act. The FTCA, enacted in 1946, provides for recovery for torts, providing for tort liability of the federal government "in the same manner and to the same extent as a private individual under like circumstances."[147] The Tucker Act, first enacted in 1855, provides for recovery of damages in "cases not sounding in tort," meaning primarily government contracts cases.[148] However, in keeping with the notion that there could be no suit in the absence of a congressional waiver of sovereign immunity, Congress has made exceptions to its waiver of immunity and exempted the United States from trial by jury and punitive damages.[149]

b. Suits Against *State* Agencies in *State* Court

As stated in Chapter I, states retain whatever rights and powers they had as sovereign international states except to the extent that they gave up those rights and powers in the Constitution. Among the rights retained is a state's sovereign immunity from suit in its own courts absent consent. However, many states have allowed suit on terms similar to those allowed by the federal government, discussed above. Other states have abolished or waived their sovereign immunity completely.[150]

c. Suits Against *Federal* Agencies in *State* Court

The APA's waiver of federal sovereign immunity explicitly waives it only for suit in *federal* court. Moreover, because of the nature of the federal structure contemplated by the Constitution and particularly the supremacy of federal law, state courts have no power to review or order relief with respect to the actions of federal officials or agencies. This rule was established in *Tarble's Case*.[151] In that case, the Supreme Court held that a state court in Wisconsin could not issue a writ of *habeas corpus* against a federal army recruiting officer ordering the release of an allegedly

---

145 *See supra* note 76.

146 5 U.S.C.A. §702 (emphasis supplied). Before the APA was amended to waive immunity, suits against the United States for injunctive relief were permitted on the same basis that such suits are allowed against states, despite the 11th Amendment, as described under 3. below. *See Larson v. Domestic & Foreign Commerce Corp.*, 337 U.S. 682 (1949).

147 28 U.S.C.A. §2674.

148 28 U.S.C.A. §1491(a)(1).

149 For a discussion of the FTCA and the Tucker Act, *see* CHEMERINSKY, *supra* note 144, §§9.2.3-9.2.4.

150 *See* PROSSER & KEETON'S HORNBOOK ON TORTS, 5TH ED. §§131-132 (West 1984, 1988). More detail about the immunity of states from tort liability is set out in Chapter XI, p. 413.

151 80 U.S. (13 Wall.) 397 (1871).

underage soldier. In addition, Congress has provided that federal officials may remove any state court suits against them to federal court.[152]

d. Suits Against *State* Agencies in *Federal* Court

This category of suits is perhaps the most important of all because plaintiffs seeking redress for state violations of federal law have traditionally sought relief in federal rather than state court. The popularity of federal courts in such cases flows from the facts that federal judges are not part of the state governmental machinery, are generally more expert than state judges on issues of federal law, and are insulated from political pressure by their life tenure. As discussed in Chapter I, when the Constitution was being debated, the question of whether states gave up their sovereign immunity from suit in *federal* court arose. In the 1791 case of *Chisholm v. Georgia*,[153] the Supreme Court decided that Article III's grant of federal judicial power over suits in which a state is a party abolished state immunity from suit in the *federal* courts, regardless of whatever immunity the state might enjoy in its own courts. Congress and the states responded with passage and ratification of the 11th Amendment in 1798, reinstating that immunity. The immunity continues to exist today despite the diminution in states' rights wrought by the Civil War and the 14th Amendment's limits on state action.[154] The literal wording of the 11th Amendment does not apply to bar suits for enforcement of *federal rights* brought by citizens against their *own* states. Nonetheless, the Supreme Court in the 1890 case of *Hans v. Louisiana*, held that, notwithstanding the wording of the 11th Amendment, such suits were nonetheless barred.[155]

However, caselaw interpreting the 11th Amendment has worked a division between permissible injunctive relief and prohibited damages relief roughly similar the division created by the APA for federal court suits against the federal government. The Supreme Court in *Ex parte Young*[156] held that, while sovereign immunity prevents suits against *states*, it does not bar federal law claims against state *officials in their official capacities* at least where the suit is for prospective injunctive relief. The theory of *Young* was the fiction that an official acting contrary to superior federal law was for that reason no longer a state official and could be subjected to suit for such "individual conduct." However, this theory is pure fiction since the relief awarded in an official-capacity officer suit binds the state and thus has the same effect as relief ordered against the state itself.[157] However, the "officer-suit" fiction does not go so far as to

152 28 U.S.C.A. §1442(a)(1). *But see Mesa v. California*, 489 U.S. 121 (1989) (removal is proper only if the defendant official has some defense to the suit or prosecution based on federal law). *Tarble's Case* followed and resolved issues raised by the vigorous use of state courts to protect escaped slaves from being recaptured and sent back to the south on order of federal "slave commissioners." This history is related in the Gibbons law review article cited in note 79 of Chapter V.

153 2 U.S. (2 Dall.) 419 (1793).

154 These limits are primarily the due process and equal protection clauses. The argument has been made that the 14th Amendment of its own force repealed the 11th Amendment, but the Court avoided deciding the question. *See Millikin v. Bradley*, 433 U.S. 267, 290 n.2 (1977).

155 134 U.S. 1 (1890). Sovereign immunity under the 11th Amendment also does not bar suits against municipal subdivisions of states — cities, counties, townships and the like — unless those municipalities are acting as the "alter ego" of the state, i.e. serving simply as the agent of the state in carrying out what is really a state program. *Pennhurst State School and Hospital v. Halderman*, 465 U.S. 89 (1984).

156 209 U.S. 123 (1908).

157 The concept of suing the government by suing its officials was borrowed from English practice where a similar fiction was employed to allow some suits against the Crown. *See* Louis Jaffe, *Suits Against Governments and Officers: Sovereign Immunity*, 77 HARV. L. REV. 1 (1963).

allow an official-capacity officer suit for *damages* collectable from the state treasury.[158] Congress has the power, if it chooses, to override state sovereign immunity from damages relief by passing a statute, if it makes clear on the face of that statute its intent to abrogate state immunity. However, Congress may do so only if it acts pursuant to powers granted to it by amendments ratified after 1798 — when the 11th Amendment was ratified. Since most of Congress's powers come from Article I (ratified 1789) and it does not qualify, the most important power for abrogation purposes is in section 5 of the 14th Amendment (ratified 1868).[159]

Official capacity suits against state officials in federal court are generally asserted pursuant to 42 U.S.C.A. §1983, the Civil Rights Act of 1871, which makes "[e]very person" acting "under color of" state law liable for injunctive or damages relief in federal court for violations of federal law. Suits for relief against administrative agency heads are facilitated by the fact that there is no requirement that the §1983 plaintiffs exhaust state administrative or judicial remedies.[160] However, there are three limits on the use of §1983 as a method of judicial review of state agency action. The first is that the plaintiff can only raise federal constitutional or statutory issues since the statute is only addressed to deprivations of federal rights. Second, relief may not include any accrued retroactive money judgment against a state agency, as discussed above. Third, if the state administrative proceeding is an enforcement action brought *against* the would-be federal plaintiff by the state agency, the federal court will be required to abstain from jurisdiction to permit the state proceeding to take its course. If those proceedings are decided against the party, that party will be relegated to state court judicial review.[161]

2. Suits Against Administrative Officials for Personal Liability

Despite the sovereign immunity of governmental bodies, it is sometimes possible to recover a *personal* money judgment against an administrative *official* for bad faith illegal actions. These suits are not barred by sovereign immunity because the suit is solely against the official and does not result in any government liability.[162]

Suits Against State Officials for Violating Federal Rights It should be noted as well that personal damages suits are generally possible *only* against administrative officials. The 1871 Civil Rights Act, discussed above, provides broadly for suit in state or federal court for damages liability against "every person" acting under color of state law who violates federal rights. Howoever, there are several common law immunities that the Court has presumed that Congress meant to continue to apply despite the broad statutory language. Legislators,[163] judges[164] and prosecutors are immune for action

---

158 *Edelman v. Jordan*, 415 U.S. 651 (1974).

159 *Seminole Tribe v. Florida*, 517 U.S. 44 (1996), *overruling Pennsylvania v. Union Gas Co.*, 491 U.S. 1 (1989). One example of the exercise of this power is 42 U.S.C.A. §2000d-7 (allowing suits against states for discrimination under several civil rights laws). *See generally* CHEMERINSKY, *supra* note 144, §§7.1-7.7.

160 *Patsy v. Florida International University*, 457 U.S. 496 (1982). The plaintiff may be bound by certain findings of fact made at any trial-type state administrative hearing, if the federal plaintiff did in fact pursue state administrative remedies. *See University of Tennessee v. Elliott*, 478 U.S. 788 (1986).

161 *See Ohio Civil Rights Comm'n v. Dayton Christian Schools*, 477 U.S. 619 (1986) (federal court must abstain in favor of pending state civil rights administrative proceeding against federal plaintiff). This is part of "*Younger* abstention," discussed in Chapter V, p. 190.

162 *See Scheuer v. Rhodes*, 416 U.S. 232 (1974) (suit for personal injuries by college students against Ohio governor and National Guard soldiers called out to quell student unrest not barred by 11th Amendment). *See generally* CHEMERINSKY, *supra* note 144, §7.1-7.7.

163 *Tenney v. Brandhove*, 341 U.S. 367 (1951) (state legislators); *Eastland v. United States Serviceman's Fund*, 421 U.S. 491 (1975) (federal legislators); *Bogan v. Scott-Harris*, 523 U.S. 44 (1998) (local legislators). High-level administrators or judges who act as "legislators" by promulgating rules may taken in their capacity as such.[165] However, they are amenable to suits for personal damages when they take action in their *administrative* capacities.[166]

Administrative actors are liable only if they acted in "bad faith" — defined as action which the official reasonably should have known would violate the plaintiff's rights.[167] The determination of bad faith is an objective one and has nothing really to do with the actual state of mind of the defendant. It is a purely legal question of whether the official's actions violated clearly established federal rights. The Court has recently stated that "[t]he qualified immunity standard gives ample room for mistaken judgments by protecting all but the plainly incompetent and those who knowingly violated the law."[168] Compensatory damages may be awarded and punitive damages are available if evil motive or intent or recklessness is shown.[169]

Suits Against Federal Officials There is no statute like §1983 providing for a private right of action for damages for violation of the Constitution or federal law against *federal* officials. However, the Court in *Bivens v Six Unknown Named Agents of the Federal Bureau of Narcotics*[170] implied a private right to sue for damages for bad faith constitutional violations. All the common law immunities set out above for state officials apply to their federal counterparts.[171] For all other claims, if federal officials are acting within the scope of their official capacity, the suit is treated as if it were against the United States and is handled in accordance with the FTCA. If the federal employees involved are determined not to have been acting within the scope of their employment, then suit may proceed in state court under applicable state law.[172]

Suits Against State Officials for Violations of State Law The immunities just discussed apply only when claims based on *federal* law are asserted against state or federal officials. If the basis of the claim against a state official is state law, then any immunities applied would be solely those provided for in state law. Those vary from state to state, but are sometimes somewhat similar to the federal immunities.

---

also be entitled to legislative immunity. *See Supreme Court of Virginia v. Consumers Union*, 446 U.S. 719 (1980). Legislative immunity applies to bar not only damages, but injunctive relief as well.

164 *Stump v. Sparkman*, 435 U.S. 349 (1978) (state judge who illegally ordered sterilization of minor was immune from damages; though order was not authorized by law, it was a judicial act); *Butz v. Economu*, 438 U.S. 478 (1978) (federal administrative law judge entitled to same judicial immunity as regular judges).

165 *Imbler v. Pachtman*, 424 U.S. 409 (1976); *Buckley v. Fitzsimmons*, 509 U.S. 259 (1993). *See also Briscoe v. LaHue*, 460 U.S. 325 (1983) (police officer witnesses).

166 *See Davis v. Passman*, 544 F.2d 865 (5th Cir. 1977), *rev'd on other grounds* 442 U.S. 228 (1979) (congressman may be liable for sex discrimination in hiring his staff since that action was administrative rather than legislative); *Burns v. Reed*, 500 U.S. 478 (1991) (prosecutor not entitled to immunity for giving erroneous advice to police, since that was an administrative act not connected with representation of government in court). A clear and concise summary of the complicated law in this area can be found in CHEMERINSKY, *supra* note 144, §§8.1-8.11.

167 *See Harlow v. Fitzgerald*, 457 U.S. 800 (1982) (suit against Department of Defense officials for retaliatory discharge of plaintiff who exposed cost overruns).

168 *Hunter v. Bryant*, 502 U.S. 224, 112 S.Ct. 534, 537 (1991) (*per curiam*).

169 *Smith v. Wade*, 461 U.S. 30 (1983).

170 403 U.S. 388 (1971).

171 One that is unique to the federal context is that the President is absolutely immune from any damages liability for actions taken pursuant to his office. *Nixon v. Fitzgerald*, 457 U.S. 731 (1982). However, there is no immunity for a President, even temporary immunity while President, from suit for actions taken before becoming President. *See Clinton v. Jones*, 520 U.S. 681 (1997)

172 28 U.S.C.A. §2679.

CHAPTER VII

CIVIL PROCEDURE

Part I of this chapter will trace the course of a typical civil lawsuit. Trial procedure was discussed extensively in Chapter III, so the emphasis here will be on pre-trial procedures, relief available after trial and the effect of judgments. In Part II of this chapter, we will consider some of the complexities that a federal system creates for litigation of civil claims as a result of multiple overlapping laws and court systems. Under this heading, we will consider the question of the proper court in which suit may be filed and what law must be applied.

PART I: The Course of a Civil Lawsuit

As noted in Chapter III, procedure during trial is quite similar in civil and criminal cases. There are substantial differences in pre-trial procedure, however.[1]

The rules of civil procedure vary among the states, but most state rules are similar to the Federal Rules of Civil Procedure (FRCP). Passed in 1938, the FRCP have been adopted virtually unchanged by half of the states and states that have not adopted them unchanged have borrowed significantly from them. Consequently, in the material below, procedure will be explained by reference to the FRCP.[2]

A. The Pleading Stage of the Case

1. Plaintiff's Complaint

A civil action begins when the plaintiff files a "complaint" with the clerk of the court. The FRCP requires that the complaint contain (1) a statement of the grounds upon which subject matter jurisdiction of the court is based, (2) "a short and plain statement of the claim showing that the pleader is entitled to relief" and (3) a demand for the relief that the pleader seeks.[3]

At common law, one wrong step in pleading meant that the litigant's case was dismissed or a defense was lost. This has given way to a more liberal view that facilitates getting to the merits of the dispute — what has been called "notice pleading." Notice pleading, as the term implies, requires only enough facts, in the words of a leading case, "to give the defendant fair notice of what the plaintiff's claim is and the grounds on which it rests."[4] The appendix of forms of the FRCP sets out the following example of a complaint for negligence arising out of an automobile accident:

---

1   For more detail on civil procedure see JACK H. FRIEDENTHAL, MARY KAY KANE, AND ARTHUR R. MILLER, HORNBOOK ON CIVIL PROCEDURE, 2D ED. (West 1993); FLEMING JAMES, JR., GEOFFREY C. HAZARD, JR. & JOHN LEUBSDORF, CIVIL PROCEDURE, 4TH ED. (Aspen 1992); LARRY TEPLY & RALPH U. WHITTEN, CIVIL PROCEDURE (Foundation 1994). Student texts are JOSEPH W. GLANNON, CIVIL PROCEDURE: EXAMPLES AND EXPLANATIONS, 3D ED. (Aspen 1997) and GENE R. SHREVE & PETER RAVEN-HANSEN, UNDERSTANDING CIVIL PROCEDURE, 2D ED. (Matthew Bender 1994). See also ROGER C. PARK & DOUGLAS D. MCFARLAND, COMPUTER-AIDED EXERCISES ON CIVIL PROCEDURE, 4TH ED. (West 1995). For books that concentrate specifically on federal courts and the intricacies of their jurisdiction, see CHARLES ALAN WRIGHT, HORNBOOK ON THE LAW OF FEDERAL COURTS, 5TH ED. (West 1994) and ERWIN CHEMERINSKY, FEDERAL JURISDICTION, 2D ED. (Aspen 1994).

2   The Federal Rules of Civil Procedure, other rules and selected federal statutes related to federal courts are collected in FEDERAL RULES OF CIVIL PROCEDURE - 1998-99 EDUCATIONAL EDITION (West 1998).

3   FRCP 8(a).

4   Conley v. Gibson, 355 U.S. 41, 47 (1957).

1. Allegation of jurisdiction.

2. On June 1, 1936, in a public highway called Boylston Street in Boston, Massachusetts, defendant negligently drove a motor vehicle against plaintiff who was then crossing said highway.

3. As a result plaintiff was thrown down and had his leg broken and was otherwise injured, was prevented from transacting his business, suffered great pain of body and mind, and incurred expenses for medical attention and hospitalization in the sum of one thousand dollars.

Wherefore plaintiff demands judgement against defendant in the sum of _____ dollars and costs.

Since complaints are written by lawyers, few are quite this short and to the point, but under the regime of what has been called "notice pleading," there is no requirement that the complaint go much beyond these conclusionary allegations. The net effect of notice pleading is to make the pleadings in a case relatively unimportant. Pleadings of this sort are of limited use in determining what the facts of the claim are. This function is instead performed directly by the device of "discovery." An exchange of "notice" pleadings also does little to distill out the issues to be tried or to screen out insufficient claims. Instead, these functions are performed by pre-trial conferences and summary judgment procedures, discussed below.[5]

Service of Process After the plaintiff files the complaint with the court clerk, the clerk issues a "summons." This is an order of the court directing the defendant to respond to the complaint or suffer a "default judgment."[6] Then the plaintiff must arrange to have the summons and a copy of the complaint "served" on the defendant. There are various methods of service, but the most common are in-hand personal service and service by mail. Service of the complaint is necessary to establish the court's "personal jurisdiction" over the defendant — its power to decide the case and bind the defendant to its judgment.[7]

2. The Defendant's Response to the Complaint

The defendant responding to the complaint has two options. The first is to raise one or more of several procedural defenses that are allowed to be raised by a "motion to dismiss." The second option is to contest the complaint on its merits by filing an "answer."[8] Whichever of the two alternatives is chosen, the defendant's response must be filed with the court within 20 days after service of the complaint unless an extension of time is obtained from the plaintiff or the court.[9]

Motion to Dismiss The defendant has the option of asserting certain procedural defenses in a motion to dismiss. Those grounds are challenges to the court's

---

5 Some states, among them California, require "fact" pleading. While fact pleading is somewhat more demanding of the pleader than "notice" pleading, these systems also provide all the modern advantages of liberal discovery and pretrial procedures. In addition ,even the FRCP require that some matters be pleaded "with particularity," such as fraud, mistake and special damages. *See* FRCP 9(b), (g).

6 FRCP 55. A default judgment is a judgment entered as a result of a defendant's failure to contest a case. The amount of the judgment is determined by the clerk of the court when it is for a liquidated sum (such as a loan plus interest) and is determined by the judge in a brief hearing if it is an unliquidated amount (such as personal injuries in a tort case).

7 Personal jurisdiction was introduced in Chapter I, p. 28, and is discussed in its interstate context *infra* pp. 245-248.

8 *See* FRCP 8 and 9.

9 FRCP 12(a). Sixty days is allowed for response if the defendant agrees to waive service of process. FRCP 4(d)(3) and 12(b)(1)(B).

jurisdiction (personal or subject-matter), improper venue (place the case was filed), improper service of process, failure of the plaintiff to join an indispensable party, or failure of the plaintiff to state a legal claim.[10] Asserting these grounds by motion is not required and the defendant could just as well include them in the answer. However, proceeding by motion allows the defendant to adopt a more aggressive posture by forcing the plaintiff to respond to the motions. In addition, the court must dispose of these procedural objections before the defendant will be required to file an answer responding to the plaintiff's complaint on its merits. If the motion to dismiss is granted, of course, the defendant may never have to file an answer.

The ground of "failure to state a claim upon which relief can be granted"[11] deserves some further discussion. It is the only ground relating to the merits of the case that is allowed to be raised by motion this early in the suit. A motion made on this ground is an important early screening device for claims: it tests whether, assuming all the facts alleged in the complaint are true, the plaintiff would be able to recover.

Complaints dismissed for failure to state a claim generally fall into two categories. The plaintiff may have alleged facts that are sufficient to make out a claim if such a claim existed in the law, but the law does not provide for claims of this type. For example, a complaint alleging all the elements of intentional infliction of emotional distress would be dismissed on this basis in a state that does not recognize that particular tort.[12] Or the plaintiff may have failed to allege sufficient facts to make out all the essential elements of a claim that *is* authorized by the law. For example, the plaintiff's complaint may assert facts that otherwise sound like a case calling for the application of the well-established tort of negligence, but the acts or omissions of the defendant that are alleged do not amount to negligence.

Answer The defendant's answer contests the plaintiff's claim on the merits. The main parts of the answer are the responses to the allegations in the plaintiff's complaint and "affirmative defenses." In the responses to the allegations, the defendant is required to admit, deny or state lack of knowledge as to each allegation in the complaint (lack of knowledge is treated as a denial). Affirmative defenses stated in the answer may include such grounds as contributory negligence, satisfaction of the claim, estoppel or fraud, or them may be one or more of the procedural defenses mentioned above. Affirmative defenses are so called because alleging them usually requires that the defendant go beyond simply denying the plaintiff's allegations and set out additional affirmative facts that avoid the claim.

In a third part of the answer, the defendant may include any "counterclaims" against the plaintiff.[13] The federal courts, as well as most state courts, make counterclaims compulsory if they arise out of the same transaction or occurrence as the plaintiff's claim. Thus, failure to assert related counterclaims will bar their later assertion in a separate suit. All other counterclaims are merely "permissive counterclaims," meaning that the defendant may choose to bring them in response

---

10 *See* FRCP 12(b).

11 FRCP 12(b)(6).

12 Thus, many appellate cases that make new law are appeals from grants or denials of a motion to dismiss for failure to state a claim. If the defendant's answer states what the plaintiff believes to be a legally insufficient defense, the plaintiff may file a "motion to strike" that defense on a similar basis.

13 *See* FRCP 13(a) and (b). For simplicity's sake, the discussion in the text refers to a defendant's counterclaiming against the plaintiff in response to the plaintiff's claim. However counterclaims may be filed against *any* opposing parties.

to the plaintiff's claim or bring them later in a separate action. Also possible are "cross-claims," claims that are filed by one co-party against another co-party, usually co-defendants. For example, assume in a three-car collision between A, B, and C, that A sues B and C. If B has injuries and thinks the accident was C's fault, B may file a cross-claim against co-defendant C. If B thinks the accident was A's fault, B may counterclaim against the plaintiff A.[14]

A final method of defense applies if a defendant in a suit believes that someone not joined as a party to the lawsuit has a duty to indemnify the defendant for all or part of what the defendant may have to pay the plaintiff. In such a situation, a "third-party claim" may be asserted by way of "impleading" the responsible party into the lawsuit. For example, if P sues D because D's truck hit P and the accident happened because the brakes on the truck failed, D may implead the company that repaired the brakes on that truck as a third party defendant.[15]

Amendment of Pleadings If a motion to dismiss for failure to state a claim is granted for failure to allege sufficient facts, the plaintiff will usually be allowed to "amend" the complaint if there is reason to believe the facts exist, but were simply left out of the complaint. The defendant has a similar opportunity to amend if the defendant has omitted or has inadequately set out a defense in the answer. The rules also provide generally that permission to amend pleadings "shall be granted freely when justice so requires."[16]

"Rule 11" Duties and Sanctions Under FRCP 11, lawyers and parties who file pleadings, motions or other papers, or otherwise assert a position in court thereby certify that they have investigated the grounds for the relief requested and that the request is well-grounded in law and fact or is supported by non-frivolous arguments for a change in law. If documents filed or positions asserted in court do not live up to this standard, the judge may award "sanctions" against the attorney or party, including the full amount of the opposing party's attorney fees that were made necessary by the groundless lawsuit or defense.[17]

These provisions of FRCP 11, first approved in 1983, have been the source of some controversy. Critics have charged that the rule as applied discriminates against plaintiffs, particularly those who assert novel constitutional and other claims or those who face uncooperative defendants from whom they need information to substantiate their claim. Other criticism has been over the vast amount of "satellite litigation" it has spawned over whether and to what extent sanctions should have been imposed. As a result, the latest amendments to the rule have softened its impact somewhat. The revisions provide that sanctions are optional with the judge and will usually be paid to the court rather than the other party. There is also set a 21-day "grace period" within which a party can withdraw the offending paper. Further, unsupported

---

14 *See* FRCP 13(g).

15 *See* FRCP 14(a). There must be an indemnity relationship between the existing defendant and the third party defendant. Thus, the existing defendant generally cannot implead a third-party defendant who it maintains is directly responsible to the plaintiff instead of to the existing defendant.

16 FRCP 15(a). In addition, a plaintiff can amend a complaint without court permission before an answer is filed and an answer can be similarly amended as of right within 20 days after it is filed. To avoid problems with statutes of limitations when new claims are added by way of amendment, the federal rules provide that an amendment takes the place of the original pleading and "relates back" to the date the original was filed when the new claim arises out of the same transaction as the original claim.

17 This is an exception to the usual rule in the U.S. that each side has to bear its own legal costs regardless of outcome. *See infra* p. 239.

allegations are allowed to be made if the party making them has grounds to believe that they are likely to be have support after discovery is conducted.[18]

3. Joinder of Claims and Parties

Joinder of Claims Joinder of multiple claims is very liberal. At the plaintiff's option, a complaint may combine all the claims the plaintiff has against the defendant even if they are unrelated. Thus, claims for negligence, breach of contract and slander, all arising from different events occurring at different times, may be joined in one suit or they may be sued upon separately.[19] However, if multiple theories of recovery or forms of relief arise from the *same* transaction or occurrence, the plaintiff must combine them in the same complaint or be barred from raising them later in a separate suit. For example, claims for strict liability, negligence and breach of a warranty, as redress for a single injury from a defective product, must be asserted in the same lawsuit.[20]

Joinder of Parties Joinder of parties is somewhat more limited, but still liberal. Plaintiffs may join together or may join multiple defendants on their claims if all the claims arise out of the same transaction or occurrence and have an issue of law or fact in common. If the case becomes too complex to try in one proceeding, the court has the discretion to order separate trials.[21] Similarly, if there are separate actions pending that would be appropriate to be tried together, those cases can be consolidated or, in some circumstances, can be consolidated for pre-trial proceedings.[22]

Interpleader "Interpleader" allows a party holding a disputed sum of money to deposit that money in court and join all the claimants to it as defendants. The court will determine who is entitled to the money and has the power to enjoin all other litigation involving that particular money. The advantage of interpleader is that it forces the claimants to litigate their claims in a single suit, thus saving the stakeholder from having to defend multiple litigation in multiple forums. An example is an insurance company that is uncertain which of several beneficiaries to pay.[23]

Class Actions A "class action" is a suit in which one or more representatives of a group of people with similar claims can file suit on behalf of the entire group.[24] Class actions are often used when individual actions would be impractical because of the low value of the claims involved, such as in an action by consumers against a drug company for overcharges on medicines. They are also used as a means of redressing discriminatory or unconstitutional treatment of a group pursuant to some generally-applicable policy of a government or private company, such as in an action

---

18 *See* FRCP 11. Discovery is discussed *infra* pp. 226-231.

19 FRCP 18(a).

20 This result is compelled by the doctrine of claim preclusion or *res judicata*, which is discussed below in the section on the effect of judgments. *See infra* p. 240.

21 FRCP 20(a) and (b), and FRCP 42(b).

22 *See* FRCP 42(a) and 28 U.S.C.A. §1407. In complex cases, consolidations for pre-trial proceedings under the cited statute are administered by the Judicial Panel on Multi-District Litigation, which has the power to determine when and where cases will be consolidated. Mass disaster cases typically are processed by the Panel. *See e.g. In re Air Disaster at Lockerbie, Scotland*, 709 F.Supp. 231 (Jud.Pan.Mult. Lit. 1989).

23 Congress has passed the Federal Interpleader Act liberalizing subject-matter and personal jurisdiction for many interpleader cases. *See* 28 U.S.C.A. §1335 (minimal diversity among claimants and $500 in controversy); §2361 (nationwide service of process).

24 FRCP 23.

for racial discrimination in employment against an employer.[25] Class actions have increasingly been resorted to in mass tort cases involving personal injuries, in part for the protection from future liability that they afford defendants.[26]

A class action is started by one or more representatives of the class, called the "named plaintiffs," file suit and move for class certification. To order certification, the judge must find that the class is so large that joinder is not practicable, that their claims have common legal or factual issues and are similar in nature, and that the named plaintiffs will adequately represent the interests of the unnamed class members. Adequate representation is essential for the judgment to be binding on the unnamed class members as a matter of due process.[27] Notice must generally be provided when money damages are sought to allow class members to "opt out" of the class and file their own suit if they choose.[28] To protect absent class members' interests, notice must be given to them. All settlements are then subject to the judge determining that the agreed-to class definition complies with the rules (if the class definition is part of the settlement) and that the settlement is fair to the class.[29]

B. The Discovery Stage

After all matters of preliminary defenses and pleading are resolved, the facts of the case are investigated and developed through a pre-trial process called "discovery." In discovery, the parties have the power to require anyone who has knowledge relevant to the case, including the opposing party, to come forward and divulge that knowledge under oath. Consistent with the tenets of the adversary system, discovery is largely conducted by the lawyers themselves independently of the court or a judge.[30] Any necessary discovery meetings, including the taking of testimony, are generally held in the office of one of the discovering party's attorneys. It is routine for a lawyer *via* the discovery process and long before trial to interrogate virtually every witness the other side expects to call at trial and to obtain copies of every document and to examine all other tangible evidence the other side expects to offer as proof at trial.

The need for pre-trial discovery grows out of the fact that the adversary system in the United States uses a single, concentrated, continuous trial. It is undoubtedly useful in any system for the lawyers to know as much about a case as possible early in the proceedings. But the typical civil law system's discontinuous hearing process, which spreads the "trial" over several hearings over a period of time, makes it easier to react to surprise facts introduced by an opposing party. There is time to find rebuttal evidence and present it at a later hearing. In the United States, the single concentrated trial is the only opportunity the parties will have to prove their case and

---

25 Two of the most important constitutional cases decided by the Supreme Court, *Roe v. Wade*, 410 U.S. 113 (1973) and *Brown v. Board of Education*, 349 U.S. 294 (1955), were brought as class actions.

26 Most mass tort personal injury plaintiffs will be interested only in pursuing their own claims, but a defendant may be willing to be more generous in individual cases if future liability can be cut off. *But see Alchem v. Windsor, infra* note 29.

27 *Hansberry v. Lee*, 311 U.S. 32 (1940) (black residents of neighborhood not bound by prior judgment upholding racially discriminatory deed restrictions on residential property because representation of their interests was inadequate and violated their due process rights).

28 *Eisen v. Carlisle & Jacqueline*, 417 U.S. 156 (1974) (suit for securities fraud; notice of pendency of the class action and right to opt out must be given and named plaintiff must pay for it).

29 *See Amchem Products v. Windsor*, 521 U.S. 591 (1997) (in class action against former asbestos makers filed solely for settlement purposes, class was too broad where it included currently injured class members seeking immediate payment and exposure-only members seeking ample, inflation-protected fund for the future).

30 *See* Chapter III, pp. 84-85..

rebut the opposing party's evidence. Discovery allows the party to be completely prepared on all aspects of the case by the time the trial starts.[31]

Though discovery aids trial preparation, it has other purposes. First, pre-trial knowledge of all the facts will induce more realistic evaluation of the strength and weaknesses of claims and defenses. Thus, discovery can promote settlement. Second, if discovery shows that the facts are not really controverted, the case may be able to be resolved without trial by way of summary judgment, discussed below. Third, if trial is ultimately necessary, the trial will be simpler and fairer. It will be simpler because undisputed issues will be clear and it will not be necessary to hear proof on them. It will be fairer because the lawyers will know more and be better prepared to meet the opposing party's claims or defenses. Thus, resolution of the case will depend less on the relative skill of the parties' lawyers.[32]

1. Discovery Methods

There are five different discovery devices. Though characteristics may differ slightly from state to state, the differences are minor and the Federal Rules of Civil Procedure provide a model. All these devices may be used against parties to the case (plaintiff or defendant), while a few may be used against a non-party witness.

Depositions   The first and most widely used is the oral "deposition."[33] Any person who has information relevant to the case, can be compelled to undergo a deposition, or be "deposed." Parties to the case can be deposed without a court subpoena so long as "reasonable notice" is given. People who are not parties must be served with a "subpoena" (a court order to appear), but lawyers may obtain subpoenas from the court clerk easily or, in some jurisdictions, may issue subpoenas themselves.[34] Depositions usually take place in the office of one of the attorneys in the case. A court reporter who is a notary is present to swear the deponent (the person being deposed) and to make a verbatim record of the examination as in court. The deponents are interrogated by the lawyers just as they would be in court. Any objections to testimony will be on the record for later ruling by the judge should a party seek to use the deposition at trial.

Answers given in depositions are hearsay. However, at trial a deposition of a *party* may be used for any purpose by the adverse party since all the statements therein are party admissions.[35] The deposition of a non-party witness may be used at trial only if it is inconsistent with the witness's trial testimony.[36] However, the Federal Rules of Evidence provide that the deposition of any witness may be used as a substitute for live testimony if the witness is unavailable, most often when the witness

---

31 FRCP 26-37 regulate discovery. For a comparison of the differences between the civil law and common law systems' approach to pre-trial and trial procedure in civil cases, *see* ARTHUR T. VON MEHREN, LAW IN THE UNITED STATES: A GENERAL AND COMPARATIVE VIEW 75-82 (Kluwer 1988).

32 Discovery may also be used to preserve testimony for later use at trial if the witness will not be available to testify. *See* FRCP 27.

33 *See* FRCP 30. Written depositions are possible as well, but are rarely used.

34 *See* FRCP 45.

35 Hearsay and other limitations on evidence were discussed in Chapter III, pp. 106-112.

36 The Federal Rules of Evidence also define all inconsistent deposition testimony as non-hearsay, thus allowing the inconsistent deposition of any testifying witness to be used as substantive evidence. *See* FRE 803(d)(1).

is dead or too ill to testify, cannot remember what happened, or cannot be subpoenaed.[37]

Depositions are useful tools for preparing for trial. They allow the lawyers to directly question the opposing witnesses and party well before trial, the better to evaluate how they will perform at trial. The oral format facilitates finding out information, since the witness's answers are uncoached and the questioner can follow up on the answers given with further questions. However, depositions are expensive since a court reporter must be hired and a transcript of the deposition prepared.[38]

Interrogatories The second most used device are "interrogatories" sent to the opposing party.[39] Interrogatories are written questions that must be answered under oath in writing. They may be addressed only to a party, and parties usually respond only after consultation with their attorney. At the later trial, an interrogatory can be used for any purpose, whether as substantive evidence or as a means of impeaching a party's testimony. The advantage of interrogatories is that they are cheap and easy to use. All one needs is a typewriter and an imagination. On the other hand, written interrogatories are a much more cumbersome way to obtain information than depositions, where the questioner can immediately follow up on unclear answers. Moreover, interrogatory answers are invariably filtered through the opposing party's attorney, who has time to think up ways of answering that will impart as little useful information as possible.

Requests to Produce Documents and Things Like interrogatories, "requests for production of documents" can be sent only to an opposing party.[40] This device is often used in conjunction with interrogatories, thus allowing a party to ask about documents and then require that appropriate copies be attached. To get documents from a *non-party*, a subpoena must be issued, either in conjunction with a deposition or separately. This device is also the method by which a party can inspect land or real evidence in the possession of the opposing party.

Order for Physical or Mental Examination An order of this type is used to verify a party's physical condition by requiring that the party be examined by a doctor chosen by the opposing party. Because such examinations are very invasive, they are permitted only with special court permission. The Court will grant permission only if the mental or physical condition of the party is truly "in controversy" and there is "good cause" for the examination.[41] These requirements effectively require that the issue of the party's health be essential to proper resolution of the lawsuit. The most common occasion when examinations are ordered is in suits for personal injuries when the defendant seeks to verify the extent of the plaintiff's injuries by means of an independent examination. An order for physical or mental examination applies only to parties and cannot be used to determine the physical or mental condition of a non-party witness, no matter how useful such information might be.

---

37 FRE 804(b)(1). Other instances of unavailability include the witness's refusal to testify or exemption from testifying at trial by the court on grounds of a privilege.

38 Recent amendments make this somewhat easier by allowing videotaped depositions. FRCP 30(b)(7).

39 FRCP 33.

40 FRCP 34.

41 FRCP 35(a). *See Schlagenhauf v. Holder*, 379 U.S. 104 (1964).

Requests for Admissions The final form of discovery discussed here is final in another sense, because it is generally used after all the other discovery devices have uncovered the facts of the case. "Requests for admissions" are written requests asking that the opposing party admit the truth of certain facts which discovery shows are essentially undisputed.[42] While a party may refuse to admit a fact, an unreasonable refusal will be grounds for reimbursing the requesting party for the costs of proving that fact at trial. Failure to respond to a request for admissions is taken as an admission of the matters sought to be admitted. An admission is viewed as conclusively establishing the matter admitted, though only for the purposes of that particular case.

2. Scope of Discovery

Relevance and Privilege The scope of discovery is very broad: the parties "may obtain discovery regarding any matter, not privileged, which is relevant to the subject matter involved in the pending action."[43] Even if the information or material being sought would not be admissible in evidence at trial, discovery may still be had if the information is "reasonably calculated to lead to admissible evidence." The only absolute exception to the broad notion of "relevance" is information protected by a "privilege" — information given in confidence in the course of a special relationship, such as doctor-patient, lawyer-client, priest-penitent or spousal relationships, or others established by law.[44]

Protection of Confidential Commercial Information Even if material is not privileged, there may be some basis for protecting it from discovery through use of a "protective order." Trade secrets and other confidential commercial information are specifically mentioned in the rule as properly subject to a protective order. Such information is not completely exempt from discovery if it is directly relevant to the lawsuit, but even if it must be disclosed to the opposing party, a protective order can be used to prevent disclosure outside the lawsuit.[45]

Attorney Work Product Potentially exempt from discovery is "attorney work product" material.[46] Work product includes much of the materials that lawyers produce when they prepare a case for trial, such as witness interviews, analyses of the facts and law applicable to the case, witness and trial preparation notes, and observations and impressions of the strengths and weaknesses of the case. Allowing discovery of such materials is thought to be unfair and disruptive of the trial preparation process. The attorney's mental impressions, conclusions, and legal theories can never be discovered. However, the lawyer may be required to share some factual work product material with the other side if the other side cannot, without "undue hardship," acquire the materials from another source. For example, if the defendant's lawyer finds and interviews an eyewitness right after an accident,

---

42 FRCP 36.

43 FRCP 26(b)(1).

44 Issues of federalism complicate the privilege question in federal courts. Privilege is determined according to state law for state-law claims and according to federal common law for federal claims. *See* FRE 501.

45 FRCP 26(c). *See Coca-Cola Bottling Co. of Shreveport, Inc. v. Coca-Cola Co.*, 110 F.R.D. 363, 366 (D.Del. 1986) (secret formula for Coca-Cola ordered to be revealed because essential to determining lawsuit; when Coca-Cola Co. refused to comply, all inferences from the formula would be assumed to be in plaintiff's favor at trial).

46 FRCP 26(b)(3) and (4). *See also Hickman v. Taylor*, 329 U.S. 495 (1947) (discussing the basis for the work product exception).

that witness' statement is generally not discoverable by the plaintiff since it is work product and the plaintiff can simply obtain the same information from the witness by way of a deposition. However, if the plaintiff's lawyer got involved in the case late and the witness, on being deposed by the plaintiff, cannot recall the details of the incident because of the passage of time, the defense would probably have to give the witness's written statement to the plaintiff.

The work product exception does not exempt a party from disclosing all relevant *information* that party may have found if it is requested by the opposing party. Parties and their lawyers are always required to reveal the names and location of anyone they know about who has information relevant to the lawsuit so that the opposing party can depose the person if they want. This is so even if finding the witness involved took major investigative efforts. They must also disclose what information they have as a result of interviewing that witness since that is information about the subject of the lawsuit that is within the knowledge of the party. What is protected is the very document that the lawyer has produced in working with the witness.

Expert Witnesses Expert witnesses present a special problem for the lawyer who must cross-examine them since their testimony deals with specialized knowledge and complex concepts. This is particularly true of medical experts. To aid in cross-examination by the other side, a party is required to disclose the name of any expert witness it plans to use at trial and provide a report describing the expert's probable testimony at trial. After receiving the report, the opposing party is permitted to depose the expert. However, disclosures and depositions are allowed only for experts whom the party has decided to call to testify at trial. Discovery is generally not allowed with respect to experts whom the party has decided not to call to testify at trial.[47]

3. Enforcement of Discovery

Discovery is generally conducted without court supervision and relies heavily on voluntary compliance with the discovery rules. When problems arise, they may be taken up with the court. The purpose of having discovery take place without involving the judge is to avoid wasting court time. Consequently, judges will often be impatient with recalcitrant parties who are not cooperating in divulging information or who are overreaching by seeking to gain information to which they are not entitled under the rules. Also discouraging parties from taking discovery disputes to the judge is a provision in the rules that requires — unlike the general "American rule" under which each side absorbs its own litigation costs — that the loser in a discovery proceeding before the judge pay the costs incurred by the winner unless the loser's position was "substantially justified."[48]

Compelling Discovery The primary way that enforcement issues are raised is through a "motion to compel discovery" filed by the discovering party after an objection to particular discovery is made.[49] This can arise in a variety of situations. Instead of answers, a party may receive objections to interrogatories. A witness or

---

47 FRCP 26(b)(4). A party may be especially interested in finding out about experts that the other side has consulted, but has decided not to call as witnesses. This is because the party probably decided not to call them because they gave an opinion that undercut the party's case. Exempting non-testifying experts from discovery is based on the ideas that one side should not be able to "freeload" off work done by the other side and that parties should be encouraged to consult a wide variety of experts without fear that the other side will be able to have access to their opinions. The non-discovery rule is relaxed in "exceptional circumstances," such as where one party has consulted all the experts in a given field.

48 FRCP 37(a)(4). Attorneys fees as part of the costs are discussed *infra* p. 239.

49 *See* FRCP 37.

party may refuse to answer deposition questions or refuse to be deposed at all. Requests for documents may not be honored. In all these situations, a motion to compel answers may be filed with the court. If the motion is granted, an "order compelling discovery" will be issued and the recalcitrant party will have to submit to the discovery and may have to pay for the costs of obtaining the order, including attorney fees. Parties or other persons who do not comply with an order compelling discovery may be held in contempt of court and fined or even incarcerated.[50] Additional sanctions are available against a party. The court may order that the facts sought to be established by discovery are deemed to be proven for the purposes of the litigation. If the recalcitrant party is a plaintiff, it may dismiss the case or, if a defendant, it may enter a default judgment.

Protective Orders The other way that issues of the propriety of a discovery request get before the court is for the party *against whom* discovery is sought to raise the issue by seeking a "protective order." When the court grants a protective order, it has broad discretion to order that no discovery be conducted at all as to a particular subject, that discovery be done only at certain times and places, or that the method of discovery be limited only to certain discovery devices.

Abuse of Discovery and Recent Reforms Because discovery is conducted mostly without court supervision, it can be misused to harass the opposing party or to drive up the opposing party's costs of litigating. Perceived abuse of discovery and its failures to live up to its original purposes have been foremost in the minds of the Supreme Court and the Advisory Committee on the Federal Rules. Amendments in 1983 addressed discovery abuse somewhat. In addition, the growth of the number and powers of magistrate judges has helped. Virtually all discovery matters are now handled by magistrate judges in the first instance, since they have more time to devote to supervision of the discovery process than do district judges.[51]

New amendments make even more radical changes in discovery. They require that the parties meet early in the case and disclose to each other, without the need for any request, all the principal evidence they have to support their claims or defenses to the extent that any claim or defense is stated with particularity.[52] The rules also limit the total number of interrogatories in a given case to 25 and the depositions to 10. These changes have been severely criticized by many as contrary to adversary principles and as imposing impossible burdens.[53] However, the required disclosure provisions may be overridden by local rule or agreement of the parties. As of this writing, over half of all federal judicial districts have "opted out" of these requirements and in other districts party agreements avoiding these and other requirements are common.[54]

---

50 Contempt is discussed *infra* p. 239.

51 Federal magistrate judges are described in Chapter V, p. 181.

52 *See* new FRCP 26(a)(1).

53 Three justices dissented from promulgation of the federal automatic disclosure requirements on the ground the such rules do not "fit comfortably within the American judicial system, which relies on adversarial litigation to develop the facts." *See* dissenting statement of Scalia, J., with whom Justices Thomas and Souter concurred. *See* 146 F.R.D. 401, 507 (1993).

54 Not all agree that discovery abuse is a problem. *See* Linda S. Mullinex, *The Persuasive Myth of Pervasive Discovery Abuse and the Consequences for Unfounded Rulemaking*, 46 STAN. L. REV. 1393 (1994).

C. Motion for Summary Judgment and the Final Pre-Trial Conference

1. Summary Judgment

Earlier we discussed the motion to dismiss for failure to state a claim as a rough screening device for claims on the merits. The dismissal motion looks only at the pleadings, however. All the facts alleged in the complaint are assumed to be true. Once there has been the opportunity for some discovery, there is a second screening device that tests whether the plaintiff has evidence to support the claims stated. That device is the "motion for summary judgment."

Summary judgment is based on the principle that the primary purpose of the trial is to determine the facts of the case. If the facts of a case are not in dispute, there is no need for trial and at least the liability portion of the case can be disposed of summarily by the judge alone. Thus, summary judgment will be granted if "there is no genuine issue as to any material fact and . . . the moving party is entitled to judgment as a matter of law."[55] The defendant filing for summary judgment will attach affidavits in support — written statements of witnesses sworn to under oath — or the defendant may simply refer to evidence given in depositions or other discovery that negates the plaintiff's claim. Then the plaintiff must respond by bringing forth facts in support of the claim that contradict the defendant's evidence, either by presenting counter-affidavits from witnesses or by reference to discovery, so as to show that there is a genuine factual dispute for trial.[56]

The standard for granting summary judgment is the same as the standard for a directed verdict at a trial — if there is sufficient evidence for a rational jury to decide the case in favor of the plaintiff, then summary judgment should be denied and a trial ordered.[57] The difference between summary judgment and a directed verdict is that the summary judgment decision is made on the basis of *written versions* of the evidence set out in the affidavits and discovery materials, while the directed verdict motion is decided based on the judge's evaluation of *actual trial testimony and evidence*. If, after considering the written evidence, the judge is convinced that, if such evidence were presented at trial, no rational jury could decide for the plaintiff, then the judge should enter summary judgment for the defendant. On the other hand, if there is evidence on both sides of the case, the judge must deny summary judgment and order a trial.

For example, assume that P sues D in an automobile accident case, claiming that D ran a red light, which D denies in an answer. D moves for summary judgment, attaching affidavits of three witnesses who state, contrary to what P has alleged, that they saw the accident and that D had a *green* light at the time. If P files a counter-affidavit from another witness who saw the accident stating that the light was *red* for D, then the judge should deny summary judgment and set the case for trial, since there is conflicting evidence on the issue. But if P is not able to produce any proof to support his allegation that D ran the red light, then the judge should grant summary judgment to D. In looking at the proof on both sides, the judge must give the benefit of the doubt to the party defending against the motion, in this example, to P. This is

---

55 FRCP 56(c). The rule allows summary judgment to be entered if liability is clear even if the amount of damages is still in dispute. This simply means that there will be a later trial, but it will be limited to the issue of damages.

56 *See Celotex Corp. v. Catrett*, 477 U.S. 317 (1986) (discussing the parties's responsibilities on summary judgment).

57 The standard for a directed verdict is discussed in more detail in Chapter III, pp. 99, 105.

essential to preserve the constitutional right to a trial by jury.[58]

2. Pre-Trial Conferences

As a means of managing a case, most judges hold pre-trial conferences, which all the lawyers are required to attend. Under the Federal Rules, the purpose of pre-trial conferences is to manage the case in such a way as to assure that all settlement opportunities are explored, that wasteful pre-trial activities are avoided, and that the quality of the trial is improved through more open discovery and better case preparation.[59]

Issues Raised There is no limit on the number of pre-trial conferences that may be ordered. Pre-trial conferences held early in a case will tend to focus on settlement and discovery, including setting "discovery cut-off" dates. Later pre-trial conferences and particularly the final pre-trial conference are devoted to expediting and simplifying the trial of the case, including the possibility of obtaining stipulations (agreements) regarding uncontested facts to avoid wasting time on unnecessary presentations of evidence. The parties are typically required to exchange lists of all the witnesses they will call at trial and copies of all the documents they will present at trial. They will also be required to agree to as many issues of admissibility of evidence as possible. The judge will then decide as many remaining evidence issues as possible before the trial begins so that the trial is not unnecessarily interrupted by objections.

Role of the Judge The individual personality of the judge determines to a large extent how active the judge is in pre-trial conferences. Variability between judges is substantial in terms of how much the judge will "push" the parties to settle or to agree on limiting the issues to be tried. In general, federal judges are quite active. This level of activism has been fueled by complaints about the slow pace of civil cases caused by insufficient case management by the lawyers. In this respect, U.S. judges are starting to resemble more their civil law system counterparts than the traditionally passive referees of the past.[60] However, U.S. judges are not supposed to put forward legal issues or defenses the parties have not asserted as some civil law system judges are required to do.[61]

Final Pretrial Order After the final pre-trial conference, the judge enters a "final pre-trial order." Again, styles vary from judge to judge, but this order is usually comprehensive. It will recite all the facts and law applicable to the case that are not in dispute (including matters settled by stipulation or by pre-trial rulings of the court), set out the remaining issues to be tried, and list the witnesses to be called and exhibits to be presented at trial. No witnesses may be called except those listed in the pre-trial order. No exhibits may be offered except those ruled admissible or designated as eligible to be offered at trial in the pre-trial order. No legal or factual issues and

---

58 The most common summary judgment situation is where the defendant seeks to test the plaintiff's claim and the examples used is this discussion reflect this. However, a plaintiff may also move for summary judgment on a claim if the defendant has raised an insubstantial defense or the facts are otherwise overwhelmingly in the plaintiff's favor.

59 *See* FRCP 16(a).

60 This relatively new function of judges has been dubbed "managerial." *See* Judith Resnik, *Managerial Judges*, 96 HARV. L. REV. 374 (1982).

61 In addition to the degree of activism varying from judge to judge, the setting may vary as well. Some judges hold their pretrial conferences in chambers (in the judge's office), a practice common in federal court, while others hold them in open court in the same way that a formal hearing might be.

theories may be gone into at trial beyond those set out in the order. The order may be changed only as necessary to "prevent manifest injustice."[62]

D. Trial Procedure

Chapter III provided a full description of the procedures involved in an adversary jury trial as well as a discussion of various trial techniques used by lawyers in such trials.[63] Most of the examples given there were from a criminal trial, but civil trials are virtually identical in their overall form and structure. However, two matters should be discussed here in addition to what was said in Chapter III: the impact of civil pre-trial procedures on civil trials and the scope of the right to a jury trial in civil cases.

1. Impact of Civil Pre-Trial Procedures on Trials

Despite the similarities between civil and criminal trials, discovery and the other extensive pre-trial procedures available in civil cases alter some aspects of the trial. First, these procedures, and particularly the final pre-trial conference before an active judge, can focus the civil trial more specifically on the issues that are disputed. Often it is possible to submit much of the case to the jury on stipulated facts, reserving testimony and other evidence only for disputed issues. At the very least, it is possible to shorten or eliminate laying foundations for many exhibits, since most judges will have required that the parties agree on the admissibility or at least the authenticity of all exhibits at the pre-trial conference. Second, witness examinations even as to disputed issues should go much more smoothly since the lawyers will have already questioned the witness once in deposition. Copies of depositions are available to be used to impeach the witness, should the witness contradict or "improve upon" what was said in the deposition. Third, as discussed earlier, if a witness is not available, a deposition may be used in place of live testimony and a deposition of a party may be used for any purpose by an opposing party.[64] Answers to interrogatories or responses to requests for admissions operate as party admissions and may completely remove the need for proof on some issues. In keeping with the oral tradition of the adversary trial, if these written substitutes for testimony form a part of the proofs in the trial, they are usually read to the jury rather than being given to them to read.[65]

2. Scope of the Right to a Jury Trial in Civil Cases

Law vs. Equity Distinction   The 7th Amendment to the Constitution "preserves" the right to a trial by jury for civil cases only"[i]n Suits *at common law.*" This makes all important a distinction that would otherwise be largely of historical interest only: the distinction between "law" and "equity." Law and equity at one time defined two separate court systems in England and in some of the United States. There were the common law courts staffed by common law judges and equity or chancery courts staffed by "chancellors." The procedures followed in law and equity were quite different. Common law courts used juries to decide contested fact issues. The equity

---

62 FRCP 16(e). Modern pre-trial practice renders somewhat unlikely a favorite dramatic technique in movies about lawyers in the United States: the "surprise witness" who appears at the last moment in what seems to be a hopeless trial, and saves the case. While this might happen in a criminal case or in some state court systems, the modern pre-trial order makes it virtually impossible in federal and most state civil cases in the United States.

63 *See* Chapter III, p. 88-106.

64 *See supra* p. 227.

65 Another distinction between the criminal and civil jury trial rights is that in criminal cases, trial by jury is assumed unless the defendant affirmatively waives the right to a jury. In civil cases, the party must make a timely demand for jury trial. FRCP 38. Most of the time, jury trials are requested by the plaintiff in the complaint and by the defendant in the answer.

chancellors sat alone and without a jury.[66]

Consequently, to determine whether the right to a jury trial exists in a given civil case, a court must refer to the division between law and equity as it existed in 1791 — the date the 7th Amendment was ratified. This was not difficult when law and equity were administered by two different courts. But the dual court systems of law and equity have been merged into one. There is only one form of action, the unified "civil action."[67] Matters are further complicated by the fact that legislatures and courts have been active in the last 200 years in creating a variety of new claims beyond the limited number authorized common law writs and settled forms of equity actions of the 18th century. For these new claims, a historical approach is employed which requires that courts consult ancient history and determine what common law or equitable cause of action is most directly *analogous* to the claim before them.[68]

A general rule of thumb that will work in most situations is that an action will be classified as "legal" if money damages are sought and will be classified as "equitable" if some other form of relief is sought. The rule works in most cases because money damages were the traditional form of relief offered in the courts of law. However, there are exceptions going both ways. Money can be awarded in an action for breach of fiduciary duty, but the action is historically equitable, so no jury is possible[69] And actions for replevin (return of personal property wrongfully taken) and suits to evict a tenant from property are "legal" even though they entail court orders for specific non-monetary relief, so a jury is available as of right.

Civil Jury Size Juries of less than 12 and non-unanimous verdicts are permitted under the Seventh Amendment and are common in civil cases in both federal and state court.[70] A variety of winning verdict votes exist in the states, from unanimous 12-person jury verdicts (9 states) to 5 members of a 6-person jury (6 states) and even 6 members of an 8-person jury (5 states).[71]

---

66 The 7th Amendment applies only to civil cases in *federal* court, as it has not been "incorporated" against the states *via* the due process clause of the 14th Amendment. Incorporation is discussed in Chapter VIII, p. 271. However, state constitutional provisions, the source of the right to a jury trial in state courts, almost uniformly make the same distinction between law and equity.

67 *See* FRCP 1 and 2. Some states preserve some vestige of separate systems or law and equity by having the same judges sit as "chancellors" or "judges" depending on the nature of the claim they are hearing.

68 The analysis demanded sometimes borders on the absurd as the sides trade abstruse historical references. For example, *Chauffeurs, Teamsters & Helpers, Local No. 391 v. Terry*, 494 U.S. 558 (1990), involved a suit against union for breach of duty of fair representation by failing to pursue the plaintiff's rights granted under collective bargaining agreement. The majority opinion found the action to be analogous to the equitable action against a trustee for breach of fiduciary duty despite the fact that in 18th century England collective bargaining was illegal. The majority rejected the analogy to the "legal" common law action for attorney malpractice, but found a right to a jury trial anyway because plaintiff sought money damages, a traditional form of "legal" relief.

69 *See also Curtis v. Loether*, 415 U.S. 189, 196 (1974) (finding that claim for back pay in employment discrimination case would be "equitable restitution," but that damages for discrimination in housing would be "legal").

70 *Colgrove v. Battin*, 413 U.S. 149 (1973) (federal court). *See supra* note 65.

71 Source: Center for Jury Studies, National Center for State Courts (1998). Federal courts now select any number of jurors between 6 and 12 in civil cases, with the whole number selected to hear the case and to participate in the deliberations. This way no juror who endures to the end of the trial will be prevented from participating in the deliberations, as alternates were when their services proved unnecessary because no regular jury member had dropped out.

E. Judgments in Civil Cases: Money Damages, Equitable Relief and Costs

After the trial, a "judgment" is entered on the jury verdict, subject to any post trial motions.[72] In a bench trial, the judge must deliver an opinion or findings of fact and conclusions of law on the basis of which a judgment is entered.[73] There are several kinds of relief that may be granted in a judgment.[74]

1. Money Judgments

Types of Damages Money judgments may reflect damages of three types: compensatory, punitive and nominal. Compensatory damages are designed to compensate — to place the party in the position the party would have been in but for the actions of the defendant. Compensatory damages are available in all kinds of cases. The question of what elements are included in compensatory damages varies with the type of claim and is discussed in the appropriate substantive law chapters.[75]

Punitive damages may sometimes be awarded to punish the defendant beyond the requirement of paying compensation. They may be awarded only in intentional tort cases as a rule. However, if a breach of contract also constitutes an intentional tort, punitive damages may be awarded. In addition, a breach of the implied covenant of good faith and fair dealing established in a contract relationship is considered an intentional tort and it thus remediable by punitive damages.[76]

A judge or jury may award a plaintiff nominal damages in the amount of one dollar. Nominal damages are not often awarded, but are possible in cases where the jury determines that the plaintiff has made out a claim and proved the defendant wrong, but the plaintiff has not suffered any real harm. Some jurisdictions (including federal law) allow punitive damages to be awarded even when there are no compensatory damages. In cases in those jurisdictions, where the defendant has acted very badly, but the plaintiff was lucky to suffer no injury, an award of one dollar in nominal damages plus a large sum in punitive damages is possible. Other jurisdictions require that there be proof of some compensatory damages before any award for punitive damages can be made.

Enforcement of Money Judgments If a defendant fails to pay a judgment, the party that won the judgment must take action to enforce it. One common way to enforce a judgment against an employed person is to use a writ of garnishment, an order to the defendant's employer to pay a percentage of the defendant's wages to the plaintiff until the judgment is satisfied.[77] If liquid assets are not available, but the defendant has property, a "writ of execution" must be obtained from the court authorizing a sheriff to seize the defendant's nonexempt property and sell that property in order to satisfy the judgment. Any proceeds in excess of the judgment are then returned to the defendant.[78]

---

72 *See* Chapter III, pp. 105-106.

73 FRCP 52.

74 *See generally* DAN B. DOBBS, HORNBOOK ON THE LAW OF REMEDIES, 2D ED. (West 1993), a single-volume treatment, or the 3-volume version of the same.

75 *See* Chapter X, pp. 381-383 (contract breaches) and Chapter XI, pp. 429-434 (torts).

76 *See* Chapter X, p. 382; Chapter XI, p. 431 (torts) and pp. 432-433 (constitutional limits).

77 Federal law limits the weekly amount to 25% of wages. 15 U.S.C.A. §1673(a).

78 Each state has laws which identify property that is exempt from execution. Most provide that clothing and other personal items and tools of the defendant's trade are exempt, as well as a portion of the value of the defendant's home, if the defendant owns a home. Exemptions vary widely from state to state.

The plaintiff can find out if the defendant owns any property by using supplemental discovery proceedings that require the defendant to appear in court at a hearing to determine his assets and ability to pay the judgment. At the hearing, the defendant may be required to reveal the location of property or to turn over certain property for execution. Failure to comply with such an order could be either civil or criminal contempt of court and could result in imprisonment. But the defendant cannot be imprisoned for refusing to pay a judgment debt just as a person cannot be imprisoned for failure to pay any legal debt. The defendant can be imprisoned only for failing to comply with a court order and even then imprisonment ends when he agrees to comply or is no longer able to comply.[79]

2. Equitable Relief

Forms of Equitable Relief Damages provide a money substitute for what is usually impossible: actually preventing or undoing the harm suffered by the plaintiff. But where a court is able by order to stop the very harm of which plaintiff is complaining or to restore to the plaintiff the rights that have been violated, the plaintiff may be entitled to such "specific" equitable relief. The distinction between law and equity was discussed above when the right to a jury trial was discussed.

The most common form of equitable relief is the injunction. An injunction can be simple, such as an order to the defendant not to come onto the plaintiff's property. Other forms of equitable relief include "reformation" or "rescission" of a contract, and "specific performance" — an order requiring the breaching party to perform obligations required under the contract.[80] But the possible forms of equitable relief are almost infinite. Historically, the power of equity courts was developed to avoid the rigid strictures on relief imposed on common law courts.[81] Consequently, the key to equitable relief has always been flexibility and the forms of equitable relief that may be awarded are as diverse as the wrongs it is used to remedy. The equitable relief granted in some cases may be very complex, such as an order completely restructuring a company or reorganizing a school system to stop racial discrimination and to eradicate its continued effects.[82]

Grounds for Equitable Relief There are two preconditions for equitable relief: (1) that the plaintiff has "no adequate remedy at law" and (2) that the relief is appropriate, necessary and fair under the circumstances. The inadequacy of a "remedy at law" generally means the plaintiff must show that money damages would not fully compensate for the harm. This prerequisite for equitable relief is inherited from a compromise worked out between the common law courts and the chancery courts in 17th century England to avoid conflicts: chancery would not step into a dispute unless the common law courts could not afford adequate relief. Today, the same court and judge consider what relief is appropriate, so conflicting jurisdiction is no problem. Instead, the requirement today serves to impose a hierarchy of relief in

---

79 *See supra* pp. 234-235 (development of equity) and *infra* p.239 (enforcement of equitable relief).

80 *See* Chapter X, p. 383. Perhaps the most numerous invocations of equitable powers are in divorce cases from the decree itself to orders for child support, restraining orders and other ancillary relief.

81 For a history of the development of equity, *see* ALFRED H. MARSH, HISTORY OF THE COURT OF CHANCERY AND OF THE RISE AND DEVELOPMENT OF THE DOCTRINES OF EQUITY (Carswell, Toronto 1890, reprinted 1985).

82 For an example of such a detailed "structural" injunction in a school desegregation case, *see Carr v. Montgomery County Bd. of Education*, 289 F.Supp. 647 (M.D.Ala. 1968), *aff'd* 395 U.S. 225 (1969). *See generally* OWEN FISS, INJUNCTIONS (Foundation 1972). Among the equitable actions that are possible are actions which damages is "ordinary" relief, while equitable relief is the "extraordinary" relief.[83] Especially given that specific relief can be intrusive and disruptive in some cases, courts will often emphasize that an injunction is not a step to be taken lightly and that one should be ordered only if it is necessary and will afford an appropriate resolution of the dispute.

The first requirement that the legal remedy be inadequate, then, shades into the second requirement that the relief be shown to be appropriate, necessary and fair. This second precondition reflects equity's tradition of flexibility. In injunctive cases, the requirement is sometimes stated as one of "balancing the hardships" on the plaintiff if the relief is denied against the hardship on the defendant if relief is granted.[84] Consistent with the flexibility of equity, equitable decrees are generally modifiable at a later time if circumstances change. Thus, an order granting equitable relief in cases involving prospective and ongoing judicial supervision of the defendant's conduct may be modified as necessary to assure that it is still fair and is accomplishing what it was intended to accomplish. In a recent Supreme Court case involving an injunctive order regarding jail conditions, the Court allowed the sheriff in that case to seek a modification of the order several years after it was entered on the ground that interim changes in the factual circumstances and law made it inequitable to continue the decree.[85] If the purposes of the decree have been carried out, the defendant may even have the decree rescinded.[86]

There are inherited verbal nuances used in suits for equitable relief that should be mentioned. How often they appear in a case varies from jurisdiction to jurisdiction. There has been a marked decrease in their use in recent years. The initial pleading in a suit in equity is often called a "petition" instead of a complaint. The judgment rendered is often called a "decree" rather than a judgment. Judges discussing what relief to order will sometimes refer to their powers "as chancellor." Finally, ancient equity "maxims" may sometimes appear in opinions. For example, a judge may deny relief under the "clean hands doctrine, under which a petitioner "who seeks equity, must do equity," meaning that the petitioner will not get any relief from the court unless his own conduct in the controversy with the defendant has been morally right. It is more likely today that a judge will simply "balance the equities" of the case without any felt need to invoke equity maxims.

Provisional Relief The flexible nature of equity allows for certain kinds of provisional relief to be entered, mainly relief aimed at preserving the *status quo* until a final trial of the dispute can be held. Thus, a "preliminary injunction" preventing a defendant from taking certain action may be entered. Generally the plaintiff must show a reasonable likelihood of success on the merits of the claim and a clear need for protection pending a decision on the merits.[87] A "temporary restraining order" is

---

83 This notion of a remedial hierarchy has been challenged in view of the ease with which courts give injunctions in certain kinds of cases without much inquiry into the actual effectiveness of substitutionary relief. *See* and *compare* Douglass Laycock, *The Death of the Irreparable Injury Rule*, 103 HARV. L. REV. 688 (1990) *and* Doug Rendleman, *The Inadequate Remedy at Law Prerequisite for an Injunction*, 33 FLA. L. REV. 346 (1981).

84 *See, e.g., Sigma Chemical Co. v. Harris*, 605 F.Supp. 1253 (E.D.Mo. 1985) (entering injunction enforcing agreement not to compete), *injunction modified on appeal* 794 F.2d 371 (8th Cir. 1986).

85 *Rufo v. Inmates of the Suffolk County Jail*, 502 U.S. 367 (1992).

86 *Board of Education v. Dowell*, 498 U.S. 237 (1991) (court-ordered remedy to end *de jure* racial segregation of schools should be terminated when the effects of *de jure* discrimination have ended).

87 *See William Inglis & Sons Baking Co. v. ITT Continental Baking Co., Inc.*, 526 F.2d 86 (9th Cir. 1975) (discussing alternative formulations of the preliminary injunction test).

also possible to avoid immediate serious irreparable harm to the plaintiff until a hearing can be held on a motion for a preliminary injunction.[88] For example, a temporary restraining order would be appropriate in a divorce case to keep a husband who has threatened physical violence away from the wife.

Enforcement of Equitable Decrees If the losing party in a suit for equitable relief refuses to comply with an order, that party is said to be "in contempt of court" and can be fined or imprisoned. It is important to note that imprisonment for civil contempt is not a means of punishment; it is a coercive measure. Thus, the imprisoned party "carries the keys to the prison in his own pocket," meaning that his compliance will "purge" his contempt and result in immediate release.[89]

3. Declaratory Relief

Another form of relief similar to an injunction and often awarded along with it is "declaratory relief." A declaratory judgment establishes the rights of the parties based on the facts and law, but does not require either party to do anything.[90] Perhaps the most common declaratory judgment actions are actions filed by insurance companies seeking a determination that an insured who suffered a loss arguably covered in an insurance policy has no claim under the policy. This issue would normally be determined in a suit by the insured against the company for money, but if the insured does not sue and the company wants the matter settled, a declaratory judgment is the appropriate way to get a definitive ruling. Declaratory judgments are also used when laws or practices are sought to be declared unconstitutional and there is no need for injunctive relief. Thus, if there is an ordinance of a city that the plaintiff contends violates the Constitution and there is no indication of any immediate harm to the plaintiff that requires injunctive relief, the court may simply enter a judgment declaring that the ordinance is unconstitutional and declaring what conduct the plaintiff has a right to engage in.

The Supreme Court has been less than clear as to the precise effect of a declaratory judgment:

> [E]ven though a declaratory judgment has the "force and effect of a final judgment," it is a much milder form of relief than an injunction. Though it may be persuasive, it is not ultimately coercive; noncompliance with it may be inappropriate, but is not contempt [of court].[91]

Whatever the effectiveness of declaratory relief by itself, it can form the basis for an injunction should the trial court deem that necessary.[92]

4. Awards of Costs

Costs Recoverable Most judgments award "court costs" to the prevailing party. In the U.S. legal system, these costs include fees of the clerks and marshals, fees for the witnesses, and docket fees.[93] Unlike the "English rule" on fees and costs and the prevailing rule in many civil law countries, the "American rule" on costs recoverable

---

88 *See* FRIEDENTHAL, KANE & MILLER, *supra* note 1 §15.4. *See also* FRCP 65.

89 *See* RONALD L. GOLDFARB, THE CONTEMPT POWER (Anchor Books, Garden City, N.J. 1971).

90 The federal Declaratory Judgment Act is found at 28 U.S.C.A. §§2201-2202.

91 *Steffel v. Thompson*, 415 U.S. 452, 471 (1974), quoting from *Perez v. Ledesma*, 401 U.S. 82, 126 (1971) (separate opinion of Brennan, J.). In *Steffel*, the Court approved entry of a declaratory judgment that held that a state statute against hand-billing could not be constitutionally enforced against an anti-Vietnam War protester.

92 28 U.S.C.A. §2202.

93 28 U.S.C.A. §1920 (allowable costs in federal court).

by a prevailing party is that attorney fees are not normally included in the absence of some specific statutory authorization. Thus, both parties must normally pay their own attorney fees, which will usually represent the largest portion of litigation expenses.[94] However, the FRCP and analogous state court rules have "offer of judgment" rules. If a party offers to settle the suit by entry of judgment in a particular amount, the offeree rejects the offer and the result at trial is not at least as favorable as the offer, the rejecting offeree is liable for the actual costs incurred by the offeror after the date of the offer. Thus, if a prompt realistic offer is made early in the suit, successful parties can recover almost all their attorney fees.[95]

Attorney Fees Award Statutes There are several special statutory authorizations for attorney fee awards in both state and federal law. These statutes generally relate to claims that the government wants to encourage people to bring because successful individual suits benefit society in general. Common among these are civil rights claims, suits to protect consumer rights, actions to gain redress for stock market manipulation, antitrust suits, and suits to protect the environment.[96]

F. Effect of Judgments

Judgments not only award relief. They also settle claims, defenses and issues that were in dispute between the parties. The system needs to avoid litigating these claims and issues a second time, both because doing so is unfair to the defending parties and because it would be a waste of valuable judicial resources. The law that defines the effect that final judgments will have on any subsequent litigation is the common law doctrine of "*res judicata*."

All American courts, both state and federal, follow *res judicata*. *Res judicata* is divided into two separate doctrines, claim preclusion and issue preclusion.[97] The traditional name for claim preclusion is "*res judicata*" and the traditional name for issue preclusion is "collateral estoppel."

1. Claim Preclusion (*Res Judicata*)

Claim preclusion means that the plaintiff gets only one chance to sue the defendant based on a single transaction or occurrence.[98] Thus in a case where there could be several legal theories upon which to base a claim, all such theories must be included in one lawsuit. For example, assume the plaintiff is injured when hit by the defendant's truck and sues based on *negligence*. Once that suit is over, that plaintiff cannot sue the defendant again based on the same accident even if a new theory of recovery is alleged, such as *strict liability* (liability without fault) based on the fact that the defendant's truck was overloaded. Plaintiff is barred by the first judgment whether plaintiff won or lost the first suit. This application of *res judicata* is called the rule against "claim splitting." Similarly, a plaintiff may not "split" damages. This means that the plaintiff must assert a claim for the entire loss in one suit and may not generally claim property damage in one suit and personal injuries in another. *Res*

---

94 *See Alyeska Pipeline Service v. Wilderness Society*, 421 U.S. 240 (1975) (reaffirming "American Rule" against attorney fee awards in the absence of statute).

95 *See* FRCP 68. However, the rule does not apply if the defendant offeror prevails. *Delta Air Lines, Inc. v. August*, 450 U.S. 346 (1981) (defendant offered $450 and plaintiff lost; plaintiff is not liable for costs).

96 *See, e.g.* 42 U.S.C.A. §1988 (civil rights suits) and the numerous consumer protection statutes discussed in Chapter X, pp. 394-401.

97 *See generally* RESTATEMENT OF JUDGMENTS, 2D (American Law Institute 1982-1988) [hereafter "RESTATEMENT"] and FRIEDENTHAL, KANE AND MILLER, *supra* note 1, §§14.1-14.15.

98 *See* RESTATEMENT §§18-20.

judicata also operates against defendants.   Compulsory counterclaims — counterclaims that arise out of the same transaction or occurrence — are barred if not asserted by the defendant in response to a claim.[99]

2. Issue Preclusion (Collateral Estoppel)

Defensive and Offensive Uses of Issue Preclusion Issue preclusion does not bar relitigation of entire claims. It bars relitigation of certain *issues* that have already been litigated in an earlier lawsuit. If an issue of fact or law has been (1) actually litigated and determined (2) by a final and valid judgment and (3) the determination was essential to the judgment, then that determination binds the parties in any later proceeding (4) as the same issue, whether it arises on the same or a different claim.[100] For example, assume that P holds a patent and sues D Co. for infringement. The court finds that P's patent is invalid and enters judgment for D Co.   P then files suit for infringement of the same patent against X Co.   X Co. can use the doctrine of issue preclusion to have the second suit dismissed.   The issue of the validity of P's patent has already been determined against P, so P is precluded from re-litigating that issue. This is *defensive* use of issue preclusion, i.e., its use by the defendant in the second suit to defeat a claim.[101]

In some jurisdictions, issue preclusion can be used *offensively*, i.e., by the plaintiff to establish a claim.   Assume that there is a plane crash and 100 passengers are injured. If a passenger, P1, sues and wins, the judge or jury necessarily determined that the airline was negligent and that the negligence led to the plane crash. P2, P3, P4 and all the rest of the passengers through P100 can now sue and use issue preclusion offensively against the airline on the issues of negligence and causation. Effectively this means that the only thing remaining for P2 through P100 to prove at trial is the amount of their damages.[102]

Mutuality of Estoppel A common limitation on the application of issue preclusion is the requirement of "mutuality of estoppel." Mutuality requires that the parties in the first and any later suits be identical before the losing party in the first suit will be bound in the later lawsuit. Thus, if a jurisdiction follows mutuality, in neither of the examples given above (the patent infringement or the plane crash cases) would issue preclusion be allowed to be used.   The second patent case involved a different defendant company and the later plane crash cases involved different plaintiffs. Mutuality is based on the principle that a person should not be bound by the results of a contest in which that person risked nothing. Thus, supporters of mutuality would argue that the second company sued in the patent case, X Co., should not be allowed to use the determination in the first case *against P*, because if P had *won* in the first case and the patent was declared to be *valid*, P could not have used that determination *against X Co.* Similarly, passengers P2 through P100 should not be able to use P1's victory over the airline, because if the airline had *won* the case against P1, the airline could not have used that judgment to bar claims by the remaining passengers.[103] Mutuality is not required for federal court judgments, nor is it a requirement for preclusion as

---

99 *See* RESTATEMENT §22.

100 RESTATEMENT §27.

101 *See Blonder-Tongue Laboratories, Inc. v. University of Illinois Foundation*, 402 U.S. 313 (1971).

102 *See In re Air Crash at Detroit Metropolitan Airport*, 776 F.Supp. 316 (E.D.Mich. 1991).

103 Fundamental due process notions prohibit a person from being bound by the result of proceedings to which that person was not a party.

explicated in the second Restatement of Judgments.[104] However, several states require it in some form or another.[105]

Exceptions to Issue Preclusion Whatever the scope of basic issue preclusion, there are exceptions to it. For issue preclusion to apply to a litigated issue, it must have been "fully and fairly litigated."[106] This means that if the procedural protections available in the first court were not very good or for some other reason the party was limited in its ability to fully litigate the issue, then re-litigation may be allowed. For example, the determination of a small claims court where no lawyers are permitted and no appeal is allowed would not be given issue preclusion effect. Also, application of issue preclusion will not be allowed if the issue comes up again in an unusual and unanticipated context, if its application would have an adverse impact on the public interest, if the standard of proof in the first action was lower (as where the first case is civil and the second criminal), or if prior determinations of the issue are conflicting.[107]

G. Resolving Cases Without Litigation

Litigation according to the procedures outlined above can take a great deal of public and private time and money, and each year approximately 18 million civil cases are filed. The judicial system could not long survive if even a substantial minority of these cases went to trial. In the state courts of the 75 most populous counties in the U.S. in 1992, about 75% of civil cases were disposed of by agreed settlement or dismissal, while only 3% went to trial.[108] Courts have for years encouraged the use of non-litigatory means for disposing of cases. Such encouragement has increased in recent years with increasing numbers of cases and increasing costs of litigating. The movement is called alternative dispute resolution (ADR). Recently courts and legislatures have gone beyond merely encouraging ADR methods, and have taken some steps to require that those methods be pursued.[109]

1. Voluntary Settlements

Private Negotiation and Settlement Negotiation and voluntary settlement is the oldest and most commonly used dispute resolution technique. Parties can reach negotiated settlements at any time in the litigation process, including during trial or appellate review. Unless a minor child or other dependent person is a party or the case is a class action, there is no need for the judge to scrutinize the settlement.

Lawyers representing clients in negotiation must evaluate their clients' legal position and advise them of the probable trial outcome. Though it is sometimes difficult to shake clients from an overly optimistic view of their chances of success,

---

104 *See Blonder-Tongue Laboratories v. University of Illinois Foundation*, 402 U.S. 313 (1971) (defensive use) and *Parklane Hosiery v. Shore*, 439 U.S. 322 (1979) (offensive use) and RESTATEMENT, *supra* note 97, §27.

105 *See Howell v. Vito's and Trucking and Excavating Co.*, 191 N.W.2d 313 (Mich. 1971) (criticizing and rejecting offensive non-mutual issue preclusion). Typically, states that have relaxed the mutuality requirement have done so first for defensive use.

106 RESTATEMENT §28.

107 *See* RESTATEMENT §§28 and 29 (setting out these and other exceptions). Section 29 exceptions only apply if the person seeking to use issue preclusion was not a party to the first action, as was the case in both the examples above of the patent infringement and the plane crash.

108 Source: Bureau of Judicial Statistics, U.S. Dept. of Justice.

109 For an overview, *see* JACQUELINE NOLAN-HALEY, ALTERNATIVE DISPUTE RESOLUTION IN A NUTSHELL (West 1992). *See also* ABRAHAM P. ORDOVER, ALTERNATIVES TO LITIGATION (Nat'l Inst. for Trial Adv., Notre Dame U. 1993)

ultimately the decision is the client's to make after considering the advice of the lawyer. Lawyers are ethically bound to communicate all offers to their clients for their consideration.[110] It is some measure of the importance that negotiation and settlement have attained that there are now courses at some law schools and many continuing legal education programs for lawyers that focus on negotiating skills.[111]

Mini-Trials A twist on voluntary settlement procedure that has recently gained popularity is the "mini-trial." This process follows a trial-like procedure and is often used in disputes involving highly technical or complex matters that are otherwise hard to evaluate. During a mini-trial, counsel for both parties present a shortened version of their client's case before their clients and a "jury" hired for the occasion. What happens next can vary. In some instances, the lawyers simply continue to negotiate, having been informed of what at least one jury would determine were the case to come to trial. In other instances, and especially where the clients are resistant to settlement, the lawyers may leave and allow their clients and a neutral advisor to discuss the possibility of a settlement. The mini-trial is beneficial because it gives the parties and the lawyers a realistic view of the strength of their case and makes them more aware of the risks involved in going to trial. As with informal negotiations, the mini-trial is usually a private affair and does not involve the court system.

Mediation Mediation is similar to private negotiation except that the settlement is facilitated by an impartial third party, or mediator. The mediator does not decide the dispute for the parties; the mediator simply acts as a supervisor of the negotiation between the parties by convening the negotiations and helping to find common ground. The fact that parties maintain control over the process means that mediation, like negotiation, has no rules except those that the parties decide to set up for themselves in the process. Mediation is a popular method of resolving disputes between parties who have an ongoing relationship and want to maintain that relationship, whether it is husband and wife, management and labor, or manufacturer and supplier. Once the parties reach a settlement, it is incorporated into a written agreement that has the same effect as a contract between two parties.

Arbitration Unlike a mediator, an arbitrator decides the dispute between the parties. The arbitration hearing is generally conducted like a trial. Attorneys for both sides present their evidence and arguments to the arbitrator and the arbitrator renders a decision, usually in written form. Though arbitration is similar to judicial resolution of the case, it has the advantage of being less formal, less expensive, and less time-consuming. A major advantage of arbitration is that the parties can design their own procedure and choose a decision-maker who has specialized knowledge useful in deciding their dispute. Arbitration clauses in contracts or other agreements to arbitrate will often set out in detail how the arbitrator or arbitration committee is to be chosen, the procedures to be followed, and the precise standard to be applied in resolving the dispute.[112] Arbitration can be binding or non-binding. If the parties have

---

110 ABA Model Rules of Professional Conduct, MR 1.4(a) and (b) and comments.

111 Two texts are DONALD G. GIFFORD, LEGAL NEGOTIATION: THEORY AND PRACTICE (West 1989) and MARK SCHOENFIELD & MICK SCHOENFIELD, THE MCGRAW-HILL 36-HOUR NEGOTIATION COURSE (McGraw-Hill, N.Y. 1991). For an interesting book on negotiation not limited to the legal context, *see* ROGER FISHER, GETTING TO YES (Penguin Books, New York, N.Y. 1991).

112 An unusual procedure was approved in *Ferguson v. Writers Guild of America, West, Inc.*, 277 Cal. Rptr. 450 (Cal.App. 1991) (in dispute over screen-writing credits for film, *Beverly Hills Cop II*, parties filed written submissions to arbitrators whose identities were unknown both to the litigants and to each other).

agreed that the arbitration decision is to be binding, most courts will honor that agreement and will refuse to review a dispute that has been settled by arbitration.[113]

While arbitration can be used for resolving any dispute, it is most commonly used to resolve contract disputes, since it is usually only in those contexts that the parties agree beforehand to arbitrate. Arbitration clauses are common and arbitration is used extensively for resolving labor-management disputes and disputes over commercial contracts.[114]

2. Judicially Sanctioned Settlement Procedures

Because of the increase in litigation and the resulting docket backlog, many states have developed "court-annexed" arbitration programs, meaning that the court sponsors and to some extent requires use of these programs. By 1987, 22 states had some form of court-annexed arbitration introduced through legislation.[115] Similar systems have been introduced in ten federal court districts and during 1990, 38,434 civil cases were filed in these ten districts with 3,970, or roughly 10% of those cases referred to arbitration.[116] This was expanded in late 1998, when Congress passed a law requiring that litigants in all civil cases consider the use of ADR, and requiring the federal courts to provide litigants with at least one ADR process including, but not limited to, mediation, early neutral evaluation, mini-trials, and arbitration.

Arbitration programs follow different models. Some programs are similar to trials where both sides present their cases, including sworn witnesses, before a panel of lawyers. In others, the sides present an abbreviated version of their case. After the presentation, the panel often meets with each side and to try to negotiate a settlement. If a settlement cannot be reached, the panel renders a decision. If both parties accept the decision, the case is settled. If either side rejects, the case will go to trial. However, in most jurisdictions, if one side accepts and the other rejects the panel's decision, and the rejecting side does not win at least as much as the panel recommended, the rejecting side must pay the attorney fees and costs of the accepting side. The shifting of attorney fees is an important occurrence in a system in which the normal rule is that each side absorbs its own attorney fees.

PART II: The Complicating Effects of Federalism on Civil Procedure

The concepts discussed so far have considered court systems in isolation. However, as noted in Chapter I, federalism complicates the legal system. Two coordinate *judicial systems* with substantial overlapping jurisdiction — state and federal — coexist on the same territory. Furthermore, *50 state lawmaking and judicial* systems exist side by side. In cases involving parties, transactions or occurrences that concern more than one state, the reach of these laws and court power often overlaps. This can make litigation in some cases very complex.[117]

---

113 Federal courts are required by the Federal Arbitration Act to enforce agreements to arbitrate in all cases where it is agreed to. *See* 9 U.S.C.A. §§2 *et seq.* and *Shearson-American Express, Inc. v. McMahon*, 482 U.S. 220 (1987). State courts are required by the Act to give enforce arbitration agreements if the underlying transaction involved interstate commerce. *Southland Corp. v. Keating*, 465 U.S. 1 (1984).

114 The American Arbitration Association, a private organization that serves as a clearinghouse for arbitrators, reported that over 60,000 cases were filed with their association in a recent year. American Arbitration Association, *Annual Report 1990-1991* 3 (1991).

115 SUSAN M. LEESON AND BRYAN M. JOHNSTON, ENDING IT: DISPUTE RESOLUTION IN AMERICA 78 (Anderson Pub. Co., Cincinnati 1988).

116 *Annual Report of the Administrative Office of the United States Courts 1990*, 9 (1991).

117 Some of these problems were introduced briefly in Chapter I, pp. 32-36.

There are four areas of the law that deal with these problems of conflicts of laws and court power. The first is the law of personal jurisdiction. It defines which courts have the power to adjudicate the liability of a given defendant. Personal jurisdiction is usually based on the defendant's connection to the territory of the state where the action is filed. The second area is the law of *forum non conveniens*. Under this doctrine, a court may decline to exercise jurisdiction it otherwise has, because a court in another judicial system (another state or country) is much more convenient and has a greater interest in handling the case. The third is the law of interstate recognition of judgments. This is sometimes called "full faith and credit" after the choice of words used in the constitutional provision that sets the general rule of recognition. The fourth area, which is the most difficult, is "choice of law." Choice-of-law rules determine what law a court will apply to resolve a particular case on the merits when the law of more than one jurisdiction has been identified as potentially applicable. Each of these areas has international as well as interstate implications.

A. Personal Jurisdiction in State and Federal Courts

1. Personal Jurisdiction in State Courts

One example given in Chapter I of the legal blurring of state boundaries that has occurred in the 20th century has been the growth of state courts' powers of "personal jurisdiction" over out-of-state defendants. Personal jurisdiction is a court's authority "to determine the personal rights and obligations of the defendant."[118]

Personal Jurisdiction and Territoriality   At its most basic level, personal jurisdiction is founded on the concept of territoriality. It starts with the proposition that a state or country has power to adjudicate only matters that concern the persons and property within its borders. The concept of territorial limits on a court's jurisdiction is most often associated with *international* states, but the same concept applies to the states in the United States. Under a strict view of territoriality, personal jurisdiction can exist only if (1) the defendant or any property in dispute is physically located in the state where suit it filed and (2) the defendant is appropriately served with process in the state or the property is properly seized by state authorities.

The "Contacts" Test   The Supreme Court, in its seminal 1945 decision in *International Shoe Co. v. Washington*,[119] departed from this strict territorial view of personal jurisdiction. It formulated a test that focused instead upon the *fairness* of the particular state court's exercise of jurisdiction over the defendant in light of the defendant's connection with the state. For personal jurisdiction to exist over an out-of-state defendant, the *International Shoe* test required only that there be "certain minimum contacts" with the forum state such that exercising jurisdiction over the defendant would "not offend traditional notions of fair play and substantial justice" embodied in the 14th Amendment due process clause. Under this rubric, the Court has approved exercises of personal jurisdiction pursuant to state statutes establishing "long-arm" jurisdiction over out-of-state defendants based on certain kinds of past actions taken by them or effects caused by them in the forum state.

How many contacts are sufficient to constitute the requisite "minimum contacts" clearly depends on the circumstances. Only one contact will do if it is the right kind

---

[118] *Pennoyev v. Neff*, 95 U.S. 714, 727 (1877). The term "jurisdiction," then, is used in several ways. Subject matter jurisdiction (discussed in Chapter V, pp. 183-185) differs from personal jurisdiction in that subject matter jurisdiction grants power to hear a particular *type of case*. For more detail on personal jurisdiction, *see* FRIEDENTHAL, KANE & MILLER, *supra* note 1, §§3.1-3.28.

[119] 326 U.S. 310, 316 (1945).

and the claim is related to that contact, such as driving into a state and hitting a state resident with ones car.[120] Or, if a person owns land in a state and the dispute is related to that land, the presence of that land in a state is enough of a contact to permits its courts to adjudicate that claim.[121]

"General" and "Specific" Jurisdiction Later refinements of the doctrine have divided personal jurisdiction into "general" and "specific" jurisdiction. If general jurisdiction exists, then the defendant may be sued on any claim regardless of whether it arises out of the defendant's contacts with the state. For an individual person, general jurisdiction exists if the person is served with process while physically in the state or if the person is domiciled in the state.[122] For corporations, general jurisdiction exists if the defendant has its principal place of business in the state, is incorporated there or does a substantial and continuing part of its general business in the state.[123] "Specific" jurisdiction exists if contacts are more limited, but the claim involved *arises out of* those contacts. An example of this is the one given above of a claim arising out of an automobile accident in another state.

The Requirement of "Directed" Contacts Specific jurisdiction cases are by far the most numerous ones in which personal jurisdiction is contested. Cases involving manufactured goods that travel across state lines and injure consumers are among the most difficult. In the years following the establishment of the *International Shoe* contacts test, due process constraints on personal jurisdiction seemed to grow without limit. However, in recent years the Supreme Court has carefully scrutinized the contacts required for specific personal jurisdiction. The Court has emphasized that these contacts must be truly "voluntary" and "purposefully directed" toward the forum state. Thus, there will be jurisdiction when a manufacturer, retailer seller or distributor has intentionally targeted the market in the forum state and sells a substantial number of units of the product there. Similarly, where the distributor or manufacturer has placed those products into the "stream of commerce" with the expectation that they will be carried to and purchased by consumers in other states, they cannot be heard to complain.[124] Such defendants should fully expect that, if there is a problem with their product, they will be sued in the courts of the states so targeted. On the other hand, if the only contact with the state is that the *consumer-plaintiff brought* the product into the forum state or only a few units of the product coincidentally happen to be sold in the forum state, personal jurisdiction is more difficult. The idea behind requiring voluntary and purposeful direction of contacts toward the forum state is that potential defendants should be able to structure their conduct in such a way as to know where they will be subject to suit and where they will not.

---

120 *Hess v. Pawloski*, 274 U.S. 352 (1927) (using a consent theory of jurisdiction based on road use).

121 *Shaffer v Heitner*, 433 U.S. 186 (1977).

122 *Burnham v. Superior Court*, 495 U.S. 604 (1990) (upholding constitutionality of "transient jurisdiction," service on defendant who is only temporarily in the state); *Milliken v. Myer*, 311 U.S. 457 (1940) (domiciliary of state is subject to personal jurisdiction even if living out of state); *Blackmer v. United States*, 284 U.S. 421 (1932) (U.S. citizen domiciled abroad is subject to subpoena power of U.S. federal court).

123 *See Helicopteros Nacionales de Columbia, S.A. v. Hall*, 466 U.S. 408 (1984) (discussing what level of business activity is needed for general jurisdiction).

124 The Supreme Court is not of one mind as to what the "stream of commerce" idea means. *See Asahi Metal Industry Co., Ltd. v. Superior Court*, 480 U.S. 102 (1987) (4-4 split of the Justices on this point).

The facts of a principal products liability case will illustrate the new, more limited approach. In *Worldwide Volkswagen Corp. v. Woodson*,[125] a couple bought a car from a seller in New York and a design defect in the car caused serious injury in an accident in Oklahoma. The Supreme Court held that there was no personal jurisdiction over the New York seller, which did business only in New York and neighboring states. Under these circumstances, the contacts with Oklahoma were the product of the buyer's voluntary action and the seller could not have reasonably foreseen that it would be subjected to suit in Oklahoma. Clearly, if a seller or manufacturer has service facilities or other agents in the forum state, the foreseeability requirement is satisfied. For that reason, the Oklahoma court clearly had jurisdiction over Audi, the *manufacturer* of the car, even though it did not have jurisdiction over the seller.[126]

The Overall Fairness Factor Another refinement of the test for specific jurisdiction has also been used to limit its scope. The Court has divided the test into two separate questions: not only must there be "minimum contacts," but the assertion of jurisdiction must in some overall sense comport with "traditional notions of fair play and substantial justice." This second general fairness factor has been used as a separate basis for denying jurisdiction in only one Supreme Court case. That case also suggests that personal jurisdiction will be particularly difficult to establish when the defendant is a manufacturer from another country. In the 1987 case of *Asahi Metal Industry Co. v. Superior Court*, a products liability case, the Court was unable to agree on whether the sufficient "minimum contacts" existed, but agreed 8-1 that assertion of jurisdiction by the California courts in that case over foreign manufacturers would be "unreasonable and unfair."[127]

In contract cases, the contacts and fairness test is applied in a similar manner. If the contract has connections with more than one state, the course of negotiation and performance of the contract are considered, along with any other indications of reasonable expectations of the parties about where suit might be filed.[128] However, forum selection clauses in contracts often govern the question of what courts have personal jurisdiction and the Supreme Court has generally upheld their validity.[129]

---

125 444 U.S. 286 (1980).

126 *Compare Gray v. American Radiator & Sanitary Corp.*, 176 N.E.2d 761 (Ill. 1961) (Illinois courts had jurisdiction over manufacturer of defective valve, installed by water heater manufacturer, that caused injury to consumer in Illinois).

127 480 U.S. 102 (1987)(suit for injuries caused by defective tire on motorcycle). It should be stated, however, that in *Asahi Metal*, the products liability claim of the plaintiff California resident had been settled, and the only live dispute was between the Japanese and Taiwanese defendants over who would pay for the loss, thus reducing considerably California's interest in the suit. *See also Hapner v. Rolf Brauchli, Inc.*, 273 N.W.2d 822 (Mich. 1987) (no personal jurisdiction over Swiss manufacturer of hair dryer that injured the plaintiff where only a few were exported and there was no evidence of manufacturer targeting the Michigan market).

128 *Burger King Corp. v. Rudzewicz*, 471 U.S. 462 (1985) (Michigan franchisees were subject to personal jurisdiction in Florida federal court because they voluntarily entered into long-term contractual relationship with Florida corporation and received benefits from it).

129 *National Equipment Rental, Ltd. v. Szukhent*, 375 U.S. 311 (1964) (appointment of agent in New York for service of New York court process on Michigan defendants with no New York contacts upheld against constitutional attack). Forum selection clauses in some consumer contracts might be held invalid based on the disparity in bargaining power. *But see Carnival Cruise Lines, Inc. v. Shute*, 499 U.S. 585 (1991) (in admiralty suit against cruise ship company for injury sustained on ship, passenger from Washington was held bound by forum selection clause requiring suit in Florida courts that was printed on back of ticket). *Shute* was overruled by statute in 46 U.S.C.A.App. §183c (prohibiting limitations on the right to sue in any court of competent jurisdiction), but is still good law on the constitutional issue.

2. Personal Jurisdiction Powers of Federal Courts

In contrast to the state courts, the "territory" of federal courts is the entire country. Consequently, one might think that federal courts would have nationwide personal jurisdiction powers and that the complexities posed by state borders would be inapplicable to suits in federal court. However, Congress and the Supreme Court in the Federal Rules of Civil Procedure have chosen a more limited view that draws a distinction between diversity cases and federal question cases.

Diversity Cases In diversity cases, state-law claims are being asserted and the Federal Rules of Civil Procedure provide that a federal court may exercise no more power of personal jurisdiction than may a *state court* of the state where the federal court is located.[130] Thus, a plaintiff would gain no advantage in terms of personal jurisdiction by filing a diversity suit in the New York federal court rather than in the New York state court. Keeping federal courts on a par with state courts when they handle state-law claims discourages forum-shopping — turning to federal courts solely to extend the reach of personal jurisdiction on a state claim.

Federal Question Cases When the case arises under federal law, federal courts are not so confined and "may exercise jurisdiction in any manner not inconsistent with the Constitution and laws of the United States."[131] The Court has formally reserved judgment on the precise constitutional limits of jurisdiction as it relates to federal courts. However, by analogy to territorial concepts and the *International Shoe* test, this provision would presumably mean that, if the general fairness test is met, federal courts in federal question cases have personal jurisdiction over all defendants residing in the United States and all foreign defendants who have the appropriate contacts with any part of the United States.[132]

B. *Forum Non Conveniens*

The common law doctrine of *forum non conveniens* allows a court to decline to handle a case over which it otherwise has jurisdiction if it determines that a court in another judicial system — the judicial system of another state or country — is much more convenient and has a greater interest in handling the case.

Forum Non Conveniens in Perspective It is important to place *forum non conveniens* in context. Personal jurisdiction, like *forum non conveniens*, relates to location of the suit and convenience. In addition, both state and federal judicial systems have "venue" requirements that assure that trial in the case is held at a place *within that system* that is convenient parties and witnesses. The state and federal court systems allow for free transfer within them for this purpose.[133] Together personal jurisdiction and venue thus have a "funneling" effect: personal jurisdiction

---

130 FRCP 4(k)(1).

131 FRCP 4(k)(2). This is a change from the prior rule which imposed the same restriction on federal courts handling federal law claims as it imposed on them when they handled state-law diversity claims.

132 *See Omni Capital International v. Rudolf Wolff & Co., Ltd.*, 484 U.S. 97, 103 n. 5 (1987) (reserving the question of what the precise constitutional limits of federal court personal jurisdiction are). Congress has provided for nationwide service of process in certain special kinds of cases. *See, e.g.* 28 U.S.C.A. §1391 (suits against officials and agents of the U.S. government); 28 U.S.C.A. §2361 (interpleader cases, where there are several claimants to a single fund of money). The Court has upheld interpleader jurisdiction provision as constitutional. *State Farm Fire & Cas. Co. v. Tashire*, 386 U.S. 523 (1967). The applicable due process limitation would be the due process clause of the *5th* Amendment rather than the due process clause of the 14th Amendment, since the 14th Amendment applies only to state courts. *See* Chapter VIII, p. 285.

133 Federal venue requirements are found in 28 U.S.C.A. §1391 and 28 U.S.C.A. §1404 provides for transfer for convenience among permissible venues.

narrows the decision of where suit can be filed to a particular state and venue then narrows it down further. For federal court cases, venue narrows it down to a particular federal district and for state court cases, it narrows the location to a particular county in the state. Where *forum non conveniens* comes in is when the *most* convenient place within a particular judicial system has been found, but it is *still* inconvenient as compared to a place *within another judicial system* (another state or another country). In such a case, *forum non conveniens* permits the court to dismiss the lawsuit so that it can be brought in that more convenient judicial system.[134]

Forum-Shopping and Forum Non Conveniens The key to understanding *forum non conveniens* is to understand why a plaintiff would choose to file a case in an inconvenient place. Usually the plaintiff is seeking to obtain more favorable substantive or procedural law. The incentives to "shop" for better law have increased as the revolution in choice-of-law rules has increased the number of instances when a forum court will apply its own law to a dispute.[135]

In the United States, *forum non conveniens* issues can arise in both an interstate and in an international context and in both federal and state courts. However, because federal courts have the power to transfer a case between districts throughout the country,[136] *forum non conveniens* issues usually arise in federal court only where the competing jurisdiction is a foreign country.

An example of *forum non conveniens* in an interstate situation would be where a plaintiff from *Michigan*, slips and falls in an *Ohio* restaurant. The plaintiff files suit in his own *Michigan* state court, hoping to avoid Ohio law, which limits the amount of non-economic damages that can be recovered for personal injuries in that state.[137] A well-known example of the application of *forum non conveniens* in the international context is the case involving the Union Carbide chemical disaster in Bhophal, India. Instead of suing in the courts of India, where the disaster took place and most of the witnesses were located, the Indian plaintiffs sued in the federal court in New York City. The main reason was the more advantageous procedural and substantive law that would be applied by the New York federal court, particularly the procedural advantages of liberal discovery and the right to a jury trial.[138]

Forum Non Conveniens Factors A court considering whether to dismiss a case for *forum non conveniens* must consider a wide variety of factors. These are summarized and discussed in the seminal case of *Gulf Oil Corp. v. Gilbert*.[139] However, the Supreme Court in more recent years established an important limitation on the ability of a federal court to retain a case in the face of a *forum non conveniens*

---

134 Dismissal rather than transfer is the appropriate remedy for *forum non conveniens*. Transfer of cases from one system to another would be considered a violation of the transferee state's sovereignty in the absence of agreement between transferring and transferee jurisdictions or appropriate legislation. There is no such agreement or legislation allowing for transfers between state courts in different states or between federal courts and state courts.

135 *See* discussion of trends in choice-of-law doctrine *infra*, pp. 254-258.

136 *See supra* note 133.

137 Personal jurisdiction exists because the Ohio restaurant is part of a nationwide chain, so there is general personal jurisdiction. Venue would exist because plaintiff residence venue is allowed in many state courts.

138 *See supra*, pp. 226-231 (discovery) and 234-235 (jury trial right). One might add that juries in large cities, such as New York, tend to be more favorably disposed toward plaintiffs in personal injury cases and generally toward awarding large verdicts, than are juries from suburban or rural areas.

139 330 U.S. 501 (1947). They include both "public" administrative difficulties the court would have and general appropriateness of handling the case and "private" factors related to the effect difficulties with access to evidence and other practical problems.

challenge. It ruled that the possible loss of advantageous procedural or substantive law should dismissal be granted "should ordinarily not be given conclusive or even substantial weight in the *forum non conveniens* inquiry."[140]

Applying the relevant factors to the interstate situation posited above, the suit should probably be dismissed by the Michigan court so that it can be brought in Ohio. In the international situation involving India, the federal appeals court ordered the action dismissed so that it could be refiled in India. Among other things, it considered the fact that virtually all the witnesses were in India, all the plant records were in Hindi and Indian law would undoubtedly govern liability in the case.[141] Conditional dismissals are possible in order to deal with problems of personal jurisdiction or the running of statutes of limitations. Thus, the federal court in Union Carbide Bhophal disaster case made its dismissal conditional upon Union Carbide consenting to the jurisdiction of the Indian courts and waiving any applicable statute of limitations.[142]

C. Recognition of Judgments: The "Full Faith and Credit" Requirement

1. Enforcement and Effect of Out-of-State Judgments

Means of Enforcement The "full faith and credit" clause of the Constitution states that "Full Faith and Credit shall be given in each State to the public Acts, Records, and judicial Proceedings of every other State."[143] This requires states to enforce judgments rendered in other states.[144] The state in which the judgment was obtained is called the "rendering" state, while the state in which the plaintiff seeks enforcement is called the "enforcing" state. The plaintiff must usually file a "suit on the judgment" to convert the rendering state's judgment into a judgment of the enforcing state. Once this is done, the plaintiff can proceed against the defendant's property under the laws of the rendering state. Several states provide a registration procedure for judgments from other states, which eliminates the need for filing a suit on the judgment. A typical registration act which has been adopted in some states is the Uniform Enforcement of Foreign Judgments Act.[145]

Res Judicata Effect The second "full faith and credit" effect of a judgment is that it settles claims and issues that could arise in later litigation. In determining what

---

140 *Piper Aircraft Co. v. Reno*, 454 U.S. 235, 247 (1981) (in suit arising out of a plane crash in Scotland, the absence of strict liability under the law of Scotland and lower damage awards in its courts afford no basis to keep case in Pennsylvania federal court). This decision affects only federal courts, as state courts can have their own standards. For a more detailed discussion of venue and *forum non conveniens*, *see* FRIEDENTHAL, KANE & MILLER, *supra* note 1, §§2.15-2.17.

141 *In re Union Carbide Corp. Gas Plant Disaster*, 809 F.2d 195 (2d Cir. 1987). A by-product of the case was a political problem for the Indian government. It argued in the trial court that the case should stay in the U.S. courts because Indian courts could not handle such a large, complex case. However, it changed sides and argued for dismissal on appeal after negative reaction in India to its original argument.

142 Statutes of limitations provide time periods within which a person with a claim must bring that claim or be barred.

143 Article IV §1. *See also* 28 U.S.C.A. §1738 (judgements "shall have the same full faith and credit in every court within the United States . . . as they have by law and usage in the courts of such State.")

144 The procedure for enforcing judgments within a state was discussed *supra* p. 236.

145 13 UNIF.L.ANN. 149-180 (1964). *See* Sara L. Johnson, *Validity, Construction, and Application of the Uniform Enforcement of Foreign Judgements Act*, 31 A.L.R. 4th 706 (1984). On the subject of recognition and enforcement of sister-state judgments, *see* EUGENE F. SCOLES & PETER HAY, HORNBOOK ON CONFLICT OF LAWS, 2D ED. §§24.8-24.32 (West 1992, 1995).

those effects are, the preclusion law of the *rendering* state generally governs its effect.[146]

2. Exceptions to Full Faith and Credit

Direct and Collateral Attacks   The grounds for avoiding the effects of the rendering state's judgment in the courts of the enforcing state are few and narrow. Generally a distinction is made between "direct" attacks on a judgment and "collateral" attacks. A direct attack is a challenge to a judgment that is mounted in the original lawsuit, such as a timely appeal. A collateral attack is any challenge to the validity of a judgment that is mounted in a different proceeding. A defense against a suit on the judgment in the enforcing state would be a collateral attack. Generally, states do not permit a collateral attack when the party once had the opportunity to file a direct appeal. Since no collateral attack is generally permitted in the *rendering* state's courts, full faith and credit would prohibit the *enforcing* state from affording the opportunity for one. This rule against collateral challenges applies even if the judgment sought to be enforced violates the public policy or laws of the enforcing state. Thus, in *Fauntleroy v. Lum*,[147] the Court required Mississippi courts to enforce a Missouri judgment based on a gambling debt incurred in Mississippi, a debt that would have been illegal and unenforceable under Mississippi law. The Court noted that, "as the jurisdiction of the Missouri court is not open to dispute, the judgment cannot be impeached in Mississippi even if it went upon a misapprehension of Mississippi law."

The Jurisdiction Exception   As the above quotation suggests, a major exception to the rule against collateral attacks is personal jurisdiction. The enforcing state is required by the Constitution to entertain arguments that the rendering court did not have personal jurisdiction. However, this is permitted only if the defendant did not appear in the original action, since this would have afforded the defendant an opportunity to mount a direct attack on jurisdiction.[148] A challenge based on the allegation that the judgment was procured by fraud is possible as well.[149]

The principles discussed above require *federal* courts to recognize *state* court judgments, though this results not from constitutional requirements, but from a statute.[150] Federal courts in one part of the country give preclusive effect to judgments of federal courts in other parts of the country because they are all part of the same court system.

3. Recognition of Foreign-Country Judgments

The full faith and credit clause of the Constitution does not require states to recognize judgments of the courts of foreign countries. Nonetheless, most states recognize and enforce foreign money judgments as a matter of course so long as the procedures followed are compatible with due process. They do so despite old

---

146 *See supra*, pp. 240-242, and RESTATEMENT OF JUDGMENTS, 2D, *supra* note 97, §86 (effect of state court judgment in another state) and §87 (effect of federal court judgment in state court) and RESTATEMENT OF CONFLICTS, 2D §103 (American Law Institute 1969) (effect of judgment of one state in another state).

147 210 U.S. 230 (1908).

148 *See Pennoyer v. Neff*, 95 U.S. 714 (1877). Collateral challenges to *subject-matter* jurisdiction are also possible, but only if the rendering jurisdiction permits them to be raised collaterally after judgment. *Aldrich v. Aldrich*, 378 U.S. 540 (1964). However, this sort of challenge is rarely provided for under state law. Federal subject-matter jurisdiction is generally not subject to collateral challenge. *See Chicot County Drainage Dist. v. Baxter State Bank*, 308 U.S. 371 (1940) and WRIGHT, *supra* note 1, at 84-85.

149 *See* SCOLES & HAY, *supra* note 145, §24.17.

150 28 U.S.C.A. §1738.

Supreme Court authority requiring proof of reciprocal recognition by the foreign country.[151] To date, 21 states have subscribed to the Uniform Foreign Money-Judgments Recognition Act, which provides in §1(2) that foreign-country judgments be enforced "in the same manner as the judgment of a sister state which is entitled to full faith and credit."[152]

D. Choice of Law Rules

In Chapter I, we observed that the fact that 50 coordinate state lawmaking jurisdictions exist side-by-side can complicate litigation. Thus, in lawsuits involving people, transactions or occurrences connected with more than one state, it may be necessary to determine which state's law applies to the case. It would be useful if this issue — even when arising in state courts — were governed by *federal* law, since that would mediate between the competing state interests. However, Congress has enacted no federal conflicts statute. And as discussed in Chapter V, when conflicts issues arise in *federal* courts in connection with state-law claims, the Court has held that choice of law rules are "substantive" because they affect outcome, thus calling for the federal court to apply the choice of law laws of the state where it sits.[153]

We will first review briefly the modest constitutional limitations on choice of law and then proceed to consider the variety of conflicts rules that exist in the states.[154]

1. Constitutional Limitations on State Choice-of-law Rules

Choice of law decisions would seem to implicate issues of state sovereignty since the forum state commonly seeks to "reach out" to apply its law to a dispute having a substantial connection with another state. There are also concerns about fairness since a party could be surprised when the law from an unexpected source is suddenly applied to that party's conduct. Based on these considerations, one might expect that constitutional limitations related to interstate federalism or due process would play a major role in limiting the content of state choice-of-law rules. In fact, they do not, and the permissive constitutional climate that has resulted has made possible a bewilderingly wide variety of state choice-of-law rules.

The modest constitutional limits on choice of law today come from the due process clause of the 14th Amendment.[155] When a dispute has *no connection at all* to a given state (other than the fact suit was filed there), it is unconstitutional to apply

---

151 *Hilton v. Giyot*, 159 U.S. 113 (1895).

152 13 UNIF.L.ANN. 261 (1962). Unlike full faith and credit, the Act does provide a "public policy" exception. Though this exception is in most cases narrowly construed, it has been given an expansive reading on occasion. *See Stein v. Siegel*, 377 N.Y.S.2d 580 (App.Div. 1975) (Austrian decree dismissing case not a bar to bringing the claim in New York since New York law would not prevent re-litigation). *See generally* SCOLES & HAY, *supra* note 145, §§24.33-24.45.

153 *See* Chapter V, p. 187 and *Klaxon Co. v. Stentor Electric Mfg. Co.*, 313 U.S. 487 (1941).

154 A standard treatise on choice of law discussing in depth many of the issues covered in this section is SCOLES & HAY, *supra* note 145. A previous edition of an introductory chapter of this book, written for a European audience, appeared as PETER HAY & RONALD ROTUNDA, THE AMERICAN FEDERAL SYSTEM (Giuffrè, Milan, Italy and Oceana Press, Dobbs Ferry, N.Y. 1982). For a more succinct summaries *see* LEAH BRILMAYER, CONFLICT OF LAWS, 2D ED. (Aspen 1991); and WILLIAM M. RICHMAN & WILLIAM L. REYNOLDS, UNDERSTANDING CONFLICT OF LAWS (Matthew Bender 1993).

155 The Court at one time considered that the full faith and credit clause of Article IV provided an independent, stricter limitation on a state's refusal to apply the law of another state, but in it has since abandoned the idea, essentially merging it into the due process test. *See* SCOLES & HAY, *supra* note 145, §3.24.

the law of that state.[156] However, the required connection between the dispute or the parties and the state is minimal, and it does not matter that there is another state with comparatively greater contacts. Thus, in *Allstate Ins. Co. v. Hague*,[157] the Supreme Court permitted Minnesota to apply its own law to a claim against an insurance company arising out of a motorcycle accident that caused the death of the insured. The contract of insurance was taken out in Wisconsin, the accident was in Wisconsin and both people involved in the accident were residents of Wisconsin. However, the Supreme Court found three sufficient "contacts" between the suit and Minnesota: the insured victim had worked in Minnesota for years before his death, the plaintiff widow had moved to Minnesota *after* his death, and the defendant insurance company did business (unrelated to the suit) in Minnesota. The test as stated in the plurality opinion in *Hague* is that, for a state's substantive law to be selected, "that State must have a significant contact or significant aggregation of contacts, creating state interests, such that choice of its law is neither arbitrary nor fundamentally unfair."[158]

2. The Variety of State Choice-of-Law Rules

Freed from significant constitutional or federal statutory restraints, states have taken three basic types of approaches to choice of law: the traditional "vested rights" doctrine, the various "interest" and "policy" analysis approaches, and the "most significant relationship" theory of the Second Restatement.

Vested Rights Approach to Conflicts   The traditional "vested rights" view dominated the view of courts in the United States during the period 1900-1950 and was the approach taken by the 1934 First Restatement of the Conflict of Laws. It was based on the notion of "legislative jurisdiction" of a particular sovereign — the idea that a state has the power to prescribe rules of conduct for transactions or occurrences taking place on its own territory. Once the "last event" of the transaction or occurrence takes place on the territory of that state, the parties to it acquire vested rights under the law of that jurisdiction that cannot be taken away. For instance, in the case of an airplane crash, if the crash occurred in California and the plaintiff sued claiming that the pilot was negligent, the law of California would govern because that was where all the acts or omissions constituting the tort took place (*lex loci delicti*). In contract cases, the place the offer was accepted and, therefore, where the contract was formed, would govern. Similarly, the law of the jurisdiction where a marriage was performed determined its validity, and the law of the place where land was located determined title.[159]

One problem with the vested rights approach is its malleability. Under the vested rights approach, what law applies depends on how the claim is characterized. Often, equally plausible multiple characterizations of the claim are possible. For example, a suit by the passenger-survivor of an airplane crash could be characterized as a *tort*

---

156 *Home Insurance Co. v. Dick*, 281 U.S. 397 (1930) (Texas could not apply its own law to a dispute over an insurance policy where nothing in any way relating to the policy sued on was done or required to be done in Texas). *See also Phillips Petroleum Co. v. Shutts*, 472 U.S. 797 (1985) (Kansas could not constitutionally apply its own law to claims of class members in class action who had no connection with Kansas).

157 449 U.S. 302 (1981).

158 449 U.S. at 313. While this "contacts" test sounds similar to the test for personal jurisdiction over out-of-state defendants, the contacts needed are much less, as the facts of the *Hague* case make clear. *Compare* discussion, *supra* pp. 245-247.

159 *See generally* SCOLES & HAY, *supra* note 145, at 430-926 (applying of the "vested rights" and other choice of law theories over a wide spectrum of subject-matter areas). *See also* RESTATEMENT OF CONFLICTS (American Law Institute 1934) §377 (torts), §311 (contracts), §§215, 255 (property).

claim, pointing to the law of the place of crash. But it might also be characterized as a suit for *breach of contract* for transportation, pointing to the law of the place the ticket was purchased — often and not coincidentally the forum state and the state where the plaintiff resides.[160] By approaching choice-of-law issues by *issue*, called "*dépeçage*," even more manipulation was possible. Thus, in one case, the court avoided a defense of interspousal immunity to a tort claim by characterizing the issue as one of *family* law calling for application of law of place of marriage, while applying a different body of *tort* law to remaining aspects of the claim.[161] Vested rights can thus be manipulated to provide "escape devices" to allow application of the forum state's law or some other law favorable to one or the other party.

A more fundamental criticism of the "vested rights" theory is that it focuses on a territorial connection to some state is artificial and often coincidental. Too often it points the forum court away from its own law, despite the existence of strong forum state interests in having its law applied. In tort cases, victims and survivors of torts suffered in other states often seek to sue in the courts of their own state. Since the forum state will be responsible for supporting those victims should they be unable to obtain adequate compensation, it has a strong interest in having its law applied. In light of this interest, many would argue that, in the case of an interstate airplane flight that crashed in California, it is a mere fortuity that the crash took place in California, or in any other state the plane might have flown over on its way to California.

Interest Analysis and Policy Approaches to Choice of Law Dissatisfaction with the vested rights approach led to the formulation of several different theories by academic commentators, some of which or some parts of which have been adopted by some state courts. There are many varied descriptions of these approaches, but most of them require the judge to resolve choice-of-law questions by (1) determining the policies behind the laws involved and (2) deciding the extent to which the states involved have an interest in applying law reflecting those policies to the issue presented in the suit.[162]

Primary among the interests asserted in many of these theories are the interests of the forum state. Thus, the net result of most such analyses is to increase the number of occasions when a *forum* court will apply its *own* law. Setting the tone for many of these interest-oriented reactions to vested rights is Professor Currie's "nihilist" statement: "We would be better off without choice-of-law rules. Normally, even in cases involving foreign elements, the court should be expected as a matter of course to apply the rules of the forum."[163]

One contribution to interest analysis, provided by Professor Currie, is the concept of "false conflict," which has gained "almost unanimous acceptance."[164] A "false conflict" describes the situation when an analysis of the *policies* underlying apparently conflicting laws discloses that those *policies* do not conflict. For example, assume that in the California airplane crash hypothetical posited earlier a wrongful death suit is brought in New York against a Minnesota-based airline company. Assume further that

---

160 This characterization was attempted, but rejected by the court in *Kilberg v. Northeast Airlines, Inc.*, 172 N.E.2d 526 (N.Y. 1961), which reached the same result by characterizing the foreign jurisdiction's limitation on suit as "procedural." *See also Levy v. Daniels' U-Drive Auto Renting Co.*, 143 A. 163 (Conn. 1928) (tort claim re-characterized as contract claim).

161 *See Haumschild v. Continental Cas. Co.*, 95 N.W.2d 814 (Wis.1959).

162 For an overview of these various theories, *see* SCOLES & HAY, *supra* note 145, at 15-33.

163 Brainerd Currie, *Notes on Methods and Objective in the Conflict of Laws*, 1959 DUKE L.J. 171, 177.

164 SCOLES & HAY, *supra* note 145, at 583.

New York law allows recovery by the surviving children of the present value of the decedent's future earnings, while California, the place of the crash, does not allow recovery of that element of damages.[165] A court could well decide that the two different rules present a false conflict. If the purpose of California's damages limitation is to protect *California courts* from speculative computations of future damages and to protect *California defendants* from excessive verdicts, then that purpose is inapplicable where suit is brought outside of California and against a non-California corporation. Since there is no "true" conflict, the forum state (New York) should apply its own law.[166]

The false conflict idea does not invariably point to the forum state's law, however. This is illustrated by a recent New York case, where a Boy Scout was sexually assaulted by a supervisor on an outing. The suit against the Boy Scout organization alleged that it was negligent in selecting the offending supervisor. The issue was whether New Jersey's charitable immunity would bar suit.   The defendant organization and the plaintiffs were from New Jersey and the negligent selection of the supervisor took place in New Jersey. However, the incident and the outing were in New York, and the plaintiffs brought suit in New York, probably in an attempt to avoid New Jersey law. The New York court nonetheless applied New Jersey charitable immunity to bar suit despite New York's abolition of such immunity. It determined that the policy underlying immunity — regulating or encouraging charities — was solely an interest of New Jersey. Thus, the apparent conflict with New York's abolition of charitable immunity was a false one.[167]

In the case of a "true conflict," an interest analysis approach attempts to weigh the interests of the various states involved.[168] These interests may reflect such policies as protecting local victims, protecting local defendants, or other more specific interests arising from the particular wrong involved. One method of weighing competing states' interests is California's "comparative impairment" test. Under this test, a court will compare the extent of damage that application of one or the other legal rule to the case would inflict on the competing states' interests. The court should choose the rule that causes the *lesser* degree of impairment. A leading case involved liability of a bar for injuries caused by drunk customers (referred to as "dram shop" liability). California plaintiffs were injured by a drunk patron of a Nevada bar and sued the bar in the California courts. The bar claimed that Nevada law, which did not provide for liability in such a case, applied. The California Supreme Court first identified the respective interests: California's interest was in protecting its residents from the acts of intoxicated individuals while Nevada's policy was to protect its bar owners from ruinous liability. The court concluded that California's interests would suffer greater impairment from *not* imposing liability than Nevada's interest would suffer from *imposing* liability. California's interest was greater, the court said, because its interest extended to harm caused by persons who became intoxicated *both in*

---

165 These assumptions should not be taken as representing the true state of the law in any of the states mentioned.

166 *See Griffith v. United Airlines*, 203 A.2d 796 (Pa. 1964).

167 *Schultz v. Boy Scouts of America*, 480 N.E. 2d 679 (N.Y. 1985). The other situation where a "false conflict" exists is where the non-forum state explicitly disclaims an interest in applying its own law outside its borders by providing for a *renvoi* to the forum state's law or an *envoi* to the law of a third jurisdiction. There is substantial overlap in the functions performed by these two doctrines and the "false conflict" idea. *See* SCOLES & HAY, *supra* note 145, at 70-72 and *infra* p. 257.

168 Professor Currie's approach would refuse to resolve "true" conflicts since it assumes that it is a legislative rather than judicial function to weigh truly conflicting interests.

California and out of state. It seemed to the court that Nevada's attempt to protect *local* businesses was much less seriously impaired since the defendant Nevada bar in that case had advertised in California to attract California residents. The court noted that there might be more serious impairment of Nevada's local interests if the case involved a truly "local" bar that did no advertising and did not otherwise seek to attract California residents.[169]

When freely evaluating competing states' interests, there is clearly the tendency of a forum court to prefer its own state's interests. An even stronger "homing tendency" is provided by theories that state a preference for the "better rule of law."[170] In the absence of objective criteria for determining when one legal rule is "better" than another, the chances are great that the forum state, which has chosen to adopt the legal rule it has over all other choices, will modestly find its own law to be "better" than others. It is true that there are often other "choice-influencing considerations" that might counterbalance any "homing tendency," but these factors tend to be vague and contradictory. Professor Leflar's factors would take into account predictability of results, maintenance of interstate and international order, simplification of the judicial task, advancement of the forum's governmental interests, as well as the application of the better rule of law.[171]

Second Restatement Approach to Conflicts The most recent approach to choice of law is the Second Restatement of Conflicts, promulgated in 1971. It attempts to consolidate and refocus all that has gone before. The Second Restatement approach seeks to determine which state has the "most significant relationship" to the case. It seeks to accomplish this by providing specific rules for certain kinds of cases, while at the same time stating a number of interests to be balanced by a court in ultimately resolving choice-of-law questions. The "rules" are in essence rebuttable presumptions that are to be applied in the absence of strong countervailing indications pointing toward the law of different state. Many of the rebuttable presumptions indicate an overall attempt to return to some of the security of the old "vested rights" approach. This is also reflected in the fact that departures from the presumptive rules are to be made "under the principles of §6." That section lists factors similar to those stated by Professor Leflar set out above. However, there are two significant differences: the "better rule of law" factor is omitted and a "protection of justified expectations" factor has been added.[172]

Clearly, the thrust of the Second Restatement is to edge away from the overwhelming tendency of the forum court to favor application of its own law and to provide more stability to choice of law rules than existed with interest analysis. For example, §146 on torts states that "the local law of the state where the injury occurred determines the rights and liabilities of the parties, unless, with respect to the particular issue, some other state has a more significant relationship under the principles of §6 to the occurrence and the parties." What contacts are counted to determine a "more

---

169 *Bernhard v. Harrah's Club*, 546 P.2d 719 (Cal.1976).

170 *See* SCOLES & HAY, *supra* note 145, §2.11.

171 SCOLES & HAY, *supra* note 145, §2.9 and authorities cited. *Many* more approaches, factors and rules are summarized in SCOLES & HAY, *id.* at 15-33 and later developed throughout the book.

172 The factors which the Second Restatement requires to be considered are the needs of the interstate and international system, the relevant policies of the forum, the relevant policies of the other interested states and their interests in the determination of a particular issue, the protection of justified expectations, the basic policies underlying the particular field of law, and the certainty, predictability and uniformity of result.

significant relationship" are set out in a non-exhaustive list in §145(2): place of the injury, place of the conduct causing the injury, residence or place of business or incorporation of the parties, and the place where any relationship between the parties is centered.   Regarding contracts, §188 lists as appropriate contacts generating interests the place of negotiation, formation or performance of the contract, the place where the object of the contract is located, and the parties' domicile, nationality, residence place of business or incorporation.   Similar to torts, it provides a presumptive rule that, whenever the place of negotiation and performance are in the same state, that state "will *usually* be the state that has the greatest interest in the determination of issues arising under the contract."[173]   Later sections provide presumptive rules for different kinds of contracts.[174]

If the forum state's choice of law rules point to the law of another state, that other state's choice of law rules may sometimes point back to the forum state's law, "returning" the case or issue back to the forum state. For example, State A's choice of law rules may indicate that State B's standard of liability (strict liability) should apply, but State B's choice of law rules, if applicable, would apply State A's standard of liability (negligence). This "return" of the case to State A, called *"renvoi,"* is generally not applicable in the United States.[175] However, some of the purposes of *renvoi* are accomplished through the device of the "false conflict": if State B's law points back to State A's law, that could be seen as a disclaimer by State A of any interest in applying its own law. In addition, §8 of the Second Restatement of Conflicts, allows for *renvoi* when "the objective of the particular choice of law rule is that the forum reach the same result on the very facts involved as would the courts of another state" or "when the state of the forum has no substantial relationship to the particular issue or the parties."

3. Trends in Conflicts Law in the Courts

Unclarity in the Courts Courts have lagged behind the commentators in the conflicts area. Some courts still apply some version of "vested rights," some use a pure interest analysis approach, while yet others have adopted the Second Restatement. In many states, it is not clear what the state of the choice-of-law approach is. Confusion is increased by the fact that academic commentators advocating conflicting theories lay claim to the same judicial decisions as representing their approach. New York has employed an approach that combines elements of straight policy choices, interest balancing and the notion of a "center of gravity" of the lawsuit.[176] But later New York cases demonstrate more certainty through use of specific rules distilled from policy analysis.[177]

While the vested rights theory had its faults, many are coming to realize that even more damage is done to a legal system by the inexorable move toward applying the

---

173 §188(3) (emphasis added).

174 The 1980 Convention on the Law Applicable to Contractual Obligations of the European Communities adopts a test similar to the Second Restatement, providing that the law of the "most closely connected" country should apply and setting out rebuttably presumptive rules. *See* SCOLES & HAY, *supra* note 145, §18.40.

175 This has been criticized. *See* SCOLES & HAY, *supra* note 145, §3.13. Similarly, there can be an *envoi*, a direction by a non-forum state to follow the law of a third state.

176 *See Babcock v. Jackson*, 191 N.E.2d 279 (N.Y. 1963).

177 See *Neumeier v. Kuehner*, 286 N.E.2d 454 (N.Y. 1973) (rules for liability of car drivers to passengers) and *Cooney v. Osgood Machinery, Inc.*, 612 N.E.2d 277 (N.Y. 1993) (law governing contribution between joint tortfeasors is the law of the state where the insurance to cover the loss was taken out). *See* Symposium on *Cooney v. Osgood Machinery, Inc.*, 59 BROOKLYN L. REV. 1323 (1994).

forum state's law. When the result in litigation depends on the place suit is filed, both respect for law's integrity and the business climate suffer. Since the Supreme Court has effectively abdicated any constitutional control over choice of law and has abandoned choice of law to state prerogatives,[178] the answer to this problem will come slowly, if at all.

Some Stability for Contracts and Property The problem of unpredictability of choice of law is less in contracts situations, since the parties can and often do agree on what law will apply in the event of a breach. For example, §1-105 of the Uniform Commercial Code provides that "when a transaction bears a reasonable relationship to this state and also to another state or nation the parties may agree that the law of either this state or of such other state or nation shall govern their rights and duties." Similar party autonomy is recognized in §187 of the Second Restatement.[179] Choice of law is also more predictable in property cases, since the rule that the law of the place where the property is located will govern, is well established.[180]

Other Mitigating Factors It should also be pointed out that the problem of over-application of the forum's law is somewhat ameliorated by "minimum contact" requirements of personal jurisdiction, which limit the number of states in which a plaintiff may sue.[181] The doctrine of *forum non conveniens* provides some protection as well.[182] However, for companies whose products or services bring them into contact with residents of every state in the United States, it is possible that the law of any of the fifty states could be applied to judge their conduct.

---

178 *See* discussion *supra* p. 252.

179 *See generally* SCOLES & HAY, *supra* note 145, at 673-678.

180 *See* SCOLES & HAY, *supra* note 145, §19.2.

181 *See supra* pp. 245-248.

182 *See supra* pp. 248-250.

CHAPTER VIII

CRIMINAL PROCEDURE

This chapter is divided into two parts. Part I outlines the procedural steps in the criminal justice process. Part II deals with constitutional criminal procedure law — limitations on the criminal justice process imposed by the Constitution.

PART I: An Outline of the Criminal Justice Process

The system of criminal procedure in the United States is both adversarial and accusatorial.[1] The adversarial aspects have been discussed: the parties themselves develop and present the evidence for their side before the jury, and the judge acts only as necessary to assure overall fairness of the contest between the sides.[2] Accusatorial principles are not the same as adversarial principles, but they complement each other. Accusatorial principles require the "government in its contest with the individual to shoulder the entire load,"[3] while adversarial principles require that the prosecutor, as the government's representative, present the case against the defendant. Thus, the prosecutor generally must bear the entire burden of proving the defendant's guilt on every element of the crime without the compelled assistance of the accused or the helping hand of the judge. The U.S. system allows for exceptions to the accusatorial principle, just as it contemplates exceptions to the adversarial principle, but it remains primarily accusatorial and adversarial.[4]

A. Arrest, Formal Charges, and the First Appearance

Crimes are divided into "felonies" and "misdemeanors." The classification is determined by the potential sentence: felonies are crimes punishable by death or by imprisonment for a year or more, and misdemeanors are punishable by less than a year in jail. However, some states have what are called "high misdemeanors," crimes punishable by up to two years in jail. The felony-misdemeanor distinction has an impact upon the nature of pre-trial procedure, as noted below.[5]

Police Investigation and Arrest As in most countries, the police are usually the first to arrive at the scene of a crime or to receive a report of one.[6] If the report is

---

1 *See generally* JOHN H. MERRYMAN, THE CIVIL LAW TRADITION, 2D ED. 126-128 (Stanford University 1985);. WAYNE R. LAFAVE & JEROLD H. ISRAEL, HORNBOOK ON CRIMINAL PROCEDURE, 2D ED. 32-43 (WEST 1992, 1997). LAFAVE & ISRAEL is the standard hornbook on criminal procedure. Other useful books include JOSHUA DRESSLER, UNDERSTANDING CRIMINAL PROCEDURE, 2D ED. (Matthew Bender 1997); CHARLES H. WHITEBREAD & CHRISTOPHER SLOBOGIN, CRIMINAL PROCEDURE, 3D ED. (Foundation 1993, 1998). *See also* ROBERT M. BLOOM AND MARK S. BRODIN, CONSTITUTIONAL CRIMINAL PROCEDURE: EXAMPLES AND EXPLANATIONS, 2D ED. (Aspen 1996). *See also* WAYNE R. LAFAVE & AUSTIN W. SCOTT, HORNBOOK ON CRIMINAL LAW, 2D ED. §1.6(a) (West 1986, 1997).

2 *See* Chapter III, pp. 78-83.

3 *See Murphy v. Waterfront Commission*, 378 U.S. 52, 55 (1964). *See* LAFAVE & ISRAEL, *supra* note 1, at 37-39.

4 Examples of exceptions from the pure form of accusatorial justice include requiring the defendant to give pretrial notice of certain defenses (such as alibi and insanity), to bear the burden of proof on some defenses, and to supply blood, handwriting samples, and fingerprints. *See infra* note 28 and *infra* p. 307 and note 187.

5 Violations of traffic regulations and city ordinances constitute a third category: offenses that do not normally result in arrest and are often considered "civil infractions," rather than crimes. These violations are usually disposed of by the payment of a fine, often by mail.

6 The description here presents a composite picture of procedure that would be typical in most states, with occasional references to federal procedure. *See generally* LAFAVE & ISRAEL, *supra* note 1, 1-29. For a detailed description of the federal criminal process, complete with transcripts of hearings and

based upon police observation and the police believe that they have "probable cause" to believe the suspect committed a crime, the suspect is immediately arrested.[7] If the report is based upon information provided by a victim, the police will conduct a pre-arrest investigation to determine if there is sufficient evidence to support charges against a suspect. The police may also seek an arrest warrant from a judge if they submit written affidavits (sworn statements under oath) showing that there is probable cause to believe the accused committed the crime. However, the vast majority of arrests are made based on probable cause, without a judicial warrant. Warrants are still sought on a regular basis since, when the issue of probable cause to arrest is a close one, the legality of the arrest is more likely to be upheld if a warrant was obtained. After an arrest, the police will also carry out any necessary investigation to gather further evidence against the person arrested.

Once an arrest is made, a higher police official and then the prosecutor will informally review the sufficiency of the evidence to determine whether to charge the accused with the crime, but these reviews are not impartial or even quasi-judicial. The only information provided comes from the police working on the case, usually in the form of an arrest report and any additional evidence discovered. The arrestee does not appear. In some jurisdictions, police will decide not to file charges in 10%-15% of their arrests, most of them misdemeanors. The prosecutor will also review the charges. As a result of the prosecutor's screening, between 30% and 50% of felony cases will be dropped at this stage.

Police Independence In general, the police carry out both pre-arrest and post-arrest investigations without any direct supervision by or assistance from the prosecutor. The police eventually have to justify their arrests and criminal charges to the prosecutor before the latter will institute a criminal case in court, but the prosecutor does not normally get directly involved in the police investigation, except in very important cases.[8] Judicial involvement is also episodic and only at the request of the police. It mainly takes the form of the issuance of search warrants or arrest warrants as needed, for which the police apply directly to a judge, again without the involvement of the prosecutor. No judge or any other judicial officer has any responsibility for overall supervision of the investigation.

Police investigators do not have the power to issue subpoenas or otherwise compel unwilling witnesses or victims to give statements to them (or even to talk to them). Instead, they must resort to persuasion, pressure or charm, as the situation demands. Court subpoenas are not available to investigators because they are issued only to compel witness attendance at trials or other hearings. Prosecutors also have no subpoena power. The only way that witnesses can be compelled to come forward is if a grand jury conducts the investigation and it issues a subpoena. But in most jurisdictions grand juries do not routinely investigate ordinary criminal cases. The principal reason is that their investigations, compared to police investigations, are

---

forms, *see* HARRY L. SUBIN, CHESTER L. MIRSKY, AND IAN S. WEINSTEIN, THE CRIMINAL PROCESS: PROSECUTION AND DEFENSE FUNCTIONS (West 1993).

7   In this context "probable cause" is defined as facts sufficient to establish a reasonable belief that a crime has been committed and that the person to be arrested committed that crime. *Brinegar v. United States*, 338 U.S. 160, 175-76 (1949).

8   The police may occasionally seek the prosecutor's legal advice on how to proceed, but even this degree of involvement is rare.

"expensive, time consuming, and logistically cumbersome."[9] Generally, grand juries are resorted only in organized crime cases, in which a complicated criminal structure must be unraveled and victims and potential witnesses are particularly wary of cooperating; in cases involving political figures (e.g., corruption), in which use of the grand jury would allay any public suspicions about the objectivity and thoroughness of the investigation; and in cases involving abuse of private corporate power (e.g., price-fixing cases), both because they are complicated and because there is substantial public interest in them.[10]

Prosecutorial Discretion   Once prosecutors do become involved in a criminal case, they enjoy a great degree of discretion in their decision to drop charges or dismiss cases (called *nolle prosequi*), and in their overall control of the case throughout judicial proceedings. Under the fundamental concept of "prosecutorial discretion," the prosecutor is not required by law to prosecute a case, even if there is sufficient evidence to support a conviction. Prosecutors in the U.S. never lose control of their cases and can drop charges at any time prior to final judgment and sentencing. Cases can be dropped even during an appeal.[11]

Filing the Complaint Against the Defendant   If charges are authorized by the prosecutor, a "complaint" is filed in court. A judge or magistrate then conducts an *ex parte* review of it and supporting information to assure that there is sufficient incriminating information to establish probable cause. This must take place within 48 hours after the arrest.[12] *Ex parte* in this context means that the prosecutor may participate, but neither the defendant nor the defendant's lawyer is present. The judge reviews the evidence from reports and information in the complaint or may require that the victim or arresting officer fill in details. If the supporting information is not sufficient, the judge will direct the prosecutor to produce more information or release the arrestee.

The complaint operates as the initial charging instrument. In the case of a misdemeanor, the complaint serves as the charging instrument throughout the proceedings. If the crime is a felony, the complaint is replaced by an indictment or information, as discussed below.

The First Appearance   The next stage is the defendant's "first appearance" before a judge or magistrate.[13] This first appearance has several purposes. One is to assure that the person arrested is actually the person named in the complaint. Another is to advise the defendant of the charge against him or her and to provide information

---

9   LaFave & Israel, *supra* note 1, p. 382. The more common use of the grand jury to screen charges to determine whether there is sufficient evidence to indict and subject the defendant to trial is discussed *infra* pp. 262-264.

10   Even if called before the grand jury, a person has the right to decline to testify on grounds of self-incrimination under the 5th Amendment. If the prosecutor and grand jury believe the testimony is crucial to the investigation of others, it must then grant the witness immunity from prosecution for any crimes revealed by the testimony before it can force the witness to testify. The law related to this and other issues that arise when the grand jury does investigate, is explained *id.* at 375-458.

11   There is generally no judicial review of the exercise of prosecutorial discretion. But if clear and convincing evidence of selective prosecution based on race, religion or other impermissible factors can be shown, such actions may be reviewed for possible violations of equal protection. *See United States v. Armstrong*, 517 U.S. 456 (1996) (there must be evidence of both discriminatory effect and purpose; for a race-based claim, defendant must show that similarly situated individuals of a difference race were not prosecuted). "Desuetude,"an objection to prosecution because of the law's long and continued nonuse, is generally not a basis for contesting the decision to prosecute.

12   *Gerstein v. Pugh*, 420 U.S. 103 (1975); *County of Riverside v. McLaughlin*, 500 U.S. 44 (1991).

13   This step is also called an "arraignment on the warrant" or "initial presentment" in some states.

about rights the accused will have in future proceedings. These include the right to a lawyer. For most defendants, this is the point at which a lawyer is appointed.

The judge also decides whether the defendant may be released pending trial. Pre-trial release has traditionally been referred to as "release on bail." "Bail" is money that the defendant forfeits if he or she fails to appear at later hearings in the case. To gain release, defendants generally must pay a certain amount of money to the court and obligate themselves to pay an even larger amount if they do not appear at later hearings. Factors affecting the amount of bail a judge will set include the nature and circumstances of the offense, the evidence against the accused, the character of the accused, and the ability of the accused to make bail. However, financial inability to post bail is not a reason for release without bail.[14]

Financial conditions are not the only type of conditional pre-trial release. Particularly in misdemeanor cases, defendants in many states are routinely "released on recognizance," meaning that they simply sign a promise to return for any later hearings and to obey any other court orders or conditions of release. The federal system uses a similar process of "release on condition" for felony cases, in which the defendant signs an agreement to abide by certain conditions that are a substitute for financial conditions. The technology revolution has created the option of using an "electronic tether" — a device worn by the defendant that informs police where the defendant is at any given moment and, when it is tampered with, alerts them that the defendant is probably trying to flee.

If the case is a felony, the judge sets a date for a "preliminary examination," discussed in the next section. If the case is a misdemeanor, preliminary examination is not necessary, and the case may be tried immediately. However, often there is no time for a trial that day because of other cases or the need for trial preparation, so a pre-trial conference date or trial date is set for some future time.

B. Preliminary Hearings, Indictments or Informations, and Pre-Trial Motions

In felony cases, the next step is to screen the evidence against the defendant to see if it can support a formal charge. This is done in one of two ways: (1) by a judge or magistrate after a preliminary hearing or (2) by a grand jury. If the preliminary hearing route is used and the case survives scrutiny, a "prosecutor's information" is filed. If the case passes muster with the grand jury, a "grand jury indictment" is filed. The two documents are similar in setting out the formal charges against the defendant. The only difference is who signs them. The 5th Amendment to the Constitution requires that federal prosecutors proceed by grand jury indictment in all felony cases. Currently, 19 states also require grand jury indictments, while 27 are "information states" with a preliminary hearing system. The remaining 4 states permit proceeding by information for all felony cases, except those punishable by life imprisonment or the death penalty.[15]

14　LaFave & Israel, *supra* note 1, pp. 602-604. In minor cases, the defendant may be able to obtain release by means of "stationhouse bail," i.e. by posting cash as security with the police at the police station and promising to appear before the judge at the next hearing date in the case. *Id.* p. 20. A recent study of cases in state courts in 1992 discloses that in serious felony cases, 63% of defendants were released. About 25% of them did not appear as required and 8% were arrested for a new offense. Of the 25% who failed to appear, about one-third were still at large after 1 year. Source: U.S. Dept. of Justice.

15　*See* LaFave & Israel, *supra* note 1, pp. 686-687. The arguments for and against grand jury indictments are outlined *id.* pp. 692-695. England has abolished its grand jury.

Preliminary Hearings and Prosecutor's Information The preliminary examination or hearing takes place before a judge or magistrate a few weeks after the first appearance. Both sides are present and represented by counsel. The issue at the preliminary hearing is whether there is enough evidence to "bind over" the defendant for trial.[16] For a "bind-over," the court must find that (1) a crime has been committed and (2) there is "probable cause" to believe that the defendant committed it. "Probable cause" in this context is generally defined as sufficient evidence to hold the defendant for trial. As a practical matter, it means that there must be reasonable and trustworthy information sufficient to show a good probability that the defendant committed the crime.

Charges are rarely dismissed as a result of the preliminary hearing. The defendant has the right to present evidence, but also has a constitutional right not to say anything or to produce any evidence, and will rarely do either at this stage.[17] The prosecutor, however, is required to present enough of the government's case against the defendant to establish probable cause. This provides the defendant and defense counsel with a "preview" of the evidence that will face them at trial and the opportunity to test its strength through cross-examination. Because of this, the preliminary hearing is an important indirect form of "discovery" for the defense.[18]

Because the preliminary examination is designed for the protection of the defendant, the defendant can waive it. Despite the discovery value of a preliminary hearing, it is not uncommon for defendants to waive it and proceed directly to the arraignment, described below. This often occurs when the prosecutor has offered a concession to the defendant for his waiver in a "plea bargain."[19] It may also take place when the defense is aware of a curable defect in the prosecution's case and does not want to alert the prosecutor to it, or if the defense feels that a preliminary hearing will strengthen the resolve and memory of the prosecution's witnesses by putting their testimony on record. However, the most common situation in which a preliminary hearing does not take place is where a grand jury indictment has preceded it, as is explained next. Of course, this would take place only a jurisdiction with a grand jury system.

Grand Jury Indictments The grand jury is a group of 23 private citizens selected to review criminal cases for a period of several months to one year. To return an indictment, the grand jury must determine, by a majority vote, that there is probable cause to believe that the defendant committed a crime. Thus, the grand jury has a function roughly equivalent to that of the judge at the preliminary hearing. However, the grand jury hears only the prosecution's evidence, and the defendant and defense counsel have no right to attend, to present evidence or to cross-examine the prosecution's witnesses.[20] Although on rare occasions grand juries exercise independence and refuse to issue an indictment, they usually follow the wishes of the

---

16 The preliminary hearing in state cases is usually conducted by a lower level trial court. Thus, in a state that vests trial jurisdiction over felonies in the circuit or superior courts, the district or municipal court will usually hold preliminary examinations. *See* Chapter V, pp. 169-170.

17 The defendant has the absolute right not to testify in this or any other proceeding based on the right against self-incrimination under the 5th Amendment of the Constitution. *See infra,* pp. 293-293.

18 Compare the procedures for discovery in civil cases. *See* Chapter VII, pp. 226-231.

19 Plea bargaining is discussed *infra,* pp. 268-269.

20 Some states allow counsel to attend and to ask questions. Even states that do not so provide, give the defense the right to a copy of the testimony of any witness who testified before the grand jury.

prosecutor. The number of refusals to indict is even lower than judge refusals to bind the defendant over following a preliminary hearing.

Where the grand jury procedure is required or available as an option, a preliminary hearing date will be set, but the prosecutor will seek and obtain a grand jury indictment *before* any preliminary hearing is held. Since grand jury review is considered to be an adequate screening of the charges, this makes the preliminary hearing unnecessary. If given a choice, prosecutors prefer the grand jury route to formal charges for perhaps obvious reasons. Often a grand jury indictment is obtained even before the defendant is arrested, which allows the prosecutor to proceed directly to the arraignment.

Arraignment on the Indictment or Information Within a short time after the indictment or information has been filed with the trial court, the defendant is "arraigned" before that court. This means that the defendant is brought before the court to be formally charged with the crime as specified in the indictment or information. At the arraignment, the defendant is informed of the charges and asked to plead guilty or not guilty or, in some circumstances, *nolo contendere* (no contest). The vast majority of cases that reach this stage (70%-90%, depending on the jurisdiction) do not go to trial because the defendant at some point pleads guilty to these or lesser charges.[21] Plea bargaining is discussed below in the section of this chapter dealing with the methods of resolving cases without trial. If the defendant does not plead guilty at the arraignment, the judge sets a date for a trial.

Pre-Trial Motions Prior to the trial, a defendant has the right to raise several motions.[22] A common motion is a *Brady* motion, a motion for discovery of the prosecution's evidence. Prosecutors are not required to turn over their entire file to the defendant. And the extensive discovery devices available in civil cases are not applicable to a criminal case. However, the due process clause, as interpreted in *Brady v. Maryland*,[23] requires that the prosecution at least turn over all the *exculpatory* evidence in its possession.[24]

Prominent among important pre-trial motions are motions to suppress evidence obtained through unconstitutional police methods. The grounds for many such motions are discussed in Part II of this chapter on constitutional criminal procedure.[25] The defense may demand a hearing on any such issues and has the right to compel the attendance of any necessary witness, including the police. These hearings are usually held several weeks before trial.

C. Trial

The procedures for a jury trial were discussed in Chapter III.[26] As stated there, civil and criminal trials are conducted very similarly. However, the standard of proof in a criminal case requires that the case be proven "beyond a reasonable doubt," in contrast to the civil standard of "preponderance of the evidence." In addition, the

---

21 LaFave & Israel, *supra* note 1, p. 10.

22 A motion is simply an application to the court for an order.

23 373 U.S. 83 (1963) *See also United States v. Bagley*, 473 U.S. 667 (1985) (standard for reversal for failure to disclose). *See* Chapter III, p. 87, n. 14.

24 *See, e.g., Kyles v. Whitley*, 514 U.S. 419 (1995) (reversing death sentence because of prosecution's failure to disclose various items, including initial statements of eyewitnesses with conflicting descriptions of the murderer).

25 *See infra*, Part II, pp. 285-314.

26 *See* pp. 88-106.

defendant in a criminal case, consistent with accusatorial principles, has an absolute right not to testify.

There are major differences, however, in the extensiveness of civil and criminal *pre-trial* procedures and these have an impact on the trial. The comprehensive formal civil discovery procedures are inapplicable to a criminal case.[27] Although, as just discussed, the defendant can obtain discovery of any *exculpatory* evidence, there is generally no right to discover *incriminating* in the hands of the prosecution. Because of the defendant's constitutional right against self-incrimination, the prosecutor has only limited rights of discovery from the defendant.[28] Generally the only statements of the defendant that may be used at trial are whatever statements the defendant might have given to police investigators voluntarily after appropriate warnings on the right to remain silent.[29] The only evidence the defense will have other than evidence the prosecution is required to turn over is what the defense is able to find out through its own investigation. Since the trial lawyers in a criminal case often know less about the other side's evidence than in a civil case, the trial of the average criminal case can hold more surprises for the lawyers involved.[30]

The prosecution at trial has the duty to prove each and every element of the offense against the defendant beyond a reasonable doubt and that burden may not be shifted to the defendant.[31] As a result, another difference between civil and criminal trials is that it is less common in a criminal trial to have "stipulations," voluntary. Stipulations are agreements between the parties, which obviate the need to present proof on some elements of the case or which concede the admissibility of evidence, particularly exhibits. Stipulations are routine in civil trials and are often entered into under pressure from the trial judge who does not want to waste time on unnecessary proofs. This is generally inappropriate in a criminal trial. The absence of stipulations will often mean that the lawyers in a criminal trial will have to spend more time laying the necessary foundation for admission of evidence.

D. Sentencing Procedures in Criminal Cases

Sentencing Hearings Upon the defendant pleading guilty or being found guilty after a trial, the next step is to determine what punishment is appropriate — to impose a "sentence." In some systems the judge sentences the defendant immediately after the trial is over. In the U.S. the judge will set a separate date for sentencing and order the preparation of a "pre-sentence report." This report is prepared by an agency attached to the court, generally the "probation department." The report addresses the defendant's background as it relates to factors relevant to

---

27 For example, depositions, which are routine in civil cases (discussed in Chapter VII, p. 227), may be ordered only in exceptional circumstances to preserve testimony for trial. FRCrP 15(a).

28 The defendant may be required to notify the prosecution of the intent to rely on certain defenses that require substantial pre-trial investigation to rebut. Thus, notices of a claim of alibi (that the defendant was elsewhere during the crime) or a claim of insanity are typically required. *See* Federal Rule of Criminal Procedure (FRCrP) 12.1, 12.2. In addition, the defendant may be compelled to provide handwriting samples, fingerprints, and blood samples for comparison purposes. Also, if the defense seeks discovery, it may have to submit to reciprocal discovery of any exhibits or scientific analyses that it plans to introduce at trial. *See* FRCrP 16(b).

29 *See infra*, pp. 283-285.

30 Criminal defense attorneys sometimes employ private investigators to assist them in investigating the facts of a case. *See* Chapter III, p. 87, note 13.

31 *See In re Winship*, 397 U.S. 358 (1970), discussed *infra* p. 294. However, the burden of proof on defenses may be shifted to the defendant. *See infra* p. 295.

sentencing. Some jurisdictions allow the jury to decide or recommend a sentence, but most leave sentencing determinations to the judge.

On the date set for sentencing, the defendant appears once more before the judge and has the right to address the judge personally or through defense counsel on the question of sentence. A prime determinant of the severity of the sentence is the defendant's prior history of crime. But the judge may consult all kinds of evidence, including hearsay and lay opinions, and even evidence of uncharged crimes or crimes of which the defendant was acquitted.[32] In serious cases, the judge may hear witness testimony or statements.

Victim Impact Statements   Traditionally, the victim's role at the sentencing hearing has not been very important, since the focus is not on what to do for the victim, but what to do with the defendant. However, this is changing. A recent movement in favor of greater victims' rights has arisen and has convinced some states to enact statutes allowing or requiring the use of "victim impact statements." The Supreme Court initially held such evidence unconstitutional, but it reversed itself almost immediately and held that such statements are permitted.[33] Restitution to victims can be ordered by the court as part of the sentence, but victims have no right to demand it, as is often the case in civil law countries. Instead, victims wishing an award of damages for a crime committed against them must file a separate civil suit. The finding in the criminal case that the defendant is guilty often will automatically prove liability in the civil case because of the effects of issue preclusion.[34] Civil suits are not often filed, mainly because criminal defendants rarely have money or property from which a judgment could be collected.

The Jury's Role in Death Penalty Cases   The jury generally has no role in sentencing, so its work is completed when it determines that the defendant is guilty. However, it is common for the jury to participate in the decision whether the death penalty should be imposed. Usually there is a two-part procedure. The first stage of the trial is the guilt stage, during which the issue of potential punishment is irrelevant. Indeed, evidence relating to possible punishment the defendant could receive is inadmissible. If the jury decides that the defendant is guilty, then the same jury is reconvened for a punishment stage of the trial. At this stage of the trial any additional evidence bearing on punishment may be brought in, including evidence on the defendant's background, character and other crimes. The jury considers all of the evidence presented in the case in deciding whether the death penalty should be imposed. In some states the jury has only advisory input, in others it decides the question, and in yet others death is imposed only if both judge and jury agree.[35]

E. Appellate Review of Convictions

Direct Appeal   Defendants convicted in a state trial court generally have a statutory right to one appeal, usually to the intermediate appellate court of the state. If the state's intermediate appellate court affirms the conviction, they have the right

---

32 *See* 18 U.S.C.A. §3661 and *United States v. Watts*, 519 U.S. 148 (1997) (use of acquitted conduct does not violate the ban on multiple prosecution for the same offense and may be proven by the prosecution by a preponderance of the evidence, not beyond a reasonable doubt).

33 *See Payne v. Tennessee*, 501 U.S. 808 (1991), (overruling *Booth v. Maryland*, 482 U.S. 496 (1987) and *South Carolina v. Gathers*, 490 U.S. 805 (1989)).

34 *See* Chapter VII, pp. 241-242 where preclusion is discussed.

35 *See* Model Penal Code §210.6, providing states a choice of differing versions of this procedure that vary depending on how much control the judge or jury have. Methods of execution and statistics are discussed in Chapter XIV, p. 530. Ranges of imprisonment are discussed in Chapter XIV, pp. 527-529.

to petition for leave (permission) to appeal to the state supreme court. Defendants may also file a petition for *certiorari* in the United States Supreme Court in an effort to gain review of any federal issues raised. Defendants convicted in a federal district court have a statutory right to appeal to the United States Court of Appeals for the circuit in which they were convicted. If unsuccessful in the circuit court, they may petition for *certiorari*.[36]

Review on Federal Habeas Corpus Under certain circumstances, a prisoner, after exhausting all direct appeals, may be able to gain additional review of federal constitutional issues by filing a *habeas corpus* case in the federal District Court.[37] *Habeas corpus* is not an appeal. It is an entirely new civil lawsuit filed against the warden of the prison where the prisoner is confined. It is thus a "collateral attack" on the prisoner's conviction. What is sought is a "writ of *habeas corpus*" — an ancient common law remedy that requires the authorities to justify why a particular prisoner is being held. If detention is determined to be illegal, the writ is issued and the prisoner is released. The reasons for confinement are usually that the prisoner was properly convicted of a crime and sentenced to prison. Consequently, to gain release the prisoner must show that the conviction was obtained in violation of the Constitution.

The overall purpose of federal *habeas corpus* review has been to assure enforcement of federal constitutional rights by allowing anyone held in confinement to test the constitutionality of that confinement at any time. State courts have the power to adjudicate prisoners' claims of constitutional error and will have done so on the prisoner's direct appeal. But releasing convicted felons is not a popular thing for a judge to do. Federal judges' lifetime tenure insures a more dispassionate review of constitutional issues. In addition, some feel that federal judges are more sensitive to and often more knowledgeable about issues of federal law. Not surprisingly, many of the important constitutional criminal procedure decisions the Supreme Court has made — some of which are discussed below — have been in *habeas corpus* cases.[38]

But despite the illustrious history of the "Great Writ," as it has been called, there has been a recent trend in both the Court and Congress to limit its scope and availability. Some years ago, the Supreme Court removed all issues of unconstitutional searches and seizures from *habeas* review, by limiting review to cases in which the state court denied the opportunity for full and fair litigation of the

---

36 The scope of appellate review was discussed in Chapter V, pp. 166-167.

37 28 U.S.C.A. §§2254-2255. *See also* Art. I §9 cl. 2 of the Constitution ("The Privilege of the Writ of Habeas Corpus shall not be suspended, unless when in Cases of Rebellion or Invasion the public Safety may require it.") For an excellent summary of *habeas corpus* law, *see* ERWIN CHEMERINSKY, FEDERAL JURISDICTION, 2D ED. §§15.1-15.5 (Aspen. 1994). *See also* LAFAVE & ISRAEL, *supra* note 1, §§28.1-28.7. It is estimated that the success rate for prisoners who file for *habeas corpus* is about 4%.

38 This explains why many of the Supreme Court cases on constitutional criminal procedure have the names of two natural persons as the parties rather than a state and the defendant's name. Because *habeas corpus* is an action to "bring forth the body" of the prisoner, it is brought against the *warden of the prison* in which the prisoner is held, rather than against the state. The state, however, is the real party in interest and its criminal appellate lawyers defend the action.

issue.[39] The Court recently effectively limited prisoners to only one *habeas* petition.[40] It has also held that the prisoner's lawyer's failure to raise a constitutional issue on direct appeal in state court will usually bar later arguing that issue on federal *habeas corpus*.[41] A more serious limitation — only recently imposed — is that relief is available only to redress violations of federal constitutional rights that were clearly established at the time of the prisoner's trial, unless the new right is one that would be applied retroactively to other cases.[42] Congress recently codified several of these restrictions and imposed an additional one of its own: limiting the time period during which a writ of *habeas corpus* can be sought to one year after all state appeals (if any) are exhausted.[43]

F. Resolving Criminal Cases Without Trial

One of the consequences of an adversary system giving the parties control over litigation is that parties can choose to give up their right to litigate. In criminal cases, this most often happens when defendants choose to waive their right to contest the charges at a trial and instead admit their guilt. Guilty pleas are not only consistent with adversary principles; they are a matter of necessity for the criminal justice system. If even a third of criminal defendants actually insisted on having a trial, especially a trial by jury, the system would collapse. Of the 47,556 criminal defendants convicted in federal court during 1995, 91.7% pleaded guilty. Similar results obtain in state court.[44]

Procedure for Guilty Pleas The process for accepting a guilty plea is summary. The defendant stands at the lectern with defense counsel and the judge questions the defendant personally about his plea. The judge's purpose in inquiring is twofold: to assure that the guilty plea is voluntary and to set out sufficient facts to show that the defendant is in fact guilty of the offense. Without establishing both these matters on the record, the plea cannot be accepted by the court and the case will be set for trial.

No Contest Pleas It is also possible for a defendant to plead *nolo contendere* or "no contest" to charges. This means simply that the defendant is choosing not to contest the charges. This plea has the same result as a guilty plea — a finding of guilt by the court. The main advantage is that the admission inherent in the no contest plea, unlike a guilty plea, is not admissible to prove any element of the offense in a civil trial.[45] This consideration is of no consequence to most defendants who, because they have no money, will probably not be sued civilly. But civil liability can be a serious consequence of a guilty plea to some business crimes, such as antitrust

---

39 *Stone v. Powell*, 428 U.S. 465 (1976). *Stone* is based on the theory that the exclusionary rule has little deterrent effect when applied several years after a conviction on *habeas corpus* review. Somewhat inconsistently, the Court has declined to extend the doctrine of *Stone* to federal court review of *Miranda* violations despite the fact that the exclusionary rule is involved in both confession and search and seizure cases. *Withrow v. Williams*, 507 U.S. 680 (1992) (distinguishing *Stone* largely on the ground that the evidence excluded in 4th Amendment cases is reliable, while there may be some doubt as to reliability of confessions obtained in violation of *Miranda*).

40 *McCleskey v. Zant*, 499 U.S. 467 (1991) (second petition that was filed after death row prisoner found out that police had placed an informant in his cell should be dismissed even though government had withheld information about informant at time of first petition).

41 *Coleman v. Thompson*, 501 U.S. 722 (1991) (fact that death penalty defendant missed state court appeals time limit by 3 days prohibits federal habeas review of possible constitutional errors).

42 *Teague v. Lane*, 489 U.S. 288 (1989) (plurality opinion). *See also Penry v. Lynaugh*, 492 U.S. 302 (1989) (majority opinion applying *Teague* to death penalty case). *See* Chapter II, pp. 45-46 (discussing retroactivity of caselaw decisions).

43 *See* 28 U.S.C.A §§2244, 2253, 2254, 2255, 2261-66.

44 Source: Bureau of Justice Statistics, U.S. Dept. of Justice.

45 This effect, called issue preclusion or collateral estoppel, is discussed in Chapter VII, pp. 241-242.

violations, or in some criminal offenses involving automobile accidents if the defendant has insurance or other assets sufficient to pay a civil judgment. No contest pleas are possible only with the approval of the prosecution and the judge.

1. Plea Bargaining

Although defendants sometimes plead guilty without receiving anything in return, and often do in misdemeanor cases, guilty pleas in most felony cases are the result of a "plea bargain" struck by the prosecution and the defendant. A plea bargain is an agreement by which the defendant agrees to plead guilty in return for either a reduction in the charge or some special dispensation regarding the sentence. The advantage from the defendant's position is clear: the disposition of the case is made more certain and usually more lenient than if the defendant went to trial. The advantage of plea bargaining from the standpoint of the prosecutor and the court is that the plea agreement saves time and resources since, once a defendant pleads guilty, there is no need for a trial.

The Bargaining Process Bargaining often occurs at some time prior to the arraignment on the indictment or information, though in the federal system, it is usually after indictment. The prosecution may approach the defense, or the defense may suggest a plea to the prosecution. There can be charge bargaining and sentence bargaining (or a combination of both). An example of charge bargaining is where the defendant is charged with armed robbery, but is permitted to plead guilty to unarmed robbery, a lesser offense, because the case is weak or there are special considerations. In a sentence bargain, on the other hand, charges are not reduced. Instead, the prosecutor and the defendant agree on a sentence range or a particular recommendation the prosecutor is willing to make in return for a guilty plea. To start in as strong a bargaining position as possible, many prosecutors initially charge a defendant with the greatest number of the most serious charges warranted by the facts, with the idea that some of the weakest of them can be traded away in bargaining.[46]

Role of the Judge in Plea Bargaining In both charge bargaining and sentence bargaining, the judge is informed of the bargain before taking the guilty plea and must agree. However, the judge does not usually become involved in the plea bargaining discussions and most often allows the prosecutor and defendant to reach whatever agreement will dispose of the case.[47] As with all other guilty pleas, when defendants plead guilty, they must state on the record facts that show that they are guilty of the bargained offense or it must otherwise be shown that the evidence is consistent with guilt. Otherwise, the judge will reject the plea and the case will be set for trial. If the judge accepts the plea bargain, but the defendant does not receive what was promised, the defendant can compel specific performance of the plea agreement in accord with basic contract principles.[48]

Criticisms of Plea Bargaining Plea bargaining has come under considerable attack. Some critics feel that plea bargaining is too lenient on the criminal. Others

---

46 If the highest charge possible has not been filed, it is even permissible for the prosecutor to threaten to file more serious charges in order to "persuade" the defendant to plead guilty. *Bordenkircher v. Hayes*, 434 U.S. 357 (1978).

47 Some controversy exists over whether the court should participate in any discussion of plea bargaining. The Federal Rules of Criminal Procedure prohibit court involvement in any plea discussion, as do many state court rules. *See* Richard E. Gerstein, *Plea Bargaining: An Overview*, reprinted in the Association of Trial Lawyers of America Education Fund, *Settlement and Plea Bargaining* 282-283 (1981).

48 *Santobello v. New York*, 404 U.S. 257, 260 (1971).

fear that it induces defendants who may be innocent or have a defense to the charge to plead guilty anyway for fear that they might nonetheless be convicted at trial.[49] But a series of U.S. Supreme Court rulings has upheld plea bargaining as constitutional. Plea bargaining, it has declared, "is an essential component of the administration of justice" and, "[p]roperly administered, it is to be encouraged."[50]

2. Programs for Diversion from the Criminal Justice System

Several programs are available to divert the offender from being processed through the criminal justice system. Many of these programs were developed because it was felt that incarceration of first offenders and juvenile offenders for non-violent crimes is often too harsh. These programs represent attempts to rehabilitate offenders, instead of punishing them. They have the added benefit of helping to reduce case backlogs and relieving overcrowding in prisons.

Programs for diversion from the criminal justice system can be an alternative to prosecution or they can be a substitute for incarceration. Programs that are an alternative to prosecution usually are directed toward juvenile offenders and adult first-time offenders, who often have drug or alcohol addiction problems. Programs vary from city to city, but offenders are generally required to attend private counseling or psychotherapy, or drug or alcohol treatment and vocational training as a condition for dropping the criminal charges. Offenders can be diverted into these programs prior to prosecution if their characteristics and background meet the criteria of the program and they have been referred by the local prosecutor. Similar programs are also available for offenders who may be rehabilitated through a vocational and job placement program.[51]

Most of the programs mentioned above are also available as an alternative to incarceration for convicted offenders. Thus, a first-time offender found guilty of a nonviolent crime is often given the choice of serving time in prison or completing substance abuse treatment or vocational training.

PART II: Constitutional Criminal Procedure

A. Introduction and Preliminary Comments

Among the most important rights that suspects and defendants enjoy in the criminal process are federal constitutional rights.[52] The law in this area is complicated. It is governed exclusively by court decisions and the number of published appellate decisions is staggering. While many Supreme Court cases are

---

49 *Cf. North Carolina v. Alford*, 400 U.S. 25 (1970) (defendant's plea of guilty to second degree murder to avoid death penalty is proper if it is intelligently and voluntarily made and if there is sufficient evidence to support guilt, even though defendant later protested his innocence).

50 *Santobello v. New York*, *supra* note 48. *See also Brady v. United States*, 397 U.S. 742 (1970) (voluntary plea bargaining is constitutional). The defendant also has a right to effective assistance of counsel in the plea bargaining process. *See infra* note 210.

51 For a description of one such program in Colorado, *see* Herbert C. Covey and Scott Menard, *Community Corrections Diversion in Colorado*, 12 J. Crim. Just. 1 (Winter 1984). A study of a community correctional program in Allegheny County, Pennsylvania, showed that in 1984, 38% of all criminal cases filed in that county were disposed of through a program called Accelerated Rehabilitation Disposition. This program offered both drug and alcohol treatment, as well as educational and vocational training. *Comment*, 24 DUQUESNE L.REV. 253 (1985).

52 State constitutions, to the extent that they provide more or different protection to defendants, can be important on some issues. *See* Chapter II, p. 35, and *infra* note 122 and accompanying text. However, state constitutional provisions largely track federal constitutional provisions and court decisions, so constitutional criminal procedure remains overwhelmingly federal.

cited or discussed below, there are many more Supreme Court decisions that are not mentioned. And virtually no mention is made here of any of the many decisions of United States Courts of Appeals, both in direct appeals and *habeas corpus* cases, or the intermediate appellate or supreme courts of the states.

Before delving into the substance of the law, a few preliminary points should be made.

Constitutional Source of Criminal Procedural Rights The content of the federal constitutional criminal procedure rights applied in federal and state legal systems is virtually the same. However, the immediate constitutional source of those rights is different. For federal prosecutions, the major sources are (1) the specific Bill of Rights guarantees in the 4th, 5th, 6th, and 8th Amendments and (2) separate rights protected by the general wording of the due process clause of the 5th Amendment, such as the requirement of proof beyond a reasonable doubt. For state prosecutions, the Bill of Rights does not apply since it was intended by its drafters and the ratifying states to apply of its own force only to the *federal* government.[53] However, in a series of decisions beginning in the 1960s, the Supreme Court has held that the 14th Amendment due process clause "incorporates" most of the protections of the Bill of Rights. In addition, parallel to the rights secured by the due process clause of the 5th Amendment, the due process clause of the 14th Amendment directly protects more general rights for criminal defendants.[54]

State Action The United States Constitution defines and limits the power and authority of the government (be it federal or state) and in all but one instance its provisions are applicable only to government actors.[55] This limitation has an important significance for constitutional criminal procedure. Private citizens acting on their own initiative could break into someone's home, retrieve evidence, and give it to the police, and the 4th Amendment provides no protection.[56] However, if government officials knew and approved of the private conduct and the private actor intended to assist the police, private action is considered to be state action.[57]

General Trends in the Law The Supreme Court is the ultimate interpreter of the Constitution, so the history of criminal due process rights has largely been a history of the views of particular majorities of the Supreme Court, subject to the effects of *stare decisis*. Under the Court's influence, the United States, like many other countries, has moved back and forth between the two "models" of a criminal procedure system: "crime control model" and "due process model."[58] The Court under Chief Justice Earl Warren in the 1960s leaned more toward the due process model, emphasizing the

---

53 *Barron v. City of Baltimore*, 32 U.S. (7 Pet.) 243 (1833). *See* Chapter I, p. 4.

54 *See generally* LAFAVE & ISRAEL, *supra* note 1, §§2.1-2, and *infra* pp. 294-296. Some provisions of the Bill of Rights have not been incorporated at all. They are the 2nd Amendment's right to keep and bear arms, the 3rd Amendment's protection against quartering troops in private homes, the 5th Amendment's requirement of grand jury indictment, and the 7th Amendment's right to a jury trial in civil cases. Incorporation is important beyond the question of criminal procedural rights, as it applies to the entire Bill of Rights. Indeed, the first Bill of Rights provision to be incorporated was the 1st Amendment right of freedom of speech. *See Gitlow v. New York*, 268 U.S. 652 (1925).

55 Only the 13th Amendment has been interpreted to apply to private actors. The 13th Amendment, enacted after the Civil War, bans slavery and involuntary servitude.

56 *Burdeau v. McDowell*, 256 U.S. 465 (1921).

57 *United States v. Leffall*, 82 F.3d 343 (10th Cir. 1996)(insufficient government involvement when airline employee thought is was airline policy to open all suspicious packages, became suspicious of an air express package and called airport police, who witnessed him open it).

58 *See* HERBERT PACKER, THE LIMITS OF THE CRIMINAL SANCTION 149-246 (Stanford University Press 1968).

rights of individuals against the government. A drift in the opposite direction began under Chief Justice Warren Burger in the 1970s, and the Court under Chief Justice William Rehnquist in the 1980s and 1990s had sharply turned toward the "crime control" end of the spectrum.[59]

B. Limitations on Investigative Techniques and Apprehension of Suspects

1. Search and Seizure

The 4th Amendment provides that "[t]he right of the people to be secure in their persons, houses, papers, and effects, against unreasonable searches and seizures, shall not be violated, and no Warrants shall issue, but upon probable cause, supported by Oath or affirmation, and particularly describing the place to be searched, and the persons or things to be seized." There are two issues that must be resolved in a challenge to police investigative action alleged to constitute an unconstitutional search or seizure. The first is whether the action constituted a "search" or a "seizure." If there was a search or seizure, then the second issue is whether that search or seizure was "unreasonable," considering among other things whether prior judicial approval in the form of a warrant was obtained.

a. What is a "Search"?

One might think that determining whether a search has taken place would be a simple matter. It is not.

The Katz Test At one point, "search" was defined in terms of a physical intrusion into a "constitutionally protected area."[60] The Supreme Court in 1928 held that a telephone wiretap, whereby incriminating conversations were recorded and used against the defendant, was not a search because a conversation was not a physical object and there was no physical penetration of any constitutionally protected area.[61] In *Katz v. United States*,[62] a 1967 case, the Court abandoned its property-oriented approach. It held that an electronic listening device attached to the outside of a public telephone booth to record a defendant's telephone conversations *did* constitute a search subject to 4th Amendment protections. The Court held that the 4th Amendment is designed to protect *people*, not *places*. What people seek to keep private should be protected without reference to whether a "public" place or a physical trespass was involved. Conversely, what people "knowingly expose to the public, even in [their] own home[s] or office[s]" is outside the protection of the 4th Amendment. Since Mr. Katz had a reasonable expectation that his telephone conversations would be private, the interception of them was a search, and the police had to first obtain a search warrant. Under the *Katz* rule then, when law enforcement officials have invaded a person's "reasonable expectation of privacy," there is deemed to be a search subject to 4th Amendment protections.

"False Friends" When one has a confidential conversation with a trusted friend, one undoubtedly expects privacy, and that "expectation" on some level might be thought to be "reasonable." However, the Supreme Court has held that people cannot reasonably expect that their conversation partner will not relay the conversation to the

---

59 Only trends since the 1960s are mentioned because it was only in the 1960s that the Supreme Court began to develop and protect individual rights in earnest.

60 *Boyd v. United States*, 116 U.S. 616 (1886).

61 *Olmstead v. United States*, 277 U.S. 438 (1928).

62 389 U.S. 347 (1967).

police.[63] Nor may they reasonably expect that their conversation partner is not an agent sent by the police.[64] Similarly, the Supreme Court has held that the 4th Amendment is not violated when the police equip an informer with a recording device or a transmitter by which the police can hear the conversation.[65] In a similar vein, the Supreme Court held that use of a "pen register" device, which records numbers dialed from a particular telephone, but does not record conversations, does not constitute a search. It explained that this is because there was no reasonable expectation that the telephone company did not keep records of the numbers dialed and would not turn such information over to the police.[66]

"Open Fields" Doctrine Despite the Supreme Court's rejection in *Katz* of a property-based concept of "search," in *Oliver v. United States* it reaffirmed the so-called "open fields" doctrine established before *Katz*.[67] An open field is any land outside the "curtilage" of a house. The "curtilage" of a house is, in the city, the lot upon which the house is located and all other things on the lot — sidewalks, garages, porches, driveways and lawns. The curtilage of a farm house includes some land around the house, but does not include the entire acreage of a farm. The notion is that "open fields do not provide the setting for those intimate activities that the Amendment is intended to shelter from government interference or surveillance." Thus, on the facts of *Oliver* it was held not to be a search when police ignored "no trespassing" signs, got around a locked gate and stone wall and observed marijuana plants that were not visible without trespassing on the land.[68] A large part of the justification for assuming that activity in "open fields" is beyond 4th Amendment protection is that the general public regularly trespasses on such areas, even though such intrusions are technically illegal. Moreover, the decision in *Oliver* noted, police and non-police alike could have flown over the property in an airplane and looked at it lawfully, so the fact they viewed it by illegally trespassing on foot did not matter.

Aerial Surveillance The last comment suggests that aerial surveillance is not a search. Aerial photography of an industrial plant did not constitute a search of an industrial plant due to the nature of the premises, but the Supreme Court has indicated that such surveillance of the curtilage of a home, "where privacy expectations are most heightened," might constitute a search.[69] Yet, where police officers flew in an airplane at 1,000 feet over a defendant's residence within public navigable airspace and observed marijuana plants growing within the curtilage of the defendant's home, no search occurred. This was so even though six-foot high fences surrounding the curtilage prevented the officers from observing the marijuana from the ground.[70] The defendant had no reasonable expectation of privacy, because "any member of the public flying in this airspace who glanced down could have seen everything that these officers observed." In a case involving a police helicopter flying

---

63 *United States v. White*, 401 U.S. 745 (1971).

64 *Hoffa v. United States*, 385 U.S. 293 (1967) (defendant's acquaintance in a hotel room was paid government informant; defendant assumed the risk that his "false friend" would inform on him).

65 *United States v. White*, 401 U.S. 745 (1971).

66 *Smith v. Maryland*, 442 U.S. 735 (1979).

67 466 U.S. 170 (1984). *Hester v. United States*, 265 U.S. 57 (1924) (original "open fields" case).

68 *See also United States v. Dunn*, 480 U.S. 294 (1987) (holding no search took place when federal agents went to defendant's farm, climbed over an outer fence that enclosed the entire farm, then climbed over an inner fence around a barn, smelled the odor of drug manufacturing coming from the barn, went to the barn and peered inside without entering the barn and saw incriminating evidence).

69 *Dow Chemical Co. v. United States*, 476 U.S. 227 (1986).

70 *California v. Ciraolo*, 476 U.S. 207 (1986).

lower, the Court held there was no search, but indicated that the result might have been different if the helicopter had interfered with the normal use of the curtilage by causing excess noise, wind, or dust, or had allowed the police to observe "intimate details connected with the use of the home or curtilage."[71]

Other Enhanced Senses A theory similar to that involved in the aerial surveillance cases allowed police to use a "beeper" tracking device, an instrument attached to an object in the suspect's possession that emits signals enabling police to track the location and movement of the suspect and the object.[72] The theory is that the defendant was traveling on public roads and was there for anyone to see as he drove along, if they wished to pay any attention.

Allowing a dog trained for drug-detection to sniff luggage in a public airport when government agents had reasonable suspicion that the luggage owner possessed illegal drugs was held not to be a search.[73] The dog sniff disclosed the presence of contraband only, and not the nature of any noncontraband items in the luggage. Similarly, a government agent's in-the-field chemical test of a substance he suspected was cocaine was held not to be a search.[74] Where possession of the substance in question is outlawed, no "legitimate interest in privacy" is "compromise[d]" when the field test merely reveals its contraband nature.

Undoubtedly technology will present more questions to be answered in the future. One investigatory technique is "thermal imaging." Police use a device to determine whether the heat generated by a house is excessive, which could possibly be caused by high-intensity lamps used to grow marijuana.[75] A sophisticated weapons detection device under development would permit police to electronically "frisk" anyone for weapons from a distance of 3 to 7 meters.[76]

Trash One's trash is not protected by the 4th Amendment, because "plastic garbage bags left on or at the side of a public street are readily accessible to animals, children, scavengers, snoops, and other members of the public," and the owners have no "subjective expectation of privacy" in garbage "that society accepts as objectively reasonable." Where police suspected a homeowner of drug law violations, their inspection of trash bags left outside the curtilage for garbage collection was held not to be a search.[77]

Premises of Others The Court has held that a person who is present briefly in another person's apartment for commercial (drug-dealing) purposes with no other connection to the householder has no legitimate expectation of privacy. Consequently, no 4th Amendment interests were infringed when police officers looked in the window through a gap in the closed blind and observed the defendants and the apartment's lessee bagging cocaine.[78]

---

71 *Florida v. Riley*, 488 U.S. 445 (1986) (helicopter flying at lawful altitude of 400 feet, from which marijuana plants were observed in greenhouse within curtilage of house).

72 *See also United States v. Knotts*, 460 U.S. 276 (1983). *But see United States v. Karo*, 468 U.S. 705 (1984) (illegal search when beeper tracked item in suspect's possession into homes).

73 *United States v. Place*, 462 U.S. 696 (1983).

74 *United States v. Jacobsen*, 466 U.S. 109 (1984).

75 *See United States v. Cusumano*, 67 F.2d 1497 (10th Cir. 1995), *vacated en banc* 83 F.3d 1247 (10th Cir. 1996).

76 *See* David Harris, *Superman's X-Ray Vision and the Fourth Amendment: The New Gun Detection Technology*, 69 TEMPLE L.REV. (1996).

77 *California v. Greenwood*, 486 U.S. 35 (1988).

78 *Minnesota v. Carter*, ___ U.S. ___, 119 S.Ct 469 (1998).

b. Whether a Search is "Reasonable"

If it is determined that a search took place, it must next be determined whether the search was "reasonable" within the meaning of the 4th Amendment. Generally, for a search to be reasonable, there must be "probable cause" to search and a search warrant. "Probable cause" to search in the context of the 4th Amendment exists when there is reasonable and trustworthy information indicating that particular evidence will be found in a particular place.[79] Search warrants are judicial orders permitting a search. However, there are exceptions to both these requirements. Thus, "reasonable" searches may be categorized as (1) searches requiring both probable cause and a warrant, (2) searches requiring probable cause, but no warrant and (3) searches requiring neither probable cause nor a warrant.

(1) Searches With Probable Cause and a Warrant

The Warrant Requirement According to the Supreme Court, "searches outside the judicial process, without prior approval by a judge or magistrate, are *per se* unreasonable under the 4th Amendment — subject only to a few specifically established and well-delineated exceptions."[80] The burden is on the government to show that the search came within one of the exceptions. This general rule is based on the fact that the "reasonableness clause" and the "warrant clause" of the 4th Amendment are linked. The Amendment provides that the right "against unreasonable search and seizure shall not be violated, *and no Warrants shall issue* but upon probable cause, supported by Oath or affirmation, and particularly describing the place to be searched, and the persons or things to be seized." At the same time, the 4th Amendment could not reasonably be read to require that a warrant be obtained in *every* instance, since the police often have no time to get a warrant. But the Court has read this wording of the 4th Amendment as expressing a clear preference for searches with warrants.[81]

Warrant Procedure To get a warrant, the police must submit an application for a warrant to a judicial officer. No assistance, permission, or request from the prosecutor is required. In most states, that judicial officer is a lower-level trial court judge. Whatever the judicial officer's title, that officer must qualify as a "neutral and detached magistrate" who is independent of the police.[82] The warrant application must describe the place, person, and the things to be searched and seized and must be supported by an affidavit (a statement made under penalty of perjury). In that

---

79 *Carroll v. United States*, 267 U.S. 132, 162 (1925). The issue of probable cause is subject to *de novo* review on appeal. *Ornelas v. United States*, 517 U.S. 690 (1996).

80 *Katz v. United States*, 389 U.S. 347, 357 (1967). *See also Chimel v. California*, 395 U.S. 752 (1969); *Mincey v. Arizona*, 437 U.S. 385, 390 (1978).

81 Some members of the Court read the warrant clause differently. They maintain that it was directed at assuring that *warrants that are issued* are not like the abusive "general warrants" issued by colonial judges that allowed searches of general areas for any evidence of criminal activity. Thus, only warrants that "particularly describ[ed] the place to be searched, and the persons or things to be seized" are permitted. For proponents of this view, failure to get a warrant is only one factor to consider in deciding whether a search is reasonable and any *per se* requirement of a warrant is "judicially created" and not constitutionally compelled. For proponents of this position, the "constitutional test is not whether it is reasonable to procure a search warrant, but whether the search was reasonable." *Robbins v. California*, 453 U.S. 420 (1981) (Rehnquist, J., dissenting), overruled by *United States v. Ross*, 456 U.S. 798 (1982).

82 *Johnson v. United States*, 333 U.S. 10, 14 (1948). *See Coolidge v. New Hampshire*, 403 U.S. 443 (1971) (state attorney general could not issue search warrant acting as Justice of the Peace); *Connally v. Georgia*, 429 U.S. 245 (1977) (magistrate without regular salary, who was paid a fee for each warrant issued, but was paid nothing for each warrant denied, was not neutral and detached).

affidavit the police or a witness must explain the circumstances constituting "probable cause." If the "totality of the circumstances" discloses probable cause, the magistrate or judge should issue the warrant.[83]

In large metropolitan areas, police officers often seek out "easy" judges who do not make pointed inquiries as to the precise nature of the evidence supporting probable cause. Often, judges consider warrant applications while on the bench presiding over a trial or other hearing. The question arises whether the warrant procedure provides much protection. Some judges do deny warrants, but the simple fact that a warrant *application* must be made provides some protection. Since the application stands as a *record* of the facts allegedly constituting probable cause as they existed *before* the search is carried out, there can be no dispute over what the facts constituting probable cause were. When there is no warrant application, it is open to the police to exaggerate the amount of evidence they had *before* the search by adding incriminating facts they in fact learned as a result of or after the search.

(2) Searches With Probable Cause, But No Warrant

Exigent Circumstances Most of the exceptions to the warrant requirement come under the general category of "exigent circumstances," meaning that there was an emergency situation that made it impracticable for the police to get a warrant. Any emergency will suffice, but in every such situation, the trial judge on motion of the defendant must review whether there was an emergency and whether the police had probable cause.

The "Automobile Exception" The Court has recognized that when police stop a car and suspect criminal activity in the car, the car and the evidence in it can rapidly be moved out of the jurisdiction.[84] As a result, the automobile exception to the warrant requirement might seem to be included in the above general "exigent circumstances" category. However, the presence of exigent circumstances need not be shown in every case involving an automobile. The only thing that need be shown is probable cause to believe that it contains contraband or other evidence of a crime.[85] If an additional justification for an automobile exception is needed, it is that people have a reduced expectation of privacy in automobiles. This arises from the facts that there is extensive regulation of motor vehicles[86] and that such vehicles are used only for transportation and not for residential or personal storage purposes.[87]

The most common automobile search occurs when a person is stopped for traffic violations and during the stop evidence of non-traffic offenses are observed, thus leading to a search of the car. Often narcotics or other officers will look for traffic violations to use as a basis for stopping a motorist suspected of a non-traffic offense. This tactic was approved by the Court recently. In *Whren v. United States*,[88] it

---

83 For an example of the kind of information that constitutes probable cause, *see Illinois v. Gates*, 462 U.S. 213 (1983) (approving issuance of search warrant based on anonymous tip with some corroboration from police sources).

84 *Carroll v. United States*, 267 U.S. 132 (1925). Any vehicle comes within this exception: mobile homes, boats, trucks, and airplanes are included. *California v. Carney*, 471 U.S. 386, 393 n.2 (1985).

85 *Pennsylvania v. Labron*, 518 U.S. 938 (1996).

86 *Cady v. Dombrowski*, 413 U.S. 433 (1973).

87 *Cardwell v. Lewis*, 417 U.S. 583 (1974).

88 517 U.S. 806 (1996). *Compare United States v. Botero-Ospina*, 71 F.3d 783 (10th Cir. 1995) (Seymour, C.J., dissenting) (such a rule "frees a police officer to target members of minority communities for the selective enforcement of otherwise unenforced statutes"). *See also* Henry Louis Gates, Jr., "Thirteen Ways of Looking at a Black Man," THE NEW YORKER 56, 59 (Oct. 23, 1995) ("there's a moving unanimously held that if there is probable cause to stop for a traffic violation, it does not matter that the officer has a non-traffic motive for the stop or that a reasonable traffic officer would not have stopped a motorist under the circumstances. An automobile search may include any part of the automobile that contains criminal evidence, including any container found therein that is large enough to hold the object of the search.[89] In addition, officers making a traffic stop can order the driver and any passengers out of the car.[90]

An automobile may be searched where it is stopped or parked, if not parked in a residential setting (e.g., in a parking lot or on a street).[91] Or the vehicle may be seized and removed to another location for search. Removal for search is permitted whenever a law enforcement officer would have been permitted to search the automobile where it was stopped or first discovered.[92]

Plain View Doctrine This warrantless search situation comes into play whenever a police officer is conducting a lawful search or is otherwise present at a place the officer has a right to be and observes incriminating evidence in "plain view." If so, the officer may seize it without getting a warrant. The three requirements of the doctrine are: (1) the officer's presence in the area where the item is seen must be lawful; (2) the officer must have lawful access to the item; and (3) it must be immediately apparent to the officer that the item is contraband in nature or evidence of a crime. A typical case would involve officers who enter a home pursuant to a warrant to search for a murder weapon. While searching the living room of the home, they see several clear plastic bags full of what looks like rock cocaine on top of a coffee table. The officers may seize the bags. The officers' presence in the home was lawful because they had a search warrant authorizing them to enter and search the home; they had lawful access to the bags because the bags were in plain view for all who entered the living room to see, and it was not necessary to disturb anything in order to see the bags; and finally, it was immediately apparent to the officers that the bags were filled with contraband, so they had probable cause to seize them.

If it is not immediately apparent that the item is contraband, then the seizure is improper. In one case, the occupant of an apartment reported that a bullet came through the ceiling and injured him. Officers entered the apartment above looking for the shooter, other victims, or guns. While there, one officer saw two expensive stereo sets and suspected that they were stolen. The officer lifted up a stereo turntable to check its serial number, called the police station and matched the number with that of a stolen item, and then seized the turntable. The Supreme Court held that reading serial numbers that were in plain view would be justified, but that the act of picking up the turntable to see and record the number constituted a separate search, for which the officers needed separate probable cause.[93]

[traffic] violation that many African-Americans know as D.W.B. — Driving While Black").

89 *California v. Acevedo*, 500 U.S. 565 (1991). This includes containers that clearly belong to passengers. *Wyoming v. Houghton*, ___ U.S. ___, _1999 WL181177 (1999).

90 *Pennsylvania v. Mimms*, 434 U.S. 106 (1977) (driver); *Maryland v. Wilson*, 519 U.S. 408 (1997) (passenger).

91 *California v. Carney*, 471 U.S. 386 (1985). If the automobile is parked within the curtilage of a residence, a warrant generally must be obtained. *Coolidge v. New Hampshire*, 403 U.S. 443 (1971).

92 *Chambers v. Maroney*, 399 U.S. 42 (1970). The vehicle should be searched within a few days of its seizure. *Chambers, supra; Cardwell v. Lewis*, 417 U.S. 583 (1974); *United States v. Johns*, 469 U.S. 478 (1985).

93 *Arizona v. Hicks*, 480 U.S. 321 (1987). The state conceded that the officer's initial suspicions before checking the serial number did not amount to probable cause.

Like the automobile exception to the warrant requirement, "plain view" seems like just another example of "exigent circumstances," since evidence in "plain view" situations could easily be removed or tampered with by someone before the police could return with a search warrant. However, as with the automobile exception, the police need not show in each case that it was essential that they seize the evidence immediately to prevent its being lost.

(3) Searches Without Probable Cause or a Warrant

Inventory Searches The police often have authority to impound vehicles for non-investigatory reasons. These might include instances when vehicles are improperly parked and blocking traffic, the owner has a mass of unpaid parking tickets, or the vehicle has been abandoned for some period of time on a public street. When police impound a car, they have a right to inventory its contents. If in the process of such inventory criminal evidence is found in "plain view," such evidence may be seized.[94] Inventory searches should not be a pretext for investigative searches and are reasonable only if conducted pursuant to established, uniformly-applied law enforcement department procedures.[95] Similarly, the police have the right to inventory the possessions of an arrested person in preparation for jailing.[96]

Search Incident to Lawful Arrest A search incident to (i.e., in connection with) a lawful arrest may be made without a warrant. Under this exception to the warrant requirement, the arrested person and the area within the arrestee's immediate control may be searched. This exception has been justified by law enforcement agents' need to protect themselves and others by preventing an arrestee from acquiring a weapon, and to prevent the destruction of evidence.[97] While searching an arrestee, law enforcement agents may seize anything (not just a weapon) that they have probable cause to believe is evidence of a crime, even a crime unrelated to the arrest.[98] When arresting someone in a private home, law enforcement agents may automatically conduct a "sweep" of "spaces immediately adjoining the place of arrest" to ensure that the arresting officers will not be attacked by others present in the home.[99]

The "search incident" exception has expanded beyond its original rationale of protecting officers or preserving evidence of the crime for which the defendant was arrested. It was used to justify a full search of a person subject to a full custody arrest for a traffic violation and seizure of heroin capsules which the officer felt inside a cigarette pack and then emptied out during a pat-down search of the defendant.[100] The Court rejected arguments that whatever the officer felt in the cigarette package was obviously neither a weapon nor evidence of the traffic violation, observing broadly that it was not necessary to tie authority for a search to one of the reasons behind the exception. The Court also used the "search incident" exception to permit the police, when arresting any occupant of an automobile (not just the driver), to search the passenger compartment of the automobile, and any clothes or containers

---

94 *South Dakota v. Opperman*, 428 U.S. 364 (1976).

95 *Colorado v. Bertine*, 479 U.S. 367 (1987); *Florida v. Wells*, 495 U.S. 1 (1990).

96 *Illinois v. Lafayette*, 462 U.S. 640 (1983).

97 *Chimel v. California*, 395 U.S. 752 (1969).

98 *United States v. Robinson*, 414 U.S. 218 (1973).

99 *Maryland v. Buie*, 494 U.S. 325 (1990). This right flows from the fact of arrest. There need not be separate probable cause for this search. *See* DRESSLER, *supra* note 1, §68[C].

100 *United States v. Robinson*, 414 U.S. 218 (1973). A pat-down search is explained *infra* p. 281, where "*Terry*" stops" are discussed.

found in it.[101] However, the Court has drawn the line at searches incident to issuance of a traffic citation or "ticket." An Iowa statute permitted police officers who have stopped a motorist and issued a citation to conduct a full search of the person and car. This blanket authorization would not be justified, a unanimous Court held, either by concern for the officer's safety or by the need to search for evidence. Officer safety is less a concern when a citation is being issued than when there is a full custody arrest and officers who have a reasonable suspicion that a particular motorist may be armed already have authority to order that person out of the car and conduct a pat-down search. As for evidence, it is hard to imagine what further evidence of the traffic violation would be found in the car.[102]

Consent Searches Searches conducted with the suspect's consent similarly require neither probable cause nor a warrant. However, consent to a search must be voluntary. Consent may not be obtained through coercion (threats, intimidation, shows of force). Consent obtained as a result of the police falsely informing a person that they have the right to search is not valid. For example, in *Bumper v. North Carolina*,[103] the police falsely claimed to a homeowner that they had a warrant to search her home. She opened the door and said "go ahead." When no warrant was ever produced, the prosecutor claimed that the homeowner had consented to the search. The Supreme Court found that her consent was invalid, as it was obtained through coercion, by "acquiescence to a claim of lawful authority." However, police officers need not inform people of their right to refuse consent.[104] Similarly, a search conducted during a traffic stop pursuant to consent is not invalid because before consent was given the police officer did not tell the defendant that he was "free to go."[105] Consent is determined based on all the surrounding facts and circumstances.

c. Means of Executing Searches: The "Knock and Announce" Rule

The police have the right to break down the door of a dwelling to carry out a search or an arrest. However, issues have recently arisen as whether they need to knock and announce their presence first. In *Wilson v. Arkansas*,[106] the Court unanimously held that the common law rule that officers must "knock and announce" is part of 4th Amendment law. There may be "countervailing law enforcement interests" that could create exceptions to the rule, but the Court in *Wilson* did not indicate what these might be. What is clear, however, is that a blanket exception for police officers executing a warrant in a felony drug investigation is not constitutional. A unanimous Court invalidated this in *Richards v. Wisconsin*.[107]

d. Unreasonable "Seizures" of Persons: Illegal Arrests

The Significance of the Illegality of an Arrest The fact that an arrest is illegal will not result in a suspect being released from custody if the illegality can be cured. Once it is cured, the suspect can simply be "rearrested" while in custody. The legality of the

---

101 *New York v. Belton*, 453 U.S. 454 (1981). "Passenger compartment" would not include the trunk or engine compartment.

102 *Knowles v. Iowa*, ___ U.S. ___, 119 S.Ct. 484 (1998). Pat-down searches based on reasonable suspicion are authorized by the "stop and frisk" rule of *Terry v. Ohio*, discussed *infra* p. 281.

103 391 U.S. 543 (1968).

104 *Schneckloth v. Bustamonte*, 412 U.S. 218, 248 (1973). As discussed *infra*, pp. 396-398, police *are* required to inform suspects of their 5th Amendment right against self-incrimination.

105 *Ohio v. Robinette*, 519 U.S. 33 (1996).

106 514 U.S. 927 (1995).

107 520 U.S. 385 (1997).

original arrest is important mainly because it affects the application of two warrantless search categories just discussed: the "search incident to arrest" exception and the "plain view" exception. Searches incident to arrest cannot be valid if the arrest to which they are "incident" was illegal. Similarly, evidence is often in "plain view" of a police officer only because that officer is in a particular place making an arrest. If the arrest is illegal, there may be no other justification for the officer's presence at that place.

For the arrest to be "reasonable," there must be probable cause and, in some instances, an arrest warrant. Whether a warrant is required depends in large part on where the arrest takes place.[108]

Arrests in the Home Because "physical entry of a home is the chief evil against which the wording of the 4th Amendment is directed," police officers may not enter a person's home to arrest that person unless they have an arrest warrant and good reason to believe that the suspect is there, unless there is consent or "exigent circumstances."[109] Exigent circumstances exist if (1) the police are in "hot pursuit" of a fleeing felon;[110] (2) there is probable cause to believe that evidence will be destroyed if the police do not enter the home immediately; (3) the suspect will escape if police do not enter the home immediately; or (4) harm will occur to the police or others if the police do not enter the home immediately.[111]

Because the sanctity of the home is so important, the police, in seeking to arrest a suspect, may not enter the home of an acquaintance of the suspect in order to arrest that suspect, even if they have an arrest warrant. To enter any house other than the suspect's, they must have a *search* warrant allowing them to enter that house to search for the suspect. Otherwise, police officers could use the arrest warrant as a pretext for a search by waiting to arrest the suspect until he visited a house the police wanted to search based on mere suspicions that illegal activity was taking place there.[112]

Arrests Outside the Suspect's Home Outside the home, although a warrant is preferred, suspects may generally be arrested without a warrant, but on probable cause. The Supreme Court approved a federal statute authorizing the warrantless arrest of suspected felons based on probable cause. In that case, federal agents had probable cause to arrest the suspect, who was in a restaurant. The arrest was valid, even though federal agents had plenty of time to obtain an arrest warrant, but did not do so.[113] However, under common law principles, misdemeanants may not be arrested without a warrant, unless the misdemeanor occurs in the arresting officer's presence.[114]

Reasonableness of Means of Arrest The means used to effectuate an arrest must be reasonable. This can include the application of deadly force, such as a gun. However, "use of deadly force to prevent the escape of all felony suspects, whatever the circumstances, is constitutionally unreasonable." Application of deadly force is

---

108 *See* the discussion of warrant procedures *supra*, p. 260.

109 *Payton v. New York*, 445 U.S. 573 (1980).

110 *Warden v. Hayden*, 387 U.S. 294 (1967); *United States v. Santana*, 427 U.S. 38 (1976).

111 *Minnesota v. Olson*, 495 U.S. 91 (1990).

112 *Steagald v. United States*, 451 U.S. 204 (1981).

113 *United States v. Watson*, 423 U.S. 411 (1976). This is consistent with the common law rule which did not require a warrant to arrest suspected felons.

114 *See* WAYNE R. LAFAVE, SEARCH & SEIZURE, 2D ED. §5.1(c) (West 1987).

justified only if "the officer has probable cause to believe that the suspect poses a threat of serious physical harm, either to the officer or to others."[115]

"Terry" Stops and Other Lesser Seizures An important form of temporarily detaining individuals that is permissible under the 4th Amendment is the *"Terry* stop," named for *Terry v. Ohio*.[116] For purposes of crime prevention and detection, a police officer may stop a person if the officer has a "reasonable suspicion" that "criminal activity is afoot." "Reasonable suspicion" is less than probable cause, which would be sufficient for a full arrest and search. Reasonable suspicion is defined as specific and articulable facts which form a basis for suspecting that the detainee may be involved in criminal activity. If an officer also has reasonable suspicion that a detainee is armed, the officer may "frisk" the detainee. A frisk, also called a "pat-down," is when an officer pats the outside of a person's clothing all over the person's body feeling for objects that might be weapons. *Terry* frisks were originally limited to officers searching for and seizing weapons in order to protect themselves. However, the Supreme Court held in 1993 that a police officer could, while conducting a proper *Terry* frisk for weapons, seize an item that the officer could immediately tell was contraband. Thus, the Court engrafted a "plain feel" rule onto *Terry* analogous to the "plain view" rule. However, if an object felt through the clothing is obviously not a weapon and it is only after squeezing, sliding or otherwise manipulating the object that it became apparent that it was contraband, then the seizure is invalid.[117]

An issue for *Terry* stops is the use of "drug courier profiles." In one case, a nervous young man paid cash for an airline ticket from Miami to New York under an assumed name and carried heavy bags. He was stopped and his bags were searched. The Court suppressed the evidence. It held that the defendant could be stopped by police and they had grounds to temporarily detain him and his luggage while they attempted to verify or dispel their suspicions that he was a drug courier. However, the police exceeded the limits of an investigative stop where they asked the defendant to accompany them to a small police room, and retained his ticket and driver's license and indicated in no way that he was free to depart.[118] In a later case, the Court refused to suppress drugs found in a search following a similar stop. In this case the defendant paid $2,100 for two round-trip plane tickets between Honolulu and Miami, a source city for illicit drugs, with a roll of $20 bills; he traveled under a name that did not match the name under which his telephone number was listed; he stayed in Miami for only 48 hours, even though a round-trip flight from Honolulu to Miami takes 20 hours; he appeared nervous during his trip; and he checked none of his luggage. Upon stopping the defendant, having a dog sniff defendant's luggage and obtaining a warrant, they found evidence of involvement in drug trafficking in one bag, which led them to search the other bags.[119]

Administrative Searches and Seizures The government is allowed to detain and search people in circumstances that would otherwise violate the 4th Amendment if it has a "special interest" in doing so for administrative reasons, i.e., for reasons other

---

115 *Tennessee v. Garner*, 471 U.S. 1 (1985).

116 392 U.S. 1 (1968).

117 *Minnesota v. Dickerson*, 508 U.S. 366 (1993). One problem with *Terry* stops is that they can be used disproportionately against minorities. *See* David A. Harris, *Factors for Reasonable Suspicion: When Black and Poor Means Stopped and Frisked*, 69 IND. L.J. 659 (1994).

118 *Florida v. Royer*, 460 U.S. 491 (1983).

119 *United States v. Sokolow*, 490 U.S. 1 (1989).

than investigating crimes.[120] In determining the validity of such searches or seizures, the Court requires only that they be "reasonable," determined "by balancing the need to search against the invasion which the search entails."[121] Thus, in *Michigan Department of State Police v. Sitz*, the Court approved of police detaining persons for a few minutes at random checkpoints on the highway in order to determine whether those persons were driving while intoxicated. While drunk driving was a criminal offense, the roadside checkpoints also served the administrative purpose of removing drunk drivers from the road.[122] Similar fixed Border Patrol checkpoints were approved 66 miles inland from the border with Mexico for the purpose of checking for illegal aliens.[123] Also falling into this category are airport security checks. If evidence of a crime is found as a result of the administrative detention or search, it may be used in a criminal prosecution.

The Court has also approved a public school official searching the purse of a 14-year-old student whom the school official suspected of selling marijuana. The Court held that such searches of public school students were permissible if made on "reasonable grounds" for suspecting a violation of school rules of the law and if "the measures adopted are reasonably related to the objective of the search and not excessively intrusive in light of the age and sex of the student and the nature of the infraction."[124] The Court also approved as a proper administrative search random urinalysis drug tests of high school athletes in public schools.[125] However, in a later case, it invalidated a state statute that required that all candidates for public office submit to drug testing. It observed that the state had no "special interest" in such testing, because there was "no evidence of a drug problem among the State's elected officials," such officials did not perform tasks that were "safety sensitive," the tests were not necessary to prevent drug trafficking and elected officials are subject to intense day-to-day scrutiny, unlike others who have been subject to such tests.[126]

2. The Law of Confessions

Voluntariness Requirement The self-incrimination clause of the 5th Amendment provides that no person "shall be compelled in any criminal case to be a witness against himself." At the very least, this clause and the due process clauses of the Constitution prohibit involuntary confessions.[127] Whether a confession was given voluntarily or involuntarily depends on the "totality of the circumstances" surrounding

---

120 *See generally* LaFave & Israel, *supra* note 1, §3.9. Sometimes these searches are called "regulatory or "inspections."

121 *Camara v. Municipal Court*, 387 U.S. 523 (1967) (routine inspections of housing for fire, health and safety code violation are proper if made pursuant to a warrant based, not on probable cause, but on passage of time, the nature of the building and the condition of area where the building is located), *followed in Marshall v. Barlow's, Inc.*, 436 U.S. 307 (1978) (worker safety inspections).

122 496 U.S. 444 (1990). The Michigan Supreme Court subsequently held the same alcohol check points unconstitutional under the *Michigan* Constitution. *Sitz v. Dept. of State Police*, 506 N.W.2d 209 (Mich. 1993). *See* Chapter II, p. 35 and note 3.

123 *United States v. Martinez-Fuerte*, 428 U.S. 543 (1976).

124 *T.L.O. v. New Jersey*, 469 U.S. 325 (1985). The Court pointedly did not address the issue of what standards might apply to searches of students' lockers, desks or other storage facilities.

125 *Vernonia School District 47J v. Acton*, 515 U.S. 616 (1995).

126 *Chandler v. Miller*, 520 U.S. 305 (1997). *Compare Treasury Employees v. Von Raab*, 489 U.S. 656 (1989)(drug testing of federal customs officers who carry guns approved); *Skinner v. Railway Labor Executives' Assoc.*, 489 U.S. 602 (1989)(drug testing of railroad train drivers approved). *See also Griffin v. Wisconsin*, 483 U.S. 868 (1987)(search of convict on probation without warrant and on less than probable cause approved due to "special interests" of the state); *United States v. Biswell*, 436 U.S. 307 (1972) (warrantless unannounced inspection of firearms dealer's business during working hours proper).

127 *Bram v. United States*, 168 U.S. 532 (1897); *Brown v. Mississippi*, 297 U.S. 278 (1936).

the confession. In general, a confession is voluntary if it is the product of an essentially free and unconstrained choice of its maker. These circumstances include any coercive conduct by police, and the characteristics and status of the confessor. Physical brutality, such as beating, or deprivation of food, water, or sleep, or threats of violence, can constitute coercive police conduct without regard to the defendant's individual characteristics.[128] Extended periods of incommunicado interrogation can also be coercive. Promises of leniency can invalidate a confession, as can some forms of police deception, usually misrepresentations of law. For example, telling suspects that their fingerprints were found at the scene, or that accomplices have already confessed and implicated them, are deceptions that are tolerated by courts. But telling suspects that their confession cannot be used against them is not proper.

Miranda Warnings In *Miranda v. Arizona*,[129] the Supreme Court decided that the voluntariness test was an insufficient protection against police overreaching in interrogating suspects and extracting involuntary confessions. The Court held that statements obtained during custodial interrogation may not be used against the suspect in a criminal trial unless the police first provide procedural safeguards to ensure that the privilege against self-incrimination is not violated. Under *Miranda*, the police are required, upon arresting and interrogating a suspect, to advise the arrestee of certain rights, or as police shows on television have popularized it, to "read him his rights." The suspect must be advised: "You have the right to remain silent. Anything you say can and will be used against you in a court of law. You have the right to consult an attorney and have an attorney with you during questioning. If you cannot afford an attorney, one will be appointed for you."

As the *Miranda* warnings suggest, a suspect may waive the right to remain silent, as well as the right to have an attorney present during interrogation, but such a waiver must be knowing and voluntary.[130] Studies show that most suspects do choose to talk. But a voluntary waiver of the right to remain silent is one made without threats, trickery, or cajoling by police. A "lengthy interrogation or incommunicado incarceration before a statement is made is strong evidence" of an involuntary waiver of the suspect's rights. A knowing and intelligent waiver can only be made if the suspect is given the *Miranda* warnings. Circumstantial evidence that the suspect was aware of his rights will not suffice.[131]

A suspect's waiver of *Miranda* rights need not be expressly made. When a police officer reads a suspect the *Miranda* warnings, the suspect apparently understands the warnings, and the suspect then makes incriminating statements, waiver can be inferred.[132] However, once a suspect "indicates in any manner, at any time prior to or during questioning, that he wishes to remain silent, the interrogation must cease."[133] If the suspect indicates a desire to speak to a lawyer, then the suspect must

---

128 *Brown v. Mississippi, supra* (first case to bar use of a confession in a state court; police brutally beat suspects).

129 384 U.S. 436 (1966).

130 *Miranda, supra; see Johnson v. Zerbst*, 304 U.S. 458 (1938).

131 After *Miranda* warnings are given and waived, police trickery and deceit are more tolerated. It is not at all unusual that the police will lie to the suspect to try to induce a confession. *See Frazier v. Cupp*, 394 U.S. 731 (1969) (suspect falsely told co-defendant said something); *State v. Barner*, 486 N.W.2d 1 (Minn.App. 1992) (suspect falsely told his fingerprints were found on a knife).

132 *North Carolina v. Butler*, 441 U.S. 369 (1979).

133 *Miranda, supra* note 129; *but see Michigan v. Mosley*, 423 U.S. 96 (1975) (no violation when suspect cut off questioning and 2 hours later a different officer asked about a different crime after giving *Miranda* warnings again).

not be subjected to further interrogation until counsel is supplied, unless the suspect initiates further communications.[134] This ban includes questioning about an offense different from the subject of the initial interrogation.[135] Once the suspect consults with a lawyer, questioning cannot be reinitiated without the lawyer present.[136] These strict "bright-line" rules regarding reinitiating questioning were deemed essential to prevent possible police-coerced waivers of *Miranda* rights.[137]

The *Miranda* warnings are required only if there is "custodial interrogation." This is defined as "questioning initiated by law enforcement officers after a person has been taken into custody or otherwise deprived of his freedom of action in any significant way."[138] The prerequisite that the suspect be in custody means that statements elicited in casual contact between the police and citizens or statements volunteered by a person on the street are unaffected by *Miranda*. Also, no *Miranda* warnings are needed before police interrogate a suspect in the suspect's home if the suspect is not under arrest, but is free to leave or ask the police to leave.[139] "Interrogation" includes express questioning or its "functional equivalent," i.e., "any words or actions on the part of police (other than those normally attendant to arrest and custody) that the police should know are reasonably likely to elicit an incriminating response from the suspect."[140]

Miranda Exceptions In recent years, the Supreme Court has created exceptions to the requirement that *Miranda* warnings be given before a defendant's statements may be used against him in a criminal trial. The Supreme Court recognized a "public safety exception" to the *Miranda* requirement in *New York v. Quarles*.[141] There, police had been informed that a rapist had fled into an all-night grocery store armed with a weapon. When police found him in the store, they frisked him and found his holster empty. Without reading *Miranda* warnings to him, an officer asked where the gun was, and the defendant indicated its location. Because this "custodial interrogation" occurred under circumstances posing a threat to public safety, the Supreme Court reversed the lower courts' suppression of the statement about the gun. The Court reasoned that the defendant's right to his *Miranda* warnings was outweighed by the interest in public safety.

---

134 *Edwards v. Arizona*, 451 U.S. 477 (1981). *But see Davis v. United States*, 512 U.S. 452 (1994) (no violation where defendant initially waived his rights, then after some interrogation said "Maybe I should talk to a lawyer," but then, when asked to clarify his intentions, said "No, I don't want a lawyer.").

135 *Arizona v. Roberson*, 486 U.S. 675 (1988); *McNeil v. Wisconsin*, 501 U.S. 171 (1991).

136 *Minnick v. Mississippi*, 498 U.S. 146 (1990).

137 An interesting issue is whether a statute passed by Congress and intended to "overrule" *Miranda* is valid. That statute, 18 U.S.C.A. §3501(c), provides that a confession "shall be admissible in evidence if it is voluntarily given." The theory of its validity is that *Miranda* warnings are not a constitutional requirement, but only a judicially created "prophylactic" rule to prevent potential 5th Amendment violations. *See infra* p. 288. However, the issue has never been decided because successive presidential administrations for the past 25 years have avoided relying on it.

138 *Miranda, supra* note 129. The fact that the person interrogated is the "focus" of the investigation is irrelevant, if this fact is not communicated to the person and custody is not involved. *Stansbury v. California*, 511 U.S. 318 (1994) (per curium).

139 *Beckwith v. United States*, 425 U.S. 341 (1976).

140 *Rhode Island v. Innis*, 446 U.S. 291 (1980) (conversation between police officers within hearing of suspect that it would be bad if handicapped children from nearby school were to find weapon defendant had abandoned did not constitute interrogation). *Compare Brewer v. Williams*, 430 U.S. 387 (1977), discussed *infra* p. 286.

141 467 U.S. 649 (1984).

Another exception is the "covert custodial interrogation" exception established in *Illinois v. Perkins*:[142] "*Miranda* warnings are not required when a suspect is unaware that he is speaking to a law enforcement officer and gives a voluntary statement." In *Perkins*, an undercover police officer was placed in a jail cell with the defendant and engaged the defendant in a conversation in which the defendant made incriminating statements. The rationale of this exception is that the purpose of *Miranda* is to protect against the coercion that can inhere in the "interplay between police custody and police interrogation." When the suspect does not know that he is speaking to a police officer, there is no such interplay and therefore no coercion.

A "routine booking exception" has also been made according to a plurality of justices in a recent case. "Booking" is the process by which a suspect who has been arrested is processed administratively through the collection of personal information and taking of fingerprints and photographs. Under this exception, *Miranda* warnings need not be given prior to asking questions designed to elicit "biographical data necessary to complete booking or pre-trial services." Thus, incriminating statements given in response to such questions are admissible in evidence against the defendant, so long as the booking questions were not designed to elicit incriminating information.[143]

3. Pre-Trial Right to Counsel

The 6th Amendment provides that "[i]n all criminal prosecutions, the accused shall enjoy the right . . . to have the Assistance of Counsel for his defence." Although an important part of this right to counsel is the right to a lawyer to defend the accused in court at trial, as discussed below, the right to counsel must be afforded at all "critical stages" of a criminal prosecution. This includes the important period between pleading not guilty to the formal charge and trial. During this period, the right to counsel includes the right to have a lawyer present whenever there is any contact with government agents or officials outside the context of court hearings.

In a seminal case in this area, *Massiah v. United States*,[144] the defendant, indicted on federal narcotics charges, retained counsel, pleaded not guilty, and was released. A codefendant was cooperating with the federal authorities, but Massiah did not know about it. The co-defendant allowed government agents to install a listening device in his car, and he engaged the defendant in an incriminating conversation, tapes of which were used against the defendant at his trial. The Supreme Court held that the 6th Amendment was violated by the government's "deliberate elicitation" of incriminating statements after indictment and in the absence of counsel. The Court reasoned that the period after indictment and before trial was "the most critical period of the proceedings," and denial of counsel at this stage would be denial of "effective representation by counsel at the only stage when legal aid and advice would help him," hence, a violation of the 6th Amendment right to counsel. The *Massiah* rule

---

142 496 U.S. 292 (1990).

143 *Pennsylvania v. Muniz*, 496 U.S. 582 (1990) (plurality opinion) (statements by drunk driver whose processing was videotaped at police station with his knowledge, but without *Miranda* warning, is admissible). A battle has raged recently over the issue of whether *Miranda* has had an adverse effect on law enforcement. *See* Richard A. Leo, *Inside the Interrogation Room*, 86 J.Crim.L & Criminology 263 (1996) (study of three California cities "does not support the assertion that *Miranda* has exercised an adverse impact on law enforcement"), Paul G. Cassell, *Miranda's Social Costs: An Empirical Reassessment*, 90 Nw.L.Rev. 387 (1996) ("*Miranda* has led to lost cases against almost 4% of all criminal suspects how are questioned") and Stephen J. Schulhofer, *Miranda's Practical Effect: Substantial Benefits and Vanishingly Small Social Costs*, 90 Nw.L.Rev. 500 (1996) (lost case rate is "*at most* only 0.78%").

144 377 U.S. 201 (1964).

attaches "at or after the time that judicial proceedings have been initiated against [the accused] — whether by way of formal charge, preliminary hearing, indictment, information, or arraignment."[145] From *Massiah* it can be seen that the 6th Amendment right to counsel takes over where *Miranda* leaves off. *Miranda* protects against interrogation without counsel *before* formal charges have been brought, while the 6th Amendment protects against interrogation without counsel *after* they have been brought.[146]

In a controversial 1977 case on "deliberate elicitation," *Brewer v. Williams*,[147] a defendant in the case of the murder of a little girl was being transported between jails. His appointed counsel had instructed the police officers transporting the defendant not to question his client. However, one of the officers started talking to the defendant about the victim of the crime. The officer did not ask any questions, but lamented that the murdered child's parents would not be able to give the girl a proper "Christian burial," as it was winter and her body would soon be covered by snow. The defendant, an escaped mental patient who was deeply religious, was overcome with emotion and told the police where the little girl's body was. The Court held that this evidence had to be suppressed at trial.

4. The Exclusionary Rule

Basis for Exclusionary Rule As can be gleaned from the cases discussed above, the remedy that is usually applied if evidence is obtained in violation of constitutional rights is that the evidence is excluded from trial. This is accomplished by the defendant filing a "motion to suppress evidence" thereby invoking the "exclusionary rule." The exclusionary rule was first announced in 1914 in *Weeks v. United States*,[148] but it applied only to federal trials. The rule was extended to the states in 1961 in *Mapp v. Ohio*.[149] The *Mapp* Court set out two justifications for the exclusionary rule: (1) to deter law enforcement officers from violating Constitutional rights by removing their incentive to do so; and (2) to preserve "judicial integrity," i.e., to ensure that courts do not become accomplices in the violation of constitutional rights by accepting and relying on evidence derived from such violations.

Criticism of the Exclusionary Rule The exclusionary rule has been under attack in recent years as pressures for a more "crime control" regime in criminal procedure have grown. Part of that attack has come from members of an increasingly conservative Supreme Court. The criticisms of the rule emphasize the enormous social costs when criminals are released. Moreover, the truth-finding process of courts is seriously retarded, and public respect for judicial institutions correspondingly is eroded when criminals are set free "on a legal technicality." Supporters of the exclusionary rule argue that exclusion of unconstitutionally seized evidence is the only

---

145 *Brewer v. Williams*, 430 U.S. 387 (1977).

146 There is also a parallel between "deliberate elicitation" of incriminating statements for *Massiah* purposes and "interrogation" for *Miranda* purposes. *See supra* p. 284.

147 *Id.*

148 232 U.S. 383 (1914). Before *Weeks*, the Court had wavered on the issue. In *Boyd v. United States*, 116 U.S. 616 (1886), it held that certain papers of the defendant in that case seized in violation of the 4th Amendment had to be suppressed. However, in *Adams v. New York*, 192 U.S. 585 (1904), it declared that the "weight of authority as well as reason" supported application of the common law view that all evidence, whatever its source and however obtained, should be admissible. Nonetheless, U.S. courts have always followed the English rule that *coerced confessions* were not admissible. *See The King v. Warickshall*, 168 Eng. Rep. 234 (K.B. 1783).

149 367 U.S. 643 (1961). *Mapp* thus "incorporated" 4th Amendment rights into the due process clause of the 14th Amendment so that they could be applied against the states. *See* discussion *supra* p. 271.

effective redress for the person whose rights were violated and the only means of insuring that 4th Amendment and other constitutional rights are respected. They also point out that there are social costs imposed when *illegal police* conduct is routinely tolerated by the courts. Moreover, abolishing the rule would create even greater cynicism about judicial institutions, since it is hard to justify the notion that one has a particular *right*, but has no effective *remedy* for its violation.[150] Even apart from what the true measure of the relative social costs would be, supporters of the rule assert, the balance struck by the Constitution is clearly in favor of protection of individual rights.[151]

Instead of abolishing the exclusionary rule, the current Supreme Court has chosen to preserve it, but to narrow its application. Most of these limitations have been tied to the first reason given in the *Mapp* case — deterrence of police misconduct. The result has been that, unless the application of the rule to a particular kind of case directly and substantially furthers the policy of deterrence, the rule will not be applied to bar the evidence involved. As the Court observed in a recent case, "The exclusionary rule operates as a judicially created remedy designed to safeguard against future violations of Fourth Amendment rights through the rules general deterrent effect. As with any remedial device, the rule's general application has been restricted to those instances where its remedial objectives are thought to be efficaciously served."[152] The second basis of *Mapp* — that "judicial integrity" is compromised when courts use unconstitutionally obtained evidence — has been largely forgotten.

"Good Faith" Exception   Primary among the exceptions linked directly to deterrence is the "good faith" exception. Under this concept, if the police officers did not know or could not reasonably have been expected to know that their actions were unconstitutional, the evidence is admissible. This exception has so far been applied only to search warrants, but could well spread to other kinds of cases. In *United States v. Leon*,[153] a police officer obtained evidence in reliance on a warrant that seemed valid on its face, but which was later determined to be invalid. The Court created the "good faith" exception and held that the evidence could be admitted.[154] And, in a recent case, the defendant was searched incident to an arrest that was made based on a computer mistake. The computer in the police car indicated that an arrest warrant existed when in fact it had been quashed. The Court held the exclusionary rule did not apply, in part because the computer mistake was made by court personnel rather than by the police.[155]

---

150 According to a study of California cases, the frequency with which the exclusionary rule actually results in freeing the defendant is between 0.6% and 2.35% of felony arrests, though in drug cases, the number rose to 7% or 8%. NATIONAL INSTITUTE OF JUSTICE, THE EFFECTS OF THE EXCLUSIONARY RULE: A STUDY IN CALIFORNIA (1982), cited in *United States v. Leon*, 468 U.S. 897, 907 & n.6 (1984).

151 For a cogent summary of the exclusionary rule debate, *see* DRESSLER, *supra* note 1, §120. Two cases in which various justices debate the merits of the exclusionary rule are *Stone v. Powell*, 428 U.S. 465 (1976) and *United States v. Leon*, 468 U.S. 897 (1984). *See also Bivens v. Six Unknown Named Agents*, 403 U.S. 388 (1971) (Burger, C.J., dissenting) (arguing for monetary compensation to innocent victims in place of an exclusionary rule).

152 *Arizona v. Evans*, 514 U.S. 1 (1995).

153 *United States v. Leon*, 468 U.S. 897 (1984).

154 The decision in *Leon* sparked a spirited dissent that defended the exclusionary rule against much of the criticism to which it has been subjected. *See supra*, note 128.

155 *Arizona v. Evans*, *supra* note 152.

The Impeachment Evidence Exception   Even when the exclusionary rule applies to bar use of unconstitutional evidence as proof of guilty, it may be used on cross-examination to impeach the defendant's credibility in front of the jury if the defendant chooses to testify at trial and makes any statement that is inconsistent with that illegal evidence.[156] In the case of a confession obtained in violation of *Miranda*, this means that a defendant who takes the witness stand in his own defense and testifies that he was not involved in the crime must anticipate that the jury will also hear his illegally-obtained confession. The rationale the Court has given for the impeachment exception is that violations of constitutional rights do not give defendants the right to commit perjury. The value of truthful testimony outweighs "the speculative possibility" that using suppressed evidence to impeach a defendant would encourage police to violate the constitution.[157] Illegally obtained evidence may not be used to impeach other defense witnesses, however.[158] In addition, despite the impeachment exception, an *involuntary* confession is inadmissible in evidence for any purpose.[159]

Exceptions for Derivative Evidence   Important to the operation of the exclusionary rule is the notion that any additional evidence that is derived from the evidence unconstitutionally obtained should also be excluded at trial. This is the doctrine of the "fruit of the poisonous tree."[160] Under this doctrine, if the tree is "poisoned" (i.e., evidence is unconstitutionally obtained), then the "fruits" of that tree (any items or information derived from the use of the unconstitutional evidence) are also "poisoned." For example, if an unconstitutional search reveals an address book which contains a map describing where other evidence is located, the court must exclude not only the address book, but also the other evidence described in it.

Major exceptions exist, however. If the prosecution can demonstrate that the derivative evidence has a source independent of the tainted source, it will be permitted to use it.[161] The Supreme Court has also held that the derivative evidence portion of the exclusionary rule does not apply at all to evidence derived from statements elicited in violation of *Miranda*.[162] The rationale is that the *Miranda* rule is not a rule compelled by the Constitution, but simply a "prophylactic" rule designed to *prevent* 5th Amendment violations. More recently, the Court in *Nix v. Williams*[163] created a new "inevitable discovery" exception to the derivative evidence rule: if the prosecutor can prove by the civil *preponderance of the evidence* standard that the challenged evidence "ultimately or inevitably would have been discovered by lawful means," then the evidence is admissible. The prosecutor in *Nix* admitted that the police secured information from the defendant about the location of the murder victim's body in violation of the defendant's 6th Amendment right to counsel. The Supreme Court held that the evidence was admissible because, under the circumstances in that case, the police had organized an extensive search, were only

---

156 *See Walder v. United States*, 347 U.S. 62 (1954) (4th Amendment violations); *Harris v. New York*, 401 U.S. 222 (1971) (*Miranda* violations).

157 *Harris v. New York, supra*.

158 *James v. Illinois*, 493 U.S. 307 (1990).

159 *Mincey v. Arizona*, 437 U.S. 385 (1978); *New Jersey v. Portash*, 440 U.S. 450 (1979).

160 *Nardone v. United States*, 308 U.S. 338 (1939).

161 *Murray v. United States*, 487 U.S. 533 (1988).

162 *Michigan v. Tucker*, 417 U.S. 433 (1974) (defendant gave names of witnesses, who testified against him at trial, during interrogation in violation *Miranda*).

163 467 U.S. 431 (1984).

a few miles from the body, and would have eventually found the body without relying on the unconstitutionally-obtained information.

Exception for Proceedings Other Than Criminal Trials While the exclusionary rule applies to some forfeiture proceedings in which criminal activity is alleged,[164] it does not apply to civil tax proceedings[165] or to deportation hearings.[166] Unconstitutionally obtained evidence may also be presented to grand juries,[167] at preliminary hearings,[168] parole revocation proceedings[169] and in bail determination proceedings.[170]

C. Rights at the Charging Stage and Pre-Trial Release

Charging Procedures The 5th Amendment requires "presentment or indictment of a Grand Jury" in all felony cases. However, this provision is one of the few provisions of the Bill of Rights that has not been incorporated into the due process clause and applied against the states.[171] Thus, states may bring charges by using grand juries, or by filing a prosecutor's information.[172] Some states either require, or allow as an option, indictment by a grand jury as a matter of state law.

Pre-Trial Release Procedures for pre-trial release on bail were discussed earlier.[173] The 8th Amendment guarantees that "[e]xcessive bail shall not be required."[174] Traditionally, persons charged in all non-capital crimes had a right to be considered for release on bail pending trial. The Supreme Court has stated that bail set in an amount higher than that which would secure a defendant's appearance at trial may be excessive.[175] However, in the 1980s "preventive detention" of defendants who were not a flight risk, but who might commit other crimes while on bail began to be used. For example, the 1984 amendments to the Federal Bail Reform Act of 1966[176] gave federal magistrates the power to hold without bail any defendant as to whom "no condition or combinations of conditions [of release] will reasonably assure the appearance of the person as required *and the safety of any other person and the community*."[177] The act lists offenses that imply high flight and community safety risks. The preventive detention provisions of the Act were held constitutional in *United States v. Salerno*.[178]

---

164 *One 1958 Plymouth Sedan v. Pennsylvania*, 380 U.S. 693 (1965).

165 *United States v. Janis*, 428 U.S. 433 (1976).

166 *Imm. & Naturalization Service v. Lopez-Mendoza*, 468 U.S. 1032 (1984).

167 *United States v. Calandra*, 414 U.S. 338 (1974).

168 *Giordenello v. United States*, 357 U.S. 480 (1958).

169 *Pennsylvania Board of Probation v. Scott*, 524 U.S. 357 (1998).

170 18 U.S.C.A. §3142(f) (applicable to federal cases).

171 *Hurtado v. California*, 110 U.S. 516 (1884). *See* discussion *supra* p. 271.

172 *See supra* pp. 262-264, where indictments and informations are discussed.

173 See *supra* p. 262.

174 The Supreme Court has never squarely held, though it has observed in passing that the excessive bail clause of the 8th Amendment is applicable to the states through the due process clause of the 14th Amendment. *Schlib v. Kuebel*, 404 U.S. 357 (1971).

175 *Stack v. Boyle*, 342 U.S. 1 (1951).

176 18 U.S.C.A. §§3146-3152, repealed in part, 18 U.S.C.A. §§3141-3150.

177 18 U.S.C.A. §3142(b).

178 481 U.S. 739 (1987).

D. Rights at Trial

1. Right to Speedy Trial

The 6th Amendment provides that "[in] all criminal prosecutions, the accused shall enjoy the right to a speedy . . . trial." In *Smith v. Hooey*, the Supreme Court noted three purposes of the speedy trial guarantee: "(1) to prevent undue and oppressive incarceration prior to trial, (2) to minimize anxiety and concern accompanying public accusation and (3) to limit the possibilities that long delay will impair the ability of an accused to defend himself."[179]

The right to a speedy trial attaches at the time of arrest or formal charge, whichever comes first. The remedy for violation of the right to a speedy trial is dismissal of the charges.[180] The issue comes up most often in the context of "detainers." Detainers notify prison officials in one state that authorities in another state want the prisoner turned over to them for trial on other criminal charges at the end of the prisoner's current sentence. A prisoner against whom detainers have been "lodged" is likely to be treated differently in prison. Detainers also affect eligibility for parole. Consequently, upon a prisoner's demand, the state must make a diligent effort to bring the prisoner to trial.[181]

Outside the detainer area, speedy trial issues do not come up often as a constitutional matter because Congress passed the Speedy Trial Act of 1974 for the federal system,[182] and the states have implemented rules of court or statutes that require prompt trials.[183] Issues do arise in unique situations, however. In *Klopfer v. North Carolina*,[184] the defendant's trial ended in a hung jury and the prosecutor failed to bring the defendant to a prompt retrial, instead deciding to take a *"nolle prosequi with leave"* — a device by which the defendant remained under indictment, but was released, subject to the prosecutor retrying the defendant at any time in his discretion. The Court held that this violated the right to a speedy trial.

2. Right to Public Trial

The 6th Amendment guarantees the right to a "public trial." The defendant's right extends to all criminal prosecutions and all phases of them, from jury selection to the final verdict. It has even been held to extend to pre-trial evidence suppression hearings.[185] The Supreme Court has stated that the right to a public trial safeguards against attempts to use "courts as instruments of persecution" and as checks on "possible abuse of judicial power." In addition, a public trial may encourage potential witnesses to come forward and may make testifying witnesses more truthful, for fear of contradiction by others with knowledge of the case who are sitting in the audience

---

179 393 U.S. 374, 377 (1969), quoting *United States v. Ewell*, 383 U.S. 116, 120 (1966).

180 *Strunk v. United States*, 412 U.S. 434 (1972).

181 *Smith v. Hooey*, 393 U.S. 374 (1969). Parole is conditional release before the end of the prisoner's sentence. *See* Chapter XIV, p. 528.

182 18 U.S.C.A. §§3161-3174. This act provides that information or indictment is to be issued 30 days after a defendant is arrested or served with a summons, and trial is to commence within 70 days of the filing of the information or indictment. There are numerous exceptions to the time requirements. The remedy for a violation of the Act is dismissal of the charges, sometimes with and sometimes without the right to reinstate charges.

183 LAFAVE & ISRAEL, *supra* note 1, at 797-798. States typically require trials to commence anywhere from 75 to 180 days arrest, indictment, or the filing of an information, whichever comes first. In most states, where a defendant has shown by timely motion that the time required by the statute or court rule has elapsed, the remedy for violating the statute or court rule is dismissal with prejudice.

184 *Klopfer v. North Carolina*, 386 U.S. 213 (1967)

185 *Waller v. Georgia*, 467 U.S. 39 (1984).

and might come forward.[186] The public trial requirement is met so long as the public in general has free access to a defendant's criminal trial. The right is not violated just because all persons who wish to attend a trial cannot be accommodated.

To show that the right has been violated, a defendant need not show prejudice to his case; he need only show that the public was improperly excluded, and he will be granted a new trial.[187] The 6th Amendment right to a public trial is the defendant's alone, and exclusion of the public is not a violation if the defendant has waived his right. However, the press and members of the public may have a separate *1st Amendment* right of access to court proceedings.[188]

3. Right to a Jury Trial

In NM, 12 person jury in criminal trial

The 6th Amendment guarantees the right to trial by jury in criminal prosecutions for all "non-petty" offenses, defined as crimes for which the potential punishment is more than 6 months.[189] Historically, the number of jurors on a jury was 12. However, the Supreme Court has held that it is constitutional for states to convene juries of as few as 6 in criminal cases, concluding that having 12 jurors was nothing more than "historical accident."[190] Today, 33 states have authorized juries of less than 12 in at least some kinds of criminal cases.[191] The number of jurors for federal criminal cases remains at 12 as a matter of non-constitutional law, so there has never been the occasion to determine definitively if the federal government is required to use a jury of 12. Although the right to a jury trial is generally thought to be for the protection of the defendant, the prosecution has a right to a jury trial even if the defendant does not want one in the federal system and in 25 states.[192]

As for the vote margin needed to decide a case, the Supreme Court has held that unanimity is not a constitutional requirement for states. The Court has approved a 10-2 vote as sufficient for conviction, and certain members of the Court have hinted that a 9-3 vote might be constitutional.[193] However, if the state uses six-person juries, unanimity is required.[194] Notwithstanding the constitutional latitude states enjoy with criminal juries, all but 5 states require unanimous verdicts as a matter of their own law, as does the federal government.[195]

4. Right to an Impartial Jury

In *Duncan v. Louisiana*,[196] the Supreme Court held that the 6th Amendment right

---

186 *In re Oliver*, 333 U.S. 257 (1948).

187 *Waller v. Georgia*, 467 U.S. 39 (1984).

188 *See, e.g., Gannett Co., Inc. v. DePasquale*, 443 U.S. 368 (1979); *Richmond Newspapers, Inc. v. Virginia*, 448 U.S. 555 (1980); *Globe Newspaper Co. v. Superior Court*, 457 U.S. 596 (1982). *See also* Chapter IX, p. 353.

189 *Bloom v. Illinois*, 391 U.S. 194 (1968). Multiple petty offenses may not be added together to reach the six-month period. *Lewis v. United States*, 518 U.S. 322 (1996).

190 *Williams v. Florida*, 399 U.S. 78 (1970). In *Ballew v. Georgia*, 435 U.S. 223 (1978), the Court disapproved use of a five-person jury.

191 Empirical studies have shown that 6-person juries are substantially worse than 12-person juries in their ability to decide cases properly. *See* Lempert, *supra*, Chapter III, p. 126, note 144. *See also* p. 119 (greater diversity improves jury accuracy more than greater average education).

192 *Singer v. United States*, 380 U.S. 24, 34 (1965). Stated another way, there is no right to a judge trial.

193 *Apodaca v. Oregon*, 406 U.S. 404 (1972); *Johnson v. Louisiana*, 406 U.S. 356 (1972).

194 *See Burch v. Louisiana*, 441 U.S. 130 (1979) (5-1 vote for conviction held unconstitutional).

195 As with the issue of the required size of the jury, the fact that unanimous verdicts have always been required by statute and common law has made it unnecessary to determine if a federal jury is required to be unanimous as a constitutional matter.

196 391 U.S. 145 (1968).

to an "impartial jury" was applicable to the states through the 14th Amendment's due process clause. In *Taylor v. Louisiana*,[197] the Court held that all defendants are entitled to be tried by juries drawn from a pool representing a fair cross-section of the community. A "jury pool made up only of segments of the populace [or excluding] large, distinctive groups" does not serve the purpose of a jury, which is "to guard against the exercise of arbitrary power." Though the jury *pool* must represent a cross-section, the actual jury that is eventually selected need not represent a fair-cross section.[198] However, if peremptory challenges are being used to exclude prospective jurors on grounds of their race, ethnic or national heritage, or gender, such action by either the prosecution or the defense is unconstitutional. To succeed in peremptorily challenging any juror, the prosecutor or the defense may be called upon to justify the challenge as based on a non-discriminatory reason.[199]

The 6th Amendment also states that defendants have the right to be tried by a jury "in the State and district wherein the crime shall have been committed." State constitutions often provide that trial by jury should take place in the county where the crime charged was alleged to have been committed.

5. Right to Confront Accusers

The 6th Amendment also guarantees that the accused "shall enjoy the right . . . to be confronted with the witnesses against him . . . ." This right stems from the long adversary tradition that recognizes the value of giving a defendant the opportunity to see his or her accusers publicly and to cross-examine them. A paradigm case is *Pointer v. Texas*,[200] in which a robbery victim had testified against the defendant at the preliminary hearing, but subsequently moved out of state.[201] At trial, the prosecution introduced a transcript of the victim's testimony and the defendant was convicted. This, the Court held, violated the right of confrontation.

The right to confront one's accusers includes the right to cross-examine them. Thus, in *Davis v. Alaska*,[202] the prosecution witness, a juvenile delinquent on probation for burglary, testified against the defendant, but the trial court entered a protective order prohibiting the witness from being cross-examined. The Supreme Court held this to be a violation of the right of confrontation. And in *Bruton v. United States*,[203] Bruton was implicated in his co-defendant Evan's confession, but Bruton was unable to cross-examine Evans because Evans had exercised his right not to take the stand. Although the jury was told that Evans's confession should be considered solely as evidence of his guilt and not Bruton's, the Supreme Court held that this was insufficient protection. If such a co-defendant confession is used, it must be edited remove any reference to the defendant.[204]

---

197 419 U.S. 522 (1975).

198 *Fay v. New York*, 332 U.S. 261 (1947); *Lockhart v. McCree*, 476 U.S. 162 (1986); *Holland v. Illinois*, 493 U.S. 474 (1990).

199 *See Batson v. Kentucky*, 476 U.S. 79 (1986) (race); *Hernandez v. New York*, 500 U.S. 352 (1991) (Latin American heritage); *J.E.B. v. Alabama ex rel. T.B.*, 511 U.S. 127 (1994) (sex). The Court extended the prohibition to defense challenges in criminal cases in *Georgia v. McCollum*, 505 U.S.42 (1992). *See also*, *Purkett v. Elem*, 514 U.S. 765 (1995) (clarifying procedures for implementing *Batson*). Peremptory challenges were discussed in Chapter III, p. 90.

200 380 U.S. 400 (1965).

201 Preliminary hearings, at which the prosecutor must present enough evidence to bind the defendant over for trial, were discussed *supra* p. 263.

202 415 U.S. 308 (1974).

203 391 U.S. 123 (1968).

204 *See also Gray v. Maryland*, 523 U.S. 185 (1998) (using "[deleted]" for defendant not enough).

It is possible for the accused to waive the right of confrontation by obstreperous behavior in the courtroom. Consequently, it did not violate any confrontation right when the trial judge excluded the defendant from his own trial after he had used vile language and engaged in other disruptive behavior, had been repeatedly warned and was told he could return to the trial anytime if he agreed to behave himself.[205]

6. Right to Counsel at Trial

Relying on the 6th Amendment right to counsel, the Supreme Court has held that state and federal governments must appoint an attorney for anyone accused of a felony who cannot afford an attorney. The Court held that "lawyers in criminal courts are necessities, not luxuries," and that "in our adversary system of criminal justice, any person haled into court, who is too poor to hire a lawyer, cannot be assured a fair trial unless counsel is provided for him."[206] Counsel must also be appointed for one accused of a misdemeanor where a conviction on the misdemeanor could result in even one day in jail.[207]

A person has the right to waive his right to the assistance of counsel and represent himself at his criminal trial, no matter how ill-advised that choice might be. In *Faretta v. California*,[208] the defendant had been granted permission to represent himself. Later, the trial judge appointed a public defender, because he felt that the defendant was not knowledgeable enough to defend himself. The defendant was convicted, but the Supreme Court reversed the conviction, holding that "the right to defend is given directly to the accused."

The right to counsel means the right to the *effective* assistance of counsel. As the Supreme Court observed in *Strickland v. Washington*,[209] the mere fact "[t]hat a person who happens to be a lawyer is present at trial alongside the accused" will not alone meet the requirements of the 6th Amendment. However, the 6th Amendment standard for counsel's performance is rather low. A conviction will be reversed only where "counsel's conduct so undermined the proper functioning of the adversarial process that the trial cannot be relied on as having produced a just result."[210]

7. Right Not to Testify

The 5th Amendment's self-incrimination clause has been discussed as it applies to interrogations by the police. The clause is also applicable at the trial stage, where it prevents the defendant from being forced to testify at trial. The right also applies and the 5th Amendment privilege may be asserted in any setting where the testimony could be used against the person in a criminal proceeding. The setting in which the

---

205 *Illinois v. Allen*, 397 U.S. 337 (1970).

206 *Gideon v. Wainwright*, 372 U.S. 335 (1963) (state); *Johnson v. Zerbst*, 304 U.S. 458 (1938) (federal).

207 *Argersinger v. Hamlin*, 407 U.S. 25 (1972). However, if the case involves a misdemeanor for which only a fine is to be imposed, there is no right to appointed counsel. *Scott v. Illinois*, 440 U.S. 367 (1979). Moreover, the uncounseled conviction may be used to enhance the sentence of a later crime. *Nichols v. United States*, 511 U.S. 738 (1994) (drunk driving conviction punished only by a fine used to enhance prison sentence on conviction of later federal drug charges).

208 422 U.S. 806 (1975).

209 466 U.S. 668, 685 (1984).

210 A defendant's right to effective assistance of counsel applies to plea bargaining as well. *Hill v. Lockhart*, 474 U.S. 52 (1985); *United States v. Gordon*, 156 F.3d 376, 380 (2d Cir. 1998) (attorney breached his duty as a criminal defense lawyer "to advise his client fully on whether a particular plea to a charge appears desirable" when the attorney "grossly underestimat[ed his client's] sentencing exposure") privilege may be claimed may be anywhere — at a police station, a civil trial, a legislative or administrative hearing, or a grand jury proceeding.[211]

The right not to testify necessarily includes within it the right not to have that silence used against the defendant. The trial court must instruct the jury on this point and the prosecutor is not allowed to comment on the defendant's silence. For example, in *Griffin v. California*,[212] the trial judge had instructed the jury that when a defendant does not testify in his own defense, but it is reasonable to expect him to deny or explain evidence presented against him because of facts within his knowledge, the jury may consider his failure to testify as proof against him. The prosecutor argued at the close of the case that the defendant "certainly" knew what had happened to the victim, but had refused to tell the jury what he knew. The Supreme Court held that comment on a defendant's refusal to testify, made by either a court or a prosecutor, violated the self-incrimination clause.[213]

Despite these advantages of the right against self-incrimination, defendants who choose to take the stand must take the same oath to tell the truth as any other witness. Theoretically then, a criminal defendant could be prosecuted for perjury for taking the stand and falsely denying involvement in the crime. This rarely happens in practice, however, as prosecutors are usually satisfied with the verdict of guilty in the principal case and know the difficulties of proving perjury beyond a reasonable doubt.[214]

The right against self-incrimination applies to everyone, not just to defendants in criminal cases. However, witnesses may be forced to testify against a defendant if the prosecutor has granted those witnesses "immunity" from prosecution based on the evidence they give.[215] Since immunity removes any self-incriminating effect of their testimony, witnesses may not decline to testify. If a witness still refuses to testify even after being granted immunity, that witness can be held in contempt of court and punished accordingly. One method of enforcing orders to testify is to jail the witness until the witness agrees to testify.[216]

8. Burden of Proof

Closely related to the right not to testify is the due process requirement articulated in *In re Winship*:[217] that the prosecution has the burden of proof as to "every fact necessary to constitute" the charged crime and that those facts must be proved "beyond a reasonable doubt." It is perhaps strange that so fundamental a right is not set out explicitly in the Bill of Rights, but instead had to be inferred from the due process clauses of the Constitution. The *Winship* requirement imposes two different requirements. First, it imposes a quantum of proof requirement on judge and jury,

---

211 Fear of prosecution under the laws of a foreign country are not sufficient to invoke the privilege. *United States v. Balsys*, 524 U.S. 666 (1998) (suspected Nazi collaborator could not refuse to testify in a investigation that could lead to his deportation and prosecution in Lithuania or Israel).

212 380 U.S. 609 (1965).

213 *See also Carter v. Kentucky*, 450 U.S. 288 (1981) (jury instruction on defendant's silence).

214 Not only may perjury be prosecuted, an untrue denial of guilt under questioning by a Federal investigator can be prosecuted as a crime under the Federal false-statements law. *Brogan v. United States*, 522 U.S. 398 (1998).

215 Such a grant of immunity is only from *use* of the compelled statements to prosecute the person; it does not bar a prosecution that is based on evidence *independent* of the compelled statements. *Zicarelli v. New Jersey*, 406 U.S. 472 (1972).

216 Imprisonment until the person complies would be civil contempt. *See* Chapter VII, p. 238.

217 397 U.S. 358 (1970).

prohibiting them from using any lower standard of proof of facts necessary for conviction than proof "beyond a reasonable doubt."[218] Second, it assures that the burden of proof on the elements of an offense may not be shifted to the defense in a way that forces defendants to prove their innocence.[219]

This shifting may not be done indirectly through presumptions either.[220] Thus, in *Sandstrom v. Montana*,[221] the Court held invalid a jury instruction given in a deliberate homicide case that stated that "the law presumes that a person intends the ordinary consequences of his voluntary acts." This violated the *Winship* rule because it could be understood by the jury as shifting the burden to the defendant to disprove intent once the prosecution had proved his voluntary act of causing the death of the victim. Even more problematic are mandatory presumptions. Thus, in *Carella v. California*,[222] the Court unanimously held invalid under *Winship* a California law providing that anyone who fails to return a rental vehicle within 5 days of its due date is presumed to have stolen it.

Despite *Winship*'s close regulation of burden shifting as to the *elements* of an offense, it does not prevent the state from placing the burden of proof on the defendant as to *defenses*.[223] What standard of proof the defense may constitutionally be required to meet in proving defenses is not completely clear. The issue does not often come up, since most jurisdictions impose a "preponderance of the evidence" standard — the most lax standard and the one used in civil cases.[224] The Court in a 1952 case approved Oregon's requirement that the defense prove insanity "beyond a reasonable doubt," but that case predates the due process revolution of the 1960s.[225] Moreover, the Court in 1996 held that the defense's burden of proving mental incompetence *to stand trial* may not be higher than the civil "preponderance of the evidence" standard.[226]

The Court has also made clear that the *Winship* requirement does prevent a state from preventing the defense from introducing certain kinds of evidence in defense of a criminal charge. In *Montana v. Egelhoff*,[227] the defendant in an intentional homicide case sought to prove that he was so intoxicated that he was unable to form the intent to kill, but he was barred from doing so by a statute prohibiting any evidence of a

---

218 *See* Chapter III, p. 108, where jury instructions explaining the criminal standard of "beyond a reasonable doubt" and the civil standard of "preponderance of the evidence" are set out.

219 *Mullaney v. Wilbur*, 421 U.S. 684 (1975) (in murder prosecution, defendant could not be required to negate malice by proving sudden provocation). *Compare Patterson v. New York, infra* note 223.

220 *Winship* also does not affect either the burden or the standard of proof in suppression hearings. *See Colorado v. Conelly*, 479 U.S. 157 (1986) (prosecution need only prove waiver of *Miranda* rights by a preponderance of evidence).

221 442 U.S. 510 (1979).

222 491 U.S. 263 (1989).

223 *Patterson v. New York*, 432 U.S. 197 (1977) (state may require that defendant in a murder prosecution prove the affirmative defense of extreme emotional disturbance that reduces the crime to manslaughter).

224 This was the case in *Patterson, supra* note 223.

225 *Leland v. Oregon*, 343 U.S. 790 (1952).

226 *Cooper v. Oklahoma*, 517 U.S. 348 (1996). *But see United States v. Amos*, 803 F.2d 419 (8th Cir. 1986) (upholding on authority of *Leland* federal statute's imposing on the defense the burden of proving insanity by "clear and convincing"). The different treatment of insanity as a defense to a crime and incompetence to stand trial may lie in the fact that the insanity defense is not constitutionally required, while it violates due process to try a person who is so incompetent to stand trial.

227 518 U.S. 37 (1996). The case is also discussed in Chapter XIV, p. 517.

defendant's state of alcohol intoxication. The Court upheld the statute.[228]

9. Other Constitutional Protections

Other rights not explicitly mentioned in the Bill of Rights — like the right in *Winship* — have been found in the 14th Amendment and the 5th Amendment due process clauses. Some of the practices prohibited that are not discussed elsewhere in this chapter include: defense discovery rights,[229] improper closing argument by the prosecutor,[230] violation of the right to counsel at parole revocation proceedings,[231] prohibiting a defendant's access to evidence,[232] entrapment,[233] improper conduct of the prosecutor in grand jury proceedings,[234] judicial bias,[235] prejudicial publicity,[236] and charges motivated by prosecutorial vindictiveness.[237] Since due process is a flexible concept, this list is not exhaustive.[238]

E. The Effect of Prior Proceedings: The Double Jeopardy Guarantee

The 5th Amendment provides that no one may "be subject for the same offence to be twice put in jeopardy of life or limb."[239] Double jeopardy problems typically occur in two instances: (1) when the prosecution is disappointed in an acquittal and seeks to try the defendant once again for the same crime, or (2) when the prosecution obtains a conviction, but is dissatisfied with the severity of that conviction or sentence and wishes to try a second time to convict the defendant of a more serious crime, or to obtain a higher or additional sentence. The essence of double jeopardy's protection against retrial is not just the possibility of a worse result for the defendant in the second trial, however. It is also the "continuing state of anxiety and insecurity" and the "embarrassment, expense, and ordeal" of a second trial.[240]

---

228 A plurality of four justices held exclusion of relevant evidence was constitutional because it did not offend any "principle of justice so rooted in the traditions and conscience of our people as to be ranked as fundamental." Justice Ginsberg, the fifth vote necessary for a majority, reasoned more simply that the state had a broad constitutional right to define the elements of criminal offenses and could change its concept of the moral culpability of defendants to equate sober and intoxicated defendants. Justice Ginsberg's opinion suggests a difficulty with the *Winship* doctrine: that it seems to turn on whether the state defines a given issue as an *element* of the offense or as a *defense*. If this is correct, then the state could presumably avoid the *Winship* problem by simply redefining the offense in most cases.

229 *Pennsylvania v. Ritchie*, 480 U.S. 39 (1987).

230 *Donnelly v. DeChristoforo*, 416 U.S. 637 (1974).

231 *Morrissey v. Brewer*, 408 U.S. 471 (1972) (appointed counsel required only under certain circumstances).

232 *Arizona v. Youngblood*, 488 U.S. 51 (1988).

233 *United States v. Russell*, 411 U.S. 423 (1973) (dictum). Entrapment is a defense based on the claim that the police caused the defendant to commit a crime he would not otherwise have committed. *See* Chapter XIV, p. 523.

234 *Bank of Nova Scotia v. United States*, 487 U.S. 250 (1988).

235 *Turney v. Ohio*, 273 U.S. 510 (1927) (fees paid to judge for each conviction); *Mayberry v. Pennsylvania*, 400 U.S. 455 (1971) (defendant insulted judge and same judge held defendant in contempt).

236 *Sheppard v. Maxwell*, 384 U.S. 333 (1966).

237 *Blackledge v. Perry*, 417 U.S. 21 (1974).

238 *See* Chapter VI, pp. 200-202, where the question of what procedural protections due process requires is discussed.

239 *See generally* LAFAVE & ISRAEL, *supra* note 1, §§25.1-25.5. Despite the somewhat archaic reference to "jeopardy of life or limb," double jeopardy applies to all crimes, from misdemeanors to capital felonies. *Ex parte Lange*, 85 U.S. 163 (1873).

240 *Green v. United States*, 355 U.S. 184 (1957). *See also United States v. DiFrancesco*, 449 U.S. 117 (1980) (discussing at length the purposes and history of the double jeopardy clause). Double jeopardy applies only to criminal prosecutions, so it has no effect on an ordinary civil suit following conviction. In addition, if the first acquittal was the result of bribing the judge in the first trial, a second trial is not barred on the theory that the defendant had never truly "in jeopardy" of conviction the first time.

1. When Jeopardy Attaches

It is important to know when jeopardy "attaches" to the first prosecution, since it is only if the first prosecution is terminated after that point that it "counts," and thus will bar a second trial. If the case is tried to a jury, jeopardy attaches when the jury is empaneled and sworn.[241] When the case is tried before the judge alone, jeopardy attaches when the prosecution begins its opening statement.[242] Therefore, multiple criminal complaints based on the same crime that are dismissed *before the trial stage* do not violate the prohibition against double jeopardy.

2. Retrial After a Completed Trial or Other Ruling on the Merits

Once a trial has started and jeopardy has attached, a jury *acquittal* presents the clearest bar to a second prosecution.[243] A dismissal by the judge for lack of sufficient evidence or any other form of judicial acquittal also bars re-prosecution.[244] A *conviction* after trial also bars retrial for the same offense. However, if after a conviction, a new trial takes place because the trial judge set aside the original verdict at the defendant's request, double jeopardy will not bar the second trial because the defendant sought the new trial.[245] Similar waiver results when a defendant wins a reversal of a conviction on appeal.[246] Nonetheless, double jeopardy *bars* retral if the defendant wins reversal of the first verdict from the trial or appellate court because there was insufficient evidence to support that verdict.[247]

Double jeopardy necessarily means that the prosecution cannot appeal an acquittal regardless of what errors were committed at trial, since a reversal of the acquittal would result in a second trial.[248] However, double jeopardy does not prevent the prosecution from appealing a *trial judge's order setting aside* a jury conviction — even one that is on grounds of insufficiency of the evidence. The reason for this is that reversal of the judge's order would not subject the defendant to a second trial: it would simply reinstate the original jury conviction.[249] In addition, the double jeopardy clause is not violated when the prosecution appeals the imposition of a particular *sentence* (as opposed to a judgment of guilt) that the prosecution thinks is illegal or

---

241 *Crist v. Bretz*, 437 U.S. 28 (1978).

242 *See* Chapter III, pp. 89-92, for a description of trial procedure as it relates to empaneling the jury and opening statements.

243 *See also Green v. United States*, 355 U.S. 184 (1957) (where defendant was charged alternatively with first and second degree murder, conviction for second degree murder operated as an acquittal of first degree murder); *Bullington v. Missouri*, 451 U.S. 430 (1981) (where jury had convicted defendant, but declined to impose the death penalty in first trial, death could not be imposed on retrial after defendant successfully appealed because first verdict was tantamount to a partial acquittal).

244 *Smalis v. Pennsylvania*, 476 U.S. 140 (1986). This is so regardless of how erroneous the judge's determination of lack of evidence might be. In *Smalis*, the judicial direction of acquittal was based on an erroneous understanding of the applicable law. For a discussion of the circumstances under which a judge may direct the verdict or judgment in the defendant's favor, see Chapter III, pp. 99,105.

245 *United States v. Scott*, 437 U.S. 82 (1978).

246 *Ball v. United States*, 163 U.S. 662 (1896). *See also North Carolina v. Pearce*, 395 U.S. 711 (1969) (any more severe sentence imposed after retrial must be based on conduct occurring since the first sentence).

247 *Burks v. United States*, 437 U.S. 1 (1978). *Cf. United States v. Watts*, 519 U.S. 148 (1997).

248 *Ball v. United States*, 163 U.S. 662 (1896); *Fong Foo v. United States*, 369 U.S. 141 (1978).

249 *See United States v. Wilson*, 420 U.S. 332 (1975). Thus, a distinction is drawn between a judicial acquittal *following* a jury verdict (usually referred to as a judgment notwithstanding the verdict) and one ordered mid-trial *before* a jury verdict (directed verdict of acquittal). Only if the trial is aborted *before* the verdict is retrial necessary, so that is the only situation in which double jeopardy bars a prosecution appeal from a judicial acquittal. *See* Chapter III, pp. 99, 105, for the distinction in general between judgment notwithstanding the verdict and a directed verdict.

too lenient, when that is permitted by statute. The rationale is that no retrial of the case is needed. Also, re-sentencing does not involve the same sort of government oppression as successive trials on the issue of guilt.[250]

3. Retrial After a Mistrial

Not all trials end in convictions or acquittals. Trials can abort for many other reasons, resulting in the judge declaring a mistrial.[251] If the defendant moves for or consents to the mistrial, this is often deemed a waiver of double jeopardy protections,[252] but there is no waiver when the prosecution's actions at trial provoked the defense motion for a mistrial.[253] But even mistrials granted over the defendant's objection will not bar re-prosecution of the defendant if there was "manifest necessity" for the judge to stop the trial. Such necessity exists whenever "an impartial verdict cannot be reached, or if a verdict of conviction could be reached, but would have to be set aside on appeal due to an obvious procedural error in the trial."[254] But consistent with the concern for prosecutorial oppression underlying double jeopardy, retrial is not allowed after a mistrial granted on a ground that "lend[s] itself to prosecutorial manipulation" and could "allow the prosecution the opportunity to strengthen its case."[255]

4. What is the "Same Offence"

For double jeopardy to apply, the second prosecution must be for the "same offence." A single criminal action can violate several criminal statutes, thus raising the possibility that prosecutions brought and tried separately for each "offense" would violate double jeopardy. The overall test of whether the second prosecution is the same offense was set out in *Blockburger v. United States*.[256] That test states that crimes under different statutes are different offenses if any element is different: if each offense "requires proof of an additional fact which the other does not." This would mean at the very least that a crime and any of its "lesser-included offenses" would be considered to be the same offense. A lesser-included offense of a crime is any offense that is less serious than that crime and whose elements are all included within the definition of the more serious crime. Thus, the Supreme Court has held that it violated double jeopardy to try a defendant first for operating a car without permission and then to charge him with stealing the same car, because operation of a car without permission is included within the definition of auto theft.[257]

---

250 *United States v. DiFrancesco*, 449 U.S. 117 (1980).

251 *See* Chapter III, p. 103, for a discussion of mistrials.

252 *United States v. Dinitz*, 424 U.S. 600 (1976).

253 *Dinitz, supra; Oregon v. Kennedy*, 456 U.S. 667 (1982) (second trial not barred after defense motion for mistrial was granted based on prosecutor asking witness whether witness did not do business with the defendant "because [he] is a crook?").

254 *Illinois v. Somerville*, 410 U.S. 458 (1973) (indictment did not allege essential element and could not be amended under state law; retrial allowed). For examples of cases involving "manifest necessity," *see United States v. Perez*, 22 U.S. (9 Wheat.) 579 (1824) (jury deadlocked); *Simmons v. United States*, 142 U.S. 148 (1891) (juror was found to have known the defendant personally): *Brock v. North Carolina*, 344 U.S. 424 (1953) (prosecution witnesses unexpectedly invoked their right against self-incrimination).

255 *Downum v. United States*, 372 U.S. 734 (1963) (retrial barred after mistrial granted to prosecution on ground that prosecution had not subpoenaed one of its witnesses).

256 284 U.S. 299 (1932). *See also United States v. Dixon*, 509 U.S. 688 (1993).

257 *Brown v. Ohio*, 432 U.S. 161 (1977). However, *Brown* made clear that if the lesser included offense were prosecuted first before facts constituting the more serious offense developed, then a second prosecution on the more serious charge is not barred. For example, if a defendant is convicted of attempted murder for shooting the victim and the victim dies from those injuries, a second prosecution for murder is not barred.

5. Collateral Estoppel

The classic *Blockburger* definition of "same offense" would make kidnaping, robbery, and murder arising out of a *single* criminal episode all "different offenses." Thus, it would seem that the prosecution could proceed to trial on the kidnaping charge first and, if the defendant is acquitted, it could follow up with a second prosecution for robbery or even a third trial for murder, should the defendant be acquitted of robbery. What may prevent this is the doctrine of issue preclusion or collateral estoppel.[258] The leading case is *Ashe v. Swenson*,[259] where the defendant was prosecuted for robbing one of 6 players at a card game.[260] At his first trial, his defense was that he was elsewhere at the time of the crime, and he was acquitted by a jury. The prosecution then tried to prosecute him for robbery of the second card player. The Supreme Court held that, since it was clear that the jury acquitted the defendant because it was convinced that the government had not shown that the defendant participated in the robbery, the government was bound by that determination in any later proceedings involving that defendant.[261] However, the Court has also held that evidence of a defendant's participation in a burglary for which he was acquitted may be introduced in a later trial for bank robbery to bolster identification of the defendant as the bank robber and to show his connection with another person implicated in the bank robbery.[262]

6. Double Jeopardy and Dual Sovereignty

Successive prosecutions by *state* and *federal* governments for criminal offenses arising out of the same criminal episode are not barred by double jeopardy. These are permitted under the "dual sovereignty" doctrine. That doctrine is based on the notion that "an act denounced as a crime by both national and state sovereignties is an offense against the peace and dignity of both and may be punished by each."[263] The federal government may prosecute a defendant for the same conduct for which the defendant had already been convicted by a state,[264] and a state may prosecute a defendant for the same conduct for which the defendant had already been convicted by the federal government.[265] However, when the first prosecution was in state court, federal policy requires that a later federal prosecution should be undertaken only if there is a compelling federal interest in pursuing it.[266] A recent example of the operation of the "dual sovereignty" doctrine was the prosecution of Los Angeles police officers in federal court for civil rights violations for the beating of motorist Rodney King following their acquittal on state assault charges in state court. Issues of dual sovereignty are likely to increase as the number of federal crimes increases.

---

258 For a general discussion of collateral estoppel or issue preclusion, *see* Chapter VII, pp. 241-242

259 397 U.S. 436 (1970).

260 The robbery of each card player was a different offense because each was committed against a different victim.

261 The prosecution cannot *take advantage* of a prior finding against the defendant. *Simpson v. Florida*, 403 U.S. 384 (1971). *Compare* Chapter VII, pp. 241-242 (offensive use allowed in civil cases)..

262 *Dowling v. United States*, 493 U.S. 342 (1990). FRE 404(b) permits proof of other wrongful acts if offered to prove, not bad character, but identity. *See* Chapter III, p. 108.

263 *United States v. Lanza*, 260 U.S. 377 (1922). *See generally* LaFave & Israel, p. 1083.

264 *Abbate v. United States*, 359 U.S. 187 (1959)

265 *Bartkus v. Illinois*, 359 U.S. 121 (1959)

266 LaFave & Israel, *supra* note 1, p. 1084, n.8, citing U.S. Attorneys' Manual §9-2.142. *See also Petite v. United States*, 361 U.S. 529, 530 (1960) (*per curiam*).

The same notion of dual sovereignty permits two states to prosecute the defendant for the same conduct. In *Heath v. Alabama*,[267] the victim had been kidnaped in Alabama, taken to Georgia and murdered. The Court held that it did not violate double jeopardy for the defendant to be convicted of felony murder in Alabama and ordinary murder in Georgia. However, dual sovereignty does not work where there is a violation of both state law and a city or county ordinance, since cities are subdivisions of the state and are considered to be the same sovereign. In one case, the defendant stole a mural from the city hall and damaged it. He was prosecuted and convicted under city ordinances for destruction of city property and for disorderly breach of the peace. Then he was prosecuted and convicted of felony grand larceny under state law. The Court held that conviction on the city ordinance charges barred the state larceny prosecution. [268]

F. Limitations on Punishment

1. The Death Penalty

The Eighth Amendment states that "cruel and unusual punishments [shall not be] inflicted." Based upon this, the Supreme Court in 1972 banned the use of capital punishment.[269] The reasoning for the decision was that the death penalty was selectively invoked on an arbitrary basis by judges and juries. By 1976, however, states had revised their laws to limit the discretion of judges and juries and to require them to consider relevant aggravating and mitigating circumstances specified by statute. The Court held that these new laws did not violate the Constitution. While the Court admitted that the death penalty was "cruel" punishment, it denied that it was "unusual" — either today or in 1791, when the 8th Amendment was ratified.[270]

While the constitutional problem with many death penalty laws has been the wide discretion permitted, death as an *automatic* punishment upon conviction for certain crimes has also been struck down. The Supreme Court has struck down statutes providing for mandatory death for all first-degree murder[271] and for killing a police officer or firefighter.[272] A plurality of the Court has also held that a death sentence was not acceptable for rape of an adult woman because it did not involve the killing of another human being.[273] The Court also reversed the death sentence of a defendant who had committed a murder when he was only 15 years old. A plurality opinion thought that "evolving standards of decency" under the 8th Amendment would prevent the execution under any circumstances of a person for a crime committed before the age of 16.[274] And the ancient common law principle that an insane person may not be put to death has been held to be enshrined in the 8th Amendment.[275]

---

267 474 U.S. 82 (1985)

268 *Waller v. Florida*, 397 U.S. 387 (1970).

269 *Furman v. Georgia*, 408 U.S. 238 (1972).

270 *Gregg v. Georgia*, 428 U.S. 153 (1976). *See also McCleskey v. Kemp*, 481 U.S. 279 (1987) (rejecting challenge to death penalty based on it being invoked in a racially discriminatory manner).

271 *Woodson v. North Carolina*, 428 U.S. 280 (1976).

272 *Roberts v. Louisiana*, 431 U.S. 633 (1977).

273 *Coker v. Georgia*, 433 U.S. 584 (1977). Commentators believe that this nonetheless leaves open the possibility that a death sentence is constitutional for some non-murder offenses, such as treason, airplane hijacking or kidnaping, as pointed out by the dissenters in *Coker*. *See* LAFAVE & SCOTT, *supra* note 1, at 180-181.

274 *Thompson v. Oklahoma*, 487 U.S. 815 (1988).

275 *Ford v. Wainwright*, 477 U.S. 399 (1986). This results in what has been called a "cure-to-kill" situation, whereby a prisoner is treated in order to be sufficiently sane to be executed.

2. Other Forms of Cruel and Unusual Punishment

Arguments that the 8th Amendment prohibits terms of imprisonment that are disproportionately long in light of the offense have generally been difficult to win. In *Harmelin v. Michigan*,[276] the Supreme Court held 5-4 that it did not violate the 8th Amendment for a state to impose a sentence of mandatory life imprisonment without parole for simple possession of 650 grams (1.56 pounds) of cocaine. The majority did not agree on a rationale. The four dissenters vehemently disagreed with the judgment, finding the sentence to be disproportionate to the offense.[277]

3. Civil Forfeitures

Prior to 1970, civil forfeiture of property was available as an additional remedy in criminal cases, but was not often used. Its increased popularity among prosecutors recently has raised several constitutional questions. For constitutional purposes, a distinction must be drawn between *in personam* civil penalties and *in rem* forfeiture actions.

In personam civil forfeitures are for the purpose of punishing the owner for transgressions against the criminal law and typically involve seizure of property unrelated to the offense. In pursuing them the government must afford the property owner the same panoply of due process rights applicable to a criminal case.[278] In addition, any such punitive forfeiture that is "grossly disproportional" to the offense violates that 8th Amendment's ban on "excessive fines." The Court recently so held in a case where federal prosecutors sought the forfeiture of $357,144 in cash from a man and his family, who tried to bring it with them on a flight to Cyprus in order to repay a family debt. He had failed to report it in accordance with a Federal law requiring that all currency being taken out of the country in excess of $10,000 be declared. Given that there was no evidence that the money was the product of any illegal conduct, the Court affirmed the lower court's determination that $15,000 was sufficient.[279]

By contrast, *in rem* civil forfeitures are actions directly against "guilty" property —property used in the commission of crime. Such actions are "remedial" rather than punitive since their purpose is simply to remove the offending property from circulation without regard to any sanction against a criminal defendant. As remedial procedures, they are not subject to the excessive fines clause because the forfeiture, not being punishment, is not a fine.[280] In addition, it does not matter that innocent owners or co-owners of the property may lose their interest as a result of the forfeiture. This was demonstrated in a recent case where Michigan seized an automobile a man had used to have sex with a prostitute. The car was titled in both the man's and his wife's names and the wife sought to claim at least her half of the

---

276 501 U.S. 597 (1991).

277 *But see Solem v. Helm*, 463 U.S. 277 (1983) (requiring sentences to be proportional to the offense). It is interesting to note that the Michigan Supreme Court, reviewing the same law in question under the *Michigan* Constitution, held such a sentence unconstitutional. The Michigan Constitution forbids "cruel *or* unusual" punishments, unlike the "cruel *and* unusual" punishments prohibited by the federal Constitution. *People v. Bullock*, 485 N.W.2d 866 (1992).

278 *One 1958 Plymouth Sedan v. Pennsylvania*, 380 U.S. 693 (1969).

279 *United States v. Bajakajian*, 524 U.S. 321 (1998).

280 *See United States v. Ursery*, 518 U.S. 267 (1996) (*in rem* civil forfeiture of property used in a crime does not constitute double punishment for purposes of the double jeopardy clause). A purportedly remedial forfeiture may become a punitive one if it goes beyond instrumentalities of the crime to those that merely "facilitate" the crime, in which case it is subject to the excessive fines limitation. *Austin v. United States*, 509 U.S. 602 (1993). *See also United States v. Bajakajian*, *supra* note 279.

car. The Supreme Court determined that the state's deprivation of her interest did not violate due process. The Court did note that if the property used was stolen from the owner or if the owner did everything possible to avoid having the property put to the unlawful use, a constitutional question about forfeiture might arise, but there was no general "innocent owner" defense.[281]

G. Rights on Appeal

Right to Appeal The United States Supreme Court has said in *dictum* that criminal defendants have no constitutional right to appeal their convictions.[282] However, state and federal defendants by statute have the right to at least one appeal, so there has been no need to decide the issue definitively.

Right to Counsel on Appeal Even if the right to appeal is only statutory, the Supreme Court held in *Douglas v. California*[283] that the 14th Amendment requires that states provide counsel to convicted indigent criminal defendants on their first appeal of right. *Douglas* involved a California rule that gave appellate courts the discretion to appoint or deny counsel to indigent appellants, depending on the appellate court's determination of whether or not the appointment of appellate counsel would be advantageous to the appellant or "helpful" to the court. No such preliminary review of the necessity of appellate counsel was made when an appellant could afford to hire appellate counsel. The Supreme Court found that the rule discriminated between rich and poor appellants, thus violating the 14th Amendment, relying on both the due process and equal protection clauses of that Amendment. Beyond the first appeal as of right, however, there is no right to counsel.[284] There is similarly no right to appointed counsel for collateral attacks on convictions by way of federal *habeas corpus*[285] or state discretionary post-conviction remedies,[286] even when a death sentence is involved.[287]

Appeals by the Government As discussed earlier, because of the double jeopardy clause, the government does not have the right to appeal an acquittal. It may, however, appeal sentences, reversals of convictions and orders for new trials.[288]

Harmless Error Just because a defendant is able to show on appeal that constitutional violations took place at the trial level, this will not result automatically in the reversal of the defendant's conviction. Such violations might have constituted "harmless error." Because of accusatorial principles and the importance of constitutional rights, the burden is generally on the prosecutor to show that the error was harmless and was harmless beyond a reasonable doubt.[289] Certain kinds of constitutional errors will automatically call for reversal despite the *Chapman* rule,

---

281 *Bennis v. Michigan*, 516 U.S. 442 (1996). *See also Calero-Toledo v. Pearson Yacht Leasing Co.*, 416 U.S. 663 (1974) (innocent lessor-owner of yacht used in drug smuggling has no defense to forfeiture). The Court has held that procedural due process requires prior notice and opportunity for hearing before seizure if there is no emergency. *United States v. James Daniel Good Real Property*, 510 U.S. 43 (1993).

282 *McKane v. Durtson*, 153 U.S. 684 (1894) and *Jones v. Barnes*, 463 U.S. 745 (1983).

283 372 U.S. 353 (1963).

284 *Ross v. Moffitt*, 417 U.S. 600 (1974).

285 *Pennsylvania v. Finley*, 481 U.S. 551 (1987). *Habeas corpus* was discussed *supra* p. 267-268.

286 *Pennsylvania v. Finley*, 481 U.S. 551 (1987).

287 *Murray v. Giarratano*, 492 U.S. 1 (1989) (plurality opinion). States, however, must make legal materials reasonably available so that inmates can prepare their own petitions. *Bounds v. Smith*, 430 U.S. 817 (1977).

288 *See supra*, p. 309.

289 *Chapman v. California*, 386 U.S. 18 (1970).

however. This is particularly true of errors that could have affected the fact-finding process.[290]

---

[290] *See Sullivan v. Louisiana*, 508 U.S. 275 (1993) (constitutionally deficient jury instruction on reasonable doubt required reversal despite harmless error argument by the state).

CHAPTER IX

CONSTITUTIONAL LAW

Constitutional law pervades virtually every area of law in the United States, As should be clear from the number of constitutional issues already discussed.[1] This chapter will deal with some of the important areas of constitutional law that have not been discussed. The discussion here is necessarily a cursory one. As with the constitutional criminal procedure area, the cases cited or discussed in this chapter represent only a small portion of the relevant caselaw.[2]

PART I: Judicial Review, Structure and Powers

A. Judicial Review

Judicial review was officially recognized in 1803 in *Marbury v. Madison*.[3] The rationale of *Marbury* and some pitfalls of judicial review were mentioned in Chapter I and will not be repeated here. What is needed here are some more specific comments on the nature of judicial review and constitutional interpretation.

1. The General Nature of Judicial Review

Constitutional Review as a By-Product of Private Litigation The basic idea behind *Marbury* is that constitutional judicial review of laws is nothing extraordinary. As the Court observed, the first "province and duty" of all courts is to determine "what the law is" in any case before them. "The law" includes the Constitution and, in particular, its supremacy clause setting the hierarchy of laws. Consequently, when a court discovers that a statute violates the Constitution, it simply engages in a "choice-of-law" determination, applying the Constitution and ignoring the statute.

This rationale for judicial review has three effects on how such review is carried out. First, unlike some countries, the United States has no special constitutional tribunal separate from the ordinary courts that effectuates judicial review. Any court at any level may and indeed every court at every level *must* engage in constitutional judicial review — from the lowest municipal court to the U.S. Supreme Court. Thus, judicial review in the United States is a decentralized rather than a centralized system of constitutional review.[4]

---

1 Constitutional law issues discussed elsewhere in this book: judicial review (pp. 9-11), separation of power (pp. 4-9), federalism and Congressional power (pp. 21-27), jury trial right in civil cases (pp. 291-292), jury trial right in criminal cases (pp. 234-235), constitutional doctrines affecting the legal profession (pp. 137, 138); appointment and impeachment of federal judges (pp. 212-214), procedural due process (pp. 198-202), separation of powers and agencies (pp. 211-215), due process limits on state court power (pp. 245-248, 252-258), full faith and credit (pp. 250-252), defendants' rights in the investigation and prosecution of criminal cases (pp. 270-303), constitutional limits on tort recovery for libel by public officials (pp. 426-428) and constitutional limits on condemnation of property (pp. 449-451).

2 Standard one-volume treatises on constitutional law are JOHN E. NOWAK & RONALD D. ROTUNDA, HORNBOOK ON CONSTITUTIONAL LAW, 5TH ED. (West 1995) and ERWIN CHEMERINSKY, CONSTITUTIONAL LAW: PRINCIPLES AND POLICIES (Aspen 1997). An unusually useful casebook is DANIEL FARBER, WILLIAM ESKRIDGE AND PHILIP FRICKEY, CONSTITUTIONAL LAW, 2D ED. (West 1998). *See also* Robert A. Sedler, "Constitutional Law of the United States," in INTERNATIONAL ENCYCLOPEDIA OF LAWS (Kluwer Int'l and Taxation 1994); JEROME A. BARON & C. THOMAS DIENES, CONSTITUTIONAL LAW IN NUTSHELL (West 1999).

3 5 U.S. (1 Cranch.) 137 (1803).

4 Separate constitutional tribunals are the norm in Europe. *See* Louis Favoreau, "Constitutional Review in Europe," in LOUIS HENKIN AND ALBERT J. ROSENTHAL, EDS., CONSTITUTIONALISM AND RIGHTS: THE INFLUENCE OF THE UNITED STATES CONSTITUTION ABROAD 40-42, 56 (Columbia U. Press 1990); MAURO CAPPELLETTI, THE JUDICIAL PROCESS IN COMPARATIVE PERSPECTIVE 132-143 (Oxford U. 1989).

Second, courts decide constitutional issues when they arise in ordinary lawsuits. Any person may challenge the constitutionality of any law or other governmental action that adversely affects that person. The right is not limited just to certain public officials or entities as it is in some countries.[5] And at least the federal courts may decide constitutional issues *only if* they arise in an actual "case or controversy."[6] Federal courts and the courts of most states may not render advisory opinions.[7]

Finally, judicial review is supposed to be judicial in the sense that a court deciding a constitutional question makes a legal rather than a political determination. And it does so by doing what courts normally do — by interpreting enacted law. Indeed, the "political question" is designed to prevent courts from doing anything else.[8]

Judicial Review as a Special Public and Political Process   Despite the above, there is evidence to undercut each of the three points made above. While it is true that judicial review is decentralized and thus available in any court, and that the U.S. Supreme Court is simply another "ordinary" court, there is a reverence with which lawyers and lower court judges treat even *obiter dictum* in Supreme Court constitutional decisions that gives those decisions the aura of being, not just the "final word," but the "only word" on the meaning of the Constitution. The feeling is that an issue of constitutional law is not *really* settled until the Supreme Court resolves it and that the decisions of the lower federal and state courts (not to mention the opinions of legislators or executive officials) are somehow only "best guesses" about what the Constitution means.

The Supreme Court has not exactly discouraged this impression. For example, in the 1992 decision reaffirming its 1973 abortion decision, the Court spoke of the abortion case as involving "the sort of intensely divisive controversy" that "has a dimension that the resolution of the normal case does not carry." Such "rare precedential force" occurs when "the Court's interpretation of the Constitution calls the contending sides of a national controversy to end their national division by accepting a common mandate rooted in the Constitution." Whatever this statement means, it goes beyond what the normal preclusive and precedential effects a judicial decision would have in an ordinary non-constitutional case.[9]

Second, any attempt to pass of judicial review as a by-product of ordinary litigation does not take into account "test case" litigation that is routinely brought today in the Supreme Court and the lower federal courts. Many suits are truly "public law litigation" that go beyond the private interests of any party.[10] The focus instead is

---

5 *See* Favoreau, *supra* note 4, at 51-53. Even though the suit may not include the government as a party, its views are always made known where needed by way of *amicus curiae* briefs. *See* Chapter II, p. 41, note 26.

6 *See Liverpool, N.Y. & P. Steamship Co. v. Comm'rs of Emigration*, 113 U.S. 33, 39 (1885) (federal courts may not "pronounce any statute . . . void, because irreconcilable with the constitution, except as it is called upon to adjudge the legal rights of litigants in actual controversies.") and *infra* pp. 310-312.

7 *See* NOWAK & ROTUNDA, *supra* note , at 55 (describing the Court's 1793 refusal to answer a list of legal questions involving the United States' attempts to remain neutral in the war between France and England) and *infra* pp. 310-312. *But see* Mass. G. L. A. Const., pt. 2, c. 3. art. 2, Amend., Art. 85 and Mich. Const. Art. 3 §8 (empowering courts of Massachusetts and Michigan to render advisory opinions).

8 The political question doctrine is discussed *infra* p. 313.

9 *Planned Parenthood of Southeastern Pennsylvania v. Casey*, 505 U.S. 833, 866 (1992). The Court evinced a similar attitude with regard to its racial desegregation decision in *Brown v. Board of Education*, 347 U.S. 483 (1954). *See Cooper v. Aaron*, 358 U.S. 1 (1958).

10 *See* Abram Chayes, *Public Law Litigation and the Burger Court*, 96 Harv. L. Rev. 4 (1982). Class actions were discussed in Chapter VII, p. 225.

almost exclusively on the issues raised and their impact on the public at large. An example is the class action suit, in which the original plaintiff and his or her problem may be all but forgotten, but the lawsuit continues anyway on behalf of an undetermined class of persons similarly situated.[11]

Finally, as will be discussed in the next section and demonstrated in the cases, interpretation of constitutional provisions is quite different from more "ordinary" interpretations of enacted law that courts engage in. Indeed, some have suggested that constitutional review in the United States is not "judicial" at all — that it is more accurately described as a political function that has been "carefully disguised" behind the "fiction" of courts determining the law.[12] We have already seen how "judicial philosophy" is perceived to play an important role in judicial decision-making. It is clear that many of the elements of "judicial philosophy" touch on basic political values. If evidence of this is needed, one need look no further than the judicial selection process, particularly at the Supreme Court level, which is as almost as politicized and rancorous as a partisan election campaign.[13]

It is for readers to determine for themselves which of the competing models of constitutional judicial review is more accurate after considering the remaining materials in this chapter. There is abundant evidence on both sides of the question.

2. Constitutional Interpretation

Modes of Interpretation Constitutional interpretation takes various forms.[14] Sometimes it is textual and is similar to the approach courts take when interpreting statutes. In other cases, the Court will use a "functional" approach, moving to a higher level of generalization than the text employs and seeking only to give effect to the overall functions served by a particular provision or structural limitation. We saw an example of this when the caselaw dealing with separation of powers objections to administrative agencies was discussed in Chapter VI.[15] Other cases have been the subject of a "structural" approach, in which the Court reasons from the overall structure and purpose of the entire Constitution. This technique was used to some extent by the Court in *Marbury v. Madison*. In part, the type of analysis employed depends on the clarity of the Constitution's text — the clearer the text, the greater the attention to its wording. But different members of the Court have different views as to what constitutes a "clear" textual command.

Flexibility of Interpretive Methods Whatever labels might be applied to the Court's approaches to constitutional interpretation, a characteristic of most of them is that

---

11 *See Sosna v. Iowa*, 419 U.S. 393, 397-403 (1974) (determining the constitutionality of the waiting period for divorce long after the original plaintiff had obtained a divorce elsewhere because the case was certified as a class action). Class actions were discussed in Chapter VII, p. 225. *See also infra* p. 312. *See also U.S. Parole Board v. Geraghty*, 445 U.S. 388 (1980) (an action brought on behalf of a class does not become moot upon expiration of the named plaintiff's substantive claim, even though class certification has been denied; prisoner had been released from prison, but was allowed to appeal class action issue).

12 CAPPELLETTI, *supra* note 4, at 149.

13 *See* Chapter V, pp. 175-176.

14 For books discussing and excerpting principal works on constitutional theory, *see* JOHN H. GARVEY & T. ALEXANDER ALIENIKOFF, MODERN CONSTITUTIONAL THEORY: A READER, 3D ED. (West 1994) and MICHAEL GERHARDT AND THOMAS D. ROWE, CONSTITUTIONAL THEORY: ARGUMENTS AND PERSPECTIVES (Lexis 1993). *See also* PHILIP BOBBITT, THE MODALITIES OF CONSTITUTIONAL ARGUMENT 12-22 (Blackwell, Oxford 1991) and WALTER E. MURPHY, JAMES E. FLEMING & SOTIRIOS A. BARBER, AMERICAN CONSTITUTIONAL INTERPRETATION, 2D ED. (Foundation Press 1995)

15 *See* pp. 211-215.

they are very flexible.[16] As a result, much of the body of constitutional law cannot be traced to the text of the Constitution by any traditional means used interpreting other forms of enacted law.[17] In many cases, it is more accurate to say, not that a particular statute violates *the Constitution*, but that it violates a principle that *courts say* the Constitution *represents*. In the process of a court ascertaining what principles underlie the Constitution, there is ample room for judges — consciously or unconsciously — to inject all manner of political, economic or social theory into their constitutional decision-making. This often leads commentators to criticize courts in general, and the Supreme Court in particular, for engaging in "political activism" rather than applying the law.

But at least two characteristics of the Constitution invite such judicial activism. First, much of the Constitution's text is very general. And many of those general terms, such as "liberty," "due process" and "equal protection of the laws," are of a type that would require anyone seeking to define them to draw on one or another political vision or tradition. Second, the Constitution is 200 years old. Issues deemed important by the Framers have become non-issues today and new important problems have arisen that the Framers could not have foreseen. Amendment is not a realistic option for changing basic constitutional values, given the Constitution's extremely difficult amendment process, so the task of "updating" the Constitution has fallen to the courts. One could add as well that the tendency toward such "updating" is accelerated by the nature of the job of the judge, who in the process of hearing cases, is presented daily with concrete examples of laws and government practices that seem to operate in an unjust way. And common law judges are especially comfortable with judicial law-making.[18]

The tendency toward a flexible and expansive approach to constitutional interpretation is most often associated with the constitutional "rights explosion" of the 1960s, but in many ways it has existed virtually from the beginning. In 1819, in *McCulloch v. Maryland*, Chief Justice Marshall found "implied powers" behind those specifically enumerated to sustain the constitutionality of a federal statute. Further, he reasoned from the overall structure of the Constitution to find an immunity of the federal government from oppressive state taxation. He felt it sufficient to justify such action by his famous statement: "we must never forget that it is *a constitution* we are expounding."[19] He emphasized that the Constitution does not have the "prolixity" of a statute. Many parts of it are written in generalities, the better to endure for the "ages to come."

Debate Over Interpretive Methods In recent years, the question has been raised whether it is legitimate for judges interpreting the Constitution to rely on values not directly traceable to its text or its history. "Originalists" argue that it is illegitimate to go beyond the "original intent" of the Framers of the Constitution. Similar to original-

---

16 This is in sharp contrast to the approach common law courts take in their interpretation of *statutes*. *See* Chapter II, pp. 47-50.

17 The lack of close connection to text is shown by the fact that in the average constitutional law course in law school, the Constitution itself is usually not even assigned to be read, while hundreds of pages of caselaw must be digested.

18 *See* Chapter II, pp. 38-45. It is interesting to observe that the aging Codes of some continental European countries have similar problems of obsolescence and similarly general provisions, thus leading to greater judicial activism. CAPPELLETTI, *supra* note 4, at 45.

19 17 U.S. (4 Wheat.) 316 (1819) (emphasis in original). *McCulloch*'s holding is discussed in Chapter I, p. 21.

ists are "strict interpretivists."[20] Both argue that referring to the text and intent of the Framers is logical, since that is the approach courts use in interpreting statutes. Moreover, they assert, once text and original intent are abandoned, there are no limits to what values judges could ascribe to constitutional provisions. And the pre-1937 "Lochner Era" illustrates starkly the danger of judges choosing the "wrong" values.[21]

These views are controversial, however. One difficulty with originalism is that the original intent of the Framers is undiscoverable. There is no official history of what the Framers discussed during the constitutional convention in 1787, and unofficial sources — mainly James Madison's notes — account for perhaps 10% of what went on during the convention. And there is no guarantee that Madison's account is an accurate or balanced one. Madison had strong views on many issues and his views often did not prevail. His views and his participation in the debates could well have biased his report.[22] Moreover, Madison's notes show that the Framers often exchanged a wide range of opposing views and then approved compromise wording, leaving us to wonder *which* Framers' original intentions to follow. A pragmatic argument is that originalism and close textual interpretivism are not practical. They will result in the Constitution not reaching many important questions that the Framers could not have foreseen, but which are as important today as any issues the Framers deemed worthy of constitutional treatment in their day. And if the Constitution is not invoked to upset a legislative rule or executive action unless it can be shown to be clearly contrary to the text and original intent of the Framers, then the Constitution will seldom be invoked to deal with the problems of modern society.

Coming from the opposite end of the spectrum from originalists and strict interpretivists are "non-interpretivists" or "fundamental rightists." Non-interpretivists maintain that it is proper for judges to "find" in the general provisions of the Constitution "fundamental rights" that must be respected by the government, and to use contemporary notions of fairness and rights in determining what those fundamental values are. Non-interpretivists point to the fact that the Framers placed several "open-ended" provisions into the Constitution — the "due process" clause being only one of them — that could only have been intended to be applied with a contemporary frame of reference. This, they claim, is supported by the 9th Amendment, which proclaims that "[t]he enumeration in the Constitution, of certain rights, shall not be construed to deny or disparage others retained by the people." In this respect, non-interpretivists claim essentially to be both "originalists" and "strict interpretivists." They assert that both the text of the Constitution and the "original understanding" of the Framers show that unwritten fundamental principles should have constitutional status.[23]

---

20 A unique public debate on the question of using extra-textual constitutional values took place during the hearings before the Senate Judiciary Committee on the (non) confirmation of Robert Bork to be a Supreme Court justice. *See* Chapter V, p. 308 and note 56. For development of Bork's views, *see* Robert Bork, *Neutral Principles and Some First Amendment Problems*, 47 IND.L.J. 1 (1971). A large part of the Senate's decision not to confirm Bork was his disapproval of any approach to constitutional adjudication other than that of an originalist or strict interpretivist.

21 *See* Chapter I, pp. 11-12.

22 Interestingly enough, Madison intended that his notes be destroyed upon his death because he was concerned that they might be misused by succeeding generations. RALPH L. KETCHAM, JAMES MADISON: A BIOGRAPHY 660-671 (U. Va. Press 1990).

23 *See* Thomas C. Grey, *Do We Have an Unwritten Constitution?*, 27 STAN.L.REV. 703 (1975). For a challenge to originalism and a response, *see* Paul Brest, *The Misconceived Quest for the Original Understanding*, 60 BOSTON U.L.REV. 204 (1980) and Richard A. Kay, *Adherence to the Original Intentions in Constitutional Adjudication: Three Objections and Responses*, 82 NW.U.L.REV. 226 (1988). These and

The debate between the originalists and strict interpretivists on the one hand and fundamental rightists and non-interpretivists on the other, is often overshadowed by the political views of their adherents. It is no coincidence that most originalists and strict interpretivists are political conservatives who believe that courts should defer to the majority will as represented by the legislature. Thus, it is argued, originalism is just a mask for a conservative political agenda. On the other hand, originalists and strict interpretivists charge that open non-interpretivism, at least as practiced in the 1960s and 1970s, is no less "result-oriented" and is designed to advance a "leftist" political vision. It is interesting to note as well that, in the *Lochner* era, the political positions were reversed: the political conservatives of that time supported the Court's intervening to strike down "leftist" business regulation by Congress and the state legislatures to protect workers, while the "progressive" forces of the time condemned the conservative "activism" of the "nine old men" on the Supreme Court.

As will be seen as we discuss specific cases in this chapter, the Supreme Court has decided cases using all these modes of interpretation and several in between. In addition, both it and commentators have utilized several other modes of constitutional decision-making that could be classified as hybrids of the types just discussed.

B. Separation of Powers and the Federal Judiciary

Both state and federal courts at all levels exercise the power of constitutional judicial review. However, litigants have traditionally resorted to the federal courts for protection of federal constitutional rights. Moreover, the United States Supreme Court, the final arbiter of federal constitutional issues coming from state or federal court, is a federal court subject to separation of powers limits. Consequently, it is appropriate to start our discussion of separation of powers issues with a review some of the limitations on federal judicial power that can affect judicial review. The principal doctrines discussed here are standing and its associated doctrines of ripeness and mootness, and the political question bar on judicial review. In addition, the potential constitutional power of Congress to limit judicial review through its power to regulate federal court jurisdiction should be explored.

Standing and other justiciability doctrines arise out of the requirement that federal courts determine only actual "cases" and "controversies." Some have provided additional justifications for them, primarily notions of "judicial restraint" — the concept that in a democracy, courts insulated from the political process should not be too active in holding actions of the political branches unconstitutional.[24] But much of the ultimate reason for requiring that all constitutional issues be decided solely in the context of a lawsuit can be traced to the original rationale for judicial review explicated in *Marbury v. Madison*: courts engaging in constitutional judicial review are simply "doing their job" of applying the law at the request of the parties in an ordinary lawsuit.[25]

---

other articles on constitutional theory are excerpted in GARVEY & ALEINIKOFF, *supra* note 14.

24 The assumption that "anti-majoritarian" courts with appointed judges do not fit well in a democracy underlies one of the more influential modern theories of judicial review that counsels judicial restraint in all but a few "democracy-reinforcing" areas. *See* JOHN HART ELY, DEMOCRACY AND DISTRUST (Harvard Univ. Press 1980) *and* ALEXANDER BICKEL, THE LEAST DANGEROUS BRANCH 16-26 (Bobbs-Merrill, Indianapolis 1962). For a general discussion of the problem, *see* CAPPELLETTI, *supra* note 4, at 40-46.

25 Other justifications relate to the importance of adversary litigation and nature of caselaw development. *See infra*, pp. 323-324 .

1. Standing

Standing requires that plaintiffs in any case in federal court be able to demonstrate that they have some "personal stake" in the outcome of the controversy: (1) a "distinct and palpable injury" (2) caused by the defendant.[26] Standing is generally a problem only in cases seeking injunctive or declaratory relief, since a claim for damages will always allege a sufficient tangible injury caused by the defendant's conduct.

Injury in Fact The Court has not set out a clear theory of how to determine what constitutes appropriate injury. It is clear that ideological or philosophical satisfaction or disappointment will not qualify. This is so no matter how upset or jubilant the plaintiff might be over the court's decision one way or the other. Injury to a citizen's interest in the government acting legally is also insufficient for standing.[27] Congress is even without power to bestow such "citizen standing." Congress passed a federal environmental statute that granted "any person" the right to enjoin violations of the statute. But the Court viewed the violation of this "abstract, self-contained, non-instrumental 'right' to have the Executive observe the procedures required by law" as an insufficient injury.[28] Members of Congress challenging the constitutionality of the Line Item Veto Act, which allowed the President to "cancel" certain spending and tax benefit measures he disagreed with after he had signed them into law, rather than having to veto the whole bill, were held not to have standing to challenge the Act. Their alleged injury was insufficient because it was not personal, but common to all members of Congress and because it amounted to an abstract dilution of institutional legislative power rather than palpable personal injury.[29] However, where the harm is concrete, though widely shared, there is injury in fact.[30]

At the same time, the injury required for standing is not limited to concrete, economic interests. It includes some intangible injury, such as injury to the "aesthetic, conservational and recreational interests" of users of a national park. Such users suffered injury and had standing to challenge the proposed construction of an entertainment facility in a park when that facility would have interfered with their use of the park.[31]

Causation and Redressability Turning to the second requirement that the injury be *caused* by the illegal conduct, the injury must not only bear a "fairly traceable causal connection" to the challenged law or governmental action: it must be shown that the injury is likely to be redressed by a favorable decision invalidating the law or governmental action. For example, the Court in *Warth v. Seldin*,[32] denied standing to

---

26 *Simon v. East Kentucky Welfare Rights Org.*, 426 U.S. 26, 41 n.2 (1976).

27 *United States v. Richardson*, 418 U.S. 166 (1974) (no "citizen" standing to challenge law that prohibited public disclosure of CIA expenditures).

28 *See Lujan v. Defenders of Wildlife*, 504 U.S. 555 (1992) (Endangered Species Act bestowing on "any person" the right to commence a civil suit for violations of the law). *But see Bennett v. Spear*, 520 U.S. 154 (1997) (ranchers could use citizen suit provisions where injury from reduced water for irrigation could result from drawing water from reservoir).

29 *Raines v. Byrd*, 521 U.S. 811 (1997).

30 *Federal Election Commission v. Akins*, 524 U.S. 11 (1998) (where citizens challenged the government's classification of an organization not being a "political committee," which meant it would not have to disclose its membership, contributions and expenditures, citizens suffered the injury of denial of information).

31 *See Sierra Club v. Morton*, 405 U.S. 727 (1972). *But see Lujan v. Defenders of Wildlife*, *supra* note 28 (rejecting injured interest in observing endangered species) and Chapter XV, note 330.

32 422 U.S. 490 (1975).

low-income residents living in an urban area adjoining a suburban area, who sued the suburb for refusing to grant permits for the construction of low-income housing, claiming discrimination. The plaintiffs were denied standing because they could not point to any tangible injury that the suburb's action had caused them. They could not identify a particular housing project that the suburb had blocked and could not show that, if such a project had been approved and constructed, they would have been able to move into it. Such a showing *was* made in *Arlington Heights v. Metropolitan Housing Development Corp.*,[33] where the intended residents of a particular project that had been denied approval by a suburb had standing to challenge the denial of approval for that project as being racially discriminatory.[34]

On the other hand, the Court recently held in *Northeastern Florida Chapter of the Association of General Contractors of America v. City of Jacksonville*[35] that injury in fact may be the deprivation of the *opportunity to compete* for a governmental benefit. It held that it is not necessary that the party show that, if the challenged law or governmental action is declared unconstitutional, the party would actually receive the benefit. Thus, a contractor that regularly bid on government contracts had standing to challenge the constitutionality of a law that would prevent it from bidding on a certain percentage of the contracts that were "set aside" for contracting firms owned by racial minorities and women.[36]

Taxpayer Standing   As a general proposition, a federal taxpayer lacks standing as a taxpayer to challenge the constitutionality of the expenditure of federal funds, and the same is true of a state taxpayer seeking to the challenge the constitutionality of the expenditure of state funds. The individual taxpayer's interest in the expenditure of such funds is said to be "comparatively minute and indeterminate."[37] However, older cases that have never been overruled by the Supreme Court have held that a taxpayer of a *local* governmental unit, such as a city, does have a "direct and immediate" interest in the expenditure of local funds.[38] The Supreme Court has also allowed taxpayer standing to challenge the expenditure of governmental funds in aid of religion as constituting an impermissible "establishment of religion," in violation of the 1st Amendment.[39] While this exception is difficult to reconcile with the "distinct and palpable injury" requirement, the causation-redressability requirement and the Court's rejection of "citizen standing," it nonetheless remains viable at the present time.

Rationale for Standing   Standing is said to be justified by Article III's "case or controversy" limitation. To this have been added policy concerns about the properly restrained role that courts should play in a democratic society.[40] Thus, courts should

---

33   429 U.S. 252 (1977).

34   See also *Simon v. Eastern Kentucky Welfare Rights Organization*, 426 U.S. 26 (1976) (fact that tax authorities had lowered the amount of free medical care hospital had to give to the poor to retain its tax exemption was not shown to be causally related to any denial of care to poor plaintiffs).

35   508 U.S. 656 (1993).

36   *See also Duke Power Co. v. Carolina Environmental Study Group*, 438 U.S. 59 (1978) (plaintiffs had standing to challenge limitation on liability of nuclear plants in event of catastrophe despite fact no catastrophe had taken place and no one had been denied recovery based on the challenged limitation).

37   *Frothingham v. Mellon*, 262 U.S. 447 (1923) (federal); *Asarco, Inc. v. Kadish*, 490 U.S. 605 (1989) (state).

38   *See Crampton v. Zabriskie*, 101 U.S. 601 (1879).

39   *Flast v. Cohen*, 392 U.S. 83 (1968).

40   For a debate on this general subject, *see generally and compare* BICKEL, *supra* note 24 *with* Gerald Gunther, *The Subtle Vices of the "Passive Virtues" — A Comment on Principle and Expediency in Judicial Review*, 64 COLUM. L. REV. (1964).

become involved in making decisions, particularly constitutional decisions, only when necessary to resolve an actual concrete dispute. Correspondingly, the presence of specific facts in each case will serve to limit courts only to a narrow decision of that case, rather than the declaration of broad abstract principles. Further policy justification is found in the tenets of the adversary system: concrete injury to the parties to a case is necessary to insure the requisite motivation to fully explore and present all facts and law on both sides to allow the court to make a fully informed decision.[41] However, it has been pointed out in response that parties motivated by purely ideological concerns, such as environmental activists (who would *not* have standing) are much more likely to vigorously pursue a lawsuit than someone who stands to lose only $25.00 (who *would* have standing). The Court's standing doctrine has been widely criticized by many commentators as unprincipled and a disguised method of deciding the merits of the case.[42]

2. Ripeness and Mootness

Ripeness and mootness issues are related to standing and might be understood simply as standing in a time frame. Ripeness issues arise in cases where the plaintiff may in time face redressable harm, but that harm has not yet come to fruition. Thus, plaintiffs who seek to challenge the validity of an ordinance against handing out political leaflets may not sue until they have engaged in the activity and have been threatened with arrest for a violation.[43]

Mootness issues arise when the redressable harm is over and the case therefore no longer presents a live controversy. In a leading "mootness" case, an applicant to a state university law school challenged the law school's refusal to admit him as unconstitutional. He prevailed in the lower court, and was ordered admitted. By the time the case reached the United States Supreme Court, he was in his final term at the law school, and the school stipulated that he would be permitted to graduate regardless of the outcome of the case in the Supreme Court. The Supreme Court held the case was moot.[44]

Despite its connection to constitutionally based standing doctrine, the Court views mootness as a non-constitutional "prudential" limitation on federal court power. This means that the Court has the discretion in some circumstances to decide a case that is really moot. The most common exception to mootness occurs when an issue is "capable of repetition, yet evading review." The 1973 abortion case, *Roe v. Wade*,[45] is an illustration of this. The state defendants argued that the case was moot because the plaintiffs were no longer pregnant. The Court rejected this, reasoning that, since pregnancy lasts only nine months, it would be impossible for anyone challenging an anti-abortion law to stay pregnant until the case is finally decided by the Supreme

---

41 *See* Chapter III, pp. 78-83. For an argument that this is not an essential ingredient for constitutional cases, *see* Abram Chayes, *Foreword: Public Law Litigation and the Burger Court*, 96 HARV. L. REV. 4 (1982).

42 *See, e.g.*, Gene Nichol, *Causation as a Standing Requirement: The Unprincipled Use of Judicial Restraint*, 69 KY. L. J. 185 (1981). Another standing limit that was discussed in the chapter on administrative law and is used exclusively in administrative law cases is the "zone of interests" test. *See* Chapter VI, pp. 204-204.

43 *Steffel v. Thompson*, 415 U.S. 452 (1974). *See also Socialist Labor Party v. Gilligan*, 406 U.S. 583 (1972) (political party's challenge to loyalty oath requirement not ripe since they had not yet been denied place on ballot). *Compare Duke Power Co. v. Carolina Environmental Study Group*, 438 U.S. 59 (1978) (challenge to law providing limited liability for nuclear power companies in event of disaster held ripe despite fact there had not been a disaster that exceeded those limits).

44 *DeFunis v. Odegaard*, 416 U.S. 312 (1974).

45 410 U.S. 113 (1973).

Court. In this and other situations, the Court has not deemed a case to be moot if the issue presented is "capable of repetition, yet evading review." In the normal course of things in the *Roe* case, the plaintiffs could again become pregnant and could again seek an abortion, which would continue to be prohibited by the challenged law. Consequently, the Court deemed the case to present a live controversy.

3. The "Political Question" Doctrine

Under this doctrine, the Court has stated that it will refuse to decide some disputes on the ground that they present a *political* question incapable of judicial resolution — as opposed to a *legal* question which a court can resolve. While this seems appropriate as far as it goes, it is not clear what the precise distinction is between a non-justiciable political question and a justiciable legal one.[46] It is hard to see how some of the issues the Court has dismissed as "political" are any less political than other issues it routinely decides. As Justice Jackson once commented, "all constitutional interpretations have political consequences."[47] Nonetheless, the Court has identified two primary situations where a question will be considered political rather than judicial.[48]

Lack of Judicially Manageable Standards The first situation is where there is a lack of manageable standards which a court could apply to resolve the issue. An example of the problem of a lack of standards for decision was the Court's decision in *Coleman v. Miller*.[49] There the Court was called on to resolve the question of whether an amendment to the Constitution prohibiting child labor was properly ratified by the states where it was claimed that Kansas had ratified it too late. Congress had imposed no time limit on ratification, as it had done for some other proposed amendments. The issue on the merits of the cases was whether this meant that there was a limit of a "reasonable time" and, if so, whether Kansas's ratification some 13 years after passage by Congress was too late. Instead of deciding the case, the Court dismissed it on political question grounds. Part of the reason for doing so was the lack of judicially ascertainable standards to determine what a reasonable time was. In deciding that question, the Court would essentially be making a political judgment reserved for the other two branches.[50] A lack of standards is also said to underlie the Court's decision in *Luther v. Borden*[51] that the determination of whether a particular government of a state constituted a "Republican Form of Government," as required by Article IV §4, presented a non-justiciable "political" question.

---

46 One noted commentator has suggested that there is really no such thing as a political question doctrine since all decisions in the area can be explained according to well-accepted axioms already applicable to courts. *See* Louis Henkin, *Is there a "Political Question" Doctrine?*, 85 YALE L.J. 597, 622-623 (1976).

47 ROBERT JACKSON, THE SUPREME COURT IN THE AMERICAN SYSTEM 56 (1955).

48 *See generally Baker v. Carr*, 369 U.S. 186, 217 (1962). *Baker* was a voting rights cases decided under the equal protection clause of the 14th Amendment in which the Court rejected arguments that the case seeking reapportionment of state legislative districts presented a political question. *Baker* was discussed briefly in Chapter I, p. 20.

49 307 U.S. 433 (1939)

50 The latest amendment to the Constitution is perhaps proof of how "political" a question the issue was in *Coleman v. Miller*. No time limit was imposed for the 27th Amendment and it languished over 200 years before it was ratified by 38 states. The amendment, proposed in 1789, but not ratified until 1992, prevents Congress from voting itself an immediate pay raise by prohibiting congressional pay raises from taking effect until after the next election for the House of Representatives. Congress, concerned about voter reaction if it showed itself unwilling to accept a limit on its ability to give itself a raise, immediately voted to "accept" the ratification.

51 48 U.S. (7 How.) 1 (1849). *Luther v. Borden* was discussed briefly in Chapter I, p. 20.

Commitment to a Political Branch The second way that a question can be political occurs when the Constitution entrusts its resolution to one or the other of the two "political" branches of government. The Court has held that Article I's grant to the Senate of the "sole Power to try all Impeachments" granted an unreviewable power to determine what procedure to follow.[52] It dismissed a federal judge's challenge to the Senate's decision to conduct his impeachment trial by appointing a committee of 12 Senators to hear the evidence and to report that evidence to the full Senate, which then voted on the impeachment charge.[53] On the other hand, Article I §5 provides that each House of Congress is to be the "judge of the elections, returns and qualifications of its own members." Yet, in *Powell v. McCormack*,[54] the Court held that *this* provision was *not* a grant of an unreviewable power to the House to decide whether to seat a Member who had been elected by the voters and met age, citizenship and residency qualifications imposed by the Constitution.[55]

Foreign policy disputes between Congress and the President often fall into the political question category. When Congress and the President disagree on foreign policy, they often use the powers given by the Constitution to advance those views — Congress through its "power of the purse" and the President through his various foreign policy powers, including his power as commander-in-chief of the armed forces.[56] In *Goldwater v. Carter*[57] some Senators brought suit against the President, contending that the President lacked the power to terminate a treaty with Taiwan without Congressional approval. The Supreme Court dismissed the suit, but disagreed on its reasons. A plurality of four Justices found it to present a non-justiciable political question, since the courts were being asked to settle a dispute between "coequal branches of our government, each of which has resources available to protect and assert its interests." The plurality also emphasized the lack of judicially manageable standards given the absence of any constitutional provision on treaty termination. One justice gave a similar reason, but under a "ripeness" rubric: Justice Powell argued that the courts should not intervene *until* each branch has "taken action asserting its constitutional authority." Since neither House of Congress had expressly taken action rejecting the President's claim of authority to terminate the treaty, Powell would hold that the constitutional issue was not "ripe."

4. Congressional Power Over Federal Court Jurisdiction

Article III specifies that the judicial power of the Supreme Court in its appellate form is subject to "such Exceptions, and under such Regulations as the Congress shall make." It also gives Congress the right to decide whether to "ordain and establish" the lower federal courts and, if so, to specify what their jurisdiction will be.[58] Some have read the "regulations and exceptions" clause and Congress's plenary power over the existence and jurisdiction of lower federal courts effectively to give it absolute control over the content of court decisions — in essence, having the last word on constitutional judicial review. Under this theory, if Congress does not like what the Supreme Court or lower federal courts are doing in particular kinds of cases, it can

---

52 Art. I §3 cl. 6.

53 *See Nixon v. United States*, 506 U.S. 224 (1993).

54 395 U.S. 486 (1969).

55 *See* Art. I §2 cl. 2.

56 Foreign policy powers of the President and Congress are discussed *infra* pp. 316-318.

57 444 U.S. 996 (1979).

58 The federal court system Congress has created is discussed in Chapter V, pp. 170-173.

simply deprive those courts of jurisdiction over that category of disputes. Such "jurisdiction-stripping" legislation has perennially been proposed. In the 1950s bills were aimed at decisions striking down anti-subversion laws, loyalty oaths and other practices, in the 1960s, at expansions of criminal due process rights, and in the 1970s and 1980s at decisions on abortion rights and religious activities in public schools.

No such bill has ever passed, but the academic commentary on the issue of the constitutionality of jurisdiction-stripping has been described as "choking on redundancy." Professor Gunther and others maintain that this control over jurisdiction is proper and is simply one of the "checks and balances" provided for in the Constitution to check the unrestrained exercise of judicial review. Others disagree and have suggested that this cannot be correct on several grounds.[59]

Essential Function Theory Some opponents of jurisdiction-stripping argue that the terms used, "regulations" and "exceptions," denote only "procedural" kinds of rules that address administrative problems or increase the efficiency of the courts.[60] They argue that "the exceptions must not be such as will destroy the essential role of the Supreme Court in the constitutional plan."[61] The followers of this "essential function" theory further argue that it is not likely that the purpose of the regulation and exceptions clause was to provide control over the substantive content of Supreme Court decisions, since the form of control it provides is clumsy and counterproductive. First, depriving the Court of jurisdiction in *future* cases does not wipe away the effect of the decision already made and that decision would continue to govern the lower courts. Indeed, depriving the Court of jurisdiction would have the *opposite* effect to the one desired. It would assure that the Court would *not* have jurisdiction to accept review of a *future* case to *overrule* the decision Congress did not like. Second, these commentators read the Constitution as requiring at the very least that Congress leave *state* courts free to decide the issues it has removed from Supreme Court jurisdiction. This would result in different states' courts taking conflicting positions on what the Constitution means with no means of resolving those conflicts.

Limits Imposed by Substantive Rights Another view, identified with Professor Tribe, does not reason from Article III, but points out that jurisdictional statutes, no less than any other statute, may violate the rights-securing provisions of the Constitution if they unduly burden the exercise of a constitutional right.[62] For example, it would

---

59 The points of view are set out and discussed and criticized in Gerald Gunther, *Congressional Power to Curtail Federal Jurisdiction: An Opinionated Guide to the On-Going Debate*, 36 STAN. L.REV. 201 (1984). The comment in the text on redundancy is Professor Gunther's.

60 Congress has the power to control other procedural aspects of the Supreme Court's operations, such as its size, which has fluctuated between 5 and 10 justices. The "procedural" nature of this aspect of the Court has not prevented Congress from manipulating it for political purposes. Congress reduced the Court's number from 10 to 6 in 1866 in part to prevent President Andrew Johnson from filling a vacancy. Angry about Johnson's opposition to Congress's post-Civil War policies toward the south, Congress had earlier impeached Johnson, but conviction was avoided by one vote.

61 Henry Hart, *The Power of Congress to Limit the Jurisdiction of Federal Courts: An Exercise in Dialectic*, 66 HARV. L.REV. 1362, 1365 (1953). *See also* Leonard G. Ratner, *Congressional Power Over the Appellate Jurisdiction of the Supreme Court*, 109 U.PA.L.REV. 157 (1960). For the application of a similar theory to the lower federal courts, *see* Lawrence Sager, *Forward: Constitutional Limitations on Congress's Authority to Regulate the Jurisdiction of the Federal Courts*, 95 HARV. L. REV. 17 (1981).

62 *See* Lawrence Tribe, *Jurisdictional Gerrymandering: Zoning Disfavored Rights Out of the Federal Courts*, 16 HARV. C.R.-C.L.L.REV. 129 (1981). The term "Gerrymandering" actually refers to drawing legislative districts in a manner that allows one to promote the election of one party's candidates — a tactic identified with Governor and later Vice President Elbridge Gerry of Massachusetts (1744-1814). This is ironic, given that Gerry had nothing to do with the politically-shaped Massachusetts election districts. Racial gerrymandering is discussed *infra*, p. 343.

certainly violate equal protection for Congress to pass a statute denying federal courts jurisdiction over all suits brought by black people. Similarly, a statute depriving the Court of the power to hear cases involving abortion would impermissibly burden the rights of women to obtain an abortion no less than a law that provided some other obstacle to realization of the right to an abortion, such as a law requiring a woman's husband's consent for an abortion.[63]

The Court has never squarely faced and decided the question of validity of jurisdiction-stripping statutes. Two Civil War-era cases are inconclusive. One upheld the jurisdiction-stripping statute, but it was clear that the statute left other jurisdictional routes to appeal open.[64] The other struck down the statute, but the Court gave reasons for doing so that would have been sufficient even without considering its jurisdiction-stripping aspects.[65] *Dictum* statements in the opinions in these two cases speak broadly of Congress's plenary power under the regulations and exceptions clause. More recently, however, the Court construed a federal statute to allow a government employee to sue for violation of his constitutional rights "in part to avoid the 'serious constitutional question' that would arise if a federal statute were construed to deny any judicial forum for a colorable constitutional claim."[66]

The Supreme Court has never faced the issue squarely because no such statute has ever been passed, though several have been introduced. Some argue that the lack of clarity on the issue is healthy. On the one hand, the argument in favor of the power to pass such a statute is sufficiently strong that a congressional threat to do so is credible. Therefore, it can be a serious means of Congress communicating its displeasure with the Court's decisions. On the other hand, there is enough basis for the Supreme Court to strike the statute down that Congress will probably never go past the "communication" stage and actually pass one.

C. Separation of Powers Issues Between Congress and the President

1. Domestic Affairs

The nature and extent of presidential power in domestic affairs and the limits thereon were explored briefly in Chapter I.[67] In addition, some issues of separation of powers as it affects the power of the President, executive branch officials and agencies were reviewed in the chapter on administrative law.[68] Those discussions are sufficient for our purposes and will not be repeated here.

2. Foreign Affairs

In foreign affairs, the President as head of state has broad authority.[69] But the Framers provided for a shared responsibility with Congress for foreign policy by giving to Congress the power to regulate foreign commerce and to decide whether and to what extent to maintain and regulate armies, ratify treaties, or fund foreign involvements. This shared responsibility imposed by the constitutional text requires

---

63 *Planned Parenthood of Southeastern Pennsylvania v. Casey*, 505 U.S. 833 (1992) (striking down husband consent law).

64 *Ex parte McCardle*, 74 U.S. (7 Wall.) 506 (1868).

65 *United States v. Klein*, 80 U.S. (13 Wall.) 128 (1872).

66 *See Webster v. Doe*, 486 U.S. 592, 603 (1988), discussed in Chapter II, p. 57.

67 *See* pp. 12-14.

68 *See* Chapter VI, pp. 211-215.

69 *See* Chapter I, pp. 7, 12.

congressional approval to validate many presidential actions.[70]

Executive Orders and Executive Agreements Executive orders and executive agreements are widely used in foreign affairs. The Constitution requires that treaties be ratified by the Senate, but it says nothing about executive agreements. Many of the country's most important international commitments are still made by way of the formal treaty process, but many have been made by way of executive agreement implemented by executive orders.[71] The approach of the Court had been that these devices are permitted since the Constitution does not make treaties the exclusive form of international agreement. Executive agreements are not generally used to avoid Senate opposition to the agreement. The power to make executive agreements has often been authorized by ratified treaties or willingly delegated or otherwise approved by Congress.

The evidence of Congressional approval of given executive actions may be rather weak. In *Dames & Moore v. Regan*,[72] President Carter negotiated an end to the Iranian hostage case at the American Embassy in Teheran. Embassy employees were released pursuant to a complex agreement that included an agreement on the part of the United States to "nullify all attachments and judgments" against Iranian assets in the United States and to "prohibit litigation based on such claims, and to bring about the termination of such claims through binding arbitration" before an international claims tribunal. The Court held that the executive order transferring the encumbered assets was valid on the ground that Congress had given the President emergency economic powers in a statute it had passed earlier, and that the purpose of that statute was to permit the President to use the foreign assets as a "bargaining chip" when negotiating with a hostile nation. Although there was no such statutory support for nullifying claims in U.S. courts, the Court relied on the "long continued practice" of the President settling international claims of citizens "acquiesced in by Congress." It determined that this "raises a presumption that the action has been taken in pursuance of [Congress's] consent."[73]

War Powers and Military Intervention The Constitution gives both Congress and the President specific powers in the area of war and military intervention. Under Art.I §8, Congress has the power to "declare War, grant letters of Marque and Reprisal, and make Rules concerning Captures on Land and Water," to "raise and support Armies," to "provide and maintain a Navy," to "make Rules for the Government and Regulation of the land and naval Forces," and to regulate the state militias and to call them into federal service. The President under Article II §2 is the "Commander in Chief of the Army and Navy of the United States, and of the militia of the several States when called into the actual Service of the United States."

This mix of powers has raised the issue many times in history of the ability of the President to engage in military action abroad without a formal declaration of war from

---

70 The "political question" limitation on justiciability (discussed *supra*, pp. 313-314) presents some difficulty in gaining answers to questions about the extent of presidential powers in foreign affairs.

71 For example, U.S. participation in the General Agreement on Tariffs and Trade (GATT) was accomplished by way of an executive agreement. *See generally* NOWAK & ROTUNDA, *supra* note 2, at 215-220.

72 453 U.S. 654 (1981).

73 The Court did made clear, however, that the general legality of the executive agreement and order did not affect the constitutional duty to pay "just compensation" for any private claims invalidated. This is based on the 5th Amendment requirement that every "taking" of private property by the government must be compensated.

Congress. Certainly a concurrent resolution (a resolution passed by a majority of both houses) granting authority to the President to take military action is sufficient, and such resolutions were passed before commencement of the Gulf War in 1991 and in several other interventions before it. But the President has used American troops several times in history without going to Congress for a declaration of war, and it was largely the result of the President leading and Congress following that the United States became involved in the disastrous Vietnam War.[74] It is not likely that the extent of the President's power in this area will be clarified by the Supreme Court, as it would likely consider it to be a non-justiciable political question.[75]

It is significant, however, no President has ever asserted the authority to expend appropriated funds contrary to a restriction specifically imposed on the use of such funds by Congress pursuant to its "power of the purse." This would seem to be a permissible way for Congress to preserve its sole power to declare war.[76] However, legislation containing such a restriction must be signed by the President or passed over his veto.[77] While this might seem to be an insurmountable hurdle for Congress when only a simple majority opposes presidential action, the President may feel compelled to sign the bill despite the funding restriction in it because of other positive provisions it contains.

The Commander-in-Chief power probably allows the President to order some military action without Congressional authorization on a short-term emergency basis, such as an armed attack on the United States or a threat to American citizens or property in a foreign country. This basis for military intervention was relied on by President Reagan when he sent American troops into Grenada in 1983, claiming that the safety of Americans attending a medical school in Grenada was in danger. Such power to launch short-term interventions could also be argued to support the bombing of Libya by President Reagan in 1986 in reprisal for a terrorist attack in Germany that killed American military personnel, and the invasion of Panama by President Bush in 1990 to capture General Noriega and bring him to trial in the United States for alleged violations of American drug laws.[78]

D. The Relationship Between the States and the Federal Government: Vertical Federalism Limits

Federalism most often limits *state* power. This aspect of federalism was outlined

---

74 Vietnam and later incursions were only the latest in a long line of presidential military actions taken without a declaration of war. Between 1789 and 1970, one author counted 130 transfers of troops or war matériel abroad without Congressional involvement. *See* NOWAK & ROTUNDA, *supra* note 2, at 223.

75 *See supra* pp. 313-314. The constitutionality of the Vietnam War was raised in the lower federal courts, but most held the issue non-justiciable under the political question doctrine. The Supreme Court avoided deciding either the political question issue or the constitutionality of the war by exercising its discretionary power to deny review. *See Mora v. McNamara*, 389 U.S. 934 (1967) (denying certiorari over two dissents). *But see Orlando v. Laird*, 443 F.2d 1039 (2d Cir. 1971) (finding the issue justiciable and finding sufficient congressional authorization). Certiorari was also denied in *Orlando*.

76 A recent example of this was Congress specific prohibition any use of appropriated funds to provide assistance to the "contras" in Nicaragua. Congress's action forced certain officials in the Reagan administration to seek to fund the "contras" by means other than appropriated funds. One method was by selling arms to Iran, which led to the "Iran-Contra" scandal.

77 For this reason, the section of the War Powers Resolution of 1973 which allowed Congress to halt military action ordered by the President by way of a joint resolution of Congress not subject to the presidential signature requirement, is unconstitutional. *See* Chapter VI, p. 210, where *Immigration and Naturalization Service v. Chadha*, 462 U.S. 919 (1983), the "legislative veto" case, is discussed.

78 Whether such action is constitutional is separate from the question of whether such military intervention comports with international law.

in Chapter I when we discussed the scope of federal legislative power,[79] the preemption doctrine,[80] and conditional spending programs.[81] In addition, the structural limitations of federalism prohibit states from taxing federal instrumentalities. *McCulloch v. Maryland*,[82] discussed in another respect in Chapter I, prohibited the State of Maryland from taxing a federal bank.[83] But federalism also limits the *federal* government's ability to act in some circumstances.

There are two types of federal laws passed pursuant to the commerce clause: laws that regulate the activities of the *states themselves* and laws that regulate *private conduct within* states. In general, federalism limits in recent years have been imposed only on laws that regulate the states themselves.

1. Regulating the States Themselves

The "Clear Statement" Rule Since 1985, the Court has taken the position that federalism limits were essentially self-enforcing. In *Garcia v. San Antonio Metropolitan Transit Authority*[84] the Court held that the federal Fair Labor Standards Act, which governs minimum wages and payment for overtime work, applied to state employees despite arguments that it invaded powers reserved to the states. Any federalism-based objections to the use of the federal commerce power, it held, have already been factored in "through state participation in federal government action." In this way "[t]he political process ensures that laws that unduly burden the States will not be promulgated."[85] Consequently, the Court reasoned, there is no need for the Court to further protect states with a *judicial* doctrine of federalism limitations.[86]

Nonetheless, the Court in *Gregory v. Ashcroft*[87] recognized the value of requiring a "clear statement" by Congress of its intention to affect state governmental functions. *Gregory* involved the issue of whether the federal Age Discrimination in Employment Act applied to bar mandatory retirement of state judges at age 70. Given the central role of the state judiciary in state government, the Court presumed that Congress did not mean to include state judges, since it did not mention them specifically in the Act. The Court noted that there was an exception for state employees who are "appointee[s] on the policy-making level" and determined that state judges fell within that exception. *Gregory* is only a rule of statutory interpretation. It assumes that Congress

---

79 *See* Chapter I, pp. 21-27.

80 *See* Chapter I, p. 29 and note 123.

81 *See* Chapter I, p. 25.

82 17 U.S. (4 Wheat.) 316 (1819). *See* Chapter I, p. 21.

83 State taxation of federal employees' income is permitted so long as it is even-handed. *See Davis v. Michigan Department of Treasury*, 489 U.S. 803 (1989) (state exemption of state, but not federal, retirement pay is impermissibly discriminatory).

84 469 U.S. 528 (1985).

85 469 U.S. at 556. *See* Herbert Wechsler, *The Political Safeguards of Federalism: The Role of the States in the Composition and Selection of the National Government*, 54 COLUM. L.REV. 543 (1954). Some evidence that political safeguards may be working is found in the fact that Congress has refrained from exercising its considerable power to regulate private conduct in states, thus leaving vast areas of conduct to be governed by state law. *See* Chapter I, pp. 28-30.

86 Before 1937 and for a 10-year period from 1976 to 1985, the Court used the federalism policies embodied in the 10th Amendment to invalidate federal legislation affecting states in areas of "traditional state functions." *See National League of Cities v. Usery*, 426 U.S. 833 (1976) (holding that Fair Labor Standards could not be applied to state and local government workers). *Usery* was overruled by *Garcia*. Nonetheless, the 10th Amendment probably remains a bar to some federal legislation affecting states. *See Coyle v. Smith*, 221 U.S. 559 (1911) (Congress may not dictate location of the Oklahoma's capital city).

87 501 U.S. 452 (1991).

could pass an amendment to the Act specifically making state judges subject to the Act and federalism would not stand in the way.[88]

"Commandeering" State Governmental Bodies and Officials This doctrine concerns attempts by Congress to force state officials to pass laws or perform other tasks. In *New York v. United States*,[89] Congress tried to deal with the growing problem of states refusing to allow development of in-state disposal sites for hazardous radioactive waste generated by private companies in the state, and instead shipping it to other states for disposal. One part of the law provided economic incentives for states that permitted private development of safe waste disposal sites within the state. But behind such persuasion were more coercive consequences. The federal law provided that states that did not enact laws permitting regulated disposal within their borders would become the owners of all wastes generated in the state and would become liable for all damages suffered as a result of failure to take possession of "their" wastes. The Court held this latter provision unconstitutional. Though it did not directly compel states to pass in-state disposal laws, the "choice" of the state taking possession of all wastes produced within its borders was undesirable enough to say that the state was effectively being coerced into enacting those laws.

While many thought that the *New York* rule applied only to "commandeering" the state *legislature*, the Court in 1997 applied the doctrine to officials of the *executive* branch of state government. In *Printz v. United States*,[90] federal gun control legislation required local police officials to investigate the background of all prospective purchasers of handguns to determine whether they satisfied federal requirements for such purchase. Among those federal requirements were that the prospective purchaser be over age 21, be a resident of the state where the gun is being purchased and have no criminal felony record. The Court held that Congress could not require local police officials to perform such "background checks." It distinguished *Garcia* and similar cases as involving the "incidental application to the States of a federal law of general applicability," while "here, it is the whole object of the law to direct the functioning of the state executive."

The Impact of the New York and Printz Cases It bears emphasizing what the Court's decision in *New York* and *Printz* do *not* do. First, they do not affect Congress's right to regulate directly the conduct of *individual waste producers or waste management companies* who are located *in* the states. So, if Congress *itself* passed the regulatory program it had tried to force the states to enact as *federal* legislation and provided for *federal* enforcement of its provisions, it could attain the same goal.[91] Second, the decision did nothing to affect Congress's power to accomplish the same thing through a conditional spending program — offering federal funding contingent on state acceptance of federal conditions. The financial impact of not receiving federal funds is not considered to be a form of "coercion" of states, even if the state feels compelled to participate in the federal program in order to try to recoup federal

---

88 The Court had earlier held that the Act applied to bar mandatory retirement of more ordinary state employees in *Equal Employment Opportunity Comm'n v. Wyoming*, 460 U.S. 226 (1983).

89 505 U.S. 144 (1992).

90 521 U.S. 98 (1997).

91 In the event it did so, Congress would also have to set up a mechanism to administer it. Avoiding the need for creating a new federal bureaucracy could well have been the reason for Congress choosing to pass the statute in the form that it did.

tax money paid by its citizens and even if a condition of receipt of federal money is that the state pass certain laws.[92]

2. Federal Regulation of Private Conduct Within States

As just noted, cases such as *New York* and *Printz* have no effect on federal power to regulate private conduct that takes place in states. At one point, the Court did impose strict limits. However, this doctrine disappeared in the 1937 changes in justices and philosophy surrounding the dispute with the Roosevelt administration, a brief history of which was recounted in Chapter I.[93] The post-1937 commerce clause cases have established the rule that federal legislation is valid under the Commerce Clause so long as Congress could have had a "rational basis" to believe that the activity it chose to regulate affected interstate commerce in some way. Congress need not have conducted a study and reached such a conclusion and it did not seem to matter what the immediate object of Congressional regulation was or in what area of law Congress was seeking to pre-empt state law. Thus, in *Katzenbach v. McClung*,[94] the Court sustained the application of the Civil Rights Act of 1964, which banned private racial discrimination in all public accommodations, to a small local restaurant. The Court concluded that Congress could have rationally decided that the cumulative effect of local incidents of racial discrimination could affect interstate commerce and that some of the food served there had moved in interstate commerce. Similarly, in *Perez v. United States*,[95] the Court employed a similar "cumulative effect" theory to uphold a federal law prohibiting extortion by local racketeers threatening violence to recover loan payments from local citizens.[96]

This cornerstone of modern federal power was thrown into doubt in the recent case of *United States v. Lopez*.[97] *Lopez* involved Congressional reaction to a growing problem of violence in the nation's public schools. Congress passed the "Gun-Free School Zones Act," which prohibited the possession of any firearm within 1,000 feet (307 meters) of any public or private school. The Supreme Court struck it down as not within the commerce power because it "is a criminal statute that by its terms has nothing to do with 'commerce' or any sort of economic enterprise, however broadly one might define those terms." The government argued that possession of a firearm in a school zone may result in violent crime and that violent crime can be expected to affect the functioning of the national economy because the medical and other costs of violent crime are substantial, and, through the mechanism of insurance, are spread throughout the entire population of the country. It also maintained that violent crime reduces the willingness of individuals to travel to areas within the country that are perceived to be unsafe. Moreover, violent crime can impede the educational process, thus resulting in a "less productive citizenry." The Court rejected these arguments, observing that acceptance would allow Congress to regulate all violent crime and all the activities that might lead to it, as well as any activity that related to the economic productivity of citizens, including marriage and divorce.

The Court admitted that its commerce clause cases had upheld legislation before that regulated "activities that arise out or are connected with a commercial

---

92 *See* Chapter I, p. 25.

93 *See* pp. 11-12, 24.

94 379 U.S. 294 (1964).

95 402 U.S. 146 (1971).

96 *See* Chapter I, p. 24.

97 514 U.S. 549 (1995).

transaction." But the gun law "is not an essential part of a larger regulation of economic activity, in which the regulatory scheme could be undercut unless the intrastate activity were regulated." The defendant in *Lopez* "was a local high student at a local school; there is no indication that he had recently moved in interstate commerce, and there is no requirement [in the statute] that his possession of the firearm have any concrete tie to interstate commerce."

The Court also noted that there were no congressional findings in either the law or the legislative history demonstrating the connection Congress had found between gun possession near schools and interstate commerce. The Court admitted that it had not generally required this before, but that such findings would assist it "in evalu-at[ing] the legislative judgment that the activity in question substantially affected interstate commerce."

It is as yet difficult to know what the effect of *Lopez* will be. Almost immediately, Congress passed and President Clinton signed an amendment to the law adding the requisite congressional findings.[98] The Court offered little guidance on how to define what are "commercial" and what are "non-commercial" activities. In addition, there are several federal laws that include what have traditionally been state crimes: extortion, possession of a machine gun, "car-jacking" (stealing a car at gunpoint) and several anti-drug laws. The constitutionality of at least one of these was explicitly upheld in the *Perez* case.[99]

3. Congressional Power Under §5 of the 14th Amendment

The 14th Amendment to the Constitution prohibits states from depriving anyone of life, liberty or property without due process of law or denying equal protection of the laws. Section 5 of that Amendment states that "Congress shall have power to enforce, by appropriate legislation, the provisions of this article." While this power does not assist in battling economic crises, one might well wonder why Congress did not rely on it instead of the commerce clause in passing laws prohibiting racial discrimination. The big question regarding §5 has been whether Congress's power under it is limited to passing "procedural" laws that provide the *means* of redressing violations of *existing* due process and equal protection rights, or whether Congress could by legislation create additional *substantive rights* beyond those declared by the Court to be part of due process or equal protection.

Katzenbach v. Morgan[100] upheld a federal prohibition on literacy tests despite the fact that the Court had never held such tests constituted racial discrimination. The Court followed a rational-basis approach, holding that "it is enough that we perceive a basis upon which Congress might predicate a judgment that the application of New York's literacy requirement to deny the right to vote to [Puerto Ricans fluent in Spanish] constituted an invidious discrimination in violation of the Equal Protection Clause." This was thought by some to authorize Congress to go beyond the rights already declared by the Court to exist under the 14th Amendment so long as there was a rational basis to believe that those additional rights were appropriate to supplement existing constitutional rights.

---

98 The *Lopez* Court noted this, but deemed it irrelevant since the government did not rely on this after-the-fact justification in arguing the validity of the version of the law in question. *Id.* at 563 n. 4.

99 *See supra* p. 321.

100 384 U.S. 641 (1966).

In the recent case of *City of Boerne v. Flores*,[101] however, the Court took a narrow and more procedural view of congressional power under §5. The Court considered the validity of the Right to Freedom of Religion Act (RFRA). Congress passed RFRA out of its disagreement with a Supreme Court decision that narrowed the scope of the 1st Amendment guarantee of the "free exercise" of religion. The Court had changed the free exercise test to remove 1st Amendment protections for any religiously motivated conduct that was made criminal by a state law of general applicability.[102] Congress wished to reestablish as a federal *statutory* matter the earlier constitutional test of state laws, providing in RFRA that a state law of general applicability that burdens religious practices is valid only if it "(1) is in furtherance of a compelling governmental interest, and (2) is the least restrictive means of furthering that compelling interest." In *City of Boerne*, the archbishop of a Catholic church in Texas sued under RFRA when the city, acting under a local historic preservation ordinance, denied the church a building permit to enlarge the church.

The Court held that RFRA was beyond Congress's power. There was a difference, it held, "between measures that remedy or prevent unconstitutional actions and measures that make a substantive change in the governing law." The anti-literacy-test law in *Katzenbach v. Morgan* was of the former type, while RFRA was of the latter. The Court noted that before enacting RFRA there was no study done by Congress finding a need to prevent state laws passed out of religious bigotry. In *Katzenbach*, there was "evidence in the record reflecting the subsisting and pervasive discriminatory — and therefore unconstitutional — use of literacy tests." Further, RFRA "reflects a lack of proportionality or congruence between the means adopted and the legitimate end to be achieved." The Voting Rights Act involved in *Katzenbach* and other cases required pre-implementation administrative approval of electoral practices targeted at states with a long history of intentional discrimination in voting designed to ferret out discriminatory practices, and even those targeted states were relieved of the burdens of such review after 7 years had passed. RFRA was not so focused in time, geographical area or design. It allowed anyone who could show some substantial burden on his or her religious practices to force the state to demonstrate both a "compelling interest" in its law and that its law was "the least restricted means of furthering [that] interest."

E. The Relationship Between the States: Horizontal Federalism

States retain all the powers of international states except for those given up in the Constitution and, in exercising some of the independent powers they have in the federal system, act in many ways like separate countries. However, in other instances the Constitution requires them to act more like simple subdivisions of a single country. In Chapter I, we discussed how the right to interstate travel, the "dormant" commerce clause, state court jurisdiction over out-of-state defendants, the "full faith and credit" clause and the extradition clause have had a blurring effect on state boundaries.[103] In Chapter VII we considered in more detail the issues of personal jurisdiction and the "full faith and credit" due federal and state court judgments.[104] Two topics should be discussed here. The "dormant" commerce clause doctrine should be reviewed in

---

101 521 U.S. 507 (1997).

102 The "free exercise" clause is discussed in more detail *infra* this chapter, pp. 362-365. The Supreme Court case in question is the *Smith* case, discussed *infra* p. 362, in which was fired for using drugs as part of religious observances in the Native American Church.

103 *See* pp. 26-28.

104 *See* pp. 245-248 and 250-252.

more detail and the related requirement that states respect the privileges and immunities clause of those from out-of-state should be mentioned.

1. The "Dormant" Commerce Clause

Source and Purpose   The interstate commerce clause provides Congress with broad powers to pass legislation and such legislation preempts state law whenever the two conflict. But even when Congress has not acted, the commerce clause has a limiting effect on state regulation. Its mere existence, in its "dormant" state, gives rise to a negative implication that states may not interfere with interstate commerce in certain ways. Its purpose is to prevent a state from engaging in economic protectionism — from "establishing an economic barrier against competition with the products of another state or the labor of its residents."[105]

Tests Applied to State Laws   The Court's current dormant commerce clause doctrine has two tests: it invalidates state laws that "discriminate against interstate commerce" without substantial justification or that impose an "undue burden" on interstate commerce. The clearest cases of discrimination are where the state regulation discriminates on its face. But even neutral laws that have a discriminatory effect will be invalidated if either a discriminatory motivation can be detected or "reasonable non-discriminatory alternatives adequate to conserve legitimate local interests are available."[106] The "undue burden" test will invalidate state action that impedes commerce when "the burden imposed on such commerce is clearly excessive in relation to the putative local benefits," considering as well "whether [local interests] could be promoted as well with a lesser impact on interstate activities."[107]

In recent years, the Court has shown a preference for the "discrimination" test over the "undue burden" test.[108] But from the above statements of the tests, it can be seen that the two tests amount essentially to the same thing. A state law that imposes an "undue burden" on interstate commerce because it brings few legitimate (i.e., non-protectionist) local benefits can be understood as being discriminatory, since the small measure of non-protectionist local benefit suggests strongly that it is simply a pretext for discrimination. Similarly, a law that discriminates on its face or has a discriminatory impact on interstate commerce without any substantial local non-protectionist benefits imposes an "undue burden," since the non-protectionist local interests will seldom outweigh the burden imposed.

Three General Categories of State Practices   Most dormant commerce clause cases can be placed in three general categories.

The first is where a state tries to "fence out" items of commerce that compete with local products. A state may bar "harmful" products from another state, such as excluding cattle with disease that could infect in-state herds.[109] However, barring non-health-threatening out-of-state products based on their origin is prohibited. For

---

105 *Philadelphia v. New Jersey*, 437 U.S. 617, 624 (1978).

106 *Dean Milk Co. v. City of Madison*, 340 U.S. 349, 354 (1951). *Dean Milk* also demonstrates that the dormant commerce clause prohibition applies to the laws of local governments and how local governments cannot justify burdening out-of-state interests by pointing out that its law also discriminates against in-state residents from other parts of the state.

107 *Pike v. Bruce Church, Inc.*, 397 U.S. 137, 141 (1970).

108 *See generally* Don Regan, *The Supreme Court and State Protectionism: Making Sense of the Dormant Commerce Clause*, 84 MICH. L. REV. 1091 (1986).

109 *Mintz v. Baldwin*, 289 U.S. 346 (1933).

example, the Court invalidated New York's prohibition of the sale of milk purchased from farmers in other states at lower prices than the New York minimum price.[110]

A second category of cases involves states "fencing in" valuable local resources. Among the laws in this category that have been struck down are laws prohibiting a privately owned hydroelectric power located in the state from exporting power to other states,[111] prohibiting exportation of certain fish caught in the state,[112] prohibiting exportation of ground water to adjoining states that grant no reciprocal water rights[113] and prohibiting giving licenses to milk processing facilities that would divert local milk supplies to other states.[114] Also included in this category are laws fencing out unattractive out-of-state items, such as garbage and other wastes, in order to preserve the state's landfill space to handle its own wastes. Thus, in *Philadelphia v. New Jersey*,[115] the Court struck down New Jersey's prohibition on private landfills taking in out-of-state waste. Except for the waste's out-of-state origin, it was no different from New Jersey waste. Less-than-complete or "indirect" restrictions on interstate commerce also run afoul of the dormant commerce clause.[116] Recently the Court relied on this line of cases to strike down a state law granting a general exemption from real estate taxes solely to state residents. In the Court's view, this amounted to giving state residents "a preferred right of access" to land in the state.[117]

The third category is where states use means short of prohibition either to burden out-of-state or to prefer in-state businesses or products. An example is *Hunt v. Washington State Apple Advertising Commission*,[118] in which the Court invalidated a North Carolina law on advertising for apples. The law in effect prohibited the display of Washington state apple grades on packages of apples shipped to North Carolina. Washington state had developed a grading system that was considered in the industry to be superior to the federal Department of Agriculture grading system. Since the Washington grade marked superior apples, prohibiting its display on apple containers had the effect of depriving Washington apples of the competitive advantage they would otherwise enjoy.[119]

Dealing With Discriminatory Effect In all three categories above, to base a finding of discrimination on improper discriminatory *effect*, one must be able to identify benefitted and burdened groups that are similarly situated except for the identification of one with interstate commerce or out-of-state location. The fact that the regulation benefits one kind of *economic interest* at the expense of another does not make it

---

110 *Baldwin v. G.A.F. Seelig, Inc.*, 294 U.S. 511 (1935). *See also Lewis v. B.T. Investment Managers ,Inc.*, 447 U.S. 27 (1980) (state prohibition on out-of-state banking institutions controlling in-state investment advisory firms invalid).

111 *New England Power Co. v. New Hampshire*, 455 U.S. 331 (1982).

112 *Hughes v. Oklahoma*, 441 U.S. 322 (1979).

113 *Sporhase v. Nebraska*, 458 U.S. 941 (1982).

114 *H.P. Hood & Sons v. DuMond*, 326 U.S. 525 (1949).

115 *Supra* note 105.

116 *See Chemical Waste Management, Inc. v. Hunt*, 504 U.S. 334 (1992) (higher fee for disposal of out-of-state hazardous waste). It is also no excuse that a state is retaliating for discriminatory treatment by another state. *Great A.& P. Tea Co. v. Cottrell*, 424 U.S. 366 (1976).

117 *Camps Newfound/Owatonna, Inc. v. Town of Harrison,* 520 U.S. 564 (1997).

118 432 U.S. 333 (1977).

119 *See also Pike v. Bruce Church*, 397 U.S. 137 (1970) (requirement that cantaloupes picked in Arizona be packed there violates dormant commerce clause). *Pike* was decided on the ground that the packing requirement was an "undue burden," rather than on discrimination grounds. But it is easily understood as a discrimination case when one realizes that requiring packing in the state attracts additional business to the state at the expense of other states.

"discriminatory" for negative commerce clause purposes, even though the benefitted economic interest is primarily local while the burdened economic interest is primarily interstate. Thus, in *EXXON Corp. v. Maryland*,[120] Maryland law prohibited oil refining companies from owning retail service stations. The Court held that the law did not violate the dormant commerce clause, even though its effect was to favor retail service station owners, most of whom were local, over oil companies, all of which were out-of-state.[121] Maryland also had a relatively strong non-discriminatory reason for its law: in the oil crisis of 1973, the oil refining companies favored their own service stations over independents, selling gasoline to them while not filling orders from the independents.

Why a Preference for a Discrimination Test If a state law burdens both out-of-state and in-state interests, a discrimination charge is harder to prove even if there is some disproportionate impact. But if *in-state* interests are *also* affected, "a State's own political processes will serve as a check against unduly burdensome regulations."[122] This is one reason why the Court's prefers the discrimination rather than the "undue burden" test. With the "undue burden" test, the *Court itself* must evaluate the burden, a task for which a court is not well equipped. With the discrimination test, it need only insure that—whatever burden there is on out-of-state interests — that burden is imposed equally on in-state interests. This leaves it to the political process of the state to evaluate the burdens and benefits of the law in response to complaints from in-state residents also affected by it.[123]

"Tentative" Judicial Review Judicial review of legislation on dormant commerce clause grounds differs somewhat from review on other constitutional grounds. Because Congress's power to regulate interstate commerce is plenary, it has the power to authorize any form of state regulation of commerce that it chooses, including discriminatory or burdensome state laws that would otherwise violate the dormant commerce clause. As a result, a Supreme Court case striking down state regulation is really a form of "tentative" judicial review: even though the Court has struck down the state regulation as violative of the dormant commerce clause, Congress has the power to "overrule" the Court and determine that the state's regulation *is* an appropriate regulation of interstate commerce.[124]

Market Participant Exception One category of discriminatory state action that does not violate the dormant commerce clause consists of cases in which the state acts as a "market participant." Thus, when the state purchases goods from suppliers or sells goods produced at state-owned facilities or distributes its own property, it can give preference to its own residents. For example, in *Reeves v. Stake*[125] South Dakota

---

120 437 U.S. 117 (1978).

121 *See also Minnesota v. Clover Leaf Creamery Co.*, 449 U.S. 456 (1981) (Minnesota regulation barring use of plastic non-refillable milk containers not discriminatory even though permitted use of paperboard non-refillable milk containers favored instate pulpwood industry).

122 *Kassel v. Consolidated Freightways Corp. of Delaware*, 450 U.S. 662, 675 (1981).

123 *See CTS Corp. v. Dynamics Corp. of America*, 481 U.S. 69, 94-97 (1987) (Scalia, J., concurring in part and concurring in the judgment).

124 *See e.g.*, *Prudential Ins. Co. v. Benjamin*, 328 U.S. 408 (1951) (state regulation of insurance); *Northeast Bankcorp, Inc. v. Board of Governors of Federal Reserve System*, 472 U.S. 159 (1985) (state regulation of interstate banking). However, Congress must clearly state its intention to approve the state regulation. *See South-Central Timber Dev., Inc. v. Wunnicke*, 467 U.S. 82, 91 (1984). Also, a separate challenge to the state statute could be made under the equal protection clause of the 14th Amendment. *See Metropolitan Life Ins. Co. v. Ward*, 470 U.S. 869 (1985), discussed *infra*, text at note 175.

125 447 U.S. 429 (1980).

owned its own cement-producing facility and properly limited sales to state residents. The notion is that a state is using its tax revenues to provide benefits for its own people and need not share those resources with non-citizens of the state. Another market participant situation was *White v. Massachusetts Council of Construction Employers, Inc.*,[126] where the Court upheld a city's rule requiring that contractors on city-funded projects employ at least 50% city residents in their work force.

2. The Privileges and Immunities Clause of Article IV

The "privileges and immunities" clause of Art. IV §2 cl. 1, has a non-discriminatory policy similar to the dormant commerce clause, but it protects "basic rights," not just commerce rights. It provides that "[t]he citizens of each State shall be entitled to all Privileges and Immunities of Citizens of the several States." Generally the difficulty is in identifying some "basic right" that is affected.[127] But even as to "basic rights," a "substantial reason" for the discrimination based on the fact of the person's non-resident status is sufficient to justify different treatment. For example, the right to vote in state and local elections is a "basic" one, but a state can properly restrict non-residents from voting. But it may not restrict admission to the practice of law solely to residents of the state.[128] And it may not subject out-of-state residents to higher taxes.[129]

Moreover, a state has the right to reserve its tax funds and the resources it owns for its own residents. The justification for this is perhaps self-evident: taxes revenues of a state would not last long if everyone in the country had an equal right to them. Consequently, a state may charge non-resident students higher tuition to attend its public universities.[130] However, preservation of the resources *of the state* must be directly involved. Discriminatory state regulation of *private* conduct violates the privileges and immunities clause. For example, a state may not require *private* employers to give employment preference to state residents in all oil and gas operations connected with state-owned oil and gas reserves.[131] Yet, state-required hiring preferences for state residents on *state-funded* construction projects so long as it can show that the preference is based on a welfare motive, such as the need to provide employment for unemployed workers.[132]

PART II: Individual Rights Protected by the Constitution

The subject of individual rights and liberties protected by the Constitution is a vast one. The discussion here will be limited to the most important constitutional

---

126 460 U.S. 204 (1982).

127 *Baldwin v. Fish & Game Commission of Montana*, 436 U.S. 371, 383 (1978) (elk hunting for sport was not a "basic right," so state may charge higher hunting license fee for non-residents).

128 *Supreme Court of New Hampshire v. Piper*, 470 U.S. 274 (1985), discussed in Chapter IV, p. 137

129 *Lunding v. New York Tax Appeals Tribunal*, 522 U.S. 287 (1998) (invalidating a New York law permitting only New York residents a tax deduction of alimony payments).

130 *See Vlandis v. Kline*, 412 U.S. 441 (1973). *See also McCready v. Virginia*, 94 U.S. 391 (1877) (upholding a state's exclusion of non-residents from planting oysters in state-owned tidelands).

131 *Hicklin v. Orbeck*, 437 U.S. 518 (1978).

132 *United Building and Construction Trades Council v. City of Camden*, 465 U.S. 208 (1984). Art. IV privileges and immunities overlap somewhat with the dormant commerce clause. However, there are some differences: under Art. IV, discrimination must be overt (not just in effect), only "basic rights" are protected, corporations are not "citizens" protected, there is no "market participant" exception and Congress cannot validate discriminatory state action. *See* FARBER, *supra* note 2, at 899-900.

provisions and doctrines outside the areas of procedural due process rights and criminal due process rights, which have already been discussed in other chapters.[133]

A. Rights to Equal Protection of the Laws

The equal protection clause of the 14th Amendment provides that no *state* shall "deny to any person within its jurisdiction the equal protection of the laws." Though there is technically no equal protection clause applicable to the *federal* government, the Supreme Court has held that the *due process* clause of the 5th Amendment contains an equal protection component that imposes the same limitations on the federal government that the 14th Amendment imposes on the states.[134] Consequently, everything that follows applies equally to actions and laws of the federal government and the states.

Modern equal protection doctrine is really three different doctrines, since there are three levels of judicial scrutiny applied to determine if particular legislation or other government action denies equal protection of the laws. In short, they are as follows: (1) for a classification that burdens fundamental rights or affects "suspect classes" of people (primarily racial groups), the Court applies "strict scrutiny" and requires a compelling governmental interest to justify it, (2) for a classification that relates to business, economic or welfare matters that does not burden particular races or fundamental rights, the Court applies lax scrutiny and requires only that the legislature have had some conceivable "rational basis" for the classification, and (3) for classifications that distinguish on grounds of sex, the Court applies "middle-level scrutiny" and requires that the classification bear a substantial relationship to an important governmental interest to be sustained. These three tests are addressed in the next three sections.

1. Strict Scrutiny for Suspect Classifications and Burdens on Fundamental Rights

Under this strict scrutiny test, a law that draws distinctions along "suspect" lines or that discriminates with regard to a "fundamental right" will be held to be unconstitutional, unless it is necessary to promote a compelling governmental interest. This test thus has both an "ends" and a "means" aspect: the end sought to be achieved must be extremely important and the means chosen to achieve it (the classification in the challenged statute) must be one that involves the least possible burden on the suspect class or the fundamental right. Thus, even given a compelling governmental interest, if there is an alternative means of achieving that interest that would be less burdensome to the fundamental right or the suspect class, the classification will be struck down.[135]

a. Suspect Classifications   *also religion & national origin*

Because the equal protection clause of the 14th Amendment was a part of one of the three post-Civil War amendments designed to assure the benefits of full citizenship to the newly freed slaves (it was ratified in 1868), race was always considered to be at the core of the "equal protection of the laws" that it guaranteed.

---

133 *See* Chapter VI, pp. 198-202 (procedural due process) and Chapter VIII, pp. 270-303 (criminal due process rights).

134 *Bolling v. Sharpe*, 347 U.S. 497 (1954). This holding, of course, is nonsensical as an interpretation of constitutional text. However, the Court has shown no inclination to retreat from it.

135 The requirement of a close ends-means "fit" is a common characteristic of other constitutional tests, such as 1st Amendment rights. *See infra*, p. 348 (freedom of expression) and pp. 362-363 and note 374 (free exercise of religion).

Consequently, almost all government discrimination based on race or ethnicity violates equal protection.[136]

Discriminatory Purpose and Discriminatory Effect For discrimination to be a violation of equal protection, it must be shown to have been intentional.[137] When the discrimination results from an explicit classification set out on the face of the law itself, there can be no doubt that the different treatment is intentional. The Court will in most all circumstances invalidate explicit suspect classifications, since there can be few compelling justifications for them.[138] However, when the statute or regulation is neutral on its face, but has a disproportionate impact on a suspect class, intent to discriminate may be difficult to prove. Of course, substantially disproportionate effect and a lack of a racially-neutral explanation for that effect is good circumstantial evidence of intent to discriminate.[139]

Where there is a neutral statute, but the discretion of an administrator is broad, a finding of discrimination is more likely. In *Yick Wo v. Hopkins*,[140] a law prohibited laundries from being located in wood buildings without a special permit. The city consistently refused permits to Chinese laundries while granting them to others. Since the authorities could offer no racially neutral explanation for their conduct, the Court held that it could only have been based on an intent to discriminate against Chinese.[141] On the other hand, where disproportionate racial impact resulted from administration of a written objective test for employment, that in and of itself was not sufficient to show discriminatory purpose for equal protection purposes.[142]

There are special difficulties with proving intent when the challenged law is a statute enacted by a legislature, since inquiry into the motives of legislative bodies is a "sensitive inquiry." In such cases, the general historical background for the law, the prevalence of other prior discriminatory laws, the sequence of events leading to this particular law, and statements of lawmakers are all considered. In *Hunter v. Underwood*,[143] the question was whether a section of the Alabama constitution, adopted in 1901, constituted intentional discrimination against blacks when it provided that those convicted of crimes of "moral turpitude" lost their right to vote. The Court held that the history of the constitutional convention and other historical studies demonstrated an intent to disqualify blacks from voting.[144]

---

136 *Strauder v. West Virginia*, 100 U.S. 303 (1880) (law prohibiting blacks from serving on grand or petit juries unconstitutional); *Yick Wo v. Hopkins*, 118 U.S. 356 (1886) (discriminatory denial of laundry license to Chinese); *Hernandez v. Texas*, 347 U.S. 475 (1954) (exclusion of Mexican-Americans from jury service);

137 *Arlington Heights v. Metropolitan Housing Development Corp.*, 429 U.S. 252, 267 (1977) (racially disproportionate impact of zoning ordinance not sufficient to show intent).

138 *But see infra*, p. 330 -332 (affirmative action programs).

139 *Compare* dormant commerce clause discrimination. *See supra*, p. 324. Both equal protection and dormant commerce clause challenges are discussed in a case involving a law having disproportionate impact on interstate commerce in *Minnesota v. Clover Leaf Creamery*, *supra* note 121.

140 118 U.S. 356 (1886).

141 *See also Louisiana v. United States*, 380 U.S. 145 (1965) (literacy tests for prospective voters in the south were discriminatory; they were administered loosely and the results were invariably that blacks failed in large numbers while whites did not).

142 *Washington v. Davis*, 426 U.S. 229 (1976). Disproportionate effect is sufficient to prove discrimination under federal statutes prohibiting discrimination in some instances. *See* Chapter XV, pp. 569-570 (employment discrimination in violation of Civil Rights Act of 1964).

143 471 U.S. 222 (1985).

144 Though the Court found that the lawmakers had an *additional* motive of discriminating against poor *whites*, this was not sufficient to save the provision because it was clear that it would have been adopted in any event to disenfranchise blacks, the overwhelming majority of whom were poor.

Racial Segregation Racial segregation was not held to violate equal protection until 1954. In 1896, the Court settled on a definition of equality in the case of *Plessy v. Ferguson*,[145] that allowed "separate but equal" treatment of minorities. In *Plessy*, it upheld a Louisiana law separating train passengers according to race. *Plessy* was not overruled until *Brown v. Board of Education*.[146] Only in *Brown*, then, did the Court finally accept the idea that separate treatment based on race constitutes racial discrimination regardless of how equal the separate facilities are, because such segregation — being imposed by the majority to insulate itself from the minority — stigmatizes the minority group. *Brown* involved racial segregation of public schools.

It is impossible to overemphasize the dehumanizing effects of the racial segregation system which the "separate-but-equal" doctrine allowed states to impose on black people in the United States until more than half way through the 20th century. Especially in the southern states, these laws and a multitude of customary practices that accompanied them operated to perpetuate an entire separate system of inferior schools, housing, churches, businesses, transportation, and hotels. A black person seeking to find a place to eat would have to find a "black" eating place. Public restrooms were divided into "Men," "Women," and "Colored." There were even "White" and "Colored" public drinking fountains. In the Northern states, there were fewer petty indignities and not as many segregative practices were enshrined in law. But because of the uniformity of the private choices of businesses and individuals, such practices might as well have been law. An ironic result was that it was often the case that famous black musicians, such as Lena Horne and Louis Armstrong, would not be allowed to stay overnight in the very hotel where they were performing.

It is similarly impossible to over-emphasize the importance of the Court's 1954 decision in *Brown v. Board of Education*. Whenever lawyers in the United States are asked to name the single most important decision of the Supreme Court, for most it is the *Brown* case. *Brown* invalidated the dual system of public schools which was either mandated by law or established and maintained through consistent practices of school administrators. But it applied by analogy to all other governmental racial segregation.[147]

Affirmative Action Given this history, it is perhaps ironic that the most important issue in the area of racial discrimination today concerns discrimination against whites. "Affirmative action" programs — programs designed to give advantages to minorities for jobs, school admissions, government contracts and any number of other areas — have been under attack as explicit, intentional racial discrimination against whites violative of the equal protection clause.

The Court has held that affirmative action programs are subject to strict scrutiny analysis since they classify based on race. However, this does not mean that all such programs are *per se* unconstitutional as laws disadvantaging minorities are. The Court has suggested that there may be the government interest may be sufficiently compelling to justify discrimination in favor of minorities in some circumstances. However, the Court has not clarified precisely what those circumstances might be.

---

145 163 U.S. 537 (1896).

146 347 U.S. 483 (1954).

147 The equal protection clause has no effect on racially discriminatory action by *private* individuals since the Constitution generally applies only to governmental action. Private discrimination is outlawed by several federal statutes starting with the Civil Rights Act of 1964. Title VII of this law, which prohibits discrimination in employment, is discussed in Chapter XV, pp. 569-573. Other title prohibit discrimination in private housing, public accommodations and credit extensions, and in any federally-funded activity.

One thing that is clear is that a general desire by the government to remedy past "societal discrimination" is not sufficiently compelling. This was the holding of *Richmond v. J.A. Croson Co.*, in which the Court struck down a program that required that prime contractors who received contract awards from the city, subcontract at least 30% of the work to minority-owned construction firms.[148] The Court dismissed as insufficient a general history disclosing that few minority contractors were ever used by the city's general contractors. The Court in *Croson* conceded that a program that was "narrowly tailored to remedy the effects of prior discrimination" would be valid. Clearly this would include a "program" awarding contracts to those minority contractors who can show that they personally had been denied contracts in the past on racial grounds. But it is unclear how much further the city could go.

It remains to be seen whether other governmental interests might be considered sufficiently compelling to justify preference programs for minorities. For example, one might argue that creating racial diversity in critical areas of public concern is a sufficiently compelling interest. There are suggestions in the cases that this might justify using race as a factor in admissions to state law or medical schools[149] and choice of teaching personnel in secondary schools,[150] though there is no agreement among the members of the Court on the point.[151]

Racially-Conscious Decisions Affecting Voting Rights A similar area of current controversy is the use of race in drawing the boundaries of Congressional and state legislative districts to assure proportionate minority representation. The federal Voting Rights Act[152] prohibits "diluting" the political power of racial minorities. Consequently, states have frequently drawn legislative district borders in such a way that racial minorities will constitute a majority of the voters in a percentage of districts equal to as the percentage of minority voters in the general population of the state. The Supreme Court has approved this deliberate creation of "minority-majority" districts where the purpose is to provide minority voters with a fair share of political power.[153] However, a recent case suggests that there is a constitutional limit to such efforts. In *Shaw v. Reno*,[154] a 5-4 majority invalidated a rather improbably shaped "majority-minority" Congressional district. It was 160 miles long and for much of that length no wider than a highway. If race was found on remand to have been the "predominant factor" in drawing the district, then it would violate equal protection.[155]

In a later effort to clarify the standard, the Court emphasized that there is a strong presumption that the line-drawing was proper. It indicated that an attack on racial grounds would succeed only if the plaintiff was able to show "that the legislature subordinated traditional race-neutral districting principles, including but not limited

---

148 488 U.S. 469 (1989). Recently, the Court made clear that the *Croson* standard applies to affirmative action programs of the federal government. *Adarand Constructors, Inc. v. Pena*, 515 U.S.200 (1995) (preference program for contractors owned by "socially and economically disadvantaged persons").

149 *See Regents of the University of California v. Bakke*, 438 U.S. 265 (1978).

150 *See Wygant v. Jackson Board of Education*, 476 U.S. 267 (1986).

151 The Court of Appeals for the Fifth Circuit has explicitly rejected this argument, holding that the use of race as a factor in admission to the University of Texas Law School was "per se proscribed. *Hopwood v. Texas*, 78 F.3d 932 (5th Cir. 1996). The Supreme Court denied certiorari. 518 U.S. 1033 (1996).

152 42 U.S.C.A. §1971.

153 *United Jewish Organizations of Williamwburgh v. Carey*, 430 U.S. 144 (1977).

154 509 U.S. 630 (1993).

155 In an second appeal following a remand, the Supreme Court held the district invalid, noting that it was not narrowly tailored to serve any compelling state interest. *Shaw v. Hunt*, 527 U.S. 899 (1996).

to compactness, contiguity, respect for political subdivisions or communities defined by actual shared interests, to racial considerations."[156]

Discrimination Based on Alienage   Distinctions based on alienage are treated differently depending on whether it is the federal government or state or local government that is discriminating. If it is a state or local government that is treating aliens differently, the Court applies strict scrutiny. When the *federal* government deals with aliens, the classifications it makes will be subject only to rational basis scrutiny.[157] This double standard is based on the federal government's plenary power over immigration and naturalization.[158] However, the rational basis standard is also applied to state or local exclusion of aliens from certain government jobs that are "intimately related to the process of democratic self-government."[159] Thus, the Court has applied strict scrutiny and struck down state laws disqualifying aliens from obtaining welfare benefits or from becoming lawyers or civil servants.[160] However, states *may* prohibit aliens from becoming state policemen, probation officers, and public school teachers.[161]

b. Classifications Affecting Fundamental Rights

Strict scrutiny will be applied to classifications that are drawn in such a way as to affect the exercise of "fundamental rights." The relevant rights include any of the rights set out in the Constitution explicitly (such as in the 1st Amendment),[162] plus any that are not set out explicitly, but have been held to be fundamental under the general provisions of the constitution (such as the right to vote or the right to privacy).[163] Like suspect classifications, these classifications based on the exercise of a fundamental right will be struck down unless the government can show that they are necessary to pursue a compelling governmental interest. The major issue in many cases then is whether the classification burdens fundamental rights. Thus, even though abortion is a fundamental right, a federal welfare statute prohibiting federal funding for medical costs of abortions while continuing to fund the cost of live births was not judged according to strict scrutiny. The Court determined that classification was not one that affected the right to an abortion, since it did not place any obstacles in the path of a woman seeking one. Consequently, the statute was subjected to rational-basis review and was upheld.[164]

---

156 *Miller v. Johnson*, 515 U.S. 900 (1995).

157 *See, e.g., Mathews v. Diaz*, 426 U.S. 67 (1976), as explained in *Nyquist v. Mauclet*, 432 U.S. 1, 7 n.8 (1977) (upholding durational residency requirements for medical welfare benefits imposed on aliens, but not citizens, by Congress).

158 Art. I §8 cl. 4.

159 *Bernal v. Fainter*, 467 U.S. 216, 220 (1984).

160 *Graham v. Richardson*, 403 U.S. 365 (1971) (welfare benefits); *Application of Griffiths*, 413 U.S. 717 (1973); *Sugarman v. Dougall*, 413 U.S. 634 (1973) (civil service jobs).

161 *Foley v. Connelie*, 435 U.S. 291 (1978) (police officer); *Cabell v. Chavez-Salido*, 454 U.S. 432 (1982) (probation officer); *Ambach v. Norwick*, 441 U.S. 68 (1979) (public school teacher).

162 *See e.g. Carey v. Brown*, 447 U.S. 455 (1980) (statute prohibiting all picketing near residences unless related to a labor dispute violates both 1st Amendment and strict scrutiny equal protection).

163 *See Shapiro v. Thompson*, 394 U.S. 618 (1969) (state welfare residency requirement violates strict scrutiny equal protection because it affects fundamental right to travel). *See also Attorney General of New York v. Soto Lopez*, 476 U.S. 898 (1986) (both right to travel and equal protection violated by employment preference solely for veterans living in the state when they entered military service).

164 *See Harris v. McRae*, 448 U.S. 297 (1980).

Perhaps the seminal case in fundamental-rights equal protection is *Skinner v. Oklahoma*.[165] Skinner was convicted of larceny for the third time and the state sought to apply a law allowing it to sterilize habitual criminals convicted of certain crimes. The Supreme Court held the law unconstitutional as a violation of equal protection. The reason given was that the law provided that persons convicted multiple times of some offenses, such as robbery, burglary, larceny, manslaughter, could be sterilized, while people convicted of other crimes, such as fraud or embezzlement, could not be. The Court seemed to admit that there could be a rational basis for the distinction and that it might be sustainable under the lax equal protection test usually used. However, the classification in the statute had to do with sterilization, an action that affected the fundamental right to procreate. [166]

2. Lax "Rational Basis" Scrutiny for Economic and Business Regulation or Social Welfare Programs

A "rational basis" test is applied in all classifications involving economic, social welfare or business regulation, which do not otherwise relate to the exercise of fundamental rights or suspect classifications. As the Court has recently stated, under the rational basis test, the law will be sustained "if any state of facts reasonably may be conceived to justify it."[167] It is not necessary for the legislature to have actually had such facts in mind. The rational basis can be suggested by counsel later in the process of the lawsuit challenging the legislation or can be supplied by the court examining the legislation. In essence, unless the classification is completely irrational, it will be sustained. The reason for a lax test is that "[t]he Constitution presumes that . . . even improvident decisions will eventually be rectified by the political process and that judicial intervention is generally unwarranted no matter how unwisely we may think a political branch has acted."[168] As an "ends-means" test, then, the end need only be a legitimate one and the means chosen need only be one that a rational person might conceive of as furthering that end.

Under these conditions, it is relatively easy to think up a rational basis for a classification, so this test has the effect of presuming the validity of the legislation. In this respect, it is the opposite of the suspect classification test which presumes that the legislation is invalid. Thus, in these two areas, the battle over the validity of a challenged classification is largely over once it is determined into what category the legislation falls.

A recent example of the application of the rational basis test is *Dallas v. Stanglin*,[169] in which the Court unanimously upheld a city ordinance that limited the use of certain dance halls to persons between the ages of 14 and 18. The Court first found that the law was not one limiting any rights to association protected by the 1st Amendment or the due process clause and thus did not warrant strict scrutiny. It then applied the rational basis test. In response to the argument that there was no rational basis for the distinction between dance halls and other gathering places (such as roller rinks) in terms of the city's purpose of preventing corrupting influences of

---

165 316 U.S. 535 (1942).
166 Other fundamental rights are discussed *infra* pp. 352-355.
167 *Sullivan v. Stroop*, 496 U.S. 478 (1990).
168 *Vance v. Bradley*, 440 U.S. 93 (1978).
169 *Dallas v. Stanglin*, 490 U.S. 19 (1989).

persons over 18, the Court observed that the difference "may not be striking, but the differentiation need not be striking in order to survive rational basis scrutiny."[170]

The rational basis test is indeed a lax one and — given a legitimate legislative purpose — it is hard to win an argument that the classification could not conceivably be thought to further it. However, the legislative purpose must be *legitimate*. In *City of Cleburne v. Cleburne Living Center*,[171] the city denied a permit for use of a home as a place for a group of mentally-retarded persons to live together. However, it would have permitted an identical number of *non-retarded* unrelated persons to live together. While rejecting the argument that mentally retarded persons were a "suspect" class, it nonetheless found that the ordinance violated equal protection. This was because the only conceivable basis for the ordinance was the city's desire to keep retarded persons out — a purpose that was not legitimate. Similar reasoning was used in *Romer v. Evans*.[172] There the Court struck down a popular referendum in Colorado that prohibited the state or local governments from enacting any law that would give protected status or other preference to persons based on their sexual orientation. Since homosexuals do not constitute a suspect class and there is no fundamental right to engage in homosexual activities,[173] only rational basis scrutiny was called for. However, the referendum did not pass the rational basis test because "imposing a broad and undifferentiated disability on a single named group" is an "invalid form of legislation." "[A]nimus toward [that] class" lacks any rational relationship to *legitimate* state interests.[174]

The Court used similar reasoning in the business context in *Metropolitan Life Insurance Co. v. Ward*.[175] That case involved a state law that imposed a higher tax on *out-of-state* insurance companies doing business in the state than on *in-state* insurance companies. The Court held that the law would be invalid if the sole reason for the distinction was a desire to protect local businesses from out-of-state competition, since this was not a permissible governmental purpose. Dissenters in the case asserted that a possible reason for favoring local companies could be consumer protection: i.e., local companies would be more likely to have local offices through which companies could help local consumers. The consumer protection rationale was not even argued by the city in the appeal. The Supreme Court thought of it and remanded the case to the lower court to consider it as a possible rational basis for sustaining the law.[176]

3. The Middle-Level Test for "Semi-Suspect" Classifications

Why a Middle-Level Test Before the 1970s, the Court seemed satisfied with only two levels of scrutiny for legislative classifications. However, as it was faced with more and more challenges to classifications based on sex, it became clear that neither the strict nor the lax test would work too well. For example, in one case, a Michigan law prohibited women from working as bartenders unless they were the daughter or wife of the bar owner. A rational basis was found in the assertions that

---

170 490 U.S. at 28.

171 473 U.S. 432 (1985).

172 517 U.S. 620 (1996).

173 *See Bowers v. Hardwick*, 478 U.S. 186 (1986) (plurality) and *infra* p. 342.

174 517 U.S. at 632 (emphasis added).

175 470 U.S. 869 (1985).

176 Incidentally, there was no dormant commerce clause problem with the law because Congress has given states the power to regulate the insurance industry, even if such regulation burdens interstate commerce, as it has the power to do under the commerce clause. *See* discussion, *supra* p. 326.

it is mainly men who frequent bars and the atmosphere would be detrimental to women, and that the law cut down on instances of prostitution. One could readily criticize this basis for the law by pointing out that bars are no worse in these respects than any other places that the legislature allows women to work, but it probably satisfies the rational basis test.[177] If strict scrutiny is applied, this law would clearly be invalidated. But then so might many other laws, such at those that exempt women from compulsory military service or protect them from sexual exploitation, since the government would have to show a compelling interest in the classification and prove that it could not achieve that interest in any other way.

The common law has discriminated against women for centuries. A married woman had few rights.[178] The common law treatment of women carried over into constitutional law. In an 1873 case, *Bradwell v. Illinois*,[179] the Court held that it was constitutional for Illinois to deny women the right to practice law in the state. A concurring justice was moved to write:

> The natural timidity and proper timidity and delicacy which belongs to the female sex unfits it for many of the occupations of civil life . . . . The paramount destiny and mission of woman are to fulfill the noble and benign offices of wife and mother. This is the law of the Creator.[180]

Much has happened in constitutional law since 1873. Indeed, exactly 100 years after *Bradwell*, four members of the Court were in favor of holding that classifications on the basis of sex were suspect and called for the application of strict scrutiny.[181]

The Standard Today In the end, however, the Court settled upon a middle-level scrutiny test halfway between strict scrutiny and rational basis. Under this test, a law drawing distinctions based on sex must meet a middle-level scrutiny test: the law must "serve important governmental objectives and must be substantially related to achievement of those objectives."[182] Unlike rational basis, the governmental objective cannot be an after-the-fact justification, but must have actually been relied upon in drawing the distinction.[183] As a test of "ends" and "means," the end must be a substantial one — halfway between a "compelling" one and a merely "legitimate" interest — and the "fit" between that end and the means to accomplish it must be that the classification chosen "substantially" furthers it. Recently, the Court emphasized that this means that the state must show an "exceedingly persuasive justification" for differing treatment based on sex.[184] This is halfway between the "fit" required for a suspect classification and rational basis. By contrast, a suspect classification must be the only reasonable way to achieve the governmental end while the rational basis test requires only that it be rationally possible that the means chosen will advance the governmental interest.

---

177 *See Goesaert v. Cleary*, 335 U.S. 464 (1948).

178 *See* p. 476.

179 83 U.S. 130 (1873).

180 *Id.* at 141 (Bradley, J., concurring). Ms. Bradwell was not deterred from a legal career, For 30 years she was the editor and publisher of a very influential legal journal, The Chicago Law Journal. Ms. Bradwell was admitted to the Illinois bar after her death, as Illinois and several other states finally began to abolish their bans on women becoming lawyers. *See* JANE M. FRIEDMAN, AMERICA'S FIRST WOMAN LAWYER: THE BIOGRAPHY OF MYRA BRADWELL (Prometheus Books, N.Y. 1993).

181 *Frontiero v. Richardson*, 411 U.S. 677 (1973).

182 *Craig v. Boren*, 429 U.S. 190 (1976).

183 *United States v. Virginia*, 518 U.S. 515 (1996).

184 *Id.* at 523.

Using this intermediate standard, the Court held invalid an Oklahoma law that set the legal age for drinking at 18 for females and 21 for males.[185] It also struck down an Idaho law providing a preference for men over women among the relatives of a deceased person in the choice of an administrator for the estate of that decedent,[186] rejecting generalizations about women's lesser ability to understand law, business or commerce as a basis for the irrebuttable preference. In *Mississippi University for Women v. Hogan*, the Court struck down a state "women-only" nursing school admissions policy as based on "archaic and stereotypic notions" concerning the abilities of males and females.[187] In *United States v. Virginia*, the Court required that a state military academy with a reputation for tough training admit women, despite arguments that the presence of women would disrupt its "adversative" approach to training. The Court equated these arguments to those made in the 19th century against women becoming lawyers. It observed that "generalizations about 'the way women are,' estimates of what is appropriate for *most women*, no longer justify denying opportunities to women whose talent and capacity place them outside the average description."[188] In *Orr v. Orr*, the Court struck down a statute that provided for alimony to be awarded to wives, but not to husbands. It found that presuming that husbands were never as needy as wives was based on impermissible sexual stereotypes.[189] Similarly, the Court invalidated statutes based on assumptions that when both spouses were employed, the husband is the superior wage-earner, and that men have a need for more education than women.[190]

Laws Disadvantaging Men As the *Orr* and *Hogan* cases indicate, men as well as women can use the equal protection clause to strike down distinctions based on sex. Thus, the Court invalidated a law providing child support benefits to the surviving *wife* of a deceased male worker, but not to the surviving husband of a deceased female worker[191] and a law providing survivors' benefits to all wives of deceased male workers without a showing of actual dependency on the deceased spouse, but providing such benefits to the husband of a deceased female worker only upon a showing that he was actually dependent on his wife's earnings.[192] However, statutes drawing distinctions based on sex that give *advantages* to women are valid, if designed to compensate women for *past unequal treatment by society.* Thus in *Kahn v. Shevin*, the Court held valid a Florida law that gave property tax exemptions to widows, but not to widowers.[193] Similarly, in *Califano v. Webster*,[194] federal Social Security laws permitted women to disregard more years of lower earnings than men in determining the rate of payment of their retirement benefits. The Court noted that it was a well-known fact that working women have historically been paid much less

---

185 *Craig v. Boren, supra* note 182.

186 *Reed v. Reed*, 404 U.S. 71 (1971).

187 458 U.S. 718 (1982).

188 518 U.S. at 549.

189 440 U.S. 268 (1979).

190 *Frontiero v. Richardson*, 411 U.S. 677 (1973) (invalidating federal law that automatically gave military men a "dependency allowance," but required military women to prove actual dependency of their spouse in order to qualify); *Stanton v. Stanton*, 421 U.S. 7 (1975) (invalidating state law that required parents to support male children until age 21, but female children only until age 18).

191 *Weinberger v. Weisenfeld*, 420 U.S. 636 (1975).

192 *Califano v. Goldfarb*, 430 U.S. 199 (1977). These laws could also be viewed as discriminating against the female workers involved by not providing them with the protection that male workers get.

193 *Kahn v. Shevin*, 416 U.S. 351 (1974).

194 430 U.S. 313 (1977).

than men and Congress's attempt to correct this imbalance was a sufficiently substantial governmental objective. These cases would seem to make the constitutionality of affirmative action programs for women less problematic than they would be for racial minorities.

Permissible Sex-Based Distinctions Laws based on true biological differences, sometime referred to as "sex-specific traits," will also be upheld so long as they satisfy the less restrictive "rational basis" standard of review. For example, the biology of human reproduction is such that the mother of a child is easily identified by the birth process, while the father is not so easily identified. Consequently, the state may permit the unmarried *mother* of a child to bring an action for the child's wrongful death, but deny that right to the *father* unless the father has "legitimated" the child by acknowledging that he is the father.[195] The Court has also held that the state may constitutionally exclude pregnancy from its medical insurance plan for state workers even though it is only women who get pregnant.[196] Finally, the Court has upheld the constitutionality of Congress's limiting the draft (compulsory military service) to males.[197] From that decision, it appears likely that the Court would hold that military regulations banning women from frontline combat duty are constitutional. In the draft case, the Court approved Congress's reliance on the lesser physical strength of women, the difficulties of maintaining separate facilities under combat conditions, as well as the effect on public morale that sending women into combat might entail.[198]

Differing Views of Women's Rights and Equality Criticisms of the Court's approach in the women's rights area are as varied as the points of view about women's position in society. Even feminists are divided. Some feminists believe that the Court should have determined that sex was a suspect classification and should strike down all sex-based classifications, even those that are designed to assist women. The theory is that such protections, while they provide some temporary assistance to some women, are in the long run harmful because they perpetuate the stereotype of women as being dependent and inferior. They argue that these meager advantages become excuses for perpetuating even greater disadvantages. They also serve to encourage women to follow the traditional dependent path of homemaker, rather than to seek their way in the working world.

On the other hand, other feminists support statutes that provide women with special protections on the ground that they are necessary as a practical matter. Such statutes are needed to counteract disabilities imposed by society both in the past and at the present time. They argue that treating women the same as men simply allows those societal inequalities to continue to oppress women until such time as society changes its expectations of women, something that could be a long time in coming.

This conflict in views was evident in a case raising the question of the validity of a California law that required employers to provide all female employees with an unpaid pregnancy leave of up to four months and the right to be reinstated into a "substantially similar job" upon return from that leave. *Amicus curiae* briefs filed by

---

195 *Parham v. Hughes*, 441 U.S. 347 (1979). *But see Caban v. Mohammed*, 441 U.S. 380 (1979) (mother-only consent to adoption unconstitutional where biological father had lived with mother and child and established a relationship with the child).

196 *Geduldig v. Aiello*, 417 U.S. 484 (1974). However, Congress has provided statutory protection against such discrimination with the Pregnancy Discrimination Act, 42 U.S.C.A. §2000e(k).

197 *Rostker v. Goldberg*, 453 U.S. 57 (1981).

198 Women receive more effective protection from sex discrimination from Title VII of the Civil Rights Act of 1964, 42 U.S.C.A. §2000e *et seq. See* Chapter XV, pp. 569-573.

two feminist organizations, the National Organization for Women (NOW) and the Equal Rights Advocates, took opposing positions on the validity of the law. NOW argued that the law should be struck down because it was yet another piece of "protective" legislation based on assumptions about the weakness of women. Equal Rights Advocates argued that the law should be upheld, claiming that the special treatment afforded by the statute was not discrimination; it was necessary to *assure equality* of employment opportunity given the disadvantages that women face in the workplace. The Court upheld the law.[199]

True sex-neutrality would have presumably been required by the Equal Rights Amendment had it been ratified. The ERA, as it is known, would have provided that "[e]quality of rights under the law shall not be denied or abridged by the United States or by any State on account of sex." It was passed by Congress in 1972 after a 55-year struggle and was sent to the states for ratification with a 7-year limit. Though 30 of the necessary states quickly ratified the ERA, a more conservative mood later swept the country and the ratification process was stalled. Five more states ratified, but three that had previously ratified, sought to withdraw their approval. Though Congress extended the time for ratification until 1982, no additional states ratified and the amendment died for lack of support.

Discrimination Against "Illegitimate" Children The Supreme Court has held that a middle-level test like that used to strike down some sex-based classifications applies to discrimination against "illegitimate" children or children born of parents who are not married to each other. The Court has invalidated many of the traditional legal disabilities imposed on such children. It has held unconstitutional the denials of the right to inherit from the father,[200] the right to receive workers' compensation benefits,[201] the right to wrongful death recovery for the death of a parent,[202] the right to welfare benefits,[203] and the right to child support from the natural father.[204] The Court has held, however, that if governmental benefits are based on past "actual dependency" on a deceased parent, the government may require that illegitimate children establish actual dependency even though it presumes that *legitimate* children were dependent on the father.[205] It also rejected a challenge to a federal statute bestowing U.S. citizenship automatically upon birth to a child born out of wedlock to an American citizen *mother*, though not to the same child born of a citizen *father* unless a paternity decree was entered before the child turned 18.[206]

B. Substantive Due Process Rights

The Varieties of Due Process As pointed out in the chapter on criminal procedure,[207] there are two due process clauses in the Constitution: one is found in

---

199 *See* FARBER, *supra* note 2, at. 353-356 (briefs) and *California Federal Savings and Loan Association v. Guerra*, 479 U.S. 472 (1987).

200 *Trimble v. Gordon*, 430 U.S. 762 (1977).

201 *Weber v. Aetna Casualty & Surety Co.*, 406 U.S. 164, 175 (1972).

202 *Levy v. Louisiana*, 391 U.S. 68 (1968).

203 *New Jersey Welfare Rights Organization v. Cahill*, 411 U.S. 619 (1973).

204 *Gomez v. Perez*, 409 U.S. 535 (1973). *See also Clark v. Jeter*, 486 U.S. 456 (1988) (6-year limitation on the time for filing paternity action was constitutionally impermissible). *But see Lalli v. Lalli*, 439 U.S. 259 (1978) (state may require that paternity be established in a judicial proceeding during the father's lifetime as precondition for inheriting from father).

205 *Mathews v. Lucas*, 427 U.S. 495 (1976).

206 *Miller v. Albright*, 523 U.S. 420 (1998). *See also* Chapter XIII, p. 483 note 45.

207 *See* Chapter VIII, p. 271.

the 5th Amendment and applies only to the federal government and the other is found in the 14th Amendment, which is applicable to the states. Collectively they provide a person may not be "deprived of life, liberty or property without due process of law" by any governmental body in the United States.

The generality of this wording has led to the Court use due process for many purposes. In the area of individual rights, due process is understood as establishing three distinct sets of rights. The first, "incorporated" due process rights, have already been discussed in the criminal procedure chapter.[208] The second are "procedural" due process rights, which were discussed in the chapter on administrative law.[209] The third set of rights, which will be discussed here, are "substantive" due process rights.

Definitions "Substantive due process" would seem to be a contradiction in terms. In fact, the doctrine has little to do with "process" and a great deal to do with "substance." While the due process clause states that the government shall not "deprive any person of life, liberty or property *without due process of law*," substantive due process holds that there are certain rights encompassed within the term "liberty" that may not be infringed by the state no matter what "process" it provides. Indeed, the rights protected in this area might more accurately be described, not as *due process* rights, but as "*no process*" rights. If the "without due process" portion of the clause means anything, it can only be that a court presumes that there was a failure in the *legislative* process if it produced a law that violates fundamental rights. However, the Court has simply ignored the "process" reference and has never explained what role it plays in the substantive due process context.

Overlap With Equal Protection There is considerable and perhaps complete overlap between substantive due process and the top and bottom levels of three-tier equal protection law discussed earlier. "Fundamental rights" substantive due process corresponds to strict scrutiny equal protection in that it requires a compelling governmental interest to sustain any infringement on fundamental rights.[210] There is also a lax form of substantive due process identical to rational basis equal protection: it applies to business, welfare or economic legislation and invalidates a law only if it is completely irrational. As such, it is rarely used and even more rarely used successfully.[211] Today, the validity of business, welfare and economic laws is almost always judged under the equal protection rubric rather than due process. Consequently, only the fundamental rights side of substantive due process will be discussed here.[212]

Substantive Due Process and Judicial Review Substantive due process has become the major source of unwritten "fundamental rights" generation outside the more specific rights-bestowing provisions of the Constitution. As such, it raises — more than any other constitutional doctrine — the question of the legitimate role of

---

208 *See* Chapter VIII, pp. 270-303

209 *See* Chapter VI, pp. 198-202. While procedural due process standards are most often applied to administrative action, they also apply to judicial action. *See* Chapter VI, p. 201. As discussed in Chapter VII, due process is also used to test the limits of personal jurisdiction (*see* pp. 245-248) and choice of law (pp. 252-253).

210 *See supra* p. 332.

211 *See, e.g. North Dakota State Board of Pharmacy v. Snyder's Drug Stores, Inc.* 414 U.S. 156 (1973) (law requiring pharmacies to be controlled by pharmacists is not completely irrational and thus does not violate due process). *Compare supra* pp. 333-334 ("rational basis" equal protection).

212 At one point it seemed that strict scrutiny equal protection rather than substantive due process would be the major vehicle for protecting fundamental rights. Some texts reflect this in their organization. *See* NOWAK & ROTUNDA, *supra* note 2, §14.29 (discussing the abortion cases under equal protection).

the Court in applying its power of judicial review to invalidate governmental action through what has been called "non-interpretivist" methods.[213]

Substantive due process has a history that dates from the embarrassing 1900-1937 period, discussed in Chapter I.[214] Cases in this era, the most famous (or infamous) being *Lochner v. New York*, "found" in the "liberty" guaranteed by the due process clause the tenets of 19th-century *laissez faire* capitalist philosophy. Today, the Court's elaborations on what is included in "liberty" have largely been confined to the right of privacy. Whether this revised return to substantive due process is any better than *Lochner* is hotly debated.[215]

1. The Right to Privacy

Birth Control and Abortion   The initial step in developing a right to privacy pointedly avoided any reliance on substantive due process analysis. In *Griswold v. Connecticut*,[216] the Court struck down a state statute that prohibited all use of birth control devices on grounds of a right to privacy. The majority opinion relied on the cumulative effect of the Bill of Rights — "penumbras, formed by emanations from" Bill of Rights guarantees — as defining "zones of privacy" that protected the right of a married couple to use birth control devices. It explicitly rejected arguments "suggest-[ing] that *Lochner* be our guide," disavowing any power to "sit as a super-legislature to determine the wisdom, need, and propriety of laws."   A concurring opinion emphasized the 9th Amendment's reservation of unspecified "other [rights] retained by the people."   Two concurring opinions relied on substantive due process.   But despite its disclaimers, the majority opinion relied on two cases from the *Lochner* period: *Meyer v. Nebraska*[217] and *Pierce v. Society of Sisters*.[218]   In *Meyer*, the Court struck down a Nebraska law that prohibited teaching young children any language other than English in any public or private school.   The Court held that "liberty" in the due process clause included "certain fundamental rights which must be respected."   In *Pierce*, the Court followed *Meyer* in striking down an Oregon law that required all children to attend public schools based on the right of the parents to choose a private school for their children if they wanted.

In *Roe v. Wade*,[219] the abortion decision, the majority relied directly on a substantive due process rationale.   As if to make sure that it was choosing the "correct" set of values to infuse into the term "liberty," Justice Blackmun's opinion undertook an exhaustive examination of the history of abortion law, beginning with the time of the ancient Greeks, and considered all manner of medical, philosophical and religious input on the questions involved.   The opinion held that the right to privacy included the right to an abortion, but recognized two countervailing interests of the state: an interest in the mother's health and an interest in "potential human life."   Based on this and medical information on fetal development, the Court divided

---

213 *See supra* p. 308.

214 *See* pp. 11-12.

215 The opinions of Justices O'Conner and of Chief Justice Rehnquist and Justice Scalia in dissent in a recent abortion case constitute a classic debate about the role of the Court in "fundamental rights" substantive due process doctrine and what dangers to its authority exist in light of its experiences in the pre-1937 years. *See Planned Parenthood of Southeastern Pennsylvania v. Casey*, 505 U.S. 833 (1992).

216 381 U.S. 479 (1969).

217 262 U.S. 390 (1923).

218 268 U.S. 510 (1925).

219 410 U.S. 113 (1973).

pregnancy into three trimesters.[220] Because in the first trimester childbirth is more of a threat to the woman's health than an abortion and the fetus is not viable outside the mother's body, neither of the two state interests is very strong. At the other end of the gestation period, last trimester abortions involve both a substantial threat to the mother's health and destroy a fetus capable of surviving outside the mother's body. Thus, the state's interest in regulating abortions in this final three-months of pregnancy becomes "compelling" and it can prohibit abortions altogether except to save the life or health of the mother. During the middle trimester, the state's interest in the health of the mother is stronger than in the first trimester, so it can regulate as necessary to protect that interest, such as requiring that the procedure be performed in an adequate medical facility like a hospital or clinic.

Since *Roe*, there has been almost endless litigation over the issues it raised. Several state regulations attempting to make abortions more expensive and requiring them to be performed in hospitals were struck down.[221] The Court invalidated on vagueness grounds a statute requiring a doctor to determine viability of the fetus before performing an abortion,[222] but then later approved a more specific viability test requirement aimed at abortions past the 20th week of pregnancy.[223] In other cases it struck down consent requirements that required the father's consent or the mother's parents' consent if she was a minor,[224] but later approved a statute requiring that a minor either notify both parents or obtain judicial approval before getting an abortion.[225] The Court also rejected challenges to federal and state welfare laws that prohibited funding for abortions for poor women, while allowing such funding for live childbirth. The Court held that the government may not place obstacles in the path of a woman seeking an abortion, but it is not required to *fund* her exercise of her right.[226] Finally, after almost 20 years of *Roe* and increasing anti-abortion protests across the country, the Court agreed to consider the question of overruling *Roe* in 1992 in the case of *Planned Parenthood of Southeastern Pennsylvania v. Casey*.[227]

In *Planned Parenthood*, the joint opinion of the Court affirmed two limits on the right to an abortion contained in the Pennsylvania law. One, which had been approved in earlier cases, was a requirement of parental consent or judicial approval for minors. The other was a 24-hour waiting period after the doctor had provided specified information about abortions and fetal development, a limitation that the Court had previously invalidated as an undue burden on exercise of the right.[228] However, a bare majority of the Court refused to overrule *Roe*. In doing so, the Court relied heavily on *stare decisis*. The opinion for a majority of the Court by Justice O'Conner observed that "[a]n entire generation has come of age free to assume *Roe*'s concept of liberty in defining the capacity of women to act in society" and that *Roe*'s doctrinal basis is "not at odds with other precedent for the analysis of personal

---

220 A trimester is one of the three three-month periods that make up the 9 months of gestation in the normal pregnancy.

221 *See Planned Parenthood v. Danforth*, 428 U.S. 52 (1976) and *Akron v. Akron Center for Reproductive Health*, 462 U.S. 416 (1983).

222 *Colautti v. Franklin*, 439 U.S. 379 (1979).

223 *Webster v. Reproductive Health Services*, 492 U.S. 490 (1989).

224 *Danforth, supra* note 221.

225 *Hodgson v. Minnesota*, 497 U.S. 417 (1990).

226 *Maher v. Roe*, 432 U.S. 464 (1977); *Harris v. McRae,* 448 U.S. 297 (1981).

227 505 U.S. 833 (1992).

228 *See Akron, supra* note 221.

liberty." Consequently, "the stronger argument is for affirming *Roe*'s central holding, with whatever degree of personal reluctance any of us may have . . . ." The Court also referred to the public protests against its decision that had taken place in recent years, but considered that factor, not just irrelevant, but a reason not to overrule *Roe*. Being seen to "surrender to political pressure" would hurt the Court's moral authority and prestige.[229]

2. Other Privacy Rights

Beyond protecting abortion decisions and access to contraception, the right to privacy has expanded somewhat to cover other aspects of family life and marriage. Zoning laws that prohibited a grandmother from living with her grandsons was struck down for its interference with family privacy.[230] The Court also struck down a law that required as a precondition of marriage that a parent show that he or she did not owe unpaid child support, declaring the right to marry to be fundamental.[231] However, the Court has declined to extend the right to privacy to protect homosexuals engaging in consensual sodomy in their own home.[232]

The right to privacy has been argued to be broad enough to include a "right to die." In *Cruzan v. Director, Missouri Dept. of Health*,[233] Nancy Cruzan was in an irreversible coma and her parents sought have her feeding tube removed to let her die of natural causes. The Missouri Supreme Court held that they could not because they had failed to meet Missouri's "clear and convincing evidence" standard for showing that Nancy would have so decided if she could. The U.S. Supreme Court held that (1) artificial feeding is a form of medical treatment that may be terminated to fulfill the patient's desire to die with dignity, but (2) Missouri had a strong state interest in preserving human life and assuring against hasty decision-making, so it high standard of proof was not unconstitutional.[234] In 1997, the Court faced the right-to-die issue again when mentally competent patients sought to be able to receive lethal medicine from their doctors. The case involved a Washington state law that prohibited causing or aiding a suicide. The lower federal court found the law unconstitutional on privacy grounds. The Supreme Court reversed, recasting the issue, not as a "right to die," but as a "right to *assistance*" in dying. Relying on a long history of states prohibiting assisted suicides and what it saw as abuses in the practice of euthanasia in the Netherlands, it concluded that Washington had the right to ensure against the risks of abuses by totally banning rather than regulating assisted suicides.[235]

---

229 *Planned Parenthood*, 505 U.S. at 860-860 (joint opinion). Justice Scalia's dissent argued that the Court's prestige and authority was undermined more by continuing to operate in an "area, where we have no right to be, and where we do neither ourselves nor the country any good by remaining." *Id* at 1002.

230 *Moore v. City of East Cleveland, Ohio*, 431 U.S. 494 (1977). The Court had upheld a more inclusive city ordinance in *Belle Terre v. Boraas*, 416 U.S. 1 (1974) that limited a "family" to not more than two unrelated persons.

231 *Zablocki v. Redhail*, 434 U.S. 374 (1978). *See also supra* p. 333 (right to procreate).

232 *Bowers v. Hardwick*, 478 U.S. 186 (1986). The same Georgia statute was held unconstitutional on state constitutional grounds by the Georgia Supreme Court in *Powell v. State*, 510 S.E. 2d 18 (Ga. 1999).

233 *Cruzan v. Director, Missouri Dept. of Health*, 497 U.S. 261 (1990).

234 Most states only require a preponderance of the evidence. *But see Washington v. Harper*, 494 U.S. 210 (1990) (liberty interest in refusing unwanted medical treatment did not allow prisoner to refuse administration of antipsychotic drugs).

235 *Washington v. Glucksberg*, 521 U.S. 702 (1997); *Vacco v. Quill*, 521 U.S. 793 (1997). *See Symposium: Physician-Assisted Suicide*, 82 MINN. L.REV. 885 (1998).

C. First Amendment Freedoms of Expression

The 1st Amendment protects the rights of free speech, press and assembly — the freedoms of expression. Included in freedom of expression are not only oral, written and other direct modes of expression, but also "symbolic speech" — conduct intended to express a point of view, such as wearing armbands or burning flags.[236]

Why Protect Free Expression There are several reasons typically given for protecting free expression. Principal among them is the notion that in a democracy people must be informed to govern themselves and that freedom of expression is essential to this informing function.[237] Coupled with this idea is the conviction that the free flow of discussion and criticism of the performance of those in power serves as a check on abuses of governmental power.[238] Another theory is the "marketplace of ideas" theory — the idea that "[t]he best test of truth is the power of the thought to get itself accepted in the competition of the market."[239] Repression of expression causes "market distortion" and does so in two different ways. If it is successful, it removes some points of view from the "market." If it is not successful, it may give "forbidden" points of view more appeal than they would otherwise have.[240] A related idea that has been suggested concentrates on perhaps the most immediate benefit of free expression: it is healthy for people — it allows them to express their individuality and to "blow off steam." People will make speeches in the park instead of making revolution in the streets. As Justice Brandeis observed in *Whitney v. California*, "it is hazardous to discourage thought, hope, and imagination; . . . repression breeds hate; . . . hate menaces stable government; . . . the path of safety lies in the opportunity to discuss freely supposed grievances and proposed remedies."[241]

These various theories have their detractors. If limited to their rationales, the self-government and the information and the "marketplace of ideas" theories would presumably protect only "idea" speech or perhaps only "political idea" speech.[242] And some have noted that the "marketplace of ideas" theory posits a peculiarly archaic *laissez-faire* form of the marketplace that was long ago abandoned as unworkable for goods and services. After all, dangerous *consumer products* are banned in the *real* market, so why not ban dangerous *ideas* — such as racial hatred and genocide — from the marketplace of *ideas*. As for the idea of people "blowing off steam," critics charge that we have ignored the real harm that words can cause. The use of "free expression" to degrade women or members of racial minorities, thus keeping them "in their place," is a serious social, economic and political problem.[243] At least at the present time, these objections have not prevailed in 1st Amendment law.

---

236 For a lucid and thought-provoking explanation of 1st Amendment law *see* DANIEL A. FARBER, THE FIRST AMENDMENT (Foundation 1998).

237 *See* ALEXANDER MEIKLEJOHN, FREE SPEECH AND ITS RELATION TO SELF-GOVERNMENT (Harper, New York, N.Y. 1948).

238 *See* Vincent Blasi, *The Checking Power of the First Amendment Theory*, 1977 AM. BAR FOUND. RES. J. 521.

239 *Abrams v. United States*, 250 U.S. 616, 630 (1919) (Holmes, J.). *See* JOHN STUART MILL, ON LIBERTY (Hacket Pub. Co., Indianapolis, Ind. 1978) (originally published in 1859).

240 *See* NOWAK & ROTUNDA, *supra* note 2, at 939-941 for a discussion of this and other justifications for freedom of speech, with appropriate citations to original sources.

241 274 U.S. 357 (1927) (Brandeis, J., concurring).

242 *See* Robert Bork, *Neutral Principles and Some First Amendment Problems*, 47 IND. L. J. 1 (1971).

243 *See* Richard Delgado, *Words that Wound: A Tort Action for Racial Insults, Epithets and Name-Calling*, 17 HARV. CIV. RTS.-CIV. LIB. L. REV. 133 (1982) and Catherine MacKinnon, *Pornography, Civil Rights, and Speech*, 20 HARV. CIV. RTS.-CIV. LIB. L. REV. 1 (1985). *See also infra* p. 347 (discussion of obscenity and feminist view of pornography).

Content Neutrality A first principle of government regulation of expression is that it must be content neutral. "If there is any fixed star in our constitutional constellation, it is that no official, high or petty, can prescribe what shall be orthodox in politics, nationalism, religion, or other matters of opinion or force citizens to confess by word or act their faith therein."[244] Content regulation requires the greatest burden of justification — a compelling governmental interest. Thus, the Court held in *Boos v. Barry*,[245] that a law that prohibited the display of any sign in front of a foreign embassy that "tends to bring the foreign government into public odium or public dispute," while allowing signs praising the foreign government, violates the First Amendment, since it directly regulates based on content. This principle of content neutrality underlies cases holding "anti-flag-burning" laws unconstitutional. Those laws punish burning the U.S. flag as a sign of contempt or desecration, but allow burning as a respectful means of disposal of a worn or soiled U.S. flag.[246]

A second "bedrock principle underlying the First Amendment" that is related to content neutrality is that "the government may not prohibit the expression of an idea simply because society itself finds the idea itself offensive or disagreeable."[247] Just as the government cannot itself condemn speech for its content, it cannot use its offensiveness to the *public* as a basis for prohibiting it. Consistent with this principle, the Court in *Cohen v.* California[248] held that Mr. Cohen could not be arrested for wearing a jacket in a courtroom corridor that displayed the "unseemly expletive" of "Fuck the Draft." Similarly, the Court in *R.A.V. v. St. Paul*[249] disapproved the prosecution of a juvenile for engaging in action expressing racial hatred when he burned a cross on the lawn of a black family. Even self-styled Nazis, who sought to march in uniform with swastikas in a section of town where survivors of Nazi concentration camps lived, cannot be prohibited from marching just because it would be offensive to residents.[250]

1. Content Regulation

In view of the almost *per se* rule of invalidity of government regulation of expression based on content, prohibiting expression based on content can generally take place only in areas of expression that do not fall within the 1st Amendment's protections at all. Despite the 1st Amendment's absolute command that there shall be *"no Law . . .* abridging the freedom of speech," there are several categories of speech that are not protected at all by the 1st Amendment. The Supreme Court has taken the view that the Framers of the Constitution had in mind that there would be exceptions.[251]

---

244 *West Virginia State Board of Education v. Barnette*, 319 U.S. 624, 642 (1943) (state could not require school children of Jehovah's Witnesses faith to salute the American flag). The difficulty and controversial nature of the case is shown by the fact that *Barnette* overruled a 3-year-old precedent, *Minersville School District v. Gobitis*, 310 U.S. 586 (1940), and was decided during the war, when feelings of patriotism were high.

245 485 U.S. 312 (1988).

246 *See Texas v. Johnson*, 491 U.S. 397 (1989); *United States v. Eichman*, 496 U.S. 310 (1990).

247 *Texas v. Johnson*, 491 U.S. 397, 414 (1989) (burning of the American flag).

248 403 U.S. 15 (1971).

249 505 U.S. 377 (1992).

250 *See Collin v. Smith*, 578 F.2d 1197 (7th Cir.), discussed in Chapter IV, p. 154.

251 According to some, this is reflected in the language chosen. The 1st Amendment says that *freedom* of speech may not be abridged, not that *speech* may not be abridged. The *freedom* of speech excludes several categories of speech. *See* MEIKLEJOHN, *supra* note 237, at 19.

Speech as Illegal Conduct The fact that many crimes are carried out by way of speech does not make their prosecution unconstitutional. For example, speech is used to carry out the crimes of perjury, bribery, fraud and solicitation to commit murder. Yet, the 1st Amendment is clearly no barrier to prosecution. In a less extreme situation, it does not violate freedom of speech to prohibit a newspaper from publishing sex-designated employment opportunity advertisements, since publication amounts to sex discrimination prohibited by federal law.[252]

Fighting Words Developed in the 1942 case of *Chaplinsky v. New Hampshire*, "fighting words" are words that are of the sort that are "likely to provoke the average person to retaliation and thereby cause a breach of the peace."[253] A problem with the "fighting words" exception is that it is based on the probable *reaction of the listener*. Unless limited carefully solely to face-to-face personal insults of an especially confrontational type, the doctrine could be used to punish speech just because it represents an unpopular point of view. A case that emphasized the need for a face-to-face confrontation that could escalate to violence was *Cohen v. California*, discussed above.[254] The Court admitted that the message conveying Mr. Cohen's sentiments about compulsory military service on his jacket might well offend some veterans, but it was not the kind of direct face-to-face statement that would qualify under the "fighting words" exception.

Seditious Speech Since the central purpose of freedom of expression is to foster spirited political debate, the problem of seditious speech must be handled carefully. Unfortunately, regulation of sedition got off to a bad start in the United States — actually it got off to two bad starts. The first of these was the Sedition Act of 1798, which provided for fines and imprisonment *inter alia* for making any "false, scandalous and malicious writing against the government or members of the government with intent to defame . . . or to bring them . . . into contempt or disrepute." The Act was passed on the eve of war with France by a Congress controlled by the Federalist Party to use as a tool for suppressing its Democratic-Republican opponents. Several opponents of Federalist government policy were fined and imprisoned. Although the Sedition Act was condemned by Madison and Jefferson, it was never subject to challenge in the Supreme Court and it expired in 1801. However, as the Court noted in a 1964 case, "the attack upon its validity has carried the day in the court of history."[255] Fines levied in its prosecution were repaid by Act of Congress on the ground that it was clearly unconstitutional.

The second "bad start" with regard to sedition laws was over a hundred years later and involved the Espionage Act of 1917, enacted and applied during a period of "Red hysteria" following the Russian Revolution and in the midst of World War I. In *Schenck v. United States*,[256] the Court upheld the conviction of Schenck, a socialist, who published and distributed leaflets opposing U.S. involvement in World War I, attacking the draft as slavery and encouraging young men to resist. Similarly, in *Abrams v. United States*,[257] the Court upheld the conviction and 20-year sentence of Abrams, who was passing out leaflets opposing U.S. involvement in the Russian

---

252 *Pittsburgh Press v. Pittsburgh Comm. on Human Rights*, 413 U.S. 376 (1971).

253 315 U.S. 568, 574 (1942).

254 403 U.S. 15 (1971).

255 *New York Times v. Sullivan*, 376 U.S. 254 (1964).

256 249 U.S. 47 (1919).

257 250 U.S. 616 (1919).

Revolution. Both cases used a "clear and present danger" test. Under this test, the government has the right to punish those who advocate the overthrow of government if their advocacy represents a clear and present danger that such overthrow will happen. It is difficult today to see how Schenck's leafleting could have satisfied this test.[258]

The current standard for judging seditious advocacy is set forth in the 1969 case of *Brandenberg v. Ohio*.[259] The *Brandenberg* test is a revised "clear and present danger" test. The Court held that a state may not "forbid or proscribe advocacy of the use of force or of law violation except where such advocacy is directed to inciting or producing imminent lawless action and is likely to incite or produce such action." Relying on the "marketplace of ideas" theory, the Court justified governmental interference with a speaker's calls to *immediate* action on the ground that the immediate incitement left no time for more speech to counteract it. At the Ku Klux Klan meeting in *Brandenberg*, crosses were burned and some people had weapons, and they talked about marching to Washington, but there was no indication that they were immediately going from their meeting to attack a government installation.[260] Consequently, their expression was protected.

Obscenity Obscenity is excluded from 1st Amendment protection not so much on a theory that it presents a danger to society, but because of historical understandings that the Framers of the 1st Amendment would not have thought it to be protected.[261] The most difficult question has been the issue of how to define what is obscene. The Court cannot seem to come up with a workable definition. Whatever definition it has come up with, the test is so vague that some prosecutor in some city or town somewhere in the country has used it to suppress books and films that are recognized as good literature or even classics.[262]

In the 1960s, a court in Boston found an 18th century book, John Cleland's *Fanny Hill: Memoirs of a Woman of Pleasure*, obscene. The Court reversed. It was also forced to reverse a number of similar decisions in the 1960s. In each case, it had to watch the movie or read the book to see if it met the test of obscenity. Some justices, in reaction, after several attempts to define what was obscene, essentially gave up.

---

258 *See also Gitlow v. New York*, 268 U.S. 652, 658 (1925). The anti-communist hysteria of the 1950s provided another occasion for suppression of political expression. In *Dennis v. United States*, 341 U.S. 494 (1951) and *Scales v. United States*, 367 U.S. 203 (1961), the Court approved convictions of member of the Communist Party of USA, because it thought they represented a real threat. The fact that all these cases were decided in the 20th century should not be taken as suggesting that suppression of speech and political activity did not take place until recent times. In fact there is considerable evidence that it did on a regular basis between the 1798 and 1917 acts. *See generally* David Rabban, *The First Amendment in Its Forgotten Years*, 90 YALE L. J. 514 (1981).

259 395 U.S. 444 (1969).

260 *See also Hess v. Indiana*, 414 U.S. 105 (1973) (threats made by university students during an anti-war demonstration to "take the fucking street later" did not reach the point of "likely to incite or produce imminent lawless action").

261 *Roth v. United States*, 354 U.S. 476, 484-485 (1957). Another important point resolved in *Roth* was that novels and other artistic works are protected by the 1st Amendment even though they do not directly relate to the self-governance policies behind protecting free expression. A summary of the history of obscenity regulation is recounted in NOWAK & ROTUNDA, *supra* note 2, §16.56.

262 Interestingly enough, though the government may punish *distribution* of obscene materials, a person has a substantive due process right of privacy that protects private possession of such materials in one's home. *Stanley v. Georgia*, 394 U.S. 557 (1969). How one gets those materials to one's home is a problem, however. *See United States v. 12,200 Ft. Reels*, 413 U.S. 123 (1973) (not unconstitutional to punish mailing, transporting or importing obscene materials even if they are for private use).

Justice Potter Stewart is famous for his statement that he was unable to define obscenity, but "I know it when I see it."[263]

The current test applied is the test of *Miller v. California*.[264] Under the *Miller* test, a book, magazine or film will be considered to be obscene if: (1) the "average person, applying contemporary community standards," would find that the work as a whole, "appeals to the prurient interest" in sex; (2) the work depicts "in a patently offensive way" sexual conduct specifically defined by the applicable state law; and (3) the work, taken as a whole, "lacks serious literary, artistic, political, or scientific value." Aside from its vagueness, this test has at least three problems. First, it requires judges and local juries to determine what the local "community standards" are regarding sex and to engage in literary criticism — matters about which they are not necessarily experts. Second, the Court has never explained what it means by the phrase "appeals to the prurient interest" in sex. In a recent case, it held that the phrase does not include appeals to "normal" interest in sex, only to "shameful or morbid interest in sex." However, there is no clue as to how one is to distinguish between the two.[265] Third, the reference to "contemporary community standards" means *local* standards. As a result, the Constitution effectively has a different meaning in rural Georgia than it does in New York City.

All these difficulties with the *Miller* test surfaced almost immediately after *Miller* was decided, when a Georgia jury found a highly-acclaimed film, *Carnal Knowledge*, starring Jack Nicholson and Arthur Garfunkel, to be obscene. The Supreme Court reversed, pointing out that the nudity and "ultimate" sex acts depicted were not what it had in mind in *Miller* and that "there was no exhibition of the actors' genitals."[266]

A new approach to defining obscenity has emerged in recent years. This basis for suppressing obscenity is not based on traditional morality. It asserts that obscenity should be curbed because it "is central in creating and maintaining the civil inequality of the sexes," from employment opportunities to crimes directed at women, such as rape, battery and prostitution.[267] These new laws suppress "pornography," defined as "the sexually explicit subordination of women, graphically depicted, whether in pictures or words." Several examples of pornography are listed, such as where "women are presented dehumanized as sexual objects, things or commodities" or as enjoying being raped or beaten or otherwise degraded or humiliated. Many of these laws would give any woman the right to sue various persons trafficking or otherwise responsible for pornography for damages arising from their activities. However, in one case involving such an ordinance enacted in Indianapolis, the federal Court of Appeals held that it violated the 1st Amendment on the ground that it regulated material that was not obscene under the *Roth* test and did so based on its content. That decision was summarily affirmed by the Supreme Court.[268] The definition of pornography discussed has met with better favor in Canada. The Canadian Supreme

---

263 *Jacobellis v. Ohio*, 378 U.S. 184 (1964).

264 413 U.S. 15 (1973).

265 *Brockett v. Spokane Arcades, Inc.*, 472 U.S. 491 (1985).

266 *Jenkins v. Georgia*, 418 U.S. 153 (1974)

267 Proposed ordinance of the City of Minneapolis, Minnesota.

268 *American Booksellers Assoc. v. Hudnut*, 771 F.2d 323 (7th Cir. 1985), *aff'd mem.* 475 U.S. 1001 (1986). A summary affirmance is considered to have precedential value. For opposing viewpoints of commentators, *see* MacKinnon, *supra* note 243, and Nadine Strossen, *The Convergence of Feminist and Civil Liberties Principles in the Pornography Debate* (Book Review), 62 N.Y.U. L.Rev. 201 (1987).

Court recently adopted a similar definition in defining the limits on freedom of expression under the Canadian constitution.[269]

The difficulties of defining what is obscene has caused a shift in policy in the states in dealing with sexually explicit expression. Instead of trying to close "adult" establishments under anti-obscenity laws, cities and prosecutors are concentrating on regulating through licensing and zoning where they can be located — an area in which they enjoy considerable power even with regard to protected expression.[270]

2. Time, Place and Manner Restrictions on Protected Expression

Different Rules for Different Places of Expression The categories of expression just discussed may be prohibited completely. However, even if expression is protected in general by the 1st Amendment, the government may be able to regulate it depending on the setting in which it occurs. If expression takes place on one's own private property, there are no restrictions beyond those already stated. If expression takes place on the private property of another, the private owner may prohibit the expression.[271] Most commonly, however, speakers will use public property for expression. In such cases, some regulation may be constitutionally proper. To what degree expression may be regulated depends on whether it takes place in a "traditional public forum," a "designated public forum," or a "non-public forum." These three categories of public property were established by the Court in *Perry Education Association v. Perry Local Educators' Assoc.*[272]

Traditional Public Forums A traditional public forum includes public streets and parks, which "have immemorially been held in trust for the use of the public and time out of mind, have been used for purposes of assembly, communicating thoughts between citizens, and discussing public questions."[273] The right to expression is at its broadest in public forums. The government generally may not prohibit any form of expression protected by the 1st Amendment. It may impose reasonable time, place and manner regulations unrelated to content, but then only if those restrictions leave open sufficient alternative means for expression.

The most common content-neutral governmental interest affected by expressive conduct is disruption of traffic. However, laws allowing denial of permits must be narrowly drawn to prevent abuse under the pretext of time, place and manner regulation.[274] In *Heffron v. International Society for Krishna Consciousness,*[275] religious proselytizers sought to distribute their literature by walking among the crowd at a state fair ground. A state fair regulation required that distribution of all merchandise,

---

269 *See Butler v. Regina*, 134 Nat'l Rep. 81 (Sup. Ct. of Canada 1992).

270 *See infra* p. 356, where the use of zoning and other incomplete prohibitions are discussed. Strict laws and vigorous prosecution continue against purveyors and consumers of child pornography, however. The 1st Amendment standard for child pornography is more absolute. The government can ban all photographic depictions of children in sexual situations on the theory of protecting the children involved in the making of the films or pictures. *See New York v. Ferber*, 458 U.S. 747 (1982).

271 *See Lloyd Corp. v. Tanner*, 407 U.S. 551 (1972) and *Hudgens v. Nat'l Labor Relations Bd.*, 424 U.S. 507 (1976) (expressive activity properly prohibited by owners of private shopping malls despite their having some of the characteristics of a public forum).

272 460 U.S. 37 (1983).

273 *Hague v. Congress of Industrial Organizations*, 307 U.S. 496 (1939).

274 *See and compare Cox v. New Hampshire*, 312 U.S. 569 (1941) (upholding denial of permit for religious organizers to parade to advertise a religious meeting) *with Shuttlesworth v. Birmingham*, 394 U.S. 147 (1969) (holding unconstitutional city's denial of a permit for a civil rights march organized by Martin Luther King).

275 452 U.S. 640 (1981).

including written materials, take place only from approved booths on the fairground. The Court held that crowded conditions at the relatively confined area of the fairground were a sufficient reason for such regulation. The Court noted that the rule regulated only one means of communication — distribution of merchandise and materials — thus leaving other means of communication free.[276]

Some complete prohibition of expressive activity is possible if not content based and supported by substantial governmental interest. The Court held in *Boos v. Barry*[277] that a law prohibiting critical picketing of foreign embassies (but permitting more positive picketing) was content-based and therefore invalid. However, the Court also approved in that same case a complete ban on congregations of persons within 500 feet of a foreign embassy if such gatherings posed a security threat to the embassy. The absence of any such substantial interest led the Court to hold unconstitutional a federal law prohibiting all signs and leaflets on the sidewalk in front of its own building.[278]

Picketing in residential areas has been a controversial issue recently in part because it has been used by anti-abortion activists to "expose" doctors who perform abortions. Streets and sidewalks of a residential area, no less that the streets in a business district, are traditional public forums. However, the Court held in *Frisby v. Schultz*[279] that a city can ban "all focused picketing taking place solely in front of a particular residence." The rationale was for this was that "focused" picketers "do not seek to disseminate a message to the general public, but to intrude upon the targeted resident, and to do so in an especially offensive way."

Designated Public Forums A designated public forum is any public property other than a natural public forum that the government has designated as a public forum by opening it up for use by the public as a place for expressive activity. Designated public forums are generally governed by the same rules as traditional public forums. However, the government has more control over designated public forums than traditional public forums in two ways. First, it may "undesignate" the forum, i.e., cancel its designated status as a public forum, thus rendering it subject to the less speech-permissive rules applicable to non-public forums. The second is that the government may limit the groups of people who will have access. For example, a state university can limit its public forum facilities solely to its own students.[280] However, to whatever extent access to facilities might be limited, the limitations cannot be based on the viewpoint of the expression. Thus, it violated the 1st Amendment when a public school district's regulation permitted after-hours use of school facilities for "social, civic and recreational purposes" by private organizations, but denied access to a religious organization that wanted to show a film on family values and child rearing that represented a religious viewpoint. The Court held that it discriminated on the basis of viewpoint because it permitted the presentation of all views about family issues and child rearing except those dealing with the subject from a religious standpoint.[281] Similarly, in *Rosenberger v. Rector and Visitors of the*

---

276 *See also Grayned v. City of Rockford*, 408 U.S. 104 (1972) (a ban on loud picketing on sidewalk near schools is permissible); *Ward v. Rock Against Racism*, 491 U.S. 781 (1989) (city noise regulation of sound system at outdoor concert is permissible).

277 485 U.S. 312 (1988).

278 *United States v. Grace*, 461 U.S. 171 (1983).

279 487 U.S. 474 (1988).

280 *Widmar v. Vincent*, 454 U.S. 263 (1981).

281 *Lamb's Chapel v. Center Moriches Union Free School District*, 508 U.S. 384 (1993).

University of Virginia, the Court held unconstitutional a state university's policy of excluding religious groups from a program funding student organization publications.[282]

Non-Public Forums A non-public forum is any other government property accessible to the public that is not generally suited for expressive activities, but is capable of being used that way. The government may "reserve [such non-public forum property] for its intended purposes . . . as long as the regulation on speech is reasonable and not an effort to suppress expression merely because public officials oppose the speaker's views."[283] Thus, the Court has allowed a ban on all partisan political activity on a military base[284] and has upheld prohibition of non-profit political advocacy groups from charitable solicitation drives in federal government offices.[285] The reason for the bans was the government's interest in avoiding the appearance of political favoritism. This means that the government may constitutionally impose content-based, but viewpoint-neutral category-type restrictions on access to a non-public forum, so long as the restriction is reasonably related to the purpose for which the property is being used. The non-public forum in the *Perry Education Association* case was the school district's interschool mail system. The Court found nothing wrong with the school district allowing the union that represented its teachers to send materials through the system, while denying access to other groups, including a rival union.

Problems with the Perry Test The *Perry* three-category test seems tidy, but there are problems, both in deciding what kind of forum is involved and how to apply the test for that forum. Two recent cases will illustrate. In a 1990 case,[286] the Court tried to apply the *Perry* test to a sidewalk connecting a post office to a parking lot. A badly split Court held that the post office could ban solicitations on the sidewalk, but could not agree on whether the particular sidewalk was public forum or non-public forum property. In a1992 case, it held that Hare Krishna proselytizers could be prohibited from soliciting funds and handing out leaflets in the New York airports.[287] A majority of the Court viewed the test of "traditional public forum" to be a purely *historical* one and denied that status to airports generally, since passenger aviation is a relatively recent phenomenon. The restrictions on soliciting funds was thus reasonable because passengers would have to stop, engage the solicitor in conversation and perhaps reach into a pocket or purse, thus disrupting passenger pedestrian traffic. However, a different majority of the Court struck down the airport's ban on *distributing leaflets* as unreasonable since leafleting is not as problematic as soliciting of funds. The dissent by four members of the Court argued that an airport was a public forum, since "expressive activity has been a commonplace feature of our Nation's airports for many years." However, despite its public forum status, the dissent agreed that solicitation of funds *could* be banned, thus appearing to endorse a test for public forums that is more restrictive than that underlying *Perry* and other cases.

Other crucial issues relating to designated public forums are what power the government has *in its designation* to deny access to certain categories of persons or

---

282 515 U.S. 819 (1995).

283 *Perry Education Association, supra* note 272, 460 U.S. at 46.

284 *Greer v. Spock*, 424 U.S. 828 (1976).

285 *Cornelius v. NAACP Legal Defense & Education Fund*, 473 U.S. 788 (1985).

286 *United States v. Kokinda*, 497 U.S. 720 (1990).

287 *International Society for Krishna Consciousness Inc v. Lee*, 505 U.S. 672 (1992).

organizations, and precisely what are "content-neutral," as opposed to "viewpoint-neutral," regulations.[288] These issues arose in the Court's most recent use of the *Perry* test. In *Arkansas Education Television Commission v. Forbes*,[289] it held constitutional a state-owned public television station's decision to exclude a candidate from a televised debate because he had little popular support. The debate was a non-public forum, from which the station could exclude him "in the reasonable, viewpoint-neutral exercise of its journalistic discretion." The *Perry* test was used, but not exactly wholeheartedly endorsed.[290] Dissenters objected that the station had created a designated public forum for political discourse and could not "undesignate" certain ballot-qualified candidates except pursuant to clear, objective, predetermined standards, not by way of an *ad hoc* decision, as it had done. Otherwise, officials could exclude a speaker based on viewpoint and then to make up a viewpoint-neutral category to cover its real reason for the exclusion.

3. Regulating Symbolic Expression

Words are clearly a form of expression, but one can express a political or other point of view by engaging in conduct. Such action is commonly referred to as "symbolic speech." But not all expressive conduct is protected. A politically motivated assassination is clearly expressive conduct, but no one would suggest that it is protected by the 1st Amendment. In a prominent symbolic expression case, the Court in *United States v. O'Brien*[291] held that the government could constitutionally punish burning a draft registration card — a popular form of protest against the Vietnam War. According to the Court, draft-card burning involved more than just expressive activity; it also involved disruption of an administrative system. In *O'Brien*, the Court developed a test for judging activity that involves both protected symbolic "speech" and unprotected "non-speech elements." Regulation of non-communicative elements of conduct will be valid (1) "if it furthers an important or substantial governmental interest" and that interest is "unrelated to the suppression of free expression" and (2) if the "incidental restriction" on claimed 1st Amendment protected activity "is no greater than is essential to the furtherance of that interest."

The requirement that the government interest involved be "unrelated to suppression of free expression" has been the basis for striking down several laws punishing particular conduct. For example, in *Johnson v. Texas*,[292] the defendant was prosecuted for burning a U.S. flag. Texas's asserted interest was that it was seeking to preserve the flag as a symbol of nationhood and national unity. However, the Court rejected it as directly "related to the suppression of free expression." It reasoned that, if destruction of a flag had a negative impact on these interests, it was *precisely because* the conduct communicated a message of casting contempt on the flag.[293] There was a spirited dissent in the case and a public furor over the decision that included calls to amend the Constitution to overrule the Court. Congress passed a federal "anti-flag-burning" statute that punished the simple act of destroying or

---

288 *See* the duel between the majority and the dissent in *Rosenberger, supra* note 282.

289 523 U.S. 666 (1998).

290 In discussing the applicable law, the Court in *Forbes* noted dryly: "[f]or our purposes here, it will suffice to employ the [*Perry*] categories of speech for a . . ."

291 391 U.S. 367 (1968).

292 491 U.S. 397 (1989).

293 *See also Tinker v. Des Moines School District*, 393 U.S. 503 (1969) (secondary school's ban on students wearing black armbands to protest Vietnam War, but not on wearing other political symbols was improper regulation of expression not otherwise justified).

defacing without reference to casting contempt or "desecrating" — in essence an attempt to come within the *O'Brien* guidelines. The Court nonetheless held the statute unconstitutional.[294]

4. Some Special Issues in Freedom of Expression

Regulation of Electronic Media   Because the airwaves needed for broadcasting television and radio signals are limited and belong to the public, the 1st Amendment does not prohibit the Federal Communications Commission (FCC) from regulating broadcasting "in the public interest," as Congress has authorized it to do. Thus, many forms of governmental regulation that would be unconstitutional as applied to newspapers or books can be properly applied to the broadcast media. For example, broadcast media can be required to provide "equal time" to political spokespersons with differing views, even though newspapers may not.[295] The FCC's power is considerable. In *FCC v. Pacifica Foundation*, the Court upheld the FCC's power to ban "patently offensive" (but not obscene) words , noting the special nature of radio transmission, which "confronts the citizen, not only in public, but also in the privacy of the home."[296] One the other hand, the Court in 1996 struck down a federal statute that required cable television operators to "block and segregate" all sexually explicit programs, meaning that they were required to provide a separate channel for such broadcasts and block transmission of them unless they received a written request from a cable subscriber. While protection of children was a "compelling interest," the Court concluded that the government could protect that interest using less restrictive means.[297] Finally, in a 1997 case, *Reno v. American Civil Liberties Union*,[298] the Court addressed the constitutionality of the Communications Decency Act of 1996, which prohibited transmitting indecent communications to persons under age 18 on the Internet. The Court held that the Internet was fully subject to the 1st Amendment, observing that is it not as invasive as radio or television, nor could a person come across sexually explicit materials by accident without prior warning.

Political Campaign Regulation   Recent scandals in political campaigning have led Congress and the states to seek to impose limitations on various campaign practices. Because speech involving the electoral process is at the heart of the 1st Amendment, some such restrictions have had a difficult time in the Supreme Court. Thus, a federal law limiting the amount of money that could be *spent* on a campaign was held unconstitutional. However, limits on campaign *contributions* were upheld based on the interest in avoiding the skewing effect on elections of large contributions.[299] In general, the ability to limit corporate contributions is greater, since the corporate form generates immense wealth that is unrelated the degree of political support that exists for ideas espoused by the corporation. The corporations general

---

294 *United States v. Eichman*, 496 U.S. 310 (1990).

295 *Compare Red Lion Broadcasting Co. v. Federal Communications Comm'n.*, 395 U.S. 367 (1967) ("fairness doctrine" for broadcast media) *with Miami Herald Publishing Co. v. Tornillo*, 418 U.S. 241 (1969) (rejecting "fairness" limits on print media). *See also Turner Broadcasting System v. Federal Communications Comm'n*, 520 U.S. 180 (1997).

296 438 U.S. 726 (1978).

297 *Denver Area Education Telecommunications Consortium, Inc. v. Federal Communications Comm'n*, 518 U.S. 727 (1996).

298 521 U.S. 844 (1997). *Cf. Sable Communications v. Federal Communications Comm'n*, 492 U.S.115 (1989) (holding unconstitutional a federal law that prohibited "sexually oriented prerecorded telephone messages," because the messages did not come into the home involuntarily).

299 *Buckley v. Valeo*, 424 U.S. 1 (1976). *But see Fed. Elections Comm'n v. Nat'l Conservative Political Action Comm.*, 470 U.S. 480 (1985) (limit of $1,000 on spending by political action committees invalid).

funds may not be used, but the corporation may, like any individual, raise money for political expenditures separately.[300]

Press Access to Criminal Trials The press and the public have a right under the 1st Amendment to attend criminal trials even over a defendant's objection. At the same time, the accused in a criminal case has the right to an impartial jury and a fair trial.[301] However, control over the press may not be exercised in a way that infringes on 1st Amendment rights unless that is absolutely essential to prevent a serious threat to the fairness of the proceedings.[302] A "prior restraint" on publication of information adduced at trial will be presumptively invalid.[303] Privacy interests of participants are an insufficient justification for closing a proceeding or prohibiting publicity. Thus, in *Globe Newspaper Co. v. Superior Court*,[304] the Court invalidated the routine exclusion of press and public during testimony of child victims of sexual abuse. A state may even permit television broadcast of a criminal trial over a criminal defendant's objection.[305] Today, in Florida, California and some other states, one can watch court proceedings on television. A separate television network, called Court TV, has even been founded.

Reporter Privileges Another clash of rights of the press and the courts occurs when prosecutors seek evidence of criminal acts that is in the possession of journalists. In *Branzburg v. Hayes*,[306] a reporter was jailed for refusing to comply with a subpoena for his notes on a news story on illegal drug manufacturing. The reporter argued that he had promised his sources confidentiality and that no one would talk to him if the police could get his notes. The Court held that the interest of the police in investigating criminal activity justified the interference with his interest in reporting the news. However, a concurring opinion of Justice Powell necessary for the majority of 5 justices, while purporting to endorse the majority opinion, adopted a case-by-case balancing test suggesting that, where the needs of law enforcement were small and infringements on freedom of the press great, a court should decline to enforce such a subpoena. Similarly, in *Zurcher v. Stanford Daily*,[307] police obtained a warrant to search a student newspaper for photos of a student riot in an effort to identify the participants. A similar alignment of justice upheld the legality of the search, rejecting 1st Amendment arguments. Again, Justice Powell's "swing" vote suggested qualifications on the right to conduct such searches. In response to the *Zurcher* case, Congress passed a federal statute prohibiting searches of newsrooms and seizures of "work product" of reporters except as "necessary to prevent the death of, or serious bodily injury to, a human being" and in other exceptional circumstances.[308]

---

300 *See Federal Elections Commission v. National Right to Work Committee*, 459 U.S. 197 (1982) (upholding a ban on use of general corporate funds); *Austin v. Michigan Chamber of Commerce*, 494 U.S. 652 (1990) (same; statute also permitted expenditure of funds separated from political contributions).

301 *See Sheppard v. Maxwell*, 384 U.S. 333 (1966) (conviction of prominent doctor for murder of his wife reversed where press was so unrestrained that "carnival atmosphere" was created).

302 *Waller v. Georgia*, 467 U.S. 39 (1984).

303 *Nebraska Press Assoc. v. Stuart*, 427 U.S. 539 (1976). *See also infra* p. 355 (prior restraints).

304 *Globe Newspaper Co. v. Superior Court*, 457 U.S. 596 (1982).

305 *Chandler v. Florida*, 449 U.S. 560 (1981).

306 *Branzburg v. Hayes*, 408 U.S. 665 (1972).

307 436 U.S. 547 (1978).

308 Privacy Protection Act of 1980, 42 U.S.C.A. §2000aa. o search for or seize any work product materials possessed by a person reasonably believed to have a purpose to disseminate to the public a newspaper, book, broadcast, or other similar form of public communication, there is reason to believe that the immediate seizure of such materials

Commercial Speech   Before 1976, speech involving the exchange of goods or services for profit, called "commercial speech," belonged among the categories of speech excluded from the protections of the 1st Amendment, along with obscenity and seditious speech. However, the Supreme Court opened up an entirely new area of 1st Amendment law when decided, in *Virginia State Board of Pharmacy v. Virginia Citizens Consumer Council*, that a ban on pharmacists' advertising prices of prescription drugs violated free speech.[309] Shortly thereafter it decided a case of even greater interest to lawyers, *Bates v. Arizona State Bar*,[310] in which it struck down an absolute ban on lawyer advertising. The reasons for deciding to protect commercial speech were set out in the *Virginia Consumers Council* case: commercial speech is no less valuable than expression of ideas and other forms of protected speech. The Court considered it ironic that the same information about relative prices of prescription drugs would clearly be protected if the pharmacist "cast himself as a commentator on store-to-store disparities in drug prices, giving his own and those of a competitor as proof." Commercial advertising, however tasteless it might be at times, contains information and, as such, is important in a system of free enterprise. It relates both to the private economic decisions of the purchasing public and to formation of intelligent opinions of voters as to how the economic system should be changed or regulated.

To qualify for protection, however, the commercial speech must concern lawful activity and must not be misleading. In addition, the government may regulate based on a substantial governmental interest if "the regulation directly advances" that interest and is "not more extensive than is necessary to serve that interest."[311] Thus, the justification of aesthetics and traffic safety is sufficient to prohibit all commercial billboards.[312] However, in a recent case, *City of Cincinnati v. Discovery Network, Inc.*,[313] the Court required a rather strict justification when it invalidated a city ordinance. The city ordinance permitted news racks containing newspapers to be placed on public sidewalks, but prohibited news racks containing advertising and promotional materials. The Court found that there was no valid basis for distinguishing between news racks based on the content of the material in them.

Advertising is relatively impersonal and can be ignored easily by consumers. More personal, direct in-person solicitation of business also raises 1st Amendment issues. In the recent case of *Edenfield v. Fane*,[314] the Court held unconstitutional a ban on certified public accountants' direct in-person solicitation of prospective business clients. However, it has held that the state *may* prohibit *lawyers* from engaging in direct in-person solicitation of prospective clients. The Court viewed this as necessary because of the peculiar dangers inherent in direct solicitation by lawyers.[315] And in a recent case evincing more concern about the abuses of lawyer solicitation even by mail, the Court upheld a Florida ban on "targeted mailings." These are letters to a

---

309 425 U.S. 748 (1976). *See also 44 Liquormart v. Rhode Island*, 517 U.S.484 (1996) (striking down state statute banning price advertising for alcoholic beverages except at the store selling them).

310 433 U.S. 350 (1977). *See also* Chapter IV, p. 138.

311 *Central Hudson Gas & Electric Co. v. Public Service Commission*, 447 U.S. 557 (1980) (prohibition on advertising by state-regulated monopoly utility company struck down).

312 *Metromedia, Inc. v. City of San Diego*, 453 U.S. 490 (1981).

313 507 U.S. 410 (1993).

314 507 U.S. 761(1993).

315 Public interest lawyers are permitted to solicit on behalf of their organizations since the profit motive is absent. *Ohralik v. Ohio State Bar Association*, 436 U.S. 447 (1978); *In re Primus*, 436 U.S. 412 (1978). Public interest lawyers were discussed in Chapter IV, pp. 152-155.

specific person injured in an accident or to the survivor in case of death, offering legal services. Florida did not completely ban them; it only prohibited their being sent within 30 days after the accident, a rule properly designed "to forestall the outrage and irritation with the state-licensed legal profession that the practice of direct solicitation only days after accidents has engendered."[316]

5. Means of Regulating Expression

Prior Restraints There are various ways that the government can seek to regulate expression. Most often the expression is not anticipated. But when it is anticipated, the government sometimes seeks some form of injunction. In general, any such form of "prior restraint" is unconstitutional. Possible civil or criminal liability *after* expression takes place is normally the only means of obtaining redress for harm done. This is the import of *Near v. Minnesota*.[317] In *Near*, a newspaper planned to publish an article accusing city officials and the mayor of corruption. A state court issued an injunction against publication, finding that the charges in the article were unsubstantiated. The Supreme Court reversed the injunction. It held that, if the statements in the article were not true, city officials could sue later for libel. But even untrue publication could not be enjoined beforehand.

Another landmark case on prior restraint was *New York Times v. United States*,[318] the "Pentagon Papers" case. There the Court held unconstitutional an injunction prohibiting publication, during the Vietnam War, of a secret government study on the war that had been leaked to the press by a disgruntled defense department employee. The Court rejected the government's argument that national security would be endangered or that it would cause problems and embarrassment for U.S. allies. Absent the government proving that the study contained specific information on movements of troops or the like that could have been used by an enemy, an injunction was impossible.

Injunctions have been permitted in other areas. For example, an injunction may properly be entered against dissemination of obscenity since it is not protected expression at all,[319] so long as there is an opportunity for a prior hearing on the issue of whether the material is obscene under the 1st Amendment.[320] Injunctions have also been approved against anti-abortion protesters seeking to disrupt the operations of abortion clinics and to discourage patients from going there. In one case, there had been numerous blockades and disruptions of clinic operations. Certain disruptive conduct specified in the injunction was banned and all demonstrations were banned within a "buffer zone" of 15 feet around clinic facilities. However, a "floating buffer zone" around all patients entering or leaving the clinic was struck down as burdening more speech than necessary. The reasons why the normal rule against prior restraints was inapplicable were because the injunction was unrelated to content, left other channels of communication open and was based on prior unlawful conduct of the demonstrators.[321]

---

316 *Florida Bar v. Went For It, Inc.*, 515 U.S. 618 (1995).

317 283 U.S. 697 (1931).

318 403 U.S. 713 (1971).

319 *Paris Adult Theatre v. Slaton*, 413 U.S. 49 (1973).

320 *Kingsley Books, Inc. v. Brown*, 354 U.S. 436 (1957); *Freedman v. Maryland*, 380 U.S. 51 (1965).

321 *Schenck v. Pro-Choice Network of Western New York*, 519 U.S. 357 (1997). *See also Madsen v. Women's Health Center*, 512 U.S. 753 (1994) (36-foot buffer zone in front of clinic and noise restrictions upheld; restriction on approaching patients within 300 fee of the clinic invalid).

Taxation and Forfeiture of Profits The government is limited in its ability to impose financial burdens on speech based on its content. In *Arkansas Writers' Project v. Ragland*,[322] the Court invalidated a tax scheme that taxed "general interest" publications, but did not tax religious, professional, trade or sports publications. The law was unconstitutional because it was content-based even though it was not shown that the state had any purpose to hinder expression by the burdened category of publications. Also held unconstitutional was a New York law that allowed the state Crime Victims Compensation Board to seize all profits made from publication of a book about a crime written by an author who had committed that crime. In *Simon & Schuster, Inc. v. Members of the N.Y. State Crime Victims Comm.*, the Court held the law unconstitutional because it singled out certain publications based on content.[323]

Private Tort Actions The 1st Amendment prohibits the government, through its courts, from enforcing certain kinds of claims for damages pressed by private parties. In *New York Times Co. v. Sullivan*,[324] the Court held that defamation and other similar tort actions brought by public officials and "public figures" implicate 1st Amendment concerns because they could be used as a means of "chilling" or discouraging discussion of public issues. Any such action brought by public officials or public figures must fail unless the plaintiff can prove with "convincing clarity" that the defendant writer or publisher's statement was knowingly false, or was made with "reckless disregard" for its truth or falsity.[325]

Zoning At least in the area of sexually explicit expression, the Court has approved broad government power to regulate where shops exhibiting sexually explicit materials may locate — even though the materials they are selling are not obscene. The Court has approved a city ordinance prohibiting adult theaters within 1,000 feet of any residence, church, park or school based on the government interest in regulating the "secondary effects" of such theaters, such as crime, lowered property values and spoiling the quality of neighborhoods.[326] Nude dancing, though not necessarily obscene, may be completely banned at least in state-regulated bars. In *Barnes v. Glen Theaters*, the Court admitted that there was undoubtedly some 1st Amendment protection for nude dancing, but the Indiana law was content-neutral in its prohibition of all public nudity and applied only to bars, thus permitting such activities in other establishments. It should also be added that states enjoy broad power when it comes to liquor regulation because of the 21st Amendment of the Constitution.[327] It should be remembered, however, that all protected expression is not equal in this regard. Protected sexually explicit expression probably ranks lower than other protected forms of expression. One would have difficulty imagining a state

---

322 481 U.S. 221 (1987).

323 502 U.S. 105 (1991). *But see Snepp v. United States*, 444 U.S. 507 (1980) (per curiam) (approving government seizure of profits from book published by a former CIA employee in violation of pre-employment agreement to obtain prepublication clearance).

324 376 U.S. 254 (1974). *See also Philadelphia Newspapers, Inc. v. Hepps*, 475 U.S. 767 (1986); *Gertz v. Robert Welch, Inc.*, 418 U.S. 323 (1974) (cases involving public figures rather than public officials). The *New York Times* rule applies as well to actions for invasion of privacy and for infliction of emotional distress.

325 *Time, Inc. v. Hill*, 385 U.S. 374 (1967); *Hustler Magazine, Inc. v. Falwell*, 485 U.S. 46 (1988). For more detail on the *New York Times* standard, *see* Chapter XI, pp. 426-428.

326 *City of Renton v. Playtime Theaters*, 475 U.S. 41 (1986).

327 *California v. LaRue*, 409 U.S. 109 (1972). The 21st Amendment repealed the 18th Amendment, which had established "prohibition," a complete ban of alcoholic drink in the entire United States, which existed from 1920 to 1933. Despite efforts to enforce it, liquor was widely sold and consumed in the country. The 21st Amendment ended prohibition by giving liquor control to the states.

being allowed to ban political debates in bars or within 1,000 feet of any school or residence.

Unconstitutional Conditions and Conditional Funding   The Court has prohibited the government from "penalizing" the exercise of constitutional rights by withholding benefits. However, the Court sustained as constitutional a funding program for family planning services projects that prohibited employees of funded projects (primarily doctors and other health-care professionals) from "provid[ing] counseling concerning the use of abortion as a method of family planning" or from referring a pregnant woman to an abortion provider, even upon her specific request. It held that this funding condition did not impermissibly burden the free speech rights of clinics or their staff. The program sought to fund only family planning services prior to pregnancy and excluded abortion as a method of family planning, thus rendering advice about abortion beyond the scope of the program.[328] In *National Endowment for the Arts v. Finley*,[329] the Court held constitutional a federal statute passed in reaction to the National Endowment for the Arts (NEA) funding art projects that many members of Congress considered offensive.[330] The statute, passed after bitter debate, required that the NEA, in making its funding decision, "tak[e] into consideration general standards of decency and respect for the diverse beliefs and values of the American public," as well as the "artistic worth" of proposed projects. It observed that it did not matter that the NEA decision was subjective or that funding was denied to a large amount of constitutionally protected expression.

Indirect "Chilling" of 1st Amendment Rights   Whenever the government passes criminal laws, those laws must be specific and clear. If a law is either vague or is so broad as to include some activity that *may* be protected by the 1st Amendment, then the doctrines of "overbreadth" and "vagueness" can be used to invalidate them on that basis alone under the due process clause, without directly using the 1st Amendment. Thus, a city ordinance that prohibited anyone from standing on a sidewalk in the city and "there conduct[ing] themselves in a manner annoying to persons passing by" was held unconstitutional on its face as overly broad.[331] Though some such activity might be punishable consistent with the Constitution, much of this kind of activity could well be protected by the 1st Amendment.

The Court has resorted to overbreadth and vagueness when it is not yet ready to specify the boundaries of protected 1st Amendment behavior. For example, flag-burning has been with us for some time as a means of protest. Yet, it was only in 1986 in *Johnson v. Texas* that the Court provided a definitive answer to the 1st Amendment question. The Court had sidestepped the 1st Amendment issue several years earlier using vagueness. It reversed the flag desecration conviction of a man who had sewed a flag on the seat of his pants. But it did so on the ground that the statutory phrase involved — "treats contemptuously" — was unconstitutionally vague under the due process clause.[332] Similarly, in 1987 the Court held that a resolution banning all "First Amendment activities" in an airport terminal was unconstitutionally overbroad, thus

---

328 *Rust v. Sullivan*, 500 U.S. 173 (1991). The Court did note that the doctor or other health care professional was "free to make clear that advice regarding abortion is simply beyond the scope of the program."

329 524 U.S. 569 (1998).

330 Among the works were *The Perfect Moment*, which included homoerotic photographs, and *Piss Christ*, a photograph of a crucifix immersed in urine.

331 *See Coates v. Cincinnati*, 402 U.S. 611 (1971).

332 *See Smith v. Goguen*, 415 U.S. 566 (1974).

making it unnecessary to decide whether the activities involved would have been protected by the 1st Amendment. Then in 1992, the Court in the *Hare Krishna* case discussed earlier, decided the question of what expressive activities in airport terminals are protected by the 1st Amendment.[333]

D. First Amendment Religious Freedoms

There are two "religion clauses" of the 1st Amendment. One guarantees a right to the "free exercise" of religion, while the other prohibits any "law respecting the establishment of religion." One problem with interpreting these clauses in light of their history is that the Framers had divergent views on what they meant.[334] Another complicating factor is that "free exercise" and "establishment" are ultimately contradictory. For example, if the government provides fire and police services to churches, it could be accused of supporting religious institutions, but if it denied such services, it could be accused of interfering with the free exercise of religion. What has emerged from this essential dilemma has been the notion that the government must be *neutral* in its attitude toward religion.[335] However, as the example just given suggests, it is difficult to define what that position of neutrality is in many instances.

1. The Establishment Clause

The test of whether a law or practice has the required neutrality toward religion is determined according a three-part test developed in *Lemon v. Kurtzman*:[336] (1) the law or action must have a secular purpose, (2) the primary effect of it must be that it neither advances nor inhibits religion, and (3) it must not foster "excessive government entanglement" with religion. It is often said that the establishment clause establishes a "wall of separation between Church and State."[337] However, both the statement of the *Lemon* test and the cases recognized that complete non-involvement with religion is impossible.

By far, the greatest number of establishment clause issues that have arisen have involved the nexus of religion and schools. This has two aspects. First, since the public school system in the United States is run by the government, it may not be used to "establish" any particular religion or even to encourage religion in general. Second, there is a healthy system of private schools responsible for the education of a substantial minority of children in the country. Many of these schools are run by religious institutions. To the extent that the government assists those schools in teaching children, it can be accused of aiding that religion.

Religion in Public Schools While public school students may be required to study religion or the Bible as part of a secular program on that subject, a public school may not require religious exercises in class. It does not matter whether the exercises are denominational (associated with one or another religious group) or non-

---

333 *See and compare Board of Airport Commissioners of Los Angeles v. Jews for Jesus*, 482 U.S. 569 (1987) and *International Society for Krishna Consciousness v. Lee*, 505 U.S. 672 (1992).

334 *See* ARLIN ADAMS & CHARLES EMMERICH, A NATION DEDICATED TO RELIGIOUS LIBERTY: THE CONSTITUTIONAL HERITAGE OF THE RELIGION CLAUSES 6-26 (U. of Philadelphia Press, Philadelphia, Pa. 1990). For a succinct review of the religion clauses, *see* THOMAS C. BERG, THE STATE AND RELIGION IN A NUTSHELL (West 1998) and FARBER, *supra* note 236, at 243-285.

335 *See Wallace v. Jaffree*, 472 U.S. 38 (1985).

336 403 U.S. 602 (1971). Though the *Lemon* decision stated the test, it was derived from several earlier cases as well. Nonetheless, it is commonly referred to as "the *Lemon* test." For a more complete discussion of the religion clauses, see NOWAK & ROTUNDA, *supra* note 2, §§17.1-17.16.

337 *Everson v. Board of Education*, 330 U.S. 1, 16 (1947) (quoting Thomas Jefferson).

denominational.[338] The same applies to prayers offered at graduation ceremonies.[339] All such exercises coerce religious observance. Even a period of silence for "meditation or voluntary prayer" is prohibited, at least when it is implemented in order to "return voluntary prayer to the public schools."[340] Excusing objecting children from such activities is not a solution. In fact, excluding students exacerbates the problem, since the objecting students' relationship with their classmates and teacher may be affected, and the effect would be based on religious differences.[341] Though a school has broad discretion in the selection of its curriculum, it may not use that discretion to advance religion. Thus, a state statute prohibiting the teaching of Charles Darwin's theory of evolution of humans from lower animals was held to violate the establishment clause.[342] In reaction, some states passed statutes allowing the teaching of evolution, but requiring that equal time be devoted to "creation science," the notion that a supernatural being created humankind. But the Court held that this violated the secular purpose part of the 3-part Lemon test since it was clear that the purpose of the requirement was to counterbalance the teaching of evolution, thus advancing the religious viewpoint.[343]

Religious instruction in school is prohibited even if done by teachers who come in from outside the school.[344] However, other "accommodations of religion" by public schools are not prohibited, such as releasing children from their schoolwork for a period of time during the school day to attend religious classes off school premises.[345] And as pointed out earlier when freedom of expression was discussed, when public schools open their facilities to community groups for use as a public forum, it may not exclude religious groups.[346] It follows that permitting such access does not violate the establishment clause.[347] On the other hand, it was held to be a violation of the establishment clause when New York "accommodated" a community of ultra-Orthodox Jews, the Satamar Hassidim, by authorizing them to form their own school district so their children would not have to attend the normal public schools.[348]

Financial Assistance to Religious Schools Cases dealing with governmental assistance to religious schools (also called "parochial" schools) have followed a tortuous path, as members of the Court sharply divide on the proper approach. The requisite neutrality under the Lemon test was found in state programs that provided reimbursement to parents for the expense of public bus transportation to private

338 *See Engel v. Vitale*, 370 U.S. 421 (1962) (New York statute required prayer: "Almighty God,we acknowledge our dependence upon Thee, and we beg Thy blessings upon us, our parents, our teachers and our Country"). *See also Stone v. Graham*, 449 U.S. 39 (1980) (posting of 10 commandments from Old Testament of Bible violated establishment clause).

339 *Lee v. Weisman*, 505 U.S. 577 (1992).

340 *See Wallace v. Jaffree*, 472 U.S. 38 (1985). Presumably, such a moment of silence, which is not religious by itself, would have to be sustained if it was not enacted for a religious purpose.

341 *School District of Abington Twp. v. Schempp*, 374 U.S. 203 (1963).

342 *Epperson v. Arkansas*, 393 U.S. 97 (1968).

343 *Edwards v. Aguillard*, 482 U.S. 578 (1987).

344 *Illinois ex rel. McCollum v. Board of Education*, 333 U.S. 203 (1948).

345 *Zorach v. Clausen*, 343 U.S. 306 (1952).

346 *See supra*, p. 349.

347 *Widmar v. Vincent*, 454 U.S. 263 (1981). *Widmar* involved a state college, but Congress passed an Equal Access Act in 1984 extending *Widmar* to public secondary schools. In *Board of Education of Westside Community Schools v. Mergens*, 496 U.S. 226 (1990), the Court held that the Act did not violate the establishment clause.

348 *Board of Education of Kiryaz Joel Village School District v. Grumet*, 512 U.S. 687 (1994).

schools,[349] loans of state-approved secular textbooks to children in religious schools,[350] and state funding of state-required standardized tests.[351] However, the Court disapproved state salary supplements for private (including religious) school teachers of secular subjects. Though the purpose was secular and it did not promote religion as such, there was "excessive entanglement." Religious school teachers were subject to religious supervision by their schools and the aid was a continuing close involvement of the government with religious schools.[352]

An area of sharp disagreement in recent years has been the issue of offering public school programs on the premises of a religious school. In *School Dist. of Grand Rapids v. Ball*,[353] remedial and enrichment programs were being taught to *religious* school students at public expense in *public* classrooms, and a community education program was being taught by *public* school teachers in *religious school* classrooms. In that case the Court worried that teachers would become inadvertently involved in teaching particular religious beliefs, that the program might provide a "crucial symbolic link between government and religion" in the "eyes of impressionable youngsters," and that the programs would in general assist indirectly in the "primary religious mission" of the religious institutions whose programs and students were assisted. However, in *Zobrest v. Catalina Foothills School Dist.*[354] a school district supplied sign-language interpreters for deaf students in public schools. A deaf student wished to continue to have such an interpreter after transferring to a parochial school. A sharply divided Court held 5-4 that it did not violate the establishment clause for the school district to continue to provide the interpreter. Most recently, the Court, in an extraordinary move, granted a motion to vacate an injunction it had affirmed earlier preventing New York City from sending public school teachers into parochial schools to provide remedial education. It set aside the injunction, overruled its previous decision and overruled such parts of the *Ball* decision as prevented secular public school programs from being offered in religious schools. This decision was 5-4 as well.[355]

Because college student minds are not as "impressionable," the Court has been more forgiving of governmental aid to religious colleges, so long as there is assurance that the funds will be used for secular purposes.[356] If the process for assuring such secular use requires on-going monitoring by the government, that may be an "excessive entanglement" with religion. Nonetheless, funding for sex counseling services for adolescents in religious schools and other institutions was approved, the Court dismissing as inconsequential problems with religious school counselors promoting religious views on sex.[357]

---

349 *Everson v. Board of Education,* 330 U.S. 1 (1947).

350 *Board of Education of Central School Dist. No. 1 v. Allen,* 389 U.S. 1031 (1968).

351 *Committee for Public Education and Religious Liberty v. Regan,* 444 U.S. 646 (1980).

352 *Lemon v. Kurtzman,* 403 U.S. 602 (1971).

353 *School Dist. of Grand Rapids v. Ball,* 473 U.S. 373 (1985).

354 509 U.S. 1 (1993).

355 *Agostini v. Felton,* 521 U.S. 203 (1997).

356 *See Tilton v. Richardson,* 403 U.S. 672 (1971) (20-year limit on the assurance of secular use of property deemed insufficient to avoid an establishment clause challenge). *See also Roemer v. Board of Public Works of Maryland,* 426 U.S. 736 (1976) (grants to private colleges, including sectarian schools, with assurances of secular use of funds upheld).

357 *Bowen v. Kendrick,* 487 U.S. 589 (1988).

Financial benefits that do not go to religious schools, but directly to students or to their parents, are more likely to be upheld. Tax deductions for school expenses granted to parents of both public and private schoolchildren do not violate the establishment clause. This is so even if it can be shown that the greatest beneficiaries will be parents sending their children to religious schools.[358] A specific deduction for tuition paid to parochial or other private schools alone is unconstitutional.[359] Similarly, a state educational grant to a blind student which was used by him to attend a Christian college was not unconstitutional because it went directly to the student who made the choice, it was unlikely that any large portion of the grant would be spent to support religious education, and the state program applied equally to students at non-religious colleges.[360]

Establishment Clause Issues Outside the Educational Context Government recognition of religious holidays has been permitted as satisfying the *Lemon* test's second requirement that government action be supported by a secular purpose. Common in some parts of the United States are "blue laws," which require that businesses be closed on Sundays. These laws were originally based on Sunday being the day of worship for Christians and a "day of rest." Despite this original religious purpose, the Court's view is that Sunday closing laws are constitutional because their *present* purpose is the secular one of having a uniform day of rest. Any benefits to religion are incidental.[361] Secular purpose also justifies government recognition of Christmas, the most important holiday of the year in the United States for most people. As the Court has noted, despite its religious origins, Christmas is really observed as a holiday of gift-giving and other secular activities. However, the government may not "endorse" the original Christian religious significance of Christmas by way of public display of a nativity scene of Jesus's birth on public property.[362] On the other hand, displaying a nativity scene as part of an overall "holiday display" of a Santa Claus, toy animals, gifts and other secular symbols of Christmas, has been held not to endorse Christianity. The Court has noted more broadly that there is no establishment problem with "the government's acknowledgment of our religious heritage and government sponsorship of graphic manifestations of that heritage."[363]

A long history of routine use of religious symbols may demonstrate their secular purpose. Thus, the Court upheld on historical grounds the practice of having a state-paid chaplain open the legislative session with a prayer. It observed that the first United States Congress at the time the 1st Amendment was adopted did the same and did not see legislative prayer as a violation of the establishment clause.[364] Similar reasoning would presumably support the approval of numerous routine religious references and symbols in government activities. United States currency has "In God We Trust" on it, "God Save This Honorable Court" concludes the official announcement of the opening of all federal courts, including the Supreme Court, and "one nation under God" is part of the Pledge of Allegiance. It is probably the case that

---

358 *Meuller v. Allen*, 463 U.S. 388 (1983).

359 *Committee for Public Education v. Nyquist*, 413 U.S. 756 (1973).

360 *Witters v. Washington Dept. of Services for the Blind*, 474 U.S. 481 (1986).

361 *McGowan v. Maryland*, 366 U.S. 420 (1961). However, a state law giving employees the right not to work on the sabbath of their choice does violate the establishment clause because it has the primary effect of advancing religion. *Estate of Thornton v. Caldor, Inc.*, 472 U.S. 703 (1985).

362 *Allegheny County v. American Civil Liberties Union*, 492 U.S. 573 (1989).

363 *Lynch v. Donnelly*, 465 U.S. 668 (1984).

364 *Marsh v. Chambers*, 463 U.S. 783 (1983).

these references are "interwoven so deeply into the fabric of our civil polity that [their] present use may well not present the type of involvement which the First Amendment prohibits."[365]

2. The Free Exercise Clause

The paradigm violation of the free exercise clause occurs when the government acts to disadvantage people because of their religion.[366] Laws that do this explicitly are rare. Most free exercise claims instead involve laws that pursue some permissible public purpose, but which burden religious beliefs *indirectly*. What the challenger seeks is an *exemption* from a *general* law. While the Court has been quite solicitous of accommodating religion in the past, some recent cases suggest a trend toward the view that any law that is of general applicability will be sustained even though it interferes with the religious practices of some people.

Traditional vs. New Free Exercise Standards For years, the Court applied a strict scrutiny test under which it would first determine whether the burden on religious beliefs was significant and, if it was, would sustain the law only if it was narrowly drawn to achieve a *compelling* state interest. In determining the question, the availability of less restrictive alternatives was to be considered.[367] Thus, in *Sherbert v. Verner*,[368] the state denied unemployment benefits to a woman who had been fired because she refused to work on Saturday, the Sabbath day of her religion. This denial of benefits was taken pursuant to a general prohibition on awarding unemployment benefits to those who refuse offers of "suitable work." The Court held that the law as applied violated her right of free exercise of religion because it forced her to choose between getting unemployment compensation and following her religious beliefs — something the state had no compelling interest in doing.[369] However, in the recent case of *Employment Division, Department of Human Resources v. Smith*,[370] the Court announced that it will no longer follow this process of balancing the burden on religion against a compelling state interest. Instead, so long as the *purpose* of the law is not to burden the exercise of religion, a "generally applicable and otherwise valid law" will be sustained regardless of its "incidental" effects on religious practices. In *Smith*, the Court upheld Oregon's denial of unemployment benefits to a drug counselor who was fired for using peyote (a naturally occurring hallucinogenic drug) as part of his religious practices as a member of the Native American Church. Peyote use violated state drug laws and those laws made no exception for religious uses. The Court did not overrule the *Sherbert v. Verner* line of cases. It noted, however, that the Oregon case involved violation of a *criminal* law, unlike its earlier cases.[371]

---

365 *Abington Township School District v. Schempp*, 374 U.S. 203, 304 (1963) (Brennan, J., concurring).

366 *See, e.g. McDaniel v. Pay*, 435 U.S. 618 (1978) (striking down law prohibiting clergy from serving as legislators) and *Torasco v. Watkins*, 367 U.S. 488 (1961) (law requiring declaration of belief in God as a condition of public office unconstitutional).

367 This test is similar to the test involved in strict scrutiny equal protection (*supra*, pp. 339, 344-345), substantive due process (*supra*, p. 352), and 1st Amendment freedom of expression (*supra* p. 366).

368 *Sherbert v. Verner*, 374 U.S. 398 (1963).

369 To the same effect are *Thomas v. Indiana Employment Security Comm.*, 450 U.S. 707 (1981) and *Hobbie v. Unemployment Appeals Comm.*, 480 U.S. 136 (1987). *Thomas* rejected asserted state interests in preventing unemployment and avoiding probing inquiries into religious beliefs of applicants for unemployment as not compelling enough. It also rejected the state's claim that *paying* unemployment compensation would violate the *establishment* clause.

370 494 U.S. 872 (1990).

371 In an analogous case decided in 1878 before much of today's free exercise doctrine was established, the Court decided that the 1st Amendment was not offended when the government prosecuted a Mormon for bigamy despite the fact that his faith required that he have more than one wife.

The strict scrutiny test was similarly declined in *Lyng v. Northwest Indian Cemetery Protective Assoc.*[372] *Lyng* was a challenge by Native Americans to the federal government's decision to permit timber harvesting and road construction in a National Forest. Native Americans used an area of forest that was owned by the government, but open to public use, for religious purposes. The proposed development would virtually destroy the religious use of the forest. The Court declined to apply the strict scrutiny test, pointing out that such an incidental effect on religion was far from a government "prohibition" of the free exercise of religion. Matters have not cleared up since *Smith* and *Lyng*. In *Church of Lukumi Babalu Aye, Inc. v. Hialeah*,[373] a church that had animal sacrifice as one of its religious rituals claimed that city ordinances prohibiting such practices were unconstitutional. All the justices agreed that strict scrutiny applied in that case because the ordinances, while neutral on their face, were passed for the purpose of stopping the religious practice in question. The Court rejected as not a sufficiently "compelling governmental interest" the city's interest in public health and preventing cruelty to animals. Concurring opinions in the case debated the propriety of the *Smith* standard and demonstrated how *Smith* could have been based on the state's compelling interest in prohibiting use of hallucinogenic drugs.[374]

Past Uses of the Traditional Test Whatever the status of the strict scrutiny test after *Smith* and *Lyng*, a long line of pre-*Smith* cases has used the compelling state interest test to invalidate application of neutral statutes or policies that affect religion. Principal among them was *Wisconsin v. Yoder*.[375] In *Yoder*, the Court held that neutral compulsory education laws that required that children go to school until they are 16 years old could not be applied to children of the Amish faith, which considered any formal education beyond 8 years to be an interference with religious training. The state's interests in assuring children would be productive members of society and protecting their well-being were deemed insufficient in view of the fact that the Amish system of home-based vocational training prepared children for life. The Court has also exempted religious organizations from federal civil rights laws prohibiting employment discrimination based on religion, on the ground that forcing religious employers to hire non-adherents to their faith violated the free exercise clause.[376] The Court has also held that church-affiliated schools are not subject to federal unemployment compensation laws[377] and has construed federal labor laws narrowly, making them inapplicable to protect unionization activities of lay faculty at religious schools on the ground that government intervention would present "serious constitutional questions."[378]

Reynolds v. United States, 98 U.S. (8 Otto) 145 (1878).

372 *Lyng v. Northwest Indian Cemetery Protective Assoc.*, 485 U.S. 439 (1988).

373 508 U.S. 520, (1993).

374 Congress responded to *Smith* by passing the Religious Freedom Restoration Act of 1993, imposing the pre-*Smith* standard as a *statutory* matter. However, the Court struck down the Act in 1998 in *City of Boerne v. Flores*, as discussed *supra* p. 323.

375 *Wisconsin v. Yoder*, 406 U.S. 205 (1972).

376 *Corporation of the Presiding Bishop of the Church of Jesus Christ of Latter-Day Saints v. Amos*, 483 U.S. 327 (1987). But the Court has sustained the application of federal wage and hour laws to commercial businesses operated by religious organizations. *Tony and Susan Alamo Foundation v. Secretary of Labor*, 471 U.S. 290 (1985). General employment discrimination laws are discussed in Chapter XV, pp. 569-573.

377 *St. Martin Evangelical Lutheran Church v. South Dakota*, 451 U.S. 772 (1981).

378 *Nat'l Labor Relations Bd. v. Catholic Bishop of Chicago*, 440 U.S. 490 (1979). For a discussion of law relating to labor organizing, *see* Chapter XV, pp. 563-568.

On the other hand, the Court has used the traditional free exercise test to *reject* claims for exemptions from generally applicable governmental requirements. These cases are most certainly still good law after *Smith*. Thus, the Court has upheld forcing an Orthodox Jewish merchant who closed his store on Saturday to comply with a Sunday closing as well on the grounds of a governmental need for a uniform day of rest for all employees,[379] a military regulation prohibiting an Orthodox Jewish officer from wearing a yarmulke while in uniform,[380] state child labor laws as applied to a child distributing religious literature with her guardian,[381] a law requiring immunization of children despite a parent's religious objections,[382] and a law requiring that children be assigned Social Security numbers against the religious wishes of their parents.[383]

Taxation and Free Exercise Many free exercise cases have dealt with tax policy. The Court has upheld the application of a general sales tax to religious goods and literature offered for sale,[384] denied exemption from Social Security taxes to the Amish who do not believe in compulsory insurance programs,[385] and upheld denial of tax exemptions to non-profit religious organizations that practice racial discrimination, even if it is done for religious reasons.[386] On the other hand, in a pair of older cases, the Court, on free exercise grounds, prohibited cities from applying a flat-fee licensing tax (charged all "solicitors") to persons distributing religious literature and from applying a flat "bookseller" fee to a minister who earned his living selling religious literature.[387]

In some taxation cases, free exercise claims meet the countervailing force of the establishment clause. For example, the Court held that a state tax *exemption* given to all religious publications violates the *establishment* clause.[388] Yet, it has held that exempting church property from taxes based on market value — along with the property of other educational and charitable institutions — does not violate the establishment clause. Such an exemption represents a neutral position toward religion that would be destroyed by the "entanglement" that would result from government determining the value of church property and enforcing the tax.[389]

Government Resolution of Religious Questions The need for government neutrality is most starkly presented when in lawsuits that turn on the resolution of a religious question. In one case, two competing religious groups sought possession of church property. Under the church charter, the group that was the follower of the "true faith" was entitled to the property. The Supreme Court held that it would violate the 1st Amendment for the state court to decide this issue. Instead, the court must defer to the determination of the highest tribunal of the church.[390] If no such definitive

---

379 *Braufeld v. Brown*, 366 U.S. 599 (1961).

380 *Goldman v. Weinberger*, 475 U.S. 503 (1986).

381 *Prince v. Massachusetts*, 321 U.S. 158 (1944).

382 *Jacobson v. Massachusetts*, 197 U.S. 11 (1925).

383 *Bowen v. Roy*, 476 U.S. 693 (1986).

384 *Jimmy Swaggart Ministries v. Board of Equalization*, 493 U.S. 378 (1990).

385 *United States v. Lee*, 455 U.S. 252 (1982).

386 *Bob Jones University v. United States*, 461 U.S. 574 (1983).

387 *See Murdock v. Pennsylvania*, 319 U.S. 105 (1943); *Follett v. McCormick*, 321 U.S. 573 (1944).

388 *Texas Monthly, Inc. v. Bullock*, 489 U.S. 1 (1989).

389 *Walz v. Tax Commission*, 397 U.S. 664 (1970).

390 *Presbyterian Church v. Hull Church*, 393 U.S. 440 (1969). The Court noted, however, that the decisions of church tribunals *are* reviewable by civil courts if they are based on "fraud, collusion, or arbitrariness." *Id.* at 450 n. 7, quoting from *Gonzalez v. Roman Catholic Archbishop of Manila*, 208 U.S. 1 at 16 (1929).

tribunal exists and the court can apply neutral principles of contract and property law to the dispute, it may do so.[391] If not, neither the state court nor any federal court can become involved.

Another fundamental potential "entanglement" with religion occurs when a court must decide what constitutes a "religion" either for 1st Amendment or other purposes. The Court has not limited religion to theistic beliefs and has held that it is not required that a person claiming an exemption on religious grounds be a member of an organized religion or a particular sect.[392] In cases involving claims of exemption from military service on religious grounds, the Court has held that the test of whether a belief is religious is whether the belief is "sincere and meaningful . . . [and] . . . occupies in the life of its possessor a place parallel to that filled by the God of those admittedly qualifying for the exemption."[393]

---

391 *Jones v. Wolf*, 443 U.S. 595 (1979).

392 *Frazee v. Illinois Dept. of Employment Security*, 489 U.S. 829 (1989) (unemployment claimant with "sincerely held" religious views on Saturday work entitled to *Sherbert v. Verner* protections).

393 *Welsh v. United States*, 398 U.S. 333 at 339 (1970), quoting from *United States v. Seeger*, 380 U.S. 163 at 176 (1965).

CHAPTER X

CONTRACTS AND COMMERCIAL LAW

Contract law originated in the English common law courts and remains today largely governed by common law. However, as in other areas of the law, state and federal statutes play an increasing role. For example, every state has adopted most or all of the Uniform Commercial Code (UCC) which sets out a standardized set of rules for many types of commercial agreements, such as the sale of goods. In addition, federal and state governments have created consumer protection laws which regulate many consumer transactions.[1] The result is a mix of common law and federal and state statutes. Transactions often have to be examined carefully to determine what laws apply.[2]

PART I: The Common Law of Contracts

A. Formation of Contracts

A contract is a promise between two or more parties that the law recognizes as binding by providing a remedy in the event of breach. The common law states that for promises to be enforceable there must be "mutual assent" between the parties. Mutual assent exists if there was an offer and an acceptance of the offer, supported by mutual consideration, defined below. When focusing on offer and acceptance, it is common to refer to the parties as the "offeror" and the "offeree." An offeror is a person who makes an offer and the offeree is a person to whom the offer is made.

Although mutual assent is frequently referred to as a "meeting of the minds" and courts speak freely of the "intent" of the parties, actual subjective intent is irrelevant. Instead, an objective test is used and the intent that a reasonable person would infer from a party's words and acts is assigned to the parties. For example, an offeree may receive an offer and, without reading it, send an acceptance without any additional terms. Since the acceptance would lead a reasonable offeror to conclude that the offeree had read and accepted the offer's terms, there is a contract with all of the offeror's terms, despite the fact that the offeree could not possibly have intended subjectively to accept those terms. One result of an objective standard is that an offer which is made in jest can be enforced if a reasonable person would have concluded that a real offer was intended, unless the offeree actually knew that the "offer" was a joke.[3]

1. Offer and Acceptance

Offers An offer is "a manifestation of willingness to enter into a bargain so made as to justify another person in understanding his assent to that bargain is invited and will conclude it."[4] An offer must be sufficiently definite such that, if accepted, there would be a sufficient "basis for determining the existence of a breach and for giving

---

1   *See infra* pp. 394-398, where Truth in Lending and other federal consumer laws are discussed.

2   The UCC is discussed *infra* pp. 384-392. Standard single-volume treatises on contract law are E. ALLAN FARNSWORTH, CONTRACTS, 2D ED. (Aspen 1990), JOHN D. CALAMARI & JOSEPH M. PERILLO, HORNBOOK ON CONTRACTS, 4TH ED. (West 1998); BRIAN A. BLUM, CONTRACTS: EXAMPLES AND EXPLANATIONS (Aspen 1998).

3   *See Lucy v. Zehmer*, 84 S.E.2d 516 (Va. 1954) (seller claimed he "was high as a Georgia pine" and that the transaction "was just a bunch of doggoned drunks bluffing to see who could talk the biggest and say the most"; written contract to sell his farm was valid nonetheless as a "serious business transaction").

4   RESTATEMENT (SECOND) CONTRACTS §24 (American Law Institute 1981) [hereafter RESTATEMENT]. Restatements were discussed in Chapter II, p. 72.

an appropriate remedy."[5] This will often require that the offer specify essential elements such as quantity and price. The offeror must manifest an intent to give the offeree the power to "close" the deal by accepting the offer. Thus, the statement "I will sell you my car for $300" is an offer. The offeree can accept by promising to pay the $300 or by paying it.

Agreements are often arrived at only after a series of negotiations. In such cases, a party might make a statement which is not an offer, but a manifestation of an intent to negotiate. For example, a person might say: "It would not be possible for me to sell my old car to you for less than $300." Viewed objectively, this statement is not an offer to sell for $300, but an intent to open negotiations.

Often statements resemble offers but do not meet the necessary requirements. For example, advertisements are generally not offers, in part because they do not contain sufficient language of promise or commitment to sell. Instead, they are usually considered invitations to bid or make an offer. But some advertisements may be offers. For example, in one case, a retail store's advertisement read: "Saturday, 9 A.M., . . . 1 black lapin stole, . . . $1, First come first served." It was held to be an offer because the words "First come first served" are promissory, there is a price and quantity element, and it is directed toward a particular person — the first person to tender $1 on Saturday after 9 A.M.[6]

Acceptance The offeree accepts the offer by agreeing to the proposed bargain. At common law the acceptance must be a "mirror image" of the offer; that is, the acceptance cannot add terms or change any terms of the offer. If it does, then it is not an acceptance at all, but a rejection of the original offer and a counteroffer. In one well-known case, the seller sent an offer on its form, which listed the terms of sale. The buyer responded with its order form. That form corresponded to the seller's form with one minor exception. The buyer wanted out of the contract for other reasons and the court permitted it to do so because of the discrepancy.[7]

Means of Acceptance The common law makes a distinction between "bilateral" contracts (where the offeror seeks acceptance through a *promise* of performance) and "unilateral" contracts (where the offeror seeks acceptance through actual *performance*). The offeror, as the master of the offer, may prescribe the method by which the offer will be accepted. For example, if an offeror promises to sell a car to the offeree for $300, the offeror can specify whether the acceptance will be by a promise to pay the $300 or by actual payment of the $300. If the offeror does not specify the mode of acceptance, the offeree can accept "in any manner and by any medium reasonable in the circumstances."[8] In a unilateral contract, where the offer specifically invites acceptance by performance, the offer can be accepted only by full performance. For example, assume an offeror promises to pay $100 if the offeree walks across the Brooklyn Bridge. The offeree cannot accept this offer by *promising* to walk across the bridge, nor can the offeree accept by starting to walk across. The offeree can accept the offer only by *crossing* the bridge. Until the offeree has walked completely across, there is no acceptance and therefore no contract. This rule may cause unfair results by allowing the offeror to receive partial performance and then revoke the offer before the acceptance is complete. Consequently, it is generally held

---

5 RESTATEMENT §33(2).

6 *Leftkowitz v. Great Minneapolis Surplus Store, Inc.*, 86 N.W.2d 689 (Minn. 1957).

7 *See Poel v. Brusnwick-Balke-Collender Co.*, 110 N.E. 619 (N.Y. 1915).

8 RESTATEMENT §30(2).

that once the offeree has started to perform, the offer becomes an "option contract" (discussed below) which cannot be revoked until the offeree has had a chance to perform.

Time for Acceptance The power to accept an offer does not belong to the offeree forever. The period of acceptance can be terminated by lapse, rejection, revocation, or the death of a party. Often the offer specifies the amount of time in which the offer may be accepted by the offeree. If the offeree does not accept within that time, the offer has lapsed, and the offeree can no longer exercise the power to accept and close the deal. If no period is specified in the offer, it lapses after a reasonable time or until the offeror revokes the offer. What is a reasonable time depends on the circumstances. For example, unless specified otherwise, an offer made in a face-to-face conversation is usually deemed to continue only to the close of the conversation, and cannot be accepted thereafter.[9]

The power to accept an offer also ends when the offeree rejects the offer. After rejecting the offer, the offeree cannot reconsider and accept. An offeree's counteroffer terminates the power of acceptance just as if the offeree had rejected the offer, unless the original offer is irrevocable (discussed below). An offeree can avoid this result by using language which does not reject the offer. For example, the offeree can keep the original offer open by replying "we are considering your offer. In the meantime, would you consider . . . ."

Before the offeree accepts or rejects the offer, the offeror can terminate the offeree's power of acceptance by revoking the offer. A revocation sent by the offeror is effective upon receipt by the offeree. Thus the issue of when the acceptance becomes effective may be an important question in determining if the offeror still has the power to revoke the offer or if it has already been accepted. The common law follows the "mailbox rule," whereby the acceptance becomes effective upon mailing the acceptance. Since the acceptance is effective when mailed, the contract is concluded at that time. Thus the offeror will only learn of the acceptance and existence of the contract when the offeror actually receives it. If an offeree mails an acceptance, but later reconsiders and communicates a rejection, the rejection is not valid even if it arrives before the acceptance. This rule prevents an offeree from accepting an offer using, for example, slow mail service, while knowing that if market prices suddenly change or a better offer is submitted by someone else, the offeree can quickly dispatch an overtaking rejection. But if a rejection is sent first and the offeree after reflection sends an overtaking acceptance, the acceptance will be effective if it arrives before the rejection.

Option Contracts For the protection of the offeree, there are some situations in which an offer is irrevocable for a period of time. An offer is irrevocable if the offeree gives the offeror "consideration" for a promise not to revoke the offer for a period of time. Giving consideration means that the offeree pays or otherwise gives value to the offeror to keep the offer "open" for some period of time. An offeree in this position is said to have an "option contract," and may consider the offer for the period of time agreed upon without fear of revocation.[10]

---

9 *See Akers v. J.B. Sedberry, Inc.*, 286 S.W.2d 617 (Tenn.App. 1955) (employer's acceptance of employees' offers to resign after the end of the face-to-face conversation was too late).

10 Consideration is discussed more generally in 2. below.

Another occasion when an option contract is formed is when the offeror wants acceptance by performance and the offeree begins the invited performance.[11] The length of this option contract is a "reasonable time." Since an offer for a unilateral contract has not been accepted until the offeree has fully performed, this rule protects the offeree from revocation after beginning performance in reliance on the offer. Returning to the Brooklyn Bridge hypothetical mentioned earlier, the offeree would be protected from revocation if already part way across the bridge.

Under some circumstances, an offer can be irrevocable when the offeree *relies* on the offer, but has not yet begun performance. Thus, "an offer which the offeror should reasonably expect to induce action or forbearance of a substantial character on the part of the offeree before acceptance and which does induce such action or forbearance is binding as an option contract to the extent necessary to avoid injustice."[12] For example, assume a general contractor receives an offer from a subcontractor — often called a "bid" — to do the electrical work of a building that the general contractor is seeking to build. The general contractor uses the subcontractor's bid to calculate its own bid to construct the building. If the subcontractor were then able to revoke the offer, and the general contractor wins the contract, the general contractor would be responsible for completing the building at the contract price but would likely have to hire a more expensive electrician. The quoted rule protects the general contractor in this situation by making the subcontractor's bid irrevocable.[13]

2. Consideration

General Requirement Consideration was introduced above when the option contract was discussed. It plays a broader role in contracts than just that. Generally, no promise is enforceable unless it is supported by consideration. Consideration is a bargained-for exchange between the promisor and the promisee. "Promisee" refers to the person benefitting from a given promise, while the "promisor" is the person who made the promise and is being called on to carry it out. Generally, anything that is given in exchange for a promise will constitute consideration, as long as it was bargained for.[14] Thus, a promise or performance given by the promisee to the promisor must be "sought by the promisor in exchange for his promise and . . . given by the promisee in exchange for that promise."[15] Therefore, the mere fact that the promisee gave something to the promisor does not in itself satisfy the requirements of consideration.

All legal systems look for a serious intent to be bound when determining which promises will be enforced as contracts. But the requirement of consideration is unique to the common law countries and it may sometimes restrict what the law considers to be an enforceable contract. The consideration requirement reflects a discomfort that common law judges feel in determining parties' subjective intent. Consideration provides an objective manifestation of agreement.

Promises to Make a Gift One situation affected by the consideration requirement is a promise to make a gift. Such a promise is usually unenforceable. This is because

---

11 RESTATEMENT §45.

12 RESTATEMENT §87(2)

13 *See, e.g, Drennan v. Star Paving Co.*, 333 P.2d 757 (Cal. 1958) (paving subcontractor's bid is binding even if based on a mistake, in the absence of the bid stating a specific right to revoke it).

14 The modern view is that the consideration need not convey a benefit to the promisor or a detriment to the promisee. RESTATEMENT §79.

15 RESTATEMENT §71(2).

the whole nature of a gift is that the promisor wants nothing in return for the promise. Sometimes it may sound as if the promisor of a gift wants something in return. For example, a man may tell a neighbor: "If you come over to my house, I'll give you some suits that I have outgrown." By going to the house, the neighbor has performed an action to get the suits. However, performing this act is not really sufficient consideration to make the promise binding because the promisor was probably not seeking a visit to his or her house in exchange for the promise to hand over the suits. Instead, the promisor probably meant, "you can have the suits but you have to come and get them." In other words, the promisor probably did not make the promise in exchange for the neighbor's act of going to the house. If this is the case, there is no consideration for the promise and it is unenforceable.

Illusory Promises   A promise which appears to promise something, but in fact does not commit the promisor to anything at all, is known as an "illusory" promise and is insufficient consideration. For example, it has been held that the promise of a creditor not to collect the debt "until such time as I want my money" is illusory.[16] A promise is similarly illusory when one of the parties reserves an unrestricted right to terminate the agreement at any time. With such a reservation, the party has not committed to anything and the promise is void for lack of consideration. On the other hand, a termination clause that requires the party to give notice some period of time before the termination becomes effective does not make the promise illusory, because the duty to give notice is a detriment. There are some cases, however, that have enforced seemingly illusory promises by implying a duty to use "good faith" in performing the promise. In one case, an employee in a contract promised to work only as much "as he in his sole judgement shall deem necessary." This promise was not illusory, since there was an implied promise to "render some substantial services" and that he was required "to act in good faith."[17]

Pre-Existing Duty Rule   Consideration may be absent when the promise is in exchange for performing a "pre-existing duty." A promise to do something that is already legally required is not valid consideration for a new promise. The pre-existing duty rule seeks to prevent extorted modifications of contracts. For example, if a builder agrees to construct a place of business for one price and the parties later agree that the price is to be increased, the additional amount is generally not enforceable. The promise to build the structure is not consideration for the owner's promise to pay the additional amount since the builder was already obligated to build the house in accordance with their first agreement. Thus a promise to pay an additional amount requires "fresh" consideration. If, for example, the builder agrees in return for the higher amount to complete the structure one month earlier than originally agreed or to expand it, the additional amount is enforceable.[18]

The pre-existing duty rule has been criticized because it interferes with the parties' freedom to modify their agreements as they see fit. As a result, some jurisdictions have found exceptions to the rule, and a few have abolished the rule

---

16 *Strong v. Sheffield*, 39 N.E. 330 (N.Y. 1895).

17 *See Seymour Grean & Co. v. Grean*, 82 N.Y.S.2d 787 (App. Div. 1948) (dictum; court held other consideration sufficient).

18 *See* RESTATEMENT §73. *W.E.Koeler Construction Co. v. Medical Center of Blue Springs*, 670 S.W.2d 558 (Mo.App. 1984) (subsequent agreement allowing contractor to substitute cheaper materials and promising to award later work to that contractor were not enforceable in return for contractor keeping bid price firm, because contractor already had a duty to complete the building for the bid amount).

altogether. The modern trend is to enforce modifications to contracts not fully performed that are fair and equitable in view of unanticipated circumstances.[19]

Promissory Estoppel At first glance it may appear that the requirement of consideration could lead to rather harsh results. For example, it may seem unfair to allow a promisee, thinking a binding contract existed, to incur an expense, only to discover later that the law would not enforce the contract for lack of consideration. Such problems are dealt with through a doctrine known as "promissory estoppel." Promissory estoppel provides that reliance on a promise can make the promise binding or enforceable to some extent, even without consideration, but only if it was foreseeable to the promisor that the promisee would rely on the promise.[20]

3. Formal Requirements

Once there is mutual assent supported by consideration, an enforceable contract exists. There is no requirement for any formal ceremony to make the agreement "official," no requirement for a seal (an embossed marker), and, in some cases, no requirement that the contract even be in writing. If the contract is in writing it does not have to be in any particular form. However, some types of contracts are required to be in writing under the "Statute of Frauds."

a. The Statute of Frauds

All of the states (except Louisiana) have adopted a close form of the English Statute of Frauds (1677), which requires that certain types of contracts be in writing in order to be enforceable. The primary purpose of the Statute of Frauds is to ensure that certain contracts are not enforced unless there is sufficient proof that the contract exists. There are four types of contracts that typically fall within the Statute of Frauds and must therefore be in writing. These are (1) a suretyship contract (a contract to answer for the debt or obligation of another), (2) a contract to transfer or buy any interest in land, (3) a contract that cannot be performed within one year of its making, and (4) a contract for the sale of goods worth more than $500.

Under both the common law and the UCC, the Statute of Frauds requires that the writing must be "signed by the party against whom enforcement is sought."[21] This generally means that the signature must be written on a paper copy of the contract. However, the Information Security Committee of the American Bar Association's Science and Technology Section has proposed a relaxation of the requirement that signatures be written on paper. The Committee suggests that digital signatures could replace physical signatures and would facilitate global commerce by avoiding having mail hard copies of the written contract back and forth.[22]

When it would be extremely unfair to one of the parties to hold a contract invalid due to its failure to satisfy the Statute of Frauds, courts have made exceptions. For example, courts have enforced oral agreements for the sale of land if the purchaser

---

19 RESTATEMENT §89. *See Angel v. Murray*, 322 A.2d 630 (R.I. 1974) (upward modification of compensation under garbage collection contract due to unexpected increase in number of residential units served was effective).

20 RESTATEMENT §90. *See State Dept. of Highways v. Woolley*, 696 P.2d 828 (Colo.App. 1984) (landowners were estopped from revoking their promise to grant state highway department right to enter their land where department spent money and labor in reliance on promise). *But see Local 1330, United Steel Workers v. United States Steel Corp.*, 631 F.2d 1264 (6th Cir. 1980) (not foreseeable that the union would rely on a promise to keep plants operating if fixed costs of the plants were met).

21 UCC §2-201

22 Information Security Committee, American Bar Ass'n, *States' Role in Developing Digital Signatures Policies and Standards* (July 31,1997) *See* <http:// www.abanet.org/scitech/ec/isc/stateds.html>.

has paid a considerable portion of the price or made significant improvements to the land.[23]

b. Resolving Problems with Incomplete or Indefinite Written Agreements

The Parol Evidence Rule A frequent problem occurs when a contract has been reduced to writing, but one of the parties claims that their actual agreement included a term which is not in the writing. The "parol evidence rule" generally prohibits the introduction of extrinsic evidence that contradicts terms of a written contract. The purpose of the parol evidence rule is to promote certainty by preventing written agreements from being contradicted by less reliable accounts of the agreement and by encouraging parties to make their written agreements complete.[24]

The parol evidence rule applies only if a written contract is intended to be the final expression of the entire agreement and to include all of the terms and details of the agreement. If the contract is not intended to include all the details of the agreement, evidence of terms that *contradict* the written contract will *not* be allowed, but the party may show evidence of *additional* terms that do not contradict the writing. If the writing is not intended to constitute the full agreement, then parol evidence can be used to supplement or even contradict the terms of the writing. In the past the decision of the question of whether a written contract embodies the complete agreement of the parties was made by looking solely at the document and determining if the terms sought to be added by parol evidence would naturally and normally have been left out of the writing. But under the more modern approach a judge balances the actual intentions of the parties against the document itself.[25]

The parol evidence rule applies only to extrinsic agreements that were made prior to or contemporaneous with the written agreement. It does not bar evidence that the contract was orally modified after the writing. It also does not prevent the introduction of evidence that would show that no valid contract exists or that the contract is voidable, so parties may show evidence of fraud, duress, lack of consideration, or anything else that would make the contract void or voidable.

B. Interpretation of Contracts

Plain Meaning Rule One approach to interpretation, called the "plain meaning rule," provides that the meaning of any writing or term which appears to be plain and unambiguous on its face will be determined without using any extrinsic evidence whatsoever. The plain meaning rule does not allow the parties to show what they thought the term meant, and does not even allow evidence of trade usage to interpret the words. Although this rule is widely criticized, "it is undoubtedly still employed frequently or on occasion by the great majority of the jurisdictions in this country."[26]

---

23 *See, e.g., Holt v. Katsanevas*, 854 P.2d 575 (Utah App. 1993) (oral modification of contract for the sale of land enforceable notwithstanding the statute of frauds if the party has performed in part in reliance on the modification).

24 Although "parol" literally means "oral," the parol evidence rule acts to exclude not only oral evidence, but all forms of evidence extrinsic to the written agreement.

25 *See Sierra Diesel Injection Service, Inc. v. Burroughs Corp.*, 890 F.2d 108 (9th Cir. 1989) (computer seller's printed form contract was not a final complete statement of the agreement despite the fact that it so stated; most important factor was the parties' intent). *See generally* CALAMARI & PERILLO, *supra* note 2, §3-2.

26 CALAMARI & PERILLO, *supra* note 2, at 167. The "plain meaning" rule in contract law is similar to the "plain meaning" maxim of statutory interpretation. It has many of the same benefits and difficulties as does the statutory interpretation maxim, noted in Chapter II, pp. 51-54.

Interpretation Focusing on the Parties' Intent   The common law maintains a strong position that terms of a contract should be interpreted by their external expression and not by the subjective intentions of one party. Even so, recognizing the importance of the parties' intentions and the imprecisions of language, a more modern approach allows the parties to introduce evidence of what they subjectively thought the terms in the writing meant.[27] Parties may have directly conflicting ideas about what the terms meant. When this happens, the court may find that there was no mutual assent and therefore no contract. But if one party knows of or should have known of the meaning attached by the other party to a term, a court will find that there was mutual assent.[28]

When parties have conflicting interpretations of a term in the contract, courts may also make use of some general principles of law, or maxims, in deciding which interpretation should be followed. The Restatement suggests some of these general principles. For example, an ambiguous term will be construed against the drafter of the agreement.[29] All terms will be interpreted, where possible, to have a reasonable, lawful, and effective meaning.[30] A term that has been negotiated between the parties will control over one that is part of the standardized, non-negotiated part of the contract, or "boilerplate."[31] Another maxim, the primary purpose rule, provides that if the court can determine what the parties' "primary purpose" for making the contract was, that purpose should be given great weight in the interpretation of the terms.[32]

Court-Supplied Terms   Often parties enter into contracts without expressly or implicitly providing all the terms of their agreement. When this occurs, courts are often willing to supply the missing term. "When the parties to a bargain sufficiently defined to be a contract have not agreed with respect to a term which is essential to a determination of their rights and duties, a term which is reasonable in the circumstances is supplied by the courts."[33] Such court-supplied terms usually deal with an issue that the parties never even thought about. A reasonable supplied term is one that the parties would have agreed to or which conforms to commercial standards of fairness. For example, if a person hires a painter to paint a house but the parties did not discuss price, the court may supply the term "reasonable price," and define it as the painter's usual charges. Thus a court will look to trade usage, course of performance, and course of dealings when deciding what is a fair term.[34]

Courts are often unwilling to supply certain kinds of missing terms. For example, quantity terms will generally not be filled in, because an objective standard is difficult to find for this usually subjective expectation.

---

27   The parol evidence rule does not bar the use of parol evidence to interpret or explain terms contained in a complete written agreement, but the use of extrinsic evidence to interpret or explain terms may be limited by rules of contract interpretation.

28   RESTATEMENT §§18, 20, 201. *See Wells v. Weston*, 326 S.E.2d 672 (Va. 1985) (property settlement agreement providing for spousal support payments to wife for as long as she lived valid as written; husband's uncommunicated intent that payments stop upon her marriage was not part of the contract).

29   RESTATEMENT §206.

30   *Id.*, §203(a).

31   *Id.*, §203(d).

32   *Id.*, §202(1).

33   RESTATEMENT §204. *See Barco Urban Renewal Corp. v. Housing Authority*, 674 F.2d 1001, 1007 (3d Cir. 1982) (right of first refusal deemed to continue for a commercially reasonable time where no time was stated by contract).

34   *See, e.g., Columbia Nitrogen Corp. v. Royster Co.*, 451 F.2d 3 (4th Cir. 1971) (evidence of trade usage allowing phosphate buyers to ignore contractually stipulated minimum quantities should have been allowed by court).

C. Issues in Performance of Contracts

1. Order of Performance

Ideally, parties to a contract will tender their promised performances simultaneously. This preferred order provides the security that both parties' expectations will be met because both parties can defer their performance until there is adequate certainty that the other party will perform. It is especially common for parties to follow this order of performance when selling and buying real estate. On the agreed date for performance, the seller tenders a deed and the buyer tenders the purchase price. This is referred to as "closing" the transaction.

Often circumstances make it impractical for parties to tender their performance at the same time. This is the case where the performance of one party will take longer than the other party's. This is especially true of construction contracts where the builder's promised performance is providing a completed building and the owner's performance is payment for that completed building. But under such circumstances the builder can regain the security of simultaneous performance by requesting payments at stated intervals for work completed. It is also very common for one party to tender performance first in reliance on the other party's promise to tender its performance at a later date. This often happens when one party has lesser bargaining power and has no choice but to perform first. This is common when parties have dealt with each other before and one party is willing to perform first.

2. Conditions and Duties

Although a party to a contract has a duty to perform the tasks promised, that duty to perform may be conditional. A "condition" is "an event, not certain to occur, which must occur, unless its nonoccurrence is excused, before performance under a contract becomes due."[35] A party whose performance is conditional does not have to perform the promised act until and unless the condition has been satisfied or excused.

Explicit Condition When the parties have agreed to the condition (expressly or impliedly), the condition is an express condition. For example, suppose a party has contracted to buy a house "subject to and conditional upon" obtaining a mortgage to finance the $100,000 sale price. If no bank will approve such a mortgage, the buyer's duty to perform does not arise. Explicit conditions are applied strictly. Thus, even if a bank is willing to lend $90,000 and the seller is willing to make separate arrangements for the remaining $10,000, the buyer does not have a duty to perform.[36]

Presumption Against Forfeiture Strict application of explicit conditions can cause some hardship where one party has substantially relied on the other party's apparent ability to satisfy the condition. Because of this, the law has a "presumption against forfeiture" — a presumption that the contract is not forfeited for failure of the condition. Under this rule, a court might try to interpret the contract language so as not to impose a condition. If there is clearly a condition, the court might seek to avoid forfeiture by concluding that the condition has been satisfied. For example, in one case an insurance policy for a store owner's safe provided that the insurance company's duty to pay for loss resulting from a burglary was conditional upon a forceful entry into the safe evidenced by "visible marks made by tools, explosives,

---

35 RESTATEMENT §224. These conditions are sometimes called "contingencies."

36 *See Luttinger v. Rosen*, 316 A.2d 757 (Conn. 1972) (purchases unable to find mortgage at a certain rate, so contract condition was not satisfied).

electricity or chemicals upon the exterior of . . . the doors of the vault or the safe . . . ."
A burglar opened the safe by manipulating the combination lock of the outer door and punching out the lock of the inner door, making no visible marks on the exterior of either door. The court held that the only real condition was that the safe be burglarized by physical force to protect the insurance company from "inside jobs" and that that condition had been satisfied.[37]

Excuse of Conditions In some cases, the party who must perform the condition, but cannot do so, wishes to enforce the contract. This is permitted if that party is somehow excused from performing the condition. One instance of an appropriate excuse is where the party is prevented from performing the condition by the other party's wrongful conduct. In one case, for example, a nephew agreed to live with his uncle and take care of him for the rest of his life in exchange for payment after the uncle died. The nephew performed his part of the agreement for several years, during which the uncle was constantly drunk and abusive to the nephew. The uncle eventually forced the nephew to leave. The nephew was still permitted to recover under the contract, even though he did not care for the uncle for the rest of the uncle's life. The condition (lifetime care) that qualifies the uncle's performance was prevented from occurring by the uncle's wrongful conduct, so the condition is excused and the uncle must perform even though the condition did not occur.[38]

Difference Between Condition and Duty A condition is different from a duty. A duty results from a promise, and the breach of a promise will give the other party a cause of action for damages. For example, an insurance policy agreement provides that the homeowner *must notify* the insurance company of any fire within seven days. The homeowner has made a promise and therefore has a duty to inform the insurance company. If the homeowner fails to notify the insurance company within seven days after a fire, the homeowner has breached the contract. The insurance company may sue for damages for that breach (if there are any). But it still has to perform, i.e., it must still pay the agreed-upon insurance coverage amount. If, however, the agreement had provided that the insurance company will pay the coverage amount *if and only if* it is notified of the fire within seven days, then there is a condition. The condition qualifies the insurance company's duty to perform. If the homeowner does not inform the insurance company within seven days, the insurance company does not have to pay the coverage amount.[39]

Constructive Conditions A promise might not be expressly conditional on performance by the other party. In the absence of the doctrine of "constructive conditions," a party would be obligated to perform his or her promise even though the other party has not performed. Beginning in the 18th century, courts recognized the unfairness of a party who was in breach of a contract suing to enforce the other party's performance. In response, courts began to imply conditions into agreements where the parties have not expressly agreed otherwise.[40] Thus, where A and B have a

---

37 *Ferguson v. Phoenix Assurance Co.*, 370 P.2d 379 (Kansas 1962).

38 *Barron v. Cain*, 4 S.E.2d 618 (N.C. 1939). Another way of analyzing the uncle's conduct is that it breached an implied promise of cooperation. Under this analysis, his failure to cooperate was a material breach, which excuses the nephew from performing, and entitles the nephew to damages for breach. *See* discussion of constructive conditions below.

39 An agreement could contain both a condition and a duty. For example, the agreement could provide that the homeowner *promises* to inform the insurance company, *and* the insurance company must pay the coverage amount *if and only if* the homeowner notifies it within the specified time period.

40 *See Kingston v. Preston*, 99 Eng. Rep. 437 (K.B. 1773) (seller of shop not obligated to deliver possession if the buyer has not paid).

contract and their promises can be performed at the same time, performance by A need not take place until B tenders performance.[41] A constructive condition must be substantially performed while an explicit (express) condition must be strictly complied with. If B fails to substantially perform the condition, then there is a material breach of the contract and A's duty to perform never arises. However, if B substantially performs, then A's duty to perform arises. Although B substantially performed, B did not tender full performance therefore there is a breach, but the breach is immaterial so A must perform. After B's substantial performance gives rise to A's duty to perform, A may sue B for breach of contract (discussed below).

The necessary result of the constructive conditions rule is that it may create an inequity where A's promise would take longer to perform than B's. In that case, A would be required to complete performance before B's performance is due. For that reason, the rule has been criticized. This is because, in effect, it requires the party whose performance happens to take more time to extend credit to the other party. Under this rule, for example, a laborer who was hired for the summer could end up in the position of not getting paid until the end of the summer, since it takes less time to hand over money than to work an entire summer. Nonetheless, the employer under the contract as agreed would not be required to pay the laborer until all the work was completed.[42]

D. Grounds for Nonperformance of Contracts

1. Mistake

A party may be released from a contract if the contract was based upon a mutual mistake, and the party seeking release did not bear the risk of that mistake. The mistake must concern a basic assumption on which the contract was made, such as the nature, identity, or existence of the subject matter. For example, if a buyer unfamiliar with livestock sees a steer and thinks it is a cow, and agrees to buy it, the buyer will still have to perform. The mistake here was not mutual; it was unilateral. Also, the buyer bore the risk of this mistake, since the buyer admittedly knew little about livestock, but chose to proceed anyway. On the other hand, if two parties agree to the sale of a cow, but unknown to them, the cow had died before their agreement, the mistake is mutual and the seller will not have to perform.[43]

2. Changed Circumstances: Impossibility and Frustration of Purpose

Impossibility A party might also be released from a contract where, through no fault of the parties, the performance has become impossible or the principal purpose of one of the parties in entering into the contract has become frustrated. For example, assume a painter is hired to paint a building. Through no fault of either party, the building burns down before the painter starts painting. The painter is excused from performing because of impossibility.

---

41 The doctrine of constructive conditions might apply to the hypothetical about the duty to notify the insurance company. If the failure to notify the insurance company within seven days is determined to be a *material* breach, then the homeowner has failed to substantially perform. Because the insurance company's duty to perform is qualified by the constructive condition of substantial performance, and that condition was not satisfied, the insurance company would not have to pay.

42 The laborer's problem in most employment situations is taken care of by statutory wage and hour regulations, which generally require that the laborer be paid on a regular basis throughout the summer for work as it is performed.

43 *See Sherwood v. Walker*, 33 N.W. 919 (Mich. 1887) (seller of cow could avoid contract for sale of cow when both buyer and seller erroneously believed the cow to be infertile).

Impracticability In some cases, the performance has not become literally impossible, but unforeseeable circumstances have made performance extremely costly or burdensome. This is known as "impracticability," and the modern trend is to release a party from a contract if performance becomes extremely impracticable. But impracticality requires that the economic loss be both substantial and unforeseen at the time the contract was made. Many of the modern cases dealing with impracticability have involved drastic increases in energy costs resulting from the oil embargo of the 1970s. These cases show that courts are generally unwilling to release parties from their obligations simply because of lost profits.[44]

Frustration of Purpose   Frustration of purpose occurs when a change in circumstances makes one party's performance virtually worthless to the other. For example, the parties enter into a lease of a building. The lease specifies that the building is to be used for the sole purpose of operating a casino. During the period of the lease, gambling is declared illegal. The lessee cannot claim any right to discontinue paying rent due to impossibility, because it is still legal for the lessee to rent the building. But the main purpose of the lease has been frustrated, so the lessee might be excused from continuing to perform.[45]

Reformation of Contracts Instead of declaring the contract invalid because of changed circumstances, a court may try to "reform" it. However, U.S. courts generally feel that they have no power to impose unbargained-for terms upon parties when the parties agreed on different terms. Such action is seen as a direct interference with a free market and the right of parties to contract freely to guarantee their own expectations. One can nonetheless find occasional cases where contracts have been reformed.[46]

3. Lack of Capacity: Minors and Mental Incapacity

Persons lacking legal capacity include those who are too young (below the age of majority) or mentally incompetent. A person who lacks the legal capacity to enter into an agreement can be released from the duty to perform.

Minors A minor may enter into a contract, but may disaffirm the contract at any time during minority or within a reasonable time after majority, even if the other party has fully performed. To disaffirm a contract, the minor has only to indicate an intent not to be bound by the contract. For example, a minor may buy a car, drive it for a few months, and then decide to disaffirm the contract. The minor can return the car for a refund even if the car has been damaged.

There are limitations on the minor's power to disaffirm. One limitation concerns contracts for necessaries. In most jurisdictions, if the minor disaffirms after having already received the necessary, the seller can recover the reasonable value of the

---

44 *Laclede Gas Co. v. Amoco Oil Co.*, 522 F.2d 33 (8th Cir. 1977). *See also Missouri Public Service Co. Peabody Coal Co.*, 583 S.W.2d 721 (Mo.App. 1979) (upholding specific performance of contract to supply coal to utility after price had increased dramatically, because change was foreseeable).

45 *But see Scottsdale Road General Partners v. Kuhn Farm Machinery*, 909 P.2d 408 (Ariz. App. 1996) (doctrine did not excuse non-payment for resort facilities after organizer canceled convention because participants were canceling due to fear of flying during the Gulf War).

46 *See ALCOA v. Essex Group, Inc.*, 499 F.Supp. 53 (W.D. Pa. 1980) (long term contract for aluminum ingots held to have failed of its essential purpose due to energy price increases; it was reformed by changing the price to reflect the original intentions of parties and court's sense of fairness).

necessary, which will likely be lower than the contract price.[47] Contracts to pay child support, military enlistments, and educational loans are other areas where a minor's power to disaffirm is usually limited. Additionally, even when the contract can be avoided, some courts hold the minor liable for the benefit received from the subject matter of the contract or for the deterioration of its value.[48]

After reaching the age of majority, the former minor can ratify the contract that was previously voidable, and make it enforceable. Failure to disaffirm is considered ratification of the contract. The former minor can also ratify the previously voidable contract by words, even oral, after reaching the age of majority. Finally, the former minor can ratify the contract by conduct, such as by insisting that the other party perform, or by beginning to perform after reaching the age of majority.

Mental Deficiency Like a minor, a person who is mentally infirm lacks legal capacity. A person lacks capacity who, because of mental disease or defect, does not have the ability to understand the contract. Some jurisdictions also deem persons to lack capacity if they are unable to make a reasonable judgement, even if they understand the contract.[49] A contract is voidable by a party who contracted while mentally infirm. In close cases, the court looks at the "substance of the bargain" to see whether the bargain was fair.

4. Duress and Undue Influence

Duress A contract entered into under duress is voidable at the option of the victim of the duress. If the victim has already performed, damages or other suitable relief may be obtained in court. Duress is an action that compels another to do something that person would not otherwise do, so there can be no mutual assent when duress is present. Duress can be committed by violence, imprisonment, wrongful taking and keeping of a person's property, or the threat of any of those acts. Under some circumstances, a threat to breach a contract unless it is modified may be duress. The modern rule is that such a threat is duress if the threat would result in irreparable injury and if it is made in "breach of the duty of good faith and fair dealing." The same applies to threats to exercise legal rights in an oppressive way. For example, an employer employs duress by threatening to fire an at-will employee (which the employer has a legal right to do) unless the employee signs an agreement to sell back all shares of stock the employee has in the company. Under the circumstances, the contract to sell the stock is unenforceable.[50]

Undue Influence This defense is like duress in that it involves pressure on a party. But it is generally invoked only when someone takes advantage of the party's

---

47 This would not be a recovery under a contract, since the contract cannot be enforced against the minor. Instead, the recovery would be in "quasi-contract" (discussed *infra* p. 384), which is not a contract at all, but a term that refers to recoveries that are imposed in the absence of enforceable contracts when justice so requires.

48 *See Dodson v. Shrader*, 824 S.W.2d 545 (Tenn. 1992) (minor who bought and wrecked pickup truck allowed to avoid the contract and could only recover the price paid, but truck's deterioration in value and the benefit received would be deducted from recovery); *Vichnes v. Transcontinental & Western Air, Inc.*, 18 N.Y.S.2d 603 (1940) (minor could not disaffirm contract to purchase airline ticket where she received benefit of ticket purchased). *But see Adamowski v. Curtiss-Wright Flying Service, Inc.*, 15 N.E.2d 467 (Mass. 1938) (money paid for flying lessons must be refunded because they are not necessaries).

49 *See, e.g., Lloyd v. Jordan*, 544 So.2d 957 (Ala. 1989) (annuity owner suffering from dementia held incapable of understanding change of beneficiary form, so change was void).

50 RESTATEMENT §176(D) *See Reiver v. Murdoch & Walsh, P.A.*, 625 F.Supp. 998, 1011-1014 (D.Del. 1985) (law firm's threats to fire at-will employee to force release of part of employee's bonus could support claim of economic duress).

particular vulnerability to pressure. In one case, a teacher had been arrested and had not slept for 40 hours when the principal of his school and the district superintendent arrived at his house and persuaded him to resign his position. The court held that the physical and mental condition of the teacher, the intrusion into the home and the lack of time given to think about it or consult a lawyer showed undue influence.[51]

5. Misrepresentation

A party to a contract that was procured by misrepresentation or concealment may avoid the contract. Only misrepresentations of fact, not of opinion, qualify, and the victim of the misrepresentation must have justifiably relied on the misrepresentation. Generally the misrepresentation must have been intentional. But if it concerns a material fact, unintentional misrepresentation may be sufficient.

Concealment of a fact, rather than the misrepresentation of it, is tolerated, because there is generally no duty to disclose anything to the contracting party. But there are several exceptions that result in the party's having a duty to disclose. If only part of the truth is told such that an overall misleading impression is created, this non-disclosure of the entire truth may constitute misrepresentation. Positive action taken in concealment, such as sweeping up evidence of termites and painting the affected area just before the sale of a house, can also constitute misrepresentation. Disclosure of a fact is also required where it is needed to prevent some previous assertion from being misleading. For example, if the seller of a house truthfully states that the house has no termites, but later discovers termites before the sale takes place, the seller must disclose this later discovery. A party who knows that the other is making a mistake as to a basic assumption also has a duty to disclose. The party's failure to correct that misunderstanding constitutes a misrepresentation if the non-disclosure amounts to a failure to act in good faith.

6. Unconscionability

A party may be excused from performance under a contract if the contract is found to be unconscionable. A contract may be unconscionable if there was "an absence of meaningful choice on the part of one of the parties together with contract terms which are unreasonably favorable to the other party."[52] For example, if there is a gross inequality of bargaining power, if one of the parties has an obvious lack of education, or if the contract contains important terms that are hidden in fine print and are minimized by deceptive sales practices, these circumstances might indicate an absence of meaningful choice. If the parties enter into a contract under these circumstances and the contract is grossly unfair and one-sided, a court may conclude that all or part of the contract is unconscionable. If so, the court may refuse to enforce the unconscionable part or the whole contract, or may reform the contract so that it is no longer unconscionable. The Restatement provides generally that where one party has reason to believe that the other party agreeing to the contract "would not do so if he knew that the writing contained a particular term, the term is not part of the agreement."[53]

Unconscionability often arises as a result of standardized contracts, which are now commonly used in many types of transactions. Often parties signing these

---

51 *Odorizzi v. Bloomfield School District*, 54 Cal.Rptr. 533 (Cal.App. 1966).

52 *Williams v. Walker-Thomas Furniture Co.*, 350 F.2d 445 (D.C.Cir. 1965).

53 RESTATEMENT §211(3). *Mills v. Agrichemical Aviation, Inc.*, 250 N.W.2d 663 (N.D. 1977) (voiding exclusion of liability for crop spraying in insurance policy because insured would reasonably expect coverage for crop spraying in such a policy).

contracts, especially private consumers, are unaware of the meaning of the terms contained in them or are unable to negotiate the terms because of an unequal bargaining power. The UCC does provide for the obligation of good faith in all contracts[54] and for the removal of unconscionable terms.[55] However, it must be remembered that the UCC applies only to contracts for the sales of goods.

7. Illegal Contracts and Contracts Against Public Policy

A contract that involves illegal subject matter or illegal means of performance is void for illegality. Examples are contracts for gambling debts or prostitution or a contract to gain a competitive advantage by destroying the property of a competitor. The illegality may also spring from civil law. Thus, contracts to defame another person or to infringe on someone's trademark are also void. In addition, courts have found contracts void simply because they are against the "public policy" of the state. For example, in some states, agreements by employees who leave their employment not to compete with their former employer are void because of the public policy in favor of free competition and full productivity of its citizens.[56]

E. Contract Breaches and Remedies

1. Breach and Repudiation

Traditionally a party who has not performed by the time that performance is due has breached. Today, the other party does not always have to wait until performance is due to see whether the first party will breach. When one party clearly communicates unwillingness or inability to perform the contract and the threatened breach is material, the other party may treat this potential breach as a "repudiation" of the contract. For example, assume a landowner enters into a contract under which that owner is to convey the land to the buyer on May 1st. On April 15, the landowner tells the buyer that he or she will not be conveying the land after all. The owner has not yet breached the contract because the duty to convey the land has not yet arisen, but there has been a repudiation. When one party repudiates, the other party may suspend performance and may sue for damages immediately as if a breach had already occurred. Allowing the innocent party to act based on a repudiation prevents the unnecessary accrual of damages that could take place while the innocent party waited until the performance was due.

Repudiation must be unequivocal, so there is no repudiation if one party merely states vague doubts about willingness or ability to perform or if circumstances make it appear that performance may not be forthcoming. However, since such circumstances may give the other party reasonable ground for insecurity, the other party may demand an assurance of due performance. For example, if a seller finds out that the buyer is having financial difficulties and is failing to perform its contracts with other sellers, the seller may demand that the buyer provide some kind of assurance of performance. If the buyer fails to provide the demanded assurance, this failure will be considered a repudiation entitling the seller to suspend performance and sue for damages.[57]

---

54 UCC §1-203.

55 UCC §2-302.

56 *See Diaz v. Indian Head, Inc.*, 402 F.Supp. 111 (N.D. Ill. 1975) (applying New York law).

57 *See Kaiser Francis Oil Co. v. Producer's Gas Co.*, 870 F.2d 563 (10th Cir. 1989) (where contract required buyer to make certain payments and buyer did not do so when demanded by seller, seller was entitled to suspend performance). UCC §2-609 and §2-610

2. Remedies for Breaches of Contracts

Compensatory Damages and Their Limitations The most common kind of relief that is awarded in a suit for breach of contract are "expectation damages," so called because they seek to remedy the unfulfilled expectations of a party by awarding an amount of money that will put the aggrieved party in the same position that party would have been if the contract had been fully performed. But the award will not compensate for all losses that the aggrieved party may sustain from the breach. Two limits on this general rule are "mitigation" and "foreseeability."

Mitigation of Damages Injured parties are under an obligation to take reasonable steps to mitigate or minimize their damages to the extent that this can be done without "undue risk, burden or humiliation."[58] For example, when a seller fails to deliver components needed to manufacture a product, the manufacturer-buyer must try to get the components elsewhere if this can reasonably be done. This is called "cover" and if a price higher than the contract price must be paid, the difference is recoverable as damages. The buyer may not simply do nothing and let its manufacturing plant remain idle and then sue for the shut-down of production. The theory of mitigation is that the additional damages a non-mitigating injured party allows to accumulate are the fault of that party and not of the breaching party.

Foreseeability Damages are not recoverable for loss that the party in breach did not have reason to foresee as a probable result of the breach when the contract was made. For example, assume once again a seller who fails to deliver components of a product to the manufacturer-buyer. The buyer is able to purchase the components from another seller and production is resumed after a one-week delay. However, unknown to the seller, the buyer was counting on taking that very week's production to a major trade fair at which it usually concludes several contracts with prospective purchases. Because the plant had to be shut down, the buyer had no products to take to the trade fair and could not go. The breaching seller should have foreseen that the buyer would "cover," by buying the components elsewhere, and must pay the buyer the difference between the contract price and the price of the cover. And, if the buyer covered as promptly as possible, the seller is liable for the normal loss of profits during one-week halt in production. But the seller is not liable for the loss of the contracts that the buyer could have signed at the trade fair because such a consequence was not foreseeable by the seller. A breaching party may be liable for unusual losses that result from special circumstances, but only if the party had actual notice of the possibility of these special losses.[59]

Recovery Beyond Expectation Damages As we will see when recovery of tort damages is discussed, the elements of compensatory damages for torts is quite broad and includes such items as compensation for emotional distress.[60] Generally, the plaintiff cannot recover any compensatory damages beyond the foreseeable benefits of the contract bargain — the expectation damages discussed above. This rule arises from the basic difference between contract and tort law: whereas "[c]ontract actions are created to protect the interest in having promises performed," "[t]ort actions are created to protect the interest in freedom from various kinds of harm. The duties of

---

58 RESTATEMENT §350.

59 RESTATEMENT §351. *Hadley v. Baxendale*, 156 Eng. Rep. 145 (1854) (shipper not liable for its negligent delay in delivering a miller's shaft for repair because it was not foreseeable that the miller would not have another shaft).

60 *See* Chapter XII, pp. 429-431.

conduct which give rise to [tort liability] are imposed by law, and are based primarily on social policy, not necessarily upon the will or intention of the parties."[61]

Similarly excluded from recovery for breach of contract are the punitive damages that may be awarded in some tort cases to punish a wrongdoer who has intentionally or recklessly injured the plaintiff.[62] No matter how intentional the breach of contract, punitive damages are not available. As Justice Holmes remarked, "[t]he duty to keep a contract at common law means a prediction that you must pay damages if you do not keep it — and nothing else."[63] Economists argue that the rule against punitive damages in contracts cases is justified by the fact that intentional breaches of contract may benefit society. This would be so when the gain to the breaching party exceeds the loss to the party suffering the breach, thereby causing optimal use of resources.[64]

However, there are two circumstances when the same actions that constitute a breach of a contract can give rise to punitive damages. The first situation is when the breach of contract also constitutes a tort independent of the contract. A simple example is if a car dealer sets back the odometer on a used car and misrepresents the car to the buyer as being new. The tort of fraud may be punished by punitive damages despite the fact that it probably also constitutes a breach of the contract for sale of the car.[65] This overlap of traditional tort obligations and contractual obligations is nothing unusual. Most cases of the architect, attorney or doctor being sued by a client or patient involve a contractual relationship. The mere fact of the relationship between the professional and the plaintiff gives rise to tort duties independent of any contract between them. Though it is not typically the case, if the actions of the professional are intentional or reckless, punitive damages may be awarded.[66]

The second category of punitive damage contract cases consists of those where tort liability arises exclusively out of the contractual relationship. These are cases of "bad faith breach of contract." The basis for this liability is that all contracts contain an "implied covenant of good faith and fair dealing."[67] A party to a contract breaches this duty when it utilizes its discretionary rights under a contract to inflict harm or otherwise acts unreasonably with regard to rights under the contract. Since such actions are most commonly intentional or reckless, liability for an intentional tort may result, with the potential for punitive damages. The most common cases have been against insurance companies which unreasonably fail to settle or resolve claims by their insureds.[68] The California Supreme Court at one point extended such liability beyond the insurance context, but recently overruled itself.[69] However, other courts have expanded the concept to include actions of a contracting party that coerce or

---

61 *Applied Engineering Corp. v. Litton Saudi Arabia Ltd.*, 869 P.2d 454, 460 (Cal. 1994).

62 *See* Chapter XI, pp. 431-437.

63 O.W. Holmes, Jr., *The Path of the Common Law*, 10 HARV. L. REV. 457, 462 (1897).

64 RICHARD POSNER, ECONOMIC ANALYSIS OF LAW 107-108 (1986).

65 *Boise Dodge, Inc. v. Clark*, 453 P.2d 551 (Idaho 1969).

66 A common intentional tort that arises in the medical malpractice area is a battery, the result of unconsented to treatment. *See Gragg v. Calandra*, 696 N.E.2d 1282 (Ill.App. 1998). *See also Smith v. Welch*, 967 P.2d 717 (Kansas 1998) (doctor who repeatedly fondled patient's breasts during physical exam could be sued for the intentional tort of "outrage" and receive punitive damages).

67 RESTATEMENT §205.

68 *See Egan v. Mutual of Omaha Ins. Co.*, 620 P.2d 141 (Cal. 1979).

69 *Seaman's Direct Buying Service, Inc. v. Standard Oil Co. of California*, 686 P.2d 1158 (Cal. 1984) (liability for bad faith breach based on party denying the existence of the contract causing the other party to go out of business); *overruled by Freeman & Mills, Inc. v. Belcher Oil Co.*, 900 P.2d 669 (Cal. 1995).

deceive another party into foregoing its contractual rights,[70] intentional breaches that are especially injurious to the other party,[71] and bad faith terminations of employment.[72]

Specific Performance   Another possible remedy for a breach of contract is specific performance. Specific performance is an equitable remedy in which the court orders the breaching party to perform duties under the contract. This remedy is usually used only where remedies at law will not adequately compensate the innocent party for the breach of the contract.[73] For example, if a contract to sell goods is breached by the seller, a legal remedy is adequate because damages awarded to the buyer will cover the cost of replacing the goods. But the buyer will not be adequately compensated by money if the contracted-for item is unique and irreplaceable.[74] In this case, the court may order the seller to deliver that item in accordance with the terms of the contract. Land is also considered "unique" and specific performance is appropriate in real estate contracts. In contracts involving services, specific performance will generally not be ordered, because ordering a person to perform a service is considered to be imposing "involuntary servitude" prohibited by the 13th Amendment. However, a defendant may be enjoined from performing services *elsewhere*. For example, a professional athlete who refuses to play for the team he or she has contracted to play for cannot be ordered to play, but can be enjoined from playing for any other team.[75]

Restitution Remedies   In some contract cases, "restitution" may be ordered as an equitable remedy.[76] Restitution is based on the principle that "one person is accountable to another on the ground that otherwise he would unjustly benefit or the other would unjustly suffer loss."[77] There are two distinct uses of restitution. The first is to "undo" a contract that is void or voidable for fraud, duress, mistake, non-compliance with the Statute of Frauds, or any of the other such reasons. The purpose is to place the parties back in the positions they were before the contract.

The second use of restitution is as an alternative to suing for damages for breach of contract. However, restitution is an option only if there is a complete breach of the contract, i.e., one that goes to the essence of the contract. If there is, instead of suing for damages for breach of contract, the innocent party can elect to "cancel" the contract and sue for restitution. The advantage of restitution over damages is that the amount awarded in restitution may exceed the contract price if the value that the breaching party has received is more than the contract price. The basic difference between restitution and expectation damages, is that restitution is measured by the

---

70 *See, e.g. Adam's v. Crater Well Drilling, Inc.*, 556 P.2d 679, 681 (Ore. 1976) (punitive damages justified when contracting party used threat of criminal prosecution to obtain more than it owed under the contract); *Jones v. Abriani*, 350 N.E.2d 635, 649 (Ind.App. 1976) (punitive damages proper where mobile home salesman threatened to forfeit buyers' down payment if buyers did not accept delivery of mobile home with defects).

71 *See, e.g., Hilder v. St. Peter*, 478 A.2d 202, 210 (Vt. 1984) (punitive damages permitted against landlord who failed to repair defect in apartment essential to health and safety after notice of the defect); *Romero v. Mervyn's*, 784 P.2d 992 (1989) (punitive damages proper against department store which promised to pay injured customer's medical expenses and then reneged).

72 *See* Chapter XV, p. 575, and *supra* note 50.

73 Equitable relief was discussed in Chapter VII, pp. 237-239.

74 UCC §2-716

75 *See Dallas Cowboys Football Club v. Harris*, 348 S.W.2d 37 (Tex.Civ.App. 1961).

76 *See generally* DAN B. DOBBS, HORNBOOK ON THE LAW OF REMEDIES, 2D ED. §12.7 (West 1993).

77 *See* RESTATEMENT OF RESTITUTION 1 (American Law Institute 1937).

gain the breaching party obtains, while expectation damages are measured by the benefit the innocent party should expect according to the contract. The difference is said to be justified because wrongdoers should suffer the consequences of their own wrongdoing and should not be permitted to be protected by the very contract that they breached.[78]

For example, suppose a builder enters a contract to build a building for $100,000. When the builder is halfway through and has been paid $25,000, the owner refuses to pay any more on the contract and orders the builder off the premises — a total breach of the contract. The owner then sells the uncompleted building for $200,000. If the builder sued for expectation damages, they would amount to only $75,000, the balance of the contract price not yet paid. However, restitution would total $175,000, the value of the building that the builder built minus what the builder had already been paid.[79] However, if the owner's breach was a delay in making an installment payment on time, the builder would not be justified in canceling the contract and suing for restitution, since this is not a total breach of the contract.[80]

Quasi-Contract Theories of Recovery In cases where there is no contract, but the defendant has nonetheless been enriched by the plaintiff's action, the plaintiff may recover under "quasi-contract." For example, if a physician happens upon an injured child and renders medical assistance, the physician can recover against the child's parents for the value of that assistance in quasi-contract. Despite the terminology, quasi-contractual recovery has nothing to do with contracts. Such recovery comes from duties imposed by the law as a means of ensuring justice by preventing one party from being unjustly enriched at the expense of another.[81]

PART II: Commercial Law

A. The Uniform Commercial Code

1. Adoption and General Applicability of the UCC

There have been attempts in the past to codify commercial law,[82] but none has succeeded like the Uniform Commercial Code (UCC).[83] The UCC's principal purposes are "to simplify, clarify and modernize the law governing commercial transactions"

---

78   *See* CALAMARI & PERILLO, *supra* note 2, §15-1-15-15-4.

79   *See Boomer v. Muir*, 24 P.2d 570 (Cal.App. 1933) (affirming judgment for contractor of $258,000 when contract rate would have yielded only $20,000).

80   *Integrated, Inc. v. Alec Fergusson Electrical Contractors*, 58 Cal.Rptr. 503, 509 (Cal.App. 1967) ("slight deviation either in time or amount of progress payments should not justify rescission or abandonment"; only "an extended and unreasonable delay, imposition of new and onerous conditions to payment, outright refusal, or a total repudiation of the contract" is sufficient to justify cancellation).

81   *See* CALAMARI & PERILLO, *supra* note 2, §1-12. Quasi-contract is to be distinguished from actual implied contracts. Thus, if the parents of an injured child asked a physician to treat their child, they would be liable to pay, but it would not be on a quasi-contract theory. There was an actual contract, because the request for treatment implied that they would pay for that treatment.

82   *E.g.*, Uniform Sales Act (1906) and the Negotiable Instruments Law (1896).

83   The UCC is a joint product of the National Conference of Commissioners on Uniform State Laws and the American Law Institute and was finished in 1952. All states except Louisiana have adopted it virtually unchanged and Louisiana has adopted large parts of it, though not Article 2 on sales. Excellent succinct treatments of the UCC are JOHN F. DOLAN, COMMERCIAL LAW: ESSENTIAL TERMS AND TRANSACTIONS (Aspen 1995) and LAYTON P. GILLETTE & STEVEN D. WALT, SALES LAW: DOMESTIC AND INTERNATIONAL (Foundation 1999) (also discussing the U.N. International Sales of Goods Convention). The standard treatise is JAMES J. WHITE & ROBERT S. SUMMERS, UNIFORM COMMERCIAL CODE, 4TH ED. (West 1995). The UCC and many other statutes are in SELECTED COMMERCIAL STATUTES (West 1998). An extensive survey of the UCC is found in UCC Survey, 51 BUSINESS LAWYER 1339 (1996).

and "to make the law uniform among the various jurisdictions."[84] In this section, we will focus on some of the principal ways in which the UCC's Article 2 on sales of goods alters the common law rules of contracts outlined earlier.[85] If there are gaps in its provisions, then the normal common law rules apply.[86]

2. Contracts for Sales of Goods Under the UCC

Article 2 of the UCC applies only to sales of goods, not to sales of real property, services and securities.[87] Issues of coverage arise when there are "mixed" contracts for sales, usually sales of both goods and services, such as a builder who installs cabinets and appliances. Usually courts seek to determine whether the "predominant purpose" of the contract was the provision of services or sale of goods.[88] However, it may be a mistake to try to categorize the entire contract. Often the predominant purpose of the *contract* and the *nature of the breach* involved are quite different. In the case of a "mixed" contract, it would seem to make sense to apply Article 2 to breaches that concern the quality of any goods supplied and to apply common law to breaches that concern how the goods were installed or applied. Thus, if the contract calls for repairs to an airplane that involve replacing parts, claims that a part was defective would be governed by Article 2, while a claim regarding improper installation of that part would be governed by non-UCC law. Similar reasoning can be applied to mixed sales of real property and goods.[89]

a. Special Rules for "Merchants"

To assure that the UCC works for both the business community and ordinary consumers, it defines a special class of "merchants" and applies different standards of conduct to them. "Merchants" are those who "deal in the goods" involved or who "hold themselves out as having knowledge or skill peculiar to the practice or goods involved."[90] The UCC's comments disclose an intent to distinguish between a "professional in business" and the "casual or inexperienced seller or buyer." Typical merchants would include the jewelry or hardware store and their owners, car dealers and others who sell from normal inventory, as well as the plumber or carpenter who has the requisite "knowledge or skill" and sells a sink or a cabinet. However, proper application of the definition is not self-apparent. Litigation has arisen, for example, over whether farmers selling their crops are merchants. One could argue that farmers may be knowledgeable about growing crops, but are hardly "professionals in

---

84 UCC §1-102(2).

85 Article 9 of the UCC governing security interests in goods is covered *infra*, pp. 392-394. Other Articles are 2A (leases), 3 (negotiable instruments), 4 (bank deposits and collections), 4A (funds transfers), 5 (letters of credit), 6 (bulk sales), 7 (documents of title) and 8 (investment securities).

86 UCC §1-103.

87 In addition, as of 1988 the United States is subject to the United Nations International Sale of Goods Convention, so the UCC does not apply to international sales of goods when the other country is also a party to the Convention. *See generally* GILLETTE & WALT, *supra* note 83, at 25-41 and *passim*.

88 *See Bonebrake v. Cox*, 499 F.2d 951, 960 (8th Cir. 1974) (applying the test to determine that installation of bowling lanes and equipment was a sale of goods). *But see Ward v. Purego Co.*, 913 P.2d 582 (Idaho 1996) (contract for application of fertilizer on crops was one for services, not goods).

89 *See Foster v. Colorado Radio Corp.*, 381 F2d 222 (10th Cir. 1967) (in sale of radio station, UCC applied to goods, but not to non-goods, such as good will, real estate, studios and transmission tower). *But see Hudson v. Town & Country True Value Hardware*, 666 S.W.2d 51 (Tenn. 1984) (applying two different measures of damages would pose "insurmountable problems of proof").

90 UCC §2-104(1).

business." It is also unclear what number of sales will turn a "casual or inexperienced seller or buyer" into someone who "deals in the goods" involved.[91]

b. Contract Formation

Elimination of Consideration   The UCC eliminates the requirement of consideration for some option contracts for merchants. Thus, a merchant's signed written offer to buy or sell goods that assures that it will be held open is a "firm offer" that is irrevocable for the period of time stated or for a reasonable time.[92] The UCC also abolishes any need for fresh consideration for modifications in contracts, thus rejecting the common law "pre-existing duty" rule. This makes it easier for parties to adjust their contracts to meet commercial exigencies. The problem of extortionate modifications, as where a builder threatens to slow down construction unless the contract price is raised, is thought adequately dealt with by the UCC's unconscionability (§2-302) and good faith (§1-203) requirements.[93]

Formation and the Requirement of a Writing   The UCC's "statute of frauds" requires that all contracts for sales of goods over $500 be in writing, but not much writing is required. An enforceable contract exists if there is some writing "signed by the party against whom enforcement is sought" that "indicates" that a contract was made and that sets out the quantity of goods involved.[94] And between merchants, oral agreements are enforceable if "within a reasonable time a writing in confirmation of the contract . . . is received" and no "written notice of an objection to its contents is given within 10 days."[95] In addition, under §2-204(1), "conduct . . . which recognizes the existence of a contract" is sufficient — most often performance by the parties. Under §2-204, missing terms will not invalidate a contract if the parties had intended to enter a binding agreement.

Acceptance of Offers   Under §2-206(1), acceptance of an offer may be made in "any reasonable manner" unless the offeror has made it "unambiguously" clear that the offer may be accepted only in a certain manner. Section 2-207(1) provides that an acceptance is effective even if it contains terms "additional to or different from those offered, unless the offeror has expressly limited acceptance to the terms of the offer." Thus, the UCC rejects the common law "mirror image" rule.[96] However, there must be some "definite and seasonal expression of acceptance," so if an "acceptance" differs so much from the offer as to indicate absence of agreement on basic terms, no contract is formed. For example, in an attempted sale of surplus factory equipment, there was an exchange of telegrams that agreed on price, but the seller proposed a

---

91 *See Nelson v. Union Equity Cooperative Exchange*, 548 S.W.2d 352 (Tex. 1977) (farmer selling his wheat to silo held to be a "merchant"; dissent argued farmer made only one "casual sale" a year). Most cases agree with the majority. *See also infra* note 95. *Compare Dixon v. Roberts*, 853 P.2d 235 (Okla. App. 1993) (amateur ostrich raisers with little experience in that business are not merchants).

92 UCC §2-205. A three-month limit on irrevocability is imposed.

93 UCC §2-209. *See Roth Steel Products v. Sharon Steel Corp.*, 705 F.2d 134 (6th Cir. 1983) (modifications must be consistent with commercial standards of fair dealing in the trade and the modifier must have a valid commercial reason for seeking the modification; raising steel prices because of market changes not a proper modification on facts of the case). Pre-existing duty was discussed *supra* p. 370.

94 UCC §2-201(1). There need not be a single writing; an exchange of letters will do.

95 UCC §2-201(2). It was this provision that underlay the dispute over whether the farmer in the *Nelson* case was a merchant. *See supra* note 91. Nelson had an oral agreement to sell his wheat to a silo at a stated price. The silo followed this up with a §2-201(2) confirmatory letter. The price of wheat suddenly increased, Nelson refused to perform and the silo sued him and won. Another exceptions to the writing requirement is where goods specially ordered have begun to be manufactured or there is part performance. *See* §2-201(3).

96 *See* discussion *supra* p. 367.

sale "as is — where is," while the buyer proposed "F.O.B. our truck your plant loaded." The buyer's F.O.B. (free on board) statement meant that the seller would be required to load the equipment on the buyer's truck. The Court held there was no contract.[97]

c. Determining Contract Content Under the UCC

Some sales contracts are fully negotiated in a deliberate manner, reduced to an integrated writing and signed by the parties. When this occurs, contract content is easily determined. As just seen, however, the UCC recognizes an enforceable contract in many situations where contract terms are incomplete or unclear. Moreover, as just discussed, even when the parties' correspondence is insufficient to demonstrate agreement to conclude a contract, confirmatory conduct of the parties that recognizes the existence of a contract, usually performance, is sufficient to establish a contract. So, the UCC is usually called upon to determine the content of the contract in two situations: (1) when the parties' communications reflect an agreement, but the terms of it are not clear and (2) when the parties' correspondence does not reflect any true agreement, but the parties nonetheless perform.

Missing Terms Any missing terms in the contract are supplied by a set of gap-filler default terms set out in the Code. Part 3 of Article 2 provides gap fillers for such basic terms as price, place for delivery, time for performance and duration and time and place of payment, based on prevailing commercial practices.[98] It also imposes standard quality requirements through an implied warranty of merchantability and special quality standards through a warranty of fitness for a particular purpose, as well as rules for creating express warranties and for excluding implied warranties.[99] In addition, Part 3 provides definitions for standard terms, such as F.O.B., C.I.F., Ex-Ship, "letter of credit"and "sale on approval." Part 5 sets out standards for performance, including issues of risk of loss in transit. Parts 6 and 7 set out default rules for breaches and remedies.[100]

Additional and Different Terms A more complicated problem than missing terms are "additional" and "different" terms. This problem results from widespread use of standard business form contracts. Sellers' forms favor sellers and buyers' forms favor buyers. When the offer is on one such form and the acceptance is on a different one, there is usually agreement on the basic terms actually negotiated and a contract is formed based on those terms. But it is only by sheer chance that any of the other terms on the opposing forms agree. When a dispute arises, the parties will pull out their forms and actually read them — perhaps for the first time — to see what they "agreed"to. Disputes of this type are called the "battle of the forms" and are governed by §2-207.[101]

---

97 *Koehring Co. v. Glowacki*, 253 N.W.2d 64 (Wis. 1977). *Compare Idaho Power Co. v. Westinghouse Electric Corp.*, 596 F.2d 924 (9th Cir. 1979) (acceptance containing additional warranty disclaimer was "seasonable expression of acceptance").

98 UCC §2-305 (reasonable price); UCC §2-308 (delivery at the seller's place of business); UCC §2-309 (reasonable time for performance); UCC §2-310 (payment due at time and place buyer is to receive the goods or documents of title; other provisions govern inspection and goods shipped on credit).

99 Warranties are discussed in greater detail *infra* pp. 389-392.

100 *See infra* p. 392.

101 Only a few of the types of "battles of the forms" can be discussed here. White and Summers discuss 8 common types and warn that many other combinations are possible. WHITE & SUMMERS, *supra* note 83, §1-3. Also, as will be seen, §2-207's meaning and application are not self-apparent. The Kansas Supreme Court has dubbed it a "murky bit of prose." *Southwest Engineering Co., Inc. v. Martin Tractor Co.*, 473 P.2d 18, 25 (Kan. 1970). *See also Roto-Lith, infra* note 107 (§2-207 "not too happily drafted")

An "additional term" is a term set out in a form offer or acceptance for which there is no corresponding term on the other form. For example, the offer may provide that the parties will submit all disputes to arbitration, while the acceptance is silent on the subject. Under §2-207(2), *additional* terms are treated as "proposals for addition to the contract." They become part of the contract unless the offeror objects to them within a reasonable time.[102]

A "different term" is a term in the offer or acceptance that conflicts with a counterpart term in the other. For example, the offer may provide for arbitration, but the acceptance provides that there will be no arbitration. Most courts agree that *conflicting* terms cancel each other out and are "knocked out" of the contract.[103]

Express Terms at Odds With Gap Fillers When different terms are knocked out of the contract, a UCC default gap filler will be inserted if there is one on the subject. In the arbitration case above, arbitration is not covered by a gap filler, so the contract is not subject to arbitration. However, if the UCC has a gap filler on the subject and an express term conflicts with it, the question arises as to whether this makes the express term a "different" term that is then knocked out of the contract. For example, assume an offer includes a limitation on damages ordinarily available under the UCC, while the acceptance is silent on the question. An argument could be made that the acceptance necessarily includes the gap filler — full consequential damages. Therefore, as with the collision between *express* "different" terms on the subject, the *implied* gap filler term of the acceptance knocks the damages limitation out of the contract.   However, this argument has been rejected by courts and most commentators. The express term in the offer is simply an "additional" term that becomes part of the contract for lack of objection to it within a reasonable time.[104]

A different result may obtain if it is the *acceptance* that introduces a term at odds with a gap filler. Returning to the damages waiver example, assume the *offer* is silent as to damages, while the *acceptance* seeks to limit damages. Since we know that a term that conflicts with a gap filler is an "additional" term rather than a "different" term, the disclaimer should ordinarily become part of the contract unless the offeror objects.[105] However, §2-207(2) sets out a second exception for acceptance terms in addition to objection by the offeror: additional terms in an *acceptance* do not become part of the contract if they "materially alter" the terms of the offer.[106] Comments to the Code indicate that a limitation on damages is usually not such a material alteration. Examples of material alterations are a warranty disclaimer and a term securing

---

102 UCC §2-207(2). *See Polyclad Laminates, Inc. v. VITS Maschinenbau GmbH*, 749 F.Supp. 342 (D.N.H. 1990) (arbitration clause in seller's offer accepted by buyer's form that did not address the issue). In a merchant-consumer situation, any additional or different terms do not become part of the contract unless the consumer expressly consents to them.

103 *See Daitom, Inc. v. Pennwalt Corp.*, 741 F.2d 1569, 1580 (10th Cir. 1984) (disclaimer of warranty knocked out; knock-out rule essential to avoid giving unfair advantage to the person who sent the first form and it at least results in a Code gap filler being applied). Oddly enough, the two major experts on the UCC, White and Summers, disagree on how even this basic issue of conflicting terms should be resolved. *See* WHITE & SUMMERS, *supra* note 83, at 8-12.

104 *Idaho Power Co.*, *supra* note 97 The court also held that the statement in the acceptance that it would be "deemed to constitute an agreement to the conditions named hereon and supersedes all previous agreements" did not make the buyer's acceptance of the offer conditional on the seller's assent to its terms.

105 This assumes that the acceptance evinces sufficient agreement with the offer to form a contract or that the parties' conduct in performing the contract indicates an contract exists. *See supra* text at note 97, where the *Koehring* case is discussed.

106 *See* §2-207(2), discussed in text *supra* at note 102.

cancellation rights or a very short time period for complaints to be made. However, a remedy limitation can be deemed a "material alter[ation]" of the terms of the offer if it is a severe limitation.[107] If deemed a material alteration, the additional term in the acceptance stands as a *proposal* for an addition to the contract, but, like any other offer, it cannot become part of the contract without the other side expressly accepting it. The contract made then is the agreed-to terms plus any applicable gap fillers.

Expressly Conditional Acceptances So far in this discussion, none of the acceptances involved has been one that was conditioned on the offeror assenting to additional or different terms. Under §2-207(1), if "acceptance is made expressly conditional on [the offeror's] assent to an additional or different term," there is no acceptance and no contract is formed unless offeror gives such "assent." Mere lack of objection is not sufficient to add the term. However, this provision is narrowly interpreted to require absolutely unambiguous expression of the conditional nature of the acceptance that "clearly reveals that the offeree is unwilling to proceed with the transaction unless he is assured of the offeror's assent to the additional or different terms therein." For example, in the case setting out the quoted rule, the seller responded to the buyer's order-offer by accepting the proposed price, quantity and other negotiated terms, but stating that "this acceptance is subject to all the terms and conditions on [this form], including arbitration." The seller then shipped the goods and the buyer accepted them. The seller's shipment and buyer's acceptance of the goods was conduct indicating a binding contract was formed. But the court held that the buyer's acceptance of the goods was not "assent" to the arbitration term.[108]

d. Warranties

The UCC goes well beyond the common law in its provisions on "warranties." Warranties are promises of the seller about the quality of goods that become part of the contract for sale under Article 2. Warranties may be express or implied.

Express Warranties Under §2-313, "[a]ny affirmation of fact or promise made by the seller to the buyer which relates to the goods and becomes part of the basis of the bargain creates an express warranty that the goods shall conform to the affirmation or promise." The assertion of fact can be written or oral. It may include a description of the goods (e.g., "1989 Ford Mustang") or even a nonverbal affirmation, such as showing the buyer a sample of the goods. The seller need not use "formal words such as 'warrant' or 'guarantee'" nor need there be "a specific intention to make a warranty." However, "an affirmation merely of the value of the goods or a statement purporting to be merely the seller's opinion or commendation of the goods" — generally called "puffing" — is not a warranty.[109]

---

107 *See Altronics of Bethlehem, Inc. v. Repco, Inc.*, 957 F.2d 1102 (3d Cir. 1992) (in sale of security systems, seller's acceptance which limited remedies solely to repair or replacement was a material alteration; therefore not part of the contract). *But see Roto-Lith, Ltd. v. F.P. Bartlett & Co.*, 297 F.2d 497 (1st Cir. 1962) (acceptance with warranty disclaimer held to be expressly conditional and assented to by buyer's acceptance of goods).

108 *See Dorton v. Collins & Aikman Corp.*, 453 F.2d 1161 (6th Cir. 1972) (involving quoted language). *See also Idaho Power Co., supra* note 97 (noting that the expressly conditional acceptances provision "has been construed narrowly") *Compare Roto-Lith* case, *supra* note 107 (buyer's acceptance of goods was assent). Once more, it is somewhat unsettling that not only the courts, but White and Summers disagree on how this situation should be resolved. *See* WHITE & SUMMERS, *supra* note 83, at 13-20.

109 UCC 2-313(2). *See Fitzner Pontiac-Buick-Cadillac v. Smith*, 523 So.2d 324 (Miss. 1988) (description of used car as in "first class shape" was not a warranty); *But see Hauter v. Zogarts*, 534 P.2d 377 (Cal. 1975) ("Golfing Gizmo" statement "completely safe ball will not hit player" held an express warranty that was breached when golf ball hit the plaintiff) and *Acme Equipment Corp. v. Montgomery Cooperative Creamery Ass'n.*, 138 N.W.2d 729 (Wis. 1966) ("in good shape and good working order" a warranty as

The requirement that the seller's warranties be "part of the basis of the bargain" has given courts some trouble. The official comments to §2-313 and some courts deny that it means the buyer must rely on the warranty statements, but others disagree.[110] Some courts state that "basis of the bargain" is met in the case of an advertisement or a brochure so long as there is evidence the plaintiff read the item before the deal was concluded.[111] Issues arise where there is evidence that the buyer had independent knowledge that the seller's representations were not true. In the case of the sale of a painting, the seller argued that the buyer had known about authenticity challenges to the painting at the time of the sale, so he could not have relied on the seller's representations that there had been no challenges. The court rejected this argument, holding that representations form a "basis of the bargain," not just when "the buyer believe[s] in the truth of the warranted information," but when the buyer believes he is "purchasing the [seller's] promise as to its truth."[112] It has even been argued that statements of the seller made *after* the goods are sold are enforceable warranties, at least where the buyer could return the goods and the post-contract additional assurances forestalled or prevented such return.[113]

Implied Warranties of Merchantability   Section 2-314's "implied warranty of merchantability" is perhaps the most important warranty under the UCC. It arises automatically in any sale of goods by a merchant seller. However, "merchantable" is defined as goods that are "fit for . . . ordinary purposes," are of "fair average quality" and "pass without objection in the trade." Goods can meet these standards and yet fall short of perfection. If a certain level of defects is reasonably to be expected with regard to a good, it is merchantable even if it injures someone. For example, fresh New England fish chowder is not "unfit" for eating just because it has fish bones in it, even if those bones cause personal injury.[114] The usage of the trade may have to be consulted to determine the appropriate standard of merchantability. Hormone additives in cattle feed make it unmerchantable only in light of trade usage establishing that such additives are not usually included unless requested and that their addition is always disclosed on the label.[115] It must also be proven that the manufacturer caused the defect. For example, a drug manufacturer was not liable for injuries caused when poison was injected into its medicine by a third person, even though the medicine clearly was unfit for its intended purposes.[116]

Implied Warranty of Fitness for Purpose   Under §2-315, if a seller "has reason to know any particular purpose for which the goods are required and that the buyer is

---

applied to dairy equipment).

110 *Compare Speed Fastners, Inc. v. Newsom*, 382 F.2d 395 (10th Cir.1967) (sale of stud fasteners; plaintiff not entitled to recover in breach of express warranty where there was no evidence that plaintiff's employer relied on statements in seller's pamphlet before purchase) *with Hawkins Constr. Co. v. Matthews Co.*, 209 N.W.2d 643 (Neb. 1973) (sale of scaffolding; express warranty created even if buyer did not rely on statements in seller's brochure).

111 *Interco v. Randustrial Corp.*, 533 S.W.2d 257 (Mo.App. 1976) (advertising statement in brochure that flooring "will absorb considerable flex" read by buyer was a warranty).

112 *Rogath v. Siebenmann*, 129 F.3d 261 (2d Cir. 1997) (applying New York law). Reliance has been an issue in tobacco litigation based on manufacturers' warranties that cigarettes did not harm one's health. *Compare Cipollone v. Liggett Group*, 893 F2d 541 (3d Cir. 1990) (only knowledge of advertising claims required) *with American Tobacco Co. v. Grinnell*, 951 S.W.2d 420 (Tex. 1997) (reliance on advertising claims required and negated by showing plaintiff had other reasons for starting to smoke).

113 WHITE & SUMMERS, *supra* note 83, at 342-343.

114 *See Webster v. Blue Ship Tea Room*, 198 N.E.2d 309 (Mass. 1964) (plaintiff choked on bones).

115 *Kassab v. Central Soya*, 246 A.2d 848 (Pa. 1968).

116 *Elsroth v. Johnson & Johnson*, 700 F.Supp. 151 (S.D.N.Y. 1988).

relying on the seller's skill or judgment to select or furnish suitable goods," an implied warranty arises that the goods the seller selects will be fit for that purpose. Unlike the implied warranty of merchantability, there is no requirement that the seller be a merchant.[117]

Third Party Beneficiaries of Warranties   One principle of the common law of contracts is the notion of "privity of contract." This means that in general, only persons who are parties to a contract may claim its benefits. This presents a problem in recovery under warranties when the person injured by a breach of warranty is someone other than the buyer. The UCC generally abolishes privity as a requirement for warranty recovery. However, in deference to the controversy over third-party recovery, it provides three alternatives that offer different options in terms of what third parties may sue (natural persons or anyone), what injuries are compensable (personal injury or property damage) and who may recover (only household members or any bystander).[118] In addition, none of the options includes recovery for "pure economic loss," such as lost profits, making abolition of privity of limited use to businesses which did not actually purchase the defective goods that damaged them.[119]

Warranty Disclaimers   A seller may disclaim any of the above warranties or may limit what remedies are available in case of breach.[120] Disclaimer can be accomplished by words in the contract such as "the buyer takes the item as is" or "the seller disclaims any warranties express or implied." However, any disclaimer of merchantability must "mention merchantability" and must be "conspicuous," meaning that it must be in type that is larger than the rest of the contract or is in a contrasting color.

"Unconscionability" is a specific limit on remedy limitations. An important and common remedy limitation is the exclusion of any recovery for "consequential damages." However, the UCC presumes that limiting "consequential damages for injury to the person in the case of consumer goods" is unconscionable.[121] Unconscionability is more difficult when it comes to warranty disclaimers. There is a general provision on unconscionability in UCC §2-302, but most courts have held that it is "preempted" by the more specific provisions of §2-316 describing how a seller can properly disclaim warranties.[122] But some courts have held warranty disclaimers unconscionable even when the provisions of §2-316 have been satisfied.[123] Typically, a seller will disclaim all implied warranties, provide a one-year express warranty of

---

117 *Leal v. Holtvogt*, 702 N.E.2d 1246 (Ohio App. 1998) (selling chronically lame stallion when seller knew that buyers were interested in a horse good for breeding beached implied warranty of fitness).

118 UCC §2-318, Alternatives A, B, and C.

119 *See Minnesota Mining and Manufacturing Co. v. Nishika Ltd.*, 565 N.W.2d 16 (Minn. 1997) (plaintiff camera manufacturer, who never bought chemicals from manufacturer, could not recover for lost profits unaccompanied by personal injury or property damage when chemicals failed to develop film properly). This demonstrates a similarity to the torts ban on "pure" economic loss. *See* Chapter XI, p. 430.

120 UCC §2-316 (disclaimers of warranties); UCC §2-719 (limitations of remedies).

121 UCC §2-719(3). *See Collins v. Uniroyal*, 315 A.2d 16 (N.J. 1964) (warranty against tire "blow-outs" limited to tire replacement or repair held presumptively unconscionable as applied to death caused by blow-out). The presumption does not apply to limits on commercial losses, so few are set aside. *But see Majors v. Kalo Laboratories, Inc*, 407 F.Supp 20 (M.D.Ala. 1975) (limiting warranty claims to those raised within 10 days of sale was unconscionable where hidden defect in soybean seeds caused loss of farmer's crop).

122 *Marshall v. Murray Oldsmobile Co.*, 154 S.E.2d 140 (Va. 1967) (disclaimer upheld in new car sale).

123 *Martin v. Joseph Harris Co.*, 767 F.2d 296, 299 (6th Cir. 1985) (waiver of cabbage seed warranties that complied with §2-316 was unconscionable when seeds contained "black leg" disease).

freedom from defects in design and manufacture, and limit remedies to replacement or repair, and courts routinely uphold such disclaimers and limitations on remedies.

Remedies Buyers who are faced with a breach of warranty have several possible remedies, but the most common is a suit for damages.[124] Damages are available both for personal injury and for commercial loss or property damage. As discussed in the next chapter, warranty theories of recovery for consumers injured by defective products form a significant part of "products liability."[125] Indeed, in some ways warranty liability is broader.[126]

3. Security Interests in Goods Under the UCC

Nature of a Security Interest Article 9 of the UCC governs "security interests" in goods.[127] A security interest is an interest in property granted by a debtor to a creditor which secures a debt, thus allowing the creditor to take the secured property in the event that the debtor does repay the debt.[128] The encumbered property is referred to as the "collateral." Security interests are used in a variety of contexts. A manufacturer may give a security interest in its machinery to borrow money to purchase raw materials needed in manufacturing. The supplier of goods to a retail store may insist on retaining a security interest in those goods as inventory of the store until they are sold. Or a consumer may borrow money from a bank or credit union to purchase an automobile and grant a security interest in the car to secure the loan. If the security interest secures the loan used to purchase the collateral, it is called a "purchase money security interest" (PMSI).

To have a valid enforceable security interest, three requirements must be met: (1) the parties must sign an agreement that describes the collateral or the debtor must give possession of the collateral to the creditor, (2) the creditor must give value for the security interest (normally a loan of money), and (3) the debtor must have an interest in the property.[129] Once these requirements are met, the security interest has "attached," i.e. it is enforceable. In order for the creditor to have "priority" over other creditors, buyers and other third parties, the creditor must "perfect" the security interest. A creditor normally perfects the security interest by taking steps to give the world notice of the security interest.[130] Such steps include filing a financing statement (discussed below),[131] taking possession of the collateral[132] or, in the case of an automobile, noting a lien on the certificate of title.[133]

---

124 UCC §§2-714, 2-715. Rejection and revocation of acceptance are also possible. *See* §§2-601-2-605 and §2-608. The buyer can then recover any price paid, the costs of purchasing substitute goods, called "cover," and consequential damages. §§2-711(1), 2-712. However, the seller has the right to "cure" the defect under §2-508 in the event of rejection and revocation of acceptance is possible only when the goods' "non-conformity substantially impairs [their] value." §2-608(1).

125 *See* Chapter XI, pp. 417-419. In addition to the warranties discussed, the UCC provides for a warranty of title, under which sellers automatically warrant that they own the goods and have a legal right to sell them and that the goods do not infringe upon any patent or trademark. UCC §2-312.

126 *See* Chapter XI, p. 419, note 95. Other warranty remedies for consumers may be available under the federal Magnuson-Moss Warranty Act, discussed *infra* p. 399.

127 Security interests in real property are discussed in Chapter XII, p. 451.

128 UCC §1-201(37).

129 UCC §9-203(2).

130 UCC §9-303.

131 UCC §9-302(1).

132 UCC §9-305.

133 UCC §9-302(2), (3). In some limited cases, perfection is automatic. *See, e.g.* §9-302(1)(d) (financing statement is not required to perfect a purchase money security interest in consumer goods).

Disputes Between Secured Creditor and Debtor   If the debtor fails to repay the creditor and does not voluntarily give up the property, the creditor has the right to take the collateral upon default by either judicial or non-judicial means. Judicial means involve an action for "replevin" or "claim and delivery" — a claim used in any situation where one seeks to gain possession of personal property that is in the possession of another.[134] The secured party may also seize the property without going to court if the seizure can be accomplished without a "breach of the peace."[135] Clearly non-judicial means are simpler and less expensive, so many creditors regularly use them. Since security interests are regularly taken in sales of automobiles, some creditors resort to such "self-help repossession" on a regular basis and employ persons who are specialists in the art of locating cars of defaulting debtors and then driving or towing them away.[136]

Disputes Between Secured Creditors   When a debtor gives conflicting security interests in the same property, the question arises as to which creditor's security interest will prevail — which creditor has "priority." Priority is given to the creditor who has perfected the security interest and, if both have perfected, to the one who perfected first. The most common means of perfecting a security interest is by filing a short form, called a "financing statement," with the office of the Secretary of State of that state. The financing statement indicates a security interest in particular property owned by the debtor. As a general rule, priority is given to the first secured creditor to file a financing statement.[137] Before lending money, a creditor can research the public record for prior financing statements. If no financing statement is found, the creditor can be sure that it will have first priority in the collateral when it files its financing statement.[138]

Disputes Between the Creditor and Purchasers From the Secured Party The UCC provides that a security interest continues in the property even if it is sold,[139] so the creditor with a security interest will win a dispute with someone who buys the collateral from the debtor. However, the purchaser takes goods free of any security interest if the purchaser buys the encumbered goods "in the ordinary course of business."[140] This means that the debtor must be one who ordinarily sells goods of that kind. Thus, a clothing store may give a security interest in its inventory of clothes to a bank in order to obtain a loan. If the store sells a sweater, the purchaser will take that sweater free of the secured creditor's security interest because the purchaser is a buyer in the ordinary course of business. However, if the clothing store has granted a security interest in its office equipment and it sells a computer used by the store manager's secretary, the purchaser will not be protected because the clothing store does not ordinarily sell computers.[141]

---

134 *See* Chapter XI, p. 408. Procedural due process requires that the debtor be given notice before judicial seizure and an opportunity for a hearing. *See* Chapter VI, p. .

135 UCC §9-503.

136 In some states, this a more dangerous job than in others. *See* Chapter XIV, p. 518, note 101.

137 UCC 9-312(5)(a). In fact, creditors may and often do file a financing statement before the loan is made or the debtor has signed a security agreement in order to ensure that they will have priority.

138 Sometimes local filing in a county office is required as well.

139 UCC §9-306(2).

140 UCC §9-307(1).

141 Most sales of secured property between consumers are valid against the secured creditor, unless the creditor has filed a financing statement or, in the case of an automobile, a lien is noted on the document of title. UCC §9-307(2).

Disputes Between Secured Creditor and Bankruptcy Trustee   Bankruptcy is a judicial proceeding in which a debtor whose debts exceed assets can apply remaining assets to those debts and be discharged from any further obligation on those debts.[142] It is the job of the bankruptcy trustee to gather together all the assets of the debtor on behalf of the *unsecured* creditors. In the process, the trustee seeks to enlarge the pool of money available to pay unsecured creditors (the bankrupt's "estate"). One way to do so is to contest and invalidate the security interests of secured creditors.

In a contest between the trustee and the secured creditor, a secured creditor with a fully valid and perfected security interest will generally have priority over the bankruptcy trustee. If the creditor has not perfected its interest (usually by failing to file a financing statement), it will lose to the trustee.[143] The creditor will also lose if the creditor's transaction amounted to a voidable "preference" or a "fraudulent transfer" of an interest in property, including a security interest. These concepts prevent creditors from using their leverage with the debtor to gain an advantageous position shortly before bankruptcy. The "preference" rule allows the trustee to avoid (invalidate) any transfers made by debtor to creditors within 90 days before the bankruptcy was filed. The "fraudulent transfer" rule permits the trustee to avoid any transfers made by the debtor within the *year* before filing, if made with the intent to defraud or if less than reasonable value was given to the debtor and the debtor was or would be come insolvent as a result. Commonly avoided are debtors giving new security interests to a creditor to secure an old debt.[144]

B. Consumer Protection Laws

By distinguishing between merchants and consumers and making commercial transactions subject to the unconscionability doctrine, the UCC makes some effort to protect consumers in their purchases of goods. Other laws go even further.

1. Consumer Credit Transactions

The consumer economy of the United States runs on credit. Not only does the United States have one of the lowest savings rates in the industrialized world, the use of credit to live beyond one's immediate means is taken for granted. The eagerness of consumers to obtain credit often means that they do not shop for it and those who extend consumer creditors often will not bargain over credit terms. This makes the area of consumer credit transactions particularly subject to abuse by lenders and therefore the object of several consumer protection laws.

a. Federal Laws

The Truth in Lending Act   Since 1968, consumer credit transactions have been subject to the Truth in Lending Act (TILA), part of the Consumer Credit Protection Act (CCPA).[145] The TILA does not regulate the actual terms of credit, such as how much

---

142 Bankruptcy is discussed in Chapter XV, pp. 554-556.

143 *See* 11 U.S.C.A. §544 (trustee has the status of a lien creditor); UCC §9-301(1)(b) (lien creditor has priority over an unperfected secured party). One might wonder why a secured creditor would ever fail to file a financing statement. But a creditor whose debtor is having difficulty may intentionally refrain from filing because it could prevent the debtor from borrowing new money to pay off old debts.

144 11 U.S.C.A. §547 (preferences) and §548 (fraudulent transfers). Liens with priority over preexisting fully perfected security interests include tax liens, 26 U.S.C.A. §§6321-6323, and mechanics liens — statutory liens to protect persons who have repaired property. UCC §9-310.

145 15 U.S.C.A. §1601 *et seq.* Also of importance is Regulation Z, promulgated under the TILA by the Federal Reserve Board. 12 CFR §226.1 *et seq.* The TILA, Regulation Z and virtually the entire CCPA are set out in SELECTED COMMERCIAL STATUTES, *supra* note 83.

interest a lender can charge.[146] Instead, the states regulate these. TILA requires that, whatever the terms of an extension of credit are, they must be disclosed clearly and in a uniform way so that prospective consumer borrowers can shop for the lowest cost credit. The principal disclosures are the "finance charge" — defined broadly to include not just interest, but many of the "hidden" costs of borrowing, such as loan application fees, mortgage broker fees, and required insurance — and the resulting "annual percentage rate," expressed as a percentage of the "amount financed."[147] In addition, in one-time closed end credit transactions the lender must disclose the sum of the amount financed and the finance charge as the "total of payments," late payment fees and how the finance charge will be rebated in the event of an early payoff of the debt. In the case of credit cards and other open-end credit accounts, the TILA requires disclosure of the rate of the finance charge and the conditions under which it will be imposed.[148]

Another provision of the TILA is the right of any consumer to cancel within 3 days any transaction that involves a security interest in the consumer's home, other than a purchase money mortgage. If the creditor does not properly disclose the 3-day rescission right at the time of the transaction as required by TILA, the 3-day period become 3 years.[149] This provision of the TILA has as its focus home improvement contractors and bill consolidators peddling "home equity loans" to pay off other debts, both of whose extensions of credit have high rates and high fees.[150] The rationale behind the right to rescind this kind of transaction is that borrowers need to understand and think particularly seriously about the terms of a transaction that could ultimately lead to the loss of their home if they are unable to repay the loan.[151]

The TILA is enforceable by a consumer suit in federal court without regard to diversity of citizenship or amount in controversy. Actual damages or a statutory penalty of double the finance charge, but not less than $100 nor more than $1000, plus actual attorney fees, may be recovered.[152] Various federal agencies responsible for supervising different classes of creditors can also sue to enforce compliance and may also themselves order institutions under their supervision to adjust accounts of consumers so that they do not pay a higher finance charge than was disclosed.[153]

Credit Card Issuance, Liability and Billing It used to be a prevalent practice for merchants or credit card companies to simply send out cards to potential users. The

---

146 *But see* 15 U.S.C.A. §1615 (outlawing the "Rule of 78s," a method of computing the unearned portion of the finance charge to be rebated to the debtor in the event the debt is paid off early that allows creditors to receive a high amount of unearned interest) and §1639 (certain terms of home equity loans).

147 *First Acadiana Bank v. Fed. Deposit Ins. Corp.*, 833 F.2d 548 (5th Cir. 1987) (when bank required all car loan applicants to use bank-approved attorneys to draw up loan documents, attorney fees paid were part of the finance charge); *Lawson v. Reeves*, 537 So.2d 15 (Ala. 1988) (difference in price between cars sold for cash and cars sold on installment contracts was a hidden finance charge).

148 *See* 15 U.S.C.A. §1638 (closed end) and §§1637 and 1637a (open end).

149 15 U.S.C.A. §1635. *See Jenkins v. Landmark Mortgage Corp.*, 696 F.Supp. 1089 (E.D. Va. 1988).

150 Development of home equity loans was also spurred by changes in that tax laws that prohibited deductions for interest on consumer debts, but continued to permit deduction of mortgage interest.

151 *See also* 15 U.S.C.A. §1637a (home equity loan disclosures). For an example of a successful class action attacking many of the excess "garbage fees" in home equity loan transactions, *see Rodash v. AIB Mortgage Co.*, 16 F.3d 1142 (11th Cir. 1994). Class actions of this type were so successful that Congress established stricter standards for them in 1995. *See* 15 U.S.C.A. §§1640(1), 1649.

152 15 U.S.C.A. §1640(a). This changes the normal "American rule" on fees. *See* Chapter VII, p. 239.

153 *See, e.g., Acadiana Bank, supra* note 147. TILA advertising requirements may be enforced only by a federal agency, the Federal Trade Commission. Consumer leasing is also covered by the TILA, which imposes requirements similar to those discussed here. *See* 15 U.S.C.A. §1667 *et seq.*

CCPA puts a stop to this by prohibiting the issuance of any credit card except at the request of the consumer.[154] The CCPA also limits the liability of consumers whose credit cards are used fraudulently to the first $50 of such charges if the consumer reports loss of the card or other evidence of unauthorized use.[155] As for credit card billing, the CCPA provides a procedure for card holders to protest errors on their credit card bill within 60 days of the error appearing. The credit card issuer must make the required corrections, including crediting any finance charges imposed, or send the card holder an explanation of why it believes the account is correct. If the billing error is the result of goods not being delivered, the card issuer may not deem the amount correct unless it verifies that the goods were sent. No action may be taken to collect the disputed amount nor may the card issuer restrict or cancel the account while the dispute is being investigated.[156]

An interesting feature of the Act with regard to credit cards is that it allows card holders to assert against the credit card issuer any claims they have against the seller of goods as to the quality of any good purchased. However, the right is limited to transactions exceeding $50 in which the seller is located in the same state or within 100 miles of the card holder.[157]

Electronic Funds Transfers Electronic funds transfer (EFT) cards and other EFT deductions from bank accounts are becoming increasingly popular as a means of making payments. The CCPA has provisions on EFT billing errors that are similar to those on credit card billing errors. A $50 consumer liability limit is imposed as well.[158]

Consumer Credit Reporting Gathering and reporting information on consumer creditworthiness is a big business. In response to widespread abuses in the industry, the CCPA (1) limits the type of information that may be included in a consumer's file, particularly old information, such as bankruptcies more than 10 years old and judgments against the debtor, accounts placed for collection or arrests or convictions of crime that are more than 7 years old, (2) restricts the uses to which reports can be put, usually only for credit transactions, insurance applications and employment; (3) requires notification whenever a report is or may be requested; (4) provides consumers the right to view their file, to challenge the accuracy of information in it, to force deletion of unverifiable information and to add statements disputing the accuracy or completeness of any information that is then required to be included in any future reports; (5) requires disclosure of the sources of information and who has requested a credit report in the previous year; and (6) imposes verification requirements for particularly sensitive information, such as public records of convictions, and for potentially suspect sources of information, such as personal interviews with the consumer's neighbors, friends or associates.[159] Civil suits by

---

154 15 U.S.C.A. §1642. Given the present-day rate of default on credit card bills, perhaps this prohibition is not needed today.

155 15 U.S.C.A. §1643. The Act also makes fraudulent use a federal crime punishable by 10 years in prison or a $10,000 fine. 15 U.S.C.A. §1644.

156 *See* 15 U.S.C.A. §1666 *et seq.*

157 15 U.S.C.A. §1666i. The holder in due course rule would normally prevent this. *See infra* p. 397.

158 Civil liability provisions similar to the TILA also apply.

159 *See* 15 U.S.C.A. §1681 *et seq.*

consumers may be filed in federal court on the same basis generally as under the TILA.[160]

Equal Credit Opportunity   The CCPA also provides for "Equal Credit Opportunity."[161] It prohibits any discrimination against applicants for credit on grounds of (1) race, color, religion, nationality, origin, sex or marital status, or age, (2) because all or part of the applicant's income is from public assistance or (3) because the applicant has exercised rights under the CCPA. In the event credit is denied, lenders are also required to give applicants a written statement of reasons for the denial as well as the name and address of any credit reporting agency relied on.

Debt Collection   The CCPA also includes a Fair Debt Collection Practices Act.[162] It regulates practices of debt collectors, sometimes called "collection agencies," which have as their business collecting debts. The Act prohibits collectors from contacting debtors at any unusual or inconvenient time (usually a time other than between 8:00 AM and 9:00 PM) or place, including their place of work, or from contacting any debtor at any time after being told in writing that the debtor will not pay the debt or wishes that no further contact be made. Contact with anyone else regarding the debt is prohibited, except when the debt has been reduced to a court judgment and such contact is necessary. Harassment and abuse of the debtor are prohibited, such as threats of violence or injury to the debtor's reputation, use of obscene or profane language, publishing a "shame list" of debtors who allegedly refuse to pay their debts or repeated use of the telephone to annoy or harass any person. Further, debt collectors may not do anything that would give the false impression that they are law enforcement officers or lawyers, that nonpayment of the debt could result in arrest or imprisonment or that documents they use in collection efforts are legal process from a court. In the event of a dispute, collection agencies must inform debtors of their right to seek a "validation" of the debt from the creditor. States have regulated collection agencies for a long time, requiring among other things that they get a license from the state.[163] Consequently, another possible remedy for a consumer is to complain against the license of the offending collection agency. The CCPA does not preempt state debt collection laws.[164]

Federal Trade Commission "Holder in Due Course" Regulations   Whenever a consumer finances the purchase of goods, the financing contract or note is negotiable, meaning that it can be sold to another party, usually a bank or other financial institution, which then has the right to collect on it from the consumer. This is a useful device for sellers, who are in the business of selling goods, not financing credit, and need the money tied up in credit sales to purchase more goods to sell and expand their markets. The difficulty comes in when a problem with the goods develops and the consumer wants to stop making payments on the contract. If the seller of the goods is still the holder of the contract, the consumer can put pressure on the seller

---

160 For an example of a successful suit, *see Stevenson v. TRW, Inc.*, 987 F.2d 288 (5th Cir. 1993) (credit reporting company's placing burden on consumer to deal with fraudulent accounts it was reporting was inadequate reinvestigation; damages of $30,000 and attorney fees of $20,700 approved).

161 15 U.S.C.A. §701.

162 15 U.S.C.A. §1692 *et seq.*

163 *See Miller v. Payco-General American Credit*, 943 F.2d 482 (4th Cir. 1991) (printing notice of validation right in gray ink on reverse of letter demanding immediate payment was not proper disclosure).

164 In a decision that caused some consternation in the legal profession, the Supreme Court held that lawyers who normally collect debts for clients through litigation are subject to the Act. *See Heintz v. Jenkins*, 514 U.S. 291, 115 S.Ct. 1489, 131 L.Ed.2d 395 (1995). Congress then amended the act to provide that litigation papers need not set forth the disclosures required for all communications with a debtor.

by withholding payment if the problem is not taken care of. However, if the seller has sold the contract and the new holder has purchased it without notice of any difficulties with the goods, the purchaser of the contract is a "holder in due course" (HDC) under the UCC. The HDC can enforce payment even if the goods are defective or the original seller engaged in fraud when it sold the goods to the consumer.[165] The HDC rule is based on a policy of promoting free trade in negotiable instruments. While this is fine when only merchants and banks are involved, it often leaves consumers victimized by shoddy goods without a meaningful remedy.

Some states have simply passed laws or state courts have held on various bases that the consumer can assert any defenses against a later holder that could be asserted against the seller. However, much of this state law has been rendered moot by regulations of the Federal Trade Commission (FTC). The FTC has not changed state law. Instead it has proclaimed that the use of the HDC rule to shield a holder from the buyer's defenses is an "unfair trade practice." FTC rules prohibit any seller from taking or receiving any consumer credit contract that does not include a notice that "any holder [of the contract] is subject to all claims and defenses which the debtor could assert against the seller of the goods or services obtained." This language then becomes one of the contract terms and is enforceable as a matter of state contract law.[166]

b. State Laws

The Uniform Consumer Credit Code The Uniform Consumer Credit Code (UCCC or "U-triple-C") was first promulgated in 1968, with major revisions in 1974. It is in effect in some form in only 9 states. Its unpopularity with states is largely because many of the consumer protections it affords have either already been enacted as separate state laws or implemented nationally by FTC rules, such as federal limitations on the "holder in due course" rule and debt collection practices, and the various disclosure requirements in consumer credit and lease transactions already discussed, as well as limitations on garnishment and "cooling-off periods" for home solicitation sales, discussed below. While the UCCC adopts a maximum ceiling rate for consumer credit of 24%, many states had long ago imposed even lower ceilings. UCCC provisions not generally duplicated elsewhere prohibit contract provisions that require consumer payment of creditors' attorney fees, take excessive collateral as security for payment, and impose "balloon payments," default charges and excessive charges for credit life, property and liability insurance. In addition, the UCCC establishes unconscionability as a basis for rescinding consumer credit transactions.[167] Also provided are statutory penalties and attorney fees for successful private suits and administrative enforcement, similar to the provisions of the federal TILA.

Other State Laws on Consumer Credit Before Congress got involved in consumer credit in 1969 with the TILA, states regulated the area, imposing both licensing and disclosure requirements. State licensing and regulation continue unaffected by federal law. Often state law requires disclosures that supplement TILA.

---

165 *See* UCC §2-305 and §2-306.

166 16 CFR §433.2. *See Ford Motor Credit Co. v. Morgan*, 536 N.E.2d 587 (Mass. 1989) (buyer of car permitted to use defense of misrepresentations of seller against holder, but a buyer's affirmative claim for rescission of the contract is possible only if the goods are not delivered or are totally worthless).

167 Unlike the UCC, the UCCC sets out 5 "considerations" to guide courts in determining unconscionability. They are applied in *Besta v. Beneficial Loan Co.*, 855 F.2d 532 (8th Cir. 1988).

2. Deceptive and Unfair Trade Practices

a. Federal Laws

The Federal Trade Commission Act and Regulations As noted above when HDC was discussed, the FTC has stepped in to regulate various aspects of consumer credit transactions. But its authority extends even more broadly to policing all "unfair and deceptive trade practices."[168] In addition, where it appeared necessary, Congress has passed statutes dealing with consumer protection problems unrelated to credit.

Home Solicitation Sales Sales by a salesperson who has come to the consumer's home present a difficult psychological dimension for many people. The consumer is not expecting the salesperson or the sales pitch and all but the most intrepid consumers are likely to feel "cornered" in their own home.   Federal Trade Commission regulations and many state laws provide a mandatory "cooling-off" period to permit affected consumers to reconsider their decision and cancel the sale without any penalty. The cooling-off period mandated by federal law is three days, but federal law provides that state laws with more protection apply instead.[169]

Mail or Telephone Transactions The FTC regulates all mail order sales and any sales using telephone lines that are initiated by the buyer — including computer shopping. Sellers are required to ship orders within a reasonable time, to notify the buyer promptly if the order cannot be shipped on time and to provide prompt refunds when the consumer cancels.[170]

Magnuson-Moss Warranty Act Warranties on consumer products continue to be regulated primarily by state law, principally the UCC. However, Congress deemed it necessary to step in with the Magnuson-Moss Warranty Act to improve on state law as it relates to *express written* warranties on consumer products.[171] The Act creates no new warranties. Like the TILA, it primarily regulates how warranty terms are used and disclosed to facilitate comparison shopping. The Act provides that, if a written warranty is given, its terms and conditions must be "fully and conspicuously disclose[d] in simple and readily understood terms" and must be available for inspection before sale. The Act defines what terms a warranty must have to be a "full warranty" and requires that anything less be "conspicuously designated" a "limited warranty." A full warranty (1) must provide for prompt remedy of any defect or other failure to conform to the warranty without charge, (2) may not limit the duration of implied warranties and must conspicuously disclose any limitations on remedies, (3) must provide a refund-or-replacement guarantee if a reasonable number of attempts at repair do not succeed, (4) must extend to all consumers who use the product, not

---

168 15 U.S.C.A. §45.

169 16 CFR §429 *et seq.* As mentioned earlier, if the door-to-door sale involves granting s security interest in the consumer's home, other recission laws may apply as well. *See supra* p. 395.

170 16 CFR §§435.1-435.2. Other FTC actions are the Used Motor Vehicle Regulation Rule, 16 CFR §§455.1-455.5 and Regulation of Funeral Industry Practices, 16 CFR §§453.1-453.9. In addition to making rules, the FTC can pursue unfair and deceptive practices whether or not contained in a rule, adjudicate whether they are unfair or deceptive and, if so, order appropriate relief. *See Arthur Murray Studio of Washington v. Fed. Trade Comm'n*, 458 F.2d 622 (5th Cir. 1972) (enjoining high-pressure tactics and long-term contracts in selling of dance lessons).

171 15 U.S.C.A. §2301 *et seq.;* 16 CFR §700 *et seq.* The Act and regulations are set out in SELECTED COMMERCIAL STATUTES, *supra* note 83. UCC warranties were discussed *supra* pp. 389-392.

just the immediate buyer, and (5) must require no action other than consumer notification to effectuate its terms.[172]

The Act importantly creates remedies for violations of the Act and any breach of consumer warranties, including express and implied warranties created under the UCC. But unlike the UCC, the Act provides for the award of attorney fees in successful suits.[173] The Act also shifts the burden of proof to the warrantor on the defense of consumer misuse. Once the consumer proves that the product does not conform to the warranty, the burden of proof shifts to the warrantor to prove that the failure of the product was caused by abuse by the consumer.[174]

Warrantors are encouraged to enter into agreements with third parties, such as consumer groups, to set up an informal dispute resolution mechanism as specified in the Act. As an incentive for doing so, the Act provides that the seller can require that the consumer go through that mechanism before suing in court if such a requirement is stated in the seller's warranty.[175]

Labeling Laws   Federal labeling laws range from those on fur, wool and flammable fabrics to smokeless tobacco and butter.[176] Smokers will be most familiar with the federally mandated Surgeon General's warnings on cigarette packages.[177] Everyone is familiar with the little boxes with standardized information on the nutritional content of food products in grocery stores.[178] Perhaps the most important of the labeling laws are those applicable to medicines, where incorrect labels can have deadly effects.[179] However, a drawback of many federal labeling laws is that they do not provide consumers with a right to sue for damages. Instead, the injured person must invoke a state-law-based right to sue for negligence and argue that the fact that the mislabeling violated federal standards — like any other violation of a regulatory statute — means that it is considered *per se* negligence.[180]

Limitations on Garnishment   One method of executing on a civil judgment is garnishment, the process whereby the judgment creditor can obtain an *ex parte* order

---

172 15 U.S.C.A. §2304(a)-(b). In addition, if the seller also sells the buyer a service contract for servicing and repair, then the seller may not disclaim any implied warranties. For a used car case involving a service contract that generally shows the interrelationship between the federal Act and the UCC, *see Ismael v. Goodman Toyota*, 417 S.E.2d 290 (N.C.App. 1992).

173 *See generally* 15 U.S.C.A. §2310(d). Suit is possible in federal court only if individual claims total at least $25 and all claims in the case total at least $50,000. Otherwise suit must be in state court. Despite the right to sue for damages under this section, courts have construed another section of the Act to bar suits for personal injuries that are otherwise available under state law. *See*, *e.g.*, *Gorman v. Saf-T-Mate, Inc.*, 513 F.Supp. 1028 (N.D.Ind.1981) (noting the "poor drafting" of the Act made decision difficult).

174 15 U.S.C.A. §2304(c); *Universal Motors v. Waldock*, 719 P.2d 254 (Alaska 1986) (consumer's proof that BMW engine failed because of damaged timing tensioner was sufficient to shift the burden to the defense to prove that that damage was cause by consumer's overreving the engine; jury verdict for consumer affirmed).

175 15 U.S.C.A. §2310(a).

176 *See*15 U.S.C.A. §69 (fur products); 15 U.S.C.A. §68 (wool); 15 U.S.C.A. §4401 *et seq.* (smokeless tobacco); 21 U.S.C.A. § 321a (butter).

177 15 U.S.C.A. § 1331 *et seq.*

178 15 U.S.C.A. §1451 *et seq.*

179 21 U.S.C.A. §331.

180 Despite the need to determine whether the drug was mislabeled under federal law, such a suit is not a "federal question" suit that can be brought in federal court. *See Merrill Dow Pharmaceuticals. v. Thompson*, 478 U.S. 804 (1986), discussed in Chapter V, p. 184, note 83. Another difficulty with federal labeling laws is that manufacturers can argue that they preempt state law remedies. *See Cipollone v. Liggett Group, Inc.*, 505 U.S. 504 (1992) (state law failure-to-warn claims are preempted by federal cigarette warning requirements; misrepresentation and other claims are not).

from the court requiring the debtor's employer to pay a portion of the debtor's wages directly to the creditor.[181] Because such disruption of the debtor's household budget can be devastating to the debtor's family, the CCPA limits garnishment to 25% of "disposable" wages (after taxes and other mandatory deductions).[182] Garnishment is not popular with employers, who must report the debtor's wages to the court, calculate the withheld amount and reprocess checks to make payment to both creditor and debtor in the correct proportions. Consequently, the CCPA makes it illegal for an employer to discharge an employee by reason of garnishment for any one indebtedness.[183]

Unsolicited Merchandise A tactic used by some unscrupulous sellers by mail was to send consumers unordered goods and then to bill them when the goods were not returned. A federal statute has provided since 1970 that consumers may keep any such goods or throw then away without incurring any obligation to pay for them.[184]

Telemarketing Telephone solicitation of sales, referred to as "telemarketing," was subjected to regulation in 1991. Prohibited practices are use of automatic telephone dialing systems and the playing of prerecorded messages. In contrast to some other federal laws, a private right of action is provided for and actual damages with a minimum of $500 may be sought in state or federal court, with the additional possibility of the court granting treble damages in the event of wilful or knowing violations.[185]

b. State Laws

Consumer Protection Acts Many states have comprehensive consumer protection acts that provide protections to consumers for a wide variety of deceptive and unfair practices. Representative of some of these laws is the Uniform Consumer Sales Practices Act (UCSPA).[186] The Act has been adopted in only three states and the reasons for its lack of success parallel those that apply to the UCCC — many states have their own consumer protection acts that borrow to a greater or lesser degree the text or ideas and purposes of the UCSPA and the FTC has covered some of the more urgent consumer protection issues. Aside from their substantive provisions, one of the hallmarks of an effective consumer protection act is its provision of a right to recover minimum damages and actual attorney fees expended in suing and the right to use the class action device to represent an entire groups of similarly situated consumers. Without these remedies, the vast majority of consumer protection violations do not involve enough money to make them worthwhile pursuing.[187]

The Importance of State Law in Enforcing Federal Rights Some of the rights set out above are secured by FTC rules. But the rules can be difficult to enforce because the only enforcement remedy provided in the FTC Act is an enforcement proceeding

---

181 *See* Chapter VII.

182 15 U.S.C.A. §1673. *See* SELECTED COMMERCIAL STATUTES, *supra* note 83, at 1396.

183 15 U.S.C.A. §1674. This section makes such discharge a criminal offense (misdemeanor). No explicit private right of action is created.

184 39 U.S.C.A. §3009.

185 47 U.S.C.A. §227. The Act's constitutionality under the 1st Amendment has been sustained by at least one Circuit Court of Appeals. *Moser v. Fed. Communications Comm'n.*, 46 F.3d 970 (9th Cir. 1995).

186 &A UNIF.L.ANN. 208 (1970). The Uniform Act has been adopted only by Kansas, Ohio and Utah, but other states have "borrowed" portions of it. *See, e.g.*, §§V.T.C.A.Bus. & C. 17.41 to 17.63 (Texas);

187 *See, e.g.*, UCSPA §§11-13. Mich.Comp.L.Ann. 445.911(2) ("actual damages or $250.00, whichever is greater, together with reasonable attorneys' fees")

brought by the FTC itself.[188]   The FTC can prosecute only a tiny fraction of the complaints that are brought to its attention,[189] so state laws become crucial for effective relief. Some state statutes use language similar to the "deceptive and unfair trade practices" language of the FTC Act and state that "[i]t is the intent of the legislature that . . . the courts will be guided by the interpretations given by" the FTC of the federal Act. Other state laws provide that any practice that is subject to an FTC cease and desist order affirmed by a federal court is a violation of the state law.[190]

---

188 There is general agreement that this means that there is no private right of action by a consumer to enforce FTC rules or the FTC Act itself. *Holloway v. Bristol-Myers Corp.*, 485 F.2d 986 (D.C. Cir. 1973). *But see Guernsey v. Rich Plan of the Midwest*, 408 F.Supp. 582 (N.D. Ind. 1976) (FTC had found that this very seller's practices violated federal law, so a consumer affected by those practices had a right to sue).

189 An example of an FTC prosecution is *Kraft v. Fed. Trade Comm'n*, 970 F.2d 311 (7th Cir. 1992) (cheese maker deceptively advertised amount of calcium in its cheese). See also *supra* note 170.

190 Mass.Gen.L.Ann. 93A § 2(quoted language); Mich.Comp.L.Ann. 445.911(2)(c) (FTC cease and desist order). An FTC rule that is quite effective without a right to sue to enforce it is the HDC rule, since it is most commonly used by the consumer as a defense when the creditor sues. *See supra* p. 397.

CHAPTER XI

TORT LAW

The word "tort" simply means "wrong." The law of torts concerns civil wrongs: wrongful acts which injure the body, property, or reputation of a person that can result in civil liability.[1]

A. Torts in Perspective

Torts Distinguished from Contracts Tort law in the Anglo-American tradition is distinguished from contract law, which enforces duties set out in parties' agreements. This is in contrast to the civil law's unified approach that considers both contractual and non-contractual civil wrongs under the heading of the "law of obligations." Tort law requires no express agreement between the parties for a duty to arise, but instead simply assumes that all members of society have a common, unspoken duty to refrain from behavior that creates an unreasonable risk of harm to other people.

Though tort law and contract law are distinct, there is some overlap. Parties to a contract owe certain duties to each other as specified in the contract, but parallel obligations may flow from tort law which would apply to them even in the absence of a contract. Consequently, in many cases both tort and contract theories of recovery can be alleged. A tort theory of recovery will in most instances provide broader relief and will be the primary claim pressed. Generally, in a contract case, the plaintiff may not receive damages for emotional distress or punitive damages, while in some tort cases, such categories of damages are permitted. A common example of overlap is in the area of liability for personal injuries caused by defective products — "products liability" — where the plaintiff may often sue either in tort for strict liability or negligence, or in contract for breach of warranty.[2]

Torts Distinguished from Criminal Law Torts and criminal law are similar in that both focus on wrongful acts and those wrongful acts can often be both criminal and tortious. Torts also has some elements of concern with society's and the government's interests, particularly with respect to the question of deterring future wrongful behavior. The nexus is felt particularly strongly in tort cases where punitive damages are allowed.[3] However, close examination shows significant differences. The most common type of tort is negligence, while most crimes require intent or at least recklessness. Punitive damages are not allowed in negligence cases. Moreover, tort law's primary focus is the relationship between private parties and assuring that compensation is paid to the injured individual, while criminal law is concerned with vindicating society's interests. Symbolic of the separation between criminal law and

---

1   A standard hornbook on torts is DAN DOBBS, ROBERT E. KEETON & DAVID G. OWEN, PROSSER & KEETON ON TORTS, 5TH ED. (West 1984, 1988). A more concise summary is provided in KENNETH S. ABRAHAM, THE FORMS AND FUNCTIONS OF TORT LAW (Foundation 1997). *See also* EDWARD J. KIONKA, TORTS IN A NUTSHELL, 2D ED. (West 1992) and LEVINE & DIAMOND, UNDERSTANDING TORTS (Matthew Bender 1996). An excellent comparative work explanation with many good sources cited is JOHN G. FLEMING, THE AMERICAN TORT PROCESS (Clarendon Press, Oxford 1988). Two books providing an interdisciplinary perspective on the tort system are SAUL LEVMORE, FOUNDATION OF TORT LAW (Oxford U. Press 1994) and ROBERT L. RABIN, PERSPECTIVES ON TORT LAW, 4TH ED. (Aspen 1995).

2   *See* Chapter X, pp. 381 and 401, and *infra* p. 417. The options in electing either tort or contract remedies are discussed in PROSSER & KEETON, *supra* note 1, §92 and KIONKA *supra* note 1, §10-1. *See also* Chapter X, p. 575, where the possibility of *tort* liability based on breach of an implied "covenant of good faith dealing" inherent in all *contracts* is discussed.

3   *See infra* pp. 431-437.

torts is the fact that, unlike some countries, a civil claim for damages cannot be appended to a criminal prosecution. Instead a crime victim who wishes to get monetary compensation must file a separate civil lawsuit.[4]

Sources of Tort Law Tort law in the U.S. is largely common law. This means that courts have the power to shape and change the elements of claims and defenses of existing torts and the power to create new torts.[5] Statutes have been passed, particularly in recent years, in attempts to "reform" the tort system, but most of those have related to procedural matters and amounts and categories of damages.[6] With a few exceptions, legislatures appear content to leave basic tort elements and defenses to the courts.[7]

State and federal legislatures regularly create new civil wrongs by passing regulatory statutes and providing a private claim for damages for their breach. Examples are federal statutes on employment discrimination or various consumer protection acts.[8] However, these statutory wrongs are generally not referred to as "torts." Similarly, persons injured by violations of constitutional rights can sue the government officials involved for civil liability.[9] This area is sometimes referred to as "constitutional torts," but it is generally considered part of civil rights or constitutional law rather than torts.[10]

As common law, tort law is primarily state law and there is some variation from state to state. However, most of the bases for civil liability came from a common core of common law and are roughly similar in all states. Yet, despite relative uniformity among states, torts remains an area that does not contain an overall unifying principle. This is in large measure the result of the common law development of tort law: *seriatim* recognition by courts of rights to recover damages under specific headings — trespass, slander, conversion, and others — each containing its own unique requirements for recovery.

Organization of this Chapter It is traditional to divide torts into three categories based on the degree of fault attributable to the tortfeasor: intentional torts, negligent torts, and liability without fault.[11] After this, we will consider torts vindicating particular kinds of interests, which involve more than one state of mind. Following that will be a consideration of relief available in tort cases and an overall view of the tort system of compensation, including the role played by liability insurance, recent efforts at "tort reform" and substitutes for tort recovery that have been developed.

---

4 The criminal victim as civil plaintiff in a later suit for damages will have little trouble establishing liability because of the doctrine of issue preclusion or collateral estoppel. *See* Chapter VII, pp. 241-242. Because many criminals have no money, some states have instituted crime victim compensation boards before which a crime victim can file an administrative claim for compensation from a state fund. *See, e.g.* N.Y. Exec. Law §622 *et seq.*; Cal. Gov. Code §13959 *et seq.*

5 Examples of relatively new torts include intentional and negligent infliction of mental suffering, infliction of prenatal injuries and the alienation of the affections of a parent. *See* PROSSER & KEETON, *supra* note 1, §1.

6 *See infra* p. 435.

7 In recent years in the United States, however, some courts have expressed hesitancy in making judicial changes in tort law. *See* discussion in Chapter II, p. 43.

8 *See* Chapter XV, pp. 569-573 (employment discrimination) and Chapter X, pp. 394-401 (consumer protection).

9 The basis for suit in these situations was discussed in Chapter VI, p. 218-220.

10 In fact, the line between constitutional and regular common law torts is sometimes difficult to discern. *See* William Burnham, *Separating Constitutional and Common law Torts: A Critique and a Proposed Constitutional Theory of Duty*, 73 MINN. L. REV. 515 (1989).

11 "Tortfeasor" simply means the person who committed the tort.

B. Types of Torts by Degrees of Fault

1. Intentional Torts

Intent is defined in terms of the tortfeasor's probable attitude toward the *consequences* of an act. Thus, a person acts *intentionally* with respect to injury when that person desires to cause a certain injury or where that person is substantially certain that the injury would occur.[12] This definition of intent is subjective to the extent that the defendant must have at least been aware that the injury was substantially certain to occur. Since many defendants will not admit to such intent, however, it may be proved by circumstantial evidence. The test of intent is ultimately objective since the law presumes that a defendant intends the natural and probable harmful consequences of his or her acts. Thus, a person who fires a gun directly at someone may testify to their fervent hope that the bullet would not injure the victim, but it is not likely that such testimony would be believed, and liability for the intentional shooting would be properly imposed.[13]

In general, intentional conduct is more morally reprehensible than negligent conduct, so the law tends to impose greater responsibility on intentional tortfeasors. Thus, the amount of compensation, degree of causation and the issue of who bears the burden of proof required will often be more liberal for the plaintiff in intentional tort cases than in negligence cases.

a. Most Common Types of Intentional Torts

Battery   A battery is an intentional harmful or offensive contact the defendant makes with the plaintiff.[14] The nature of intent has already been discussed. It is further relevant to emphasize, however, that battery does not require that the defendant intended a *particular injury*, only that the person intended the contact. For example, assume a victim's leg is peculiarly susceptible to injury because of prior injury. Not knowing this, the defendant kicks the victim's leg in a way that would not seriously injury a healthy leg, but causes serious injury in this case. The defendant is liable even though there was no intent to cause an injury that serious.[15]

The contact required for battery must be "harmful or offensive." Harmful contact is obvious when the defendant physically attacks the plaintiff causing injury. Offensive contact is contact that would be considered offensive by the average person and that the defendant knows will be offensive to the plaintiff. Examples of offensive contact include being spit upon, being kissed by a stranger, or being pushed. The circumstances of the situation help define whether the contact is "offensive."[16] It is irrelevant that the defendant intended the contact to benefit the plaintiff if it was not

---

12   RESTATEMENT (SECOND) OF TORTS §8A (American Law Institute 1965) [hereafter RESTATEMENT].

13   *See* PROSSER & KEETON, *supra* note 1, at 35-36.

14   *See* RESTATEMENT §13.

15   *Vosburg v. Putney*, 50 N.W. 403 (Wis. 1891).

16   *See Estate of Berthiaume v. Pratt*, 365 A.2d 792 (Me. 1976) (doctor who moved dying patient's head to get a better photograph of it over patient's objections held liable for battery and invasion of privacy); *Fidler v. Murphy*, 203 Misc. 51, 113 N.Y.S.2d 388 (1952) (cause of action for assault and battery properly stated when police officer had plaintiffs photographed and fingerprinted when this was not allowed by law); *Gallela v. Onassis*, 353 F.Supp. 196 (S.D.N.Y. 1972) (bumping and touching Jackie Kennedy Onassis while attempting to take photographs was offensive contact and therefore battery). *See also* RESTATEMENT §§15, 18, 19.

consented to. For example, a doctor who operates on a plaintiff without informed consent commits a battery.[17]

The contact required for battery is generally actual contact with another person's body. American courts have, however, allowed battery claims where the contact was only with an extension of the body. For example, knocking off a hat or striking a car in which someone is riding may be sufficient to constitute contact.[18] The contact does not need to be violent. All that is required is harmful contact of something against the body of the plaintiff. For example, poisoning someone's food is considered a battery, as is transmission of a sexual disease and withdrawal medical treatment.[19]

Assault Assault is closely related to battery but does not require contact. An assault occurs when the defendant intentionally acts in a way that is sufficient to cause reasonable apprehension of an immediate battery. The required apprehension of battery must be such that a normal person would feel threatened. This generally means that the defendant must have the apparent ability to carry out the threat. However, actual fear on the plaintiff's part is not required. Thus, plaintiffs who are too brave to be frightened can still recover if they perceived a threat. However, plaintiffs must be aware of the threatening act at the time.[20] Generally, mere words alone, unaccompanied by a physical act, will not be enough to establish reasonable apprehension. For the threatened contact to be immediate, there must be a manifestation of the threatened act. Thus, a threat to injure someone tomorrow is not immediate. Similarly, a threat to shoot someone, when it is clear that no gun is present, is not an "immediate" threat sufficient for an assault claim.[21]

It is common for people to refer to "assault and battery," as if they were the same thing or always go together. This is not the case. They often do go together, but there can be an assault without a battery and a battery without an assault.

False Imprisonment False imprisonment is the unlawful intentional confinement of a person against that person's will.[22] The essence of the tort is the natural mental harm that results when one's freedom is restricted without justification. The confinement may be a result of physical force or of a threat to person or property. Confinement may be the result of withholding or failing to provide a means of escape.[23] The threat or physical barrier that restrains the plaintiff must be one that would restrain a reasonable person. For example, false imprisonment would not

---

17 *See, e.g., Ballard v. Kellum*, 975 S.E.2d 922 (Tenn. 1998) (battery suit proper where patient was not informed by dentist that all 32 of her teeth would be pulled in one sitting). Usually the duty to obtain informed consent is imposed by statute. The duty requires that all the risks and alternative, non-experimental procedures be explained. *See Moore v. Baker*, 989 F.2d 1129 (11th Cir. 1993) (doctor's failure to explain alternative therapy that was not a generally accepted did not vitiate consent).

18 *See Crossman v. Thurlow*, 143 N.E.2d 814 (Mass. 1957) (battery when defendant rammed police officer's car with his car while officer was in it).

19 *See Kathleen K. v. Robert B.*, 198 Cal.Rptr. 273 (Cal.App. 1984) (battery when genital herpes contracted through sexual relations with the defendant who knew he had the disease); *Causey v. St Francis Medical Center*, 719 So.2d 1072 (La.App. 1998) (battery when physician and hospital withdrew life-sustaining care to comatose patient over strongly expressed objections of patient's family).

20 RESTATEMENT §22.

21 *See, e.g., Brooker v. Silverthorne*, 99 S.E. 350 (S.C. 1919) (statement made over telephone that defendant would break plaintiff's neck not an assault because defendant was not in close proximity to plaintiff). *See also* RESTATEMENT §24.

22 *See* RESTATEMENT §35.

23 *See Whittaker v. Sandford*, 85 A. 399 (Me. 1912) (defendant leader of a religious cult agreed to take a defecting follower back to America aboard his private yacht; upon arrival he told plaintiff she was free to leave but refused to provide a boat to take her ashore).

occur if a person was told to stay in a room but there was no threat of harm or physical barrier to prevent the person from leaving. A common suit for false imprisonment involves merchants detaining people suspected of shoplifting. Recovery is often made more difficult, however, by state statutes granting immunity if the merchant had probable cause to detain and detained in a reasonable manner.[24]

Trespass to Land Trespass to land involves entry onto the land of another.[25] The intent requirement for trespass is only that the trespasser intended to enter the property. It is irrelevant whether the trespasser knew that the property belonged to the plaintiff, or even if the trespasser believed it was his or her own property. There is also no requirement of actual damages. Damages are presumed. The strict rules of trespass reflect the high value that was placed on land ownership in feudal times. They also reflect the fact that at common law an action for trespass was the only way to determine title to land. Today that can be done by way of a suit to quiet title, though trespass actions are used even today to prevent a habitual trespasser from acquiring title through adverse possession or an easement by prescription — methods of gaining property rights through continued usage.[26]

A trespass can also occur when the defendant causes an inanimate object to enter plaintiff's land. Courts have allowed claims of trespass in cases where smoke or pollution has entered the plaintiff's land and has caused damage.[27] Thus, the ancient torts of trespass and nuisance have been adapted to provide a common law basis for modern environmental protection. Even objects crossing over or under plaintiff's land may, in some cases, constitute a trespass. This rationale developed from the common law rule that the property owner owned the piece of land from the center of the earth all the way up to "the heavens." This view of property has changed in modern times, especially with the advent of aircraft which requires the ability to fly freely over privately owned land.[28]

Conversion Conversion is one of the many common law torts that relate to interferences with possessory interests in personal property, called "chattels." It is closely associated with a "trespass to chattels" and is a more serious version of it. Thus, trespass to chattels is available for any intentional interference with personal property of any substantial kind, while conversion is an interference so serious that the value of the personal property is essentially lost to the original owner. Whenever personal property is wrongfully taken or retained, the owner is entitled to appropriate damages. The measure of damage is determined by the length of time the defendant had control over the property, whether the defendant acted in good faith, how much

---

24 *See Hainz v. Shopko Stores, Inc.*, 359 N.W.2d 397 (Wis.App. 1984) (reversing jury verdict for plaintiff on basis of such a statute).

25 The original common law understanding of trespass imposed liability without fault. Even today, reckless or negligent trespass are actionable as well. However, most trespass actions involve an intentional entry onto land and the only real question is whether that entry was lawful. RESTATEMENT §166.

26 *See* Chapter XII, p. 454, for a discussion of title by adverse possession.

27 *See Borland v. Sanders Lead Co., Inc.*, 369 So.2d 523 (Ala. 1979) (lead smelting company held liable in a trespass case for damages caused to a farmer's crops when airborne lead particles escaped from their plant).

28 RESTATEMENT §159(2) states that "[f]light by an aircraft in the air space above the land of another is a trespass if, but only if, (a) it enters into the immediate reaches of the air space next to the land and (b) it interferes substantially with the other's use and enjoyment of the land." In one case, the court held that poison sprayed from an airplane that otherwise was at the appropriate altitude was part of the flight and its invasion of the lower reaches of the plaintiff's airspace constituted a trespass because it interfered with his use of his land. See *Schronk v. Gilliam*, 380 S.W.2d 743 (Tex.Civ.App. 1964).

actual damage was done, and the amount of inconvenience inflicted upon the true owner.[29]

Replevin As an alternative remedy, the owner whose personal property has been taken may seek a court order requiring return of the property by way of an action for "replevin," sometimes called "claim and delivery." A plaintiff will seek replevin when it is especially difficult to assign a price to a chattel or the chattel is unique and irreplaceable. However, replevin is most often used by creditors who sell personal property on credit and retain a security interest in the property. When the debtor fails to pay, the creditor can regain possession or "repossess" the item though replevin.[30]

b. Defenses to Intentional Torts

Consent Consent can be used as a defense against any intentional tort when the plaintiff has expressly or impliedly agreed to the harm inflicted. Consent can also be implied when plaintiffs place themselves in situations where it is obvious that harm will result. For example, boxers consent to being struck just by entering the ring and could not successfully claim assault and battery. However, they do not consent to their opponents using bricks inside their gloves. This exceeds the scope of the consent given.[31]

Most states follow the rule that a person who consents to a criminal act is barred from bringing a tort action arising from the criminal act. But if a statute exists to prevent harm to a certain class of individuals, such as children, from their inability to appreciate the consequences of the act, consent will not bar a tort action.[32]

Self-Defense Self-defense, defense of others, and defense of property are used as defenses to assault, battery and false imprisonment and can be used if the party claiming the defense responded in a reasonable manner and in a manner proportionate to the threat presented. Therefore, a person who is the victim of a beating cannot shoot the batterer and claim self defense unless the victim reasonably fears for his or her life. The victim may use only such force as is necessary to stop the battery. In other words, deadly force can be used only to meet deadly force.[33] Use of deadly force is generally not allowed to protect property unless there is some threat of harm to the owner. Defense of property is available only to protect it or to recover it immediately after it has been stolen so long as the response is reasonable.

Necessity The defense of necessity is sometimes used as a defense to trespass and conversion. Necessity is the privilege to use, and damage if necessary, a person's property in order to prevent greater harm to a person or the public as a whole. There are two categories of necessity — public necessity and private necessity.

---

29 *See* RESTATEMENT §222A.

30 Security in and repossession of personal property are discussed in Chapter XII, p. 392-394.

31 *See Hackbart v. Cincinnati Bengals Inc.*, 601 F.2d 516 (10th Cir. 1979) (after the referee in a football game had stopped play, one football player struck another player in the back of the head, causing his neck to be broken; injured player never consented to being struck after the play was over).

32 An example of statutes enacted to protect a certain class of persons is statutory rape. Under statutory rape laws a female under a certain age may sue for battery even if she consented to sexual intercourse. *See* Chapter XIV, p. 515.

33 RESTATEMENT §65 states that deadly force is never allowed unless there is a threat of death and no means of retreat. But there is a great deal of variation among the states as to when deadly force is authorized. *See Silas v. Bowen*, 277 F.Supp. 314 (D.S.C. 1967) (self-defense held proper where the defendant shot the plaintiff in the foot after the plaintiff verbally threatened him; situation was such that the defendant could well have perceived himself in danger of death even though the defendant never threatened to kill the plaintiff).

Public necessity occurs when it appears reasonably necessary that an individual's property will have to be damaged to prevent greater damage to the community. A famous case from the American Civil War illustrates what "reasonably necessary" can include. Upon learning that Union Troops were approaching, the citizens of a town in Tennessee destroyed all the whiskey of a local distillery for fear that the Union troops get drunk on the whiskey and pillage the town. The distillery sued in conversion to recover the value of the whiskey, but the town successfully raised the defense of public necessity.[34]

Private necessity is similar to public necessity except that an individual's property is harmed in order to prevent a greater harm to another individual or to property. Private necessity prevents property owners from resisting the use of their property by claiming trespass.[35] However, a person who exercises private necessity will be required to pay for any actual damages caused.[36]

2. Negligence

To qualify as intentional injury, the injury must be substantially certain to occur. By contrast, negligence involves actions (or omissions) that create an *unreasonable risk* that the injury will occur. Negligence, like intent, might be thought of as reflecting a tortfeasor's mental attitude toward the consequences of his or her actions, thus ensnaring only careless or inattentive people. But we *presume* that everyone, by virtue of their living in society, knows what acts or omissions create unreasonable risks of harm. As a result, negligence is best understood as conduct that falls below the *standard of care deemed by the law* as necessary to protect others from unreasonable risks of harm — regardless of the actor's actual subjective state of mind.[37] Negligence, then, is generally expressed as a "breach of a duty."[38]

a. Negligence as the Breach of a Duty of Care

Reasonable Person Standard The standard of care to which people are expected to conform their conduct is defined in terms of how a "reasonable person" would have acted. Any special traits of the tortfeasor are taken into account, but the standard otherwise remains unchanged. Thus, a child or a person with a disability will be held

---

34 *Harrison v. Wisdom*, 54 Tenn. 99 (1872). If the *city itself* had taken the property today based on public necessity, it would have to pay reasonable compensation under the "just compensation" clause of the 5th Amendment to the Constitution. *See* Chapter XII, p. 449-451.

35 *See Ploof v. Putnam*, 71 A. 188 (Vt. 1908) (boat moored to a dock to avoid a storm was set adrift by the owner of the dock; dock owner was liable for damages because the boat owner was exercising private necessity).

36 *See Vincent v. Lake Erie Transp. Co.*, 124 N.W. 221 (Minn. 1910) (defendant owner of cargo ship that had moored to plaintiff's pier to ride out a violent storm was liable for damage caused by ship during the storm when ship smashed against the pier). These forms of necessity bear some resemblance to the defense of necessity in the criminal law. *See* Chapter XIV, p. 521.

37 RESTATEMENT §282.

38 Somewhere between intent and negligence is "reckless" or "grossly negligent" conduct. RESTATEMENT §8A, comment b. In certain categories of negligent torts, for social policy reasons, tortfeasors qualify for some greater protection than the negligence standard affords. For example, in automobile torts, although negligence is usually sufficient to hold a driver liable for injuries resulting from an accident, some states have enacted "guest" statutes protecting a driver from liability except for reckless or grossly negligent driving when sued by a "guest" passenger in the car, a protection designed to encourage giving rides to people. *See, e.g., Roe v. Lewis*, 416 So.2d 750 (Ala.. 1982) (explaining basis for guest statute). However, many such statutes have been held unconstitutional as denying equal protection to injured riders in cars. *Manistee Bank & Trust v. McGowan*, 232 N.W.2d 636 (Mich. 1975).

to the standard of a "reasonable person" of that age or with that disability.[39] The standard of what a reasonable person would do is most commonly established by examining prior judicial decisions, by referring to standards of conduct set out in regulatory statutes (e.g., safety codes for construction or traffic laws). But there need not be any prior decision on similar facts or a statutory standard, as the jury (or trial judge) may determine even in a unique case whether the risk of injury was one that a reasonable person would have foreseen.[40]

Violation of a Regulatory Statute In most jurisdictions, if the defendant has violated a statutory duty of care, the mere violation of the statute is *per se* negligence. The classic example is the driver who runs a red light, in violation of traffic laws. However, the statute must have as its purpose protecting against the type of harm that resulted from its violation.[41] In most tort cases, this means that the statute must have been enacted for a public safety purpose. For example, it has been held that "[t]he evident purpose of requiring motor vehicles to be locked is not to prevent theft for the sake of owners or the police, but to promote the safety of the public in the streets." Consequently, failure to do so is negligence *per se* in a personal injury action against the car owner by a person injured by the stolen vehicle following its theft.[42]

Negligence of Professionals When the negligence standard is applied to a professional, such as in a medical malpractice case, a "professional version" of the reasonable person standard is applied. The standard becomes that of a reasonable professional in that field possessing the training and skills of a member in good standing of that profession.[43] Just as in a negligence case involving a non-professional defendant, the standard of care in a medical malpractice case can be established by prior court decisions and any applicable regulatory rules. But if the doctor follows what was ordinary and customary in the profession, it is rare that a court will view that conduct as negligent.[44] The standard of care is further limited in some jurisdictions by requiring that the standard be that of reasonably qualified physicians *in the locality where the defendant practices*, though the trend is away from this limitation. The appropriate standard of care is most often determined with the assistance of expert witnesses, such as other doctors in the field who can give their opinion as to whether the care met appropriate standards.[45]

---

39 *See, e.g., Roberts v. Ring*, 173 N.W. 437 (Minn. 1919) (child plaintiff not contributorily negligent for walking in front of moving car because a reasonable child of the same age and maturity would have behaved the same way).

40 RESTATEMENT §285. *See Weirum v. RKO General, Inc.*, 539 P.2d 36 (Cal. 1975) (radio station liable for actions of radio listeners who drove their cars recklessly to arrive first at radio station to claim prize).

41 *Gorris v. Scott*, L.R. 9 Ex. 125 (1874) is the principal case applying this limitation. The owner of sheep that were washed overboard and lost at sea during shipment sued the shipper. The owner claimed the shipper was negligent because he failed to place the sheep in pens as required by law. However, the court held that the owner could not rely on violation of the law as proof of negligence. While penning would have prevented the sheep from being washed overboard, the penning law was enacted to prevent the transmission of disease, not to protect the animals from being washed overboard.

42 *Ross v. Hartman*, 139 F.2d 14, 15 (D.C.Cir. 1943). *See also Elliott v. Michael James, Inc.*, 559 F.2d 759, 764 (D.C.Cir. 1977) (stabbing of restaurant employee; escape prevented because doors were unlawfully locked on inside contrary to industrial safety board regulations).

43 *See* PROSSER & KEETON, *supra* note 1, at 185-192.

44 *But see Helling v. Carey*, 519 P.2d 981 (Wash. 1974) (holding ophthalmologist negligent as a matter of law for failing to give test for glaucoma despite expert testimony that standard practice was not to give it to patients under age 40).

45 *See* Chapter III, p. 107, for a discussion of expert witnesses.

Res Ipsa Loquitur Proof of negligence can be accomplished directly or through circumstantial evidence. The concept of *res ipsa loquitur* ("the thing speaks for itself") is sometimes used to shift the burden of proof to the defendant in situations where the facts constituting negligence are more accessible to the defendant.[46] Thus, where the defendant had control of the situation or instrumentality that injured the plaintiff and harm of this type would not ordinarily occur without the defendant being negligent, the jury may be instructed that it may infer that the defendant was negligent as long as the plaintiff was not contributorily negligent.[47]

The Nature and Extent of Tort Duties Generally, the law imposes duties to refrain from acting, but it tends not to impose affirmative duties to take action. One area where such questions have arisen is in "failure to aid" cases. In the United States, a person generally owes no duty to aid or rescue another person in peril. However, such a duty may arise if there is a special relationship, such as an innkeeper's duty to aid guests in case of fire or a school's duty to aid its pupils.[48] Special relationships can also be created if the rescuer placed the person in the predicament.[49] Also, a person who begins rendering aid may not discontinue that aid if it would place the victim in a worse position than if no aid had been rendered.[50]

The duties of land owners to people who enter their property are discussed when property law is outlined. However, special mention should be made here of suits for "attractive nuisances" because of their prevalence. A land owner is liable for injury even to trespassing children that results from a dangerous condition on the land, which is particularly attractive to children, such as a flooded gravel pit "swimming hole." In essence, however, the "attractive nuisance" doctrine is nothing more than a negligence standard imposing a duty on property owners to take into account the special circumstances of their property's allure to children and children's lack of judgment.[51]

b. Causation in Negligence Cases

To prove the element of causation, the plaintiff must prove that the defendant's act or breach of duty was both the "cause-in-fact" and the "proximate cause" of the plaintiff's injuries.

Cause-in-Fact Cause-in-fact is usually determined by applying a "but for" test: if the plaintiff would not have been injured "but for" the act of the defendant, the defendant's act is determined to be a cause-in-fact of the injury. Another standard for determining actual cause is the "substantial factor" test, which attempts to determine if the defendant's action was a substantial factor in causing the injury. Cause-in-act

---

46 *See* RESTATEMENT §328D.

47 *See Ybarra v. Spangard*, 154 P.2d 687 (Cal. 1944) (*res ipsa loquitur* applied to claim of plaintiff who sustained traumatic injury to his shoulder while unconscious during appendectomy surgery performed by defendants; burden of proof shifted to defendants).

48 *See* PROSSER & KEETON, *supra* note 1, at 376. *But see Parra v. Tarasco, Inc.*, 595 N.E.2d 1186 (Ill. App. 1992) (restaurant not liable for failing to aid diner who choked to death on food because it was not responsible for putting him in danger).

49 *But see Yania v. Bigan*, 155 A.2d 343 (Pa. 1959) (no liability where defendant incited victim to jump into water and then stood by while he drowned). *See* PROSSER & KEETON, *supra* note 1, at 375-376 for other "unappetizing" decisions.

50 *See Zelenko v. Gimbel Bros.*, 287 N.Y.S. 134 (Sup.Ct.1935) (store liable where customer became ill, employees took her to store's infirmary and left her there unattended for six hours resulting in injury).

51 *See* RESTATEMENT §339. *See, e.g., Gregory v. Johnson*, 289 S.E.2d 232 (Ga. 1982) (unfenced swimming pool 3 blocks from elementary school). *See also* Chapter XII, pp. 446-447 (other duties of landowners to those who come on their property).

is very broad in its scope. If this were the only type of causation required, liability would be extended to some absurd situations. Thus, people could say that whoever introduced their parents to each other is a "but for" cause of everything that happens to them in life. The broad scope of cause-in-fact is narrowed by applying the concept of proximate cause.

Proximate Cause   Some argue that proximate cause has little to do with proximity or nearness of the defendant's conduct to the result. Rather it is better thought of as *legal* cause — the sort of causal relationship the law will accept as sufficient. As such, proximate cause may have less to do with "cause" than with the scope of the defendant's duty. The case of *Palsgraf v. Long Island R.R.* discusses this very issue.[52] A railroad's employees assisted a passenger to get on board a moving train. That action knocked loose a package the passenger was carrying, which contained fireworks. The fireworks exploded causing shock waves that knocked over a heavy scale at the end of the railroad platform which fell on Mrs. Palsgraf injuring her. Judge Cardozo of the New York Court of Appeals wrote the majority opinion reversing a judgment for the plaintiff on the ground that the actions of the employee were not negligent since the employee did not owe a duty to Mrs. Palsgraf for such unforeseeable consequences. Judge Andrews in dissent viewed the issue more traditionally as one of proximate cause and found liability.

Whether viewed as a matter of duty or of proximate cause, courts in situations like the *Palsgraf* case usually consider the question to be one of the foreseeability of the injury. If the injury was a foreseeable consequence of the defendant's actions, the law will deem it to be proximately caused by those actions. The question is not whether the defendant *in fact* foresaw the harmful results. It is sufficient if a *reasonable person would have* foreseen the harmful results. Another test of proximate cause that has been suggested is a test of the "directness." The question under this test is whether there is an unbroken sequence of events between the act and the harm.[53] The directness test and the foreseeability test have been criticized as not being tests at all, but simply restatements of the court's intuitive conclusion that liability would be fair or unfair under the circumstances.

Intervening Cause A complicating factor in causation is "intervening cause." An intervening cause is an event which occurs after the defendant's negligent act has occurred and which contributes to the injury. If the intervening cause was the *proximate* cause of the plaintiff's injury, the defendant's act will not be considered the proximate cause. But if the intervening cause was a foreseeable consequence of the defendant's conduct, the defendant will often be held liable for this additional harm. For example, a person who allows gasoline to spill on the sidewalk may be liable for the resulting harm if a third person drops a lighted cigarette into the gas. This is because a reasonable person could foresee such a thing happening. A defendant may even be held liable for injury resulting from an Act of God as long as it is foreseeable.[54]

---

52 162 N.E. 99 (N.Y. 1928). The exchange between Judges Cardozo and Andrews is perhaps the most famous judicial exchange of views in all of tort law.

53 *See In re Polemis and Furness, Withy & Co.*, [1921] 3 K.B. 560, All E.R. Rep. 40 (defendant's act of dropping plank on a ship which caused a spark which ignited fuel which destroyed a ship was proximate cause of ship's destruction regardless of whether fire was foreseeable consequence of dropping plank).

54 *See Chase v. Washington Water Power Co.*, 111 P.2d 872 (Idaho 1941) (power company spaced wires close enough that it was foreseeable that something could connect them, so it was liable when wingtips of two hawks connected wires causing a fire that destroyed the plaintiff's barn).

c. Defenses to Negligence

The defendant facing a negligence action will seek to negate causation and breach of duty, but may also assert affirmative defenses. Affirmative defenses to a negligence action include "contributory negligence" and "comparative negligence," "assumption of the risk" and various immunities.

Contributory and Comparative Negligence   At least beginning in 1809, the common law defense of contributory negligence provided that plaintiffs who contribute to their injury through their own negligence, however slight, are completely barred from any recovery.[55] This all-or-nothing rule shifts the loss even to plaintiffs who are less at fault than the defendant. The feeling has grown in the last 35 years that this produces unfair and harsh results. Beginning in the 1970s, state courts began modifying their common law and state legislatures passed statutes adopting comparative negligence.   Today, 46 states follow some form of comparative negligence. In 34 states, the change was made legislatively and in 11 it was made judicially.[56]

There are two forms of comparative negligence, pure and modified. Pure comparative negligence apportions liability between the plaintiff and the defendant exactly in accord with their relative percentages of fault. For example, if a jury finds that the plaintiff's negligent act accounted for 30% of his or her injury, the plaintiff will still be allowed to recover the remaining 70% from the defendant. If the plaintiff was 70% negligent and the defendant 30%, plaintiff can still recover 30%. Pure comparative negligence is the form most commonly adopted by judicial opinion and endorsed by commentators.[57]

Modified comparative negligence is the most common legislative approach. There are different versions of it, but the most common is to provide that the plaintiff may recover for that percentage that the defendant was at fault, but only if the plaintiff's degree of fault is 50% or less. Other versions employ an "equal fault bar" rule, under which a 50%-50% tie will bar any recovery.[58]

Assumption of Risk The defense of assumption of risk applies as a defense when the plaintiff voluntarily consented to take the risk that a certain harm would occur. To invoke this defense, the defendant must prove that the plaintiff knew and appreciated the potential danger but consented to take the risk. This consent can be either express or implied. For example, the plaintiff in one case used a motel's side door where the ice has obviously not been cleared away to bring things in from her car.

---

55 For a review of the history of contributory negligence, *see Hoffman v. Jones*, 280 So.2d 431 (Fla. 1973), the Florida Supreme Court case that changed Florida law from contributory to comparative negligence, which was discussed in Chapter II. *See* Appendix, p. A4.

56 The states that retain contributory negligence as a complete bar are four southeastern states: Maryland, Virginia, North Carolina and Alabama. *See McIntyre v. Balentine*, 833 S.W.2d 52 (Tenn. 1992), which collects citations to all the relevant cases and statutes as of 1992.

57 *Hoffman v. Jones, supra* note 55, and the majority of judicial adoptions of comparative negligence have been in pure form. *See* Appendix, pp. A8-A9. *But see McIntyre v. Balentine, supra* note 56 (adopting comparative negligence, but barring recovery if the plaintiff is more at fault than the defendant). For a recent case deciding to retain contributory negligence as a complete bar, *see William v. Delta International Machinery*, 619 So.2d 1330 (Ala. 1993). An interesting empirical study on jury reaction to modified comparative fault is set out in Jordan H. Leibman, Robert B. Bennett Jr. and Richard Fetter, *The Effect of Lifting the Blindfold from Civil Juries Charged with Apportioning Damages in Modified Comparative Fault Cases: an Empirical Study of the Alternatives*, 35 Am. Bus. L.J. 349 (1998) (concluding jurors find greater fault on the defendant's part when the know the result of their finding).

58 For a guide to the debate over pure versus modified comparative negligence, *see* David C. Sobelsohn, *"Pure" vs. "Modified" Comparative Fault: Notes on the Debate*, 34 Emory L. Rev. 65 (1985).

She made one trip without mishap, but fell and broke her ankle during the second. She was held to have assumed the risk.[59]   A spectator at a baseball game, by sitting in the stands, assumes the risk of being hit by a ball hit into the stands.[60] But a person does not assume risks not reasonably contemplated. So if a spectator at a baseball game is trampled by an unruly crowd chasing a baseball hit into the stands, the spectator cannot be said to have consented to that type of risk, because most people would not anticipate that type of risk at a baseball game.[61]

A person can assume a risk by signing a written agreement. Such agreements are commonly upheld where there is open and free bargaining between the parties. However, if one party is at an obvious disadvantage in terms of bargaining power, courts may refuse to recognize the agreement.[62] Courts also consider the degree to which the consenting person actually understood the consent form.[63]

Immunities An immunity is a defense to tort liability that is granted to a particular class of people for reasons of social policy. The most common immunities in tort law are husband and wife immunity, parent and child immunity and governmental immunity. While these immunities were created by common law, many have been eliminated or modified by statute or overruled by judicial decisions.

At common law husbands and wives could not sue each other because they were considered to be the same person in the eyes of the law.[64] The same reason was given for child and parent immunity. But today this distinction has eroded to the point that most states allow suits between husbands and wives or children and their parents.[65]

Governmental immunity came from English common law and was based on the notion that "the king can do no wrong." Both the United States and state governments enjoy common law sovereign immunity. In 1946, however, Congress enacted the Federal Tort Claims Act (FTCA) waiving federal sovereign immunity except for intentional torts. The state's immunity extends to local municipalities at least to the extent that they are exercising governmental (as opposed to proprietary) functions. Governmental acts include functions that are uniquely governmental and could not be provided by a private organization. For example, police and fire departments are uniquely governmental and enjoy a wide range of immunity. County hospitals or airports, on the other hand, are not so uniquely governmental and are, therefore, not usually extended immunity.

With the widespread introduction of liability insurance, many states abolished state and municipality immunity in the 1960s and 1970s. Some saw this as a positive

---

59 *Schroyer v. McNeal*, 592 A.2d 1119 (Md.App. 1991). Clearly, cases like this could also be decided on the basis of contributory negligence.

60 *Arbegast v. Board of Education, South New Berlin Cent. School*, 480 N.E.2d 365 (N.Y. 1985) (plaintiff admitted she was told that "participants are at their own risk" before she participated in basketball game played while riding donkeys).

61 *Lee v. National League Baseball Club of Milwaukee, Inc.*, 89 N.W. 2d. 811 (Wis. 1958).

62 *Union Pacific Railroad Co. v. Burke*, 255 U.S. 317 (1921) (where shipper was offered only one price, waiver of liability would not be honored, since no off-setting benefit was offered in return for it).

63 *Conservatorship of Estate of Link, Inc.*, 205 Cal.Rptr. 513 (Cal.App. 1984) (convoluted 193-word disclaimer sentence in fine print held insufficient). The validity of consent forms parallels the unconscionability defense in contract actions. *See* Chapter X, p. 379.

64 *See* Chapter XIII, p. 476.

65 *See Self v. Self*, 376 P.2d 65 (Cal. 1962) (abolishing interspousal tort immunity) discussed in Chapter II, p. 59. *See generally* John DeWitt Gregory, Peter N. Swisher & Sheryl L. Scheible, Understanding Family Law §§6.01, 6.02.(Matthew Bender 1993)

step toward government being accountable for its wrongs and as a proper application of the same loss-spreading and compensation policies applicable to private tortfeasors.[66] However, there has been a backlash against this trend and immunity has reappeared in recent years.[67] But states that have governmental immunity generally make exceptions for some of the most common kinds of torts, such as personal injuries caused by traffic accidents involving state vehicles or improperly maintained public buildings. In addition, many states do not extend their immunity to their *employees* who can be held personally liable. And in many situations where there is employee liability, the government routinely steps in to pay any judgment.[68]

d. Some Special Issues in Negligence Liability

(1) Joint Torts

Nature of Joint Tortfeasor Liability   Conduct of more than one person may lead to injury. When this is the case, it is possible that there will be "joint tortfeasors." The issue of whether multiple wrongdoers are joint tortfeasors is important because joint tortfeasors are "jointly and severally" liable for injury that was caused by *all* of them. This means that any *one* of several joint tortfeasors can be held liable for the full amount of the plaintiff's injury. Thus, the plaintiff needs to sue only one of several joint tortfeasors to obtain a judgment for the entire amount of the damage caused by all of them. The hapless joint tortfeasor who is sued alone has a "right of contribution" from the other joint tortfeasors, meaning that he or she can obtain a judgment against the other joint tortfeasors for their proportional share.[69] However, the other tortfeasors may well be "judgment-proof" — without assets sufficient to pay any judgment.[70]

Concurrent Action   There are two circumstances in which persons acting concurrently will be deemed joint tortfeasors. First, if their concurrent acts are independent of each other, they are joint tortfeasors only if the injury is not "divisible," meaning that it cannot be shown which part of the injury was caused by one actor and which by the other. Thus, where a fire of unknown origin merged with a fire set by the defendant and the combined fires destroyed the plaintiff's home, it is impossible to divide the damage between the two fires and a single defendant is liable for the entire amount of the damage.[71] A more common example of an indivisible single injury is where the passenger in a car is injured in a crash caused by the concurrent negligence of the driver of the passenger's car and the driver of another vehicle. If the injury *is* divisible, the concurrent actors will not be joint tortfeasors. For example, assume that A and B, members of two different hunting groups, fire their guns simultaneously and negligently in P's direction while shooting at game. A's shot hits

---

66 *See infra* pp. 434-435, where the role of liability insurance is discussed.

67 Usually the courts will abolish common law governmental immunity and the legislature will reestablish it by statute. *See, e.g. Pittman v. City of Taylor*, 247 N.W.2d 512 (Mich. 1976) (abolishing common law governmental immunity) and Mich.Comp.L.Ann. §691.1401 (reasserting immunity).

68 *See* PROSSER & KEETON, *supra* note 1, §§131-132. *See generally* Chapter VI, pp. 215-220, where sovereign immunity and its exceptions are discussed.

69 Thus, the defendant joint tortfeasor in a lawsuit has the right to implead the other tortfeasors in the same suit. *See* the discussion of impleader in Chapter VII, p. 224.

70 *See* Chapter VII, p. 236. Another reason for not suing all joint tortfeasors is that some of them may be relatives or friends. For example, the negligence of the driver of one car may combine with the negligence of the driver of another car to injure the passenger in the first car. If the driver of the first car is the passenger's teenage son, the passenger may not wish to include him as a defendant.

71 *See Kingston v. Chicago & N.W. R. Co.*, 211 N.W. 913 (Wis. 1927).

P in the leg and B's shot hit P in the arm. P's injury is divisible, so A is liable for the leg injury and B for the arm injury.[72]

Action in Concert   The second joint tortfeasor situation is where two tortfeasors act "in concert," meaning that they cooperate or coordinate their actions. They are considered joint tortfeasors regardless of whether the injury is divisible. Thus, modifying the example above, if A and B are in the same hunting party and agree that they will fire their guns in P's direction to scare him, but their shots accidentally hit P in the arm and leg, A and B are joint tortfeasors. This is so even though it is possible to determine which injury A caused and which injury B caused.

Multiple Serial Actions   Where the actions of tortfeasors are not concurrent, but take place one after the other, joint and several liability may also be imposed. For example, A injures P and P is taken to the hospital where Dr. B aggravates P's injury with negligent treatment. Since negligent medical treatment is a risk that is a foreseeable consequence of injury, A is liable to P for the entire injury and Dr. B is jointly and severally liable with A for the aggravated portion of the injury.

(2) Vicarious Liability for the Negligence of Others

Respondeat Superior   A person has "vicarious liability" when that person is responsible for injury caused by the tortious actions of another. Most often this is based on some relationship between them. The most common kind of vicarious liability is *respondeat superior* — the liability of an employer for the torts of its employees committed while acting within the scope of their duties.

Liability of Owners of Cars   Owners of automobiles are also responsible for the negligence of persons driving their car with their permission. Most often, this form of liability is imposed by statute.[73] As with *respondeat superior*, the principal tortfeasor remains liable, but it is generally more fruitful to sue the employer or owner, since they are more likely to have insurance.

(3) Dram Shop Liability

Many states have passed "Dram Shop" acts, which establish liability for taverns for injuries inflicted by a person who became intoxicated at a given tavern or who was already intoxicated when served by that tavern.[74] And even in states without such special statutes, a negligence action can be brought, assisted by regulatory prohibitions on serving drunk patrons.[75] This form of liability has been extended by judicial decision to social hosts of parties, though the trend is against it.[76]

3. Liability Without Fault

Liability without fault, or strict liability, occurs when the law imposes liability without requiring proof of intent, negligence, recklessness or any other fault. The defendant in a strict liability action may even have taken all precautions possible to prevent an injury to the plaintiff.

---

72 If there is only one injury, such as where only one shot hits P, and P cannot prove whose shot it was, the courts have shifted the burden of proof to the defendants on the issue of causation, imposing liability on both unless they can prove their innocence. *See Summers v. Tice*, 199 P.2d 1 (Cal. 1948).

73 *See* KIONKA, *supra* note 1, §8-16.

74 "Dram shop" is an 18th century term for a tavern used today only to refer to this kind of liability.

75 *Rong Yao Zhou v. Jennifer Mall Restaurant, Inc*, 534 A.2d 1268 (D.C. 1987). Violations of regulatory statutes as *per se* negligence were discussed *supra* p. 410.

76 *See, e.g., Kelly v. Gwinnell*, 476 A.2d 1219 (N.J. 1984) *superceded by* N.J.S.A. 2A:15-5.6a.

a. Abnormally Dangerous Activities

Strict liability was first applied in cases involving owners of dangerous animals. The theory was later expanded to cover abnormally dangerous activities. The origin of this branch of the doctrine was the famous English case of *Rylands v. Fletcher*.[77] That case imposed strict liability on the owner of a water reservoir when the water broke through a mine shaft and flooded adjacent land. In determining whether an activity is abnormally dangerous, courts have considered the degree of risk of some harm, the likelihood that the harm that results from it will be great, the inability to eliminate the risk by exercise of reasonable care, the extent to which the activity is not a matter of common usage, the inappropriateness of the activity to the place where it is carried on, and the degree to which the dangerous nature of the activity outweighs any value of the activity to the community.[78] To the extent that each of these factors is rated high, a given activity is more likely to be declared eligible for strict liability treatment. Modern examples of ultra-hazardous activity are fumigation of residences, fireworks displays and gasoline storage.[79]

b. Products Liability

Nature of Liability Strict liability is applied commonly to dangerously defective or unsafe products.[80] It was pioneered by a California Supreme Court decision in 1963 and the Second Restatement of Torts §402A in 1964.[81] Under this concept, a supplier of a product (manufacturer, distributor or seller) is liable for personal injury or property damage suffered by the ultimate consumer or user of that product as a result of the product being "in a defective condition unreasonably dangerous to the user."[82] A manufacturer can be held liable even if it maintained reasonable quality control and there was no negligence in the design process. A retail seller can be held liable even though it was in no way involved in the manufacturing or design process. However, the seller can pass on the liability to the manufacturer.[83]

The policy reasons behind strict liability for products are numerous. As products and production methods have become more complex, consumers are less able to inspect products and determine their safety. Strict liability will also motivate manufacturers to make their products safer. Moreover, the cost of injuries from defective products can be spread over all of society by imposing that cost on suppliers,

---

77 L.R. 3 H.L. 330 (1868).

78 RESTATEMENT §520.

79 *Old Island Fumigation v. Barbee*, 604 So.2d 1246 (Fla.App. 1992) (fumigator held liable for residents becoming ill even though the reason fumes reached them was a defect in the buildings that the fumigator could not have noticed); *Klein v. Pyrodyne Corp.*, 810 P.2d 917 (Wash. 1991) (spectators injured by fireworks display put on by pyrotechnic company); *Yommer v. McKenzie*, 257 A.2d 138 (Md. 1969) (maintaining underground gasoline tank that contaminated water in nearby well was ultra-hazardous activity). *But see Arlington Forest Assoc. v. Exxon Corp.*, 774 F.Supp. 387 (E.D. Va. 1992) (applying Virginia law to conclude use of underground gasoline tanks is not ultra-hazardous).

80 *See* JERRY J. PHILLIPS, PRODUCTS LIABILITY IN A NUTSHELL, 5TH ED. (West 1998).

81 *Greenman v. Yuba Power Products, Inc.*, 377 P.2d 897 (Cal. 1963).

82 RESTATEMENT §402A. Limitations on this sweeping liability are that (1) it applies only to merchant suppliers, meaning suppliers who regularly deal in the product, and (2) the product must not have been altered after it left the supplier's control and must be used in a normal and proper manner. All but 6 jurisdictions (Delaware, Massachusetts, Michigan, North Carolina, Virginia and the District of Columbia) have adopted some version of the Restatement formulation. So have many European civil law countries. *See* Jon R. Maddox, *Products Liability in Europe; Towards a Regime of Strict Liability*, 19 J. WORLD TRADE LAW 508-521 (1985).

83 To conserve legal resources, some states provide by statute that if the manufacturer is solvent and can be sued, other suppliers in the distribution chain may not be joined.

because they then pass that cost on to all consumers by purchasing insurance and increasing prices of the product to reflect the cost of the premiums.[84]

Defining "Defective"   A product is considered defective if it contains some irregularity that renders it not reasonably safe.   The defect can exist through (1) defective manufacturing, (2) defective design or (3) a failure to warn of a potential hazard associated with the product.   Defective manufacturing occurs when one item of a line of products is improperly built, making it different from the rest.   Examples are a jar of baby food with glass in it or missing bolts on an airplane wing.[85]   With defective design, an entire line of products contains the same harmful quality making it unnecessarily dangerous.   Examples are a lack of proper support bars on a scaffold or exposed electrical wires.[86]   Failure to warn of a potential hazard in using a product is a defect when the risk of harm is foreseeable and a warning to the consumer or user would substantially reduce the risk of that harm occurring.[87]

These three categories of defects were developed over the years by courts refining the definition of "defective" in §402A of the Second Restatement.   In 1997, a Third Restatement was promulgated.   Its §2 explicitly divides defects into the three categories and seeks to provide a clearer definition of design and warning defects.[88]   Product design is defective "when the foreseeable risks of harm posed by the product could have been reduced or avoided by the adoption of a reasonable alternative design . . . and the omission of the alternative design renders the product not reasonably safe."[89]   Some have criticized this definition as departing from the strict liability regime of §402A in its apparent requirement that it be shown that a "reasonable design alternative" was available.   However, §2 is not the only route to a finding of defectiveness.   Under §3, there need not be proof of any specific defect if it can "be inferred that the harm sustained by the plaintiff was caused by a product defect . . . when the incident that harmed the plaintiff . . . was of a kind that ordinarily occurs as a result of product defect."   Thus, if the back of the driver's seat of a car suddenly collapses causing the driver to lose control of the car, the plaintiff need not prove as a prerequisite to recovery that specific alternative designs were available to the manufacturer that would have made the seat less likely to collapse.   Also a plaintiff can recover for "manifestly unreasonable design" — a design that is so unreasonably dangerous that the product simply should not be marketed at all.   For example, if someone is injured by an exploding cigar, the novelty company that manufactured the exploding cigar could be held liable without the plaintiff having to prove that an alternative design would not have been as dangerous, but would have been equally effective as a prank.

The Third Restatement approach to the issue of warnings is that a product "is defective because of inadequate instructions or warnings when the foreseeable risks

---

84 *See* PROSSER & KEETON, *supra* note 1, §98. For an early influential judicial articulation of this view, *see Escola v. Coca-Cola Bottling Co.*, 150 P.2d 436, 440-444 (Cal.1944) (Traynor, J. concurring).

85 *See also Embs v. Pepsi-Cola Bottling Co.*, 528 S.W.2d 703 (Ky.App. 1975) (several bottles of 7-Up carbonated soft drink exploded injuring bystander; recovery allowed).

86 *See, e.g., Leichtamer v. American Motors Corp.*, 424 N.E.2d 568 (Ohio 1981) ("roll bar" on jeep not strong enough to protect passengers when jeep pitched over in an accident).

87 *See Jackson v. Coast Paint and Lacquer Co.*, 499 F.2d 809 (9th Cir.1974) (failure to warn of inflammability of epoxy paint fumes in enclosed areas could render paint unreasonably dangerous).

88 Section 2, RESTATEMENT (THIRD) OF TORTS: PRODUCT LIABILITY (American Law Institute 1997). Because of the breadth of tort law, the ALI has decided to update the torts restatement in segments.

89 *See,* e.g., *Uniroyal Goodrich Tire Co. v. Martinez*, 977 S.W.2d 328 (Tex. 1998) (possible alternative tire design in case where tire exploded, causing brain damage to mechanic trying to mount it).

of harm posed by the product could have been reduced or avoided by the provision of reasonable instructions or warnings . . . and the omission of the instructions or warnings renders the product not reasonably safe." Comments make clear, however, that warnings alone are not sufficient to make a product reasonably safe if other measures, such as alternative design, could have been used to reduce its danger. This is a variance from the Second Restatement, which provided in its comment j that a product bearing a warning "which is safe if the warning is followed, is not in a defective condition."[90]

The question of whether a product is "reasonably safe" enters into all categories of allegedly defective products. This determination clearly involves a balancing of the risk involved against the social utility of the product. A car that will only go 25 miles per hour is infinitely safer than one capable of going 70-plus miles per hour, but the social utility of the faster car saves it from being held defective. On the other end of the social utility spectrum is the hypothetical on the exploding cigar. The low social utility of playing pranks using explosives is a key consideration in determining that all exploding cigars are probably "unreasonably dangerous."

"Misuse" can be a complete defense to a products liability claim. For example, a person might use a kitchen knife to try to pry the top off a jar. The blade breaks and a piece of it shoots into the person's eye. The knife maker might claim this was misuse. However, if the particular misuse was a foreseeable one, the defendant will usually be liable.[91] On the other hand, if the plaintiff knowingly assumed the risk of the foreseeable misuse, the misuse is not a defense. The plaintiff's contributory negligence may also be used to assess comparative fault or to permit the defendant to prove that it was the plaintiff's conduct that was the proximate cause of the plaintiff's injuries, not any defect in the product.[92] By whatever name the plaintiff's misconduct goes, the overall issue is whether it is fair in light of all the facts to place the responsibility on the plaintiff user or the manufacturer.

Other Product Liability Theories   Strict liability in tort is not the only theory that a plaintiff can pursue if injured by a defective product. Two others are a contract theory of recovery based on implied or express warranties[93] and a tort theory claiming negligent design or manufacture.[94] Usually, strict liability is the easiest of the three available theories of recovery. Indeed, it was developed because of dissatisfaction with the difficulties of recovery under a warranty or negligence theory. But these other methods of recovery are a matter of necessity for plaintiffs from jurisdictions that do not have strict liability.[95]

---

90 An example of the Third Restatement approach being used to hold a tire manufacturer liable even when the user ignored a warning, *see Uniroyal Goodrich Tire Co. v. Martinez, supra* note 89.

91 *Price v. BIC Corp.*, 702 A.2d 330 (N.H. 1997) (parent could maintain action for child's injury because butane lighter lacked child restraint device; misuse by another child was foreseeable).

92 *Madonna v. Harley Davidson, Inc.*, 708 A.2d 507 (Pa. 1998) (intoxication of driver of motorcycle). One defective product for which strict liability and warranty liability have been excluded in most states is bad blood, usually blood contaminated with the AIDS virus. *See Kozup v. Georgetown University*, 663 F.Supp. 1048 (D.D.C. 1987). However, some states allow recovery on a negligence theory. *United Blood Services v. Quintana*, 827 P.2d 509 (Colo. 1992).

93 *See Goldberg v. Kollsman Instrument Corp.*, 191 N.E.2d 81 (N.Y. 1963) and Chapter X, p. 401.

94 *See supra* pp. 409-412.

95 *See supra* note 82. Other reasons to use a warranty theory are (1) warranty claims have a 4-year statute of limitations, UCC §2-725(1), which is longer than the typical tort limitations period; (2) economic damages may be recoverable if not disclaimed (*see supra* p. 430 and note) and (3) §402A provides for recovery only by the ultimate *consumers and users* of products, while Alternatives B and C of UCC 2-318 (enacted in 14 states) permit recovery by anyone "who may *reasonably be expected to . . . be affected*

A federal statutory remedy may exist for products with designs regulated by federal product safety standards. In 1972, Congress passed the federal Consumer Product Safety Act (CPSA)[96] establishing the Consumer Product Safety Council (CPSC), a 5-person regulatory body that sets safety standards for various products, including required warnings labels where appropriate. The CPSC regulations cover many products, to name but a few, swimming pool slides, cribs and pacifiers for babies, power lawn mowers, bicycles, cigarette lighters, paint, products propelled by chlorofluorocarbons, toys, pajamas and fireworks. Like the Food and Drug Administration and other federal agencies, the CPSC has the power to conduct research and investigations into possibly dangerous products, to order recalls and to sue to enjoin distribution. Unlike federal food and drug standards, however, a violation of CPSA and CPSC product standards forms the basis for damages liability for any resulting injury if the violation was a "knowing" one.[97]

Market-Share Liability In some product liability cases it is not possible to tell what company manufactured the defective product. In such cases, under limited circumstances "market-share" liability may be imposed in some states. If the products of all manufacturers are identical and the plaintiff cannot reasonably be expected to identify the particular manufacturer, the plaintiff can hold liable *all* the manufacturers who produced a substantial amount of the product in question when the plaintiff was exposed to it, with each manufacturer being liable for the proportion of the judgment that corresponds to its share of the market. The facts of the first case to impose this form of liability, *Sindell v. Abbott Laboratories*,[98] illustrates its application. *Sindell* involved DES, a drug marketed from 1941 to 1971 and given to pregnant women to prevent miscarriages. While the drug did not harm the mother and had no immediate effect on the fetus or child, it did cause female children to develop certain kinds of cancers when they reached adulthood. Because all the DES marketed was made from the same formula and the passage of time made it impossible to tell which manufacturer made any given dose of DES, the California Supreme Court held that liability would be shared by all manufacturers on a market-share basis, unless a particular manufacturer could prove that it could not have made the product that injured the plaintiff. Market-share liability remains controversial and many states do not impose it. And even courts that agree with it in principle have been reluctant to extend it to products other than drugs with latent effects.[99]

C. Torts Vindicating Particular Interests

The torts discussed so far have dealt with general interests in freedom from phyisical harm or property damage. There are other torts, however, that are designed to protect special kinds of interests.

... by the goods." *But see Giberson v. Ford Motor Co.*, 504 S.W.2d 8 (Mo. 1974) (§402A liability applied to bystanders injured when car motor exploded in traffic causing collisions).

96 15 U.S.C.A. §§2051 *et seq.* Regulations of are found at 16 CFR §1000 *et seq.*

97 15 U.S.C.A. §2072. Food and drug standards are not enforceable by a private civil suit, except indirectly where they afford a basis for tort liability under state tort law, *See* Chapter X, p. 400, note 180. The CPSA is not a complete boon for plaintiffs, however. If the CPSC has promulgated a standard for a particular product, any state-law-based suit seeking to impose a higher standard is preempted. *See* 15 U.S.C.A. §2075(a) and *Moe v. MTD Products*, 73 F.3d 179, 182 (8th Cir. 1995) (in lawn mower injury case, federal standards preempted state-law failure-to-warn claim, but not defective design claim).

98 607 P.2d 924 (Cal. 1980).

99 *See Smith v. Eli Lilly & Co.*, 560 N.E.2d 624 (Ill. 1990) (encyclopedic opinion rejecting market-share liability for drugs and citing cases rejecting its application to drugs in other states and to other products).

1. Injuries to Economic Interests

a. Fraud and Misrepresentation

Fraud   The common law action for fraud or deceit is the intentional version of the tort of misrepresentation. Its elements are (1) a misrepresentation by the defendant, (2) knowledge by the defendant that the statement was false, (3) intent to induce plaintiff's reliance upon the false statement, (4) reasonable reliance by the plaintiff, and (5) actual damages resulting from plaintiff's reliance.

Misrepresentation can be either false statements or the intentional concealment or failure to disclose information. For example, if a seller knows that a home is termite-infested, but tells the buyer it is not infested, the seller has made a false statement. If the seller, on the other hand, covers up any evidence of termite infestation and does not tell the buyer of the termites, this action could be considered intentional concealment or failure to disclose information.[100]

Negligent Misrepresentation   Negligent misrepresentation is a relatively new tort. Courts were at first reluctant to allow recovery, permitting such actions to proceed only when tangible injury to person or property had occurred. As the concept gained more recognition and support, however, courts allowed the action where the damages were intangible economic interests such as lost profits or a disadvantageous contract. Today, negligent misrepresentation cases are often brought in situations involving business relations when one party relies on wrong information supplied by another party. An action for negligent misrepresentation requires the same elements as any other negligence action.[101]

Innocent Misrepresentation   In a few jurisdictions, innocent misrepresentations are actionable. This is based on the judgment that, as between the injured party and the innocent representor, it is fair to require that the latter absorb the loss.[102] This strict liability theory is now accepted in the majority of jurisdictions when the misrepresentation involves the sale of an item or service. Thus, a manufacturer of an item may be held strictly liable for physical harm if a product does not meet performance standards advertised, even if the manufacturer thought in good faith that the claims were true.[103]

b. Interference with Economic Advantage

Intentional Interference with Contract Rights   This tort has its origin in the English case of *Lumley v. Gye*, in which the defendant induced an opera singer to breach her contract to perform at the Queen's Theater.[104] The interference must be shown to be intentional and for an improper purpose, including economic benefit to the defendant.

---

100 *Obde v. Schlemeyer*, 353 P.2d 672 (Wash. 1960). Because fraud is a serious allegation, even liberal "notice" pleading regimes often require that the circumstances constituting the fraud be stated "with particularity" in the complaint. *See* FRCP 9(b) and Chapter VII, p. 222.

101 *See Seagraves v. ABCO Manufacturing Co.*, 164 S.E.2d 242 (Ga.App.1968) (defendant held to reasonable person standard where he stated that tank was clean before plaintiff made repairs, when in fact it had been used to store flammable materials).

102 *See* RESTATEMENT §552C and Alfred Hill, *Damages for Innocent Misrepresentation*, 73 COLUM. L. REV. 679 (1973). Clearly many misrepresentation cases will overlap with contract law imposing express or implied warranties. *See* Chapter X, p. 389.

103 *See e.g., Hawkinson v. A.H. Robbins*, 595 F.Supp. 1290 (D.Colo. 1984) (manufacturer of inter-uterine contraceptive device that seriously injured users held strictly liable for misrepresentation that its product was a "carefree contraceptive device").

104 118 Eng.Rep. 749 (Q.B. 1853).

A noted recent case was *Texaco, Inc. v. Pennzoil*,[105] in which Texaco was sued for interfering with a deal whereby Getty Oil would purchase Pennzoil. The case was primarily noted for its award of major damages against Texaco: $7.53 billion in actual damages and $1 billion in punitive damages.

Interference with Prospective Economic Advantage It is also tortious to otherwise interfere with another's prospects for commercial success even when those are not secured by contract if such action is wrongful or undertaken solely to cause harm. For example, standing in the door a store and seeking to persuade customers to go to one's own store would be actionable. However, it should be noted that "fair" economic competition that is designed to disadvantage a competitor is proper. Also close to the boundaries of this tort are other actions for economic wrongs under antitrust laws, unfair competition laws, and trademark, copyright and patent infringement.[106]

2. Misuse of Legal Procedures

Misuse of legal procedure occurs when a person is unjustifiably subjected to legal action. Under this heading are the three torts of malicious prosecution, wrongful institution of civil proceedings, and abuse of process.[107]

Malicious Prosecution Malicious prosecution takes place when a person is subjected to criminal proceedings, those proceedings terminate in that person's favor, and the defendant instituted those proceedings without probable cause and for an improper purpose, defined as a purpose other then bringing a criminal to justice. A common example is where a store has the plaintiff prosecuted for shoplifting even though there was no reasonable basis for it.[108] The final requirement of improper purpose is sometimes referred to as a requirement of "malice." Although it is analytically distinct from the question of absence of probable cause, malice or improper purpose can be inferred from the absence of probable cause.[109]

Wrongful Institution of Civil Proceedings Wrongful institution of civil proceedings is similar to malicious prosecution but applies when the defendant brings an unfounded *civil* lawsuit. As with malicious prosecution, this tort is established by showing that the action terminated in favor of the plaintiff and was brought for an improper purpose.[110] Thus a suit brought to harass a person or to solicit a settlement with no real chance of success, is brought for an improper purpose.[111]

Abuse of Process Abuse of process occurs when a civil or criminal suit is warranted, but a party uses the litigation for an improper purpose. An example of this would be threatening to subpoena a person to testify in an ongoing suit unless the person pays a debt or performs some service.[112]

---

105 729 S.W.2d 768 (Tex.App. 1987).

106 Another use of the tort is to sue departing lawyers who "steal" firm clients. *See* Chapter IV, p. 162. An encyclopedic opinion on the tort is *Della Penna v. Toyota Motor Sales*, 902 P.2d 740 (Cal. 1995).

107 *See* PROSSER & KEETON, *supra* note 1, §§119-121.

108 *Tweedy v. J.C. Penny Co.*, 221 S.E.2d 152 (Va. 1976).

109 *Martin v. City of Albany*, 364 N.E.2d 1304 (N.Y. 1977).

110 RESTATEMENT §676 states that the only proper purpose for bringing a civil law suit is to adjudicate the issue upon which the claim is based.

111 Summary sanctions may be ordered against litigants and lawyers who file suits or assert positions in lawsuits that are groundless or are asserted for improper purpose. *See* Chapter VII, p. 224.

112 *See, e.g., Czap v. Credit Bureau of Santa Clara Valley*, 86 Cal.Rptr. 417 (Cal.App. 1970) (plaintiff stated a cause of action for abuse of process where credit agency sought to execute on debtor's property in order to pressure her to use funds that were exempt by law from seizure by creditors to pay her debt).

3. Invasions of Dignitary Interests

a. Defamation

Elements Defamation is concerned with injury to the reputation of another person. The elements are (1) the defendant made a defamatory statement concerning the plaintiff; (2) the statement was "published"; and (3) the statement damaged the plaintiff's reputation. The damaging statement need not be shown to be intentional or negligent; if caused to be published, it is actionable. "Publication" is a special term that does not have its usual meaning, but simply means that the statement was communicated to some other person. Defamation can either be written (libel) or oral (slander). One who "re-publishes" (repeats) a defamation is subject to liability equally with the original person who uttered it. Consequently, the author, editor and owner of a newspaper, journal, book or radio or television company are all subject to liability, as are radio and television broadcasters.[113] The original source of the defamation will usually be held responsible for the damage caused by such re-publication.[114]

A "defamatory" statement is a statement that damages a person's reputation by lowering the person in the estimation of the community or deterring other people from associating with that person.[115] What counts is not so much the plaintiff's own feeling about the statement, but whether others would consider it a mark of disgrace. Some statements are defamatory on their face, such as accusing a person of committing a crime. Others depend on the context in which they are uttered. Unlike English law, U.S. law considers a statement defamatory that injures the plaintiff's reputation within any subgroup, not just the community in general.[116] Pure expression of opinion and simple name-calling — as opposed to an assertion of fact — can never be defamatory.[117] The question of whether a statement is defamatory is one of law for the judge to determine, not the jury.[118] However, if language used is fairly susceptible of two different meanings only one of which is defamatory, then that is a question of fact for the jury.[119]

Defenses One defense to defamation is "privilege." "Absolute privilege" protects the speaker who is carrying out certain important duties, regardless of that person's motive or the truth or falsity of the statement. Absolute privilege usually arises from involvement in judicial or legislative proceedings, or by virtue of being a high-level

---

113 RESTATEMENT §578. *See also* §581(2) (radio or television broadcaster).

114 RESTATEMENT §§576, 622A.

115 RESTATEMENT §559.

116 *Ben-Oliel v. Press Publishing Co.*, 167 N.E. 432 (N.Y. 1929) (complaint was sufficient when it alleged that plaintiff was defamed when false statements about the customs of Palestine were attributed to her even though her reputation would be tarnished only among those familiar with those customs).

117 RESTATEMENT §566. *See Curtis Publishing Co. v. Birdsong*, 360 F.2d 344 (5th Cir. 1966) ("bastards"). However, if the ridicule or insult is serious enough, an action for infliction of emotional distress may be proper. *See infra* p. 428.

118 *See Great Coastal Express v. Ellington*, 334 S.E.2d 846 (Va. 1985) (whether accusation of commercial bribery was an accusation of a crime involving moral turpitude is an issue for court, not jury); *Nichols v. Item Publishers*, 132 N.E.2d 860 (N.Y. 1956) (reversing a jury determination that a statement that a pastor had been removed from his office in church was defamatory). *See* Chapter III, p. 84 (division of labor between judge and jury)..

119 *See Rovira v. Boget*, 148 N.E. 534 (N.Y. 1925) (jury question whether "cocette," which can mean either a prostitute or a poached egg, is defamatory).

governmental official.[120] Also, husband and wife are absolutely privileged to defame each other.[121] An important special privilege that affects the media is the privilege of fair reporting of an official action or proceeding, or of meetings open to the public that deal with matters of public concern.[122]

"Qualified privilege" may also be a defense to defamation. Qualified privilege is qualified in that it will not defeat a defamation claim if the defendant claiming it made the defamatory statement with actual malice, recklessness, or knowledge of falsity. Qualified privilege applies to communication related to a matter of public interest or where it is necessary to protect one's own interest. For example, defendants who reasonably believe that the plaintiff has stolen their property may communicate that belief to the police without incurring liability. Qualified immunity is also granted to protect the interest of a third person, such as reporting suspicions that the plaintiff stole someone else's property. Reports by former employers are also covered by qualified immunity in many states. Thus a former employer who tells a potential employer that the plaintiff was a bad worker is protected, so long as the communication was made without malice, recklessness or knowledge that the statement is false.[123]

A defamatory statement must be false to be actionable.[124] But the common law has considered truth to be a *defense* to defamation rather than an element of the plaintiff's case. Thus, the defendant has the burden of proving the statement was true rather than the plaintiff having to prove that it was false. However, this rule is modified by 1st Amendment considerations in cases involving "public concern," as discussed below.

Damages Generally, if defamation is shown, damages are presumed and if the defamation was intentional, then punitive damages may be assessed. However, like placing the burden of proving truth on the defendant, this rule is modified by 1st Amendment considerations in cases involving "public concern," as discussed below.

b. Infliction of Emotional Distress

Infliction of emotional distress is a relatively new tort and the limits of liability are still being defined. In the past, for a plaintiff to recover for emotional distress, there had to have been some kind of physical contact involved (a battery). The modern tort of infliction of emotional distress does not require actual physical contact. Although this tort is sometimes discussed with intentional torts, the mental state required can be intent or recklessness and, most recently, even negligence.[125]

Intentional Infliction Intentional infliction of emotional distress occurs whenever a defendant's behavior toward the plaintiff is so outrageous and extreme that it causes serious emotional distress. Proof of actual damages is often a barrier to a plaintiff attempting to bring an emotional distress case. It is not sufficient to prove that the

---

120 *See* RESTATEMENT §§585-591. *See, e.g., General Electric Co. v. Sargent and Lundy*, 916 F.2d 1119, appeal after remand, 954 F.2d 724 (6th Cir. 1992) (absolute privilege extends to comments made by defendant in anticipation of litigation regarding allegedly defective anti-pollutant devices).

121 RESTATEMENT §592.

122 RESTATEMENT §611.

123 See e.g., *Russell v. American Guild of Variety Artists*, 497 P.2d 40 (Haw. 1972) (union official's letter to plaintiff's booking agent stating that plaintiff had been committed to mental facility covered by qualified privilege because not made in bad faith or with malice).

124 RESTATEMENT §581A.

125 RESTATEMENT §46.

defendant's actions were extreme and outrageous; the plaintiff must prove that the acts caused severe distress. While there is generally no requirement that the emotional distress manifest itself as a physical symptom, courts will sometimes look to see whether the plaintiff has sought medical attention.

There is some disagreement among jurisdictions as to when a third person, such as a person who witnesses an outrageous act, can recover for emotional distress. For example, a person may witness a murder and become ill as a result. The Restatement requires generally that the third party suffer some kind of physical symptoms in order to recover damages. A close family member, however generally need not prove physical symptoms.[126]

Negligent Infliction   Negligent infliction of emotional distress is a new concept and has met with a varied reception. Most of the states that allow this cause of action require that the act which causes the distress be in some way directed toward the plaintiff and that the resulting distress be reasonably foreseeable. For example, courts have allowed recovery in a case where a mother witnessed a car running over her child. This is because people who are driving negligently should reasonably foresee that, if they run over a child, the child's mother may be nearby and witness the accident, and that witnessing the injury would upset the mother.[127] However, under the same circumstances most courts will not allow a stranger to recover after seeing the same accident nor do they allow a parent to recover if the parent does not actually witness the injury.[128]

In contrast to intentional infliction of emotional distress, *negligent* infliction usually requires that the plaintiff suffer a physical symptom as a result of the emotional distress.[129] But some states, most notably California, have allowed recovery even when there is no physical symptom.[130] It remains to be seen whether this is a growing trend.

c.   Invasion of Privacy

Four Component Torts of Invasion of Privacy   Invasion of privacy is divided into four separate torts: "appropriation," "intrusion," "publicity of private life," and "displaying in a false light."[131] "Appropriation" is the use of a person's name or picture for financial gain without his or her consent, such as where a famous person's name or picture is placed in an advertisement for a product without consent.[132] "Intrusion" is the invasion of a person's solitude which would be highly offensive to the reasonable person, such as taking a photograph of a person through a window of the person's house. However, it is not an actionable intrusion to take another's picture

---

126 *See* RESTATEMENT §46(2).

127 *See Dillon v. Legg*, 441 P.2d 912 (Cal. 1968) (mother who witnessed her daughter being struck by a car allowed to recover).

128 *Thing v. LaChusa*, 771 P.2d 814 (Cal. 1989) (mother who learned of her child's accident and rushed to the scene may not recover because she was not actually present when the accident occurred).

129 RESTATEMENT §436(A). *See Johnson v. West Virginia University Hospitals*, 413 S.E.2d 889 (W.Va. 1991) (policeman who was bitten by AIDS-infected patient whom he tried to subdue was allowed to recover from hospital for emotional distress over his exposure to AIDS when hospital negligently failed to inform him of the patient's infected status when they called on him to assist).

130 *See Molien v. Kaiser Foundation Hospitals*, 616 P.2d 813 (Cal. 1980) (husband allowed to recover for emotional distress when defendant misdiagnosed him as having syphilis and wife's suspicions of marital infidelity caused their marriage to break up).

131 *See* RESTATEMENT §§652A-652E.

132 *See Midler v. Ford Motor Co.*, 849 F.2d 460 (9th Cir. 1988)(advertising firm which had singer sing in a way that resembled Bette Midler's voice liable for appropriation).

in a public place, such as a public beach, or with permission in a private place.[133] "Publicity of private life" involves making public details of a person's private life. "Displaying in a false light" occurs when the plaintiff is placed before the public in a way that would be offensive to a reasonable person. "False light" cases are similar to defamation cases. However, recovery for being displayed in a false light does not require that it be proven that the portrayal would injure a person's reputation, as is the case with defamation.

d. Constitutional Limits on Dignitary Torts

(1) The 1st Amendment and Defamation

The policy behind the 1st Amendment is to encourage robust public debate of issues affecting society. If the normal common law of defamation applied, with its strict liability, its requirement that the defendant prove truth and its rule of presumed damages, defamation actions or the threat of them could "chill" the exercise of 1st Amendment rights. Though not entirely free from doubt, the amount of protection due an alleged defamatory statement has generally depended on the extent to which the victim of that defamation is a "public figure" and the extent to which the subject of the libel involved a matter of "public concern." "Public figures" are all public officials in supervisory positions and any private persons who voluntarily "thrust themselves to the forefront of particular public controversies in order to influence the resolution of the issues involved."[134] What is an issue of "public concern" is less clear, though it clearly includes government officials' performance of their duties or criticism of the views of other public figures on the subject matter that made them a public figure.

Public Figure, Public Concern   When a *public figure* sues regarding defamation related to a matter of *public concern* the 1st Amendment severely restricts that figure's ability to recover. The principal case of this type is *New York Times v. Sullivan*.[135] In that case, a city police commissioner sued several black ministers and the New York Times when the ministers published an advertisement in the paper seeking support for their civil rights struggles. The advertisement made critical comments about law enforcement's handling of civil rights demonstrators. It also contained some factual errors.[136] *New York Times* held that the 1st Amendment has three effects on the common law elements of defamation when public figures sue: (1) it shifts the normal common law burden of proof on truth to require that the *plaintiff* prove *falsity*, (2) it imposes a higher degree of culpability by requiring the plaintiff to prove that the defendant acted with "actual malice" and (3) it requires a higher proof standard, requiring that the plaintiff prove such actual malice "with convincing clarity."[137] To

---

133 *But see Dieteman v. Time, Inc.*, 449 F.2d 245 (9th Cir. 1971) (actionable claim where reporter took photograph from concealed camera while in plaintiff's house under a false pretenses).

134 *See Rosenblatt v. Baer*, 383 U.S. 75 (1966) (supervisor of county-owned ski resort). On non-government public figures, *compare Gertz v. Robert Welch, Inc.*, 418 U.S. 323, 345 (1974) (attorney representing plaintiffs in civil rights suit against a city police officer was not a public figure) *with Curtis Publishing v. Butts*, 388 U.S. 130 (1967) (athletic director of a privately incorporated athletic association attached to a state university, who was accused of "fixing" football games, was a public figure).

135 376 U.S. 254 (1964). *See also* Chapter IX, p. 356.

136 Perhaps influencing the decision was the fact that the mistakes were minor. For example, the advertisement said that civil rights leader Martin Luther King had been arrested 7 times, when he had in fact been arrested only 4 times.

137 The "convincing clarity" standard is somewhere in between the normal civil standard of "preponderance of the evidence" and the criminal standard of "beyond a reasonable doubt." *See* Chapter III, p. 102, where standards of proof are compared. At the very least, *New York Times* holds that this prove actual malice, the plaintiff must prove that the defendant either knew that the statement was false or evinced a reckless disregard for whether it was true or false. The standard is subjective, meaning that it must be proven that the editor or writer "in fact entertained serious doubts as to the truth of his publication."[138]

Private Figure, Public Concern   Where a *private figure* sues regarding alleged defamation that relates to what is clearly a *public concern*, the 1st Amendment has a limiting effect, but not to the extent that it does in the case of public figures. The principal case in this category is *Gertz v. Robert Welch, Inc.*[139] In that case, a police officer had been convicted of murdering a young man. Elmer Gertz, a private lawyer, represented the family in a highly publicized civil rights suit against the policeman. A John Birch Society publication accused Gertz of orchestrating a "communist frame-up" of the policeman for murder. It also claimed falsely asserted that Gertz had a criminal record and asserted that Gertz, as a "Leninist" and "communist fronter," was participating in a communist conspiracy to discredit local police departments, apparently an essential step in a communist conspiracy to enslave the country. The Court held that Gertz was a private figure and that the *New York Times* standard would not apply. Nonetheless it held that the 1st Amendment (1) shifts the common law burden of proof as to truth to the plaintiff, as discussed above, (2) permits recovery of compensatory damages only if the plaintiff actually proves such damages based on at least a standard of negligence, and (3) prohibits any award of presumed or punitive damages unless the plaintiff proves "actual malice" in compliance with the *New York Times v. Sullivan* standard.

Similarly, in *Philadelphia Papers, Inc. v. Hepps*,[140] a private businessman sued a newspaper that had accused him of having links to organized crime and using them to influence legislation. The state court imposed the common law burden of proof that required the defendant to prove truth. The Court disagreed and applied the *Gertz* standard to the case, labeling the subject matter of the defamation "speech of public concern" and noting that it was "against a media defendant."

One might criticize *Gertz* and *Hepps* for distinguishing between public and private figures, at least when the defamation deals with matters of public concern, since vigorous discussion of public concerns is at the core of 1st Amendment protections regardless of whether a public figure is involved. The *Gertz* court found different treatment of public and private figures to be warranted for two reasons. First, people who become public figures do so voluntarily and assume the risk of sharp public criticism. Second, public figures' celebrity status and high positions give them a ready access to the media that private figures do not have. This allows public figures to

---

requires that the plaintiff prove he was referred to directly by name or title —something not done in that case. *See also Bose Corp. v. Consumers Union of the United States*, 466 U.S. 485 (1984) (appellate court must scrutinize facts on actual malice carefully to assure that it is has been established with convincing clarity).

138 *St. Amant v. Thompson*, 390 U.S. 727, 731 (1968). *See also Harte-Hanks Communications v. Connaughton*, 491 U.S. 657 (1989) (newspaper accused judgeship candidate of using "dirty tricks" to influence a witness by offering her and her sister a trip to Florida; evidence was sufficient to support jury finding of actual malice where the paper failed to attempt to contact the witness's sister, the editor refused to listen to taped interviews of the witness, and jury rejected testimony that the paper thought that the witness was credible). *But see Masson v. New Yorker*, 501 U.S. 496 (1991) (fact that quotations ascribed to plaintiff public figure were fabricated was not sufficient to show actual malice unless fabricated quotes substantially change the meaning of what was actually said).

139 418 U.S. 323 (1974).

140 475 U.S. 767 (1986).

respond publicly to defamatory attacks, thereby reducing their need to resort to defamation suits for protection.[141]

Private Figure, Private Concern   In the absence of evidence that the plaintiff is a public figure or that the defamation related to a public concern, the 1st Amendment has not effect. Thus, in *Dun & Bradstreet v. Greenmoss Builders*,[142] the private figure plaintiff sued over a false credit report disseminated to only 5 business clients that incorrectly asserted that the plaintiff company had filed for bankruptcy. A plurality of the Court maintained that the case involved only a matter of private concern, so no 1st Amendment protections were due, and a majority of the Court affirmed a judgment for presumed compensatory and punitive damages without compliance with the *Gertz* standard.

Public Figure, Private Concern   Few cases have involved this category, perhaps because it is hard to imagine any aspect of a public figure's life that would not be automatically be a public concern. Certainly, the Clinton sex scandal suggests that today most any private matter can be related to an official's fitness for office.

A Caveat   Although the various combinations of public and private figures and issues are set out neatly above, it must be stated that things are not quite this clear. The principal problem is that the Court has not been clear on what a "public concern" is and if it is relevant. In the *Gertz* case, the Court specifically denied that there was any public-private concern distinction, thus suggesting that the *Gertz* protections apply to all private issue defamation. Another source of uncertainty is the phrase quoted above from *Hepps* — the suggestion that it made a difference that the suit was "against a media defendant." *Gertz* also stated that it was imposing a minimum negligence standard for compensatory damages in defamation suits against "a broadcaster or publisher." Yet, the Court has not attempted to define who is belongs to the "media" nor has it taken the position that the media are somehow different because "the press" is mentioned in the 1st Amendment.

Protection of Opinion   One thing the Court has made clear is that there is no general privilege for all expressions of *opinion* on matters of public concern. Some have argued that, since name-calling, epithets and rhetorical hyperbole are a normal part of the discussion of matters of public concern, such a privilege based on the 1st Amendment should be afforded. The Supreme Court has rejected any such blanket rule, noting that rephrasing "Jones is a liar" as "in my opinion, Jones is a liar" does little to change its effect on Jones's reputation. Thus, even a statement of opinion is actionable if it contains some provable false factual implication.[143]

(2) The 1st Amendment and Other Dignitary Torts

Intentional Infliction of Emotional Distress   Most defamation is intended to hurt its target, so public figures could easily avoid *New York Times* limitations in many defamation cases by simply switching to the tort of intentional infliction of emotional distress instead. Consequently, it is essential that the *New York Times* standard apply to this tort as well. Thus, in *Hustler Magazine, Inc. v. Falwell*,[144] Falwell, a nationally known minister and founder of the "Moral Majority," could not recover for emotional

---

141 *Gertz*, 418 U.S. at 344-345.

142 472 U.S. 749 (1985) (plurality opinion).

143 *Milkovich v. Lorain Journal Co.*, 497 U.S. 1 (1990) (newspaper columnist's statement that high school coach, a private figure, committed perjury presents factual issue of whether it was true; there is no separate constitutional privilege for "opinion").

144 485 U.S. 46 (1988).

distress caused by mock interview with him in which he stated that his first sexual encounter was a drunken incestuous rendezvous with his mother in an outhouse. Falwell's defamation claim failed because the jury found that no reasonable person would have believed the "facts" in the mock interview to be true. However, the jury awarded substantial damages for intentional infliction of emotional distress. The Court reversed, holding that intentionally inflicting emotional distress on public figures is a time-honored tradition in the United States and that the 1st Amendment prohibits any liability in suits by public figures regarding issues of public interest unless a false statement of fact is made and the *New York Times v. Sullivan* "actual malice" standard is met with regard to it.

Invasions of Privacy   The four components of invasion of privacy have been handled somewhat differently in terms of 1st Amendment protections. The *New York Time* rule has been applied to cases where the public figure plaintiff claims to have been portrayed in a false light, requiring proof that the defendant acted with "actual malice."[145] But appropriation cases have not been held subject to 1st Amendment limitations. It has likened them to copyright suits, in which the appropriation decreases the commercial value of someone else's speech and invades "the right of the individual to reap the reward of his endeavors."[146] As for publicity of private life, if the private details are already part of the public record, any prohibition of further dissemination violates the 1st Amendment rights of free speech and press. In one case, the Court reversed a judgment for damages in favor of a rape victim whose name had been published by a newspaper in its "Police Reports" section, based on a state statute prohibiting publication of the name of any victim of a sexual assault. If a newspaper "lawfully obtains truthful information about a matter of public significance," it violates the 1st Amendment to prohibit or penalize its publication.[147] No 1st Amendment issues have yet arisen in intrusion cases.

D. Relief Available in Tort Cases

What damages are recoverable for torts varies by jurisdiction. In general, aside from nominal damages, two types of damages are available in tort cases: compensatory damages and punitive damages.[148] A plaintiff may recover both compensatory and punitive damages in the same case.

1. Compensatory Damages

Awards of damages are generally made in a lump sum, not by way of periodic payments, as is the case with most administrative compensation systems. The elements of compensatory damages available vary from state to state, but the overall purpose of compensatory damages everywhere is to compensate the plaintiff monetarily for the actual damage suffered. This is generally subject to a duty of the plaintiff to "mitigate damages," meaning that the plaintiff must take steps to prevent

---

145 *Time, Inc. v. Hill*, 385 U.S. 374 (1967) (holding *Sullivan* standard applicable to false light cases). The actual holding in *Hill*, that non-public figure plaintiffs had to meet the *Sullivan* standard, has since been undercut by the *Gertz* case, as discussed above under defamation. Consequently, lower courts are divided over what approach to use for private figures.

146 *Zacchini v. Scripps-Howard Broadcasting Co.*, 433 U.S. 562, 573 (1977) (television station broadcast a 15 second tape of plaintiff's "human cannonball" act, which was the entire performance). The Court rejected 1st Amendment limits on copyright suits in *Harper & Row v. Nation Enterprises*, 471 U.S. 539 (1985) (copying 300 words from a 200,000 word manuscript of President Ford's memoirs).

147 *Florida Star v. B.J.F.*, 491 U.S. 524 (1989). *See also Cox Broadcasting Corp. v. Cohn*, 420 U.S. 469 (1975) (rape victim's name made public by open records of the trial proceedings) and *Smith v. Daily Mail Publishing Co.*, 443 U.S. 97 (1979) (name of juvenile delinquent lawfully obtained).

148 *See* Chapter VII, p. 236.

damages from continuing or getting worse if that can be done by reasonable action. Compensatory damages include both economic and non-economic losses resulting from personal injury or property damage.[149]

Economic Loss Economic losses are the actual expenses that the plaintiff incurred. Damaged property, medical bills, and lost wages are typical examples. Medical expenses can be substantial in a country that has no free national health program.[150] Property damage and past medical expenses and lost wages are relatively easy to measure. Future medical expenses and future employment income losses are more difficult to determine. To project these losses, expert testimony from doctors and economists is required. An injured homemaker, most often the female spouse who is not employed outside the home and takes care of the home, may claim for the cost of replacement services.

Until recently, it was a universal rule that benefits received by a plaintiff from a "collateral source" may not be used to reduce the defendant's liability for damages. Consequently, a plaintiff who is out of work for a period of time may recover lost wages for that period even if the employer paid the plaintiff wages under a disability or sick leave benefit for all or part of that time. A plaintiff can also recover for medical expenses even if they have been paid by a medical insurance policy or were provided free of charge. While this may seem like overcompensation, one theory behind the rule is that the wrongdoing defendant should not be the beneficiary of the plaintiff's or plaintiff's employer's foresight in purchasing insurance. Today, about half the states have enacted statutes modifying or abolishing the collateral source rule in at least some categories of cases. Thus, the amount of a judgement is reduced by any amount the plaintiff has received from insurance policies or governmental compensation programs such as worker's compensation.[151]

The "Pure" Economic Loss Rule In negligence cases, a plaintiff usually cannot recover for what are called "pure" economic losses — lost profits or other financial opportunities. These may be recoverable for *intentional* torts designed to remedy such losses, such as interference with contractual relations.[152] And even in negligence, even pure economic losses can be recovered if they are the result of personal injury or property damage. For example, wages lost or medical expenses incurred as a result of injury are recoverable, as just discussed. The rationale for the pure economic loss rule is largely based on the fear that there is no good stopping point for cutting off such losses. If an airline flight full of business people is canceled or even delayed because of mechanical difficulty resulting from negligence, one can only imagine how extensive the liability would be if economic losses were recoverable — from lost work time to lost clients to missed deadlines for bids.[153]

---

149 *See generally* DAN B. DOBBS, LAW OF REMEDIES §8.1 (West 1993).

150 *See* Chapter XV, p. 576 (cost of private medical insurance).

151 Some of these statutes have been held unconstitutional. *Denton v. Con-Way Southern Express, Inc.*, 402 S.E.2d 269 (Ga. 1991). The impact on the plaintiff of deducting private medical or disability insurance proceeds from the judgment is often negligible. Most of the deducted amounts would have gone to the plaintiff's medical or disability insurance carriers anyway because of subrogation agreements — agreements under which insureds agree to reimburse their insurance carrier from any recovery they received in order to reimburse the carrier for payments it has made to the insured.

152 *See supra* pp. 421-422.

153 *See Seely v. White Motor Co.*, 403 P.2d 145, 151 (Cal. 1965) (defective truck; recovery of economic loss from loss of use permitted on warranty, but not on negligence or product liability theory). *But see Union Oil Co. v. Oppen*, 501 P.2d 558 (9th Cir. 1974) (major oil company negligently cause oil pollution on the California coast killing many fish; commercial fishermen allowed to recover economic losses.)

Non-Economic Loss The largest component of non-economic loss is "pain and suffering." As the phrase indicates, this category of damages is designed to compensate the plaintiff for the conscious physical pain and mental suffering involved with physical injury. Not only physical pain, but mental anguish over disfigurement or (in some states) shorter life expectancy and other consequences of the injury are recoverable. Also included within pain and suffering are loss-of-enjoyment-in-life damages, such as the inability without pain or complete inability to have sex, play the violin, jog or any other customary activity that gave the victim pleasure in life before the injury. It is often difficult to place a dollar value on these losses and it is thought that this amount is best evaluated by a jury.

An interesting limit on damages is applied in most "wrongful pregnancy" cases, where there is negligent sterilization of a woman by her doctor. Most such cases that permit recovery allow for "direct" expenses to be recovered — expenses of pregnancy, lost wages, medical expenses and even pain and suffering — but deny recovery for the expenses of raising a normal child. The rationale is that the intangible emotional benefits of having a child offset these expenses.[154]

2. Punitive Damages

a. Nature of Award and Grounds

Punitive damages are awarded only for particularly egregious behavior and are designed to punish the tortfeasor and deter a repetition of that conduct.[155] They are usually awarded in addition to compensatory damages, though some jurisdiction permit an award of punitive damages despite the absence of compensatory damages. For a punitive damage award, the plaintiff generally must prove either an intentional tort or, in some jurisdictions, reckless, willful or wanton behavior. The size of punitive damage awards is usually determined by a jury, though it is subject to review by the judge. Punitive damages are typically awarded in intentional tort cases, but have also been awarded in some products liability actions where the manufacturer knew of a defect in its product and the potential for serious injury and death, and yet made a conscious decision not to correct the defect. For example, in *Grimshaw v. Ford Motor Co.*,[156] a woman was badly burned when the car she was riding in burst into flames when it was struck in the rear end. Evidence introduced at the trial showed that the defendant was aware of the defect before the car was introduced on the market, but chose not to remedy the defect. The jury awarded the plaintiff $2,500,000 in compensatory damages and $125,000,000 in punitive damages. This amount was later reduced to $3,500,000 by the court because of the gross disparity between the compensatory and punitive damages.

Despite popular belief to the contrary based on the publicity given to punitive awards, punitive damages are somewhat of a rarity. For example, in Cook County (which includes the City of Chicago), the number of punitive damage awards per year averaged 1.8 during the 1960s and 1970s and 2.8 per year during 1980-1984. During the entire 25-year period of 1960-1984, only 50 punitive damage awards were made. San Francisco averaged even fewer: 0.2 awards per year from 1960 to 1980, 1.2 per year from 1980 to 1984, and an overall total of 10 over the 25 years. Also contrary to popular

---

154 *See Rouse v. Wesley*, 494 N.W.2d 7 (Mich.App. 1992). *But see Lovelace Medical Center v. Mendez*, 805 P.2d 603 (N.M. 1991) (full costs of rasing child not offset by intangible emotional benefits; also rejecting defense argument that the plaintiffs should have mitigated their damages by having an abortion).

155 *See generally* DOBBS, *supra* note 149, §3.11.

156 174 Cal. Rptr. 348 (Cal.App. 1981).

belief, the amounts of punitive awards have not "skyrocketed" as some have asserted. Awards have increased, but have obviously not reached the height most assume. In the same 25-year period, the average punitive damage award in Cook County increased from $1,000 to $43,000 and the average San Francisco award increased from $17,000 to $63,000.[157]

b. Constitutional Objections

In recent years, the Supreme Court has become sensitive to constitutional objections to punitive damage awards. It has rejected the notion that such awards violate the Amendment's prohibition on excessive fines, holding that that Amendment does not apply to suits between private parties.[158] However, it has held that awards are subject to scrutiny under the due process clause. The due process objection can apply either to the procedure used in arriving at the amount of the award or to the amount itself.

Procedure The Court held in *Pacific Mutual Life Insurance Co. v. Haslip*[159] that due process requires that the jury be given specific standards as the grounds for awarding punitive damages and the amount, but it upheld the award in that case. *Haslip* was a suit against an insurance company for bad faith denial of medical insurance coverage. The Court pointed out that evidence of the defendant company's wealth was excluded from evidence, that jury instructions gave guidance as to the nature and function of punitive damages, and that both the trial and appellate courts had supervisory power to revise such awards. Judicial supervision is also required. In *Honda Motor Co., Ltd. v. Oberg*,[160] the Court stuck down an Oregon constitutional provision that prohibited any judicial review of a jury's punitive damages award unless there was a complete absence of evidence to support it.

Amount In the *Haslip* case above, the Court approved an award of $800,000 punitive damages and $200,000 compensatory damages. This was a 4:1 ratio of punitive to compensatory damages and a 200:1 ratio of punitive damages to out-of-pocket expenses. As such, it was much in excess of the criminal fine that the state could have imposed for insurance fraud. The Court indicated that such a ratio "may be close to the line of constitutional propriety." However, in a 1993 case, a plurality of the Court affirmed a judgment of $10 million in punitive and $19,000 in compensatory damages for a ratio of 526:1 in a slander of title case.[161]

The Court finally reversed an award on this basis in *BMW v. Gore*.[162] *Gore* holds that such awards may not be "grossly excessive" in relation to the state's "legitimate

---

157 MARK A. PETERSON, CIVIL JURIES IN THE 1980S: TRENDS IN JURY TRIALS AND VERDICTS IN CALIFORNIA AND COOK COUNTY, ILLINOIS 12 (Rand Corp. 1987), as discussed in Michael T. Saks, *Do We Really Know Anything About the Behavior of the Tort Litigation System—and Why Not?* 140 U.PA.L.REV., 1147, 1254-1258 (1992).

158 *Browning-Ferris Industries of Vt., Inc. v. Kelco Disposal, Inc.*, 492 U.S. 257 (1989). The excessive fines clause does apply to civil forfeiture actions brought by the government. *See* Chapter VIII, p. 301.

159 499 U.S. 1 (1991).

160 512 U.S. 415 (1994).

161 *TXO Productions v. Alliance Resources Corp.*, 509 U.S. 443 (1993). Slander of title is an intentional tort in which the plaintiff owner of property suffers damages (usually in the form of loss of business) because the defendant has in bad faith cast doubt on the plaintiff's title to property. A colorful opinion by an eccentric West Virginia Supreme Court Justice approved the award and divided punitive damages cases into those involving "really mean defendants," "really stupid defendants," and "really stupid defendant who could have caused great harm by their actions but who actually caused minimal harm." *See TXO Productions v. Alliance Resource Corp.*, 419 S.E.2d 870 (W.Va. 1992).

162 517 U.S. 559 (1996).

interests" in punishing unlawful conduct and deterring its repetition. *Gore* involved BMW's practice of repainting cars damaged in transit and then selling them as new cars without telling the purchaser that the car had been damaged and repainted. The award must be judged by the application of three "considerations": (1) the degree of reprehensibility of the defendant's conduct, (2) the disparity between the harm or potential harm suffered by the plaintiff and the award amount and (3) the disparity between the punitive damage award and other civil and criminal penalties authorized by state law. In striking down the award in *Gore*, the Court determined on the facts of *Gore* that the damage inflicted was purely economic and in the amount of only $4,000, that the $2 million award was 500 times actual damages and that it was greatly in excess of the $2,000 fine and penalties imposed by the state for similar conduct. The Court also noted that in some states, BMW's policy was legal. This was relevant to the amount because a state's "legitimate interests" in punitive damages awards do not extend to seeking to affect conduct in other States.

3. Wrongful Death and Survival Actions

At common law, a plaintiff's claim expired on the death of the plaintiff. Thus, it was, as some said, "cheaper to kill than to maim." To counter this rather harsh common law rule, most states have enacted statutory modifications providing for "wrongful death" claims and "survival" actions to be prosecuted beyond death by certain designated relatives.[163]

Wrongful Death Claims Wrongful death statutes generally provide that the entity or person who would have been liable had the victim not died continues to be liable despite that death. Only certain "heirs at law" of the victim can sue — those who according to statute would inherit from the deceased should the deceased die intestate, i.e., without a will. Usually, those heirs at law are the spouse, children and parents of the deceased.[164] The damages that may be recovered are the damages suffered by the heirs at law, not those suffered by the deceased before death. This would include economic losses, such as medical bills and loss of support in the form of income the deceased would have received. It also includes non-economic damages, such as emotional loss in the form of loss of companionship. Because the measure of damages is the effect on the surviving plaintiff, it can vary considerably depending on how significant the deceased was, actually or potentially, in the life of the plaintiff. Thus, a 12-year-old girl who loses her mother will be awarded considerably more than the adult brother of the deceased who has been out communication with the deceased for years.

A wrongful death claim exists only if the deceased would have had a claim had death not ensued, so claims are subject to all the various defenses applicable to live victims. Most commonly, the issue is the contributory negligence of the deceased.

Survival Actions All states have enacted survival statutes. Unlike wrongful death statutes which permit recovery of losses suffered by surviving relatives, these statutes provide for the *estate* of the deceased person to recover damages for losses the *deceased* suffered before dying. This includes all the economic and non-economic damages outlined above that a live plaintiff can recover, including pain and suffering the deceased experienced before death. The rationale of survival statutes is that it is

---

163 In at least one instance, a wrongful death claim was created by judicial decision, though that decision was inspired by enactment of wrongful death statutes. *See Moragne v.* States Marine Lines, Inc., 398 U.S. 375 (1970), discussed in Chapter II, p. 59.

164 This is so even if there was a will. Intestate succession is discussed in Chapter XIII, p. 471.

only fair for the estate of the deceased to recover the amount the deceased would have had, had death not intervened. Some states have gone further than this and allow recovery for what the estate of the deceased would have been had the deceased died a natural death after a normal life span.

4. Specific Relief

In situations where monetary damages are inadequate to remedy a civil wrong, a court may instead grant specific relief rather than money damages. Injunctions are commonly granted in trespass cases or to "abate" a nuisance.[165] Otherwise injunctions will be awarded only when monetary damages are difficult to fix. However, an action for replevin for recovery of property is commonly used as a remedy to repossess personal property pledged as security.[166]

E. Administration of the Tort System of Compensation

1. The Role of Liability Insurance

Most potential defendants purchase liability insurance under which an insurance company agrees to pay for losses for which the insured may be held liable, up to a given policy limit. Without tort liability, insurance would not be needed. But just as clearly, without insurance coverage, tort liability would largely be unavailing, as few would have assets sufficient to pay judgments.[167]

Spreading Costs Insurance coverage provides a way to spread the costs of accidents and other injuries over the entire society. The tort system shifts costs to defendants, and insurance further shifts and spreads the loss over all in society when prospective defendants pass on the cost of the insurance premiums by raising the price of the products and services they sell. Viewed broadly then, the expenses of accidents are just one of the costs of living in an industrialized society. Since we all reap the benefits of having that kind of society, it is fair that we all share its costs.

Duty to Defend Clauses As important as the insurance company's obligation to pay liability is its "duty to defend" — its obligation to provide the insured with legal representation in defending any lawsuit for liability insured under the contract. Disputes arise over the duty to defend, mainly over the question of whether the claims made are for liability that is covered under the policy. The general rule is that if *any* of the claims made are for a liability compensable under the policy, then the insurance company must defend the entire suit.[168] Because the insurance company is in charge of the defense of the lawsuit, the presence of insurance increases the number of out-of-court settlements. While individual defendants' pride may cause them to balk at settling a case by paying the plaintiff something on the claim, insurance companies look at it as a simple business question of whether the risk of losing plus the costs of defending are greater than the cost of settling. In a dispute between the insured and the insurance company over whether to settle, the company will generally win out because most insurance policies contain a clause that allows the insurance company to settle without the consent of the insured. However, there

---

165 Trespass and nuisance are discussed in Chapter XII, pp. 446-447.

166 *See supra* p. 408 and Chapter XII, p. 393 (repossession through replevin).

167 For more on liability insurance, *see* PROSSER & KEETON, *supra* note 1, §§82-85.

168 *See Maryland Casualty Co. v. Peppers*, 355 N.E.2d 24 (Ill. 1976) (both intentional and unintentional bases of liability were alleged; policy covered only unintentional wrongs, but company had a duty to defend both).

are numerous conflict-of-interest situations that can arise between the company and the insured in the settlement process.[169]

Prevalence of Liability Insurance   The development and widespread use of the automobile have been the catalyst for the widespread use of liability insurance. Whenever a business engages in an activity that might cause serious personal injury, it purchases the requisite insurance. It is common as well for individuals to purchase a comprehensive "homeowner's insurance" policy, a broad policy that insures home owners against loss of their home, but also insures against liability for torts connected with ownership of the property and "off-premises" torts committed by the insured. Most on and off-premises torts covered by liability insurance policies cover only negligent acts and not intentional acts of the insured. Other common types of liability insurance include insurance for landlords and other property owners, medical and legal malpractice and other professional insurance, and commercial liability insurance.

2. The "Crisis" in the Tort Compensation System and Recent Attempts at Reform

The Litigation "Explosion"   In recent years, many have argued that society's burden in absorbing the cost of injuries through insurance has become too great. Led by the insurance industry, objections have been heard most often in the area of medical malpractice cases where the cost of insurance is very high and adds to the already high cost of health care in the United States. In the area of products liability, critics argue, increased awards and numbers of suits have posed a severe impediment to the growth of business and scientific research within the United States. The constant fear of liability makes insuring high risk ventures almost impossible and thwarts the development of new research that developers fear could expose them to liability. They argue that this is the result of easy liability rules, contingent fees for lawyers, the presence of insurance, "runaway juries" and a culture in which everyone with even the hint of injury sues for compensation without thinking twice about it.

Types of Tort Reform Measures   Based on these perceptions and arguments, numerous "tort reform" measures have been pushed through state legislatures. While most of the basic grounds for liability have remained untouched, there have been numerous limits in the amount that can be recovered and other procedural aspects, such as modification of joint and several liability, modification or elimination of the collateral source rule, limits on recoveries of both compensatory and punitive damages and regulation of attorney contingent fees. In 1997, Congress debated a "Products Liability Reform Act" that would establish uniform laws and procedures for resolving and compensating parties injured by defective products that would be generally much more restrictive that the law existing in the states now.[170] A Model Punitive Damages Act was adopted in 1996 by the National Conference of Commissioners on Uniform State Laws that would, if adopted, further restrict punitive damage awards. While the Act largely codifies current law on the subject as set out in the *BMW v. Gore* case, it would change the law in most states by requiring a

---

169 *See Merritt v. Reserve Insurance Co.*, 110 Cal.Rptr. 511 (Cal.App. 1973) (discussing conflicts).

170 Products Liability Reform Act, Senate Report No. 105-32, 105th Cong. 1st Sess. (1997), For the reader interested in the arguments on both sides of the issue on the need for and advisability of such reforms, the majority reports and minority statement set out much of the arguments and data.

heightened standard of "clear and convincing" evidence that the defendant "maliciously injured" the plaintiff.[171]

Validity of Assumptions About Tort Litigation Despite these enactments and proposals, decisions on reforms are being made without any solid information about how the tort system of compensation works and what needs fixing. An article surveying studies about the tort litigation system demonstrates that what everyone assumes is the case is not necessarily the true state of things. The article concludes that there is much about the tort system that is simply unknown, but the data that exist undercut the popular conceptions about it.[172] As for the complaint of a "litigation explosion" and the propensity of Americans to "sue at the drop of a hat," the evidence shows that tort filings have actually decreased in the last 7 years and that, barring automobile accident cases, only a tiny fraction of accidental deaths and injuries become claims for compensation. Studies further show that most cases filed are settled and on average these settlements undercompensate plaintiffs.[173] In medical malpractice, studies consistently show that only a small percentage who receive seriously unsatisfactory medical care sue and plaintiffs win such suits only 30% of the time.[174] As for "runaway" juries, as discussed in Chapter III, in the great majority of cases that are tried, the extent of disagreement between judge and jury on amount of recovery is not that great. The "problems" with punitive damages have already been discussed: such awards are infrequent and modest in amount.[175]

Most studies conclude that there is a problem with the cost of the tort litigation and with the fact that it undercompensates most successful litigants and does not compensate at all the vast majority of people with deserving claims. But the tort reform packages that have been enacted attack the perception of "too many suits and runaway juries" rather than seeking to address what should be the focus of such reform — how to compensate deserving injured people more fairly and more efficiently.[176]

3. Substitutes for Tort Recovery

Workers' Compensation A relationship with enormous potential for tort litigation is the employer-employee relationship. For years, however, strict enforcement of contributory negligence, assumption of the risk and the "fellow servant" rule[177] kept the chances of recovery low. Even cases of clear liability were difficult to litigate against the superior legal resources of the employer and in any event the litigation

---

171 *See* Model Punitive Damages Act, 14 UNIF.LAWS ANN. 49 (Supp. 1998).

172 *See generally* Saks, *supra* note 157.

173 An in-depth study completed by the Rand Corporation in 1991 indicates that only about 10% of accident victims in the study sought some form of compensation. While 7% of these did so by contacting an attorney, only 4% actually hired the attorney and only 2% filed suit. DEBORAH R. HENSLER ET AL., COMPENSATION FOR ACCIDENTAL INJURIES IN THE UNITED STATES 121-22 (Rand Corp. 1991).

174 In a 1990 study, researchers examined the cases of a group of patients whom medical experts determined were subjected to seriously deficient medical care. Of them, 26% did nothing, 46% changed doctors, 25% complained directly to the doctor and 9% contacted a lawyer, but none actually filed suit. Marylynn L. May & Daniel B. Stengel, *Who Sues Their Doctors? How Patients Handle Medical Grievances*, 24 Law & Soc'y Rev. 105, 107-108 (1990).

175 *See supra*, p. 431.

176 A strong critic of the existing tort system of compensation evan makes this point and agrees that the Reagan-Bush administration initiatives to "reform" the tort system have been "one-sided." Stephen D. Surgarman, *Doctor No*, 58 U. CHI. L. REV. 1499, 1513 (1991) (reviewing PAUL C. WEILER, MEDICAL MALPRACTICE ON TRIAL (1991).

177 Under this rule, if the immediate cause of an injury at work was the action or omission of a fellow employee, the employer could not be sued. *See Priestley v. Fowler*, 150 Eng. Rep. 1030 (Ex. 1837).

process consumed years before the injured worker would actually receive any money. As a result, states began to pass "workers' compensation" acts at the turn of the 20th century.[178]   These laws set up an employer-financed administrative system for compensating work-related injuries without the need for the worker to prove fault. The amounts paid are limited to wage loss and medical expenses, with no provision for pain and suffering, punitive damages or other elements of damages recoverable in tort. The remedy is exclusive of any tort remedy against the employer that might otherwise arise out of the employment relationship.   The advantage of worker compensation awards to the employee is that money is paid quickly shortly after the injury — when it is most needed — and recovery is assured without any need to show fault. The advantage of worker compensation to employers is that the costs of industrial accidents are made certain and predictable.[179]

No-Fault Automobile Insurance Systems   The no-fault concept has been applied as well to automobile accidents, the most numerous tort cases in the courts. About half the states have laws that provide that, instead of proving fault and collecting damages from the *other* party's insurance company, all parties involved in an accident are compensated by *their own* insurance company. This eliminates the need for litigation to gain compensation for most traffic accidents — litigation that often did little more than shuttle money back and forth between insurance companies, pursuant to subrogation agreements.[180]

Most no-fault plans allow an injured motorist to receive payment of medical costs and lost wages caused by injury in an automobile accident and for any property damage.   These amounts reflect only economic compensatory damages.   Non-economic damages, such as pain and suffering, are not allowed for most ordinary injuries. However, there is an exception for injuries that result in death or serious disfigurement or permanent impairment of bodily functions. For those, the traditional tort remedies are available against the defendant directly as they existed before. No-fault statutory schemes have been challenged as unconstitutional in several states, but have generally been upheld.[181]

No-Fault Tort Systems?   Florida and Virginia have tried to apply the no-fault concept to babies who suffer neurological damage during delivery. Congress has done the same with regard to injuries resulting from vaccinations. However, there is disenchantment with no-fault systems for various reasons, including their high cost

---

178 For a more detailed discussion of Worker's Compensation, *see* MARK A. ROTHSTEIN ET AL., EMPLOYMENT LAW §§7.1 *et seq.* §§10.6 *et seq* .(West 1994) and JACK B. HOOD, BENJAMIN A HARDY, JR., & HAROLD S. LEWIS, JR., WORKER'S COMPENSATION AND EMPLOYEE PROTECTION LAWS IN A NUTSHELL 1-140 (West 1990).

179 The constitutionality of worker's compensation systems was upheld in *New York Central R.R. v. White*, 243 U.S. 188 (1917). Within in 3 years of the *White* decision, all but 8 states had adopted workers' compensation laws. For an account of the interesting history of workers' compensation, *see* Richard A. Epstein, *The Historical Origins and Economic Structure of Workers' Compensation Law*, 16 GA. L. REV. 775 (1982).

180 An essential ingredient for the success of a no-fault system, however, is that automobile insurance coverage be mandatory. Subrogation agreements were discussed supra note 151.

181 The basis for attack has generally been equal protection or due process. However, when the subject of regulation is economics, welfare and business and does not involve invidious discrimination or infringement on a fundamental right, all that is needed is a rational basis to uphold it. *See* Chapter IX, pp. 333-334. The first major decision upholding the constitutionality of a no-fault law was *Pinnick v. Cleary*, 271 N.E.2d 592 (Mass. 1971). In addition to discussing the various constitutional objections, the case outlines in detail the operation of Massachusetts's no-fault law.

and workability in an area as complicated as injuries from medical treatment, especially given the greater number of claims such a system would entail.[182]

---

182 *See and compare* MAXWELL J. MEHLMAN, SAYING "NO" TO NO-FAULT: WHAT THE HARVARD MEDICAL MALPRACTICE STUDY MEANS FOR MEDICAL MALPRACTICE REFORM (1991) (costs would be greater than the current tort system) *with* William G. Johnson et al., *The Economic Consequences of Medical Accidents*, 267 J. Am. Med. Assoc. 2487 (1992) (costs would not be significantly costlier than tort system).

CHAPTER XII

PROPERTY LAW

The chapter is devoted to discussing property in the United States and the legal forms it takes. Included will be discussions of real and personal property of all kinds, including the basics of intellectual property. Also discussed will be issues of property taxation, zoning and other land use restrictions, government takings of property for public purposes, and mortgages and other security interests in property. To provide a practical context for understanding property law as applied, aspects of real estate purchase transactions and landlord-tenant relations will be explored, as well as more recent forms of home ownership, such as condominiums and cooperatives. Gifts, testamentary transfers and trusts are also discussed.

A. Nature and Forms of Property

The Nature of Property Rights Most people think of property as an object, such as a car or a piece of land. More precisely, property law concerns the rights and obligations of *people with respect to* such objects. The aggregate of such rights and obligations is sometimes analogized to bundle of sticks. Each "stick" can be seen as a specific right: (1) the right to possess, (2) the right to use, (3) the right to exclude others and (4) the right to alienate (sell). The right of possession allows a person to possess property, but does not give that person the right to sell it. For example, a landowner may give another person the right to possess his or her land for a limited time pursuant to a "lease." In effect, the landowner transfers to the other person the "right-to-possession stick," but keeps all the other rights. Once the term of the lease expires, the right to possess expires and the "stick" is returned to the bundle.

A fundamental principle of property conveyance is that an owner generally may not convey a greater interest than that owner has. Thus, in the example of the owner above who leased property, if that owner sells the property, the buyer of the property would still be subject to that lease.

Real and Personal Property The U.S. legal system, like most others, distinguishes between "real property" and "personal property." Real property, also called "realty," is land and the structures built upon it. All other property is personal property or "personalty." These correspond roughly to the civil law notions of immovable and movable property. The manner in which the law views these two types of property varies, especially in regard to transfer or sale. Because of this difference, each will be discussed separately, starting with real property. However, the nature of interests or rights in property discussed in this first section applies generally to both. The examples given relate primarily to real property, but most definitions of interest and rights have their counterpart in personal property. Special features that relate to personal property will be indicated.[1]

B. Defining Interests in Real Property

A person who owns or possesses a piece of real property is said to have an "estate" or an "interest" in the property. From the following outline, it can be seen

---

1 A standard treatise on property law is ROGER A. CUNNINGHAM, WILLIAM B. STOEBUCK & DALE A. WHITMAN, HORNBOOK ON THE LAW OF PROPERTY, 2D ED. (West 1993). *See also* ROGER BERNHARDT, REAL PROPERTY IN A NUTSHELL, 3D ED. (West 1993); BARLOW BURKE, JR., PERSONAL PROPERTY IN A NUTSHELL, 2D ED. (West 1993); RAY A. BROWN, THE LAW OF PERSONAL PROPERTY, 3D ED. (Raushenbush Pub. 1975).

that U.S. property law is very flexible in its ability to define property interests — to allocate the "sticks" in the "bundle." Property interests can be defined in terms of (1) the degree of control the owner of that interest has, (2) the duration of the interest (time), (3) physical space allocated to the owner, and (4) the way the ownership interest is held (single or shared title).

1. Property Interests Defined by Degree of Ownership or Control

Ownership Interests: Fee Simple Absolute The greatest interest in terms of degree of control over the property is called "fee simple absolute" or "fee simple" ownership.[2] The owner of the fee simple estate holds all the possible rights and interests associated with property in a single bundle. The fee simple estate is freely transferable during the life of the owner/holder and can be passed from generation to generation by inheritance. A fee simple estate may thus be transferred by a "deed" or a "will." A deed is a written document that conveys title and ownership, either through sale or gift. A will is a written instrument that passes property upon the death of a person according to the wishes of the deceased.

Fee simple ownership is the most common interest in land. Consequently, the rights, limitations and obligations associated with it will be discussed in more detail in a later section.[3] In addition, sales of fee simple ownership are the most common method by which interests in real estate are transferred, so modern real estate sales transactions will also be discussed.[4]

Possessory Interests in Property: Leases The owner of a property can convey to another person the right to possess the property for a limited period of time. The owner of the property is called the "lessor" or "landlord." The person using the property is called the "lessee" or "tenant." The interest of the tenant is called the "leasehold" and it is generally created by way of a document called a "lease." At the end of the lease term, the right to possess the property returns to the landlord and the tenant's rights are extinguished. During the term of the lease the tenant can transfer or assign the tenant's possessory interests to another or may sublease or sublet the premises. In an assignment, the transferee tenant takes the place of the original tenant. In a sublease situation, the lessee conveys the right of possession to the sub-lessee, but remains liable to the landlord under the lease. Because of this, the original lessee retains the right to intervene and even evict the sub-lessee should the sub-lessee act contrary to the original lessee's interests. The landlord also has a similar right to intervene. Leases between landlords and tenants often restrict the tenant's ability to transfer all or part of the tenant's interest.[5]

The landlord may convey ownership interests in leased land. However, when the property is leased, all the landlord retains is a "reversionary" interest in the property. This means that the possessory rights that the owner-landlord conveyed to the tenant will return to the owner only at the end of the leasehold. Thus, a landlord who sells leased property conveys only this reversionary interest, so the buyer takes the land subject to the lease.

---

2 The holder in fee simple holds the property for the longest period of time — an indefinite period.

3 *See infra* pp. 444-448.

4 *See infra* pp. 451-453.

5 Because many people rent their place of residence in the U.S., modern landlord-tenant law will be addressed later in a separate section. *See infra* pp. 455-457.

Leasing personal property — from cars to heavy equipment — has become an increasingly common substitute for outright ownership, which can entail a greater outlay of money and other burdens. Personal property leases follow the same basic concepts as real property leases. Because of the greater frequency of leasing, the authors of the Uniform Commercial Code have added a new Article 2A that parallels Article 2's regulations of sales of goods.

Use and Access Rights: Easements   An easement is the right to use land owned by another. Easement rights to land are discussed under the heading of limitations on ownership rights.[6]

Splitting Legal and Equitable Title: Trusts   A fee simple owner of property can transfer property into a "trust." The transferor is referred to as the "settlor," "trustor" or "grantor." When this is done, one person, the "trustee," controls and manages the property, while another person, the "beneficiary," is entitled to receive the benefits from the property. The trustee receives "legal title" to the property, but must manage and allocate its benefits according to the terms of the trust agreement. The beneficiary, on the other hand, has the beneficial interest in the property and is generally considered to have "equitable title" to the property.

Trusts are widely used to give someone — often the settlor's children or other relatives — some of the benefits of ownership of property (such as the income from property) without the burdens or rights of such ownership. Because of their widespread use, trusts are discussed in greater detail later in this chapter.[7]

2. Property Interests Defined by Physical Limits

Boundaries of Land   The most common way that interests in real property are defined is by the physical boundaries of the land owned. Thus, interests in land are confined to the physical boundaries of the property in question. Historically, the owner of land was said to possess the space below the surface of the land "to the center of the earth" and the space above the land as well "up to the heavens." However, the invention of the airplane has made ownership of air space infeasible.[8]

Physical Structures on Land   Physical structures located on land, such as buildings, are part of the real property. Included as well are items of personal property that have been affixed to those structures, called "fixtures." Despite the fact that such items of property might otherwise be considered personal property before they became affixed, they become part of the realty when they become fixtures. For example, before being installed, a roll of carpeting is personal property. After that roll of carpeting is cut and tacked down as wall-to-wall carpeting, it becomes a fixture.[9]

Space Inside Buildings: Condominiums   Real property interests are not limited to the ownership of land and buildings, but may also include ownership of space inside a building. A building can be divided into "condominiums" — separate units in a building, each of which is separately owned. The owners own both the space between the interior walls of the unit and a part interest in the building by way of their membership in an association which owns the entire building. Because of the

---

6   *See infra* p. 445.

7   *See infra* pp. 471-473.

8   *See* Chapter XI, p. 407 and note 28, concerning the question of what interference with the airspace above land is considered wrongful.

9   *See, e.g., Dean Vincent, Inc. v. Redisco, Inc.*, 373 P.2d 995 (Or. 1962) (carpeting a fixture where there is "annexation, adaption, and [the] functional intention" for it to be a permanent part of the structure).

increasing popularity of condominiums, they will be discussed in more detail, along with the somewhat similar "cooperative," in a later section of this chapter.[10]

3. Property Interests Defined by Time

Present Indefinite Continuous Ownership   Fee simple ownership is for an indefinite period of time.

Property Interests of Limited Definite Duration   Leasehold interests terminate at the end of the leasehold period. At that point the possessory right which the tenant had "reverts" back to the owner. Commercial leases for business property are almost always leases of a definite duration (sometimes with an option to renew), as are most residential leases.

Interests of Periodic Renewable Duration   Despite the fact that most leases have a definite end date, it is common to have a "periodic" tenancy. Such a tenancy is for a certain period of time, but that period of time automatically renews unless notice is given by either landlord or tenant of an intention to terminate the tenancy. Thus, in a "month-to-month" tenancy, the time period of the tenancy is one month, but each month a new tenancy arises unless notice is given. Many people remain in apartments for years under a month-to-month tenancy arrangement.

Life Estates Terminating Upon Death   A life estate is a possessory property interest that terminates on the death of the estate holder. Upon such death the interest returns to the grantor or goes to another person in accord with the wishes of the grantor as expressed in the instrument that created the life estate. Life estates are usually freely transferable. But the basic principle of property transfer — that a transferor can transfer no greater estate than that possessed — means that the life estate will terminate upon the death of the person who transferred the interest. Thus, life estates have little commercial value. They are often used, however, by elderly parents who sell or give their home to their children while reserving a life estate in themselves so that they may continue to live there until their death.[11]

Future Interests   A future interest is an interest in property that comes into being sometime in the future. The holder of a future interest does not presently possess the property, but only has the right to possess it sometime in the future. Future interests are true property rights in that they are inheritable and generally freely transferable. A simple example of a future interest is the landlord's reversionary interest during a lease, as just described. The landlord's "reversion" presently exists, but does not give the landlord the right to possession of the property until the term of the lease expires. Another example is the remainder interest of the owner of property subject to a "life estate" just discussed.[12]

Discontinuous Periodic Ownership Interests: Time-Share Properties   A "time-share" interest is an ownership in property that grants the owner the right to possession of that property for a specific period of time every year. For instance, an owner may buy a time-share interest in a condominium located at a ski resort for the third week in January every year. Time-share units are usually furnished and managed

---

10 *See infra* pp. 454-455.

11 Today, this arrangement is more likely to be accomplished through a trust, since it provides for more flexibility. *See infra* pp. 471-473.

12 For more information on future interests, see CHARLES I. NELSON AND PETER T. WENDEL, A POSSESSORY ESTATES AND FUTURE INTERESTS PRIMER (West 1996); THOMAS F. BERGIN & PAUL G. HASKELL, PREFACE TO ESTATES IN LAND AND FUTURE INTERESTS, 2D ED. (Foundation 1984).

by the condominium developer. Owners of units often have the right to trade their time share (period of possession) with another owner.[13]

4. Property Interests Defined by the Way the Interest Is Held

Single Ownership   A property interest may be held by one person or entity. Included are natural persons, partnerships, corporations or trusts.[14] Fee simple single ownership gives the person or entity full rights to the entire property for an indefinite period. As such, it is the highest form of property ownership.

Joint Tenancy   In a joint tenancy, owners ("joint tenants") own an undivided, equal portion of the property. A joint tenancy creates "concurrent estates" in more than one person. This means that all the owners have the right to possess and enjoy the entire piece of property. Joint tenants also enjoy the "right of survivorship." In other words, if a joint tenant dies, that tenant's interest in the property does not descend to the tenant's heirs, but is extinguished.[15] As a result, the interests of the surviving joint tenants expand in equal proportions. For example, if three people own a property as joint tenants, and one of the owners dies, the surviving owners will each own an undivided one-half interest in the property. If joint tenants cannot agree about how to manage or use the land, a joint tenancy may be extinguished by court action called a "partition" action. This action may be brought by one of the joint tenants. A partition of the property can result in an actual physical division of the property giving each joint tenant an undivided fee simple interest in a physical portion of the property, or in a court-ordered sale of the entire property, with a division of the proceeds of the sale. If a joint tenant sells that tenant's partial interest in the property, the joint tenancy is severed and it is converted into a tenancy in common, described below.

Tenancy by the Entirety   Tenancy by the entirety refers to the method by which a husband and wife may jointly own property. It is similar to a joint tenancy because when one spouse dies the surviving spouse takes the entire estate in fee simple. However, unlike a joint tenancy, there is no unilateral right to division of the property. Divisions can be made only in a divorce action or by mutual agreement.[16] A major advantage of tenancy by the entirety is that the creditors of an individual spouse cannot reach the entireties property.

Tenancy in Common   A tenancy in common establishes a concurrent estate in land and is similar to a joint tenancy, but tenants in common do not enjoy the right of survivorship. Thus, if a tenant in common dies, that tenant's interest descends to his or her heirs and the tenancy in common continues. When the ownership interest is ambiguous, the law prefers a tenancy in common over a joint tenancy. In general, absent the expressed intent of a grantor to create a joint tenancy, a court will presume that the grantor intended to create a tenancy in common.[17]

---

13 The common law provided for only a limited set of leaseholds. Today, contract law governs creations of interests in land, thus allowing the parties to create whatever interests they want.

14 For a discussion of partnerships and corporations, *see* Chapter XV, pp. 532-551.

15 "Heirs" are the persons who have rights to the property upon the death of the owner. *See infra* pp. 470-471.

16 *See* Chapter XIII, pp. 466-468, for a discussion of property division in divorce actions.

17 Some commentators reason that this presumption is justified because the right of survivorship that would attach to a joint tenancy would have the effect of cutting off the rights of the joint tenant's heirs. However, the law's preference for tenancies in common is probably more historical than rational.

Like real property, personal property can be held by multiple owners by means of the concurrent ownership interests mentioned above. For example, a joint tenancy bank account is useful because it gives the right to survivorship to the other tenant.

C. Rights and Obligations of Owners of Real Property

1. Rights Included in Ownership of Real Property

Right of "Quiet Enjoyment" An owner has the right to possession and control of the property. This right is called a right of "quiet enjoyment" of the premises. This includes the right to exclude trespassers (anyone who comes on land without permission). Multiple owners of real property, such as joint tenants, tenants in common and tenants by the entireties, are entitled to equal and undivided possession of the property. Thus, each owner has the right to possess the whole property unless that possession interferes with the possessory rights of the other owners.[18]

Oil, Gas and Mineral Rights Fee simple ownership of a property includes the ownership of resources both below and above the surface of the land. Not only can the resources themselves be conveyed by the owner, but the right to enter the land and remove these resources may be conveyed separately by the owner. An owner may convey the outright ownership of subsurface resources to another by deed. More commonly, an owner will grant, by means of a lease, the right to remove resources for a limited period of time. Obviously, the process of actually extracting oil, gas or minerals from land can involve a major disruption of the possessory rights to the surface of the land. Thus, an owner who has granted mineral rights to another has substantially reduced the value of the land.

Water Rights As a general rule, landowners have the right to use the water that is located on their property. The terms "riparian rights" (rivers) and "littoral rights" (seas, oceans and lakes) refer to the rights of a landowner with respect to bodies of water bordering on the landowner's property. The nature of water rights in the United States varies depending on whether the property is East or West of the Mississippi River.

The climate east of the Mississippi River is relatively wet and humid, and there are numerous rivers and a high water table. The climate West of the Mississippi River is drier with fewer rivers and a lower water table. East of the Mississippi River there was sufficient water to meet the needs of human consumption, agriculture and manufacturing. Consequently, a rule of riparian rights developed that provides that water be shared equally. No priority is given to the first user of the water. West of the Mississippi River there was often not enough water to satisfy the needs of all property owners in a particular area. As a result, a "prior appropriation" rule developed. Under this rule, the first user of the water was allowed to use all the water he or she needed. Subsequent settlers could not demand that the water be shared. The prior appropriation rule was developed as an incentive to settle the land. It assured the first settlers to arrive that they would not have to worry about later settlers demanding that they share scarce water.

Right to Lateral and Subjacent Support Landowners have a right to the support afforded their land through adjacent or subterranean land. If a person removes either the lateral or subjacent support from another person's property, either through excavation or mining, that person is liable for any damage should the property slide

---

18 The right of an owner to sue another for trespass is discussed in the chapter on torts. *See* Chapter XI, p. 407.

or fall. The liability arising from the removal of lateral or subjacent support is "strict liability" so long as the damaged property was in its natural state. If there is a building or other structure on the property and the weight of that building contributes to the movement of the land, the person who removed the support will only be liable if negligent in the removal of the support.

2. Consensual Limitations on Ownership

Easements An easement is the right to *use* part of another person's land for a specific purpose without actually owning it.[19] For example, a landowner may grant the gas or electric utility company the right to use part of the landowner's property so that the utility company can lay gas pipes or install electric cables. The landowner maintains ownership of the property while the utility company has a right to use the land for the specified purpose. The landowner cannot take any action that would prevent the utility company from using the property. An easement can be perpetual or for a limited period of time. If it is perpetual, the right to use it remains with the easement holder even if the property is sold. However, for this to occur the easement must be recorded. An easement may be terminated by a written agreement between property owner and the easement holder.[20]

Licenses A license is the permission of a landowner to use his or her property in some specific way. A license can be distinguished from an easement in that it is generally revocable by the grantor at any time. An easement cannot be revoked by the grantor without the agreement of the grantee.   Licenses and easements both differ from leases in that they only grant the right to engage in some sort of activity on the land, not the right to possession. Although a license is considered an interest in land,[21] it need not comply with the Statute of Frauds and may therefore be granted orally.[22]

Covenants and Equitable Servitudes "Covenants" and "equitable servitudes" are promises made by landowners with respect to use of their land. These promises usually appear in deeds to the property or in subdivision plans. Covenants may be classified as either affirmative or negative. An affirmative covenant is a promise made by a landowner to do an affirmative act. For example, a promise to pay dues to a homeowners' association is an affirmative covenant. Negative covenants, also known as "equitable servitudes," are promises not to use a piece of property in a certain way. For example, a landowner may promise not to build a house above a certain height. The most common use of covenants is to establish "building and use restrictions" which bind all the homeowners in a neighborhood to a set of rules for building and living in that neighborhood. The building restrictions are established for the purpose of ensuring that all homes in the area are of similar size, quality and esthetic value. A covenant generally "runs with the land." This means that a covenant binds all subsequent landowners.[23]

---

19 *See* STEPHEN A. SIEGEL, A STUDENT'S GUIDE TO EASEMENTS, REAL COVENANTS AND EQUITABLE SERVITUDES (Matthew Bender 1988).

20 In limited situations, an easement may be established "by prescription" through long-standing use or "by necessity," as where the owner of a land-locked parcel must cross other property to gain access.

21 RESTATEMENT OF PROPERTY §512 (1944, 1998) Comment C.

22 *See* Chapter X, p. 371, for a discussion of the Statute of Frauds.

23 One difference between a covenant and an equitable servitude is the remedy. In general, money damages are awarded for breach of a covenant, while breach of an equitable servitude is remedied by an injunction to induce or prevent further action. *See* Chapter VII, pp. 236-239.

At one point in the United States, "racially restrictive covenants" were used to keep homeowners from selling their houses to members of a minority race. The Supreme Court held these invalid as a violation of the equal protection clause of the Constitution in the 1948 case of *Shelley v. Kraemer*.[24]

3. Duties of Owners of Real Property

Nuisance   Every person has a duty to refrain from creating or allowing a "nuisance" to exist on property that person controls. A nuisance is any activity that adversely affects adjacent owners or the general public, such as a factory that releases toxic fumes into the atmosphere.

The most common remedy is for a court to "abate" the nuisance. This means that it grants an injunction ordering the property owner who is creating the nuisance to cease the activity that is interfering with the rights of others. In rare cases, however, the courts have awarded money damages and allowed the nuisance to continue when an injunction would stop a factory from operating thereby causing great detriment to the community through the loss of jobs and revenue.[25] In deciding whether to abate a nuisance, courts balance the importance of the interfering activity against the harm caused by it. What is a nuisance and the extent of its interference are situational. For example, noise and air pollution are expected to be encountered in a large city and are not necessarily unreasonable. On the other hand, a person who lives in the country may reasonably expect quiet and clean air. A factory emitting smoke and noise that is erected near a residence in a rural area is more likely to be considered a nuisance that should be abated.[26]

Owners' Duties to Persons Who Enter the Property   An owner has duties with regard to persons who enter his or her property and may be injured. Traditionally, what duties are owed has been categorized based on the relationship between the person who enters the property and the owner of it. "Invitees" are persons whom the owner has explicitly or implicitly invited to come onto the premises to make purchases or to work there, such as the customers or employees of a business. Since invitees are there for the benefit and profit of the owner, the owner owes the highest duty to them — a duty to protect them from all unreasonable risks. "Slip-and-fall" cases are a common example of lawsuits involving invitees. For example the owner of a store has a duty to promptly clean up any spilled liquids or other hazards in the aisles of the store.[27] "Licensees" are people who enter the property with the owner's permission, but are not there for the profit of the owner, such as party guests. The owner's duty to them is not to protect them from all unreasonable risks of harm, but only to warn them of any risks of injury that the property presents.[28] "Trespassers" generally have not right to be on the owner's property, but even as to them the owner must keep the property free from unreasonable dangers that the trespasser might not

---

24   334 U.S. 1 (1948).

25   *See Boomer v. Atlantic Cement Co.*, 257 N.E.2d 870 (N.Y. 1970).

26   *See Spur Industries, Inc. v. Del E. Webb Development Co.*, 494 P.2d 700 (Ariz. 1972) (feed lot located next to a residential neighborhood, with odor and flies from the feed lot made living in the neighborhood unhealthy; injunction forcing lot to move). For general law on injunctions and other equitable relief, *see* Chapter VII, pp. 237-239.

27   Invitees may include persons other than paying customers. *See Bray v. Kate, Inc.*, 454 N.W.2d 698 (Neb. 1990) (plaintiff can recover for slipping on ice in front of restaurant even though he fell just as he was about to open the door to enter).

28   *Thacker v. J.C. Penny Co.*, 254 F.2d 672 (5th Cir. 1958) (store owner could be liable for actions of child climbing on balcony and falling).

expect. However, the owner has no duty to warn of any hidden dangers. And in any event, the owner of land may not set a trap employing deadly force to repel a trespasser.[29]

Courts have increasingly expressed dissatisfaction with this "trichotomy" approach based on the status of the person entering the property. The main reason has been the difficulty of classifying the injured persons. Nearly one half of all jurisdictions have either abandoned or substantially modified the trichotomy approach in favor of a unified analysis based on reasonableness of the owner's action or inaction in light of all the surrounding circumstances.[30]

A special duty applies to owners of hotels or motels. Innkeepers have had a special duty to protect guests under the common law from the time of the Middle Ages. This duty extends to protection against intentional actions of third parties under some circumstances. Thus, an innkeeper can be held liable for injuries to guests caused by robbers who broke into the guests' room, shot the husband, caused the wife emotional distress and robbed them, where there was evidence that a prudent innkeeper would have installed better doors and locks.[31]

Liability of Owners and Creditors for Environmental Cleanups Several state and federal laws mandate the clean up of hazardous waste, and some impose the costs of the cleanup on those landowners or those involved with the contamination of the property. An example is the federal Comprehensive Environmental Response Compensation and Liability Act (CERCLA).[32] Under CERCLA, any present or past owner of contaminated property is liable for the costs incurred in the cleanup of hazardous waste on the property. There is, however, a defense for subsequent purchasers of contaminated property who were ignorant of the contamination when they purchased the property. This defense is only available to those purchasers who have made adequate inquiries about the ownership and uses of the land.[33]

4. Property Taxes on Ownership of Real Property

Most states and municipalities impose taxes on real property. These local taxes are used to support community services and are due at least once every year. They are based on the value of the property as determined by a municipal tax assessor, so they are often called "*ad valorem*" taxes. To determine the amount of the tax, the "assessed value" of the property is multiplied by the tax rate, called the "millage rate" because it is expressed in "mills."[34] The millage rate is usually determined by community vote in general elections. The rate of property tax differs significantly from state to state depending on how much funding for local governmental functions is derived from property taxes. Such taxes can cost homeowners anywhere from a few hundred to several thousand dollars a year depending on the region of the country and the value of the homes in the area. Tax revenues generally fund education, parks, police and fire departments and other city services. The largest part of local property taxes generally goes to fund the local public school system.

---

29 *See Katko v. Briney*, 183 N.W.2d 657 (Iowa 1971) (trespasser on unoccupied house injured by trap with gun set by owner may recover for injuries).

30 North Carolina most recently did so in an opinion that reviews the entire area, the competing authorities and difficulties with the old approach. *Nelson v. Freeland*, 507 S.E.2d 882 (1998).

31 *Kveragas v. Scottish Inns*, 733 F.2d 409 (6th Cir. 1984) (applying Tennessee law).

32 42 U.S.C.A. §§9601-9675.

33 *See generally* KATHRYN R. HEIDT, ENVIRONMENTAL OBLIGATIONS IN BANKRUPTCY (West 1993, 1998).

34 A "mill" is one tenth of a cent.

Since the tax is based on the value of the real property in a given locale, richer communities often have both a lower millage rate and more money to spend on their public schools than poorer communities. The result can be inferior educational opportunities for children in poor communities. The Supreme Court has rejected constitutional challenges to the unequal educational opportunities that result.[35] However, some state courts have held such systems for financing public schools unconstitutional as discriminatory under their own state constitutions.[36]

D. Government Control Over Real Property

1. Regulating Land Use

Some land use regulation occurs at the federal level. For example, there are federal regulations designed to preserve the quality of the environment. But the majority of land use regulation is by local governments.[37] Although the right to regulate land is considered to be among those "reserved" by the states, states generally delegate most of their regulatory power to local municipal governments. However, some states have adopted comprehensive land use management acts in order to assure that local regulation is consistent with statewide planning goals.[38]

Zoning Zoning is the principal means of land use regulation in America today. A typical municipal zoning ordinance divides the municipality into "zones." The ordinance specifies which uses are permitted in each zone and which uses are prohibited there. For example, one zone may be designated as a "single family housing" zone, while another zone might be designated as an "industrial use" zone. This means that a factory may not be built in the single family housing zone and that a residence may not be built in an industrial zone. Zoning ordinances have been held to be a constitutionally valid use of the state's authority to regulate land use as long as they promote the public, health, safety, morals and general welfare.[39]

Building Requirements In most areas of the country, a building permit is needed before beginning any construction or demolition of structures on land. Plans must be submitted and methods of construction must comply with complex regulations. All these are local regulations imposed by counties and cities. However, most all of them are based on a model code promulgated by the Building Officials and Code Administrators International, Inc. (BOCA). There is variation depending on the special needs of particular areas. For example, earthquake-resistant construction methods and design are required in California and hurricane-resistant methods are required in Florida.

Subdivision Regulation Subdivision regulation is directed at developers who subdivide large tracts of land into smaller lots. The developer is usually required to submit a plan showing how a subdivision will connect with existing utilities and streets. In addition, the developer may be required by the municipality to "dedicate" (donate) a part of the land for a community purpose, such as for a school or a park. However, as indicated below when regulatory takings are discussed, there are some limits to what state and local governments can require.

---

35 *San Antonio Independent School District v. Rodriguez*, 411 U.S. 1 (1973) (rejecting equal protection challenge under 14th Amendment).

36 *See, e.g., Serrano v. Priest*, 557 P.2d 929 (Cal. 1976) (school financing by property taxes invalid under the equal protection clause of California's constitution).

37 *See generally* DANIEL R. MANDELKER, LAND USE LAW, 3D ED. (Lexis 1993, 1996).

38 *See, e.g.*, Oregon's statute, Ore.Rev.Stat. §§197.005-197.860, passed in 1991.

39 *Village of Euclid v. Amber Realty Co.*, 272 U.S. 365 (1926).

2. Governmental Takings of Land: Eminent Domain and Condemnation

The government's power to take private property for public use is known as the power of "eminent domain." The government most often exercises its power of eminent domain to "condemn" property needed for public improvements, such as for the construction of a highway or a park. However, the 5th Amendment's "takings" clause provides that "private property [may not] be taken for public use, without just compensation."[40] This means that in every case of condemnation, the government must show that the "taking" of property is for a public purpose *and* it must pay the owner adequate compensation.

The "Public Purpose" Requirement If a court finds that the government's taking of private property is not for a public purpose, it will strike down the government's action and may require the property to be returned. However, the public purpose requirement is generally easy to meet. Often it will be apparent from the nature of the project, such as construction of a highway or government building. Public purposes less direct or obvious have also been approved. In one unusual case, a state supreme court found that a city's condemnation of an entire neighborhood to allow the construction of a privately-owned factory was for a public purpose since the factory would create new jobs and reduce unemployment in a depressed area.[41] And the United States Supreme Court recently held that Hawaii's taking of the property of certain landlords and transferring that property in fee simple to their tenants was for a public purpose. The Court reasoned that, because most of Hawaii's land was controlled by a small group of landowners, it was in the public's interest to have real estate more widely distributed.[42]

The "Just Compensation" Requirement The "just compensation" requirement has as one of its primary purposes barring the government "from forcing some people alone to bear public expenses which, in all fairness and justice, should be borne by the public as a whole."[43] By requiring that the government pay for what it takes, the burden of public improvements is spread to all taxpayers.

3. Regulatory "Takings"

Generally the government need not compensate a property owner for any loss in the value of land that is caused by changes in *zoning* or other forms of *regulation*. Otherwise, the government would have to compensate many people almost every time it passed a law. However, the Supreme Court has held that it is possible for a regulation to be so extensive that it constitutes a compensable "taking" under the 5th Amendment. This type of taking, where the government does not explicitly invoke its power of eminent domain, is known as a "regulatory taking."[44] When property owners sue contending that government regulation of their property constitutes a taking, the suit is referred to as an action for "inverse condemnation." The condemnation is "inverse" because in essence the property owners are seeking to

---

40 Although the 5th Amendment technically only applies to the federal government, this protection for "takings" applies equally to state and local governments because it has been "incorporated" against the states through the due process clause of the 14th Amendment. *See* Chapter VIII, p. 271.

41 *See Poletown Neighborhood Council v. City of Detroit*, 304 N.W.2d 455 (Mich. 1981).

42 *Hawaii Housing Authority v. Midkiff*, 467 U.S. 229 (1984). The facts of this case are unusual given Hawaii's unique land ownership problem.

43 *Armstrong v. United States*, 364 U.S. 40 (1960).

44 *See generally, Lucas v. South Carolina Costal Council*, 505 U.S. 1003 (1992) (discussion of regulatory takings).

force the government to condemn the property.

The problem with regulatory takings is how to tell when restrictions on the use of property constitute a taking. The general rule that has been developed through a series of U.S. Supreme Court cases is that "land use regulation can effect a taking if it does not substantially advance legitimate state interests, or denies an owner viable use of his land."[45] This means that the government can impose serious limitations on property owners' rights and yet the action will not be deemed a taking if it appropriately advances state interests. Two cases with similar facts demonstrate this. In an early case, *Pennsylvania Coal Co. v. Mahon*,[46] a coal company sold land, but retained its mineral rights to mine coal at a later time. Thereafter a state law prohibited mining beneath the surface of a residence. The Supreme Court held that the law effected a taking that must be compensated since it seriously diminished the value of the company's interest in the coal deposits. However, in *Keystone Bituminous Coal Association v. DeDenedictis*,[47] the Court held that a similar statute did not constitute a compensable taking of the coal company's property rights, because the state was acting to protect the owners of buildings located on the surface of the land above the coal deposits.

In a pair of recent cases, the Court has shown an increased willingness to scrutinize regulatory laws or administrative decisions that affect property rights. In *Nollan v. California Coastal Commission*,[48] the owner of beachfront property sought a building permit to demolish a house and construct a larger one in its place. The Commission was inclined to grant the permit, but required in exchange that the owner give a public easement across his property in order to allow the public to walk between two public beach areas that were on each side of the owner's property. The asserted connection of the easement to the grant of building permit was that the larger house the owner planned to build would block the public view of the ocean. Although the Court agreed that this was a legitimate state interest, it thought that there was no reasonable connection between simply *viewing* the ocean and granting a public easement all the way across the owner's property. Requiring that the owner agree to this degree of interference with his property to get his permit, the Court maintained, converted the otherwise valid regulation into "an out-and-out plan of extortion."

In a more recent case, *Dolan v. City of Tigard*,[49] the owner of a commercial property wished to expand her building and add a paved parking lot, so she applied for a permit from her city. The city required in return that the owner deed a portion of the property to the city for use as a "public greenway" along an adjoining creek and that the owner grant a pedestrian and bicycle pathway easement across a portion of the property. The Court struck down these conditions. In the process, it established a new test which required that the city demonstrate "rough proportionality" between the nature and extent of the harm caused by the owner's new land use and the conditions the city wished to require. The city must make "some sort of individualized determination" of the connection. On the facts of *Dolan*, the owner *could* be required to keep her land along the creek a "greenway" since that would assist in preventing

---

45 *Keystone Bituminous Coal Association v. De Denedicts*, 480 U.S. 470 (1987).
46 260 U.S. 393 (1922).
47 *See supra*, note 34.
48 483 U.S. 825 (1987).
49 512 U.S. 374 (1994).

the increased danger of flooding from water running off the owner's new parking lot. But the Court could find no reason why the city had to *own* that greenway. As for the bicycle and pedestrian easement, the Court admitted that the property owner's expanded store would create more traffic, but found that the city's generalized conclusion that the easement "could offset some of the traffic demand" did not comply with the required "individualized determination."

It should be kept in mind that none of the regulatory takings cases prevents the governments involved from doing exactly what they wished to do with the owners' property. They could simply condemn the property, take possession of it and use it for the stated purposes. However, if they do so, they must pay compensation to the owner. In the past, local governments with limited budgets have often resorted to attaching conditions to building or use permits as an economical way to make public improvements that benefit the community. Clearly, *Nollan* and *Dolan* will make that more difficult in the future.

E. Real Estate Purchase Transactions

The steps in a typical real estate residential purchase are outlined here. Commercial real estate transactions follow much the same process except that financing may be more complicated.[50]

1. The Purchase Contract

An interested buyer will make a written offer in the form of a proposed agreement. The Statute of Frauds requires that all agreements related to real estate be in writing.[51] The modern purchase agreement is governed by the same rules as is any other contract: there must be offer, acceptance and consideration. Once the seller and the purchaser have agreed on the terms and signed the agreement, the agreement becomes a binding legal contract. After the purchaser has had an opportunity to investigate the condition of the property, research the status of the title of the property, and obtain financing, then the parties arrange for the "closing" or "settlement" of the sale. The closing is the final step in the sale when the title of the property (deed) is given by the seller to the purchaser in exchange for the balance of the money due the seller.

2. Financing

Because of the amount of money involved in the purchase of real estate, most buyers have to seek financing from a third party such as a bank, or less frequently, arrange for installment payments with the seller.[52] If the buyer obtains a mortgage loan, the buyer pays the seller a down payment, usually 10 to 20 percent of the purchase price. The balance is paid to the seller from the proceeds of the buyer's loan from the bank. The seller thereby receives the entire purchase price and conveys the deed to the buyer. The buyer uses the purchased property as security for the loan and makes regular payments to the bank until the loan is repaid. The three principal documents signed at the closing are (1) the deed, which the seller signs conveying the title of the property to the purchaser, (2) the note, which is the purchaser's promise

---

50 For more information, *see* GRANT S. NELSON & DALE A. WHITMAN, LAND TRANSACTIONS AND FINANCE, 3D ED. (West 1998); (D. BARLOW BURKE, JR., REAL ESTATE TRANSACTIONS: EXAMPLES AND EXPLANATIONS, 2D ED. (Aspen 1999).

51 *See* Chapter X, p. 371, for a discussion of the Statute of Frauds.

52 The document used when installment payments are made is generally referred to as a "land contract." For a fuller discussion of these and other methods of financing real estate transactions, *see* GRANT S. NELSON & DALE A. WHITMAN, HORNBOOK ON REAL ESTATE FINANCE LAW (West 1994).

to pay the loan back to the bank, and (3) the mortgage which pledges the property as collateral for repayment of the note.

The buyer is given the deed which grants legal title to the property. However, as long as there is an outstanding balance on the loan, any ownership interest granted is subject to the bank's right to "foreclose" on the mortgage and take possession of the property if the purchaser fails to make payments. In a foreclosure action, the bank may have the property sold at a "sheriff's sale" and have the proceeds used to pay off the loan. This is generally subject to a statutory right of the purchaser to "redeem" the property up to a certain time after the sheriff's sale — to get the property back by paying all past due payments.[53]

3. Merchantable or Marketable Title

The seller must deliver "marketable" title upon closing the sale or the buyer has the right to rescind the purchase contract. In order to provide a means by which a buyer can be certain that no one else has any claim to a property, all states have enacted "recording statutes." Under these statutes, when a buyer receives a deed he may record the document at a governmental office, usually at the office of the "register of deeds." This recording gives "notice" to the world that the purchaser is now the owner of the property. The records in which the deeds are recorded also show the presence of liens, mortgages and covenants to which the property is subject.

The system for determining whether a seller has good title to a property has changed over the years. Originally the purchaser would hire an attorney "to do a title search" — to trace the history of the property at the register of deeds, examining all deeds, mortgages, liens and covenants that affect the property. In most states today there is no need for the purchaser's lawyer to trace the title in this manner. A purchaser is now able to purchase a "title insurance" policy at the closing of the sale that insures that the purchaser is getting good title to the property. Of course, the title insurance company will be willing to guarantee good title only after it has had its lawyers do the necessary title search.

4. Transfer Taxes on the Sale of Property

The sale or transfer of real property is taxed on both the state and federal level. Typically, states will levy a "transfer tax," similar to a sales tax, at the time of sale of a property. This can vary from state to state and can be a set sum of a few hundred dollars or a percentage of the sale price of the property, running into the thousands of dollars. The revenues from these transfer taxes usually are included in the state's "general revenues." This means that these tax revenues are not dedicated for a particular purpose, but may be spent by the state for any legitimate state function. Transfer taxes are usually lower than the annual *ad valorem* property taxes discussed earlier.

5. RESPA Disclosures to the Purchaser-Borrower

All the above procedures result in a broad array of charges made to the purchaser at the closing — attorney fees, taxes, property insurance, title insurance and brokers' fees. In an effort to insure that purchasers are fully informed as to these charges, Congress passed the Real Estate Settlement Procedures Act (RESPA), which requires that lenders give prospective borrowers a booklet prepared by the U.S. Housing and Urban Development agency (HUD) and a good faith estimate of what the charges that

---

53 The buyer's pre-foreclosure right of redemption has traditionally been protected by the common law. Post-foreclosure redemption rights have been added by statute.

will be made at the closing within 3 days after they apply for their mortgage. The HUD booklet explains procedures for the closing, explains the charges made and the applicants' rights. The finance charge for the loan, expressed as an "Annual Percentage Rate" (APR) as defined by federal law must also be disclosed. In reaction to lenders steering the borrower to certain lawyers or title insurers, who charged inflated rates and "kicked back" part of it to the lender, RESPA prohibits any "kickback" payments and requires clear disclosure of any persons or companies the consumer is required to use for legal and other real estate services.[54]

6. Income Tax on Gains Realized From Sale of Real Property

Federal and state governments provide substantial income tax incentives to support home ownership, which is view by many as an essential part of the "American dream." Of the approximately 105 million residences in the United States, approximately 64% are owned by the occupants. Annual property taxes the homeowner pays on the residence are deductible from income received in calculating each year's federal income tax. Further, although personal interest is not deductible, interest paid on a loan for a personal residence is deductible.

Profit from the sale of property is taxable as income under the federal income tax laws. However, there is a major exclusion that permits most homeowners to keep their gains tax-free. Recent changes in the tax code provide an exclusion of gains up to $250,000 for a single person and $500,000 for a couple.[55] And even when there is a sale of investment property or property used for business purposes, the proceeds of such a sale can be reinvested in "like-kind" property and taxation of any gain will be deferred until the new property is sold.[56] Many states also have income taxes. If so, a state would also potentially tax the gain from the sale of property. However, the rates of state income taxes are generally much lower than the federal rates.[57]

7. Other Methods of Acquiring or Transferring Real Property

Gift or Succession Real property, like all other property, may be given away. Gifts are discussed further in Part II below, where personal property is discussed. However, unlike gifts of personal property, real property gifts — like all other transactions involving real estate — must be in writing. This generally means that the person making the gift must execute the deed to the donee (the person receiving the gift).

Succession This type of transfer occurs when the owner of property dies and it passes to the owner's heirs, either by will or by statutory provision. Succession is discussed in detail later in this chapter.[58]

Judicial Sale Judicial sales of property are sales which are ordered and supervised by a court. The most common judicial sales are sales to satisfy civil

---

54 12 U.S.C.A. §2601 *et seq.* APR disclosures are required in other extensions of credit by the Truth in Lending Act, which was discussed in Chapter X, p. 394.

55 26 U.S.C.A. §121. The taxpayer must own and use the property for 2 of 5 years before sale. Excellent concise guides to federal income tax law are MARVIN CHIRELSTEIN, FEDERAL INCOME TAXATION, 8TH ED. (Foundation 1997), HOWARD E. ABRAMS & RICHARD L. DOERNBERG, FEDERAL CORPORATE TAXATION (Foundation 1998); JOSEPH BANKMAN, THOMAS D. GRIFFITH & KATHERINE PRATT, FEDERAL INCOME TAX: EXAMPLES AND EXPLANATIONS, 2D ED. (Aspen 1999).

56 26 U.S.C.A. §1031. The process by which a taxpayer exchanges or replaces investment or business property is commonly referred to as a "section 1031 transaction" or a "1031 exchange."

57 Federal income tax rates vary from 15% to 39% of income after deductions. *See generally* Chapter XVI, where income taxation is discussed in detail.

58 *See infra*, pp. 469-471.

judgments. These sales are sometimes called "sheriff's sales."[59]

Adverse Possession Adverse possession is a means of gaining ownership of real property without the consent of the owner. The elements of an adverse possession claim are that the possession must be actual, hostile to the owner's interests, open and notorious, exclusive and continuous for the statutory period, typically 15 or 20 years.[60] The theory of adverse possession is that it is essentially a time limitation (statute of limitations) on the owner's right to sue for trespass. Once the land has been possessed for the required period of time and all the elements of adverse possession have been fulfilled, the adverse possessor can bring an action to "quiet title." If the action succeeds, the adverse possessor will be awarded title to the property. The policy behind adverse possession is to prevent land from remaining unused and to assure that owners are vigilant in protecting their rights. It is relatively rare that a person would acquire an entire parcel of land through adverse possession. More typically adverse possession issues involve small encroachments on land, usually by improper placement of a fence or driveway. A property owners facing such an encroachment must take action before the statutory period runs on pain of losing that part of their land.

F. Condominiums and Cooperatives

1. Condominiums

The basic concept of a condominium was introduced in the first section of this chapter. A condominium is typically a building that has been divided into individual "units," with the space between the interior walls of each unit being owned separately. The building itself, including the land, exterior walls, mechanical systems, hallways, and any other common facilities, called the "common elements," are owned by an association of the unit owners as tenants in common. Unit owners become members of the association by virtue of owning their unit.[61] This entitles them to vote on association matters. The association is responsible for the maintenance, repair and management of the common elements of the building, such as halls, walks, elevators and roof. Owners are charged a monthly assessment for these services. In addition to the monthly association assessment, owners are responsible for property tax assessed on their unit.

Condominium development is governed by state statute. Typically the statute requires condominium documents, including the "master deed," the bylaws of the condominium association, and the condominium subdivision plan, to be prepared and recorded with the register of deeds. The documents must describe the units and common elements, the rules by which the association is run, and the restrictions for the use of the units. Owners are bound by these restrictions and rules, which can be quite specific. Typical are restrictions on the size, type, and number of pets allowed, parking regulations, rental restrictions, and rules for use of the common areas of the building. In recent years, courts have started to limit the types of restrictions that can be imposed. Usually contracts provide that owners cannot transfer their interest to anyone not approved by the owners' association. However, there are limits to this.[62]

---

59 *See* Chapter VII, p. 236, where execution of civil judgments is discussed.

60 *See* CUNNINGHAM ET AL., *supra* note 1, §11.7 (discussing adverse possession requirements)..

61 Association members are often called co-owners.

62 *See Nahrstedt v. Lakeside Village Condominium Ass'n*, 878 P.2d 1275 (Cal. 1994) (discussing restrictions in general and citing cases) and *Laguna Royale Owners' Ass'n v. Darger*, 174 Cal.Rptr. 136 (Cal. App. 1981) (striking down association disapproval of transaction; association "must act reasonably,

Condominium projects can be older buildings that were formerly apartments, new buildings designed as condominiums, office condominiums, vacant-land or "site" condominiums, and vacation condominiums, including "time-share" properties.[63]

2. Cooperatives

A "cooperative" is a form of ownership in real estate in which the owner does not own the specific space the owner occupies, but rather owns an interest in the whole building or complex. This lack of an ownership interest in the specific space occupied is the principal difference between a cooperative and a condominium. An organization (usually a corporation) actually holds title to the property. The individual owns an interest in the organization, usually in the form of shares in the corporation. The individual unit is then leased on a long term lease to the individual "owner." This type of lease — usually known as a proprietary lease — typically gives tenants possessory rights that are so extensive that they are effectively the same as condominium ownership. However, the sale of the shares or stock, and the owners' right to sublet their units are extremely restricted by the organization and often involve the organization's approval of purchasers. "Rent" is usually based on the expenses of the corporation. "Financing" to purchase shares, similar to mortgage financing, is available to the individual unit owner.

Despite their legal differences, condominiums and cooperatives may seem to be quite similar in practical effect. However, there is a significant practical difference. Condominium units are usually purchased by owners obtaining their own mortgage financing for their own unit, just as is the case with the sale of any other real property. Condominium owners are responsible for the payment of the mortgage, taxes and association fee for *their unit alone*, and if those payments are not made, only their unit is subject to foreclosure. Cooperatives are financed by mortgaging the entire project. Thus, owners are each liable for the payment of the mortgage on the *entire* property. If cooperative unit owners fail to make their payments on the cooperative, the other owners are responsible for the share of the non-paying owner. If full payment is not made on the mortgage on the building, then the *entire building* may be foreclosed.

G. Landlord-Tenant Law

Landlord-tenant law is important because many individuals and entities rent (lease) their homes or places of business. The basic concepts of leasing are the same for both residential and commercial leasing, but there are several important differences in the legal protections afforded the tenant.[64]

1. Residential Leasing

Since residential tenants are on the whole less sophisticated in business affairs and often in a far weaker bargaining position than landlords, most states and localities have enacted special laws designed to protect residential tenants. For example, nearly all localities have local laws requiring that a landlord have the property inspected and approved by local housing officials before it may be rented, and at regular times every few years. Many jurisdictions regulate the content of residential leases to assure that tenants are not subject to unfair agreements.

It was not always the case that residential tenants had such protections. Until the

---

exercising its power in a fair and nondiscriminatory manner and withholding approval only for a reason or reasons rationally related to the protection, preservation and proper operation of the property").

63 Time-shares were discussed *supra* p. 442.

64 *See* DAVID S. HILL, LANDLORD AND TENANT LAW IN A NUTSHELL (West 1995).

1960s, leaseholds tended to be viewed as "interests in property" and lease terms tended to be construed under the rules of property law. A fundamental rule of property law that affected residential tenants' ability to protect their rights was the doctrine of "independent covenants." Under this doctrine, promises made by the landlord and the tenant were independent rather than "mutually dependent." Consequently, even if landlords promised to make necessary repairs, but failed to do so, tenants were not relieved of their agreement to pay rent. Since tenants were not permitted to withhold rent, they were often without any recourse to force the landlord to maintain the premises.

By the 1960s, however, the common landlord-tenant relationship in the United States had changed significantly. Courts began to analyze leases under contract law rather than property law and ignored the independent covenants doctrine.[65] Today, the landlord's promises under a lease are mutually dependent upon the lessee's duty to pay rent. Thus, if the landlord does not keep the premises in reasonable repair, the tenant is generally permitted to withhold rent until the landlord makes necessary repairs.

The changes of the 1960s resulted in what is sometimes referred to as a "revolution" in the law governing the landlord-tenant relationship. Primary among the changes was an implied "warranty of habitability" in all residential leases. This warranty generally means that a landlord, as a matter of law, must maintain rented premises in a safe and habitable condition. If the premises do not meet these standards, the landlord will have breached the implied warranty of habitability and the tenant may withhold rent until the breach is cured.[66]

A modern lease is also subject to an implied covenant of quiet enjoyment. This covenant gives the tenant the right to possess and use the property. A landlord may also have the duty under *tort* law to make necessary repairs to the premises. A landlord who fails to fulfill this obligation may be liable in a tort action for injuries suffered by tenants as a result of unrepaired dangerous conditions or as a result of faulty repairs.[67]

2. Commercial Leases

The commercial tenant is considered to be more sophisticated and has greater bargaining power. And, in any event, the commercial tenant is probably better able than the residential tenant to inspect the premises and demand that any defects be repaired before signing the lease. As a result, the implied warranty of habitability and many of the other covenants discussed above do not generally apply to a commercial lease. Commercial leases are often much longer in duration than residential leases and often give the tenant greater rights to make changes on the property. A condition of a long-term commercial lease will often be that the landlord will remodel the property to suit the tenant's planned business use of it.

---

65 See *Brown v. Southall Realty*, 237 A.2d 834 (D.C.App. 1968) (housing regulations were implied part of the lease and landlord's non-compliance relieved the tenant of the obligation to pay rent).

66 *See Javins v. First National Realty Corp.*, 428 F. 2d 1071 (D.C.Cir. 1970).

67 *See Sargent v. Ross*, 308 A.2d 528 (N.H. 1973) (landlord held liable for death of child where landlord had exposed tenants to unreasonable risk of harm due to faulty design of stairs and his failure to correct the dangerous condition).

H. Personal Property

1. Types of Personal Property

Personal property is all property that is not real property or "fixtures," as defined earlier. Examples of personal property are books, utensils, cars, furniture, stocks, bonds, patents and copyrights. Personal property may be either "tangible" or "intangible." "Tangible" personal property consists of material objects that have intrinsic value — objects that are valuable in and of themselves, such as jewelry. "Intangible" property is made up of those "things" that lack material form. Examples of intangible property are stocks in corporations, copyrights, patents, and bank accounts.[68] The documents that these are printed on are only evidence of the ownership interest and are not in themselves the "thing" possessed. However, an item of personal property may embody both tangible and intangible property rights. For example, educational materials such as books and films have the tangible property qualities of a physical existence as well as the intangible property qualities of ownership of the ideas that go into them.[69]

2. Acquiring and Transferring Interests in Personal Property

Gifts   As noted earlier, a gift is the transfer of title to property without an exchange of consideration for the property. For a gift to be valid, it must be made with the "donative intent" on the part of the grantor, the intention to make a gift. The grantor must also intend present transfer of the item.[70] Additionally, for a gift to be valid, there must be delivery and acceptance of the item. The general rule on delivery is, if the item is capable of being manually delivered, it must be so delivered.[71] However, some goods, because of inaccessibility or large size, cannot feasibly be delivered. If so, symbolic delivery of something that represents the item is sufficient, such as handing over the key to a car.

Finders   Ownership interests in personal property may also be acquired by finding an item. The ownership interest that the finder receives depends on how the true owner became separated from his or her property. Once lost property is found, the finder receives an ownership interest in the property which is inferior only to the interest of the original owner. If the personal property has been abandoned, the finder gets title superior to that of all others, including the original owner. If the personal property has been mislaid (the property has been put in a specific location purposefully and inadvertently left there), the owner of the real property on which it is found generally has the right to the item, not the finder.

Adverse Possession   Adverse possession of personal property, like adverse possession of real property, can be a means of acquiring ownership, and the same requirements apply. The adverse possessor must fulfill those requirements for the

---

68 Coins and other currency are considered tangible, however. Intellectual property, which includes patents, copyrights and trademarks, is intangible personal property.

69 *Simplicity Pattern Company, Inc. v. State Board of Equalization*, 161 Cal.Rptr. 558 (Cal.App. 1980) (sale of collection of original film negatives was not a sale of "tangible personal property" because the value of the negatives was in their content), *opinion vacated by*, 615 P.2d 555 (Cal. 1980) (court held that sale of film negatives was a sale of tangible personal property because the negatives were physically useful in making the finished product).

70 Of course, a testamentary gift may be made by will. In that case, all of the formalities of a will must be fulfilled. *See infra* p. 469.

71 *See Newman v. Bost*, 29 S.E. 848 (N.C.1898).

statutory period.[72] However, difficulties arise with personal property in that it may be hard for the adverse possessor to prove that his or her possession was open and notorious because of the small size and easily transportable nature of much personal property. Some courts avoid this problem by rejecting adverse possession in the case of personal property and basing their inquiry instead upon the diligence of the true owner in trying to recover the property.[73]

Bailments A bailment exists when one person leaves property in the possession of another for safekeeping or some other temporary purpose. This could include leaving one's car in a parking garage or leaving one's watch at a jeweler's shop to be repaired. Problems with bailments arise when the "bailee," the person keeping the property, loses it, conveys it, or damages it. There are different standards of care that apply depending on the nature of the bailment. For bailments that are for the benefit of the bailee, as where the bailee charges for the service, the bailee is held to a higher standard of care than where the bailment is gratuitous (where no fee is charged), or where the bailment is for the benefit of the property owner.

Accessions and Improvements Under the doctrine of accession, an owner of property gains title to any natural or artificial increases in or additions to that property. For example, the owner of a cow would gain title to any milk produced by that cow. Woodworkers who turn their own wood into a table are entitled to the increased value of the wood. A more complicated scenario arises when a person unites his or her labor or property with the property of another person. In that case, ownership of the finished product is determined on the basis of such factors as the difference in value as a result of the labor, the degree of change in the form of the original property, and the ease with which the personal property of the laborer can be removed from the other's property.[74]

3. Intellectual Property

Intellectual property is an important form of personal property. It is composed of three distinct bodies of law: copyright law, patent law and trademark law.[75]

a. Copyright Law

What is Copyrightable Copyright is a form of legal protection provided to "original works of authorship" that are fixed in some tangible form.[76] Works can be literary, dramatic, scientific, musical, artistic or architectural, and can be any form of pictorial or sculptural representations, recorded sounds or computer programs. A work is protected by copyright law as soon as it assumes such tangible fixed form. It

---

72 *See supra* p. 454.

73 *See, e.g., O'Keeffe v. Snyder*, 416 A.2d 862, 869 (N.J. 1980) (the statute of limitations of an action for return of the property begins to run when the true owner "discovers or should have discovered facts which form the basis of a cause of action").

74 See e.g. *Austrian Motors, Ltd. v. Travelers Insurance Co.* 275 S.E. 2d 702 (Ga.App. 1980) (tires and other easily removable parts innocently added to another's car remain the property of the trespassing laborer, but materials such as paint that cannot be easily removed as well as the labor employed become the property of the car owner).

75 For more information on intellectual property, *see* SELECTED INTELLECTUAL PROPERTY AND UNFAIR COMPETITION STATUTES, REGULATIONS AND TREATIES. (West 1998); DONALD S. CHISUM & MICHAEL A. JACOBS, UNDERSTANDING INTELLECTUAL PROPERTY (Matthew Bender 1992).

76 The 1976 Copyright Act, 17 U.S.C.A. §§101 *et seq.* is the basic current law. The constitutional basis is Art. I §8 cl. 8 of the Constitution, which authorizes "securing for limited times to authors and inventors the exclusive right to their respective writings and discoveries."

need not be registered nor have a copyright notice © on it.[77]

The "originality" requirement demands only minimal contributions of the author, but it is not satisfied when the work is a mere compilation of otherwise uncopyrightable information. Thus, there is no "sweat-of-the-brow" copyright doctrine protecting the significant amount of work that goes into compiling information.[78] The requirement that the work be in some tangible form excludes from protection such things as improvisational speeches, choreography or other performances that have not been recorded in some manner. Copyright law protects the specific form of expression the author has adopted, not the underlying ideas themselves, which may be freely used by others.[79]

Copyright Owner's Rights The law protects various rights to copyrighted works, including the right to reproduce or copy the work, to prepare or control preparation of derivative works from them (e.g., films based on novels), to distribute copies (free or for sale), and, in the case of musical and other audio-visual works, to perform, display or transmit such works. The period of protection of a copyright is 70 years beyond the death of the author of the work. The period may not be renewed.[80]

Public Domain A work that is in the "public domain" has no copyright protection and may therefore be used by anyone for any purpose, including commercial purposes. A work may pass into the public domain if it was once copyrighted, but the copyright period has expired. Or the author of the work may have expressly dedicated or abandoned the work to the public domain. However, abandonment cannot be implied from failure to assert the right against infringers.[81] And, contrary to popular belief, placing one's work on the Internet is not abandonment. Other categories of works in the public domain are works of the U.S. government and names, titles, slogans or short phrases that cannot be copyrighted.[82]

Fair Use "Fair use" is an exception to the normal protections of copyright. It is based on the theory that preventing anyone from copying even the shortest excerpt

---

77 17 U.S.C. §102(a). A work is fixed when it is "sufficiently permanent or stable to permit it to be perceived, reproduced, or otherwise communicated for a period of more than transitory duration." 17 U.S.C. §101. A work produced on a computer is fixed as soon as it is saved. It need not be printed out. The presence of a copyright symbol on the work, though not needed to gain protection, makes it hard for the infringer to claim "innocent infringement," which might reduce the amount of damages recoverable for infringement. 17 U.S.C.A. §§401(d), 402(d).

78 *Feist Publications v. Rural Telephone Service Co.*, 499 U.S. 340 (1991) (compilation of names and numbers in telephone directory "not remotely creative"). *But see Bellsouth Advertising & Publishing Corp. v. Donnelley Information Publishing, Inc.* 933 F.2d 952 (11th Cir. 1991) ("yellow page" business directory protected because business classifications were created and listings categorized). *See also Matthew Bender & Co. v. West Publishing Co.*, 158 F.3d 674 (2d Cir. 1998) (selection and ordering of caption and other aspects of non-copyrightable judicial decisions is not copyrightable).

79 *See Baker v. Selden*, 101 U.S. 99 (1879) (method of accounting is not copyrightable, although the explanation of it is); *Reyher v. Children's Television Workshop*, 533 F.2d 87 (2d Cir. 1976) (idea for television program not copyrightable). *But see infra* p. 464 (computer programs patentable).

80 17 U.S.C.A. §302(a). Congress added 20 years to the previous 50-year term in 1998. Works produced between 1964 and 1977 enjoy copyright status for 95 years. Works from 1923 through 1963 have 28-year initial and 67-year renewal terms. 17 U.S.C. §304(a).

81 *National Comics Publications v. Fawcett Publications*, 191 F.2d 594, 598 (2nd Cir. 1951) (1939 copyright to comic strips, including "Superman," not abandoned by failure to affix copyright symbol or enforce); *Micro Star v. Formgen, Inc.*, 154 F.3d 1107 (9th Cir. 1997) (copyright owner encouraging players themselves to make other "levels" of computer game "Duke Nukem 3D" and providing editing program to assist in doing so was not abandoned).

82 *Matthew Bender & Co. v. West Publishing Co.*, 158 F.3d 674 (2d Cir. 1998) (captions of court decisions not copyrightable). Titles, slogans and short phrases may in some cases qualify as trademarks, however. *See infra* pp. 466-469.

from a copyrighted work would stifle the very sort of creativity that copyright laws are supposed to encourage. Fair use is not clearly defined and courts have struggled with its boundaries. Before the 1976 Act, fair use was a common law doctrine. It is now set out in the Act, but the intent of Congress was to codify the common law. Unfortunately, the Act does not provide a definition of fair use, only examples and four "factors" to consider. The examples are "criticism, comment, news reporting, teaching (including multiple copies for classroom use), scholarship, or research." The factors to consider are: "(1) the purpose and character of the use, including whether such use is of a commercial nature or is for nonprofit educational purposes; (2) the nature of the copyrighted work; (3) the amount and substantiality of the portion used in relation to the copyrighted work as a whole; and (4) the effect of the use upon the potential market for or value of the copyrighted work."[83]

Under the factor of "character and purpose" of the copying, the presence of a profit motive has been important in determining that the use was not a fair use.[84] On the other hand, copying for private non-profit home use tends to be considered fair use, as in the case of consumers recording movies with their home video recorders.[85] Educational use, even outside the context of formal education, has been deemed important as well. One court upheld a vacuum cleaner company's reprinting without permission an independent consumer group's favorable review of its product. Among other factors, the court noted that circulating the review served to educate consumers.[86]

On the question of the "nature of the work" involved, one distinction made by some courts is between fact and fiction, with fiction receiving the greater protection on the ground that there are fewer if any uncopyrightable facts involved with fiction.[87] Other courts have used a "published/unpublished" distinction, protecting unpublished works much more completely on the grounds that there is a unique value to first publication involved and that the very decision whether to publish may be affected by the distribution of copies.[88] A recurring fair use issue is the copying of copyrighted works as materials for courses at educational institutions. While the statute expressly refers to "teaching" and "multiple copies for classroom use," there are limits. When class materials are reproduced, not by the educational institution itself, but by commercial duplicating establishments that sell the materials to students at a profit, fair use has not been found.[89]

The "amount and substantiality" of copying is a factor that some have attempted to quantify. A typical editor's guide might list such limits as no more than 300 words from a scholarly text, no more than 150 words from popular books, no more than 2

---

83 17 U.S.C.A. §107.

84 *Henry Holt & Co. v. Liggett & Myers Tobacco Co.*, 23 F.Supp. 302 (E.D.Pa. 1938) (portions of scientific book used to advertise cigarettes).

85 *Sony Corp. of America v. Universal City Studios, Inc.*, 464 U.S. 417 (1984). Audio music recordings may also be copied for personal use. *See* Audio Home Recording Act of 1992, 17 U.S.C.A. §1001 *et seq.*

86 *Consumers Union v. General Signal Corp.*, 724 F.2d 1044 (2nd Cir. 1983).

87 Even with non-fiction, the case can be made that the author's particular description of uncopyrightable facts is a large part of the appeal of the work. *See Harper & Row v. Nation Enterprises*, 471 U.S. 539 (1985) (copying former President Ford's memoirs is not fair use).

88 *Salinger v. Random House*, 811 F.2d 90, 97 (2d Cir. 1987) (paraphrase of famous author's unpublished letters in biography of that author was not fair use). *But see* 17 U.S.C.A. §107 ("The fact that a work is unpublished shall not itself bar a finding of fair use if such finding is made upon consideration of all the [fair use] factors.")

89 *Princeton University Press v. Michigan Document Services,* 99 F.3d 1381 (6th Cir. 1996) (*en banc*).

lines of song lyrics, and no more than 1 sentence from a newspaper. However, as the Copyright office warns, "[t]here is no specific number of words, lines or notes that may safely be taken without permission."[90] The issue of the amount of a work that can be copied often comes up in parody cases. The Supreme Court recently made clear that parody copying may be substantial since copying even of the "heart" of the original may be necessary to the work's parodic purpose.[91]

The factor of "the effect of the use upon the potential market for or value of the copyrighted work" has been described as "undoubtedly the single most important element of fair use."[92] Especially where the copier uses the work in precisely the market it was created for, this factor weighs heavily, such as where material copied for educational use was itself written for educational use.[93]

Ownerships and Transfers of Copyrights   Authors may sell or otherwise assign their rights to someone else, typically to the publisher of their work.[94] However, if the author is an employee and the work is created within the scope of employment, then the work is a "work made for hire" and the employer is considered the author, unless there is a contrary written agreement.[95] Further, even if the work is not made for hire and the author owns the copyright, the author may have created an implied non-exclusive license in the person for whom the author created the work. This allows the party who ordered the work to use and distribute it to others.[96]

The assignment of the copyright gives the publisher or other assignee the full rights the author had in the work. There have been notable cases of authors who sold their works cheaply early in their careers and then faced relative poverty later in life, while the publisher continued to reap profits from selling their work. In reaction to this, Congress in the 1976 Act created a non-waivable right in authors to "recapture" their copyright by canceling the transfer of the copyright after the expiration of 35 years following the original transfer.[97]

The First Sale Doctrine   Once the copyright owner sells copies of the work, the new owner may treat the copies it purchased as its own and may resell them even if the original owner prohibits resales. This is called the "first-sale" doctrine.[98] The sale does not permit the buyer to make further copies of the work, but even resale of the very copies sold may create problems for the original owner. The problem is illustrated by the facts of a recent Supreme Court case, *Quality King Distributors Inc.*

---

90 Copyright Office Document FL102. Law reviews in the United States typically give copying permission without charge. Other academic journals and commercial publications usually insist on a fee.

91 *Campbell v. Acuff-Rose Music, Inc.* 510 U.S. 569, 589 (1994) (copying of the "heart" of Roy Orbison's "Oh, Pretty Woman" by 2 Live Crew rap group in parody may not necessarily be excessive, but remand ordered to determine whether repetition of the bass riff was excessive copying).

92 *Harper & Row, supra* note 87, at 566.

93 *See McMillan v. King*, 223 F. 862 (D. Mass. 1914) (teacher copying of substantial portions of an economics text written for the classroom is not fair use).

94 Any assignment must be in writing.   17 U.S.C.A. §204.   *See also* 17 U.S.C.A. §201(d)(1) (testamentary and other transfers of copyright).

95 17 U.S.C.A. §201(b). *But see CCNV v. Reid*, 490 U.S. 730 (1989) (sculpture was not a "work made for hire"; sculptor was an independent contractor rather than a "employee" despite some supervision).

96 *See Effects Associates v. Cohen*, 908 F.2d 555 (9th Cir. 1990) (copyright to special effects film footage that depicted "alien yoghurt oozing out of a defunct factory" belonged to the company that made it, not the film producer who ordered it, but the company impliedly granted a license to the producer to use the footage and distribute it to others).

97 17 U.S.C.A. §203.

98 Sold copies may be leased as well, except for sound recordings and computer programs. 17 U.S.C.A. §109(b)(1).

v. L'Anza Research International Inc.[99] In *Quality King*, a manufacturer made all of its products in the United States, but sold them at lower prices to distributors overseas. Some of these distributors imported the products back to the United States and they were sold in discount houses at lower prices. The manufacturer attempted to stop the sales on the ground that the importation violated its copyright in the labels on the product. A unanimous Supreme Court held that, because of the first-sale doctrine, copyright law was no barrier to importation. It noted that such importation might be prohibited through enactment of an international trade law or conclusion of an international agreement with the importer's country, but that copyright laws afforded no protection.[100] Goods like those in *Quality King* are sometimes called "gray-market" goods, thus implying there is something illegal about their sale, but *Quality King* shows that such sales are completely legitimate, as least as a matter of copyright law.

Registration As noted earlier, no particular procedure need be followed to obtain copyright protection for a work. However, registration of the copyright with the Copyright Office is available and it is encouraged since it establishes an official public record of the copyright. Registration is also necessary as a precondition for a suit for infringement, though this can be done after the infringement and just prior to filing suit. Registration by a U.S. author within 5 years of publication of the work establishes *prima facie* evidence in court of the validity of the copyright. Registration within 3 months after publication of the work and before infringement entitles the author to statutory damages and attorney fees in any infringement suit.[101]

Infringement To prove infringement, a party must prove (1) its ownership of a valid copyright and (2) copying of constituent elements of the work that are original. Copying is proven usually by showing similarities between the works and access by the infringer to the original. Infringement need not be intentional to be actionable. A famous case on this point was the successful suit against George Harrison of the Beatles, whose song, "My Sweet Lord," was held to be an unconscious infringement of an earlier song.[102] Experts are often called to testify on the issue of similarity. In musical pieces, similarity may be found in certain sequences of notes. For literary copying, it must be kept foremost in mind that ideas are not copyrightable, only particular expressions of ideas are. However, the line is difficult to draw. Verbatim copying of dialog or descriptions from a novel is clearly improper. But copying plots, incidents or characters may also be protected depending on the circumstances. A character is copyrightable if the character is not a stereotypical figure, is well developed and figures prominently in the work.[103] Clearly, characters depicted visually provide an added dimension for comparison.

Computer programs are copyrightable under the Computer Software Copyright Act of 1980.[104] This includes both the programmer-written (source code) and the

---

99 523 U.S. 135 (1998).

100 The Court noted that executive agreements had been reached with 5 countries on the subject.

101 17 U.S.C. §§411-412. Registration is not a precondition for suit if the origin of the work is a foreign country that is a signatory of the Berne Convention. Statutory damages are "not less than $500 or more than $20,000 as the court considers just." Actual damages in the form of lost profits are also available.

102 The infringed song was "He's So Fine" by the "Chiffons." *Bright Tunes Music Corp. v. Harrisongs Music, Ltd.*, 420 F.Supp. 177 (S.D. N.Y. 1976).

103 *Denker v. Uhry*, 820 F.Supp. 722 (S.D.N.Y. 1992), *aff'd* 996 F.2d 301 (2d Cir. 1993) (play "Driving Miss Daisy" depicting relationship between elderly, bigoted white woman and her black chauffeur did not infringe novel about crusty, bigoted, elderly Jewish man and his black physical therapist)

104 17 U.S.C.A. §117. *See also infra* p. 464.

converted computer-readable (binary code) versions of the program.[105] However, a programmer can avoid copying the very codes used and yet come up with a result that performs the same functions and has the same structure and organization — sometimes called "look and feel" — of the original program. Courts in some cases have held that structure and organization are protectable by copyright, not just the literal computer code. This is by analogy fictional works, from which it is prohibited, not just to copy verbatim, but also to copy plots, incidents and characters.[106] However, recent cases have tended to treat computer programs — even those with audiovisual animation — more like non-fiction than creative works. As such, virtual identity of the programs will have to be found for there to be infringement. In a case affirmed by an equally divided Supreme Court, the First Circuit Court of Appeals held that Borland's Quatro Pro spread-sheet program did not infringe Lotus's 1-2-3 program even though Borland copied exactly the 1-2-3 menu command terms and hierarchy, and despite the fact that Lotus developers made some expressive choices in arranging the Lotus command terms. The menu, as a "method of operation," could not be copyrighted.[107]

International Copyright Protection   International copyright protection does not really exist. It is only through the laws of individual countries that copyrights are protected, if at all. However, there are two major treaties on copyright protection: the Berne Union for the Protection of Literary and Artistic Property (Berne Convention) and the Universal Copyright Convention (UCC). These treaties extend the protection of each signatory country's laws to authors from other signatory countries or to works published in other signatory countries. In addition, several bilateral treaties may apply to countries that are not signatories of these two treaties. However, there are still several countries with which the United States has no copyright treaty.

b. Patent Law

Scope of Patentability   A patent is the right granted by Federal statute to an inventor to exclude others in the U.S. from making, using, or selling his or her invention for a limited period of time. In return for the grant, the inventor must disclose the patent completely to the public. This *quid pro quo* promotes the practice of science. Complete disclosures encourage further inventions and the limited exclusionary right serves as an incentive to disclose.

Patents are granted for processes, machines, manufactures, or compositions of matter that meet the Patent Act's requirements of novelty, utility and non-obviousness.[108] Novelty has to do with whether the challenged invention was included within a prior invention.[109] Utility simply means that the invention has some

---

105 *See Apple Computer v. Franklin Computer Corp.*, 714 F.2d 1240, 1246-1249 (3d Cir. 1983).

106 See, *e.g.*, *Whelan Associates v. Jaslow Dental Laboratory*, 797 F.2d 1222 (3d Cir. 1986) (dental laboratory infringed software copyright of consulting company that developed record keeping program for laboratory; program structure similar despite use of another computer language).

107 *Lotus Development Corp. v. Borland International*, 49 F.3d 807 (1st Cir. 1995), *aff'd by an equally divided Court*, 516 U.S. 233 (1996). *See also Apple Computer, Inc. v. Microsoft Corp.*, 35 F.3d 1435, 1441-1447 (9th Cir. 1994) (in dispute over "Windows" interface, infringement exists only if Microsoft used virtually identical selection and arrangement of windows; no infringement found). Possible *patent* protection for software installed on a computer as a patented "process" is discussed *infra* p. 464.

108 *See* 35 U.S.C.A. §101 *et seq.* Actually, there are three classes of patents: utility (§101), design (§171)and plant (§161) patents. The only type discussed here are utility patents, which make up over 90% of all issued patents. Design patents cover new and ornamental designs of useful articles, such as furniture and shoes. Plant patents are issued for new plant varieties, such as flowers and fruit trees.

109 *See, e.g.*, *In re Donahue*, 766 F.2d 531 (Fed.Cir. 1985) (chemical compound not novel; journal disclosed how it was made and person of ordinary skill could have made it).

function of benefit to humanity. This may be important for establishing an invention date. When two inventors have been simultaneously working on the same process for producing a chemical compound, it is not the first to develop it, but the first to discover a practical utility for it who wins. Except in the case of new medicines, the utility requirement is usually no hard to meet.[110] Obviousness is present where the invention would have been clear to a person of ordinary skill in the field.[111]

Patents may be issued for "anything under the sun that is made by man,"[112] but not for "laws of nature, natural phenomena, and abstract ideas." Nonetheless, a naturally occurring substance may be patented if the discoverer has made it in purified or altered form. Thus, a new life form of bacteria genetically altered to eat petroleum wastes was held patentable.[113]

Computer technology has presented some challenges with regard to patentability, as it has with regard to copyright. The 1984 Semiconductor Chip Protection Act protects computer circuitry, including the code fixed in ROM (read-only memory) chips.[114] And as discussed earlier, Congress amended the Copyright Act to make software programs copyrightable.[115] Nonetheless, creators of software programs have continued to assert their patentability, arguing that such programs, when properly installed on computers, constitute patentable "machines." Patentability is sought because a patent protects against copying the *process* and the *result* the installed program produces, while copyright protects only the particular way the software program produces that result.[116] The difficulty in patenting such "machines" lies in the fact that software programs are in essence nothing more than a series of mathematical calculations, and thus simply "abstract ideas."[117] But the Federal Circuit Court of Appeals recently held that a software program installed on a computer can be patented. In that case, the program as installed transformed stock price data through a series of mathematical calculations to produce a waveform display on a monitor. The court held that this was patentable as a practical application of an abstract idea since it produced a "useful, concrete and tangible result." The Court emphasized that the Patent Act expressly includes "processes" as a category of inventions.[118]

Registration Procedures A person wishing to obtain a patent must file a patent

---

110 *Brenner v. Manson*, 383 U.S. 519 (1966) (process for making a known steroid compound not shown to have utility where possible uses were being investigated and a related chemical was useful in treating tumors in mice).

111 *Graham v. John Deere Co.*, 383 U.S. 1 (1966) (improvements on plow obvious).

112 *Diamond v. Chakrabarty*, 447 U.S. 303, 309 (1980).

113 *Diamond v. Chakrabarty, supra. See also Amgen, Inc. v. Chugai Pharmaceutical Co.*, 927 F.2d 1200 (Fed.Cir. 1991) (concentrated amino acid proteins that stimulate red blood cell production).

114 *See* 17 U.S.C.A. §902 *et seq.* Protection is provided for 10 years. This might seem to be a short time period, but it is substantial considering the speed of developments in computer technology.

115 17 U.S.C.A. §117. *See supra* p. 462.

116 *See* discussion *supra* p. 462.

117 *See Gottschalk v. Benson*, 409 U.S. 63 (1972) (algorithm that converted binary-coded decimals into binary numerals could not be patented because it was an abstract idea). Computer programs may also suffer from lack of novelty and obviousness, since many such programs simply do more quickly what can already be done manually.

118 *State Street Bank & Trust Co. v. Signature Financial Group*, 149 F.3d 1368 (Fed.Cir. 1998). This decision was foreshadowed by *Diamond v. Diehr*, 450 U.S. 175 (1981), where the Court held that a process for curing synthetic rubber that utilized a computer to process temperature information and recalculate curing time could be a potentially patentable "new and useful process." It did not matter that the process used a well-known mathematical formula that expressed the relationship between temperature, time and cure. The issues of obviousness and lack of novelty were left open.

application, which includes (1) a description of how to make and use the invention in the best way known to the inventor and (2) "claims," which set out the innovative features of the invention. Usually, an inventor will seek the services of a "patent attorney" or "patent agent" who is experienced in preparing patent applications.[119] The attorney or agent sends the application to the Patent Office in Washington, D.C., where it is examined by a patent examiner to ensure that it meets the statutory requirements for patentability. The examiner will either reject the application or issue a "Notice of Allowance." If the application is rejected, the applicant has the right to respond formally to each rejection to persuade the Examiner that the claims are indeed patentable. Alternatively or additionally, the applicant can amend the claims. However, the applicant cannot introduce subject matter that is not already set forth in the application. If an application is twice rejected, the applicant may appeal the Examiner's decision to the Patent Office's Board of Appeals; if such appeal fails, the applicant can then appeal to the Court of Appeals for the Federal Circuit or the federal District Court for the District of Columbia. A patent holder gives notice to all that the invention is patented by placing the word "Patented" or "Pat.," plus the patent number on the item. This is important because the holder can recover damages only for infringements that occur after the infringer is given notice.[120]

Priority Among Inventors In contrast to most other countries, the United States determines priority of inventorship by a "first to invent" standard instead of a "first to file" standard. And, as the Supreme Court has observed, the "meaning of 'invention' in the Patent Act unquestionably refers to the inventor's conception rather than to a physical embodiment of that idea."[121] Thus, even though one inventor may win the race to the Patent Office or may produce a working model sooner, another inventor can prevail by proving that he or she first conceived of the invention and showed diligence in reducing the invention to practice.[122]

Rights Protected If the patent application is approved, the inventor has the right to exclude others from making, using or selling the invention for the period of the patent, currently 20 years from the date of filing.[123] A patent cannot be renewed, so it enters the "public domain" at the end of the stated period. During the patent period, the patentee can sell it to another or license others to develop it on either an exclusive or non-exclusive basis, or the patentee may choose not to develop the device at all.[124] The right to make, use, or sell one's own invention is not absolute, however. It is possible, and not uncommon, for a patentee to be prohibited from practicing his or

---

119 Patent agents are nonlawyers who have the right to prepare, file and argue patent applications with the U.S. Patent Office and Board of Appeals. However, agents do not have the right to give legal advice or appear in court. A patent lawyer is a regular lawyer who has passed the patent bar examination — an exception to the usual "generalist" nature of the license to practice law. *See* Chapter IV.

120 The patent owner must give the infringer actual notice. *Lemelson v. Fisher Price Corp.*, 545 F.Supp. 750 (S.D.N.Y. 1982) (holder only gave notice 2 years after patent had expired, so suit dismissed).

121 *Pfaff v. Wells Electronics, Inc.*, ___ U.S. ___, 119 S.Ct. 304 (1998) (invention date was when drawings were sufficient to produce it). In the most famous example of this, the Court upheld a patent issued to Alexander Graham Bell even though he had filed his application before constructing a working telephone. *See The Telephone Cases*, 126 U.S. 1 (1888).

122 This definition of "invention" presents a pitfall for inventors in connection with the Act's provision that an invention that has been on sale more than one year before filing a patent application may not be patented. *See Pfaff, supra* note 121 (inventor concluded sales contracts based on drawings).

123 35 U.S.C.A. §154(2). Certain patented inventions that are subject to considerable delay in being approved by the government for distribution, such as new drugs and medical devices, are given an additional 5 years under certain conditions. 35 U.S.C.A. §156.

124 The lack of a requirement that the patentee "work" the patent distinguishes U.S. patent law from that in many other countries.

her own invention, if doing so would infringe an unexpired patent. For example, if inventor A invented aspirin, and received a patent for this invention, A could, for the lifetime of the patent, keep inventor B from making, using or selling *buffered* aspirin, even though it may be patentable and represents a major improvement in the state of the art of painkillers. In practice such problems are usually resolved by a cross-licensing agreement between the patent holders.

Infringement A patent owner can sue anyone who infringes any or all of the claims of the patent without authorization.[125] If successful, the owner is entitled to invoke the same injunctive and damages remedies available in copyright cases.[126] The owner who sues for infringement may be confronted with a defense that the patent is invalid because the Patent Office erred in finding novelty, utility or non-obviousness. Other ways of raising the issue of the validity of a patent are by way of a suit for a declaratory judgment by the party wishing to use the patent and a request to the Patent Office to re-examine the patent application it has approved.[127]

c. Trademark Law

Trademarks and Their Role A trademark is a distinctive mark that identifies the origin of particular goods sold in the marketplace. It can be a word ("Sprite"), phrase ("Kentucky Fried Chicken"), symbol (the scallop shell of Shell Oil Co.), design (the McDonald's "golden arches") or even a product's overall appearance and shape or its color.[128] A primary policy behind trademark protection is protection of the public from mistake, deception and confusion with regard to the origin of a product. At the same time, consumer preference for a good of a particular origin allows the trademark to be used as a marketing and advertising device.

Source of Trademark Law Trademark law originated as common law, but has since been adopted and modified by federal statute. That statute, the Lanham Act, also provides procedures for protection of trademarks.[129] Among other things, it provides a national system for registration of trademarks.

Distinctiveness A mark must be distinctive to be a proper trademark. Generic or purely descriptive terms are not distinctive, since they do no more than state what the item is. Thus, "banana" could never be a trademark for bananas. Aside from creating confusion, merchants would be unable to describe the bananas they have for sale for fear of infringement.[130]

Courts have recognized points on a spectrum of distinctiveness. From most distinctive to least distinctive they are (1) fanciful or arbitrary marks, (2) suggestive

---

125 35 U.S.C.A. §281.

126 35 U.S.C.A. §§284-285.

127 35 U.S.C.A. §302.

128 *See Two Pesos, Inc. v. Taco Cabana, Inc.*, 505 U.S. 763 (1992) (restaurant's "Mexican trade dress" that included a "festive eating atmosphere" protected). *Qualitex v. Jacobson Products*, 514 U.S. 159 (1995) (green-gold color of manufacturer's dry clearing press pads can be registered). Also protected are "service marks," which are essentially trademarks attached to services instead of goods and "certification marks," such as "UL Tested" or "Good Housekeeping Seal of Approval." 15 U.S.C.A. §§1053-1054.

129 15 U.S.C.A. §§1051 *et seq.* The Lanham Act was passed pursuant to interstate commerce clause. Consequently, it is supposed to affect only the interstate use of trademarks. However, as with other exercises of the commerce clause power, the statute is read broadly by courts. *See* Chapter I, p. 24.

130 For similar reasons, geographical marks are not proper trademarks unless they are more than merely descriptive (e.g. London Fog). Immoral or offensive terms or phrases may not become trademarks. *See Bromberg v. Carmel Self Service, Inc.*, 198 U.S.P.Q. 176 (T.T.A.B. 1978) (mark for a chicken restaurant, "Only a breast in the mouth is better than a leg in the hand," disallowed).

marks, (3) descriptive marks and (4) generic marks.[131] Fanciful or arbitrary marks may be made-up words (e.g., "Kodak" cameras or "Exxon" gasoline) or ordinary words with a fanciful or arbitrary association (e.g., "Apple" computers or "Camel" cigarettes). Such marks are automatically distinctive. Suggestive marks suggest a particular quality of the product (e.g., "Diehard" car batteries or "Ivory" soap). A leap of imagination is required to associate them with the product involved, so suggestive marks, like fanciful marks, are presumptively distinctive. Descriptive terms are presumed not to be distinctive, but may be if, through use, they have acquired a "secondary meaning." Thus, "Realemon" as a mark for a *particular* reconstituted lemon juice that supposedly tastes like real lemons, "Animal Crackers" as a mark for *particular* cookies shaped like animals and "Instant Breakfast" as a mark for a *particular* powdered breakfast substitute that can be prepared instantly, are all distinctive trademarks. The question as to descriptive marks is whether "the primary significance of the term in the minds of the consuming public is not the product, but the producer."[132] If so, they are sufficiently distinctive.

A trademark may, through use, lose its distinctiveness and become generic or purely descriptive. Perhaps the best-known example of this is the term "aspirin," which went from a trademark of the Bayer Company to a generic description of the drug.[133] Other examples are "cellophane,"[134] "shredded wheat,"[135] and "escalator."[136] Though it is rare, sometimes a mark that has become generic or descriptive can be "recaptured" by the owner.[137]

Surnames Surname marks usually describe an establishment, product or service as being that of a particular person, such as Smith's Café. Like other descriptive marks, however, if a secondary association has been established through the public associating the surname with a particular product or service, a surname can become a trademark. For example, "McDonald's" evokes in the minds of most people a particular fast-food restaurant chain. As a result, no other persons named McDonald may use their name to market fast-food, though they could use their name for a different kind of business. But even when the same type of business is involved, courts are reluctant to prevent people from using their own names to promote their businesses because of the inherent unfairness of it. An acceptable compromise is to permit use, but to require a disclaimer.[138] But if the later surname-user is trying to deceive the public or to exploit the first user's success, even use of one's own surname will be prohibited.[139]

---

131 *Abercrombie & Fitch v. Hunting World*, 537 F.2d 4 (2d Cir. 1976) (Friendly, J.). *See also Two Pesos, Inc. v. Taco Cabana*, 505 U.S. 763, 768 (1992) (approving this approach).

132 *Kellogg Co. v. National Biscuit Co.*, 305 U.S. 111, 118 (1938) (long exclusive use of term "shredded wheat" not sufficient to give it a secondary meaning necessary for trademark status).

133 *Bayer Co. v. United Drug Co.*, 272 F. 505 (2d Cir. 1921).

134 *DuPont Cellophane C. v. Waxed Products Co.*, 85 F.2d 75 (2d Cir. 1936).

135 *Kellogg Co. v. National Biscuit Co.*, *supra* note 132 at 116.

136 *Haughton Elevator Co. v. Seeberger*, 85 U.S.P.Q. 80, 83 (Comm'r of Patents 1950).

137 *See Singer Manufacturing Co. v. June Manufacturing*, 163 U.S. 169 (1896) ("Singer," while originally distinctive, is now a generic term for all sewing machines) and *Singer Manufacturing Co. v. Briley*, 207 F.2d 519 (5th Cir. 1953) (continuous use the term of "Singer" as a trademark for over 50 years after 1896 ruling has made it once again a distinctive mark).

138 *See Taylor Wine Co. v. Bully Hill Vineyards, Inc.*, 569 F.2d 731 (2d Cir. 1978) (grandson of Taylor Wine's founder may use his name Taylor in selling his own competing wines, but only with a disclaimer).

139 *See Sardi's Restaurants v. Sardie*, 755 F.2d 719 (9th Cir. 1985) (Sardie using his own name in California to denote his restaurant did not infringe rights of famous Sardi's Restaurant in New York City when his use was "honest and straightforward with no intent to confuse the public").

Infringement Suits The owner of an infringed mark may sue for injunctive relief and for damages for wilful infringements in federal court.[140] Infringement occurs when there is a "likelihood of confusion" among an appreciable number of "ordinarily prudent purchasers."[141] Actual confusion, while not required, is highly probative of likelihood, so consumer surveys are often performed and used as evidence. The degree of similarity of marks and similarity of the products involved is also important. For example, a motion sickness drug called "Bonamine" is likely to be confused with "Dramamine," a preexisting motion sickness drug,[142] but there is little likelihood of confusion with "Bonamine" computers. How goods are marketed also matters. For example, goods with competing trademarks that are stacked together in a supermarket and subject to "impulse buying" will be treated differently than an expensive item, such as a car, which is purchased only after considered deliberation.

Fair Use Fair use is a defense to infringement. A common example of fair use is where a manufacturer includes a component in another product and advertises the product as containing that part using its trademark. For example, the label on a computer may proclaim "Intel Inside" in referring to its CPU. Reconditioned goods can be advertised with the trademark of the original manufacturer so long as they are not sold as new items. In addition, as with copyright, parody can be fair use.[143]

Registration Registration with the U.S. Trademark Office is available to owners of trademarks, but registration is not necessary to acquire protectable rights in a trademark. All that is required is actual use of the mark. There must be evidence of "use in commerce," defined as "bona fide use in the ordinary course of trade, and not merely to reserve a right in the mark."[144] While not required, registration is useful for at least two reasons. First, a certificate of registration of a mark on the principal register "shall be prima facie evidence of the validity of the registered mark"[145] and registration plus five years continuous use thereafter makes the mark "incontestable" for so long that it is in actual use.[146] Among other things, this means that an infringer cannot raise the defense that a descriptive mark has not acquired its necessary "secondary meaning."[147] Second, registration provides constructive notice to the entire country, thus avoiding the normal common law limits on a trademark that confine rights in it to the geographical areas where it is being used.[148] Thus, a manufacturer that uses the trademark only in the eastern U.S. can gain protection

---

140 15 U.S.C.A. §1117(2).

141 *See Mushroom Makers, Inc. v. R.G. Barry Corp.*, 580 F.2d 44, 46 (2d Cir. 1978) (Friendly, J.).

142 *G.D. Searle & So. v. Chas. Pfizer & Co.*, 265 F.2d 385 (7th Cir. 1959).

143 *Jordache Enterprises v. Hogg Wyld, Ltd.*, 828 F.2d 1482, 1486 (10th Cir. 1987) (no confusion likely between "Jordache" jeans and alleged infringing "Lardache" jeans). *See also Reddy Communications v. Environment Action Foundation*, 477 F.Supp. 936 (D.D.C. 1979) (use of "Reddy Kilowatt," an electric utility industry trademark, in pamphlets critical of electric utilities held not an infringement; critical point of view made confusion unlikely).

144 15 U.S.C.A. §1127. *See also La Societe Anonyme des Parfums Le Galion v. Jean Patou*, 495 F.2d 1265 (2d Cir. 1974) (registration of mark as part of a "trademark maintenance program" without any "serious effort to merchandise" and with only minimal sales was ineffective to show ownership).

145 15 U.S.C.A. §1057(b).

146 15 U.S.C.A. §1065.

147 *Park 'N Fly v. Dollar Park and Fly, Inc.*, 469 U.S. 189 (1985). However, even an incontestable mark may be merely descriptive, thus affecting its strength as a mark and whether it is infringed. *See Petro Stopping Centers v. James River Petroleum, Inc.*, 130 F.3d 88, 92 (4th Cir. 1997) (incontestable mark "Petro" is largely descriptive as applied to gas stations and therefore is not a strong mark for purposes of determining likelihood of confusion). Secondary meaning was discussed *supra* p. 467.

148 15 U.S.C.A. §1072.

against infringement in California by registering the mark.[149]

Registration is permitted if the mark is in use and meets the requirements for trademarks discussed earlier. But registration will be denied if the mark so closely resembles a prior user's mark that it would create a likelihood of confusion, deceit or mistake. Registration is often approved despite prior use, because the earlier user has not registered the mark. If so, the rights of the prior user must be recognized and protected. For example, if A uses a mark extensively in 6 western states, but does not register it, and then B starts using the same mark nationally and registers it, A will be permitted to continue as before in the 6 western states, while B owns the mark in the other 44 states. Disputes over registrability of a mark often arise between the applicant and the federal Trademark Office. Such disputes are resolved through an examiner's decision and an administrative appeal to the Trademark Trial and Appeal Board. Thereafter, judicial review is possible in the Court of Appeals for the Federal Circuit and under some circumstances in the federal district court. Once an application has been approved, the mark is published in the Official Gazette of the Trademark Office. Any person who "believes he would be damaged by the registration" is permitted to file an opposition proceeding within 30 days, which is then handled by the Trademark Trial and Appeal Board, subject to judicial review.[150]

Contingent Registration As just noted, rights in trademarks are established only by actual use. However, the Act set up in 1988 a system of "contingent" registration based on intent to use a trademark. Such registration establishes "constructive use" and provides priority over except over earlier users and contingent filers. Contingent registration can ripen into full registration if the applicant files a statement of actual use within 6 months (extendable for additional 6-month periods to 24 months) after notice that the contingent registration has been allowed.[151] Contingent registration later ratified by actual use may well become the standard method for establishing rights in trademarks in the future.

International Trademark Protection As with copyrights, there is no such thing as international trademark protection. With the exception of certain treaties, the owner must comply with the laws of each foreign country to gain protection in that country. The closest thing to international protection is afforded by the Madrid Arrangement of 1891, which provides that registration with a Central Registration Bureau in Berne, Switzerland, extends to all other signatory countries. But the U.S. is not a signatory. It is possible that the subsidiary or division of a U.S. company located in a Madrid country could take advantage of the treaty. In addition, most countries allow for registration of trademarks without evidence of prior use, so rights can be established without a major financial commitment to marketing efforts. As for registration of foreign trademarks in the U.S., foreign owners can avail themselves of the registration process on the same basis as U.S. owners based on actual use or registration in the foreign owner's home country may be sufficient.[152]

---

149 Registration also entitles the trademark owner to more extensive damages, including treble damages, plus attorney fees. 15 U.S.C.A. §1117. Registration lasts 10 years and is renewable for a like period. A "use affidavit" must be filed each 6 years or the mark will be canceled. 15 U.S.C.A. §1058(a).

150 Trademark cases may be brought in federal court. 15 U.S.C.A. §1121.

151 15 U.S.C.A. §1051(b)-(d).

152 *See generally* 15 U.S.C.A. §1126 for international aspects of trademarks.

I. Disposition of Property Upon Death of the Owner

Interests in real and personal property are transferred upon the death of the owner.[153] The transfer, called "succession," can be either "testamentary," meaning by way of a "will" or by way of "intestate succession," which means without a will.[154]

1. Testamentary Succession of Property

Testamentary succession of property is disposition of that property upon death through a will. If a person writes a will, then the property that person owns at the time of his or her death will go to the persons named in the will. If real property passes, beneficiaries are called "devisees"; if personal property passes, they are called "legatees."

The "testator," the person writing the will, may generally designate whomever he or she wishes to receive the property. The formalities of proper execution of a will by a testator are governed by state laws. These laws generally require that testators be "competent" (that they understand what they are doing), that the will be in writing, that it be signed by the testator, and that the signing be witnessed by at least two witnesses.[155] A will may be changed or revoked by the testator at any time during his or her life. Changes to a will are often made by drafting an additional document known as a "codicil." A codicil, or any change in a will, must be made with the same formalities as the original will itself.

One constraint on the power of testators to bequeath property is that they may not choose to leave their spouse nothing at all. Typically, state laws allow a spouse one-third of the testator's property even if the testator has designated a smaller amount in the will. The decision to take a "statutory share" of the property rather than the amount designated in the will is generally known as "electing against the will." Such a share for the surviving spouse is often referred to as a "statutory elective share." The statutory share idea was an effort to protect women, whose economic welfare was often completely dependent on their husband's wishes.[156]

After the testator dies, the mechanics of the distribution of the testator's property are generally supervised by a special court, usually called a "probate" court.[157] Probate courts are responsible for seeing that the property of a testator is promptly distributed and all of the testator's debts are paid. The process of overseeing and certifying the distribution is called "probate," sometimes referred to as "probating an estate." When a will is involved, the court will appoint an "executor" to oversee the distribution process. The executor is a person whom the testator trusts, who is named in the will itself. The executor is personally responsible for insuring that the debts are paid and the property distributed to the correct persons.

---

153 For more information on wills and testamentary dispositions, *see* WILLIAM M. MCGOVERN, JR., SHELDON F. KURTZ, & JAN ELLEN REIN, HORNBOOK ON WILLS, TRUSTS AND ESTATES (West 1988), MARK REUTLINGER, WILLS, TRUSTS AND ESTATES: ESSENTIAL TERMS AND CONCEPTS, 2D ED. (Aspen 1998), and ROBERT L. MENNELL, WILLS AND TRUSTS IN A NUTSHELL, 2D ED. (West 1994). *See also* UNIFORM PROBATE CODE, OFFICIAL TEXT WITH COMMENTS, 11TH ED. (West 1994).

154 A will is a document in which an owner can specify to whom property should go after death. The terms "testamentary" and "intestate" are derived from the term "testament." "Testament" is a somewhat antiquated term referring to a "will." Even today, however, many wills are entitled "Last Will and Testament."

155 In general, these witnesses should have no interest in receiving any property under the will. If a witness is an interested party, the will, in general, will not be invalidated. However, the witness risks losing his or her interest under the will.

156 Marital property rights are discussed in Chapter XIV, pp. 476-477.

157 Such courts may have different names in different states. *See* Chapter V, p. 169.

2. Intestate Succession

Decedents who die without a will are said to have died "intestate" and their property passes by way of "intestate succession." In such cases, the probate court appoints an "administrator" to oversee the distribution and debt-payment process, whose responsibilities are generally the same as an executor, described above.

The property of people who die intestate goes to their "heirs at law."[158] These heirs are determined by state law. These laws vary somewhat, but strongly favor distributing the decedent's estate to a surviving spouse, children and, in their absence, to parents. State "intestacy" statutes tend to follow a pattern of awarding one-third of the decedent's property to the decedent's spouse and two-thirds to the couples' children. However, the surviving spouse generally makes out much better than the statutory division would seem to indicate. This is because most of the important property of the decedent — such as a house, bank accounts, stocks and bonds — are owned jointly with rights of survivorship by husband and wife. Thus, the surviving spouse automatically becomes the sole owner such property upon the decedent's death and the property is not included in the decedent's estate.

J. Trusts

The concept of a trust was introduced at the beginning of the chapter.[159] As stated there, settlors can convey their property to a trustee, who will have legal title to it, and convey a beneficial interest in that property to on other persons, called beneficiaries. This allows the beneficiaries to receive the benefits of the property, but relieves them of the obligations and rights of ownership. Trusts that come into being at the death of a person, usually as part of a plan coordinated with a will, are referred to as "testamentary trusts." Trusts created during the lifetime of a person are called "inter-vivos trusts."

1. The Establishment and Operation of a Trust

An example of a typical family trust might be as follows. A owns considerable stocks and bonds and wishes to have A's children, B, C, and D, receive the income from them. However, managing a securities portfolio takes some skill and time. A is also somewhat concerned that D, the youngest, may not appreciate the value of the securities and may sell them if A gave them as a gift outright. A might wish to set up a trust for the children and transfer the securities to that trust. A can choose anyone to be "trustee" of the trust. Under the terms of the trust, B, C, and D, the "beneficiaries" of the trust, will receive all of the net income from the securities every year. However, the "legal title" to the securities is actually transferred to the trustee. Since B, C and D have the right to enjoy the benefits of the property in the trust, it is sometimes said that they have "equitable title." This separability of legal and equitable title has been a feature of Anglo-American law for several centuries.

A might name First State Bank & Trust as "trustee." As trustee, the bank owes a "fiduciary duty" to the beneficiaries — the highest duty of care to protect their interests. The bank must manage the property competently and must distribute the net income from the property in accord with A's wishes as expressed in the trust document. The distributions can be in accord with any division A wishes. For example, if A wanted B to receive one-half of the net income and C and D the

---

158 Technically, in most states, "heirs at law" or "heirs" describes only those who receive real property. Recipients of personal property are referred to as "next of kin."

159 *See supra*, p. 441. For more material on trusts, *see supra*, note 153.

remaining half, then all A would need to do is to specify that division in the trust document. The beneficiaries have no right to interfere with the trustee's management of the trust property. For instance, if D wanted the trustee to sell all the gold mining stock in the portfolio because the mining company involved has been polluting the air, D would have no authority to order the trustee to do so. Only the trustee would have that authority. In general, the trustee must manage the property in the way that a "prudent businessperson" would manage it.

It is not unusual for the trust agreement to provide for certain limited withdrawal rights in beneficiaries. In other words, in addition to paying out the income from the securities, the trustee may be authorized to make lump sum payments up to a certain limit upon request of a beneficiary for certain special needs. Thus, A might provide that B, C, or D may receive up to $10,000 additional money per year for each year that they are enrolled in college, or in the event of an emergency.

2. Avoiding Probate with a Revocable *Inter-Vivos* Trust

Trusts are commonly used, along with wills, as part of "estate planning." Estate planning involves preparing for the distribution of a person's property upon death. *Inter-vivos* trusts are trusts established during the lifetime of the settlor and are commonly used to avoid making the distribution of the decedent's property subject to the probate process described earlier. A trust will avoid probate because the legal title to the property in the trust was already transferred to the trustee during the settlor's lifetime. As a result, there is no distribution of property upon the death of the decedent. Thus, there is nothing for the probate court to supervise.

Trusts designed to avoid probate may be either revocable by the settlor or "irrevocable." In revocable inter-vivos trusts, the settlor has the right to end the trust at any time during the settlor's life and assume the direct ownership of the property. Inter-vivos trusts designed primarily to avoid probate are usually revocable by the settlor while living in order to provide maximum flexibility. If the trust is not revoked by the time of the settlor's death, the property therein is not part of the settlor's probate estate, despite the fact that the settlor could have ended the trust and retaken the property while living. However, since a revocable trust effectively allows the settlor the full benefit of the property (if the settlor so wishes) while living, federal income tax must be paid by the settlor on all the *income* from such a trust, just as if the settlor owned the property outright. In addition, federal *estate* taxes will be imposed on the value of the trust at the time of the settlor's death. The federal estate tax laws follow the "substance" rather than the "form" of trust arrangements. Consequently, while this form of trust avoids the probate process, it does not avoid estate taxes upon the settlor's death or income taxes while living.

3. Avoiding Taxes with an Irrevocable *Inter-Vivos* Trust

Avoiding Income Taxes If the settlor wishes to avoid income taxes on income from trust property, the *inter-vivos* trust must be irrevocable so that the settlor cannot regain ownership of the trust property. The *beneficiaries* must pay income taxes on payments they receive, but they are often subject to a lower rate of taxation than the settlor. This is because they have less income and therefore fall into a lower "tax bracket." Often the beneficiaries in a lower tax bracket will be the settlor's children.

Avoiding Estate Taxes Irrevocable inter-vivos trusts are also used to avoid federal estate taxation upon the death of the settlor. However, a transfer to such an irrevocable trust is "complete" at the time of the transfer, so the transfer is subject to the federal *gift tax* at the time of the transfer. Despite the fact that the federal estate and gift taxes are coordinated, the gift tax will produce a lower effective rate of tax than the estate tax. On the other hand, gift tax must be paid currently, whereas the estate awaits payment until the death of the settlor. Estate planning generally requires the help of sophisticated lawyers who specialize in taxation. A proper estate plan must not only minimize the effects of federal and state gift, estate and income taxes, but must also assure that the client has an adequate income to live on.[160]

4. Testamentary Trusts and the Use of a Pour-Over Will in Conjunction with an *Inter Vivos* Trust

Tax and Probate Treatment of Testamentary Trusts   A settlor may wish to set up a "testamentary" trust — a trust that comes into being upon the testator's death. While such a trust provides the benefits of having a trustee control distribution to beneficiaries, testamentary trusts have none of the tax or probate avoidance benefits outlined above. The entire corpus of the trust will be taxed and will be included in the estate to be probated.

Pour-Over Wills and Inter Vivos Trusts   To avoid some of the tax and probate disadvantages of a testamentary trust, the settlor may wish instead to place part of the property into a revocable (or irrevocable) *inter vivos* trust and use a "pour-over" will to dispose of the remainder of the property. A pour-over will is so named because the will provides that the remainder of the estate is to be given to a trustee under a trust established in the will.[161] The existence of the trust agreement will be recognized in the will and the trust will come into existence when the will is executed. Using this device, the settlor-testator is able to gain the benefits of having a trust after death to provide on-going control of distribution of property and to make outright unrestricted testamentary bequests as well.

---

160 For more on the details of estate and gift tax, *see* JOHN K. MCNULTY, FEDERAL ESTATE AND GIFT TAXATION IN A NUTSHELL, 5TH ED (West 1994).

161 *See* John R. Cohan and Geraldine Hemmerling, INTER VIVOS TRUSTS: PLANNING, DRAFTING AND TAXATION, §4.7 (McGraw-Hill 1975). *See also*, 79 Am. Jur. 2d §209 (discussing wills).

CHAPTER XIII

FAMILY LAW

Family law has traditionally been considered the special province of the states. However, as discussed in the chapter on constitutional law, federal constitutional law has increasingly played a role, especially in the development of the fundamental right to privacy in family matters.[1] Moreover, Congress has intervened with the power and resources of the federal government in some family law areas, notably in providing assistance to needy families and in enforcing child support obligations.[2] The Uniform Law Commissioners have been active the family law area, but have had mixed success in attracting states to adopt uniform laws, undoubtedly because of the strong feeling that family law policy issues generate in state legislatures.[3] As a result, the law can vary considerably from state to state.[4]

Most state law governing family matters is statutory. Yet, court decisions are of paramount importance because statutory provisions tend to be general. At most, statutes will list factors courts are to consider in making decisions, thus leaving much to the discretion of the court and making much depend on the facts of each case.

A. Marriage

Couples usually marry for intangible, personal reasons and romantic love plays a major role in the decision to marry in the United States. But there are also certain tangible benefits and legal rights that accrue to those in a valid marriage, primarily property ownership rights. Further, if one spouse dies intestate, the surviving spouse is entitled to some or all of the decedent's estate under intestacy laws. Similar legal rights exist with respect to social security benefits, pension plans and health care benefits.

1. Ceremonial Marriages

Legal capacity to marry is fulfilled when an individual is of legal age, mentally competent, and not already married. Age requirements vary among states, ranging generally from 16 to 18 years old. Mental competence, which requires that a person understand the nature and consequences of marriage at the time of the act, is presumed unless it is proven that a person either was mentally ill or was involuntarily intoxicated. In the case of someone who is mentally ill, a legal guardian must give consent to the marriage.[5] Both parties must freely consent to the marriage. If one party is coerced under duress to marry the other, the marriage is invalid. Free and voluntary consent may also be vitiated by fraud, jest or some other ulterior motive.

---

1 *See* Chapter IX, pp. 340-342.

2 *See infra* this chapter, pp. 491-492.

3 *See, e.g.*, UNIFORM MARRIAGE AND DIVORCE ACT, 9A UNIF. L. ANN. 91 (1979) (UMDA); UNIFORM PARENTAGE ACT, 9B UNIF.L.ANN. 287 (1987)(UPA); UNIFORM RECIPROCAL ENFORCEMENT OF SUPPORT ACT, 9A UNIF.L.ANN. 747 and REVISED UNIFORM RECIPROCAL ENFORCEMENT OF SUPPORT ACT, 9A UNIF.L.ANN. 643 (1979); UNIFORM STATUS OF CHILDREN OF ASSISTED CONCEPTION ACT, 9B UNIF.L.ANN. 152 (Supp. 1994); UNIFORM CHILD CUSTODY JUDGMENT ACT, 9 UNIF.L.ANN. 123 (1968); UNIFORM PREMARITAL AGREEMENT ACT, 9B UNIF.L.ANN. 371 (1983); UNIFORM ADOPTION ACT, 9 UNIF.L.ANN. 72 (1988); UNIFORM MARITAL PROPERTY ACT, 9A UNIF.L.ANN. 97 (1987). Many of these and other statutes are reprinted in DOCUMENTS AND STATUTES IN FAMILY LAW (West 1994).

4 For a hornbook treatment of family law *see* HOMER H. CLARK, JR., THE LAW OF DOMESTIC RELATIONS IN THE UNITED STATES, 2D ED. (West 1986, 1988). See also JOHN DeWITT GREGORY, PETER N. SWISHER & SHERYL L. SCHEIBLE, UNDERSTANDING FAMILY LAW (Matthew Bender 1993).

5 A legal guardian is a person appointed by a court to supervise the affairs of persons who are mentally or physically incompetent to manage their own affairs. *See infra* p. 500.

The procedure for marrying begins with the couple obtaining a marriage license issued by the county clerk. This requirement is typically perfunctory unless the applicants have a close blood relationship[6] or are of the same sex,[7] or one or both lack legal capacity, such as where one of the parties is already married. After an application for a marriage license is submitted, most states impose a brief waiting period, usually 3 days to a week, before a license is issued. Many states require a blood test to check for sexually transmitted diseases, such as syphilis or gonorrhea, though the right to marry is not denied based on the results. Some states have imposed testing requirements for acquired immune deficiency syndrome (AIDS), while other states view AIDS testing as an invasion of an individual's right to privacy.

Finally, the parties must solemnize their marriage through someone authorized by law to do so. A religious representative will do, such as a priest, rabbi, or minister. Some civil officials have that power, such as a judge or the mayor of a city. Most commonly solemnization involves a ceremony during which the couple announces their intent and desire to be married. The secular purposes for this requirement are to give public notice and to impress upon the parties the serious nature of the commitment they are making to the other person.

2. Common Law Marriages

Approximately one-fourth of the states recognize "common law" marriages which, technically, meet none of the formal requirements described above. Thirty-seven states have either passed statutes or decided by case law to abolish common law marriages.[8] These informal marriages are entered into by the parties pursuant to an agreement to be married, but without the formalities of a license and solemnization. The agreements are almost never written and are rarely agreed to in explicit detail by the parties. In fact, most often they are implied after the fact by courts, which draw inferences about the existence of an agreement from the conduct of the parties. If a valid common law marriage can be proven, then it will entitle the spouses or children to the same benefits and legal rights outlined above for a ceremonial marriage. The most common situation where common law marriage is sought to be proven is where one partner dies and the other seeks to claim a share of the estate or some form of other benefits tied to marriage, such as workers' compensation payments or Social Security benefits.

Courts determining whether a common law marriage existed will consider whether the couple held themselves out to the public as husband and wife, whether they cohabited, filed joint tax returns, maintained a joint bank account or undertook any other actions which indicated their intent to be married. The couple must also have manifested a present intent to be husband and wife and must have the capacity to marry. An intent to ceremonially marry in the *future* may preclude a finding of a present intent to be husband and wife.[9]

---

6 Many states prohibit an uncle and niece and aunt and nephew from marrying. Only a few states forbid first cousin marriages. CLARK, *supra* note 4, at §2.9. The issue of whether relatives are "marriageable" also determines whether sexual relations between them will be considered incest. *See Tapscott v. State*, 684 A.2d 439 (Md. 1996) (defendant's sexual liaison with his half-blood niece violated prohibition against incest; case cites many sources and traces history of incest laws).

7 *But see infra*, p. 493.

8 Some of these states qualify this restriction. For example, in Indiana, a common law marriage may be recognized for worker's compensation purposes if it both occurred before 1958 and was open and notorious for five years before the party's death. West's Ann. Ind. Code §22-3-3-19 (1991, 1998). For a complete listing of state statutes, see CLARK, *supra* note 4, at §2.4. n. 9 and n. 11.

9 *In re Estate of Shepherd*, 646 N.E.2d 561 (Ohio App. 1994) (co-habitant not a "surviving spouse").

A common law marriage will be recognized by all states if it was valid where and when it was entered into. This follows from the conflicts of law rule that the law of the place of the marriage controls, regardless of where the couple travels thereafter. Consequently, a common law marriage legally formed in one state will be recognized as valid even by the states that do not permit common law marriages.[10]

3. Marriage and Property Rights

Common Law At common law, single women had legal capacities similar to men's. But upon marriage, that all changed. As Blackstone described it, "[b]y marriage, the husband and wife are one person in law; that is, the very being or legal existence of the woman is suspended during the marriage, or at least is incorporated and consolidated into that of the husband."[11] A married woman could neither enter into contracts, nor could she sue or be sued. Any real or personal property belonging to the wife was controlled by the husband upon marriage. The wife's personal property actually became the property of her husband, and on his death passed to his personal representative. Even such items as clothing and jewelry were owned by the husband, although these did come back to the wife if the husband died. While the wife retained the right to direct to whom real property owned by her *prior* to the marriage would go upon her death, the husband had control over that property, including any rents or profits generated by land, for the duration of the marriage.[12]

Married Women's Property Acts In England, as early as the 1600s and 1700s, equity courts began to develop exceptions to common law rules limiting women's legal capacities. This resulted in creation of the *feme sole* estate. This device permitted married women to control their separate property much like a single woman could, and shielded it from the husband's creditors. The more pervasive solution, however, were the many "Married Women's Property Acts" (MWPAs). By 1900, all states had enacted one. However, the laws fell far short of granting married women full legal capacity. Also, courts had a tendency to interpret the statutes as narrowly as possible. Eventually, the MWPAs provided full rights and responsibilities to the married woman, permitting her to own, convey or sell property, to contract, engage in business, seek employment and keep her own earnings. A married woman could sue or be sued, make a will and testify in court. Finally, she became fully responsible for her own criminal and tortious conduct.

The MWPAs, however, did not undermine the husband's position as head of the household or the wife's duty to provide him with household services. Moreover, by providing that the property of each spouse, whether acquired before or during the marriage, remained that spouse's property, MWPAs hurt most women. Most women

---

10 Thus, a marriage satisfying the requirements of the state where entered into is valid everywhere, "unless it violates the strong public policy of another state which had the most significant relationship to the spouses and the marriage at the time of the marriage." RESTATEMENT (SECOND) OF CONFLICTS §283. Section 284 provides that a state usually gives the same incidents to a valid foreign marriage that it gives to a marriage contracted within its territory. RESTATEMENT §284. *See also* Chapter VII, p. 253. The Constitution's "full faith and credit" clause may also require it. *See* Chapter VII, p. 250. *Cf. infra* p. 494.

11 1 WILLIAM BLACKSTONE, COMMENTARIES ON THE LAWS OF ENGLAND 445 (1765-1769) (William S. Hein & Co. 1992).

12 Upon death of the husband, the fact that his property went to his heirs often left the widow destitute. The common law developed the concepts of dower and curtesy to protect surviving spouses. These doctrines permitted the wife to claim a certain portion of the husband's estate (dower) or the husband to claim a certain portion of the wife's estate (curtesy) regardless of the deceased spouse's will. Later these became the "statutory elective share" a spouse can choose instead of what is provided for in the deceased spouse's will. *See* Chapter XII, p. 470.

had no property of their own. For them, the only effect of a MWPA was the negative one of assuring that wives had no property interest in their husbands' earnings.

The Common Law Separate Property Approach Upon Divorce The vast majority of the states follow the common law separate property approach, as adjusted by MSPAs. But this approach is modified by divorce laws that require, upon divorce, that there be an "equitable distribution" of the property acquired during marriage to achieve a fair settlement between the spouses. This is based on the idea that marriage is a shared enterprise and the assets of this enterprise should accrue to both partners in light of the contributions of each, including homemaking services.

Community Property Approach A minority of the states has adopted what is called a "community property" approach, borrowed from the civil law systems in Europe. Under this concept, all property acquired during the marriage is community property and both spouses share an ownership interest in it from the time that it is acquired. Property acquired prior to marriage, gifts or inheritances either spouse acquires during marriage and any profits earned on separate property remain separate property, unless commingled. Upon divorce, spouses retain their separate property and the community property is divided equally. While the community property concept seems simple, much litigation has arisen on its application to the many different forms of property acquired during marriage, such as veterans' benefits, damages for personal injuries, and property acquired before marriage but paid for in part with community funds. Rebuttable presumptions have developed that property acquired during the marriage, regardless of who acquired it, is community property.

Premarital Agreements In most states, the parties may predetermine contractually what marital property or support rights will accrue upon marriage. This is done by means of a premarital agreement, sometimes called a "prenuptial" or "antenuptial" agreement. Traditionally such agreements could affect property rights only upon death of a spouse. Common situations were a marriage of people with grossly disproportionate financial assets or marriage of two older people who wanted to protect the inheritance rights of children from previous marriages. In recent years, however, premarital agreements have had the broader purpose of affecting property distribution upon divorce. Not all courts will recognize agreements in contemplation of divorce, usually on the ground that they encourage divorce.[13] But some courts maintain that there is no real evidence that premarital agreements encourage divorce and that, given that divorce is "such a commonplace fact of life," it makes sense to permit the parties to agree on what property and alimony rights should accrue to the parties "in the event that their marriage, despite their best efforts, should fail."[14]

Even in states that honor premarital agreements, however, courts tend to require that there be complete disclosure of both parties' assets and liabilities and that the agreement be "fair." Courts will refuse to enforce an agreement that is grossly unfair or one-sided, especially when it is evident that one party took advantage of the other party's ignorance or lack of knowledge in business affairs. They will also take into account the fact that it may be difficult for the parties to predict what their circumstances will be at the time of divorce, and equity will step in if necessary to

---

13 *See Mulford v. Mulford*, 320 N.W.2d 470 (Neb. 1982) (ignoring premarital agreement that waived any right to alimony, support or property in the event of divorce).

14 *Posner v. Posner*, 233 So.2d 381, 384 (Fla. 1970). *See generally* J. Thomas Oldham, *Premarital Agreements Are Now Enforceable Unless* . . . , 21 HOUSTON L. REV. 757 (1984).

adjust for such changes.[15]   The courts are more willing to enforce a prenuptial agreement when the weaker partner (traditionally the wife) had independent counsel.[16] In 1983, the Uniform Premarital Agreement Act was drafted and has since been adopted in 16 states. It makes such agreements enforceable, but codifies the caselaw exceptions just described.[17]

B. Dissolution of Marriages

1. Divorce

Grounds   A divorce action is a civil lawsuit in equity.[18] Traditionally, to obtain a divorce in the United States, one party was required to show that the other party was at fault. While state statutes have varied somewhat, the traditional grounds have been similar: habitual drunkenness, adultery, physical cruelty, mental cruelty, abandonment, and insanity. However, a revolution in divorce law was spurred by California's enactment in 1969 of a "no-fault" divorce statute. The "grounds" stated were "irreconcilable differences which have caused irremediable breakdown of marriage."[19] The Uniform Law Commissioners approved §302 of the Uniform Marriage and Divorce Act in 1970, providing as the sole ground for divorce "that the marriage is irretrievably broken."[20]   The policy behind no-fault divorces is that they avoid invading the family's privacy, reduce the acrimony between the couple and, where both parties want the divorce, eliminate the need to "create" grounds that meet the requirements of the law. However, while all states have some form of no-fault divorce, many states also retain traditional fault grounds. Most important, fault can be taken into account in determining child custody, property settlements and spousal support. Fault issues can be especially hard fought when proof of marital fault disqualifies the offending party from receiving any spousal support.[21]

In most no-fault states, the proof necessary to show a no-fault "ground" for divorce is not very demanding. For example, the complaint may simply recite the words of the statute, and the testimony of one spouse affirming that the statutory definition applies to the marriage is sufficient proof. However, no-fault statutes do not remove all the impediments to divorce or totally banish fault from the process. First, many statutes impose a waiting period before a divorce judgment can be entered. Typical periods are 60 days for couples with no children and 6 months for couples with children.[22] However, some states impose waiting periods of up to two years. Second, some states have read the requirement that the marital relationship be *truly* irretrievably broken to require that there be some evidence of unsuccessful attempts

---

15 *Reilling v. Reilling*, 474 P.2d 327 (Or. 1970) (distinguishing premarital agreements from separation agreements, since the latter affect present, known financial circumstances).

16 *Del Vecchio v. Del Vecchio*, 143 So.2d 17 (Fla. 1962) (where wife had no counsel and full disclosure of the extent of the husband's assets was not made, agreement will not be honored on his death and a court must order adequate provision for wife).

17 UNIFORM PREMARITAL AGREEMENT ACT, *supra* note 3.

18 Equity is discussed in Chapter VII, pp. 234-235. Divorces were first handled in ecclesiastical courts.

19 West's Ann.Cal.Civ.Code §4506, enacted in 1969 and effective in 1970. *See* CLARK, *supra* note 4, §12.1 for a brief history of divorce law.

20 UMDA §302.

21 *See* Va. Code Ann. §20-107.1 (adultery is an absolute bar to spousal support unless "manifest injustice" would result). Fault grounds and defenses for divorce will not be discussed here. *See* GREGORY, SWISHER & SCHEIBLE, *supra* note 4, §7.03 for more information. The role of fault in other aspects of divorce is discussed *infra* p. 481.

22 Mich. Comp. L. Ann. §552.9f. *See also* Cal. Fam Code App. §4514 (6 months for all couples).

to work out problems or to reconcile. Counseling is usually made available for couples who might be able to reconcile.[23]

Procedural Requirements for Divorce   Most states require in general that at least one spouse be "domiciled" in the state where the complaint for divorce is filed, meaning that the state must be the permanent home of that spouse.[24] States generally impose a "durational residency" requirement, mandating that the plaintiff live in the state continuously for a given length of time. This period varies with the state and ranges from 6 weeks to 2 years. The most common length is 6 months.[25] The main reason for the requirement is to provide objective evidence of a party's domicile in a state as proof that that state's court has proper jurisdiction over the divorce action.[26]

Settlement and Alternative Dispute Resolution   Many feel that it is a mistake to give the judicial system the primary task of handling marital breakups. Among the reasons are that the judicial setting encourages an adversarial relationship between the two spouses, even when the parties approach it amicably, and that it gives the advantage to the party with the greater resources, a serious concern in marital breakups where one party (usually the wife) is in a much worse financial circumstance than the other. In addition, it is a waste of precious judicial resources, given that over half the civil cases filed in state courts of general jurisdiction are divorces.

No state has taken courts completely out of divorce cases, but courts routinely "lean on" the parties to settle as many issues as possible out of court and efforts have been made to use non-judicial resources whenever possible. Out of court settlement efforts often do little to reduce acrimony, as settlement negotiations can often be as contentious as contested court proceedings.[27] However, mediation has been touted as one option for settling marital settlement disputes in a less hostile environment. Arbitration, like mediation, is an informal procedure that offers the advantage of saving time and money. However, in the family law area, enforceability of arbitration decisions is less sure than in other areas of the law. Courts have been careful to assure that the best interests of all concerned, particularly any children involved, are protected in divorce cases. Thus, courts are not likely to approve arbitration decisions without first reviewing them.[28]

2. Annulment and Legal Separation

Annulments   When a couple has obtained a license and solemnized the

---

23 *See Riley v. Riley*, 271 So.2d 181 (Fla. App. 1972) (imposing a three-month period for possible reconciliation and counseling).

24 The Supreme Court has likewise assumed that domicile is necessary for jurisdiction in a divorce case. *See Williams v. North Carolina*, 325 U.S. 226, 229 (1945). For a discussion of jurisdiction and procedural issues in divorce actions see CLARK, *supra* note 4, §§12.2-12.5 and Chapter 14.

25 Residency requirements of up to one year have been held constitutional. *Sosna v. Iowa*, 419 U.S. 393 (1975). *Compare Shapiro v. Thompson*, 394 U.S. 618 (1969) (durational residence requirement for need-based welfare eligibility violates fundamental right to travel).

26 A county residency requirement is also imposed usually. It is shorter in duration than the state residency requirement, usually between seven and ten days. It is imposed to deter parties from flocking to a particular court in the state perceived as more favorable to certain interests and to spread the divorce docket rationally among the courts of the state.

27 See CLARK, *supra* note 4, §14.8 for a complete discussion of alternative methods of dispute resolution.

28 Mediation and arbitration in civil cases were discussed in Chapter VII, p. 243. At least one commentator has protested use of mediation in divorces as disadvantageous to women. Trina Grillo, *The Mediation Alternative: Process Dangers for Women*, 100 YALE L.J. 1545 (1991).

marriage, but has failed to meet the other requirements for a valid marriage, such as consent or capacity, the couple may be eligible for an annulment. An annulment is a legal recognition that the marriage was invalid. Despite annulments declaring that no valid marriage took place, courts usually treat them just as they would a divorce — apportioning property, assets and debts, and determining the custody and support of children. Alimony, however, is generally not awarded. Courts deem such action necessary to restore the parties to the same position they were in prior to the invalid marriage and to protect any children involved. Nearly all states' laws provide that any children on the union will not be made illegitimate as a result of the annulment. However, some states require good faith intent to enter into a valid marriage.[29] Because divorce has become more prevalent, more socially acceptable, and easier to get, fewer legal annulments are sought or granted by the courts.[30]

Legal Separations   Couples may choose legal separation as a way to gain a perspective on their marriage while deciding whether to divorce. Others, for various reasons, may wish to live apart on a permanent basis, but to remain married. A permanent legal separation of this type is known as a "divorce from bed and board" or divorce *a mensa et thoro*, and is recognized in about half the states. In such cases, a court order is entered specifying the terms of the separation, including resolution of property and child-related issues, much like a divorce. The main difference is that the parties may not remarry. If the parties later decide to divorce, another legal proceeding is necessary. For this reason, many lawyers advise their clients to forego legal separations and either file for divorce or separate without a court order.[31]

3. Alimony and Property Settlement

a. Distinction Between Alimony and Property Settlements

"Alimony," sometimes called "spousal support," is money paid by one spouse to the other for financial support pursuant to court order. Payment can be made either in a lump sum or periodically. Periodic payments can be for a definite or indefinite period of time. Generally, the death of the payer or payee will terminate the obligation to pay alimony. The remarriage of the payee or other major changes in the financial circumstances of either party may be grounds for modifying alimony, unless the alimony order expressly states otherwise.[32]

In contrast to alimony, property settlements try to achieve an equitable division of the *assets* of the marriage and typically divide those assets by way of lump-sum payments or specific awards of particular items of property to one or the other party. Assets are determined and evaluated based on several factors, typically the parties' contributions, including homemaking and child rearing services, and other equities, such as what property the parties brought to the marriage and the duration of the marriage.

---

29 In the absence of statute, the common law considered all such children to be illegitimate. Because of recent cases holding much discrimination against illegitimate children unconstitutional, the consequences of illegitimacy are not as serious as they used to be. *See* Chapter IX, p. 350..

30 Religious annulments are different. Most commonly a religious annulment is sought by a Roman Catholic who wishes to remarry in a Catholic church. Religious annulments and not recognized by law, so the parties to them have usually already obtained a civil divorce.

31 Couples are also considered legally separated pursuant to a formal agreement or a temporary order of the court while the divorce case is pending.

32 Historically, the husband's legal duty to provide for his wife was the basis for the right to alimony, so many state alimony statutes provided that only wives could receive alimony. However, the Supreme Court has held such statutes to be unconstitutional sex discrimination in violation of the equal protection clause of the 14th Amendment. *See Orr v. Orr*, 440 U.S. 268 (1979) and Chapter IX, p. 336.

Both property settlements and alimony may consist of periodic payments or a lump sum and the payments could well be classified as one or the other. But how they are characterized can have important ramifications. First, a property settlement is not taxable income to the *recipient* under federal income tax laws. Similarly, the transfer of property does not create a tax deduction for the *payer*. Alimony, however, *is* taxable income to the *recipient* and can be *deducted* from the *payer's* gross income in calculating income tax due. Second, although a property settlement may have more favorable tax consequences for the recipient, there are some disadvantages. The obligation to comply with a property award is dischargeable in bankruptcy, while the obligation to pay alimony is not. Finally, while property settlements generally cannot be modified, alimony awards may be modified where warranted by a change in circumstances, as discussed above. Modifiability is a risk factor that may positively or negatively affect a dependent spouse's standard of living in the future. The paying spouse may argue for the entire settlement to be treated as a property settlement so that the receiving spouse cannot modify it in the future. In contrast, the receiving spouse may wish to include some alimony in the settlement to preserve the right to future modification.

b. Determining the Amount of Alimony Awards and Property Settlements

As noted earlier, some states, while retaining no-fault grounds for *divorce*, effectively provide for "fault" grounds to be considered in resolution of issues of alimony, property division and child custody. But these are often the only issues the parties fight about, so reintroducing fault undercuts the purposes of no-fault legislation. Consequently, some states prohibit consideration of fault at any point in the divorce. For example, the UMDA provides that the amount and duration of spousal support is to be determined "without regard to marital misconduct."[33]

Alimony States statutes typically grant the courts broad discretion in determining the amount of an alimony award and provide only factors to be considered. The UMDA[34] is typical in listing in §308 the following factors: (1) the financial resources of the party seeking alimony including marital property received in a settlement, any child support payments which include a sum for the party as custodian, and the party's earning potential; (2) the time necessary for the spouse seeking alimony to acquire sufficient education or training to enable that spouse to re-enter the job market; (3) the standard of living established during the marriage; (4) the duration of the marriage; (5) the age and physical and emotional condition of the spouse seeking alimony; and (6) the financial status of the spouse from whom alimony is sought.

Courts today award alimony less often than in the past and for shorter periods of time. One state, Texas, does not allow alimony under any circumstances.[35] Other state statutes strictly limit the situations in which alimony can be awarded. The property settlement is replacing alimony as the principal means of adjusting the parties' financial relationship in most states.

Property Settlements In all states — whether common law separate property or community property states — courts seek to divide property equitably and have wide discretion in determining which spouse gets what property. The UMDA, for example,

---

33 UMDA §308. The factors to be considered are discussed below.

34 *See supra* note 3.

35 *See, e.g., Tinsley v. Tinsley*, 512 S.W.2d 74 (Tex.Civ.App. 1974).

requires the court to consider all the assets of the parties, whenever acquired, and (1) the duration of the marriage; (2) prior marriages of either party; (3) any prenuptial agreements; (4) the age, health, occupation, earning power, and employability of the parties; (5) the liabilities and needs of each party; and (6) any alimony received.

c. Agreements on Alimony and Property Settlement

In most cases, the parties will agree to particular financial and other arrangements and present the agreement to the court for approval. One ground for avoiding the effect of a settlement agreement is that it is "unconscionable."[36] Courts have tended to insist that such agreements not only be free of fraud and coercion, but also that they be "fair and sufficient in light of the station in life and circumstances of the parties."[37] Invalidation of a settlement agreement is most likely to be invoked successfully at the behest of the traditionally weaker party, the wife. Husbands have more difficulty arguing that they were forced into one-sided agreements.[38]

If approved by the court, settlement agreements are often incorporated into the divorce decree. This may be done either by referring to a separate agreement or by simply copying the agreement's terms into the divorce judgment. Either procedure allows the agreement to be enforced in the same manner as any other judgment.

d. Property Subject to Division

Virtually any thing that can be evaluated and the value divided between the parties is potentially property that may be divided upon divorce. Divisible property includes not only houses, cars, business property, cash, stocks, bonds, and accounts, but also pension rights, disability payments and medical insurance.[39] Even more intangible things, such as the "good will" generated by a business or professional practice, are considered in most states to be marital property. Such property may be evaluated and part of its value ordered paid to a party.[40]

Recently, there has been a trend to expand the concept of divisible property to include "career assets" or "human capital." These terms refer to a college or professional degree which one spouse earned during the marriage while the other spouse worked and supported the family. The essence of this development is to allow the court to reach future earnings, which many believe is the only way to achieve economic fairness when one spouse has sacrificed to put the other through school. Traditionally, alimony was awarded to remedy inequities of this sort. However, the growing antipathy toward alimony has caused courts to categorize some professional degrees acquired during marriage as a marital asset that can be divided as part of the property settlement. In *O'Brien v. O'Brien*,[41] a New York court found that the wife had

---

36 UMDA §306.

37 *Crawford v. Crawford*, 350 N.E.2d 103 (Ill.App. 1976).

38 *Compare Jameson v. Jameson*, 239 N.W.2d 5 (S.D. 1976) (though the agreement was "harsh" from the husband's standpoint, it would not be invalidated on grounds of unconscionability) *with In re Marriage of Hitchcock*, 265 N.W.2d 599 (Iowa 1978) (agreement invalidated at wife's request even though she was represented by counsel and advised by her brother).

39 *See Schober v. Schober*, 692 P.2d 267 (Alaska 1984) (state policeman's unused personal leave time from work was deemed to be a divisible marital asset by analogy to a pension). *But see Boyd v. Boyd*, 323 N.W.2d 553 (Mich.App. 1982) (refusing to evaluate and divide husband's seniority at work).

40 *See Wisner v. Wisner*, 631 P.2d 115 (Ariz.App 1981) (community property state) and *Rostel v. Rostel*, 622 P.2d 429 (Alaska 1981) (common law state). *But see Nail v. Nail*, 486 S.W.2d 761 (Tex. 1972) (good will of medical practice is an attribute of a particular person that cannot be transferred, so it is not community property).

41 489 N.E.2d 712 (N.Y. 1985).

contributed 76% of the household's income during the period the husband pursued his medical degree, determined that the present value of the degree was $188,000 and that the wife was entitled to 40% of that amount.[42] Other courts have refused to categorize professional and college degrees as marital property because degrees are not property that can be transferred, inherited or acquired by merely paying money[43] or because alimony provides the better method of dealing with the issue.[44] But even in these states the contributions of a spouse toward the other spouse's acquisition of an advanced degree is taken into account in determining property settlements or alimony.

4. Custody of Children

The issue of the custody of children most often comes up when there is a divorce, but it may arise in other contexts as well. In general, courts treat custody disputes in an identical fashion whether the parents are married to each other or not.[45]

Legal custody of a child includes the right to make all decisions pertaining to the child's upbringing, including education, health care, religion, growth and development. It usually includes physical custody of the child as well. Thus, the child will live with the custodial parent and is under that parent's physical supervision. Custody generally lasts as long as the child remains a minor; it may extend beyond the age of majority for a mentally disabled child.

a. Presumptions and Factors in Awarding Custody

Presumption in Favor of Birth Parents Contests between a natural parent and a non-parent do not often arise in divorce child custody disputes, but when they do and in other contexts, there is a clear presumption in favor of the natural parent. This presumption can be overcome, but given its probable constitutional underpinnings, it requires "extraordinary circumstances."[46] One such circumstance has been a determination that a stranger-caregiver of the child has become the psychological parent of the child.[47]

Presumptions As Between Parents Under traditional common law in the 19th century, custody of children was granted to the father. In the first half of the 20th century, this changed to the "tender years" doctrine, under which it was presumed that the mother was best qualified to care for children in their pre-teenage years. The

---

42 *See also Woodworth v. Woodworth*, 337 N.W.2d 332 (Mich.App. 1983) (plaintiff-wife worked to support the family while the husband was in law school; law degree was the product of a concerted family effort and the result of mutual sacrifices and efforts by both the husband and wife).

43 *See In re Marriage of Graham*, 574 P.2d 75 (Colo. 1978) and *In re Marriage of Weinstein*, 470 N.E.2d 551 (Ill.App. 1984).

44 *McLain v.McLain*, 310 N.W.2d 316 (Mich.App. 1981). *See also Graham, supra* and *In re Marriage of Sullivan*, 691 P.2d 1020 (1984) (community property jurisdictions).

45 To some extent, this is required by constitutional considerations. *See Stanley v. Illinois*, 405 U.S. 645 (1972) (law presuming unwed father to be unfit parent and depriving him of custody after mother's death was unconstitutional). *Compare Quilloin v. Walcott*, 434 U.S. 246 (1978) (state may deny putative father veto right over adoption of child by future stepfather, when birth father had no relationship with child) and *Lehr v. Robertson*, 463 U.S. 248 (1983) (not unconstitutional for adoption to take place without notice to putative father who had established no custodial, personal, or financial relationship with the child) *with Caban v. Mohammed*, 441 U.S. 380 (1979) (mother-only consent to adoption unconstitutional where biological father had lived with mother and child and established a relationship with the child). *See also infra* note 82.

46 *Bennett v. Jeffries*, 356 N.E.2d 277, 281 (N.Y. 1976) (contest between natural mother and friend of child's grandmother to whom grandmother had entrusted custody).

47 This was the determination of the trial court on remand in *Bennett, id. See also Painter v. Bannister*, 140 N.W.2d 152 (Iowa 1966) (custody awarded to maternal grandparents on this basis).

father could overcome this presumption only by proving that the mother was unfit or far less capable than he of caring for the children. Today, the explicit preference for mothers has disappeared because of the dramatic increase in the number of mothers working outside the home, a greater willingness of fathers to be custodial parents, and concerns about its constitutionality.[48] Instead, courts consider the "best interests of the child" without regard to the sex of the competing parents. Nonetheless, this often amounts to a *de facto* custody presumption in favor of the mother, since courts often presume that the best interests of children facing the disruption of divorce are served by maintaining continuity in their care. This presumption in favor of the "primary caregiver" during the marriage in most cases points to the mother.[49] The component factors in determining the "best interests" of the child are (1) the demonstrated ability of each parent to care for the child personally; (2) the nature of the relationship between the child and the competing parents as revealed by the past conduct of parent and child; (3) the desires of the parents for custody; (4) maintenance of the stability of the child's current environment, especially with respect to home, school and friends; and (5) the desires of the child.[50]

Religion and Race It has been traditional for courts to take into consideration the religious beliefs, or lack thereof, of the parents. However, increased sensitivity to 1st Amendment issues has led courts typically to consider a parent's religious views only if they threaten the health or well-being of a child. The issue of religion arises in its extreme form when a parent refuses to consent to medical treatments for a child on religious grounds. Even then, however, the 1st Amendment allows religion to be considered as a factor only when there is "an immediate and substantial threat to the child's well-being" because of the religious practices.[51] Similarly, race has been routinely considered as a factor in child custody disputes. However, the Court has made clear that the Constitution prohibits using race as the sole basis for a custody award even when based on anticipated difficulties of the child living with a parent of a different race and public attitudes toward interracial families.[52]

Lifestyles of Parents The most difficult questions that arise in many custody cases involve the character and "lifestyles" of the parents and their possible effect on the child. Traditionally, the courts closely scrutinized the moral fitness and character of each parent, particularly as it related to sexual behavior. In the past, an adulterous parent had very little chance of gaining custody. The current trend is to place less emphasis on the parent's morality, except where the parent's behavior or activities

---

48 Some courts have held the "tender years" doctrine invalid as violative of the equal protection clause of the 14th Amendment. *Ex Parte Devine*, 398 So.2d 686 (Ala. 1981); *Pusey v. Pusey*, 728 P.2d 117 (Utah 1986). *But see J.B. v. A.B.*, 242 S.E.2d 248 (W.Va. 1978). State constitutional equal rights amendments are a common basis for this conclusion. *See* Annotation, 90 A.L.R.2d 158, 186 (1979).

49 *See Garska v. McCoy*, 278 S.E.2d 357 (W.Va. 1981) (in addition observing that the primary caretaker preference is necessary to prevent non-custodial parents from using their possible custody claim as bargaining leverage in divorce negotiations). *But see Wolf v. Wolf*, 474 N.W.2d 257 (N.D. 1991) (concluding that the primary caretaker factor is not a presumption; only one of many factors to consider).

50 *See* CLARK, *supra* note 4, §19.4.

51 *Osier v. Osier*, 410 A.2d 1027 (Me. 1980) (trial court acted improperly in granting custody to the father by giving too much weight to the fact that the mother, a Jehovah's Witness, refused to consent to a blood transfusion for her child).

52 *Palmore v. Sidoti*, 466 U.S. 429 (1984) (award of custody of white child to white father after white mother married a black man was unconstitutional racial discrimination).

could have a detrimental effect upon the child.[53] This is also the view adopted by the UMDA.[54] However, there are many cases with the traditional view. Some courts have refused to grant custody to a parent who is cohabiting with a lover, and they have prohibited overnight visitation. In *Jarrett v. Jarrett*,[55] the Illinois Supreme Court granted the father custody after he proved that the mother was living with her boyfriend. The court stated that the moral values the mother was representing to her children "contravened statutorily declared standards of conduct and endanger the children's moral development."

Homosexual parents face even more difficulty gaining or retaining custody. While society appears increasingly willing to extend rights to homosexuals and lesbians in certain areas, public opinion is less favorable when it comes to child custody and care issues. Thus, in *Roe v. Roe*,[56] the court found that the father's exposure of his 9-year-old daughter to his "immoral and illicit homosexual relationship rendered him an unfit and improper custodian as a matter of law." But court decisions have sometimes been based on more than simple moral judgments. Courts have denied custody to a homosexual parent and limited visitation rights because of fears that the child would become homosexual,[57] and that the "children upon reaching puberty would be subject to either overt or covert homosexual seduction."[58] However, other courts have deemed the homosexual relationship of a parent irrelevant to either custody or visitation rights in the absence of some indication of actual harm to the child.[59]

Preference of the Child   The child's preference is usually elicited by the judge in chambers rather than in the open court. Although some state statutes set a minimum age for children to state a preference, others leave it to the discretion of the judge. How much weight to give to a child's preference is left to the discretion of the trial court. The greatest weight is given when all the other factors are equal.[60]

b. Visitation Rights

Visitation by the Non-Custodial Parent   The court will generally grant the non-custodial parent visitation rights in order to maintain as much stability in the child's life as possible following the marital breakup, and to enable the non-custodial parent to continue his or her involvement with the child.[61] Only in the event that visitation is found to be of serious harm to the child will it be denied altogether.[62] In such an

---

53 *See Feldman v. Feldman*, 358 N.Y.S.2d 507 (N.Y.App. 1974) (reversing trial court for "punishing this sexually-liberated divorced woman for her life-style and personal beliefs" and noting that sexually active unmarried men are not so harshly judged).

54 UMDA §401.

55 400 N.E.2d 421, 425 (Ill. 1979).

56 324 S.E.2d 691 (Va. 1985). The court also prohibited any visitation in the father's home or in the presence of his lover.

57 *Dailey v. Dailey*, 635 S.W.2d. 391 (Tenn.App. 1981); *In re J.S. & C.*, 324 A.2d 90 (N.J.Super. 1974).

58 *In re J.S. & C.*, *id.* at 96. *See also*, *J.L.P.(H.) v. D.J.P.*, 643 S.W.2d 865, 867 (Mo.App. 1982).

59 *S.N.E. v. R.L.B.*, 699 P.2d 875 (Alaska 1985) (change of custody denied when based on mother having a live-in lesbian lover); *Conkel v. Conkel*, 509 N.E.2d 983 (Ohio App. 1987) (visitation).

60 *See Goldstein v. Goldstein*, 341 A.2d 51 (R.I. 1975) (preference for father of 9 ½ girl, very intelligent of her age, given substantial weight where other evidence was "so clearly in a state of equipoise").

61 *See generally* Steven Novinson, *Post-Divorce Visitation: Untying the Triangular Knot*, 1983 U.Ill.L.Rev. 119.

62 *See French v. French*, 452 So.2d 647 (Fla.App. 1984) (fact husband failed to recognize the effect of his extramarital affair on the children was not enough to ban all visitation; sexual intercourse in front of the children might be). *See also* UMDA §407.

event, the courts may require that the non-custodial parent see the children in the presence of a social worker or the child's grandparents or that the child not visit overnight.

In most cases courts will leave visitation open-ended, dictating only that the visitation rights be "reasonable." In amicable divorce situations this may be the best approach because it gives the parents flexibility and decreases the court's involvement. However, the court may dictate a visitation schedule with specific times and arrangements. This may be the best approach where the parties are hostile and are unwilling to work together to facilitate visitation. Also, this type of definite and routine arrangement may be better for young children because it gives them a sense of stability.

Interfering with a non-custodial parent's visitation rights is a violation of a court order that renders the violator potentially subject to contempt of court sanction, such as a jail sentence or fine.[63] However, the difficulties and expense of going to court often make minor interferences with visitation not worth pursuing.

A difficult issue of visitation rights and custody is presented when the custodial parent wishes to leave the state, since this will radically alter the ability to visit the children and may even, as a practical matter, terminate visitation. Courts may deny custody to the moving parent if the move is for the purpose of frustrating visitation and has few countervailing benefits for the moving parent or the child. More difficult decisions are where the custodial parent's move is a good faith attempt to improve the custodial parent's life. Nonetheless, many courts have flatly made custody dependent on the custodial parent continuing to live in a particular place[64] or have enjoined the custodial parent from moving.[65]

Visitation by Others   Concern for the relationship of children to their extended family has caused courts and legislature to give attention to the possibility of visitation rights for grandparents or other relatives. In the last 10 years, nearly all states have passed statutes recognizing the potential for granting independent visitation rights to grandparents or other non-parent relatives. The overall test is the best interests of the child. Courts will typically consider pre-divorce involvement of the grandparents in the child's life and the psychological bond that may have resulted, plus the child's preferences. The most difficulty is created when the custodial parent is hostile to such visitation, usually to visitation by the ex-spouse's parents.[66] Some courts have even ordered visitation for grandparents when the custodial parent has remarried, despite the objections of the natural parent and stepparent.[67]

c.   Joint Custody Arrangements

"Joint custody" entails the child living alternatively with one parent and then the other on a rotating basis, such that the parents share both decision-making and actual custodial care responsibilities. For example, the child many live at the father's home certain days of the week and at the mother's home on other days. The facts that

---

63 For a brief discussion of the contempt power, *see* Chapter VII, p. 238.

64 *See Carlson v. Carlson*, 661 P.2d 833 (Kan.App. 1983) (custody dependent on living in the county).

65 *Weiss v. Weiss*, 418 N.E.2d 377 (N.Y. 1981) (mother enjoined from moving to Las Vegas where she planned to seek employment).

66 *Compare In re Robert D.*, 198 Cal.Rptr. 801 (Cal.App. 1984) (granting visitation over parent's objections) *with Commonwealth ex rel. Zaffarano v. Genaro*, 455 A.2d 1180 (Pa. 1983) (denying visitation based on friction between parent and grandparent).

67 *See e.g. Roberts v. Ward*, 493 A.2d 478 (N.H. 1985).

divorce is more commonplace, that it is granted without regard to fault, and that the traditional roles of fathers and mothers have begun to break down, have generally meant greater cooperation between the separating marital partners regarding care of their children. Proponents of joint custody argue that it helps to assure children that they are loved by both parents and to avoid the sense of loss the non-custodial parent feels, as well as to provide a beneficial effect that both parents share in the pleasure and burdens of raising their children. Opponents argue that joint custody undermines the stability that children of divorce need and that the difficult logistical demands of joint custody make strife between the parents more likely, resulting in unnecessary damage to the children. The desirability of joint custody is still a hotly debated topic and there are indications recently of lessened enthusiasm for it.[68]

Whatever the ultimate benefits or detriments of joint custody, a majority of states have legislation that permits it. In some states, joint custody is the preferred custody arrangement and is presumed to be in the best interests of the child. Courts in a few states have held that joint custody is not in the child's best interest except in extraordinary circumstances.[69] The key consideration in determining whether joint custody is in the best interest of the child is the parents' ability and willingness to cooperate in daily decisions affecting the child's welfare. In many cases, the need for cooperation presents an insurmountable barrier to joint custody.

Distinctions between joint *legal* custody and joint *physical* custody can create difficulties. An order for joint legal custody gives an equal say to both parents on all major decisions affecting the child, while an order for joint physical custody allocates the actual times that the child is in the custody of each parent. It is possible for there to be joint *legal* custody, but physical custody in only one parent. In such cases, the physical custodian often resents having to consult with the non-custodial parent, who is not sufficiently involved in the child's life to properly participate in daily decision-making for the child.

d. Interstate Enforcement of Custody Decrees

Custody orders of state courts do not have a direct effect beyond the borders of a state. Problems regularly arose in the past where a parent simply took a child into another state to avoid a custody ruling. However, in 1980 Congress passed the Parental Kidnaping Prevention Act (PKPA),[70] which makes clear the applicability of the full faith and credit clause to child custody decrees and requires states to enforce the custody decrees of other states.[71] In addition, almost all states have adopted the Uniform Child Custody Judgment Act (UCCJA), which requires enforcement.[72]

Though strict enforcement of custody decrees discourages the reprehensible "forum-shopping" that often occurred, some have argued that there should be more flexibility for a court in the second state in appropriate cases to reconsider the issue of custody. However, in a recent case under the federal act involving an attempted adoption that attracted national attention, the Michigan Supreme Court took a strict

---

68 *See* Susan Steinman, *Joint Custody: What We Know, What We Have Yet to Learn, and the Judicial and Legislative Implications*, 16 U.C.D. L.REV. 739 (1983).

69 *See, e.g., Trimble v. Trimble*, 352 N.W.2d 599 (Neb. 1984); *Lumbra v. Lumbra*, 394 A.2d 1139 (Vt. 1978).

70 28 U.S.C.A. §1738A.

71 Art. IV §1. *See* Chapter VII, pp. 250-251. Doubts about the enforceability of child custody decrees arose because equitable decrees are always modifiable and then only by the court that rendered them.

72 *See supra* note 3.

view of the matter. It held that an Iowa court's award of custody to the natural father prevailed regardless of the best interests of the child and even if it meant removing the child from the would-be adoptive parents with whom the child had lived virtually since birth.[73]

5. Child Support

a. Nature and Duration of the Support Obligation

Traditionally, it was the father's obligation to provide adequate support for his children. The mother became liable for support upon the father's failure or refusal to furnish support. Today both parents have a duty to provide for their children to the extent that they are financially able.[74] This obligation continues even in the event of divorce. It is generally enforced in a divorce case by way of a child support order requiring that the non-custodial parent make periodic payments in a certain amount to the custodial parent.

The parents' support obligation normally runs until the child reaches the age of "majority," usually 18 years of age.[75] The statutes in some states limit support awards to support of "minor children," while others refer simply to "children." Some courts have held that support can be ordered beyond the age of 18 for children with physical or mental disabilities.[76] More controversial have been orders for the expenses of a child's college education. The traditional view is not to impose such an obligation because college is not a "necessity." Today most states by statute or judicial decision allow orders for college education when the parents can afford it and the child is making academic progress.[77] In other states, such an order will be made if there are "special circumstances," though the circumstances in the cases often seem to be rather ordinary.[78] The change in approach reflects the belief that a college education is very important and that children from divorced families should have the same advantages as those from non-divorced families.[79]

Minor children who become "emancipated" are no longer owed a duty of support. Emancipation occurs when the child marries or enlists in the army before the age of majority or whenever the child is capable of self-support. In some states there is a procedure for emancipation.[80] The support duty also terminates when parental rights are terminated by a court proceeding. Unlike the duty to pay alimony,

---

73 *In re Clausen*, 502 N.W.2d 649 (Mich. 1993).

74 In some states, a stepparent has a duty to support stepchildren. *See Washington Statewide Organization of Stepparents v. Smith*, 536 P.2d 1202 (Utah 1975) (rejecting constitutional objections).

75 It is unconstitutional for a state to have different ages of majority for males and females that results in differential support obligations. In *Stanton v. Stanton*, 412 U.S. 7 (1975), the Court rejected arguments that girls tend to mature earlier and marry young while boys need extended time to get a good education or training to prepare them for a job. For a discussion of sex discrimination, *see* Chapter IX, pp. 334-338.

76 *See Grapin v. Grapin*, 450 So.2d 853 (Fla. 1984) (based on common law).

77 *Greiman v. Friedman*, 414 N.E.2d 77 (Ill.App. 1980) (order to pay college expenses upheld even though child's academic record was not outstanding); *Childers v. Childers*, 575 P.2d 201 (Wash. 1978) (state statute makes support obligation turn on "dependency," not minority).

78 *In re Marriage of Plummer*, 735 P.2d 165 (Colo. 1987) (order based on finding that both parents have college degrees and "a college education is to be expected in this family").

79 Even graduate school has been included. *See Ross v. Ross*, 400 A.2d 1233 (N.J.Super. 1979). *But see Brown v. Brown*, 474 A.2d 1168 (Pa.Super. 1984) (no obligation to fund law school). Law school in the United States is graduate study that follows four years of college study. Chapter IV, p. 126.

80 *See* Cal.Civ.Code §60 *et seq.* Such procedures have been used in some notable cases where a child actor or athlete wishes to gain control of his or her own money. The press has touted such actions as the child "divorcing" the parents and the accompanying acrimony is similar.

however, the duty to pay child support does not always expire upon the death of the parent and is not dischargeable in bankruptcy.[81]

b. Determining Parentage for Support Purposes

Presumptions and Acknowledgments   Children born during a marriage are presumed by the law to be the children of the couple.[82]   Consequently, in most divorce situations, the identity of the parents who owe the obligation of support is not in question.   Outside of marriage, paternity is usually determined by voluntary "legitimation" by the father.   The father simply signs and files a form with a state agency, usually the county clerk.   In other states, less formal methods may be acceptable as well, such as written and even oral contracts[83] or the putative father taking the child into his home.

Paternity Suits   When the parents are not married and paternity is disputed, a paternity suit must be filed.   This is a civil suit filed by the mother seeking a judgment declaring the defendant to be the father (an order of "filiation") and a child support order.[84]   In the past, crude means of proof were used, such as having the jury look at the baby and the putative father to see how much they look alike, but today blood tests can play a key role and the state must pay for blood tests for indigent putative fathers.[85]   Depending on the type of test, blood tests can be effective both for excluding and including a particular putative father.[86]   The focus of paternity proceedings is the welfare of the child, so the actions of the parents are irrelevant. Consequently, it is no defense that the father was tricked into intercourse by the mother's false statement that she was using contraceptive pills.[87]   Recognizing that the original nature of the action was criminal and that claims of paternity are difficult to defend against, some states require proof beyond a reasonable doubt or clear and convincing evidence, but others impose only the normal civil standard of a preponderance of the evidence.[88]

c. The Amount of Support Orders

Guidelines and Discretion   The amount of child support orders, whether temporary — during the pendency of the divorce case — or permanent, lies within the discretion of the trial court.   Since both parents are responsible for the support of their children, the court will consider the finances of both in making its determination,

---

81   *See Bailey v. Bailey*, 471 P.2d 220 (Nev. 1970) (order must specifically provide that it is enforceable against the estate); 11 U.S.C.A. §523(a) (bankruptcy). Courts in some states may also require a parent to maintain a life insurance policy payable to the children.

82   *See* Uniform Parentage Act, §4(a), *supra* note 3, which provides a rebuttable presumption of paternity if the child is born during the marriage or within 300 days after its termination. *See also Mock v. Mock*, 411 So.2d 1063 (La. 1982) (rebuttable by preponderance of the evidence); *P.B.C. v. D.H.*, 483 N.E.2d 1094 (Mass. 1985) (rebuttable only by proof beyond a reasonable doubt). The Supreme Court has held (with no majority opinion) that it did not violate due process for a state to prohibit anyone but the married couple who are the presumed parents to contest the presumption, thus disallowing a challenge by the putative father. *Michael H. v. Gerald D.*, 491 U.S. 110 (1989).

83   *See T. v. T.*, 224 S.E.2d 148 (Va. 1976) (oral contract valid where there had been part performance and detrimental reliance); *Peterson v. Eritsland*, 419 P.2d 331 (Wash. 1966) (written contract).

84   Some states and the Uniform Parentage Act §6 permit the child to bring the action (by the child's guardian or "next friend") and some states permit the state agency providing welfare assistance to the child to sue as well.

85   *Little v. Streater*, 452 U.S. 1 (1981).

86   For a summary of the types of tests *see* GREGORY, SWISHER & SCHEIBLE, *supra* note 4, §5.02[F].

87   *See Pamela L. v. Frank S.*, 449 N.E.2d 713 (N.Y. 1983).

88   Though rare, fathers sometimes sue to establish their paternity and the trend is toward allowing such suits. Constitutional aspects were discussed in note 45, *supra*. *See also* note 82 *supra*.

along with any division of property or awards of alimony provided for in the divorce decree. Federal law requires states to develop and follow guidelines for support amounts, but guidelines vary considerably from state to state.[89] The overall test of a child support amount is that it be "reasonable" considering the limits of the parents' financial abilities.[90] Reasonable needs of the child include clothing, food, education, medical care, and entertainment. The court may also consider the standard of living to which the child had become accustomed prior to the divorce.[91]

Modifications in Amount   Most child support orders provide for periodic payments to be made to the custodial parent. The amount of such payments can be modified if circumstances warrant. Such circumstances might include changes in either party's financial condition, the needs of the child or the cost of living. Decrease is possible where the parent has changed careers or otherwise can no longer pay the amount ordered.[92] A strong case can be made that a change in a parent's career that results in a lower standard of living is possible in an intact family, so it should have a similar effect on the child support order. However, courts will closely scrutinize such cases with some skepticism to determine whether the career change was made for the purpose of lowering the child support amount.[93] While support orders are supposed to reflect the obligor's ability to pay, many cases in this area seem to consider what the obligor *should have* been able to pay.[94] Increases are possible when there is an increase in the child's needs, such as an increase in education or medical expenses. However, an increase may also be ordered based solely on an increase in the non-custodial parent's ability to pay.[95] To discourage parties from constantly seeking modifications, many statutes require that the change in financial circumstances be a major one. For example, the Uniform Marriage and Divorce Act requires that to warrant modification the change in circumstances be "so substantial and continuing as to make the terms [of the order] unconscionable."[96]

The problem of the adequacy of support orders is often less one of sudden changes than one of gradual erosion of the value of the amount ordered resulting of inflation. Some states have addressed this problem by permitting an "escalation

---

89   42 U.S.C.A. §667. The guidelines are part of the federal government's intervention to ensure child support enforcement. *See infra* p. 492.

90   Common formulas for computing support payments are discussed in GREGORY, SWISHER & SCHEIBLE, *supra* note 4, §8.06[C].

91   *See White v. Marciano*, 235 Cal.Rptr. 779 (Cal.App. 1987) (when the child's parent is wealthy, :the child is entitled to, and therefore 'needs,' something more than the bare necessities of life"). *But see State v. Hall*, 418 N.W.2d 187 (Minn.App. 1988) (despite father's monthly income of $16,000, child's actual expenses did not exceed $1000 per month, so ordering the standard amount was sufficient; any excess would only go to increase the mother's standard of living).

92   *See Guyton v. Guyton*, 602 A.2d 1143 (D.C. 1992) (reduction required when father lost his job).

93   *Compare Curtis v. Curtis*, 442 N.W.2d 173 (Minn.App. 1992) (father who quit job of 10 years to attend school to be electronic repairman one month after support order entered acted in bad faith and was not entitled to a reduction) *with Diagre v. Diagre*, 527 So.2d 9 (La.App. 1988) (father's quitting real estate job to go to law school was not an attempt to evade support obligations, so decrease in order was proper). Courts are generally less sympathetic to lessened ability to pay that results from remarriage and a new family. *See Berg v. Berg*, 359 A.2d 354 (R.I. 1976) (father stopped paying support after he adopted three children of his new wife; contempt sentence affirmed; remand to determine issue of bad faith).

94   *Compare Pierce v. Peirce*, 412 N.W.2d 291 (Mich.App. 1987) (amount should abate while father in jail where he has no resources) *with In re Phillips*, 493 N.W.2d 824 (Iowa 1992) (inability to pay resulting from imprisonment for father's voluntary conduct does not warrant modification).

95   *See Graham v. Graham*, 598 A.2d 355 (D.C. 1991) (allowing downward adjustment when financial ability declined, but denying upward adjustment when it increases, would be unfair to children, who have a right to a higher standard of living when the parent's finances improve).

96   Uniform Marriage and Divorce Act, §316(a), *supra* note 3.

FAMILY LAW

clause" that ties the amount of the order to the Consumer Price Index (CPI) calculated periodically by the United States Department of Labor.[97]

d. Welfare Programs for Needy Families

When child support and the resources of the custodial parent are not sufficient to support the child, a "safety net" of welfare programs is available. From 1935 until 1996, the federal government funded and supervised a cooperative state-federal program that provided cash and in-kind payments to needy families with children deprived of support as a result of the absence, disability or, in some cases, the unemployment of a parent, called Aid to Families with Dependent Children (AFDC). The purpose of the program was to provide a stable source of income at a subsistence level to allow the needy children involved to be cared for at home by their parent or parents. But in 1996 Congress replaced the program with one called the Family Assistance Program. Congress determined that single parents with children at home should work and that financial assistance should be temporary until they can become self-sufficient. A two-year limit was imposed on financial assistance and various work requirements were imposed.[98] It remains to be seen what will happen to the families involved once they get to the end of their two-year periods.

In addition to cash assistance, "food stamps" — coupons redeemable for food — are available to low-income households,[99] as is medical assistance (called "Medicaid").[100] Also, totally disabled people, including children, are entitled to support under the Supplemental Security Income program.[101]

e. Enforcement of Child Support Orders

Non-payment of child support is a major problem in the United States that is only now getting better. Statistics vary from state to state, but one set of data shows that at one point less than half of all custodial parents awarded child support received payment in full.[102] The main problem has been that the custodial parent must hire a lawyer to pursue collection.

One method of collection is to seek to have the defaulting parent held in civil contempt of court. This could lead to the jailing of the non-supporting parent until the order is paid.[103] A second remedy is "garnishment" of the obligor's wages or an order that property be seized and sold. Indeed, federal law requires that wage withholding be included in support orders.[104] Finally, where the party has willfully defaulted on a support obligation, he or she may be charged with criminal contempt or criminal non-support, often a felony. However, these remedies, if they result in a long prison term, generally do not result in the immediate collection of more money.

---

97 *See In re Marriage of Nesset*, 345 N.W.2d 107 (Iowa 1984) (indexing support to CPI approved).

98 *See* Title IV-A of the Social Security Act, 42 U.S.C.A. §§601 *et seq.*

99 *See* 7 U.S.C.A. §§2011 *et seq.*

100 42 U.S.C.A. §§601 *et seq.* Also of assistance to families with children are federal programs providing for free or reduced-price hot lunches (and sometimes breakfasts) in public schools.

101 *See* 42 U.S.C.A. §1382 *et seq.*

102 CLARK, *supra* note 4, at 734, citing LOUISE WEITZMAN, THE DIVORCE REVOLUTION: THE UNEXPECTED SOCIAL AND ECONOMIC CONSEQUENCES FOR WOMEN AND CHILDREN IN AMERICA 283 (1985).

103 Civil contempt was discussed in Chapter VII, p. 238. The indigent non-supporter's right to counsel was initially held not to be constitutionally required, but in recent years this trend has been reversed. *See Mead v. Batchlor*, 460 N.W.2d 493 (Mich. 1990), *overruling Sword v. Sword*, 249 N.W.2d 88 (Mich. 1976).

104 42 U.S.C.A. §§666(a)(8), (b)(2), (b)(3).

A major problem with collection remedies is that individuals bent on avoiding their court-ordered support obligations often leave the state where it was ordered. To meet this problem, all states have adopted the Uniform Reciprocal Enforcement of Support Act (URESA) and the Revised Uniform Reciprocal Enforcement of Support Act (RURESA)[105] which require each state to enforce the support obligations of other states. These acts, then, supplement the Constitution's requirement that states give "full faith and credit" to judgments from other states.[106] However, the acts have not been as successful as hoped, largely because of the lack of public resources.

In response to this, Congress in 1975 decided to devote federal resources to the problem of non-support.[107] The federal law originally sought only to recoup federally funded welfare benefits paid to custodial parents, but many of its provisions now apply to all support orders. The federal law now provides for a Parent Locator Service to assist in finding absent parents and an Office of Child Support Enforcement to assure that state support enforcement programs live up to federal standards. Those federal standards require states to implement numerous administrative reforms in their child support enforcement systems to keep better track of non-supporting parents and to provide for more efficient processing of support orders. In addition, the law authorizes intercepting federal or state income tax refunds.

C. Non-Traditional Relationships and Family Law

1. Unmarried Heterosexual Couples

The increase in the number of couples living together outside of wedlock can be attributed to the rise in the divorce rate and an accompanying skepticism about the institution of marriage, plus a general tendency for couples to wait longer before getting married.[108] While 40 years ago the cohabitation of unmarried couples was shocking, today it is accepted. In fact, with the high incidence of divorce, some view living together as a prudent and cautionary measure and as a way to avoid the complicated and costly divorce process in the event the relationship breaks up.

One legal advantage which marriage holds that is not available to the unmarried couple is judicial protection of the financial interests of the partners. This situation may be changing, however. Some courts have applied equitable principles to the breakup of unmarried couples and have held that they may order property divisions and support for unmarried couples who break up in a manner similar to that used in divorces. Awards of property or maintenance payments in these circumstances are sometimes referred to as "palimony" — "alimony" payments by one former "pal" to another.[109]

Marvin v. Marvin[110] established the right of an unmarried partner to seek such relief. Marvin and his female companion, Michele Triola, lived together for six years. The court held that Triola could seek to recover support or property from Marvin by

---

105 *See supra* note 3.

106 *See* Chapter VII, p. 250, where the full faith and credit clause is discussed.

107 *See generally* Title IV-D of the Social Security Act, 42 U.S.C.A. §§651 *et seq.* These provisions and other interstate support collection issues are discussed in GREGORY, SWISHER & SCHEIBLE, *supra* note 4, §8.06[F][3]-[4].

108 CLARK, *supra* note 4, at §2.1, n. 36.

109 The option of arguing that a common law marriage existed is often unavailable. It been abolished in many states and there is usually more than ample evidence that the couple had the specific intention not to be married. *See* discussion of common law marriage, *supra* p. 475.

110 557 P.2d 106 (Cal. 1976).

showing either an explicit oral agreement or an implied agreement based on a tacit understanding so long as the consideration for the contract was not solely sexual. On remand to the trial court, Triola was unable at trial to prove either theory of recovery, but the legal basis for such recovery was established for other cases.

Many states are skeptical about the *Marvin* doctrine and have rejected it altogether even when there were compelling facts.[111] Critics reason that, had the couple wanted legal interference in their separation, they would have gotten married in the first place. The issue is far from settled and will continue to face the courts until, perhaps, state legislatures formulate a position on the issue.

2. Homosexual Couples

Marvin-Type Grounds for Protection The *Marvin* rationale has been extended to same-sex couples in California at least. It is, of course, subject to all the requirements of that case, including the requirement that sex not be the sole basis for the agreement.[112]

Legality of Same-Sex Marriages Virtually all states prohibit same-sex marriages. However, in *Baehr v. Lewin*,[113] the Hawaii Supreme Court held that the state's same-sex marriage ban constituted sex discrimination, thus calling for strict scrutiny under the equal protection clause and equal rights amendment of the state constitution.[114] It noted that the ban effectively denied homosexuals and lesbians access to many rights and benefits such as tax breaks, public assistance, community property rights, inheritance rights, child custody rights and alimony.[115] The direct precedential effects of this case are confined to Hawaii, but conflict-of-law and "full faith and credit" requirements would have compelled other states to recognize the same-sex marriages of their own residents so long as they had been validly concluded in Hawaii.[116] However, Congress prevented this effect by passing the "Defense of Marriage Act," relieving states of any duty to recognize homosexual marriages.[117]

Other Decisions and Issues Affecting Homosexual Couples Some courts have bypassed the legal issue of marriage and instead extended some of the benefits of marriage to same-sex couples. The concept of "family" was held broad enough to include homosexual couples in *Braschi v. Stahl Associates Co.*[118] There the New York Court of Appeals prevented the eviction of a gay man from his deceased partner's

---

111 *See, e.g., Hewitt v. Hewitt*, 394 N.E.2d 1204 (Ill. 1979) (court concluded woman had no rights to alimony or property even though she lived with her partner, a dentist, for fifteen years and had borne and raised their three children).

112 *Whorton v. Dillingham*, 248 Cal.Rptr. 405 (Cal.App. 1988) (where sex was an explicit part of the agreement, if there was other adequate consideration for agreement and non-sexual part of agreement was severable, it is valid)

113 852 P.2d 44 (Hawaii 1993).

114 For a discussion of application of the strict scrutiny standard in federal equal protection, *see* Chapter IX, pp. 328-333. Hawaii's equal protection and equal rights amendments are more protective of equal rights than the federal equal protection clause.

115 The state had argued that the statute did not discriminate based on sex, because it only distinguished between *opposite-sex* and *same-sex* couples and applied equally to males and females. The court rejected the argument by analogy to cases holding that statutes prohibiting racially mixed marriages, which apply both to whites and minorities, constituted race discrimination. *See Loving v. Virginia*, 388 U.S. 1 (1967).

116 *See* Chapter VII, p. 253 (conflicts rule for marriages).

117 28 U.S.C.A. §1738C. The Act also defined marriage for all federal statutes to mean "only a legal union between one man and one woman as husband and wife," thus assuring that benefits based on marriage secured by federal statutes would not be available to same-sex partners. 1 U.S.C.A. §7.

118 543 N.E.2d 49 (N.Y. 1989).

rent-controlled apartment in Manhattan, finding him to be a "member of the deceased tenant's family." While the holding was restricted to the New York city ordinance governing rent-controlled apartments, the majority did recognize that "a more realistic and certainly equally valid view of a family includes two adult lifetime partners whose relationship is long term and characterized by an emotional and financial commitment and interdependence."[119] It is reported by mid-1995, 36 municipalities, 8 counties, 3 states, 5 state agencies, and 2 federal agencies extended some benefits to same-sex domestic partnerships, or registered them for some official purposes.[120] More than 25 private companies, including Levi-Strauss and Co., offer health plans to domestic partners, and the number of public and private employers who do so is increasing.

D. Child Custody Issues Outside Divorce

1. Adoption

In adoptions, a child in essence gets a new parent or set of parents in place of their birth parent or parents. The parental rights of both natural parents must be terminated before a child can be adopted. This can be accomplished voluntarily, by having the parent(s) sign a document agreeing to termination, or involuntarily, through court proceedings in which neglect or abuse has been shown. Where reliance is placed on voluntary release of the child for adoption, most states have waiting periods before an adoption can become final, and some require counseling of the birth parent(s) before parental rights are voluntarily relinquished. If the birth mother is acting alone or if the birth father is not known, certain due process rights of notice are required before his rights can be terminated.[121] Like other family law matters, other aspects of adoption laws vary widely among the states, but in general two types of adoptions are possible: "agency" and "private" adoptions.

Agency Adoptions Every state has a system of agency adoptions, either as the sole means of adopting or in addition to private adoptions. Agency adoptions are administered through a public agency or private agencies licensed by the state. In the typical agency adoption, the birth parents' parental rights have already been terminated and the adopting parents have no contact with them. Records are sealed for the privacy of the family and the child. In general, the idea behind agency adoptions is to assure that adoptive parents are carefully screened by professionals before adoption can take place. This is more difficult to assure in private adoptions. In some states, screening is thought so important that all forms of private adoption are banned. A disadvantage of agency adoptions is that they typically take much longer than private adoptions and impatient adoptive parents who live in an "agency state" often consider going to a state or country with private adoptions to get a child.[122] Similarly, some birth parents prefer private adoptions because they have more control over who the adoptive parents will be.[123]

Private Adoptions In private adoptions, no state agency is involved. Many private adoptions involve birth and adoptive parents who know each other or are related to each other, or the birth and adoptive parents might be "matched" by an intermediary, usually a lawyer, a physician or a private company specializing in such matches. The

---

119 *Compare* the German Constitutional Court decision discussed in Chapter II, text at note 58.

120 Lynn D. Wardle, *A Critical Analysis of Constitutional Claims for Same-Sex Marriages*, 1996 B.Y.U. L. Rev. 1, 54 (1996).

121 *But see Lehr v. Robertson*, 463 U.S. 248 (1983), summarized *supra* note 44.

122 Interstate adoptions are subject to the Interstate Compact on Placement of Children.

123 *See generally* Mitchell A. Charney, *The Rebirth of Private Adoptions*, 71 A.B.A.J. 52 (1985).

amount of regulation of private adoptions varies in terms of whether a home study must be conducted, the degree to which counseling is required for any of the parties involved and other issues. Most states prohibit profiteering by intermediaries, regulating fees they can charge and permitting lawyers only to charge for the legal services involved. However, such regulations are hard to enforce especially given the eagerness of the adoptive couples to get a baby. As a result, the boundary between permitted adoption and prohibited baby selling is not a bright line, and there is considerable room for the shady intermediary to cross it.

Requirements for Adoptive Parents Usually the statutes require only that the adopting person be an adult, that an adopting couple be married and jointly adopt the child, and in some states age restrictions are imposed to assure a "normal" spread in age between the adoptive parents and the child. But in "agency" adoption states at least, there are various "rules" in the form of standards set by the agency and long-standing practices that are sometime very specific. Traditionally, agencies have looked for "ideal" married couples of similar backgrounds to the birth parents, for placing adoptive children. This has been criticized by some who argue that agencies' criteria are too narrow and result in some children not being adopted who should be or in turning down non-traditional adoptive parents who would be excellent parents.

2. Reproductive Technology and Child Custody

Artificial Insemination The simplest and most common case involving reproductive technology is artificial insemination of the mother with sperm from a donor. If the mother is married when insemination occurs and the husband agrees, the husband is considered the father rather than the donor of the sperm.[124] The logical result of this rule is that, if the husband did not consent, then the child is considered illegitimate, though this result has been criticized.[125] Where an unmarried woman has a child through artificial insemination, the donor, if identified, is considered to be the father of the child. However, some states provide that if the insemination is done by a doctor, the donor is not considered the father; if no doctor is used, then the donor is the father.[126] This rule applies to "natural insemination" situations as well — where an unmarried woman agrees with a man to get her pregnant and she agrees to waive any right to child support from him. The Indiana Supreme Court refused to allow such an agreement to affect the father's support obligation, holding it invalid on general public policy grounds.[127]

In Vitro Fertilization Medical science is also able to conceive a child in the laboratory and then implant the fertilized egg in the mother's body. In such a case, the legal implications are no different from where there is natural or artificial insemination within the mother's body. However, not all such fertilized eggs may be used and they may be frozen and placed in storage for future use. In a recent case, the Tennessee Supreme Court was faced with the question of the "custody" of such frozen embryos upon the couple's divorce. Because of the husband's constitutional right to decide whether to procreate was involved, the court held that there must be *joint* "custody." This overrode the wife's desire to keep the embryos or donate them to a childless

---

124 *People v. Sorensen*, 437 P.2d 495 (Cal. 1968) (husband can be prosecuted for non-support); Uniform Parentage Act §5. Consent can be implied. *In re Baby Doe*, 353 S.E.2d 877 (S.C. 1987).

125 *See* CLARK, *supra* note 4, p. 154.

126 *See, e.g.*, Cal. Family Code §7613 and *Jhordhan C. v. Mary K.*, 224 Cal.Rptr. 53 (Cal.App. 1986).

127 *Straub v. B.M.T. by Todd*, 645 N.E.2d 597 (Ind. 1994).

couple.[128] In a similar case, the California Court of Appeals held that the unmarried woman partner of a man who died was entitled to possession of his frozen sperm over the claims of his estate.[129]

Surrogate Mothers More difficult legally than artificial insemination is the situation is presented by so-called "surrogate mother" agreements.[130] In a typical situation, a childless couple will hire a woman to bear a child for them. The husband, as provider of the sperm, is the biological father and the surrogate mother consents to adoption by the wife. Difficulties arise when there is a dispute, typically when the surrogate mother refuses to give up the child as agreed to in the contract. When this happens, traditional legal principles dictate the unsatisfactory result of the legal parents of the child being the surrogate mother and the husband.

A famous New Jersey case, *Matter of Baby M*,[131] illustrates the difficulties. The trial court in that case upheld the validity of the contract, awarding custody to the husband and authorizing adoption by the wife, thus terminating the parental rights of the biological surrogate mother. On appeal, the New Jersey Supreme Court held that surrogacy contracts were unenforceable because they violated public policy by determining custody without regard to the child's best interests and for their lack of true voluntariness, given the potential for exploiting the poor. It ruled that the case should be treated like any other custody dispute. Consequently, it affirmed the award of custody to the father alone, but granted visitation rights to the surrogate mother. Other states have reached different results. The Kentucky Supreme Court, for example, has held that the state's prohibition on sale of children for adoption did not apply to void a surrogate contract and declined to revoke the charter to do business of a surrogacy agency.[132]

Even more complex are cases where the surrogate mother is essentially a "gestation surrogate" because she is implanted with an embryo produced by the husband and wife. The surrogate is truly the "birth mother" of the child, but the child has none of her genetic material. In a California case, after a dispute arose and the surrogate threatened not to give up the child, the California court had to determine who the parents of the child were. It determined that the married couple were the only parents of the child and ordered that the surrogacy contract be enforced.[133] However, a New York court reached the opposite conclusion.[134] In a case even more complicated case, a husband and wife used anonymous sperm and egg donors and had a surrogate mother implanted with the embryo. The California court in this case declared that the husband and wife were the parents of the child.[135]

Since the *Baby M* case, there has been a flurry of legislative activity to deal with surrogacy, with states taking divergent paths. Most have completely prohibited paid

---

128 *Davis v. Davis*, 842 S.W.2d 588 (Tenn. 1992). *See also Kass v. Kass*, 693 N.E.2d 194 (N.Y. 1998) (enforcing contract requiring consent of both by husband and wife and, if no agreement, donation to medical research).

129 *Hecht v. Superior Court*, 20 Cal.Rptr.2d 275 (Cal.App. 1993).

130 *See generally* CLARK, *supra* note 4, §20.8. The term "surrogate mother" is not technically correct, since the woman is the child's biological mother, but the terminology has stuck and is used here.

131 537 A.2d 1227 (N.J. 1988). *See also* 542 A.2d 52 (Super.Ct. 1988) (decision on remand).

132 *Surrogate Parenting Associates, Inc. v. Kentucky ex rel. Armstrong*, 704 S.W.2d 209 (Ky. 1986).

133 *Anna J. v. Mark C.*, 286 Cal.Rptr. 369 (Cal.App. 1991).

134 *Andres A. v. Judith N.*, 591 N.Y.S.2d 946 (N.Y. Fam. Ct. 1992) (N.Y. artificial insemination law precluded declaring wife, whose embryo was implanted, the mother of the child).

135 *Buzzanca v. Buzzanca*, 72 Cal.Rptr.2d 280 (Cal.App. 1998).

surrogacy arrangements[136] while others have chosen to permit, but closely regulate them.[137] Regardless of the legality of surrogacy contracts, however, courts nonetheless will undoubtedly scrutinize very closely the custody arrangements contemplated by the contract to assure that they are in the best interests of the child involved.

E. Problems in the Intact Family

1. Spouse Abuse

Domestic violence against women is a serious problem in the United States. Crime statistics show that 34% of all female homicide victims older than 15 years are killed by their husbands or other intimate male partners.[138] Over 4 million acts of domestic violence are perpetrated each year and as many as 40% of all police calls concern matters of domestic violence.[139] Despite the prevalence of abuse, it is only recently that measures have begun to be taken to deal with it.

Historical Roots of Spousal Abuse The delayed reaction of society to domestic violence finds its roots in the common law. At common law, a man had the right to "discipline" his wife (or child) through application of moderate physical violence. And the common law definition of rape excluded even forcible sexual assault by a husband of his wife.[140] In the late 1800s, states legislated specific punishments for batterers, but these laws were seldom enforced. It was only in the 1960s that the advent of the women's movement brought the issue of domestic violence into the national spotlight. Still, courts are reluctant to interfere in family situations; unless the abuse is blatant and serious, and police find domestic violence situations to be among the most dangerous, distasteful and frustrating parts of their job.

Law Enforcement Policy on Domestic Violence A large part of the solution to the problem has been major revisions in law enforcement policy. In 1984, the Minneapolis police department issued an order requiring police officers "to aggressively utilize arrest powers" in domestic violence situations.[141] This order resulted from the outcome of a National Institute of Justice study analyzing over 300 cases of domestic violence. The study evaluated the three methods police most often use to prevent further domestic violence — arrests, mediation, and ordering the assailant out of the house to "cool off." The most effective method was found to be arrest. Statutes have also been enacted requiring the police to inform victims of available resources to help them extricate themselves from a violent relationship.[142] Other statutes require police to offer transportation to a shelter or other safe place.[143] Where police policy fails to treat domestic abuse complaints on par with other

---

136 *See* N.Y. Dom. Rel. §122; Mich.Comp.Laws §722.855. The Michigan statute was held constitutional in *Doe v. Attorney General*, 487 N.W.2d 484 (Mich.App. 1992).

137 *See* Va. Code. Ann. §20-156 *et seq. See* GREGORY, SWISHER & SCHEIBLE, *supra* note 4, §5.07[B].

138 Source: Federal Bureau of Investigation data, 1976-1987.

139 *Developments in the Law — Legal Responses to Domestic Violence*, 106 HARV.L.REV. 1498, 1501 (1993). In 1992, the Massachusetts courts issued an estimated 60,000 civil restraining orders to protect women from their abusive partners.

140 *See also* Chapter XIV, p. 514.

141 *Arrests of Wife-Beaters Rise In New Policy in Minneapolis,* N.Y.TIMES, July 24, 1984.

142 *See, e.g.,* Mont.Code Ann. §46-6-602.

143 Tenn. Code Ann. §40-7-103(7).

complaints of crime, battered women have sued, arguing that it constitutes impermissible sex discrimination in violation of the 14th Amendment.[144]

Personal Protection Orders   Often more useful than the criminal process are "personal protection orders" for the wife. If a divorce case is pending, a temporary restraining order can be issued by the court forbidding the husband from having contact with the wife. In recent years, a similar remedy has been authorized in virtually all states for unmarried partners. In addition, the enforcement process has been streamlined. Though any battery on the partner is clearly a violation of the court order, traditionally restraining orders could be enforced only by filing a complaint with the court and seeking a contempt of court remedy. Now many states allow the police to arrest violators of restraining orders immediately based upon a reasonable belief that the order has been violated.

2. Child Abuse and Neglect

Civil Abuse and Neglect Proceedings   Child abuse and neglect is often a crime, but more commonly remedial civil proceedings are pursued against the parents instead. Such proceedings are usually brought in the juvenile or family court, most often a division of the state probate court. Once the court takes jurisdiction of the case upon proof of neglect or abuse, it has broad discretion to take whatever action it deems necessary to protect the children and plan for their future. The court cooperates closely with the state department of child welfare services. A social worker is assigned to the case to make recommendations and supervise any court disposition. The court may return the child to the custody of the parents under supervision and conditions, place the child in a foster home until the conditions improve in the home, require counseling or parenting classes for the parents, require therapy or other treatment for the child, or any combination of these measures.[145]

Terminating Parental Rights   When it appears unlikely that any of these measures will improve the child's home sufficiently to permit the child's return, the state may terminate parental rights and make the children "wards of the court." Thereafter, if the child is very young, adoption is a good possibility. However, older children who are permanent wards of the court are difficult to place for adoption. Often the child drifts from one foster home to another, never establishing any real familial ties. Because of these risks and the drastic nature of termination, agencies usually make every effort to return the child home if this is at all possible.[146] The question in such cases is not whether the child would be better off in foster care than in their parents' home, but whether the parents are unfit. As one state supreme courts put it, "even though it might be in a child's best interests to live with a family of comfortable means rather than a poorer family, this standard may not justify the state's intervention absent a finding of parental unfitness."[147]

---

144 *Watson v. City of Kansas City*, 857 F.2d 690 (10th Cir. 1988) (reversing summary judgment dismissing complaint).

145 *See generally* GREGORY, SWISHER & SCHEIBLE, *supra* note 4, §5.08.

146 Termination can also result from parental abandonment, mental illness, chronic non-support or from an absent parent unreasonably withholding consent to adoption. *See* Uniform Adoption Act, §19(c), *supra* note 3.

147 *In re Kristina L.*, 520 A.2d 574, 581 (R.I. 1987). *See also New Jersey Division of Youth and Family Services v. A.W.*, 512 A.2d 438 (N.J. 1986) ("[p]arents are not to be adjudged unfit because of the lack resources or intelligence, but only by reason of conduct detrimental to the physical and mental health of the child").

Due Process Rights Abuse or neglect proceedings, while they are civil, have very serious potential consequences for the parents. Consequently, the Supreme Court has held that due process requires that, despite the fact that termination proceedings are civil, the proof standard must be "clear and convincing evidence" rather than the normal civil standard of "preponderance of the evidence."[148] On the other hand, the Court has held that such proceedings are not so much like criminal cases or other cases involving deprivations of liberty that due process requires appointment of counsel for indigent parents at state expense in every case.[149] State law often secures this right, however, as well as other procedural protections beyond those afforded in an ordinary civil case.[150] It is also common for the juvenile court to appoint a *guardian ad litem* for the child to directly assert the child's interests in court to the extent that they can be ascertained.

A controversial question involving neglect and abuse statutes has been whether drug-addicted or alcoholic women who give birth to an addicted fetus have committed child neglect or abuse. In *Matter of Smith*[151] a New York court answered this question in the affirmative, holding that an unborn fetus is a child. On the other hand, in *Reyes v. Superior Court in and for San Bernardino County*,[152] the California Court of Appeals refused to view the birth of a drug-addicted baby as evidence of neglect by the mother, because at the time the mother ingested the drugs, she was carrying a fetus, not a developed child. The court felt that neglect or abuse of a child could take place only after birth because the child abuse statutes do not include fetuses within their definition of "child." If the legislature meant to include a fetus in the definition, it could have specifically stated so, as in the murder statute which specifically defines murder as the unlawful killing of a "human being or fetus."

3. Medical Care

Parents have a duty to provide necessary medical care to their children and a pattern of not doing so may constitute child neglect. However, there are also situations where parents are not providing needed care for a sick child for religious reasons. If the medical procedures indicated involve little risk to the child, courts have not hesitated to step in.[153] If the authorities do not act in time and a child dies, the parents can be convicted of homicide.[154] On the other hand, if the medical procedure is at all risky or the risks associated with non-treatment are speculative, courts are less likely to intervene to overturn a parent's decision. Each case is decided on its own facts.

Another issue that has arisen is the medical treatment of newborn children with severe birth defects. Parents in two cases in New York and Indiana withheld consent for lifesaving medical treatment for their severely disabled newborn on the non-

---

148 *Santosky v. Kramer*, 455 U.S. 745 (1982). Standards of proof are explained in Chapter III, p.102.

149 *Lassiter v. North Carolina Dept. of Social Services*, 452 U.S. 18 (1981) (due process may require appointment of counsel in certain cases where the parents are unable to assert their interests, but not all).

150 *See V.F. v. State*, 666 P.2d 42 (Alaska 1983) (state constitution requires appointment of counsel).

151 492 N.Y.S.2d 331 (N.Y.Fam.Ct. 1985). *But see Matter of Fletcher*, 533 N.Y.S.2d 241 (N.Y.Fam.Ct. 1988) (questioning decision in *Smith*).

152 141 Cal. Rptr. 912 (Cal.App. 1977).

153 *Jehovah's Witnesses v. King County Hospital*, 278 F.Supp. 488 (W.D. Wash), *aff'd* 390 U.S. 598 (1968) (blood transfusion necessary to save children ordered despite religious opposition of parents).

154 *See Walker v. Superior Court*, 763 P.2d 852 (Cal. 1988) (parents convicted of manslaughter by denying child medical treatment; religious reasons are no defense). However, some states have made religion-based actions exceptions to child endangerment. *See, e.g.,* Ohio Rev.Code § 2919.22.

religious ground that it was better for them to die. Because of the resulting public clamor, Congress enacted a federal law requiring equal necessary medical for such newborns.[155] Nonetheless, some suspect that where the parents do not object to withholding treatment, there is an unofficial policy of benign neglect in many hospitals.

4. Juvenile Delinquency

A "juvenile delinquent" is a child who has committed an act that would be a crime if the child were an adult or an act that manifests anti-social inclinations, such as repeatedly missing school or disobeying parents. For years the interests of the delinquent and the juvenile court were thought to be identical, so no due process rights were needed like those for adults facing criminal prosecutions. Delinquency was treated as a species of child neglect or abuse in which the court was seen not really a court, but as a social services agency helping to give guidance to a troubled or confused child. In 1969, this myth was exploded and the Supreme Court held that juveniles who are subject to confinement for committing an act that would be a crime if committed by an adult, are entitled to the same due process rights as any adult prosecuted for a crime.[156] Since most juvenile delinquency proceedings involve criminal charges, the law of criminal procedure rather than family law is the applicable body of law.[157]

One difference between ordinary criminal proceedings and juvenile delinquency proceedings is the result of the proceeding. If the state proves beyond a reasonable doubt that the minor committed a crime,[158] the court does not apply the penalties set out in the statute. Instead, a "disposition" is ordered that is designed to rehabilitate the delinquent minor or otherwise seek to overcome whatever it was that led the minor to commit the offense in the first place. Sometimes this means that in a serious felony case such as murder, a minor could often receive a "sentence" that is much less severe than would be the case with an adult. However, the juvenile court has the option of "waiving jurisdiction" to the normal criminal courts for older minors who do not appear to be amenable to the rehabilitative measures that the court has at its disposal for juveniles. Juveniles in recent years have been committing progressively more serious crimes and presenting a hardened attitude toward changing their conduct. This has resulted in an increased number of instances of juvenile courts waiving jurisdiction to the ordinary criminal courts.

5. Mentally or Physically Disabled People

a. Guardianships of the Estate and the Person

Guardianships of the Estate Adults who are mentally or physically incapable of taking care of their financial affairs can be the subject of a guardianship or wardship "of the estate," under which another person is appointed guardian and makes whatever financial arrangements are necessary to provide for them. Petitions for guardianships are most often filed in the probate or surrogate's court. Often the guardian is a close relative of the ward, the person in need of assistance. The duty

---

155 29 U.S.C.A. § 794 (prohibiting discrimination against the handicapped); 45 C.F.R. § 84.55 (requiring public notice that "nourishment and medically beneficial treatment . . . should not be withheld from handicapped infants solely on the basis of their present or anticipated mental or physical impairments).

156 *In re Gault*, 387 U.S. 1 (1967).

157 *See* Chapter VIII, pp. 270-303.

158 Proof beyond a reasonable doubt is required in juvenile proceedings. *In re Winship*, 397 U.S. 358 (1970).

imposed is a fiduciary duty in which the highest degree of loyalty and care is required. To insure that the ward is protected from improper actions or neglect of the ward's affairs, guardians are usually required to file reports with the court and to purchase a bond to cover any losses they cause. In some states, a guardianship can be established, not just when there is full mental incapacity, but where the ward is a "spendthrift."

Guardianship of the Person This form of guardianship is also used when the ward is mentally or physically disabled, but its purpose is not to deal with the ward's finances. A guardian of the person can in general make decisions for the ward with respect to non-financial matters, such as decisions as to medical treatment. Often guardianships of both the estate and the person are established.[159]

b. Civil Commitment of Mentally Ill Persons

All states have some procedure for involuntary commitment of mentally ill persons to a psychiatric facility. Usually the petitioner seeking commitment is a relative of the respondent or a public agency or social worker. However, more than just mental illness must be proven. Constitutional principles permit involuntary commitment only of persons who are a danger to themselves or others, or who cannot take care of their basic needs. In addition, though the proceeding is a civil one, the grounds for commitment must be proven by "clear and convincing evidence" rather than the normal civil "preponderance of the evidence" standard.[160]

c. Issues Involving the Mentally Retarded

Civil Commitment to an Institution The adult mentally retarded are in most states subject to the same procedures for involuntary commitment to an institution as are the mentally ill, although the nature of their institutional surrounding and care is different Most often, however, the mentally retarded are diagnosed as such early in life and are committed voluntarily by their parents as infants. However, a major effort at "de-institutionalizing" the less severely mentally retarded has come about since the 1970s and more and more of them are taken care of in small group homes or are in independent living situations.

Sterilization of the Mentally Retarded At the turn of the century, the eugenics movement was strong in the U.S. and its followers believed that one means by which "science" could improve the human species was to eliminate "defective" genes from the overall human gene pool. One method of doing this was to sterilize those who suffered from mental retardation, mentally illness, epilepsy and other "defective" conditions, and many states passed laws permitting it. The U.S. Supreme Court was called on in 1927 to pass on the constitutionality of these laws. It upheld them by analogy to compulsory vaccinations against smallpox, with Justice Holmes for the majority reflecting the eugenics theory in his opinion: "It is better for all the world, if instead of waiting to execute degenerate offspring for crime or to let them starve for their imbecility, society can prevent those who are manifestly unfit from continuing

---

159 For more on guardianships, *see* DONALD H.J. HERMANN, MENTAL HEALTH AND DISABILITY LAW IN A NUTSHELL 214-233 (West 1997).

160 *O'Connor v. Donaldson*, 422 U.S. 563, 576 (1975) ("a State cannot constitutionally confine . . .a non-dangerous individual who is capable of surviving safely in freedom by himself or with the help of willing and responsible family members or friends"); *id.* at 432 (proof standard). *See also supra* note 148. For more on mental commitments, *see* HERMANN, *supra* note 159, at 142-183..

their kind."[161] In 1942, the Supreme Court decided *Skinner v. Oklahoma*, in which it declared that an Oklahoma statute that provided for mandatory sterilization of "habitual criminals" was unconstitutional because it interfered with the "fundamental right" to procreate.[162] However, *Skinner* did not invalidate involuntary sterilization in all cases. It only required that there be "strict scrutiny" of such laws, thus requiring that they be justified by a "compelling state interest."[163]

Today, involuntary sterilization is possible in many states, either by statute or as an exercise of courts' inherent equity powers. In general, mentally disabled persons who are sexually active, are unwilling or unable to employ other contraceptive methods and are unable to care for a child, will probably be ordered sterilized and that result is probably constitutional.[164]

---

161 *Buck v. Bell*, 274 U.S. 200, 207 (1927). One sentence later he uttered his now-famous dictum "Three generations of imbeciles is enough."

162 316 U.S. 535 (1942). *Skinner* is also discussed in Chapter IX, p. 333.

163 Strict scrutiny and compelling state interest are discussed in Chapter IX, pp. 328-333, 339.

164 *See North Carolina Ass'n of Retarded Citizens v. North Carolina*, 420 F.Supp. 451 (M.D.N.C. 1976); *See also In re Moe*, 432 N.E.2d 712 (Mass. 1982) (sterilization is proper exercise of equity powers; concept of "substituted judgment" to be used, whereby court determines what the retarded person would want were he or she mentally competent).

CHAPTER XIV

CRIMINAL LAW

Crimes usually have private victims, but criminal actions are considered to be offenses against the state and society. As a result, the state has an interest in prosecuting offenders beyond the rights or wishes of any private person.[1]

A. General Considerations

1. Sources and Variety of Criminal Law

State and Federal Law Criminal law in the United States has traditionally been the domain of the state law. Most "ordinary" criminal offenses, such as murder, assault, rape, larceny and robbery are governed exclusively by state law, while federal crimes have historically limited to conduct having a direct relationship to federal property or legislative programs or interstate aspects of crime.[2] However, just as non-criminal federal legislative activity has grown in recent decades, there has been an increased "federalization" of criminal law. Again like non-criminal federal law, federal crimes do not preempt state law on the same subject, so the result is a mix of state and federal criminal laws that might apply to the same conduct of a person or enterprise.[3] But beyond the creation of new federal crimes pursuant to Congress's broad commerce power, there has been an increased willingness to prosecute "old" federal crimes based on the perception that some crimes present a national problem that states alone cannot handle. The prime example of this is the federal government's "War on Drugs," declared by President Reagan and continued in successive administrations.

Statutory and Common Law Crimes Crimes in England were originally defined by the common law. Given the lack of sufficient notice of potential criminal sanctions involved when criminal offenses are set out exclusively in case law, most states have chosen to adopt a statutory approach. However, statutes have tended to codify the common law. This means that there is considerable similarity in crimes among the states. It also means that common law definitions of elements of offenses and defense are still important. Indeed, many state statutes use general common law terms without defining them, such as "murder," because it is expected that courts will give those terms their settled common law meaning.[4] A few states retain common

---

1 Standard criminal law texts are WAYNE R. LAFAVE AND AUSTIN W. SCOTT, JR., HORNBOOK ON CRIMINAL LAW, 2D ED. (West 1986, 1997) and JOSHUA DRESSLER, UNDERSTANDING CRIMINAL LAW, 2D ED. (Matthew Bender 1995). An outline with more than average detail is PETER W. LOW, CRIMINAL LAW (West 1990).

2 *See, e.g.* 18 U.S.C.A. §2312 (transportation of stolen vehicles across state lines) and 18 U.S.C.A. §1073 (interstate flight to avoid prosecution or giving testimony).

3 The general federalization of the law and the resulting mix was discussed in Chapter I, pp. 21-26, 28-30.

4 *See, e.g.*, Mich.Comp.L.Ann. §§750.317 (punishing "murder" without defining it).

law crimes to the extent that they do not conflict with statutes.[5] Federal crimes are completely statutory, however.[6]

Civil penalties can also be set out in state and federal administrative regulations or orders pursuant to legislative delegation of authority.[7] However, agencies adjudicating violations are limited solely to imposing a fine and may not order imprisonment as a sanction.[8]

The Importance of the Model Penal Code A major step toward greater uniformity and rationality of state criminal codes was taken in 1962 when the American Law Institute adopted the Model Penal Code (MPC).[9] Spurred by the MPC, nearly 40 states have enacted new criminal codes during the past 30 years. Some states have used the MPC almost in its entirety except for certain provisions they believe need modification. Other states have utilized only certain provisions from the MPC which they feel appropriately fit within their pre-existing statutory scheme.

Unlike the Uniform Commercial Code (UCC), which stresses the necessity for uniformity in commercial practices, the MPC is intended to be a "model" for state legislatures to help identify the major issues, and the alternatives to these issues, in criminal law. In fact, it is considered appropriate by many scholars that states should have significant variations in their penal laws, based upon differences in local conditions or points of view.[10]

Because criminal law in the United States is a mixture of the MPC and common law concepts, it has become necessary for students of the criminal law to learn both. Consequently, both common law and MPC approaches will be discussed in this chapter where their differences are major.

Categories of Criminal Offenses A crime can be either a "felony" or a "misdemeanor." Generally, crimes punishable by imprisonment for more than one year or by death are felonies. Those punishable by incarceration for less than a year or solely by a fine are misdemeanors. Some states, however, have a classification of "high misdemeanor," which are crimes punishable by more than one year, but not more than two years of imprisonment.[11] Some states have "civil infractions" that have

---

5 *See, e.g., Gervin v. State*, 371 S.W.2d 449, 454 (Tenn. 1963) (common law misdemeanor offense of solicitation to commit a crime was not merged into attempt statute and is still prosecutable as an offense separate from attempt); *State v. Palendrano*, 293 A.2d 747 (N.J. 1972) (common law offense of "common scold," a chronically difficult and argumentative woman, was preempted by statutory offense with common elements). Common law offenses come into the law by way of state statutes or constitutional provisions formally "receiving" English common law. *See* Chapter II, p. 40.

6 *United States v. Hudson and Goodwin*, 11 U.S. (7 Cranch.) 32 (1812) (Article III's vesting judicial power in federal courts did not include the authority to create common law crimes). The reasons for limiting federal court common law powers are discussed in Chapter I, pp. 32-33. One federal crime is defined in the Constitution. Art. III §3 defines treason as "levying War against [the United States] . . . or in adhering to their Enemies, giving them Aid and Comfort."

7 *See also Atlas Roofing Co. v. Occupational Safety and Health Review Comm.*, 430 U.S. 442 (1977) (no right to jury trial in civil penalty administrative proceeding for violation of worker safety rules).

8 *See Wing Wong v. United States*, 163 U.S. 228 (1896) (judicial trial necessary before sentence of 1 year at hard labor could be imposed). For federal agencies at least, part of the reason that agencies cannot punish criminal offenses is that crimes are said to involve "private rights" that must be adjudicated by an Article III judge. *See* Chapter VI, pp. 212-214. On the question of administrative powers regarding these issues, *see generally* BERNARD SCHWARTZ, ADMINISTRATIVE LAW, 3D ED., §§2.24, 2.28, 2.29, 9.17 (Aspen 1991).

9 MODEL PENAL CODE, PROPOSED OFFICIAL DRAFT (American Law Institute 1962).

10 *See* LAFAVE AND SCOTT, *supra* note 1, at 4.

11 MPC §1.04.

only monetary penalties and are not considered to be criminal offenses. These include parking and other minor traffic offenses.

2. Constitutional Considerations

Both the federal and state governments have broad powers to criminalize a wide range of behavior, but these powers must give way if they violate constitutional liberties. Many of the cases discussed in the chapter on constitutional law grew out of criminal prosecutions.[12] However, there are other constitutional limitations specifically applicable to criminal statutes that should be mentioned here.

The Constitution prohibits bills of attainder and *ex post facto* laws.[13] A bill of attainder is a law passed by a legislature that specifically identifies a person or an easily identifiable person within a group and punishes that person without a trial.[14] An *ex post facto* law operates to make conduct criminal that was not criminal when it occurred. Also included in the definition are laws that increase the punishment for crimes that have already been committed or that change the rules of evidence for such crimes.[15] The prohibition against *ex post facto* laws applies only to legislatively enacted law, not judicially created law.[16]

B. Elements of a Crime

Generally, for there to be a criminal offense, there must coexist (1) a wrongful act or omission, (2) a guilty state of mind, and (3) in some cases, causation of injury. The burden is on the prosecution to prove each applicable component "beyond a reasonable doubt."[17]

1. The Wrongful Act

Nature of Requirement of a Wrongful Act Bad thoughts alone are an insufficient basis of criminal liability. Instead, there must be some wrongful or criminal act (*actus reus*), whether it be an actual physical action taken by the defendant or an omission. In order for an omission to constitute an "act," there must be some duty to act on the part of the defendant. Generally there is no duty to aid another person in peril, even when such aid can be given without inconvenience. One need not reach out to save a drowning child in a pool, nor give warning to a person who is about to fall into an open manhole.[18] A duty to act generally exists only when there is some special relationship created by contract or statute. Thus a parent has affirmative duties to care for and protect a child, one person may voluntarily assume the care of another, a person may create some peril by his or her unlawful act that creates a duty to act, and a landowner may have a duty to business invitees.[19]

---

12 *See* Chapter IX.

13 Art. I §§9, 10.

14 *See, e.g. United States v. Brown*, 381 U.S. 437 (1965) (federal act that made it a criminal offense for a member of the Communist party to be a labor organization officer held unconstitutional).

15 See *Calder v. Bull*, 3 U.S. (3 Dall.) 386 (1798) (listing types of laws covered by the constitutional prohibition against *ex post facto* laws and determining that a Connecticut law granting a new trial regarding a will was not such a law).

16 See *Ross v. Oregon*, 227 U.S. 150 (1913) (*ex post facto* prohibition does not apply to judicial construction of a state statute).

17 *See* Chapter VIII, p. 259.

18 *See, e.g., State v. Ulvinen*, 313 N.W.2d 425 (Minn. 1981) (defendant not criminally liable for daughter-in-law's death when he knew of son's plan to kill her and did not warn her).

19 *See, e.g., State v. Benton*, 187 A. 609 (Del. 1936) (railway gateman guilty of criminal homicide for failing to lower gate to prevent an automobile from colliding with a train).

Voluntariness Requirement The defendant's act must have been voluntary to qualify as criminal.[20] The requirement of voluntariness is based on the principle that criminal liability only attaches to conduct that the defendant can control.[21] But what is meant by "voluntary" is not entirely clear. The MPC does not define the term. But it does list acts which are not voluntary: reflex or convulsion, bodily movement during sleep, conduct during hypnosis, and bodily movement that otherwise is not a product of the effort or determination of the actor, either conscious or habitual.[22]

Punishment of Status In *Robinson v. California*,[23] the Supreme Court held it was unconstitutional to punish a defendant for *being* a drug addict. It reasoned that addiction is an illness that can be acquired involuntarily and punishing involuntary status would amount to "cruel and unusual punishment," contrary to the 8th Amendment. However, in *Powell v. Texas*[24] the Court upheld the conviction of a chronic alcoholic for public drunkenness. A synthesis of these two cases suggests that a defendant can be punished for the possession or use of substances to which the defendant is addicted, but cannot be punished for the status of being addicted.[25]

2.　Fault or Guilty Mind (*Mens Rea*)

Generally, there can be a crime only if a criminal act (*actus reus*) is combined with some guilty state of mind (*mens rea*). Nonetheless, at least in certain circumstances, liability is possible without regard to fault.

a.　The Levels of Fault

Although guilty mind requirements have been variously stated, the modern view is that there are three levels: intent, recklessness and negligence. The greatest fault is assigned when defendants act intentionally. A person is said to act with intent to bring about certain harm if that person either (1) acts with the purpose (i.e., desire or design) of causing the harm or (2) voluntarily acts with the knowledge that the harm will almost certainly occur as a result of that act.[26] An example of acting with the intent to kill would be where a person aims and shoots another with a gun.[27] "Recklessness" can be defined as acting with the awareness that one's conduct is creating a significant unjustified risk of harm. For example, a person who fires a gun in the direction of a group of people assembled on the street acts recklessly. Criminal recklessness requires that the defendant actually be aware of the risk of harm. "Criminal negligence" embraces somewhat lesser culpability than recklessness. It is reserved for defendants whose behavior would otherwise be reckless, but who are not subjectively aware of the significant unjustified risk of harm that they are creating. Negligence exists if a "reasonable and prudent" person *would* have been aware of the

---

20 MPC §2.01(1).

21 *See, e.g., Fain v. Commonwealth*, 78 Ky. 183 (1879) (person who kills while in a state of sleep or between waking and sleep not guilty of murder).

22 MPC §2.01.

23 370 U.S. 660 (1962).

24 392 U.S. 514 (1968).

25 *See also United States v. Moore*, 486 F.2d 1139 (D.C. Cir. 1973) (declining to recognize addiction as a defense because there is no consensus that addiction overrides free will).

26 The MPC does not use the term "intent." Instead, it distinguishes between (1) and (2) in the text above explicitly as (1) "purposely" and (2) "knowingly." MPC §2.02.

27 Knowledge includes a suspicion that a fact exists with the deliberate avoidance of learning that the suspicion is correct, sometimes referred to as "wilful blindness." *See, e.g., United States v. Jewell*, 532 F.2d 697 (9th Cir. 1976) (where defendant knew of a secret compartment in a car which he acquired under suspicious circumstances, this was sufficient to establish the knowledge requirement for importing marijuana even if he did not actually know that it was in the compartment).

risk. Thus, negligence is better understood, not as defining a state of mind, but as setting a standard of conduct to which people must adhere regardless of their state of mind. An example of criminal negligence would be firing a gun out a window without looking to see whether there was anyone there.[28]

b. General and Specific Intent

General and Specific Intent The requirement of fault demands that at least "general intent" be shown to make out a crime. General intent is satisfied by showing a voluntary act done with an awareness of the probable consequences of that act — essentially the standard of recklessness.[29] "Specific intent" may also be required for some crimes.[30] This extra mental element is essentially a requirement that the defendant have a purpose to accomplish a particular harmful result. A specific intent requirement is usually imposed when the law wishes to single out particular types of behavior for more serious treatment. Usually the basic conduct involved is already punishable, but higher punishment is specified if the conduct is carried out with a particular purpose in mind. For example, a state might punish simple possession of narcotics, but punish more severely the very same act of possession if it is coupled with the intention to sell those narcotics. Similarly, the law may wish to punish more severely assault with intent to do serious bodily harm than a simple assault, even when the same injury is inflicted in both cases. For a conviction on the more serious version of the crime, the prosecution must prove both general intent and the specific intent.[31]

"Transferred" Intent Situations occur where the defendant acts with the intent to cause one result and another result takes place instead. For example, if the defendant shoots at one person intending to kill that person and hits and kills another person instead, the defendant has the requisite *mens rea* for the murder of the person actually killed because the defendant intended to kill *some* person, and therefore satisfied the fault requirement for murder.[32] Because the harm that resulted (killing a person) was the same *type* of harm the defendant intended, then the requisite *mens rea* exists. In such cases, it is said that the intent is "transferred" from the intended victim to the actual accidental one. However, if the defendant shoots at a teacup sitting on a table intending only to destroy it and instead accidentally hits a person, the same type of harm was not intended, so intent cannot be "transferred" from the cup to a person.[33]

---

28 These definitions correspond generally with that in tort law. *See* Chapter XI, p. 405.

29 The MPC states that when no intent is specified for a crime, it is understood that at least a level of recklessness is required. MPC §2.02(3).

30 The MPC does not make this distinction.

31 Specific intent is shown by circumstantial evidence. *See, e.g., United States v. Wilson*, 432 F.Supp. 223 (S.D.Tex.1976) (possession of 493 pounds of marijuana is sufficient to presume intent to distribute. See also *Defries v. State*, 342 N.E.2d 622 (Ind. 1976) ("if one throws a piece of chalk at the legendary victim with an eggshell skull, and the chalk strikes the victim and fractures his skull, the perpetrator would be guilty [of assault with intent to do great bodily harm] even though he did not intend to do great bodily harm").

32 *See, e.g., Mayweather v. State*, 242 P. 864 (Ariz. 1926) (defendant found guilty of murder for shooting one person while intending to kill another).

33 If the teacup was close to the person shot, the defendant might be deemed to have acted intentionally toward the victim, i.e. with knowledge that the resulting injury was almost certain to occur. Depending on the distance, the defendant might also be deemed to have acted recklessly, i.e. creating an unjustifiable risk of harm.

c. Liability Without Fault

The common law traditionally requires some level of fault to make out a criminal offense. However, legislatures have dispensed with the requirement in three situations. One is where there is a "public welfare offense" for which strict liability is imposed. A second is where the fault of one person is vicariously attributed to a different person. A third type of liability without fault is the criminal liability of a corporation, which has no mind and thus can have no guilty mind.

Public Welfare Offenses Most "public welfare offenses" are minor offenses for which it is difficult to prove intent or other fault. Traffic offenses are the most numerous type.[34] Others involve liquor sales.[35] These offenses are often not thought of as "real" crimes since they usually do not involve morally blameworthy conduct and are usually punished only by fines. Reflecting this sentiment, some states have decriminalized some of them, calling them "civil infractions."[36] This movement for change is not universal, however, and in any event not all such offenses have been decriminalized. In many countries such matters are handled administratively, so it is sometimes a shock when visitors to the U.S. find out first hand that they are crimes.

Other public welfare offenses are more serious, but still remove the need to prove fault at least as to some elements. The theory operating with these offenses is that the threat to health and safety posed by the activity in question is so obvious that this is sufficient notice to the defendant that it is regulated, thus excusing the need to prove fault. The nature of the object or activity punished, then, may affect the degree of fault required. For example, the Supreme Court held it proper to convict a defendant of illegal possession of an unregistered hand grenade based solely on the defendant's knowledge that what he possessed was a hand grenade. However, conviction for possession of an unregistered machine gun required that it be proven that the defendant knew that the weapon he possessed was capable of firing multiple rounds with one trigger pull, the salient characteristic of a machine gun.[37] In both cases, the person was held strictly liable for knowing that the item needed to be registered, but the characteristics of the item that required its registration differed in terms of their obviousness. For some public welfare offenses, then, it must be proven that the defendant's conduct as to *operative facts* of the offense was undertaken knowingly, though it need not be proven that the defendant knew the consequences of that conduct or its unlawfulness.[38]

Vicarious Liability Vicarious liability is liability imposed on a person without regard to personal fault or even personal conduct. It is automatic liability that results from the conduct of another. The largest number of vicarious liability situations involve the employer-employee relationship, as where a clerk in a store sells liquor

---

34 *See People v. Caddy*, 540 P.2d 1089 (Colo. 1975) (speeding is a strict liability crime, so defective speedometer is no defense).

35 *City of Dickinson v. Mueller*, 261 N.W.2d 787 (N.D. 1977) (strict liability for sale of liquor to minor).

36 *See* MPC 2.05, which calls such strict liability offenses "violations." rather than crimes. Often the decriminalization is not so much out of concern for the stigma attached as it is about avoiding giving defendants jury trials. Many state constitutions provide for the right to a jury in "all criminal prosecutions."

37 *United States v. Freed*, 401 U.S. 601, 609 (1971) (hand grenade); *United States v Staples*, 511 U.S. 600, 612 (1971) (machine gun).

38 Environmental laws present similar problems and a similar approach has been taken by the lower federal courts. *See United States v. Wilson*, 133 F.3d 251, 264-265 (4th Cir. 1997) (Clean Water Act case with a thoughtful discussion of the issues). *See also* Chapter XV, p. 582 (environmental offenses).

to a minor and the employer is held responsible.[39] Corporate officers can also be held vicariously liable for crimes committed by their corporation if they had a "responsible relation" to the relevant actions and the power to prevent them.[40] Laws imposing vicarious liability on parents for the acts of their children have had a more difficult history.[41] And even employer-employee situations have their limits. The Supreme Court held it was unconstitutional to convict a store owner of "knowingly and willfully" contributing to the delinquency of a minor just because one of his employees sold a button with an indecent slogan on it to a minor.[42]

3. Causation

Some criminal offenses require proof that the defendant's conduct caused harm to a victim. For example, to be convicted of any form of homicide, the prosecutor must prove that the defendant's actions were the legal or "proximate" cause of the victim's death.[43]

Cause-in-Fact and Proximate Cause   There are two steps in determining causation. The first is to determine if the defendant's action was a "cause-in-fact" of the harmful result. Cause-in-fact is a cause that is sufficient for the result to occur, a *sine qua non* test. It is most often stated as "but-for" causation: "but for" the defendant's conduct (i.e., without the defendant's conduct), the result or harm would *not* have taken place. If cause-in-fact cannot be shown, then the inquiry is over and causation is not satisfied. If cause-in-fact is shown, then the second step is to determine whether that cause-in-fact was the "proximate cause" of the harm. There can be many "but-for" causes of harm, but the law can punish a defendant's behavior only if it was a *proximate* cause of the harm. In general, "proximate cause" means that there is an uninterrupted causal chain between the defendant's act and the harm. In most cases this is easily determined. For example, if the defendant shoots the victim and the victim dies immediately, there is obviously nothing breaking the causal chain. However, the causal link is sometimes less clear.[44]

Intervening Cause   An intervening act can "break the chain" of causation. Whether it will depends in most situations on whether it was a *coincidence* unrelated to the defendant's actions or a *response* to the actions of the defendant. As might be expected, the law permits a longer chain of causation for response than coincidence.

A coincidence will break the chain of causation only if its intervention and result were not foreseeable. For example, assume that the defendant inflicts a non-fatal wound on the victim and leaves the victim lying unconscious in the middle of a road at night. If a passing motorist runs over the victim causing death, then the defendant can be said to have caused the death because such a consequence was a foreseeable

---

39 *But see Commonwealth v. Koczwara*, 155 A.2d 825 (Pa. 1959) (in liquor sale case, held that due process does not permit imprisonment of employer for acts of employee, only a fine).

40 *United States v. Park*, 421 U.S. 658 (1975) (not unconstitutional to hold president of national food store chain liable for corporation's shipments of adulterated food).

41 *State v. Akers*, 400 A.2d 38 (N.H. 1979) (law making parents vicariously liable for offenses committed by their children in the operation of snowmobiles is unconstitutional).

42 *Vachon v. New Hampshire*, 414 U.S. 478 (1974) (button proclaiming "copulation, not masturbation" sold to 14-year-old girl).

43 *See, e.g., People v. Dlugash*, 363 N.E.2d 1155 (N.Y. 1977) (murder conviction reduced to attempted murder where defendant shot victim five times in the face after victim had been shot in the chest by another; prosecution did not show that victim was alive at the time the defendant shot him).

44 *See, e.g., Commonwealth v. Berggren*, 496 N.E.2d 660 (Mass. 1986) (proximate cause existed based on foreseeable chain of events in motor vehicle homicide case when defendant on his motorcycle led police car on a high-speed chase and police office died in accident when his car hit a tree).

result of leaving the victim on the road.[45] On the other hand, if the defendant left the victim on a *sidewalk* and a drunk driver lost control and drove onto the sidewalk and ran over the victim, this would not be foreseeable.

In the case of an intervening *response* to conditions created by the defendant, causation will be found in some cases even if the response was not foreseeable. Only if the response is completely abnormal will the defendant be said not to have caused the ultimate result. An example is provided by the cases involving negligent treatment of the crime victims' wounds by health care professionals. Generally, "ordinary" negligent medical treatment is considered "normal" and does not break the causation chain,[46] while grossly negligent or intentional malpractice will be deemed an intervening cause.[47]

Response actions by the *victim* may also be part of a proper causation chain as when the victim, whom the defendant has beaten, dragged to a river and threatened with further beatings, "voluntarily" jumps into the river and drowns.[48] Responsibility for the result of a victim's suicide is sometimes imposed. Where the defendant has seriously wounded the victim and the victim commits suicide for reasons unrelated to his wounds, the defendant will not be held responsible for the victim's death. But it is not considered abnormal that a victim could commit suicide out of extreme pain from the wounds the defendant inflicted or from mental incompetence caused by those wounds. In such a case, the defendant has been held responsible.[49]

The Common Law "Year and a Day" Rule The common law rule that is still followed by many jurisdictions is that a defendant cannot be found guilty of murder if the victim lives for more than a year and a day after the defendant's act. This rule is based on the premise that it is too difficult to prove that the act of the defendant was the cause of the death after too much time has passed. Due to advances in the medical field, this is clearly no longer the case and many jurisdictions have abandoned the rule.[50]

Other Causation Situations Intervening acts aside, the lack of foreseeability of the *particular* resulting harm does not always break the causal chain. For instance, an illness of the victim that causes the victim to suffer greater harm than was foreseeable to the defendant at the time of the crime does not bar the act from being considered the proximate cause of the harm.[51] As the Indiana Supreme Court once noted, "if one throws a piece of chalk at [a] victim with an eggshell skull, and the chalk strikes the victim and fractures his skull, the perpetrator would be guilty" of aggravated assault

---

45 *People v. Fowler*, 174 P. 892 (Cal. 1918).

46 *People v. Fite*, 627 P.2d 761 (Colo. 1981) (doctor's discontinuance of antibiotics not gross negligence, so causation chain not broken).

47 *People v. Stewart*, 358 N.E.2d 487 (N.Y 1976) (failure of anesthesiologist to provide oxygen to patient in operation to repair hernia following surgery for knife wound defendant inflicted held to break causation chain).

48 *State v. Myers*, 81 A.2d 710 (N.J. 1951).

49 *See also United States v. Hamilton*, 182 F.Supp. 548 (D.D.C. 1960) (defendant responsible for death where non-fatal wound he inflicted sent victim to hospital and victim while there ripped out life-supporting tubes causing death).

50 *See, e.g., Commonwealth v. Lewis*, 409 N.E.2d 771 (Mass. 1980) (rule is an anachronism in light of advances in showing cause of death and in prolonging life).

51 See e.g., *Hopkins v. Commonwealth*, 80 S.W. 156 (Ky. 1904) (it was murder when defendant killed victim weakened by prior illness who perhaps would not have died if completely healthy).

with intent to inflict great bodily harm, even though he did not intend to do this amount of bodily harm.[52]

C. Specific Offenses

1. Criminal Homicide

Murder Murder is a common law crime which is traditionally defined as an unlawful killing of a human being with "malice aforethought."[53] The meaning of malice aforethought has never been entirely clear, but a common formulation is that malice aforethought includes unjustified intent to kill, intent to cause serious bodily harm, and recklessly causing death or serious bodily harm. These coincide with the intent and recklessness levels of *mens rea* discussed earlier.[54] In defining malice for juries, some courts have used such terms as "wilful and wanton disregard for the value of human life" or "abandoned and malignant heart," while others have stated more simply that intent to kill from any "unlawful and unjustified motives" is sufficient, leaving the matter for the jury to determine.[55]

It is common for criminal codes to divide murder into degrees. This was originally done to single out first degree murder for capital punishment. For example, a statute might classify murder perpetrated by means of poison, lying in wait, or other wilful, deliberate, and premeditated killing, or which is committed in the perpetration of any felony, as murder in the first degree, and provide that all other murder is in the second degree. The MPC provides that a criminal homicide constitutes murder when it is committed purposely, knowingly, or recklessly under circumstances which manifest an extreme indifference to the value of human life.[56] The MPC does not divide murder into degrees.

Felony Murder One of the more controversial forms of murder is "felony murder," which exists in most states: if any death occurs during the commission of a felony, the defendant committing the felony can be convicted of murder without the requisite mental state for murder and even without directly causing the death of the victim.[57] In theory, the requisite mental state can be imputed to the defendant from the defendant's intent to commit the felonious act.[58] Felony murder is said to deter criminals from committing felonies, or at least to encourage them to commit them safely. However, felony murder has been criticized by scholars, and many courts have limited it. Courts have (1) required that the felony be inherently dangerous, (2) required the prosecutor to prove malice in addition to proof of a killing and a felony, (3) required that the felony be independent from the act that caused the victim's death, and (4) tightened the causal chain by requiring that the death be at least

---

52 *Defries v. State*, 342 N.E.2d 622, 629-630 (Ind. 1976).

53 *See* LaFave & Scott, *supra* note 1, §7.1.

54 *See supra* p. 506. Negligence is insufficient for murder.

55 *See also People v. Woods*, 331 N.W.2d 707 (Mich. 1982) (substituting intent to kill or do great bodily injury for the term "malice," which court considered to be meaningless and confusing to juries).

56 MPC §210.2(1)(b).

57 *See, e.g., People v. Stamp*, 82 Cal.Rptr. 598 (Cal.App. 1969) (defendant properly found guilty of murder when, during a robbery, a person died of fright). *Compare Commonwealth v. Redline*, 137 A.2d 472 (Pa. 1958) (defendant not guilty of murder where co-felon was shot and killed by a policeman) *with Commonwealth v. Moyer*, 53 A.2d 736 (Pa. 1947) (defendant properly guilty of murder where one victim accidentally shot another victim after being wounded by defendant).

58 *But cf. People v. Dillon*, 668 P.2d 697 (Cal. 1983) (malice is not an element of felony murder, so there is no unconstitutional presumption).

foreseeable and take place close in time to the time of the felony.[59] In addition, some statutes limit felony murder to deaths that take place only during specific felonies enumerated in the statute. The MPC largely rejects felony murder and instead substitutes an evidentiary presumption of malice from commission of certain enumerated felonies.[60] Despite the MPC's stand, most states retain some form of felony murder.

Manslaughter Manslaughter includes homicide which is less serious than murder. There are two major types of manslaughter: voluntary manslaughter, which involves intentional killings, and involuntary manslaughter, which involves unintentional killings. Usually a more severe punishment attaches to voluntary manslaughter than to involuntary manslaughter. The MPC and some states do not make a distinction between voluntary and involuntary manslaughter. However, many jurisdictions maintain the distinction. Other states disregard the distinction between voluntary and involuntary, and, instead, divide manslaughter into degrees.

In the common law understanding, voluntary manslaughter is an intentional killing which is reduced from murder when the defendant is provoked so as to be said to be acting in the "heat of passion." In determining what constitutes an adequate provocation, courts ask whether "reasonable" persons would have had their passions aroused. Moreover, the killing must follow shortly after the provocation. A homicide committed after adequate provocation, but after a sufficient "cooling-off" period intervened would not be considered manslaughter, but murder.[61]

Involuntary manslaughter may be divided into two types. The first type is negligent involuntary manslaughter. The majority of jurisdictions have *mens rea* requirements for involuntary manslaughter that are similar to either the criminal negligence or the recklessness standards discussed earlier.[62] However, a few jurisdictions use a civil negligence standard.[63] The second type of involuntary manslaughter, "misdemeanor-manslaughter," parallels the felony-murder rule. Under this concept, an unintended homicide that occurs in the commission of a misdemeanor constitutes involuntary manslaughter.[64] However, like felony murder, misdemeanor manslaughter has been limited by courts because they deem it too harsh.

2. Burglary

Burglary was defined at common law as breaking and entering the dwelling of another in the nighttime with the intent to commit a felony therein.[65] At common law,

---

59 *See generally* LAFAVE & SCOTT, *supra* note 1, §7.5.

60 MPC §210.

61 *See, e.g., Sheppard v. State,* 10 So.2d 822 (Ala. 1942) (defendant killed wife several days after finding out about her adulterous behavior; conviction of first degree murder, not manslaughter, is proper).

62 *See supra* p. 506. *Compare Commonwealth v. Welansky,* 55 N.E.2d 902 (Mass. 1944) (awareness of high risk of harm not necessary for conviction of manslaughter when 490 people died in fire due to inadequate precautions) *with Bussard v. State,* 288 N.W. 187 (Wis. 1939) (defendant found not to have realized the high risk of harm created by driving negligently and therefore was not guilty of involuntary manslaughter for resulting death).

63 *See, e.g., State v. Williams,* 484 P.2d 1167 (Wash.App. 1971) (civil negligence standard was sufficient for involuntary manslaughter conviction of parents who caused the death of their infant child by failing to get medical care).

64 *See, e.g., People v. Nelson,* 128 N.E.2d 391 (N.Y. 1955) (defendant-landlord's misdemeanor of failing to provide adequate fire precautions in his apartment building which resulted in two deaths held to support manslaughter conviction).

65 *See* LAFAVE & SCOTT, *supra* note 1, §8.13.

"breaking" meant that the burglar had to create an opening to enter the dwelling. Going through an open window or door was insufficient. The rationale was to ensure that homeowners secured theirs windows and doors. However, modern criminal codes rarely require "breaking." Instead, such terms like "unlawfully" are used to describe the type of entry necessary for burglary.[66] Modern statutes do not require much "entering" either. It has been held that as small an entry as a foot entering through a kicked-in window satisfies the requirement.[67] Moreover, if one enters premises when open and remains there surreptitiously until after the premises are closed, that is also counted as an entry.[68]

Part of the theoretical basis of burglary was the need for special protection of homes. Any building used for habitation is considered a dwelling, even if only part of the building is so used. The requirement that the burglary take place at nighttime is based on the notion that such intrusions will terrorize residents more than daytime entries. Most modern burglary statutes punish both day and nighttime entries as burglary, but some states punish nighttime entries more severely.

Common law burglary also required that the burglar intend to commit a felony within the dwelling. If the intruder merely intended to trespass, then there was no burglary. However, modern criminal codes no longer make it necessary to intend a felony. Instead, all that is required is an intent to commit some offense. Where intent to commit an offense is a required element, proof of specific intent is required.[69]

3. Theft Offenses

Traditionally, larceny, false pretenses and embezzlement make up the three major forms of theft. "Larceny" has been defined as the "trespassory taking and carrying away of the personal property of another with the intent to deprive the other of the property permanently."[70] Larceny includes improperly retaining the lost, mislaid or mistakenly delivered property of another, as well as actually taking property.[71] False pretenses can be defined as knowingly obtaining the property of another, with the purpose to defraud the other, through factual misrepresentation.[72] Embezzlement involves the wrongful conversion to one's own use of the property of another that is already in one's possession. An example is an employee who handles money or property of his or her employer and takes some of it.[73]

---

66 The Model Penal Code deals with the problem by simply excluding all entries onto premises when they are open to the public or by a person who is licensed or privileged to enter. MPC §221.1.

67 *People v. Roldan*, 241 N.E.2d 591 (Ill.App. 1968) (defendant's act of kicking in store window, which enabled others to loot store, sufficient for burglary).

68 MPC §221.1.

69 Specific intent was discussed *supra* p. 507.

70 *United States v. Waronek*, 582 F.2d 1158, 1161 (7th Cir. 1978) (dictum). *See also People v. Khoury*, 166 Cal.Rptr. 705 (Cal.App 1980) (defendant guilty of sufficiently carrying away tools when he concealed them in a chandelier box and wheeled them back into the store when the cashier insisted on inspecting the box before accepting payment for the chandelier).

71 *See, e.g., State v. Hector*, 402 A.2d 595 (R.I. 1979) (defendant who retained money after bank teller misread check and overpaid him was guilty of larceny).

72 LaFave & Scott, *supra* note 1, §8.7. *See, e.g., Rex v. Barnard*, 173 Eng. Rep. 342 (1837) (defendant who purposefully created the erroneous understanding that he was an Oxford student by wearing a cap and gown found guilty of false pretenses for obtaining goods on credit).

73 *United States v. Faulkner*, 638 F.2d 129 (9th Cir. 1981) (embezzlement occurred when truck driver displayed and tried to sell refrigerators he was transporting even though he never took the goods off the truck or sold any of them; possession and control with the intent to convert goods is sufficient).

Intent to permanently deprive the owner of the property is an essential element of theft and an intent to return property to the lawful owner will absolve the defendant.[74] However, abandoning the property with nothing more than a hope that the owner will find it will not negate intent to permanently deprive the owner of the property.[75] Problems with young people taking cars temporarily to go "joyriding" have caused many states to pass statutes that remove the need to show permanent deprivation intent in the case of motor vehicles and punish simple taking without permission of the owner.[76]

Modern theft offenses include blackmail, bribery and money laundering. Blackmail involves the threat to expose private information or accuse another of a crime with intent to extort money or certain acts from that person.[77] Bribery of public officials is payment of money or other valuable consideration to seek to influence the official in the discharge of his or her duties. International bribery connected with business deals has recently become a great concern for governments and businesses.[78]

Of most recent vintage is money laundering. Money laundering is undertaken in order to be able to openly spend the proceeds of an illegal business operation, such as drug dealing. The money is "dirty" both because it is from drug sales and because it has never been declared as income and no taxes have been paid on it. Spending the money openly would likely alert the tax authorities, who are always on the alert for people who seem to be spending beyond their official declared means. Typically, to launder the money, a person will affiliate with a legitimate business person who runs a business, preferably one that operates on a cash basis, such as a restaurant. The "dirty" money is added little by little to legitimate profits of the business, profits are declared and taxes paid on what seems to be a successful legitimate business. It is difficult to tell what is legitimate income taken in by the business and what is "dirty" money.[79] Often offenses such money laundering and bribery, embezzlement and tax evasion are referred to as "white collar" crimes, since they are often perpetrated by persons in business suits and white shirts.[80]

4. Rape (Criminal Sexual Conduct)

Common Law Rape and Modern Definitions The common law defined rape as

---

74 *Impson v. State*, 58 P.2d 523 (Ariz. 1936) (larceny conviction not proper where facts showed defendant took car with intent to use it and return it). *But see Chapman v. State*, 212 P.2d 485 (Okla. App. 1949) (larceny conviction proper where defendant fraudulently rented the car and did nothing to disclose its whereabouts until he saw escape was impossible).

75 *See* MPC §223.0(1) (including as part of "deprive" disposing of property "so as to make it unlikely that the owner will recover it."); *State v. Davis*, 38 N.J.L. 176 (1875) (defendant-students who took professor's horse and buggy and left it abandoned had requisite intent).

76 *See* LaFave & Scott, *supra* note 1, at 724-725.

77 *See State v. Harrington*, 260 A.2d 692 (Vt. 1969) (blackmail conviction proper where evidence showed defendant intended to extort money by threatening to expose private information). *See generally*, Wendy J. Gordon, *Truth and Consequences: The Force of Blackmail's Central Case*, 141 U.Pa.L.Rev. 1741 (1993).

78 *See generally* Shada Islam, *Investment: Kickback Setback: OECD Bolsters Fight Against International Corruption*, Dec. 11, 1997 Far E. Econ. Rev. 69.

79 18 U.S.C.A. §1956. *See United States v. Jensen*, 69 F.3d 906 (8th Cir. 1995) (conviction of accepting money from a drug deal to purchase a car held constitutional). *See United States v. Cleveland*, 951 F.Supp. 1249 (E.D.La. 1997) (federal money laundering statute properly passed under Congress' taxing power).

80 *See generally* Ellen S. Podgor & Jerold H. Israel, White Collar Crime in a Nutshell (West 1997). *See also infra* pp. 525-527, where "enterprise criminality" is discussed.

sexual penetration by a man of a woman who is not his wife, which is accomplished through force or otherwise without her consent. This definition has been abandoned in virtually all states.[81] Each state rape statute differs slightly, but most address forcible penetration of another person without that person's consent.[82] Some states have expanded and revised sexual offenses. For example, Michigan has created four degrees of "criminal sexual conduct" and punishes a variety of forms of "sexual contact" that include more than just actions by males against females. The statute also specifies that resistance on the part of the victim is not necessary.[83]

"Rape Shield" Laws A major change in the law that affects prosecutions for rape has been a modification in the law of evidence. Traditionally, the sexual history of the rape victim was admissible to show that the victim consented to the sexual intercourse and to undermine the reliability of her testimony. Presently, the rules of evidence of all states and the federal court system limit such evidence.[84] Behind such "rape shield" laws is a desire to encourage victims to report rapes and a judgment that the sexual history of the victim is generally irrelevant.

The Husband Exemption A few states still follow the common law rule that non-consensual sexual intercourse between a husband and wife is not rape. Even the MPC states that the victim must not be the wife of the defendant.[85] The "husband exemption" has its origin in the common law treatment of women as not much better than their husbands' property, coupled with the idea that, when a woman marries a man, she has given blanket consent to sexual intercourse with him. Modern justifications for the exemption include the difficulty of proving rape within a marital context, the potential for false claims of rape in divorce, the societal interest in maintaining marital privacy, and the idea that spousal rape is a less serious crime than other forms of rape.[86] Most states have abandoned the husband exemption and some courts have even held it unconstitutional.[87]

Statutory Rape Most states also have what is called "statutory rape," which prohibits even consensual sexual relations with a female under a certain age, often 16 or 18. This is a strict liability offense in that it does not require that the defendant know or even have reason to suspect that his sexual partner is underage.

D. Defenses to Criminal Liability

It is useful to divide defenses into two categories: "failure-of-proof" (FOP) defenses and affirmative defenses. FOP defenses are defenses which tend to negate

---

81 *See* DRESSLER, *supra* note 1, §33.02. There has been much recent attention to the issue of rape in non-legal as well as legal circles. Some of the literature is collected in DRESSLER, *supra*, §33.03-33.04.

82 *See State v. Baker*, 441 S.E.2d 551,553 (N.C. 1994) (defendant convicted of first-degree rape for forcing the victim on the bed and penetrating her vagina with his fingers and genitals). *See Wisdom v. State*, 708 S.W.2d 840, 842, 843 (Tex.Cr.App. 1986) (Court held that the Legislature recognized that forceful and violent sexual penetration is non-consensual and is therefore a crime of violence per se). *See generally*, 65 Am. Jur. Rape §1 (1972, 1998)

83 Mich.Comp.L.Ann. §§750.520(a)-.520(l). Sexual contact includes the "intentional touching of the victim's . . . intimate parts . . . [if it] . . . can be construed to be for the purpose of sexual arousal or gratification." *Id.* §750.520a(k). The Michigan law is discussed in DRESSLER, *supra* note 1, §33.09(A).

84 *See, e.g.*, Federal Rules of Evidence 412 (limiting evidence regarding the sexual past of the victim, unless "good cause" is shown, such as to show that the defendant was not the source of semen found in the victim). *Cf.* Federal Rules of Evidence 413-415 (permitting evidence of the defendant's commission of another sexual assault or child molestation in either a civil or criminal case).

85 MPC §213.1(1).

86 For more on spousal rape, *see* DRESSLER, *supra* note 1, §33.07.

87 *See People v. Liberta*, 474 N.E.2d 567 (N.Y. 1984) (husband exemption rule denies equal protection of the law to unmarried men and is therefore unconstitutional).

some element of the offense, typically the mental element of *mens rea*. Affirmative defenses essentially concede all the elements of the crime and rely on some additional reason as an excuse or justification of the offense.

1. Failure-of-Proof Defenses

Foremost among FOP defenses are "mistake of fact" and "mistake of law." A mistake of fact or law defense is invoked by defendants to show that they lacked the requisite intent to commit the crime because they were mistaken as to the circumstances of the crime.[88] A mistake as to whether something is punishable under the criminal law is not a defense even when that mistake is based on advice from one's attorney. The maxim *ignorantia legis neminem excusat* (ignorance of the law excuses no one) is deeply imbedded in Anglo-American jurisprudence. Other FOP defenses are "diminished capacity" and "intoxication." Diminished capacity, where recognized as a defense, may be used to show that, due to a mental defect short of insanity, the defendant was deluded, mistaken or otherwise may not have formed the requisite *mens rea*.[89] The defense of voluntary intoxication is sometimes used to negate the presence of the requisite specific intent due to the intoxication.[90]

FOP defenses are treated differently at common law than they are under the MPC. Generally, the common law takes a stricter view than the MPC, allowing FOP defenses only to negate specific intent, never general intent.[91] The result of this limitation is that FOP defenses generally only *reduce the seriousness* of criminal conduct; they do not completely excuse it. For example, while voluntary intoxication can negate premeditation in a first degree murder prosecution, it does not negate malice, the general intent requirement for murder. Thus, regardless of how drunk the defendant was in a homicide case, that defendant can be convicted of murder, a general intent crime.[92]

Limiting FOP defenses to specific intent elements has been criticized as illogical.[93] After all, intoxication or mistake of fact can just as easily be seen as negating the general intent element of murder (malice aforethought) as the specific intent of premeditation. Certainly the degree of "specificity" of the intent in question is irrelevant. For example, in the case of burglary, mistake of fact would *not* be allowed to negate the intent *to break into* an occupied dwelling, but *could* be used to negate the rather general "specific" intention *to commit some felony* once inside. The limitation to specific intent elements can best be explained, not logically, but as a policy decision that persons with these types of defenses deserve some leniency, but should not be completely exonerated. Consequently, the MPC, which does not adopt

---

88 *See, e.g., Green v. State*, 221 S.W.2d 612 (Tex.Cr.App. 1949) (in larceny prosecution, defendant did not have the intent to permanently deprive another of several hogs because he mistakenly thought that they belonged to him). *Cf. Lambert v. California*, 355 U.S. 225 (1957) (due process violated by punishing defendant for violating law requiring convicted felons to register with police when she did not know of that requirement).

89 The MPC and about a dozen states recognize diminished capacity for all crimes. MPC §4.02(1). A few jurisdictions do not recognize it at all. *Bethea v. United States*, 365 A.2d 64 (D.C.App. 1976). Others reserve it solely for murder prosecutions. *State v. Cooper*, 213 S.E.2d 305, 319 (N.C. 1975). Yet others limit it to specific intent elements of offenses. *United States v. Brawner*, 471 F.2d 969 (D.C. Cir. 1972), *United States v. Gonyea*, 140 F.3d 649 (6th Cir. 1998). *See* DRESSLER, *supra* note 1, §§26.01-26.03.

90 *See, e.g., Heideman v. United States*, 259 F.2d 943 (D.C.Cir. 1958) (defendant did not have intent to steal due to intoxication and therefore not guilty of robbery).

91 *See supra* p. 507, where specific and general intent were discussed.

92 *See, e.g., People v. Langworthy*, 331 N.W.2d 171 (Mich. 1982) (intoxication not a defense to a charge of rape, a general intent crime).

93 See DRESSLER, *supra* note 1, at 279-280.

the distinction between general and specific intent, allows use of FOP defenses to negate *any* element of culpability of a crime. However, it makes one exception: voluntary drug or alcohol intoxication may not negate recklessness — the MPC's threshold "general intent" requirement for basic criminal liability.[94] Clearly, the exception for intoxication is a policy choice designed to limit defendants' ability to negate culpability based on use of drugs or alcohol.

In recent years, courts have become increasingly reluctant to allow excuses based on impaired capacity for self-control through addiction to drugs or alcohol. The general theory behind this movement is that, while people may not act voluntarily when they are addicts, they did make a voluntary choice when they first decided to use drugs or alcohol, and this is sufficient to impose criminal liability. In *Montana v. Egelhoff*, the Supreme Court affirmed the constitutional validity of this approach when it held constitutional a Montana law that prohibited the defendant from introducing and the jury from considering *any* evidence of voluntary intoxication.[95]

2. Affirmative Defenses

The successful assertion of an affirmative defense exonerates the defendant even though the prosecution has proven all of the elements of the offense. These defenses are "affirmative" in the sense that new additional facts beyond those placed in issue by denial of the elements must be affirmatively proven for the defense to succeed. In addition, the law often places the burden of proof on affirmative defenses on the defendant. As with other aspects of criminal law, the common law and the MPC versions of these defenses differ somewhat and these differences will be noted.[96]

a. Defensive Violence

Self-Defense One can use force to defend against attack if one actually *and* reasonably believes that there is an imminent threat of death or serious bodily harm such that force is necessary to prevent that harm. This defense most often applies to homicide and assault cases. The majority of courts hold that where the threat is this serious, there is no duty to retreat, even when a retreat can be safely accomplished. The rationale for this belief is the notion that people should be able to stand their ground and not be forced to back down. If the defendant subjectively believes that force is necessary, but the belief is not reasonable, it may be sufficient to negate specific intent, thereby reducing murder to manslaughter. However, objective reasonableness is required to constitute a complete defense to homicide.[97]

Defense of Others and Property Force may also be used to defend another person, to defend property, to stop crimes, and to apprehend criminals. Most courts permit defense of others only if the person the defendant is protecting would have

---

94 MPC §2.08.

95 518 U.S. 37 (1996). *Egelhoff* is also discussed in Chapter XIV, p. 517.

96 It has been customary to categorize affirmative defenses as either "justifications" or "excuses." Justifications are defenses that focus on the conduct of the defendant and exonerate the defendant because that *conduct* is not a crime (e.g. self-defense). Excuses focus on the defendant and exonerate based on a judgment that the defendant is not blameworthy (e.g. insanity). However, these distinctions have no real practical meaning, so they are ignored here. *But see* Joshua Dressler, *Justifications and Excuses: A Brief Review of the Concepts and the Literature*, 33 WAYNE L. REV. 1155 (1987) (arguing the utility of the distinction).

97 *See People v. Humphrey*, 921 P.2d 1, 6 (Cal. 1996) ("If the belief subjectively exists but is objectively unreasonable, there is 'imperfect self-defense,' i.e., 'the defendant is deemed to have acted without malice and cannot be convicted of murder,' but can be convicted of manslaughter.").

been justified in using the same force in self-defense.[98] In a minority of states, however, defense of others is proper if the defendant *reasonably believed* that the other person would have been justified in the same force in self-defense.[99] Property may be defended with the use of reasonable, non-deadly force if the defendant reasonably believed that it is necessary to do so to avoid imminent theft or trespass to the property. Generally, because human life is more important that property, one can never use *deadly* force in the defense of property, except as permitted in those states with the "castle doctrine." Under it, a person's dwelling house is a "castle of defense" for its occupants and an assault on it with intent to injure the occupants may justify the use of deadly force as protection.[100] Other courts limit this to a threat of "forcible" felonies (e.g., rape, murder) or serious bodily harm.[101] Finally, non-deadly force may be used by both police officers and private citizens to prevent the commission of a crime and to apprehend criminals.[102]

Battered Women Cases In order to have a valid claim of self defense, one must have a reasonable belief of an *imminent* threat of serious harm. These limits on self defense have been severely tested by recent cases in which an abused woman has killed her abusive husband or boyfriend at a time when he was not actively attacking her, often while he slept. Some scholars advocate that courts, instead of applying the traditional self-defense standard, should consider whether the woman's actions were reasonable given a history of repeated beatings or whether she suffered from "battered woman syndrome," which made it impossible for her to resolve the abuse problem in any other way.[103] Others oppose this trend, arguing that if courts consider each defendant's circumstances, this will leave judge and jury without any guide as to what is reasonable and will permit them to acquit on the improper ground that the defendant "deserved" to be killed.[104]

b. Insanity and Other Mental Illness

The Right or Wrong Test The traditional common law test for legal insanity was the *M'Naghten* test, or "right and wrong" test.[105] Under this test, defendants are considered insane if, as a result of some form of mental disease, they did not know

---

98 *See, e.g., People v. Young*, 183 N.E.2d 319 (N.Y. 1962) (defendant's use of force to defend a person who was being arrested by a plainclothes policeman not justified because the arrest was lawful).

99 *See, e.g., State v. Menilla*, 158 N.W. 645 (Iowa 1916) (defendant's reasonable belief that her husband would imminently kill her son justified her use of deadly force against her husband even though her son would not have been so justified because he did not know he was in danger).

100 *Falco v. State*, 407 So.2d 203 (Fla. 1981).

101 *Morrison v. State*, 371 S.W.2d 441 (Tenn. 1963) (defendant was justified in using deadly force when intoxicated victim attempted to enter defendant's house). *Cf. State v. Terrell*, 186 P. 108 (Utah 1919) (burglary of a rabbit pen described by court as a forcible felony, justifying the use of deadly force by the defendant). In Texas, secured creditors trying to repossess automobiles for failure to make installment payments were shot by the debtors. Prosecutors refused to prosecute on the ground that the debtor's action was justified under Texas law. *Cf.* Uniform Commercial Code §9-503 (self-help repossession permitted if it can be accomplished without a breach of the peace) and Chapter XII, p. 393.

102 The Supreme Court has held that it is unconstitutional for police officers to use deadly force to apprehend a felony suspect unless it is necessary to prevent the escape and the suspect poses a threat of death or serious physical injury to the officer or others. *See Tennessee v. Garner*, 471 U.S. 85 (1985).

103 *See e.g., State v. Hodges*, 716 P.2d 563 (Kan. 1986) (jury could consider "the history of violence" and circumstances leading up to the use of force in battered women syndrome cases); *State v. Kelly*, 478 A.2d 364 (N.J. 1984) (describing the nature of the battered woman syndrome); Cal.Evid.Code §1107 (permitting expert testimony on "the physical, emotional, or mental effects upon the beliefs, perceptions, or behavior of victims of domestic violence").

104 James R. Aker & Hans Toch, *Battered Women, Straw Men and Expert Testimony: A Comment on State v. Kelly*, 21 CRIM. L. BULL. 125 (1985).

105 *Daniel M'Naghten's Case*, 8 Eng.Rep. 718, 10 Cl. & Fin. 200 (1843).

what they were doing or failed to realize that what they were doing was wrong. The *M'Naghten* test has been criticized because it focuses on cognitive impairment and ignores cases where defendants knew what they were doing, but were unable to control themselves. In response to this criticism, courts have adopted other tests. One is the "irresistible impulse" test, under which defendants were unable, due to a mental disease, to refrain from engaging in the prohibited conduct, though they realized that their conduct was wrong.[106] Another has been the "product" or *Durham* test, which allows the defense whenever a causal connection can be shown between a mental disease and the criminal conduct. The *Durham* test has been criticized for its heavy reliance on expert evidence. It is not presently followed in any jurisdiction.[107]

The MPC's "Substantial Capacity" Test   Under this test, defendants are not responsible for their crimes if they lacked the substantial capacity either to appreciate the wrongfulness of that conduct *or to conform their conduct to the requirements of the law*. The substantial capacity test was used in the federal system until failed presidential assassin John Hinckley used it successfully in the prosecution against him for shooting President Reagan. As a result, Congress limited insanity as a defense to cases in which the defendant, "as a result of a severe mental disease or defect, was unable to appreciate the nature and quality or the wrongfulness of his acts." Moreover, "the defendant has the burden of proving the defense of insanity by clear and convincing evidence," as opposed to the lesser "preponderance of the evidence" standard.[108]

Guilty But Mentally Ill   In recent years an increasing number of states have by statute adopted a new verdict option of "guilty but mentally ill" (GBMI).[109] Traditionally, if a defendant raised an insanity defense the jury had only three possible verdicts: guilty, not guilty, or not guilty by reason of insanity. With a guilty-but-mentally-ill verdict, the jury may find beyond a reasonable doubt that the defendant did the criminal acts charged and was mentally ill, but *not* legally insane. The result of a GBMI verdict is that the defendant is sent to prison, but is supposed to get psychiatric treatment there. However, critics point out that psychiatric treatment is generally not available in prisons and that, in any event, overcrowded prisons are hardly an atmosphere conducive to recovering from mental illness. Moreover, the GBMI option will cause jurors not to seriously consider an insanity defense, since they will think that the defendant will get treatment under either option and at least will be sent to prison if the verdict is GBMI.[110]

It should be emphasized that defendants acquitted by reason of insanity do not go free. Instead, they are committed to a psychiatric hospital and may not be released until and unless cured and no longer a danger to themselves or others.[111] An example is would-be presidential assassin John Hinckley, who to date remains in a mental hospital. Even defendants who have been convicted and have completed their prison

---

106 *Parsons v. State*, 2 So. 854 (Ala. 1887).

107 *See Durham v. United States*, 214 F.2d 862 (D.C. Cir. 1954) *overruled by United States v. Brawner*, 471 F.2d 696 (D.C. Cir. 1972).

108 18 U.S.C.A. §17(a). The constitutionality of the "clear and convincing" standard of proof has not been passed on by the Supreme Court. *See infra* text at note 114 and Chapter VIII, p. 295.

109 *See* 71 A.L.R.4th 702 (1992) (reviewing GBMI statutes).

110 *See* Linda C. Fentiman, *"Guilty But Mentally Ill": The Real Verdict Is Guilty*, 26 B.C.L.Rev. 601 (1985) and Project, *Evaluating Michigan's Guilty But Mentally Ill Verdict: An Empirical Study*, 16 U. Mich. J. L. Ref. 77 (1982).

111 MPC §4.08(1).

sentences may be confined in a psychiatric facility. In the recent case of *Kansas v. Hendricks*,[112] Hendricks was a repeat child sex offender who was scheduled for release from prison following completion of his latest sentence, but whose pedophilia had not been cured and who continued to harbor sexual desires for children that he admitted he could not control when he was "stressed out." The Supreme Court rejected constitutional objections to his confinement in a psychiatric facility under Kansas's Sexually Violent Predator Act, which permitted civil commitment of any person who suffered a "mental abnormality" or a "personality disorder" that made them likely to engage in "predatory acts of sexual violence."

Mental Incompetence to Stand Trial It is also possible that a defendant will not be able even to stand because of mental incompetence. The standard generally applied is whether the defendant "lacks capacity to understand the proceedings against him or to assist in his own defense."[113] A state may presume competence and require the defendant to prove incompetence by a preponderance of the evidence.[114] If incompetence is found, the criminal proceedings are suspended and the defendant is committed to a mental health facility until competence is restored. Then the criminal case can resume, unless the court determines that "so much time has elapsed since the commitment of the defendant that it would be unjust to resume the criminal proceeding."[115]

c. Duress, Necessity and Other Pressures on Free Will

Duress Duress applies when a defendant commits a crime under a threat of death or serious bodily injury. The threat may be to the defendant, a family member or other person, but it must in any event be a real threat and its consequences must be imminent. Relevant on this point is the defendant's ability to escape (if being physically held) or to report the threats to the authorities.[116] Duress does not apply if the person had a role in creating the coercive situation.[117]

Most states limit duress to situations where the harm threatened is greater than the harm the defendant is coerced into inflicting. So if the defendant participates in a robbery on threat of being killed, the defense applies.[118] This limit and the inapplicability of duress to murder — effective in about half the states — make duress inapplicable where a defendant kills because threatened with death.[119] However, the MPC provides that a defendant has a duress defense when coerced into performing

---

112 *Kansas v. Hendricks*, 521 U.S. 346 (1997).

113 MPC §4.04.

114 *Cooper v. Oklahoma*, 517 U.S. 348 (1996). For a discussion of the various standards of proof, *see* Chapter III, p. 102.

115 MPC §4.06(2). Another issue regarding insanity arises when a defendant sentenced to death become insane after conviction and sentence. States have uniformly prohibited execution of an insane prisoner and the Supreme Court has held the principle to be a constitutional one. *See* Chapter XIV, p. 300.

116 *United States v. Lee*, 694 F.2d 649 (11th Cir. 1983) (defendant who claimed to have been forced to join drug conspiracy because of threats to friend had numerous reasonable chances to inform police). *But see United States v. Riffe*, 10 F.3d 682 (9th Cir. 1993) (opportunity to report drug ring to authorities was not real for prisoner coerced into participating by threats of death, since protective segregation had failed to protect informants in the past).

117 *See* MPC §2.09(2) and *Williams v. State*, 646 A.2d 1101 (Md.App. 1994) (defendant who was allegedly coerced by gang into robbery could not claim duress because he had borrowed money from gang leader and participated in crimes to pay it back).

118 *People v. Merhige*, 180 N.W.2d 418 (Mich. 1920) (defendant forced to drive getaway car; not guilty of robbery or felony murder when robber he assisted shot a bank patron during the robbery).

119 *State v. Nargashian*, 58 A. 853 (R.I. 1904) (A threatened B with death unless B helped hold C so A could kill C; duress instruction refused).

any crime if a person of "reasonable firmness" in the defendant's situation would not have been able to resist.[120] Under the MPC, then, duress might apply when X threatens to kill D if D does not hold Y while X stabs Y to death.[121]

Necessity While duress deals with psychological pressure applied by another *person*, the defense of necessity involves the effects of *physical circumstances* on a defendant's will. For necessity to apply, (1) defendants must face some force that threatens imminent harm to themselves or others, (2) their committing a criminal act is the only way to prevent that harm, (3) they did not place themselves in that position of danger and (4) the criminal conduct involves less harm than the harm threatened. For example, if a person is lost in a snowstorm facing death from exposure and starvation, it is not a crime to break into a cabin to seek shelter and food. The law places a higher value on human life than on property.

Economic necessity does not justify a crime, such as where a person steals food out of hunger.[122] Necessity has also been routinely rejected in cases of "civil disobedience" — where protesters violate the law for the purpose of preventing certain conduct from occurring. For example, protesters against abortion cannot assert that their blocking entrances to abortion clinic was necessary to prevent the killing of unborn children, nor can opponents of nuclear power claim necessity based on the dangers of nuclear power. In these cases, the law has already anticipated the choice involved and determined the balance to be struck between the competing values. Consequently, defendants and courts are precluded from reassessing those values to determine whether certain conduct is justified.[123]

Another important limitation on the necessity defense is that it does not excuse intentional homicide. In a famous English case, the defense was rejected when shipwrecked seamen killed a youth to eat his flesh to survive.[124] U.S. law is in agreement.[125] Critics doubt the wisdom of this limit on necessity. They argue that *duress* sometimes permits trading a life for a life and the only real difference between duress and necessity is the source of the threat — duress involves a threat from a person while necessity involves a threat from nature.

MPC "Choice of Evils" Defense The MPC's version of the necessity defense is the "choice of evils" defense. It is interesting for its effort to generalize the fundamental social issue involved in duress and necessity. The defense is established if it is shown that, in committing a crime, (1) the defendant believed his conduct was necessary "to avoid a harm or evil to himself or to another" and (2) "the harm or evil sought to be avoided by such conduct [was] greater than that sought to be prevented by the law."[126] Notable differences from common law necessity and duress are the lack of a requirement of "imminent" necessity, the lack of an exception for cases where the

---

120 MPC §2.09.

121 *See* LaFave & Scott, *supra* note 1, §5.3(b). *Compare State v. Nargashian, supra* note 119

122 *State v. Moe*, 24 P2d 638, 640 (Wash. 1933) (mob of unemployed looted grocery store owned by head of relief committee who had refused to increase their flour allotment; no necessity defense).

123 *Cleveland v. Municipality of* Anchorage, 631 P.2d 1073 (Alaska 1981) (trespass at abortion clinic); State *v. Warshow*, 410 A.2d 1000 (Vt. 1979) (nuclear power plant). *See also State v. Tate*, 505 A.2d 941 (N.J. 1986) (necessity did not excuse paraplegic's use of marijuana to relieve pain).

124 *Regina v. Dudley & Stephens*, 14 Q.B.D. 273 (1884).

125 *United States v. Holmes*, 26 F.Cas. 360 (C.C.E.D. Pa. 1842) (crew members of sunken ship, who threw 14 male passengers overboard to keep lifeboat afloat, guilty of manslaughter).

126 MPC §3.02. The MPC also requires that it be clear that the legislature did not intend to exclude the choice made by the defendant, such as in the civil disobedience cases just discussed.

defendant had a role in creating the difficult choice presented, and its applicability to choices imposed both by the forces of nature and by another person.

Like common law necessity and duress, "choice of evils" does not apply to excuse intentional homicide even if the defendant is threatened with death. The rationale is that the choice is between two innocent lives involved — the victim's and the defendant's — which have equal value.[127] It has been argued, however, that if the choice of evils is between taking one life and saving *several* other lives, then the defense should apply.[128]

Situational Coercion Some argue in favor of a defense even broader than duress and the MPC's "catch-all" choice of evils defense. A defendant, it is asserted, should be able to choose the *greater* of two evils if there was some understandable reason for doing so. Such a "situational coercion" defense would be available if a person of reasonable firmness would bend under the pressure and choose the greater evil. Mercy killing is an example. If a person takes the life of his or her spouse, who is suffering tremendous pain from terminal cancer, after being repeatedly requested to do so, many would not consider such a person morally blameworthy. Such conduct does not qualify for the choice of evils defense because intentional killing is the greater evil. Yet, critics argue, most would understand how a loving spouse of reasonable firmness could well act the same way under the circumstances.

d. Entrapment

It is common for the police to use various undercover methods of operation to catch criminals. These range from simple police purchases of narcotics to more elaborate "sting" operations, such as setting up complete, bogus businesses. For example, police might set up a fake "chop shop," an underground enterprise which purchases stolen automobiles and dismantles them to sell the parts. Such a scheme allows the police to catch offenders in the entire distribution chain of stolen car parts. Even "reverse stings," as where the police sell illegal drugs, are common. Yet, the police should not become so involved in arranging crimes that they pressure or induce innocent people into committing crimes they would not otherwise commit. The doctrine of entrapment deals with this issue.

Subjective Test There are two approaches to entrapment: subjective and objective. The majority of states and the federal courts use what has been called the "subjective" approach. Both tests require that it be proven that the idea for the crime originated with the police, i.e., that the police offered the narcotics for sale, delivered the bribe or offered to buy the stolen car. Beyond this, the subjective test focuses on whether the defendant was "predisposed" to commit the type of offense charged — whether the defendant was "ready and willing to commit the crimes such as are charged in the indictment, whenever the opportunity was afforded."[129] One difficulty with the subjective approach is that it opens the door to introducing evidence of the defendant's character, reputation and criminal history. Such evidence is generally not admissible at trial against the defendant except under limited circumstances, because

---

127 This is in contrast to self-defense, where the judgment of the law is that the aggressor's life is worth less than an innocent person's.

128 *See* Comment to MPC §3.02, Tentative Draft No. 8, at 15.

129 LAFAVE & SCOTT, *supra* note 1, at 280; *Sherman v. United States*, 356 U.S. 369 (1958) (entrapment established as a matter of law where government informer met the defendant while both were undergoing treatment for narcotics addiction, repeatedly badgered the defendant into assisting him in obtaining narcotics, paid for the drugs and the taxi to go get them).

of the risk that the jury will convict the defendant, not for committing this particular crime, but for being a generally bad person.[130] Another problem with the subjective approach is that, if it is followed strictly, there is no limit to how shocking the level of police deceit or badgering is in a given case — it is tolerated so long as the defendant was predisposed to commit the offense. Indeed, the police can single out "predisposed" suspects for outrageous treatment, confident that "anything goes" with them.

Objective Test In reaction to these criticisms, an alternative "objective" approach, used by a minority of jurisdictions, has developed. It does not focus on the particular defendant and his or her criminal propensities. Instead, it looks at the effect that the police conduct in question would have had on the *average innocent* person. The particular defendant's character and predisposition are irrelevant. The objective test, then, seeks to determine how bad the police practices were, rather than how bad a person the defendant is.[131]

A recent Supreme Court case imposes an additional limit on the subjective test. In *Jacobson v. United States*,[132] a child pornography case, the government spent some two-and-a-half years trying to persuade the defendant to order sexually explicit materials, using five different fictitious organizations and a bogus "pen pal." After finally receiving a missive from one of the "organizations" decrying international censorship, he ordered a magazine — doing so, he testified later, because he was curious about "all the trouble and the hysteria over pornography and I wanted to see what the material was." The Court reversed his conviction. It held that the predisposition of the defendant must be "independent and not the product of the attention" the government had directed at him over the two-and-a-half years.

Some have argued that entrapment, like many other limits on police investigation techniques, should be constitutionally based — that entrapment is an unfair tactic that violates due process of law. In general, the Court has rejected this idea. The Court has suggested in dictum that truly outrageous police entrapment behavior might violate due process, though no such case has yet reached the Court.[133]

E. Peripheral Actors, Anticipatory Crimes and Enterprise Criminality

1. Accessories and Accomplices

The legal system views as criminals those who assist principal criminal actors. An "accessory before the fact" is someone who helps the principal out beforehand, but is not present when the crime is committed. An "accomplice" is someone who assists in the commission of the crime. Both are treated the same as principals. In

---

130 The general inadmissibility of bad character evidence against criminal defendants was discussed in Chapter III, p. 108. The difficulties are compounded by the fact that the subjective test requires that the *jury* rather than the judge determine the defendant's predisposition. *See Sherman v. United States, supra.*

131 The objective test also differs from the subjective test in that it is the judge rather than the jury that determines what the effect of the police practices would be on the average person.

132 503 U.S. 540 (1993).

133 *See* Chapter VIII, p. 296, note 233. Because *Jacobson* is not constitutionally based, it is only binding on the federal courts. The extent to which "sexual entrapment" is proper has divided the lower federal courts. *Compare United States v. Simpson*, 813 F.2d 1462 (9th Cir. 1987) ("deceptive creation and/or exploitation of an intimate relationship does not exceed the boundaries of permissible law enforcement tactics) *with United States v. Cuervelo*, 949 F.2d 559 (2d Cir. 1991) (hearing required to examine allegations that federal drug agent had sexual relations with the defendant on 15 occasions, had given her gifts of money, clothes and jewelry, had written her "a number of love letters," and had induced her to come to the U.S. to participate in drug smuggling by procuring a visa for her and paying her way).

effect then, the acts of the principal participant are imputed to them.[134] Consequently, the driver of the "get-away" car that brought the robbers to a bank is subject to the same criminal liability as the robbers who actually went in and robbed the bank and shot the bank manager. What must be shown is that the accomplice rendered some form of assistance to the principal and intended to promote the crime. Clearly, providing a weapon or transportation or standing as a lookout qualify, but it is also sufficient if the accessory or accomplice does not supply any assistance, but is standing by to render assistance if necessary. The relevant *mens rea* requirement is equal to that of the principal actor for the relevant crime, plus having the purpose to promote or facilitate the principal's commission of the crime.[135]

An "accessory after the fact" is someone who helps the principal actor after the crime. Accessories after the fact are usually not held equally accountable with the principal. Generally they are punished separately for crimes such as "obstruction of justice" or "aiding and abetting" an escape.

2. Solicitation, Attempts and Conspiracies

Because of the harmful consequences of criminal activity, society need not wait for a complete crime to take place before acting. "Solicitation" of a crime — encouraging or engaging another to commit a crime — can be punished.[136] Similarly, an "attempt" to commit a crime is punishable, typically by one-half the penalty for the completed crime. An attempt takes place when the defendant has the intent to commit a completed crime and takes a substantial step toward doing so, such as the robber who points a gun at the victim, but then runs away without taking anything.[137] Solicitation merges into attempt once some step toward undertaking the crime takes place and an attempt merges into the offense itself once the offense is completed. This means that the defendant cannot be prosecuted for both the attempt and the completed offense.

A "conspiracy" exists when two or more people agree to commit a criminal act and take some overt step toward committing it. Conspiracy laws have been justified on the theory that groups of criminals are more dangerous in part because, once formed to commit one crime, they are likely to plan and commit other crimes as well.[138] Conspiracy remains a separate crime regardless of whether the planned crime is carried out. However, if offenses are committed, then every coconspirator is liable for all crimes committed by every other coconspirator that are "within the scope of the conspiracy, are in furtherance of it, and are reasonably foreseeable as a necessary or natural consequence of the conspiracy."[139]

---

134 *See* MPC 2.06(3).

135 *See* MPC §2.06(3) (defining when a defendant is "legally accountable" for conduct of another). Accomplices and accessories before the fact may also be conspirators. The difference between conspiracy and accomplice or accessory liability is that conspirators are responsible for their act of conspiracy — a separate crime by itself — even if the planned crime does not take place.

136 MPC §5.02.

137 MPC §5.01(1)(c). *State v. Smith*, 621 A.2d 493 (N.J.App. 1993) (defendant, who had tested positive for HIV, could be found guilty of attempted murder upon proof that he intended to kill corrections officer by biting him; it was sufficient that defendant himself believed he could cause death by biting his victim).

138 *United States v. Rabinowich*, 238 U.S. 78, 88 (1915); *Pinkerton v. United States*, 328 U.S. 640, 644 (1946) (reaffirms the conspiracy rule defined in *Rabinowich*).

139 *State v. Walton*, 630 A.2d 990, 997 (Conn. 1993), *citing Pinkerton*, *supra* note 138; *State v. Bridges*, 628 A.2d 270 (N.J. 1993) (conspiracy was to return to party with loaded guns to intimidate party-goers from beating a friend; although killing was not within the scope of the conspiracy, it was foreseeable that things would escalate and someone would fire into the crowd). *But see Commonwealth v. Wilson*, 296 A.2d 719, 721 (Pa. 1972) (reversing conviction for voluntary manslaughter when Wilson's friends stabbed

3. Enterprise Liability

a. Criminal Liability of Corporations

Vicarious strict criminal liability of business entities based on the actions of employees were discussed earlier. As stated there, liability is generally limited to social welfare offenses of a minor type, which generally do not require any *mens rea* on the part of the employee.[140] However, there are more serious offenses for which a corporation or other entity can be punished.

The common law's requirement that a criminal actor have the requisite *mens rea* to commit a crime traditionally excluded corporations from criminal liability, since they have no human mind. Today, corporations can be convicted of criminal offenses. The MPC provides, for example, that the corporation is liable when any one of the following applies: (1) the conduct made criminal is performed by the corporation's agents within the scope of their employment and the statute's purpose is to impose criminal liability on the corporation, (2) the crime is a failure to act when the law requires the corporation to act or (3) the criminal inaction was authorized or "recklessly tolerated" by "high managerial agents" of the corporation.[141] Though some states limit liability of corporations, crimes for which corporations have been convicted range from theft to homicide. Many of the corporate criminal cases have been for violations of workplace safety requirements that injured employees.[142]

b. Criminal Liability for Racketeering Activities: RICO

RICO Elements The Racketeer-Influenced and Corrupt Organizations Act (RICO), passed by Congress in 1970, imposes criminal and civil liability for various actions related to enterprises.[143] RICO outlaws four things: (1) investing income that was derived from a "pattern of racketeering activity" in any "enterprise," (2) the acquisition or maintenance of any interest in such an enterprise "through a pattern of racketeering activity," (3) participating in the conduct of an enterprise "through a pattern of racketeering activity" and (4) conspiring to do any of the preceding.[144] "Racketeering activity" is defined broadly as the commission of or threat to commit any of a list of generic types of state crimes set out in the Act or any "indictable" acts proscribed by numerous federal criminal provisions, including mail and wire fraud, bankruptcy offenses, securities fraud or drug-related offenses. A "pattern" of racketeering is defined as commission of 2 such acts in the last 10 years that are related and continuous. "Related" means that the offenses were linked by having a common goal or by some other logical connection. "Continuity" means that the acts must continue or constitute a threat of continuation.[145] An "enterprise" can be a formal organization, such as any normal business organization, or it can simply be

---

and killed someone with whom Wilson had been engaged in a barroom brawl where Wilson did not encourage or acquiesce in nor was he even aware of his friend's use of a knife).

140 *See supra* p. 508.

141 MPC §2.07(1).

142 *People v. Pymm*, 563 N.E.2d 962 (N.Y. 1990) (sustaining convictions of corporation and officers for assault and conspiracy based on mercury poisoning of employees; prosecution not preempted by federal law). *See generally The Corporation's Criminal Liability for Homicide*, 45 ALR4th 1021 (1987).

143 18 U.S.C.A. §§1961-1968.

144 18 U.S.C.A. §1962. The enterprise must affect interstate commerce.

145 *See* 18 U.S.C.A. §1961(a)(1), (5); *H.J., Inc. v. Northwestern Bell Telephone Co.*, 492 U.S. 229 (1983) ("only few weeks or months with no possibility of continuation beyond that" is not sufficient); *Religious Tech. Center v. Wollersheim*, 971 F.2d 364, 367 (9th Cir. 1992) (12-month rule of thumb). *But see Allwaste Inc. v. Hecht*, 65 F.3d 1523, 1528 (9th Cir. 1995) (12-months not a per se rule).

"any group of persons associated together for a common purpose of engaging in a course of conduct."[146]

Up to 20 years imprisonment and substantial fines are possible under RICO. Serious forfeiture sanctions are also possible. The statute provides that convicted RICO defendants forfeit any interest they may have in the relevant "enterprise" and "any property constituting, or derived from, any proceeds which the person obtained, directly or indirectly, from racketeering activity."[147]

Criminal Uses of RICO   The primary focus of RICO was organized crime's infiltration and use of legitimate business enterprises as a "front" for their criminal activities or for money laundering. Examples are where a "loan-sharking" extortion operation is run out of a bar owned by organized crime figures or where a drug dealing group takes over a bank for money laundering purposes. RICO responded to the concern that the traditional approach of arresting and imprisoning individual members of organized crime groups is not fully effective. RICO was designed to get at the entire organization itself, its assets and the top leaders who run it. It has been used effectively against the mafia and other organized crime groups.[148] It has also been used to fight political corruption, white collar crime and violent groups.[149]

The broad reach of RICO, however, goes beyond organized crime groups. This is especially apparent in the civil RICO suits filed by private plaintiffs, as discussed below. Use of interstate wire communications or the mails to perpetuate fraud is a federal crime that qualifies as "racketeering," so any multiple acts of fraud that involve interstate use of the telephone or fax or use of the postal service can qualify as "racketeering" under RICO if the requisite relatedness and continuity can be shown. In *Sedima SPRI v. Imrex Co., Inc.*,[150] a Belgian company filed a RICO claim against its joint venture partner for the latter's continued over-billing of expenses for locating aircraft parts. The RICO connection was the fact that the bills were mailed and thus constituted mail fraud. The Supreme Court held that a RICO claim was properly alleged. In so holding, the Court expressly rejected the concerns of the lower court, which was distressed that RICO, "instead of being used against mobsters and organized criminals, . . . has become a tool for everyday fraud cases brought against 'respected and legitimate 'enterprises'" that are then branded "racketeers."

A conspiracy to violate RICO also casts a wide net. In *Salinas v. United States*,[151] a Texas sheriff arranged for a federal prisoner held in his jail to have unsupervised visits with his wife and girlfriend for $6,000 per month and $1,000 per visit. There was no question of the sheriff's RICO liability, but a question arose regarding the sheriff's deputy. The deputy had been acquitted of RICO charges, but was convicted of conspiracy to violate RICO. The issue was whether the deputy's continuing to permit the visits while in charge of the jail during the sheriff's absence was sufficient for the conspiracy conviction or whether the deputy had to have personally committed the 2 criminal acts required for a "pattern of racketeering activity." According to the Court,

---

146 *United States v. Turkette*, 452 U.S. 576, 583 (1981).

147 18 U.S.C.A. §1963(a).

148 *See United States v. Brooklier*, 685 F.2d 1208 (9th Cir. 1982) (La Cosa Nostra extortion operation).

149 *United States v. Bustamante*, 45 F.3d 933, 935 (5th Cir. 1995) (congressman convicted of running bribery scheme); *United States v. Yarbrough*, 852 F.2d 1522, 1526-28, 1540, 1546 (9th Cir. 1988) (members of radical right-wing, white-supremacist group, the "Order," convicted); *United States v. Marubeni America Corp.*, 611 F.2d 763 (9th Cir. 1980) (contractors convicted in bid-rigging bribery scheme).

150 473 U.S. 479, 499 (1985).

151 522 U.S. 52 (1997).

all that was necessary was proof that the deputy was involved in the scheme as a co-conspirator and that the *sheriff* had accepted the bribes. The Court observed broadly that, if conspirators have a plan which calls for some conspirators to perpetrate the crime and others to provide support, the supporters are as guilty as the perpetrators and are liable for the acts of their co-conspirators.

Cases like *Salinas* raise the question of the potential RICO liability of "outsiders" — lawyers, accountants, bankers and other professionals — who may be hired to perform services for a business that is violating RICO. Outsiders present an attractive "deep pocket" both for the government and civil RICO plaintiffs, especially when the principal offenders involved have no assets. The Supreme Court has made clear that outsiders are guilty of a RICO violation only if they are involved in the "operation or management" of the RICO enterprise. Consequently, lawyers and other professionals avoid liability by sticking solely to providing services.[152] However, *Salinas* teaches that a *conspiracy* to violate RICO may be made out so long as the outsider had knowledge of what the principal was doing and through providing professional services rendered assistance in what was later determined to be a RICO violation.[153]

Civil Uses of RICO As already alluded to, civil suits under RICO are also possible. Private persons or organizations "injured in [their] business or property by reason of a violation" of the Act may obtain treble damages and attorney fees — substantial incentives for civil plaintiffs.[154] A civil suit is proper even though no prior criminal action has been brought.[155] And, as seen from the *Sedima* case discussed above, the fact that ordinary business fraud and a legitimate business are the target is irrelevant. Civil RICO has even expanded beyond economic "racketeering" to target non-profit political "racketeering." In *National Organization for Women v. Scheidler*,[156] the Court permitted a RICO suit by abortion clinics against an anti-abortion group. The suit claimed that the anti-abortion group was a racketeering "enterprise" that on a continuous basis used and threatened violence to induce clinic doctors and other employees to give up their jobs and patients to give up their right to obtain clinic services, thus injuring the clinics' business and property interests.[157]

F. Criminal Sanctions

The most common criminal sentences are fines and imprisonment. In addition, the death penalty is possible in some states for first degree murder.[158]

1. Imprisonment

Range of Sentences for Particular Offenses The range of sentences varies considerably from state to state. To give a general idea of the ranges for certain offenses, the following prevail in California: 1st degree murder, 25 years to life in

---

152 *Reves v. Ernst & Young*, 507 U.S. 170 (1993) (accounting firm not liable for understating value of assets where its role was limited to preparing financial reports).

153 W.B. Markowitz, *Expanding Rico Civil Liability for Lawyers and Other "Outsiders": Perspectives of a Plaintiff's Lawyer*, 45 FED. LAWYER 35 (1998).

154 18 U.S.C.A. § 1964(c). The federal court is empowered in § 1964(a) to grant appropriate injunctive relief ordering divestiture or limits on future activities of enterprises or persons or dissolution of enterprises. However, the use of injunctive relief in private RICO suits is not well-developed.

155 *Sedima*, 473 U.S. at 486-493. The Court strongly hinted that the normal civil "preponderance of the evidence" standard of proof would apply, but did not decide the question. *Id.* at 491.

156 510 U.S. 249 (1994).

157 The Court reserved the question of whether some applications of RICO to abortion protesters could violate their 1st Amendment free speech and association rights.

158 For discussion of the procedure for determining sentences, *see* Chapter VIII, pp. 265-266.

prison or death; 2nd degree murder, 15 years to life in prison; kidnaping, 3 to 8 years in prison; armed robbery, 3 to 9 years; rape, 3 to 8 years; arson of an inhabited structure, 5 to 9 years; and burglary, 2 to 6 years in prison.

Indeterminate Sentences Most states still utilize "indeterminate" sentences. Under this method, the statute determines a minimum and maximum term of imprisonment for each crime. Judges then use their discretion and impose a minimum and maximum sentence term which fall within the statutory sentence range. An administrative body called a "parole board" then decides the actual date of release somewhere between the minimum and maximum term set by the judge and releases the defendant "on parole." In deciding on a release date, the parole board considers the offender's behavior while in prison and other factors bearing on the offender's ability to avoid involvement in further crime, if released.

Determinate Sentences While indeterminate sentences are still used by a majority of states, there are concerns that indeterminate sentencing results in defendants serving different sentences for the same crime. Concern over such sentence disparity has led several states to enact legislation that imposes set determinate sentences for each crime. Judges in these states impose a sentence for a specific term falling within a narrow range set by legislation. This system of determinate sentencing, now used in about 10 states,[159] not only restricts a judge's discretion in deciding the length of a sentence, but also prevents prisoners from being released by parole boards until they have served their entire sentence.

Regardless of what sentencing method is used, the time actually served by prisoners is usually less than the maximum sentence imposed. For example, while prisoners convicted of all forms of homicide received average maximum sentences of 12 years, five months, they actually served only 5 years, 11 months. Sentences of 7 years, 11 months were imposed on those convicted of robbery, while they actually served only 3 years, 8 months. The average sentence for assault was 5 years, 1 month, while only 2 years, 5 months was actually served. Even in systems with determinate sentencing, such "discounted" sentences exist because it is often possible for prisoners to earn "good time," a system of counting prison time whereby good behavior allows them to count more days than have actually gone by.

Mandatory Minimum Sentences Some jurisdictions have introduced a mandatory sentencing system that gives the judge no discretion. These have typically been imposed in drug trafficking cases and felony cases in which a gun is used.[160] For example, at the federal level, Congress has imposed mandatory minimum sentences for the manufacture or distribution of narcotics.[161] These sentences are currently set at 5 and 10 years, depending on the quantity of the drug involved.

Limits on Judicial Discretion California has declared that "the purpose of imprisonment for crime is punishment" and that this purpose "is best served by terms [of imprisonment] proportionate to the seriousness of the offense with provisions for uniformity of sentences of offenders committing the same offense under similar

---

159 2 U.S. Department of Justice, Bureau of Judicial Statistics, *Report to the Nation on Crime and Justice* 91 (1990).

160 *See, e.g.,* Mich.Comp.L. Ann. §750.227(b) (Michigan's mandatory 2-year sentence, to be added to any felony involving a firearm); 18 U.S.C.A. §924(c) (mandatory sentences of varying lengths for using different kinds of guns in the commission of a drug offense).

161 *See, e.g.,* 21 U.S.C.A. §841.

circumstances."[162] Accordingly, in the sentence ranges given above as examples from California, what actually is provided for most offenses is a "menu" of three choices of terms of imprisonment. For example, rape is punishable by terms of 3, 6, or 8 years in prison. The judge must impose the middle term of imprisonment "unless there are circumstances in aggravation or mitigation of the crime," in which case the higher or lower term is to be used. The judge must articulate the reasons for the sentence chosen on the record.

Federal Sentencing Guidelines More precise methods of calculating sentences are found in the federal sentencing guidelines enacted by Congress in 1984.[163] These guidelines produce a range of sentence that is a function of two factors: the adjusted offense level and the defendant's criminal history category. The judge focuses first on the "base offense level" for the particular crime and adjusts that level upward or downward for specific aggravating and mitigating factors that are specified in the guidelines. This results in an "adjusted offense level." For example, larceny has a base level of 4. However, if more than $10,000 (but less than $20,000) is taken, the judge would increase the level by 5 levels to 9. If the theft involved more than minimal planning, the judge would further increase it by 2 levels to 11. If the crime involved the exploitation of a vulnerable victim, the judge would increase the level by 2 to 13. This would be the "final adjusted offense level." Next, the judge looks at the criminal history category into which the defendant falls. Assuming the defendant has one previous conviction, even for an unrelated crime, for which a sentence of more than a year in prison was imposed, the defendant would be classified in "criminal history category II." This would produce a sentencing range of 15-21 months. The judge is prohibited from sentencing this defendant to less than 15 months or more than 21 months in the absence of certain extraordinary circumstances specified in the guidelines, usually rendering substantial assistance to the authorities in uncovering other crimes or turning in other offenders. The mandatory guideline system remains controversial. Judges tend to oppose it because they feel that the long prison terms it uniformly requires result in injustice in individual cases.

Rates of Incarceration The most commonly articulated policies behind sanctions in criminal law are deterrence of crime, incapacitation of offenders and rehabilitation of offenders. As the statement quoted above from California's sentencing statute indicates, recent years have seen a decline in the rehabilitative function and a greater emphasis on punishment, incapacitation and deterrence through long prison sentences. The change in emphasis is reflected in the percentage of population in the United States behind bars. While Germany in 1994 had a rate of incarceration of 80 inmates per 100,000 population, England had 93 per 100,000, and Japan had 36 per 100,000, the rate in the United States was 519 per 100,000. The rate of incarceration in the United States increased 22% from 1989 to 1994.[164] Despite its high prison

---

162 Cal. Penal Code §1170(a)(1).

163 Federal Guidelines Sentencing Reform Act, 18 U.S.C.A. §3551. The guidelines are explained with appropriate examples in HARRY L. SUBIN, CHESTER L. MIRSKY, AND IAN S. WEINSTEIN, THE CRIMINAL PROCESS: PROSECUTION AND DEFENSE FUNCTIONS §§19.1-19.12 (West 1993).

164 Source: The Sentencing Project, as reported in the New York Times, September 13, 1994, p. A8. Only Russia, with 558 inmates per 100,000 population, had a higher incarceration rate than the United States in 1994. Of the states, Texas in 1996 had the highest rate at 686 prisoners per 100,000 population. This represented a 156% increase over 1991, the highest rate of increase among the states and over twice that of the state with the next highest increase.

population, the United States continues to have among the highest crime rates among developed industrialized countries.[165]

2. Probation

Sentencing statutes often allow the judge to sentence an offender to a term of "probation" if a judge feels that the circumstances of the crime and the defendant's background would make a prison sentence too harsh or that it would not serve any good purpose. Offenders on probation are returned to the community under the nominal supervision of a "probation officer." They will avoid prison if they comply with certain conditions, such as avoiding bad behavior, reporting regularly to their probation officer, and perhaps other more specific conditions, such as payment of restitution or performance of some community service. If offenders on probation do not fulfill the conditions, probation can be revoked, and they will begin serving their prison sentence. Probation is a common alternative to incarceration. In 1996 over 3 million adults, or 57.6% of all offenders under correctional control, were on probation.[166] Use of probation in a greater number of cases is facilitated by the use of an "electronic tether." The device is attached to a defendant's leg and it "reports" on whether the defendant is at home as required by probation conditions and whether the tether has been removed.

3. The Death Penalty

The death penalty has been widely available as a punishment for certain serious crimes in the United States since colonial times. However, from 1966 to 1976, there was a moratorium on use of the death penalty that resulted in large part from doubts about the constitutionality of a number of state death penalty statutes. The Supreme Court's view since 1976 has been that the death penalty is not unconstitutional *per se* when applied to defendants convicted of first-degree murder.[167] Today, 38 states and the federal government have adopted laws allowing capital punishment that conform to the Supreme Court's constitutional requirements. Methods of execution include the gas chamber, electrocution, lethal injection, hanging, and firing squads. The federal government and 13 states use lethal injection, 12 states use electrocution, one state uses the gas chamber, and 10 states allow criminals to choose among all five of the listed methods. Almost 60% of the prisoners executed in 1996 were executed by means of lethal injection.[168] At year-end 1996, 3,046 inmates were on death row and 56 inmates had been executed that year.[169] In 1997, 74 were executed and in 1998, there were 67. In 1998, the states passed the 500 mark in the number of executions completed since they became constitutional again in 1976.

---

165 It should be mentioned, however, that the crime rate in the U.S. has been decreasing in recent years. There was a 3% decrease in serious crime from 1995 to 1996, which followed decreases of 1% in 1995, 1% in 1994, 2% in 1993 and 3% in 1992. The largest decrease in 1996 was a 7% fall in violent crime (with murder down 9%, aggravated assault down 6% and robbery down 8%), while property crime decreased by only 2%. Source: *Uniform Crime Reports*, Federal Bureau of Investigation (1996). Preliminary reports for 1997 indicate a further drop in homicide of 8% and a 7% drop in all violent crime.

166 Christopher J. Mumola and Thomas P Bonczar, *Substance Abuse and Treatment of Adults on Probation, 1995* 2 (1998).

167 Constitutional aspects of the death penalty were discussed in Chapter VIII, pp. 311-300.

168 Committee on Ethical Affairs, American Medical Association, *Physician Participation in Capital Punishment*, J. AM. MED. ASSOC. 365 (July 21, 1993).

169 U.S. Dept. of Justice, Bureau of Justice Statistics, *Capital Punishment Statistics* (1998). California was the state with the highest number of prisoners on death row (420), though it executed no one in 1996. Texas, with 404 on death row, executed 19 prisoners in 1996.

The MPC takes no position on the death penalty, but instead provides criteria and procedures for its implementation that states can enact if they choose. Its factors and bifurcated jury procedure have widely influenced state procedure.[170]

Despite the trend toward reinstatement of the death penalty, it remains controversial. Active lobbying both for and against the death penalty takes place when the issue comes up in a particular state. In states that have the death penalty, each execution is an occasion for both supporters and opponents to express their feelings in demonstrations at the prison where the execution takes place.

---

170 *See* MPC §210.6 and Chapter VIII, p. 266.

CHAPTER XV

BUSINESS LAW

This chapter will outline some of the more important legal aspects of doing business in the United States: the law of business organizations, securities law, antitrust law, bankruptcy, labor and employment law and environmental law. Sources for further study are cited in each section.

A. Business Organizations

Most business enterprises are organized in one of three ways: as a sole proprietorship, as a partnership (general or limited), or as a corporation. In addition, a new form of business entity, the limited liability company, has recently emerged. Each business organization shares some common aspects with others, but differs in method of ownership, the degree of personal liability of the investors for the enterprise's debts and in the complexity of the structure. Business organizations are governed primarily by state law, with a few areas governed by federal law.[1]

1. Sole Proprietorships

A sole proprietorship is a business enterprise owned solely by one individual. It is the most elementary organizational form of business. Small new businesses often begin as sole proprietorships because they are the simplest and least expensive to form and operate. Local accountants or attorneys in business for themselves or small retail shops are likely to be sole proprietorships.

The formation, operation, and management of sole proprietorships are generally simple. It is not necessary to file any documents with any governmental office other than local requirements (by a city or county) that the owner register the name of the business to prevent fraud. This registration would notify the public, for example, that John Smith is "doing business as Smith's Hardware Store."

The owner has total control, making all decisions concerning the business. Employees may be hired, and some management authority may be delegated to them, but the sole proprietor maintains ultimate control. Businesses that are sole proprietorships are not considered separate legal entities apart from the owner. Thus, the owner of the business is personally liable for all of the business' debts out of the owner's personal assets. However, the owner also reaps all the fruits of the business and need not pay partners or shareholders anything.

The identity of owner and business entails a tax advantage as well. Unlike corporations, sole proprietorships are not considered to be separate taxable entities by the Internal Revenue Service (IRS), the federal income taxing agency. Therefore, unlike the corporation, the sole proprietorship business itself does not have to pay

---

1 Two texts that survey business law for undergraduate students in college are RICHARD A. MANN & BARRY S. ROBERTS, BUSINESS LAW, 8TH ED. (West 1991) and KENNETH W. CLARKSTON, ET.AL., WEST'S BUSINESS LAW 4TH ED. (West 1989). *See also* ROBERT W. HAMILTON & RICHARD BOOTH, BUSINESS BASICS FOR LAW STUDENTS, 2D ED. (Aspen 1998). Law student guides to the legal aspects of business include WILLIAM A. KLEIN & JOHN C. COFFEE, JR., BUSINESS ORGANIZATION AND FINANCE: LEGAL AND ECONOMIC PRINCIPLES, 6TH ED. (Foundation Press 1996). For more detail on corporations, *see* HARRY G. HENN AND JOHN R. ALEXANDER, LAW OF CORPORATIONS, 3RD ED. (West 1983, 1986) or ROBERT C. CLARK, CORPORATE LAW (Aspen 1986). Succinct guides to many of the issues discussed here are ROBERT W. HAMILTON, THE LAW OF CORPORATIONS IN A NUTSHELL (West 1996); ROBERT W. HAMILTON, BUSINESS ORGANIZATIONS: UNINCORPORATED BUSINESSES AND CLOSELY HELD CORPORATIONS (Aspen 1997); and LEWIS D. SOLOMON & ALAN R. PALMITEV, CORPORATIONS: EXAMPLES AND EXPLANATIONS, 2D ED. (Aspen 1994).

federal income taxes. Instead, the income and deductible expenses of the business are reported on the owner's personal tax return.[2]

2. General Partnerships

Nature of General Partnerships A partnership is an association of two or more persons to carry on a business for profit as co-owners.[3] There are two kinds of partnerships, general and limited. General partnerships (GP) are discussed here and limited partnerships (LP) are discussed in the next section.

An agreement to operate as a partnership can be written, but unlike a corporation or limited partnership, there is no requirement that any documents be filed with any governmental authority. The agreement may even be oral and a partnership agreement may even be implied from conduct despite a written agreement to the contrary. For example, a business subject to a "partnership agreement" was held not to be a partnership and a business not formally described as a partnership was deemed to be one.[4] Thus, people in business together often may not realize that they are partners subject to all the rights and obligations arising out of a partnership, including the important principle that one partner can bind the entire partnership to debts.[5]

Reasons for Choice of Form Like the sole proprietor, partners in a GP are exposed to unlimited liability and the partnership does not have to pay income taxes separate from its owners. Instead, the income or loss of the business is reported on the partners' personal individual tax returns. The choice of the partnership form rather than a sole proprietorship is made because two or more people want to go into business together. A partnership is chosen over a corporation to avoid the complexities involved in forming and running a corporation.

Formation The Uniform Partnership Act (UPA) governs the formation, operation, and structure of partnerships in almost all states.[6] Partners may agree to almost any arrangement between them that is not illegal or contrary to public policy. Thus, much of the UPA provides simply a "default provision" — applicable only in the absence of express agreements in the partnership agreement.[7] However, some UPA provisions cannot be changed by agreement of the partners. Among them are provisions declaring that each partner is personally liable for all of the partnership's debts[8] and that each partner owes a "fiduciary duty" to the partnership and the other partners.[9]

---

2   *See* HENN & ALEXANDER, *supra* note 1, §18. As explained *infra* p.541, it is possible to reduce the tax disadvantage of the corporate form with closely held corporations by "zeroing out" income through distributions to employees.

3   Uniform Partnership Act (UPA) §6, 6 UNIF.L.ANN. 1 (1969). All states except Louisiana have adopted the UPA, with some local variations from it. *See generally* HENN & ALEXANDER, *supra* note 1, §§19-27. Copies of this act, the Uniform Limited Partnership Act and various statutes and rules related to business enterprises are set out in EDWARD S. ADAMS & JOHN H. MATHESON, EDS., SELECTED CORPORATION AND OTHER BUSINESS ASSOCIATIONS: STATUTES, RULES AND FORMS (West 1998).

4   *Cutler v. Bowen*, 543 P.2d 1349 (Utah 1975) (owner of furnishings, equipment and lease of bar must share compensation for harm to business with bartender-manager because they were partners pursuant to oral agreement to share profits); *Chaiken v. Employment Security Commission*, 274 A.2d 707 (Super. Ct Del. 1971) (nature of agreement showed that barbers working in shop were employees for whom unemployment tax was due, not partners).

5   UPA §9.

6   *See supra* note 3.

7   UPA §4.

8   *Id.* §15.

9   *Id.* §21.

This fiduciary duty means that each partner must abide by the highest standards of loyalty, good faith, and integrity when engaging in matters pertaining to the partnership.[10] Any partner who fails to act in the best interest of the partnership or who acts in personal self interest is liable to the partnership. Thus a partner who uses partnership assets for personal gain is liable to the partnership for all the resulting profits.[11]

Each partner is required to make an initial contribution to the business in the form of cash, property, services, or some combination of these. The amount of each partner's contribution need not be the same. For example, in forming the ABC partnership, partner A might contribute $10,000 in cash, partner B might contribute $5,000 in cash and a $15,000 building, and partner C might agree to perform $20,000 worth of management services as an initial capital contribution. If a written partnership agreement exists, it will usually detail each partner's contribution.

Operation and Management Pursuant to the UPA, all general partners have an equal voice in the operation and management of the business, unless otherwise agreed, regardless of the amount of capital contributions made by the individual partners. Thus, each partner is entitled to one vote on management matters, and decisions are made on a majority basis.[12] The act of any partner in the name of the partnership binds the partnership.

Partners can agree in the partnership agreement that decision-making authority will be granted to only one or a given group of the partners. Or the partners may agree to afford management powers in proportion to the capital contributions of each partner. For example, in the ABC partnership formed above, the partnership agreement might specify that A gets one vote, while B and C get two votes each. In the absence of such a partnership agreement, A, B, and C would each have one vote.[13]

Sharing Profits and Losses and Compensation Rights In the absence of an agreement to the contrary, all partners share in the profits and losses of the partnership equally, regardless of the amount of cash, property, or services contributed by each partner to the partnership. The equal sharing rule is often altered by an appropriate provision in the partnership agreement, which makes the distribution of profits proportional with the amount of capital contribution of each partner. For example, the ABC partnership, in its written partnership agreement, might provide that A is entitled to 20% of the partnership's profits, while B and C are each entitled to 40% of its profits. But partners can elect to allocate profits and losses in any manner they wish, regardless of the partners' initial capital contribution.

The partnership's losses and income can be distributed among the partners in any way they wish. This may be done to provide tax benefits to certain partners, because losses are often deductible on the partners' personal tax returns. If no provision is made for the distribution of losses, the UPA requires that losses be distributed in the same manner as profits are shared.[14]

---

10 A classic discussion of fiduciary duty is set out in *Meinhard v. Salmon*, 164 N.E.2d 545 (N.Y. 1928) (Cardozo, J.).

11 *Clement v. Clement*, 260 A.2d 728 (Pa. 1970) (fraud not necessary for recovery by one partner against another; all that need be shown is that second partner freely converted partnership assets to his own personal use).

12 UPA §18.

13 *Id.* §18. HENN & ALEXANDER, *supra* note 1, §§20-22.

14 UPA §18. The partnership's flexibility in allocating income and losses a particular way is a useful way to "shelter" income from taxes, a practice widely used in limited partnerships, as discussed below.

The partnership agreement can provide that some partners will be compensated for services rendered to the partnership. However, if the partnership agreement does not specifically say so, no partner is entitled to any compensation, regardless of any services provided. Absent express agreement to the contrary, the partners' shares of the profits are considered to be their full compensation.[15]

Dissolution Each partner has the inherent power to withdraw from the partnership and cause a dissolution, and the death or bankruptcy of a partner automatically causes dissolution.[16] The UPA states that the withdrawing partner or the partner's estate has the power to cause the partnership to wind up its affairs and liquidate its assets, and pay each partner a sum representing that partner's interest.[17] But the partnership agreement will typically state that the business will continue and that the withdrawing partner or the partner's estate will be entitled to a sum of money representing the partner's interest in the partnership upon death or withdrawal. Even when liquidation is an option with the withdrawing partner or a partner's estate, it is often in everyone's best interest to continue operations and pay off the withdrawing partner or estate.[18]

Withdrawal of Partners A partnership agreement may limit a partner's intentional withdrawal from the partnership for a period of time. Thus, if money has been borrowed, partners may not be permitted to withdraw until the loan is paid off. These provisions cannot stop a partner from exercising the right to withdraw and cause dissolution. But the partnership can continue the business by posting a bond to secure payment of the withdrawing partner's share at the end of the time period set in the agreement. Moreover, the withdrawing partner could be liable for damages for wrongful termination of the partnership and will in any event not receive full value upon distribution of assets.[19]

3. Limited Partnerships

Nature and Business Reasons for Choice of Form A limited partnership (LP) has both general and limited partners. It differs from a general partnership in the fact that the limited partners are not subject to unlimited liability for the debts of the business and risk only the loss of their initial capital contribution to the partnership. Correspondingly, limited partners have little control over the running of the business, which is run by the general partner or partners. Thus, an LP is often the choice of a businessperson who wishes to raise capital, but does not wish to give up control over the business as would happen with a general partnership.

Today, *general* partnerships are often small- to medium-sized businesses operating within the local community and generally have relatively few partners. LPS, on the other hand, are usually much larger because, among other reasons, the LP is popular with investors as a tax shelter device, as discussed below. LPS will often have one general partner and hundreds or thousands of limited partners.[20]

---

15 *Id*. See HENN & ALEXANDER, *supra* note 1, §23.

16 These and other grounds for dissolution are listed in UPA §31.

17 *Id*. §37.

18 *See generally* HENN & ALEXANDER, *supra* note 2, §26.

19 UPA §38(c). A recent practical article on how to mediate "business divorces" in partnerships and small corporations is James C. Freund, Anatomy of a Split-Up: Mediating the Business Divorce, 53 BUSINESS LAWYER 479 (1997).

20 *See generally* HENN & ALEXANDER, *supra* note 1, §§28-36.

Formation LPS can be formed only by compliance with state statutory requirements. Most all states have adopted the Uniform Limited Partnership Act (ULPA)[21] or the Revised Uniform Limited Partnership Act (RULPA)[22] to govern the formation and operation of limited partnerships. To form an LP, a certificate of limited partnership must be filed with a designated state official. This certificate must include specified information concerning the LP, such as the names and addresses of the general and limited partners, the amount of each partner's capital contribution, and the manner in which profits are to be shared.[23] LPS are also required to have a written partnership agreement.[24] In most cases, the certificate of limited partnership and the written partnership agreement are the same thing.

Operation and Management Every LP must have at least one general partner and one limited partner. In most circumstances, the general partners in an LP have the same rights and duties as partners in a general partnership and manage the business as provided in the agreement.[25] Limited partners, on the other hand, are treated as investors. They have no rights to participate in the management of the business, to use partnership property, or to conduct business on behalf of the partnership. However, they are entitled to share in the profits of the business as specified in the partnership agreement.[26]

The exact extent to which limited partners can participate in the business without losing their limited liability status is often undefined. The ULPA states that a limited partner becomes liable as a general partner if the partner "takes part in the control of the business."[27] The RULPA has a list of "safe harbor" activities in which a limited partner may engage without losing limited liability.[28] As a general rule, any limited partner who engages in management decisions on an ongoing basis will lose limited partner status and will be subject to unlimited liability. Some gross control over management is permitted. Thus, the agreement can give limited partners the right to remove the general partner. In addition, under some circumstances limited partners have been allowed to sue to contest the propriety of the general partner's management decisions, similar to the right of shareholders in a corporation.[29]

Dissolution Unlike the withdrawal or death of any general partner in an LP, a limited partner's withdrawal or death does not cause dissolution. Upon withdrawal or death, limited partners or their estates are entitled to the value of their interest in the LP.

Special Tax Aspects of Limited Partnerships As stated earlier, the partnership form has great flexibility in allocating income and losses among partners. This characteristic has been capitalized upon to provide a "tax shelter" for money.

---

21 6 Unif.L.Ann. §§1-31 (1969).

22 6 Unif.L.Ann. §§101-1106 (Supp. 1993).

23 ULPA §2.

24 *Id.* §2.

25 *Id.* §9.

26 *Id.* §§10, 17.

27 *Id.* §7. *See Alzado v. Blinder, Robinson & Co., Inc.*, 752 P.2d 544 (Colo. 1988) (holding activities of limited partner in promoting boxing match were not sufficient to render him liable).

28 RULPA §303. These include working as a contractor for the partnership or consulting and advising the general partner with respect to the business.

29 *See* RULPA §§1001-1004. In such cases, the managing general partner is judged under the same "business judgment rule" applicable to corporate managers, discussed *infra* p. 546. *See Wyler v. Feuer*, 149 Cal.Rptr. 626 (Cal.App.1978) (finding no basis for suit by limited partners when partnership's movie did not make money).

Typically two groups come together for mutual benefit: entrepreneurs with skill, but no money, and taxpayers with high incomes seeking business losses to claim on their tax returns to offset income.[30] For example, assume that a developer believes that there is a need for an office building in a big city, but it has no money. Often the developer will seek out people with high incomes taxed at a high rate to invest their money as limited partners in a partnership formed to build and then rent out and manage the building. The developer uses the investment to build the building, takes the rents from the building as income and allocates the losses (primarily in the form of depreciation of the building) to the limited partner investors. These losses, taken each year for several years, serve to reduce the amount of income from other sources on which the investors must pay taxes. The developer gets the money needed to build the building, and the investors are protected by limited liability from losing more than their investment, and get a substantial tax savings.[31]

4. Corporations

a. General Nature

Corporations are recognized as legal entities distinct from their owners — "shareholders," so-called because they "hold" a "share" of the overall ownership of the corporation. Corporations can sue and be sued, enter into contractual relations, and own property. Corporations even have constitutional rights separate from their owners or management: since 1868 corporations have been able to sue for violations of their 14th Amendment due process and other rights.[32] One of the principal values of the corporate form of doing business is its limited liability. Absent exceptional circumstances, the shareholders in the corporation cannot be held personally liable for debts incurred or liability imposed on the corporation. However, this is only one feature of the corporation that must be weighed in deciding whether to incorporate, as discussed below.

Corporations law is principally state law. It is largely statutory, but the common law is often relied upon, especially when defining the fiduciary duties of management. Federal law governs trading in publicly-offered corporate securities[33] and federal income taxation law drives some corporate decision-making.[34] There is a Model Business Corporation Act (MBCA) and Revised Model Business Corporation Act

---

30 The federal income tax system is moderately "progressive," meaning that as income goes up, the rate of taxation does as well. In general, the tax rate is between 15% and 40%.

31 The losses taken on the investors tax returns do not relieve the limited partners of tax liability for the benefits of the value of the building. They will pay for the gain their investment has produced when the building is sold years later. But such a "tax deferral," generally for a number of years, provides the limited partners with real benefit. First, they have the *use* of the money that would otherwise have been paid in taxes over several years. Second, their overall tax liability is less when the building is sold years later, because the investors will often be retired and therefore have less income. Taxpayers with lower incomes pay a smaller percentage of their income in taxes. For more detail, *see* sources cited in note 44, *infra*, and *see generally* Chapter XVI, where income and other federal taxes are discussed.

32 *See Paul v. Virginia*, 75 U.S. (8 Wall.) 168 (1868) (corporation is a "person" as that term is used in the 14th Amendment). Corporations have been responsible for raising most of the issues of 1st Amendment commercial speech. *See* Chapter IX, pp. 354-355. Strangely enough, while it is a "person," a corporation is not a "citizen" protected by the privileges and immunities clause of the 14th Amendment or Article IV. *See* Chapter IX, p. 327. This is so despite the fact that a corporation can be a citizen of a state for purposes of diversity of citizenship. *See* Chapter V, p. 185.

33 *See infra* p. 551.

34 *See infra* p. 540.

(RMBCA) promulgated by a committee of the American Bar Association.[35] However, the MBCA and RMBCA have not gained as wide acceptance by state legislatures as the uniform partnership laws have.

The corporate law of the state of Delaware is very important. Generally, the laws of the state where the company was incorporated control issues of governance of a corporation even when all the corporation's offices and facilities are in other states. Delaware has tried its best to be an attractive state for incorporation by providing perhaps the greatest flexibility for corporate governance. Thus, Delaware has won what some have called "the race to the bottom" that began in the early 20th century — a competition among states to pass corporate laws that least restrict corporate management prerogatives.[36] As a result, over one-third of the corporations listed on the New York Stock Exchange are incorporated in Delaware. The great number of Delaware corporations has in turn produced a great number of cases decided under Delaware law. As a result, Delaware corporate law is by far the most well-developed and therefore the most predictable.[37]

b. Types of Corporations

There are all sizes of corporations, but it is generally helpful to distinguish between two types: publicly held corporations and closely-held corporations. Both are created by state statute and are subject to the same basic rules. Both can conduct the same types of business. But they inhabit different worlds in terms of ownership and operation. Among the differences is the fact that publicly held corporations are subject to federal regulation to a much greater extent.

Publicly Held Corporations Publicly held corporations are those whose shares are traded by the general public in organized markets, such as the New York Stock Exchange, other national exchanges or in the "over-the-counter" markets. These are the largest corporations, such as Exxon, General Motors and IBM. Their stockholders are numerous, widely dispersed and constantly changing. Most shareholders purchase shares as an investment and have no desire to become involved in management decisions or even to attend stockholders' meetings or vote. However, some holders of major blocks of stock serve as directors or managers, are active at shareholder meetings or otherwise seek to affect management decisions.

Closely-Held Corporations Closely-held corporations, called close corporations, are corporations that have relatively few shareholders. Often shareholders will be close business associates or family members. Most often, the shareholders have managed the business from its inception and do not want outside investors involved in the business. There is no market for shares of a close corporation. Moreover, shareholders often agree to restrict transfers of their stock to any outside investors to ensure that the corporation continues to run as the original shareholders want.

---

35 *See* MODEL BUSINESS CORPORATION ACT ANN., 3D ED. (Prentice Hall Law & Bus. 1985-present). The RMBCA and the corporation acts of several states (including Delaware) are set out in SELECTED CORPORATION AND OTHER BUSINESS ASSOCIATIONS: STATUTES, RULES AND FORMS, *supra* note 3. Professor Hamilton, author of the Nutshell on corporations, *supra* note 1, was the reporter for the RMBCA.

36 *See* William L. Cary, *Federalism and Corporate Law: Reflections Upon Delaware*, 83 YALE L.J. 663 (1974). *But see* Daniel R. Fischel, *The "Race to the Bottom" Revisited: Reflections on Recent Developments in Delaware Corporation Law*, 76 NW. L.REV 913 (1982).

37 Delaware's incentive to provide a hospitable environment for corporations is at least in part financial. Currently, 20% of Delaware's state budget comes from fees charged to corporations incorporated there, thereby allowing the state to abolish its sales tax and to lower its residents' income tax.

The shareholders in close corporations are usually directly involved in the management and daily operations of the business and generally serve as directors and officers. Because of this direct shareholder involvement in the business, close corporations sometimes resemble sole proprietorships or partnerships. In fact, closely-held corporations are often businesses that were once sole proprietorships or partnerships, but have since incorporated to obtain benefits offered by the corporate form, such as limited liability or advantageous treatment of corporate retirement pension plans. Most close corporations are small businesses, but there are some large ones that rival the size of some of the publicly traded corporations. Whatever their size, though, close corporations must still comply with the same state statutory requirements as publicly held corporations. Thus, even though the shareholders and officers may be the same people, the corporation must elect directors, appoint officers, conduct board and stockholders' meetings, and comply with other statutory requirements.[38] Many states have passed special close corporation statutes that attempt to deal with some of the unique features of the close corporation. For example, the shareholders may be able to manage the corporation without having a board of directors. The goal of these statutes is to allow for internal flexibility within the close corporation, much like that in a partnership.[39]

c. Formation of the Corporation

Despite variations in law from state to state, the basic rules for formation are substantially the same everywhere.[40] The first step is to file "articles of incorporation" with the appropriate state official and to pay a fee. Exactly what these papers must contain varies among the states, but at a minimum they must include the name of the corporation, the number of shares the corporation is authorized to issue, the address of the corporation's registered office in the state, and the incorporators' names and signatures. When these papers are in the proper form, a state official will issue a certificate of incorporation, and the corporation comes into legal existence.[41]

After obtaining a certificate of incorporation, the incorporators must adopt the corporation's bylaws. The bylaws are a set of rules that govern the internal affairs of the corporation. However, rules contained in the articles of incorporation control over contrary bylaws. The articles of incorporation are a matter of public record, whereas the bylaws are not accessible to the general public for inspection.

d. Business Reasons for Choosing to Incorporate

For many large businesses, the corporate form is the most efficient way to carry on the business. Many small partnerships and sole proprietorships, however, will consider incorporation when they wish to expand their businesses. For these businesses, it is often said that the best advice on whether to incorporate is "when in doubt, don't." It is useful to review some of the advantages and disadvantages of incorporation now before getting into some of the details of corporate operation.

Limited Liability The first advantage of incorporation is the limited liability the corporate form provides for all of its shareholders. If a corporation has 1,000 shares

---

38 *See* discussion of powers and duties of board of directors *infra* pp. 544-546.

39 *See generally* HENN & ALEXANDER, *supra* note 1, §§257-290.

40 *Id.*, §§116-133.

41 States enacted general incorporation statutes starting in the early 1800s in response to the growth in business activity at that time. Before then, corporations generally could only be created by action of the legislature and then only for limited public or semi-public purposes (such as to build a toll road or canal). *See* HENN & ALEXANDER, *supra* note 1, §12.

of stock and a shareholder owns 250 shares, that shareholder has a 25% ownership interest in the corporation. Shareholders stand to lose no more than the amount represented by the value of their shares, regardless of the corporation's outstanding debts. Such limited liability allows corporations to raise capital easily since purchasers of shares can own part of a business without incurring its liabilities.[42] While limited partners in an LP also enjoy limited liability, LPs are required to have at least one general partner who remains personally liable for all the partnership debts.

But limited liability is not always as important as it might seem. Liability insurance can often be purchased to cover all but the most unusual losses. Or liability exposure may not be a major worry in a given business. Moreover, banks and other creditors lending money to new and often undercapitalized corporations often insist that shareholders give *personal* guarantees for loans to the corporation. Obtaining loans is often a more efficient method of raising capital than selling shares, since it is often difficult to attract investors in the rather limited market for shares in most small corporations.

Perpetual Existence A second reason for choosing to incorporate is the advantage of the perpetual existence of the corporation. A partnership can dissolve at the insistence of any partner and, absent contrary agreement, the withdrawing partner can insist on payment to each partner of the appropriate share of the enterprise.[43] A shareholder in a corporation generally cannot unilaterally dissolve the entity and withdraw his investment. Yet, a partnership may be almost as durable as many corporations. While the partnership's *legal* continuity is disrupted by various occurrences, its *economic* continuity generally is not. In most cases, as noted earlier, the business continues unchanged while the partnership is reformed.

Ease of Transfer of Shares A third advantage of incorporation is the fact that the ownership interests represented by shares of stock in a corporation can be easily transferred with no effect on the corporation. If a shareholder dies, the shares pass to the estate and then to heirs. If a shareholder wishes to sell to a new investor, this transaction will not affect the corporation. But, while easy transfer is true of publicly-traded companies, small businesses often restrict transfers of shares to maintain control and commonly have the right to buy back shares of deceased or withdrawing shareholders.

Centralized Structure Another reason often given for incorporating is that the corporation is more centrally governed since management power is vested in directors and officers. In a partnership, all general partners usually participate in management decisions. But this is only a default position. Partnership agreements can provide for centralized control in managing partners.

Tax Treatment A major consideration in choice of the corporate form is tax treatment of corporate earnings.[44] Consistent with their separate legal existence, corporations must pay their own federal income taxes. Corporate earnings then are effectively subject to a double tax: earnings are taxed once through *corporate* income

---

[42] *See* discussion of corporate financing and structure *infra* pp. 541-542.

[43] UPA §§31(1)(b), 38(1).

[44] *See generally* Chapter XVI and DOUGLAS KAHN & JEFFREY LEHMAN, HORNBOOK ON CORPORATE INCOME TAXATION, 4TH ED. (West 1994). Excellent concise guides to federal income tax law are MARVIN CHIRELSTEIN, FEDERAL INCOME TAXATION, 8TH ED. (Foundation 1997), HOWARD E. ABRAMS & RICHARD L. DOERNBERG, FEDERAL CORPORATE TAXATION (Foundation 1998); JOSEPH BANKMAN, THOMAS D. GRIFFITH & KATHERINE PRATT, FEDERAL INCOME TAX: EXAMPLES AND EXPLANATIONS, 2D ED. (Aspen 1999).

taxation and then taxed again through *individual* income taxation when the corporation distributes part of those earnings to its shareholders by way of dividends.

But the double taxation problem is not as serious as it might seem for many corporations. In most cases, a closely-held corporation can avoid double taxation. If it is an independent domestic and domestically-owned corporation with no more than 75 shareholders and only one class of stock, it may qualify for special tax treatment as an "S corporation" under the Internal Revenue Code (IRC).[45] Such corporations may opt to have corporate income taxed directly to the shareholders. This "pass-through" or "conduit" form of taxation operates much like taxation of partners in a partnership.

Corporations not covered by the exception just explained are called "C corporations."[46] In many relatively small C corporations, shareholders are also employees or creditors of the corporation. Such C corporations may be able to obtain "pass-through" tax advantages similar to an S corporation. The C corporation could make distributions of corporate income by way of payments of reasonable salaries or interest on loans to shareholder-employees or shareholder-creditors. Such "non-dividend" distributions are deductible from corporate earnings. If the C corporation is able to thus "zero-out" its earnings, corporate income ends up being taxed only once — when it is received by the shareholder-employees and shareholder-creditors — just as in the case of partnership or subchapter S distributions.[47]

Whatever the benefits of incorporation, they come at the price of increased complexity. There is much more paperwork and formal requirements must be observed. Annual reports must be filed and shareholder meetings held and a host of other additional work done (including preparation of separate tax returns) that is not involved when the business is a partnership. And one must add to this the lawyers' and accountants' fees in dealing with these complexities. An additional aspect of the various corporate filing formalities is that the filings become public record, thus making the corporate form a less private way of doing business. Not surprisingly, small businesses that have recently incorporated have a natural tendency to continue the business in the same informal way they did when it was a sole proprietorship or partnership. But the consequences of failure to follow essential corporate formalities can be serious because such failures might allow a creditor to disregard the corporate form and reach shareholders' or officers' personal assets.[48]

e. Corporate Finance and Ownership

Corporations raise capital primarily by issuing "securities." Securities are evidence of the obligation to pay money or of the right to participate in earnings. Most corporations issue two types of securities to investors: (1) equity securities or shares of stock (already encountered) and (2) debt securities or bonds.[49]

---

45   26 U.S.C.A. §§1361 *et seq.* "S Corporation" comes from subchapter S of Chapter 1 of subtitle A of title 26 of the United States Code where these requirements are found. Changes in 1996 raised the number of stockholders from 35 to 75, allowed S corporations to own subsidiary corporations under certain circumstances and have them treated as S corporations, and permitted non-profit S corporations.

46   26 U.S.C.A. §§301 *et seq.* Subchapter C of the IRC governs corporate taxation in general.

47   Yet, this device may be difficult to use where some C corporation shareholders are not employees and the amount that needs to be distributed in this way is so large that payment in salary or bonuses may violate IRC limits on the reasonableness of compensation for employees that can be deducted.

48   *See* discussion *infra* p. 546.

49   *See generally* Henn & Alexander, *supra* note 2, §§154-161.

Stocks As mentioned earlier, shares of stock represent ownership interests in the corporation. In public corporations, shares are generally freely transferable, meaning that shares can be bought and sold by investors without the consent of the corporation and without affecting corporate operations. Similarly, the death of a shareholder matters little to the corporation, as the shareholder's heirs become the new owners.[50] The purchasers of stock do not actually "own" the assets of the corporation. All of the business' assets are owned by the corporation itself. Instead, shareholders are granted certain rights, depending upon the type of stock owned, as outlined below.

Corporate shares are usually divided into two categories, "common stock" and "preferred stock." Common stock is the most basic type of stock and must be issued by every corporation. It confers upon its holders two fundamental rights: (1) the right to vote for the directors of the corporation and on other matters requiring stockholder approval, such as a merger, and (2) the right to the net assets of the corporation upon dissolution of the corporation. Dividends are discretionary payments made by the corporation to the stockholders out of the earnings of the business. Dividends are declared by the board of directors and are usually paid on a quarterly basis. The receipt of dividends is one way for stockholders to earn a profit on their investment in the corporation. However, the board of directors is not required to declare a dividend, and shareholders have no inherent right to the payment of dividends. The other way they profit is by the increase in the market value of their shares. But there is no guarantee that the stock will increase in value. Its value will depend on the profitability of the business.

Shares of preferred stock also represent an ownership interest in the corporation. However, the owners of preferred stock are entitled to certain rights and privileges that are superior to those of common stock owners. The most common feature of preferred shares is a dividend preference over common stock. This preference does not guarantee the payment of a dividend, but it does guarantee that any dividends declared by the board will be paid first to the preferred stock owners. Preferred stock holders also are given priority over common stockholders in the event of a liquidation of the corporation, though neither class of shareholders can be paid before the corporation's creditors, including bondholders, discussed next.

Bonds In addition to equity securities, most corporations also issue debt securities, or bonds, which represent the borrowing of money. In other words, instead of purchasing an ownership interest in the corporation, the bondholder is making a loan to the corporation. The bond represents an unconditional guarantee by the corporation to pay the bond holder a specific amount on a certain date. In addition, the bondholder is generally entitled to periodic interest payments. For example, the ABC Corporation might issue a $1,000 ten-year bond, paying 6% interest. To obtain this bond, the purchaser will pay the corporation $1,000. In return, the corporation agrees to repay the purchaser the $1,000 in ten years. During the ten-year period, the corporation agrees to pay the bondholder annually 6% of the face value of the note, or $60 a year. Unlike shareholders, bondholders are not entitled to voting rights, nor do they receive dividends. Instead, a debtor-creditor relationship is established between the corporation and the bondholder.

---

50 As noted earlier in the discussion of closely held corporations, the articles of incorporation may restrict the transferability of shares to assure that control of the business is not lost.

f. Organizational Structure and Powers

Ownership and management of a corporation consists of three tiers: (1) shareholders, (2) directors, and (3) officers. Directors and officers, and occasionally controlling shareholders, comprise the management. Each group has defined powers within the enterprise.

Shareholders' Rights and Duties   Shareholders' rights are established in the articles, bylaws and the state's general incorporation law. Shareholders have either the absolute or qualified right to inspect the corporate books and records for proper purposes, such as to become informed of corporate affairs.[51] Shareholders do not actually run the business, nor do they have the power to act individually on behalf of the corporation. Instead, their powers must be exercised collectively along with the other shareholders by way of voting, usually at the stockholders' meeting. Most states require a yearly stockholders' meeting with advance written notice.

Each shareholder is entitled to one vote per share of common stock owned. Shareholders do not have to be present at the stockholders' meeting to vote. Through the use of a document called a "proxy," shareholders can appoint someone else to cast their vote on a specific subject. Because of the large number of shareholders in most publicly held corporations and the impracticability of attending shareholders' meetings, voting by proxy is common.

Through their voting powers, shareholders have control over the corporation in three primary ways: (1) they can elect or remove the directors;[52] (2) they can amend the articles of incorporation or bylaws; and (3) they have the right to approve or disapprove extraordinary changes to the corporation, such as a merger with another corporation.[53]

The obligations of shareholders are few. Because of the principle of limited liability, shareholders are not responsible for any of the corporation's debts or other actions, with the extraordinary exception of "piercing the corporate veil" discussed below.[54] If the corporation fails, its shareholders lose only their investments.[55]

Shareholder Rights in Publicly Traded Corporations   In large publicly traded corporations, the governance powers of shareholders is virtually nonexistent. Shareholder proxies are delivered to the corporate managers, who elect directors that often reappoint the incumbent managers. Most shareholders do not choose to exert any control over corporate managers. First, they usually view themselves as passive investors, not owners. Second, they often doubt whether they can improve corporate performance by intervening or controlling the choice of managers. Third, even if they did want to be more active, a great deal of time, money and energy is needed to inform themselves about corporate matters and to persuade and solicit proxies from other shareholders.[56] Consequently, when shareholder meeting announcements are

---

51 An improper purpose would be to learn business secrets, to aid a competitor of the corporation, or to secure prospects for personal business.

52 Directors usually serve their full term. If the shareholders are unhappy with a director's performance, the director is simply not reelected. However, the shareholders have the power to remove a director from office *for cause* and some laws expressly provide that shareholders can vote by majority to remove a director at any time *without cause*. *See* RMBCA, *supra* note 35, §8.08(a).

53 *See infra* p. 548.

54 *See infra* pp. 546-548.

55 *See generally* HENN & ALEXANDER, *supra* note 2, §§199-203.

56 A proxy is a document executed by shareholders appointing someone else to vote their shares for them.

sent out, along with management proxy forms requesting shareholders to vote their shares as it has recommended, most shareholders simply vote with by proxy in favor of the management or throw the entire announcement away.

If shareholders wish to be come active in exerting control over corporate actions, however, federal law is of some assistance. Section 14 of the Securities Exchange Act and regulations thereunder regulate the procedures by which proxies are obtained from shareholders of publicly traded corporations.[57] In addition to prohibiting fraud and misrepresentation in management communications to shareholders, the Act and regulations require that an annual report be sent that conforms to particular specifications. The content of proxy statements is regulated. Management is required to include in any proxy statement certain shareholder proposals and supporting statements, and to afford shareholders the opportunity to vote for or against management or shareholder proposals in the management proxy. Section 14 has been viewed as embodying a policy of "corporate democracy" and a desire to prevent management from treating corporations as their own personal property.[58]

Directors Directors are responsible for the management of the corporation and for creating corporate policy. The initial directors are usually named in the articles of incorporation or elected by the incorporators, and serve until the first annual shareholder meeting or until their successors are elected and qualified. Thereafter, directors are elected by majority vote of the shareholders and usually serve a term of one year.[59] The number of directors of a corporation varies; some states require at least three, while others require only one.

Directors meet regularly at board meetings to conduct the corporation's business. Directors do not have the power to act individually for the corporation; they can act only as an entire board. Thus, unlike employees, whose acts in the name of the corporation bind it, directors can bind the corporation only by actions approved by an affirmative vote of the board. They have the responsibility for all major policy-making decisions necessary for the management of all corporate affairs: declaring and paying corporate dividends to shareholders, authorizing major corporate policy and appointing, supervising, and removing officers and employees; and making financial decisions.

Directors, as persons in control of the property of others, are "fiduciaries" who have duties to both shareholders and the corporation. The directors' fiduciary duties include the duty of care and the duty of loyalty. The duty of care entails being honest and using prudent business judgment when conducting corporate affairs. Directors must exercise the degree of care that a reasonably prudent person would use when conducting personal business affairs, including the duty to become informed about corporate affairs.[60] The duty of loyalty prevents directors from, among other things, using corporate funds or confidential corporate information for their personal advantage, competing with the corporation, usurping a corporate opportunity,

---

57   15 U.S.C.A. §78n.

58   *Medical Committee for Human Rights v. Securities & Exchange Comm.*, 432 F.2d 659 (D.C. Cir. 1970), *vacated as moot*, 404 U.S. 403 (1972).

59   Directors usually serve from annual meeting to annual meeting, but longer or staggered terms are permissible under most state statutes.

60   *Smith v. Van Gorkom*, 488 A.2d 858 (Del. 1985) (rescission of merger allowed in shareholder suit where merger was approved quickly based on a 20-minute presentation by the chairman and without review of merger documents).

engaging in insider trading, or selling control over the corporation.[61] A director who breaches either the duty of care or the duty of loyalty may be held answerable to the corporation and to the shareholders.

Officers The corporate officers are responsible for the day-to-day operation of the corporation. They are most often selected and removed by the board of directors. Traditional titles include "chief executive officer," "president," "vice-president," "treasurer," and "secretary." The officers carry out the board's decisions and conduct the day-to-day operations of the business. The tenure of the officers is generally pursuant to a contract, though it may also be at the board's discretion.

Officers are viewed as having the same fiduciary duty of care and loyalty to the corporation and its shareholders as directors do when conducting business affairs, as well as the same obligations concerning corporate opportunities and conflicts of interest.[62] Like directors, officers purporting to contract on behalf of the corporation without the authority to do so may be personally liable on the contract or to the corporation. Even authorized officers may be liable on contracts if they do not advise that they are contracting as an agent of the corporation.

Shareholder Lawsuits Many of the above duties of the management of the corporation can form the basis for a shareholder suit for breach of duty. Shareholders may file either a "direct" or a "derivative" shareholder suit. A common example of a direct shareholder suit is a suit to compel the management to declare and pay a dividend.[63] It is "direct" because it enforces a duty owed directly to shareholders.

A shareholder "derivative" suit is one to enforce a duty owed to the *corporation*. Shareholders in such a suit are suing *on behalf of* the injured corporation. In cases where the wrongdoing of officers or directors has injured the corporation itself, the *corporation* has a right to sue its own officers or directors. However, since those very officers or directors control the corporation, they will probably decide that it is "not in the best interests of the corporation" for it to sue them. A derivative shareholder's suit remedies this problem by allowing the shareholders to "step into the shoes" of the corporation and sue on its behalf. Thus, even one shareholder is able to sue on behalf of the corporation, demanding that the corporation be repaid millions of dollars, even though the individual shareholder's loss may be nominal or nonexistent. When the derivative suit is successful and benefits the corporation, the plaintiff-shareholder is entitled to be reimbursed by the corporation for reasonable expenses, including attorney fees.[64]

Because shareholders may not have much personally at stake in a derivative suit, legislatures and courts have imposed limitations on such suits to prevent abuse. For instance, the plaintiff in a derivative action must be a shareholder both when suing and at the time of the alleged misconduct. This means that a person cannot buy shares after the alleged misconduct simply for the purpose of bringing a law suit. Also, shareholders wishing to sue must give management the opportunity to take action to remedy the problem by serving them with a formal demand. Finally, if

---

61 *See* HENN & ALEXANDER, *supra* note 1, §234; *see also* RMBCA, *supra* note 35, §8.30. *See, e.g., Globe Woolen Co. v. Utica Gas & Electric*, 121 N.E. 378 (N.Y. 1918) (Cardozo, J.) (contract to supply power that grossly favored textile company voided where same person was director and chairman of the executive committee of electric company and chief stockholder and director of textile company).

62 RMBCA, *supra* note 35, §8.42; HENN & ALEXANDER, *supra* note 1, at §§219-243.

63 *See* HENN & ALEXANDER, *supra* note 1, §360. *See, e.g., Godley v. Crandell & Godley Co.*, 105 N.E. 818 (N.Y. 1914) (suit over payment of dividends).

64 *See generally* HENN & ALEXANDER, *supra* note 1, §§361-367.

disinterested directors have determined that the suit is not in the best interests of the corporation, the court may dismiss the action.[65]

Business Judgment Rule   If shareholders sue the directors or officers of a corporation, those directors and officers are entitled to the benefit of the "business judgment rule."[66]   The business judgment rule is a "presumption that in making a business decision the directors of a corporation acted on an informed basis, in good faith and in the honest belief that the action taken was in the best interests of the company."[67]   A hallmark of the business judgment rule is that a court will not substitute its judgment for that of the board if the latter's decision can be "attributed to any rational business purpose."[68]   This rule allows for honest mistakes and reasonably poor business decisions. However, if the directors permit the corporation to violate the law, the business judgment rule does not apply.[69]   On the other hand, directors in a large corporation who are effectively relegated to making broad policy decisions are not required to monitor employees closely to discover illegality absent some cause for suspicion.[70]

g.   "Piercing the Corporate Veil"

The separate legal existence of the corporation and the limited liability it affords shareholders serve important social and economic purposes. However, there are instances where courts may ignore the corporate structure and its protections for compelling reasons of public policy. This is called "piercing the corporate veil." The conditions under which the law permits it to be done vary considerably from state to state.[71]   Whatever test is used, it is easy to exaggerate the importance of veil-piercing. Only when stockholders of officers are using the corporate structure to perpetuate a fraud, to evade the law or to escape obligations will "piercing" generally be successful. And when piercing is used, the corporation involved is almost always a closely-held one.

Formalistic Approach   Under one approach, identified with New York, courts will disregard the corporate structure only when there has been noncompliance with the corporate formalities, such as failing to complete the incorporation process or to hold directors' meetings, or where shareholders treat corporate property as their own.[72]   This is a rather permissive test. But even so, the conservative "formalistic" approach can trap shareholders and officers of close corporations run by friends or family

---

65 *See* HENN & ALEXANDER, *supra* note 1, §362. *See also* Federal Rule of Civil Procedure 23.1 (requiring a verified complaint and specific pleading).

66 *See generally*, CLARK, *supra* note 1, §3.4.

67 *Aronson v. Lewis*, 473 A.2d 805, 812 (Del. 1984).

68 *Sinclair Oil Corp. v. Levien*, 280 A.2d 717, 720 (Del. 1971). *See Schlensky v. Wrigley*, 237 N.E.2d 776 (Ill.App. 1968) (rejecting challenge to management decision not to install lights at baseball field to permit games to be played at night); *Herald Co. v. Seawell*, 472 F.2d 1081 (10th Cir. 1972) (rejecting challenge to purchase by corporation of its own shares for use in employee trust plan).

69 *Miller v. American Telephone & Telegraph Co.*, 507 F.2d 759 (3d Cir. 1974) (shareholder suit allowed to contest corporation's failure to collect $1.5 million debt owed by political party, a violation of federal election laws).

70 *Graham v. Allis-Chalmers Manufacturing Co.*, 188 A.2d 125 (Del. 1963) (directors not liable for damage to corporation caused by criminal price-fixing activities of middle-level executive employees).

71 *See* HENN & ALEXANDER, *supra* note 1, §146.

72 *See Walkovsky v. Carlton*, 223 N.E.2d 6 (N.Y. 1966) (refusing to disregard corporate form where separate corporations were set up for one or two taxis in a fleet, thus protecting shareholders-owners of fleet from tort liability).

members, who run the business on an informal basis, ignoring corporate formalities and routinely mixing corporate and personal assets.

Undercapitalization Approach   Other states have given less weight to legal formalities and emphasize "undercapitalization" — where the assets of the company are "trifling compared with the business to be done and the risks of loss."[73] But even under this test, Courts are often unwilling to disregard the protections of the corporate shell when the creditor is a *business creditor* (such as a bank). The reason is that the business creditor voluntarily enters into the relationship with the company, can investigate the company's ability to pay beforehand and require additional security as needed. Most situations where the veil is pierced are where the creditors are injured tort victims.[74]

"Dummy" Corporations Often the shareholder of a company whose corporate form is sought to be disregarded is another corporation and the creditor seeks to reach the assets of the "parent" or owner corporation. If the subsidiary is treated as a "dummy" and controlled in every way by the parent corporation, the subsidiary's corporate form can be disregarded to reach the assets of the parent. This will be particularly so if the subsidiary is used to carry on particularly risky functions of a business.[75]

In theory, the piercing doctrine applies to publicly held as well as closely held corporations. However, research reveals no case in which the *shareholders* of a corporation whose stock was publicly traded or widely held were found personally liable for the obligations of the corporation. Instead, when courts pierce the corporate veil of a publicly traded corporation, liability is usually imposed on the individuals who *managed* the enterprise, on a parent corporation that gave orders, or on a group of corporations that were operating as an economic unit.[76]

Choice of Law in Veil-Piercing "Internal affairs" of the corporation are usually governed by the law of the state of *incorporation*. However, some courts resolve issues of veil-piercing according to the law of the state where the corporation *operates*.[77] This is especially so if the state of incorporation is one of convenience. Also, there is a growing *federal* common law of veil-piercing. For example, federal environmental laws impose environmental cleanup obligations on "owners" and "operators." The Supreme Court has rejected the view that this includes shareholders and any parent corporation that were heavily involved in the operations of the company that caused the contamination. However, it instructed lower courts to determine "whether, in degree and detail, actions directed to the facility by an agent

---

73 *See Minton v. Cavaney*, 364 P.2d 473, 15 Cal.Rptr. 641 (Cal. 1961) (dictum). In this case, there was also evidence that many of the basic corporate formalities had not been followed, including the serious omission of failing to complete the formation of the corporation.

74 *See Consumer's Coop v. Olsen*, 419 N.W.2d 211 (Wis. 1988) (declining to disregard limited liability for business creditor). *But see Victoria Elevator Co. v. Meriden Grain Co.*, 283 N.W.2d 509 (Minn. 1979) (holding major shareholder liable where wide variety of wrongful acts occurred).

75 *But see Craig v. Lake Asbestos of Quebec*, 843 F.2d 145 (3d Cir. 1988) (applying New Jersey law, declining to hold parent liable in tort case where asbestos production had been transferred to wholly-owned overseas corporation for lack of complete "alter ego" control). *Craig* contains a good discussion of controlling authorities.

76 David Barber, *Piercing the Corporate Veil*, 17 WILLAMETTE L. REV. 371, 372 (1981).

77 This is consistent with the general notion that the state of operation has the greater contacts and interest in the issue. *See* Chapter VII, pp. 254-257.

of the parent alone are eccentric under accepted norms of parental oversight of a subsidiary's facility."[78]

h. Extraordinary Corporate Transactions

Events that transcend ordinary business matters generally require shareholder approval. These extraordinary matters include: (1) mergers, (2) purchases of assets other than in the regular course of business, and (3) terminations.[79]

Mergers A merger is the legal combination of two (or more) corporations, whereby one corporation transfers all of its assets and liabilities to the other, called the "surviving" corporation. After merger, the surviving corporation automatically acquires all of the merged corporation's rights, privileges, and assets, as well as its debts and obligations. The former shareholders of the merged corporation may receive cash, bonds or shares in the surviving corporation, depending on what the merger agreement provides.[80] Both director and shareholder approval of all the merging corporations is generally required. However, shareholders who disapprove of a merger that has been approved by the majority usually have a statutory right of "dissent" and "appraisal," whereby shareholders can require that the corporation buy their stock at the value it had immediately prior to the approval of the merger. However, exceptions to this are often made when the new stock is publicly traded.[81]

Sale of Assets When a corporation acquires all or substantially all of the assets of another corporation, it does not alter the legal status of the acquiring corporation. Thus, shareholder approval of the acquiring corporation may not be required for such a transaction. However, the corporation that is selling substantially all its assets is substantially changing its structure, so that corporation's board of directors and shareholders must approve the transaction. Generally, acquiring all the assets of a corporation does not transfer legal responsibility for its liabilities. Exceptions to this rule exist when the purchasing corporation impliedly or expressly assumes the acquired entity's liabilities, when the sale is truly a merger, when the purchaser continues the seller's business and retains the same management staff, and when the sale is fraudulently executed to escape liability.[82]

Termination The termination of corporate life begins with "dissolution," the legal death of the corporate entity. Following that is "liquidation," the process of selling corporate assets and distributing the cash among creditors and shareholders. Typically, shareholder approval is required for dissolution, and no right of dissent and appraisal is ordinarily provided. Dissolution can be brought about voluntarily, usually by the approval of the shareholders and the board of directors or by unanimous shareholder action, or involuntarily, by court decree.[83] Involuntary judicial dissolution may occur, for example, when a board of directors is deadlocked or in the event of serious mismanagement.   However, courts are hesitant to order dissolution. Whenever dissolution does take place, the directors are responsible for handling liquidation for the benefit of creditors and shareholders. This includes selling the

---

78 *United States v. Bestfoods*, 524 U.S. 51 (1998) *See generally* KATHRYN R. HEIDT, ENVIRONMENTAL OBLIGATIONS IN BANKRUPTCY ¶10.04 (West Group 1993-1998). *See also Anderson v. Abbott*, 321 U.S. 349 (1944) (bank holding company).

79 Though filing bankruptcy is also an extraordinary event, shareholder approval is not required.

80 *Id.* §346. *See also* RMBCA §§11.01-11.07.

81 HENN & ALEXANDER, *supra* note 1, §349.

82 *Id.* at 967-968.

83 *Id.* at 746-747.

assets, paying the expenses involved, satisfying creditors' claims, and distributing the net proceeds.[84] Corporate creditors are paid first, followed by preferred shareholders (if any) and then common stockholders.[85]

i. Tender Offers

"Friendly" and "Hostile" Corporate Takeovers A method of acquiring a corporation without dealing with its management is to seek to purchase a sufficient number of the voting shares of the corporation's stock to take control of it. This can be done through market purchases or through a "tender offer" made directly to shareholders. A tender offer is the means by which a would-be acquirer invites shareholders of the "target" corporation to tender their stock for purchase. The purchase price offered is generally higher than the market price of the target stock. If the takeover is against the wishes of the managers of the corporation, it is a "hostile" takeover; if management is in favor of the takeover, it is considered a "friendly" takeover.

Federal Regulation of Tender Offers Because publicly-traded securities are involved, several aspects of tender offers are controlled by federal law, notably the Williams Act.[86] The Act requires any market purchaser of more than 5% of the stock of a publicly traded company to disclose that fact to the federal Securities Exchange and Commission (SEC). In addition, any tender offeror who proposes to purchase at least 5% of a company must disclose that fact and state the purpose of its tender offer and its plans for the target corporation should the offer be successful. Other parts of the Williams Act govern closely the terms, duration, and circumstances of tender offers.[87]

Tactics to Counter Hostile Takeovers A successful hostile takeover generally means that the managers of the target corporation will lose their jobs. With their careers at stake, managers often vigorously oppose takeover bids with various tactics. They may try to persuade shareholders that the takeover is not in the best interest of the corporation. They may file a lawsuit alleging violations of applicable federal securities and antitrust laws, although this is often done primarily to gain time to employ some other device to prevent the takeover. Another tactic is to seek out a "white knight" — a rival tender offeror who has promised to treat the managers and shareholders well after the takeover. Another tactic is the "poison pill" plan. This tactic involves giving shareholders extraordinary rights against the target corporation that are triggered by a takeover. This serves to make the target corporation less valuable to the tender offeror. Yet another defense is a "turnabout," under which the target corporation responds with a tender offer of its own for the tender offeror's shares. An expensive method of ending a hostile takeover is for the target company to pay "greenmail" by buying the shares purchased by the tender offeror at a premium, with the understanding that the offeror will stop the takeover.[88]

---

84 *Id.* at 1155.

85 *Id.* at 990. Court supervision is generally not required during liquidation.

86 15 U.S.C.A. §§78m(d)-(e), 78n(d)-(f). *See also infra*, pp. 551-554.

87 There is little state law regulating tender offer because most of it is either preempted by the Williams Act or violates the dormant commerce clause by imposing an undue burden on interstate commerce. *See Edgar v. MITE Corp.*, 457 U.S. 624 (1982) (holding Illinois anti-takeover law violative of dormant commerce clause). *See generally* Chapter IX, pp. 324-327.

88 These and other tactics are discussed in CLARK, *supra* note 1, §13.6.

Duties of Management in Hostile Takeovers There is a potential for conflicts of interest to arise between management and the shareholders of the target corporation during a takeover attempt. This raises the question of how far management may go to resist takeover efforts.[89] The answer that has emerged is the *"Revlon* duty," based on the Delaware Supreme Court's opinion in *Revlon, Inc. v. MacAndrews & Forbes Holdings, Inc.*[90] The "business judgment rule" applies generally to management actions in a takeover. However, in a takeover situation a court will scrutinize defensive action of management for signs that it was taken out of self interest rather than in the pursuance of the corporation's or shareholders' best interests.[91] And if defensive tactics fail and sale of the company becomes inevitable, the duty of the management changes from one of preserving the corporate entity to one of maximizing the company's value and assuring that its shareholders get the best deal possible for their shares.[92]

5. Limited Liability Companies

The limited liability company (LLC) is a relatively new form of business organization in the United States, borrowed from abroad. First developed in 1977 in Wyoming, LLCs are now provided for in all 50 states and the District of Columbia.[93] Similar to limited partnerships, LLCs are a non-corporate business form that provides its members (owners of the company) with limited liability.

The LLC has several advantages over other enterprise organizations. Comparing it to the limited partnership, it has the same taxation and limited liability advantages for limited partners, but LLC members, unlike limited partners, have the right to participate in control of the business. Further, there is no need for a general partner subject to unlimited liability.[94] The LLC has advantages over the close corporation. First, LLCs are simpler to create and operate. All that is needed is an operating agreement, similar to a partnership agreement. State LLC statutes typically abandon the corporation statutes' mandatory structure and hierarchy of shareholders, directors, and officers, and the attendant rules relating to meetings and voting rights. Second, there is much greater flexibility with LLCs. The operating agreement can set up capital structure and management in whatever way the members wish. Members can choose to manage the LLC directly themselves or indirectly through managers. The LLC can even be used in some states in place of a sole proprietorship, thus providing its single "member" with limited liability protection. Delaware, New York, Texas, Virginia and Wisconsin allow single-member LLCs.

Perhaps the most important advantage over a corporation is that LLCs can be taxed on a "pass-through" basis like partnerships, thus avoiding the double taxation imposed on corporations.[95] Favorable tax treatment is facilitated by a new "check-

---

89 *Id.* §13.6.3.

90 506 A.2d 173 (Del. 1985).

91 *Revlon, id.; Unocal Corp. v. Mesa Petroleum, Inc.*, 493 A.2d 946 (Del. 1985).

92 *Revlon, supra; Paramount Communications Inc. v. QVC, Inc.*, 637 A.2d 34 (Del. 1994).

93 *See generally* J. WILLIAM CALLISON AND MAUREEN A. SULLIVAN, LIMITED LIABILITY COMPANIES: A STATE-BY-STATE GUIDE TO LAW AND PRACTICE (West 1994-1997). The Delaware Act is set out in CORPORATIONS AND OTHER BUSINESS ASSOCIATIONS: STATUTES, RULES AND FORMS, *supra* note 3.

94 A limited liability partnership (LLP) similarly has no general partner requirement. However, states often allow LLPs only for certain professionals, provide protection only from certain liabilities and require a certain level of liability insurance coverage or a designated fund for payment of claims.

95 *See supra*, pp. 519-520.

the-box" procedure implemented by the IRS and effective January 1, 1997.[96] This approach allows LLCs, including one-member LLCs, to elect how they wish to be treated for tax purposes: as a corporation or as a partnership or association. This election can be changed, though not more than once in any 5-year period unless there is more than a 50% change in ownership and the IRS gives permission. Even if no election is made, the rules provide the default position that the LLC with two or more members will be treated as a partnership and the LLC with only one member will be disregarded for tax purposes, i.e., it will be treated as a sole proprietorship.[97]

Despite all of their flexibility, LLCs are not completely informal. The statutes all require an official filing for an LLC to be formed. Some of the statutes require the filings to make fairly substantial disclosures with respect to the entity's financing. Another drawback of the LLC form, is that its members' interests cannot be publicly traded, as shares of corporations can be. This limits the LLC's ability to accumulate capital from the general public as corporations can.[98] It is generally assumed that LLCs will be treated like corporations for purposes of "veil-piercing," and fiduciary duties of management.

Some predict that LLCs will soon make partnerships and subchapter S corporations obsolete. However, several issues remain to be worked out before LLCs win universal acceptance.[99]

B. Regulation of Offers and Sales of Corporate Securities

1. Federal Securities Regulation

Much of the federal law that relates to public corporations involves regulation of issuance and trading in securities.[100] The primary goal of regulation is to protect the investors who purchase them. This is done in two ways. First, issuing corporations are required to disclose accurate and current information about themselves. Unlike most goods, securities have no intrinsic value and can be issued virtually without cost and in unlimited amounts. The value of a security is dependent on the profitability or the future prospects of the entity that issues it. Consequently, accurate information about the company is essential to make a decision on purchase. Second, the federal laws seek to insure that information about the corporation is *equally* available to all shareholders. Thus, those laws penalize those who use special "inside" information about the issuing corporation to make advantageous trades of that company's stock.

Principal Federal Statutes Federal regulation of securities began soon after the stock market crash of 1929, which was viewed as a failure of the securities market.[101] The two main federal statutes are the Securities Act of 1933 (SA) and the Securities

---

96 Sections 301.7701-1 through 301.7701-3, 61 FR 66584 (December 18, 1996).

97 However, some states treat LLCs like corporations for *state* taxation purposes.

98 Subchapter S corporations are similarly limited. *See supra* p. 541.

99 Several of these issues are outlined in Larry E. Ribstein *The Emergence of The Limited Liability Company*, 51 BUSINESS LAWYER 1 (1995) and Symposium, Check-the-Box and Beyond: The Future of Limited Liability Entities, 52 BUSINESS LAWYER 605 (1997). Also of interest is the recent UNIFORM LIMITED LIABILITY COMPANY ACT (ULLCA) (1995), which also seeks to remedy deficiencies in state statutes.

100 Other federal laws relating to public corporation are those governing proxy solicitations (*supra* p. 544) and tender offers (*supra* p. 549). Securities were defined *supra* p. 541. The federal securities acts and rules discussed here and earlier in this chapter are compiled in THOMAS L. HAZEN, ED., SECURITIES REGULATION: SELECTED STATUTES, RULES AND FORMS - 1998 EDITION (West 1998).

101 For a readable up-to-date summary of the law in this area, *see* LARRY D. SODERQUIST & THERESA A. GABALDON, SECURITIES Law (Foundation 1998). *See also* David L. RATNER, SECURITIES REGULATION IN A NUTSHELL, 2D ED. (West 1998); CLARK, *supra* note 1, §§17.1-17.5; THOMAS L. HAZEN, HORNBOOK ON THE LAW OF SECURITIES REGULATION (West 1996).

Exchange Act of 1934 (SEA). Although these two acts are closely related, they affect different stages of the securities market. The SA mainly regulates the issuance of new securities. This act requires that all material facts related to that issuance be publicly filed in a "registration statement" and presented to potential buyers in a "prospectus."[102] The SEA mainly regulates the buying and selling of securities already in the public markets.[103] The SEA requires disclosure of all important information that shareholders and prospective purchasers should know. It imposes a duty of continuous disclosure for all corporations with securities traded on the securities exchanges and for those companies with assets of more than $5 million and 500 or more shareholders. The 1934 Act also established the federal Securities and Exchange Commission (SEC), which is responsible for administering all federal securities law. The 1934 Act authorizes the SEC to prohibit by rule any "manipulative or deceptive devices or contrivances" in connection with the purchase and sale of securities.[104]

Enforcement of Securities Regulations Violations of securities laws and rules are subject to public enforcement by way of criminal prosecutions or civil actions brought by the SEC. However, the primary means of enforcement is private litigation, encouraged by incentives provided in the federal and some state statutes.

Rule 10b-5 Rule 10b-5, promulgated by the SEC pursuant to the 1934 federal Act, forms the basis for much litigation about unlawful corporate disclosures or non-disclosures.[105] The rule makes unlawful any "untrue statement of a material fact" or misleading omission and "any act, practice, or course of business which operates or would operate as a fraud or deceit upon any person, in connection with the purchase or sale of any security." Any shareholder can sue for damages. The liability of a corporation can be substantial when the class action device is used to recover for all shareholders who lost money as a result of a violation of 10b-5.[106] After several years of growth in this area of the law, the Supreme Court cut down on the number of cases by imposing a "scienter" requirement, requiring that plaintiff shareholders prove that every untrue statement or omission was made or done with the *intent* to deceive or manipulate.[107]

Still, the issues of fraud and intent can be decided by the judge or jury only after a full trial. Defendant companies often feel pressured to settle even groundless suits. There are the costs of litigation to consider, as well as possible bad publicity for the company and the possibility, however slim, of ruinous class action damages. Complaints about such "strike" suits prompted Congress to react in 1995 with the most extensive changes in the SA and SEA since their original enactment.[108] There is

---

102 15 U.S.C.A. §§77a-77aa. The law is codified here, but virtually everyone uses the section numbers of the original act. That convention will be honored here.

103 15 U.S.C.A. §§78a-78hh-1.

104 15 U.S.C.A. §78j(b). The 1934 Act also provides for SEC registration and regulation of securities brokers and dealers. Other important federal securities laws are the Investment Company Act of 1940, 15 U.S.C.A. §80a (regulating publicly-owned companies engaged in investing and trading securities), the Investment Advisors Act of 1940, 15 U.S.C.A. §80b (regulating and requiring registration of investment advisors); and the Securities Investors Protection Act of 1970, 15 U.S.C.A. §78aaa *et seq.* (providing measures to protect against financial failures of securities firms).

105 *See* 17 C.F.R. §240.10b-5. *See* Ratner, *supra* note 101, §§18-20.

106 *See* Chapter VII, p. 225, where class actions are discussed.

107 *See Ernst & Ernst v. Hochfelder*, 425 U.S. 185 (1976). The scienter requirement applies to suits for injunctive relief as well as to damage suits. *Aaron v. Securities & Exchange Comm'n.*, 446 U.S. 680 (1980). *See generally* Ratner, *supra* note 101, §18.

108 Private Securities Litigation Reform Act of 1995, codified at 15 U.S.C.A. §77z-2(c).

now a "safe haven" for predictive statements accompanied by "meaningful cautionary statements" and the plaintiffs must prove that the predictive statements were "made with actual knowledge" that they were "false or misleading." There are also severe limits on plaintiffs' discovery while a motion to dismiss or for summary judgment is pending, thus protecting defendants from the expense of responding to discovery requests before the court has determined that the suit has merit.[109] In addition, there are mandatory sanctions on plaintiffs for groundless suits, limits on damages recoverable, limits on attorney fees to a certain percentage of the class recovery and qualifications for who can be the member of the plaintiff class, presuming that it will be the plaintiff owning the most shares in the defendant company rather than the plaintiff who filed first.[110]

Insider Trading   Less obvious than the use of Rule 10b-5 to police misleading predictive statements by companies is its use to police "insider trading." Insider trading is the buying and selling of securities by persons who have received important "inside" confidential information about the company's condition or business that could have a bearing on the value of its securities. In a series of administrative decisions and injunctive actions starting in the 1960s and culminating in the well-known case of *Securities & Exchange Comm'n v. Texas Gulf Sulphur Corp.*,[111] the SEC convinced the courts that the disclosure requirements of Rule 10b-5 impose a duty on persons with inside information either to disclose the information or to abstain from trading in those securities until the information is disclosed publicly. In *Texas Gulf Sulphur*, corporate officers made substantial purchases of stock after learning — but before announcing publicly — promising news about exploratory drilling on some of the company's oil and gas properties.

Liability attaches under Rule 10b-5 only to persons who have such a duty to "disclose or abstain." This clearly applies to corporate officers and employees who owe a fiduciary duty to their company. However, persons not employed by the issuer of stock misappropriate information may be liable when they trade on information gathered in the course of their employment, thus violating a duty to their employer. For example, in a recent case, a lawyer came upon nonpublic information in the process of working on a planned tender offer and traded based on it. The Supreme Court held that this constituted a breach of the duty he owed to his law firm and its client and not to take advantage of inside information acquired in the course of the attorney-client relationship. Therefore, this constituted a fraudulent device in connection with the purchase and sale of securities.

Other Liability of Insiders   Vigorous enforcement action against insiders has also revolved around §16 of the 1934 Act.[112] Rule 16(b) is designed to discourage insider trading by penalizing "short-swing" profits — profits from securities transactions that take place within a 6-month period — received by officers, directors and 10% shareholders of a public corporation. Suit can be filed by the corporation or by any shareholder. Proof that the defendant actually used insider information is not a prerequisite for recovery. Unlike Rule 10b-5 violations, no intent is required and many if not most 16(b) violations are inadvertent. All that is required is proof of a purchase

---

109 Discovery and pre-trial motions in civil cases were covered in Chapter VII, pp. 226-231, 232-233.

110 A symposium on the Act discusses these and other aspects of the changes it makes. *Symposium on the Private Securities Litigation Reform Act of 1995*, 51 BUSINESS LAWYER 975 (1996).

111 401 F.2d 833 (2d Cir. 1968). *See generally* CLARK, *supra* note 1, §§8.9-8.10.

112 15 U.S.C.A. §78p. *See* RATNER, *supra* note 101, §16.

and a sale (the order is irrelevant) within a 6-month period and a profit as determined by a rather liberal method of accounting. Persons subject to potential 16(b) liability must report their trades to the SEC and the reports are published, thus making violations easy to spot and prove. Indeed, there are lawyers who support themselves quite well reading the SEC reports, notifying the corporation whenever there has been an improper trade, and, if necessary, filing suit on behalf of the corporation. Improper profits recovered against insider violators are payable to the corporation, but attorney fees may be awarded to the plaintiff's lawyer out of profits recovered in successful litigation.[113]

"Tippees" — persons outside the corporation who are "tipped" about inside information and use it to their advantage — may also be liable. However, for tippees to be liable, the tipper must have profited in some way from the tipping, whether through pecuniary or indirect "reputational" benefit.[114]

At the urging of the SEC, Congress in the 1980s made insider trading information more serious by authorizing the SEC to recover up to three times the trading profit from the participants, increasing criminal penalties, and providing a further incentive in the form of a 10% "bounty" for private plaintiffs of any amounts recovered.[115]

2. State "Blue Sky" Laws

In addition to the federal laws governing securities, every state has its own set of securities laws regulating offers and sales of securities that take place within their borders, referred to as "blue sky" laws.[116] Similar to their federal counterparts, blue sky laws require disclosure by issuers and sellers of securities and contain anti-fraud provisions. Typically, these laws step in where federal laws do not apply, requiring registration and qualification of securities that are not covered by federal laws. Blue sky laws vary widely from state to state, though most are similar to the Uniform Securities Act, which has been passed in 30 states.[117]

C. Bankruptcy

Debtors who file for bankruptcy are usually debtors whose obligations far exceed their ability to pay and who are in massive default. Bankruptcy can result either in a reorganization of the finances of the debtor so that the debtor can continue in business or in liquidating the debtor's assets and applying the proceeds to pay outstanding debts. Bankruptcy law is federal, passed pursuant to Congress' specific authority in Article I §8 of the Constitution to prescribe "uniform bankruptcy laws" for the country. The principal law is the federal Bankruptcy Code. However, it is the law of contracts, property and torts that often defines obligations and property rights in bankruptcy and this law is overwhelmingly state law. Consequently, federal

---

113 The principal financial interest in suing is thus that of the lawyer rather than any client. Courts have ruled that this does not violate the ethical prohibition on lawyers acquiring a personal interest in litigation, since Congress must have intended to authorize such an incentive to assure vigorous enforcement. *See Magida v. Continental Can Co.*, 176 F.Supp. 781 (S.D.N.Y. 1956).

114 *See Dirks v. Securities & Exchange Comm'n*, 463 U.S. 646 (1983) (where tippers were motivated by a desire to expose that fraud, and received no monetary or personal benefit from revealing the information, tippee was not liable when he did not profit either, but communicated the information to some stockholders, who then sold their stock). In one case, the tipper's "profit" was that his inside information impressed his mistress.

115 *See* Insider Trading Sanctions Act of 1984, 15 U.S.C.A. §78u-1.

116 "Blue Sky" comes from the purpose of the laws, which is prevent "speculative schemes which have no more basis than so many feet of 'blue sky'." *Hall v. Geiger-Jones Co.*, 242 U.S. 539, 550 (1917).

117 7B Unif.L.Ann. 69-132 (Supp. 1992).

bankruptcy law adopts or necessarily contemplates the application of state law.[118] Federal courts have exclusive jurisdiction over bankruptcy proceedings.[119]

Both businesses and individuals can file for bankruptcy.[120] A person operating as a sole proprietorship files as an individual and corporations, partnerships and LLCs file as entities. Whether business or personal, the policy behind bankruptcy is debtor rehabilitation — to give the debtor a "fresh start" — and to provide a fair means of distributing a debtor's assets among all its creditors.[121] Bankruptcy can be either voluntary (commenced by the debtor) or involuntary (commenced by creditors).

There are two principal types of bankruptcies that relate to businesses. They are commonly referred to by the chapters of the Bankruptcy Code that regulate them. A Chapter 7 bankruptcy results in liquidation of the debtor's assets and distribution of the corporation's assets to creditors. Chapter 11 provides a procedure for reorganization of an entity which could continue to function if adjustments were made in its debts and structure agreeable with its creditors.[122] All forms of bankruptcy provide the debtor with the immediate relief of immunity from suit by creditors for the duration of the bankruptcy proceedings.

Chapter 7 In a Chapter 7 proceeding, a trustee in bankruptcy is appointed to administer and liquidate the debtor. A trustee is a private person, often a lawyer, who is appointed by the court and is paid by the court. The trustee's job is to gather the assets of the debtor, to notify creditors to file their claims, to adjudicate any matters of dispute involving assets or obligations of the debtor's estate, and finally to pay out the bankrupt's estate to creditors on an equal basis. Individual debtors are permitted to retain certain personal and real property.[123] Individual debtors receive a discharge of their debts — complete relief from the obligation to pay those debts — unless they have engaged in certain fraudulent or wrongful acts, such as concealing assets, making a false statement under oath or violating a bankruptcy court order.[124] Other exceptions to discharge are listed in the federal statute.[125] A partnership or corporation does not receive a discharge, but simply goes out of business and may

---

118 For more complete treatment of bankruptcy, *see* DAVID G. EPSTEIN, STEVE H. NICKLES & JAMES J. WHITE, BANKRUPTCY (West 1993); BRIAN BLUM, BANKRUPTCY AND DEBTOR-CREDITOR:EXAMPLES AND EXPLANATIONS (Aspen 1993). *See also* BANKRUPTCY CODE, RULES AND OFFICIAL FORMS, LAW SCHOOL EDITION (West 1998).

119 *See* 11 U.S.C.A. §§101-1330. The federal bankruptcy court is attached to the federal District Court in each district and has a separate Bankruptcy Judge who is appointed for 14-year terms. *See* Chapter V, p. 181. Bankruptcy judges are Article I, not Article III judges, and are limited in the powers they can exercise. *See* Chapter VI, pp. 212-214 and note 129.

120 An individual can file an individual bankruptcy because of personal rather than business debts and much the same procedure is followed as outlined here. However, since the topic of this chapter is business law, the examples and descriptions of procedures will focus on the individual doing business.

121 *See Local Loan Co. v. Hunt*, 292 U.S. 234 (1934) and *In re Chicago, Milwaukee, St. Paul and Pac. R.R.*, 974 F.2d 775 (7th Cir. 1992) (discussing bankruptcy policies).

122 There is a Chapter 13 "reorganization" option as well for individual debtors who have regular income. However, it is used almost exclusively by consumers rather than businesses, who use Chapter 11. In 1991, 69% of cases filed were under Chapter 7, 38% were under Chapter 13, and 3% were under Chapter 11. The total number of all cases filed under the Bankruptcy Code that year was 943,987.

123 *See* 11 U.S.C.A. §522(b). Exemptions specified in either federal or state law or both will apply, depending on state option. Typical state exemptions for individual debtors are for tools of the trade, household goods, clothes and jewelry, and certain farm animals, as well as a "homestead exemption" in a limited amount for the house in which the debtor lives. There is considerable variation in exemption laws from state to state and some states, Florida in particular, have extremely liberal exemption laws.

124 11 U.S.C.A. §727(a).

125 Completely non-dischargeable are certain taxes, debts contracted under false pretenses, alimony and child support, and most educational loans for students. *See* 11 U.S.C.A. §523(a).

dissolve itself under state law. Most Chapter 7 bankruptcies proceed without difficulties and are over in a matter of months.

Chapter 11 The purpose of Chapter 11 proceedings is to reorganize the debtor's debt structure in such a way as to enable the business to continue, if that is possible. Reorganization is encouraged since it will allow the business to continue to employ people, pay taxes and otherwise contribute to the economy. This makes the course of Chapter 11 proceedings less predictable and more complex than Chapter 7 proceedings.

Upon filing the Chapter 11 case, the debtor's current management remains in control as the "debtor-in-possession" and continues to run the business.[126] But in this capacity, the managers of the debtor take on the "fiduciary responsibilities of a trustee" to preserve the estate for the benefit of the creditors.[127] A "creditor's committee" is appointed, which consists of the largest creditors of the debtor willing to serve. The creditors' committee's job is to protect the interests of the "general creditors" — creditors who do not hold security or collateral for their debts. However, general creditors' claims to the bankrupt's assets are subject to security interests in those assets (real estate mortgages and liens on personal property). There is also a priority for employees' unpaid wages and any taxes owed.

To successfully conclude a Chapter 11 reorganization, the court must "confirm" a "plan of reorganization." The plan of reorganization will substitute new obligations for the debtor's old obligations. The debtor usually submits a proposed plan of reorganization. To be confirmed, the plan must meet a number of requirements not discussed here.[128] But an important one is that the plan must give each creditor at least what that creditor would receive under a Chapter 7 distribution unless the affected creditor consents to a different arrangement. Further, the court may confirm a plan only if it is either (1) approved by a vote of all classes of creditors[129] or (2) determined by the bankruptcy court to be a "fair and equitable" plan that pays creditors in accordance with the "absolute priority rule."[130] Under the absolute priority rule, all classes of claims must be paid in full first before the shareholders receive anything. Unless the creditors are paid in full or agree otherwise, the result of this rule is that the creditors become the owners of the company.

In practice, most Chapter 11 plans that are confirmed are plans negotiated between creditors and the shareholders and approved by them. Under such a compromise, creditors are paid something less than what they are due and stockholders get to keep some of their stock. In only 17% of cases are reorganization plans finally confirmed. In the remainder of the cases, the case is converted to a Chapter 7 proceeding and the debtor's assets are liquidated.[131]

---

126 11 U.S.C.A. §§1101(1), 1107.

127 *Commodity Futures Trading Comm'n v. Weintraub*, 471 U.S. 343 (1985). *See, e.g.*, *In re Tudor Associates, Ltd.*, 20 F.3d 115 (4th Cir. 1994) (manager of limited partnership violated fiduciary duty when he arranged to buy partnership assets through separate company he owned).

128 *See* 11 U.S.C.A. §1129(a).

129 11 U.S.C.A. §1129(a)(8). Approval does not mean a unanimous vote. Two-thirds in debt amount and over one-half in number of each class of creditors voting must approve. 11 U.S.C.A. §1126(d).

130 11 U.S.C.A. §1129(b). The legal slang term for this court-imposed plan is a "cram-down plan" — since it is effectively "crammed down the throats" of the creditors.

131 Edward M. Flynn, "Statistical Analysis of Chapter 11", Administrative Office of U.S. Courts, Statistical Analysis and Reports Division 10 (October 1989) (unpublished).

D. Antitrust Law

The core of federal antitrust law is set out in the Sherman Act, the Clayton Act, and the Federal Trade Commission Act.[132] Most states have their own antitrust statutes, which are not preempted by the federal statutes.[133] But by far it is federal law that is more important, so in this short summary we will deal only with it.[134]

1. Applicable Law

The Sherman Act   The Sherman Act dates from 1890.[135] Its language is uncommonly broad and vague. Section 1 prohibits "every contract, combination . . . or conspiracy in restraint of trade."   Section 2 prohibits actions, attempts or conspiracies to "monopolize."[136] None of these terms is defined in the act. All business contracts limit the freedom of the parties by imposing obligations on them and thus "restrain" free trade. Consequently, the Court has held that Congress intended that the Sherman Act prohibit only *unreasonable* restraints of trade. Since it is up to the courts to define what business practices come within this "rule of reason," judicial decisions define much of federal antitrust law.[137]

The Clayton Act   The general language of the Sherman Act as originally interpreted by the Supreme Court led to some dissatisfaction with its lack of effect on monopolies. This resulted in passage of the Clayton Act.[138] That Act prohibits specific activities and mergers that tend to monopolize or that demonstrate a reasonable likelihood of substantially lessening competition.[139] As will be pointed out later, most practices specifically prohibited by the Clayton Act's provisions are banned under the Sherman Act as well.

The Federal Trade Commission Act   The Federal Trade Commission Act of 1914[140] established the Federal Trade Commission (FTC). Under §5 of the FTC Act, the FTC can initiate administrative proceedings against those who engage in any "[u]nfair methods of competition in or affecting commerce."[141] Business conduct that tends to restrain trade or create a monopoly under the Sherman Act often amounts to an

---

132 *See generally* HERBERT HOVENKAMP, FEDERAL ANTITRUST POLICY: THE LAW OF COMPETITION AND ITS PRACTICE (West 1994); ERNEST GELLHORN AND WILLIAM E. KOVACIC, ANTITRUST LAW AND ECONOMICS IN A NUTSHELL, 4TH ED. (West 1994); ABA SECTION ON ANTITRUST, ANTITRUST LAW DEVELOPMENTS, 3D ED. (ABA 1992) (two volumes).

133 For a summary of the law that covers unfair trade practices generally, including state law, *see* CHARLES R. MCMANIS, UNFAIR TRADE PRACTICES, 3D ED. (West 1993). *See also* HOVENKAMP, *supra* §20.8 for a discussion of state antitrust law and its relationship to federal antitrust law and ABA ANTITRUST SECTION, STATE ANTITRUST PRACTICE AND STATUTES 44-53 (ABA 1990).

134 Federal law may be applied only to transactions that affect interstate commerce, but, as has been discussed elsewhere, this includes almost any economic activity. *See* Chapter I, p. 24, and *Summit Health, Ltd. v. Pinhas*, 500 U.S. 322 (1991) (Sherman Act held to apply to alleged conspiracy by local hospital to exclude eye surgeon because conduct would have effect on interstate commerce).

135 The word "antitrust" comes from the cartels and groups of firms that were then called "trusts."

136 15 U.S.C.A. §§1-7.

137 *Standard Oil Co. of New Jersey v. United States*, 221 U.S. 1 (1911) (holding rule of reason did not encompass oil company's pattern of acquisition of rivals, illegal rebates from railroads, industrial espionage and predatory pricing that led to controlling almost 90% of country's oil refining capacity). *See also National Society of Professional Engineers v. United States*, 435 U.S. 679, 688 (1978) (Congress intended phrase in statute prohibiting all agreements "in restraint of trade or commerce" would be "shape[d]" by "drawing on common law tradition").

138 15 U.S.C.A. §§12-27. *See* HOVENKAMP, *supra* note 132, at 56-57.

139 15 U.S.C.A. §13.

140 *Id.* §§41-58. The FTC is also authorized to issue regulations on and investigate unfair and deceptive trade practices that affect the consumer. *See* Chapter X, pp. 397, 399, and note 170.

141 *Id.* §45.

unfair method of competition. Consequently, the FTC can proceed against violators of the Sherman Act. In addition, it has joint civil enforcement authority with the Department of Justice to proceed against violators of the Clayton Act. Moreover, it may intervene and conduct administrative proceedings even when there has technically been no violation of antitrust laws if a particular business activity appears to violate the "spirit" of the antitrust laws.[142]

2. Prohibited Practices

These three Acts, when taken together, prohibit principally four kinds of anti-competitive activity: restraints on trade, monopolization, mergers and acquisitions, and price discrimination. When the "rule of reason" is used, anticompetitive effects from the challenged practice must be shown. However, some activities "have such predictable and pernicious anticompetitive effect, and such limited potential for procompetitive benefit, that they are deemed unlawful per se."[143]

Restraints on Trade Restraints on trade may be horizontal or vertical. Horizontal restraints are attempts to restrain competition between companies on the same level of production or distribution, such as agreements by companies not to compete on each other's territories.[144] Vertical restraints involve attempts by companies at one level to control what happens at a lower level, such as where a manufacturer seeks to control the price at which the distributor or retailer sells its product.[145] With vertical restraints, a distinction must be made between setting minimum and maximum prices. At one point, the Court held that maximum price restraints were *per se* violations. Recently, it overruled that case, finding that the anticompetitive effects of such restraints were less serious than it originally thought and that such restraints often result in lower prices for consumers.[146]

Another vertical restraint is the "tying arrangement." If a seller has good market position for one of its products or services, it may try to promote a second product or service by "tying" its purchase to the purchase of the first, i.e., by selling the first only on the condition that the buyer purchase the second.[147] Not all tying arrangements are unlawful. Liability attaches only if the seller has market power in the market for the tying product and the tying arrangement affects a substantial amount of commerce for the tied product. Even then, the need for quality control or other business justifications can be a defense.[148]

---

142 *See Fed. Trade Comm'n v. Brown Shoe Co.*, 384 U.S. 316 (1966).

143 *State Oil Co. v. Khan*, 522 U.S. 3 (1997). *See United States v. Socony-Vacuum Oil Co.*, 310 U.S. 150 (1940) (scheme of oil companies to buy up surplus gas from independent suppliers to prevent them from "dumping" it on depressed market at reduced prices). There is some dispute, however, as to what a *per se* rule is. *See* discussion in HOVENKAMP *supra* note 132, at 226-240.

144 *Palmer v. BRG of Georgia, Inc.*, 498 U.S. 46 (1990) (agreement of competing companies dividing up territory where each would offer bar review course to bar examinees *per se* violation of Sherman Act).

145 *Dr. Miles Medical Co. v. John D. Park & Sons Co.*, 220 U.S. 373 (1911) (drug manufacturer may not use resale price maintenance agreement specifying minimum price for which resellers can sell product).

146 *See State Oil Co. v. Khan, supra* note 143, *overruling Albrecht v. Herald Co.*, 390 U.S. 145 (1968) In commenting on *Albrecht*, the Court noted that the defendant newspaper's refusal to sell to the plaintiff distributor because it resold papers to customers at above suggested retail price could well protect consumers from price gouging by monopolist distributors.

147 Section 3 of Clayton Act regulates tying arrangements of goods, while §1 of the Sherman Act covers goods or services.

148 *See, e.g., Eastman Kodak Co. v. Image Technical Services, Inc.*, 504 U.S. 451 (1992) (illegal tying when copy machine manufacturer with 23% market share sold repair parts only to buyers who purchased repair service for it). *But see Jefferson Parish Hosp. Dist. No. 2 v. Hyde*, 466 U.S. 2 (1984) (no illegal tying arrangement where hospital required patients to use its staff anesthesiologists; justification shown).

Yet another vertical restraint is the "exclusive dealing" contract. An exclusive dealing contract is a sales contract in which the buyer agrees not to purchase a competitor's or group of competitors' goods or services. Such agreements, like tying arrangements, are often an effort to use economic power as to one product to promote sales of another.[149] But liability results only if the agreement causes some substantial foreclosure of the market. Concerted refusals to deal in an effort to affect price are *per se* violations.[150]

Monopolization In prohibiting any activities that "monopolize" or "attempt to monopolize," §2 of the Sherman Act outlaws only certain monopolistic *activities,* not the mere existence of monopoly power. It is the *abuse* of monopoly power and the *acquisition* of such power *through unreasonable means* that is prohibited, as distinguished from the attainment of such power through prudent business tactics and innovative products. Abuse of monopoly power generally entails preventing others from entering a field or running competitors out of business.

A description of three practices from recent cases will provide a flavor of the kind of conduct that is the focus of §2.[151] The first practice is "predatory pricing" — selling at below cost to squeeze out competitors. But to prove predatory pricing, it must be shown that the defendant has a reasonable prospect of "recouping its investment in below-cost prices."[152] A second practice is a monopolist's development of a new product that is incompatible with the products of rivals whose business depends on their ability to adapt to industry standards. Yet, courts have been forgiving in this area if the monopolist's new products are improvements, even though rivals are hurt, on the ground that to do otherwise would stifle innovation.[153] A third practice, refusing to deal with weaker competitors, is improper, but only if it can be shown that there is no reason for it other than an anti-competitive one.[154] A variant of refusal to deal is refusal by a monopolist to share facilities with a competitor. But this is improper only if the facility is essential and the competitor cannot feasibly duplicate the facility.[155]

The government has won many monopolization cases, but it is significant that it has rarely succeeded in breaking large companies with monopoly power into competing smaller ones. A significant failure was the suit against International Business Machines (IBM) — abandoned in 1982 after 13 years of litigation and 700

---

149 *See, e.g., Standard Oil Co. of California v. United States,* 337 U.S. 293 (1949) (agreement that retail gas stations only purchase oil company's products illegal since it foreclosed competition in 7% of retail gas sales, deemed a "substantial share" of the market); *compare Tampa Electric Co. v. Nashville Coal Co.,* 365 U.S. 320 (1961) (effect on coal market of exclusive dealing agreement for coal was not substantial, so no violation).

150 *Fed. Trade Comm'n v. Superior Court Trial Lawyers Assoc.,* 493 U.S. 411 (1990) (lawyers' boycott, refusing to accept criminal appointment from court because compensation rates were too low, was *per se* violation of §5 of FTC Act).

151 For a readable summary of this complex area, *see generally* GELLHORN & KOVACIC, *supra* note 132.

152 *Brook Group Ltd. v. Brown & Williamson Corp.,* 509 U.S. 209 (1993) (reversing jury finding that manufacturer's below-cost pricing of name-brand cigarettes undercut plaintiff's generic cigarette sales in the absence of proof that manufacturer would recoup its investment in low prices).

153 *Berkey Photo, Inc. v. Eastman Kodak Co.,* 603 F.2d 263 (2d Cir. 1979) (monopolist Kodak need not disclose new camera designed for exclusive use with its new film because disclosure would retard innovation); *California Computer Products v. IBM Corp.,* 613 F.2d 727 (9th Cir. 1979) (new computer design not §2 violation even though it was incompatible with rival manufacturer's peripheral products).

154 *Aspen Skiing Co. v. Aspen Highlands Skiing Corp.,* 472 U.S. 585 (1985) (refusal to continue joint ski ticket program with one of three competing ski slopes held unlawful).

155 *MCI Communications Corp. v. American Tel. & Tel. Co.,* 708 F.2d 1081, 1150-53 (7th Cir. 1983) (monopolist must share communications interconnections, but need not provide the latest equipment).

days of trial.[156] But a notable success was the breakup of American Telephone & Telegraph, which many have credited with lowering prices and improving service in the telecommunications industry.[157]

Mergers and Acquisitions Section 7 of the Clayton Act prohibits mergers and acquisitions that tend to lessen competition substantially or tend to create a monopoly in any line of commerce.[158] The Act mandates government approval for certain kinds of mergers and requires merging entities to notify the Federal Trade Commission and the Justice Department before specified transactions can be completed.[159] Complex guidelines, issued by those agencies, set out criteria by which they will determine what mergers to challenge.[160]

There are three main categories of mergers which the antitrust laws address. The first is the horizontal merger, defined as a company acquiring a competitor company that is in the same geographic area and market.[161] Regulators will examine the resulting market concentration and what barriers exist to new competitors entering the market.[162] The second kind of merger is the vertical merger, defined as a company starting to perform itself some function it would otherwise employ others to do. An example is a manufacturer acquiring a supplier of components for its product.[163] Vertical mergers in recent years have not been condemned except in the most extreme circumstances, because courts have come to view most of them as efficient and not seriously anti-competitive.[164] The third category is the conglomerate merger. This includes all other types of acquisitions not covered in the other two categories. It often deals with potential anti-competitive effects of joint ventures between large companies[165] or mergers of companies whose businesses are not in direct competition.[166]

---

156 *See United States v. IBM Corp.*, 687 F.2d 591 (2d Cir. 1982), GELLHORN & KOVACIC, *supra* note 132, at 134-136.

157 *United States v. American Tel. & Tel. Co.*, 552 F. Supp. 131 (D.D.C. 1982), *aff'd sub nom Maryland v. United States*, 460 U.S. 1001 (1983).

158 15 U.S.C.A. §7.

159 15 U.S.C.A. §18A requires a pre-merger notification process when a party to the proposed merger has annual net sales or total assets in excess of $100 million and the other merging party has annual net sales or total assets in excess of $10 million and the acquisition price or value of the acquired entity is greater than $15 million. See generally, GELLHORN & KOVACIC, *supra* note 132, at 400-402.

160 *See* 1992 Horizontal Merger Guidelines, 57 Fed. Reg. 41552 (Sep. 10, 1992), discussed in HOVENKAMP, *supra* note 132, §§3.8, 12.4d, 13.5. While the guidelines are not binding, courts give deference to them, *See, e.g., Fed. Trade Comm'n v. Cardinal Health, Inc.* 12 F.Supp.2d 34 (D.D.C. 1998).

161 *See, e.g., Boyertown Burial Casket Co. v. Amedco, Inc.*, 407 F.Supp. 811 (E.D.Pa. 1976) (preliminary injunction entered against tender offer by one casket company to purchase another where there was concentration in the market).

162 *See* 1992 Horizontal Merger Guidelines, *supra* note 160. *See and compare United States v. Philadelphia National Bank*, 374 U.S. 321, 363 (1963) (emphasizing concentration where merging banks would have one-third of Philadelphia market) and *United States v. Phillipsburg National Bank & Trust Co.*, 399 U.S. 350, 368-369 (1970) (relying on high entry barriers to condemn bank merger).

163 *See, e.g., Ford Motor Co. v. United States*, 405 U.S. 562 (1972) (automobile manufacturer acquisition of spark plug manufacturer illegal vertical merger).

164 *Hovenkamp, supra* note 132, §9.4.

165 *United States v. Penn-Olin Chemical Co.*, 378 U.S. 158 (1964) and 386 U.S. 906 (1967) (chemical companies' joint venture to build plant not shown to be violation of Clayton Act).

166 *See, e.g., Federal Trade Comm. v. Procter & Gamble Co.*, 386 U.S. 568 (1967) (violation of §7 when household product manufacturer that did not make bleach acquired bleach manufacturer because buyer was a potential competitor). *See generally* HOVENKAMP, *supra* note 132, §§9.1-9.5 (vertical mergers); 12.1-12.10 (horizontal mergers); and §§13.1-13.5 (conglomerate mergers).

BUSINESS LAW

Price Discrimination Section 2 of the Clayton Act and the Robinson-Patman Act prohibit sellers from engaging in price discrimination — charging different buyers different prices — if competition may be adversely affected. Buyers are also prohibited from inducing or receiving discriminatory prices.[167] Prohibition of price discrimination was designed largely to help small retailers who were being priced out of their markets by large "chain stores." However, it has been widely criticized as overly complex and ineffective at curbing price discrimination. Some also condemn it as hurting rather than helping smaller businesses, as where small businesses band together to negotiate a lower price from a supplier.[168] In addition, a seller can escape liability by showing that it charged a lower price in a good faith effort to "meet competition."[169] The fundamental problem with the Act is that it penalizes low prices, thus making price competition more difficult. It also sometime works at cross purposes with the prohibition against price-fixing. For example, any conversation with a competitor about price could be a *Sherman Act* violation. To avoid this conflict, the Court held that there was no need to verify competitors' prices in order to assert a "meeting competition" defense to price discrimination.[170] Government suits aimed at price discrimination have been significantly reduced since 1977, though private enforcement does continue.[171]

3. Federal Antitrust Remedies and Enforcement Powers

Public Enforcement The federal antitrust laws are unique in that they provide for dual civil enforcement powers in two federal agencies — the Department of Justice and the FTC. In civil actions, equitable relief is usually sought, such as an injunction or a "cease and desist" order. Only the Department of Justice has authority to bring criminal actions for violations of the federal antitrust laws, and it brings many of them. Nearly all of them are for §1 horizontal restraints, such as price-fixing and market division agreements. Under the Sherman Act, the maximum criminal sanction is a $10 million fine, and any antitrust felony can result in fines up to double the corporate defendant's monetary gain or double the victim's monetary loss, whichever is greater. Individual violators of the Sherman or Clayton Acts may be fined up to $350,000 and imprisoned for up to three years.[172]

Private Enforcement Private persons and companies by far file the greatest number of antitrust actions. Congress has sought to encourage private enforcement

---

167 15 U.S.C.A. §§13(a), (f), 14, as amended by the Robinson-Patman Act in 1936. *See, e.g., Best Brands Beverage, Inc. v. Falstaff Brewing Corp.*, 653 F. Supp. 47 (S.D.N.Y. 1985) (preliminary injunction entered rolling back price hike imposed by brewery on only one beer distributor on grounds of price discrimination); *Rose Confections, Inc. v. Ambrosia Chocolates Co.*, 816 F.2d 381 (8th Cir. 1987) (seller's "meeting competition" defense to price discrimination was rejected where seller relied on "assumption and speculation" that competitors were charging lower prices). *See generally* Robert M. Klein, *The Robinson-Patman Act: Jurisdictional Aspects and Elements*, 59 ANTITRUST L.J. 777 (1991).

168 *See* William F. Baxter, *A Parable*, 23 STAN. L. REV. 973 (1971) and HOVENKAMP, *supra* note 132, §14.6. *See, e.g., Mid-South Distributors v. Fed. Trade Comm'n.*, 287 F.2d 512 (5th Cir. 1961) (it was illegal price discrimination for cooperative buying group of small manufacturer-suppliers to buy auto parts at reduced cost through volume rebates in order to compete with larger competitors).

169 *See United States v. United States Gypsum Co.*, 438 U.S. 422 (1978) (holding that "good faith" in charging lower price is all that is required, but discussing problem of the "untruthful buyer") and *Falls City Industries, Inc. v. Vanco Beverage, Inc.*, 460 U.S. 428 (1983) (Congress "intended to allow reasonable pricing responses on an area-specific basis where competitive circumstances warrant them").

170 *See United States v. United States Gypsum Co.*, *supra*, and HOVENKAMP, *supra* note 132, at 523 ("while [the Act] is hostile toward economic competition, it is nevertheless disguised as an antitrust law.").

171 *See* U.S. Dept. of Justice, Report on the Robinson-Patman Act (1977).

172 15 U.S.C.A. §§1-3; 18 U.S.C.A. §3623.

by providing substantial incentives. Section 4 of the Clayton Act provides that private plaintiffs may sue for "treble damages" — three times their actual damages. In addition, states can bring actions for treble damages on behalf of their citizens as consumers. Prevailing private plaintiffs can recover reasonable attorneys' fees, while prevailing defendants ordinarily may not.[173]

4. Exemptions and Reach of Federal Antitrust Laws

Exemptions from federal antitrust regulation are provided for labor unions and regulated industries. Thus, each deregulation of an industry expands the reach of antitrust laws. This was true for the airline industry, which was deregulated in 1976. Another exemption is a "state action" doctrine, which exempts most state or local government regulation from federal antitrust laws. The exemption applies even if the regulation at issue requires what is clearly anti-competitive activity, so long as that activity is actively supervised by a state regulatory agency. Thus, monopoly private electric power utility companies regulated by states that supply most of the power in the country are exempt, even though their prices are controlled and entry into the market is restricted.

The 1st Amendment protects the right to petition government for redress of grievances, so attempts by businesses to influence government action are exempt despite their anti-competitive effects. This includes not just attempts to influence legislation or rules, but also the filing of lawsuits or counterclaims in lawsuits so long as they are legitimate and not merely a sham.[174] The "sham" distinction is difficult to define. In some recent cases, fine distinctions were made based on intent, while more recently the Court seems to have opted for a more objective test.[175]

The Sherman Act explicitly refers to actions that restrain trade or commerce "with foreign nations." This has been held to mean that foreign companies are subject to the Act if their actions were intended to and in fact did affect commerce in the United States.[176] The Department of Justice and the FTC have issued revised proposed international guidelines explaining how antitrust laws apply abroad.[177] The international reach of U.S. antitrust laws is subject to discretionary comity requirements, meaning that courts may decline to enforce U.S. law where it would conflict with the domestic policy of the foreign state, out of respect for that policy.[178]

---

173 15 U.S.C.A. §15.

174 *Eastern Railroad Conference v. Noerr Motor Freight, Inc.*, 365 U.S. 127 (1961) and *United Mine Workers v. Pennington*, 381 U.S. 657 (1965) (applying 1st Amendment immunity to activity aimed at influencing a government agency's purchasing decision).

175 *Compare City of Columbia v. Omni Outdoor Advertising, Inc.*, 499 U.S. 365 (1991) (subjective test applied to efforts to influence zoning, because they were aimed at the ultimate product, i.e. zoning ordinances, rather than as a means of imposing cost and delay on its rival) *with Professional Real Estate Investors, Inc. v. Columbia Pictures Industries, Inc.*, 508 U.S. 49 (1993) (objectively reasonable legal claim filed in court is immune regardless of subjective intent).

176 *United States v. Aluminum Co. of America*, 148 F.2d 416, 444 (2d Cir. 1945) (L. Hand, J.) (U.S. law applied to conspiracy between U.S. and foreign insurance companies to refuse to agree to reinsurance contracts without certain limited liability provisions). The Supreme Court has approved and applied the doctrine, most recently in *Hartford Fire Insurance Co. v. California*, 509 U.S. 764 (1993) (also involving reinsurance agreements). Congress has, by negative implication, approved it as well. *See* 15 U.S.C.A. §6a (prohibiting federal court jurisdiction except where there is intent and effect *vis-a-vis* U.S. commerce).

177 Draft Antitrust Enforcement Guidelines for International Operations, 59 Fed. Reg. 52810-03 (Oct. 19, 1994).

178 *See Hartford Insurance Co., supra* note 180 (denying comity claim of British reinsurance companies based on the fact the conduct in question was only *permitted* by British law; only if conduct is *compelled* by foreign law is comity required).

Also relevant is the "Act of State" doctrine, under which non-commercial acts of foreign states cannot form a basis for suit.[179] Despite the limits of comity, U.S. antitrust law is more aggressive than that of some other countries and its application has surprised some foreign firms. Because the focus is effects in the *United States*, however, the Sherman Act has been held not to apply to a *U. S. company's* actions *in the United States* that had an effect only in *Europe*.[180]

E. Labor Laws

Three areas touching on the employment relationship will be discussed here: protection of employee rights to unionize and engage in concerted and collective activity, employment discrimination based on race, sex and other discriminatory grounds, and the continuing evolution of the law of "wrongful discharge" limiting the employer's right to discharge even for non-discriminatory reasons.

1. Rights to Unionize and to Act and Bargain Collectively

Workers' collective action to improve working conditions has progressed from criminal conspiracy to a federal statutory right.[181] In 1935, Congress passed the National Labor Relations Act (NLRA),[182] which guaranteed the right of employees to form unions, to strike and to bargain collectively with an employer. The NLRA also created the National Labor Relations Board (NLRB), a five-member federal agency that supervises and enforces the NLRA. The NLRB is one of the "independent" administrative agencies discussed in Chapter VI. Its five members are appointed by the President and confirmed by the Senate for overlapping 5-year terms. The NLRB tends to be more "political" than most independent agencies, with Republican members tending to side with employer's and Democratic members inclined to side with unions. The result has been several reversals and modifications of policy, especially in the area of unfair labor practices. Clarity and stability of the law are further hindered by the fact that the NLRB generally makes policy through case-by-case adjudication rather than by regulation.[183]

Workers Covered Private employers whose activities affect interstate commerce are the principal group regulated by the NLRA. The NLRA applies to employees, other

---

179 *See* Foreign Sovereign Immunity Act, 28 U.S.C.A. §1330(a), and *International Assn. of Machinists v. Organization of Petroleum Exporting Companies*, 649 F.2d 1354 (6th Cir. 1981) (OPEC cartel cannot be sued based on Act of State doctrine). *See also* Stephen Calkins, *The October 1992 Supreme Court Term and Antitrust: More Objectivity Than Ever*, 62 ANTITRUST L.J. 327 (1994).

180 *Eurim-Pharm GmbH v. Pfizer*, 593 F.Supp. 1102 (S.D.N.Y. 1984) (territorial restraints imposed in Europe by U.S. drug exporter are not a violation). On the issue of extra-territorial application of antitrust laws, *see* HOVENKAMP, *supra* note 132, §§21.1-21.2. *But cf.* U.S. Department of Justice, Statement of Enforcement Policy Regarding Anticompetitive Conduct that Restricts U.S. Exports, reprinted in 62 Antitrust & Trade Reg. Rep. (BNA) 483 (Apr. 9, 1992) (reversing prior policy so that the Department will now enforce the U.S. antitrust laws against foreign cartels who collude to harm U.S. exports even if there is no direct harm to U.S. consumers).

181 *See* DOUGLAS L. LESLIE, LABOR LAW IN A NUTSHELL 1-4 (West 1992), citing *Commonwealth v. Pullis* (Philadelphia Mayor's Court 1806) (workers refusing to work except for specified wage and seeking to prevent others from doing so guilty of criminal conspiracy). LESLIE, *supra*, provides a succinct overview of U.S. labor law as does WILLIAM B. GOULD, A PRIMER ON AMERICAN LABOR LAW, 3D ED. (M.I.T. Press, Cambridge, Mass. 1993). More comprehensive coverage is provided by the two-volume AMERICAN BAR ASSOCIATION SECTION ON LABOR LAW, THE DEVELOPING LABOR LAW: THE BOARD, THE COURTS AND THE NATIONAL LABOR RELATIONS ACT (Bureau of National Affairs, Washington ABA 1992). A Nutshell that covers both labor organizing rights and individual employment rights is ROBERT N. COVINGTON & KURT H. DECKER, INDIVIDUAL EMPLOYMENT RIGHTS IN A NUTSHELL (West 1995).

182 29 U.S.C.A. §§151-168.

183 *See* Chapter VI, p. 198. Some stability results the presidential tradition, from Franklin D. Roosevelt to the present, for the President to name no more than 3 members from his own party to the Board.

than supervisors and managers, and not to independent contractors. Employees of railroads and airlines are governed by the somewhat different provisions of the Railway Labor Act.[184] Public sector workers (employees of federal, state and local governments and agencies) are not covered by the NLRA, except for federal postal workers. Agricultural workers are outside the protection of the NLRA. Often employees not covered by federal labor laws are covered by similar state laws. California, for example, has an elaborate system governing farm workers.[185]

General Policy Unlike some countries where the *content* of collective bargaining agreements is specified by law or administrative action, U.S. labor laws generally take a "procedural" approach in that they do not dictate the substance of agreements. Instead, they provide the appropriate arena for the union and the employer to "fight it out" with each other using their respective economic weapons, and to come to an agreement if they can.

a. Union Organizing

The most important right that the NLRA protects is the right of employees to form and join unions and to collectively bargain with their employer through their union representatives.[186] When employees want to form a union, they typically must first seek support from a majority of workers in a "bargaining unit" — a group of employees defined by either particular job categories or a particular industry. Employees signal their desire for a union usually by getting other workers to sign authorization cards designating the union as their representative. When 30% of the employees in a bargaining unit have signed such cards, a union election may be required by the NLRB. In such elections, the union organizers will campaign for unionization and the employer often will campaign against the union, but the employer cannot coercively interfere with the union's organizing efforts or the election process.[187] The NLRB oversees elections to ensure that they are fair.[188] If the union already represents a majority of employees, the employer may (but need not) voluntarily recognize the union without the need for an election, although most employers request an election.

Once the union wins recognition from the employer, it becomes the exclusive representative of all workers in its bargaining unit, whether members of the union or not.[189] It will seek to conclude a collective bargaining agreement governing wages and working conditions for its bargaining unit. "Closed shop" agreements, requiring union membership to get a job are illegal.[190] However, the union may and often does negotiate a "union security clause" in the collective bargaining agreement, under which all non-members are required to pay union dues or an amount that represents the portion of union activity related to collective action benefitting all employees in the

---

184 This Act is enforced by a different agency. The reason for having a separate law and bureaucracy for railroad and airline employees is largely one of historical accident.

185 *See* Cal. Labor Code §§1140-1167. Some believe it is superior to the federal NLRA.

186 29 U.S.C.A. §157. However, it also protects some worker rights separate from union activity. *See Nat'l Labor Relations Bd. v. Washington Aluminum Co.*, 370 U.S. 9 (1962) (held protected activity when seven non-union employees left work to protest cold temperatures in their shop).

187 *Id.* §158(a)(1).

188 *Id.* §§159, 160.

189 29 U.S.C.A. §159(a).

190 *Id.* §§158(a)(3), 158(b)(2).

bargaining unit.[191] If the employer has a "good faith reasonable doubt" that the union continues to enjoy the support of a majority of workers, it may poll employees to find out for sure or it may withdraw recognition or seek a Board-supervised election.[192]

b. Unfair Labor Practices

The NLRB protects fairness during elections and at other times by prohibiting certain unfair labor practices. For example, an employer is prohibited from interfering with, restraining, or coercing employees in any way in connection with their right to engage in concerted activities, to protect working conditions, and to join labor organizations for the purpose of collective bargaining.[193] Included in this prohibition are use of spies or other surveillance of union activities, interrogating employees about their union activities, and threats and promises designed to stop union activity. Similarly, the union may not restrain or coerce workers in the exercise of their right to oppose the union or other rights protected by the statute.[194]

The procedure for handling alleged unfair labor practices begins with the union, employee or employer filing a charge with the NLRB. If the NLRB issues a complaint, there is a hearing before an administrative law judge (ALJ) that is prosecuted by lawyers from the NLRB General Counsel's office.[195] If a party disagrees with the ALJ's decision, there will be a hearing before the NLRB. However, that hearing will be on the record made before the ALJ. Although the NLRB hearing sounds similar to appellate court review of a trial court, there is rarely any oral argument and the NLRB is not bound by ALJ fact-finding. After the NLRB decision is rendered, the Board can apply to the U.S. Court of Appeals for enforcement of its decision or the losing party can obtain judicial review in the same court.[196] The complaint process is long and involved and unions often complain that this has made the NLRB largely ineffective to protect the rights of unions and their members.

c. Collective Bargaining, Strikes and Other Concerted Activity

Both the employer and union are obliged to "bargain in good faith." While good faith *bargaining* is mandatory, agreement is not, and it is a difficult question whether a party who insists that particular terms be in the contract is bargaining in good faith.[197] The good faith bargaining requirement applies to mandatory subjects of bargaining — wages and conditions of work, including issues of layoffs, vacation and sick leave, and fringe benefits. Other non-mandatory subjects that have only an indirect effect on worker life may be the subject of bargaining. However, some

---

191 *Nat'l Labor Relations Bd. v. General Motors*, 373 U.S. 734 (1963). Disputes arise over how much is attributable to these activities. *See Airline Pilots Assoc. v. Miller*, 523 U.S. 866 (1998).

192 *See generally Allentown Mack Sales & Service, Inc. v. Nat'l Labor Relations Bd.*, 522 U.S. 359 (1998) (discussing the standards and sufficiency of evidence of "reasonable doubt").

193 29 U.S.C.A. §158(a). In cases of alleged discrimination against workers for union activities, the Supreme Court has held that, once it has been shown that union membership was a substantial factor in the employer action, the burden of proof shifts to the employer to prove non-discriminatory motivation. Where there are mixed motives, the employer must show that the same result would have occurred in absence of anti-union animus. *Nat'l Labor Relations Bd. v. Transportation Management Corp.*, 462 U.S. 393 (1983). This is similar to the standard used in employment discrimination cases. *See infra* p. 569.

194 *Id.* §158(b)(1).

195 Federal ALJs and administrative hearings were discussed in Chapter VI, pp. 196-198.

196 *Id.* §160(e), (f).

197 *Compare Nat'l Labor Relations Bd. v. American National Insurance Co.*, 343 U.S. 395 (1952) (insistence on broad "management functions" clause is still good faith) *with Nat'l Labor Relations Bd. v. Reed & Prince Mfg. Co.*, 205 F.2d 131 (1st Cir. 1953) (refusal of management to find any common ground with union proposals and insistence on management discretion on every issue held not good faith).

decisions of management are not mandatory bargaining issues even though there is clearly a direct impact on workers. For example, it is completely up to management whether the plant will start making a new product. Plant closings that result in layoffs have also been held to be management decisions on the basic scope and direction of the entire enterprise not subject to mandatory bargaining.[198] On the other hand, if an employer decides to subcontract out work previously done by union employees and the subcontractor will perform that work under similar employment conditions, such a management decision has been held to be subject to mandatory bargaining.[199] It is widely assumed that loss of jobs through automation is a managerial decision not subject to bargaining.

Both sides, labor and management, may use their economic power to pressure the other side into an agreement. The union's right to strike is protected by the NLRA and employees may not be discharged or disciplined for engaging in such conduct.[200] However, employers have the right to replace the striking workers and go on with business if possible.[201] Thus, the Court has drawn the line between discharge, which is not permitted, and replacement, which is. The right to replace exists only for economic strikes (wages, working conditions, etc.), not if the strike is to protest an unfair labor practice.[202]

The employer may impose a lockout (refusing to permit employees to enter the premises to work), either as a means of exerting economic pressure on workers or as a preemptive device in anticipation of a union strike or other tactic. So long as the use of the lockout is not so hostile to the union's interest in organizing and bargaining as to "destroy or frustrate the process of collective bargaining," the lockout is legal.[203] Sit-down strikes (when employees refuse to work, but stay at their work stations) are not protected and may violate state criminal trespass laws, thus making participating workers subject to discharge by the employer or arrest by the local police.[204]

Certain strikes are illegal under the NLRA. Foremost among these is the "secondary boycott."[205] Generally, workers may strike only against their own employer, known as the "primary employer." Strikes or picketing directed against companies that do business with the primary employer — in order to pressure the primary employer into concessions — are illegal secondary boycotts. However, action against a second employer is permissible if the second employer is working as an "ally" of the first by, for example, allowing a manufacturing step to be performed on its premises.[206] Similarly, the primary employer is not immune from union appeals to

---

198 *First National Maintenance Co. v. Nat'l Labor Relations Bd.*, 452 U.S. 666 (1981) (company closed division). The union may be entitled to 60-days notice under another law, 29 U.S.C.A. §2101. Moreover, the *effects* of a plant closing on workers is a mandatory bargaining subject, such as issues of the order of layoffs, rights to transfer to other divisions or plants, and the like.

199 *Fibreboard Paper Products v. Nat'l Labor Relations Bd.*, 379 U.S. 203 (1964).

200 29 U.S.C.A. §158(a)(3).

201 *Nat'l Labor Relations Bd. v. Mackay Radio and Telegraph Co.*, 304 U.S. 333 (1938). Overruling the *Mackay* doctrine has been a major legislative agenda item for organized labor for some time.

202 *See Mastro Plastics v. Nat'l Labor Relations Bd.*, 350 U.S. 270 (1956). The distinction between being fired and being replaced is one that is lost on many workers. The difference is that replaced strikers retain the right to be called back to work if positions become available.

203 *American Shipbuilding Co. v. Nat'l Labor Relations Bd.*, 380 U.S. 300 (1965).

204 *Nat'l Labor Relations Bd. v. Fansteel Metallurgical Corp.*, 306 U.S. 240 (1939).

205 29 U.S.C.A. §158(b)(4).

206 *See Nat'l Labor Relations Bd. v. Office Appliances Conference Bd. (Royal Typewriter)*, 228 F.2d 553 (2d Cir. 1955) (picketing of typewriter repair facility performing repairs for struck employer permitted).

secondary workers who come to the work site of the struck employer if they do work that is "related" to that done by the strikers.[207] It is proper for unions to appeal to consumers not to purchase a secondary employer's products if the appeal is accomplished by off-premises leafleting or newspaper advertisements. Such activity is probably protected by the 1st Amendment in any event. "Hot cargo" agreements, in which employers agree with unions not to deal with non-union companies, are also illegal secondary boycotts.[208]

From all this it is clear that the effectiveness of a strike or threat of a strike will vary depending on many factors, including the state of the economy and willingness of other workers to support the union's position. In recent bad economic times, workers' need for a job has made strikes less attractive as a weapon. When strikes do occur, replacement has been a successful technique for counteracting them. Replacement was used successfully in the 1990 New York Daily News strike and the 1992 Caterpillar Tractor Company strike, though in the Caterpillar case the replacement workers were not hired permanently. Thus, in recent years, employers have been in a better position than the union to wait out an impasse in bargaining. On the other hand, lower unemployment rates and a generally better economy made the 1997 strike against United Parcel Service a notable success for the union involved.

Regardless of who wins when there is a strike or a lockout, such disputes are costly in both economic and human terms. For this reason, some commentators have argued for mandatory arbitration when voluntary agreement is not possible, but that would require a major change in the law which Congress has been unwilling to make. The percentage of U.S. workers in private industry covered by collective bargaining agreements has declined substantially in recent years. It has gone from 33.2% in 1955 to 14.5% in 1996.[209] This decrease may be due in part to more conservative attitudes among workers in recent years and a perceived lesser need for the protection a union affords. But most of the change is probably due to changes in the global marketplace. The three most heavily unionized industries — steel, automobile and basic manufacturing — have essentially left the U.S. and moved overseas.

d. Disputes Under the Collective Bargaining Agreement

Collective bargaining agreements are governed by federal common law, the Court having concluded that Congress delegated to courts the power to develop a federal common law of labor contracts.[210] However, most disputes about the interpretation of collective bargaining agreements do not get to the courts since the parties usually agree to some form of arbitration for all disputes arising under the agreement. These disputes, called "grievances," are then decided by the private

---

207 *Local 761, International Union of Electrical Workers v. Nat'l Labor Relations Bd. (General Electric)*, 366 U.S. 667 (1961) (striking picketers could appeal to maintenance and other workers not to work when they arrived at primary employer's plant).

208 29 U.S.C.A. §158(e). In a rarely used provision of the law, the President is given special powers to end a strike in a national emergency, including the right to seek an injunction. However, presidential intervention in strikes has almost always been informal efforts to talk or "jaw-bone" the parties into ironing out their differences.

209 Source: U.S. Dep't of Labor. Public employees (employees of federal, state and local governments) have unionized at a higher rate, but the number of public employees in the U.S. is small.

210 *Textile Workers Union v. Lincoln Mills*, 353 U.S. 448 (1957); *Local 174, Teamsters v. Lucas Flour Co.*, 369 U.S. 95 (1962). For a discussion of the ordinarily limited nature of federal common law, *see* Chapter I, pp. 32-33. State courts have concurrent jurisdiction and must apply federal common law, *Charles Dowd Box Co. v. Courtney*, 368 U.S. 502 (1962), and the defendant may remove such a case to federal court because it involves an issue of federal law. *Avco Corp. v. Aero Lodge*, 390 U.S. 557 (1968).

arbitrator, whose decision is final. Courts may disturb a grievance arbitration decision only in limited circumstances.[211] Workers, the union and the employer can file grievances, though employer grievances are rare. The union may dispute such things as the meaning of a "no-strike" clause or whether the employer can contract out work. The union may seek relief for an individual worker and "grieve" such things as the proper calculation of seniority rights or severance or vacation pay for a particular worker.[212]

Courts will intervene to order arbitration if the employer or union has ignored the required grievance procedure. This issue arises often with "no-strike" clauses, where the union goes out on strike even though it has given up its right to strike and has agreed to arbitrate disagreements. A seeming obstacle to injunctions against strikes is the Norris-LaGuardia Act of 1932, which prohibits federal courts from enjoining any strike.[213] However, the Supreme Court held that the anti-injunction provision had to be accommodated to the federal labor policy of encouraging arbitration of disputes, so it read the applicable statutes as allowing injunctions against strikes that violate no-strike clauses.[214] Thus, the employer can properly seek to enjoin strikes in breach of the agreement and seek appropriate damages from the union. Consistent with this reasoning, if the strike is over an issue that is not arbitrable (such as a sympathy strike), the Norris-LaGuardia Act applies and injunctive relief is *not* available.[215] A recent illustration of a strike still within the Norris-LaGuardia prohibition on injunctions was the refusal of longshoremen working on a dock to handle cargo from the Soviet Union in protest of its military intervention in Afghanistan. This kind of work stoppage was not arbitrable under the collective bargaining agreement, so it could not be enjoined.[216]

e. The Union's Duty of Fair Representation

The union has a "duty of fair representation" requiring it to represent the interests of all the bargaining unit's employees (both members and non-members), both in collective bargaining and in pursuing grievances under any collective bargaining agreement it concludes. For breach of this duty the union may be sued for damages. Generally, the union has considerable discretion in fulfilling its bargaining duties, and can pick and choose among issues it will assert. However, racially motivated union bargaining for less favorable treatment for minority members constitutes a breach of the duty of fair representation.[217] As for its duty with regard to presenting grievances of its members, the Court has held that the union has some discretion and may refuse to pursue some grievances. However, it may not do so arbitrarily or based on personal animus or other bad faith reason.[218] The union must pursue competently those grievances it does choose to take.

---

211 *See United Paperworkers International Union v. Misco, Inc.*, 484 U.S. 29 (1987) (absent fraud by the parties or the arbitrator's dishonesty, courts cannot reconsider the merits of the award; reinstatement of employee who used drugs affirmed). Arbitration was discussed in Chapter VII, p. 243.

212 Employment discrimination claims are not subject to an arbitration requirement unless there is a clear and unmistakable waiver of the covered employees' rights to a judicial forum" in the collective bargaining agreement. *Wright v. Universal Maritime Service Corp.*, ___ U.S. ___, 119 S.Ct. 391 (1998).

213 28 U.S.C.A. §104.

214 *Boys Markets, Inc. v. Retail Clerks Local 770*, 398 U.S. 235 (1970).

215 *Buffalo Forge Co. v. United Steelworkers*, 428 U.S. 397 (1976).

216 *Jacksonville Bulk Terminals v. International Longshoremen's Union*, 457 U.S. 702 (1982).

217 *Steele v. Louisville & Nashville Ry.*, 323 U.S. 192 (1944).

218 *Vaca v. Sipes*, 386 U.S. 171 (1967) (union could decline to press grievance of employee denied the right to return to work for medical reasons where employee's medical evidence was not strong).

2. Employment Discrimination

Title VII of the Civil Rights Act of 1964 prohibits discrimination in employment or employment opportunities on account of race, color, sex, national origin, or religion.[219] The Equal Employment Opportunity Commission (EEOC) is the federal administrative agency that has power both to handle administrative complaints of violations and to sue to redress violations in cases it deems sufficiently important to pursue. Title VII applies to all employers in all industries that affect interstate commerce and, since 1972, includes state and local governments.[220]

Procedure A person with a discrimination claim may not file suit immediately, but must first file an administrative complaint with the EEOC and give it or any similar state or local agency the opportunity to investigate.[221] The agency will provide a "right-to-sue" letter if it finds no grounds for the claim or if it finds grounds, but is unable to obtain a settlement of the claim. In addition, permission to sue is granted if 180 days have expired and the claimant wishes to sue. Incredible delays in processing administrative claims have made both the EEOC and most state agencies largely ineffective in gaining administrative compliance, thus leaving enforcement by private suits as the most common avenue of relief. A plaintiff can sue for injunctive relief or for damages.[222] An important provision of the law that serves to make private enforcement a reality is the provision for a successful plaintiff's recovery of attorney fees from the defendant.[223]

Proving Discrimination   One method of proving discrimination is to point to direct evidence of discriminatory motive.[224] When direct proof of discrimination is not available, Title VII law allows inferential proof of intentional discrimination based on "disparate treatment" in a three-step process.[225] For example, job applicants need to prove only that they are members of a protected class, that they are qualified for the job for which they applied and that the employer did not hire them and continued to seek applicants with their qualifications. Once this is shown, the burden of proof shifts to the *employer* to produce evidence that the failure to hire was *not*

---

219 42 U.S.C.A. §§2000e *et seq.* For more complete treatment, *see* MARK A. ROTHSTEIN ET AL., EMPLOYMENT LAW §§3.1 *et seq.* (West 1994), a two-volume treatise providing an overview of employment law outside the area of unionization and collective bargaining. *See also* MACK A. PLAYER, FEDERAL LAW OF EMPLOYMENT DISCRIMINATION (West 1992). Other prohibitions passed in 1964 ban racial discrimination in public accommodations (Title II), federally-funded programs (Title VI), and sales or rentals of housing (Title VIII). Only Title VII will be discussed here, Title VII law is more developed and many of its features have been adopted in litigation of discrimination claims under other statutes.

220 Constitutional challenges to basing anti-discrimination laws on the interstate commerce power have been rejected. *See Heart of Atlanta Motel v. United States*, 379 U.S. 241 (1964). Power to include state and local governments is granted under §5 of the 14th Amendment. *Fitzpatrick v. Bitzer*, 427 U.S. 445 (1976). States and local governments also have anti-discrimination laws and it is clear that Congress did not intend to preempt such laws or remedies when it passed Title VII. Since 1991, Title VII has applied to U.S. citizens working abroad.

221 The time limit for filing is 180 days, unless a charge has been filed with an appropriate state or local agency, in which case it is 300 days.

222 42 U.S.C.A. §2000e-5. An EEOC determination of "no reasonable cause" is not binding on the court in a later suit, but it may be admissible in evidence at trial. *Cf.* FRE 803(8).

223 42 U.S.C.A. §2000e-5(k). Though the statute provides that the "prevailing party" is to be awarded fees, this is read as imposing a double standard, with prevailing *plaintiffs* receiving fees as a matter of course, but prevailing *defendants* receiving fees only if the plaintiff's suit was completely groundless.

224 *See, e.g. Grant v. Hazelitt Strip-Casting Corp.*, 880 F.2d 1564 (2d. Cir 1989) (in age discrimination case, employer memo stated that it was looking for a "young man . . . between 30 and 40 years old").

225 *See McDonnell Douglas Corp. v. Green*, 411 U.S. 792 (1973).

discriminatory.[226] If in response the plaintiff can then show that the non-discriminatory reason was a "pretext" for discrimination, the plaintiff has proven intentional discrimination.[227] In addition, discrimination may be shown by proving that there is "systematic disparate treatment" of minorities, as evidenced by gross under-representation of minorities in given positions.[228] In response, the employer may seek to prove that its overall record in promotions shows racial balance, but this is not a conclusive rebuttal of discrimination.

Title VII allows recovery for discrimination even when the employer has no intent to discriminate: "The Act proscribes not only overt discrimination, but also practices that are fair in form, but discriminatory in operation."[229] Where a qualification that is neutral on its face has a "disparate impact" on a protected class, it can constitute unlawful discrimination. Once disparate impact is shown, the burden is shifted to the employer to show that the qualification "is job related" and "consistent with business necessity."[230] All educational requirements or tests that have the effect of disqualifying minorities at a disproportionate rate must be determined to be job-related.[231] Similarly, even though an employer can show statistically that women live longer than men and that therefore that their pension costs are greater, that is no basis for requiring women employees to make larger contributions to its pension fund than men employees.[232]

Basing discrimination claims on discriminatory effect under Title VII has improved the chances of state and local government employees recovering for discrimination. Absent Title VII, public employees must rely solely on the equal protection clause, which requires proof of intentional discrimination.[233]

Defenses to Discrimination Other than seeking to show the non-discriminatory basis for its action, employers may rely on the defense of "bona fide occupational qualification" or BFOQ. BFOQ is narrowly construed. First, a protected group may be excluded from consideration for a job only if the relevant characteristic is closely related to the essence of the employer's business.[234] Thus, in an often-cited case, a

---

226 *Furnco Construction Corp. v. Waters*, 438 U.S. 567 (1978) (employer preference for known over unknown applicants not discriminatory). These non-discriminatory grounds may be otherwise illegitimate or even illegal; if the action was taken based on them, it is not discriminatory. *See Hazen Paper Co. v. Biggins*, 507 U.S.604 (1993) (employer fired plaintiff weeks before plaintiff's pension would have vested; not age discrimination).

227 *But see St. Mary's Honor Center v. Hicks*, 509 U.S. 502 (1993) (just because trial court disbelieves the employer's stated reason does not mean that it must find discrimination).

228 *Hazelwood School District v. United States*, 433 U.S. 299 (1977) (disparities between actual and expected representation of minorities among teachers).

229 *Griggs v. Duke Power Co.*, 401 U.S. 424 (1971) (high school diploma requirement that excluded more minorities than whites). *See also New York City Transit Authority v. Beazer*, 440 U.S. 568 (1979) (arrest record). *Compare New York Transit Authority v. Beazer, supra* (ban on employment of *methadone users* upheld despite statistics showing greater number of blacks and Hispanics are on the drug; lack of other legitimate requirements, such as education, could account for disparity).

230 42 U.S.C.A. §2000e-2(k)(1)(A)(I).

231 *See Albemarle Paper Co. v. Moody*, 422 U.S. 405 (1975).

232 *Los Angeles Department of Water & Power v. Manhart*, 435 U.S. 702 (1978).

233 *See* Chapter IX, pp. 328-338. Public employees may nonetheless have to resort to the equal protection clause if Title VII is not available, such as when the claimant has missed the 180 or 300-day limitation period for filing Title VII claims with the EEOC. The remedies are cumulative.

234 Race can never be a BFOQ. Yet, there may be jobs that require persons of a particular race, such as an acting job where racial authenticity is desired. While such a job qualification has been considered to be a "business necessity," recent changes possibly place this in doubt. 42 U.S.C.A. §2000e-2(k)(1)(C)(2) (business necessity cannot be a defense to intentional discrimination).

court rejected as not a BFOQ an airline's requirement that all airline attendants be women. The airline justified its requirement on the ground that women attendants allayed psychological fears of passengers, but the "essence" of the airline's business was providing safe transportation and this requirement had no relationship to that purpose.[235] Second, a BFOQ is proper only if the employer has a factual basis for concluding that all or substantially all applicants in the protected class lack the qualifications for that position or that it is impracticable to determine which can and which cannot perform the job.[236] This narrow definition of BFOQ has resulted in women obtaining jobs that traditionally have gone only to men because physical requirements effectively excluded women, such as police officer, firefighter and construction worker. In a recent BFOQ case, the Court invalidated a ban on fertile women working with lead in a battery plant, finding that there was no showing that fertile women were any less able to do the job. The Court found insufficient the employer's concern for tort liability should there be damage to any fetus present in the woman's body.[237] On the other hand, the Court upheld as a proper BFOQ a ban on women guards in a men's maximum security prison where sexual predators were mixed in with the general population and attacks on women guards would also present a threat to the general order in the prison.[238]

Affirmative Action The circumstances under which affirmative action plans are constitutional have been discussed.[239] In *United Steelworkers v. Weber*,[240] the Court held that Title VII permits employers to give preferential treatment based on race pursuant to a formal affirmative action plan adopted to remedy a "conspicuous racial imbalance in traditionally segregated job categories." In addition, the plan must be "reasonable" in that it must be a temporary attempt to address imbalance and must not "unduly" interfere with opportunities of white males. This last requirement means at least that no white workers may be fired to remedy an imbalance. Thus, in *Weber* the Supreme Court approved a plan agreed to between the union and an employer whereby 50% of the persons admitted into an apprenticeship program for skilled trades would be black until the proportion of black skilled trade workers approximated the black population in the area. Similarly, when courts order "affirmative action as may be appropriate" as authorized by Title VII, they must follow the same guidelines.[241]

Sexual Harassment In *Meritor Savings Bank v. Vinson*, the Supreme Court confirmed that Title VII could be used to redress sexual harassment, since sexual harassment can alter the "terms, conditions or privileges" of employment based on

---

235 *Diaz v. Pan American Airways, Inc.*, 442 F.2d 385 (5th Cir. 1971) ("While a pleasant environment, enhanced by the obvious cosmetic effect that female stewardesses provide," coupled with their women's apparently greater ability to quiet psychological fears of passengers "may all be important, they are tangential to the essence of the business involved").

236 *See Western Airlines v. Criswell*, 472 U.S. 400 (1984) (in age discrimination case, mandatory retirement of flight engineers at age 60 is not BFOQ). *See also Diaz, supra.*

237 *International Union, United Auto Workers v. Johnson Controls, Inc.*, 499 U.S. 187 (1991).

238 *Dothard v. Rawlinson*, 433 U.S. 321 (1977).

239 Chapter IX, pp. 330-332.

240 443 U.S. 193 (1979). *See* Chapter II, p. 53, where the statutory interpretation aspects of the case are discussed.

241 42 U.S.C.A. §2000e(5)(g)(1). *Local 28 of Sheet Metal Workers' Int. Ass'n v. Equal Employment Opp. Comm'n*, 478 U.S. 421 (1986). The same standards discussed here apply to affirmative action based on sex. *Johnson v. Transportation Agency, Santa Clara County*, 480 U.S. 616 (1987).

sex.[242] There are two legal theories used: "quid pro quo" and "hostile environment." The *Vinson* case was an example of the former, where giving in to the sexual demands of a supervisor was understood to be a *quid pro quo* for continued employment. In a "hostile environment" situation, usually the victim suffers no economic consequences, but unwelcome sexual advances and other acts of gender animosity or sexually charged work behavior are so "severe or pervasive" that they can be said to have altered the victim's employment conditions. In judging whether there has been such a change, the EEOC and many courts have held that an objective standard of the "reasonable victim," usually a woman, is to be applied. This is primarily because a sex-blind reasonable *person* standard "tends to be male-biased and tends to systematically ignore the experience of women."[243]

The facts of hostile environment cases are various. In one case, the court held insufficient five mild sexual advances by a supervisor.[244] In another, the court deemed insufficient "undoubtedly inappropriate" incidents of a supervisor rubbing the plaintiff's leg, kissing her and, after rejection, refusing to speak with her, teasing her about her relationship with a co-worker and being condescending toward her.[245] A situation deemed sufficient was where a supervisor called plaintiff "honey" and "dear," touched her shoulders, asked her what kind of underwear she wore and what kind of birth control she used, and said that it was his turn to have his way with her.[246] Another case deemed sufficient involved six abusive incidents during three weeks of employment including off-color jokes, comments on complainant's appearance, leaning on or rubbing her back, placing a hand on her shoulder, and calling her at home.[247] Sexual harassment by members of the same sex is also actionable, as the Supreme Court made clear in a recent case.[248] Liability was proper in a case where a male heterosexual employee was singled out for abuse because he wore an earring and otherwise did not conform to his co-workers' view of appropriate masculine behavior.[249] Recently, the Supreme Court clarified the circumstances under which sexually harassing action of a company's employees will subject the company to liability, permitting liability even when the employer lacks specific knowledge of the abuse. However, the employer can avoid liability if it has provided adequate procedures for worker complaints and the worker unreasonably failed to use them.[250]

---

242 477 U.S. 57 (1986). *See also Harris v. Forklift Systems, Inc.*, 510 U.S. 17 (1993) (no need to show psychological injury). Sexual harassment has been held by some lower courts to constitute a violation of the equal protection clause of the 14th Amendment as well. *See Bohen v. City of East Chicago*, 799 F.2d 1180 (7th Cir. 1986).

243 *Ellison v. Brady*, 924 F.2d 872, 878-79 (9th Cir. 1991).

244 *Chamberlin v. 101 Realty*, 915 F.2d 777, 782-83 (1st Cir. 1990).

245 *Saxton v. AT&T*, 10 F.3d 526, 528, 534 (7th Cir. 1993).

246 *Beardsley v. Webb*, 30 F.3d 524, 528-29 (4th Cir. 1994).

247 *Canada v. Boyd Group, Inc.*, 809 F.Supp. 771, 776 (D.Nev. 1992).

248 *Oncale v. Sundowner Offshore Services, Inc.*, 523 U.S. 75 (1998) (plaintiff forcibly subjected to sex-related, humiliating actions against him by co-workers and supervisor in the presence of the rest of the crew and to physical assaulted in a sexual manner and threaten of rape).

249 *Doe v. City of Belleville, Illinois*, 119 F.3d 563 (7th Cir. 1997).

250 *Faragher v. City of Boca Raton*, 524 U.S. 775 (1998); *Burlington Industries v. Ellerth*, 524 U.S. 742 (1998). However, the Court recently declined to extend liability for harassing actions taken against students by employees of schools unless the plaintiff can show that the school knew of the conduct and responded to it with "deliberate indifference." *Gebser v. Lago Vista Independent School District*, 524 U.S. 274 (1998). Also possible are racial harassment claims. *See Monteiro v. Tempe Union High School District*, 158 F.3d 1022 (9th Cir. 1998)

Pregnancy Discrimination While Title VII protects against sex discrimination, the Supreme Court held in 1976 that differing treatment based on pregnancy did not constitute sex discrimination.[251] Congress responded by passing the Pregnancy Discrimination Act in 1978, making clear that it considered discrimination on the basis of pregnancy to be sex discrimination.[252]

Equal Pay The Equal Pay Act requires pay for women to be equal to that earned by men who perform "equal work on jobs the performance of which requires equal skill, effort, and responsibility, and which are performed under similar working conditions" in the same place of employment.[253] Thus, in one case, female guards at a women's prison made out an Equal Pay Act violation when they showed that their retirement benefits were lower than those of male guards at a men's prison.[254]

Age and Disability Discrimination Age discrimination by private and public employers is prohibited by the 1967 federal Age Discrimination in Employment Act and applies to employees over 40.[255] Compulsory retirement at age 65 is prohibited except for certain executive and "high-level policy making" positions.[256] Discrimination against individuals with physical or mental disabilities is redressed by the Americans with Disabilities Act, which provides remedies similar to Title VII.[257] Employment discrimination laws apply to protect U.S. citizens when working for U.S. or U.S.-controlled foreign employers overseas.[258]

3. Wrongful Discharge

The employment "at-will" doctrine became well established in the late 19th century. Under it, employers could fire workers whenever they wished, absent a contractual agreement to the contrary. As the Tennessee Supreme Court stated in one case, the employer must be left without interference "to discharge or retain employees at will for good cause or for no cause, or even for bad cause without thereby being guilty of an unlawful act *per se*."[259] While the at-will doctrine continues to this day, statutes such as those discussed in the last section have limited the employer's power of dismissal for certain prohibited or discriminatory reasons. But even beyond these statutes, courts exercising their common law power have gradually

---

251 *General Electric v. Gilbert*, 429 U.S. 125 (1976) (upholding a medical disability leave plan that excluded disability based on pregnancy).

252 42 U.S.C.A. §2000e(k).

253 29 U.S.C.A. §206(d).

254 *Marcoux v. State of Maine*, 797 F.2d 1100 (1st Cir. 1986). The Equal Pay Act clearly overlaps with Title VII, but a plaintiff may wish to use the Equal Pay Act since it does not require administrative exhaustion of remedies and has a 2 or 3-year limitations period rather than 180 days. *See Washington County v. Gunther*, 452 U.S. 161 (1981) (discussing intersection of Title VII and the Equal Pay Act).

255 29 U.S.C.A. §623 *et seq. See* cases *supra* in notes 224, 226 and 236.

256 29 U.S.C.A. §631(c). Unlike other forms of discrimination, it is not clear whether discriminatory impact applies to age discrimination. *Compare Ellis v. United Airlines*, 73 F.3d 999 (10th Cir. 1996) (no) with *Smith v. City of Des Moines*, 99 F.3d 1466 (8th Cir. 1996) (yes). *See also Marks v. Loral Corp.*, 68 Cal. Rptr.2d 1 (Cal.App. 1997) (not age discrimination to prefer lower-paid workers).

257 42 U.S.C.A. §12111 *et seq.* In its first case under the ADA, the Court ruled recently that the ADA applies to people with HIV, the precursor to AIDS. *Bragdon v. Abbott*, 524 U.S. 624 (1998) (dentist who refused to treat patient with HIV cannot refuse in absence of medical evidence of harm).

258 29 U.S.C.A. §623(h) (age); 42 U.S.C.A. §2000e-1(c) (Title VII).

259 *Payne v. Western & Atlantic R.R.*, 81 Tenn. 507 (1884) (holding it proper for employer-railroad to discharge anyone who shopped at plaintiff's store). The at-will doctrine at one time was thought to be constitutionally required. *See Adair v. United States*, 208 U.S. 161 (1908) (federal statutes barring employer from firing employee for union membership violated due process).

been eroding the at-will employment doctrine by recognizing a cause of action for "wrongful discharge" in certain circumstances.[260]

Protection of Whistle-Blowers The first cases in this direction and the most widespread common law exception to the at-will employment doctrine are discharges that violate public policy. In the seminal case in this area, the California Court of Appeals held improper the firing of an employee for refusing to testify falsely as instructed by his employer.[261] Most recently, the Supreme Court permitted suit under a Civil War-era statute by an at-will employee who claimed he was fired in retaliation for obeying a grand jury subpoena and to deter him from testifying at a criminal trial.[262] Other cases have involved discharges of employees for performing a public obligation (such as jury duty),[263] or in retaliation for the employee's exercise of a constitutional or statutory right, or reporting employer violations of the law (sometimes called "whistle-blowing").[264] These examples have all served as a basis for imposing compensatory and punitive damages upon offending employers.[265]

"Just Cause" Requirements of Implied Contracts More far-reaching are cases finding an implied contract not to dismiss an employee in the absence of "just cause." For example, a company's personnel manual or handbooks may state that, as a matter of policy, the company will only dismiss workers for good and sufficient cause. If the employee is aware of this policy and continues to work for the company, a court may find that there is an implied contract, based on the terms of the company policy.[266] In the words of one court, if an employer "creates an atmosphere of job security and fair treatment with promises of specific treatment in specific situations and an employee is induced thereby to remain on the job," those promises will be enforced.[267] This kind of contract is easily avoided by an employer who could write company manuals to make it clear that the arrangement is an "at-will" arrangement. However, publicizing the employer's intention to treat employees this way will undercut efforts to attract and retain qualified employees. Moreover, companies usually have no interest in dismissing employees without any basis.

The promise of "just cause" suits has not been fully realized in part because the financial incentive is not there for lawyers to bring such suits. Unlike employment discrimination and other civil rights cases, where the statute provides that attorneys' fees can be recovered by a winning plaintiff from the defendant, suits based on a

---

260 *See generally* ROTHSTEIN ET AL, *supra* note 222, §§9.3-9.20 and COVINGTON & DECKER, *supra* note 181, at 221-272.

261 *Petermann v. International Brotherhood of Teamsters*, 344 P.2d 25 (Cal.App. 1959).

262 *Haddle v. Garrison*, ___ U.S. ___, 119 S Ct 489 (1998) (suit under 42 U.S.C.A. §1985(2) upheld).

263 *Nees v. Hocks*, 536 P.2d 512 (Ore. 1975). Now virtually all states and the federal government have statutes prohibiting this. *See* ROTHSTEIN ET AL., *supra* note 222, §4.31.

264 *Garibaldi v. Lucky Food Stores, Inc.*, 726 F.2d 1367 (9th Cir. 1984) (employee of food store reported adulterated milk after being ordered to deliver it) (applying California law). Today three quarters of the states have statutes protecting "whistle-blowers" in some situations. *See* ROTHSTEIN ET AL, *supra* note 222, §9.18.

265 See, *e.g.*, *Sheets v. Teddy's Frosted Foods*, 427 A.2d 385 (Conn. 1980) (at-will employee could sue for discharge for efforts to insure employer followed state product quality standards).

266 *See, e.g. Toussaint v. Blue Cross & Blue Shield of Michigan*, 292 N.W.2d 880 (Mich. 1980); *Duldulao v. Saint Mary of Nazareth Hosp.*, 505 N.E.2d 314, 317 (Ill. 1987) (listing 25 jurisdictions recognizing contractually binding force of employee handbooks); *Foley v. Interactive Data*, 254 Cal.Rptr. 211, 665 P.2d 373 (Cal. 1988). In some states, it is not even necessary that the employee be aware of the company policy. *But see Sabetay v. Sterling Drug, Inc.*, 506 N.E.2d 919, 923 (N.Y. 1987) (requiring express agreement to limit employer's "unfettered right to terminate at will").

267 *Thompson v. St. Regis Paper Co.*, 685 P.2d 1081, 1087-1088 (Wash. 1984).

common law claim for wrongful discharge go by the normal "American rule" on attorneys' fees.[268] Lawyers and clients in "just cause" cases would prefer to work on a contingent fee basis.[269] However, it is often the case that only dismissed employees in upper management positions will have a salary high enough that the amount of damages will be sufficient to attract legal representation.

Breach of Covenant of Good Faith and Fair Dealing A few states allow wrongful discharge claims to be based on an alternative theory that employment contracts, like all other contracts, contain an implied "covenant of good faith and fair dealing," meaning that both sides promise to abide by the contract in good faith. If the employer fires an employee for an arbitrary reason, the employee can claim that this covenant of good faith was breached.[270] The distinct advantage of this theory of recovery is that, although the duty of good faith is one implied from the existence of a contract, breach of that duty is considered a *tort* rather than a breach of contract. The importance of this is that more types of damages are recoverable for torts than for contract breach, including possible punitive damage awards for intentional breaches of good faith.[271]

Judicial activity in this area has prompted the Uniform Commissioners on State Laws to act. They proposed a Model Employment Termination Act.[272]

4. Other Laws Protecting Workers

There are several other important areas of law protecting workers that will not be discussed here: minimum wage and maximum hour requirements,[273] rights to unpaid leaves of absence for family needs,[274] workers' compensation for work-related injuries[275] unemployment compensation programs,[276] workplace safety,[277] social security insurance benefits programs covering disability[278] and federal and private retirement benefits.[279] Virtually all these areas of law date, at the earliest, from the first half of the 20th century, and most of them from depression years of the 1930s.

---

268 *See* Chapter VII, p. 239, for a discussion of awards of attorney fees.

269 *See* Chapter IV, p. 142, where contingent fees are discussed.

270 *See Dare v. Montana Petroleum Marketing Co.*, 687 P.2d 1015 (Mont. 1984). *But see Foley v. Interactive Data Corp.*, *supra* note 266 (no tort liability based on bad faith).

271 *See* the discussion in the torts chapter, Chapter XI, p. 382.

272 *See* ROTHSTEIN ET AL., *supra* note 222, §9.20 and Theodore J. St.Antoine, *A Seed Germinates: Unjust Discharge Reform Heads Toward Full Flower*, 67 NEB.L.REV. 56 (1988).

273 *See* ROTHSTEIN ET AL, *supra* note 222, §§4.1-4.13, and COVINGTON & DECKER, *supra* note 181, at 273-295, discussing the federal Fair Labor Standards Act and state statutes.

274 *See* ROTHSTEIN, ET AL., *supra* note 222, §§4.29-4.30, discussing the Family and Medical Leave Act of 1993, 29 U.S.C.A. 2601-2654, and related state laws.

275 *See* Chapter XI, p. 436.

276 *See* ROTHSTEIN ET AL., *supra* note 222, §§10.6 *et seq.* and §§7.1 *et seq. See also* JACK B. HOOD, BENJAMIN A HARDY, JR., & HAROLD S. LEWIS, JR., WORKER'S COMPENSATION AND EMPLOYEE PROTECTION LAWS 1-140, 141-161 (West 1990).

277 *See* ROTHSTEIN ET AL., *supra* note 222, §§6.1 *et seq.* and COVINGTON & DECKER, *supra* note 181, at 16-33 (discussing the federal Occupational Health and Safety Administration (OSHA), 29 U.S.C.A. §651 *et seq.*, its regulations and corresponding state and local laws).

278 *See* U.S. SOCIAL SECURITY ADMINISTRATION, SOCIAL SECURITY HANDBOOK (Gov't Printing Office, Washington 1993) and COVINGTON & DECKER, *supra* note 181, at 68-82.

279 *See* ROTHSTEIN ET AL, *supra* note 222, §§4.19 *et seq.*, and COVINGTON & DECKER, *supra* note 181, at 296-329, discussing the federal Employment and Retirement Security Act (ERISA), 29 U.S.C.A. §1001 *et seq. See also* SOCIAL SECURITY HANDBOOK, *supra*.

Notable for its absence is any national program for medical care.[280] The United States has no National Health program and attempts by President Clinton in his first term as President to persuade Congress to pass one were resoundingly rebuffed. Behind the defeat was a vigorous publicity campaign mounted by the private health insurance industry, which is the main source of health care funding in the country. Whether paid for by the individual or an employer — as is most often the case — private medical insurance policies are quite expensive. For example, the cost of an individual policy for a family of four with average coverage from Blue Cross and Blue Shield, a major medical insurance company, is approximately $7500 per year, plus various "co-pay" requirements, including 50% of the cost of all doctor visits. A trade group for the private health insurance industry estimated in 1998 that 43.5 million people in the United States have no health insurance coverage and that most say that the reason is that they cannot afford it.

Health maintenance organizations (HMOs) have been promoted as a less costly way of providing privately funded medical care. While regular private medical insurance permits patients to choose what doctor to go to and when to consult a specialist, HMOs limit the patient to a certain list of doctors who are either employed by it or who have agreed to accept referrals of patients from the HMO at a reduced fee. In addition, the patient's need for a specialist is determined by the patient's primary physician, a doctor employed by the HMO, who makes a referral only if the generalist HMO employed doctors are not able to treat the problem. Further savings are realized when HMOs use their market power to negotiate special prices from drug manufacturers. However, HMOs are not perfect. There have been several troubling cases of HMOs denying coverage for certain care that turned out to be necessary. While such improper denials of treatment are bad enough, what is truly shocking to some is that the law provides no judicial remedy for the consequences of such mistakes. In one case, an HMO approved bone marrow transplant procedures to treat a patient's cancer. After the first two of three transplants were completed, the HMO administrators changed their minds and refused to authorize the final treatment. The patient sued and the administrators acknowledged their mistake and authorized the final treatment, but because of the delay it was ineffective. Even though the patient died as a result, the federal court dismissed the wrongful death suit filed by the patient's family on the ground that the suit was preempted by federal legislation.[281] Other difficulties with HMOs have involved "gag orders" imposed on plan doctors. In some cases doctors are prevented from discussing any experimental or investigative treatment with patients and in some cases from discussing any treatment options that are not authorized by the HMO plan.[282] Federal legislation has been proposed to establish an HMO "Patient's Bill of Rights" to deal with these and other problems, but opposition from the health insurance industry is expected once again to be strong.

F. Environmental Law

Scope of Environmental Law Prior to the 1960s, industry operated without much

---

280 The poor and the aged, blind and disabled are generally covered by federally funded Medical Assistance program. *See* 42 U.S.C.A §1396a *et seq.*

281 *Spain v. Aetna Life Ins. Co.*, 11 F.3d 129 (9th Cir. 1993). The federal law is a general law regulating employee benefit plans, which contains a broad preemption. Since the purpose of the law was to strengthen worker protections, it is likely that the instant preemptive effect was an oversight.

282 *Comment*, "Tort Law: The Appropriate Vehicle to Control HMO Abuse of Gag Clauses," 29 ARIZ. ST. L.J. 1103 (1997).

regard for the detrimental effects on the environment. This changed in the 1970s.[283] Congress responded to the newfound public concern with new and ambitious legislation on air pollution, water pollution, toxic chemicals, contaminated drinking water, pesticides, hazardous waste, the environmental impact of actions of federal government agencies and protection of endangered species. Most of the efforts to control pollution are aimed at industry and, even where environmental laws focus on the actions of federal agencies, that action commonly concerns the agency's issuance of a permit for private business development or activities. Additionally, laws on endangered species have direct application to private business development on private lands when those lands are part of the critical habitat of a listed threatened or endangered species. Consequently, it is appropriate to address the topic of environmental law in this chapter on business law.

The Environmental Protection Agency   Administration and enforcement of environmental laws are the responsibility of the Environmental Protection Agency. The EPA is an independent agency within the executive branch.[284] It was created by Executive Order in 1970 and assigned responsibility for administering environmental laws, previously allocated among the Departments of Agriculture, the Interior and Health Education and Welfare. With a budget of more than $5 billion and 15,000 employees, the EPA is among the largest of federal administrative agencies. The EPA promulgates rules and the enforces the law like other agencies, but it also engages in research. Various bills, popular among environmentalists, have been introduced to elevate the agency to cabinet rank, but to date they have not been successful.

Sources of Environmental Law   As suggested by the above, the federal government and federal law have been in the forefront of environmental protection. However, state law is becoming an increasingly important source of environmental law.[285]   But on both the federal and state levels, the fundamental debate in environmental law has focused on the trade off between economic growth and environmental protection. Recent conservative trends in the Congress, presidential administrations and the country in general have led to concerns that environmental regulation is retarding business growth and limiting the ability of U.S. industries to 0compete in the international marketplace. The result has been a trend both with the EPA and the states to work with industry rather than to enforce against it. This has led to a greater number of citizen suits.[286]

1. Pesticides and Other Toxic Substances

The federal environmental market access statute dealing with pesticides is the Federal Insecticide, Fungicide, and Rodenticide Act (FIFRA).[287] The federal statute dealing with other toxics is the Toxic Substance Control Act (ToSCA).[288]   FIFRA requires any person distributing, selling, offering, or receiving any pesticide to register

---

[283] For more complete coverage of environmental law, *see* WILLIAM H. RODGERS, JR., ENVIRONMENTAL LAW, 2D ED. (West 1994, 1998). For a helpful casebook on the subject, *see* ZUGMUNT PLATER, ROBERT H. ABRAMS, WILLIAM GOLDFARB & ROBERT GRAHAM, ENVIRONMENTAL LAW AND POLICY: NATURE, LAW AND SOCIETY, 2D ED. (WEST 1998). *See also* JOHN G. SPRANKLING & GREGORY S. WEBER, THE LAW OF HAZARDOUS WASTES AND TOXIC SUBSTANCES IN A NUTSHELL (West 1997). All the statutes discussed here are collected in SELECTED ENVIRONMENTAL LAW STATUTES (West 1998).

[284] The distinction between executive and independent agencies is discussed in Chapter I, p. 15.

[285] *See infra* p. 582.

[286] Joseph J. Armao, "Private Attorneys General: The New Watchdogs,"NAT'L LAW J., p. C18, col 1 (December 1, 1997).

[287] 7 U.S.C.A. §§136-136y.

[288] 15 U.S.C.A. §§2601-2671.

the poison with the EPA. Assuming proper labeling and effectiveness of a poison, the EPA will permit its use once it determines that the pesticide will perform its functions without "unreasonable risks to humans and the environment, taking into account the economic, social, and environmental costs and benefits of the pesticides' intended use." FIFRA then imposes official "tolerance levels" — the maximum permissible exposure. Once granted, registrations serve as licenses to market the product. Registrations can be canceled or suspended. A requirement in the statute that the government compensate the manufacturer for all existing supplies of materials that could no longer be marketed was recently repealed.

ToSCA is directed at the chemical manufacturing industry. It is designed to insure testing by manufacturers to identify hazards to human health and the environment associated with chemical substances before they are permitted to be manufactured and sold. The EPA may require testing and disclosure of test results to the government. If the test results are adverse, the EPA may forbid or limit the uses made of a chemical substance. ToSCA also regulates PCB and asbestos hazards and establishes national goals for indoor radon abatement, while offering states technical and other assistance.

2. Air Pollution

The Clean Air Act (CAA), with certain important exceptions, relies heavily on a "command and control" approach in which regulators make technological judgments and determine standards and then enforce them.[289] For fixed sites, the CAA applies a harm-based ambient quality regulatory approach that treats the air as a finite commons into which only so much pollution can be emitted without posing a threat to human health or the environment. Pollution standards are set based on the overall quality of the relevant airshed into which pollution in discharged. This approach allows some pollution to occur. The political and scientific challenge lies in determining the amount of emissions that can be safely assimilated. In general, the approach of the CAA has been "cost-oblivious."[290]

Under the CAA, the EPA has authority to develop and administer an air pollution control plan for each state that has failed to adopt an adequate plan of its own.[291] Adequacy of the plans, termed State Implementation Plans (SIPs), depends upon meeting the federally set National Ambient Air Quality Standards (NAAQSs). These standards set limits on the concentration of certain pollutants allowed in the air for 247 "air quality control regions" and are updated every 5 years. The NAAQSs were intended to reduce pollution to acceptable levels, i.e., levels that do not endanger human health.[292] Clearly, the decision about what to consider a pollutant is an important one and the courts have not hesitated to order the EPA to add an element that has been shown to have a negative impact on health.[293] However, less searching review has been accorded the question of how to determine compliance with NAAQSs. Averaging exposure to pollutants and determining the period over which it should be done are issues that have been left to agency discretion.[294]

---

289 42 U.S.C.A. §§7401-7671q.

290 See RODGERS, *supra* note 283, at 164.

291 Prior to the extensive 1970 amendments, the CAA had relied almost exclusively on voluntary state efforts to control air pollution, which had not been effective. Part of the problem with state control of air quality was competition among the states to attract industry.

292 42 U.S.C.A. §§7408-7409.

293 *Natural Resources Defense Counsel v. Train*, 545 F.2d 320 (2d Cir 1976) (lead must be included).

294 *American Petroleum Institute v. Costle*, 665 F.2d 1176 (D.C.Cir. 1981) (ozone exposure).

In addition to the SIP provisions, the CAA establishes a program to prevent significant deterioration of air quality where the air is clean, such as in wilderness and other pristine areas, including state and national parks.[295] The CAA also sets strict auto exhaust pipe emission standards for cars and trucks. By most accounts, the CAA has improved air quality in the United States considerably over the last 30 years. This resulted primarily from a 90% reduction in lead by phasing out leaded gasoline, but also from significant reductions in sulfur dioxide and carbon monoxide. Ozone is the most pervasive continuing problem, an important component of the "smog" that hovers over large cities and which has become a particularly serious in Los Angeles.

3. Water Pollution

Regulation of the discharge of pollutants into water is handled under the Federal Water Pollution Control Act, commonly referred to as the Clean Water Act (CWA), enacted in 1972. The CWA set as its goal achieving "fishable and swimable" waters by 1983. This deadline has been extended several times, but the struggle, in the words of the Act, "to restore and maintain the chemical, physical, and biological integrity of the nation's waters," continues.[296] Less success has been achieved than with air quality.

NPDES Under the CWA, the EPA sets technology-based effluent limitations by category of industry, determined by the type of products manufactured, and by subcategories based on processes or raw materials utilized in producing the products. This forms the basis for a permit system, the National Pollutant Discharge Elimination System (NPDES), implemented by the states with EPA approved NPDES programs or by the EPA itself. Such permits limit effluents and set out other standards, terms and conditions, as well as numerical discharge limitations. The EPA is to incorporate into the permits increasingly strict effluent limitations. Dischargers must use the "best practicable control technology currently available" (BPCT) within an industry. EPA limitations must, for toxic pollutants, be the "best available technology economically achievable" (BAT) and, for discharge of conventional pollutants, represent the "best conventional pollution control technology" (BCT).[297]

New pollution sources in an industry must meet a separate set of standards, called "new-source performance standards."[298] These standards limit the discharge of pollutants from new sources based on the "best available demonstrated control technology" (BDT). Finally, the EPA is authorized to establish "best management practices" (BMPs) to control plant site runoff, spillage or leaks, sludge or waste disposal, and drainage from raw material storage, in order to diminish the amount of toxic pollutants flowing into receiving waters.

Permit applicants are required to test any discharge into water for toxics and other substances and to report its composition and the amount of pollutants present. The permit application will be considered in light of two primary factors. First, the state or the EPA will consider the pollution control technology used by the applicant. The applicant may be required to use either BAT, BCT or BDT depending on the nature of the pollutants discharged. Second, the pollution control authority is concerned with the quality of the water receiving the effluent. States must establish water quality standards for all bodies of water. Generally, an applicant must

---

295 42 U.S.C.A. §§7470-7491.
296 33 U.S.C.A. §§1251 *et seq.*
297 33 U.S.C.A. §1311.
298 33 U.S.C.A. §1316.

demonstrate, not only the effectiveness of the pollution control devices, but also that discharge will not cause the receiving body of water to fall below the established water quality standards.[299]

The issuance of an NPDES permit is preceded by public notice and an opportunity for the public to comment on whether the permit should be issued. The EPA retains considerable control over the state NPDES programs and can veto state permit approvals.

Enforcement The enforcement provisions under the CWA are civil, administrative, and criminal. Civil penalties range up to $10,000 per day per violation. In 1987, the CWA was amended to add criminal penalties for any person who "knowingly" violates the Act and "who knows at the time that he thereby places another person in imminent danger of death or serious bodily injury." Criminal penalties range from $2500 to $25,000 per day per violation for first offenders, plus imprisonment up to one year. Habitual criminal offenders may be subject to fines of $50,000 per day of violation and/or imprisonment for not more than two years.[300] In addition, a water polluter faces requirements that it purchase and implement pollution control technology needed to bring it within the regulatory standards. In a recent case against a steelmaker, the EPA levied the largest penalty ever under the CWA.[301] The steel company was convicted of discharging pollutants, including cyanide and ammonia, into the Ohio River in violation of its NPDES permit. The company entered into a consent decree with the EPA in which it agreed to pay $6 million in penalties and also to spend $24 million on pollution control projects.

Intent requirements under the CWA have been relaxed to permit liability even where it could not be proven that the polluter knew precisely the nature of the duties imposed by the CWA or the dangers posed by the particular dumping.[302] However, other limitations have created difficulties. In one 1990 case, a federal court convicted a corporation and its president of intentionally discharging nickel plating waste and nitric acid into a public sewer system. The president, who personally participated in the dumping, faced a maximum 15-year sentence and a $500,000 fine, and the corporation could have been fined up to $2 million. However, the Court of Appeals reversed because the only people endangered by the dumping were the 12 plant employees who were ordered to dump the chemicals, noting that a CWA conviction cannot be premised upon danger that occurs before pollutant reaches publicly owned sewer or treatment works.[303]

4. Cleanups of Sites Contaminated with Toxic Substances

The Comprehensive Environmental Response, Compensation and Liability Act (CERCLA) of 1980[304] is a statutory system for managing and funding environmental cleanups of sites contaminated with hazardous substances. CERCLA was enacted in

---

299 33 U.S.C.A. §1313.

300 33 U.S.C.A. §1319(c), §1321(b)(5).

301 *United States v. Wheeling-Pittsburgh*, 1991 WL 157355 (S.D. Ohio, May 15, 1990).

302 *United States v. Wilson*, 133 F.3d 251, 264-265 (4th Cir. 1997) (discussing CWA scienter requirements). Several lower courts have concluded that the CWA violations are public welfare offenses, which do not require proof of intent at least where the pollutants involved were inherently deleterious. See, e.g., *United States v. Sinskey*, 119 F.3d 712, 716 (8th Cir. 1997) (meat packing plant waste water containing large amounts of ammonia nitrate). *See* Chapter XIV, p. 508, where the public welfare exception to *mens rea* is discussed.

303 *United States v. Borowski*, 977 F.2d 27 (1st Cir. 1992).

304 42 U.S.C.A. §§9601 *et seq.*

large part in response to the chemical waste disaster at Love Canal, New York. Hooker Chemical, a major corporation, had buried thousands of drums of industrial solvents under land surrounding its manufacturing facility and later sold parcels of the land for residential purposes. Reports of children becoming seriously ill from playing in their own backyards helped emphasize the urgent need for government-regulated hazardous waste disposal and cleanup programs.

The "Superfund" At the center of the statutory scheme established by CERCLA is the "Superfund," the source of money for cleanups. The Superfund currently obtains its money from a surtax assessed against large companies with incomes of over $2 million per year and from taxes on petroleum and chemical feedstocks. These sums are supplemented by a relatively small amount of general revenue money and money recovered from potentially responsible parties (called PRPs). PRPs may be individuals, including corporate officers and directors, or corporations involved in the disposing, arranging for disposing or transporting hazardous waste.[305] Liability of PRPs under CERCLA was intended by Congress to be retroactive and such application has been upheld in the face of constitutional attack.[306]

CERCLA provides a procedure for identifying and ranking the hazards posed by sites of hazardous materials contamination. On the basis of that hazard ranking system, the statute establishes a national priorities list (NPL) that then functions to ensure that the most dangerous sites are remediated first. When CERCLA was first enacted, many thought there would be only a few sites that merited attention. But by 1989, over 30,000 sites had been identified and there are now close to 2,000 sites on the NPL. Governmental estimates for cleanup costs of these sites fall in the range of $300 to $700 billion, with the average cost of the cleanup of an NPL site being around $25 million.

CERCLA also requires that owners or operators of contaminated facilities notify the EPA of any release of any hazardous substances.[307] When there is contamination or a threat of contamination, the EPA can act to prevent further damage and to perform the cleanup, in which case it can obtain reimbursement for such costs from PRPs, or PRPs can perform the cleanup under EPA supervision.[308] PRPs and others who pay for or themselves clean up contaminated sites have the right to seek contribution from other responsible persons.[309] Liability under CERCLA is strict and the only defenses are Act of God, acts of war, and certain actions or omissions by third parties.[310] If there is "an imminent and substantial endangerment to the public health or welfare or the environment," the EPA can order PRPs to undertake cleanup action and enforce such an order in court.[311]

CERCLA Policy The purpose of CERCLA is to place the responsibility for environmental cleanup on PRPs. Such a policy has the appeal of fairness and it is also thought to encourage voluntary cleanup action and to assist in recovering tax dollars spent on cleanups. The problems with carrying out this policy have been the

---

305 42 U.S.C.A. §9607(a).

306 *In re Penn Central*, 944 F.2d 164, 165 (3d Cir. 1991).

307 42 U.S.C.A. §9603(a), (c).

308 42 U.S.C.A. §9604(a)(1).

309 42 U.S.C.A. §113(f).

310 42 U.S.C.A. §9607(b). *See* Elizabeth Glass, *Superfund and SARA: Are There Any Defenses Left?*, 12 HARV. ENVTL. L.REV. 385 (1988). "Act of God" means natural disasters, sometimes called *force majeure*.

311 42 U.S.C.A. §9604(a).

surprising magnitude of the hazardous waste contamination problem in the country and the difficulties of finding financially solvent PRPs to pay into the Superfund. For example, of the Superfund money spent so far on cleanups, only 9% of it has come from PRPs.[312] However, PRPs performing cleanups under EPA supervision account for a substantial percentage of sites currently being remediated — annually approximately 50 out of 90.[313]

A hotly disputed issue in the Superfund program is selection of the means of remediation. Many PRP groups argue that cost must be a major factor in deciding on an appropriate remedy and note that CERCLA requires "cost-effective" remedies.[314] However, the EPA's position is that cost may only distinguish among sufficiently protective alternatives that have already been chosen without regard to cost.[315]

5. Hazardous Waste Management

While CERCLA is aimed at cleanups of hazardous wastes already in the environment, the Resource Conservation and Recovery Act (RCRA)[316] is aimed at preventing release of such materials in the first place. The Hazardous Waste Management subchapter of the RCRA takes what has been called a "cradle-to-grave" approach to waste, regulating everything in its life cycle, from generation to treatment, storage or disposal. The Act regulates generators of the waste, transporters of waste and owners and operators of waste storage, treatment and disposal facilities. It provides a tracking system and sets standards for activities and equipment used by each category of persons to prevent hazardous waste from being introduced into the environment. The RCRA also employs a waste reduction strategy under the assumption that there will be fewer releases if there is less hazardous waste to control.

RCRA standards are enforced largely through operating permits issued by the EPA or parallel state agencies. In addition, the EPA can issue administrative orders and assess civil penalties (essentially a fine) of up to $25,000 per day for each violation of RCRA standards.[317] It may also seek injunctive relief against violators and may pursue criminal penalties of up to $50,000 per day for each day of violation and up to 5 years in prison for violation of permit requirements, and up to $250,000 per day and up to 15 years in prison for violations that endanger people.[318]

6. State Environmental Laws

The EPA and federal law have been the primary guardians on the environment.

---

312 William H. Rogers, Jr., *A Superfund Trivia Test: A Comment on the Complexity of Environmental Law*, 22 ENVTL. LAWYER 417, 421-422 (1992).

313 A Management Review of the Superfund Program (EPA). Solvency of PRPs is a question in so many cases that issues of PRPs' obligations are often determined in bankruptcy court. *See* HEIDT, ENVIRONMENTAL OBLIGATIONS IN BANKRUPTCY, *supra* note 78.

314 42 U.S.C.A. §121(a)-(b).

315 Nonetheless, a recent memorandum from the EPA allows as a consideration in determining remedial action "reasonable anticipated future land use or uses," thus implying that less stringent standards for remediation should be applied to sites that are likely to be used in the future only for industrial, as opposed to residential purposes. For an article discussing problems with this approach, *see* George Wyeth, *Land Use and Cleanup: Beyond the Rhetoric*, 25 ENVTL. L.REP. 10358 (1996).

316 42 U.S.C.A. §§6901 *et seq.*

317 42 U.S.C.A. §§6925, 6928(a)(1).

318 42 U.S.C.A. §6928(d), (e). A recent issue in hazardous wastes is racially discriminatory issuance of permits resulting in concentration of waste facilities in areas where minorities live. *See, e.g., Chester Residents Concerned For Quality Living v. Seif*, 132 F.3d 925 (3d Cir. 1997) (recognizing right to sue where minority town had disproportionate share of hazardous waste facilities in the county).

Most state law and regulatory activity have been the product of the federal-state partnerships created by the various federal laws already discussed. However, state law has significance of its own in at least three areas.

"Command and Control" Regulation Some states have statutes analogous to the federal statutes just discussed, but which impose different or stricter standards. New Jersey, for example has environmental standards that exceed those of the federal government and California, Florida and Michigan have fairly comprehensive environmental statutes. The laws of most serious consequence to industry are CERCLA-like laws imposing liability for contamination of industrial sites.[319] Perhaps most noticeable to the general public are the higher emission standards imposed on automobile by the State of California. The problem of "brownfields" is another area that has been addressed by state regulation. "Brownfields" are tracts of previously developed land that could be cleaned up sufficiently for new development so that more undeveloped "greenfields" would not have to be used. At least 38 states now have voluntary cleanup programs that offer certain benefits for voluntarily remediating brownfield properties, including clear cleanup standards, streamlined environmental review and liability caps for owners who are innocent of wrongdoing. The purpose of such programs is to try to prevent additional "urban sprawl" — inexorable expansion of development into previously undeveloped land — by making the choice of redeveloping previously developed land more attractive than purchasing farm, forest or other pristine land.[320]

Local Building, Health and Sanitation Laws State and local governments have always been the primary regulators of local building, health and sanitation. For example, sewer and septic tanks systems are regulated and controlled through the issuance of building permits and inspections. Also regulated primarily by states are landfills — sites where garbage is buried. And, as already alluded to, the same state and local governments have a role in assisting the implementation of federal requirements with regard to air and water quality.

Toxic Torts In "toxic tort" litigation, the state law of relevance is the common law, primarily the doctrines of negligence, nuisance, trespass and strict liability for ultra-hazardous activities.[321] Toxic torts have taken various forms, from asbestos exposure to residential communities built on old toxic waste dumping sites. The latter sort of case was the subject of a popular book that detailed the struggle of one private lawyer to gain redress for a neighborhood inflicted with the lingering effects of the environmentally unsound practices of a large corporation.[322] While the book illustrates a rather dramatic case where tort remedies were used to redress massive damage caused by pollution, there are thousands of smaller toxic tort actions that have been filed throughout the country.

7. Environmental Impact of Actions of the Federal Government

The National Environmental Policy Act Congress enacted the National Environmental Policy Act of 1969 (NEPA) in order to set a general policy of

---

319 *See* Lynda Butler, *State Environmental Programs: A Study in Political Influence and Regulatory Failure*, 31 WM.& MARY L.REV. 823 (1990) and Wendy E. Wagner, *Liability for Hazardous Waste Cleanup: An Examination of New Jersey's Approach*, 13 HARV.ENVTL. L.REV. 245 (1989).

320 Work has been done on a federal brownfields law, but no statute has yet been passed.

321 For a case discussing all three theories of recovery, *see National RR. Passenger Corp. v. New York City Housing Authority*, 819 F.Supp. 1271 (S.D.N.Y. 1993). The law of torts was discussed in Chapter XI.

322 JONATHAN HARR, A CIVIL ACTION (Vintage Books, NY 1995).

environmental protection for the country.[323] Among other things, it requires the President to report to the nation on the state of the environment. Aside from its bold statements of general policy, the most important requirement of NEPA is that any "recommendation or report on proposals for legislation and other major Federal actions significantly affecting the quality of the human environment" be accompanied by an environmental impact statement (EIS) on "the environmental impact of the proposed action."[324] This statement is to be produced in cooperation with the EPA. The EIS must "accompany the proposal [for federal action] through the existing agency review process" and must be circulated to interested federal, state and local agencies. This requirement of NEPA might seem irrelevant to business law. However, businesses must often seek and obtain federal agency permits or other authorization to proceed, so a wide range of proposed private business development and other activities have been scrutinized for their environmental effects under NEPA. For example, permits by the U.S. Army Corps of Engineers are needed for dredging and filling waterways and a license from the Nuclear Regulatory Commission is essential for construction and operation of a nuclear power plant. Decisions of the Civil Aeronautics Board to license private activities resulting in greater air traffic and a decision of the Food and Drug Administration to authorize use of nonreturnable plastic beverage containers require EISs.[325]

By requiring preparation and circulation of an EIS, NEPA is purely "procedural." It affects the *way* agency decisions are made by forcing the agency to consider environmental factors. It does not specify the *content* of those decisions. An agency may issue a finding of no significant environment impact (called a FONSI), but the validity of FONSIs, like the sufficiency of any EIS prepared, is reviewable both administratively and by way of a citizen suit, discussed below.

Role of the Council on Environmental Quality   The Council on Environmental Quality (CEQ) is set up by NEPA to conduct research and advise the President on the state of the environment, and to mediate between the EPA and other agencies in disputes over environmental effects. These latter functions involve it in determining the need for or sufficiency of an EIS.   The CEQ has issued highly specific rules to guide agencies in their compliance with NEPA requirements, and these rules have been accepted as authoritative by the courts.[326] Ultimately, if no resolution can be reached, the matter can be referred to the President for resolution. However, the CEQ does not have the power to stop the agency action and, barring presidential intervention, the only real threat of legal intervention is a citizen suit.

Citizen Suits   By far the most common litigation under NEPA has been citizen suits contesting failure to prepare an EIS or inadequacy of an EIS. While there is no explicit statutory right to sue, courts have implied a right of action. Since NEPA is a procedural rather than a substantive law, a court reviewing proposed agency action may enjoin it only if the agency has filed a FONSI instead of an EIS or where the EIS it has filed is inadequate. If there is an adequate EIS, the court generally has no power to enjoin the action, no matter how serious the environmental effects might be. Theoretically, the court could enjoin the proposed action if its benefits are so far

---

323 42 U.S.C.A. §4331 *et seq.*

324 42 U.S.C.A. §4332(2)(C). Smaller actions that are not "major actions" are not covered by NEPA.

325 *See* RODGERS, *supra* note 283, §9.1.

326 *See* 40 C.F.R. Pt. 1500. *See Andrus v. Sierra Club*, 442 U.S. 347, 358 (1979). Also given weight are CEQ's "Forty Most Asked Questions Concerning CEQ's National Environmental Policy Act Regulations," 46 Fed. Reg. 18026 (March 23, 1981).

outweighed by environmentally disastrous effects that it would be "arbitrary and capricious."[327] However, research discloses no case where this has happened. Quite likely, this is because of the success of NEPA's procedural "stop, think and inform" approach. Agencies whose proposed actions entail very serious environmental effects have uniformly abandoned their initial decisions or have modified them substantially to minimize the environmental consequences. This can result from internal agency concerns or intervention or pressure from Congress, the President, cabinet-level policymakers or the public. Most environmental lawyers believe that in this respect, NEPA's procedural approach has worked well. Perhaps because of this success, a similar approach has been adopted by the European Union.

A recent innovation of agencies has been to issue a FONSI with a statement of how the agency intends to mitigate the planned action to ensure that it entails only a "non-significant impact." This approach has been approved by the courts. However, one difficulty is assuring that the promised mitigating actions are actually carried out effectively. It has been held that they may not be enforced by way of a citizen suit. The same is true when mitigation action is promised as part of an EIS, discussed earlier.[328] However, if the deviation from the planned mitigation is sufficiently substantial to be considered a new "major federal action," suit could be filed to compel the preparation of a supplemental EIS (SEIS).[329]

8. Endangered Species

The Endangered Species Act of 1973 (ESA) prohibits any federal governmental or private action that "takes" threatened or endangered species anywhere in the United States or its territorial seas, and requires federal agencies to insure that any actions funded by them do not entail such consequences anywhere in the United States or the high seas.[330] Section 7 applies to governmental action while §9 applies to private action. Section 7 of the ESA was read strictly in *Tennessee Valley Authority v. Hill*, to prohibit completion of a $100 million dam because of the danger such development presented to the tiny endangered snail darter fish. Arguments that a "hardship exception" should be read into the ESA were rejected by the Court. It noted that "[t]he plain intent of Congress in enacting this statute was to halt and reverse the trend toward species extinction, whatever the cost."[331] The ESA is administered by the Departments of Interior and Commerce. Among its interesting features is that the Secretary of the Interior has the option, in cooperation with the states, of purchasing the property to prevent or mitigate a "taking."[332] In addition to its other protections, the ESA provides serious civil and criminal penalties to those who knowingly violate the Act. However, courts, while taking a firm position that ignorance of the law or the

---

327 *See* Chapter VI, p. 198.

328 *Robertson v. Methow Valley Citizens' Council*, 490 U.S. 332 (1989) (NEPA does not impose a substantive duty on agencies to mitigate adverse environmental effects, only to file a sufficient EIS).

329 *Environmental Defense Fund v. Marsh*, 651 F.2d 983 (5th Cir. 1981) (Army Secretary modified water project in a major way during implementation requiring an SEIS).

330 16 U.S.C.A. §1531 *et seq.* A good summary of the ESA and cases under it is provided in RODGERS, *supra* note 283, at 993-1023. Originally, regulations of the Secretaries of Commerce and Interior extended the scope of the ESA to federally funded projects in foreign countries, but subsequently limited the scope to the United States and the high seas. A suit challenging this limitation foundered for lack of standing. *See Lujan v. Defenders of Wildlife*, 504 U.S. 555(1992).

331 437 U.S. 153, 193 (1978). The statutory interpretation issue was discussed in Chapter II, p. 56. Unfortunately for the snail darter, Congress amended the ESA to permit completion of the dam.

332 16 U.S.C.A. §1534.

list of species is no excuse, have imposed rather light punishment in cases of conviction.[333]

Listing of Endangered and Threatened Species   The list of endangered and threatened species is determined by the Secretary of the Interior, who is required to make list determinations "solely on the basis of the best scientific and commercial data available," taking into account existing efforts to preserve the species. The list may include any plant or animal species in the world and, as of 1991, included 651 species, with an additional 600 being considered as serious candidates and an additional 3,000 identified as potentially eligible. Species may be deleted or added depending on the degree of danger of their extinction. The degree of extinction danger is obviously difficult to determine, even with the best scientific help. But the ESA's listing has served to focus public attention on the extinction threat to many species, from the 3-inch snail darter of the *Tennessee Valley Authority v. Hill* case, to sea turtles, to the lowly furbish lousewort flower of Northern Maine, to the elderberry longhorn beetle.[334]

The Scope of a "Take"   Under §9, which prohibits private actions that "take" listed species, the statutory definition of "take" includes within it "harm" to the species. The Secretary of the Interior has defined "harm" as including "significant habitat modification or degradation where it actually kills or injures wildlife by significantly impairing essential behavioral patterns, including breeding, feeding, or sheltering."[335] In areas of the United States which remain in undeveloped states, this can be a significant limitation on business development, particularly in the residential building and wood products industries. The Secretary's broad definition of taking was recently approved as within his power under the ESA by the Supreme Court in *Babbit v. Sweet Home Chapter of Communities for a Great Oregon*. In *Sweet Home*, landowners and logging companies challenged the Secretary's prohibiting "habitat modification" of the endangered red-cockaded woodpecker and the threatened northern spotted owl.[336] Despite the resulting broad scope of the ESA, a 1982 amendment was added to accommodate private development. It allows private parties to "take" a listed species provided the taking is "incidental" to otherwise lawful activity and it is accompanied by a "habitat conservation plan" approved by the Department of the Interior. The plan must specify the impact on the species, the means that will be used to "minimize and mitigate" it, and the reasons why any "alternatives" to the taking are not being used.[337]

---

333 *See, e.g., United States v. Clark*, 986 F.2d 65 (4th Cir. 1993) (sale of Siberian tiger and Bengal tiger skin rugs; sentence of 1 year supervised probation, 6 months home detention and 500 hours of community service; but rejecting as a defense reliance on advice that sales of wildlife killed before the ESA were legal).

334 *See* 50 C.F.R. §§17.11-17.12. Endangered species throughout the world are listed because of the prohibitions on possession, importation, delivery or sale of such species.. 16 U.S.C.A. §1538(a)(1).

335 50 C.F.R. §17.3.

336 515 U.S. 687 (1995). Justice Scalia dissented, noting that the Court's holding "imposes unfairness to the point of financial ruin, not just upon the rich, but upon the simplest farmer who finds his land conscripted to national zoological use."

337 16 U.S.C.A. §1539(a)(1)(B). Interestingly, some courts have permitted the species itself to be a named plaintiff. *See, e.g., Marbled Murrelet v. Pacific Lumber Co.*, 83 F.3d 1060 (9th Cir.1996), (marbled murrelet is a rare seabird which nests primarily in old-growth coastal coniferous forests; evidence supported finding that there was imminent harm to them from company's intended logging operation).

CHAPTER XVI

TAX LAW

A. Introduction

This chapter will discuss the taxes in effect in the United States. On the federal level there are taxes on income (individual and corporate income tax), taxes to support the social security system (payroll taxes), taxes on certain products (excise taxes), taxes on gratuitous transfers (estate and gift taxes), and various minor taxes. There is no federal sales tax, property tax or value added tax.[1]

The individual states also raise revenue through taxes. The 50 states collectively raise about $600 billion ($600,000,000,000) annually, an amount equal to about one-half of the federal tax revenues. The majority of state revenues are raised by sales taxes and property taxes (about 60 percent). Most states also have some form of income tax, but state income taxes tend to raise only about 25 percent of state revenues.

The principal focus of this chapter will be on the federal income tax. The reason for this is that the federal income tax by far raises the most revenue and typically imposes the most significant tax on the taxpayer. However, there will also be a discussion of some of the other forms of federal taxation.

As if the mid-1900s, the federal government, annually raises $1,300,000,000,000 (one trillion three-hundred billion dollars) in taxes. The federal income tax on individuals and corporations raises approximately 60% of all federal revenues. Of the $1.3 trillion annually collected by the federal government, about $600 billion comes from the federal income tax on individuals, about $150 billion comes from the income tax on corporations, about $500 billion comes from payroll taxes to support the social security system, about $60 billion comes from federal excise taxes, and about $60 billion comes from other sources (including about $15 billion from the federal estate and gift taxes).

B. Sources of Law and Basic Concepts in Federal Tax Law

1. Sources of Law

The Constitution The 16th Amendment of Constitution grants to the Congress the power to levy an income tax. It was ratified in 1913.[2]

The Internal Revenue Code The first income tax was enacted in 1916. Various annual revenue acts added new laws to the first income tax laws. In addition, Congress passed other acts levying other taxes, including acts setting a tax on estates

---

1   The most important federal tax statutes and regulations (except for those related to international tax) are set out in SELECTED FEDERAL TAXATION STATUTES AND REGULATIONS (West 1999). Useful sources on tax law include the following: MARVIN A. CHIRELSTEIN, FEDERAL INCOME TAXATION, 8TH ED. (Foundation 1997); JOHN K. MCNULTY, FEDERAL INCOME TAXATION OF INDIVIDUALS IN A NUTSHELL, 5TH ED. (West 1995); KAREN C. BURKE, FEDERAL INCOME TAXATION OF PARTNERS AND PARTNERSHIPS IN A NUTSHELL, 2D ED. (West 1999); KAREN C. BURKE, FEDERAL INCOME TAXATION OF CORPORATIONS AND STOCKHOLDERS IN A NUTSHELL (West 1996); DOUGLAS A. KAHN & JEFFREY S. LEHMAN, CORPORATE INCOME TAXATION, 4TH ED. (West 1994); JOHN K. MCNULTY, FEDERAL ESTATE AND GIFT TAXATION IN A NUTSHELL, 5TH ED. (West 1994); PATRICIA T. MORGAN, TAX PROCEDURE AND TAX FRAUD IN A NUTSHELL (West 1999); RICHARD L. DOERNBERG, INTERNATIONAL TAXATION IN A NUTSHELL, 3D ED. (West 1997). For more detailed information, *see* CCH Standard Federal Tax Reporter, Research Institute of America (RIA) Federal Tax Coordinator 2d, BNA Tax Management Portfolios.

2   As pointed out in Chapter I, p. 25, the use of conditional spending, backed by the increased economic power of the federal government derived from its receipt of income taxes, has been a real factor in increasing the power of the federal government *vis-a-vis* the states in the 20th century.

and gifts. These various acts were codified in 1939 into the Internal Revenue Code ("IRC"). The IRC of 1939 was amended annually and was recodified in 1954 as the Internal Revenue Code of 1954. This Code, too, was amended and revised annually. In 1986 Congress recodified the tax law into the Internal Revenue Code of 1986. This Code includes virtually all the taxes levied at the federal level. The current code, which continues to be revised and amended annually, is now about two thousand pages long. The IRC is codified in Title 26 of the United States Code.[3]

Subtitle A of the IRC, which itself is about a thousand pages long, is the primary source of law for the federal income tax. All other sources of law are directed at interpreting the language of the Code.

The Treasury Regulations The second major source of law with respect to the income tax (and all federal taxes, for that matter) are the Regulations issued by the Department of the Treasury (the "Treasury Regulations," or just the "Regulations"). The purpose of the Regulations is to interpret the language of the Code. The Regulations are issued by the Treasury pursuant to specific legislative grant of authority found in §7805 of the IRC. The Treasury Regulations are about four times as long as the Code itself, or about eight thousand pages. The Regulations themselves are codified as Title 26 of the Code of Federal Regulations.[4]

The courts give great deference to the interpretations of the Code found in the Treasury Regulations and rarely overturn a Regulation. Indeed, the standard of judicial review seems to require that a Regulation have no plausible basis as an interpretation before a court will consider overturning it.[5]

There is a second class of Regulation that is given even greater weight and is generally considered to have the force of law itself. This kind of Regulation must be promulgated by the Treasury Department pursuant to a specific grant of authority found in a specific section of the Code. These Regulations are sometimes referred to as "legislative regulations" in that they are, in effect, a delegation of the legislative authority of Congress to the Treasury Department.[6]

Revenue Rulings As discussed below, the administration of the tax law is assigned to the Internal Revenue Service (the "IRS"), which is a division of the Treasury Department. The IRS is a very large government bureaucracy which oversees the assessment and collection of federal taxes. In addition, the IRS also issues rulings on various aspects of the tax law. The most common form of ruling is called a Revenue Ruling, of which the IRS issues about 300 each year.[7] Each Revenue

---

3   The formal citation to a section of the Internal Revenue Code would refer to Title 26. In other words, §61 of the Internal Revenue Code is formally cited as "26 U.S.C.A. §61." In most circumstances, however, it is both acceptable and common to cite this section as "IRC §61." This form of citation will be used here.

4   The numbering scheme of the Treasury Regulations tracks that of the relevant IRC section. For example, the income tax regulations concerning §61 of the IRC are to be found in Part 1 of Title 26 of the Code of Federal Regulations. In general, Part 1 of the Regulations deals with the income tax. As such, the third regulation under §61 would bear the formal citation "26 C.F.R. §1.61-3." In most practice, however, this regulation would be cited as "Treas. Reg. §1.61-3" or even more simply as "Reg. §1.61-3." The "1" before the ".61" refers to Part 1 and informs us that the regulation concerns the income tax.

5   *See also* Chapter II, p. 57 (deference to administrative interpretations of statutes).

6   *See, e.g.*, IRC §385 for an example of such a grant of authority.

7   Revenue Rulings are numbered by year and the order in which they were published. For example, the 125th Revenue Ruling of the year 1997 would bear the citation, "Rev. Rul. 97-125." Revenue Rulings are published weekly in the Internal Revenue Bulletin ("I.R.B.") and are collected annually in the Cumulative Bulletin ("C.B."). If the above ruling were to be found starting at page 347 of the 1997 Cumulative Bulletin it would also carry the parallel citation, "1997 C.B. 347"

Ruling is concerned with the interpretation of a particular aspect of a section of the Code or Regulations. These rulings are issued in a general form and often include examples of particular matters of importance that the IRS has had to deal with in its administration of the tax laws. These rulings are an important source of law in that they allow one to see the current thinking of the IRS on particular matters and the IRS will generally be held to treat similar transactions in a manner that accords with the ruling. These rulings, however, are not given the weight or deference given to Regulations and may be more easily challenged in the courts.

Private Letter Rulings In addition to the general Revenue Rulings, the IRS also issues Private Letter Rulings (sometimes referred to as just "Letter Rulings") in response to a specific question asked by a specific taxpayer with respect to a specific transaction. Taxpayers will sometimes seek to get the advance approval of the IRS as to the tax consequences of a particular transaction. When the IRS responds to such a request it issues a Letter Ruling that reiterates the facts of the transaction and states the tax consequences of the transaction if it is consummated in accord with the described facts. These Letter Rulings are only applicable to the taxpayer who sought the ruling and have no precedential value. The IRS issues about 300 such rulings each year.[8] The Letter Rulings are published, but all identifying information about the taxpayer or the transaction is deleted. These Letter Rulings are useful to taxpayers in similar situations in that they show the current thinking of the IRS on a matter, but cannot be relied upon in the same way that Revenue Rulings can be relied upon.

Legislative History Since the IRC, with its various amendments and revisions, is a product of Congress, the legislative history of a given Code section is sometimes useful in helping the courts interpret arguably ambiguous language in such a Code section.[9] Of particular import are three committee reports: the report of the Ways and Means Committee of the House, where all revenue legislation originates,[10] the Senate Finance Committee, which handles all tax measure for the Senate and the report of any Conference Committee set up to reconcile differences between House and Senate versions of the bill.

There is also a standing committee of Congress called the Joint Committee on Taxation. The Joint Committee tends to be fairly active in studying various proposals for tax reform. It issues frequent studies and reports describing the current law as well as the reform proposals. Reports of the Joint Committee on Taxation are often very thorough and are often useful in getting an overview of a particular area of the tax law as well as an overview of current reform proposals.

Caselaw The various federal courts, including the U.S. Supreme Court, have had, and continue to have, a substantial number of taxpayers cases seeking interpretations of the Code or Regulations different from that enforced by the Internal Revenue Service or its agents. The body of case law in the tax area is large in comparison to many other areas of law, but the significance of judicial interpretation in contrast to other sources of law in the tax area is relatively small. The overwhelming majority of cases deal with fact-specific issues and have little relevance to other matters.

---

8 Private Letter Rulings are numbered sequentially for the year and month they are issued. For example, the 23 ruling in the month of February 1997 would bear the citation, "L.R. 9702023."

9 Legislative history is discussed in Chapter II, pp. 53-54.

10 All revenue bills must originate in the House. *See* Chapter I, p. 6, and Art. II §7 cl. 2

2. Basic Concepts in Tax Law

It is perhaps not surprising in a common law country that judicially created doctrines would be important despite the overwhelmingly statutory and regulatory nature of tax law. Certain key judicial doctrines pervade the tax law area and tax planners must be aware of these.

The Business Purpose Doctrine Roughly, the business purpose doctrine looks askance at tax-motivated transactions. It requires that there be some non-tax purpose, such as an independent business purpose, for a given transaction to be given its tax effect. Transactions that have only tax motivations are to be disregarded. The business purpose "requirement" is a well-established cornerstone of tax law. It is codified in the Treasury Regulations in several places.

The Step Transaction Doctrine In a like manner, the step transaction doctrine holds that a court may look at the end result of a series of transactions and "collapse" the intervening steps if the steps were merely steps without any independent economic significance and they were predetermined to reach the end result. In other words, if a taxpayer wants to go from situation "A" to situation "B" but doing so would incur the unfavorable tax result "X," that taxpayer may find a way to get first from "A" to "C" without any unfavorable result and then get from "C" to "B" also without any unfavorable result. The net result would be that the taxpayer got from "A" to "B" without incurring the unfavorable result "X." If the intervening steps from "A" to "C" and from "C" to "B" do not have independent economic significance and the transaction was planned to end up at "B" then the courts may invoke the step transaction doctrine to disregard the intervening steps and cause the taxpayer to suffer the unfavorable result "X" anyway.

The Substance Over Form Doctrine Although the tax laws place great weight on following the allowable form of a transaction in order to attain the desired tax result, there are circumstances in which the courts will look beyond the form of the transaction at its substance. In a sense, both the business purpose doctrine and the step transaction doctrine are applications of the substance over form doctrine in that they both will cause an otherwise proper form to be disregarded for tax purposes. In particular, a court might look to apply the substance over form doctrine where the taxpayer's motivation was solely that of avoiding paying taxes.

3. Administration of Tax Laws

The U.S. tax system is based on self-assessment of taxes made by the taxpayer in on a "tax return" form. In other words, the taxpayer calculates the amount of taxes due and submits the amount due along with the tax return to the IRS. The taxpayer generally submits these forms without submitting any of the underlying documents (such as receipts for claimed expenses). But while the honesty of individual taxpayers is important and is relied upon heavily to produce accurate taxation, the system is not a complete "honor" system. If necessary, audits and even criminal investigations may be undertaken to follow up on the taxpayers self-assessment.

Investigations of potential criminal matters are conducted by "special agents" of the IRS' Criminal Investigation Division (the "CID"). An investigation by the CID is essentially the same as an investigation by any other law enforcement agency of the government (such as the FBI) and should be treated accordingly. The general rule in normal audits is for the taxpayer to cooperate with the government's requests. If the audit turns into a criminal investigation the taxpayer should not have any further contact with the government agents before she contacts a lawyer who specializes in criminal defense.

a. Initial Screening of Returns

Tax returns are initially reviewed only for mathematical errors. They are then reviewed by sophisticated computer programs designed to highlight potential problems. If the computer finds an area of the return in which the amounts claimed for an item are outside the average range of amounts, then that area of the return is marked for further review by an IRS agent (a "revenue agent"). If the review shows potential problems, the return is marked for an "audit." An audit is an official review of the tax return by an agent of the IRS.

b. Tax Audits

In General   If the tax return is marked for audit the taxpayer will be notified by the IRS of the time and place for the review of the tax return. The notification to the taxpayer includes a list of the issues that are to be examined and a request by the IRS to see the documents supporting the taxpayer's position on the return. The notice also tells whether the audit will occur at the local IRS office (an "office audit") or at the taxpayer's place of business (a "field audit"). Audits of individuals are usually office audits and will take place at the local IRS offices and are conducted by tax auditors. Audits of businesses are usually field audits and will take place at the place of business of the taxpayer and are conducted by revenue agents. The reason for the difference in the place of the audit is that access to records is usually easier on site at a business, while the individual taxpayer can usually bring in the requisite records without difficulty.

Audits are conducted informally. Most audits start with a revenue agent, who is usually not a lawyer or accountant, looking at supporting documents, such as receipts for expenses, to support the taxpayers position on the tax return. The great majority of audits end when the revenue agent is satisfied that the taxpayer has sufficient documentation to support the item on the return. However, some audits continue beyond this factual inquiry and concern legal issues or mixed issues of law and fact.

An audit comprises both a factual part and a legal part. Among the most common issues in audits is the propriety of "deductions" from income. The allowance or disallowance of a deduction affects the important issue of how much taxable income the taxpayer had. For example, among the more common deductions that get raised in audits are those permitted for business expenses, interest paid on loans, depreciation of business property, and gifts to charities.

The "Factual" Part of the Audit   In this part of the audit, the basic facts of the claimed deduction are established. If a business deduction is questioned, the taxpayer is asked to substantiate the claim that the business-related item was in fact purchased by production a receipt and evidence of payment. If a charitable deduction is questioned, the taxpayer will be asked to produce a receipt and canceled check for the donation.

The "Legal" Part of the Audit   The legal part of the audit will involve whether the expense for which a deduction has been claimed is a legitimate one from the standpoint of the law. If the taxpayer claimed a deduction for business expenses for using his car to take his children to school and to soccer practice, this would not be allowed as a business expense as a matter of law. On other hand, if the taxpayer is a salesperson who travels by car in her business, the deduction of transportation expenses would probably be proper.

It does not matter in which "order" the audit is conducted. In practice the two "parts" are often intermixed. The legal part may be conducted first if it disposes of the issue. Thus, if it is clear that the taxpayer's deduction is for taking the children to school and soccer practice, it will not matter whether the taxpayer can substantiate the expense or method of calculating it.

c. Administrative Protests and Appeals

When the revenue agent is satisfied that there is enough information the agent will issue a report (commonly called a "revenue agent's report" or "RAR").

The "Thirty Day Letter" The RAR is attached to a letter (commonly called a "thirty day letter") to the taxpayer that gives the taxpayer thirty days to appeal the conclusions in the report to the Appellate Division of the IRS. If the taxpayer wishes to dispute the conclusions she will generally be required to file a "protest" (or "protest letter") with the IRS within thirty days.

The Appellate Division of the IRS Upon receipt of the protest the IRS will transfer the case internally to the Appellate Division where it will be assigned to an "appeals officer." The appeals officer will review the file anew and will schedule a hearing with the taxpayer and the taxpayer's representative (typically her lawyer or accountant). The original revenue agent will generally not be present. Appeals officers are generally better trained and more sophisticated that revenue agents. They also have the authority (which auditors do not have) to "settle" a dispute with a taxpayer based on the possible risk to the IRS of losing the case if it were to go to litigation. The appellate hearing will also be an informal proceeding. The taxpayer will again be allowed to present her view of the issues. Sometime after the hearing the appeals officer will issue a final report. The report typically comes in the form of a letter stating the conclusions of the appeals officer.

The "Ninety Day Letter" If the taxpayer choose not to protest the original revenue agent's conclusions, or at the end of the IRS appeals process, the IRS will send the taxpayer another letter (typically called a "ninety day letter") which will tell the taxpayer that she has ninety days to either pay the tax or to file a lawsuit in the U.S. Tax Court. As discussed below, the taxpayer may take the matter to the Tax Court and contest the findings of the IRS without first paying the claimed tax. The taxpayer may also choose to pay the tax and then sue for a refund in the U.S. District Court (where there are juries) or in the U.S. Claims Court. These courts will be discussed below.

d. Judicial Review

As mentioned earlier, if a taxpayer disagrees with the IRS as to the treatment of an issue and wishes to gain judicial review the decision of the IRS, the taxpayer can bring the matter to one of several courts. The taxpayer has the choice of three quite different tribunals: the Tax Court, the U.S. District Court and the Claims Court.[11]

The Tax Court If the taxpayer wishes to challenge the IRS's decision without first paying the tax the IRS has assess, the Tax Court is the only possibility. All cases in the tax court are tried to a single judge sitting alone. There are no jury trials in the Tax

---

[11] The Tax Court and the Claims Courts are Article I courts, while the U.S. District Court is an Article III court. This means that only the U.S. District Court has a judge with lifetime tenure. *See* Chapter VI, pp. 213-215.

Court. The judges of the Tax Court are specialists in tax matters and they hear no other kinds of cases.

Tax Court dockets tend to move quickly. Although the same types of pre-trial discovery are available in the Tax Court as in other courts, the judges tend to place great pressure on the parties to narrow the issues in the case. Indeed, Tax Court judges tend to make far more extensive use of stipulations than judges in other courts. In general, Tax Court judges will require that the parties stipulate to all facts about which there is no dispute. In this manner, trials in the Tax Court tend to be fairly streamlined. Although the Tax Court has its administrative offices in Washington, D.C., its judges hold court throughout the country. It is not uncommon for the Tax Court to hold court for several days each month in major U.S. cities.

Appeals from Tax Court rulings are taken in the U.S. Court of Appeals for the Circuit in which the taxpayer resides. It is not uncommon for the tax law on particular points may vary from Circuit to Circuit.[12]

The taxpayer also has the option of paying the tax the IRS says is due and then suing the government for a refund. A refund suit may be brought in either the District Court or the Claims Court.

District Court A suit for a refund in the District Court where the taxpayer resides is conducted in the same manner as any other civil matter. However, as in all civil jury cases, the jury will resolve only the factual issues in dispute. The District Judge will resolve any legal matters. District Judges are rarely specialists in tax matters. Depending on the nature of the case, it may or may not be to the taxpayer's advantage to have the case heard by a jury and/or by a non-specialist judge. Appeals from District Court decisions go the Court of Appeals for the circuit of which the district is a part and the District Court is bound to follow the precedents of its circuit.

Claims Court The U.S. Claims Court has jurisdiction to hear claims, including claims for tax refunds, against the United States. Cases in the Claims Court are heard by only by a judge. There are no juries. Some tax lawyers believe that the judges of the Claims Court are fairly sophisticated in handling large and business-related claims and are not as deferential to IRS interpretations of the Code as the Tax Court judges are sometimes perceived to be. Although the Claims Court is based in Washington, D.C., its judges will travel where necessary to hear evidence in a case. Unlike other courts, a trial in the Claims Court may occur in several sittings rather than all at once. These matters may make litigation in the Claims Court a more or less attractive option. Appeals from decisions of the Claims Court go to the Court of Appeals for the Federal Circuit.

From the above it can be seen that the taxpayer has the ability to make some strategy choices based on the type of issue presented and the type of tribunal involved. Among the factors to consider are the presence or absence of a jury, the state of the law in the Federal Circuit, as opposed to the taxpayer's home Circuit, and the facts that Tax Court judges are sophisticated in tax law and Claims Court judges expert in complicated business matters, while federal district judges tend to be generalists.

---

12 Although the Tax Court once tried to establish nation-wide standards for its decisions by claiming that it did not need to follow the decisions of the Court of Appeals of the circuit where the taxpayer resided, this attempt to establish an independent Tax Court jurisprudence was rejected by the Tax Court itself in *Golsen v. Comm'r of Internal Revenue*, 54 T.C. 742 (1970). Appeals of Tax Court decisions are heard in the taxpayers's circuit Court of Appeals and the Tax Court is bound to follow its precedents.

e. Tax Lawyers and Advisors

As noted in Chapter IV, despite the general nature of the license to practice law, U.S. lawyers tend to specialize in particular areas of practice. A few states have set minimum standards of competence in various specialties. Most "tax lawyers"are highly specialized and tend to do only tax-related work. It is fairly common, but by no means universal, for tax lawyers to have had additional formal post-graduate education beyond their law degrees from law school. A typical graduate tax program consists of one year of full-time course work, or three years of part-time course work, after the J.D. degree. It typically results in a Master of Laws degree, i.e., an LL.M. in Taxation. Nowadays most of the large American cities have at least one law school that offers at least a part-time graduate tax program.[13]

Most large businesses and large law firms have a separate department that deals only with tax matters. It would not be uncommon for a 200-lawyer firm to have a tax department with 20 tax lawyers. The large accounting firms also have large tax departments staffed with tax lawyers.

Tax lawyers are usually intimately involved in tax and business planning for their clients. The need for tax advice stems from the fact that there are usually several different ways to achieve the business result desired by a client. The different ways may have very different tax consequences. The tax lawyer helps the client to assess the potential impact of the various taxes on each of the different ways to accomplish the goal and advises the client of the potential risks involved in the different paths.[14]

C. Federal Income Tax

It is helpful to look at the federal income tax from several perspectives: who pays the tax (the taxable unit), what is being taxed (the tax base), and how the tax is calculated (the tax rate structure).

1. Taxpayers, the Tax Base and Taxable Income

Taxpayers The federal income tax has a broad sweep. All U.S. citizens are subject to the tax. All U.S. residents, even if they are not citizens, are subject to the tax. All U.S. corporations are subject to the tax. In addition, all individuals and business entities doing business in the U.S. or having U.S. source income are subject to the tax.

Tax Base The tax base comprises what is being taxed. Here, too, the sweep of the income tax is broad. When looking at tax base, it is helpful to divide potential taxpayers into two categories. In the first are U.S. citizens, U.S. residents and U.S. corporations. All these taxpayers are liable for income tax on all of their income from anywhere in the world. A U.S. citizen who is living in Denmark and who only has income from Danish sources is subject to the income tax in the U.S. on that Danish income. A U.S. corporation that only does business in Japan is subject to U.S. income tax on its Japanese income.

This broad rule could clearly result in double taxation for this category of taxpayers. These are dealt with in the U.S. law and tax treaties. The principal mechanism for this is the granting of a "foreign tax credit" to the U.S. citizen, resident

---

13 LLM programs in law schools were discussed in Chapter IV.

14 Not just businesses are in need of tax planning. As discussed in Chapter XII, estate planning is essential to avoid having ones heirs pay more estate, gift or income tax than necessary upon ones death. Most lawyers who practice in the estate planning area are tax specialists.

or corporation for taxes paid to a foreign government.[15] This credit will offset any U.S. income tax liability by the amount of any *income tax* paid to a foreign government. But the initial position of the U.S. income tax is that all income from any source located anywhere is taxable if the potential taxpayer is a U.S. citizen, resident or corporation.

Individuals who are neither U.S. citizens nor residents and non-U.S. corporations, form the second category. This second class of taxpayer is generally only taxed on income that comes from U.S. sources. For example, a Brazilian corporation that does business in Brazil, Argentina and the U.S. will only be subject to U.S. income tax on its income from its U.S. activities.

Taxable Income   The income tax is levied on the "taxable income" of the individual or entity. As we will see in more detail later, taxable income is defined as "gross income" (essentially all income) minus certain specified deductions. Thus, a corporation may earn $1,000,000 in gross income but if it has spent $900,000 in allowable business expenses (such as for salaries, rent, etc.), it will have a taxable income of $100,000. It is only on this $100,000 of taxable income that the income tax is levied.

2. Tax Rates

The U.S. income tax has a graduated, "progressive" rate structure. This means that as a taxpayer earns more income, the taxpayer will not only pay more tax but will pay an increasing percentage of taxable income, i.e., will pay tax at an increasing rate.

Corporate Rates The taxation rate for corporations begins at a 15% rate.[16] This applies to the first $ 50,000 of taxable income. Thus a corporation with $20,000 of taxable income will owe $3,000 in income tax (15% times $20,000 = $3,000). Taxable income above $50,000 and up to $75,000 is taxed at the rate of 25 percent. Thus a corporation with $70,000 of taxable income will owe $12,500 in income tax. This is calculated as follows: the corporation will owe a tax of 15% of its first $50,000, or $7,500 (15% times $50,000 = $7,500). In addition, since the corporation earned $70,000, it will owe a tax of 25% on the $20,000 excess of its $70,000 in taxable income over the first $50,000. This second tier of tax is thus $5,000 (25% times $20,000 = $5,000). Its total tax bill will thus be $12,500 ($7,500 plus $5,000 = $12,500). It would be common to speak of the corporation as being in the "25% bracket." This is because the last dollars that the corporation earned were taxed at the "marginal rate" of 25%.

This concept of "marginal rate" or "marginal tax bracket" is a useful shorthand. If, for example, we are told that a taxpayer is in the middle of the 25% tax bracket then we know that the federal government will take 25 cents out of the next dollar it earns. When a taxpayer is considering expanding its business it may be helpful to realize that it will only get to keep 75 cents out of every dollar that it earns.

After the 15% and 25% brackets come the 34% and 35% brackets, which are the broadest brackets. Every dollar above $75,000 and up to $10,000,000 is taxed at a rate of 34%. Then, every dollar above $10,000,000 is taxed at a rate of 35%. As can be seen, when a corporation earns more it not only pays more in taxes, but it pays "progres-

---

15 26 U.S.C.A. §§901 et seq.

16 The corporate income tax rate schedule is found in §11 of the Internal Revenue Code, 26 U.S.C.A. §11.

sively" more in taxes in that the tax rate increases as the corporate income moves into higher brackets.[17]

Individual Rates In a like manner, individuals are also subject to a progressive rate structure.[18] The first $22,100 of taxable income is taxed at a 15% rate. The next dollars above $22,100 and up to $53,500 are taxed at marginal rate of 28%. The next dollars above $53,500 and up to $115,000 are taxed at a marginal rate of 31%. The next dollars above $115,000 and up to $250,000 are taxed at a rate of 36%. Lastly, any dollars of taxable income above $250,000 are taxed at a rate of 39.6%. Thus we can speak of the highest marginal tax rate on an individual's income as being 39.6%. Again, it is important to keep in mind that only the marginal dollars earned above $250,000 are taxed at that rate. But, as we noted with respect to corporations, it is sometimes useful to be aware that an individual in this bracket only gets to keep about 60 cents out of every dollar earned.

3. Taxable Income

The federal income tax is a tax on net income only, i.e., on gross income minus specified allowable deductions. In the language of the Internal Revenue Code (the "Code"), the income tax is imposed on the "taxable income" of the taxpayer. The two principal sections imposing the tax are §1 (on individuals) and §11 (on corporations. "Taxable income" is a term of art that is defined in §63 of the Code as "gross income minus the deductions allowed by this chapter . . ."

a. Gross Income

"Gross income," also a term of art, is the starting point for determining taxable income. It is defined as "all income from whatever source derived . . ."[19] The word "income" itself is not defined in the Code, but has been consistently interpreted by the courts (including the U.S. Supreme Court) very broadly.[20] This tax concept of income is roughly equivalent to the definition used by many economists as "anything that results in an increase in net worth." For example, if Marcia, a lawyer, received a fee of $1,000 in cash, Marcia would have $1,000 of gross income. There are a few statutory exclusions from this general rule. For example, if Marcia received a birthday gift of $1,000 she would have income in the economic sense, but the Code specifically excludes gifts from gross income.[21] The statutory exclusions[22] are generally motivated by social policy concerns.

---

17 When a corporation earns more than $100,000, it starts to pay another small amount in income tax which is calculated to eliminate the benefit it received of the lower tax rates on the first dollars it earned. In effect, the taxes "saved" by virtue of the lower rates on the first dollars are "recaptured" once the corporation starts to earn more than $100,000. It is still appropriate for most purposes to think of the maximum marginal corporate tax rate as being 35%. Indeed, as a corporation earns somewhat over $100,000 one can also view its tax burden as resulting from a "flat (non-progressive) tax" of 34 or 35%.

18 The individual income tax rate schedule is found in §1 of the Internal Revenue Code, 26 U.S.C.A. §1.

19 26 U.S.C.A. §61. The U.S. Supreme Court has held that in determining whether a transfer of property is a "gift" under §102 requires looking at the subjective motivation of the donor. If that motivation is from "detached and disinterested generosity" or "out of affection...or like impulses" and *not* because of some duty and *not* with anticipation of some benefit, then a transfer should be considered a "gift" for purposes of §102. *Comm'r of Internal Revenue v. Duberstein*, 363 U.S. 278 (1960). The test for a gift under this Code section is not the same as the test for a gift under the federal gift tax (26 U.S.C.A. §§2501 *et seq.*) or the test for the making of a gift under common law. In other words, "gift" is a technical term whose "meaning" depends very much on the context in which it is found.

20 *See, e.g., Comm'r of Internal Revenue v. Glenshaw Glass*, 348 U.S. 426 (1955).

21 26 U.S.C.A. §102.

22 26 U.S.C.A. §§101-137.

Of course, if the tax system were purely based on such an economic concept of income it would be unwieldy to administer. Market values fluctuate over time. For example, assume Bill purchases a building in April for $100,000 and the building, because of market forces, is valued at $110,000 in June, but declines in value to $105,000 in July. How should he be taxed? There are several aspects of the tax system designed to deal with matters such as this one. In Bill's case, he will not be taxed until he sells the building and "realizes" the gain. This "realization requirement" has been read into the Code by the courts and will be discussed below.

b. Arriving at Taxable Income

"Horizontal Equity" Allowing of deductions is necessary for the fair application of the system. "Horizontal equity" demands that taxpayers in like situations be treated (or taxed) in a like manner, and that taxpayers in unlike situations be treated differently. For example, if Lora receives $100,000 from her business without having to spend any of her own capital and Jesse receives $100,000 from his business but only after spending $90,000 of his own money to get it, both Lora and Jesse would have $100,000 of *gross* income. But in an economic sense Jesse is only $10,000 better off while Lora is $100,000 better off. A fair system would impose a tax only on the *net* increases in their economic positions. In the example of Lora and Jesse, the Code would allow Jesse a deduction for all "ordinary and necessary" business expenses incurred by him.[23] Assuming that the $90,000 he spent was both ordinary and necessary in his business, Jesse would be allowed a deduction of that amount in computing his taxable income. In recognizing that Jesse has $10,000 of *taxable* income and Lora $100,000 of *taxable* income, the Code accomplishes a rough approximation of horizontal equity by taxing the two differently situated taxpayers in different manners. Similarly, if Charles received $500,000 of business income as a result of spending $400,000, he would be treated the same as Lora, i.e., as having $100,000 of *taxable* income.

Deductions and "Legislative Grace" While "gross income" is interpreted broadly, "deductions" are generally interpreted narrowly. Deductions are generally considered to be a matter of "legislative grace." In other words, if the item one wishes to deduct is not allowed *explicitly* by some section of the Code, it is not deductible. In dealing with deductions it is important to be able to point to a section of the Code that explicitly allows the deduction.

(1) Deductible Expenses

Allowable deductions are specifically set out in the Code.[24] Among the more common deductions available to all taxpayers are business expenses (§162), interest paid on borrowed money (§163), certain taxes (§164), certain losses (§165), and depreciation (§167). In addition, there are provisions applicable only to individuals.[25] For example, individuals are allowed to deduct ordinary and necessary expenses incurred in the production of income that is not part of a "business" (§212), and certain medical and dental expenses (§213).

---

23 26 U.S.C.A. §162.

24 26 U.S.C.A. §§161-249.

25 26 U.S.C.A. §§211-249.

It is also important to note that the sections allowing deductions are also subject to other specific Code provisions which may specifically *disallow* a deduction.[26] An example is the disallowance deductions for "capital expenditures." A capital expenditure consists of "improvements . . . made to increase the value of property."[27] For example, assume Donald spends $20,000 to put a new roof on the warehouse where he runs his business. Although the expenditure seems to fall under the category of an "ordinary and necessary" business expense, it would likely be considered to be a "permanent improvement" and thus not deductible. On the other hand, if Donald spent $7,000 merely *to repair* the old roof, it is *possible* (but not certain) that the $7,000 would be allowed as an ordinary and necessary business expense.

The difference between an "expense" (which is currently deductible) and a "capital expenditure" (which is not deductible) is often hazy. A very rough "rule of thumb" is to ask whether the item is likely to last more than one year. If it will last more than one year, its cost is likely to not be currently deductible. Thus, the cost of routine semi-annual maintenance on the heating system of a building is likely to be viewed as a currently deductible expense, whereas the cost of replacing the furnace (which is likely to last many years) is like to not be currently deductible.

However, just because the amount paid is a capital expenditure does not mean that no deduction can be claimed. The Code allows for recovery *over time* of the cost of most capital expenditures by allowing deductions for depreciation, depletion, and amortization, as discussed next.

(2) Capital Cost Recovery: Depreciation, Depletion Allowances, and Amortization

Depreciation The most basic type of depreciation allowance is calculated using the "straight line method." For example, assume Regina buys a truck for use in her business for $20,000 and expects to use the truck for four years, after which she expects to sell the truck for $12,000. Regina will be allowed a deduction for $2,000 for each of the four years she owns the truck.[28] The straight line deduction is calculated by figuring the amount of the expenditure that is expected to be "used up" and then dividing that amount by the expected "useful life" of the asset. In Regina's case, she spent $20,000 but expects to recover $12,000 when she sells the truck 4 years later.[29] In essence, Regina expects to use up $8,000 of the asset over a 4-year period. The straight line method simply allows the taxpayer to prorate this $8,000 amount over the 4 year useful life, and allows Regina her $2,000 per year deduction. The straight line method of depreciation is the touchstone for all other methods of depreciation.

The taxpayer may have the possibility of claiming greater depreciation in the earlier years of using the asset. Increased early deductions are usually more valuable to a taxpayer because they will usually result in a lower *current* tax bill and the taxpayer may invest these current tax savings. There are "accelerated" methods of depreciation available that, in special cases, can accomplish this. For instance, a taxpayer may qualify to use a "declining balance" method of depreciation. Such a method allows a taxpayer increased deductions in the early years of an asset's life and may more closely model the actual economic depreciation of the asset. The Code

---

26 Section 161 makes it clear that all of the sections following it that allow deductions are subject to the explicit *disallowance* provisions of §§261 *et seq.*

27 26 U.S.C.A. §263.

28 26 U.S.C.A. §167.

29 This $12,000 figure is referred to as the "salvage value" of the asset.

also establishes an "Accelerated Cost Recovery System" (often referred to as "ACRS") for depreciation related to tangible property.[30]

Because different kinds of capital expenditures may qualify for differing depreciation methods, it is generally wise for a business to seek the advice of a tax lawyer or tax accountant when planning any large asset acquisition. In addition to different methods of depreciation, intangible assets, such as "goodwill" or customer lists, may not be deductible if they are found to last indefinitely and thus deemed to have no calculable useful life. It is important to know the potential tax consequences of allocating values to such intangible assets when purchasing an entire business in order to estimate the amount of depreciation deductions that will be available to deduct from future income. Such allocations should be done carefully to be able to accurately assess the potential after-tax income of the business.

Depletion The Code allows for capital cost recovery in other areas (such as oil, gas, and minerals), through allowances for depletion of the asset. There are various methods of calculating such allowances. The potential tax benefits in these areas can be significant in analyzing the overall economic value of an investment. Here, too, a good lawyer will seek the advice of a tax professional.

Amortization A deduction for amortization is similar to a deduction for depreciation of an asset. It allows the taxpayer who had to "capitalize" the cost of the asset under §263 the ability to recover that cost over time by annual deductions. Sometimes the word "amortization" is used relatively loosely to mean recovery of the cost of any (usually intangible) asset. For instance, if Ed pays an up-front premium of $5,000 for the right to lease a certain office space for 10 years he will (1) be required to capitalize that expenditure (i.e., not be allowed to deduct in currently)[31], and (2) be allowed to amortize that cost over the life of the lease (i.e., be allowed annual deductions of $500 for the 10 years.)[32]

(3) Adjusted Gross Income

"Adjusted gross income" is defined [33] as gross income minus certain specified deductions (17 in all). The concept "adjusted gross income," commonly referred to as "AGI," serves only as a touchstone for calculations in other sections of the Code that are only applicable to individuals. For instance, §170 allows a deduction for charitable contributions. However, there is a limit on the amount of charitable contributions an individual may deduct in a given year. That limit (or "ceiling") is stated as a percentage of AGI. For the most preferred class of charities, that annual limit is 50% of the taxpayer's AGI (with one modification).

In a rough, conceptual sense, AGI can be seen as the economic income of the taxpayer. The specified deductions can be very loosely viewed as an indication of the economic cost of earning the gross income. AGI is also used outside the field of tax law in economic policy studies where it is sometimes used as a measure of income for comparison of individuals.

---

30 26 U.S.C.A. §168.
31 26 U.S.C.A. §263(a).
32 26 U.S.C.A. §178.
33 26 U.S.C.A. §62.

(4) The Sale or Disposition of Property

Realization and Recognition The Code requires that gross income include "gains derived from dealings in property."[34] Whether gain is included in gross income is a two-step process of determining (1) if the taxpayer had "realized" any gain and (2) if so, whether any of the realized gains are to be "recognized."[35] Most "dispositions" of property are an "event of realization." However, any gain from such a disposition will be taxable only if it is "recognized."[36]

(a) Non-Realization and Non-Recognition of Gain

Non-Realization Some kinds of dispositions, gifts, for example, are not an event of realization. For example, if Valerie mortgages a piece of real estate in exchange for a loan, this "disposition" is not an "event of realization" that will trigger gain or loss.[37]

Non-Recognition There are numerous Code sections that provide for the "non-recognition" of gain. These sections are generally motivated by policy and fairness concerns. For instance, if Nancy exchanges an office building for another office building in an even exchange (i.e., she receives no additional cash), that exchange *is* an "event of realization" which would cause realization of the gain. Normally, the Code would require recognition of that gain and its inclusion in gross income. However, forcing Nancy to recognize gain (and to thus include it in gross income) seems unduly harsh for at least two reasons. First, Nancy's position has changed little. Before the transaction she owned one building and now, after the transaction, she owns a similar building. The principle of horizontal equity could argue for her to be treated as if nothing had happened. Second, since Nancy received no cash, she would be forced to use other assets to pay any tax due or forced to mortgage the property to get cash to pay the tax. This would violate a fundamental theoretical tenet of fair tax systems — that taxes should, if possible, be "market-neutral." In other words, taxes should not unintentionally force a taxpayer to engage in a market transaction to satisfy a tax burden (or to obtain a tax benefit).

These two concerns, among others, led to the enactment of §1031 of the Code which specifically provides for non-recognition of gain when that gain was realized by an exchange of one property for a "like-kind" property.[38] Nancy would thus qualify for non-recognition treatment. Of course, §1031 also provides that any gain that Nancy had that was not recognized on the exchange will be "preserved" in the new property. When Nancy actually sells the new building for cash she will have to recognize (and be taxed on) any gain that was carried over from the original building. Thus, non-recognition provisions generally only *defer* the payment of taxes; they do not forgive the payment. The mechanisms for accomplishing this are discussed below.

---

34 26 U.S.C.A. §61(a)(3).

35 26 U.S.C.A. §1001 *et seq.*

36 26 U.S.C.A. §1001(c).

37 There are other "dispositions" of property that are also not events of realization. For example, the making of a gift can be viewed as not being an event of realization in that no gain or loss is generally triggered by that act.

38 There are many non-recognition provisions in the Code. We will see some others later in the sections on the corporate tax.

(b) Gain or Loss Realized from Disposition

Gains More common than gifts or exchanges are sales of property. If Chris buys a building for $60,000 and then sells it two years later for $80,000 cash, common sense (sometimes a rare commodity in the tax law) tells us that he should only be taxed on the $20 gain he had in the transaction. This is exactly what the Code does,[39] although not before going through several intermediate steps.[40]

Gain Defined: Amount Realized Minus Adjusted Basis Gain from a sale or other disposition is "the excess of the amount realized therefrom over the adjusted basis provided in §1011 for determining gain."[41] The terms "amount realized" and "adjusted basis" are both terms of art and are defined in the Code.

"Amount Realized" Defined The "amount realized" is defined as "the sum of any money received plus the fair market value of the property (other than money) received."[42] So, if Miles sells a building he owns for $200,000 cash plus $30,000 worth of stock in ABC Corp., Miles's amount realized on the sale is $230,000.[43]

"Adjusted Basis" Defined The "adjusted basis" is a little more complicated. It is the "original basis" "adjusted" by other provisions of the Code. Generally, the original basis is the cost of the property.[44] If Miles purchased the building four years ago for $120,000 cash, then the original basis was the building's cost of $120,000. As for adjustments to the basis, two of the most common ones are "(1) for expenditures . . . properly chargeable to the capital account . . . [and] (2) for exhaustion, wear and tear, obsolescence, amortization and depletion."[45]

Adjustments for Capital Expenditures and for Depreciation The cost of the capital expenditure is *added* to the *basis* of the building. If Miles, in the example just given, had spent $20,000 to place a new roof on the building just after he bought the building, that $20,000 would be *added* to the original basis in the building. Miles's *adjusted basis* in the building would then be $140,000. Further, assume Miles properly depreciated his $140,000 cost of the building and roof and properly took, say, $3,000 as a depreciation deduction on his taxes for each of the 4 years he owned the building. If so, Miles's basis must be *decreased* by the amount of the deduction.[46] So, every

---

39 26 U.S.C.A. §1001(a).

40 Section 1001(a) tells how to calculate the gain or loss resulting from "the sale or other disposition of property." In a sense, this is a codification (albeit a somewhat vague one) of the realization requirement discussed above. In other words, if the taxpayer has neither sold nor otherwise "disposed" of property, there will be no gain or loss to calculate. Although the term "sale" is fairly clear, the term "other disposition" is not. For instance, is the mortgaging of a property in exchange for a loan a "disposition"? Although the answer to this question is generally "No", it is less than clear why this is so. After all, the taxpayer who mortgages property does give away an interest in the property and will have cash from the loan that could be used to pay taxes. It has generally been left to the courts and the Regulations to clarify on a case-by-case basis what is and what is not a "disposition".

41 26 U.S.C.A. §1001(a).

42 26 U.S.C.A. §1004(a).

43 As discussed later, a taxpayer may also have additional amount realized if on the sale of property he is "relieved" of any liability associated with that property (such as a mortgage liability). As we will see, this is so even if the taxpayer was not personally responsible for the debt.

44 26 U.S.C.A. §1012. In addition, as discussed later, a taxpayer may also count as part of the original basis of property purchased the amount of any liability (such as a mortgage liability) assumed by him or if the property is taken subject to such a liability even if he assumes no personal responsibility for the debt.

45 26 U.S.C.A. §1016(a)(1) and (a)(2).

46 26 U.S.C.A. §1016(a)(2).

time Miles took a $3,000 depreciation deduction (in each of the four years) the basis in the building would be *decreased* by $3,000 in that year. Miles's basis would thus be decreased by a total of $12,000 (to $128,000) as of the time of the sale.

These adjustments have the proper effect. For, if Miles's building had *actually* decreased in value by $12,000 by the time Miles sold it, and he thus sold it for $128,000 cash, Miles would realize *neither gain nor loss on the sale*. His amount realized would be the $128,000 cash he received and his adjusted basis would be the $120,000 original cost plus the $20,000 cost of the roof, minus the $12,000 adjustment for depreciation deductions allowed while he owned the building (thus, also equal to $128,000) which would yield no gain or loss. This is the correct result since Miles's claimed depreciation mirrored perfectly the economic depreciation of the building and roof.

However, experience tells us that most buildings usually *increase* in value over time. Consequently, one might wonder if Miles is getting away with something by being allowed to depreciate the building. But the Code controls for this when Miles sells the building. Assume that Miles is able to sell the building (and roof) for exactly what he paid four years earlier, $140,000 total. Since his adjusted basis at the time of the sale is $128,000, he will realize (and recognize) gain of $12,000. In essence, the Code causes Miles to *recapture* the $12,000 of depreciation deductions he took earlier in the form of gain later.[47]

Other Basis Provisions There are basis provisions in the Code other than those discussed above. In general, these provisions are of two types: *transferred* and *substituted* basis.

Transferred Basis For example, assume Susan gives a gift of one share of stock of XYZ Corporation, worth $100, to her daughter Whitney as a birthday present. If Susan bought the share of stock for $80, she would have had a cost basis of $80 in the stock. Assuming no adjustments to basis, Susan's adjusted basis in the stock would be $80. In essence, Susan transferred appreciated property to Whitney, i.e., stock which had an "inherent" gain of $20. In other words, if Susan had chosen instead to sell the stock for $100 cash, she would have realized a gain of $20 and all that gain would have been recognized. However, a *gift* of property, despite its seeming to be a "disposition," has never been considered an event of realization. So, Susan would realize no gain on making the gift to Whitney.

As we saw earlier, Whitney, one receiving the gift would have no gross income under §61 because of the exclusion of gifts from gross income under §102. But, a question remains: What is *Whitney's* basis in the stock? We need to know this to determine any gain or loss to Whitney when she sells the stock. The Code provides generally that Susan's basis is "transferred" to Whitney along with the gift itself.[48] This mechanism preserves the gain inherent in the stock and insures that it will be taxed

---

47 In this manner, "excessive" depreciation deductions only give a temporary benefit to the taxpayer. They will be "recaptured" later when the taxpayer sells the property. Depreciation deductions can thus be seen as providing a potential for tax *deferral*. Of course, if all other things are equal, a taxpayer will prefer to pay tax later rather than earlier since the current tax savings can be invested. Even when the taxpayer ultimately has to pay the tax, he still gets to keep the investment returns on the tax savings. In a sense, tax deferral is like getting an interest-free loan from the government. It is not uncommon that tax benefits, such as tax deferral, may influence the economic viability of an otherwise marginal business deal.

48 26 U.S.C.A. §1015 (basis for the donee "shall be the same as it would be in the hands of the donor").

eventually. Thus, if Whitney sells the stock later that same day for $100 cash (because she would rather have the cash to buy new jeans), then Whitney will realize and recognize gain of $20.

Substituted Basis There is a similar result when there is an exchange of property, except that it is called a "substituted basis." Returning to the case of Nancy, who exchanged one office building for another, the basis of Nancy's old building is *substituted* into the new property.[49]

Apply this to Nancy's exchange of her office building, assume that the fair market value of Nancy's office building was $250,000 and that it had an adjusted basis in her hands of $210,000 (what she paid for it). If Nancy had chosen to sell the building for $250,000 cash, she would have a realized and recognized $40,000 gain. If Nancy instead exchanges her building for another office building also worth $250,000, she would *realize* a gain of $40 under section, but that gain would *not be recognized*. The basis Nancy's old building is substituted for the basis of the new building. Later, when Nancy sells the new building, Nancy's gain of $40,000 is taxed.

Thus, whenever there is an "event" which either does not cause current realization of gain (as with a gift) or does not cause current recognition of gain (as with the like-kind exchange we saw earlier with Nancy's office building) there is always going to be a provision that will preserve any inherent gain by preserving the old basis.

Discharge of Debt as Gross Income If Miles borrows $100 from his employer, Tess, he will not have any income since his net worth will not have changed. Although he has $100 more cash after the borrowing, he also has $100 more in liabilities after the borrowing. His net worth did not change. If Tess later relieves Miles of his obligation to pay that debt back to her, Miles receives an economic benefit from that act in that his net worth increased *at that moment*. At the moment of discharge of the debt by Tess, Miles's liabilities decreased by $100, thus *increasing* his net worth. The Code treats this discharge of indebtedness as gross income.[50] A similar, but even more extensive set of rules apply to debts related to property transactions.

Relief of Liabilities as Part of the Amount Realized The amount of any liability of which a taxpayer is relieved in conjunction with the sale of property constitutes an economic "benefit" to him just as in the case of any other discharge of debt. In this context it is functionally the same as if the seller were given cash by the purchaser with which to pay off the debt. Assume Joe owns a building worth $200,000 and the building was subject to a mortgage liability of $160,000. A potential purchaser might be willing to assume the $160,000 mortgage debt, but would then only be willing to give Joe an additional $40,000 cash since the building is only worth $200,000. If the sale is concluded this way, Joe would get a total economic "benefit" of $200,000 in the form of the $40,000 cash and the relief from the $160,000 liability.

---

49 26 U.S.C.A. §1031(d) ("the basis [of the new property] shall be the same as that of the property exchanged [i.e., the old property]").

50 26 U.S.C.A. §61(a)(12). Of course, if the reason for Tess's discharge of Miles's debt was that of "detached and disinterested generosity" and without any anticipation of a future benefit to her, then the discharging of the debt could be viewed as a "gift" within the purview of §102 and the *Duberstein* case discussed earlier and thus excludable from gross income. However, if the only relationship between Tess and Miles is that of employer-employee, it will be very hard to sustain this claim for "gift" treatment. Thus, one should always look at the *reason* behind an act in order to determine its significance for tax purposes. In the case of discharge of indebtedness, there is also potential direct statutory relief in §108 of the Code, where discharge of indebtedness is excluded from gross income if the taxpayer is insolvent or in formal bankruptcy proceedings (or in one of a few other narrowly defined situations).

The case law and Treasury Regulations make it clear that "the amount realized from a sale . . . of property includes the amount of liabilities from which the transferor *is discharged*."[51] This makes obvious sense if the seller is being relieved of a personal obligation. However, it is not uncommon in large commercial purchases of real estate for the potential owner to arrange mortgage financing so that *no one* is personally liable on the debt and the lender's interest is secured by the property. This type of financing is called "non-recourse" financing because the lender has no "recourse" against the borrower directly if the debt is not paid. All the lender can do in such a situation is to foreclose on its security interest in the property. The Regulations take the position (correctly, we shall see) that even if the liability that Joe was "relieved" of (in the above example) was a non-recourse mortgage liability (i.e., one for which Joe was not personally liable, but merely one which secured the property), then Joe must count the amount of that liability as part of his amount realized on the sale. The Regulations state that for purposes of calculating the amount realized, "the sale . . . of property that secures a nonrecourse liability *discharges* the transferor from the liability."[52] Such a deemed "discharge" is thus included in the amount realized.

Liabilities Assumed as Part of the "Cost" It is well-established, originally by the U.S. Supreme Court and later in Treasury Regulations, that if a taxpayer purchases property and part of the purchase price is the assumption of a liability on the property, then the amount of that liability is included in the "cost" of the property for figuring the basis of the property. For example, if Peggy purchases an apartment building for $10,000 cash plus the assumption of a $120,000 mortgage liability, then her basis in the property will be $130,000. Thus, in essence, the cost basis of includes the amount of any loans that are part of the financing. This is true *even if the liability is a non-recourse liability* (one for which she is not personally liable). Since Peggy is permitted (required, actually) to include the amount of non-recourse debt in her basis when she buys the property, she will be able to use that basis of $130,000 for purposes of figuring how much depreciation she may take on the property.[53] In essence, Peggy will be treated *just as if she had borrowed the money and was personally liable*. This principle was needed in order to treat the property of non-recourse borrowers the same as that of full-recourse borrowers. Peggy will also get to use that same basis (adjusted, of course, for depreciation and such) as her basis when she sells the property. We can now see the logic and symmetry of treatment of requiring Peggy, or indeed, any seller, to include *in her amount realized* the amount of any non-recourse liability outstanding at that time when she sells the property. She was treated for tax purposes as if she were personally liable on the loan (even though she was not) at the purchase of the property, and she will be treated the same at the sale of the property.

Losses The first step in calculating a loss is to subtract the amount realized from the adjusted basis. The adjusted basis will, by definition, always be higher than the amount realized when we have a loss. For example, if Martin buys vacant land for use in his business for $100,000 cash and later sells the land for $70,000, he would realize and recognize a loss of $30,000 since his adjusted basis would be $100,000 and his

---

51   Treas. Reg. 1.1001-2(a)(1) (emphasis added).

52   Treas. Reg. 1.1001-2(a)(4)(I) (emphasis added).

53   26 U.S.C.A. §167(c)(1).

amount realized only $70,000. Martin will be able to deduct the loss against his other income (if any).[54]

On the other hand, if Martin had bought the land *for his personal use only* (such as for camping for him and his family) for the same $100,000 and sold it for the same $70,000, then he would have a problem. The Code provides that "[e]xcept as otherwise expressly provided in this chapter, no deduction shall be allowed for personal, living, or family expenses."[55] The loss, although realized and recognized, would not be allowed because the property was being used for personal purposes rather than business purposes. This "personal" loss exception makes the treatment of gains and losses asymmetrical. If Martin had purchased the vacant land for personal use and resold it at a *gain*, he would be taxed despite the fact that he had no business use in mind.

It is worth noting that a taxpayer can change her mind and *convert* personal use property into property for use in business or held "for profit" and thus potentially qualify for a deductible loss on sale.[56] However, the courts have generally held that this conversion must be an *actual* conversion of *actual* use, and not just a change of intent. Even so, the Regulations hold that the basis for determining ultimate loss on sale is the *lower* of the taxpayer's actual basis or the fair market value at the time of conversion.[57] For example, assume Taylor bought for $100,000 a large tract of vacant land for personal use which she did use for several years that way. If she then actually converted the property to business use (say, by starting a sheep ranch) or to "profit" use (say, by leasing it to sheep ranchers) at a time when the property was worth $80,000, then Taylor's basis *for loss purposes* would be $80,000. If she ultimately sold the ranch land for $70,000 she would be allowed a $10,000 loss. This seems reason-

---

54 Losses are permitted to be deducted by §165(a) ("There shall be allowed as a deduction any loss sustained....").

55 26 U.S.C.A. §262(a). Even though §165(a) (quoted in the last footnote) would apparently allow the deduction, there are two other issues to deal with. First, §165(c) limits the losses deduction allowed to individuals to (1) "losses incurred in a trade or business"; (2) losses incurred in any transaction entered into for profit"; and (3) other losses but only if they "arise from fire, storm, shipwreck, or other casualty, or from theft." Martin could attempt to argue that he bought the land with a profit motive and thus should qualify for a deduction under §165(c)(2). However, taxpayers are usually not successful in this line of argument which often arises in the context of personal residence that is sold at a loss. Courts usually hold that if the primary purpose was for personal use there is no deduction allowed. Indeed, §161 makes it clear that the deduction allowed in the sections following §161 (Part VI of Subchapter B of Chapter 1 of Subtitle A of Title 26 of the U.S. Code) are "subject to the exceptions provided in part IX (sec. 261 and following . . .)." Since §165, which Martin hoped would allow the deduction of the loss, is in part VI, it is subject to disallowance by §262, which is in part IX. Although §262 does allow for the possibility of another section which would expressly override it somewhere in Chapter 1 (which is the whole income tax chapter), there is none. As this demonstrates, the Tax Code is inordinately complex even when it comes to trying to find the answer to simple questions. As noted before with respect to acquiring property, it is always advisable to consult with a tax lawyer before engaging in the selling of property as well.

56 26 U.S.C.A. §165(a) allows the loss, and §165(c)(1) and (c)(2), respectively, would then exempt the loss from the limitations §165(c) otherwise imposes on individuals if the property is "incurred in a trade or business" or was part of a "transaction entered into for profit." If the taxpayer actually converts the property to business use, (c)(1) would clearly govern. If the taxpayer actually converts the property "profit" use (such as by actually renting out the former personal use property), then (c)(2) would govern, although it would seem that the "transaction entered into for profit could not likely be the ultimate sale since the taxpayer would know she was going to sustain a loss. And, we already know that the original purchase was not entered into for profit but for personal use. The only other possible "transaction" is the "transaction" (using this word rather loosely) of the conversion itself. The reader can be left to decide the somewhat metaphysical question of how an individual goes about entering into a transaction with herself.

57 Treas. Reg. 1.165-9(b)(2).

able, since the property lost that amount of value since the time of its conversion. It is interesting to note that Taylor's basis for gain still remains her $100,000 cost basis. If she sold the property for $120,000, she would recognize $20,000 of gain. Of course, this leaves an interesting middle ground where Taylor would have neither gain nor loss. If she sold the property for $90,000, she would have no gain (because her basis for gain purposes was $100,000). Nor would she have a loss (because her basis for loss purposes was $80,000).

"Characterization" of Gains and Losses: Capital Gains and Losses   There is a class of gains and losses that have a long history of being given special treatment under the Code. In general, capital gains are taxed at a lower rate than other income for individuals.[58] This preferential rate for individuals is imposed only on the "net capital gain," namely the amount of capital gain left over after subtracting the capital losses for the year, and then making some minor adjustments. Over the last few decades the rate at which capital gains have been taxed has varied widely. Capital losses are very restricted as to their deductibility.

The terms "capital gain" and "capital loss" are technical ones and should not be used loosely. A "capital gain" is a gain that results from the sale or exchange of a "capital asset."[59] A capital asset is defined as all property except listed types of property. However, the listed items tend to be interpreted broadly, and thus the term "capital asset" tends to be interpreted narrowly. A typical *non-capital asset* is inventory. The sale of inventory in the regular course of business will not generate capital gain.[60] A typical *capital asset* is stock in a corporation if the stock is owned by a taxpayer who is *not* in the business of buying and selling corporate stock. If the taxpayer were in that business, then the stock would be considered to be inventory and thus excluded from the definition of capital asset. Thus, the corporate stock portfolio of an individual usually contains only capital assets.

There is also a serious downside to an asset being classed as a capital asset. Allowance of deductions for capital losses is very limited. As we have discussed, the Code generally allows a deduction for losses.[61] However, for corporate taxpayers, deductions for capital losses are allowed only to the extent of capital gains.[62] For individual taxpayers, deductions for capital losses are only allowed to the extent of capital gains plus $3,000 per year.[63] Any losses not allowed in a given year may be carried to other years under a rather complicated set of rules.[64] The debate about the propriety of a preferential rate on capital gains and limitations on the deductibility of capital losses has been going on for several decades. Congress responds by modifying the treatment of capital gains and losses every few years, sometimes radically so. It does not look like this pattern of change is going to stop any time soon.

---

58   26 U.S.C.A. §1(h). The maximum rate of tax on "net capital gain" for individuals, as of 1999, is 20 percent. This should be contrasted with the maximum rate of tax on ordinary income of nearly 40 percent. Corporations are taxed on their "net capital gain" at the same rate as they are taxed on other income. However, both corporations and individuals are subject to the limitation on deductions of capital losses discussed below.

59   26 U.S.C.A. §1221.

60   26 U.S.C.A. §1221(1).

61   26 U.S.C.A. §165(f).

62   26 U.S.C.A. §1211(a).

63   26 U.S.C.A. §1211(b).

64   *See* 26 U.S.C.A. §1212 for the rules.

(c) The Taxable Year and Accounting Methods

The "Taxable Year" The Code requires that taxable income "be computed on the basis of the taxpayer's taxable year." "Taxable year" is defined as "the taxpayer's annual accounting period."[65] In general, the annual accounting period is either the calendar year or a "fiscal year." A fiscal year is defined as "a period of 12 months ending on the last day of any month other than December."

The timing of when a taxpayer has income or loss is significant. Assume that Elizabeth, a calendar-year taxpayer, owns a manufacturing corporation that is also a calendar year taxpayer and that Elizabeth is the chief executive officer of the corporation. If the corporation receives $60,000 of cash from customer on December 31, 1999 it will have $60,000 more gross income for 1999. However, if it pays Elizabeth a compensation bonus of $60,000 on December 31, 1999 it will have a deduction for that amount and thus have no net effect because the receipt of the $60,000 from its customer will be offset by the compensation paid. Elizabeth, on the other hand, will have gross income for 1999 and will have to pay tax (around $24,000 at current maximum rates) on that income by April 15, 2000, which is the day her 1999 tax return and payment are due.

Assume, on the other hand, Elizabeth's corporation had elected to be a January 31 fiscal year taxpayer when it was formed. When it receives its $60,000 payment from its customer on December 31, 1999 it would have gross income for its fiscal year ending one month later. If, instead of paying Elizabeth her $60,000 bonus on December 31, 1999 it waits until January 1, 2000, *it* will receive a deduction for the compensation paid in the same *fiscal* year as it had income. However, when *Elizabeth* receives the income on January 1, 2000, she would have additional gross income for her calendar year *2000*, and would only have to pay tax on that income by April 15, *2001*, which is the day her 2000 tax return would be due. In other words, by virtue of having received the income *one day* later, she gets to defer the payment of the $24,000 for a *one full year*. If she could invest that money at 8% interest, this *deferral* of one year would be worth nearly $2,000 to her.

This example is intended to point out that there are sometimes deferral advantages to having a corporation and its shareholders on different taxable years. There are some limitations on the ability to defer income. For instance, Elizabeth's corporation could not have been a "personal service corporation," that is, a corporation whose "principal activity is the performance of personal services . . . by its employee-owners." In addition, Elizabeth *may* have to make an estimated tax payment on the expected tax due on the $60,000 early on in the year 2000 (which would seriously limit the deferral), but that question depends on other facts about her.

It is important to remember that a taxpayer (including a corporation) makes the election of its annual accounting period at the time of the filing of the first tax return. Any change in annual accounting period must be approved by the IRS.[66] It is thus important to choose the annual accounting period carefully at the time of the first return.

Tax Accounting Tax accounting and regular financial accounting are related, but by no means identical systems. For instance, a corporation cannot simply file its

---

[65] 26 U.S.C.A. §441(a) and (b).
[66] 26 U.S.C.A. §442.

annual financial accounting income statement as its tax return for a given year. There is thus a cost to maintaining a set of tax records as well as a set of regular financial records.

According to the Code, taxable income "shall be computed under the method of accounting on the basis of which the taxpayer regularly computes his income in keeping his books."[67] There are numerous permissible methods of accounting authorized in particular sections of the Code. However, the two most common permissible methods of tax accounting are "the cash receipts and disbursements method" and the "accrual method."[68]

The "Cash Method" Under the cash method, the taxpayer must report any income or loss only in the year in which she actually (or "constructively") receives payment. If a business deal "closes" on December 27 of a given year, but the cash-method taxpayer only receives the proceeds on January 3 of the following year, the taxpayer will have gain or loss only in the second year. In a like manner, if the cash-method taxpayer receives an invoice on December 14 for an amount due, but pays the invoice on January 12 of the next year, a deduction will only be allowed in the second year.[69] Almost all individuals use the cash method of accounting in their personal returns.

The Accrual Method Under the accrual method, a taxpayer is deemed to receive income in the taxable year "when all the events have occurred that fix the right to receive the income and the amount of the income can be determined with reasonable accuracy."[70] A like rule applies with respect to the taxable year for a deduction for a liability incurred.[71] It is irrelevant when the taxpayer actually receives money or pays the bill. All "C corporations"[72] and any business that uses inventories are required to use the accrual method of accounting.[73]

Installment Sale Method of Accounting A taxpayer may use "any other method permitted by this chapter."[74] One of those methods is the "installment sale" method of accounting. For instance, if a cash-method taxpayer sells property at a gain but is to receive installment payments which extend beyond the end of the taxable year, then the taxpayer may report a portion of the gain in each year.[75] In general, the percentage of gain to be reported in each year will be proportional to the percentage of the total price received in that year.[76] This type of installment reporting is automatic unless the taxpayer elects not to have the transaction treated in this manner. See also

---

67 26 U.S.C.A. §446.

68 26 U.S.C.A. §446(c)(1) and (2).

69 Treas. Reg. 1.446-1(c)(1)(i).

70 Treas. Reg. 1.446-1(c)(1)(ii).

71 *Id.*

72 A "C corporation" is defined in §1361(a)(2) as any "corporation which is not an S corporation." An "S corporation" is defined in §1361(a)(1) as any "small business corporation" which makes an election to be taxed under subchapter S of the Code rather than Subchapter C of the Code. As discussed later, electing the "pass-through" treatment of subchapter S is very restricted. C corporations constitute the vast majority of corporations. They are taxed under the regular corporate tax rules of subchapter C of the Code (§§301 *et seq.*).

73 26 U.S.C.A. §448(a)(1)(C) governs the limitation on C corporations. Treas. Reg. 1.446-1(c)(2)(I) addresses the limitation on businesses with inventories.

74 Under Code §446(c)(3).

75 IRC §453(a) and (b)(1).

76 IRC §453(c).

§453A for special rules relating to non-dealers, and §453B for special rules relating to gain or loss on the disposition of installment obligations.

Other Permissible Methods of Accounting   There are other specific methods of accounting permitted in the Code.[77] It is advisable to check with a tax lawyer when planning a transaction in order to see whether the method of accounting used by the taxpayer in its financial reporting is a permissible method under the Code. Whatever method is used by a taxpayer, the Code requires that the method "clearly reflect income."[78] If it does not clearly reflect income, the IRS is authorized to recompute the taxable income of the taxpayer using a method that does clearly reflect income.

(d) Tax Credits

As noted earlier, the income tax is imposed on the taxable income of the taxpayer. However, a taxpayer may receive a dollar-for-dollar *credit* against the tax liability in certain circumstances. For example, if a taxpayer has prepaid part of the tax liability through tax required to be withheld by an employer (or through required quarterly payments of estimated tax liability), then the taxpayer will be entitled to offset its tax liability by the amount prepaid.[79] In a like manner, income taxes paid to a foreign government are creditable against a U.S. income tax liability.[80] There are also various other types of credits available to some taxpayers as mechanisms of social policies.

4. Income Tax on Corporations

As seen from the examples used and general content of the above, all the basic concepts outlined apply to corporations. However, there are other aspects of the tax system that present unique issues with regard to corporations.

a. Double Taxation of Corporate Income

As already pointed out in the last chapter when choice of business form was discussed, the federal Internal Revenue Code imposes a tax on the taxable income of corporations.[81] In addition, the individual income tax, includes in gross income dividends received from corporations.[82] However, the Code does *not* allow corporations to deduct from *its* gross income dividends paid to shareholders. The result of this structure is that corporate income is in effect taxed twice – once at the corporate level and then again when the income is distributed to shareholders.

This result deserves some explanation by way of a brief detour into the philosophy of taxation. It is generally agreed that a tax system (and, in fact, government in general) should adhere at a fundamental level to at least four basic principles: horizontal equity, vertical equity, market neutrality, and economic efficiency. The U.S. corporate tax system has been criticized for running afoul of each of these principles. There have been numerous proposals to reform the system of double taxation, but none of them has ever gained much momentum. As a result, in the last decade new forms of business structures have emerged which have allowed taxpayers to have the

---

77 See 26 U.S.C.A. §446(c)(3). If a combination of methods of accounting is used by a taxpayer the taxpayer must comply with the requirements of Treasury Regulation 1.446-1(b)(2)(iv).

78 26 U.S.C.A. §446(b); Treas. Reg. 1.446-1(c)(1)(ii)(C).

79 26 U.S.C.A. §31.

80 26 U.S.C.A. §901.

81 26 U.S.C.A. §11.

82 26 U.S.C.A. §61(a)(7).

benefits of doing business in corporate form (such as limited liability for investors) without the burden of double taxation. These newer forms are discussed later.

Horizontal Equity   This principle requires that "persons in similar situations should be treated in a similar manner." The corporate tax can be viewed as treating similarly situated persons in different manners. For instance, if Victoria owns a toy store as a sole proprietor she will be taxed on the net income (taxable income) of the business. If the store generates $100,000 of taxable income, her tax liability will be maximally about $40,000, using the highest marginal rate for individuals (about 40%). If Helen uses the corporate form to run a similar toy store, with a corporation of which she is the sole shareholder actually owning the store, then the corporation will be taxed on its net income (taxable income) and when it distributes its earnings as a dividend to Helen *and* Helen will be taxed personally on the dividend. Thus, if Helen's store generates the same $100,000 of taxable income that Victoria's did, Helen's corporation will have to pay a tax of maximally about $35,000 (using the highest marginal rate for corporations, which is 35%), leaving it with $65,000. If Helen takes the $65,000 out of the corporation as a dividend, she will be taxed again. The $65,000 will be gross income to Helen. There will be a tax of about $26,000 imposed (again using the highest marginal rate for individuals of about 40%). The result is that Helen will be left with about $39,000 after all taxes are paid while Victoria ended up with $60,000. The tax rate for Helen's is 61%, while Victoria's is only 40%.[83]

Vertical Equity The principle of vertical equity in simple form requires that the burdens of a system be distributed among the members of society in a fair manner. In a sense, this principle requires us to look at *differently* situated persons and decide how to allocate the burdens of society in a fair manner. This can be seen as part of the tax concept of progressivity discussed earlier, under which rates of taxation increase as income increases. Turning to the corporate tax, one could argue that the double taxation effect unfairly burdens those doing business in corporate form. As the example of Victoria and Helen demonstrates, there would not seem to be much basis for saying that everyone who uses the corporate form is better able to bear a higher tax burden. And even if one does view corporations as meriting an additional tax, we must still ask how much additional burden should be placed on them. As the example of Victoria and Helen demonstrates, the difference is large indeed.

A second way in which vertical equity is offended has to do with the question of who *actually* pays the corporate tax. Although a tax may be imposed on a particular person or transaction, the burden of that tax may be *shifted* to another. The corporate tax falls immediately on the corporate entity. However, the corporation will often have the ability to *shift* the *burden* of the corporate tax from itself to other sectors of the economy. It can pass on the burden on to its workers in the form of lower wages, to its suppliers in the form of lower prices paid for raw materials, to its shareholders in the form of lower returns on investment or, most likely, to its consumers in the form of higher prices. To the extent that the actual burden of the corporate tax is borne by the consumer, it is arguably "regressive" because it impacts low-income consumers and taxpayers disproportionately heavily. The analysis of who actually pays the corporate income tax is a complex one and the answer will vary from industry to

---

83 This disparity is even more striking when we realize that Victoria could choose to use one of the newer entities, such as a "limited liability company," and get all of the benefits of using true corporate form (such as limited liability, centralized management, etc.) and still only be taxed once at the individual rate. The only benefit she could not easily get is the free transferability of shares, thus limiting her ability to raise capital by selling shares to the public.

industry. What is clear is that the ultimate burden of the corporate income tax may be far from what is intended.

Market "Neutrality" Ideally, taxes should not affect the market decisions of the taxpayer. If two "products" are similar but one carries with it the additional burden of paying a high tax, the consumer of the products would be inclined to avoid the taxed product and purchase the non-taxed product. A tax that forced such a decision would violate the desirable goal of market neutrality. Seen in this light, the corporate income tax is not neutral since the burden imposed by the corporate tax should lead a rational person to avoid the corporate form (all other things being equal). In addition, doing business in corporate form affects further decisionmaking (and is thus non-neutral) in several areas. One key area in which the corporate tax affects market choices is the preference for debt-based financing over equity financing in the capitalization of the corporation since interest paid on debt is deductible while dividends paid on stock are not. As is seen in the next paragraph, this distortion may also lead to market inefficiencies.

Economic Efficiency Interest payments on debts are deductible by the corporation under the Code.[84] Dividend payments to shareholders are not deductible. Thus, dividends incur a higher rate of tax than interest payments since profits that are distributed as dividends are effectively taxed twice. This is arguably encourages economically inefficiency by encouraging corporations to raise funds by borrowing rather than by seeking more investment capital. Such encouragement also violates the policy of market neutrality.

For example, assume Kate forms a corporation that needs $100,000 of capital to operate and which she expects to generate $10,000 of gross income. First, assume Kate contributes the $100,000 to the corporation as paid-in capital. If the corporation earns the expected $10,000 there will be a corporate level tax of about $3,500 (assuming the highest marginal rate for the purpose of this example). Kate's corporation will then have $6,500 to distribute to Kate as a dividend. That $6,500 will be gross income to Kate and will be subject to a tax (again at the highest marginal rate of about 40%) of $2,600. Thus, Kate will have an after-tax return of $3,900.

Now, instead, assume that Kate only puts in $1 as paid-capital, and *loans* the corporation the other $99,999 at an interest rate of 10%. When the corporation earns its expected $10,000 it will have $10,000 of *gross* income. When the corporation pays Kate the approximately $10,000 (actually $9,999.90) of interest, it will get a *deduction* under §163 for that amount. The result is that the corporation's *taxable* income will be *zero*. Kate, of course, will treat the interest as gross income under §61(a)(4) and will pay a tax of about $4,000 on that amount. Thus, Kate will have an after-tax return of $6,000.

This example shows how the corporate tax can distort market decisions by encouraging debt-based financing over equity-based financing. It is a well-established fact that most new business ventures fail early in their lives. One of the principal causes of business failure is the inability of young businesses to meet their fixed obligations (such as payment of interest on their debts). Viewed in this way, the corporate tax not only causes market distortions (by preferring debt over equity) but also arguably causes dead-weight losses in the economy at large and is thus economically inefficient. Another inefficiency and market distortion that occurs is that the

---

84 Under 26 U.S.C.A. §163.

corporate tax encourages companies to retain their earnings at the corporate level rather than distributing them to shareholders where they will be taxed again. Corporations will do so because raising financing for new projects is cheaper with retained earnings than with new capital.[85]

b. Income Tax Issues in Formation of the Corporation

Exchanges of Stock Forming a corporation often involves transferring assets into the corporation in exchange for shares of stock. This is an "exchange" of property for stock. This exchange is an "other disposition" of property and is an event of realization.[86] Thus, if the assets are appreciated (i.e., their fair market value exceeds their adjusted basis) there will be a gain *realized* on the transfer. In a like manner, the exchange of depreciated assets will cause a realized loss. However, if the corporation is controlled by the transferor of the property, there is little of substance that has changed. The transferor once owned an asset and now owns a corporation which owns the asset. Imposing an income tax at this point on the realized gain seems inappropriate if we view this as more of a change in form rather than in substance. In addition, there is a practical problem. The transferor would have to get the cash to pay any tax imposed, thus potentially forcing her to sell some of her stock or to borrow money.[87]

The Code states that "no gain or loss shall be *recognized* if property is transferred to a corporation . . . solely in exchange for stock in such corporation" but only if "immediately after the exchange" the transferor (or group of transferors) is "in control of the corporation."[88] Three important points should be made about this provision.

First, it only allows the taxpayer to receive *stock* in the corporation in order to get non-recognition treatment. If the taxpayer receives cash, bonds, or other property, then that *gain* will be recognized up to the amount of the cash or fair market value of other property received, but that no loss will be recognized. This provision makes some sense. If one of the reasons for allowing non-recognition in the first place was to avoid imposing a tax on a taxpayer who did not have the means to pay the tax, then it seems proper to impose a tax when the taxpayer does receive cash or other property. Since gain will be recognized only up to the amount of cash or other property received, the tax imposed will always be less than that amount and thus affordable. The denial of loss recognition seems somewhat less justified since the taxpayer could have sold the loss property in a separate transaction.

Second, stock issued to a transferor in exchange for *services* is not considered as having been given in exchange for property.[89] Thus, a person receiving stock for services *cannot* be counted as part of the group of property transferors for purposes of the 80 percent control tests. It is fairly common for smaller corporations to have one person who will contribute services and one person who will contribute property. The formation of such a corporation requires careful tax planning if the property

---

85 There have been many proposals over the years to eliminate the corporate tax but none has gained widespread acceptance. However, some of the difficulties have been eliminated by the advent of the relatively new limited liability company and "check-the-box" options for treatment of the entity either like or corporation or like a partnership.

86 Under 26 U.S.C.A. §1001(a).

87 This interference with market decisions would violate the tenet of "market-neutrality."

88 26 U.S.C.A. §351(a). Being "in control" means "ownership of stock possessing at least 80 percent of the total combined voting power of all classes of stock entitled to vote and at least 80 percent of the total number of shares of all other classes of stock of the corporation." §386(c).

89 26 U.S.C.A. §351(d).

transferor is to get non-recognition treatment. Of course, if the non-services transferor is only going to contribute money, the issue of non-recognition does not arise (since the basis of cash is its fair market value).[90]

Third, non-recognition, as discussed earlier, is almost always just a deferral mechanism. Any gain (or loss) will be recognized on the later disposition of the asset. As in the like-kind exchange example earlier, this inherent gain or loss is preserved by means of substituted and transferred basis provisions.

Here is an example of how this works. Assume Marjorie owns 100% of the stock of ABC Corporation and also owns an airplane with fair market value of $50,000 and an adjusted basis of $30,000. If Marjorie transfers the airplane into the corporation in exchange for $50,000 worth of stock (a fair exchange), Marjorie has a realized gain of $20,000 since this is an event of realization and her amount realized of $50,000 exceeds her adjusted basis of $30,000 by $20,000. However, since Marjorie is in control of the corporation immediately after the transfer, none of this realized gain will be recognized. Marjorie's basis in the new shares of stock will be $30,000 and she will *substitute* her basis in the airplane as her basis for the stock.[91] Marjorie's transfer of the airplane to her wholly-owned corporation will not have any *immediate* tax consequences to Marjorie.[92] However, Marjorie had $20,000 of potential gain *inherent* in the airplane before she transferred it. If she had sold the *airplane* for its value of $50,000, she would have realized (and recognized) a gain of $20,000, because her amount realized would have been $50,000 and her adjusted basis was $30,000. This is only a deferral, however. Marjorie will realize and recognize that same $20,000 of gain when she sells the new *stock* in the corporation that now owns the airplane, since Marjorie's $30,000 basis in the airplane has been substituted as the basis for the new stock.

Effect of Stock Exchanges on the Corporation   The effect of stock exchanges on the corporation are similar to those discussed for the recipient of the stock. ABC Corp. recognized no gain or loss on the issuance of its shares to Marjorie in exchange for the airplane. The corporation, however, takes a *transferred* basis of $30,000 in the airplane from Marjorie along with the airplane itself. Of course, if the corporation sells the airplane for its $50,000 fair market value it will realize and recognize a gain of $20,000, just as Marjorie would have had she sold the airplane herself.

One should note how the Code in this manner preserves the policy of double taxation of corporations. It has not only preserved Marjorie's $20,000 inherent gain for later taxation, but they have insured that it will be taxed *twice* — once when Marjorie sells her stock and once when ABC Corp. sells the airplane.

When Both Stock and Cash are Involved: "Boot"   If Marjorie were to receive, not $50,000 worth of stock, but instead $45,000 of stock and $5,000 cash from the corporation, the Code requires that Marjorie recognize her realized gain up to the amount of

   90   We should note that §351 will apply to the transfer of property not just to new corporations, but to any controlled corporation so long as "immediately after" the transfer the transferor (or group of transferors) is in control of the corporation. We should also note that the corporation itself, under §1032 of the Code, does not recognize any gain or loss on the issuance of its own stock in exchange for money or property. Finally, while taxpayers generally prefer to not recognize gain, they generally *do* like to recognize losses. Thus, some creative tax planning may be necessary if the transferor wishes to recognize her losses on depreciated property that would otherwise be transferred to the corporation.

   91   26 U.S.C.A. §358. This section is part of a larger set of sections in Subchapter C of the Code, which deals exclusively with corporations.

   92   Nor will it for the corporation. *See infra* note 92.

money and other property received.[93] Thus, Marjorie would have to recognize $5,000 of her $20,000 of realized gain. This additional money (or property) received in a non-recognition transaction is most commonly referred to as "boot."[94] Since she will now have recognized $5,000 of her $20,000 in realized gain, the basis of her stock and the corporation's basis in the airplane should reflect this. Consequently, Marjorie should increase her basis in the stock by the amount of gain recognized.[95] Thus, Marjorie's basis in the stock would be $35,000: her substituted basis of $30,000, increased by the $5,000 of recognized gain caused by her receipt of $5,000 of boot. This makes sense. If Marjorie were to sell her stock for its $50,000 value, she would recognize the remaining $15,000 of gain. In a like manner, the corporation's basis in the airplane would be $35,000: Marjorie's transferred basis of $30,000 increased by the amount of gain recognized by Marjorie, that is, increased by $5,000.[96]

This same pattern of dealing with non-recognition of gain or loss appears throughout the Code. In almost all cases the pattern is this: (1) If one engages in an exchange of something *solely* for something else, and (2) if one meets certain criteria, then (3) neither gain nor loss shall be recognized. However, (4) if one gets boot in addition to the permitted exchange property, then (5) realized gain will be recognized but only up to the amount of boot received. Moreover, (6) the basis in the new property received will be the same as the basis in the old property exchanged and (7) increased by the amount of gain recognized because of the boot received.[97]

c. Income Tax Issues in Operating the Corporation

As we have seen, a corporation, like an individual, is a taxable entity. As with an individual, gross income is reduced to taxable income by subtracting allowed deductions.[98] The most likely deductions for a corporation will be operating expenses, which includes all ordinary and necessary business expenses,[99] depreciation[100] and any interest paid on debt.[101] However, there are special issues for corporations in two areas: distributions made to shareholders and compensation of employees.

(1) Stock and Dividend Distributions to Shareholders

This subject is fairly technical, but the concepts are relatively easy to understand. First, we should briefly explore the possible sources of a distribution to a shareholder.[102]

Distributions in the Absence of Profit Assume that David forms a wholly-owned corporation to manufacture toys by contributing $100,000 as paid-in capital. He would then have a basis of $100,000 in the stock.[103] If the corporation, before earning any

---

93 26 U.S.C.A. §351(b).

94 The etymology of this term goes back to Anglo-Saxon times in England (before the 11th century) when "*bot*" was an amount paid by one person to another person in certain custom-based transactions.

95 26 U.S.C.A. §358(a)(1)(B)(ii).

96 26 U.S.C.A. §362(a).

97 Although we did not look at the issue of boot when we explored the non-recognition of like-kind exchanges under §1031, that section does the same thing.

98 26 U.S.C.A. §§61, 63

99 26 U.S.C.A. §162.

100 26 U.S.C.A. §167.

101 26 U.S.C.A. §163.

102 26 U.S.C.A. §301

103 Under 26 U.S.C.A. §358.

money distributes $10,000 back to David, then that distribution should be seen as a mere return of capital and not as income to David. Also, as we would expect, David's basis in his stock will be reduced by $10,000 to $90,000.[104]

Distributions When There is Profit If the corporation earns profits and then makes a distribution to David, the distribution will be considered to have come first from those profits. Since the corporate tax is premised on the double taxation of profits, that distribution will be taxable again to the David as a dividend. To use a concrete example, if the corporation (before any distribution to David) earns $10,000 of taxable income, it will have to pay a corporate tax of about $3,500 (assuming the maximum marginal rate of 35% for simplicity's sake). This would leave the corporation with $6,500 of after-tax profits. If the corporation then distributes $5,000 to David, the entire $5,000 amount will be included in David's gross income as a "dividend" and thus subject to the individual income tax. If, on the other hand, the corporation distributed $8,000 to David, then only $6,500 should be considered to come from its "profits" in the economic sense of the word. That is, the corporation's *economic* profit (i.e., its "after-tax profit") is only $6,500. The remaining $1,500 should be treated as a return of capital and merely reduces his basis in the stock, just as in the first part of this example, because there are no more profits out of which to make a distribution.[105]

The Definitions of "Dividend" and "Earnings and Profits" "Dividend" is a term of art in the Code and should not be confused with Wall Street's definition of a dividend. The Code provides that if a distribution is made to a shareholder, then that distribution is a "dividend"[106] if it is made out of "current earnings and profits" or out of "accumulated earnings and profits."[107]

"Earnings and profits" (commonly referred to by tax lawyers as "e&p") is also a technical tax term. It has no virtually no relationship to the financial concepts of "retained earnings" or "current earnings."[108] Some transactions increase e&p, some decrease it. In essence, the e&p of a corporation is *very roughly* equivalent to its after-tax economic profits. However, the exact calculation of earning and profits is very complex. One is well advised to consult a tax professional before making any distribution from a corporation. However, the following brief explanation is offered.[109]

The Code essentially splits the earnings and profits of a corporation into two "accounts." The first account consists of "current earnings and profits."[110] The second account consists of "accumulated earnings and profits."[111] The current earnings and profits account holds, simply, the earnings and profits for the current taxable year. The accumulated earnings and profits account holds, as it sounds, any earnings and profits that have accumulated over the years of the corporate existence. The reason for this split is mainly historical. But the essence of this section is that a distribution to a shareholder will be a "dividend" (and thus included in the shareholder's gross

---

104 As we will see below, this is exactly how §301 of the Code treats such a distribution in the absence of profits.

105 26 U.S.C.A. §301(c)(1)-(3).

106 A dividend is includable in gross income under 26 U.S.C.A. §61(a)(7).

107 26 U.S.C.A. §316(a)(2) and (1), respectively.

108 26 U.S.C.A. §312. Actually, the term "earnings and profits" is nowhere defined in the Code. Section 312 of the Code, however, does provide some guidance by giving us several pages describing the "effect on earnings and profits" of various transactions and occurrences.

109 26 U.S.C.A. §316.

110 26 U.S.C.A. §316(a)(2).

111 26 U.S.C.A. §316(a)(1).

income) to the extent that there are earnings and profits in *either* account.[112] Thus, even e&p from 50 years ago has the potential to cause a current distribution to be taxable to a shareholder.

If we take another look at David's corporation, we saw that it had earned a taxable income of $10,000 in its first year. It also paid a corporate-level tax of $3,500. Since that tax reduces the corporation's economic capacity it will also reduce the corporation's earnings and profits to $6,500. Assuming no other adjustments to the earnings and profits account, a distribution of $5,000 will be seen as first coming from the current earnings and profits and will thus be included in David's gross income as a dividend. Since the distribution itself also reduces the corporation's economic capacity, the $5,000 will further reduce the corporation's current earnings and profits to $1,500.[113]

When the first tax year ends without any further distributions, that $1,500 of current earnings and profits will be shifted over to the *accumulated* earnings and profits account. If in the next taxable year the corporation *loses* money and has a net loss and no taxable income it may very well have a *negative current earnings and profits account* for that second year. If the corporation makes a distribution to David of $4,000 in year two, David will nonetheless have a dividend of $1,500 because even though the *current* earnings and profits account is negative, there is still $1,500 in the *accumulated earnings and profits account*. The remaining $2,500 of the distribution will be treated as a return of capital and will reduce his basis in the stock by that amount.[114]

Distributions in Excess of Both E&P and Basis If a corporation has large amounts of capital available (say, because it borrowed money) but has no current or accumulated earnings and profits and it makes a distribution to a shareholder, we have seen that the distribution will go to reduce the basis of the shareholder's stock. If the distribution exceeds that basis, then the Code treats the excess as "gain from the sale or exchange of property."[115] This has two effects. First, the shareholder will have a recognized gain includable in gross income. Second, since that gain is treated as if it were from the "sale or exchange" of property, then that gain may be *characterized* as "capital gain" *if* the stock was a "capital asset" in the hands of the shareholder. If so, as discussed earlier, it may be taxed at a preferential rate afforded to "capital gains."[116]

(2) Compensation of Corporation Employees

The compensation paid to a corporate employee is deductible to a corporation if it is an "ordinary and necessary" expense and if it is "reasonable."[117] In most small corporations, the principal shareholders are often also highly placed employees of the corporation. Since compensation to those employees is potentially deductible, there is a pressure (caused by the double taxation system) to take money out of the corporation as compensation (salary and/or bonus) rather than as a dividend. As discussed earlier, one of the most highly contested areas in tax audits is that of the "reasonableness" of compensation paid to employees who are also shareholders.

---

112 26 U.S.C.A. §§301(c)(1) and 61(a)(7).

113 26 U.S.C.A. §312(a)(1).

114 26 U.S.C.A. §301(c)(2).

115 26 U.S.C.A. §301(c)(3).

116 26 U.S.C.A. §1201 *et seq.*

117 26 U.S.C.A. §162(a)(1).

Before paying high compensation to an employee-shareholder one should do some homework on comparable compensation paid to similarly situated employees whose compensation is a matter of public record. In addition, one should be ready to demonstrate the true economic value of that employee by looking at the business profits generated by her.

Loans to Shareholders: A Word to the Wise Because of the double-tax effect of the corporate tax, there is a strong tendency, especially in smaller corporations, to find ways to take money out of the corporation without paying the double tax. Large loans to shareholders should be expected to be examined closely by the IRS. Any loans to shareholders should be well documented with formal notes. Although the topic of interest-free loans is a complex one, in general a loan to a shareholder should bear market interest. Further, the shareholder-borrower should make all payments when due. The consequences of not treating this area with respect are dire ones. The entire loan may be recharacterized by the IRS as a distribution to the shareholder with respect to stock and thus be taxable as a dividend to the extent of earnings and profits.

The Deduction for Corporate Dividends Received To avoid triple and quadruple taxation of corporate profits, the Code provides a deduction for a percentage of the dividends received from another corporation.[118] The percentage amount of deduction depends on the percentage amount of stock ownership. If the receiving corporation is a member of the same "affiliated group" as the distributing corporation, then there is a 100% deduction.[119] The term "affiliated group" is a technical one. In essence, it is a group of chains of corporations owned by common parent where at least every link in any ownership chain consists of 80% of the total voting power and 80% of the total value of any subsidiary corporation.[120] If the receiving corporation is not part of an affiliated group with the distributing corporation, but owns at least 20% of its stock "by vote and value," then the Code grants a deduction of 80% of the dividend received.[121] Finally, if the receiving corporation owns less than 20% of the stock, then a deduction of 70% of the dividend received is provided.[122]

Distributions of Stock A distribution of additional stock of a corporation, commonly referred to as a "stock dividend," is generally not a dividend at all in the tax sense. The Code provides that "gross income does not include the amount of any distribution *of the stock* of a corporation made by such corporation with respect to its stock."[123] Of course, in the inimitable style of the Internal Revenue Code, there are then two pages of exceptions to this general rule. In general, however, an ordinary pro-rata distribution of common stock on common stock will not be included in gross income. If you are thinking about any other type of distribution, it would be wise to seek expert advice.

Redemptions of Stock A corporation may redeem ("buy back") some of its stock from a shareholder for any number of reasons. Since a redemption looks like a sale or exchange, it is considered to be an exchange.[124] This gives several potential tax advantages to the shareholder. First, the amount received for the stock surrendered

---

118 26 U.S.C.A. §243.

119 26 U.S.C.A. §243(a)(3).

120 26 U.S.C.A. §243(b)(2) referring to §1504(a).

121 26 U.S.C.A. §243(c).

122 26 U.S.C.A. §243(a)(1).

123 26 U.S.C.A. §305(a) (emphasis added).

124 26 U.S.C.A. §302(a) and (b).

will be treated as the amount realized and only the excess of the amount realized over the adjusted basis in the stock will be recognized as gain.[125] Indeed, if the adjusted basis exceeds the amount realized, the taxpayer will have a recognized loss which may be allowable as a deduction. Second, since the Code grants "exchange" status, if the stock is a capital asset in the hands of the taxpayer, then the gain will be capital gain and potentially taxable at a preferential rate.[126]

The rationale for treating the redemption as an exchange can be clarified by looking at what does *not* qualify for sale or exchange treatment and examining the consequences of it not being so treated. If the redemption of stock is pro-rata among all the shareholders, it will be seen as a mere subterfuge for a distribution of earnings and profits since all shareholders after the "redemption" will own exactly the same percentage of stock they owned before it, but they will have received money from the corporation. If the corporation has any earnings and profits, then the entire amount of the distribution will be treated as a dividend to the extent of earnings and profits. The consequences of failing to qualify a stock redemption as an exchange can thus be disastrous.

Since a pro-rata redemption is archetypally what is *not* accorded exchange treatment, it is reasonable to expect that a *non-pro-rata* redemption *will* qualify for exchange treatment. This is the case. For instance, if the redemption terminates the shareholder's interest in the corporation, i.e., if it is a complete redemption of all of the shareholder's stock in the corporation, then it qualifies for exchange treatment.[127] This makes sense, because such a redemption could not be a subterfuge for a distribution from e&p. Such a shareholder should be treated the same as if he "sold" his entire interest to a third party. Likewise, a "substantially disproportionate" redemption of stock will also qualify for exchange treatment.[128] This disproportionality is determined by looking at the shareholder's percentage interest in the corporation's stock after the redemption and comparing it to the percentage interest before the redemption. This test looks at both the voting stock and the common stock. If the shareholder's percentage interest in each after is less than 80% of his interest before, then the shareholder will qualify for exchange treatment. If the shareholder cannot meet either the termination test or the substantially disproportionate test, the shareholder may yet qualify under a more nebulous test if the redemption was "not essentially equivalent to a dividend."[129] There is substantial case law analyzing particular fact patterns that either meet or fail this test. Many cases focus on whether there was a "meaningful reduction" in the shareholder's interest in the corporation.[130]

Partial Liquidations There is one other type of redemption that qualifies for exchange treatment — when the redemption of stock from an individual constitutes

---

125 26 U.S.C.A. §1001(a).

126 26 U.S.C.A. §302. Capital asset is defined by §1221. Of course, if there is a recognized loss on the redemption and the stock is a capital asset in the hands of the taxpayer, then the deductibility of the loss will be limited by §1211 and §1212.

127 26 U.S.C.A. §302(b)(3).

128 26 U.S.C.A. §302(b)(2).

129 26 U.S.C.A. §302(b)(1).

130 Section 302(c) requires that in applying the substantially proportionate test of 302(b)(2) and the termination test of (b)(3) we look at not just the stock actually owned by the taxpayer, but that we look as well at the stock *constructively* owned by him before and after the redemption, as defined by §318. Section 318 is complex. Suffice it to say that stock ownership is attributed to a taxpayer from certain family members, as well as from various partnerships, estates, trusts and corporations.

a "partial liquidation."[131] This term is defined as a distribution that "is not essentially equivalent to a dividend (determined at the corporate level rather than at the shareholder level)."[132] Although "not essentially equivalent to a dividend" is the same language found in the nebulous exception just discussed, this subsection makes it clear that, in contrast to looking at the shareholder level for dividend equivalence, we are to look at the corporate level. This section and its precursor have a long history. In general, the courts look to see if there was a significant *contraction* in the size of the corporate business before finding that a distribution was not essentially equivalent to a dividend. This provision also now provides the taxpayer with a technically drafted safe harbor if a corporation is ceasing one of its long-established businesses.[133]

d. Corporate Mergers and Liquidations

Corporate Mergers and Reorganizations   Mergers and reorganizations were discussed in Chapter XV.[134] When a corporation acquires the stock or assets of another corporation in exchange for its own stock, changes its place of incorporation, or undergoes a recapitalization, each of these transactions is likely to be an event of realization that triggers realized gain or loss to at least one of the participants. But most of these transactions result in owners of stock in one corporation ending up with stock in another corporation or with different stock of the same corporation, with the same corporate assets remaining in place. Consequently, it seems *inappropriate* to impose an income tax on them. Consistent with this, the Code lists 7 basic transactions in which where the participants will be granted "reorganization" status.[135] This status ensures that every "party to a reorganization" will not recognize any realized gain or loss.[136] In the manner of the other non-recognition exchange sections we have looked at, any realized gain or loss is preserved in the form of a substituted or transferred basis.[137] Also similar to other non-recognition exchanges, any cash or other property received as "boot" will trigger recognition of realized gain up to the amount of boot received.[138]

Liquidations   Just as the Code grants "exchange" status to amounts received in a qualifying redemption or partial liquidation, it grants that same status to shareholders who receive a "distribution in complete liquidation of a corporation."[139] The shareholders will thus be treated as if they had "sold" their stock and will get to setoff their basis in the stock against the amount realized. As with a qualified partial liquidation or redemption of stock, the shareholders may also receive capital gain or capital loss treatment. At the corporate level, the corporation will be treated as if the property distributed "were sold to the distributee at its fair market value."[140] If the corporate

---

131 26 U.S.C.A. §302(b)(4).

132 26 U.S.C.A. §302(e).

133 26 U.S.C.A. §302(e)(2).

134 *See* p. 548.

135 §368(a)(1).

136 §368(b). Shareholders are covered under sections 354 or 356 and corporations under §361.

137 *See* §358 for shareholders and under §362 (for corporations).

138 26 U.S.C.A. §368(a)(2). The reorganizations area is very complex. Briefly, this Code section covers the following types of reorganizations listed according to their subparagraph in the statute: (A) statutory mergers; (B) stock for stock transactions; (C) stock for assets transactions; (D) divisive and non-divisive reorganizations; (E) recapitalizations; (F) mere changes in form; (G) bankruptcy-related reorganizations. It also has complex rules for triangular reorganizations involving subsidiaries and the use of parent (or related company) stock.

139 26 U.S.C.A. §331.

140 26 U.S.C.A. §336(a).

assets have fair market values in excess of their adjusted bases, a gain will be recognized and thus taxed.[141] In a final twist of fate, losses, although recognized and allowed, may not be able to be used at all unless there is sufficient other current income to set them off against or they can be carried back to prior taxable years under other Code sections.[142]

5. Taxation of "Pass-Through" Entities or "Fiscally Transparent" Entities

The Code has always treated certain entities as conduits for income and loss rather than as entities to be taxed. The most common of these "pass-through" entities is the partnership. In general, under the partnership tax rules of subchapter K of chapter 1 of the Code, all items of income and loss are passed through to the partners in the proportion of their partnership interests. From a business viewpoint, partnerships have long been a favorite form of doing business because of the flexibility afforded the partners in arranging the details of the partnership. Limited partnerships even afford the limited partners limited exposure to liability. In contrast to the corporate form, virtually every detail of a partnership can be a matter of agreement of the partners. From a tax viewpoint, partnerships, especially limited partnerships, were very popular entities for at least two reasons. First, they were business entities that avoided the double taxation at the corporate level. Second, their fiscal "transparency" allowed the pass-through of *tax losses* to the individual partners even if the partnership were operating at an economic profit.[143]

The most common use of this loss pass-through feature was in real estate ventures where accelerated depreciation of buildings could generate losses that passed through to the partner's tax return (to offset other income of the partner) even though at the same time the venture itself generated a positive cash flow (that was not taxed because of this loss). Of course, since the accelerated depreciation lowered the basis in the partnership property, the end of the life of the partnership usually saw the recapture of these somewhat artificial losses by causing the realization of a significant gain and its concomitant tax liability. However, the deferral of that tax liability and the use of the losses in the earlier years provided a substantial benefit to the wealthy investor who could use those losses against other income.

Because of the widespread and "creative" use of partnerships in areas such as real estate in the last three decades, a substantial body of Treasury Regulations, caselaw, and scholarly commentary has developed around the partnership rules of subchapter K. These rules have been extended to cover the newer forms of pass-through entities, such as limited liability companies, which are treated for tax purposes as if they were partnerships.

Choice of Entity: The "Check-the-box" Regulations For several decades the IRS battled with taxpayers over whether a particular entity was more like a corporation, and thus subject to double taxation, or more like a partnership, and thus allowed a pass-through of income and losses. In the mid-1990s, the IRS finally decided to allow unincorporated business organizations, such as limited liability companies, the *choice*

---

141 26 U.S.C.A. §336.

142 26 U.S.C.A. §1501 grants an "affiliated group" of corporations the privilege of filing a consolidated tax return for all members of the group instead of individual tax returns. The definition of an "affiliated group" was discussed when the deduction for dividends received was explained. The area of consolidated returns is quite complex and entails very detailed regulations.

143 Partnerships are discussed in Chapter XV, pp. 533-537.

of being taxed as an "association" (the technical classification of a corporation) or as a partnership. The so-called "check-the-box" regulations that allow this choice were issued in late 1996.[144]

S Corporations   Until the advent of the limited liability companies in the last decade, there were only two ways to both get the limited liability protection afforded to corporations *and* the pass-through tax treatment of income and losses. One way was to use a limited partnership. However, such a partnership always carried some risk of being classified by the IRS as a corporation. The other way was to use an "S corporation." The S corporation takes its name from subchapter S of chapter 1 of the Code.[145] The S corporation allows pass-through of items of income or loss to its shareholders in much the same fashion as does a partnership. However, the S corporation has a rather limiting set of requirements in order to qualify. For instance, an S corporation can have no more than 75 shareholders. All its shareholders have to be individuals (with very limited exceptions). It can only have one class of stock.[146] Despite these limitations, the S corporation played a significant role for small businesses. The limited liability company (even before the issuance of the "check-the-box" regulations) had already significantly displaced the S corporation. It remains to be seen whether it will end up replacing it entirely.

Trusts and Estates   Trusts (which are commonly used in personal "estate planning") and estates (which are used to wind up the affairs of deceased person) are technically taxable entities.[147] However, they are granted a deduction for income distributed to beneficiaries. Thus, if all their income is distributed currently they are effectively a "pass-through" entity. However, failure to distribute income may cause a tax at the level of the trust. Despite the seeming simplicity of this scheme, the area of income taxation of trusts and estates is a fairly complex one.[148]

D. International Tax Issues

1. Tax on Foreign Income of U.S. Taxpayers

General Policy   In general, the United States asserts jurisdiction to tax U.S. citizens, U.S. residents, and U.S. corporations on their worldwide income. However, the United States taxes non-resident aliens and foreign corporations only on income that has a certain connection with the United States.

In a like manner, the United States generally does not impose a tax on the income earned by a foreign corporation even if that corporation is owned by U.S. shareholders until that income is actually repatriated to the United States in the form of a dividend. However, to prevent perceived abuses of this deferral, the United States will currently tax the income of certain foreign corporations that have U.S. shareholders.

In conformity with norms of international taxation, the United States cedes to foreign governments the primary right to tax income arising in their countries. To prevent double taxation, the United States grants a tax credit against U.S. income taxes for taxes paid to a foreign government on income earned in that country.

---

144 Treas. Reg. 301.7701-1 et seq. *See also* Chapter XV, pp. 550-551.

145 26 U.S.C.A. §§1361 et seq. *See* Chapter XV, p. 541.

146 See 26 U.S.C.A. §1361(b)(1).

147 *See* Chapter XII, pp. 470-473.

148 In general, subchapter J of chapter 1 of the Code provides the rules for the taxation of trusts and estates.

Bilateral income tax treaties, which are essentially contracts between two governments, may modify these basic rules. For instance, a treaty may waive the right of a country that is the source of income to tax that income when the recipient of the income is a citizen of the other contracting party.

The Taxation of the U.S. Corporation Doing Business Overseas A U.S. taxpayer may have foreign source income in two different ways. First, it may be doing business directly in a foreign country in the form of a branch operation. Second, it may be doing business in a foreign country indirectly through a subsidiary that is incorporated in a foreign country.

Doing Foreign Business Directly The U.S. corporation that does business abroad directly is taxed currently on its domestic and foreign income in the same manner as any other domestic corporation. There are rather detailed rules regarding the matter of currency translation of the foreign operations and very complex rules regarding the application of the foreign tax credit.[149]

The foreign tax credit is an elective provision. The taxpayer may, in certain circumstances, choose to *deduct* the foreign income taxes paid.[150] In general, a credit would be preferable because it would offset U.S. taxes on a dollar-for-dollar basis. However, if the U.S. taxpayer has foreign income in one country that is taxed in that country and an equal foreign loss in another country in the same year, the Code requires that the loss be offset against the gain to determine the *net* amount of foreign income available for the credit. In this circumstance the credit for the tax paid to the first country would not be usable and a deduction would be preferred. The election to take or not take the credit is made each year.

The foreign tax credit is subject to a complex set of limitations in order to prevent the use of the credit against U.S. income taxation of U.S. source income. The Code requires the taxpayer to look at several defined categories of foreign income and losses before applying the limitation rules.[151]

The foreign tax credit is only available to offset *income* taxes imposed by foreign governments. Although the Code does not define what is an income tax, the Treasury Regulations do attempt to do so. In essence, in order to be considered an income tax the foreign tax must be "likely to reach net gain."[152] Given the wide variety of taxes in the world, the tests laid out in the regulations often do not lead to an easy answer as to whether a particular tax is an "income" tax. The creditability of particular foreign taxes is a common issue in the negotiation of bilateral treaties.

Doing Foreign Business Indirectly Through a Subsidiary When the foreign source income of a foreign subsidiary of a U.S. corporation is repatriated to the U.S. in the form of a dividend, the parent corporation will be entitled to a credit under the Code, for the foreign income taxes paid by that subsidiary with respect to that income. This credit is usually referred to as the "indirect" or "deemed-paid" foreign tax credit.[153]

In order to be eligible for the indirect credit the U.S. parent must be at least a 10% shareholder (by vote) of the foreign subsidiary paying the dividend. This same rule applies to second- and third-tier subsidiaries so long as the *product* of the ownership

---

149 26 U.S.C.A. §901.
150 26 U.S.C.A. §164(a)(3).
151 26 U.S.C.A. §904.
152 Treas. Reg. 1.901-2.
153 26 U.S.C.A. §902(a).

percentage of each corporation down the chain equals five percent.[154] The three-tier limit imposed difficult restrictions on multinational corporations with highly hierarchical structures of subsidiaries. Many such corporations needed to use additional levels of entities for business purposes as well as for compliance with local foreign rules. These corporations were thus forced to use pass-through entities, such as partnerships and limited liability companies, at levels below the third if they wished to avail themselves of the indirect credit since those entities were by their nature deemed to pass through to their owners the foreign taxes paid. Since 1997, *corporate* subsidiaries down to the sixth level are now permitted to pass indirectly back to their parent the taxes paid to a foreign government. However, in addition to also having to meet the 10% tests, there are further restrictions on the corporations in levels four through six. Among other things, any such lower-tier foreign subsidiary corporation must also be a "controlled foreign corporation."[155] Such "CFC's" are discussed below.

"Grossing Up" the Dividend   In order to create a parallel structure to the treatment of dividends from domestic corporations, the parent corporation is required to add to the actual dividend paid the amount of the foreign tax actually paid and include *both* in gross income. This "grossed-up" amount is thus equivalent to the pre-tax foreign income (i.e., the foreign income before any foreign tax was paid).[156] The U.S. tax on the U.S. parent would thus be imposed on this grossed-up amount of income, and it is against this now U.S.-taxed income that the indirect credit would be applied.

"Controlled Foreign Corporations" and the Anti-Deferral Provisions   A "controlled foreign corporation," commonly referred to as a "CFC," is any foreign corporation if U.S. persons own more than 50% of the corporation's stock (by vote or value). However, in applying the 50% test, one must take into account only those U.S. persons who own at least 10% of the stock (by vote only).[157] The stock ownership that counts here is not just direct ownership, but is also constructive ownership of stock determined by applying attribution rules for related parties and entities.[158]

The consequences of a foreign corporation being classed as a CFC are that certain classes of income, commonly called "subpart F income," are taxed *currently* to the U.S. shareholders, even if not repatriated. The CFC is thus not permitted the deferral generally accorded to other foreign subsidiaries. When a CFC earns subpart F income that income is currently taxed to the 10% U.S. shareholders in accord with their pro-rata holdings. In addition, the U.S. will also generally tax the U.S. shareholders on their share of the CFC's earnings that are invested in the United States and in certain other assets. The foreign tax credit may be available to offset some or all of the tax on these items. Subpart F income is generally income that is fairly movable from one country to another and that may thus be subject to relatively low rates of tax.[159]

Transfer Pricing   Since a U.S. parent corporation may own a foreign subsidiary completely, there is a potential for abuse in the way the two corporations set the prices for intercompany transactions and allocate items of expense and income between them. The Code gives the IRS express authority to allocate and apportion any items of income, deductions, credits or allowances between the two companies in order to

---

154 26 U.S.C.A. §902(b).

155 26 U.S.C.A. §957(a).

156 26 U.S.C.A. §78.

157 26 U.S.C.A. §957.

158 26 U.S.C.A. §958.

159 *See* 26 U.S.C.A. §§952-954 for the details of what is included in Subpart F income.

ensure that the tax returns of the companies "clearly reflect the income" of the individual companies.[160] The area of intercompany pricing is a highly contested area and results in many disputes with the IRS. Intercompany pricing analyses are typically very complex and require the services of expert economists. It is often possible and advisable to get advance rulings from the IRS in this area.

2. Tax on U.S. Source Income of Foreign Taxpayers

There are four basic schemes for the taxing of foreign taxpayers with U.S. source income.

"FDAP" Income and 30% Gross Taxation   Foreign persons (including corporations) are subject to a flat 30-percent tax[161] without regard to any deductions, on gross income derived "from sources within the United States."[162] The income subject to this tax is generally recurring income from investments. Indeed, the Code refers to this income as "fixed or determinable annual or periodical gains, profits, and income" (commonly referred to as "FDAP" income). The most common forms of FDAP income are interest, dividends, rents, and royalties. Income from personal services rendered in the U.S. is also considered as FDAP income. This 30% tax on gross income is, subject to exceptions, required to be withheld at the source by the U.S. payor.[163]

"ECI" and Net Taxation   The U.S. also taxes the income of foreign persons that is "effectively connected" with the conduct of a trade or business in the U.S., whether or not it is sourced in the U.S. This tax is imposed on a net basis, in the same way and subject to the same rates to which U.S. persons are subject.[164] The term "effectively connected" income, sometimes referred to as "ECI," is defined as including income from sales, services, and manufacturing in the U.S.[165] Some *foreign* source income of a foreign person may be effectively connected with the conduct of a U.S. trade or business and thus may also be subject to tax in the U.S.[166] Of course, such effectively connected foreign source income may also qualify for the foreign tax credit for any foreign taxes also paid on it.[167]

"Occasional" Gains and No Taxation   If a foreign person has an occasional gain that is not FDAP income (because it is not recurrent) and no "effectively connected" income, then, subject to several major exceptions, the foreign person is not subject to any tax in the U.S. The most significant exception is for the gain from the sale of U.S. real property (or the stock in a holding company owning U.S. real property). The sale of such U.S. real property (or of the stock in such a holding company) is treated as effectively connected income (ECI), discussed above. It is therefore subject to the same net taxation scheme applicable to all ECI.

Modification by Treaty   Bilateral tax treaties may reduce or eliminate some of the above taxes. For instance, it is not uncommon for a treaty to reduce or eliminate the 30% withholding tax on FDAP income. Also, U.S. tax treaties tend to *modify* the taxation scheme for effectively connected income by looking to see if the foreign person has a "permanent establishment" in the U.S. Only if one exists will the

---

160 26 U.S.C.A. §482.
161 26 U.S.C.A. §§871(a), 881.
162 26 U.S.C.A. §§861-865.
163 26 U.S.C.A. §§1441, 1442.
164 26 U.S.C.A. §§871(b), 882.
165 26 U.S.C.A. §864(c).
166 26 U.S.C.A. §864(c)(4)(A) and (B).
167 26 U.S.C.A. §864(c)(4) and 906.

"business profits" or "commercial and industrial profits" (depending on the particular treaty) be taxable in the U.S. Even then, the treaties often agree that U.S. tax will be imposed only on the business profits attributable to the permanent establishment.

Maintaining Parity with the "Branch Profits Tax" If a foreign corporation does business in the U.S. through a U.S. subsidiary, then that subsidiary would be taxed on its income as would any other U.S. corporation. When the subsidiary paid a dividend to its foreign parent that dividend would be FDAP income subject to the flat 30% withholding tax. If, on the other hand, the foreign corporation chose to do business directly in the U.S. through a "branch" operation rather than through a U.S. subsidiary, its U.S. source income would be effectively connected income and taxed in a manner similar to other U.S. corporations. However, when the U.S. branch office sends its profits back to the foreign home office, there would be no additional tax on this intra-company transfer. When the foreign corporation then pays a *dividend* to *its* shareholders, that dividend would technically be FDAP income from a U.S. source. However, it is virtually impossible for the U.S. to collect a tax from a foreign corporation on its dividend distribution. As a result, the U.S. enacted a "branch profits" tax, which imposes a 30% flat tax on the earnings repatriated (or deemed so) by the U.S. branch office to the foreign home office.[168] This tax, like the 30% tax withheld by a U.S. subsidiary on the dividends it pays, is in addition to the regular net tax paid by the branch office on the effectively connected income.

E. Other Federal Taxes

1. The Payroll Tax

The federal social security system is funded by payments from taxpayers deducted from their payroll and paid at the source by the employer. Employers are liable for about one-half of the tax and employees the other half. Self-employed individuals also must contribute to the system. The general level of tax is 15.3% of one's wages or equivalent self-employment earnings. The maximum amount of wages or earnings subject to the tax was $68,400 in 1998.

2. Excise Taxes

There are numerous federal excise taxes on particular items. Perhaps the most common of these are the taxes on sales of alcohol and tobacco.

3. The Estate and Gift Taxes

The federal estate and gift taxes of chapters 11 and 12 of the Code[169] and the tax on generation-skipping transfers of chapter 13[170] are a relatively well-coordinated set of taxes on gratuitous transfers. Although the generation-skipping tax is a relatively recent addition to the Code, the estate and gift taxes have been around almost as long as the income tax. All three taxes are imposed on gratuitous transfers. The gift tax is imposed on transfers made during life. The estate tax imposes a final tax on the transfers made after the taxpayers death. One of the premises of these taxes is that the intra-family transfer of wealth should be taxed once each generation. The generation-skipping tax, put simply, is imposed on transfers that avoid these taxes by transferring wealth in a manner that "skips" over an intervening generation.

---

168 26 U.S.C.A. §884.
169 26 U.S.C.A. §§2001 *et seq.* and 2501 *et seq.* respectively
170 26 U.S.C.A. §2601 *et seq.*

The estate and gift taxes have a unified rate structure[171] that, as of 1999, effectively taxes only those gratuitous transfers of an individual that exceed $650,000 *in the aggregate*. In other words, an individual may give up to $650,000 in the form of lifetime gifts or in the form of a transfer at death or in some combination thereof without incurring any estate or gift tax. Because of a highly progressive rate structure, the first dollar of transfer above $650,000 is taxed at the rate of 37%. The maximum marginal rate of 55% is reached at $3,000,000. Aggregate transfers more than $10,000,000 are subject to an additional surtax of 5% until an *average* tax rate of 55% is reached.[172]

F. Other State and Local Taxes

1. The Sales Tax

Sales taxes, imposed at the point of sale to the ultimate consumer, are a major source of revenue for most states. Some cities also impose sales taxes. It is fairly common to see sales tax rates of 5%, more or less. Sales taxes have been heavily criticized as being regressive in their effect since the greatest proportional burden of the tax falls of lower-income consumers. Attempts to correct this inequity are usually in the form of exempting staples such as food from the tax base.

2. The Property Tax

Property taxes are another major source of revenue for the states. These were discussed in Chapter XII.[173]

3. Franchise Taxes

Many states impose franchise taxes on the privilege of doing business in the state. These taxes are sometimes viewed as a substitute for more comprehensive income taxes.

4. State and Local Income Taxes

Many states have income taxes on the income of residents and those non-residents doing business in the state. Some cities also impose income taxes in a like manner. Many of the state income taxes are based on federal income tax or are based on the federal adjusted gross income with further adjustments. Income tax rates vary widely, but are usually less than 10%. Some states have no income tax.[174]

---

171 26 U.S.C.A. §2001.

172 As noted earlier, the recipient of the gratuitous transfer does not have gross income because the Code excludes transfers "by gift, bequest, devise, or inheritance." 26 U.S.C.A. §102(a).

173 *See* p. 447.

174 "Tax-free Day," usually in the month of May, is the day when most taxpayers in the U.S., who have been working since January 1st, stop "working for the government" and start working for themselves.

INDEX

Index-5

APPENDIX A

Contents

Philip Francis HOFFMAN, Jr., and

Pav-A-Way Corporation, a Florida corporation,

Petitioners,

v.

Hazel J. JONES, as Administratrix of the Estate

of William Harrison Jones, Jr.,Deceased,

Respondent.

No. 43443.

Supreme Court of Florida.

280 So.2d 431 (1973)[1]

78 A.L.R.3d 321[2]

Widow brought wrongful death suits both in her individual capacity and as administratrix of deceased husband's estate. The Circuit Court, Brevard County, William G. Akridge, J., denied plaintiff's requested instruction predicated on comparative negligence, and rendered judgment for defendants, and plaintiff appealed. The District Court of Appeal, 272 So.2d 529, reversed and certified decision on question of whether contributory negligence rule should be replaced with principles of comparative negligence. On writ of certiorari, the Supreme Court, Adkins, J., adopted comparative negligence rule and delineated time when such rule is to be applied at trial and appellate levels.[3]

Remanded.

Roberts, J., dissented and filed opinion.[4] . . .

---

1   All footnotes in this appendix are by the author of this book and are inserted to point out features of the opinion.

2   A.L.R.2d, the American Law Reports, second series, publishes selected cases that have an important impact on the development of the law. Such cases are followed by an annotation commenting on the significance of the decision and analyzing that area of law in depth with citations from other jurisdictions.

3   This paragraph summary of the case was written by the editors of the case reports.

4   At this point, the West edition of the opinion sets out "headnotes" of all the major points and holdings of the opinion. These are written by the case editors, not the court. Because of space considerations, I have reproduced only two of the headnotes contained in the original, which are set out on the next page. Headnotes are collected in a "digest" which the lawyer or judge can scan to decide what judicial decisions are worth reading. *See* Chapter II, p. 79.

[4]
85   COMMON LAW
85k2   Sources and Scope

85k8 k. Decisions of English courts.
Fla. 1973.
Supreme Court has power to replace rule of contributory negligence with that of comparative negligence; in view of fact that prior to 1809 English case implicitly pronouncing that rule the theory of contributory negligence was a matter of judicial thought rather than judicial pronouncement, it could not be said that the common law was clear and free from doubt so as to make it part of the statute law of Florida by virtue of statute adopting the English common law. F.S.A.Const. art. 5, §3(b)(3). . .

[6]
272 NEGLIGENCE
272III   Contributory Negligence
272III(D) Comparative Negligence
272k97 k. Nature and application of the doctrine in general.
Fla. 1973.
A plaintiff in an action based on negligence is no longer to be denied any recovery because of his contributory negligence; if it appears from the evidence that both plaintiff and defendant were guilty of negligence which was, in some degree, a legal cause of injury to plaintiff, plaintiff's recovery is not to be entirely defeated; negligence of plaintiff and that of defendant is to be apportioned with plaintiff receiving only such an amount proportionate with his negligence and negligence of defendant. . . .

Edna L. Caruso of Howell, Kirby, Montgomery, D'Aiuto, Dean & Hallowes, West Palm Beach, for petitioners.

Sammy Cacciatore of Nance & Cacciatore, Melbourne, for respondent.

E. Harper Field and Frank C. Amatea of Keen, O'Kelley & Spitz, Tallahassee, for amicus curiae, Fla. Defense Lawyers Ass'n.[5]

C. Graham Carothers and C. DuBose Ausley of Ausley, Ausley, McMullen, McGehee & Carothers, Tallahassee, for amicus curiae, Fla. Railroad Ass'n.

Kenneth L. Ryskamp, of Bolles, Goodwin, Ryskamp & Welcher, Miami, for amicus curiae, Fla. East Coast Railway Co.

William B. Killian, of McCarthy, Steel, Hector & Davis, Miami, for amicus curiae, Fla. Power & Light Co.

Sam H. Mann, Jr. and John T. Allen, Jr., of Harrison, Greene, Mann, Davenport, Rowe & Stanton, St. Petersburg, for amicus curiae, Fla. Power Corp.

Raymond Ehrlich and James E. Cobb, Jacksonville, for amicus curiae, American Mutual Ins. Alliance, American Ins. Asso., and National Asso. of Independent Insurers.

Thomas W. McAliley of Beckham & McAliley, Miami, for amicus curiae, United Transportation Union, Fla. Legislative Boards of Railroad Brotherhoods and the Fla. AFL-CIO.

---

5 Several *amicus curiae* or "friend of the court" briefs were filed by lawyers for the organizations listed. When an appellate court is faced with deciding an important issue, appearances of *amici* are one way it can get additional points of view beyond those of the plaintiff and defendant. *See* Chapter II, p. 43 note 26.

ADKINS, Justice.

This cause is here on petition for writ of certiorari supported by certificate of the District Court of Appeal, Fourth District, that its decision (Jones v. Hoffman, 272 So.2d 529) is one which involves a question of great public interest. See Fla.Const., art. V, §3(b)(3), F.S.A.[6]

The question certified by the District Court of Appeal is: "Whether or not the Court should replace the contributory negligence rule with the principles of comparative negligence?"[7]

The District Court of Appeal answered the certified question in the affirmative and reversed the trial court in the case *sub judice* for following the precedent set down by this Court in Louisville and Nashville Railroad Co. v. Yniestra, 21 Fla. 700 (1886). This early case specifically held the contributory negligence rule to be the law of Florida, and it has uniformly been followed by the courts of the State ever since. The District Court of Appeal attempted, therefore, to overrule all precedent of this Court in the area of contributory negligence and to establish comparative negligence as the proper test. In so doing, the District Court has exceeded its authority.

In a dissenting opinion, Judge Owen stated well the position of the District Courts of Appeal when in disagreement with controlling precedent set down by this Court: "(I)f and when such a change is to be wrought by the judiciary, it should be at the hands of the Supreme Court rather than the District Court of Appeal. ... The majority decision would appear to flatly overrule a multitude of prior decisions of our Supreme Court, a prerogative which we do not enjoy." Jones v. Hoffman, 272 So.2d 529, p. 534.

The other District Courts of Appeal have recognized the relationship between their authority and that of this Court. Griffin v. State, 202 So.2d 602 (Fla. App.1st, 1967); Roberts v. State, 199 So.2d 340 (Fla. App.2d, 1967); and United States v. State, 179 So.2d 890 (Fla. App.3d, 1965). To allow a District Court of Appeal to overrule controlling precedent of this Court would be to create chaos and uncertainty in the judicial forum, particularly at the trial level. Ever since the District Court rendered its opinion there has been great confusion and much delay in the trial courts of the District Court of Appeal, Fourth District, while the attorneys and judges alike have been awaiting our decision in this case.

We point out that the mere certification to this Court by a District Court of Appeal that its decision involves a question of great public interest does not vest this Court with jurisdiction. If neither party involved petitioned here for a writ of certiorari, we would not have jurisdiction to answer the question certified or to review the District Court's action.

This is not to say that the District Courts of Appeal are powerless to seek change; they are free to certify questions of great public interest to this Court for consideration, and even to state their reasons for advocating change. They are, however, bound to follow the case law set forth by this Court.[8]

---

6 A "writ of certiorari" is a discretionary order issued by a higher court to a lower court requiring it to "bring up the record" of a case the higher court wishes to review. Florida thus follows the normal pattern of state appellate courts taking cases on the Supreme Court level only at its discretion. *See* Chapter V, p. 165. *Certiorari* practice in the U.S. Supreme Court is discussed in Chapter V, p. 172.

7 The subject of recovery for negligent actions is discussed in Chapter XI, pp. 409-412. Reading the cited pages would assist in understanding this the discussion in the opinion.

8 The Florida Supreme Court was obviously somewhat upset by the Court of Appeals' going ahead and deciding to use comparative negligence — despite the fact that Supreme Court ultimately agreed with that position on the merits. It thus demonstrates the traditional relationship that exists between superior and inferior courts. However, one frustration for lower appellate courts is the possibility that issues will remain unsettled for years because the supreme court in a system chooses not to decide them.

Prior to answering the question certified, we must also consider our own power and authority to replace the rule of contributory negligence with that of comparative negligence. It has been suggested that such a change in the common law of Florida is properly within the province only of the Legislature, and not of the courts. We cannot agree.

The rule that contributory negligence is an absolute bar to recovery was — as most tort law — a judicial creation, and it was specifically judicially adopted in Florida in Louisville and Nashville Railroad Co. v. Yniestra, *supra*. Most scholars attribute the origin of this rule to the English case of Butterfield v. Forrester, 11 East 60, 103 Eng.Rep. 926 (K.B.1809), although as much as thirty years later — in Raisin v. Mitchell, 9 Car. & P. 613, 173 Eng.Rep. 979 (C.P.1839) — contributory negligence was held not to be a complete bar to recovery. Maloney, From Contributory to Comparative Negligence: A Needed Law Reform, 11 U.Fla.L.Rev. 135, 141-142 (1958). Although "contributory negligence" itself had been mentioned in some earlier cases, our research reveals that prior to 1809 (as well as for a time after that date) there was no clear-cut, common law rule that contributory negligence was a complete defense to an action based on negligence. Most probably, the common law was the same in this regard as English maritime law and the civil law — i.e., damages were apportioned when both plaintiff and defendant were at fault. See Maloney, *supra*, page 152. Many authorities declare that early references to "contributory negligence" did not concern contributory negligence as we are familiar with it — i.e., lack of due care by the plaintiff which contributes to his injuries — but that it originally meant a plaintiff's own negligent act which was the effective, *direct cause* of the accident in which he was injured. E.G., Turk, Comparative Negligence on the March, 28 Chi-Kent L.Rev. 189, p. 196 (1950).

Prior to Butterfield v. Forrester, *supra*, there was no clear-cut pronouncement of the contributory negligence rule, so it must be said that "judicial thinking" culminated in the implicit pronouncement of the contributory negligence rule in the 1809 decision of Butterfield v. Forrester, *supra*. In view of the fact that prior to Butterfield contributory negligence was a matter of judicial thought rather than judicial pronouncement, it cannot be said that the common law was "clear and free from doubt," so as to make it a part of the statute law of this State by virtue of Fla.Stat. §2.01, F.S.A.[9]

As we stated in Duval v. Thomas, 114 So.2d 791, 795 (Fla.1959), it is "only when the common law is plain that we must observe it." We also said in this case, "(W)hen grave doubt exists of a true common law doctrine . . . we may, as was written in Ripley v. Ewell, *supra*, (61 So.2d 420), exercise a 'broad discretion' taking 'into account the changes in our social and economic customs and present day conceptions of right and justice.'"

Even if it be said that the present bar of contributory negligence is a part of our common law by virtue of prior judicial decision, it is also true from *Duval* that this Court may change the rule where great social upheaval dictates. It has been modified in many instances by judicial decision, such as those establishing the doctrines of "last clear chance," "appreciable degree" and others. See Negligence: Application of the Last Clear Chance Doctrine by Kenneth M. Myers, 8 Fla.Law.Rev. 336 (1955). In a large measure the

---

What the Florida Court of Appeals did is one way to force the issue to be decided.

9   The cited statute is a "reception" statute, officially receiving the English common law as the law of the State of Florida as of July 4, 1776. *See* Chapter II, p. 42. This explains why the majority has spent the last few paragraphs determining exactly when contributory negligence came into English common law. The Florida reception statute is quoted in the dissenting opinion *infra* p. A11. The dissent asserts that contributory negligence came into English law much earlier and thus the decision to change it is one for the legislature, not the courts. *See infra* p. A12.

A4

rule has been transfigured from any "statutory creation" by virtue of our adoption of the common law (if such it were) into decisional law by virtue of various court refinements. We have in the past, with hesitation, modified the common law in justified instances, and this is as it should be. Randolph v. Randolph, 146 Fla. 491, 1 So.2d 480 (1941), modified the common law doctrine that gave a father the superior right to the custody of a child; Banfield v. Addington, 104 Fla. 661, 140 So. 893 (1932), removed the common law exemption of a married woman from causes of action based on contract or mixed contracts in tort.

In Waller v. First Savings & Trust Co., 103 Fla. 1025, 138 So. 780 (1931), this Court refused to follow the common law principle that an action for personal injuries was abated upon the death of the tort-feasor, the Court saying: "This court has expressly recognized the principle that in specific instances certain rules which were admittedly a part of the old English common law did not become a part of the Florida common law, because contrary to our customs, institutions, or intendments of our statutes on other subjects." (p. 784)

This Court receded from the common law and held, in Hargrove v. Town of Cocoa Beach, 96 So.2d 130 (Fla.1957), that a municipal corporation may be held liable for the torts of police officers under the doctrine of *respondeat superior*, saying: "Tracing the rule to its ultimate progenitor we are led to the English case of Russel v. Men of Devon, 2 T.R. 667, 100 Eng.Rep.R. 359 (1788). 'Assuming that the immunity rule had its inception in the Men of Devon case, and most legal historians agree that it did, it should be noted that this case was decided in 1788, some twelve years after our Declaration of Independence. Be that as it may, our own feeling is that *the courts should be alive to the demands of justice. We can see no necessity for insisting on legislative action in a matter which the courts themselves originated.*" (Emphasis supplied) (p. 132) Gates v. Foley, 247 So.2d 40 (Fla.1971), established the right of a wife to recover for the loss of consortium as a result of her husband's injuries. This decision receded from Ripley v. Ewell, 61 So.2d 420 (Fla.1952) and abrogated a common law principle, saying: "It may be argued that any change in this rule should come from the Legislature. No recitation of authority is needed to indicate that this Court has not been backward in overturning unsound precedent in the area of tort law. *Legislative action could, of course, be taken, but we abdicate our own function, in a field peculiarly nonstatutory, when we refuse to reconsider an old and unsatisfactory court-made rule.*" (Emphasis supplied) 247 So.2d 40, p. 43.

All rules of the common law are designed for application to new conditions and circumstances as they may be developed by enlightened commercial and business intercourse and are intended to be vitalized by practical application in advanced society. One of the most pressing social problems facing us today is the automobile accident problem, for the bulk of tort litigation involves the dangerous instrumentality known as the automobile. Our society must be concerned with accident prevention and compensation of victims of accidents. The Legislature of Florida has made great progress in legislation geared for accident prevention. The prevention of accidents, of course, is much more satisfying than the compensation of victims, but we must recognize the problem of determining a method of securing just and adequate compensation of accident victims who have a good cause of action.

The contemporary conditions must be met with contemporary standards which are realistic and better calculated to obtain justice among all of the parties involved, based upon the circumstances applying between them at the time in question. The rule of contributory negligence as a complete bar to recovery was imported into the law by judges. Whatever may have been the historical justification for it, today it is almost universally regarded as unjust and inequitable to vest an entire accidental loss on one of the parties whose negligent conduct combined with the negligence of the other party to produce the loss. If fault is to remain the test of liability, then the doctrine of comparative negligence which involves apportionment of the loss among those whose fault contributed to the occurrence is more consistent with liability based on a fault premise.

We are, therefore, of the opinion that we do have the power and authority to reexamine the position we have taken in regard to contributory negligence and to alter the rule we have adopted previously in light of current "social and economic customs" and modern "conceptions of right and justice."

Use of the terms "contributory negligence" and "comparative negligence" is slightly confusing. The two theories now commonly known by these terms both recognize that negligence of a plaintiff may play a part in causing his injuries and that the damages he is allowed to recover should, therefore, be diminished to some extent. The "contributory negligence" theory, of course, *completely* bars recovery, while the "comparative negligence" theory is that a plaintiff is prevented from recovering only that proportion of his damages for which he is responsible.

The demise of the absolute-bar theory of contributory negligence has been urged by many American scholars in the law of torts. It has been abolished in almost every common law nation in the world, including England — its country of origin — and every one of the Canadian Provinces. Some form of comparative negligence now exists in Austria, France, Germany, Portugal, Switzerland, Italy, China, Japan, Persia, Poland, Russia, Siam and Turkey. Maloney, *supra*, page 154.

Also, our research reveals that sixteen states have so far adopted some form of the comparative negligence doctrine.

One reason for the abandonment of the contributory negligence theory is that the initial justification for establishing the complete defense is no longer valid. It is generally accepted that, historically, contributory negligence was adopted "to protect the essential growth of industries, particularly transportation." Institute of Judicial Administration, Comparative Negligence-1954 Supplement, at page 2. Modern economic and social customs, however, favor the individual, not industry.

We find that none of the justifications for denying any recovery to a plaintiff, who has contributed to his own injuries to any extent, has any validity in this age.

Perhaps the best argument in favor of the movement from contributory to comparative negligence is that the latter is simply a more equitable system of determining liability and a more socially desirable method of loss distribution. The injustice which occurs when a plaintiff suffers severe injuries as the result of an accident for which he is only slightly responsible, and is thereby denied any damages, is readily apparent. The rule of contributory negligence is a harsh one which either places the burden of a loss for which two are responsible upon only one party or relegates to Lady Luck the determination of the damages for which each of two negligent parties will be liable. When the negligence of more than one person contributes to the occurrence of an accident, each should pay the proportion of the total damages he has caused the other party.

In an effort to ameliorate the harshness of contributory negligence, other doctrines have evolved in tort law such as "gross, willful, and wanton" negligence, "last clear chance" and the application of absolute liability in certain instances. Those who defend the doctrine of contributory negligence argue that the rule is also not as harsh in its practical effect as it is in theory. This is so, they say, because juries tend to disregard the instructions given by the trial judge in an effort to afford some measure of rough justice to the injured party. We agree with Dean Maloney that, "(T)here is something basically wrong with a rule of law that is so contrary to the settled convictions of the lay community that laymen will almost always refuse to enforce it, even when solemnly told to do so by a judge whose instructions they have sworn to follow. . . . "(T)he disrespect for law engendered by putting our citizens in a position in which they feel it is necessary to deliberately violate the law is not something to be lightly brushed aside; and it comes ill from the mouths of lawyers, who as officers of the courts have sworn to uphold the law, to defend the present system by arguing that it works because jurors can be trusted to disregard that very law." 11 U.Fla.L.Rev. 135, pp. 151-152 (1958).[10]

In Connolly v. Steakley, 197 So.2d 524, 537 (Fla.1967), Mr. Justice O'Connell referred to contributory negligence as a "primitive device for achieving justice as between parties who are both at fault." Even Mr. Chief Justice McWhorter, in authoring the decision which specifically held the contributory negligence doctrine to be the law of this State, referred to it as "unjust and inequitable." Louisville and Nashville Railroad Co. v. Yniestra, *supra*, 21 Fla. p. 738.

Eighty-seven years after that decision, we find ourselves still laboring under a rule of law that has long been recognized as inequitable. The Legislature did enact a statute in 1887 which applied the principle of comparative negligence to railroad accidents. We held the statute unconstitutional under the due process and equal protection clauses of the Federal and State constitutions because it was of limited scope and not of *general application*. Georgia Southern & Florida Railway Co. v. Seven-Up Bottling Co., 175 So.2d 39 (Fla.1965). Our Legislature again addressed the problem in 1943, when a comparative negligence statute of general application was passed by both houses. This bill was vetoed by the Governor and the Legislature would not override the veto. Senate Journal, Regular Session, 1943, pp. 716-717. One man thus prevented this State from now operating under a much more equitable system of recovery for negligent personal injuries and property damage. Since that "defeat," the Legislature has done little to discard the harsh and inequitable contributory negligence rule, perhaps because it considers the problem to be a judicial one.

Since we definitely consider the problem to be a judicial one, we feel the time has come for this Court to join what seems to be a trend toward almost universal adoption of comparative negligence. A primary function of a court is to see that legal conflicts are equitably resolved. In the field of tort law, the most equitable result that can ever be reached by a court is the equation of liability with fault. Comparative negligence does this more completely than contributory negligence, and we would be shirking our duty if we did not adopt the better doctrine.

Therefore, we now hold that a plaintiff in an action based on negligence will no longer be denied any recovery because of his contributory negligence.

---

10 This demonstrates how the jury, which is only supposed to decide fact questions and follow the *judge's* instructions on the law, can ultimately have a cumulative effect on the shape of the law. The division of labor between the judge and the jury and the question of jury power to judge the law is discussed in Chapter III, p. 84. This is one area where consistent jury action "bending" the law contributed to changing the law. It is also noteworthy that here and earlier in the opinion, the majority relies heavily on scholarly commentary in support of its decision.

If it appears from the evidence that both plaintiff and defendant were guilty of negligence which was, in some degree, a legal cause of the injury to the plaintiff, this does not defeat the plaintiff's recovery entirely. The jury in assessing damages would in that event award to the plaintiff such damages as in the jury's judgment the negligence of the defendant caused to the plaintiff. In other words, the jury should apportion the negligence of the plaintiff and the negligence of the defendant; then, in reaching the amount due the plaintiff, the jury should give the plaintiff only such an amount proportioned with his negligence and the negligence of the defendant. See Florida Cent. & P.R. Co. v. Foxworth, 41 Fla. 1, 25 So. 338, 79 Am.St.Rep. 149 (1899).

This rule should not be construed so as to entitle a person to recover for damage in a case where the proof shows that the defendant could not by the exercise of due care have prevented the injury, or where the defendant's negligence was not a legal cause of the damage. Stated differently, there can be no apportionment of negligence where the negligence of the defendant is not directly a legal cause of the result complained of by the plaintiff. A plaintiff is barred from recovering damages for loss or injury caused by the negligence of another only when the plaintiff's negligence is the sole legal cause of the damage, or the negligence of the plaintiff and some person or persons other than the defendant or defendants was the sole legal cause of the damage.

If plaintiff and defendant are both at fault, the former may recover, but the amount of his recovery may be only such proportion of the entire damages plaintiff sustained as the defendant's negligence bears to the combined negligence of both the plaintiff and the defendant. For example, where it is found that the plaintiff's negligence is at least equal to that of the defendant, the amount awarded to the plaintiff should be reduced by one-half from what it otherwise would have been.

The doctrine of last clear chance would, of course, no longer have any application in these cases. See Martin v. Sussman, 82 So.2d 597 (Fla.1955).

We decline herein to dissect and discuss all the possible variations of comparative negligence which have been adopted in other jurisdictions. Countless law review commentaries and treatises can be found which have covered almost every conceivable mutation of the basic doctrine. Suffice it to say that we consider the "pure form" of comparative negligence — as we have phrased it above — to be the most equitable method of allocating damages in negligence actions.

In the usual situation where the negligence of the plaintiff is at issue, as well as that of the defendant, there will undoubtedly be a counterclaim filed. The cross-plaintiff (just as plaintiff in the main suit) guilty of some degree of negligence would be entitled to a verdict awarding him such damages as in the jury's judgment were proportionate with his negligence and the negligence of cross-defendant. This could result in two verdicts — one for plaintiff and one for cross-plaintiff. In such event the Court should enter one judgment in favor of the party receiving the larger verdict, the amount of which should be the difference between the two verdicts. This is in keeping with the long recognized principles of "set off" in contract litigation. The Court's primary responsibility is to enter a judgment which reflects the true intent of the jury, as expressed in its verdict or verdicts.

In rare cases the net result of two such claims will be that the party more responsible for an accident will recover more than the party less responsible. On the surface, this might seem inequitable. However, using an extreme example, let us assume that a plaintiff is 80 per cent responsible for an automobile accident and suffers $20,000 in damages, and that the defendant — 20 per cent responsible — fortunately suffers no damages. The liability of the defendant in such a case should not depend upon what damages he *suffered*, but upon what damages he *caused*. If a jury found that this defendant had been negligent and that his negligence, in relation to that of the plaintiff, was 20 per cent responsible for causing the accident then he should pay 20 per cent of the total damages, regardless of the fact that he has been fortunate enough to not be damaged personally.

Petitioners in this cause, and various amicus curiae who have filed briefs, have raised many points which they claim we must consider in adopting comparative negligence, such as the effects of such a change on the concept of "assumption of risk," and no "contribution" between joint tortfeasors. We decline to consider all those issues, however, for two reasons. One reason is that we already have a body of case law in this State dealing with comparative negligence, under our earlier railroad statute. Much of this case law will be applicable under the comparative negligence rule we are now adopting generally.

The other reason is that it is not the proper function of this Court to decide unripe issues, without the benefit of adequate briefing, not involving an actual controversy, and unrelated to a specific factual situation.[11]

We are fully confident that the trial court judges of this State can adequately handle any problems created by our change to a comparative negligence rule as these problems arise. The answers to many of the problems will be obvious in light of the purposes for which we adopt the rule stated above: (1) To allow a jury to apportion fault as it sees fit between negligent parties whose negligence was part of the legal and proximate cause of any loss or injury; and (2) To apportion the total damages resulting from the loss or injury according to the proportionate fault of each party.

In accomplishing these purposes, the trial court is authorized to require special verdicts to be returned by the jury and to enter such judgment or judgments as may truly reflect the intent of the jury as expressed in any verdict or verdicts which may be returned.[12]

We recognize the thousands of pending negligence cases affected by this decision. In fact, the prospect of a general upheaval in pending tort litigation has always been a deterring influence in considering the adoption of a comparative negligence rule. See Annotation, The Doctrine of Comparative Negligence, 32 ALR 3d 463, p. 487. We feel the trial judges of this State are capable of applying this comparative negligence rule without our setting guidelines in anticipation of expected problems. The problems are more appropriately resolved at the trial level in a practical manner instead of a theoretical solution at the appellate level. The trial judges are granted broad discretion in adopting such procedure as may accomplish the objectives and purposes expressed in this opinion.

Determining the time when the comparative negligence rule shall be applied at the trial level presents another problem. The confusion created by the premature adoption of the comparative negligence rule by the District Court of Appeal is further exemplified

---

11 The Court adopts the traditional judicial stance of declining to declare any law beyond what is essential to resolution of this case and gives the traditional adversary system reasons for doing so — the lack of sufficient incentive for the parties to "fight it out" over an issue that does not directly affect them. *See* Chapter III, pp. 83-88, where the value of a partisan clash of views is discussed, and Chapter IX, pp. 323-324, where the adversarial basis for limitations on judicial power are discussed.

12 A "special verdict" is one that requires the jury to provide a justification for its decision by way of specific findings of fact, rather than rendering a "general verdict" stating nothing more than who wins and in what amount. *See* Chapter III, p. 104.

by the fact that some trial judges, relying on the decision, have applied the rule in the trial of many cases. Other trial judges have conducted their trials in accordance with the law of contributory negligence.

We hold that a District Court of Appeal does not have the authority to overrule a decision of the Supreme Court of Florida. In the event of a conflict between the decision of a District Court of Appeal and this Court, the decision of this Court shall prevail until overruled by a subsequent decision of this Court.

Under the circumstances, we hold that this opinion shall be applied as follows:

1. As to those cases in which the comparative negligence rule has been applied, this opinion shall be applicable.

2. As to those cases already commenced, but in which trial has not yet begun, this opinion shall be applicable.

3. As to those cases in which trial has already begun or in which verdict or judgment has already been rendered, this opinion shall not be applicable, unless the applicability of the comparative negligence rule was appropriately and properly raised during some stage of the litigation.

4. As to those cases on appeal in which the applicability of the comparative negligence rule has been properly and appropriately made a question of appellate review, this opinion shall be applicable.

5. This opinion shall be applicable to all cases commenced after the decision becomes final.[13]

The certified question having now been answered in full, this cause is remanded to the District Court of Appeal, Fourth District, to be further remanded to the Circuit Court for a new trial.

In order to finalize the determination of the question in this case as expeditiously as possible, this decision is made effective immediately and a petition for rehearing will not be allowed.

It is so ordered.

CARLTON, C.J., and ERVIN, BOYD, McCAIN and DEKLE, JJ., concur.

ROBERTS, J., dissents with opinion.

ROBERTS, Justice (dissenting).

I must respectfully dissent from the majority opinion in this cause. My primary concern is whether this Court is empowered to reject and replace the established doctrine of contributory negligence by judicial decree.

The sovereign powers of this State are divided into three coordinate branches of government — legislative, judicial and executive — by the Constitution of Florida, Article II, Section 3. Our Constitution specifically prohibits a person belonging to one of such branches from exercising any powers "appertaining to either of the other branches unless expressly provided herein." This Court has been diligent in preserving and maintaining the doctrine of separation of powers, which doctrine was imbedded in both the state and federal constitutions at the threshhold of constitutional democracy in this country, and under which doctrine the judiciary has no power to make statutory law. State ex rel. Hanbury v. Tunnicliffe, 98 Fla. 731, 124 So. 279 (1929), Carlton v. Matthews, 103 Fla. 301,

---

13 In view of the great change in the law that this decision represents, the court decides to give its decision only partial retroactive effect. *See* Chapter II, p. 45.

137 So. 815 (1931), State v. Herndon, 158 Fla. 115, 27 So.2d 833 (1946), Hancock v. Board of Public Instruction of Charlotte County, 158 So.2d 519 (Fla.1963), Holley v. Adams, 238 So.2d 401 (Fla.1970), State v. Barquet, 262 So.2d 431 (Fla.1972).

In the case of Ponder v. Graham, 4 Fla. 23, 25 (1851), this Court emphatically stated, "The fundamental principle of every free and good government is, that these several co-ordinate departments forever remain separate and distinct. No maxim in political science is more fully recognized than this. Its necessity was recognized by the framers of our government, as one too invaluable to be surrendered, and too sacred to be tampered with. Every other political principle is subordinate to it — for it is this which gives to our system energy, vitality and stability. Montesquieu says there can be no liberty, where the judicial are not separated from the legislative powers. 1 Spirit of Laws, page 181. Mr. Madison says these departments should remain forever separate and distinct, and that there is no political truth of greater intrinsic value, and which is stamped with the authority or more enlightened patrons of liberty. Federalist, 270." Applying this well established doctrine, we held that the matter of changing statutory law is not one to be indulged by the Court, but is a legislative function. Kennedy v. City of Daytona Beach, 132 Fla. 675, 182 So. 228 (1938). Therein, this Court also reaffirmed the principle that the common law, if not abrogated by statute or constitutional provision, is in full force and effect in this state. See also Bryan v. Landis, 106 Fla. 19, 142 So. 650 (1932), Wilson v. Renfroe, 91 So.2d 857 (Fla.1957), Brooks v. City of West Miami, 246 So.2d 115 (Fla. App. 1971).[14]

It is the statutory law of this state that, "The common and statute laws of England which are of a general and not a local nature, with the exception hereinafter mentioned, down to the fourth day of July, 1776, are declared to be of force in this state; provided, the said statutes and common law be not inconsistent with the constitution and laws of the United States and the acts of the legislature of this state." Florida Statutes, Section 2.01, F.S.A.

The doctrine of contributory negligence was a part of the common law of England prior to July 4, 1776, and therefore, is part of the common law of this state pursuant to Florida Statutes, Section 2.01, F.S.A., and is secure from the desires of this Court to supplant it by the doctrine of comparative negligence, provided that it is not inconsistent with the Constitution and laws of the United States and the Constitution and acts of the Legislature of this state. Ripley v. Ewell, 61 So.2d 420 (Fla.1952), Duval v. Thomas, 114 So.2d 791 (Fla.1959). Furthermore, we have held that courts are bound by the rule of state decisis to follow common law as it has been judicially declared in previously adjudicated cases. Layne v. Tribune Co., 108 Fla. 177, 146 So. 234 (1933).

The question presently before this Court is whether this Court should replace the doctrine of contributory negligence with the concept of comparative negligence. Sub judice, by applying the doctrine of contributory negligence, the trial court correctly followed the precedent set down by this Court in Louisville and Nashville Railroad Co. v. Yniestra, 21 Fla. 700 (1886), and its progeny. This Court in *Yniestra* recognized and described contributory negligence as "the law as it unquestionably stands," 21 Fla. 700, p. 737. We said, "If Mr. Yniestra was himself negligent, and that negligence was the

---

14 The dissenting justice is setting out a limited view of Florida courts' power to make common law based on the state constitutional separation of powers principles which are similar to limits on the federal courts' s common-law powers, but are unlike that of most state courts. *See* Chapter I, p. 30 and Chapter IX, pp. 321-325 (limitations on federal court power based on separation of powers).

proximate cause of his death, the *law* calls that contributory negligence, and the plaintiff could not recover."

Although the case of Butterfield v. Forrester, 11 East 60, 103 Eng.Rep. 926 (K.B.1809), is recognized as a leading case in the area of contributory negligence, such case was not the first pronouncement of the common law doctrine of contributory negligence. Lord Ellenborough wrote in Butterfield v. Forrester, *supra*, "One person being in fault will not dispense with another's using ordinary care for himself. Two things must concur to support this action, an obstruction in the road by the fault of the defendant, and no want of ordinary care to avoid it on the part of the plaintiff." 11 East 60, 61.

The brief opinions of Bayley, J. and Lord Ellenborough in *Forrester* were merely a restatement of the concept of common law contributory negligence. If this case was the origin of common law contributory negligence, then clearly it would not have been adopted as part of the statutory law of this state through Florida Statutes, Section 2.01, F.S.A., because that decision was rendered subsequent to July 4, 1776.

I note with much interest the comment by Wex S. Malone in, "The Formative Era of Contributory Negligence," 41 Illinois Law Review, 151, to the following effect: "The concise opinions of Bayley and Lord Ellenborough in Butterfield v. Forrester (1809) afford no indication that either of those judges felt at the time that he was charting new paths for law."[15]

Contributory negligence was adopted much earlier as a part of the common law. In Bayly v. Merrell, Cro.Jac. 386, 79 Eng.Rep. 331 (1606), the Court explicated, "(I)f he doubted of the weight thereof, he might have weighed it; and was not bound to give credence to another's speech; *and being his own negligence*, he is without remedy." (Emphasis supplied) Cro.Jac. 386, p. 387, 79 Eng.Rep. 331.

Charles Beach in 1882 traced the doctrine of contributory negligence back to its origin in his treatise on contributory negligence, wherein he set out, "Our Anglo-American law of Negligence, including, as of course, that of Contributory Negligence, has come down to us, in ordinary generation, from the civil law of imperial Rome. It is a part of that great debt which the common law owes to the classical and the scholastic jurisprudence." Beach on Contributory Negligence, §1, p. 1 (1882). See also: Beach on Contributory Negligence, 2d Ed., §1, p. 1 (1892), and Beach on Contributory Negligence, 3d Ed., Crawford, §1, p. 1 (1899).

Although he expressed a personal view of dislike for the operation of the principle of contributory negligence, Chief Justice McWhorter recognized in Louisville and Nashville Railroad Co. v. Yniestra, *supra*, the inability of this Court to change the common law rule of contributory negligence when he applied the existing law required to the facts of the case before him. He observed, "The law, in cases at least where human life is concerned, certainly needs *legislative* revision." (Emphasis supplied) 21 Fla. 700, p. 738.

By virtue of Florida Statutes, Section 2.01, contributory negligence is in force and said doctrine can be modified or replaced only by legislation to the contrary. Interposition of judicial power to make a legislative change in a statute which the Legislature on numerous occasions has refused to do is a clear invasion of the legislative.

Co-Operative Sanitary Baking Co. v. Shields, 71 Fla. 110, 70 So. 934 (1916), involved a personal injury suit wherein plaintiff sought to recover damages for injuries sustained through the alleged negligence of defendant. Therein, this Court stated, inter alia, that at

---

15 The dissenting judge relies on scholarly commentary in his favor to support his position. *See supra* note 10.

common law a plaintiff could not recover for injuries to himself caused by the negligence of another if he in any appreciable way contributed to the proximate cause of injury, upon the theory that there is no apportionment of the results of mutual negligence. See also German-American Lumber Co. v. Hannah, 60 Fla. 76, 53 So. 516, 30 L.R.A.(N.S.) 882. In the *Shields* case, this Court explicitly recited, "The only modification of this common-law principle which the Legislature of this state has seen fit to make is in regard to injuries occasioned by railroad companies. See sections 3148, 3149, and 3150 of the General Statutes. *If this common-law principle is to be still further modified, it must be done by the Legislature, as it is beyond the power and province of the courts.* We would also refer to Coronet Phosphate Co. v. Jackson, 65 Fla. 170, 61 So. 318, and Wauchula Manufacturing & Timber Co. v. Jackson, 70 Fla. 596, 70 So. 599, decided here at the last term, wherein we followed the principles enunciated in German-American Lumber Co. v. Hannah, *supra*. If the evidence adduced in the instant case established the fact that the plaintiff's own negligence contributed to the proximate cause of the injuries which he received, then he cannot recover, even though it is also established by the evidence that the defendant was likewise guilty of negligence, whether by acts of commission or omission, which contributed to or formed a part of the proximate cause of the injury. In order to determine this point a careful examination of the evidence is requisite." (Emphasis supplied) *supra*, 70 So. at p. 936.

In fine, the primary question is not whether or not the law of contributory negligence should be changed, but rather, who should do the changing. Contributory negligence was recognized in the common law as far back as A.D. 1606 and made a part of the statute law of this State in A.D. 1829, and thus far not changed by statute. If such a fundamental change is to be made in the law, then such modification should be made by the legislature where proposed change will be considered by legislative committees in public hearing where the general public may have an opportunity to be heard and should not be made by judicial fiat.[16] Such an excursion into the field of legislative jurisdiction weakens the concept of separation of powers and our tripartite system of government.

For the foregoing reasons, I respectfully dissent.

---

16 Here, the dissent is making an argument about the relative institutional competence of judges and the legislature to fully consider and decide on changes in the law. *See* Chapter II, p. 43.

CONSTITUTION OF THE UNITED STATES

[drafted 1787, ratified 1789][1]

PREAMBLE

WE THE PEOPLE of the United States, in Order to form a more perfect Union, establish Justice, insure domestic Tranquility, provide for the common defence, promote the general Welfare, and secure the Blessings of Liberty to ourselves and our Posterity, do ordain and establish this Constitution for the United States of America.

ARTICLE I [Legislative Power]

Section 1. [Legislative Power Vested in Congress] All legislative Powers herein granted shall be vested in a Congress of the United States, which shall consist of a Senate and House of Representatives.

Section 2. [House of Representatives] [1. Election and Term of Members] The House of Representatives shall be composed of Members chosen every second Year by the People of the several States, and the Electors in each State shall have the Qualifications requisite for Electors of the most numerous Branch of the State Legislature.

[2. Qualifications of Members] No Person shall be a Representative who shall not have attained to the Age of twenty five Years, and been seven Years a Citizen of the United States, and who shall not, when elected, be an Inhabitant of that State in which he shall be chosen.

[3. Apportionment of Representation] {Representatives and direct Taxes shall be apportioned among the several States which may be included within this Union, according to their respective Numbers, which shall be determined by adding to the whole Number of free Persons, including those bound to Service for a Term of Years, and excluding Indians not taxed, three fifths of all other Persons.}[2] The actual Enumeration shall be made within three Years after the first Meeting of the Congress of the United States, and within every subsequent Term of ten Years, in such Manner as they shall by Law direct. The Number of Representatives shall not exceed one for every thirty Thousand, but each State shall have at Least one Representative; and until such enumeration shall be made, the State of New Hampshire shall be entitled to choose three, Massachusetts eight, Rhode Island and Providence Plantations one, Connecticut five, New York six, New Jersey four, Pennsylvania eight, Delaware one, Maryland six, Virginia ten, North Carolina five, South Carolina five, and Georgia three.

[4. Vacancies] When vacancies happen in the Representation from any State, the Executive Authority thereof shall issue Writs of Election to fill such Vacancies.

[5. Speaker of the House; Impeachment Power] The House of Representatives shall chuse[3] their Speaker and other Officers; and shall have the sole Power of Impeachment.

Section 3. [Senate] [1. Composition, Election, and Term of Office] {The Senate of the United States shall be composed of two Senators from each State, chosen by the Legislature thereof, for six Years; and each Senator shall have one Vote.}[4]

---

1   Footnotes and material in square brackets [ ] are explanatory and added by the author. Material in braces { } is superseded or changed by amendment, as explained in the accompanying footnote.

2   The mode of apportionment of representatives among the several states was amended by the 14th Amendment §2. Taxes on incomes without apportionment was authorized by the 16th Amendment. The reference to "other Persons" is to slaves. *See* Chapter I, p. 5.

3   This is the 18th century spelling of "choose."

4   The paragraph in braces was superseded by the 17th Amendment.

[2. Staggered Terms and Vacancies] Immediately after they shall be assembled in Consequence of the first Election, they shall be divided as equally as may be into three Classes. The Seats of the Senators of the first Class shall be vacated at the Expiration of the second Year, of the second Class at the Expiration of the fourth Year, and of the third Class at the Expiration of the sixth Year, so that one third may be chosen every second Year; {and if Vacancies happen by Resignation, or otherwise, during the Recess of the Legislature of any State, the Executive thereof may make temporary Appointments until the next Meeting of the Legislature, which shall then fill such Vacancies.}[5]

[3. Qualifications of Senators] No Person shall be a Senator who shall not have attained to the Age of thirty Years, and been nine Years a Citizen of the United States, and who shall not, when elected, be an Inhabitant of that State for which he shall be chosen.

[4. Vice President as President of Senate] The Vice President of the United States shall be President of the Senate, but shall have no Vote, unless they be equally divided.

[5. Officers] The Senate shall chuse their other Officers, and also a President pro tempore, in the Absence of the Vice President, or when he shall exercise the Office of President of the United States.

[6. Senate's Power to Try Impeachments] The Senate shall have the sole Power to try all Impeachments. When sitting for that Purpose, they shall be on Oath or Affirmation. When the President of the United States is tried, the Chief Justice shall preside: And no Person shall be convicted without the Concurrence of two thirds of the Members present.

[7. Effect of Conviction in Impeachment] Judgment in Cases of Impeachment shall not extend further than to removal from Office, and disqualification to hold and enjoy any Office of honor, Trust or Profit under the United States: but the Party convicted shall nevertheless be liable and subject to Indictment, Trial, Judgment and Punishment, according to Law.

Section 4. [Congressional Elections and Meetings of Congress] [1. Congressional Elections] The Times, Places and Manner of holding Elections for Senators and Representatives, shall be prescribed in each State by the Legislature thereof; but the Congress may at any time by Law make or alter such Regulations, except as to the Places of chusing Senators.

[2. Meetings of the Congress] The Congress shall assemble at least once in every year, and such meeting shall begin at noon on the {first Monday in December, unless they shall by Law appoint a different Day.}[6]

Section 5. [Power of Each House Over Internal Operations] [1. Each House as Judge of Qualifications and Election of Members; Quorum] Each House shall be the Judge of the Elections, Returns and Qualifications of its own Members, and a Majority of each shall constitute a Quorum to do Business; but a smaller Number may adjourn from day to day, and may be authorized to compel the Attendance of absent Members, in such Manner, and under such Penalties as each House may provide.

[2. Rules of Proceedings; Punishment and Expulsion of Members] Each House may determine the Rules of its Proceedings, punish its Members for disorderly Behaviour, and, with the Concurrence of two thirds, expel a Member.

[3. Journal and Voting] Each House shall keep a Journal of its Proceedings, and from time to time publish the same, excepting such Parts as may in their Judgment require

---

5 The phrase in braces was superseded by 17th Amendment.
6 The material in braces was superseded by 20th Amendment.

Secrecy; and the Yeas and Nays of the Members of either House on any question shall, at the Desire of one fifth of those Present, be entered on the Journal.

[4. Consent of Each House to Adjournment] Neither House, during the Session of Congress, shall, without the Consent of the other, adjourn for more than three days, nor to any other Place than that in which the two Houses shall be sitting.

Section 6. [Compensation and Immunities; Incompatible Offices] [1. Compensation and Immunities] The Senators and Representatives shall receive a Compensation for their Services, to be ascertained by Law, and paid out of the Treasury of the United States. They shall in all Cases, except Treason, Felony and Breach of the Peace, be privileged from Arrest during their Attendance at the Session of their respective Houses, and in going to and returning from the same; and for any Speech or Debate in either House, they shall not be questioned in any other Place.[7]

[2. Incompatible Offices] No Senator or Representative shall, during the Time for which he was elected, be appointed to any civil Office under the Authority of the United States, which shall have been created, or the Emoluments whereof shall have been increased during such time; and no Person holding any Office under the United States, shall be a Member of either House during his Continuance in Office.

Section 7. [Legislative Process] [1. Revenue Bills to Originate in House] All Bills for raising Revenue shall originate in the House of Representatives; but the Senate may propose or concur with Amendments as on other Bills.

[2. Passage of Bills by Both Houses and Presentment to President] Every Bill which shall have passed the House of Representatives and the Senate, shall, before it become a Law, be presented to the President of the United States; If he approve he shall sign it, but if not he shall return it, with his Objections to that House in which it shall have originated, who shall enter the Objections at large on their Journal, and proceed to reconsider it. If after such Reconsideration two thirds of that House shall agree to pass the Bill, it shall be sent together with the Objections, to the other House, by which it shall likewise be reconsidered, and if approved by two thirds of that House, it shall become a Law. But in all such Cases the Votes of both Houses shall be determined by yeas and Nays, and the Names of the Persons voting for and against the Bill shall be entered on the Journal of each House respectively. If any Bill shall not be returned by the President within ten Days (Sundays excepted) after it shall have been presented to him, the Same shall be a Law, in like Manner as if he had signed it, unless the Congress by their Adjournment prevent its Return, in which Case it shall not be a Law.

[3. Presentment of Orders and Resolutions] Every Order, Resolution, or Vote to which the Concurrence of the Senate and House of Representatives may be necessary (except on a question of Adjournment) shall be presented to the President of the United States; and before the Same shall take Effect, shall be approved by him, or being disapproved by him, shall be repassed by two thirds of the Senate and House of Representatives, according to the Rules and Limitations prescribed in the Case of a Bill.

Section 8. [Powers of Congress] [1] The Congress shall have Power To lay and collect Taxes, Duties, Imposts and Excises, to pay the Debts and provide for the common Defence and general Welfare of the United States; but all Duties, Imposts and Excises shall be uniform throughout the United States;

[2] To borrow Money on the credit of the United States;

---

7 The 27th Amendment amended this section by adding a sentence on compensation of members of Congress.

[3] To regulate Commerce with foreign Nations, and among the several States, and with the Indian Tribes;

[4] To establish an uniform Rule of Naturalization, and uniform Laws on the subject of Bankruptcies throughout the United States;

[5] To coin Money, regulate the Value thereof, and of foreign Coin, and fix the Standard of Weights and Measures;

[6] To provide for the Punishment of counterfeiting the Securities and current Coin of the United States;

[7] To establish Post Offices and Post Roads;

[8] To promote the Progress of Science and useful Arts, by securing for limited Times to Authors and Inventors the exclusive Right to their respective Writings and Discoveries;

[9] To constitute Tribunals inferior to the supreme Court;

[10] To define and punish Piracies and Felonies committed on the high Seas, and Offences against the Law of Nations;

[11] To declare War, grant Letters of Marque and Reprisal, and make Rules concerning Captures on Land and Water;

[12] To raise and support Armies, but no Appropriation of Money to that Use shall be for a longer Term than two Years;

[13] To provide and maintain a Navy;

[14] To make Rules for the Government and Regulation of the land and naval Forces;

[15] To provide for calling forth the Militia to execute the Laws of the Union, suppress Insurrections and repel Invasions;

[16] To provide for organizing, arming, and disciplining, the Militia, and for governing such Part of them as may be employed in the Service of the United States, reserving to the States respectively, the Appointment of the Officers, and the Authority of training the Militia according to the discipline prescribed by Congress;

[17] To exercise exclusive Legislation in all Cases whatsoever, over such District (not exceeding ten Miles square) as may, by Cession of particular States, and the Acceptance of Congress, become the Seat of the Government of the United States, and to exercise like Authority over all Places purchased by the Consent of the Legislature of the State in which the Same shall be, for the Erection of Forts, Magazines, Arsenals, dock-Yards, and other needful Buildings;—And

[18] To make all Laws which shall be necessary and proper for carrying into Execution the foregoing Powers, and all other Powers vested by this Constitution in the Government of the United States, or in any Department or Officer thereof.

Section 9. [Powers Prohibited to the United States]

[1. Importing Slaves] {The Migration or Importation of such Persons as any of the States now existing shall think proper to admit, shall not be prohibited by the Congress prior to the Year one thousand eight hundred and eight, but a Tax or duty may be imposed on such Importation, not exceeding ten dollars for each Person.}[8]

[2. Suspension of Writ of Habeas Corpus] The Privilege of the Writ of Habeas Corpus shall not be suspended, unless when in Cases of Rebellion or Invasion the public Safety may require it.

---

8 Congress duly passed a prohibition of further importation. To the extent that this clause condones slavery, it is superseded by the 13th Amendment.

[3. Bills of Attainder and Ex Post Facto Laws] No Bill of Attainder or ex post facto Law shall be passed.

[4. No Direct Tax] No Capitation, or other direct, Tax shall be laid, unless in Proportion to the Census or Enumeration herein before directed to be taken.[9]

[5. No Taxes or Duties on State Exports] No Tax or Duty shall be laid on Articles exported from any State.

[6. No Preferences to Ports Nor Duties on Vessels] No Preference shall be given by any Regulation of Commerce or Revenue to the Ports of one State over those of another: nor shall Vessels bound to, or from, one State, be obliged to enter, clear, or pay Duties in another.

[7. Appropriations; Statements and Accounts] No Money shall be drawn from the Treasury, but in Consequence of Appropriations made by Law; and a regular Statement and Account of the Receipts and Expenditures of all public Money shall be published from time to time.

[8. No Titles of Nobility or Emoluments From Foreign States to Officers of United States] No Title of Nobility shall be granted by the United States: And no Person holding any Office of Profit or Trust under them, shall, without the Consent of the Congress, accept of any present, Emolument, Office, or Title, of any kind whatever, from any King, Prince, or foreign State.

Section 10. [Restrictions on the States] [1. Powers Restrictions and Rights Restrictions] No State shall enter into any Treaty, Alliance, or Confederation; grant Letters of Marque and Reprisal; coin Money; emit Bills of Credit; make any Thing but gold and silver Coin a Tender in Payment of Debts; pass any Bill of Attainder, ex post facto Law, or Law impairing the Obligation of Contracts, or grant any Title of Nobility.

[2. Import-Export Clause] No State shall, without the Consent of the Congress, lay any Imposts or Duties on Imports or Exports, except what may be absolutely necessary for executing its inspection Laws: and the net Produce of all Duties and Imposts, laid by any State on Imports or Exports, shall be for the Use of the Treasury of the United States; and all such Laws shall be subject to the Revision and Controul of the Congress.

[3. Powers Restrictions] No State shall, without the Consent of Congress, lay any Duty of Tonnage, keep Troops, or Ships of War in time of Peace, enter into any Agreement or Compact with another State, or with a foreign Power, or engage in War, unless actually invaded, or in such imminent Danger as will not admit of delay.

ARTICLE II [The Executive Power]

Section 1. [Executive Power Vested in President; Term and Election of President and Vice-President; Qualifications of President; Removal and Succession; Compensation; Oath of Office] [1. Executive Power Vested in President; Term of Office] The executive Power shall be vested in a President of the United States of America. He shall hold his Office during the Term of four Years, and, together with the Vice President, chosen for the same Term, be elected, as follows:[10]

[2. Election of President and Vice-President] Each State shall appoint, in such Manner as the Legislature thereof may direct, a Number of Electors, equal to the whole Number of Senators and Representatives to which the State may be entitled in the Congress: but

---

9 This clause, together with Art. I §2 cl. 3, was repealed by the 16th Amendment.

10 To the extent that this implies that the President may be elected to more than two terms, it is amended by the 22nd Amendment.

no Senator or Representative, or Person holding an Office of Trust or Profit under the United States, shall be appointed an Elector.[11]

[3. Method of Selection] {The Electors shall meet in their respective States, and vote by Ballot for two Persons, of whom one at least shall not be an Inhabitant of the same State with themselves. And they shall make a List of all the Persons voted for, and of the Number of Votes for each; which List they shall sign and certify, and transmit sealed to the Seat of the Government of the United States, directed to the President of the Senate. The President of the Senate shall, in the Presence of the Senate and House of Representatives, open all the Certificates, and the Votes shall then be counted. The Person having the greatest Number of Votes shall be the President, if such Number be a Majority of the whole Number of Electors appointed; and if there be more than one who have such Majority, and have an equal Number of Votes, then the House of Representatives shall immediately chuse by Ballot one of them for President; and if no Person have a Majority, then from the five highest on the List the said House shall in like Manner chuse the President, the Votes shall be taken by States the Representation from each State having one Vote; A quorum for this Purpose shall consist of a Member or Members from two thirds of the States, and a Majority of all the States shall be necessary to a Choice. In every Case, after the Choice of the President, the Person having the greater Number of Votes of the Electors shall be the Vice President. But if there should remain two or more who have equal Votes, the Senate shall choose from them by Ballot the Vice President.}[12]

[4. When Electors Vote] The Congress may determine the Time of chusing the Electors, and the Day on which they shall give their Votes; which Day shall be the same throughout the United States.

[5. Qualifications] No Person except a natural born Citizen, or a Citizen of the United States, at the time of the Adoption of this Constitution, shall be eligible to the Office of President; neither shall any Person be eligible to that Office who shall not have attained to the Age of thirty five Years, and been fourteen Years a Resident within the United States.

[6. Succession] {In Case of the Removal of the President from Office, or of his Death, Resignation, or Inability to discharge the Powers and Duties of the said Office, the Same shall devolve on the Vice President, and the Congress may by Law provide for the Case of Removal, Death, Resignation or Inability, both of the President and Vice President, declaring what Officer shall then act as President, and such Officer shall act accordingly until the Disability be removed, or a President shall be elected.}[13]

[7. Compensation] The President shall, at stated Times, receive for his Services, a Compensation, which shall neither be encreased nor diminished during the Period for which he shall have been elected, and he shall not receive within that Period any other Emolument from the United States, or any of them.

[8. Oath of Office] Before he enter on the Execution of his Office, he shall take the following Oath or Affirmation: — "I do solemnly swear (or affirm) that I will faithfully execute the Office of President of the United States, and will to the best of my Ability, preserve, protect and defend the Constitution of the United States."

---

11 This clause was altered by the provisions of the 23rd Amendment, which authorizes Presidential Electors for the District of Columbia, thus for the first time giving District residents the right to vote in presidential elections.

12 This clause was superseded by the 12th Amendment. Parts of the 12th Amendment were in turn superseded by §3 of the 20th Amendment.

13 This clause was superseded by the 25th Amendment.

Section 2. [Powers of the President] [1. Commander in Chief; Executive Opinions; the Pardon Power] The President shall be Commander in Chief of the Army and Navy of the United States, and of the Militia of the several States, when called into the actual Service of the United States; he may require the Opinion, in writing, of the principal Officer in each of the Executive Departments, upon any Subject relating to the Duties of their respective Offices and he shall have Power to grant Reprieves and Pardons for Offenses against the United States, except in Cases of Impeachment.

[2. Treaty Power and Appointments Power] He shall have Power, by and with the Advice and Consent of the Senate, to make Treaties, provided two thirds of the Senators present concur; and he shall nominate, and by and with the Advice and Consent of the Senate, shall appoint Ambassadors, other public Ministers and Consuls, Judges of the supreme Court, and all other Officers of the United States, whose Appointments are not herein otherwise provided for, and which shall be established by Law: but the Congress may by Law vest the Appointment of such inferior Officers, as they think proper, in the President alone, in the Courts of Law, or in the Heads of Departments.

[3. Recess Appointments] The President shall have Power to fill up all Vacancies that may happen during the Recess of the Senate, by granting Commissions which shall expire at the End of their next Session.

Section 3. [Powers with respect to Congress; Ambassadors; Enforcement of the Laws; Commissioning of Officers] He shall from time to time give to the Congress Information of the State of the Union, and recommend to their Consideration such Measures as he shall judge necessary and expedient; he may, on extraordinary Occasions, convene both Houses, or either of them, and in Case of Disagreement between them, with Respect to the Time of Adjournment, he may adjourn them to such Time as he shall think proper; he shall receive Ambassadors and other public Ministers; he shall take Care that the Laws be faithfully executed, and shall Commission all the Officers of the United States.

Section 4. [Impeachment of the President and Other Federal Officers] The President, Vice President and all civil Officers of the United States, shall be removed from Office on Impeachment for, and Conviction of, Treason, Bribery, or other high Crimes and Misdemeanors.

ARTICLE III [The Judicial Power]

Section 1. [Federal Judicial System and Federal Judges] The judicial Power of the United States, shall be vested in one supreme Court, and in such inferior Courts as the Congress may from time to time ordain and establish. The Judges, both of the supreme and inferior Courts, shall hold their Offices during good Behaviour, and shall, at stated Times, receive for their Services, a Compensation, which shall not be diminished during their Continuance in Office.

Section 2. [Jurisdiction of the Federal Courts] [1. The Bases of Federal Jurisdiction] The judicial Power shall extend to all Cases, in Law and Equity, arising under this Constitution, the Laws of the United States, and Treaties made, or which shall be made, under their Authority; —to all Cases affecting Ambassadors, other public Ministers and Consuls; —to all Cases of admiralty and maritime Jurisdiction; —to Controversies to which the United States shall be a Party; —to Controversies between two or more States {; —between a State and Citizens of another State}; —between Citizens of different States; —between Citizens of the same State claiming Lands under Grants of different

States {, and between a State, or the Citizens thereof, and foreign States, Citizens or Subjects.}[14]

[2. Supreme Court Jurisdiction] In all Cases affecting Ambassadors, other public Ministers and Consuls, and those in which a State shall be a Party, the supreme Court shall have original Jurisdiction. In all the other Cases before mentioned, the supreme Court shall have appellate Jurisdiction, both as to Law and Fact, with such Exceptions, and under such Regulations as the Congress shall make.

[3. Jury Trial in Criminal Cases] The Trial of all Crimes, except in Cases of Impeachment, shall be by Jury; and such Trial shall be held in the State where the said Crimes shall have been committed; but when not committed within any State, the Trial shall be at such Place or Places as the Congress may by Law have directed.

Section 3. [Treason] [1. Definition and Proof] Treason against the United States, shall consist only in levying War against them, or, in adhering to their Enemies, giving them Aid and Comfort. No Person shall be convicted of Treason unless on the Testimony of two Witnesses to the same overt Act, or on Confession in open Court.

[2. Punishment] The Congress shall have Power to declare the Punishment of Treason, but no Attainder of Treason shall work Corruption of Blood, or Forfeiture except during the Life of the Person attainted.

ARTICLE IV [States; Federal Property]

Section 1. [Full Faith and Credit] Full Faith and Credit shall be given in each State to the public Acts, Records, and judicial Proceedings of every other State. And the Congress may by general Laws prescribe the Manner in which such Acts, Records and Proceedings shall be proved, and the Effect thereof.

Section 2. [1. Privileges and Immunities] The Citizens of each State shall be entitled to all Privileges and Immunities of Citizens in the several States.

[2. Extradition] A person charged in any State with Treason, Felony, or other Crime, who shall flee from Justice, and be found in another State, shall on Demand of the executive Authority of the State from which he fled, be delivered up, to be removed to the State having Jurisdiction of the Crime.

[3. Fugitive Slaves] {No Person held to Service or Labour in one State, under the Laws thereof, escaping into another, shall, in Consequence of any Law or Regulation therein, be discharged from such Service or Labour, but shall be delivered up on Claim of the Party to whom such Service or Labour may be due.}[15]

Section 3. [1. Admission of New States] New States may be admitted by the Congress into this Union; but no new State shall be formed or erected within the Jurisdiction of any other State; nor any State be formed by the Junction of two or more States, or Parts of States, without the Consent of the Legislatures of the States concerned as well as of the Congress.

[2. Power Over Federal Property] The Congress shall have Power to dispose of and make all needful Rules and Regulations respecting the Territory or other Property belonging to the United States; and nothing in this Constitution shall be so construed as to Prejudice any Claims of the United States, or of any particular State.

---

14 The two phrases in braces in this clause were superseded by the 11th Amendment. *See* Chapter I, p. 34, and Chapter VI, pp. 217-218.

15 This clause was repealed by the 13th Amendment's prohibition of slavery and involuntary servitude.

Section 4. [Guaranty of Republican Form of Government] The United States shall guarantee to every State in this Union a Republican Form of Government, and shall protect each of them against Invasion; and on Application of the Legislature, or of the Executive (when the Legislature cannot be convened) against domestic Violence.

ARTICLE V [Amendment of the Constitution]

The Congress, whenever two thirds of both Houses shall deem it necessary, shall propose Amendments to this Constitution, or on the Application of the Legislatures of two thirds of the several States, shall call a Convention for proposing Amendments, which, in either Case, shall be valid to all Intents and Purposes, as Part of this Constitution, when ratified by the Legislatures of three fourths of the several States, or by Conventions in three fourths thereof, as the one or the other Mode of Ratification may be proposed by the Congress; Provided that no Amendment which may be made prior to the Year One thousand eight hundred and eight shall in any Manner affect the first and fourth Clauses in the Ninth Section of the first Article; and that no State, without its Consent, shall be deprived of its equal Suffrage in the Senate.

ARTICLE VI [Debts, Supremacy and Oaths]

Section 1. [Debts] All Debts contracted and Engagements entered into, before the Adoption of this Constitution, shall be as valid against the United States under this Constitution, as under the Confederation.

Section 2. [Supremacy of Federal Law] This Constitution, and the Laws of the United States which shall be made in Pursuance thereof; and all Treaties made, or which shall be made, under the Authority of the United States, shall be the supreme Law of the Land; and the Judges in every State shall be bound thereby, any Thing in the Constitution or Laws of any State to the Contrary notwithstanding.

Section 3. [Oath of Office] The Senators and Representatives before mentioned, and the Members of the several State Legislatures, and all executive and judicial Officers, both of the United States and of the several States, shall be bound by Oath or Affirmation, to support this Constitution; but no religious Test shall ever be required as a Qualification to any Office or public Trust under the United States.

ARTICLE VII [Ratification of Original Articles]

The Ratification of the Conventions of nine States, shall be sufficient for the Establishment of this Constitution between the States so ratifying the Same.

DONE in Convention by the Unanimous Consent of the States present the Seventeenth Day of September in the Year of Our Lord one thousand seven hundred and Eighty seven and of the Independence of the United States of America the Twelfth. IN WITNESS whereof We have hereunto subscribed our Names,

[signatures of delegates omitted].

AMENDMENTS TO THE CONSTITUTION[16]

AMENDMENT I [Freedom of Religion, Speech, Press, Assembly and Petition]

Congress shall make no law respecting an establishment of religion, or prohibiting the free exercise thereof; or abridging the freedom of speech, or of the press; or the right of the people peaceably to assemble, and to petition the Government for a redress of grievances.

AMENDMENT II [Militia; Right to Bear Arms]

A well regulated Militia, being necessary to the security of a free State, the right of the people to keep and bear Arms, shall not be infringed.

AMENDMENT III [Quartering of Soldiers]

No Soldier shall, in time of peace be quartered in any house, without the consent of the Owner, nor in time of war, but in a manner to be prescribed by law.

AMENDMENT IV [Searches and Seizures]

The right of the people to be secure in their persons, houses, papers, and effects, against unreasonable searches and seizures, shall not be violated, and no Warrants shall issue, but upon probable cause, supported by Oath or affirmation, and particularly describing the place to be searched, and the persons or things to be seized.

AMENDMENT V [Grand Jury Indictment; Double Jeopardy; Self-Incrimination; Due Process of Law; Taking of Property]

No person shall be held to answer for a capital, or otherwise infamous crime, unless on a presentment or indictment of a Grand Jury, except in cases arising in the land or naval forces, or in the Militia, when in actual service in time of War or public danger; nor shall any person be subject for the same offence to be twice put in jeopardy of life or limb; nor shall be compelled in any criminal case to be a witness against himself, nor be deprived of life, liberty, or property, without due process of law; nor shall private property be taken for public use, without just compensation.

AMENDMENT VI [Speedy and Public Trial; Trial by Jury; Notice of Charges; Confrontation; Assistance of Counsel]

In all criminal prosecutions, the accused shall enjoy the right to a speedy and public trial, by an impartial jury of the State and district wherein the crime shall have been committed, which district shall have been previously ascertained by law, and to be informed of the nature and cause of the accusation; to be confronted with the witnesses against him; to have compulsory process for obtaining witnesses in his favor, and to have the Assistance of Counsel for his defence.

AMENDMENT VII [Jury Trial in Civil Cases]

In Suits at common law, where the value in controversy shall exceed twenty dollars, the right of trial by jury shall be preserved, and no fact tried by a jury, shall be otherwise reexamined in any Court of the United States, than according to the rules of the common law.

AMENDMENT VIII [Bail; Cruel and Unusual Punishment]

Excessive bail shall not be required, nor excessive fines imposed, nor cruel and unusual punishments inflicted.

---

16 The year each Amendment was ratified is indicated in parentheses, except for the Bill of Rights (first 10 amendments), which were all ratified together in 1791. *See* Chapter I, p. 4.

AMENDMENT IX [Rights Retained by the People]

The enumeration in the Constitution, of certain rights, shall not be construed to deny or disparage others retained by the people.

AMENDMENT X [Powers Reserved to the States]

The powers not delegated to the United States by the Constitution, nor prohibited by it to the States, are reserved to the States respectively, or to the people.

AMENDMENT XI [Immunity of States from Suit in Federal Court] (1798)[17]

The Judicial power of the United States shall not be construed to extend to any suit in law or equity, commenced or prosecuted against one of the United States by Citizens of another State, or by Citizens or Subjects of any Foreign State.

AMENDMENT XII [Separate Electoral Vote for President and Vice-President] (1804)[18]

The Electors shall meet in their respective states and vote by ballot for President and Vice-President, one of whom, at least, shall not be an inhabitant of the same state with themselves; they shall name in their ballots the person voted for as President, and in distinct ballots the person voted for as Vice-President, and they shall make distinct lists of all persons voted for as President, and of all persons voted for as Vice-President, and of the number of votes for each, which lists they shall sign and certify, and transmit sealed to the seat of the government of the United States, directed to the President of the Senate; — The President of the Senate shall, in the presence of the Senate and House of Representatives, open all the certificates and the votes shall then be counted; — The person having the greatest number of votes for President, shall be the President, if such number be a majority of the whole number of Electors appointed; and if no person have such majority, then from the persons having the highest numbers not exceeding three on the list of those voted for as President, the House of Representatives shall choose immediately, by ballot, the President. But in choosing the President, the votes shall be taken by states, the representation from each state having one vote; a quorum for this purpose shall consist of a member or members from two-thirds of the states, and a majority of all the states shall be necessary to a choice. And if the House of Representatives shall not choose a President whenever the right of choice shall devolve upon them before the fourth day of March next following, then the Vice-President shall act as President, as in the case of the death or other constitutional disability of the President. — The person having the greatest number of votes as Vice-President, shall be the Vice-President, if such number be a majority of the whole number of Electors appointed, and if no person have a majority, then from the two highest numbers of the list, the Senate shall choose the Vice-President; a quorum for the purpose shall consist of two-thirds of the whole number of Senators, and a majority of the whole number shall be necessary to a choice. But no person constitutionally ineligible to the office of President shall be eligible to that of Vice-President of the United States.

AMENDMENT XIII [Abolition of Slavery] (1865)

Section 1. Neither slavery nor involuntary servitude, except as a punishment for crime whereof the party shall have been duly convicted, shall exist within the United States, or any place subject to their jurisdiction.

Section 2. Congress shall have power to enforce this article by appropriate

---

17 *See supra* note 14.
18 *See supra* note 12.

legislation.

AMENDMENT XIV [Citizenship; Privileges and Immunities;
Due Process of Law; Equal Protection of the Laws] (1868)

Section 1. All persons born or naturalized in the United States, and subject to the jurisdiction thereof, are citizens of the United States and of the State wherein they reside. No State shall make or enforce any law which shall abridge the privileges or immunities of citizens of the United States; nor shall any State deprive any person of life, liberty, or property, without due process of law; nor deny to any person within its jurisdiction the equal protection of the laws.

Section 2. Representatives shall be apportioned among the several States according to their respective numbers, counting the whole number of persons in each State, excluding Indians not taxed. But when the right to vote at any election for the choice of electors for President and Vice President of the United States, Representatives in Congress, the Executive and Judicial officers of a State, or the members of the Legislature thereof, is being denied to any of the male inhabitants of such State, being twenty-one years of age, and citizens of the United States, or in any way abridged, except for participation in rebellion, or other crime, the basis of representation therein shall be reduced in the proportion which the number of such male citizens shall bear to the whole number of male citizens twenty-one years of age in such State.[19]

{Section 3. No person shall be a Senator or Representative in Congress, or elector of President and Vice President, or hold any office, civil or military, under the United States, or under any State, who having previously taken an oath, as a member of Congress, or as an officer of the United States, or as a member of any State legislature, or as an executive or judicial officer of any State, to support the Constitution of the United States, shall have engaged in insurrection or rebellion against the same, or given aid or comfort to the enemies thereof. But Congress may by a vote of two-thirds of each House, remove such disability.}

{Section 4. The validity of the public debt of the United States, authorized by law, including debts incurred for payment of pensions and bounties for services in suppressing insurrection or rebellion, shall not be questioned. But neither the United States nor any State shall assume or pay any debt or obligation incurred in aid of insurrection or rebellion against the United States, or any claim for the loss or emancipation of any slave; but all such debts, obligations and claims shall be held illegal and void.}[20]

Section 5. The Congress shall have power to enforce, by appropriate legislation, the provisions of this article.

AMENDMENT XV [Prohibition Against Racial
Discrimination in Voting] (1870)

Section 1. The right of citizens of the United States to vote shall not be denied or abridged by the United States or by any State on account of race, color, or previous condition of servitude.

Section 2. The Congress shall have power to enforce this article by appropriate legislation.

---

19 The first sentence of §2 amended the provisions of Art. I §2 cl. 3 governing apportionment of representation in the House of Representatives by requiring states to count former slaves as whole persons and providing a penalty in the event that state interfered with the voting rights of newly freed slaves.

20 Sections 3 and 4 are obsolete. They concerned matters regarding the aftermath of the Civil War.

A25

AMENDMENT XVI [Income Tax] (1913)

The Congress shall have power to lay and collect taxes on incomes, from whatever source derived, without apportionment among the several States, and without regard to any census or enumeration.[21]

AMENDMENT XVII [Direct Election of Senators] (1913)[22]

[1] The Senate of the United States shall be composed of two Senators from each State, elected by the people thereof, for six years; and each Senator shall have one vote. The electors in each State shall have the qualifications requisite for electors of the most numerous branch of the State legislatures.

[2] When vacancies happen in the representation of any State in the Senate, the executive authority of such State shall issue writs of election to fill such vacancies: Provided, that the legislature of any State may empower the executive thereof to make temporary appointments until the people fill the vacancies by election as the legislature may direct.

[3] This amendment shall not be so construed as to affect the election or term of any Senator chosen before it becomes valid as part of the Constitution.

AMENDMENT XVIII [Prohibition on Alcoholic Liquor][23]

Section 1. After one year from the ratification of this article the manufacture, sale, or transportation of intoxicating liquors within, the importation thereof into, or the exportation thereof from the United States and all territory subject to the jurisdiction thereof for beverage purposes is hereby prohibited.

Section 2. The Congress and the several States shall have concurrent power to enforce this article by appropriate legislation.

AMENDMENT XIX [Women's Right to Vote] (1920)

[1] The right of citizens of the United States to vote shall not be denied or abridged by the United States or by any State on account of sex.

[2] Congress shall have power to enforce this article by appropriate legislation.

AMENDMENT XX [Presidential and Congressional Terms] (1933)

Section 1. The terms of the President and Vice President shall end at noon on the 20th day of January, and the terms of Senators and Representatives at noon on the 3d day of January, of the years in which such terms would have ended if this article had not been ratified; and the terms of their successors shall then begin.

Section 2. The Congress shall assemble at least once in every year, and such meeting shall begin at noon on the 3d day of January, unless they shall by law appoint a different day.[24]

Section 3. If, at the time fixed for the beginning of the term of the President, the President elect shall have died, the Vice President elect shall become President. If a President shall not have been chosen before the time fixed for the beginning of his term, or if the President elect shall have failed to qualify, then the Vice President elect shall act

---

21 The 16th Amendment gave Congress the power to levy an income tax. *See* Chapter I, p. 25.

22 The 17th Amendment amended Art. I §2 cl. 1-2, which had provided for election of Senators by the state legislatures.

23 The 18th Amendment, which established "Prohibition," was repealed by §1 of the 21st Amendment. *See* Chapter IX, p. 361 note 327.

24 See supra note 6.

as President until a President shall have qualified; and the Congress may by law provide for the case wherein neither a President elect nor a Vice President elect shall have qualified, declaring who shall then act as President, or the manner in which one who is to act shall be selected, and such person shall act accordingly until a President or Vice President shall have qualified.

Section 4. The Congress may by law provide for the case of the death of any of the persons from whom the House of Representatives may choose a President whenever the right of choice shall have devolved upon them, and for the case of the death of any of the persons from whom the Senate may choose a Vice President whenever the right of choice shall have devolved upon them.

Section 5. Sections 1 and 2 shall take effect on the 15th day of October following the ratification of this article.

AMENDMENT XXI [State Control Over Intoxicating Liquors] (1933)

Section 1. The eighteenth article of amendment to the Constitution of the United States is hereby repealed.

Section 2. The transportation or importation into any State, Territory, or possession of the United States for delivery or use therein of intoxicating liquors, in violation of the laws thereof, is hereby prohibited.

AMENDMENT XXII [Limitation on Presidential Terms] (1951)

Section 1. No person shall be elected to the office of the President more than twice, and no person who has held the office of President, or acted as President, for more than two years of a term to which some other person was elected President shall be elected to the office of the President more than once. But this Article shall not apply to any person holding the office of President when this Article was proposed by the Congress, and shall not prevent any person who may be holding the office of President, or acting as President, during the term within which this Article becomes operative from holding the office of President or acting as President during the remainder of such term.

Section 2. This article shall be inoperative unless it shall have been ratified as an amendment to the Constitution by the legislatures of three- fourths of the several States within seven years from the date of its submission to the States by the Congress.

AMENDMENT XXIII [Presidential Electors for the District of Columbia] (1961)

Section 1. The District constituting the seat of Government of the United States shall appoint in such manner as the Congress may direct:

A number of electors of President and Vice President equal to the whole number of Senators and Representatives in Congress to which the District would be entitled if it were a State, but in no event more than the least populous State; they shall be in addition to those appointed by the States, but they shall be considered, for the purposes of the election of President and Vice President, to be electors appointed by a State; and they shall meet in the District and perform such duties as provided by the twelfth article of amendment.

Section 2. The Congress shall have power to enforce this article by appropriate legislation.

AMENDMENT XXIV [Prohibition on Poll Tax in Federal Elections] (1964)

Section 1. The right of citizens of the United States to vote in any primary or other election for President or Vice President, for electors for President or Vice President, or for Senator or Representative in Congress, shall not be denied or abridged by the United States or any State by reason of failure to pay any poll tax or other tax.

Section 2. The Congress shall have power to enforce this article by appropriate legislation.

AMENDMENT XXV [Succession to Presidency and Vice-Presidency; Presidential Disability] (1967)

Section 1. In case of the removal of the President from office or of his death or resignation, the Vice President shall become President.

Section 2. Whenever there is a vacancy in the office of the Vice President, the President shall nominate a Vice President who shall take office upon confirmation by a majority vote of both Houses of Congress.

Section 3. Whenever the President transmits to the President pro tempore of the Senate and the Speaker of the House of Representatives his written declaration that he is unable to discharge the powers and duties of his office, and until he transmits to them a written declaration to the contrary, such powers and duties shall be discharged by the Vice President as Acting President.

Section 4. Whenever the Vice President and a majority of either the principal officers of the executive departments or of such other body as Congress may by law provide, transmit to the President pro tempore of the Senate and the Speaker of the House of Representatives, their written declaration that the President is unable to discharge the powers and duties of his office, the Vice President shall immediately assume the powers and duties of the office as Acting President.

Thereafter, when the President transmits to the President pro tempore of the Senate and the Speaker of the House of Representatives his written declaration that no inability exists, he shall resume the powers and duties of his office unless the Vice President and a majority of either the principal officers of the executive department or of such other body as Congress may by law provide, transmit within four days to the President pro tempore of the Senate and the Speaker of the House of Representatives their written declaration that the President is unable to discharge the powers and duties of his office. Thereupon Congress shall decide the issue, assembling within forty-eight hours for that purpose if not in session. If the Congress, within twenty-one days after receipt of the latter written declaration, or, if Congress is not in session, within twenty-one days after Congress is required to assemble, determines by two-thirds vote of both Houses that the President is unable to discharge the powers and duties of his office, the Vice President shall continue to discharge the same as Acting President; otherwise, the President shall resume the powers and duties of his office.

AMENDMENT XXVI [Prohibition Against Discrimination in Voting on Basis of Age] (1971)

Section 1. The right of citizens of the United States, who are eighteen years of age or older, to vote shall not be denied or abridged by the United States or by any State on account of age.

Section 2. The Congress shall have power to enforce this article by appropriate legislation.

AMENDMENT XXVII [Compensation of Senators and Representatives] (1992)[25]

No law, varying the compensation for the services of the Senators and Representatives, shall take effect, until an election of Representatives shall have intervened.

---

25 This recent amendment amended Art.I §6 cl. 1. It is notable for having the longest period between proposal and ratification — over 200 years. *See* Chapter IX, p. 325 note 50.

Structure of the Federal Government

Legislative Branch

CONGRESS

SENATE **HOUSE**

General Accounting Office
Government Printing Office
Library of Congress
Office of Technology Assessment
Congressional Budget Office
Architect of the Capitol
U.S. Botanic Garden

Executive Branch

PRESIDENT

EXECUTIVE OFFICE OF THE PRESIDENT

VICE PRESIDENT

White House Office
Office of Management and Budget
Council of Economic Advisers
National Security Council
Office of National Drug Control Policy
Office of the U.S. Trade Representative
Council on Environmental Quality
Office of Science and Technology Policy
Office of Administration

Judicial Branch

SUPREME COURT

U.S. Courts of Appeals
U.S. District Courts
Specialized and Territorial Courts
Federal Judicial Center
Administrative Office of U.S. Courts

Department of Agriculture

Department of Commerce

Department of Defense

Department of Education

Department of Energy

Department of
Health and Human Services

Department of Housing
and Urban Development

Department of the Interior

Department of Justice

Department of State

Department of Transportation

Department of the Treasury

Department of
Veterans Affairs

Department of Labor

Independent Agencies and Government Corporations

Administrative Conference of the United States
African Development Foundation
Central Intelligence Agency
Commission on Civil Rights
Commodity Futures Trading Commission
Consumer Product Safety Commission
Environmental Protection Agency
Equal Employment Opportunity Commission
Export-Import Bank of the United States
Farm Credit Administration
Federal Communications Commission
Federal Deposit Insurance Corporation
Federal Election Commission
Federal Emergency Management Agency
Federal Housing Finance Board
Federal Labor Relations Authority
Federal Maritime Commission
Federal Mediation and Conciliation Service
Federal Mine Safety and Health Review Commission
Federal Reserve System, Board of Governors
Federal Retirement Thrift Investment Board
Federal Trade Commission
General Services Administration
Inter-American Foundation
Interstate Commerce Commission
Legal Services Corporation
Merit Systems Protection Board
National Aeronautics and Space Administration
National Archives and Records Administration
National Capital Planning commission
National Credit Union Administration
National Foundation on the Arts and the Humanities
National Labor Relations Board
National Mediation Board
National Railroad Passenger Corporation (Amtrak)
National Science Foundation
National Transportation Safety Board
Nuclear Regulatory Commission
Occupational Safety and Health Review Commission
Office of Personnel Management
Office of Special Counsel
Office of Thrift Supervision
Panama Canal Commission
Peace Corps
Pennsylvania Avenue Development Corporation
Pension Benefit Guaranty Corporation
Postal Rate Commission
Railroad Retirement Board
Resolution Trust Corporation
Securities and Exchange Commission
Selective Service System
Small Business Administration
Tennessee Valley Authority
Thrift Depositor Protection Oversight Board
Trade and Development Agency
U.S. Arms Control and Disarmament Agency
U.S. Information Agency
U.S. International Development Cooperation Agency
U.S. International Trade Commission
U.S. Postal Service

A31

Diagram of State and Federal Court Systems and Hierarchy

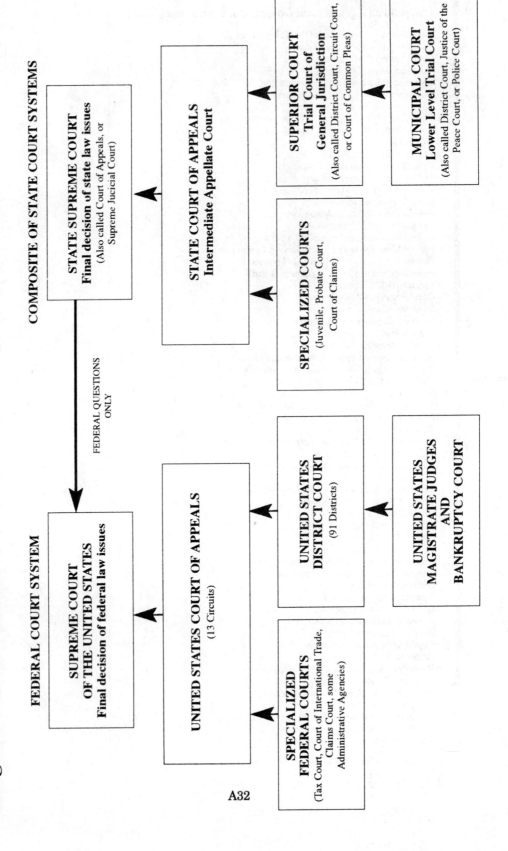

COMPOSITE OF STATE COURT SYSTEMS

STATE SUPREME COURT
Final decision of state law issues
(Also called Court of Appeals, or
Supreme Jucicial Court)

STATE COURT OF APPEALS
Intermediate Appellate Court

SUPERIOR COURT
Trial Court of
General Jurisdiction
(Also called District Court, Circuit Court,
or Court of Common Pleas)

MUNICIPAL COURT
Lower Level Trial Court
(Also called District Court, Justice of the
Peace Court, or Police Court)

SPECIALIZED COURTS
(Juvenile, Probate Court,
Court of Claims)

FEDERAL QUESTIONS
ONLY

FEDERAL COURT SYSTEM

SUPREME COURT
OF THE UNITED STATES
Final decision of federal law issues

UNITED STATES COURT OF APPEALS
(13 Circuits)

UNITED STATES
DISTRICT COURT
(91 Districts)

UNITED STATES
MAGISTRATE JUDGES
AND
BANKRUPTCY COURT

SPECIALIZED
FEDERAL COURTS
(Tax Court, Court of International Trade,
Claims Court, some
Administrative Agencies)

Typical Trial Courtroom

Door to Judge's Chambers

Judge

Bench

Witness Stand

Door to Jury Deliberation Room

Judge's Clerk

Judge's Law Clerk

Court Reporter

Jury Box

Bailiff and other Security Personnel

Lecturn

Defense Table

Prosecution or Civil Plaintiff Table

Railing (bar)

Seating for Public

A33

APPENDIX B

ADDRESSES OF MAJOR PUBLISHERS OF U.S. LEGAL EDUCATIONAL MATERIALS AND SOURCES OF U.S. LAW ON THE INTERNET

1. ADDRESSES MAJOR PUBLISHERS OF U.S. LEGAL EDUCATIONAL MATERIALS

West Group
620 Opperman Drive
Eagan, Minnesota 55123

Telephone: 651-687-7746
Fax: 651-687-7302
Web: www.westpub.com/LSchool

Foundation Press
615 Merrick Avenue
Westbury, New York 11590-6607

Telephone: 800-917-7377; 212-760-8700
Fax: 212-760-8705
Web: www.fdpress.com

Aspen Law and Business
Order Department
7201 McKinney Circle
Frederick, Maryland 21704-8356

Telephone: 800-234-1660
Fax: 301-695-7931
Web: www.aspenpub.com/lawsch/
index.htm

Matthew Bender
1275 Broadway
Albany, New York 11204

Telephone: 800-533-1646
Fax: 518-487-3584
Web: www.bender.com

Lexis Law Publishing
Attn: Customer Support
P.O. Box 7587
Charlottesville, Virginia 22906

Telephone: 800-542-0957 or 804-972-7600;
Fax: 804-972-7525
llp.customer.support@lexis- nexis.com
Web: www.lexislawpublishing.com

2. SELECTED INTERNET SITES FOR LEGAL RESEARCH AND INFORMATION

The Legal Research Sites given first provide access to basic research materials, such as cases, statutes and regulations through links to primary sources. They also provide search engines and helpful hints on how to do research on the Web, as well as legal news services. Also listed below are sites for Congress, courts and lawyers. All these sites have links to numerous other related sites.

Legal Research Sites

www.lcp.com/The-Legal-List/
www.findlaw.com/

Other Legal Search Engines

http://www.dejanews.com/
http://www.dogpile.com/

Legal News

www.ljx.com
www.counsel.com

U.S. Congress	www.thomas.loc.gov
Library of Congress	www.loc.gov
Federal Judiciary	www.uscourts.gov
National Center for State Courts	www.ncsc.dni.us
Department of Justice Bureau of Judicial Statistics	www.ojp.usdoj.gov
American Judicature Society	www.ajs.org
American Bar Association	www.abanet.org
Attorney Finders	www.abanet.org./martindale.html www.wld.com
U.S. Government Printing Office	www.access.gpo

APPENDIX C: TABLE OF CASES

C3

C16